t Distribution Critical Values

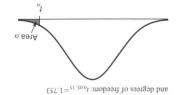

Table gives *t* values for given upper tail area α and degrees of freedom; $t_{0.05,15} = 1.753$

This table shows the *t* value that defines the given right-tail area for the stated degrees of freedom (ν).

Right-Tail Area α

ν	0.1	0.05	0.025	0.01	0.005
1	3.078	6.314	12.706	31.821	63.657
2	1.886	2.920	4.303	6.965	9.925
3	1.638	2.353	3.182	4.541	5.841
4	1.533	2.132	2.776	3.747	4.604
5	1.476	2.015	2.571	3.365	4.032
6	1.440	1.943	2.447	3.143	3.707
7	1.415	1.895	2.365	2.998	3.499
8	1.397	1.860	2.306	2.896	3.355
9	1.383	1.833	2.262	2.821	3.250
10	1.372	1.812	2.228	2.764	3.169
11	1.363	1.796	2.201	2.718	3.106
12	1.356	1.782	2.179	2.681	3.055
13	1.350	1.771	2.160	2.650	3.012
14	1.345	1.761	2.145	2.624	2.977
15	1.341	1.753	2.131	2.602	2.947
16	1.337	1.746	2.120	2.583	2.921
17	1.333	1.740	2.110	2.567	2.898
18	1.330	1.734	2.101	2.552	2.878
19	1.328	1.729	2.093	2.539	2.861
20	1.325	1.725	2.086	2.528	2.845
21	1.323	1.721	2.080	2.518	2.831
22	1.321	1.717	2.074	2.508	2.819
23	1.319	1.714	2.069	2.500	2.807
24	1.318	1.711	2.064	2.492	2.797
25	1.316	1.708	2.060	2.485	2.787
26	1.315	1.706	2.056	2.479	2.779
27	1.314	1.703	2.052	2.473	2.771
28	1.313	1.701	2.048	2.467	2.763
29	1.311	1.699	2.045	2.462	2.756
30	1.310	1.697	2.042	2.457	2.750
31	1.309	1.696	2.040	2.453	2.744
32	1.309	1.694			2.738
33	1.308	1.692			2.733
34	1.307	1.691			
35	1.306	1.690			

ν	0.1	0.05	0.025	0.01	0.005
36	1.306	1.688	2.028	2.434	2.719
37	1.305	1.687	2.026	2.431	2.715
38	1.304	1.686	2.024	2.429	2.712
39	1.304	1.685	2.023	2.426	2.708
40	1.303	1.684	2.021	2.423	2.704
41	1.303	1.683	2.020	2.421	2.701
42	1.302	1.682	2.018	2.418	2.698
43	1.302	1.681	2.017	2.416	2.695
44	1.301	1.680	2.015	2.414	2.692
45	1.301	1.679	2.014	2.412	2.690
46	1.300	1.679	2.013	2.410	2.687
47	1.300	1.678	2.012	2.408	2.685
48	1.299	1.677	2.011	2.407	2.682
49	1.299	1.677	2.010	2.405	2.680
50	1.299	1.676	2.009	2.403	2.678
55	1.297	1.673	2.004	2.396	2.668
60	1.296	1.671	2.000	2.390	2.660
65	1.295	1.669	1.997	2.385	2.654
70	1.294	1.667	1.994	2.381	2.648
75	1.293	1.665	1.992	2.377	2.643
80	1.292	1.664	1.990	2.374	2.639
85	1.292	1.663	1.988	2.371	2.635
90	1.291	1.662	1.987	2.368	2.632
95	1.291	1.661	1.985	2.366	2.629
100	1.290	1.660	1.984	2.364	2.626
110	1.289	1.659	1.982	2.361	2.621
120	1.289	1.658	1.980	2.358	2.617
130	1.288	1.657	1.978	2.355	2.614
140	1.288	1.656	1.977	2.353	2.611
150	1.287	1.655	1.976	2.351	2.609
inf.	1.280	1.645	1.96	2.33	2.575

↑ ↑ **z values**

Note: As *n* increases, critical values of Student's *t* [approach those for the *z*-] [...] this table. A common rule of thumb is to use *z* when *n* > 30, but that is not conservative.

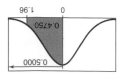

This table shows the normal area between 0 and z_0. Example: $P(0 < Z < 1.96) = 0.4750$.

z_0	0	0.01	0.02	0.03	0.04	0.05	0.06	0.07	0.08	0.09
0.0	0.0000	0.0040	0.0080	0.0120	0.0160	0.0199	0.0239	0.0279	0.0319	0.0359
0.1	0.0398	0.0438	0.0478	0.0517	0.0557	0.0596	0.0636	0.0675	0.0714	0.0753
0.2	0.0793	0.0832	0.0871	0.0910	0.0948	0.0987	0.1026	0.1064	0.1103	0.1141
0.3	0.1179	0.1217	0.1255	0.1293	0.1331	0.1368	0.1406	0.1443	0.1480	0.1517
0.4	0.1554	0.1591	0.1628	0.1664	0.1700	0.1736	0.1772	0.1808	0.1844	0.1879
0.5	0.1915	0.1950	0.1985	0.2019	0.2054	0.2088	0.2123	0.2157	0.2190	0.2224
0.6	0.2257	0.2291	0.2324	0.2357	0.2389	0.2422	0.2454	0.2486	0.2517	0.2549
0.7	0.2580	0.2611	0.2642	0.2673	0.2704	0.2734	0.2764	0.2794	0.2823	0.2852
0.8	0.2881	0.2910	0.2939	0.2967	0.2995	0.3023	0.3051	0.3078	0.3106	0.3133
0.9	0.3159	0.3186	0.3212	0.3238	0.3264	0.3289	0.3315	0.3340	0.3365	0.3389
1.0	0.3413	0.3438	0.3461	0.3485	0.3508	0.3531	0.3554	0.3577	0.3599	0.3621
1.1	0.3643	0.3665	0.3686	0.3708	0.3729	0.3749	0.3770	0.3790	0.3810	0.3830
1.2	0.3849	0.3869	0.3888	0.3907	0.3925	0.3944	0.3962	0.3980	0.3997	0.4015
1.3	0.4032	0.4049	0.4066	0.4082	0.4099	0.4115	0.4131	0.4147	0.4162	0.4177
1.4	0.4192	0.4207	0.4222	0.4236	0.4251	0.4265	0.4279	0.4292	0.4306	0.4319
1.5	0.4332	0.4345	0.4357	0.4370	0.4382	0.4394	0.4406	0.4418	0.4429	0.4441
1.6	0.4452	0.4463	0.4474	0.4484	0.4495	0.4505	0.4515	0.4525	0.4535	0.4545
1.7	0.4554	0.4564	0.4573	0.4582	0.4591	0.4599	0.4608	0.4616	0.4625	0.4633
1.8	0.4641	0.4649	0.4656	0.4664	0.4671	0.4678	0.4686	0.4693	0.4699	0.4706
1.9	0.4713	0.4719	0.4726	0.4732	0.4738	0.4744	0.4750	0.4756	0.4761	0.4767
2.0	0.4772	0.4778	0.4783	0.4788	0.4793	0.4798	0.4803	0.4808	0.4812	0.4817
2.1	0.4821	0.4826	0.4830	0.4834	0.4838	0.4842	0.4846	0.4850	0.4854	0.4857
2.2	0.4861	0.4864	0.4868	0.4871	0.4875	0.4878	0.4881	0.4884	0.4887	0.4890
2.3	0.4893	0.4896	0.4898	0.4901	0.4904	0.4906	0.4909	0.4911	0.4913	0.4916
2.4	0.4918	0.4920	0.4922	0.4925	0.4927	0.4929	0.4931	0.4932	0.4934	0.4936
2.5	0.4938	0.4940	0.4941	0.4943	0.4945	0.4946	0.4948	0.4949	0.4951	0.4952
2.6	0.4953	0.4955	0.4956	0.4957	0.4959	0.4960	0.4961	0.4962	0.4963	0.4964
2.7	0.4965	0.4966	0.4967	0.4968	0.4969	0.4970	0.4971	0.4972	0.4973	0.4974
2.8	0.4974	0.4975	0.4976	0.4977	0.4977	0.4978	0.4979	0.4979	0.4980	0.4981
2.9	0.4981	0.4982	0.4982	0.4983	0.4984	0.4984	0.4985	0.4985	0.4986	0.4986
3.0	0.4987	0.4987	0.4987	0.4988	0.4988	0.4989	0.4989	0.4989	0.4990	0.4990
3.1	0.4990	0.4991	0.4991	0.4991	0.4992	0.4992	0.4992	0.4992	0.4993	0.4993
3.2	0.4993	0.4993	0.4994	0.4994	0.4994	0.4994	0.4994	0.4995	0.4995	0.4995
3.3	0.4995	0.4995	0.4995	0.4996	0.4996	0.4996	0.4996	0.4996	0.4996	0.4997
3.4	0.4997	0.4997	0.4997	0.4997	0.4997	0.4997	0.4997	0.4997	0.4997	0.4998
3.5	0.4998	0.4998	0.4998	0.4998	0.4998	0.4998	0.4998	0.4998	0.4998	0.4998
3.6	0.4998	0.4998	0.4999	0.4999	0.4999	0.4999	0.4999	0.4999	0.4999	0.4999
3.7	0.4999	0.4999	0.4999	0.4999	0.4999	0.4999	0.4999	0.4999	0.4999	0.4999

APPLIED STATISTICS

in Business and Economics

Canadian Edition

David P. Doane
Oakland University

Lori E. Seward
University of Colorado

Yash Aneja
University of Windsor

Peter Miller
University of Windsor

McGraw-Hill
Ryerson
Connect. Learn. Succeed.

APPLIED STATISTICS IN BUSINESS AND ECONOMICS
Canadian Edition

ISBN-13: 978-0-07-081379-3
ISBN-10: 0-07-081379-5

1 2 3 4 5 6 7 8 9 10 TCP 10

Printed and bound in Canada

Vice-President and Editor-in-Chief: *Joanna Cotton*
Sponsoring Editors: *Kimberley Redhead/Jeremy Guimond*
Marketing Manager: *Cathie Lefebvre*
Developmental Editor: *Sarah Fulton*
Editorial Associate: *Jennifer Clark*
iLearning Sales Specialist: *Allison Sigurdson*
Manager, Editorial Services: *Margaret Henderson*
Supervising Editor: *Cathy Biribauer*
Copy Editor: *Michael Kelly*
Production Coordinator: *Sheryl MacAdam*
Inside Design: *Jodie Bernard/Laserwords Private Limited*
Composition: *Laserwords Private Limited*
Cover Design: *Word & Image Design Studio Inc.*
Cover Photo: *Colin Anderson/Getty Images*
Printer: *Transcontinental Printing Group*

Library and Archives Canada Cataloguing in Publication Data

Applied statistics in business & economics / David P. Doane . . . [et al.].—Canadian ed.

Includes index.
ISBN 978-0-07-081379-3

1. Commercial statistics—Textbooks. I. Doane, David P.
II. Title: Applied statistics in business and economics.

HF1017.A66 2010   519.5   C2009-905819-7

Dedication

To Robert Hamilton Doane-Solomon.
–David

To all my students who challenged me to make statistics relevant to their lives.
–Lori

To my wife, Renu; our children, Ambika and Ankur; and our granddaughter, Amaya.
–Yash

To my family and to the many thousands of my students whose fear of statistics was hopefully replaced with an appreciation of its power.
–Peter

David P. Doane

David P. Doane is Professor of Quantitative Methods in Oakland University's Department of Decision and Information Sciences. He earned his Bachelor of Arts degree in mathematics and economics at the University of Kansas and his PhD from Purdue University's Krannert Graduate School. His research and teaching interests include applied statistics, forecasting, and statistical education. He is co-recipient of three National Science Foundation grants to develop software to teach statistics and to create a computer classroom. He is a long-time member of the American Statistical Association and INFORMS, serving in 2002 as President of the Detroit ASA chapter, where he remains on the board. He has consulted with government, health care organizations, and local firms. He has published articles in many academic journals and is the author of *LearningStats* (McGraw-Hill, 2003, 2007) and co-author of *Visual Statistics* (McGraw-Hill, 1997, 2001).

Lori E. Seward

Lori E. Seward is an Instructor in the Decisions Sciences Department in the College of Business at The University of Colorado at Denver and Health Sciences Center. She earned her Bachelor of Science and Master of Science degrees in Industrial Engineering at Virginia Tech. After several years working as a reliability and quality engineer in the paper and automotive industries, she earned her PhD from Virginia Tech. She served as the Chair of the INFORMS Teachers' Workshop for the annual 2004 meeting. Prior to joining UCDHSC in 2008, Dr. Seward served on the faculty at the Leeds School of Business at CU–Boulder for ten years. Her teaching interests focus on developing pedagogy that uses technology to create a collaborative learning environment in both large undergraduate and MBA statistics courses. Her most recent article was published in *The International Journal of Flexible Manufacturing Systems,* (Kluwer Academic Publishers, 2004).

Yash Aneja

Yash Aneja is Professor of Management Science in the Odette School of Business at the University of Windsor. He received his MStat from the Indian Statistical Institute, and PhD in Mathematical Sciences from the Johns Hopkins University. Yash has published over 60 articles in leading scholarly journals such as *Management Science, Operations Research, Mathematical Programming, Networks,* and *Discrete Applied Mathematics,* among others. His current research interests include integer programming, network and combinatorial optimization, wireless sensor networks, and design and routing of flows in WDM optical networks. His main goal in teaching business statistics is to focus on the fundamentals and help students appreciate its usefulness.

Peter L. Miller

Peter L. Miller is an Assistant Professor in the Management Science area at the Odette School of Business, University of Windsor. He earned his Bachelor of Engineering degree in Electrical Engineering at McGill University, his Masters of Business Administration degree from the University of Toronto, and did some additional post-graduate studies at UCLA, earning a Candidate in Philosophy degree, majoring in business statistics and minoring in finance and urban land economics. Before becoming a faculty member at the University of Windsor over 30 years ago, he was a part-time instructor in business statistics and management science at California State University, Fullerton. His primary objectives in teaching statistics are to help students appreciate its usefulness in the business world and in their daily lives and to develop in students an understanding of why and how statistics works and not just how to apply statistical methods.

Brief Contents

Contents

Chapter Nine

Chapter Ten

Chapter Eleven

Chapter Twelve

Chapter Thirteen

Chapter Fourteen

Chapter Fifteen

Chapter Sixteen

Chapter Seventeen

Quality Management 726

Appendices

Index 810

To the Student

"How often have you heard people/students say about a particular subject, 'I'll never use this in the real world?' I thought statistics was a bit on the 'math-geeky' side at first. Imagine my horror when I saw α, R^2, and correlations on several financial reports at my current job (an intern position at a financial services company). I realized then that I had better try to understand some of this stuff."

—Jill Odette (an introductory statistics student)

As recently as a decade ago our students used to ask us, "*How* do I use statistics?" Today we more often hear, "*Why* should I use statistics?" *Applied Statistics in Business and Economics,* Canadian Edition, has attempted to provide real meaning to the use of statistics in our world by using real business situations and real data and appealing to your need to know *why* rather than just *how.*

With many years of teaching statistics between the four members of the author team, we feel we have something to offer. Seeing how you've changed has required us to adapt and seek out better ways of instruction. So we wrote *Applied Statistics in Business and Economics,* Canadian Edition, to meet four distinct objectives.

- *Objective 1: Communicate the meaning of uncertainty in a business context:* Uncertainty exists everywhere in the world around us. Successful businesses know how to measure this uncertainty. They also know how to reduce this uncertainty whenever possible. We'll show you how businesses do this.

- *Objective 2: Use real data and real business applications:* Examples, case studies, and problems are taken from published research or real applications whenever possible. Hypothetical data are used when it seems the best way to illustrate a concept. You can usually tell the difference by examining the footnotes citing the source.

- *Objective 3: Incorporate current statistical practices and offer practical advice:* With the increased reliance on computers, statistics practitioners have changed the way they use statistical tools. We'll show you the current practices and explain why they are used the way they are. We will also tell you when each technique should *not* be used.

- *Objective 4: Provide more in-depth explanation of the why and let the software take care of the how:* It is critical that you understand the importance of communicating with data. Today's computer capabilities make it much easier to summarize and display data than ever before. We demonstrate easily mastered software techniques using the common software available. We also spend a great deal of time on the idea that there are risks in decision making and those risks should be quantified and directly considered in every business decision.

Our experience tells us that you want to be given credit for the experience you bring to the classroom. We have tried to honour this by choosing examples and exercises set in situations that will draw on your already vast knowledge of the world around you, as well as knowledge you have gained from other classes you have taken. Emphasis is on thinking about data, choosing appropriate analytic tools, using computers effectively, and recognizing limitations of statistics.

Software

There are different types of software for statistical analysis, ranging from Excel's functions to stand-alone packages. Excel is used throughout this book because it is available everywhere. But calculations are illustrated using MegaStat, whose Excel-based menus and spreadsheet format offer more capability than Excel's data analysis tools. MINITAB menus and examples are also included to point out similarities and differences of these tools. To assist those of you who need extra help or "catch up" work, the Student CD contains tutorials or demonstrations on using Excel, MINITAB, or MegaStat for the tasks of each chapter. At the end of each chapter is a list of *LearningStats* and Visual Statistics demonstrations, case studies, and applications that illustrate the concepts from the chapter.

Features of the Canadian Edition

Without removing many of the well-developed American examples, the authors have added many Canadian and international examples and mini-cases that are relevant to students, not only in their current lives but also in their lives as future business leaders.

Enhanced Pedagogy

A Closer Look   These boxes, new to the Canadian Edition, are brief snapshots of a few sentences only, included throughout the text to expand on formulas and other statistical concepts.

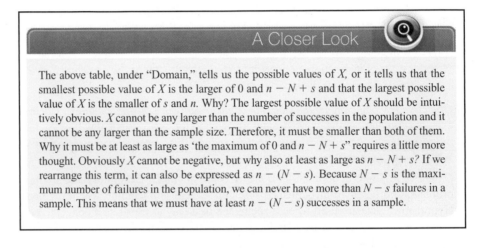

> ### A Closer Look
>
> The above table, under "Domain," tells us the possible values of X, or it tells us that the smallest possible value of X is the larger of 0 and $n - N + s$ and that the largest possible value of X is the smaller of s and n. Why? The largest possible value of X should be intuitively obvious. X cannot be any larger than the number of successes in the population and it cannot be any larger than the sample size. Therefore, it must be smaller than both of them. Why it must be at least as large as 'the maximum of 0 and $n - N + s$" requires a little more thought. Obviously X cannot be negative, but why also at least as large as $n - N + s$? If we rearrange this term, it can also be expressed as $n - (N - s)$. Because $N - s$ is the maximum number of failures in the population, we can never have more than $N - s$ failures in a sample. This means that we must have at least $n - (N - s)$ successes in a sample.

Concept Check   Also new to the Canadian Edition, these boxes expand on the material and formulas covered in a chapter or chapter section in order to give students a better understanding and insight into these materials and formulas. Solutions to each Concept Check are included in Appendix G at the end of this book.

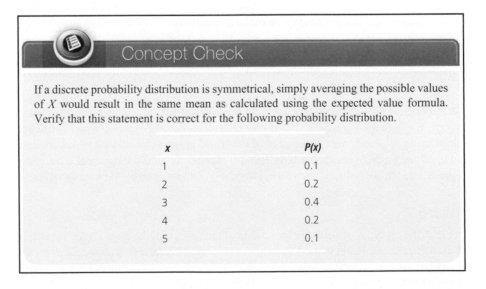

> ### Concept Check
>
> If a discrete probability distribution is symmetrical, simply averaging the possible values of X would result in the same mean as calculated using the expected value formula. Verify that this statement is correct for the following probability distribution.
>
> | x | P(x) |
> |---|------|
> | 1 | 0.1 |
> | 2 | 0.2 |
> | 3 | 0.4 |
> | 4 | 0.2 |
> | 5 | 0.1 |

Learning Objectives   Each chapter begins with a set of learning objectives designed to provide a focus for the chapter and to motivate learning. These objectives indicate what students should be able to do after completing the chapter.

Mini Cases Mini Cases interspersed throughout each chapter provide students with examples of real-world applications of statistics.

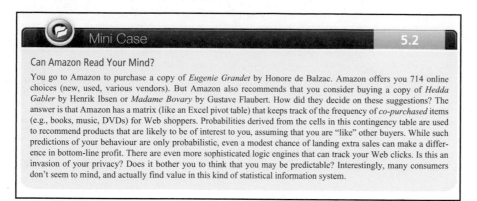

Tips Appearing throughout the text, tips offer students advice and guidance while learning the material of the chapter.

> **Tip**
>
> The mode is most useful for discrete or categorical data with only a few distinct data values. For continuous data or data with a wide range, the mode is rarely useful.

Examples Highlighted in the text to be easily spotted, examples illustrate important concepts in a real-world context.

EXAMPLE 7	
Servicing Cars at a Quick Oil-Change Shop	Consider a shop that specializes in quick oil changes. It is important to this type of business to ensure that a car's service time is not considered "late" by the customer. Therefore, to study this process, we can define service times as being either *late* or *not late* and define the random variable X to be the number of cars that are late out of the total number of cars serviced. We further assume that cars' service times are independent of each other and the chance of a car being late stays the same for each car. Based on our knowledge of the process we know that $P(\text{car is late}) = \pi = 0.10$. Now, think of this variable as satisfying the conditions of a binomial random variable and apply the binomial distribution. Suppose we would like to know the probability that exactly 2 of the next 12 cars serviced are late. In this case, $n = 12$, and we want to know $P(X = 2)$: $$P(X = 2) = \frac{12!}{2!(12-2)!}(0.10)^2(1 - 0.10)^{12-2} = 0.2301$$ Alternatively, we could calculate this by using the Excel function =BINOMDIST(2,12,.1,0). The fourth parameter, 0, means that we want Excel to calculate $P(X = 2)$ rather than $P(X \le 2)$.

Section Exercises Following each section, a set of simple exercises provides the opportunity for students to immediately apply the concepts they have just learned. Solutions to odd-numbered exercises can be found at **www.mcgrawhillconnect.ca**.

Section Exercises

6.15 Find the mean and standard deviation of four-digit uniformly distributed lottery numbers (0000 through 9999). (LO 4)

6.16 The ages of Java programmers at SynFlex Corp. range from 20 to 60. (a) If their ages are uniformly distributed, what would be the mean and standard deviation? (b) What is the probability that a randomly selected programmer's age is at least 40? At least 30? *Hint:* Treat employee ages as integers. (LO 4)

6.17 An auditor for a medical insurance company selects a random sample of prescription drug claims for evaluation of correct payment by company experts. The claims were selected at random from a database of 500,000 claims by using uniform random numbers between 1 and 500,000. To verify that the random numbers really were from a uniform distribution, the auditor calculated the mean and standard deviation of the random numbers. What should the mean and standard deviation be if these were uniformly distributed random integers? (LO 4)

6.18 (a) If the birthdays of students born in January are uniformly distributed, what would be their expected mean and standard deviation? (b) Do you think that birthdays in January really are uniformly distributed? (LO 4)

6.19 Use Excel to generate 100 random integers from (a) 1 through 2, inclusive; (b) 1 through 5, inclusive; and (c) 0 through 99, inclusive. (d) In each case, write the Excel formula. (e) In each case, calculate the mean and standard deviation of the sample of 100 integers you generated, and compare them with their theoretical values. *Hint:* Table 6.4 shows the Excel function. (LO 4)

End-of-Chapter Material

Chapter Summary   Chapter summaries aid students in their review of each chapter by condensing the most important concepts into a few paragraphs.

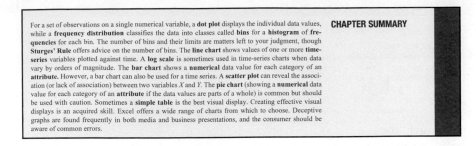

For a set of observations on a single numerical variable, a **dot plot** displays the individual data values, while a **frequency distribution** classifies the data into classes called **bins** for a **histogram** of frequencies for each bin. The number of bins and their limits are matters left to your judgment, though **Sturges' Rule** offers advice on the number of bins. The **line chart** shows values of one or more time-series variables plotted against time. A **log scale** is sometimes used in time-series charts when data vary by orders of magnitude. The **bar chart** shows a **numerical** data value for each category of an **attribute**. However, a bar chart can also be used for a time series. A **scatter plot** can reveal the association (or lack of association) between two variables X and Y. The **pie chart** (showing a **numerical** data value for each category of an **attribute** if the data values are parts of a whole) is common but should be used with caution. Sometimes a **simple table** is the best visual display. Creating effective visual displays is an acquired skill. Excel offers a wide range of charts from which to choose. Deceptive graphs are found frequently in both media and business presentations, and the consumer should be aware of common errors.

CHAPTER SUMMARY

Commonly Used Formulas   Formulas used throughout the chapter are listed at the end of each chapter for reference and review.

Commonly Used Formulas in Descriptive Statistics

Sample mean: $\bar{x} = \dfrac{1}{n}\sum_{i=1}^{n} x_i$

Geometric mean (growth rate): $GR = \sqrt[n]{(1 + x_1)(1 + x_2)\cdots(1 + x_n)} - 1$

Range: $\text{Range} = x_{max} - x_{min}$

Sample standard deviation: $s = \sqrt{\dfrac{\sum_{i=1}^{n}(x_i - \bar{x})^2}{n - 1}}$

Coefficient of variation: $CV = 100 \times \dfrac{s}{\bar{x}}$

Standardized variable: $z_i = \dfrac{x_i - \mu}{\sigma}$

Sample correlation coefficient: $r = \dfrac{\sum_{i=1}^{n}(x_i - \bar{x})(y_i - \bar{y})}{\sqrt{\sum_{i=1}^{n}(x_i - \bar{x})^2}\sqrt{\sum_{i=1}^{n}(y_i - \bar{y})^2}}$

Grouped mean: $\bar{x} = \sum_{j=1}^{k} \dfrac{f_j m_j}{n}$

Chapter Review   These questions begin the problem material at the end of each chapter and are designed to reinforce the concepts and techniques learned.

Chapter Exercises   Each chapter contains exercises, of varying levels of difficulty, giving students ample opportunity for practice. Chapter exercises are often integrative and concern more real-world situations than in-chapter exercises. The answers for odd-numbered exercises are provided at **www.mcgrawhillconnect.ca**.

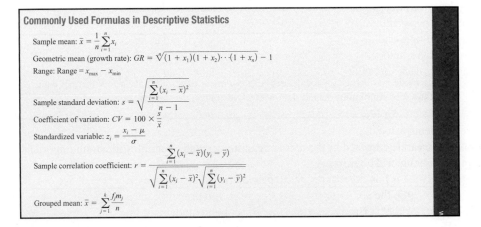

CHAPTER EXERCISES   *Note:* In these exercises, you may use a software package. Use MegaStat's Descriptive Statistics for dot plots or Frequency Distributions for histograms. Use MINITAB's Graphs or a similar software package to create the dot plot or histogram.

3.23   A study of 40 cardiac care centres showed the following ratios of nurses to beds. (a) Prepare a dot plot. (b) Prepare a frequency distribution and histogram (you may either specify the bins yourself or use automatic bins). (c) Describe the distribution, based on these displays. (LO 1 & 3)

Nurses

1.48	1.16	1.24	1.52	1.30	1.28	1.68	1.40	1.12	0.98	0.93	2.76
1.34	1.58	1.72	1.38	1.44	1.41	1.34	1.96	1.29	1.21	2.00	1.50
1.68	1.39	1.62	1.17	1.07	2.11	2.40	1.35	1.48	1.59	1.81	1.15
1.35	1.42	1.33	1.41								

3.24   The first Rose Bowl football game was played in 1902. The next was not played until 1916, but a Rose Bowl has been played every year since then. The margin of victory in each of the 87 Rose Bowls from 1902 through 2003 is shown below (0 indicates a tie). (a) Prepare a dot plot. (b) Prepare a frequency distribution and histogram (you may either specify the bins yourself or use automatic bins). (c) Describe the distribution, based on these displays. (Data are from *Sports Illustrated 2004 Sports Almanac*, and www.cbs.sportsline.com.) (LO 1 & 3)

RoseBowl

49	14	14	1	28	0	11	0	17	1	0
1	1	33	24	9	35	7	16	7	21	13
4	14	8	4	9	29	25	20	31	49	6
3	8	33	7	8	13	3	16	3	26	36
10	18	5	10	27	2	1	11	11	7	10
1	25	21	1	13	8	7	7	1	17	28
10	36	3	17	7	3	8	7	12	20	7
5	18	9	3	5	7	8	10	23	20	

Exam Review Questions   Exam review questions follow select chapters and provide opportunities for students to test their comprehension of the interrelation of important concepts over the broader scope of several chapters. Solutions to the Exam Review questions can be accessed at **www.mcgrawhillconnect.ca**.

Student Supplements

McGraw-Hill Connect™

www.mcgrawhillconnect.ca   Developed in partnership with Youthography, a Canadian youth research company, and hundreds of students from across Canada, McGraw-Hill Connect™ embraces diverse study behaviours and preferences to maximize active learning and engagement.

With McGraw-Hill Connect™, students complete pre- and post-diagnostic assessments that identify knowledge gaps and point them to concepts they need to learn. McGraw-Hill Connect™ provides students with the option to work through recommended learning exercises and create their own personalized study plan using multiple sources of content, including a searchable e-book, multiple-choice and true/false quizzes, chapter-by-chapter learning goals, interactivities, personal notes, tutorials, and more. Using the copy, paste, highlight, and sticky note features, students collect, organize, and customize their study plan content to optimize learning outcomes.

Study Plan   An innovative tool that helps students customize their own learning experience. Students can diagnose their knowledge pre- and post-test, identify the areas where they are weak, search contents of the entire learning package for content specific to the topic they're studying, and add these resources to their study plan. Students told us the act of creating a study plan is how they actually study and that having the opportunity to have everything in one place, with the ability to search, customize, and prioritize the class resources, was critical. No other publisher provides this type of tool and students told us, without a doubt, the Study Plan feature is the most valuable tool they have used to help them study.

e-Text   Now students can search the textbook online, too! When struggling with a concept or reviewing for an exam, students can conduct key word searches to quickly find the content they need.

Student CD-ROM

Every new copy of *Applied Statistics in Business and Economics,* Canadian Edition, comes with a CD-ROM featuring the software for Visual Statistics version 2.2, *LearningStats* version 3.0, MegaStat® for Excel 2007, and ScreenCam tutorials, a series of 15 screen-capture movies with voice-over introducing and showing how to use Excel, MINITAB, Visual Stats, and MegaStat for Excel.

McGraw-Hill Connect

Mc Graw Hill connect™

www.mcgrawhillconnect.ca McGraw-Hill Connect™ assessment activities don't stop with students! There is material for instructors to leverage as well, including a personalized teaching plan where instructors can choose from a variety of quizzes to use in class, assign as homework, or add to exams. Instructors can edit existing questions and add new ones; track individual student performance—by question, assignment, or in relation to the class overall—with detailed grade reports; integrate grade reports easily with Learning Management Systems such as WebCT and Blackboard; and much more. Instructors can also browse or search teaching resources and text specific supplements and organize them into customizable categories. All the teaching resources are now located in one convenient place.

Instructor Resources Available in *McGraw-Hill Connect*

Instructor Solutions Manual This manual contains the complete solutions to all exercises.

Computerized Test Bank The computerized test bank is available through EZ Test Online, a flexible and easy-to-use electronic testing program that allows instructors to create tests from book-specific items. EZ Test accommodates a wide range of question types and allows instructors to add their own questions. Test items are also available for use in Microsoft Word® (rich text format). For secure online testing, exams created in EZ Test can be exported to WebCT and Blackboard. EZ Test Online is supported at **www.mhhe.com/eztest** where users can download a Quick Start Guide, access FAQs, or log a ticket for help with specific issues.

Microsoft PowerPoint® Lecture Slides These full-colour slides include chapter objectives, definitions of key terms, graphics, and additional examples. Instructors can use them to enhance their lectures or add additional material of their own.

Lyryx Assessment for Business Statistics

LYRYX LEARNING INC
Online Learning and Assessment
lyryx.com

Lyryx is a leading-edge online homework assessment system that delivers significant benefits to both students and instructors. The assessment takes the form of a homework assignment called a Lab, which corresponds to the chapters in *Applied Statistics for Business and Economics,* Canadian Edition. The Labs are algorithmically generated and automatically graded, so students get instant scores and feedback. After registering their course with us, instructors can create labs of their choice by selecting problems based on their needs, and set a deadline for each one of these Labs. Instructors have access to all the students' marks and can view their best Labs. At any time, instructors can download the class grades for their own programs to analyze individual and class performance.

If students are doing their business statistics practice and homework, they will improve their performance in the course. Recent research regarding the use of Lyryx has shown that when Labs are tied to assessment, even if worth only a small percentage of the total grade for the course, students will do their homework—and even more than once. The result is improved success in business statistics!

*i*Learning Sales Specialist

Your Integrated-Learning Sales Specialist is a McGraw-Hill Ryerson representative who has the experience, product knowledge, training, and support to help you assess and integrate our products, technology, and services into your course for optimum teaching and learning performance. Whether it's how to use our test bank software, helping your students to improve their grades, or how to put your entire course online, your *i*Learning Sales Specialist is there to help. Contact your *i*Learning Sales Specialist today to learn how to maximize all McGraw-Hill Ryerson resources!

*i*Learning Services Program

McGraw-Hill Ryerson offers a unique services package designed for Canadian faculty. This includes technical support, access to our educational technology conferences, and custom e-courses to name just a few. Please speak to your local *i*Learning Sales Specialist for details.

Acknowledgments

The Canadian authors wish to thank the following reviewers for their invaluable insights during the development of *Applied Statistics in Business and Economics,* Canadian Edition.

Peter Au, *George Brown College*

Igor Averbakh, *University of Toronto at Scarborough*

Henry Bartel, *York University*

Richard Cho, *University of New Brunswick*

Eugene Choo, *University of Calgary*

Clare Chua-Chow, *Ryerson University*

Herbert Emery, *University of Calgary*

Ellen Fowler, *UBC/Simon Fraser*

Horand Gassmann, *Dalhousie University*

Daniel Gordon, *University of Calgary*

Paul Hobson, *Acadia University*

Chris Kellman, *BC Institute of Technology*

Stephan Kogitz, *Centennial College*

Ying Kong, *York University*

Hila Koren, *York University*

Ehsan Latif, *Thompson Rivers University*

John Nash, *University of Ottawa*

Tony Quon, *University of Ottawa*

Marie Rekkas, *Simon Fraser University*

Valerie Rochester, *Carleton University*

Rob Sorensen, *Camosun College*

George Stoica, *University of New Brunswick*

Manish Verma, *Memorial University*

Jiankang Zhang, *Carleton University*

The authors also wish to thank the team at McGraw-Hill Ryerson, including Kimberley Redhead and Jeremy Guimond, Sponsoring Editors; Sarah Fulton, Developmental Editor; Cathy Biribauer, Supervising Editor; Michael Kelly, Copy Editor; Julia Cochrane, Proofreader; Sheryl MacAdam, Production Co-ordinator; and Dr. Wayne Horn, Technical Checker.

Chapter

1

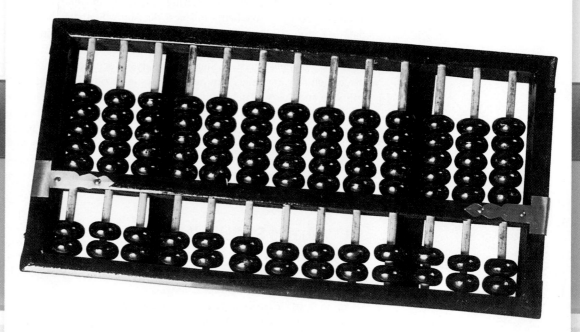

Overview of Statistics

Chapter Learning Objectives

When you finish this chapter you should be able to

1. Define statistics and explain some of its uses in business.

2. List reasons for a business student to study statistics.

3. State the common challenges facing data analysts.

4. Know the basic rules for effective writing and oral presentations.

5. List and explain common statistical pitfalls.

Prelude

When managers are well informed about a company's internal operations (e.g., sales, production, inventory levels, time to market, warranty claims) and competitive position (e.g., market share, customer satisfaction, repeat sales), they can take appropriate actions to improve their business. Managers need reliable, timely information so that they can analyze market trends and adjust to changing market conditions. Better data can also help a company decide which types of strategic information they should share with trusted business partners to improve their supply chain. *Statistics* and *statistical analysis* permit *data-based decision making* and reduce managers' need to rely on guesswork.

Statistics is a key component of the field of *business intelligence,* which encompasses all the technologies for collecting, storing, accessing, and analyzing data on the company's operations in order to make better business decisions. Statistics helps convert unstructured "raw" data (e.g., point-of-sale data, customer spending patterns) into *useful information* through online analytical processing (OLAP) and data mining, terms that you may have encountered in your other business classes. Statistical analysis focuses attention on key problems and guides discussion toward issues, not personalities or territorial struggles. While powerful database software and query systems are the key to managing a firm's data warehouse, relatively small Excel spreadsheets are often the focus of discussion among managers when it comes to "bottom line" decisions. That is why Excel is featured prominently in this textbook.

In short, companies increasingly are using business analytics to support decision making, to recognize anomalies that require tactical action, or to gain strategic insight to align business processes with business objectives. Businesses that combine managerial judgment with statistical analysis are more successful.

1.1   What Is Statistics?

Statistics is the science of collecting, organizing, analyzing, interpreting, and presenting data. Some experts prefer to call statistics *data science,* a trilogy of tasks involving data modelling, analysis, and decision making.

In contrast, a **statistic** is a single measure, reported as a number, used to summarize a sample data set. Many different measures can be used to summarize data sets. You will learn throughout this textbook that there can be different measures for different sets of data and different measures for different types of questions about the same data set. Consider, for example, a sample data set that consists of the high school GPAs of incoming first-year university business students. There could be many different uses for this data set. Perhaps the instructors of these students may be interested in the overall preparedness of their classes. The most relevant statistic in this case would be the incoming average GPA of these students. But to a student whose high school GPA is marginal at best, and who is considering applying to that program, the relevant statistic may be the minimum entering GPA. Both the average and the minimum are examples of a *statistic.*

You may not have a trained statistician in your organization, but any university graduate is expected to know something about statistics, and anyone who creates graphs or interprets data is "doing statistics" without an official title.

1.2   Why Study Statistics?

A 2006 *BusinessWeek* article called statistics and probability "core skills for businesspeople." In a *Wall Street Journal* survey, corporate recruiters said that the top five attributes they consider when recruiting business-school graduates were: (1) communication and interpersonal skills; (2) ability to work well within a team; (3) personal ethics and integrity; (4) analytical and problem-solving skills; and (5) work ethic. (See "Why Math Will Rock Your World," *BusinessWeek,* Jan. 23, 2006, p. 60; and *The Wall Street Journal,* Sept. 20, 2006.)

Knowing statistics will make you a better consumer of other people's data. You should know enough to handle everyday data problems, to feel confident that others cannot deceive you with spurious arguments, and to know when you've reached the limits of your expertise. Statistical knowledge gives your company a competitive advantage against organizations that cannot understand their internal or external market data. And mastery of basic statistics gives you, the individual manager, a competitive advantage as you work your way through the promotion process, or when you move to a new employer. Here are some more reasons to study statistics.

Communication   The language of statistics is widely used in science, social science, education, health care, engineering, and even the humanities. In all areas of business (e.g., accounting, finance, human resources, marketing, information systems, operations management), workers use statistical jargon to facilitate communication. In fact, statistical terminology has reached the highest corporate strategic levels (e.g., "Six Sigma" at GE and Motorola). And in the multinational environment, the specialized vocabulary of statistics permeates language barriers to improve problem solving across international boundaries.

Computer Skills   Whatever your computer skill level, it can be improved. Every time you create a spreadsheet for data analysis, write a report, or make an oral presentation, you bring together skills you already have, as well as learn new skills. Specialists with advanced training design the databases and decision support systems, but you must expect to handle daily data problems *without* experts. Besides, you can't always find an "expert," and if you do, the "expert" may not understand your application very well. You need to be able to analyze data, use software with confidence, prepare your own charts, write your own reports, and make electronic presentations on technical topics.

Information Management   Statistics can help you handle either too little or too much information. When insufficient data are available, statistical surveys and samples can be used to obtain the necessary market information. But most large organizations are closer to drowning in data than starving for it. Statistics can help summarize large amounts of data and reveal underlying relationships. You've heard of data mining? Statistics is the pick and shovel that you take to the data mine.

Technical Literacy   Many of the best career opportunities are in growth industries propelled by advanced technology. Marketing staff may work with engineers, scientists, and manufacturing experts as new products and services are developed. Sales representatives must understand and explain to potential customers technical products like pharmaceuticals, medical equipment, and industrial tools. Purchasing managers must evaluate suppliers' claims about the quality of raw materials, components, software, or parts.

Career Advancement   Whenever there are customers to whom services are delivered, statistical literacy can enhance your career mobility. Multibillion-dollar companies like Microsoft and Walmart use statistics to control cost, achieve efficiency, and improve quality. Without a solid understanding of data and statistical measures, you may be left behind.

Quality Improvement   Large manufacturing firms have formal systems for continuous quality improvement. The same is true of insurance companies and financial service firms. Statistics helps firms oversee their suppliers, monitor their internal operations, and identify problems. Quality improvement goes far beyond statistics, but every university graduate is expected to know enough statistics to understand its role in quality improvement.

Mini Case 1.1

Can Statistics Predict Airfares?

When you book an airline ticket online, does it annoy you when the next day you find a cheaper fare on exactly the same flight? Or do you congratulate yourself when you get a "good" fare followed by a price rise? This ticket price volatility led to the creation of an Internet start-up company called Farecast, which examines over 150 billion "airfare observations" and tries to use the data to predict whether the fare for a given ticket is likely to rise. The company's prediction accuracy so far is estimated at 61 percent (in independent tests) and 75 percent (the company's tests). In this case, the benchmark is a coin toss (50 percent). The company offers price-rise insurance for a small price. If you travel a lot and like to play the odds, such predictions could save money. With online air bookings at $44 billion, a few dollars saved here and there can add up. (See *Budget Travel,* Feb. 2007, p. 37; and *The New York Times,* "An Insurance Policy for Low Airfares," Jan. 22, 2007, p. C10.)

1.3   Uses of Statistics

There are two primary kinds of statistics:

- **Descriptive statistics** refers to the collection, organization, presentation, and summary of data (either using charts and graphs or using a numerical summary).
- **Inferential statistics** refers to generalizing from a sample to a population, estimating unknown parameters, drawing conclusions, and making decisions.

Figure 1.1 identifies the tasks and the text chapters for each.

Now let's look at some of the ways that statistics is used in business and the questions that statistics can address.

Auditing   A large firm pays over 12,000 invoices to suppliers every month. The firm has learned that some invoices are being paid incorrectly, but they don't know how widespread the problem is. The auditors lack the resources to check all the invoices, so they decide to take a sample to estimate the proportion of incorrectly paid invoices. How large should the sample be for the auditors to be confident that the estimate is close enough to the true proportion?

Marketing   A marketing consultant is asked to identify likely repeat customers for Amazon. ca, and to suggest co-marketing opportunities based on a database containing records of 5 million Internet purchases of books, CDs, and DVDs. How can this large database be mined to reveal useful patterns that might guide the marketing strategy?

Health Care   An outpatient cognitive retraining clinic for victims of closed-head injuries or stroke evaluates 100 incoming patients using a 42-item physical and mental assessment questionnaire. Each patient is evaluated independently by two experienced therapists. From their evaluations, can we conclude that the therapists agree on the patients' functional status? Are some assessment questions redundant? Do the initial assessment scores accurately predict the patients' lengths of stay in the program?

Quality Control   A manufacturer of rolled copper tubing for radiators wishes to improve its product quality. It initiates a triple inspection program, sets penalties for workers who produce poor-quality output, and posts a slogan calling for "zero defects." The approach fails. Why?

Purchasing   A retailer's shipment of 200 DVD players reveals 4 with defects. The supplier's historical defect rate is 0.005. Has the defect rate really risen, or is this simply a "bad batch"?

Medicine   An experimental drug to treat asthma is given to 75 patients, of whom 24 get better. A placebo is given to a control group of 75 volunteers, of whom 12 get better. Is the new drug better than the placebo, or is the difference within the realm of chance?

FIGURE 1.1

Overview of Statistics

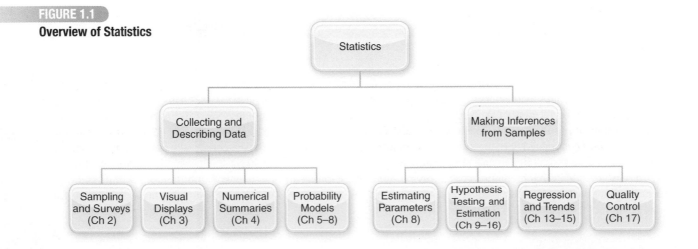

Forecasting The Home Depot carries 50,000 different products. To manage this vast inventory, it needs a weekly order-forecasting system that can respond to developing patterns in consumer demand. Is there a way to predict weekly demand and place orders from suppliers for every item, without an unreasonable commitment of staff time?

Mini Case   1.2

How Do You Sell Noodles with Statistics?

"The best answer starts with a thorough and thoughtful analysis of the data." Aaron Kennedy, founder and chairman of Noodles & Company.

Noodles & Company is the new model for the *quick casual* restaurant concept. The company is setting the standard for modern casual dining in the 21st century. Noodles & Company first opened in Colorado in 1995 and has not stopped growing since. As of June 2007, there were over 150 restaurants all across the United States.

   Noodles & Company has achieved this success with a customer-driven business model and fact-based decision making. Their widespread popularity and high growth rate have been supported by careful consideration of data and thorough statistical analysis that provide answers to questions such as:

- Should we offer continuity/loyalty cards for our customers?
- How can we increase the use of our extra capacity during the dinner hours?
- Which new city should we open in?
- Which location should we choose for the new restaurant?
- How do we determine the effectiveness of a marketing campaign?
- Which meal maximizes the chance that a new customer will return?
- Are Rice Krispies related to higher sales?
- Does reducing service time increase sales?

   Aaron Kennedy, founder and chairman of Noodles & Company, says that "using data is the strongest way to inform good decisions. By assessing our internal and external environments on a continuous basis, our Noodles management team has been able to plan and execute our vision."

   "I had no idea as a business student that I'd be using statistical analysis as extensively as I do now," says Dave Boennighausen, director of finance at Noodles & Company. In the coming chapters, as you learn about the statistical tools businesses use today, look for the Noodles logo 🍜 next to examples and exercises that show how Noodles uses data and statistical methods in its business functions.

Product Warranty   A major automaker wants to know the average dollar cost of engine warranty claims on a new hybrid engine. It has collected warranty cost data on 4,300 warranty claims during the first 6 months after the engines are introduced. Using these warranty claims as an estimate of future costs, what is the margin of error associated with this estimate?

1.4 Statistical Challenges

Business professionals who use statistics are not mere number crunchers who are "good at math." As Jon Kettenring succinctly said, "Industry needs holistic statisticians who are nimble problem solvers" (www.amstat.org). Consider the criteria listed below:

The ideal data analyst

- Is technologically current (e.g., software-wise).
- Communicates well.
- Is proactive.
- Has a broad outlook.
- Is flexible.
- Focuses on the main problem.
- Meets deadlines.
- Knows his/her limitations and is willing to ask for help.
- Can deal with imperfect information.
- Has professional integrity.

Clearly, many of these characteristics would apply to *any* business professional.

Working with Imperfect Data

In mathematics, exact answers are expected. But statistics lies at the messy interface between theory and reality. For instance, suppose a new air bag design is being tested. Is the new air bag design safer for children? Test data indicate the design may be safer in some crash situations, but the old design appears safer in others. The crash tests are expensive and time-consuming, so the sample size is limited. A few observations are missing due to sensor failures in the crash dummies. There may be random measurement errors. If you are the data analyst, what can you do? Well, you can know and use generally accepted statistical methods, clearly state any assumptions you are forced to make, and honestly point out the limitations of your analysis. You can use statistical tests to detect unusual data points or to deal with missing data. You can give a range of answers under varying assumptions. But occasionally, you need the courage to say, "No useful answer can emerge from this data."

Dealing with Practical Constraints

You will face constraints on the type and quantity of data you can collect. Automobile crash tests can't use human subjects (*too risky*). Telephone surveys can't ask a female respondent whether or not she has had an abortion (*sensitive question*). We can't test everyone for HIV (*the world is not a laboratory*). Survey respondents may not tell the truth or may not answer all the questions (*human behaviour is unpredictable*). Every analyst faces constraints of time and money (*research is not free*).

Upholding Ethical Standards

Safeguards are in place not only to protect professional integrity but also to minimize ethical breaches. All data analysts must

- Know and follow accepted procedures.
- Maintain data integrity.

- Carry out accurate calculations.
- Report procedures faithfully.
- Protect confidential information.
- Cite sources.
- Acknowledge sources of financial support.

Further, because legal and ethical issues are intertwined, there are specific ethical guidelines for statisticians concerning treatment of human and animal subjects, privacy protection, obtaining informed consent, and guarding against inappropriate uses of data.

Ethical dilemmas for a non-statistician are likely to involve conflicts of interest or competing interpretations of the validity of a study and/or its implications. For example, suppose a market research firm is hired to investigate a new corporate logo. The CEO lets you know that she strongly favours a new logo, and it's a big project that could earn you a promotion. Yet, the market data have a high error margin and could support either conclusion. As a manager, you will face such situations. Statistical practices and statistical data can clarify your choices.

Using Consultants

Someone once said the main thing you need to know about statisticians is when to call for one. An hour with an expert at the *beginning* of a project could be the smartest move a manager can make. When should a consultant be hired? When your team lacks certain critical skills, or when an unbiased or informed view cannot be found inside your organization. Expert consultants can handle domineering or indecisive team members, personality clashes, fears about diverse findings, and local politics. Large and medium-sized companies may have in-house statisticians, but smaller firms only hire them as needed. If you hire a statistical expert, you can make better use of the consultant's time by learning how consultants work. Read books about statistical consulting. If your company employs a statistician, take him or her to lunch!

Section Exercises

1.1 Select *two* of the following scenarios. Explain why you selected each, and give an example of how statistics might be useful to the person in the scenario. (LO 1)
   a. An auditor is looking for inflated broker commissions in stock transactions.
   b. An industrial marketer is representing her firm's compact, new low-power LCD screens to the military.
   c. A plant manager is studying absenteeism at assembly plants in three provinces.
   d. An automotive purchasing agent is comparing defect rates in steel shipments from three vendors of steel.
   e. A personnel executive is examining job turnover by gender in a fast-food chain.
   f. An intranet manager is studying e-mail usage rates by employee job classification.
   g. A retirement planner is studying mutual fund performance for six different types of asset portfolios.
   h. A hospital administrator is studying surgery scheduling to improve facility utilization rates.

1.2 (a) Should the average business-school graduate expect to use computers to manipulate data, or is this a job better left to specialists? (b) What problems arise when an employee is weak in quantitative skills? Based on your experience, is that common? (LO 2)

1.3 "Many university graduates will not use very much statistics during their 40-year careers, so why study it?" (a) List several arguments for and against this statement. Which position do you find more convincing? (b) Replace the word "statistics" with "accounting" or "foreign language" and repeat this exercise. (c) On the Internet, look up the Latin phrase *reductio ad absurdum*. How is this phrase relevant here? (LO 2)

1.4 How can statistics help organizations deal with (a) information overload? (b) insufficient information? Give an example from a job you have held where statistics might have been useful. (LO 2)

Lessons from NASA

Given incomplete or contradictory data, people have trouble making decisions (remember *Hamlet?*). Sometimes the correct choice is obvious in retrospect, as in NASA's space shuttle disasters. On January 28, 1986, *Challenger* exploded shortly after takeoff, due to erosion of O-rings that had become brittle in freezing overnight temperatures at Cape Canaveral, Florida. The crux of the matter was a statistical relationship between brittleness and temperature. Data on O-ring erosion were available for 22 prior shuttle flights. The backup O-rings (there were two layers of O-rings) had suffered no erosion in 9 prior flights at launch temperatures in the range of 22°C–27°C but significant erosion in 4 of 13 prior flights at temperatures in the range 12°C–21°C. However, the role of temperature was by no means clear. NASA and Morton-Thiokol engineers had debated the erratic data inconclusively, including the night before the launch.

After the *Challenger* accident, it was clear that the risk was underestimated. Two *statistical* issues were (1) the degree to which backup layer O-rings provided redundant protection and (2) the correct way to predict O-ring erosion at the *Challenger* launch temperature of 2°C when the lowest previous launch temperature had been 12°C. Two possible *ethical* issues were that NASA officials did not scrub the launch until they understood the problem better and that the astronauts, as participants in a dangerous experiment, had insufficient opportunity for informed consent. NASA's 100 percent previous success record was undoubtedly a factor in everyone's self-confidence, including the astronauts'.

On February 1, 2003, space shuttle *Columbia* burned on re-entry. The heat shield failure was apparently due to tiles damaged by falling foam insulation from the fuel tanks, loosened by vibration during launch. Prior to the *Columbia* disaster in 2003, foam-damaged tiles had been noted 70 times in 112 flights. In retrospect, review of the data showed that some previous flights may have come close to *Columbia*'s fate. This is a *statistical* issue because the heat shield had worked 70 times despite being damaged. Is it surprising that NASA officials believed that the tiles were resistant to foam damage? The statistical and ethical issues are similar to those in the *Challenger* disaster. Organizational inertia and pressure to launch have been blamed in both cases, favouring a risky interpretation of the data.

These disasters remind us that decisions involving data and statistics are always embedded in organizational culture. NASA's evaluation of risk differs from most businesses, due to the dangers inherent in its cutting-edge exploration of space. At the time of the *Challenger* launch, the risk of losing a vehicle was estimated at 1 in 30. At the time of the *Columbia* re-entry accident, the risk was estimated at 1 in 145. For non-human launches the risk is about 1 in 50 (2 percent) compared with 2 space shuttle losses in 113 flights (1.8 percent). By comparison, the risk of losing a commercial airline flight is about 1 in 2,000,000.

Sources: yahoo.com; www.nasa.gov; *The New York Times,* February 2, 2003.

1.5   Writing and Presenting Reports

Business recruiters say that written and oral communication skills are critical for success in business. Susan R. Meisinger, president and CEO of the Society for Human Resource Management, says that "In a knowledge-based economy a talented workforce with communication and critical thinking skills is necessary for organizations . . . to be successful." Yet a survey of 431 human resource officials in corporate America found a need for improvement in writing (www.conference-board.org). Table 1.1 lists the key business skills needed for *initial* and *long-range* success, as well as some common *weaknesses*.

TABLE 1.1   Skills Needed for Success in Business

For Initial Job Success	For Long-Range Job Success	Common Weaknesses
Report writing	Managerial accounting	Communication skills
Accounting principles	Managerial economics	Writing skills
Mathematics	Managerial finance	Immaturity
Statistics	Oral communication	Unrealistic expectations

Can You Read a Company Annual Report?

Many people say that company annual reports are hard to read. To investigate this claim, Prof. Feng Li of the University of Michigan's Ross School of Business analyzed the readability of more than 50,000 annual reports. One of his readability measures was the Gunning-Fog Index (GFI), which estimates how many years of formal education would be needed in order to read and understand a block of text. For company annual reports, the average GFI was 19.4. Since a student with a Bachelor's degree will have approximately 16 years of education, almost a PhD level of education is apparently required to read a typical firm's annual report. Li also found that annual reports of firms with lower earnings were harder to read. (See http://accounting.smartpros.com/x53453.xml; and *Detroit Free Press,* June 7, 2006, p. E1.)

Rules for "Power" Writing

Why is writing so important? Because someone may mention your report on warranty repairs during a meeting of department heads, and your boss may say "OK, make copies of that report so that we can all see it." Next thing you know, the CEO is looking at it! Wish you'd taken more care in writing it? To avoid this awkward situation, set aside 25 percent of your allotted project time to *write* the report. You should always outline the report *before* you begin. Then complete the report in sections. Finally, ask trusted peers to review the report, and make revisions as necessary. Keep in mind that you may need to revise more than once. If you have trouble getting started, consult a good reference on technical-report writing.

While you may have creative latitude in how to organize the flow of ideas in the report, it is essential to answer the assigned question succinctly. Describe what you did and what conclusions you reached, listing the most important results first.

Use section headings to group related material and avoid lengthy paragraphs. Your report is your legacy to others who may rely on it. They will find it instructive to know about difficulties you encountered. Provide clear data so that others will not need to waste time checking your data and sources. Consider placing technical details in an appendix to keep the main report simple.

If you are writing the report as part of a team, an "editor-in-chief" must be empowered to edit the material so that it is stylistically consistent, has a common voice, and flows together. Allow enough lead time so that all team members can read the final report and give their comments and corrections to the editor-in-chief.

Avoid Jargon   Experts use jargon to talk to one another, but outsiders may find it obscure or even annoying. Technical concepts must be presented so that others can understand them. If you can't communicate the importance of your work, your potential for advancement will be limited. Even if your ideas are good and hundreds of hours went into your analysis, readers up the food chain will toss your report aside if it contains too many cryptic references like SSE, MAPE, or 3-Sigma Limits.

Make It Attractive   Reports should have a title page, descriptive title, date, and author names. It's a good idea to use footers with page numbers and dates (e.g., Page 7 of 23—Draft of 10/10/09) to distinguish revised drafts.

Use wide margins so that readers can take notes or write comments. Select an appropriate typeface and point size. Times Roman, Garamond, and Arial are widely accepted.

Call attention to your main points by using subheadings, bullets, **boldfaced type,** *italics,* large fonts, or **colour,** but use special effects sparingly.

Watch Your Spelling and Grammar   To an educated reader, incorrect grammar or spelling errors are conspicuous signs of sloppy work. You don't recognize your errors—that's why you make them. Get someone you trust to red-pencil your work. Study your errors until you're sure you won't repeat them. Your best bet? Keep a dictionary handy! You can refer to it for both proper spelling and grammatical usage. Remember that Microsoft specializes in software, not English, so don't rely on spelling and grammar checkers. Here are some examples from student papers that passed the spell-checker, but each contains two errors. Can you spot them quickly?

Original	*Correction*
• "It's effects will transcend our nation's boarders."	(its, borders)
• "We cannot except this shipment on principal."	(accept, principle)
• "They seceded despite there faults."	(succeeded, their)
• "This plan won't fair well because it's to rigid."	(fare, too)
• "The amount of unhappy employees is raising."	(number, rising)

Organizing a Technical Report

Report formats vary, but a business report usually begins with an *executive summary* limited to a *single page.* Attach the full report containing discussion, explanations, tables, graphs, interpretations, and (if needed) footnotes and appendices. Use appendices for backup material. There is no single acceptable style for a business report but the following would be typical:

- Executive summary (1 page maximum)
- Introduction (1 to 3 paragraphs)
  - Statement of the problem
  - Data sources and definitions
  - Methods utilized
- Body of the report (as long as necessary)
  - Discussion, explanations, interpretations
  - Tables and graphs, as needed
  - Conclusions (1 to 3 paragraphs)
- Statement of findings (in order of importance)
  - Limitations (if necessary)
  - Future research suggestions
- Bibliography and sources
- Appendices (if needed for lengthy or technical material)

Writing an Executive Summary

The goal of an **executive summary** is to permit a busy decision maker to understand what you did and what you found out *without reading the rest of the report.* In a statistical report, the executive summary *briefly* describes the task and goals, data and data sources, methods that were used, main findings of the analysis, and (if necessary) any limitations of the analysis. The main findings will occupy most of the space in the executive summary. Each other item may only rate a sentence or two. The executive summary is limited to a single page (maybe only two or three paragraphs) and should avoid technical language.

An excellent way to evaluate your executive summary is to hand it to a peer. Ask him/her to read it and then tell you what you did and what you found out. If the peer cannot answer precisely, then your summary is deficient. The executive summary must make it *impossible to miss your main findings.* Your boss may judge you and your team by the executive summary alone. S/he may merely leaf through the report to examine key tables or graphs, or may assign someone to review your full report.

Tables and Graphs

Tables should be embedded in the narrative (*not* on a separate page) near the paragraph in which they are cited. Each table should have a number and title. Graphs should be embedded in the narrative (*not* on a separate page) near the paragraph in which they are discussed. Each table or graph should have a title and number. A graph may make things clearer.

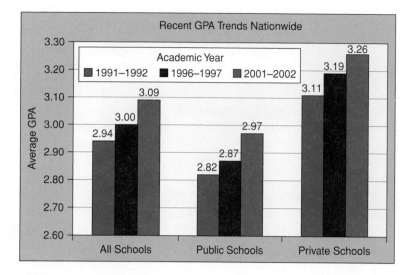

FIGURE 1.2

Pictures Help Make the Point

Source: Copyright © 2005 Stuart Rojstaczer. Used with permission.

Rules for Presenting Oral Reports

The goals of an oral report are *not the same* as those of a written report. Your oral presentation must only *highlight* the main points. If your presentation does not provide the answer to an audience question, you can say, "Good question. We don't have time to discuss that further here, but it's covered in the full report. I'll be happy to talk to you about it at the end of the presentation." Or, give a brief answer so that they know you did consider the matter. Keep these tips in mind while preparing your oral presentation:

- Select just a few key points you most want to convey.
- Use simple charts and diagrams to get the point across (as in Figure 1.2).
- Use **colour** and *fonts* creatively to emphasize a point.
- Levity is nice on occasion, but avoid gratuitous jokes.
- Have backup slides or transparencies just in case.
- Rehearse to get the timing right (don't go too long).
- Refer the audience to the written report for details.
- Imagine yourself in the audience. Don't bore yourself!

The Three Ps

Pace   Many presenters speak too rapidly—partly because they are nervous and partly because they think it makes them look smarter.

   Slow down! Take a little time to introduce yourself, introduce your data, and explain what you are trying to do. If you skip the basic background and definitions, many members of the audience will not be able to follow the presentation and will have only a vague idea what you are talking about.

Planning   Create an outline to organize the ideas you want to discuss. Remember to keep it simple! You'll also need to prepare a verbal "executive summary" to tell your audience what your talk is about. Before you choose your planned opening words, "*Our team correlated robbery with income,*" you should ask yourself:

- Is the audience familiar with correlation analysis?
- Should I explain that our data came from CSIS and the 2001 Census of Canada?
- Will they know that our observations are averages for the 10 provinces?
- Will they know that we are talking about per capita robbery rates (not total robberies)?
- Will they know that we are using per capita personal income (not median family income)?
- Should I show them a few data values to help them visualize the data?

Don't bury them in detail, but make the first minute count. If you ran into problems or made errors in your analysis, it's fine to say so. The audience will sympathize.

Check the raw data carefully—you may be called on to answer questions. It's hard to defend yourself when you failed to catch serious errors or didn't understand a key definition.

Practice   Rehearse the oral presentation to get the timing right. Maybe your employer will send you to training classes to bolster your presentation skills. Otherwise, consider videotaping yourself or practising in front of a few peers for valuable feedback. Technical presentations may demand skills different from the ones you used in English class, so don't panic if you have a few problems.

Section Exercises

1.5   Discuss and criticize each of these two executive summaries from student reports, noting both good and bad points. Is the summary succinct? Was the purpose of the investigation clear? Were the methods explained? Are the main findings stated clearly? Were any limitations of the study noted? Is jargon a problem? How might each summary be improved? (LO 4)

   a. "We weighed 10 Tootsie Rolls chosen randomly without replacement from a finite population of 290. The sample mean was calculated at 3.3048 grams and the sample standard deviation was 0.1320 grams. A 95 percent confidence interval using Student's t without FPCF was 3.2119 grams to 3.3977 grams."

   b. "The November issue of *Money* magazine contained an estimated proportion of pages with advertisements of between 53 percent and 67 percent with an estimated mean advertisements per page between 0.5 and 1.3. The November issue consisted of 222 pages, and the sample consisted of the first 100 even-numbered pages."

1.6   (a) Which of these two displays (table or graph) is more helpful in describing the salad sales by Noodles & Company? Why?
   (b) Write a one-sentence summary of the data. (*Source:* Noodles & Company) (LO 4) **NoodlesSalad**

2005 Average Daily Salads Sold by Month, Noodles & Company

Month	Salads	Month	Salads
Jan	2847	Jul	2554
Feb	2735	Aug	2370
Mar	2914	Sep	2131
Apr	3092	Oct	1990
May	3195	Nov	1979
Jun	3123	Dec	1914

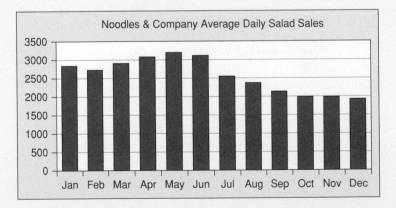

1.7   Go to the Web and use your favourite search engine to look up key words like "technical writing" or "scientific reports." Print one or two excerpts from Web sites that you found particularly interesting or useful, and write a few sentences explaining why you liked them. (LO 4)

1.8   Cite a situation from your work, daily life, or general reading where numerical facts could be presented in more than one way. What were the ethical implications for each alternative? How was it resolved? What was the result? (LO 4)

1.6 Critical Thinking

Statistics is an essential part of **critical thinking**, because it allows us to test an idea against empirical evidence. Random occurrences and chance variation inevitably lead to occasional outcomes that could support one viewpoint or another. But the science of statistics tells us whether the sample evidence is convincing. In this book, you will learn how to use statistics correctly in accordance with professional standards to make the best decision.

> "Critical thinking means being able to evaluate evidence, to tell fact from opinion, to see holes in an argument, to tell whether cause and effect has been established, and to spot illogic."
> *The Wall Street Journal,* October 20, 2006.

We use statistical tools to compare our prior ideas with **empirical data** (data collected through observations and experiments). If the data do not support our theory, we can reject or revise our theory. In *The Globe and Mail,* in *Report on Business* magazine, and on CBC you see stock market experts with theories to "explain" the current market (bull, bear, or pause). But each year brings new experts and new theories, and the old ones vanish. Logical pitfalls abound in both the data collection process and the reasoning process. Let's look at some.

Pitfall 1: Conclusions from Small Samples

"My Aunt Harriet smoked all her life and lived to 90. Smoking doesn't hurt you." Good for her. But does one case prove anything? Five customers are asked if the new product design is an improvement. If three say yes, should the company implement the new design? If 10 patients try a new asthma medication and one gets a rash, can we conclude that the medication caused the rash? How large a sample is needed to make reliable conclusions? Fortunately statisticians have developed clear rules about sample sizes. Until you learn them, it's fine to raise your Stanley Cup hopes when your favourite hockey team wins five games in a row.

Pitfall 2: Conclusions from Non-random Samples

"Rock stars die young. Look at Buddy Holly, Jimi Hendrix, Janis Joplin, Jim Morrison, John Lennon, and Kurt Cobain." But we are looking only at those who *did* die young. What about the thousands who are alive and well or who lived long lives? Similarly, we should be careful about generalizing from retrospective studies of people who have heart attacks, unless we also study those who do not have heart attacks. (From Arnold Barnett, "How Numbers Can Trick You," *Technology Review,* Oct. 1994, p. 40.)

Pitfall 3: Conclusions from Rare Events

Unlikely events happen if we take a large enough sample. Yet some people draw strong inferences from events that are not surprising when looking at the entire population.

- "Mary in my office won the lottery. Her system must have worked." Millions of people play the lottery. Someone will eventually win.
- "Bill's a sports genius. He predicted every Montreal Canadiens win last season." Millions of sports fans make predictions. A few of them will call every game correctly.
- "Tom's SUV rolled over. SUVs are dangerous." Millions of people drive SUVs, so some will roll over.

Pitfall 4: Poor Survey Methods

Did your instructor ever ask a question like "How many of you remember the simplex method from your math class?" One or two timid hands (or maybe none) are raised, even though the topic was covered. Did the math department not teach the simplex method? Or did students not "get it"? More likely, the instructor has used a poor sampling method and a vaguely worded question. It's difficult for students to respond to such a question in public, for they assume (often correctly) that if they raise a hand the instructor is going to ask them to explain it, or that their peers will think they are showing off. An anonymous survey or a quiz on the simplex method would provide better insight.

Pitfall 5: Assuming a Causal Link

In your economics class, you may have learned about the post hoc fallacy (the mistaken conclusion that if *A* precedes *B* then *A* is the *cause* of *B*). For example, the divorce rate in Mississippi fell in 2005 after Hurricane Katrina. Did the hurricane cause couples to stay together? A little research reveals that the divorce rate had been falling for the previous two years, so Hurricane Katrina could hardly be credited.

The *post hoc fallacy* is a special case of the general fallacy of *assuming causation* anytime there is a *statistical association* between events. For example, there is the "curse of the ball field," which says that teams who play in named ballparks (e.g., Citi Field for the New York Mets) tend to lose more games than they win (see *The New York Times,* Nov. 15, 2006, p. C16). Perhaps in a statistical sense this may be true. But it is actually the players and managers who determine whether a team wins. Association does not prove causation. You've probably heard that. But many people draw unwarranted conclusions when no cause-and-effect link exists. Consider anecdotes like these:

- "Murder rates were higher during the full moon in Vancouver last year. I guess the moon makes people crazy." But what about cities that saw a *decrease* in murders during the same full moon?

- "Most shark attacks occur between 12 noon and 2 p.m. Sharks must be hungrier then." Maybe it's just that more people go swimming near midday. If a causal link exists, it would have to be shown in a carefully controlled experiment.

On the other hand, association may warrant further study when common sense suggests a potential causal link. For example, many people believed that smoking was harmful decades before scientists showed *how* smoking leads to cancer, heart disease, and emphysema. A cellphone user who develops cancer might blame the phones, yet almost everyone uses cellphones, and very few get cancer. A statistical analysis should consider factors like occupation, smoking, alcohol use, birth control pills, diet, and exercise.

Pitfall 6: Generalizations about Individuals

"Men are taller than women." Yes, but only in a statistical sense. Men are taller *on average,* but many women are taller than many men. "Japanese cars have high quality." Yes, but not all of them. We should avoid reading too much into statistical generalizations. Instead, ask how much *overlap* is in the populations that are being considered. Often, the similarities transcend the differences.

Pitfall 7: Unconscious Bias

Without obvious fraud (tampering with data), researchers can unconsciously or subtly allow bias to colour their handling of data. For example, for many years it was assumed that heart attacks were more likely to occur in men than women. But symptoms of heart disease are usually more obvious in men than women, and so doctors tend to catch heart disease earlier in men. Studies now show that heart disease is the number-one cause of death in women over the age of 25. (See Lori Mosca et al., "Evidence-based Guidelines for Cardio-vascular Disease Prevention in Women," *American Heart Association* 109, no. 5 (Feb. 2004), pp. 672–93.)

Pitfall 8: Significance versus Importance

Statistically significant effects may lack practical importance. A study of over 500,000 Austrian military recruits showed that those born in the spring averaged 0.6 cm taller than those born in the fall (J. Utts, *The American Statistician,* vol. 57, no. 2 (May 2003), pp. 74–79). But who would notice? Would prospective parents change their timing in hopes of having a child 0.6 cm taller? Cost-conscious businesses know that some product improvements cannot support a valid business case. Consumers cannot perceive small improvements in durability, speed, taste, and comfort if the products already are "good enough." For example, Seagate's Cheetah 147GB disk drive already has a mean time between failure (MTBF) rating of 1.4 million hours (about 160 years in continuous use). Would a 10 percent improvement in MTBF matter to anyone?

Section Exercises

1.9 "Radar detector users have a lower accident rate than non-users. Moreover, detector users seem to be better citizens. The study found that detector users wear their seat belts more and even vote more than non-users." (a) Assuming that the study is accurate, do you think there is cause-and-effect? (b) If everyone used radar detectors, would voting rates and seat-belt usage rise? (LO 5)

1.10 A lottery winner told how he picked his six-digit winning number (5-6-8-10-22-39): number of people in his family, birth date of his wife, school grade of his 13-year-old daughter, sum of his birth date and his wife's, number of years of marriage, and year of his birth. He said, "I try to pick numbers that mean something to me." The Lottery Commissioner called this method "the screwiest I ever heard of . . . but apparently it works." (a) From a statistical viewpoint, do you agree that this method "works"? (b) Based on your understanding of how a lottery works, would someone who picks 1-2-3-4-5-6 because "it is easy to remember" have a lower chance of winning? (LO 5)

1.11 "Smokers are much more likely to speed, run red lights, and get involved in car accidents than non-smokers." (a) Can you think of reasons why this statement might be misleading? *Hint:* Make a list of six factors that you think would cause car accidents. Is smoking on your list? (b) Can you suggest a causal link between smoking and car accidents? (LO 5)

1.12 An ad for a cellphone service claims that its percent of "dropped calls" was significantly lower than its main competitor. In the fine print, the percents were given as 1.2 percent versus 1.4 percent. Is this reduction likely to be *important* to customers (as opposed to being *significant*)? (LO 5)

1.13 What logical or ethical problems do you see in these hypothetical scenarios? (LO 5)
   a. Dolon Privacy Consultants concludes that its employees are not loyal because a few random samples of employee e-mails contained comments critical of the company's management.
   b. Calchas Financial Advisors issues a glowing report of its new stock market forecasting system, based on testimonials of five happy customers.
   c. Five sanitation crew members at Malcheon Hospital are asked to try a new cleaning solvent to see if it has any allergic or other harmful side effects.
   d. A consumer group rates a new personal watercraft from Thetis Aquatic Conveyances as "Unacceptable" because two Ontario teens lost control and crashed into a dock.

1.7 Statistics: An Evolving Field

Statistics is a relatively young field, having been developed mostly during the 20th century, although its roots hearken back several centuries to early mathematicians in China and India. Its mathematical frontiers continue to expand, aided by the power of computers. Major developments of the late 20th century include exploratory data analysis (EDA), computer-intensive statistics, design of experiments, robust product design, advanced Bayesian methods, graphical methods, and data mining. In this book you will only get a glimpse of statistical methods and applications. But you can find many reference works that tell the story of statistics and famous statisticians. The Web has many resources, including university statistics Web sites and biographies of famous statisticians.

CHAPTER SUMMARY

Statistics is the science of collecting, organizing, analyzing, interpreting, and presenting data. A **statistician** is an expert with at least a master's degree in mathematics or statistics, while a **data analyst** is anyone who works with data. **Descriptive statistics** is the collection, organization, presentation, and summary of data with charts or numerical summaries. **Inferential statistics** refers to generalizing from a sample to a population, estimating unknown parameters, drawing conclusions, and making decisions. Statistics is used in all branches of business. **Statistical challenges** include imperfect data, practical constraints, and ethical dilemmas. Effective **technical-report writing** requires attention to style, grammar, organization, and proper use of tables and graphs. Business data analysts must learn to write a good **executive summary** and learn the *3 Ps* for oral presentations: pace, planning, and practice. Statistical tools are used to test theories against empirical data. Pitfalls include non-random samples, incorrect sample size, and lack of causal links. The field of statistics is relatively new and continues to grow as mathematical frontiers expand.

KEY TERMS

critical thinking, *13*
descriptive statistics, *4*
empirical data, *13*

executive summary, *10*
inferential statistics, *4*
post hoc fallacy, *14*

statistic, *2*
statistics, *2*
statistical generalization, *14*

CHAPTER REVIEW

1. Define (a) statistic; (b) statistics. (LO 1)

2. List three reasons to study statistics. (LO 2)

3. List three applications of statistics. (LO 1)

4. List four skills needed by statisticians. Why are these skills important? (LO 3)

5. List five rules for good writing. Why are good writing skills important? (LO 4)

6. (a) List some typical components of a technical report. (b) What does an executive summary include? What is its purpose? (LO 4)

7. (a) List three rules for using tables and graphs. (b) List three tips for making effective oral reports. (LO 4)

8. List three challenges faced by statisticians. (LO 3)

9. List five pitfalls or logical errors that may ensnare the unwary statistician. (LO 5)

CHAPTER EXERCISES

1.14 A survey of beginning students showed that a majority strongly agreed with the statement, "I am afraid of statistics." Why might this attitude exist among students who have not yet taken a statistics class? Would a similar attitude exist toward an ethics class? Explain your reasoning. (LO 1)

1.15 Under a recent U.S. Food and Drug Administration (FDA) standard for food contaminants, 3.5 ounces of tomato sauce can have up to 30 fly eggs, and 11 ounces of wheat flour can contain 450 insect fragments. How could statistical sampling be used to see that these standards of food hygiene are not violated by producers? (LO 1)

1.16 A statistical consultant was retained by a linen supplier to analyze a survey of hospital purchasing managers. After looking at the data, she realized that the survey had missed several key geographic areas and included some that were outside the target region. Some survey questions were ambiguous. Some respondents failed to answer all the questions or gave silly replies (one manager said he worked 40 hours a day). Of the 1,000 surveys mailed, only 80 were returned. (a) What alternatives are available to the statistician? (b) Might an imperfect analysis be better than none? (c) If you were the consultant, how might you respond to the supplier? (LO 3)

1.17 Ergonomics is the science of making sure that human surroundings are adapted to human needs. How could statistics play a role in the following: (LO 2)
   a. Choosing the height of an office chair so that 95 percent of the employees (male and female) will feel it is the "right height" for their legs to reach the floor comfortably.
   b. Designing a drill press so that its controls can be reached and its forces operated by an "average employee."
   c. Defining a doorway width so that a "typical" wheelchair can pass through without coming closer than 6 inches from either side.
   d. Setting the width of a parking space to accommodate 95 percent of all vehicles at your local Walmart.
   e. Choosing a font size so that a highway sign can be read in daylight at 100 metres by 95 percent of all drivers.

1.18 A research study showed that 7 percent of "A" students smoke, while nearly 50 percent of "D" students do. (a) List in rank order six factors that you think affect grades. Is smoking on your list? (b) If smoking is not a likely cause of poor grades, can you suggest reasons why these results were observed? (c) Assuming these statistics are correct, would "D" students who give up smoking improve their grades? (LO 5)

1.19 A research study by the Agency for Healthcare Research Quality showed that adolescents who watched more than 4 hours of TV per day were more than five times as likely to start smoking as those who watched less than 2 hours a day. The researchers speculate that TV actors' portrayals of smoking as personally and socially rewarding were an effective indirect method of tobacco promotion (*Note:* Paid television tobacco ads are illegal). List in rank order six factors that you think cause adolescents to start smoking. Did TV portrayals of attractive smokers appear on your list? (Data are from the *AHRQ Newsletter,* no. 269, Jan. 2003, p. 12.) (LO 5)

1.20 The Graduate Management Aptitude Test (GMAT) is used by many graduate schools of business as one of their admission criteria. GMAT scores for selected undergraduate majors are shown below. Using your own reasoning as well as concepts in this chapter, criticize each of the following statements. (LO 5)

    a. "Philosophy majors must not be interested in business since so few take the GMAT."

    b. "More students major in engineering than in English."

    c. "If marketing students majored in physics, they would score better on the GMAT."

    d. "Physics majors would make the best managers."

GMAT Scores and Undergraduate Major, 1984–1989 **GMAT**

Major	Average GMAT Score	Number Taking Test
Accounting	483	25,233
Computer Science	508	7,573
Economics	513	16,432
Engineering	544	29,688
English	507	3,589
Finance	489	20,001
Marketing	455	15,925
Philosophy	546	588
Physics	575	1,223

Source: Graduate Management Admission Council, *Admission Office Profile of Candidates,* Oct. 1989, pp. 27–30.

1.21 (a) Which of these two displays (table or graph) is most helpful in visualizing the relationship between restaurant size and interior seating for 74 Noodles restaurants? Explain your reasoning

    (b) Do you see anything unusual in the data? (*Source:* Noodles & Company) (LO 4)

    NoodlesSqFt

Number of Restaurants in Each Category (*n* = 74 restaurants)

Interior Seats	Square Feet inside Restaurant				Row Total
	1,000 – 1,749	1,750 – 2,499	2,500 – 3,249	3,250 – 4,000	
105 – 130	0	0	0	3	3
80 – 104	0	4	17	0	21
55 – 79	0	21	24	0	45
30 – 54	1	4	0	0	5
Col Total	1	29	41	3	74

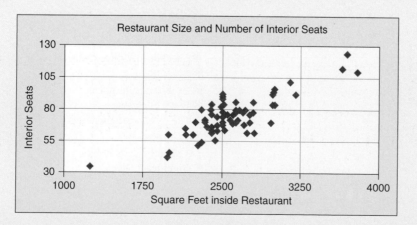

1.22 Each of the following is an actual writing sample, mostly from student projects. In each, find as many errors of spelling and/or grammar as you can, and correct them. (LO 4)

  a. "Its' R^2 value is quite close to 1 indicating it is a good fit to the actual data. I feel that G.E., one of the most respected corporations in the world, because of its' strong management and name recognition, not to mention its' valuable assets, is poised for steady growth over the next decade."

  b. "If a countries unemployment rate is to high it could cause a down swing in their economics structure."

  c. "This forecast is very unlikely, because you cannot have a negative amount of people unemployed."

  d. "It is not a well designed graph because it's title is too long and there isn't any axis labels."

  e. "This graph has no clear concise boarder to give it a sense of containment. With this graph especially since it is dealing with actually three seperate pieces of information. In this graph, the same data is presented but in a deceptive manor. Its sources weren't as specific as they should of been."

1.23 Choose *three* of the following statisticians and use the Web to find out a few basic facts about them (e.g., list some of their contributions to statistics, when they did their work, whether they are still living, etc.).

Florence Nightingale	John Wilder Tukey	Genichi Taguchi
Gertrude Cox	William Cochran	Helen Walker
Sir Francis Galton	Siméon Poisson	George Box
W. Edwards Deming	S. S. Stevens	Sam Wilks
The Bernoulli family	R. A. Fisher	Carl F. Gauss
Frederick Mosteller	George Snedecor	William S. Gosset
William H. Kruskal	Karl Pearson	Thomas Bayes
Jerzy Neyman	C. R. Rao	Bradley Efron
Egon Pearson	Abraham de Moivre	
Harold Hotelling	Edward Tufte	

LearningStats Unit 00   Basic Skills   LS

Even if you already know how to use Microsoft® Office tools (Excel, Word, PowerPoint), there may be features that you have never tried or skills you can improve. One objective of *LearningStats* is to show you how to use software applications (especially Excel) *in the context of statistics* for calculations, reports, and presentations. Excel is emphasized but there are also helpful tips on statistical reports using Word and PowerPoint. At your own pace, you should examine each demonstration. Some material will already be familiar to you, but you may pick up a few new tips. If you don't know anything about Excel, Word, or PowerPoint, you should consult additional sources, but you can still use *LearningStats.*

Topic	*LearningStats Modules*
Microsoft® Office	Excel Tips
	Word Tips
	PowerPoint Tips
	Checklist of Office Skills
Excel	Excel Basics
	Excel Embellishments
	Excel Functions
	Excel Advanced Features
Math Review	Math Review
	Using Symbols in Word
	Significant Digits

Key: = PowerPoint   = Word   = Excel

LearningStats Unit 01 Overview of Statistics [LS]

LearningStats Unit 01 introduces statistics, report writing, and professional ethical guidelines. Modules are designed for self-study, so you can proceed at your own pace, concentrate on material that is new, and pass quickly over things that you already know. Your instructor may assign specific modules, or you may decide to check them out because the topic sounds interesting. In addition to helping you learn about statistics, they may be useful as references later on.

Topic	*LearningStats Modules*
Overview	What Is Statistics?
	Web Resources
	Statistics Software
Report writing	Effective Writing
	Technical-Report Writing
	The Executive Summary
	The Oral Presentation
	Common Errors
	Writing Self-Test 1
	Writing Self-Test 2
	Writing Self-Test 3
	Gunning-Fog Index Project
Ethics	Ethical Guidelines

Key: = PowerPoint   = Word   = Excel

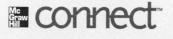

For solutions to odd-numbered exercises, Exam Review questions, and additional study tools to help you succeed in this course, visit *Connect* at www.mcgrawhillconnect.ca.

Chapter

2

Data Collection

Chapter Learning Objectives

When you finish this chapter you should be able to

1. Define terms that describe data sets.

2. Identify types of data and the mathematical operations that are appropriate.

3. Identify the basic sampling methods and their appropriate uses in a problem context.

4. Identify appropriate survey designs, survey types, and their sources of error.

5. Find everyday print or electronic data sources.

2.1 Definitions

In scientific research, data arise from experiments whose results are recorded systematically. In business, data usually arise from accounting transactions or management processes (e.g., inventory, sales, payroll). Much of the data that statisticians analyze were recorded without explicit consideration of their statistical uses, yet important decisions may depend on the data. How many pints of type A blood will be required at Toronto General Hospital next Thursday? How many dollars must State Farm keep in its cash account to cover automotive accident claims next November? How many yellow three-quarter-sleeve women's sweaters will HBC sell this month? To answer such questions, we usually look at historical data.

TABLE 2.1   **Small Multivariate Data Set (5 variables, 8 subjects)**

Case	Name	Age	Income	Position	Gender
1	Frieda	45	$67,100	Personnel director	F
2	Stefan	32	56,500	Operations analyst	M
3	Barbara	55	88,200	Marketing VP	F
4	Donna	27	59,000	Statistician	F
5	Larry	46	36,000	Security guard	M
6	Alicia	52	68,500	Comptroller	F
7	Alec	65	95,200	Chief executive	M
8	Jaime	50	71,200	Public relations	M

Subjects, Variables, and Data Sets

A subject or individual is a single member of a collection of items that we want to study, such as persons, firms, or regions. An example of a subject is an employee or an invoice mailed last month. A variable is a characteristic of the subject or individual, such as an employee's income or an invoice amount. The data set consists of all the values of all of the variables for all of the individuals we have chosen to observe. In this book, we will use data as a plural (datum is its singular), and data set to refer to a collection of observations taken as a whole. Table 2.1 shows a small data set with 8 subjects, 5 variables, and 40 observations (8 subjects times 5 variables).

A data set may consist of many variables. The questions that can be explored and the analytical techniques that can be used will depend upon the data type and the number of variables. This textbook starts with univariate data sets (one variable), and then moves to bivariate data sets (two variables) and multivariate data sets (more than two variables), as illustrated in Table 2.2.

Data Types

A data set may contain a mixture of *data types.* Two broad categories are categorical data and numerical data, as shown in Figure 2.1.

Categorical Data   *Categorical* data (also called *qualitative*) have values that are described by words rather than numbers. For example:

Structural lumber type (e.g., X = fir, hemlock, pine).

Automobile style (e.g., X = full, midsize, compact, subcompact).

Mutual fund type (e.g., X = load, no-load).

You might imagine that categorical data would be of limited statistical use, but in fact there are many statistical methods that can handle categorical data.

Using numbers to represent categories to facilitate statistical analysis is called coding. For example, a database might classify movies using numerical codes:

1 = Action, 2 = Classic, 3 = Comedy, 4 = Horror,

5 = Romance, 6 = Science Fiction, 7 = Western, 8 = Other

TABLE 2.2   **Number of Variables and Typical Tasks**

Data Set	Variables	Example	Typical Tasks
Univariate	One	Income	Histograms, basic statistics
Bivariate	Two	Income, Age	Scatter plots, correlation
Multivariate	More than two	Income, Age, Gender	Regression modelling

FIGURE 2.1

Data Types

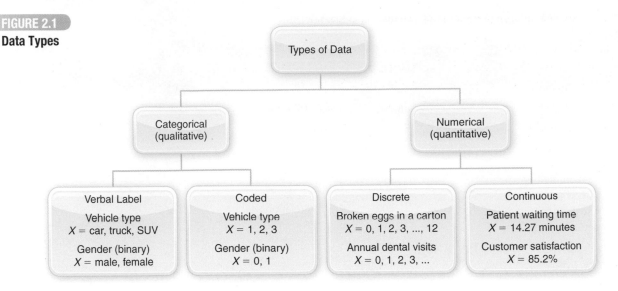

But coding a category as a number does *not* make the data numerical. Movie codes are assigned arbitrarily, and the codes generally do not imply a ranking. However, sometimes codes do imply a ranking:

1 = Bachelor's, 2 = Master's, 3 = Doctorate

Rankings may exist if we are measuring an underlying continuum, such as political orientation:

1 = Liberal, 2 = Moderate, 3 = Conservative

A **binary variable** has only two values, indicating the presence (1) or absence (0) of a characteristic of interest. For example, for an individual:

Employment	*Education*	*Marital status*
1 = employed	1 = university graduate	1 = currently married
0 = not employed	0 = not university graduate	0 = not currently married

The codes are arbitrary. A variable like gender could be coded in many ways:

Like This	*Or Like This*	*Or Like This*
1 = female	0 = female	1 = female
0 = male	1 = male	2 = male

Here again the coding itself has no numerical meaning, so binary variables are *categorical* data.

Numerical Data   *Numerical* or *quantitative* data arise from counting, measuring something, or from some kind of mathematical operation. For example:

Number of auto insurance claims filed in March (e.g., $X = 114$ claims).

Sales for last quarter (e.g., $X = \$4,920$).

Percent of mortgage applicants who are retired (e.g., $X = 22.7$ percent).

Most accounting data, economic indicators, and financial ratios are quantitative, as are physical measurements (length, weight, time, speed).

Numerical data can be further broken down into two types. A variable with a countable number of distinct values is **discrete.** Often, such data are integers. You can recognize integer data because their description begins with "number of." For example:

Number of senior citizens in a hospital waiting room (e.g., $X = 2$).

Number of takeoffs at Edmonton International Airport in a given hour (e.g., $X = 13$).

We express such data as integer variables because we cannot observe a fractional number of patients or takeoffs.

A numerical variable that can have any value within an interval is **continuous.** This would include things like physical measurements (e.g., length, weight, time, speed) and financial variables (e.g., sales, assets, price/earnings ratios, inventory turns). For example:

Weight of a package of Sun-Maid raisins (e.g., $X = 427.31$ grams).

Hourly fuel flow in a Cessna Citation V (e.g., $X = 1390.67$ pounds).

These are continuous variables because any interval (e.g., $422 < X < 428$) contains infinitely many possible values.

Apparent ambiguity between *discrete* and *continuous* is introduced when we round continuous data to whole numbers (e.g., your weight this morning). However, the underlying measurement scale is continuous. That is, a package of Sun-Maid raisins is labelled 425 grams, but on an accurate scale its weight would be a non-integer (e.g., 427.31). Precision depends on the instrument we use to measure the continuous variable. We generally treat financial data (dollars, Euros, pesos) as continuous even though retail prices go in discrete steps of 0.01 (i.e., we go from \$1.25 to \$1.26). The FM radio spectrum is continuous, but only certain discrete values are observed (e.g., 104.3) because of CRTC rules. Conversely, we sometimes treat discrete data as continuous when the range is very large (e.g., exam scores) and when small differences (e.g., 604 or 605) aren't of much importance. This topic will be discussed in later chapters. If in doubt, just think about how X was measured and whether its values are countable.

Section Exercises

2.1 Explain the difference between an observation and a variable. (LO 1)

2.2 Give an example of (a) categorical data, (b) discrete numerical data, and (c) continuous numerical data. (LO 2)

2.3 What type of data (categorical, discrete numerical, or continuous numerical) is each of the following variables? If there is any ambiguity about the data type, explain why the answer is unclear. (LO 2)
  a. The manufacturer of your car.
  b. Your major.
  c. The number of university courses you are taking.
  d. Your GPA.
  e. The kilometres on your car's odometer.
  f. The fat grams you ate for lunch yesterday.
  g. Your dog's age.

2.4 What type of data (categorical, discrete numerical, or continuous numerical) is each of the following variables? If there is any ambiguity, explain why the answer is unclear. (LO 2)
  a. Length of a TV commercial.
  b. Number of peanuts in a can of Planter's Mixed Nuts.
  c. Occupation of a mortgage applicant.
  d. Flight time from Montreal-Trudeau Airport to Pearson International Airport.
  e. Name of the airline with the cheapest fare from Vancouver to τ.
  f. Blouse size purchased by an HBC customer.

2.5 (a) Give three examples of discrete data not listed above. (b) Give three examples of continuous data not listed above. In each case, explain and identify any ambiguities that might exist. *Hint:* Do not restrict yourself to published data. Consider data describing your own life (e.g., your sports performance, financial data, or academic data). For each, show a few typical data values. (LO 2)

2.6 Look at data sets in LearningStats under Cross-Sectional Data > Cars. Find an example of (a) a univariate data set, (b) a bivariate data set, and (c) a multivariate data set. (LO 1)

2.2   Level of Measurement

Statisticians sometimes refer to four levels of measurement for data: *nominal, ordinal, interval,* and *ratio* (see Table 2.3). This typology was proposed over 60 years ago by psychologist S. S. Stevens. The allowable statistical tests depend on the measurement level. The criteria are summarized in Table 2.3 and Figure 2.2.

TABLE 2.3 **Levels of Measurement**

Characteristic	Level of Measurement			
	Nominal	**Ordinal**	**Interval**	**Ratio**
Do data values indicate the natural order of something?	No	Yes	Yes	Yes
Are differences between data values meaningful?	No	No	Yes	Yes
Is there a natural zero point that indicates the absence of something?	No	No	No	Yes
Operations allowed	Only counting allowed (e.g., frequency tally, finding the mode)	Counting and order statistics allowed (e.g., mode, median, rank tests)	Statistics that use sums or differences allowed (e.g., mean, standard deviation)	All statistical operations allowed, including ratios of numbers
Example	Eye colour (blue, brown, green, hazel)	Bond ratings (Aaa, Baa1, C1, etc.)	Temperature on Celsius scale (e.g., 17° C)	Accounts payable ($21.7 million)

FIGURE 2.2

Measurement Level Illustrated

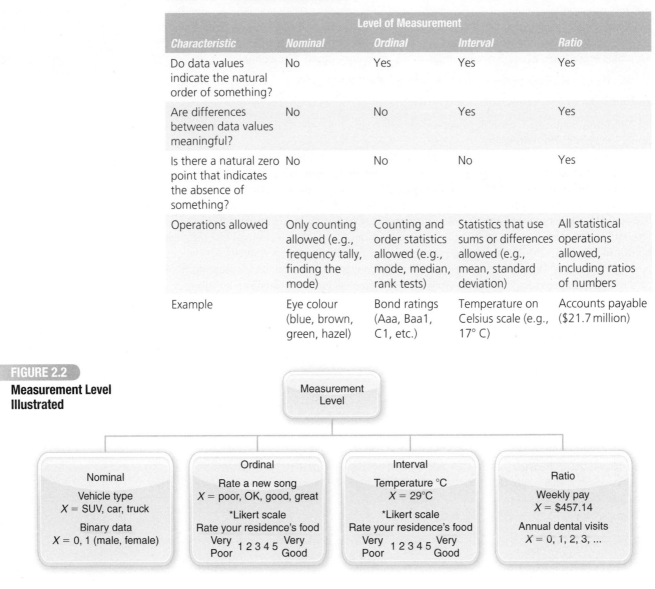

*You can treat a Likert scale as interval data if distances between scale points have meaning (otherwise, it's ordinal).

Nominal Measurement

Nominal measurement is the weakest level of measurement and the easiest to recognize. **Nominal data** (from Latin *nomen* meaning "name") merely identify a *category*. "Nominal" data are the same as "qualitative," "categorical," or "classification" data. For example, the following survey questions yield nominal data:

Did you file an insurance claim last month?
1. Yes   2. No

Which kind of laptop do you own?
1. Acer   2. Apple   3. Compaq   4. Dell   5. Gateway   6. HP
7. IBM   8. Micron   9. Sony   10. Toshiba   11. Other   12. None

We usually code nominal data numerically. However, the codes are arbitrary placeholders with no numerical meaning, so it is improper to perform most mathematical analysis on them. For example, we would not calculate the average laptop owned by averaging the number of 1s, 2s, 3s, and so on in the data set. This may seem obvious, yet people have been known to do it. Once the data are in the computer, it's easy to forget that the "numbers" are only categories.

With nominal data, the only permissible mathematical operations are counting (e.g., frequencies), converting the counts into percentages or proportions, and a few simple statistics such as the mode.

Ordinal Measurement

Ordinal data codes connote a *ranking* of data values. For example:

What size automobile do you usually drive?
1. Full-size   2. Compact   3. Subcompact

How often do you use Microsoft Access?
1. Frequently   2. Sometimes   3. Rarely   4. Never

Thus, a 2 (Compact) implies a larger car than a 3 (Subcompact). Like nominal data, these ordinal numerical codes lack the properties that are required to compute many statistics, such as the average. Specifically, there is no clear meaning to the *distance* between 1 and 2, or between 2 and 3, or between 3 and 4 (what would be the distance between "Rarely" and "Never"?). Other examples of ordinal scales can be found in a recruiter's rating of job candidates (outstanding, good, adequate, weak, unsatisfactory), S&P credit ratings (AAA, AA+, AA, AA−, A+, A, A−, B+, B, B−, etc.), job titles (president, group vice-president, plant manager, department head, clerk), or the ranking of Canadian university track and field teams. Ordinal data can be treated as nominal, but not vice versa. Ordinal data are especially common in social sciences, marketing, and human resources research. There are many useful statistical tests for ordinal data.

Interval Measurement

The next step up the measurement scale is interval data, which not only is a rank but also has meaningful intervals between scale points. Examples are the Celsius or Fahrenheit scales of temperature. The interval between 60°F and 70°F is the same as the interval between 20°F and 30°F. Because intervals between numbers represent *distances,* we can do mathematical operations such as taking an average. But because the zero point of these scales is arbitrary, we can't say that 60°F is twice as warm as 30°F, or that 30°F is 50 percent warmer than 20°F. That is, ratios are not meaningful for interval data. The absence of a meaningful zero is a key characteristic of interval data.

Likert Scales   The Likert scale is a special case that is frequently used in survey research. You have undoubtedly seen such scales. Typically, a statement is made and the respondent is asked to indicate his or her agreement or disagreement on a five-point or seven-point scale using verbal anchors. The *coarseness* of a Likert scale refers to the number of scale points (typically five or seven). For example:

"University-bound high school students should be required to study a foreign language."
(check one)

❏	❏	❏	❏	❏
Strongly Agree	Somewhat Agree	Neither Agree Nor Disagree	Somewhat Disagree	Strongly Disagree

A neutral midpoint ("Neither Agree Nor Disagree") is allowed if we use an *odd* number of scale points (usually five or seven). Occasionally, surveys may omit the neutral midpoint to force the respondent to "lean" one way or the other. Likert data are coded numerically (e.g., 1 to 5) but any equally spaced values will work, as shown in Table 2.4.

But do Likert data qualify as interval measurements? By choosing the verbal anchors carefully, many researchers believe that the *intervals* are the same (e.g., the distance from 1 to 2 is "the same" as the *interval,* say, from 3 to 4). However, ratios are not meaningful (i.e., here 4 is not twice 2). The assumption that Likert scales produce interval data justifies a wide range of statistical calculations, including averages, correlations, and so on. Researchers use many Likert-scale variants.

TABLE 2.4   **Examples of Likert-Scale Coding: "How will a change in inflation affect the investment climate?"**

Likert Coding: 1 to 5 scale	Likert Coding: −2 to +2 scale
5 = Will help a lot	+2 = Will help a lot
4 = Will help a little	+1 = Will help a little
3 = No effect on investment climate	0 = No effect on investment climate
2 = Will hurt a little	−1 = Will hurt a little
1 = Will hurt a lot	−2 = Will hurt a lot

"How would you rate your marketing instructor?" (check one)

❑ Terrible   ❑ Poor   ❑ Adequate   ❑ Good   ❑ Excellent

Respondents may prefer having verbal labels for each category but researchers who are uncomfortable with the labels can put verbal anchors only on the end points, where 1 = "very poor" and 5 = "very good."

"How would you rate your marketing instructor?" (check one)

Very Poor   ❑   ❑   ❑   ❑   ❑   Very Good

This avoids intermediate scale labels and permits any number of scale points, but lacks a concrete interpretation (what does a "3" mean?). Likert data usually are discrete, but some Web surveys now use a continuous response scale that allows the respondent to position a "slider" anywhere along the scale to produce continuous data (actually the number of positions is finite but very large). For example:

Likert (using scale points)   Likert (using a slider)

Very Poor 1 2 3 4 5 6 7 Very Good   Very Poor_____▼_Very Good

Ratio Measurement

Ratio measurement is the strongest level of measurement. **Ratio data** have all the properties of the other three data types, but in addition possess a *meaningful zero* that represents the absence of the quantity being measured. Because of the zero point, ratios of data values are meaningful (e.g., $20 million in profit is twice as much as $10 million). Balance sheet data, income statement data, financial ratios, physical counts, scientific measurements, and most engineering measurements are ratio data because zero has meaning (e.g., a company with zero sales sold nothing). Having a zero point does *not* restrict us to positive data. For example, profit is a ratio variable (e.g., $4 million is twice $2 million) yet firms can have negative profit. In cases such as this, the ratio would usually be reported as n/a (i.e., not applicable).

Zero does *not* have to be observable in the data. Newborn babies, for example, cannot have zero weight, yet baby weight clearly is ratio data (i.e., an 8-pound baby is 33 percent heavier than a 6-pound baby). What matters is that the zero is an absolute reference point. The Kelvin temperature scale is a ratio measurement because its absolute zero represents the absence of molecular vibration, while zero on the Celsius scale is merely a convenience (note that 30°C is not "twice as much temperature" as 15°C).

Lack of a true zero is often the quickest test to defrock variables masquerading as ratio data. For example, a Likert scale (+2, +1, 0, −1, −2) is *not* ratio data despite the presence of zero because the zero (neutral) point does not connote the absence of anything. As an acid test, ask yourself whether 2 (strongly agree) is twice as much "agreement" as 1 (slightly agree). Some classifications are debatable. For example, university GPA has a zero, but does it represent the absence of learning? Does 4.00 represent "twice as much" learning as 2.00? Is there an underlying reality ranging from 0 to 4 that we are measuring? Most people seem to think so, although the conservative procedure would be to limit ourselves to statistical tests that assume only interval data.

Although beginning statistics textbooks usually emphasize interval or ratio data, there are textbooks that emphasize other kinds of data, notably in behavioural research (e.g., psychology, sociology, marketing, human resources).

Changing Data by Recoding

We can recode ratio measurements *downward* into interval, ordinal, or nominal measurements (but not conversely). For example, doctors may classify systolic blood pressure as "normal" (under 130), "elevated" (130 to 140), or "high" (140 or over). The recoded data are ordinal, because the ranking is preserved. Intervals may be unequal. For example, air traffic controllers classify planes as "small" (under 41,000 pounds), "large" (41,001 to 254,999 pounds), and "heavy" (255,000 pounds or more). Such recoding is done to simplify the data when the exact data magnitude is of little interest, however, it discards information by mapping stronger measurements into weaker ones.

Section Exercises

2.7 Which type of data (nominal, ordinal, interval, ratio) is each of the following variables? Explain. (LO 2)

a. Number of goals in game 1 of the next Stanley Cup finals.
b. Toronto Maple Leafs' standing in the NHL's Northeast Division.
c. Position of a hockey player (centre, defenceman, etc.).
d. Temperature in the Air Canada Centre for game 1 (in degrees Celsius).
e. Salary of a randomly chosen NHL defenceman.
f. Gardiner Expressway traffic on the opening day of the NHL season in Toronto (light, medium, heavy).

2.8 Which type of data (nominal, ordinal, interval, ratio) is each of the following variables? Explain. (LO 2)

a. Number of employees in a Walmart store in Windsor, Ontario.
b. Number of merchandise returns on a randomly chosen Monday at a Walmart store.
c. Temperature (in degrees Celsius) in the ice-cream freezer at a Walmart store.
d. Name of the cashier at register 3 in a Walmart store.
e. Manager's rating of the cashier at register 3 in a Walmart store.
f. Social insurance number of the cashier at register 3 in a Walmart store.

2.9 Give an original example of each type of data (nominal, ordinal, interval, ratio) from your own life (e.g., your finances, sporting activities, education). (LO 2)

2.10 Which type of data (nominal, ordinal, interval, ratio) is the response to each question? If you think that the level of measurement is ambiguous, explain why. (LO 2)

a. How would you describe your level of skill in using Excel? (check one)
    ❑ Low   ❑ Medium   ❑ High
b. How often do you use Excel? (check one)
    ❑ Rarely   ❑ Often   ❑ Very Often
c. Which version of Excel do you use? (check one)
    ❑ 2000   ❑ XP   ❑ 2003
    ❑ 2007   ❑ Other
d. I spend _____ hours a day using Excel.

2.3   Time Series versus Cross-Sectional Data

Time Series Data

If each observation in the sample represents a different (usually equally spaced) point in time (years, months, days), we have **time series data.** The *periodicity* is the time between observations. It may be annual, quarterly, monthly, weekly, daily, hourly, and so on. Examples of *macroeconomic* time series data would include national income (GDP, consumption, investment), economic indicators (Consumer Price Index, unemployment rate, S&P/TSX Composite Index), and monetary data (prime rate, consumer debt, federal debt). Examples of *microeconomic* time series data would include a firm's sales, market share, debt/equity ratio, employee absenteeism, inventory turnover, and product quality ratings. For time series, we are interested in *trends and patterns over time* (e.g., annual growth in consumer debit card use from 2001 to 2008).

Cross-Sectional Data

If each observation represents a different individual unit (e.g., a person, firm, geographic area) at the same point in time, we have **cross-sectional data.** Thus, traffic fatalities in the 10 provinces for a given year, debt/equity ratios for the Fortune 500 firms in the last quarter of a certain year, last month's Visa balances for a bank's new mortgage applicants, or GPAs of students in a statistics class would be cross-sectional data. For cross-sectional data, we are interested in *summarizing the different values* (e.g., average collection period for accounts receivable in 10 Subway franchises) or in *relationships* (e.g., whether collection period correlates with sales volume in 10 Subway franchises).

Some variables (such as unemployment rates) could be either time series (monthly data over each of 60 months) or cross-sectional (January's unemployment rate in the 10 largest Canadian cities). We can combine the two (e.g., monthly unemployment rates for the 13 Canadian provinces or territories for the last 60 months) to obtain *pooled cross-sectional and time series data.*

Section Exercises

2.11 Which type of data (cross-sectional or time series) is each variable? (LO 2)
a. Scores of 50 students on a midterm accounting exam last semester.
b. Bob's scores on 10 weekly accounting quizzes last semester.
c. Average score by all takers of the province's CA exam for each of the last 10 years.
d. Number of years of accounting work experience for each of the 15 partners in a CA firm.

2.12 Which type of data (cross-sectional or time series) is each variable? (LO 2)
a. Value of TSX index at the close of each trading day last year.
b. Closing price of each of the stocks in the TSX index on the last trading day this week.
c. Dividends per share paid by General Motors common stock for each of the last 20 quarters.
d. Latest price/earnings ratios of 10 stocks in Bob's retirement portfolio.

2.13 Which type of data (cross-sectional or time series) is each variable? (LO 2)
a. Mexico's GDP for each of the last 10 quarters.
b. Unemployment rates in each of the 31 states in Mexico at the end of last year.
c. Unemployment rate in Mexico at the end of each of the last 10 years.
d. Average home value in each of the 10 largest Mexican cities today.

2.14 Give an original example of a time series variable and a cross-sectional variable. Use your own experience (e.g., your sports activities, finances, education). (LO 2)

2.4 Sampling Concepts

The retail sector is one of the most important sectors of the Canadian economy, representing 6.4 percent of total gross domestic product (GDP) or value added in the economy in 2000, with total sales exceeding $277 billion. There are over 2 million retail businesses in North America. It is unrealistic for market researchers to study every retail business in a timely way. But since 2001, a new firm called Shopper-Trak RCT (www.shoppertrak.com) has been measuring purchases at a sample of 45,000 mall-based stores, and using this information to advise clients quickly of changes in shopping trends. This application of sampling is part of the relatively new field of *retail intelligence.* In this section, you will learn the differences between a **sample** and a **population,** and why sometimes a sample is necessary or desirable.

Population	All of the items of interest to us. It may be either finite (e.g., all of the passengers on a particular plane) or effectively infinite (e.g., all of the Cokes produced in an ongoing bottling process).
Sample	A subset of the population that we will actually analyze (e.g., 20 of the passengers getting off a Boeing 747 jet arriving in Vancouver from Hong Kong).

A Closer Look

Although we define a population (all items of interest to us) essentially the same as most other statistics texts, all items of interest may be defined differently in some statistics texts. Here we define items of interest as physical entities (e.g., people, businesses); other texts may define items of interest as characteristics of these physical entities (e.g., the salaries of people, the price/earnings ratios of businesses). When discussing sampling concepts, it is easier to refer to a population as a physical entity.

Sample or Census?

A *sample* involves looking only at some items selected from the population, but a **census** is an examination of all items in a defined population. The accuracy of a census can be illusory. For example, the Census of Canada cannot locate every individual in Canada. Reasons include the extreme mobility of the Canadian population as well as the fact that some people do not want to be found (e.g., fugitives) or do not reply to the mailed census form. Further, budget constraints make it difficult to track down incomplete responses or non-responses.

When the quantity being measured is volatile, there cannot be a census. For example, the Arbitron Company tracks American radio listening habits using over 2.6 million "Radio Diary Packages." For each "listening occasion," participants note start and stop times for each station. Panelists also report their age, sex, and other demographic information. Table 2.5 outlines some situations where a sample rather than a census would be preferred, and vice versa.

Parameters and Statistics

From a sample of *n* items, chosen from a population, we compute **statistics** that can be used as estimates of **parameters** found in the population. To avoid confusion, we use different symbols for each parameter and its corresponding statistic. Thus, the population mean is denoted

TABLE 2.5 Sample or Census?

Situations Where a Sample May Be Preferred	Situations Where a Census May Be Preferred
Infinite Population No census is possible if the population is of indefinite size (an assembly line can keep producing bolts, a doctor can keep seeing more patients).	**Small Population** If the population is small, there is little reason to sample, for the effort of data collection may be only a small part of the total cost.
Destructive Testing The act of measurement may destroy or devalue the item (battery life, vehicle crash tests).	**Large Sample Size** If the required sample size approaches the population size, we might as well go ahead and take a census.
Timely Results Sampling may yield more timely results (checking wheat samples for moisture content, checking peanut butter for aflatoxin contamination).	**Database Exists** If the data are on disk, we can examine 100 percent of the cases. But auditing or validating data against physical records may raise the cost.
Accuracy Instead of spreading resources thinly to attempt a census, budget might be better spent to improve training of field interviewers and improve data safeguards.	**Legal Requirements** Banks must count all the cash in bank teller drawers at the end of each business day.
Cost Even if a census is feasible, the cost, either in time or money, may exceed our budget.	
Sensitive Information A trained interviewer might learn more about sexual harassment in an organization through in-depth interviews of a small sample of employees and confidentiality may also be improved.	

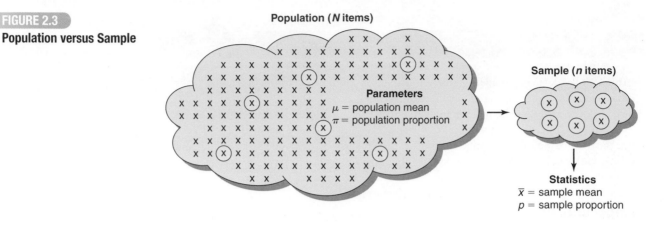

FIGURE 2.3

Population versus Sample

μ (the Greek letter *mu*) while the sample mean is $\bar{x}$. The population proportion is denoted π (the Greek letter *pi*) while the sample proportion is *p*. Figure 2.3 illustrates this idea.

Parameter	A measurement or characteristic of the population (e.g., a mean or proportion). Usually unknown as we can rarely observe the entire population. Usually (but not always) represented by a Greek letter (e.g., μ or π).
Statistic	A numerical value calculated from a sample (e.g., a mean or proportion). Usually (but not always) represented by a Roman letter (e.g., $\bar{x}$ or *p*).

For example, suppose we want to know the mean (average) repair cost for auto air-conditioning warranty claims, or the proportion (percent) of 25-year-old concert-goers who have permanent hearing loss. Because a census is impossible, these parameters would be estimated using a sample. For the sample statistics to provide good estimates of the population parameters, the population must be carefully specified and the sample must be drawn scientifically so that the sample items are representative of the population.

Target Population

A population may be defined either by a list (e.g., the names of the passengers on Flight 234) or by a rule (e.g., the customers who eat at Kelsey's). The **target population** is the population in which we are interested. Suppose we wish to estimate the proportion of potential consumers who would purchase a $20 Harley-Davidson desk calendar. Is the target population all drivers? Only male drivers over age 16? Only drivers with incomes over $25,000? Only motorcycle owners? By answering questions such as these, we not only identify the target population but also are forced to define our business goals more clearly. The **sampling frame** is the group from which we will select the sample. If the frame differs significantly from the target population, then our estimates will be of little use. Examples of frames are phone directories, voter registration lists, alumni association mailing lists, or marketing databases. Other examples might be:

- Names and addresses of all registered voters in Montreal, Quebec.
- Names and addresses of all vehicle owners in Winnipeg, Manitoba.
- E-mail addresses of all L.L. Bean Canadian customers who have placed online orders.

Finite or Infinite?

A population is *finite* if it has a definite size, *N,* even if its size is unknown. For example, the number of cars in a McDonald's parking lot or the number of MBA students enrolled at York University will be finite. A population is treated as *infinite* if it is of an indefinitely large size. For instance, assembly lines can produce indefinitely large numbers of M&Ms, Aspirin tablets, or loaves of bread. Thus, quality process control samples of *n* items usually come from *effectively infinite* populations. But if a sample comes from a particular batch and we wish to make inferences about that specific batch, we might regard the batch as a finite population. When a population is known to be very large relative to the sample, a statistician may treat the population as infinite.

Rule of Thumb

A population may be treated as infinite when N is at least 20 times n (i.e., when $N/n \geq 20$).

Mini Case | 2.1

Students—You Have a Voice in TV Ratings!

Nielsen Media Research (see www.nielsenmedia.com) conducts random sampling using a panel of 10,000 television households in order to provide viewing information to advertisers and broadcast companies. Advertising agencies use the viewing ratings to decide which programs are best for airing their commercials. Broadcast companies make decisions on advertising rates, which nights to run which shows, and which shows to keep on the air.

In 2006, Nielsen decided to add students living in residences to its National People Meter Sample. After monitoring their viewing habits, Nielsen estimated that 636,000 women age 18–24, living in residences, viewed *Grey's Anatomy* during November 2006. This implied a 50 percent jump in the program ranking and elevated *Grey's Anatomy* to a top spot in the TV rankings. But to calculate the estimates, Nielsen is extrapolating from the viewing habits of *just 130 students* around the country who have agreed to have electronic monitors installed in their rooms. That means that a handful of students can lead to a huge swing in ratings. For example, an estimated 163,000 jump in viewers for *Drawn Together* was based on only 12 people in the survey group who tuned in to the show. Later in this textbook, you will learn how to estimate the *margin of error* in a sample like this. But advertisers clearly believe that the information is reliable enough to use in making their decisions (for a discussion of Nielsen's margin of error, see *The New York Times*, Apr. 8, 2007, p. 10).

Does Nielsen accept volunteers in its National People Meter Sample? No. According to the Nielsen Web site, the firm draws its samples in a way that offers every American household with a television an equal chance of being selected. The firm goes on to say that "To include volunteers would violate basic laws of random sampling practice and skew our results. A truly representative sample of the population can only be generated using statistical methods of selection."

Section Exercises

2.15 Would you use a sample or a census to measure each of the following? Why? If you are uncertain, explain the issues. (LO 3)
  a. The model years of the cars driven by each of your five closest friends.
  b. The model years of the cars driven by each student in your statistics class.
  c. The model years of the cars driven by each student in your university.
  d. The model years of the cars driven by each professor whose classes you are taking.

2.16 Is each of the following a parameter or a statistic? If you are uncertain, explain the issues. (LO 1)
  a. The average price/earnings ratio for all stocks in the TSX index.
  b. The proportion of all stocks in the TSX index that had negative earnings last year.
  c. The proportion of energy-related stocks in portfolios owned by 50 investors.
  d. The average rate of return for stock portfolios recommended by 50 brokers.

2.17 Would you use a sample or a census to measure each of the following? Why? If you are uncertain, explain the issues. (LO 3)
  a. The mean time battery life of your laptop computer in continuous use.
  b. The number of students in your statistics class who brought laptop computers to class today.
  c. The average price paid for a laptop computer by students at your university.
  d. The percentage of disk space available on laptop computers owned by your five closest friends.

2.18 The target population is all students in your university. You wish to estimate the average current Visa balance for each student. How large would the university student population have to be in order to be regarded as effectively infinite in each of the following samples? (LO 4)
  a. A sample of 10 students.
  b. A sample of 50 students.
  c. A sample of 100 students.

TABLE 2.6   Seven Sampling Methods

Random Samples		*Non-Random Samples*	
Simple Random Sample	Use random numbers to select items from a list (e.g., Visa cardholders).	Judgment Sample	Use expert knowledge to choose "typical" items (e.g., which employees to interview).
Systematic Sample	Select every *k*th item from a list or sequence (e.g., restaurant customers).	Convenience Sample	Use a sample that happens to be available (e.g., ask co-worker opinions at lunch).
Stratified Sample	Select randomly within defined strata (e.g., by age, occupation, gender).	Focus Groups	In-depth dialogue with a representative panel of individuals (e.g., iPod users).
Cluster Sample	Define clusters (usually based on geographical areas), randomly select clusters, and randomly sample or take a census within each selected cluster.		

2.5   Sampling Methods

There are two main categories of sampling methods. In **random sampling,** items are chosen by randomization or a chance procedure. **Non-random sampling** is less scientific but is sometimes used for expediency. Seven common sampling methods are shown in Table 2.6.

Simple Random Sample

We denote the population size by N and the sample size by n. In a **simple random sample,** every item in the population of N items has the same chance of being chosen in the sample of n items, and every sample of n items has the same chance of being selected. A physical experiment to accomplish this would be to write each of the N data values on individual poker chips, and then to draw n chips from a bowl after stirring it thoroughly. But we can accomplish the same thing if the N population items appear on a numbered list, simply by choosing n integers at random between 1 and N. But we must take care not to allow any bias to creep into the selection process.

A simple random sample is easy to obtain if the population items are in a list or table. For example, suppose we want to select one student at random from a list of 48 students (see Figure 2.4). If you were asked to "use your judgment," you would probably pick a name in the middle, thereby biasing the draw against those individuals at either end of the list. Instead, we rely on **random numbers.** In this example, we used Excel's function =RANDBETWEEN(1,48) to pick a random integer between 1 and 48. The number was 44, so Stephanie was selected. There is no bias because all values from 1 to 48 are *equiprobable* (i.e., equally likely to occur).

Random Number Tables   Another method (somewhat obsolete) to select random numbers between 1 and N is to use a table of random digits. A table of random digits has the property that no matter how we pick our digits (up, down, diagonally, etc.), each digit 0 through 9 is equally likely. Table 2.7 shows 1,000 random digits arranged in 10 columns and 20 rows of five-digit blocks. All we need is a consistent rule for picking the digits.

For example, suppose that a specific Swiss Chalet restaurant wants to award cash "customer loyalty" prizes to 10 of its customers from a list of 875 who dined at its location last month. To get 10 three-digit random numbers between 001 and 875, we define *any consistent rule* for moving through the table. For example, we can point a finger at random to choose a starting point. In Table 2.7, we started in the second column in the third row. Our rule is to choose the first three digits of this five-digit block, move to the right one column, down one row, and repeat. When we reach the end of a line, we wrap around to the other side of the table and continue. We discard any number greater than 875 and move on. If we get a duplicate, we continue on. The chosen 10 three-digit random numbers are highlighted in the table:

439, 516, 201, 119, 334, 461, 388, 010, 126, 262

Random person **44**

FIGURE 2.4

Picking on Stephanie

1	Adam	17	Haitham	33	Moira
2	Addie	18	Jackie	34	Nathan
3	Anne	19	Jennie	35	Oded
4	Aristo	20	Joel	36	Pablo
5	Balaji	21	Judy	37	Pat
6	Dean	22	Kay	38	Peter
7	Dennis	23	Kristina	39	Randy
8	Diana	24	LaDonna	40	Rick
9	Don	25	Latrice	41	Sarah
10	Ellen	26	Laura	42	Shamel
11	Erik	27	Leah	43	Sid
12	Floyd	28	Lindsay	**44**	**Stephanie**
13	Frances	29	Loretta	45	Stephen
14	Gadis	30	Lou	46	Sylvia
15	Ginnie	31	Majda	47	Tara
16	Giovanni	32	Mario	48	Tim

© 2001 Scott Adams, Inc./Dist. By UFS, Inc.

By chance, no number greater than 516 was selected. Without random numbers, you might have an unconscious tendency to try to "cover" the range from 1 to 875 "evenly," but that would *not* be random.

TABLE 2.7   1,000 Random Digits   Random Digits

82134	14458	66716	54269	31928	46241	03052	00260	32367	25783
07139	16829	76768	11913	42434	91961	92934	18229	15595	02566
45056	43939	31188	43272	11332	99494	19348	97076	95605	28010
10244	19093	51678	63463	85568	70034	82811	23261	48794	63984
12940	84434	50087	20189	58009	66972	05764	10421	36875	64964
84438	45828	40353	28925	11911	53502	24640	96880	93166	68409
98681	67871	71735	64113	90139	33466	65312	90655	75444	30845
43290	96753	18799	49713	39227	15955	46167	63853	03633	19990
96893	85410	88233	22094	30605	79024	01791	38839	85531	94576
75403	41227	00192	16814	47054	16814	81349	92264	01028	29071
78064	92111	51541	76563	69027	67718	06499	71938	17354	12680
26246	71746	94019	93165	96713	03316	75912	86209	12081	57817
98766	67312	96358	21351	86448	31828	86113	78868	67243	06763
37895	51055	11929	44443	15995	72935	99631	18190	85877	31309
27988	81163	52212	25102	61798	28670	01358	60354	74015	18556
19216	53008	44498	19262	12196	93947	90162	76337	12646	26838
28078	86729	69438	24235	35208	48957	53529	76297	41741	54735
34455	61363	93711	68038	75960	16327	95716	66964	28634	65015
53510	90412	70438	45932	57815	75144	52472	61817	41562	42084
30658	18894	88208	97867	30737	94985	18235	02178	39728	66398

TABLE 2.8   Some Ways to Get 10 Random Integers between 1 and 875

Excel—Option A	Enter the Excel function =RANDBETWEEN(1,875) into 10 spreadsheet cells. Press **F9** to get a new sample.
Excel—Option B	Enter the function =INT(1 + 875*RAND()) into 10 spreadsheet cells. Press **F9** to get a new sample.
Internet	The Web site **www.random.org** will give you many kinds of excellent random numbers (integers, decimals, etc.).
MINITAB	Use MINITAB's Random Data menu with the Integer option.

With or Without Replacement?   The same number could occur more than once. If we allow duplicates, we are **sampling with replacement.** Using the bowl analogy, if we throw each chip back in the bowl and stir the contents before the next draw, an item can be chosen again. Duplicates are unlikely when the sample size n is much smaller than the population size N. People instinctively prefer **sampling without replacement** because drawing the same item more than once seems to add nothing to our knowledge. However, using the same sample item more than once does not introduce any *bias* (i.e., no systematic tendency to over- or underestimate whatever parameter we are trying to measure).

Computer Methods   Because using computers is easier, we rarely use random number tables. Table 2.8 shows a few alternative ways to choose 10 integers between 1 and 875. All are based on a software algorithm that creates uniform decimal numbers between 0 and 1. Excel's function =RAND( ) does this, and many pocket calculators have a similar function. We call these *pseudorandom* generators because even the best algorithms eventually repeat themselves (after a cycle of millions of numbers). Thus, a software-based random data encryption scheme could conceivably be broken. To enhance data security, Intel and other firms are examining hardware-based methods (e.g., based on thermal noise or radioactive decay) to prevent patterns or repetition. Fortunately, most applications don't require that degree of randomness. For example, the iPod Shuffle's song choices are not strictly random because its random numbers are generated by an algorithm from a "seed number" that eventually repeats. However, the repeat period is so great that an iPod user would never notice. Excel's and MINITAB's random numbers are good enough for most purposes.

Row/Column Data Arrays   When the data are arranged in a rectangular array, we can choose an item at random by picking a row and column at random. For example, here is a 4×3 array containing the names of 12 large merchandise companies in Canada. We select a random column between 1 and 3 and a random row between 1 and 4 so that every company has the same chance of being chosen. In this case, we used Excel's =RANDBETWEEN function to select row 3 and column 2 (Leon's).

	Col 1	Col 2	Col 3
Row 1	The Bay	Future Shop	Zellers
Row 2	Walmart	Best Buy	Sears
Row 3	The Brick	Leon's	The Source
Row 4	Mark's	People's	Ikea

Randomizing a List   To randomize a list (assuming it is in a spreadsheet) we can insert the Excel function =RAND( ) beside each row. This creates a column of random decimal numbers between 0 and 1. Copy the random numbers and paste them in the same column using Paste Special > Values to "fix" them (otherwise they will keep changing). Then sort all the columns by the random number column, and *voilà*—the list is now random! Figure 2.5 uses this method to randomize an alphabetized list of 12 students. The first n items on the randomized list can now be used as a random sample. This method is especially useful when the list is very long (perhaps millions of lines). The first n items are a random sample of the entire list, for they are as likely as any others.

FIGURE 2.5

Randomizing a List
  RandomNames

Names in Alphabetical Order				Names in Random Order			
Rand	Name	Major	Gender	Rand	Name	Major	Gender
0.382091	Claudia	Accounting	F	0.143539	Dave	Human Res	M
0.730061	Dan	Economics	M	0.229854	Marcia	Accounting	F
0.143539	Dave	Human Res	M	0.334449	Ryan	MIS	M
0.906060	Kalisha	MIS	F	0.382091	Claudia	Accounting	F
0.624378	LaDonna	Finance	F	0.402726	Victor	Marketing	M
0.229854	Marcia	Accounting	F	0.431740	Rachel	Oper Mgt	F
0.604377	Matt	Undecided	M	0.604377	Matt	Undecided	M
0.798923	Moira	Accounting	F	0.624378	LaDonna	Finance	F
0.431740	Rachel	Oper Mgt	F	0.730061	Dan	Economics	M
0.334449	Ryan	MIS	M	0.798923	Moira	Accounting	F
0.836594	Tammy	Marketing	F	0.836594	Tammy	Marketing	F
0.402726	Victor	Marketing	M	0.906060	Kalisha	MIS	F

Systematic Sample   Another method of random sampling is to choose every *k*th item from a sequence or list, starting from a randomly chosen entry among the first *k* items on the list. This is called systematic sampling. Figure 2.6 shows how to sample every fourth item, starting from item 2, resulting in a sample of $n = 20$ items.

An attraction of systematic sampling is that it can be used with unlistable or infinite populations, such as production processes (e.g., testing every 5,000th light bulb) or political polling (e.g., surveying every 10th voter who emerges from the polling place). Systematic sampling is also well-suited to linearly organized physical populations (e.g., pulling every 10th patient folder from alphabetized filing drawers in a veterinary clinic).

A systematic sample of *n* items from a population of *N* items requires that periodicity *k* be approximately *N/n*. For example, to choose 25 companies from a list of 501 companies in Mini Case 2.2 (Table 2.9), we chose every 20th stock ($k = 501/25 \approx 20$). **Systematic sampling should yield acceptable results unless patterns in the population happen to recur at periodicity *k*.** For example, weekly pay cycles ($k = 7$) would make it illogical to sample bank cheque-cashing volume every Friday. A less obvious example would be a machine that stamps a defective part every 12th cycle due to a bad tooth in a 12-tooth gear, which would make it misleading to rely on a sample of every 12th part ($k = 12$). But periodicity coincident with *k* is not typical or expected in most situations.

Stratified Sample

Suppose the federal government wants to survey 1,000 Canadians of voting age to determine what percentage of these potential voters are in favour of new legislation to make oil companies more accountable for the price of gasoline. Using simple random sampling it is possible, although unlikely, that the 1,000 Canadians could be randomly selected from only one province (e.g., Alberta or Ontario). If Canadians in different provinces have quite different opinions about this legislation, the survey may result in conclusions that are quite inaccurate. For example, if the survey consists of only Albertans, one can only expect that they would be less in favour of this legislation than the rest of Canadians. So, when the results are used to reach conclusions about the attitudes that all Canadian voters have about this legislation, the conclusions would most likely underestimate the percentage of potential voters who favour this legislation. To avoid the possibility of sampling from only one province, we can use stratified sampling.

We use stratified random samples to improve our sample efficiency (i.e., a smaller sample for the same level of accuracy, or a greater level of accuracy for the same sample size) by utilizing prior information about the population. This method is most applicable when the population is quite heterogeneous (e.g., attitudes among provinces are quite different) but can be divided into relatively homogeneous subgroups (called strata) of known size (e.g., provinces). Within each *stratum,* a simple random sample of the desired size could be taken. To

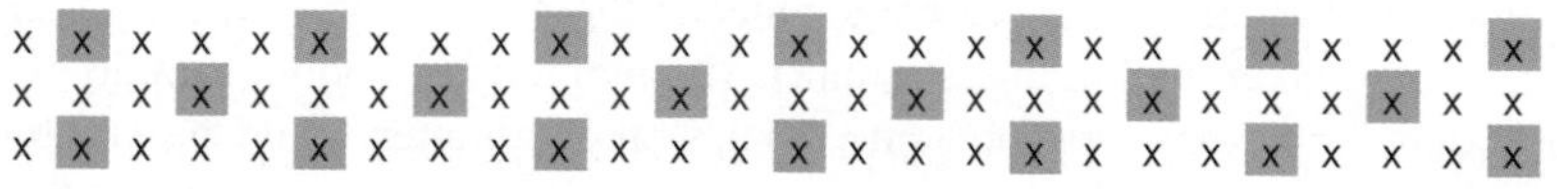

FIGURE 2.6

Systematic Sampling

Mini Case 2.2

CEO Compensation

To sample the compensation of the CEOs of the 501 largest companies in the United States listed in *Forbes'* annual survey, take every 20th company in the alphabetized list, starting (randomly) with the 13th company. The starting point (the 13th company) is chosen at random. This yields the sample of 25 CEOs, shown in Table 2.9. While it would be very time-consuming to examine all 501 executives, this sample should provide a representative cross-section.

TABLE 2.9   CEO Compensation in 25 Large U.S. Firms*   CEOComp

Observation	Firm	CEO	One-Year Total ($000)
1	Allegheny Energy	Alan J. Noia	$ 1,530
2	Analog Devices	Jerald G. Fishman	16,550
3	AutoNation	Michael J. Jackson	1,898
4	BJ Services	J. W. Stewart	23,354
5	Cendant	Henry R. Silverman	40,472
6	Coca-Cola Enterprises	Lowry F. Kline	8,725
7	Costco Wholesale	James D. Sinegal	6,078
8	DST Systems	Thomas A. McDonnell	29,644
9	EOG Resources	Mark G. Papa	785
10	Fleming Cos.	Mark S. Hansen	4,476
11	Gillette	James M. Kilts	2,840
12	Hibernia	J. Herbert Boydstun	1,231
13	ITT Industries	Louis J. Giuliano	3,022
14	Laboratory Corp. Amer.	Thomas P. MacMahon	10,385
15	Marshall & Ilsley	Dennis J. Kuester	6,510
16	Micron Technology	Steven R. Appleton	949
17	Noble Drilling	James C. Day	5,066
18	Park Place Entertain.	Thomas E. Gallagher	975
19	Principal Financial	J. Barry Griswell	2,321
20	RJ Reynolds Tobacco	Andrew J. Schindler	5,552
21	Smurfit-Stone	Patrick J. Moore	1,549
22	Synovus Financial	James H. Blanchard	1,800
23	Union Pacific	Richard K. Davidson	1,681
24	Visteon	Peter J. Pestillo	1,366
25	Wm. Wrigley, Jr.	William Wrigley, Jr.	1,697

Source: CEO Compensation, *Forbes,* May 13, 2002, pp. 116–38. Copyright © 2005 Forbes Inc. Reprinted by permission.

* Compensation is for the latest fiscal year.

get the most efficiency out of stratified sampling, the sample sizes within each stratum should be based, to a large extent, on the population size within each stratum and the homogeneity of the population within each stratum. (The larger a stratum's population, the larger the sample taken within that stratum. The more homogeneous the population is within a stratum, the smaller the sample taken within that stratum.) Alternatively, a random sample of the whole population could be taken, and then individual strata estimates could be combined using appropriate weights. This procedure, called **stratified sampling,** can reduce cost per observation and narrow the error bounds. For a population with L strata, the population size N is the sum of the stratum sizes: $N = N_1 + N_2 + \cdots + N_L$. The weight assigned to stratum j is $w_j = N_j/N$ (i.e., each stratum is weighted by its known proportion of the population).

As another illustration, suppose we want to estimate smallpox vaccination rates among employees of a provincial government, and we know that our target population (those individuals we are trying to study) is 55 percent male and 45 percent female. Suppose our budget only allows a sample of size 200. To ensure the correct gender balance, we could sample 110 males and 90 females. Alternatively, we could just take a random sample of 200 employees. Although our random sample probably will not contain *exactly* 110 males and 90 females, we can get an overall estimate of vaccination rates by *weighting* the male and female sample vaccination rates using $w_M = 0.55$ and $w_F = 0.45$ to reflect the known strata sizes.

Stratified sampling is widely used in marketing and economic surveys. For example, the Consumer Price Index is a stratified sample of 90,000 items from 364 categories, chosen from about 20,000 retail stores in 85 geographically distributed areas (strata) that are chosen to be as homogeneous as possible.

Cluster Sample

Cluster samples are taken from strata consisting of geographical regions. We divide a region (e.g., a city) into subregions (say, blocks, subdivisions, or school districts). In one-stage cluster sampling, our sample consists of all elements in each of k randomly chosen subregions (or clusters). In two-stage cluster sampling, we first randomly select k subregions (clusters) and then choose a random sample of elements within each cluster. Figure 2.7 illustrates how four elements could be sampled from each of three randomly chosen clusters using two-stage cluster sampling.

Because elements within a cluster are proximate, travel time and interviewer expenses are kept to a minimum. Cluster sampling is useful when:

- Population frame and stratum characteristics are not readily available.
- It is too expensive to obtain a simple or stratified sample.
- The cost of obtaining data increases sharply with distance.
- Some loss of reliability is acceptable.

FIGURE 2.7

Two-Stage Cluster Sampling

Although cluster sampling is cheap and quick, it is most accurate if the items within each group or cluster are quite heterogeneous while the items between groups or clusters are somewhat homogeneous. (Contrast this with stratified sampling where we would like homogeneity within each group and heterogeneity between groups.) An example of the effective use of cluster sampling is when new products are tested on a small scale before being introduced across Canada. Market testers have identified communities in Canada that represent a broad spectrum of Canadians (e.g., Peterborough, Ontario). One or more of these communities is randomly selected, and the product is introduced into the entire community. The results of this test would then determine whether the product should "die on the shelf" or be marketed nationwide.

Judgment Sample

Judgment sampling is a non-probability sampling method that relies on the expertise of the sampler to choose items that are representative of the population. For example, to estimate the corporate spending on research and development (R&D) in the medical equipment industry, we might ask an industry expert to select several "typical" firms. Unfortunately, subconscious biases can affect experts, too. In this context, "bias" does not mean prejudice, but rather *non-randomness* in the choice. Judgment samples may be the best alternative in some cases, but we can't be sure whether the sample was random. *Quota sampling* is a special kind of judgment sampling, in which the interviewer chooses the number of people to be sampled in each category (e.g., men/women) and once those numbers have been sampled, data collection is over.

Convenience Sample

The sole virtue of **convenience sampling** is that it is quick. The idea is to grab whatever sample is handy. An accounting professor who wants to know how many MBA students would take a summer elective in international accounting can just survey the class she is currently teaching. The students polled may not be representative of all MBA students, but an answer (although imperfect) will be available immediately. A newspaper reporter doing a story on perceived airport security might interview co-workers who travel frequently. An executive might ask department heads if they think non-business Web surfing is widespread.

You might think that convenience sampling is rarely used or, when it is, that the results are used with caution. However, this does not appear to be the case. Because convenience samples often sound the first alarm on a timely issue, their results have a way of attracting attention and have probably influenced quite a few business decisions. The mathematical properties of convenience samples are unknowable, but they do serve a purpose and their influence cannot be ignored.

Focus Groups

A **focus group** is a panel of individuals chosen to be representative of a wider population, formed for open-ended discussion and idea gathering about an issue (e.g., a proposed new product or marketing strategy). Typically, 5 to 10 people are selected, and the interactive discussion lasts 1 to 2 hours. Participants are usually individuals who do not know each other, but who are pre-screened to be broadly compatible yet diverse. A trained moderator guides the focus group's discussion and keeps it on track. Although not a random sampling method, focus groups are widely used, both in business and in social science research, for the insights they can yield beyond "just numbers."

Sample Size

The necessary sample size depends on the inherent variability of the quantity being measured and the desired precision of the estimate. For example, the caffeine content of Pepsi is fairly consistent because each can or bottle is filled at the factory, so a small sample size would suffice to estimate the mean caffeine content. In contrast, the amount of caffeine in an individually brewed cup of Bigelow Raspberry Royale tea varies widely because people let it steep for

We use the results of sampling to reach conclusions about some aspect of the population of interest. For example, we may use the average income of a sample of 100 households in Regina to reach conclusions about the average income of all Regina households. To reach accurate and defendable conclusions, we need to know the relationship between the information extracted from a sample (e.g., the average income in our sample) and the aspect of interest of the population (e.g., the average income of all households in Regina). To know what this relationship is, we need to select some type of random sample and we need to know the probability of each of the items in the population being selected. Non-random samples (e.g., judgment sampling, convenience sampling) do not allow us to know the relationship between our sample information and the aspect of the population of interest. Therefore, using non-random samples to reach these conclusions could be dangerous and misleading.

varying lengths of time, so a larger sample would be needed to estimate its mean caffeine content. The purposes of the investigation, the costs of sampling, the budget, and time constraints are also taken into account in deciding on sample size. Setting the sample size is worth a detailed discussion, found in later chapters.

Sources of Error

No matter how careful you are when conducting a survey, you will encounter potential sources of error. Let's briefly review a few, summarized in Table 2.10.

Non-response bias occurs when those who respond have characteristics different from those who don't respond. For example, people with call display, answering machines, blocked or unlisted numbers, or cellphones are likely to be missed in telephone surveys. Because these are generally more affluent individuals, their socio-economic class may be under-represented in the poll. A special case is **selection bias,** a self-selected sample. For example, a talk show host who invites viewers to take a Web survey about their sex lives will attract plenty of respondents. But those who are willing to reveal details of their personal lives (and who have time to complete the survey) are likely to differ substantially from those who dislike nosy surveys or are too busy (and probably weren't watching the show anyway).

Further, it is easy to imagine that dishonest replies will be common to such a survey (e.g., a bunch of university residence students giving silly answers on a Web survey). **Response error** occurs when respondents deliberately give false information to mimic socially acceptable answers, to avoid embarrassment, or to protect personal information.

Next, **coverage error** occurs when some important segment of the target population is systematically missed. For example, a survey of Simon Fraser University alumni will fail to represent non-university graduates or those who attended public universities. And **measurement error** results when the survey questions do not accurately reveal the construct being assessed,

TABLE 2.10 Potential Sources of Survey Error

Source of Error	Characteristics
Non-response bias	Respondents differ from non-respondents
Selection bias	Self-selected respondents are atypical
Response error	Respondents give false information
Coverage error	Incorrect specification of frame or population
Measurement error	Survey instrument wording is biased or unclear
Interviewer error	Responses influenced by interviewer
Sampling error	Random and unavoidable

as discussed previously. When the interviewer's facial expressions, tone of voice, or appearance influences the responses, data are subject to **interviewer error.**

Finally, **sampling error** is uncontrollable random error that is inherent in any survey. Even using a probability sampling method, it is possible that the sample will contain unusual responses. This cannot be prevented and is generally undetectable.

Section Exercises

2.19 Suppose you want to know the ages of moviegoers who attend *Spider-Man 3*. What kind of sample is it if you (a) survey the first 20 persons to emerge from the theatre, (b) survey every 10th person to emerge from the theatre, and (c) survey everyone who is wearing an earring? (LO 3)

2.20 (a) Referring to the previous question, would a simple random sample be possible? Explain. (b) Identify possible flaws and/or strengths in each of the sampling methods suggested in the previous problem. (c) Why might a survey not work at all? (LO 3)

2.21 Below is a 6 × 8 array containing the ages of moviegoers. Treat this as a population. Select a random sample of eight moviegoers' ages by using (a) simple random sampling with a random number table, (b) simple random sampling with Excel's =RANDBETWEEN( ) function, (c) systematic sampling, (d) judgment sampling, and (e) convenience sampling. Explain your methods. (LO 3)

32	34	33	12	57	13	58	16
23	23	62	65	35	15	17	20
14	11	51	33	31	13	11	58
23	10	63	34	12	15	62	13
40	11	18	62	64	30	42	20
21	56	11	51	38	49	15	21

2.22 (a) In the previous problem, what was the proportion of all 48 moviegoers who were under age 30? (b) For each of the samples of size $n = 8$ that you took, what was the proportion of moviegoers under age 30? (c) If your samples did not resemble the population, can you suggest why? (LO 4)

2.23 In Excel, type a list containing names for 10 of your friends into cells B1:B10. Choose three names at random by randomizing this list. To do this, enter =RAND( ) into cells A1:A10, copy the random column, and paste it using Paste > Special > Values to fix the random numbers, and then sort the list by the random column. The first three names are the random sample. (LO 3)

2.24 An infomercial is essentially a 30-minute "reality" commercial that tries to sell its viewers some product. It usually consists of a host, a person who is very familiar with the characteristics of the product and how to use it, several individuals who have used the product and state that the product is the greatest product ever invented, and a very enthusiastic studio audience. Why "reality"? Unlike 60-second commercials in which the vast majority of television viewers know that those in the commercials are actors and are getting paid for saying what they say, the infomercial tries to convey the appearance that it is not rehearsed and that the host, those giving testimony, and the audience are spontaneous in their words and their actions. For example, the host would act totally surprised when he or she is told how little the excellent product costs, and every individual who tried the product would appear to be giving their honest opinions about the product, which always happen to be extremely favourable. What type of sampling schemes are the producers hoping the viewers believe are being used? What type of sampling scheme is actually being used and what types of errors are probably being made? Is the deficiency of the sampling scheme used and the errors being made serious enough for a potential buyer to ignore the infomercial's content when deciding whether to purchase the product? (LO 4)

2.6   Data Sources

One goal of a statistics course is to help you learn where to find data that might be needed. Fortunately, many excellent sources are widely available, either in libraries or through private purchase. Table 2.11 summarizes a few of them.

The *Statistical Abstract of the United States* is the largest, most general, and most widely available annual compendium of facts and figures from public sources. You can purchase it at U.S. government bookstores in major U.S. cities, order it by mail, or use it for free on the Web. It covers a wide range of cross-sectional data (e.g., states, cities) as well as time series data. Subjects include population, vital statistics, immigration, health, nutrition, education, law enforcement, geography, environment, parks, recreation, elections, government, national defence, social insurance, human services, labour force, income, prices, banking, finance,

TABLE 2.11 Useful Data Sources

Type of Data	Examples
Canadian general data	Statistics Canada
Almanacs	*World Almanac, Time Almanac*
Periodicals	*Canadian Business , The Economist, BusinessWeek, Fortune,*
Indexes	*Globe and Mail ROB (Report On Business), The New York Times, The Wall Street Journal*
Databases	Census of Canada, Compustat, Citibase
World data	CIA World Factbook
Web	Google, Yahoo!, Bing

insurance, communications, energy, science, transportation, agriculture, forests, fisheries, mining, construction, housing, manufactures, and international statistics. No business statistician should be without this reference. *Statistics Canada* compiles similar data from Canadian sources.

Annual surveys of major companies, markets, and topics of business or personal finance are found in magazines such as *BusinessWeek, Canadian Business, Consumer Reports, Forbes, Fortune,* and *Money.* Indexes such as the *Business Periodical Index, The New York Times Index, Globe and Mail ROB,* and *The Wall Street Journal Index* are useful for locating topics. Libraries have Web search engines that can access many of these periodicals in abstract or full-text form.

Specialized computer databases (e.g., CRSP, Compustat, Citibase, U.S. Census) are available (at a price) for research on stocks, companies, financial statistics, and census data. An excellent summary of sources is F. Patrick Butler's *Business Research Sources: A Reference Navigator.* The Web allows us to use search engines (e.g., Google, Yahoo!, Bing) to find information. Sometimes you may get lucky, but Web information is often undocumented, unreliable, or unverifiable. Better information is available through private companies or trade associations, though often at a steep price.

Often overlooked sources of help are your university librarians. University librarians understand how to find databases and how to navigate databases quickly and accurately. Librarians can help you distinguish between valid and invalid Internet sources and then help you put the source citation in the proper format when writing reports.

2.7 Survey Research

Most survey research follows the same basic steps. These steps may overlap in time:

- Step 1:   State the goals of the research.
- Step 2:   Develop the budget (time, money, staff).
- Step 3:   Create a research design (target population, frame, sample size).
- Step 4:   Choose a survey type and method of administration.
- Step 5:   Design a data collection instrument (questionnaire).
- Step 6:   Pretest the survey instrument and revise as needed.
- Step 7:   Administer the survey (follow up if needed).
- Step 8:   Code the data and analyze it.

Survey Types

Surveys fall into five general categories: mail, telephone, interview, Web, and direct observation. They differ in cost, response rate, data quality, time required, and survey staff training requirements. Table 2.12 lists some common types of surveys and a few of their salient strengths/weaknesses.

TABLE 2.12 **Common Types of Surveys**

Type of Survey	Characteristics
Mail	You need a well-targeted and current mailing list (people move a lot). Expect low response rates and non-response bias (non-respondents differ from those who respond). Postal code lists (often costly) are an attractive option to define strata of similar income, education, and attitudes. To encourage participation, a cover letter should clearly explain the uses to which the data will be put. Plan for follow-up mailings.
Telephone	Random dialing yields very low response and is poorly targeted. Purchased phone lists help reach the target population, though a low response rate still is typical (disconnected phones, call display, answering machines, work hours, do not call lists). Other sources of non-response bias include the growing number of non-English speakers and distrust caused by scams and spams.
Interviews	Interviewing is expensive and time-consuming, yet a trade-off between sample size for high-quality results may still be worth it. Interviewers must be well-trained—an added cost. But interviewers can obtain information on complex or sensitive topics (e.g., gender discrimination in companies, birth control practices, diet and exercise habits).
Web	Web surveys are growing in popularity but are subject to non-response bias because they miss those who feel too busy, don't own computers, or distrust your motives (scams and spam). This type of survey works best when targeted to a well-defined interest group on a question of self-interest (e.g., frequent flyer views on airline security).
Direct Observation	Observation can be done in a controlled setting (e.g., psychology lab) but requires informed consent, which can change behaviour. Unobtrusive observation is possible in some non-lab settings (e.g., what percentage of airline passengers carry on more than two bags, what percentage of SUVs carry no passengers, what percentage of drivers wear seat belts).

Response Rates

Consider the *cost per valid response*. A telephone survey might be cheapest to conduct, but bear in mind that over half the households in some metropolitan areas have unlisted phones, and many have answering machines or call screening. The sample you get may not be very useful in terms of reaching the target population. Telephone surveys (even with random dialing) do lend themselves nicely to cluster sampling (e.g., using each three-digit area code as a cluster and each three-digit exchange as a cluster) to sample somewhat homogeneous populations. Similarly, mail surveys can be clustered by postal code, which is a significant attraction. Web surveys are cheap, but rather uncontrolled. Non-response bias is a problem with all of these. Interviews or observational experiments are expensive and labour-intensive, but they may provide higher quality data. Large-scale national research projects (e.g., mental health status of Canadian household members) offer financial incentives to encourage participants who otherwise would not provide information. Research suggests that adjustments can be made for whatever biases may result from such incentives. Table 2.13 offers some tips to conduct successful surveys.

Questionnaire Design

You should consider hiring a consultant, at least in the early stages, to help you get your survey off the ground successfully. Alternatively, resources are available on the Web to help you plan a survey. The American Statistical Association (www.amstat.org) offers the brochures, *What Is a Survey* and *How to Plan a Survey*. Entire books have been written to help you design and administer your own survey (see Related Reading).

The layout must not be crowded (use lots of white space). Begin with very short, clear instructions, stating the purpose, assuring anonymity, and explaining how to submit the completed survey. Questions should be numbered. Divide the survey into sections if the topics fall naturally

TABLE 2.13 Survey Guidelines

Planning	What is the purpose of the survey? What do you really need to know? What staff expertise is available? What skills are best obtained externally? What degree of precision is required? How is your budget best spent?
Design	To ensure a good response and useful data, you must invest time and money in designing the survey. Take advantage of many useful books and references so that you do not make unnecessary errors.
Quality	Care in preparation is needed. Glossy printing and advertising have raised people's expectations about quality. A scruffy questionnaire will be ignored. Some surveys (e.g., Web-based) may require special software.
Pilot Test	Questions that are clear to you may be unclear to others. You can pretest the questionnaire on friends or co-workers, but using a small test panel of naïve respondents who don't owe you anything is best.
Buy-In	Response rates may be improved by clearly stating the purpose of the survey, offering a token of appreciation (e.g., discount coupon, free gift) or paving the way with endorsements (e.g., from a trusted professional group).
Expertise	Consider working with an outside (or internal) consultant at the early stages, even if you plan to carry out the data collection and tabulation on your own. Early consultation is more cost-effective than waiting until you get in trouble.

into distinct areas. Let respondents bypass sections that aren't relevant to them (e.g., "If you answered no to Question 7, skip directly to Question 15"). Include an "escape option" where it seems appropriate (e.g., "Don't know" or "Does not apply"). Use wording and response scales that match the reading ability and knowledge level of the intended respondents. Pretest and revise. Keep the questionnaire as short as possible. Table 2.14 lists a few common question formats and response scales.

TABLE 2.14 Question Format and Response Scale

Type of Question	Example
Open-ended	Briefly describe your job goals.
Fill-in-the-blank	How many times did you attend formal religious services during the last year? _____ times
Check boxes	Which of these statistics packages have you used? ❏ SAS ❏ Visual Statistics ❏ SPSS ❏ MegaStat ❏ Systat ❏ MINITAB
Ranked choices	Please evaluate your dining experience: Excellent Good Fair Poor Food ❏ ❏ ❏ ❏ Service ❏ ❏ ❏ ❏ Ambiance ❏ ❏ ❏ ❏ Cleanliness ❏ ❏ ❏ ❏ Overall ❏ ❏ ❏ ❏
Pictograms	What do you think of the prime minister's economic policies? (circle one) ☺ ☺ 😐 🙁 ☹

Likert scale	Statistics is a difficult subject.
	
	Strongly Slightly Neither Slightly Strongly
	Agree Agree Agree Nor Disagree Disagree
	                  Disagree
	
	  ❏ ❏ ❏ ❏ ❏

Question Wording

The way a question is asked has a profound influence on the response. For example, in a *Wall Street Journal* editorial, Fred Barnes tells of a *Reader's Digest* poll that asked two similar questions:

Version 1:   I would be disappointed if Congress cut its funding for public television.

Version 2:   Cuts in funding for public television are justified to reduce federal spending.

The same 1,031 people were polled in both cases. Version 1 showed 40 percent in favour of cuts, while version 2 showed 52 percent in favour of cuts. The margin of error was ±3.5 percent (in "How to Rig a Poll," June 14, 1995, p. A18). To "rig" the poll, emotional overlays or "loaded" mental images can be attached to the question. In fact, it is often difficult to ask a neutral question without any context. For example:

Version 1:   Should provincial taxes be cut?

Version 2:   Should provincial taxes be cut, if it means reducing highway maintenance?

Version 3:   Should provincial taxes be cut, if it means firing teachers and police?

An unconstrained choice (version 1) makes tax cuts appear to be a "free lunch," while versions 2 and 3 require the respondent to envision the consequences of a tax cut. An alternative is to use version 1 but then ask the respondent to list the provincial services that should be cut to balance the budget after the tax cut.

Another problem in wording is to make sure you have covered all the possibilities. For example, how does a widowed NDP voter answer questions like these?

Are you married?	What is your party preference?
❏ Yes	❏ Liberal
❏ No	❏ Conservative

Overlapping classes or unclear categories are a problem. What if your father is deceased or is 45 years old?

How old is your father?

❏ 35–45   ❏ 45–55   ❏ 55–65   ❏ 65 or older

Coding and Data Screening

Survey responses usually are coded numerically (e.g., 1 = male, 2 = female), although some software packages can also tabulate text variables (nominal data) and use them in certain kinds of statistical tests. Most packages require you to denote missing values by a special character (e.g., blank, period, asterisk). If too many entries on a given respondent's questionnaire are flawed or missing, you may decide to discard the entire response.

Other data-screening issues include multiple responses (i.e., the respondent chose two responses where one was expected), outrageous replies on fill-in-the-blank questions (e.g., a respondent who claims to work 640 hours a week), "range" answers (e.g., 10–20 cigarettes smoked per day), or inconsistent replies (e.g., a 55-year-old respondent who claims to receive Canada Pension Plan benefits). Sometimes a follow-up is possible, but in anonymous surveys you must make the best decisions you can about how to handle anomalous data. Be sure to document your data-coding decisions—not only for the benefit of others but also in case you are asked to explain how you did it (it is easy to forget after a month or two, when you have moved on to other projects).

Data File Format

Data usually are entered into a spreadsheet or database. A "flat file" is an $n \times m$ matrix. Specifically, each column is a variable (m columns) and each row is a subject (n rows).

Case	Variable 1	Variable 2	. . .	Variable m
1	XXX	XXX	. . .	XXX
2	XXX	XXX	. . .	XXX
3	XXX	XXX	. . .	XXX
. . .	. . .	. . .	. . .	. . .
n	XXX	XXX	. . .	XXX

Spreadsheets may offer enough statistical power to handle your needs (particularly if you have an add-in like MegaStat for Excel). But spreadsheets are a general tool with limited features. You may prefer to use a professional statistical package that is designed for statistical analysis (e.g., MINITAB, SPSS, SyStat, SAS). You can copy your spreadsheet data and paste it into columns in the statistical software package, which will store the data in its own proprietary format.

Advice on Copying Data

If your data set contains commas (e.g., 42,586), dollar signs (e.g., $14.88), or percents (e.g., 7.5%), your statistics package (e.g., MINITAB or SPSS) may treat the data as text. A numerical variable may only contain the digits 0–9, a decimal point, and a minus sign. Format the data column as plain numbers with the desired number of decimal places *before* you copy the data to whatever package you are using. Excel can display a value such as 32.8756 as 32.9 if you set only one decimal digit, but it is the *displayed* number that is copied, so your Excel statistics may not agree with the package you are using.

Section Exercises

2.25 What sources of error might you encounter if you want to know (a) about the dating habits of university men, so you go to a residence meeting and ask students how many dates they have had in the last year; (b) how often people attend religious services, so you stand outside a particular church on Sunday and ask entering individuals how often they attend; (c) how often people eat at McDonald's, so you stand outside a particular McDonald's and ask entering customers how often they eat at McDonald's? (LO 4)

2.26 What kind of survey (mail, telephone, interview, Web, direct observation) would you recommend for each of the following purposes, and why? What problems might be encountered? (LO 4)
a. To estimate the proportion of students at your university who would prefer a Web-based statistics class to a regular lecture.
b. To estimate the proportion of students at your university who carry backpacks to class.
c. To estimate the proportion of students at your university who would be interested in taking a two-month summer class in international business with tours of European factories.
d. To estimate the proportion of Canadian business-school graduates who have taken a class in international business.

2.27 What kind of survey (mail, telephone, interview, Web, direct observation) would you recommend that a small laundry and dry cleaning business use for each of the following purposes, and why? What problems might be encountered? (LO 4)
a. To estimate the proportion of customers preferring opening hours at 7 a.m. instead of 8 a.m.
b. To estimate the proportion of customers who have only laundry and no dry cleaning.
c. To estimate the proportion of residents in the same postal code who spend more than $20 a month on dry cleaning.
d. To estimate the proportion of its seven employees who think it is too hot inside the building.

2.28 What would be the difference in student responses to the two questions shown? (LO 4)

Version 1: I would prefer that tuition be reduced.

Version 2: Cuts in tuition are a good idea even if some classes are cancelled.

2.29 What problems are evident in the wording of these two questions? (LO 4)

What is your race?   What is your religious preference?

❑ White   ❑ Christian
❑ Black   ❑ Jewish

CHAPTER SUMMARY

A **data set** is an array with *n* rows and *m* columns. Data sets may be **univariate** (one variable), **bivariate** (two variables), or **multivariate** (three or more variables). There are two basic data types: **categorical data** (categories that are described by labels) or **numerical** (meaningful numbers). Numerical data are **discrete** if the values are integers or can be counted or **continuous** if any interval can theoretically contain an infinite number of data values. **Nominal** measurements are unordered categories, **ordinal** measurements are ranks or ordered categories, **interval** measurements have meaningful distances between data values, and **ratio** measurements have meaningful ratios and a zero reference point. **Time series** data are observations measured at *n* different points in time or over sequential time intervals, while **cross-sectional** data are observations among *n* entities such as individuals, firms, or geographic regions measured at one point in time. Among **probability samples, simple random** samples pick items from a list using random numbers, **systematic** samples take every *k*th item, **cluster** samples select geographic regions, and **stratified** samples take into account known population proportions. **Non-probability** samples include convenience or judgment samples, gaining time but sacrificing randomness. **Focus groups** give in-depth information. **Survey design** requires attention to question **wording** and **scale definitions. Survey techniques** (mail, telephone, interview, Web, direct observation) depend on time, budget, and the nature of the questions and are subject to various sources of error.

KEY TERMS

binary variable, *22*	judgment sampling, *38*	sampling error, *40*
bivariate data sets, *21*	Likert scale, *25*	sampling frame, *30*
categorical data, *21*	measurement error, *39*	sampling with replacement, *34*
census, *29*	multivariate data sets, *21*	sampling without
cluster samples, *37*	nominal data, *24*	replacement, *34*
coding, *21*	non-random sampling, *32*	selection bias, *39*
continuous data, *23*	non-response bias, *39*	simple random sample, *32*
convenience sampling, *38*	numerical data, *21*	statistics, *29*
coverage error, *39*	observations, *21*	strata, *35*
cross-sectional data, *28*	ordinal data, *25*	stratified sampling, *37*
data, *21*	parameters, *29*	subject, *21*
data set, *21*	population, *28*	systematic sampling, *35*
discrete data, *22*	random numbers, *32*	target population, *30*
focus group, *38*	random sampling, *32*	time series data, *27*
individual, *21*	ratio data, *26*	univariate data sets, *21*
interval data, *25*	response error, *39*	variable, *21*
interviewer error, *40*	sample, *28*	

CHAPTER REVIEW

1. Define (a) data, (b) data set, (c) subject, and (d) variable. (LO 1)

2. How do business data differ from scientific experimental data? (LO 2)

3. Distinguish (a) univariate, bivariate, and multivariate data; (b) discrete and continuous data; (c) numerical and categorical data. (LO 1)

4. Define the four measurement levels and give an example of each. (LO 2)

5. Explain the difference between cross-sectional data and time series data. (LO2)

6. (a) List three reasons why a census might be preferred to a sample; (b) List three reasons why a sample might be preferred to a census.

7. (a) What is the difference between a parameter and a statistic? (b) What is a target population? (LO 1)

8. (a) List four methods of random sampling. (b) List two methods of non-random sampling. (c) Why would we ever use non-random sampling? (d) Why is sampling usually done without replacement? (LO 3)

9. List five (a) steps in a survey, (b) issues in survey design, (c) survey types, (d) question scale types, and (e) sources of error in surveys. (LO 4)

10. List advantages and disadvantages of the different types of surveys. (LO 4)

Data Types

2.30 Which type of data (categorical, discrete numerical, continuous numerical) is each of the following variables? Explain. If there is ambiguity, explain why. (LO 2)

a. Age of a randomly chosen tennis player in the Wimbledon tennis tournament.

b. Nationality of a randomly chosen tennis player in the Wimbledon tennis tournament.

c. Number of double-faults in a randomly chosen tennis game at Wimbledon.

d. Number of spectators at a randomly chosen Wimbledon tennis match.

e. Water consumption (in litres) by a randomly chosen Wimbledon player during a match.

2.31 Which type of data (nominal, ordinal, interval, ratio) is each of the following variables? Explain. (LO 2)

a. "Seed" (e.g., 20 of 128) of a randomly chosen tennis player in the Wimbledon tournament.

b   Noise level 100 metres from the Don Valley Parkway at a randomly chosen moment.

c. Number of occupants in a randomly chosen commuter vehicle on the Don Valley Parkway.

d. Number of annual office visits by a particular CPP subscriber.

e. Daily caffeine consumption by a 6-year-old child.

2.32 (a) Give *two* original examples of discrete data. (b) Give *two* original examples of continuous data. In each case, explain and identify any ambiguities that might exist. *Hint:* Do not restrict yourself to published data. Consider data describing your own life (e.g., your sports performance or financial or academic data). You need *not* list all the data, merely describe them and show a few typical data values. (LO 2)

2.33 (a) Give *two* original examples of time series data. (b) Give *two* original examples of cross-sectional data. In each case, identify the unit of observation carefully. If the data are both cross-sectional and time series, explain why. *Hint:* Do not restrict yourself to published data, and consider data describing your own life (e.g., sports performance or financial data). You need *not* list any data, merely describe them and perhaps show a few typical data values. (LO 2)

2.34 Below are 15 questions from a survey that was administered to a sample of MBA students (see *LearningStats,* Cross-Sectional Data, Surveys). Answers were recorded on paper in the blank at the left of each question. For each question, state the data type (categorical, discrete numerical, or continuous numerical) and measurement level (nominal, ordinal, interval, ratio). Explain your reasoning. If there is doubt, discuss the alternatives. (LO 2)

_____ Q1   What is your gender? (Male = 0, Female = 1)

_____ Q2   What is your approximate undergraduate university GPA? (1.0 to 4.0)

_____ Q3   About how many hours per week do you expect to work at an outside job this semester?

_____ Q4   What do you think is the ideal number of children for a married couple?

_____ Q5   On a 1 to 5 scale, which best describes your parents?
              1 = Mother clearly dominant ↔ 5 = Father clearly dominant

_____ Q6   On a 1 to 5 scale, assess the current job market for your undergraduate major.
              1 = Very bad ↔ 5 = Very good

_____ Q7   During the last month, how many times has your schedule been disrupted by car trouble?

_____ Q8   About how many years of university does the more-educated one of your parents have? (years)

_____ Q9   During the last year, how many traffic tickets (excluding parking) have you received?

_____ Q10   Which political orientation most nearly fits you?
              (1 = Liberal, 2 = Middle-of-Road, 3 = Conservative)

_____ Q11   What is the age of the car you usually drive? (years)

_____ Q12   About how many times in the past year did you attend formal religious services?

_____ Q13   How often do you read a daily newspaper?
              (0 = Never, 1 = Occasionally, 2 = Regularly)

_____ Q14   Can you conduct simple transactions in a language other than English?
              (0 = No, 1 = Yes)

_____ Q15   How often do you exercise (aerobics, running, etc.)? (0 = Not at All,
              1 = Sometimes, 2 = Regularly)

Sampling Methods

2.35 Would you use a sample or a census to measure each of the following? Why? If you are uncertain, explain the issues. (LO 3)

a. The number of cans of Campbell's soup on your local supermarket's shelf today at 6 p.m.

b. The proportion of soup sales last week in Halifax that was sold under the Campbell's brand.

c. The proportion of Campbell's brand soup cans in your family's pantry.

d. The number of workers currently employed by Campbell Soup Company.

2.36 Is each of the following a parameter or a statistic? If you are uncertain, explain the issues. (LO 1)

a. The number of cans of Campbell's soup sold last week at your local supermarket.

b. The proportion of all soup in Canada that was sold under the Campbell's brand last year.

c. The proportion of Campbell's brand soup cans in the family pantries of 10 students.

d. The total earnings of workers employed by Campbell Soup Company last year.

2.37 You can test Excel's algorithm for selecting random integers with a simple experiment. Enter =RANDBETWEEN(1,2) into cell A1 and then copy it to cells A1:E20. This creates a data block of 100 cells containing either a one or a two. In cell G1 type =COUNTIF(A1:E20," = 1") and in cell G2 type =COUNTIF(A1:E20," = 2"). Highlight cells G1 and G2 and use Excel's Chart Wizard to create a bar chart. Click on the vertical axis scale and set the lower limit to 0 and upper limit to 100. You will see something like the example shown below. Then hold down the F9 key and observe the chart. Are you convinced that, on average, you are getting about 50 ones and 50 twos? *Ambitious Students:* Generalize this experiment to integers 1 through 5.   **RandBetween**

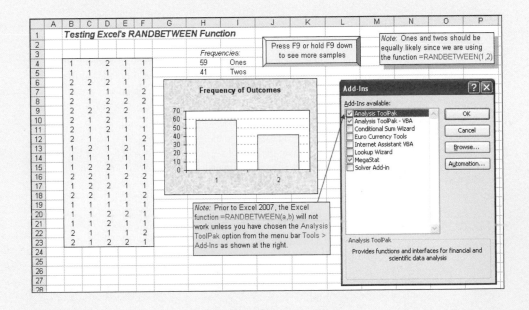

2.38 (a) To study profitability, which variables in the Fortune 1000 data set following could be used to *stratify* the sample? Name the strata for each. (b) Why might stratification be important if we wanted to study average profitability for both industries combined? (c) The Fortune 1000 list had 11 apparel companies and 39 chemical companies. If we just used the 20 companies here to estimate average profitability, what errors might we commit? (LO 3)

2.39 What sampling method would you use to estimate the percent of automobile owners who have radar detectors nationwide? Suggest several alternative methods, and discuss the strengths and weaknesses of each. Is a census possible? (LO 3)

2.40 Aflatoxin is the generic name for a family of natural poisons produced by the mould *aspergillus flavus,* which grows on peanuts and grains. Lab tests show that aflatoxin is a potent carcinogen. (a) What sampling method would you use to estimate the aflatoxin in brand-name and fresh-ground peanut butter sold in grocery stores nationwide to see whether the samples violate the U.S. Food and Drug Administration guidelines of 20 parts per billion (ppb)? (b) What is the sampling frame? Is the population finite or infinite? (c) Is a census possible? (See *Consumer Reports* 55, no. 9 [Sept. 1990], p. 591.) (LO 3)

Profitability of 20 Selected Companies from the 2003 Fortune 1000 20Firms

Company	Profit as % of Revenue	Industry	Employees (000)
Ashland	1	Chemicals	15 and Up
Cabot	4	Chemicals	Under 15
Dow Chemical	5	Chemicals	15 and Up
DuPont	4	Chemicals	15 and Up
Jones Apparel Group	8	Apparel	15 and Up
Kellwood	3	Apparel	15 and Up
Levi Strauss	−9	Apparel	Under 15
Liz Claiborne	7	Apparel	15 and Up
Lubrizol	4	Chemicals	Under 15
Nike	4	Apparel	15 and Up
Phillips Van Heusen	1	Apparel	Under 15
Polo Ralph Lauren	7	Apparel	Under 15
PPG Industries	6	Chemicals	15 and Up
Reebok International	5	Apparel	Under 15
Rohm and Haas	4	Chemicals	15 and Up
Scotts	5	Chemicals	Under 15
Terra Industries	−1	Chemicals	Under 15
VF	8	Apparel	15 and Up
W.R. Grace	−3	Chemicals	Under 15
Warnaco Group	159	Apparel	Under 15

Source: *Fortune* 1000 list 149, no. 7 April 5, 2004 issue. Copyright © 2005 Time Inc. All rights reserved.

2.41 Arsenic (a naturally occurring, poisonous metal) in home water wells is a common threat. (a) What sampling method would you use to estimate the arsenic levels in wells in a rural county to see whether the samples violate the EPA limit of 10 parts per billion (ppb)? (b) Is the population finite or infinite? (c) Is a census possible? (See *Popular Science,* Feb. 2002, p. 24.) (LO 3)

2.42 In the aftermath of the 2003 SARS outbreak in Toronto, the survey firm Wirthlin Worldwide of Reston, Virginia, found that 95 percent of men and 97 percent of women using restrooms at Toronto International Airport during August 2003 washed their hands with soap and water. At the other airports studied (O'Hare in Chicago, Kennedy in New York, Dallas/Ft. Worth, Miami, and San Francisco), the percentages of hand-washers ranged from 62 to 80 percent for men and from 59 to 92 for women. (a) Could a census have been used for this type of study? (b) Is the population finite or infinite? (c) Discuss what kind of sampling was probably used to study these questions. (d) How do you think the data were collected? (e) What biases or difficulties might be encountered? (Data are from *Science News* 164, no. 14 [Oct. 2003], p. 222.) (LO 3)

2.43 How often are "fresh wild salmon" really farm-bred? Newspaper reporters visited eight stores in New York City and bought samples of salmon sold as "wild" to a laboratory. The results showed that six of the eight samples were actually farm-bred, based on analysis of pigments known as carotenoids. (a) What kind of sampling method would you suppose was used? (b) If it was not a true random sample, does this invalidate the conclusion? (See *The New York Times,* Apr. 10, 2005.) (LO 3)

2.44 The average American male wears a size 10 shoe and spends 4 hours a year tying a tie. The average American female college student owns 3.5 pairs of jeans. The average American laughs 15 times daily, swallows 215 Aspirin tablets a year, and has a dog weighing 32 pounds. (a) Choose one of these estimates. How do you suppose it was derived? (b) What sampling method would *you* use to update each of these statistics? What problems would you anticipate? (c) Could a census be used? (d) Are the populations finite or infinite? (Data are from Mike Feinsilber and William B. Mead, *American Averages: Amazing Facts of Everyday Life* [Doubleday-Dolphin, 1980].) (LO 3)

2.45 What type of sampling schemes would you consider using in each of the following cases? If you decide to use either stratified random sampling or cluster sampling, what would your strata or clusters be? What assumptions are you making when you selected your schemes? (LO 3)

a. You want to estimate what proportion of Canadians are in favour of relaxing gun controls.

b. You want to estimate what proportion of customers who shop at a specific shopping mall spend, on average, more than $100 per visit.

c. You want to estimate what proportion of customers who shop at malls in the Vancouver area spend, on average, more than $100 per visit.

d. You want to estimate the average number of times first-year undergraduate students at Trent University skipped classes during their first term.

e. You want to sample a number of customers who shop at a particular shopping mall to determine whether the questions to a survey that you will distributing are clear and understandable.

f. You personally want to conduct personal interviews at more than one university across Canada to study students' opinions on a wide range of issues facing them now and in the future.

g. You want to study Canadian taxpayers' opinions on how our tax system can be improved.

2.46 Would you expect Noodles & Company to use a sample or census to measure each of the following? Explain.

a. The annual average weekly revenue of each Noodles restaurant.

b. The average number of weekly lunch visits by customers.

c. The customer satisfaction rating of a new dessert.

d. The number of weeks in a year that a restaurant sells more bottled beverages than fountain drinks.

2.47 *Money Magazine* published an annual list of major stock funds. In 2003, the list contained 1,699 funds. What method would you recommend to obtain a sample of 20 stock funds to estimate the 10-year percent return? If more than one method is acceptable, discuss the strengths and weaknesses of each. (Data are from *Money* 32, no. 2 [Feb. 2003], p. 166.) (LO 3)

2.48 Examine each of the following statistics. Which sampling method was most likely to have been used and why? What degree of accuracy would you imagine for each statistic? Why? (LO 3)

a. A survey showed that 30 percent of U.S. businesses have fired an employee for inappropriate Web surfing, such as gambling, watching porn, or shopping (*Popular Science,* Jan. 2007, p. 37).

b. Surveyed doctors report that 59 percent of patients do not follow their prescribed treatment (*Consumer Reports* 72, no. 2 [Feb. 2007] p. 35).

c. The Internal Revenue Service reports that, based on a sample of individual U.S. taxpayers, 80 percent of those who failed to pay what they owed did so through honest errors or misinterpretation of the tax code (*The Wall Street Journal,* Oct. 23, 2006, p. A4).

d. In Spain, per capita consumption of cigarettes is 2,274 compared with 1,230 in the United States (*The Wall Street Journal,* Mar. 23, 2006, p. B1).

e. The estimated number of illegal immigrants in the U.S. who are not working is 3.9 million (*The New York Times,* Apr. 2, 2006, p. 3).

2.49 According to a recent study, radar detector users have a lower accident rate than non-users. Moreover, detector users seem to be better citizens. The study found that detector users wear their seatbelts more and even vote more than non-users. (a) Can you suggest potential sources of coverage error? Non-response bias? Measurement error? (b) Do you agree with the conclusion that radar detector users are better citizens? Explain. (LO 4)

2.50 Prior to starting a recycling program, a city decides to measure the quantity of garbage produced by single-family homes in various neighbourhoods. This experiment will require weighing garbage on the day it is set out. (a) What sampling method would you recommend, and why? (b) Why not the others? (c) What would be a potential source of sample error? (LO 3 & 4)

2.51 As a statistics project, a student examined every cigarette butt along the sidewalk and curb along one block near his home. Of 47 identifiable butts, 22 were Marlboro. (a) What sampling method is this (if any)? (b) Is it correct to infer that 47 percent of all smokers prefer Marlboro? (c) What inferences *would* be appropriate? (d) What potential sources of error are present in this sample? (LO 3 & 4)

2.52 Devise a practical sampling method (not necessarily one of those mentioned in this chapter) to collect data to estimate each parameter. (LO 3)

a. Mean length of TV commercials during Monday night NFL games.

b. Percentage of peanuts in cans of Planter's Mixed Nuts.

c. Percentage of bank mortgages issued to first-time borrowers.

d. Mean winner-loser margin in Canadian Interuniversity Sport regular season basketball games.

e. Percentage of institutional holdings of publicly traded stocks in Canada.

2.53 Devise a practical sampling method (not necessarily one of those mentioned in this chapter) to collect data to estimate each parameter. (LO 3)

   a. Percentage of a doctor's patients who make more than five office visits per year.
   b. Percentage of commuters on your local highway who drive alone.
   c. Noise level (decibels) in neighbourhoods 100 metres from a certain freeway.
   d. Average flight departure delay for Air Canada in Regina.
   e. Average price of gasoline in your area.

2.54 (a) If the goal is to estimate the price of a particular brand of soft drink at various stores in your county, suggest several strata that might be relevant to choose the stores. (b) Suggest a feasible sampling method (not necessarily one of the standard ones). (LO 3)

2.55 What kind of bugs are killed by "mosquito zappers"? Prof. Douglas Tallamy, an entomologist at the University of Delaware, suspected that most of the carcasses were not mosquitoes. With the help of high school student volunteers, he analyzed 13,789 dead insects from six zappers from people's houses in suburban Newark, Delaware. The final count was only 18 mosquitoes and 13 other biting flies, or about 0.002 of the total. (a) Is there any alternative to sampling in this case? (b) What kind of stratification might be needed to generalize this experiment to the United States as a whole? (Data are from *Scientific American* 276, no. 6 [June 1997], p. 30.) (LO 3)

2.56 To protect baby scallops and ensure the survival of the species, the U.S. Fisheries and Wildlife Service requires that an average scallop must weigh at least 1/36 pound. The harbormaster at a Massachusetts port randomly selected 18 bags of scallops from 11,000 bags on an arriving vessel. From each bag, agents took a large scoop of scallops, separated and weighed the meat, and divided by the number of scallops in the scoop, finding a mean weight of 1/39 pound. (a) Is there any alternative to sampling in this case? (b) What kind of sampling method do you suppose was used to select the 18 bags? (Data are from *Interfaces* 25, no. 2 [Mar.–Apr. 1995], p. 18.) (LO 3)

2.57 *U.S. News & World Report* (Mar. 17, 2003) reports that the U.S. Food and Drug Administration (FDA) estimates that swordfish contains an average of 1.00 parts per million (ppm) of mercury, which exceeds the FDA guideline of 0.20 ppm. What kind of sampling method do you suppose was used to arrive at the swordfish estimate? Would more than one method be appropriate? Could a census be done? Explain. (LO 3)

2.58 A survey of 500 potential customers for new vehicles across the United States indicated that 37 percent expected their next vehicle to be an SUV. What kind of sampling method do you suppose was used to arrive at this estimate? Why not the others? (Data are from *Detroit Free Press*, Apr. 3, 2002, p. 3F.) (LO 3)

2.59 Blood lead levels exceeding 10 micrograms per decilitre have been shown to be harmful to mental and physical development in children. The U.S. Centers for Disease Control and Prevention in Atlanta say that about 500,000 children in the U.S. have blood concentrations of lead higher than this level. (a) Which sampling method do you suppose was used to measure blood levels of lead in U.S. children to reach this conclusion? (b) Which sampling methods would be infeasible in this case? (LO 3)

2.60 Households can sign up for a telemarketing "do not call list." How might households who sign up differ from those who don't? What biases might this create for telemarketers promoting (a) financial planning services, (b) carpet cleaning services, and (c) vacation travel packages? (LO 4)

2.61 "When we were kids, nobody wore seat belts or bike helmets. We used lead-based paint and didn't install ground-fault circuit protectors in our electrical circuits. Yet we survived." What kind of sampling bias(es) does this statement illustrate? (LO 4)

Surveys and Scales

2.62 Insurance companies are rated by several rating agencies. The Fitch 20-point scale is AAA, AA+, AA, AA−, A+, A, A−, BBB+, BBB, BBB−, BB+, BB, BB−, B+, B, B−, CCC+, CCC, CCC−, DD. (a) What level of measurement does this scale use? (b) To assume that the scale uses interval measurements, what assumption is required? (Scales are from *Weiss Ratings Guide to HMOs and Health Insurers*, Summer 2003, p. 15.) (LO 2)

2.63 Suggest response check boxes for these questions. In each case, what difficulties do you encounter as you try to think of appropriate check boxes? (LO 4)

   a. Where are you employed?
   b. What is the biggest issue facing the next prime minister?
   c. Are you happy?

2.64 Suggest both a Likert scale question and a response scale to measure the following: (LO 4)

   a. A student's rating of a particular statistics professor.
   b. A voter's satisfaction with the prime minister's economic policy.
   c. A patient's perception of waiting time to see a doctor.

2.65 A Web-based poll on Newsweek.com asked *Newsweek* readers the question shown below. Do you consider the wording of the responses to be neutral? Can you suggest alternative response wording? (From *Newsweek*, May 8, 2002, p. 6.) (LO 4)

Should the Boy Scouts be allowed to exclude gays?

1. No, it is wrong to discriminate.
2. No, but they should have a "don't ask, don't tell" policy regarding gays.
3. Yes, as a private group, they can determine whom they want to admit.
4. Yes, gays compromise the Scouts' moral code.

2.66 What level of measurement (nominal, ordinal, interval, ratio) is appropriate for the movie rating system that you see in *TV Guide* (☆, ☆☆, ☆☆☆, ☆☆☆☆)? Explain your reasoning. (LO 2)

2.67 A survey by the American Automobile Association is shown below. (a) What kind of response scale is this? (b) Suggest an alternative response scale. (Survey question from *Michigan Living*, Dec. 1994. Copyright © Automobile Association of America. Used with permission.) (LO 2)

New drivers under 18 should be required to complete additional hours of supervised driving beyond that provided in driver education.

❏ Strongly agree ❏ Strongly disagree

❏ Agree ❏ Undecided

❏ Disagree

2.68 A tabletop survey by a restaurant asked the question shown below. (a) What kind of response scale is this? (b) Suggest an alternative response scale that would be more sensitive to differences in opinion. (c) Suggest possible sources of bias in this type of survey. (LO 2)

Were the food and beverage presentations appealing?

❏ Yes

❏ No

Sampling Experiments

2.69 Below are 64 names of employees at NilCo. Colours denote different departments (finance, marketing, purchasing, engineering). Sample eight names from the display shown by using (a) simple random sampling, (b) sequential sampling, and (c) cluster sampling. Try to ensure that every name has an equal chance of being picked. Which sampling method seems most appropriate? (LO 3) **PickEight**

Floyd	Sid	LaDonna	Tom	Mabel	Nicholas	Bonnie	Deepak
Nathan	Ginnie	Mario	Claudia	Dmitri	Kevin	Blythe	Dave
Lou	Tim	Peter	Jean	Mike	Jeremy	Chad	Doug
Loretta	Erik	Jackie	Juanita	Molly	Carl	Buck	Janet
Anne	Joel	Moira	Marnie	Ted	Greg	Duane	Amanda
Don	Gadis	Balaji	Al	Takisha	Dan	Ryan	Sam
Graham	Scott	Lorin	Vince	Jody	Brian	Tania	Ralph
Bernie	Karen	Ed	Liz	Erika	Marge	Gene	Pam

2.70 From the display below pick five cards (without replacement) by using random numbers. Explain your method. Why would the other sampling methods not work well in this case? (LO 3)

A ♠	A ♥	A ♣	A ♦
K ♠	K ♥	K ♣	K ♦
Q ♠	Q ♥	Q ♣	Q ♦
J ♠	J ♥	J ♣	J ♦
10 ♠	10 ♥	10 ♣	10 ♦
9 ♠	9 ♥	9 ♣	9 ♦
8 ♠	8 ♥	8 ♣	8 ♦
7 ♠	7 ♥	7 ♣	7 ♦
6 ♠	6 ♥	6 ♣	6 ♦
5 ♠	5 ♥	5 ♣	5 ♦
4 ♠	4 ♥	4 ♣	4 ♦
3 ♠	3 ♥	3 ♣	3 ♦
2 ♠	2 ♥	2 ♣	2 ♦

2.71 Treating this textbook as a population, select a sample of 10 pages at random by using (a) simple random sampling, (b) systematic sampling, (c) cluster sampling, and (d) judgment sampling. Explain your methodology carefully in each case. (e) Which method would you recommend to estimate the mean number of formulas per page? Why not the others? (LO 3)

2.72 Photocopy the exhibit below (omit these instructions) and show it to a friend or classmate. Ask him/her to choose a number at random and write it on a piece of paper. Collect the paper. Repeat for *at least* 20 friends/classmates. Tabulate the results. Were all the numbers chosen equally often? If not, which were favoured or avoided? Why? *Hint:* Review section 2.6. (LO 3)

PickOne

0	11	17	22
8	36	14	18
19	28	6	41
12	3	5	0

2.73 Ask each of 20 friends or classmates to choose a whole number between 1 and 5. Tabulate the results. Do the results seem random? If not, can you think of any reasons? (LO 3)

LearningStats Unit 02 Manipulating Data LS

LearningStats Unit 02 introduces data types, sampling, random numbers, and surveys. Modules are designed for self-study, so you can proceed at your own pace, concentrate on material that is new, and pass quickly over things that you already know. Your instructor may assign specific modules, or you may decide to check them out because the topic sounds interesting. In addition to helping you learn about statistics, they may be useful as references later on.

Topic	*LearningStats Modules*
Data types	Level of Measurement
Sampling	Sampling Methods—Overview
	Sampling Methods—Worksheet
	Who Gets Picked?
	Randomizing a File
	Sampling a Large Database*
	Excel's RANDBETWEEN Function
Surveys	Survey Methods
Data sources	Web Data Sources

Key: = PowerPoint = Word = Excel

*Denotes a specialized topic.

For solutions to odd-numbered exercises, Exam Review questions, and additional study tools to help you succeed in this course, visit *Connect* at www.mcgrawhillconnect.ca.

Chapter

3

Describing Data Visually

Chapter Learning Objectives

When you finish this chapter you should be able to

1. Describe and create, either manually or by computer, commonly used statistical visual displays.

2. Determine which visual displays are appropriate for the available data and for their intended purpose.

3. Interpret the results of the created visual displays in a problem context.

4. Recognize deceptive graphing techniques.

5. Define the characteristics of good graphs in general.

3.1 Visual Description

Managers need information that can help them identify trends and adjust to changing conditions. But it is hard to assimilate piles of raw data. How can a business analyst convert raw data into relevant information? Statistics offers many methods that can help organize, explore, and summarize data in a succinct way. The methods may be *visual* (charts and graphs) or *numerical* (statistics and tables). In this chapter, you will see how visual displays can provide insight into the characteristics of a data set *without* using mathematics. We begin with a set of n observations $x_1, x_2, \ldots, x_n$ on one variable (univariate data). Such data can be discussed in terms of three characteristics: **central tendency, dispersion,** and **shape.** Table 3.1 summarizes these characteristics as *questions* that we will be asking about the data.

TABLE 3.1 Characteristics of Univariate Data

Characteristic	Interpretation
Measurement	What are the units of measurement? Are the data integer or continuous? Any missing observations? Any concerns with accuracy or sampling methods?
Central Tendency	Where are the data values concentrated? What seem to be typical or middle data values?
Dispersion	How much variation is there in the data? How spread out are the data values? Are there unusual values?
Shape	Are the data values distributed symmetrically? Skewed? Sharply peaked? Flat? Bimodal?

EXAMPLE 1
Price/Earnings Ratios

Price/earnings (P/E) ratios—current stock price divided by earnings per share in the last 12 months—show how much an investor is willing to pay for a stock based on the stock's earnings. P/E ratios are also used to determine how optimistic the market is for a stock's growth potential. Investors may be willing to pay more for a lower earning stock than a higher earning stock if they see potential for growth. Table 3.2 shows P/E ratios for a random sample of companies ($n = 57$) from Standard & Poor's 500 index. We might be interested in learning how the P/E ratios of the companies in the S&P 500 compare to each other and what the overall distribution of P/E ratios looks like within the S&P 500. Visual displays can help us describe and summarize the main characteristics of this sample.

TABLE 3.2 P/E Ratios for 57 Companies PERatios

Company	P/E Ratio	Company	P/E Ratio	Company	P/E Ratio
Ace Ltd	8	Family Dollar Stores	19	Nike Inc B	18
AFLAC Inc	14	Fed Natl Mtg Corp	11	Northrop Grumman	14
Allied Waste Inc	21	FirstEnergy Corp	14	Nucor Corp	11
AutoNation Inc	12	Fluor Corp	22	Occidental Petroleum	11
Baker Hughes Inc	13	Freeport-Mcmor-B	11	PPG Industries	13
Bank New York	16	General Electric	16	Principal Financial	16
Bank of America	11	Genzyme-Genl Div	23	Progress Energy	17
Baxter International	20	Goldman-Sachs Group	10	Radioshack Corp	24
Bear Stearns Cos	11	Hilton Hotels Co	28	Rohm and Haas Co	15
Bed Bath & Beyond	20	Ingersoll-Rand-A	12	Sara Lee Corp	25
Bemis Co	17	Jones Apparel	13	Staples Inc	20
BMC Software Inc	27	KB Home	14	Starwood Hotels	25
Burlington/Santa	14	KeySpan Corp	16	Stryker Corp	25
Chevron Corp	9	Leggett & Platt	13	Symantec Corporation	21
ConocoPhillips	8	Lexmark Intl A	17	Tribune Co	14
Constellation Energy	16	Limited Brands	16	Union Pacific Corp	15
Disney (Walt) Co	20	Mellon Financial	17	Wendy's Intl Inc	24
Electronic Data	17	Moody's Corp	29	Whirlpool Corp	18
Emerson Elec Co	17	New York Times A	19	Yum! Brands Inc	18

Source: Standard & Poor's, *Security Owner's Stock Guide*, Feb. 2007.

Measurement

Before calculating any statistics or drawing any graphs, it is a good idea to *look at the data* and try to visualize how it was collected. Because the companies in the S&P 500 index are publicly traded, they are required to publish verified financial information, so the accuracy of the data is not an issue. Because the intent of the analysis is to study the S&P 500 companies at a *point in time,* these are *cross-sectional* data. (Financial analysts also study time-series data on P/E ratios, which vary daily as stock prices change.) Although rounded to integers, the measurements are continuous. For example, a stock price of $43.22 divided by earnings per share of $2.17 gives a P/E ratio of $(43.22)/(2.17) \approx 19.92$, which would be rounded to 20 for convenience. Because there is a true zero, we can speak meaningfully of ratios and can perform any standard mathematical operations. Finally, because the analysis is based on a sample (not a census), we must allow for the possibility of *sampling error,* that is, the possibility that our sample is not representative of the population of all 500 S&P 500 firms, due to the nature of random sampling.

Sorting

As a first step, it is helpful to sort the data. This is a visual display, although a very simple one. From the sorted data, we can see the range, the frequency of occurrence for each data value, and the data values that lie near the middle and ends.

8	8	9	10	11	11	11	11	11	11
12	12	13	13	13	13	14	14	14	14
14	14	15	15	16	16	16	16	16	16
17	17	17	17	17	17	18	18	18	19
19	20	20	20	20	21	21	22	23	24
24	25	25	25	27	28	29			

When the number of observations is large, a sorted list of data values is difficult to analyze. Further, a simple list of numbers may not reveal very much about central tendency, dispersion, and shape. To see broader patterns in the data, analysts often prefer a *visual display* of the data. This chapter explains various types of visual displays, offers guidelines for effective graphs, and warns you of ways that visual displays can be deceptive.

3.2   Dot Plots

A **dot plot** is a simple graphical display of *n* individual values of numerical data. The basic steps in making a dot plot are to (1) make a scale that covers the data range, (2) mark axis demarcations and label them, and (3) plot each data value as a dot above the scale at its approximate location. If more than one data value lies at approximately the same *X*-axis location, the dots are piled up vertically. Figure 3.1 shows a dot plot for 57 P/E ratios.

Dot plots are an attractive tool for data exploration because they are easy to understand. A dot plot shows *dispersion* by displaying the range of the data. It shows *central tendency* by revealing where the data values tend to cluster and where the midpoint lies. A dot plot can also reveal some things about the *shape* of the distribution if the sample is large enough. For the P/E ratios, the dot plot in Figure 3.1 shows that:

- The range is from 8 to 29.
- All but a few data values lie between 10 and 25.
- A typical "middle" data value would be around 15 or 16.
- The sample is not quite symmetric due to a few large P/E ratios.

You can make a dot plot yourself (if the sample is small) using a straightedge and a pencil. Excel doesn't offer dot plots, but you can get them from MegaStat, Visual Statistics, or MINITAB. Figure 3.2 shows the dot plot menus and check box for MegaStat > Descriptive Statistics for the chosen data range on a spreadsheet.

FIGURE 3.1

Dot Plot of 57 P/E Ratios

P/E Ratios

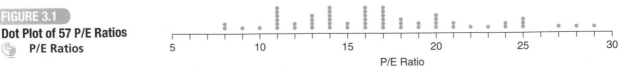

P/E Ratio

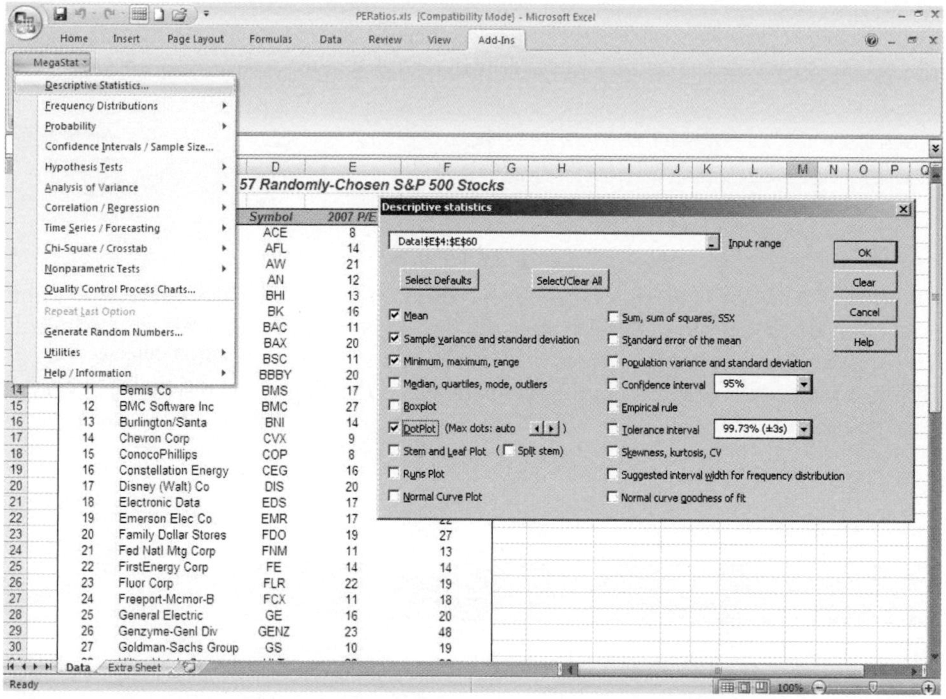

FIGURE 3.2

MegaStat Menus for Dot Plot HomePrices

Source: www.realtor.org

Section Exercises

3.1 (a) Without using a computer, make a dot plot for these 32 observations on the number of customers to use a downtown Bank of Montreal ABM during the noon hour on 32 consecutive workdays. (b) Describe its appearance. (LO 1) **BankMontreal**

25	37	23	26	30	40	25	26
39	32	21	26	19	27	32	25
18	26	34	18	31	35	21	33
33	9	16	32	35	42	15	24

3.2 Without using a computer, make a dot plot for the number of defects per 100 vehicles for these 37 brands. Describe its appearance. (LO 1 & 3)

Defects per 100 Vehicles (alphabetical by brand) **JDpower**

Brand	Defects	Brand	Defects	Brand	Defects
Acura	120	Infiniti	117	Nissan	121
Audi	130	Isuzu	191	Pontiac	133
BMW	142	Jaguar	109	Porsche	91
Buick	134	Jeep	153	Saab	163
Cadillac	117	Kia	136	Saturn	129
Chevrolet	124	Land Rover	204	Scion	140
Chrysler	120	Lexus	93	Subaru	146
Dodge	132	Lincoln	121	Suzuki	169
Ford	127	Mazda	150	Toyota	106
GMC	119	Mercedes-Benz	139	Volkswagen	171
Honda	110	Mercury	129	Volvo	133
HUMMER	171	MINI	150		
Hyundai	102	Mitsubishi	135		

Source: J. D. Power and Associates 2006 Initial Quality Study™. Used with permission.

3.3 Sarah and Bob share a 1,000-minute cellphone calling plan. Without using a computer, make a *stacked dot plot* to compare the lengths of cellphone calls by Sarah and Bob during the last week. Describe what the dot plots tell you. (LO 1 & 3)

PhoneCalls

Sarah's calls: 1, 1, 1, 1, 2, 3, 3, 3, 5, 5, 6, 6, 7, 8, 8, 12, 14, 14, 22, 23, 29, 33, 38, 45, 66

Bob's calls: 5, 8, 9, 14, 17, 21, 23, 23, 24, 26, 27, 27, 28, 29, 31, 33, 35, 39, 41

While they are easy to understand, dot plots have limitations. They don't reveal very much information about the data set's shape when the sample is small, but they become awkward to plot when the sample is large. (What if you have 100 dots at the same point?) The next section of this textbook explains some widely used methods for creating visual displays that work for any sample size.

Mini Case   3.1

U.S. Business Cycles

Although many businesses anticipated the 2001 recession that followed the long boom and stock market bubble of the 1990s, they needed to anticipate its probable length to form strategies for debt management and future product releases. Fortunately, good data are available from the National Bureau of Economic Research, which keeps track of business cycles. The length of a contraction is measured from the peak of the previous expansion to the beginning of the next expansion based on the real gross domestic product (GDP). Table 3.3 shows the durations, in months, of 32 U.S. recessions.

TABLE 3.3   U.S. Business Contractions, 1857–2001 ($n = 32$)   Recessions

Peak	Trough	Months	Peak	Trough	Months
Jun 1857	Dec 1858	18	Jan 1920	Jul 1921	18
Oct 1860	Jun 1861	8	May 1923	Jul 1924	14
Apr 1865	Dec 1867	32	Oct 1926	Nov 1927	13
Jun 1869	Dec 1870	18	Aug 1929	Mar 1933	43
Oct 1873	Mar 1879	65	May 1937	Jun 1938	13
Mar 1882	May 1885	38	Feb 1945	Oct 1945	8
Mar 1887	Apr 1888	13	Nov 1948	Oct 1949	11
Jul 1890	May 1891	10	Jul 1953	May 1954	10
Jan 1893	Jun 1894	17	Aug 1957	Apr 1958	8
Dec 1895	Jun 1897	18	Apr 1960	Feb 1961	10
Jun 1899	Dec 1900	18	Dec 1969	Nov 1970	11
Sep 1902	Aug 1904	23	Nov 1973	Mar 1975	16
May 1907	Jun 1908	13	Jan 1980	Jul 1980	6
Jan 1910	Jan 1912	24	Jul 1981	Nov 1982	16
Jan 1913	Dec 1914	23	Jul 1990	Mar 1991	8
Aug 1918	Mar 1919	7	Mar 2001	Nov 2001	8

Source: U.S. Business Contractions found at www.nber.org. Copyright © 2005 National Bureau of Economic Research, Inc. Used with permission.

Peak-to-Trough Business Cycle Duration

FIGURE 3.3

Dot Plot of Business Cycle Duration (*n* = 32)

Number of Months

From the dot plot in Figure 3.3, we see that the 65-month contraction (1873–1879) was quite unusual, although four recessions did exceed 30 months. Most recessions have lasted less than 20 months. Only 7 of 32 lasted less than 10 months. The eight-month 2001 recession was therefore among the shortest, although its recovery phase was sluggish and inconsistent compared to most other recessions.

Still, the table supplies information that the dot plot cannot. For example, during the 1930s there were actually *two* major contractions (43 months from 1929 to 1933, 13 months from 1937 to 1938), which is one reason why that period seemed so terrible to those who lived through it. The Great Depression of the 1930s was so named because it lasted a long time and the economic decline was deeper than in most recessions.

3.3   Frequency Distributions and Histograms

Bins and Bin Limits

A frequency distribution is a table formed by classifying *n* data values into *k* classes called *bins* (we adopt this terminology from Excel). The *bin limits* define the values to be included in each bin. Usually, all the bin widths are the same to prevent distorting the interpretation of this table and the histogram created from this table. The table shows the *frequency* of data values within each bin. Frequencies can also be expressed as *relative frequencies* or *percentages* of the total number of observations.

Frequency Distribution

A tabulation of *n* data values into *k* classes called *bins,* based on values of the data. The *bin limits* are cutoff points that define each bin. Bins generally have equal widths and their limits cannot overlap.

The basic steps for constructing a frequency distribution are to (1) sort the data in ascending order, (2) choose the number of bins, (3) set the bin limits, (4) put the data values in the appropriate bin, and (5) create the table. Let's walk through these steps.

Constructing a Frequency Distribution

Step 1: Find Smallest and Largest Data Values

8	8	9	10	11	11	11	11	11	11
12	12	13	13	13	13	14	14	14	14
14	14	15	15	16	16	16	16	16	16
17	17	17	17	17	17	18	18	18	19
19	20	20	20	20	21	21	22	23	24
24	25	25	25	27	28	29			

For the P/E data, we get $x_{min} = 8$ and $x_{max} = 29$. You might be able to find x_{min} and x_{max} without sorting the entire data set, but it is easier to experiment with bin choices if you have already sorted the data.

TABLE 3.4   Sturges' Rule

Sample Size (n)	Suggested Number of Bins (k)
16	5
32	6
64	7
128	8
256	9
512	10
1,024	11

Note: Sturges said that the number of classes to tabulate n items should be approximately $1 + 3.3 \log_{10}(n)$.

Step 2: Choose Number of Bins   Because a frequency distribution seeks to condense many data points into a small table, we expect the number of bins k to be much smaller than the sample size n. When you use *too many* bins some bins are likely to be sparsely populated, or even empty, making the interpretation of the distribution of the data difficult. With *too few* bins, dissimilar data values are lumped together and too much information contained in the data set is lost. Left to their own devices, people tend to choose similar bin limits for a given data set. Generally, larger samples justify more bins. According to **Sturges' Rule,** a guideline proposed by statistician Herbert Sturges, every time we double the sample size, we should add one bin, as shown in Table 3.4.

For the sample sizes you are likely to encounter, Table 3.4 says that you would expect to use from $k = 5$ to $k = 11$ bins. Sturges' Rule can be expressed as a formula:

$$\text{Sturges' Rule: } k = 1 + 3.3 \log_{10}(n) \tag{3.1}$$

For the P/E data ($n = 57$), Sturges' Rule says:

$$k = 1 + 3.3 \log_{10}(n) = 1 + 3.3 \log_{10}(57) = 1 + 3.3(1.7559) = 6.79 \text{ bins}$$

Using either Table 3.4 or Sturges' formula, we would consider using six or seven bins for the P/E data. But to get "nice" bin limits you may choose more or fewer bins. Picking attractive bin limits is often an overriding consideration (not Sturges' Rule).

Step 3: Set Bin Limits   Just as choosing the number of bins requires judgment, setting the bin limits also requires judgment. For guidance, find the approximate width of each bin by dividing the data range by the number of bins:

$$\text{Bin width} > \frac{x_{\max} - x_{\min}}{k} \tag{3.2}$$

Round the bin width *up* to an appropriate value, then set the lower limit for the first bin as a multiple of the bin width. What does "appropriate" mean? If the data are discrete, then it makes sense to have a width that is an integer value. If the data are continuous, then setting a bin width equal to a fractional value may be appropriate. Experiment until you get bins that cover the data range.

For example, for this data set, the smallest P/E ratio was 8 and the largest P/E ratio was 29, so if we want to use $k = 6$ bins, we calculate the approximate bin width as:

$$\text{Bin width} > \frac{29 - 8}{6} = \frac{21}{6} = 3.50$$

To obtain "nice" limits, we can round the bin width up to 4 and start the first bin at 8 to get bin limits 8, 12, 16, 20, 24, 28, 32. Usually "nice" bin limits are 2, 5, or 10 multiplied by an appropriate integer power of 10. As a starting point for the lowest bin, we can choose the largest multiple of the bin width smaller than the lowest data value. For example, if bin width is 5 and the smallest data value is 23, the first bin would start at 20.

Note: If there are one or two extreme values that could have a significant effect on the bin width, resulting in one of two bins containing most of the data and thus a loss of potentially

TABLE 3.5   Frequency Distribution of P/E Ratios Using Six Bins   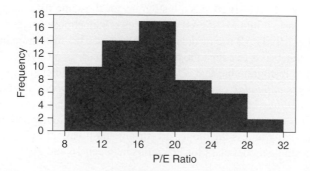 PERatios

| Bin Limits | | | | | |
From	To	Frequency	Relative Frequency	Cumulative Frequency	Cumulative Relative Frequency
8	< 12	10	0.1754	10	0.1754
12	< 16	14	0.2456	24	0.4211
16	< 20	17	0.2982	41	0.7193
20	< 24	8	0.1404	49	0.8596
24	< 28	6	0.1053	55	0.9649
28	< 32	2	0.0351	57	1.0000
	Total:	57	1.0000		

important information, you should determine the bin widths and the bin limits ignoring these extreme values. Having done this, you would then create an "open-ended" bin or two "open-ended" bins (if there are both extremely low and high values) and count these extreme values as belonging to those bins. For example, if one of the P/E ratios was 150, you should create the open-ended bin "≥ 32"

Step 4: Put Data Values in Appropriate Bins   In general, the lower limit is *included* in the bin, while the upper limit is *excluded*. MegaStat and MINITAB follow this convention. However, Excel's histogram option *includes* the upper limit and *excludes* the lower limit. (If your upper limit for a bin is stated as 20 but you don't want the value of 20 included in that bin, when setting up the bin ranges using Excel you would set the upper limit for that bin to be 19.9 if the data are recorded to one decimal place.) There are advantages to either method. Our objective is to make sure that none of the bins overlap and that data values are counted in only one bin.

Step 5: Create Table   You can choose to show only the absolute frequencies, or counts, for each bin or also include the relative frequencies and the cumulative frequencies. Relative frequencies are calculated as the absolute frequency for a bin divided by the total number of data values. Cumulative relative frequencies accumulate relative frequency values as the bin limits increase. Table 3.5 shows the frequency distribution we've created for the P/E ratio data. Sometimes the relative frequencies do not sum to 1 due to rounding.

This table tells us, for example, that 14.04 percent (relative frequency of 0.1404) of the P/E ratios in the sample are at least 20 but less than 24, and that 85.96 percent (cumulative relative frequency of 0.8596) of the P/E ratios are less than 24.

Histograms

A **histogram** is a graphical representation of a frequency distribution. A histogram is a bar chart whose *Y*-axis shows the number of data values (or a percentage) within each bin of a frequency distribution and whose *X*-axis ticks show the end points of each bin. When drawing the bars, there should be no gaps between bars (except when there are no data in a particular bin) as shown in Figure 3.4.

FIGURE 3.4

Histogram of P/E Ratios (6 bins) **PERatios**

FIGURE 3.5   **Three Histograms for P/E Ratios**   PERatios

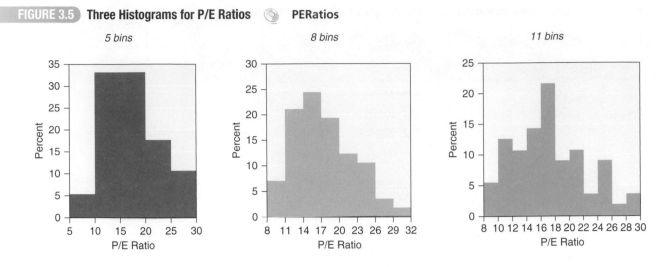

As we discussed earlier, choosing the number of bins and bin limits requires judgment on our part. The process of creating a histogram is often an iterative process. Our first choice of bins and limits may not be our final choice for presentation. Figure 3.5 shows histograms for the P/E ratio sample using three different bin definitions. Our perception of the shape of the distribution depends on how the bins are chosen. The 5-bin histogram is too coarse to give a precise view of the data. The 8-bin histogram clearly shows concentration between 11 and 20. The 11-bin histogram reveals more detail in the right tail. The question you may want to ask when looking at the 8- and 11-bin histograms is: "Which of the two shapes is more likely to occur if you had a much larger data set or the entire population data set?" Would you expect a rather smooth shape as portrayed in the 8-bin histogram or a rather disjointed shape as portrayed in the 11-bin histogram? You can use your own judgment to determine which histogram gives you a more realistic picture and which you would ultimately include in a report.

Excel Histograms

Excel will produce histograms. Click on the menu bar Data tab (if you don't see Data Analysis on the Data tab, you must click Add-Ins and check Analysis Tool Pak). You can specify a range containing the bin limits (cells E4:E60 in Figure 3.6) or accept Excel's default. The result, shown in Figure 3.6, is not very attractive. Modifying an Excel histogram is possible and not that difficult, but you may prefer using software designed for drawing histograms.

MegaStat Histograms

Figure 3.7 shows MegaStat's menu for a frequency distribution and histogram for the P/E ratios using six bins. MegaStat shows percents on the *Y*-axis instead of frequencies. You can specify the bins with two numbers (interval width and lower limit of the first interval), or you can let MegaStat make its own decisions. MegaStat also provides a frequency distribution, including *cumulative* frequencies.

MINITAB Histograms

Figure 3.8 shows how MINITAB creates a histogram for the same data. Copy the data from the spreadsheet and paste it into MINITAB's worksheet, then choose Graph > Histogram from the top menu bar. Let MINITAB use its default options. Once the histogram has been created, you can right-click the *X*-axis to adjust the bins, axis tick marks, and so on.

A **modal class** is a histogram bar that is higher than those on either side. A histogram with a single modal class is *unimodal,* one with two modal classes is *bimodal,* and one with more than two modes is *multimodal.* However, modal classes may be artifacts of the way the bin limits are chosen. It is wise to experiment with various ways of binning and to make cautious inferences about modality unless the modes are strong and invariant to binning. Figures 3.6, 3.7, and 3.8 show a single modal class for P/E ratios between 16 and 20.

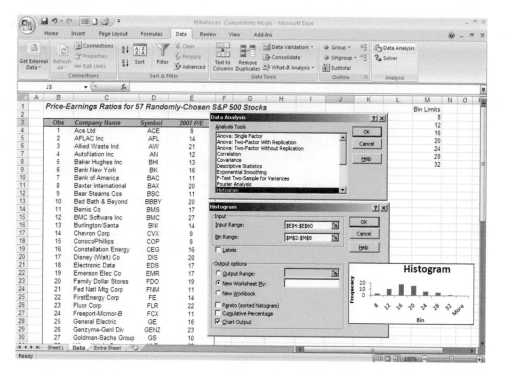

FIGURE 3.6

Excel's Histogram
PERatios

FIGURE 3.7

MegaStat Frequency Distribution and Histogram
PERatios

Frequency Distribution - Quantitative

2007 P/E						cumulative	
lower		upper	midpoint	width	frequency	percent	frequency	percent
8	<	12	10	4	10	17.5	10	17.5
12	<	16	14	4	14	24.6	24	42.1
16	<	20	18	4	17	29.8	41	71.9
20	<	24	22	4	8	14.0	49	86.0
24	<	28	26	4	6	10.5	55	96.5
28	<	32	30	4	2	3.5	57	100.0
					57	100.0		

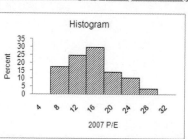

FIGURE 3.8

FIGURE 3.8

MINITAB Histogram
  PERatios

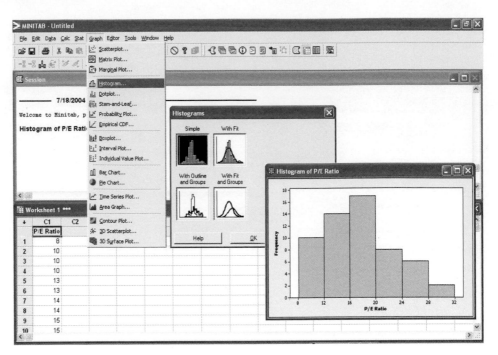

Shape

A histogram suggests the *shape* of the population we are sampling, but unless the sample is large, we must be cautious about making inferences. Our perception is also influenced by the number of bins and the way the bin limits are chosen. The following terminology is helpful in discussing shape.

A histogram's *skewness* is indicated by the direction of its longer tail. If neither tail is longer (more exactly, if one half of the histogram is a mirror image of the other half), the histogram is **symmetric.** A **right-skewed** (or positively skewed) histogram has a longer right tail, with most data values clustered on the left side. A **left-skewed** (or negatively skewed) histogram has a longer left tail, with most data values clustered on the right side. Few histograms are exactly symmetric. Business data tend to be right-skewed because they are often bounded

FIGURE 3.9

Prototype Distribution Shapes

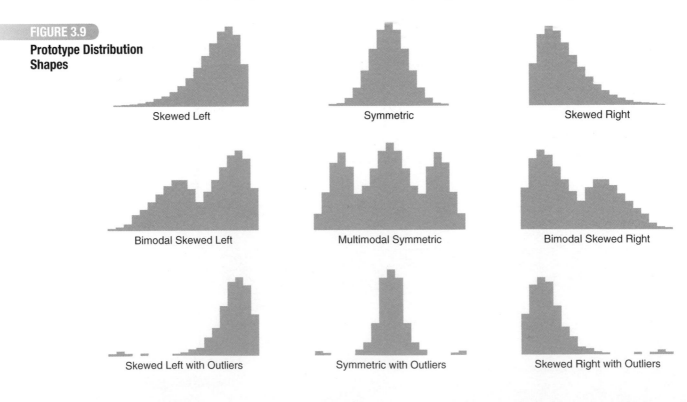

by zero on the left but are unbounded on the right (e.g., number of employees). Bimodal and multimodal distributions arise when dissimilar unimodal populations are combined into a single population. Consider, for example, two populations: heights of all Canadian adult males, and heights of all Canadian adult females. Both have unimodal distributions. According to Statistics Canada, in 2005 the average adult male height was 175 cm and the average adult female height was 161 cm. Combining these two populations will result in a bimodal distribution. You may find it helpful to refer to the templates shown in Figure 3.9.

An **outlier** is an extreme value that is far enough from the majority of the data that it probably arose from a different cause or is due to measurement error. We will define outliers more precisely in the next chapter. For now, think of outliers as unusual points located in the histogram tails. None of the histograms shown so far has any obvious outliers.

Tips for Effective Frequency Distributions

Here are some general tips to keep in mind when making frequency distributions and histograms.

1. Check Sturges' Rule first, but only as a suggestion for the number of bins.
2. Choose an appropriate bin width.
3. Choose bin limits that are multiples of the bin width.
4. Make sure that the range is covered, and add bins if necessary.

Frequency Polygon and Ogive

Figure 3.10 shows two more graphs offered by MegaStat (look at the three check boxes in the MegaStat menu in Figure 3.7), and which can also be created using Excel's line charts. A **frequency polygon** is a line graph that connects the midpoints of the histogram intervals, plus extra intervals at the beginning and end so that the line will touch the *X*-axis. It serves the same purpose as a histogram, but is attractive when you need to compare two data sets (because more than one frequency polygon can be plotted on the same scale). An **ogive** (pronounced "oh-jive") is a line graph of the cumulative frequencies. It is useful for finding percentiles or in comparing the shape of the sample with a known benchmark such as the normal distribution (that you will be seeing in the next chapter).

Mini Case   3.2

Duration of U.S. Recessions

Table 3.6 shows four "nice" ways to bin the data on the duration of 32 U.S. recessions (for details, see **Mini Case 3.1**). Most observers would think that $k = 2$ or $k = 4$ would be too few bins while $k = 13$ might be considered too many bins. Sturges would recommend using six bins, which suggests that seven bins (with nice widths of 10) would be the best choice of these four ways. However, you can think of other valid possibilities.

MegaStat's Frequency Polygon and Ogive (embellished)   PERatios FIGURE 3.10

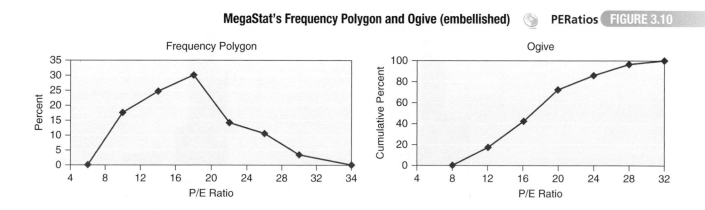

TABLE 3.6   Some Ways to Tabulate 32 Business Contractions   Recessions

k = 2 bins			k = 4 bins			k = 7 bins			k = 13 bins		
From	To	f	From	To	f	From	To	f	From	To	f
0	< 35	29	0	< 20	25	0	< 10	7	5	< 10	7
35	< 70	3	20	< 40	5	10	< 20	18	10	< 15	10
			40	< 60	1	20	< 30	3	15	< 20	8
Total		32	60	< 80	1	30	< 40	2	20	< 25	3
						40	< 50	1	25	< 30	0
			Total		32	50	< 60	0	30	< 35	1
						60	< 70	1	35	< 40	1
									40	< 45	1
						Total		32	45	< 50	0
									50	< 55	0
									55	< 60	0
									60	< 65	0
									65	< 70	1
									Total		32

All four histograms in Figure 3.11 suggest right-skewness (long right tail, most values cluster to the left). Each histogram has a single modal class, although $k = 7$ and $k = 13$ reveal modality more precisely (e.g., the $k = 7$ bin histogram says that a recession most often lasts between 10 and 20 months). The long recession of 1873–79 (65 months) can be seen as a possible outlier in the right tail of the last two histograms.

FIGURE 3.11

Histograms for 2, 4, 7, and 13 Bins

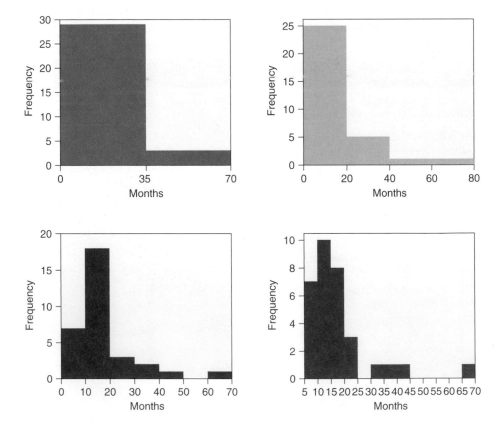

Section Exercises

3.4 (a) Without using a computer, make a frequency distribution and histogram using these 28 observations on the amount spent for dinner for four in downtown Halifax on Friday night. (b) Repeat the exercise, using a different number of bins. Which is preferred? Why? (LO 1) **Dinner**

95	103	109	170	114	113	107
124	105	80	104	84	176	115
69	95	134	108	61	160	128
68	95	61	150	52	87	136

3.5 (a) Without using a computer, make a frequency distribution and histogram for the monthly off-campus rent paid by 30 students. (b) Repeat the exercise, using a different number of bins. Which is preferred? Why? (LO 1) **Rents**

730	730	730	930	700	570
690	1030	740	620	720	670
560	740	650	660	850	930
600	620	760	690	710	500
730	800	820	840	720	700

3.6 (a) Without using a computer, make a frequency distribution and histogram for the 2003 annual compensation of these 20 randomly chosen CEOs from a list of 200 top CEOs. (b) Repeat the exercise, using a different number of bins. Which is preferred? Why? (LO 1) **CEOComp**

2003 Compensation for 20 Randomly Chosen CEOs ($ millions)

Company	CEO	Compensation (US$ millions)
Aetna	John W. Rowe	16.9
Allstate	Edward M. Liddy	14.3
American Electric Power	E. Linn Draper, Jr.	2.1
Baxter International	H. M. Jansen Kraemer, Jr.	4.5
Bear Stearns	James E. Cayne	39.5
Cardinal Health	Robert D. Walter	13.4
Cooper Tire & Rubber	Thomas A. Dattilo	2.0
Family Dollar Stores	Howard R. Levine	2.1
Fifth Third Bancorp	George A. Schaefer, Jr.	6.0
Merrill Lynch	E. Stanley O'Neal	28.1
Harley-Davidson	Jeffrey L. Bleustein	6.7
NCR	Mark V. Hurd	2.6
PG&E	Robert D. Glynn, Jr.	20.1
Praxair	Dennis H. Reilley	5.6
Sara Lee	C. Steven McMillan	10.5
Sunoco	John G. Drosdick	8.6
Temple-Inland	Kenneth M. Jastrow II	2.5
U.S. Bancorp	Jerry A. Grundhofer	10.3
Union Pacific	Richard K. Davidson	18.6
Whirlpool	David R. Whitwam	6.6

Source: *The New York Times,* Apr. 4, 2004, p. 8.

3.7   For each frequency distribution, suggest "nice" bins. Did your choice agree with Sturges' Rule? If not, explain. (LO 1)

   a.   Last week's fuel efficiency in kilometres per litre (km/L) for 35 student vehicles ($x_{min} = 9.4$, $x_{max} = 38.7$).
   b.   Ages of 50 airplane passengers ($x_{min} = 12$, $x_{max} = 85$).
   c.   GPAs of 250 first-semester university students ($x_{min} = 2.25$, $x_{max} = 3.71$).
   d.   Annual rates of return on 150 mutual funds ($x_{min} = 0.023$, $x_{max} = 0.097$).

3.8   Below are sorted data showing average spending per customer (in dollars) at 74 Noodles & Company restaurants. (a) Construct a frequency distribution. Explain how you chose the number of bins and the bin limits. (b) Make a histogram and describe its appearance. (c) Repeat, using a larger number of bins and different bin limits. (d) Did your visual impression of the data change when you increased the number of bins? Explain. *Note:* You may use MegaStat or MINITAB if your instructor agrees. (LO 1)   **NoodlesSpending**

6.54	6.58	6.58	6.62	6.66	6.70	6.71	6.73	6.75	6.75	6.76	6.76
6.76	6.77	6.77	6.79	6.81	6.81	6.82	6.84	6.85	6.89	6.90	6.91
6.91	6.92	6.93	6.93	6.94	6.95	6.95	6.95	6.96	6.96	6.98	6.99
7.00	7.00	7.00	7.02	7.03	7.03	7.03	7.04	7.05	7.05	7.07	7.07
7.08	7.11	7.11	7.13	7.13	7.16	7.17	7.18	7.21	7.25	7.28	7.28
7.30	7.33	7.33	7.35	7.37	7.38	7.45	7.56	7.57	7.58	7.64	7.65
7.87	7.97										

3.4   Line Charts

Simple Line Charts

A *simple line chart* like the one shown in Figure 3.12 is used to display a time series, to spot trends, or to compare time periods. Line charts can be used to display several variables at once. If two variables are displayed, the right and left scales can differ, using the right scale for one variable and the left scale for the other. Excel's *two-scale line chart,* illustrated in Figure 3.13, lets you compare variables that *differ in magnitude* or are measured in *different units.* But keep in mind that someone who only glances at the chart may mistakenly conclude that both variables are of the same magnitude.

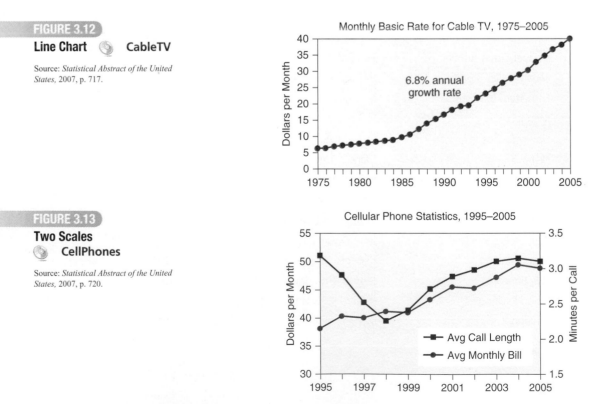

FIGURE 3.12

Line Chart   **CableTV**

Source: *Statistical Abstract of the United States,* 2007, p. 717.

FIGURE 3.13

Two Scales
CellPhones

Source: *Statistical Abstract of the United States,* 2007, p. 720.

Effect of Gridlines  **Utilities** FIGURE 3.14

Source: Author's utility bills.

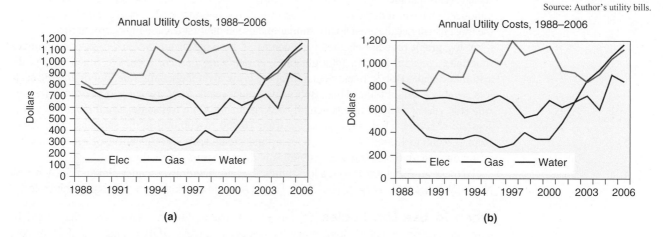

(a)   (b)

How many variables can be displayed at once on a line graph? Too much clutter ruins any visual display. If you try to display half a dozen time-series variables at once, no matter how cleverly you choose symbols and graphing techniques, the result is likely to be unsatisfactory. You will have to use your judgment.  **Utilities**

Gridlines

A line graph usually has no vertical gridlines. What about horizontal gridlines? While gridlines do add background clutter, they make it easier to establish the *Y* value for a given year. One compromise is to use lightly coloured dashed or dotted gridlines to minimize the clutter, and to increase gridline spacing, as illustrated in Figure 3.14 (a). If the intent is to convey only a general sense of the data magnitudes, gridlines may be omitted, as shown in Figure 3.14(b),

Bar charts can also be used to portray time-series data. Bars add a feeling of solidity and may hold the reader's attention, particularly if the reader is accustomed to bar charts. However, when you are displaying more than one time series, bar charts make it harder to see individual data values, so a line chart usually is preferred. In Section 3.5 we discuss rules for bar charts. Exercise judgment to decide which type of display is most effective for the audience you are addressing.

Log Scales

On the customary **arithmetic scale,** distances on the *Y*-axis are proportional to the magnitude of the variable being displayed. But on a **logarithmic scale,** equal distances represent equal *ratios* (for this reason, a log scale is sometimes called a *ratio scale*). When data vary over a wide range, say, by more than an order of magnitude (e.g., from 6 to 60), we might prefer a *log scale* for the vertical axis to reveal more detail for small data values. For example, Figure 3.15 shows the value

Same Data on Different *Y*-Axis Scales  **BobsFunds** FIGURE 3.15

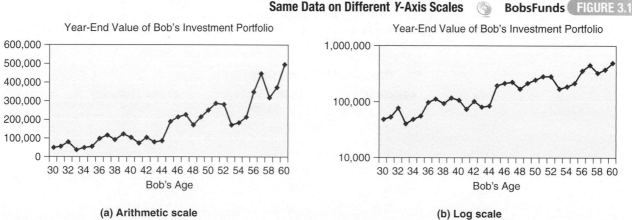

(a) Arithmetic scale   (b) Log scale

of an investment over a 30-year period. The data vary roughly from $50,000 to $500,000. The log scale reveals that there were substantial *relative* fluctuations in the first decade, which might go unnoticed on the arithmetic scale. The log scale also shows that the larger *absolute* fluctuations in the most recent decade are actually similar to those in the first decade in *relative* terms.

A log graph reveals whether the quantity is growing at an *increasing percent* (convex function), *constant percent* (straight line), or *declining percent* (concave function). On the arithmetic scale, Bob's investment appears to grow at an increasing rate, but on the log scale it is roughly a straight line. Thus, Bob's investment seems to be growing at a *constant percent rate* (the yearly average rate is actually 7.25 percent). On a log scale, *equal distances* represent *equal ratios*. That is, the distance from 10,000 to 100,000 is the same as the distance from 100,000 to 1,000,000. Because logarithms are undefined for negative or zero values (try it on your calculator), a log scale is only suited for positive data values.

To make an Excel graph with a logarithmic *Y*-scale, first draw a scatter plot (see Section 3.6). Now right-click on a *Y*-axis value, select Format Axis and check the box for Logarithmic scale.

When to Use Log Scales   A log scale is useful for time-series data that might be expected to grow at a compound annual percentage rate (e.g., GDP, the national debt, or your future income). Log scales are common in financial charts that cover long periods of time or for data that grow rapidly (e.g., revenues for a start-up company). Some experts feel that corporate annual reports and stock prospectuses should avoid ratio scales, on the grounds that they may be misleading to uninformed individuals. But then how can we fairly portray data that vary by orders of magnitude? Should investors become better informed? The bottom line is that business students must understand log scales, because they are sure to run into them.

Tips for Effective Line Charts

Here are some general tips to keep in mind when creating line charts:

1. Line charts are used for *time-series data* (never for cross-sectional data).

2. The numerical variable is shown on the *Y*-axis, while the time units go on the *X*-axis with time increasing from left to right. Business audiences expect this rule to be followed.

3. Except for log scales, a zero origin on the *Y*-axis (this is the default in Excel) is customary unless more detail is needed. The zero-origin rule is mandatory for a corporate annual report or investor stock prospectus.

4. To avoid graph clutter, numerical labels usually are *omitted* on a line chart, especially when the data cover many time periods. Use gridlines to help the reader read data values.

5. Data markers (squares, triangles, circles) are helpful. But when the series has many data values or when many variables are being displayed, they clutter the graph.

6. If the lines on the graph are too thick, the reader can't ascertain graph values.

Section Exercises

3.9   Using the following data and Excel, draw a line chart to display employment by sector in Canada between the years 2004 and 2008. Draw three lines on the same chart—one for all industries, one for the goods-producing industry, and one for the services-producing industry. Repeat the line chart using log scales. Comment on your findings. (Source: Statistics Canada, http://www40.statcan.gc.ca/l01/cst01/econ40-eng.htm) (LO 1)

	Employment by Industry (in 1000s)		
Year	*All Industries*	*Goods-Producing Sector*	*Service-Producing Sector*
2004	15,947.0	3,989.8	11,957.2
2005	16,169.7	4,002.4	12,167.3
2006	16,484.3	3,985.9	12.498.4
2007	16,866.4	3,993.0	12,873.5
2008	17,125.8	4,021.3	13,104.5

3.10 Use Excel to prepare a line chart to display the lightning death data. Modify the default colours, fonts, and so on as you judge appropriate to make the display effective. (LO 1)

Deaths by Lightning, 1940–2005   **Lightning**

Year	Deaths	Year	Deaths
1940	340	1975	91
1945	268	1980	74
1950	219	1985	74
1955	181	1990	74
1960	129	1995	85
1965	149	2000	51
1970	122	2005	38

Source: *Statistical Abstract of the United States*, 2007, p. 228; and www.nws.noaa.gov.

3.11 Use Excel to prepare a line chart to display the following transplant data. Modify the default colours, fonts, and so on to make the display effective. (LO 1)

Living Organ Transplants, 1988–2004   **Transplants**

Year	Transplants	Year	Transplants	Year	Transplants
1988	12,786	1994	18,170	2000	23,004
1989	13,471	1995	19,264	2001	23,942
1990	15,462	1996	19,566	2002	24,552
1991	15,687	1997	20,093	2003	25,083
1992	16,043	1998	21,313	2004	26,539
1993	17,533	1999	21,824		

Source: www.gsds.org.

3.5 Bar Charts

Plain Bar Charts   Tires

The **bar chart** is probably the most common type of data display in business. Attribute data are typically displayed using a bar chart. Each bar represents a category or attribute. The length or height of each bar reflects the frequency of that category (e.g., the number of students who are marketing majors) or some other quantitative aspect of that category (e.g., the average starting salary of marketing graduates). Each bar has a label showing a category or time period. Figure 3.16 shows simple bar charts comparing market shares among tire manufacturers. Each bar is separated from its neighbours by a slight gap to improve legibility (you can control gap width in Excel). *Vertical* bar charts are the most common, but *horizontal* bar charts can be useful when the axis labels are long or when there are many categories.

3-D and Novelty Bar Charts   Tires

This same data can be displayed in a *3-D bar chart,* shown in Figure 3.17. Many observers feel that the illusion of depth adds to the visual impact. The depth effect is mostly harmless in terms of bar proportions, but it does introduce ambiguity in bar height. Do we measure from the back of the bar or from the front? For a general readership (e.g., *The Globe and Mail*), 3-D charts are common, but in business they are rare. Novelty bar charts like the **pyramid chart** in Figure 3.18 are charming but should be avoided because they distort the bar volume and make it hard to measure bar height.

FIGURE 3.16 Same Data Displayed Two Ways

Source: www.mtdealer.com.

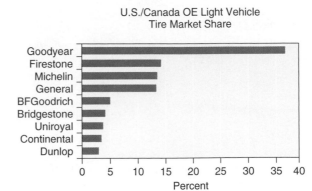

(a) Vertical bars

(b) Horizontal bars

FIGURE 3.17

3-D Bar Chart

Source: www.mtdealer.com.

U.S./Canada OE Light Vehicle
Tire Market Share

FIGURE 3.18

Pyramid Chart (avoid it)

Source: www.mtdealer.com.

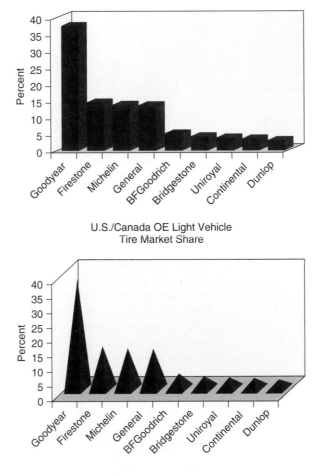

Pareto Charts

A special type of bar chart used frequently in business is the **Pareto chart.** Pareto charts are used in quality management to display the *frequency* of defects or errors of different types. Categories are displayed in descending order of frequency so that the most common errors or

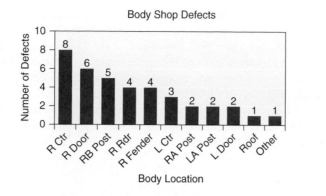

Body Shop Defects

FIGURE 3.19

Pareto Chart ⊚ Pareto

defects appear first. This helps managers focus on the *significant few* (i.e., only a few categories typically account for most of the defects or errors).

Figure 3.19 shows a Pareto chart for paint and body defects in a sample of 50 new vehicles that were inspected. Defects were recorded by body location (e.g., right front door) using a checklist of 60 possible body locations. There were 38 defects altogether (many of them minor). The "top 9" locations accounted for 95 percent of the total defects (36 out of the 38 defects). The company can concentrate its quality improvement efforts on the "top 9" body locations. The Pareto chart is attractive because it is easy to understand and is directly relevant to business tasks.

Stacked and Composite Bar Charts

EXAMPLE 2
NAFTA Attitudes

Ever since NAFTA has been in existence, the governments of Canada, the United States, and Mexico have consistently argued that this free trade agreement has been beneficial to the economies of their respective countries. Some citizens of these three countries have expressed different opinions over the years. Suppose a survey was conducted asking randomly selected adult citizens what their opinions were concerning the benefits of NAFTA and suppose the results were summarized in Table 3.7.

TABLE 3.7 Attitudes toward NAFTA by Country

	Canadian	American	Mexican	Totals
NAFTA benefited my country.	25	25	25	75
NAFTA had no overall effect on my country.	14	35	11	60
NAFTA harmed my country.	41	65	14	120
Totals	80	125	50	255

We could take the results from a particular country and construct a bar chart, such as Figure 3.20, and comment on the attitudes of that country's sample.

A simple observation based on this display would be that more Canadians in our sample have a negative opinion about NAFTA than a positive opinion.

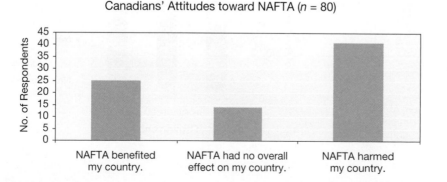

Canadians' Attitudes toward NAFTA (*n* = 80)

FIGURE 3.20

Attitudes of Canadians
toward NAFTA

In this example there are two attributes (attitude and citizenship) that were measured, and a simple bar chart could not capture the relationship between these two attributes. A stacked bar chart or a composite bar chart can. Essentially, a **stacked bar chart** has bars whose heights sum two or more subtotals without losing the individual subtotals, while a composite bar chart allows us to compare relevant subtotals with bars created side by side. Figure 3.21 shows us several different ways of presenting the results.

Figures 3.21(a) and (b) are composite bar charts, while Figures 3.21(c), (d), (e), and (f) are stacked bar charts. The horizontal axis of Figures 3.21(a), (c), and (e) are labelled by attitude while Figures 3.21(b), (d), and (f) are labelled by citizenship. In most situations with two

FIGURE 3.21 **Attitudes of North Americans toward NAFTA**

(a) Citizenship by Attitudes toward NAFTA

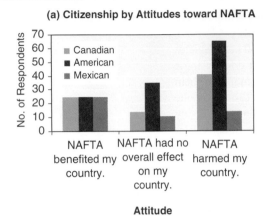

(b) Attitudes toward NAFTA by Citizenship

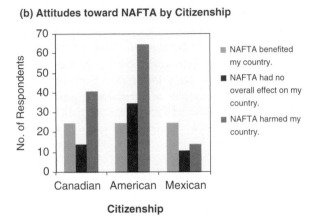

(c) Citzenship by Attitudes toward NAFTA

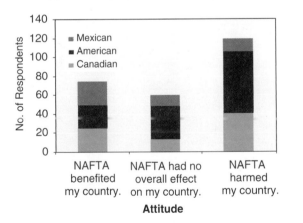

(d) Attitudes toward NAFTA by Citizenship

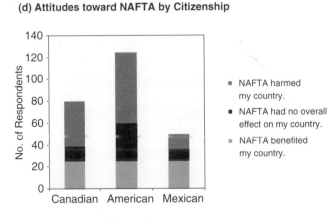

(e) Citizenship by Attitudes toward NAFTA

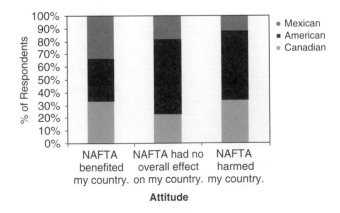

(f) Attitudes toward NAFTA by Citizenship

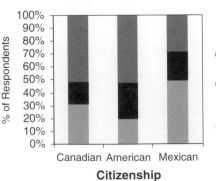

attributes, if one of the attributes is believed to affect the other attribute, it is easier to interpret the results if that attribute is listed along the horizontal axis. In this example, citizenship may be believed to affect attitudes toward NAFTA and thus it is appropriate to list citizenship along the horizontal axis. Ruling out Figures 3.21(a), (c), and (e) as charts to consider, let us look at the remaining three figures. Figures 3.21(b) and (d) look at the number of respondents within each citizenship category with particular opinions about NAFTA. Because the sample sizes are different within each citizenship category, comparing the heights of bars across citizenship doesn't give us much insight into how citizenship affects attitudes toward NAFTA. For example, the heights showing the number of respondents who said that NAFTA benefited my country were the same for all three countries. But because the total number of respondents in each of the countries were substantially different, this observation should not be interpreted as there being no difference among the three countries' samples in terms of NAFTA benefiting their countries. By converting the number of respondents into the percentage of respondents with the various attitudes within each country, as in Figure 3.21(f), we should get a better understanding of the similarities or differences among the countries. Looking at Figure 3.21(f), we can observe in the samples, for example, that Mexicans are most favourable toward NAFTA (at 50 percent), Americans are least favourable (with 20 percent stating that NAFTA benefited their country), and Canadians and Americans are equally likely (at 50 percent each) to believe that NAFTA has harmed their respective countries.

While converting this data set into percentages allowed us to best interpret the results, looking at actual values instead of percentages may be more beneficial when interpreting other data sets. For example, when comparing the annual cost of attending various universities across North America in which costs are broken down into various categories (e.g., tuition, books, student fees), it may be more insightful to look at actual costs as opposed to the percentage of costs attributed to each category.

You can use a bar chart for time-series data. Figure 3.22 shows the same data, first in a line chart, and then in a bar chart. Some people feel that the solid bars give a clearer sense of the trend. However, if you have more than one time series, it is harder to compare trends on a bar chart.

Tips for Effective Bar Charts

The following guidelines will help you to create the most effective bar charts:

1. The numerical variable of interest usually is shown with vertical bars on the *Y*-axis, while the category labels go on the *X*-axis.

2. If the quantity displayed is a time series, the category labels (e.g., years) are displayed on the horizontal *X*-axis with time increasing from left to right.

Same Data on (a) Line Chart and (b) Bar Chart CableTV **FIGURE 3.22**

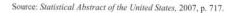

Source: *Statistical Abstract of the United States,* 2007, p. 717.

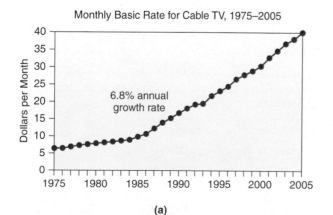

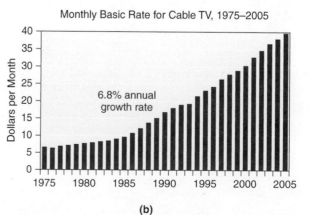

(a) (b)

3. The height or length of each bar should be proportional to the quantity displayed. This is easy, as most software packages default to a zero origin on a bar graph. The zero-origin rule is essential for a corporate annual report or investor stock prospectus (e.g., to avoid over-stating earnings). However, non-zero origins may be justified to reveal sufficient detail.

4. Put numerical values at the top of each bar, except when labels would impair legibility (e.g., lots of bars) or when visual simplicity is needed (e.g., for a general audience).

5. When a stacked or composite bar chart is appropriate, the horizontal axis should represent the attribute that is believed to affect the other attribute.

Section Exercises

3.12   The following table shows minivan sales in North America from the years 2001 to 2008, with Chrysler sales separated from the sales from other sources (Source: Ward's Automotive Data Center; and A.J. Faria, co-director, Office of Automotive Research, University of Windsor).

Year	Total Minivan Sales	Chrysler Minivan Sales
2001	1,450,940	533,573
2002	1,396,753	507,192
2003	1,299,808	451,098
2004	1,313,810	464,522
2005	1,299,102	488,287
2006	1,215,743	456,894
2007	955,282	380,591
2008	735,750	296,957

Using Excel, draw a line chart of total minivan sales over this eight-year period. Using Excel, draw two stacked bar charts, each with eight bars—one bar for each year. The first chart should show total sales broken down into Chrysler minivan sales and non-Chrysler minivan sales. The second chart should show the percentage of sales in each year broken down into the same two categories. Which of these two bar charts would be used if the objective was to show that Chrysler minivan sales are improving over time? Which bar chart would be used if the objective was to show that Chrysler sales are worsening over time? Explain. (LO 1 & 3)

3.13   (a) Use Excel to prepare a *2-D stacked bar chart* for television sales by year. Modify the colours, fonts, and so on to make the display effective. (b) Change your graph to a *2-D horizontal bar chart.* Modify the chart if necessary to make it attractive. Do you prefer the vertical or horizontal bar chart? Why? (c) Change your graph to a *3-D vertical bar chart.* Modify the chart if necessary to make it attractive. Is 3-D better than 2-D? Why? (d) Right-click the data series, choose Chart Tools, and add labels to the data. Do the labels help? (LO 1)

Television Sales, 2002–2005 ($ thousands)			TVSales
Year	Projection TV	LCD TV	Plasma TV
2002	3,574	246	515
2003	4,351	664	1,590
2004	6,271	1,579	2,347
2005	5,320	3,295	4,012

3.14   (a) Use Excel to prepare a *stacked bar chart* for in-car use and non-car use of cellphones. Modify the colours, fonts, and so on to make the display effective. (b) Right-click the data series, choose Format Data Series, and add labels to the data. Do the labels help? *Hint:* Use only the first two data columns (not the total). (LO 1)

Annual Wireless Phone Usage (billions of minutes)			Wireless
Year	In-Car Use	Non-Car Use	Total
2000	187	87	274
2001	312	191	503
2002	324	346	670
2003	400	512	912

3.15 The following table shows the forecast of vehicle production in North America by country for the years 2009 through 2012 and it also shows production for the record year, 2000. Construct a stacked bar chart (one bar for each of the five years) showing the number of vehicles forecasted by country in each of the years, and, construct a stacked bar chart (one bar for each of the five years) showing the percentage of vehicles forecasted by country in each of the years. What observations can you make looking at these two bar charts? Explain. (Source: Ward's Automotive Data Center; and A.J. Faria, co-director, Office of Automotive Research, University of Windsor.) (LO 1)

Year	U.S. Production	Canadian Production	Mexican Production
2000	12,850,000	3,055,000	2,253,755
2009	10,134,451	2,512,129	2,517,005
2010	10,575,041	2,480,727	2,568,832
2011	10,844,705	2,416,119	2,819,974
2012	10,967,704	2,439,842	3,079,641

3.6   Scatter Plots

A **scatter plot** shows *n* pairs of observations $(x_1, y_1), (x_2, y_2), \ldots, (x_n, y_n)$ as dots (or some other symbol) on an *X-Y* graph. This type of display is so important in statistics that it deserves careful attention. A scatter plot is a starting point for bivariate data analysis. We create scatter plots to investigate the relationship between two variables. Typically, we would like to know if there is an *association* between two variables and if so, what kind of association exists. As we did with univariate data analysis, let's look at a scatter plot to see what we can observe.

Table 3.8 shows the *birth rate* and *life expectancy* for nine randomly selected nations. Figure 3.23 shows a scatter plot with life expectancy on the *X*-axis and birth rates on the *Y*-axis. In this illustration, there seems to be an association between *X* and *Y*. That is, nations with higher birth rates tend to have lower life expectancy (and vice versa). No cause-and-effect relationship is implied, because in this example both variables could be influenced by a third variable that is not mentioned (e.g., GDP per capita). As with a dot plot, comments can be added. Here, nations with the lowest and highest life expectancy have been labelled. It is impractical to label all the data points.

EXAMPLE 3
Birth Rates and Life Expectancy

TABLE 3.8   Birth Rates and Life Expectancy (*n* = 9 nations)   LifeExp

Nation	Birth Rate (per 1,000)	Life Expectancy (years)
Afghanistan	41.03	46.60
Canada	11.09	79.70
Finland	10.60	77.80
Guatemala	34.17	66.90
Japan	10.03	80.90
Mexico	22.36	72.00
Pakistan	30.40	62.70
Spain	9.29	79.10
United States	14.10	77.40

Source: *The CIA World Factbook 2003*, www.cia.gov.

FIGURE 3.23

Scatter Plot of Birth Rates and Life Expectancy ($n = 9$)

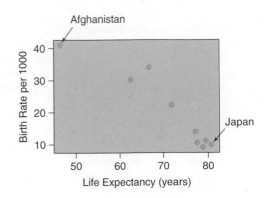

EXAMPLE 4

Aircraft Fuel Consumption

Table 3.9 shows five observations on flight time and fuel consumption for a twin-engine Piper Cheyenne aircraft. This time, a causal relationship between these two variables is assumed, because longer flights would consume more fuel.

TABLE 3.9   Flight Time and Fuel Consumption   Cheyenne

Trip Leg	Flight Time (hours)	Fuel Used (pounds)
1	2.3	145
2	4.2	258
3	3.6	219
4	4.7	276
5	4.9	283

Source: *Flying* 130, no. 4 (Apr. 2003), p. 99.

The pattern in Figure 3.24 appears to be linear. The linear pattern shows that as flight time increases, fuel consumption increases, so we say that the slope is positive. Later, you will learn about describing this relationship mathematically.

Figure 3.25 shows some scatter plot patterns similar to those that you might observe when you have a sample of (X, Y) data pairs. A scatter plot can convey patterns in data pairs that would not be apparent from a table. Compare Figures 3.26 through 3.28 with the prototypes, and use your own words to describe the patterns that you see.

Note: If you don't assume that there is a causal relationship between the two variables (e.g., between birth rate and life expectancy), it doesn't matter which variable is plotted vertically and which is plotted horizontally. If you assume that there is a causal relationship, the variable which is assumed to cause or affect the other variable (e.g., flight time is assumed to cause fuel consumption), that variable (i.e., flight time) should be plotted horizontally while the other variable (i.e., fuel consumption) is plotted vertically.

FIGURE 3.24

Scatter Plot of Fuel Consumption and Flight Time

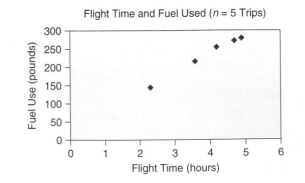

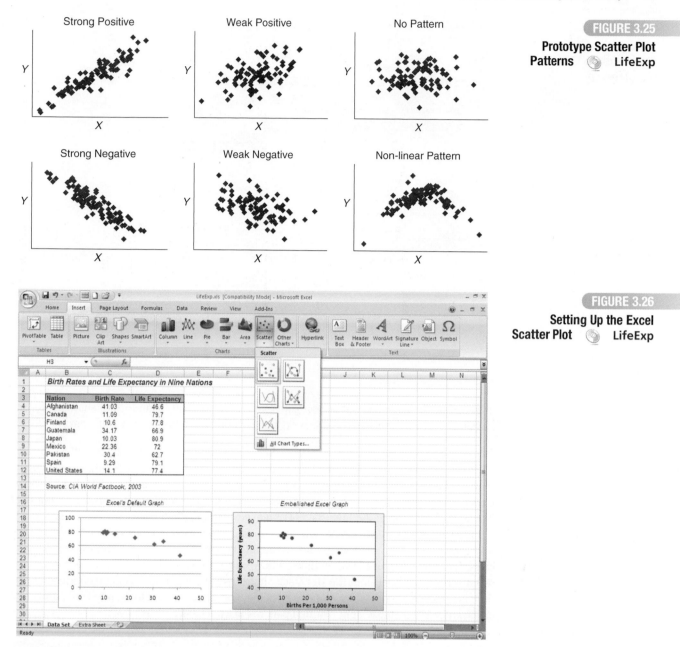

FIGURE 3.25

**Prototype Scatter Plot
Patterns** LifeExp

FIGURE 3.26

**Setting Up the Excel
Scatter Plot** LifeExp

Making a Scatter Plot in Excel

Highlight the two data columns. Then click the Insert tab in the top menu bar. Select the Scatter icon, and choose the first template, as shown in Figure 3.26. Excel assumes that the first column is X and the second column is Y, but you can change this after the graph is created, if you wish.

The resulting scatter plot is rather plain. However, you can embellish it, as illustrated in Figure 3.27 (e.g., to add labels, change colours, try different fonts). To embellish an Excel chart, click on the chart (a border will appear to show that you have selected the chart). Above the menu bar, a Chart Tools tab will appear. Click on the Chart Tools tab and choose one of the three tabs. The Design tab will let you edit the data (e.g., select new markers or change colours for the data points). The Format tab lets you select different templates for the graph. The Layout tab is probably the one you will use most often (e.g., to add a title or axis labels; edit gridlines; or annotate the graph with a text box, arrows, or shapes). Exploring these Excel menus is a "hands-on" experience that you will have to try for yourself. At first, the proliferation of menus

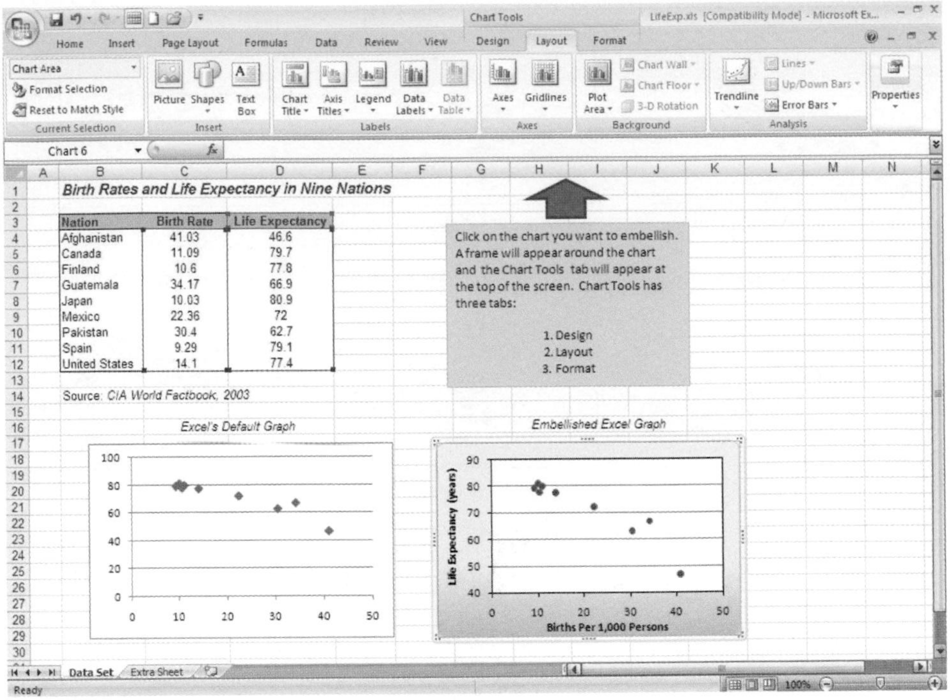

FIGURE 3.27

Using Chart Tools **to Embellish a Chart**

LifeExp

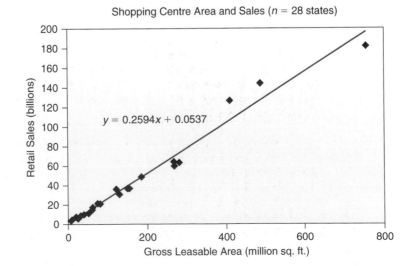

in Excel can be daunting, but as you gain experience you will begin to find shortcuts for the tasks that you are most likely to do. Soon, you will find ways to get what you want.

Excel's Fitted Trend Line   Excel makes it easy to fit a line to data on a scatter plot. Just click on the data, choose Add Trendline, choose the Options tab, and check Display equation on chart. This assumes a linear relationship between X and Y. For example, Figure 3.28 shows Excel's fitted trend for X = total gross leasable area and Y = total retail sales for a sample of 28 states. The slope of the line (0.2594) suggests that a unit change in X (each "unit" is one million square feet) is associated with an extra $0.2594 billion in retail sales, on average. The intercept is near zero, suggesting that a shopping centre with no leasable area would have no sales. Later (in Chapter 12) you will learn how Excel fits a **trend line,** how to interpret it, and when such a line is meaningful. But since almost every student discovers this option the first time he or she makes a scatter plot, we must mention Excel's fitted trend line here purely as a *descriptive tool* that may help you find patterns in (X, Y) data.

FIGURE 3.28

Excel Scatter Plot with Fitted Trend Line (n = 28 states)

RetailSales

Source: *Statistical Abstract of the United States,* 2007, p. 660.

Shopping Centre Area and Sales (n = 28 states)

$y = 0.2594x + 0.0537$

3.16 (a) Use Excel to make a scatter plot of these vehicle data, placing Weight on the *X*-axis and City MPG on the *Y*-axis. Add titles and modify the default colours, fonts, and so on as you judge appropriate to make the scatter plot effective. (b) Describe the relationship (if any) between *X* and *Y*. Weak? Strong? Negative? Positive? Linear? Non-linear? (LO 1 & 3)

Weight and MPG for 20 Randomly Selected Vehicles CityMPG

Vehicle	City MPG	Weight (lbs.)	Vehicle	City MPG	Weight (lbs.)
Acura TSX	23	3,320	Lincoln Aviator	13	5,000
BMW 3-Series	19	3,390	Mazda 6	19	3,355
Chevrolet Corvette	19	3,255	Land Rover Freelander	17	3,640
Chevrolet Silverado 1500	14	4,935	Mercedes-Benz S-Class	17	4,195
Chrysler Pacifica	17	4,660	Nissan 350Z	20	3,345
Dodge Caravan	18	4,210	Nissan Xterra	16	4,315
Ford Focus	26	2,760	Pontiac Vibe	28	2,805
Infiniti FX	16	4,295	Pontiac Grand Am	25	3,095
Jaguar XJ8	18	3,805	Toyota Sienna	19	4,120
Lexus IS300	18	3,390	Volvo C70	20	3,690

Source: © 2003 by Consumers Union of U.S., Inc. Yonkers, NY, a non-profit organization. From *Consumer Reports New Car Buying Guide, 2003–2004.* Used with permission.

3.17 (a) Use Excel to make a scatter plot of the following exam score data, placing Midterm on the *X*-axis and Final on the *Y*-axis. Add titles and modify the default colours, fonts, and so on as you judge appropriate to make the scatter plot effective. (b) Describe the relationship (if any) between *X* and *Y*. Weak? Strong? Negative? Positive? Linear? Non-linear? (LO 1 & 3)

Exam Scores for 18 Statistics Students ExamScores

Name	Midterm Score	Final Score	Name	Midterm Score	Final Score
Aaron	50	30	Joe	68	83
Angela	95	83	Lisa	75	58
Brandon	75	90	Liz	70	83
Buck	60	83	Michele	60	73
Carole	60	75	Nancy	88	78
Cecilia	63	45	Ryan	93	100
Charles	90	100	Tania	73	83
Dmitri	88	90	Ursula	33	53
Ellie	75	68	Xiaodong	60	70

3.18 (a) Use Excel to make a scatter plot of the data, placing Floor Space on the *X*-axis and Weekly Sales on the *Y*-axis. Add titles and modify the default colours, fonts, and so on as you judge appropriate to make the scatter plot effective. (b) Describe the relationship (if any) between *X* and *Y*. Weak? Strong? Negative? Positive? Linear? Non-linear? (LO 1 & 3) FloorSpace

Floor Space (sq. ft.)	Weekly Sales (dollars)	Floor Space (sq. ft.)	Weekly Sales (dollars)
6,060	16,380	5,410	15,840
5,230	14,400	4,990	16,610
4,280	13,820	4,220	13,610
5,580	18,230	4,160	10,050
5,670	14,200	4,870	15,320
5,020	12,800	5,470	13,270

3.19 (a) Use Excel to make a scatter plot of the data for bottled water sales for 10 weeks, placing Price on the *X*-axis and Units Sold on the *Y*-axis. Add titles and modify the default colours, fonts, and so on as you judge appropriate to make the scatter plot effective. (b) Describe the relationship (if any) between *X* and *Y*. Weak? Strong? Negative? Positive? Linear? Non-linear? (LO 1 & 3) **WaterSold**

Unit Price	Units Sold
1.15	186
0.94	216
1.04	173
1.05	182
1.08	183
1.33	150
0.99	190
1.25	165
1.16	190
1.11	201

3.7 Tables

Tables are the simplest form of data display, yet creating effective tables is an acquired skill. By arranging numbers in rows and columns, their meaning can be enhanced so that it can be understood at a glance.

EXAMPLE 5

School Expenditures

Table 3.10 is a *compound table* that contains time-series data (going down the columns) on seven variables (going across the rows). The data can be viewed in several ways. We can focus on the time pattern (going down the columns) or on comparing public and private spending (between columns) for a given school level (elementary/secondary or college/university). Or we can compare spending by school level (elementary/secondary or college/university) for a given type of control (public or private). Figures are rounded to three or four significant digits to make it easier for the reader. Units of measurement are stated in the footnote to keep the column headings simple. Columns are grouped using merged heading cells (blank columns could be inserted to add vertical separation). Presentation tables can be linked dynamically to spreadsheets so that slides can be updated quickly, but take care that data changes do not adversely affect the table layout.

TABLE 3.10 **School Expenditures by Control and Level, 1960–2000** Schools

Year	All Schools	Elementary and Secondary			Colleges and Universities		
		Total	Public	Private	Total	Public	Private
1960	142.2	99.6	93.0	6.6	42.6	23.3	19.3
1970	317.3	200.2	188.6	11.6	117.2	75.2	41.9
1980	373.6	232.7	216.4	16.2	140.9	93.4	47.4
1990	526.1	318.5	293.4	25.1	207.6	132.9	74.7
2000	691.9	418.2	387.8	30.3	273.8	168.8	105.0

Note: All figures are in billions of constant 2000–2001 dollars.
Source: U.S. Census Bureau, *Statistical Abstract of the United States, 2002,* p. 133.

Tips for Effective Tables

Here are some tips for creating effective tables:

1. Keep the table simple, consistent with its purpose. Put summary tables in the *main body* of the written report and detailed tables in an *appendix*. In a slide presentation, the main point of the table should be clear to the reader within *10 seconds*. If not, break the table into parts or aggregate the data.

2. Display the data to be compared in columns rather than rows. Research shows that people find it easier to compare across rather than down.

3. For presentation purposes, round off to three or four significant digits (e.g., 142 rather than 142.213). People mentally round numbers anyway. Exceptions: when accounting requirements supersede the desire for rounding or when the numbers are used in subsequent calculations.

4. Physical table layout should guide the eye toward the comparison you wish to emphasize. Spaces or shading may be used to separate rows or columns. Use lines sparingly.

5. Row and column headings should be simple yet descriptive.

6. Within a column, use a consistent number of decimal digits. Right-justify or decimal-align the data unless all field widths are the same within the column.

Pivot Tables   PivotTable

One of Excel's most popular and powerful features is the **pivot table,** which provides interactive analysis of a data matrix. The simplest kind of pivot table has rows and columns. Each of its cells shows a statistic for a row and column combination. The row and column variables must be either *categorical* or *discrete numerical* and the variable for the table cells must be *numerical* (review Chapter 2 if you do not remember these terms). After the table is created, you can change the table by dragging variable names from the list specified in your data matrix. You can change the displayed statistic in the cells (sum, count, average, maximum, minimum, product) by right-clicking the display and selecting from the *field settings* menu. We show here the steps needed to create a pivot table for a small data matrix (25 homes, 3 variables). The first table shows the *frequency count* of homes for each cell (you can pick any cell and verify the count of the number of homes in that cell). The second table was created by copying the first table and then changing the cells to display the *average* square feet of homes in that cell.

Step 1: Select the Insert tab and specify the data range.

Step 2: Drag and drop desired fields for rows, columns, and the table body.

Step 3: Now you can format the table or right-click to choose desired field setting.

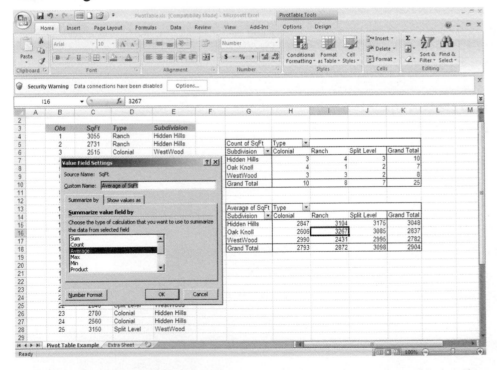

LearningStats has a more detailed step-by-step guide to creating a pivot table (see the end of this chapter list of *LearningStats* demonstrations). A pivot table is especially useful when you have a large data matrix with several variables. For example, Figure 3.29 shows two pivot tables based on tax return data for $n = 4,801$ U.S. taxpayers. The first pivot table shows the number of taxpayers by filing type (single, married joint, married separate, head of household) cross-tabulated against the number of child exemptions (0, 1, 2, . . . , 10). The second

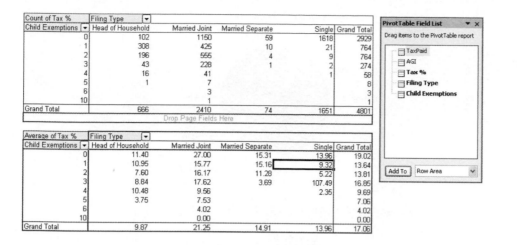

FIGURE 3.29

**Two Pivot Tables for
Income Tax Returns
(*n* = 4,801)**   Taxes

pivot table shows average tax rate (percent) for each cell in the cross-tabulation. Note that
some of the averages are based on small cell counts.

3.8   Pie Charts   PieCharts

An Oft-Abused Chart

Many statisticians feel that a table or bar chart is a better choice than a **pie chart** for several
reasons. But because of their visual appeal, pie charts appear daily in company annual reports
and the popular press (e.g., *The Globe and Mail, Financial Post, Report on Business* magazine), and on many gas station pumps indicating why you are paying so much for gasoline, so
you must understand their uses and misuses. A pie chart can only convey a *general idea of the
data* because it is hard to assess areas precisely. It should have only a few slices (e.g., two or
three) and the slices should be labelled with data values or percents. The only correct use of a
pie chart is to *portray data whose total represents 100 percent of something meaningful* (e.g.,
percent market shares). A simple 2-D pie chart is best, as in Figure 3.30. A bar chart (Figure 3.31)
could be used to display the same data.

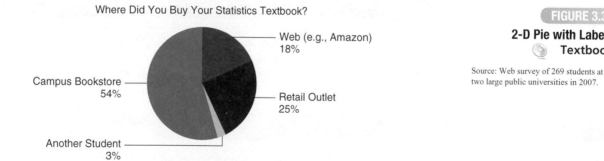

FIGURE 3.30

2-D Pie with Labels
   Textbook

Source: Web survey of 269 students at
two large public universities in 2007.

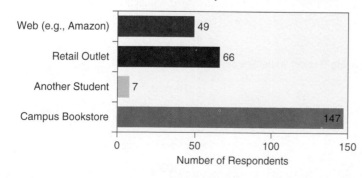

FIGURE 3.31

Bar Chart Alternative
   Textbook

Source: Web survey of 269 students at
two large public universities in 2007.

   **PieCharts**

FIGURE 3.32

Exploded Pie Chart

Source: *PC Magazine* 22, no. 4 (Mar. 11, 2003).

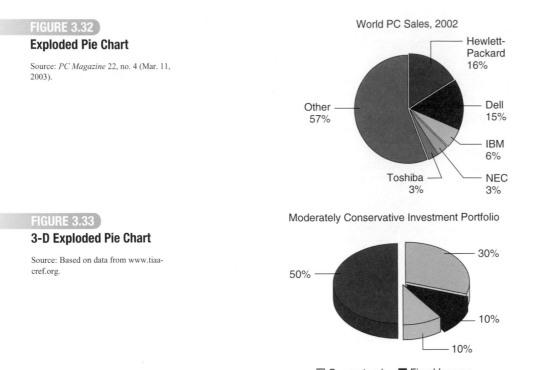

FIGURE 3.33

3-D Exploded Pie Chart

Source: Based on data from www.tiaa-cref.org.

Pie Chart Options

Exploded and *3-D pie charts* (Figures 3.32 and 3.33) add visual interest, but the sizes of pie slices are even harder to assess. Nonetheless, you will see 3-D charts in business publications because of their strong visual impact. Black-and-white charts may be used internally in business, but colour is typically preferred for customers, stockholders, or investors. Practices may change as colour copiers become more cost-effective.

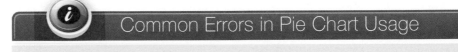

Common Errors in Pie Chart Usage

- Pie charts can only convey a general idea of the data values.
- Pie charts are ineffective when they have too many slices.
- Pie chart data must represent *parts of a whole* (e.g., percent market share)

Section Exercises

3.20 (a) Use Excel to prepare a *2-D pie chart* for these Web-surfing data. Modify the default colours, fonts, and so on as you judge appropriate to make the display effective. (b) Right-click the chart area, select Chart Type, and change to an *exploded 2-D pie chart*. (c) Right-click the chart area, select Chart Type, and change to a *bar chart*. Which do you prefer? Why? *Hint:* Include data labels with the percent *values*. (LO 1)

Are You Concerned About Being Tracked While Web Surfing?	WebSurf
Level of Concern	*Percent*
Very/extremely concerned	68
Somewhat concerned	23
No/little concern	9
Total	100

Source: *PC Magazine* 21, no. 11 (Nov. 2003), p. 146.

3.21 (a) Use Excel to prepare a *2-D pie chart* for the following Pitney-Bowes data. Modify the default colours, fonts, and so on as you judge appropriate to make the display effective. (b) Right-click the chart area, select Chart Type, and change to a *3-D pie chart.* (c) Right-click the chart area, select Chart Type, and change to a *bar chart.* Which do you prefer? Why? *Hint:* Include data labels with the percent *values.* (LO 1)

Pitney-Bowes Medical Claims in 2003 PitneyBowes	
Spent On	*Percent of Total*
Hospital services	47.5
Physicians	27.0
Pharmaceuticals	19.5
Mental health	5.0
Other	1.0
Total	100.0

Source: *The Wall Street Journal,* July 13, 2004, p. A10. © Dow Jones & Co., Inc. Used with permission.

3.22 (a) Use Excel to prepare a *2-D pie chart* for these LCD (liquid crystal display) shipments data. Modify the default colours, fonts, and so on as you judge appropriate to make the display effective. (b) Do you feel that the chart has become too cluttered (i.e., are you displaying too many slices)? Would a bar chart be better? Explain. *Hint:* Include data labels with the percent *values.* (LO 1 & 3)

World Market Share of LCD Shipments in 2004 LCDMarket	
Company	*Percent*
Sharp	34.6
Zenith	10.9
Sony	10.5
Samsung	9.6
Panasonic	8.7
Phillips	8.5
Others	17.3
Total	100.0

Source: *The Wall Street Journal,* July 15, 2004, p. B1. © Dow Jones & Co., Inc. Used with permission.
May not add to 100 due to rounding.

3.9 Effective Excel Charts

You've heard it said that a picture is worth a thousand words. Effective visual displays help you get your point across and persuade others to listen to your point of view. Good visuals help your employer make better decisions, but they also make *you* a more desirable employee and help *you* see the facts more clearly. Powerful graphics stand out in business reports, to the career benefit of those who know how to create them. This means knowing which visual displays to use in different situations. If you can make complex data comprehensible, you stand to gain a reputation for clear thinking.

The good news is that it's fun to make Excel graphs. The skills to make good displays can be learned, and the information provided here builds on the basics of Excel graphical displays that you have already learned. Excel is used widely throughout business primarily because of its excellent graphics capabilities. You say you already know all about Excel charts? That would be surprising. Professionals who make charts say that they learn new things every day.

Excel offers a vast array of charts. Although only a few of them are likely to be used in business, it is a good idea to review the whole list and to become familiar with their uses (and

FIGURE 3.34

Inserting a Chart
Fractional

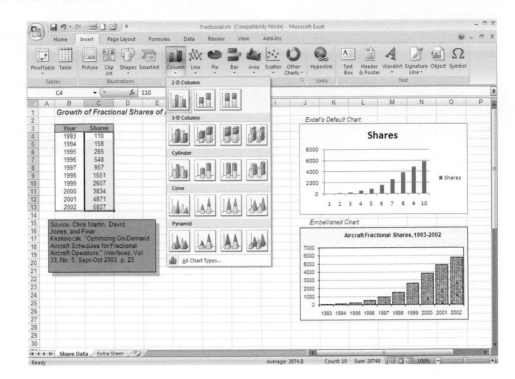

abuses). For example, Figure 3.34 shows data on fractional shares of aircraft ownership from 1993 to 2002 in cells C4:C13. Use the mouse to select the data you want to plot so that the data are highlighted. Click the Insert tab on Excel's upper menu bar, and select the icon for the type of chart you want. The appropriate chart type depends on the data. A simple bar chart is appropriate for the fractional shares time series.

Embellished Charts

Excel's default charts tend to be very plain. (See Excel's default bar chart in Figure 3.34). But business charts need not be dull. You can customize any graph to your taste. Figures 3.35 and 3.36

FIGURE 3.35

Embellished Bar Chart

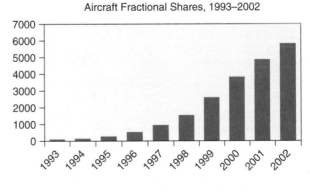

FIGURE 3.36

Over-Embellished Chart?

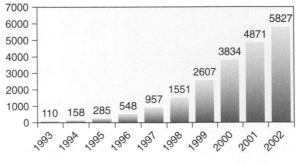

show embellished bar charts for the same data. After the chart is created in Excel, you can edit the graph to:

- Improve the titles (main, *X*-axis, *Y*-axis).
- Change the axis scales (minimum, maximum, demarcations).
- Display the data values (on top of each bar).
- Add a data table underneath the graph.
- Change colour or patterns in the plot area or chart area.
- Format the decimals (on the axes or data labels).
- Edit the gridlines (colour, dotted or solid, patterns).
- Alter the appearance of the bars (colour, pattern, gap width).

To alter a chart's appearance, click on any chart object (plot area, *X*-axis, *Y*-axis, gridlines, title, data series, chart area) to select the object, and then right-click to see a menu showing the *properties* that you can change. *LearningStats* Unit 03 gives a step-by-step explanation of how to make and edit charts in Excel. Just don't let your artistic verve overwhelm the data.

Excel offers many other types of specialized charts. When data points are connected and the area is filled with colour or shading, the result is an *area chart* (or *mountain chart*). This is basically a line chart. Its appeal is a feeling of solid dimensionality, which might make trends or patterns clearer to the reader. Figure 3.37 shows an example. A drawback is that when plotting more than one variable (e.g., especially time-series data), we can distinguish variables only if the data values "in back" are larger than the data values "in front." We might be better off using a multiple bar chart as in Figure 3.38 (or a line chart if we were showing time-series data).

Excel offers other specialized charts, including:

- *Bubble* charts (to display three variables on a two-dimensional scatter plot).
- *Stock* charts (for high/low/close stock prices).
- *Radar* or *spider* charts (to compare individual performance against a benchmark).
- *Floating bar* charts (to show a range of data values).

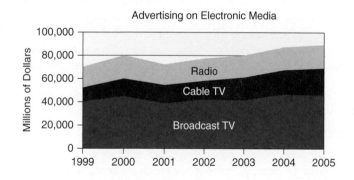

FIGURE 3.37

Area Chart
Advertising

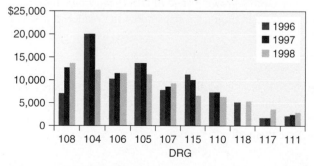

FIGURE 3.38

Multiple Bar Chart
Cardiac

Source: Standard and Poor's 500 Guide, 2004.

FIGURE 3.39

Radar Chart
MedMax

FIGURE 3.40

Floating Bar Chart
Maytag

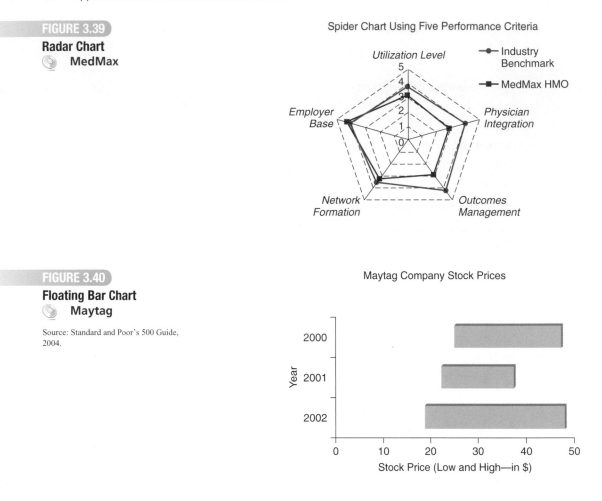

The last two are worth a closer look. Although **radar charts** (spider charts) are visually attractive, statisticians have reservations about them because they distort the data by emphasizing *areas*. In Figure 3.39, MedMax HMO seems farther below the industry benchmark on most criteria, because the eye sees *areas*. A **floating bar chart** can display low/high ranges (e.g., stock prices) as illustrated in Figure 3.40 for Maytag Company's stock.

3.10   Maps and Pictograms

Spatial Variation and GIS

Maps can be used for displaying many kinds of data, such as health statistics, demographic information, and warranty claim patterns. They are appropriate when patterns of *variation across space* are of interest. The units of observation may be provinces, counties, postal codes, school districts, or any other regions. Maps are self-explanatory and may reveal more information than a table. The rapidly growing field of GIS (*geographic information systems*) combines statistics, geography, and graphics. Maps allow the reader to assess patterns based on geography.

Pictograms

A **pictogram** (Figure 3.41) is a visual display in which data values are replaced by pictures to add visual appeal for a general audience. If done carefully, pictograms can be innocuous, but they often create visual distortion. They are entertaining art, not really graphs. The print media (e.g., *National Post*) use them often.

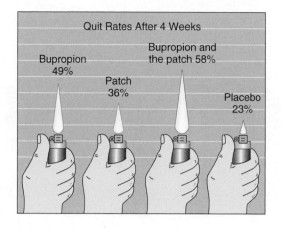

FIGURE 3.41

Cigarette Pictogram

Source: St. Joseph Mercy Oakland.

3.11   Deceptive Graphs

We have explained how to create *good* graphs. Now, let's turn things around. As an impartial consumer of information, you need a checklist of errors to beware. Those who want to slant the facts may do these things deliberately, although most errors occur through ignorance. Use this list to protect yourself against ignorant or unscrupulous practitioners of the graphical arts.

Error 1: Non-Zero Origin   Nonzero

A non-zero origin will exaggerate the trend. Measured distances do not match the stated values or axis demarcations. The accounting profession is particularly aggressive in enforcing this rule. Although zero origins are preferred, sometimes a non-zero origin is needed to show sufficient detail or to dramatize small changes when small changes are really dramatic changes. For example, when examining the value of the Canadian dollar versus the American dollar, a change of $0.01 may be considered a significant change as far as the economy of Canada is concerned. Using a zero origin would not show the change as being dramatic while starting the origin, for example, at $0.75 would show this change as being more significant. Here are two examples using the same data but different vertical scales. The first set of charts plots the daily value of the Canadian dollar versus the American dollar for the first half of the year 2009. The chart on the left (non-zero origin) shows a small change in the Canadian dollar's value as being significant, which is probably more realistic than the information conveyed in the chart on the right.

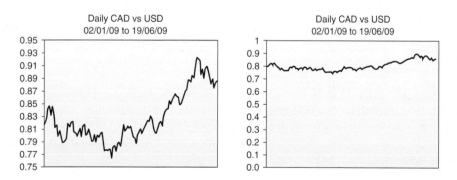

The bar chart of average length of cellphone calls on the left also shows a small change in average length as being significant, which is probably not as realistic as the information conveyed in the chart on the right. In this example, the chart on the left (non-zero origin) exaggerates the trend and may be considered deceptive.

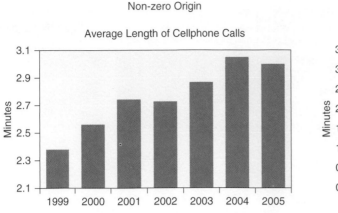
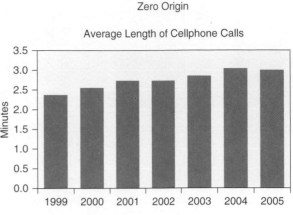

Error 2: Elastic Graph Proportions   Elastic

By shortening the *X*-axis in relation to the *Y*-axis, vertical change is exaggerated. For a time series (*X*-axis representing time) this can make a sluggish sales or profit curve appear steep. Conversely, a wide *X*-axis and short *Y*-axis can downplay alarming changes (recalls, industrial accidents). Keep the *aspect ratio* (width/height) below 2.00. Excel graphs use a default aspect ratio of about 1.8. The Golden Ratio you learned in art history suggests that 1.62 is ideal. Older TV screens use a 1:33 ratio as do older PCs (640 × 480 pixels). Movies use a widescreen format (up to 2.55), but VHS tapes and DVDs may crop it to fit on a television screen. HDTV and multimedia computers use a 16:9 aspect ratio (about 1.78). Charts with heights that exceed their width don't fit well on pages or computer screens. These two charts show the same data. Which seems to be growing faster?

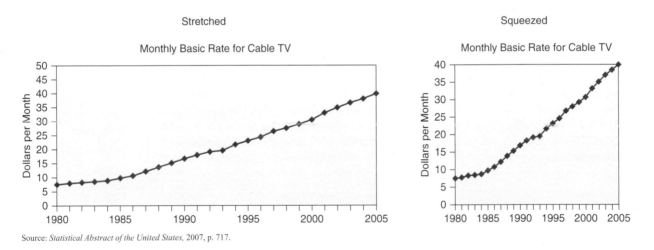

Source: *Statistical Abstract of the United States,* 2007, p. 717.

Error 3: Dramatic Title

The title often is designed more to grab the reader's attention than to convey the chart's content (Criminals on a Spree, Deficit Swamps Economy). Sometimes the title attempts to draw your conclusion for you (Inflation Wipes Out Savings, Imports Dwarf Exports). A title should be short but adequate for the purpose.

Error 4: Distracting Pictures

To add visual pizzazz, artists may superimpose the chart on a photograph (e.g., a gasoline price chart atop a photo of Middle East warfare) or add colourful cartoon figures, banners, or drawings. This is mostly harmless, but can distract the reader or impart an emotional slant (e.g., softening bad news about the home team's slide toward the cellar by drawing a sad-face team-mascot cartoon).

Error 5: Authority Figures

Advertisements sometimes feature mature, attractive, conservatively attired actors portraying scientists, doctors, or business leaders examining scientific-looking charts. Because the public respects science's reputation, such displays impart credibility to self-serving commercial claims.

Error 6: 3-D and Rotated Graphs   MedSchool

By making a graph three-dimensional and/or rotating it through space, the author can make trends appear to dwindle into the distance or loom alarmingly toward you. This example (medical school applications) combines errors 1, 3, 4, 5, and 6 (non-zero origin, dramatic title, distracting picture, authority figures, rotated 3-D look).

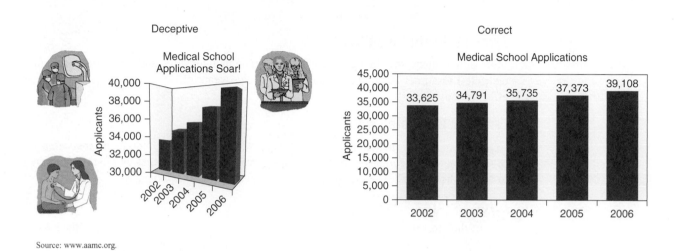

Source: www.aamc.org.

Error 7: Missing Axis Demarcations

Without "tick" marks on the axis, the reader cannot identify individual data values. Gridlines help the viewer compare magnitudes but are often omitted for clarity. For maximum clarity in a bar graph, label each bar with its numerical value, unless the scale is clearly demarcated and labelled.

Error 8: Missing Measurement Units or Definitions

Missing or unclear units of measurement (dollars? percent?) can render a chart useless. Even if the vertical scale is in dollars, we must know whether the variable being plotted is sales, profits, assets, or whatever. If percent, indicate clearly *percentage of what*.

Error 9: Vague Source

Large federal ministries or corporations employ thousands of people and issue hundreds of reports per year. Vague sources like "Ministry of Finance" may indicate that the author lost the citation, didn't know the data source, or mixed data from several sources. Scientific publications insist on complete source citations. Rules are less rigorous for publications aimed at a general audience.

Error 10: Complex Graph

Complicated visual displays make the reader work harder. Keep your main objective in mind. Omit "bonus" detail or put it in the appendix. Apply the *10-second rule* to graphs. If the message is really complex, can it be broken into smaller parts? This example (surgery volume) combines errors 3, 4, 7, 8, 9, and 10 (silly subtitle, distracting pictures, no data labels, no definitions, vague source, too much information).

Dept. of Surgery Volume
Slicing and Dicing

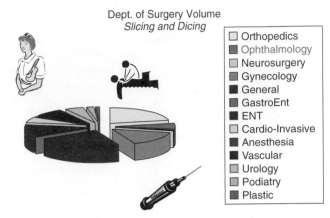

☐ Orthopedics
■ Ophthalmology
☐ Neurosurgery
■ Gynecology
■ General
■ GastroEnt
■ ENT
☐ Cardio-Invasive
■ Anesthesia
■ Vascular
☐ Urology
☐ Podiatry
■ Plastic

Source: Hospital reports.

Error 11: Gratuitous Effects

Slide shows often use colour and special effects (sound, interesting slide transitions, spinning text, etc.) to attract attention. But once the novelty wears off, audiences may find special effects annoying.

Error 12: Estimated Data

In a spirit of zeal to include the "latest" figures, the last few data points in a time series are often estimated. Or perhaps a couple of years were missing or incompatible, so the author had to "fill in the blanks." At a minimum, estimated points should be noted.

Error 13: Area Trick   ☺   **AreaTrick**

One of the most pernicious visual tricks is simultaneously enlarging the width of the bars as their height increases, so the bar area misstates the true proportion (e.g., by replacing graph bars with figures like human beings, coins, or gas pumps). As figure height increases, so does width, distorting the area. This example (physician salaries) illustrates this distortion.

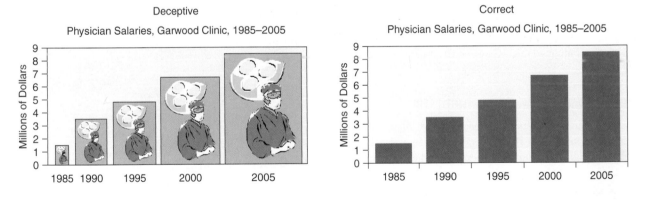

Deceptive

Physician Salaries, Garwood Clinic, 1985–2005

Correct

Physician Salaries, Garwood Clinic, 1985–2005

Final Advice

Can you trust any visual display (unless you created it yourself)? Be a skeptic, and be pleasantly surprised if the graph lives up to the best standards. Print media compete with TV and the Web, so newspapers and magazines must use colourful charts to attract reader interest. People enjoy visual displays, so we accept some artistic liberties. Mass-readership publications like *Maclean's, Time, Newsweek,* and *USA Today,* or even the more specialized business-oriented publications like *Forbes, Fortune, BusinessWeek,* and *The Wall Street Journal,* should not be judged by the same standards you would apply to an academic journal. Businesses want charts that follow the rules, because a deceptive chart may have serious consequences. Decisions may be made about products or services that affect lives, market share, and jobs (including yours). So know the rules, try to follow them, and expect your peers and subordinates to do the same. Catchy graphics have a place in selling your ideas but shouldn't dominate the data.

Further Challenges

If you enjoy playing with computers, try to learn these skills on your own:

- Copy and paste Excel charts into Word or PowerPoint.
- Copy and paste charts from other software (MINITAB, Visual Statistics).
- Use screen captures and edit the results in Paint if necessary.
- Use presentation software (e.g., PowerPoint) with transition effects.
- Know how (and when) to link Excel charts to spreadsheets.
- Use clip art and create your own simple graphics.

CHAPTER SUMMARY

For a set of observations on a single numerical variable, a **dot plot** displays the individual data values, while a **frequency distribution** classifies the data into classes called **bins** for a **histogram** of **frequencies** for each bin. The number of bins and their limits are matters left to your judgment, though **Sturges' Rule** offers advice on the number of bins. The **line chart** shows values of one or more **time-series** variables plotted against time. A **log scale** is sometimes used in time-series charts when data vary by orders of magnitude. The **bar chart** shows a **numerical** data value for each category of an **attribute.** However, a bar chart can also be used for a time series. A **scatter plot** can reveal the association (or lack of association) between two variables *X* and *Y*. The **pie chart** (showing a **numerical** data value for each category of an **attribute** if the data values are parts of a whole) is common but should be used with caution. Sometimes a **simple table** is the best visual display. Creating effective visual displays is an acquired skill. Excel offers a wide range of charts from which to choose. Deceptive graphs are found frequently in both media and business presentations, and the consumer should be aware of common errors.

KEY TERMS

arithmetic scale, *69*
bar chart, *71*
central tendency, *54*
dispersion, *54*
dot plot, *56*
floating bar chart, *90*
frequency distribution, *59*
frequency polygon, *65*
histogram, *61*
left-skewed, *64*

line chart, *68*
logarithmic scale, *69*
maps, *90*
modal class, *62*
ogive, *65*
outlier, *65*
Pareto chart, *72*
pictogram, *90*
pie chart, *85*
pivot table, *83*

pyramid chart, *71*
radar chart, *90*
right-skewed, *64*
scatter plot, *77*
shape, *54*
stacked bar chart, *74*
Sturges' Rule, *60*
symmetric, *64*
trend line, *80*

CHAPTER REVIEW

1. (a) What is a dot plot? (b) Why are dot plots attractive? (c) What are their limitations? (LO 1)

2. (a) What is a frequency distribution? (b) What are the steps in creating one? (LO 1)

3. (a) What is a histogram? (b) What does it show? (LO 1)

4. (a) What is a bimodal histogram? (b) Explain the difference between left-skewed, symmetric, and right-skewed histograms. (c) What is an outlier? (LO 1)

5. (a) What is a scatter plot? (b) What do scatter plots reveal? (c) Sketch a scatter plot with a moderate positive correlation. (d) Sketch a scatter plot with a strong negative correlation. (LO 1)

6. For what kind of data would we use a bar chart? List three tips for creating effective bar charts. (LO 2)

7. For what kind of data would we use a line chart? List three tips for creating effective line charts. (LO 2)

8. (a) List the three most common types of charts in business, and sketch each type (no real data, just a sketch). (b) List three specialized charts that can be created in Excel, and sketch each type (no real data, just a sketch). (LO 1)

9. (a) For what kind of data would we use a pie chart? (b) Name two common pie-chart errors. (c) Why are pie charts regarded with skepticism by some statisticians? (LO 2)

10. Which types of charts can be used for time-series data? (LO 2)

11. (a) When might we need a log scale? (b) What do equal distances on a log scale represent? (c) State one drawback of a log-scale graph. (LO 2)

12. (a) Why do the media like pictograms? (b) Why aren't statisticians attracted to them? (LO 2)

13. List six deceptive graphical techniques. (LO 4)

14. What is a pivot table? Why is it useful? (LO 1)

CHAPTER EXERCISES

Note: In these exercises, you may use a software package. Use MegaStat's Descriptive Statistics for dot plots or Frequency Distributions for histograms. Use MINITAB's Graphs or a similar software package to create the dot plot or histogram.

3.23 A study of 40 cardiac care centres showed the following ratios of nurses to beds. (a) Prepare a dot plot. (b) Prepare a frequency distribution and histogram (you may either specify the bins yourself or use automatic bins). (c) Describe the distribution, based on these displays. (LO 1 & 3)

Nurses

1.48	1.16	1.24	1.52	1.30	1.28	1.68	1.40	1.12	0.98	0.93	2.76
1.34	1.58	1.72	1.38	1.44	1.41	1.34	1.96	1.29	1.21	2.00	1.50
1.68	1.39	1.62	1.17	1.07	2.11	2.40	1.35	1.48	1.59	1.81	1.15
1.35	1.42	1.33	1.41								

3.24 The first Rose Bowl football game was played in 1902. The next was not played until 1916, but a Rose Bowl has been played every year since then. The margin of victory in each of the 87 Rose Bowls from 1902 through 2003 is shown below (0 indicates a tie). (a) Prepare a dot plot. (b) Prepare a frequency distribution and histogram (you may either specify the bins yourself or use automatic bins). (c) Describe the distribution, based on these displays. (Data are from *Sports Illustrated 2004 Sports Almanac,* and www.cbs.sportsline.com.) (LO 1 & 3)

RoseBowl

49	14	14	1	28	0	11	0	17	1	0
1	1	33	24	9	35	7	16	7	21	13
4	14	8	4	9	29	25	20	31	49	6
3	8	33	7	8	13	3	16	3	26	36
10	18	5	10	27	2	1	11	11	7	10
1	25	21	1	13	8	7	7	1	17	28
10	36	3	17	7	3	8	7	12	20	7
5	18	9	3	5	7	8	10	23	20	

3.25 An executive's telephone log showed the following data for the length of 65 calls initiated during the last week of July. (a) Prepare a dot plot. (b) Prepare a frequency distribution and histogram (you may either specify the bins yourself or use automatic bins). (c) Describe the distribution, based on these displays. (LO 1 & 3) **CallLength**

1	2	10	5	3	3	2	20	1	1
6	3	13	2	2	1	26	3	1	3
1	2	1	7	1	2	3	1	2	12
1	4	2	2	29	1	1	1	8	5
1	4	2	1	1	1	1	6	1	2
3	3	6	1	3	1	1	5	1	18
2	13	13	1	6					

3.26 Below are the batting averages of New York Yankees players who were at bat five times or more in 2006. (a) Construct a frequency distribution. Explain how you chose the number of bins and the bin limits. (b) Make a histogram and describe its appearance. (c) Repeat, using a different number of bins and different bin limits. (d) Did your visual impression of the data change when you changed the number of bins? Explain. *Note:* You may use MegaStat or MINITAB if your instructor agrees. (LO 1)   **Yankees**

Batting Averages for the 2006 New York Yankees

Player	Avg	Player	Avg	Player	Avg
Derek Jeter	0.343	Miguel Cairo	0.239	Sal Fasano	0.143
Johnny Damon	0.285	Bobby Abreu	0.330	Terrence Long	0.167
Alex Rodriguez	0.290	Hideki Matsui	0.302	Kevin Thompson	0.300
Robinson Cano	0.342	Gary Sheffield	0.298	Kevin Reese	0.417
Jorge Posada	0.277	Craig Wilson	0.212	Andy Cannizaro	0.250
Melky Cabrera	0.280	Bubba Crosby	0.207	Randy Johnson	0.167
Jason Giambi	0.253	Aaron Guiel	0.256	Wil Nieves	0.000
Bernie Williams	0.281	Kelly Stinnett	0.228		
Andy Phillips	0.240	Nick Green	0.240		

Source: www.thebaseballcube.com/statistics/2006/.

3.27   Concerned about a possible threat of hearing loss due to cockpit noise, airline pilots took measurements of cockpit noise levels in several aircraft during various flight phases (climb, cruise, descent). Is the cockpit noise level related to airspeed? Use the CD data set ($n = 61$) to prepare a scatter plot of X = airspeed (knots) and Y = cockpit noise level (decibels). Describe what the scatter plot tells you. *Hint:* You may need to rescale the X and Y axes to see more detail. (LO 1 & 3)   **CockpitNoise**

3.28   (a) What kind of display is this? (b) Identify its strengths and weaknesses, using the tips and checklists shown in this chapter. (c) Can you suggest any improvements? Would a different type of display be better? (LO 4 & 5)   **WomenPilots**

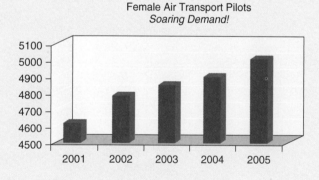

Female Air Transport Pilots
Soaring Demand!

Source: www.faa.gov.

3.29   (a) What kind of display is this? (b) Identify its strengths and weaknesses, using the tips and checklists shown in this chapter. (c) Can you suggest any improvements? Would a different type of display be better? (LO 2, 4 & 5)   **MedError**

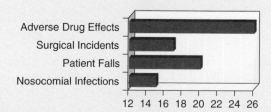

Sources of Medical Error

3.30 (a) What kind of display is this? (b) Identify its strengths and weaknesses, using the tips and checklists shown in this chapter. (c) Can you suggest any improvements? Would a different type of display be better? (LO 2, 4 & 5) 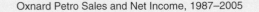 **Oxnard**

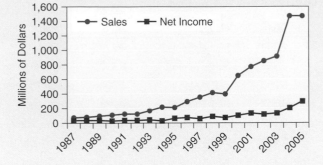

3.31 (a) What kind of display is this? (b) Identify its strengths and weaknesses, using the tips and checklists shown in this chapter. (c) Can you suggest any improvements? Would a different type of display be better? (LO 2, 4 & 5) **Advertising**

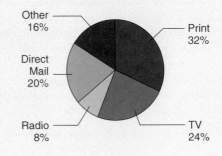

Source: *Statistical Abstract of the United States,* 2002, p. 772.

3.32 (a) What kind of display is this? (b) Identify its strengths and weaknesses, using the tips and checklists shown in this chapter. (c) Can you suggest any improvements? Would a different type of display be better? (LO 2, 4 & 5) **BirthRate**

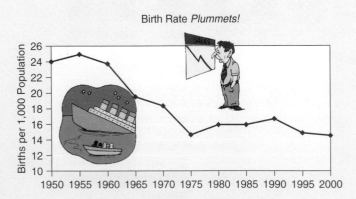

3.33 (a) What kind of display is this? (b) Identify its strengths and weaknesses, using the tips and checklists shown in this chapter. (c) Can you suggest any improvements? Would a different type of display be better? (LO 2, 4 & 5)

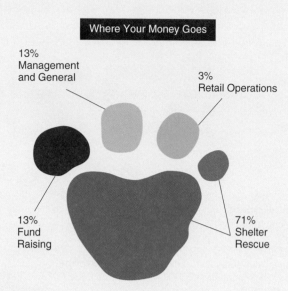

Where Your Money Goes

13%
Management
and General

3%
Retail Operations

13%
Fund
Raising

71%
Shelter
Rescue

Source: Courtesy of Michigan Humane Society.

3.34 (a) What kind of display is this? (b) Identify its strengths and weaknesses, using the tips and checklists shown in this chapter. (c) Can you suggest any improvements? Would a different type of display be better? (LO 2, 4 & 5)

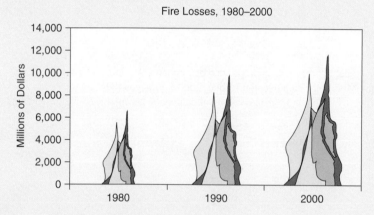

Fire Losses, 1980–2000

Source: *Statistical Abstract of the United States,* 2001, p. 340.

3.35 (a) What kind of display is this? (b) Identify its strengths and weaknesses, using the tips and checklists shown in this chapter. (c) Can you suggest any improvements? Would a different type of display be better? (LO 2, 4 & 5)  **Bankruptcies**

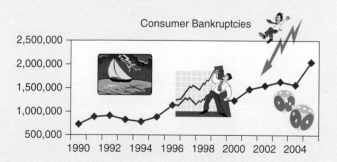

Consumer Bankruptcies

Source: American Bankruptcy Institute. www.abiworld.org.

3.36 (a) What kind of display is this? (b) Identify its strengths and weaknesses, using the tips and checklists shown in this chapter. (c) Can you suggest any improvements? Would a different type of display be better? (LO 2, 4 & 5)

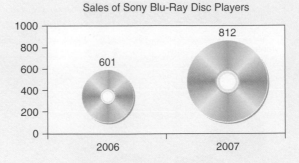

Sales of Sony Blu-Ray Disc Players

3.37 (a) Use Excel to prepare an appropriate type of chart (bar, line, pie, scatter) to display the following data. Modify the default colours, fonts, and so on as you judge appropriate to make the display effective. (b) Would more than one kind of display be acceptable? Why or why not? (LO 1 & 2)

Where Did You Purchase Your Statistics Textbook? ◎ **Textbook**

Response	Count
Campus Bookstore	147
Retail Outlet	66
Web (e.g., Amazon)	49
Another Student	7
Total	269

Source: Survey of statistics students in 2007 at two large public universities.

3.38 (a) Use Excel to prepare an appropriate type of chart (bar, line, pie, scatter) to display the following data. Modify the default colours, fonts, and so on as you judge appropriate to make the display effective. (b) Would more than one kind of display be acceptable? Why or why not? (LO 1 & 2)

How Often Do You Use an Advanced Calculator? ◎ **Calculator**

Response	Count
Frequently	75
Rarely	172
Never	44
Total	291

Source: Survey of statistics students in 2007 at two large public universities.

3.39 (a) Use Excel to prepare an appropriate type of chart (bar, line, pie, scatter) to display the following data. Modify the default colours, fonts, and so on as you judge appropriate to make the display effective. (b) Would more than one kind of display be acceptable? Why or why not? (LO 1 & 2)

How Confident Are You That You Have Saved Enough to Retire in Comfort? ◎ **Retirement**

Confidence Level	1993 (%)	2003 (%)
Very confident	18	21
Somewhat confident	55	45
Not very confident	25	33
Don't know	2	1
Total	100	100

Source: *Detroit Free Press,* Nov. 3, 2003.

3.40   (a) Use Excel to prepare an appropriate type of chart (bar, line, pie, scatter) to display the following data. Modify the default colours, fonts, and so on as you judge appropriate to make the display effective. (b) Would more than one kind of display be acceptable? Why or why not? (LO 1 & 2)

New Car Colour Preferences   CarColor

Colour	Percent
Blue	12
Green	7
Natural	12
Red	13
Silver/Grey	24
White	16
Black	13
Other	3
Total	100

Source: *Detroit Auto Scene,* 24 (2006), no. 1, p. 1.

3.41   (a) Use Excel to prepare an appropriate type of chart (bar, line, pie, scatter) to display the following data. Modify the default colours, fonts, and so on as you judge appropriate to make the display effective. (b) Would more than one kind of display be acceptable? Why or why not? (LO 1 & 2)

Age Group	Percent of Drivers	Percent of Fatal Crashes
15–19	4.7	11.0
20–24	8.5	14.3
25–34	18.2	18.1
35–44	20.5	16.5
45–54	19.7	15.6
55–64	13.8	9.8
65–74	8.2	6.3
75 and over	6.4	8.4
Total	100.0	100.0

3.42   (a) Use Excel to prepare an appropriate type of chart (bar, line, pie, scatter) to display the following data. Modify the default colours, fonts, and so on as you judge appropriate to make the display effective. (b) Would more than one kind of display be acceptable? Why or why not? (LO 1 & 2)

U.S. Market Share for Search Engines   WebSearch

Search Engine	Percent
Google	45.4
Yahoo	28.2
Microsoft	11.7
Ask	5.8
AOL/Time Warner	5.4
All Others	3.5
Total	100.0

Source: *The New York Times,* Dec. 4, 2006, p. C1.

3.43 (a) Use Excel to prepare an appropriate type of chart (bar, line, pie, scatter) to display the following data. Modify the default colours, fonts, and so on as you judge appropriate to make the display effective. (b) Would more than one kind of display be acceptable? Why or why not? (LO 1 & 2)

Fatal Complications from Liposuction   ◎   **Liposuc**

Type of Complication	Percent of Total Fatalities
Blood clots	23.1
Abdominal perforation	14.6
Anesthesia complications	10.0
Fat embolism	8.5
Cardiorespiratory failure	5.4
Massive infection	5.4
Hemorrhage	4.6
Unknown/confidential	28.0
Total	100.0

Note: Details do not add to 100 percent due to rounding.

Source: *San Francisco Chronicle,* June 30, 2002, p. A21.

3.44 (a) Use Excel to prepare an appropriate type of chart (bar, line, pie, scatter) to display the following data. Modify the default colours, fonts, and so on as you judge appropriate to make the display effective. (b) Would more than one kind of display be acceptable? Why or why not? (LO 1 & 2)

2001 Average Assembly Productivity   ◎

Firm	Hours per Vehicle
Nissan	17.92
Honda	19.78
Mitsubishi	21.82
Toyota	22.53
NUMMI	22.68
GM	26.10
Ford	26.87
CAMI	28.97
Auto Alliance	30.42
Chrysler Group	30.82

Source: *Detroit Free Press,* June 14, 2002, p. 1F.

3.45 (a) Use Excel to prepare an appropriate type of chart (bar, line, pie, scatter) to display the following data. Modify the default colours, fonts, and so on as you judge appropriate to make the display effective. (b) Would more than one kind of display be acceptable? Why or why not? (LO 1 & 2)

Average Wedding Expenses in 2002   ◎   **Wedding**

Expense	$ Amount
Rings (engagement, wedding)	4,877
Photos	1,814
Flowers	967
Reception	7,630
Attire (except bride)	1,656
Bride's attire, makeup, hair	1,523
Rehearsal dinner	875
Music	900
Other	2,118

Source: *The New York Times,* July 13, 2003, p. 17.

3.46 Suppose the following table compares the typical yearly expenditures of a family of four in a middle income neighbourhood in Montreal, Quebec.

	Year	
Category	**1998**	**2008**
Shelter	$12,000	$17,000
Transportation	$ 2,500	$ 6,000
Food	$ 5,000	$ 7,000
Education	$ 1,000	$ 4,000
Entertainment	$ 1,500	$ 2,000
Other	$ 300	$ 500
Total	$22,300	$36,500

Using Excel, create an appropriate graph which shows: (a) that more was spent on shelter in the year 2008 than in the year 1998 and (b) that less was spent on shelter in the year 2008 than in the year 1998. (LO 1, 2 & 3)

3.47 Could the following table be made into an effective chart? If so, do it. If not, explain why not. (LO 1 & 2)

Average Annual Number of Ambulatory Care Visits per Capita   **DocVisits**

Age Group	Physician Office	Outpatient Clinic	Emergency
Under 15	2.43	0.31	0.38
15 to 24	1.74	0.25	0.44
25 to 44	2.37	0.26	0.39
45 to 64	3.76	0.32	0.31
65 to 74	6.23	0.39	0.34
75 and over	7.34	0.36	0.58

Source: *Statistical Abstract of the United States, 2007*, p. 112.

3.48 The following table shows some health statistics for eight industrialized countries.

Country	Life Expectancy	Per Capita Expenditure on Health (US$)	Health Care Costs as a Percent of GDP	Percent of Government Revenue Spent on Health	Percent of Health Costs Paid by Government	Percent of Health Costs Paid by Private Insurance	Percent of Health Costs Paid by Consumer
Japan	82.5	2,662	7.9	16.8	81.0	0.4	17.2
Sweden	80.5	3,149	9.4	13.6	85.2	0.0	15.1
Canada	80.5	2,669	9.9	16.7	69.9	12.6	15.1
Australia	80.5	2,519	9.5	17.7	67.5	7.4	21.8
Germany	80.0	3,204	11.1	17.6	78.2	8.8	10.5
France	79.5	2,981	10.1	14.2	76.3	12.6	7.4
UK	79.5	2,428	8.0	15.8	85.7	0.0	14.4
USA	77.5	5,711	15.2	18.5	44.6	36.8	13.3

Construct and interpret a relevant chart that will allow you to:

(a) Compare life expectancies across these eight countries.
(b) Compare per capita expenditure on health across these eight countries.
(c) Compare health care costs as a percentage of GDP across these eight countries.
(d) Compare the breakdown of health care costs by who pays for it across these eight countries (note: the percentages paid by the three constituents [government, private insurance, consumer] do not necessarily add up to 100 percent for some unexplained reason).
(e) Compares the breakdown of health care costs between Canada and the United States (use two pie charts).
(f) Examine the relationship between per capita expenditures on health and the percentage of costs paid by private insurance companies
(g) Examine the relationship between per capita expenditures on health and life expectancy.

For parts (a), (b), and (c), construct the same types of charts, but alter them to make them misleading and then state why they are misleading. (LO 1, 2, 3 & 4)

Americans have been very resistant to more government intrusion into their health care system. Based on the evidence created above, is there justification for this resistance? Explain.

3.49 The following table compares the exports of seafood (in $mil) to Canada's five top seafood markets between 2006 and 2007 (Source: Agriculture and Agri-Food Canada, http://atn-riae.agr.ca/seafood/trade_monitor-e.htm)

	Exports ($mil)	
Country	2006	2007
United States	2,516	2,393
Japan	342	298
China	276	238
Denmark	125	130
United Kingdom	111	127

Construct the appropriate charts that allow you to compare export sales among the five countries and allow you to compare sales over the two-year period. What do you observe? (LO 1, 2, 3 & 4)

3.50 The following table shows the number of medals won by the top 20 medal-winning countries at the 2008 Beijing Olympics and the approximate populations of these countries. (LO 1, 2 & 3)

	Number of Medals				
Country	Gold	Silver	Bronze	Total	Appox. Population (mil)
United States	36	38	36	110	305.3
China	51	21	28	100	1326.4
Russia	23	21	28	72	141.9
Great Britain	19	13	15	47	61.2
Australia	14	15	17	46	21.4
Germany	16	10	15	41	82.2
France	7	16	17	40	64.5
South Korea	13	10	8	31	48.2
Italy	8	10	10	28	59.6
Ukraine	7	5	15	27	46.0
Japan	9	6	10	25	127.7
Cuba	2	11	11	24	11.3
Belarus	4	5	10	19	9.7
Canada	3	9	6	18	33.4
Spain	5	10	3	18	46.0
Netherlands	7	5	4	16	16.4
Brazil	3	4	8	15	187.8
Kenya	5	5	4	14	37.5
Kazakhstan	2	4	7	13	15.4
Jamaica	6	3	2	11	2.7

(a) Construct an appropriate graph that compares not only the total number of medals won by country but also the breakdown among gold, silver, and bronze medals.
(b) Construct an appropriate graph that indicates (or does not indicate) a relationship between population size and total medals won.
(c) Create an appropriate graph that may or may not indicate that Canada did relatively better than is simply indicated by the number of medals that it won. (**Hint:** Consider the populations of the 20 countries.)

DO-IT-YOURSELF

3.51 (a) On the Web, look up "geographical information systems" or "GIS." Do you find many references? (b) Suggest some potential applications of GIS (e.g., marketing, health care, government, military).

3.52 (a) Clip an example of a deceptive visual data presentation from a recent magazine or newspaper (if it is from a library, make a photocopy instead). Try to choose an outrageous example that violates many principles of ideal graphs. (b) Cite the exact source where you found the display. (c) What do you think is its presumed purpose? (d) Write a short, critical evaluation of its strengths and weaknesses. Be sure to attach the original clipping (or a good photocopy) to your analysis. (LO 4)

3.53 (a) Make a hand-drawn graph that presents some numerical data of your own (e.g., your GPA, earnings, work hours, golf scores) in a visual manner designed to dramatize or slant the facts. Violate the principles of ideal graphs *without actually changing any of the numbers.* (b) List each violation you tried to illustrate. (c) Now present the same data in an objective visual display that violates as few rules as possible. (d) Which took more time and effort, the deceptive display or the objective one? (LO 1 & 4)

LearningStats Unit 03 Visual Displays LS

LearningStats Unit 03 introduces tables, charts, and rules for visual displays. Modules are designed for self-study, so you can proceed at your own pace, concentrate on material that is new, and pass quickly over things that you already know. Your instructor may assign specific modules, or you may decide to check them out because the topic sounds interesting. In addition to helping you learn about statistics, they may be useful as references later on.

Topic	*LearningStats Modules*
Effective visual displays	Presenting Data—I
	Presenting Data—II
	EDA Graphics
How to make an Excel chart	Excel Charts: Step-by-Step
	Pivot Tables
	Using MegaStat
	Using Visual Statistics
	Using MINITAB
Types of Excel charts	Excel Charts: Bar, Pie, Line
	Excel Charts: Scatter, Pareto, Other
	Excel Charts: Histograms
	Wrong Chart Type?
	Gallery of Charts—1
	Gallery of Charts—2
	Gallery of Charts—3
	Gallery of Charts—4
Applications	Adult Heights
	Bimodal Data
	Data Format
	Sturges' Rule
	Stem and Leaf Plots

Key: = PowerPoint = Word = Excel

Chapter

4

Descriptive Statistics

Chapter Learning Objectives

When you finish this chapter you should be able to

1. Recognize the types of numerical measures and their symbols.

2. Demonstrate an understanding of the characteristics of common numerical statistical measures and how they can influence their usage.

3. Calculate common descriptive statistics, both manually and using Excel, and interpret the results.

4. Approximate the mean, standard deviation, and other descriptive measures from grouped data and interpret the results.

5. Determine and apply the appropriate descriptive statistics to use in a problem context.

4.1 Numerical Description

Chapter 1

The last chapter described how to create information using *visual* descriptions of data (e.g., histograms, dot plots, scatter plots). This chapter explains how to create information using *numerical* descriptions of data. Descriptive measures derived from a sample (*n* items) are referred to as *statistics,* while for a population (*N* items or infinite) these measures are called *parameters.* For a data set consisting of a single numerical variable, we are usually interested in three key characteristics: central tendency, dispersion, and shape. For a data set consisting of two or more numerical variables, we are usually interested in one additional key characteristic: the relationship between these

TABLE 4.1   Characteristics of Numerical Data

Characteristic	Interpretation
Central Tendency	Where are the data values concentrated? What seem to be typical or middle data values?
Dispersion	How much variation is there in the data? How spread out are the data values? Are there unusual values?
Shape	Are the data values distributed symmetrically? Skewed? Sharply peaked? Flat? Bimodal?

EXAMPLE 1
Vehicle Quality

Every year, J.D. Power and Associates issues its initial vehicle quality ratings. These ratings are of interest to consumers, dealers, and manufacturers. Table 4.2 shows defect rates for a sample of 37 vehicle brands. We will demonstrate how numerical statistics can be used to summarize a data set like this. The brands represented are a random sample that we will use to illustrate certain calculations.

variables. Table 4.1 summarizes the questions that we will be asking about a data set consisting of a single variable.

Preliminary Analysis

Before calculating any statistics, we consider how the data were collected. A Web search reveals that J.D. Power and Associates is a well-established independent company whose methods are widely considered to be objective. Data on defects are obtained by inspecting randomly chosen vehicles for each brand, counting the defects, and dividing the number of defects by the number of vehicles inspected. J.D. Power multiplies the result by 100 to obtain defects per 100 vehicles, rounded to the nearest integer. However, the underlying measurement scale is continuous (e.g., if 4 defects were found in 3 Saabs, the defect rate would be 1.333333, or 133 defects per 100 vehicles). Defect rates would vary from year to year, and perhaps even within a given model year, so the timing of the study could affect the results. Because the analysis is based on sampling, we must allow for the possibility of sampling error. With these cautions in mind, we look at the data. The dot plot as previously discussed in Chapter 3 and as shown in

TABLE 4.2   Number of Defects per 100 Vehicles, 2006 Model Year   JDPower

Brand	Defects	Brand	Defects	Brand	Defects
Acura	120	Infiniti	117	Nissan	121
Audi	130	Isuzu	191	Pontiac	133
BMW	142	Jaguar	109	Porsche	91
Buick	134	Jeep	153	Saab	163
Cadillac	117	Kia	136	Saturn	129
Chevrolet	124	Land Rover	204	Scion	140
Chrysler	120	Lexus	93	Subaru	146
Dodge	132	Lincoln	121	Suzuki	169
Ford	127	Mazda	150	Toyota	106
GMC	119	Mercedes-Benz	139	Volkswagen	171
Honda	110	Mercury	129	Volvo	133
HUMMER	171	MINI	150		
Hyundai	102	Mitsubishi	135		

Source: J.D. Power and Associates 2006 Initial Quality Study™. Used with permission.

NOTE: Ratings are intended for educational purposes only, and should not be used as a guide to consumer decisions.

FIGURE 4.1

**Dot Plot of J.D. Power
Data (*n* = 37 brands)**

JD Power

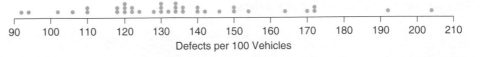

Figure 4.1, offers a visual impression of the data such as where the values are concentrated, how spread out the values are, and whether there are any extreme values, which may warrant further investigation. From this figure, we can roughly estimate that the values are concentrated somewhere between 120 and 140, that the values are quite dispersed, and that the values above 190 are extreme values compared to the other values in the data set.

Sorting   A good first step is to sort the data. Except for tiny samples, this would be done in Excel, as illustrated in Figure 4.2. Highlight the data array (including the headings), right click, choose Sort > Custom Sort, choose the column to sort on, check the My data has headers box, and click OK. Table 4.3 shows the sorted data for all 37 brands.

Visual Displays   The sorted data in Table 4.3 provide insight into central tendency and dispersion. The values range from 91 (Porsche) to 204 (Land Rover), and the middle values seem to be around 130. The next visual step is a histogram, shown in Figure 4.3. Sturges' Rule suggests 7 bins, but we use 7 and 12 bins to show more detail. Both histograms are roughly symmetric (maybe slightly right-skewed) with no extreme values. Both show modal classes near 130.

Chapter 5

FIGURE 4.2

Sorting Data in Excel

JD Power

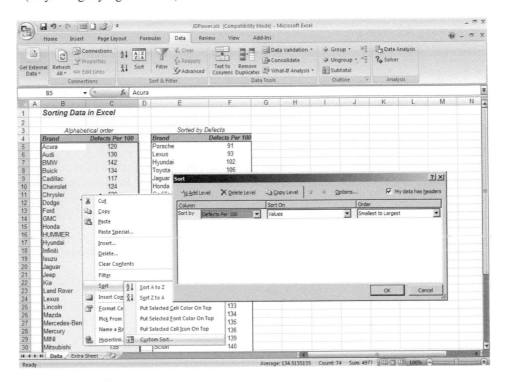

FIGURE 4.3 **Histograms of J.D. Power Data (*n* = 37 brands)**   **JD Power**

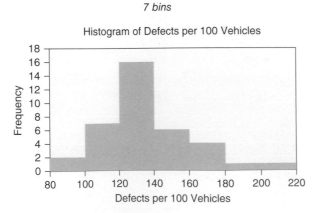

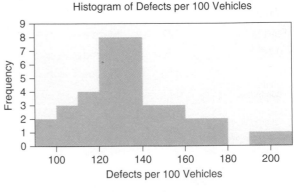

TABLE 4.3   Number of Defects per 100 Vehicles (2006 Model Year) Ranked Lowest to Highest
🔘 JD Power

Brand	Defects	Brand	Defects	Brand	Defects
Porsche	91	Chevrolet	124	BMW	142
Lexus	93	Ford	127	Subaru	146
Hyundai	102	Mercury	129	Mazda	150
Toyota	106	Saturn	129	MINI	150
Jaguar	109	Audi	130	Jeep	153
Honda	110	Dodge	132	Saab	163
Cadillac	117	Pontiac	133	Suzuki	169
Infiniti	117	Volvo	133	HUMMER	171
GMC	119	Buick	134	Volkswagen	171
Acura	120	Mitsubishi	135	Isuzu	191
Chrysler	120	Kia	136	Land Rover	204
Lincoln	121	Mercedes-Benz	139		
Nissan	121	Scion	140		

Source: J.D. Power and Associates 2006 Initial Quality Study™. Used with permission.

4.2 Central Tendency

When we speak of *central tendency* we are trying to describe the middle or typical values of a distribution. You can assess central tendency in a general way from a dot plot or histogram, but numerical statistics allow more precise statements. Table 4.4 lists six common measures of central tendency. Each has strengths and weaknesses. We need to look at several of them to obtain a clear picture of central tendency.

TABLE 4.4   Six Measures of Central Tendency

Statistic	Formula	Excel Formula	Pro	Con
Mean	$\dfrac{1}{n}\displaystyle\sum_{i=1}^{n} x_i$	=AVERAGE(Data)	Familiar and uses all the sample information.	Influenced by extreme values.
Median	Middle value in sorted array.	=MEDIAN(Data)	Robust when extreme data values exist.	Ignores extremes and can be affected by gaps in data values.
Mode	Most frequently occurring data value.	=MODE(Data)	Useful for attribute data or discrete data with a small range.	May not be unique, and is not helpful for continuous data.
Weighted mean	$\dfrac{\displaystyle\sum_{i=1}^{n} x_i w_i}{\displaystyle\sum_{i=1}^{n} w_i}$	=SUMPRODUCT(Data, Weights)/SUM(Weights)	Uses all the sample information and useful when more weight should be placed on different observations.	
Geometric mean (G)	$\sqrt[n]{x_1 x_2 \cdots x_n}$	=GEOMEAN(Data)	Useful for growth rates and mitigates high extremes.	Less familiar and requires positive data.
(growth rate formula)	$\sqrt[n]{(1 + x_1)\cdots(1 + x_n)} - 1$		Special case of geometric mean.	
Trimmed	Same as the mean except omit highest and lowest k% of data values (e.g., 5%)	=TRIMMEAN(Data, Percent)	Mitigates effects of extreme values.	Excludes some data values that could be relevant.

Chapter 1

Mean

The most familiar statistical measure of central tendency is the **mean** (sometimes referred to as the *arithmetic mean*). It is the sum of the data values divided by number of data items. For a population we symbolize it by μ (read as "mu"), while for a sample we use the symbol $\bar{x}$ (read as "x bar"). We use Equation 4.1 to calculate the mean of a population:

$$\mu = \frac{\sum_{i=1}^{N} x_i}{N} \quad \text{(population definition)} \tag{4.1}$$

Because we rarely deal with populations, the sample notation of Equation 4.2 is more commonly seen:

$$\bar{x} = \frac{\sum_{i=1}^{n} x_i}{n} \quad \text{(sample definition)} \tag{4.2}$$

We calculate the mean by using Excel's function =AVERAGE(Data) where Data is an array containing the data. So for the sample of $n = 37$ car brands:

$$\bar{x} = \frac{\sum_{i=1}^{n} x_i}{n} = \frac{91 + 93 + 102 + \cdots + 171 + 191 + 204}{37} = \frac{4{,}977}{37} = 134.51$$

Characteristics of the Mean

The arithmetic mean is the "average" with which most of us are familiar. The mean is affected by every sample item. It is the balancing point or fulcrum in a distribution if we view the *X*-axis as a lever arm and represent each data item as a physical weight, as illustrated in Figure 4.4 for the J.D. Power's data.

The mean is the balancing point because it has the property that distances from the mean to the data points *always* sum to zero:

$$\sum_{t=1}^{n} (x_i - \bar{x}) = 0 \tag{4.3}$$

This statement is true for *any* sample or population, regardless of its shape (skewed, symmetric, bimodal, etc.). Even when there are extreme values, the distances below the mean are *exactly* counterbalanced by the distances above the mean. For example, Bob's scores on five quizzes were 42, 60, 70, 75, 78. His mean is pulled down to 65, mainly because of his poor showing on one quiz, as illustrated in Figure 4.5. Although the data are asymmetric, the three scores above the mean exactly counterbalance the two scores below the mean:

$$\sum_{t=1}^{n} (x_i - \bar{x}) = (42 - 65) + (60 - 65) + (70 - 65) + (75 - 65) + (78 - 65)$$
$$= (-23) + (-5) + (5) + (10) + (13) = -28 + 28 = 0$$

FIGURE 4.4

Mean as Fulcrum ($n = 37$ vehicles)   JD Power

FIGURE 4.5

Bob's Quiz Scores ($n = 5$ quizzes)

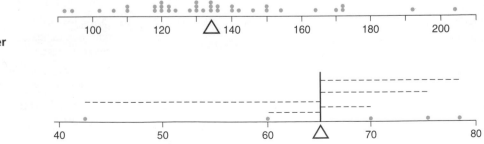

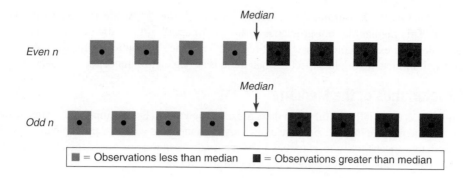

FIGURE 4.6

Illustration of the Median

Median

The **median** (denoted M in this text) is the 50th percentile or midpoint of the *sorted* sample data set $x_1, x_2, \ldots, x_n$. It separates the upper and lower halves of the sorted observations:

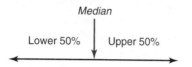

The median is the middle observation in the sorted array if n is odd, but is the average of the middle two observations if n is even, as illustrated in Figure 4.6. For example, if we have an even n, say $n = 6$, then the median is halfway *between* the third and fourth observations in the sorted array:

$$M = (x_3 + x_4)/2 = (15 + 17)/2 = 16$$

Median

$$11 \qquad 12 \qquad 15 \quad \downarrow \quad 17 \qquad 21 \qquad 32$$

But for an odd n, say $n = 7$, the median is the fourth observation in the sorted array:

$$M = x_4 = 25$$

Median

$$12 \qquad 23 \qquad 23 \qquad (25) \qquad 27 \qquad 34 \qquad 41$$

The *position* of the median in the sorted array is $(n + 1)/2$, so we can write:

$$\text{Median} = x_{(n+1)/2} \text{ for odd } n \text{ and Median} = \frac{x_{n/2} + x_{(n/2+1)}}{2} \text{ for even } n \qquad \textbf{(4.4)}$$

Excel's function for the median is =MEDIAN(Data) where Data is the data array. For the 37 vehicle quality ratings (odd n) the *position* of the median is $(n + 1)/2 = (37 + 1)/2 = 19$, so the median is

$$M = x_{(n+1)/2} = x_{(37+1)/2} = x_{19} = 132$$

It is tempting to imagine that half the observations are less than the median, but this is not necessarily the case. For example, here are 11 exam scores in ascending order:

Median

$$51 \quad 66 \quad 71 \quad 78 \quad 78 \quad (78) \quad 81 \quad 82 \quad 82 \quad 91 \quad 99$$

Their median is 78. But only three data values are *below* 78, while five data values are *above* 78. This median did not provide a clean "50-50 split" in the data, because there were several identical exam scores clustered at the middle of the distribution. This situation is not so unusual. In fact, we might expect it when there is strong central tendency in a data set.

Characteristics of the Median

The median is especially useful when there are extreme values. For example, government statistics use the median income, because a few very high incomes will render the mean atypical. The median's insensitivity to extremes may seem advantageous or not, depending on your point of view. Consider three students' scores on five quizzes:

Tom's scores: 20, 40, 70, 75, 80   Mean = 57, Median = 70

Jake's scores: 60, 65, 70, 90, 95   Mean = 76, Median = 70

Mary's scores: 50, 65, 70, 75, 90   Mean = 70, Median = 70

Each student has the same median quiz score (70). Tom, whose mean is pulled down by a few low scores, would rather have his grade based on the median. Jake, whose mean is pulled up by a few high scores, would prefer the mean. Mary is indifferent, because her measures of central tendency agree (she has symmetric scores).

The median lacks some of the mean's useful mathematical properties. For example, if we multiply the mean by the sample size, we always get the total of the data values. But this is not true for the median. For instance, Tom's total points on all five quizzes (285) are the result of the sample size times his mean ($5 \times 57 = 285$). But this is not true for his median ($5 \times 70 = 350$). That is one reason why instructors tend to base their semester grades on the mean. Otherwise, the lowest and highest scores would not "count."

A Closer Look

Although the median can obviously be used with quantitative data, it can also be used when the data are qualitative and *ordinal*. Because the median is based on the ordering of data and because ordering has significance with *ordinal* data, we can use the median to determine which value or category separates the midpoint of the data. As an example, suppose a university issues only five grades—A, B, C, D, and F—for each and every course, and in one particular course of 20 students, the grades were

F, F, D, D, D, C, C, C, C, C, C, B, B, B, B, B, A, A, A, A

With 20 observations, the median, *M,* is the value of the $(20 + 1)/2$ ordered observation, or it should be the average of the 10th and 11th ordered observations. In this case these two observations are both Cs. So, we can state that the median grade is a C, which, although not numeric, does convey important information. (If one of these grades was a C and the other a B, we could say that the median was between a C and B.)

Mode

The **mode** is the most frequently occurring data value. It may be similar to the mean and median, if data values near the centre of the sorted array tend to occur often. But it may also be quite different from the mean and median. A data set may have multiple modes or no mode at all. For example, consider these four students' scores on five quizzes:

Lee's scores: 60, 70, 70, 70, 80   Mean = 70, Median = 70, Mode = 70

Pat's scores: 45, 45, 70, 90, 100   Mean = 70, Median = 70, Mode = 45

Sam's scores: 50, 60, 70, 80, 90   Mean = 70, Median = 70, Mode = none

Xiao's scores: 50, 50, 70, 90, 90   Mean = 70, Median = 70, Modes = 50, 90

Each student has the same mean (70) and median (70). Lee's mode (70) is the same as his mean and median, but Pat's mode (45) is nowhere near the "middle." Sam has no mode, while Xiao has two modes (50, 90). These examples illustrate some quirks of the mode.

The mode is easy to define, but is *not* easy to calculate (except in very small samples), because it requires tabulating the frequency of occurrence of every distinct data value. For example, the sample of $n = 37$ brands has seven modes (117, 120, 121, 129, 133, 150, 171), each occurring twice:

91	93	102	106	109	110	**117**	**117**	119	**120**
120	**121**	**121**	124	127	**129**	**129**	130	132	**133**
133	134	135	136	139	140	142	146	**150**	**150**
153	163	169	**171**	**171**	191	204			

Excel's function =MODE(Data) will return #N/A if there is no mode. If there are multiple modes, =MODE(Data) will return the first one it finds. In this example, because our data are already sorted, =MODE(Data) will return 117 as the mode. But if the data were in alphabetical order by car brand (as in Table 4.2), Excel would return 120 as the mode. Sometimes the mode is far from the "middle" of the distribution and may not be at all "typical." Indeed, for the car defects data, one has the feeling that the modes are merely a statistical fluke. For *continuous* data, the mode generally isn't useful, because continuous data values rarely repeat. To assess central tendency in continuous data, we would rely on the mean or median.

But the mode is good for describing central tendency in *categorical data* such as gender (male, female) or university major (accounting, finance, etc.). Indeed, the mode is the *only* useful measure of central tendency for *nominal* data. The mode is also useful to describe a *discrete* variable with a *small range* (e.g., responses to a five-point Likert scale).

> ## Tip
>
> The mode is most useful for discrete or categorical data with only a few distinct data values. For continuous data or data with a wide range, the mode is rarely useful.

EXAMPLE 2

Price/Earnings Ratios and Mode

Table 4.5 shows P/E ratios (current stock price divided by the last 12 months' earnings) for a random sample of 68 Standard & Poor's 500 stocks. Although P/E ratios are continuous data, *The Wall Street Journal* rounds the data to the nearest integer.

TABLE 4.5   P/E Ratios for 68 Randomly Chosen S&P 500 Stocks   PERatios2

7	8	8	10	10	10	10	12	13	13	13	13	13	13	13	14	14
14	15	15	15	15	15	16	16	16	17	18	18	18	18	19	19	19
19	19	20	20	20	21	21	21	22	22	23	23	23	24	25	26	26
26	26	27	29	29	30	31	34	36	37	40	41	45	48	55	68	91

Source: *The Wall Street Journal*, July 31, 2003.

Note: The data file has company names and ticker symbols.

Excel's Descriptive Statistics for this sample are:

Mean:	22.7206	Minimum:	7
Median:	19	Maximum:	91
Mode:	13	Sum:	1545
Range:	84	Count:	68

For these 68 observations, 13 is the mode (occurs 7 times) suggesting that it actually is somewhat "typical." However, the dot plot in Figure 4.7 also shows local modes at 10, 13, 15, 19, 23, 26, and 29 (a local mode is a "peak" with "valleys" on either side). These multiple "minimodes" suggest that the mode is not a stable measure of central tendency for this data set, and that these modes may not be very likely to recur if we took a different sample.

Looking at a histogram, its appearance may not indicate that the distribution of the data is symmetrical, yet the median and mode may have very similar values. This can occur when the set of data does not exactly conform to one of the skewness prototypes in Figure 4.10. In these situations, individuals are more likely to compare the mean and median when determining whether a distribution is theoretically symmetrical or not.

For the sample of J.D. Power quality ratings, the mean (134.51) exceeds the median (132), which suggests right-skewness. However, this small difference between the mean and median may lack practical importance. The histograms in Figure 4.3 suggest that the skewness is minimal. Business data tend to be right-skewed because financial variables often are unlimited at the top but are bounded from below by zero (e.g., salaries, employees, inventory). This is also true for engineering data (e.g., time to failure, defect rates) and sports (e.g., scores in soccer). Even in a Likert scale (1, 2, 3, 4, 5) a few responses in the opposite tail can skew the mean if most replies are clustered toward the top or bottom of the scale.

For each of the following four sets of data, determine mean, median, and mode, and using these measures, describe the shapes of the distributions. Then assume that the last observation in each data set was incorrectly recorded as 15 when it should have been recorded as 35. Repeat your calculations of the means, medians, and modes. What do you observe?

Data set A: 5, 7, 10, 10, 13, 15
Data set B: 5, 6, 7, 8, 9, 10, 11, 12, 13, 14, 15
Data set C: 1, 5, 9, 11, 15, 15
Data set D: 5, 5, 7, 7, 13, 15

Descriptive Statistics in Excel

As shown in Figure 4.12, select the **Data** tab and click the **Data Analysis** icon (on the far right side of the top menu). When the **Data Analysis** menu appears, select **Descriptive Statistics**. On the **Descriptive Statistics** menu form, click anywhere inside the **Input Range** field, then highlight the data block (in this case C4:C41). Specify a destination cell for the upper left corner of the output range (cell K1 in this example). Notice that we checked the **Labels in first row** box, because cell C4 is actually a column heading that will be used to label the output in cell K1. Check the **Summary Statistics** box and then click **OK**. The resulting statistics are shown in Figure 4.12. You probably recognize some of them (e.g., mean, median, mode), and the others will be covered later in this chapter.

Descriptive Statistics Using MegaStat

You can get similar statistics (and more) from MegaStat as illustrated in Figure 4.13. Click the **Add-Ins** tab on the top menu, and then click on the **MegaStat** icon (left side of the top menu in this example). On the list of MegaStat procedures, click **Descriptive Statistics**. On the new menu, enter the data range (in this case C4:C41) in the Input range field (or highlight the data block on the worksheet). You can see that MegaStat offers you many statistics, plus some visual displays such as a dot plot, stem-and-leaf, and other graphs. We have only chosen a few of them for this illustration. MegaStat output normally appears on a separate worksheet, but the results have been copied to the data worksheet so that everything can be seen in one

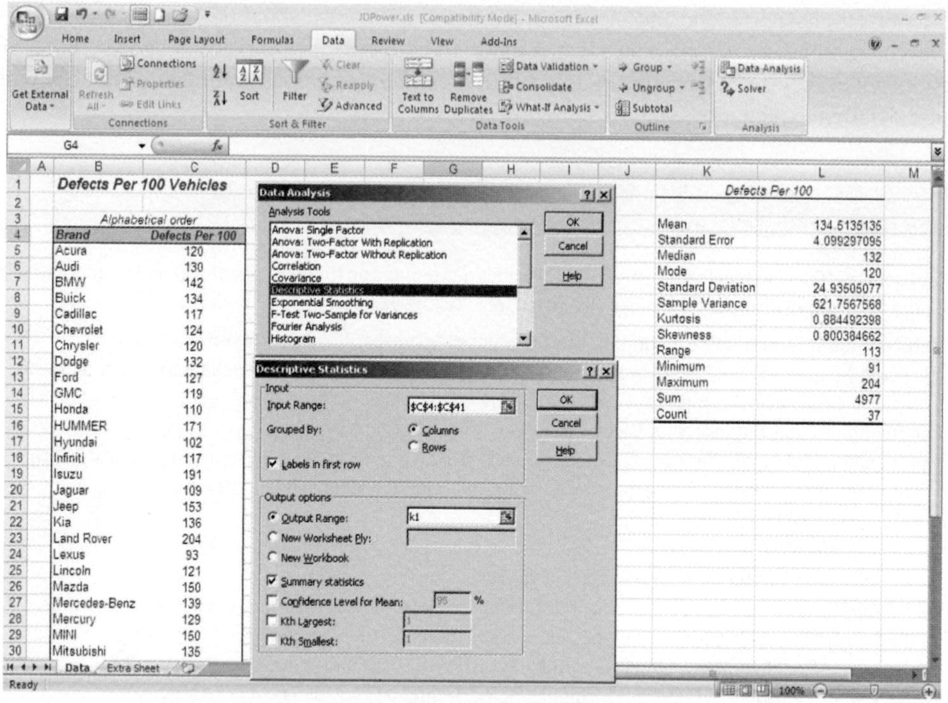

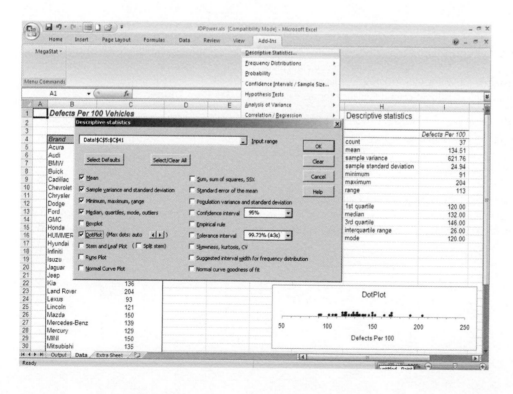

FIGURE 4.12

Excel's Data Analysis and Descriptive Statistics JD Power

Note: If Data Analysis does not appear on the upper right of the Data tab, click the multicoloured Office icon in the extreme upper left corner, select Add-Ins, and then check the box for Analysis ToolPak.

picture. Try using both Excel and MegaStat to see the similarities and differences in their interfaces and results. *LearningStats* has PowerPoint demonstrations with more detailed explanations of how to use Excel and MegaStat for statistical data description.

Descriptive Statistics Using MINITAB

MINITAB is a comprehensive software system for statistical analysis. It has nothing to do with Excel, although you can copy data from Excel to MINITAB's worksheet (and vice versa). You can get a wide range of statistics and attractive graphs from MINITAB. Although MINITAB is not on the textbook CD, it is widely available at colleges and universities. This

FIGURE 4.13

MegaStat's Descriptive Statistics JD Power

Note: MegaStat is on your textbook CD. You will be prompted to install it when you insert the CD in your computer. If MegaStat does not appear on the Add-Ins tab, click the multicoloured Office icon in the extreme upper left corner, select Add-Ins, and then check the box for MegaStat.

textbook emphasizes Excel and MegaStat, but it is wise to learn about other software that may give you just the result you want (or in a more attractive form), so we will show MINITAB results when they are appropriate. Also, *LearningStats* has a PowerPoint demonstration with more detailed explanations of how to use MINITAB.

Section Exercises

4.1 For each of the following data sets, indicate whether you would use the mean, median, or mode to measure central tendency. Explain why this measure would be more useful than the other two measures? (LO 2 & 5)

  a. The starting salaries of 10 recent nursing graduates beginning their careers at Montreal General Hospital.

  b. The starting salaries of 10 recent business school graduates, one of which will be employed as a basketball centre with the Toronto Raptors.

  c. The shoe sizes of 10 recent customers at a Payless ShoeSource outlet in Windsor, Ontario.

4.2 For each data set, find the mean, median, and mode. For each data set, compare the three measures and discuss why their values are either the same or different. What, if anything, affects the usefulness of each statistic as a measure of central tendency? (LO 2 & 3)

  a. Class absences (12 students)   0, 0, 0, 0, 0, 1, 2, 3, 3, 5, 5, 15

  b. Exam scores (9 students)   40, 40, 65, 71, 72, 75, 76, 78, 98

  c. GPAs (8 students)   2.25, 2.55, 2.95, 3.02, 3.04, 3.37, 3.51, 3.66

4.3 Professor Hardtack gave four Friday quizzes last semester in his 10-student advanced tax accounting class. (a) Without using Excel, find the mean, median, and mode for each quiz. (b) Do these measures of central tendency agree? Explain. (c) For each data set, note strengths or weaknesses of each statistic of central tendency. (d) Are the data symmetric or skewed? If skewed, which direction? (e) Briefly describe and compare student performance on each quiz. (LO 2 & 3)   **Quizzes**

    Quiz 1: 60, 60, 60, 60, 71, 73, 74, 75, 88, 99

    Quiz 2: 65, 65, 65, 65, 70, 74, 79, 79, 79, 79

    Quiz 3: 66, 67, 70, 71, 72, 72, 74, 74, 95, 99

    Quiz 4: 10, 49, 70, 80, 85, 88, 90, 93, 97, 98

4.4 CIBC recorded the number of customers to use a downtown ABM during the noon hour on 32 consecutive workdays. (a) Use Excel or MegaStat or MINITAB to find the mean, median, and mode. (b) Do these measures of central tendency agree? Explain. (c) Make a histogram and dot plot. (d) Are the data symmetric or skewed? If skewed, which direction? (e) Note strengths or weaknesses of each statistic of central tendency for the data. (LO 2 & 3)   **CIBC**

25	37	23	26	30	40	25	26
39	32	21	26	19	27	32	25
18	26	34	18	31	35	21	33
33	9	16	32	35	42	15	24

4.5 On Friday night, the owner of Chez Pierre in downtown Toronto noted the amount spent for dinner for 28 four-person tables. (a) Use Excel or MegaStat or MINITAB to find the mean, median, and mode. (b) Do these measures of central tendency agree? Explain. (c) Make a histogram and dot plot. (d) Are the data symmetric or skewed? If skewed, which direction? (e) Note strengths or weaknesses of each statistic of central tendency for the data. (LO 2 & 3)   **Dinner**

95	103	109	170	114	113	107
124	105	80	104	84	176	115
69	95	134	108	61	160	128
68	95	61	150	52	87	136

4.6 An executive's telephone log showed the lengths of 65 calls initiated during the last week of July. (a) Sort the data. (b) Use Excel or MegaStat or MINITAB to find the mean, median, and mode. (c) Do the measures of central tendency agree? Explain. (d) Make a histogram and dot plot. (e) Are the data symmetric or skewed? If skewed, which direction? (LO 2 & 3)   **CallLength**

1	2	10	5	3	3	2	20	1	1
6	3	13	2	2	1	26	3	1	3
1	2	1	7	1	2	3	1	2	12
1	4	2	2	29	1	1	1	8	5
1	4	2	1	1	1	1	6	1	2
3	3	6	1	3	1	1	5	1	18
2	13	13	1	6					

4.7 In Chapter 3, we looked at the following data concerning the North American minivan market.

Year	Total Minivan Sales	Chrysler Minivan Sales
2001	1,450,940	533,573
2002	1,396,753	507,192
2003	1,299,808	451,098
2004	1,313,810	464,522
2005	1,299,102	488,287
2006	1,215,743	456,894
2007	955,282	380,591
2008	735,750	296,957

Use Excel to calculate the mean, median, and mode for both total minivan sales and Chrysler minivan sales. Comparing the means with their respective medians, describe the theoretical shapes of the distribution of sales. (LO 2 & 3)

Mini Case 4.1

ABM Deposits

Table 4.7 shows a sorted random sample of 100 deposits at an ABM located in the student union on a university campus. The sample was selected at random from 1,459 deposits in one 30-day month. Deposits range from $3 to $1,341. The dot plot shown in Figure 4.14 indicates a right-skewed distribution with a few large values in the right tail and a strong clustering on the left (i.e., most ABM deposits are small). Excel's Descriptive Statistics indicates a very skewed distribution, because the mean (233.89) greatly exceeds the median (135). The mode (100) is somewhat "typical," occurring five times. However, 40 and 50 each occur four times (mini-modes).

Figure 4.15 shows one possible histogram for this severely skewed data. Using seven equal bins (Sturges' Rule) with a nice bin width of 200, we don't get very much detail for the first bin. Figure 4.16 shows that even doubling the number of bins still does not show much detail in the first bin. This example illustrates some of the difficulties in making good frequency tabulations when the data are skewed (a very common situation in business and economic data).

TABLE 4.7 100 ABM Deposits (dollars)  **ABMDeposits**

3	10	15	15	20	20	20	22	23	25	26	26
30	30	35	35	36	39	40	40	40	40	47	50
50	50	50	53	55	60	60	60	67	75	78	86
90	96	100	100	100	100	100	103	105	118	125	125
130	131	139	140	145	150	150	153	153	156	160	163
170	176	185	198	200	200	200	220	232	237	252	259
260	268	270	279	295	309	345	350	366	375	431	433
450	450	474	484	495	553	600	720	777	855	960	987
1,020	1,050	1,200	1,341								

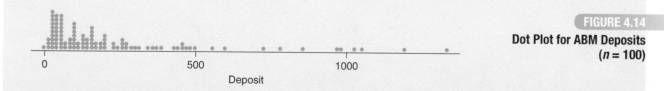

FIGURE 4.14

Dot Plot for ABM Deposits
(*n* = 100)

FIGURE 4.15

Histogram with 7 Bins

FIGURE 4.16

Histogram with 14 Bins

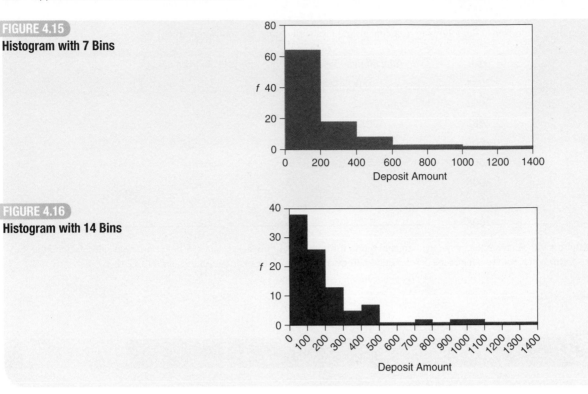

FIGURE 4.15

Histogram with 7 Bins

FIGURE 4.16

Histogram with 14 Bins

Weighted Mean

An Application Tom and Jerri are both taking an introductory statistics course. Their final grades were based on their scores on two quizzes, two midterms, two assignments, and one final exam. Their respective percentages received in each were as follows:

	Tom	*Jerri*
Quiz 1	60%	40%
Quiz 2	80%	60%
Midterm 1	75%	65%
Midterm 2	70%	55%
Assignment 1	95%	85%
Assignment 2	90%	85%
Final exam	55%	85%

To determine his overall percentage in this course, Tom averaged his percentages using the formula for the mean, resulting in a mean mark of

$$\bar{x} = \frac{\sum\limits_{i=1}^{n} x_i}{n} = \frac{60 + 80 + 75 + 70 + 95 + 90 + 55}{7} = \frac{525}{7} = 75\%$$

Jerri used the same formula for her scores and she determined her mean mark of

$$\bar{x} = \frac{\sum\limits_{i=1}^{n} x_i}{n} = \frac{40 + 60 + 65 + 55 + 85 + 85 + 85}{7} = \frac{475}{7} = 67.9\%$$

Yet when they received their final grades, Jerri received a higher grade than Tom. Why? Although their grades were determined based on their performances in each of the seven components, the professor felt some scores were more important than others and thus she weighted those scores more heavily.

If you have values $x_1, x_2, \ldots x_n$ and some values are more important than others, instead of calculating the simple mean, you should calculate the **weighted mean**,

$$\bar{x}_w = \frac{\displaystyle\sum_{i=1}^{n} x_i w_i}{\displaystyle\sum_{i=1}^{n} w_i}$$

where w_i measures the importance or the weight attached to value x_i. (You will observe that the denominator is simply the sum of the weights.)

Continuing with this application and assuming that each quiz was worth 5 percent of the final mark, each midterm was worth 15 percent of the final mark, each assignment was worth 5 percent of the final mark, and the final exam was worth 50 percent of the final mark, Tom's final percentage would actually be

$$\bar{x}_w = \frac{\displaystyle\sum_{i=1}^{n} x_i w_i}{\displaystyle\sum_{i=1}^{n} w_i} = \frac{60(5) + 80(5) + 75(15) + 70(15) + 95(5) + 90(5) + 55(50)}{5 + 5 + 15 + 15 + 5 + 5 + 50} = \frac{6{,}550}{100} = 65.5\%$$

Using the same formula, Jerri's final percentage would be

$$\bar{x}_w = \frac{\displaystyle\sum_{i=1}^{n} x_i w_i}{\displaystyle\sum_{i=1}^{n} w_i} = \frac{40(5) + 60(5) + 65(15) + 55(15) + 85(5) + 85(5) + 85(50)}{5 + 5 + 15 + 15 + 5 + 5 + 50} = \frac{7{,}400}{100} = 74.0\%$$

Note: From a practical standpoint, it may be easier to calculate the weighted mean by means of a table. For Tom's final score, the table would look like:

	x_i	w_i	$x_i w_i$
Quiz 1	60	5	300
Quiz 2	80	5	400
Midterm 1	75	15	1,125
Midterm 2	70	15	1,050
Assignment 1	95	5	475
Assignment 2	90	5	450
Final exam	55	50	2,750
		100	**6,550**

And the weighted mean is now simply

$$\bar{x}_w = \frac{\displaystyle\sum_{i=1}^{n} x_i w_i}{\displaystyle\sum_{i=1}^{n} w_i} = \frac{6{,}550}{100} = 65.5\%$$

A common use of the weighted mean is when stratified random sampling is used and some characteristic (e.g., average income) is calculated for each stratum. To get an estimate of the average for the entire population, the values obtained from the various strata would be weighted by the population size of each stratum.

There is no one universally recognized symbol for the weighted mean. We used our symbol to differentiate it from the symbol for the simple mean.

The symbol x_i used in this formula does not necessarily represent the value of a single observation. It could represent, for example, average income in a specific community or the percentage of adults in a specific province who favour some government control over gasoline prices.

Geometric Mean

The **geometric mean** (denoted G) is a multiplicative average, obtained by multiplying the data values and then taking the nth root of the product. This is a measure of central tendency used when all the data values are positive (greater than zero) and when the arithmetic mean is of not much use. The most often used type of example that illustrates the meaninglessness of the arithmetic mean is the following: You invest $100 today and you earn 100 percent return in year 1. In year 2, your return is −50 percent. Using the arithmetic mean, your average annual return can easily be calculated to be 25 percent. Not a bad average of return! But if you compare the money you had after the second year with the money you started with, the results of your investment are not that exceptional. With the 100 percent return in the first year, the money you have at the end of the first year is $200. With the loss of 50 percent in the second year, your $200 is now worth only $100 at the end of the second year, the same amount of money that you started with. So, although your average rate of return was calculated to be 25 percent, your actual average rate of return happens be 0 percent.

In general, the formula for the geometric mean is

$$G = \sqrt[n]{x_1 x_2 \cdots x_n} \tag{4.5}$$

For example, the geometric mean for $X = 2, 3, 7, 9, 10, 12$ is

$$G = \sqrt[6]{(2)(3)(7)(9)(10)(12)} = \sqrt[6]{45{,}360} = 5.972$$

The product of n numbers can be quite large. For the J.D. Power quality data:

$$G = \sqrt[37]{(91)(93) \cdots (201)(204)} = \sqrt[37]{3.21434 \times 10^{78}} = 132.38$$

The calculation is easy using Excel's function =**GEOMEAN(Data)**. Scientific calculators have a y^x key whose inverse permits taking the nth root needed to calculate G. However, if the data values are large, the product can exceed the calculator's capacity.

There is virtually no obvious practical interpretation of a geometric mean in a business context when the data are cross-sectional. Geometric means, in a business context, are generally reserved for situations when we want to measure the growth rate of some quantitative variable over time.

Growth Rates

We can use a variation on the geometric mean to find the *average growth rate* for a time series (e.g., sales in a growing company). Two formulas that can be used to determine this average growth rate are

$$GR = \sqrt[n]{\frac{x_n}{x_0}} - 1 \ \text{(average growth rate of a time series)} \tag{4.6}$$

where x_n represents the ending amount, x_0 represents the beginning amount, and n represents the number of periods (years, if we have yearly data).

Or,

$$GR = \sqrt[n]{(1 + x_1)(1 + x_2)\cdots(1 + x_n)} - 1 \tag{4.7}$$

where n represents the number of periods and x_i represents the growth rate in period i.

Either formula will result in the same answer. Which formula is best depends upon which data are readily available. Both formulas will be illustrated in the following example.

EXAMPLE 3

JetBlue Airlines

From 2002 to 2006, JetBlue Airlines' revenues grew dramatically, as shown in Table 4.8.

TABLE 4.8 JetBlue Airlines Revenue ☉ JetBlue

Year	Revenue ($mil)
2002	635
2003	998
2004	1,265
2005	1,701
2006	2,363

Source: http://moneycentral.msn.com

The *average growth rate* is given by taking the geometric mean of the ratios of each year's revenue to the preceding year. However, using Equation 4.6 only the first and last years are relevant:

$$GR = \sqrt[n]{\frac{x_n}{x_0}} - 1$$

where $n = 4$ (although five numbers are given, only four annual growth rates can be calculated—i.e., the growth rate between 2002 and 2003, the growth rate between 2003 and 2004, etc.), $x_0 = 635$, and $x_n = x_4 = 2{,}363$.

Or,

$$GR = \sqrt[n]{\frac{x_n}{x_0}} - 1$$

$$= \sqrt[4]{\frac{2{,}363}{635}} - 1 = \sqrt[4]{3.7213} - 1$$

$$= 1.389 - 1$$

$$= 0.389, \text{ or } 38.9\% \text{ average annual rate of growth}$$

In Excel, we could use the formula $=(2363/635)^{(1/4)} - 1$ to get this result.

Using the formula

$$GR = \sqrt[n]{(1 + x_1)(1 + x_2)\cdots(1 + x_n)} - 1$$

we would first need to determine each year's growth. By doing so,

$$1 + x_1 = \frac{998}{635} = 1.5717$$

or $x_1 = 0.5717$. The remaining x_i's are similarly calculated to be 0.2675, 0.3447, and 0.3892 respectively, and,

$$
\begin{aligned}
GR &= \sqrt[n]{(1 + x_1)(1 + x_2)\cdots(1 + x_n)} - 1 \\
&= \sqrt[4]{(1 + 0.5717)(1 + 0.2675)(1 + 0.3447)(1 + 0.3892)} - 1 \\
&= \sqrt[4]{3.7214} - 1 \\
&= 0.389, \text{ or } 38.9\%.
\end{aligned}
$$

Obviously, with the way the data were presented, the first formula is preferred in this case.

An Application Two mutual fund managers are each trying to convince a wealthy potential investor that their mutual fund is better than the other fund. The manager of Fund A mentions that over the past two years, his fund had a return of 100 percent two years ago although its return was –60 percent this past year. The manager of Fund B quotes a return of 20 percent two years ago and a return of 10 percent this past year. Calculating the mean return for each of the funds over this two-year period, the mean return for Fund A was 20 percent while the mean return for Fund B was 15 percent. Does this mean that Fund A outperformed Fund B over this two-year period? This wealthy investor decided to determine what would have happened to his money if he decided to invest $10,000 in each of the two funds two years ago.

He determined that after the first year, the money he invested in Fund A would have increased to $20,000 but after the second year, his money would have decreased to only $8,000. Surely an average return of 20 percent would have increased his money, not decreased it! Using the same analytical skills, he determined that the money he invested in Fund B would have increased to $12,000 after the first year and would have increased to $13,200 at the end of the second year. So actually, Fund B performed better than Fund A, yet the mean returns showed the opposite. Why? When measuring average rate of return or average growth rate with time series data, the arithmetic mean is not necessarily the proper measure to use. The better measure to use is a variation of the geometric mean, called the *average growth rate,* which for time series data is:

$$
GR = \sqrt[n]{(1 + x_1)\cdots(1 + x_2)} - 1
$$

where n is the number of periods (e.g., 2 years) and the x_i's are the growth rates or rates of return over each of the periods (e.g., each year) expressed in decimal form (e.g., a rate of return of 50 percent converts to a value of x of 0.5). Applying this formula to both Fund A and Fund B, Fund A's average growth rate is

$$
GR = \sqrt[n]{(1 + 1.00)(1 - 0.60)} - 1 = \sqrt[n]{0.80} - 1 = 0.8944 - 1 = -0.1056 = -10.56\%
$$

and Fund B's average growth rate is

$$
GR = \sqrt[n]{(1 + 0.20)(1 + 0.10)} - 1 = \sqrt[n]{1.32} - 1 = 1.1489 - 1 = 0.1489 = 14.89\%
$$

Using this measure, we observe that Fund A lost an average of 10.56 percent per year while Fund B had an average rate of return of 14.89 percent. What is the meaning of these averages? One interpretation is this: A person investing a certain amount of money in a fund that returned 14.89 percent in each of two years would end up with the same amount of money after the two years if he or she invested in a fund which had a rate of return of 20 percent in the first year and a rate of return of 10 percent in the second year.

In this example, suppose we didn't have the rates of return in each of the years, but we determined that Fund A would have an ending amount of $8,000 on an initial investment of $10,000 while Fund B would have an ending amount of $13,200 for the same initial investment. Using this information and the alternate formula for the geometric mean, the geometric average return for Fund A is

$$
GR = \sqrt[n]{\frac{\text{ending amount}}{\text{beginning amount}}} - 1 = \sqrt[2]{\frac{8,000}{10,000}} - 1 = 0.8944 - 1 = -0.1056 = -10.56\%
$$

and the geometric average return for Fund B is

$$
GR = \sqrt[n]{\frac{\text{ending amount}}{\text{beginning amount}}} - 1 = \sqrt[2]{\frac{13,200}{10,000}} - 1 = 1.1489 - 1 = 0.1489 = 14.89\%
$$

Trimmed Mean

The **trimmed mean** is calculated like any other mean, except that the highest and lowest k percent of the observations are removed. For the 68 P/E ratios (Table 4.5), the 5 percent trimmed mean will remove the three smallest and three largest ($0.05 \times 68 = 3.4$ observations). Excel's function for a 5 percent trimmed mean would be =TRIMMEAN(Data, 0.10) because $0.05 + 0.05 = 0.10$. As shown below, the trimmed mean mitigates the effects of extremely high values, but still exceeds the median.

Mean: 22.72	=AVERAGE(Data)
Median: 19.00	=MEDIAN(Data)
Mode: 13.00	=MODE(Data)
5% Trim Mean: 21.10	=TRIMMEAN(Data,0.1)

The U.S. Federal Reserve uses a 16 percent trimmed mean to mitigate the effect of extremes in its analysis of trends in the Consumer Price Index (CPI), as illustrated in Figure 4.17.

Another popular use of a variation of the trimmed mean is in international athletic competitions (such as gymnastics and diving) in which the athletes are subjectively judged on their performances. To try to lessen the impact of politics on the scoring of these athletes, the lowest and highest scores are usually dropped and the remaining scores are totalled (and possibly multiplied by the level of difficulty of the routine). Although the remaining scores are totalled instead of averaged, the positioning of the athletes (i.e., first, second, etc.) would have been the same if their scores had been averaged.

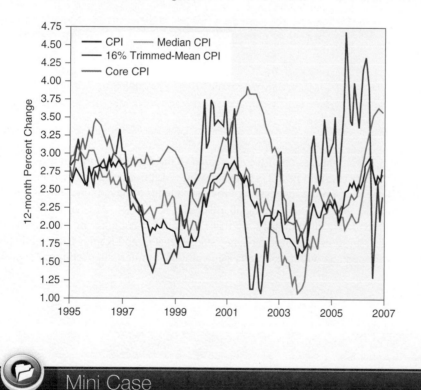

FIGURE 4.17

16 Percent Trimmed-Mean for CPI

Source: Federal Reserve Bank of Cleveland, www.clevelandfed.org

Mini Case 4.2

Prices of Lipitor®

Prescription drug prices vary across the United States and even among pharmacies in the same city. Table 4.9 shows prices for a 30-day supply of Lipitor® (a cholesterol-lowering prescription drug) in three U.S. cities from a random sample of pharmacies. Attention has recently been focused on prices of such drugs because recent medical research has suggested more aggressive treatment of high cholesterol levels in patients at risk for heart disease. This poses an economic issue for the American government because Medicare is expected to pay some of the cost of prescription drugs. It is also an issue for Pfizer, the maker of Lipitor®, which expects a fair return on its investments in research and patents. Finally, it is an issue for consumers who seek to shop wisely.

TABLE 4.9   Lipitor® Prices in Three Cities   Lipitor

New Orleans,	62.91	69.61	68.00	66.49	71.79	75.09	73.30	71.79	71.79	60.45
LA (n = 12)	73.57	66.49								
Providence,	71.99	78.50	67.15	79.79	80.00	80.00	76.00	76.00	77.00	83.69
RI (n = 20)	69.49	79.00	79.79	79.79	83.16	78.00	69.00	91.21	69.49	81.75
Grand Rapids,	77.99	69.19	71.98	72.91	71.56	65.73	76.89	76.89	61.33	64.84
MI (n = 15)	74.49	64.90	60.39	71.57	65.29					

Source: Survey by the Public Interest Research Group (www.pirg.org) in March/April 2003. Prices were studied for 10 drugs in 555 pharmacies in 48 cities in 19 states. Data used with permission.

FIGURE 4.18

Dot Plots for Lipitor® Prices

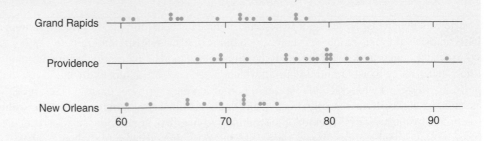

TABLE 4.10   Measures of Central Tendency for Lipitor® Prices   Lipitor

Statistic	New Orleans	Providence	Grand Rapids
Sample size	12	20	15
Mean	69.27	77.54	69.73
Median	70.70	78.75	71.56
Mode	71.79	79.79	76.89
5% Trim mean	69.57	77.36	69.81

From the dot plots in Figure 4.18, we gain an impression of the *dispersion* of the data (the *range* of prices for each drug) as well as the *central tendency* of the data (the middle or typical data values). Lipitor® prices vary from about $60 to about $91 and typically are in the $70s. The dot plots suggest that Providence tends to have higher prices, and New Orleans lower prices, though there is considerable variation among pharmacies.

In Table 4.10, the measures of central tendency unanimously say that Providence has higher prices. New Orleans and Grand Rapids are similar, although the measures of central tendency suggest that Grand Rapids has slightly higher prices than New Orleans. The means and medians within each city generally are similar, suggesting no significant skewness.

Section Exercises

4.8   Two of the many casinos (slot machines only) at racetracks across Ontario allow gamblers to bet on 1¢ slots, 5¢ slots, 25¢ slots, 50¢ slots, and $1 slots. Suppose both casinos' average daily profit is $250 per machine on the 1¢ slots, $400 per machine on the 5¢ slots, $600 per machine on the 25¢ slots, $200 per machine on the 50¢ slots, and $420 on the $1 slots. Calculate the average daily profit per slot machine for Casino A if that casino has 150 1¢ slot machines, 250 5¢ slot machines, 200 25¢ slot machines, 100 50¢ slot machines, and 200 $1 slot machines. Calculate the average daily profit per slot machine for Casino B, which has 100 1¢ slot machines, 450 5¢ slot machines, 300 25¢ slot machines, 50 50¢ slot machines, and 300 $1 slot machines. Assuming neither casino has more space to add slot machines, which casino is making better use of its available space? Explain. (LO 3 & 5)

4.9   Spirit Airlines kept track of the number of empty seats on flight 308 (DEN–DTW) for 10 consecutive trips on each weekday. (a) Sort the data for each weekday. (b) Without using Excel, find the mean, median, mode, and 10 percent trimmed mean (i.e., dropping the first and last sorted observation) for each weekday. (c) Do the measures of central tendency agree? Explain.

(d) Note strengths or weaknesses of each statistic of central tendency for the data. (e) Briefly describe and compare the number of empty seats on each weekday. (LO 2 & 3)   **EmptySeats**

Monday:	6, 1, 5, 9, 1, 1, 6, 5, 5, 1
Tuesday:	1, 3, 3, 1, 4, 6, 9, 7, 7, 6
Wednesday:	6, 0, 6, 0, 6, 10, 0, 0, 4, 6
Thursday:	1, 1, 10, 1, 1, 1, 1, 1, 1, 1

4.10 On Friday night, the owner of Chez Pierre in downtown Toronto noted the amount spent for dinner at 28 four-person tables. (a) Use Excel or MegaStat to find the mean, median, and 10 percent trimmed mean (i.e., dropping the first three and last three observations). (b) Do these measures of central tendency agree? Explain. (LO 2 & 3)   **Dinner**

95	103	109	170	114	113	107
124	105	80	104	84	176	115
69	95	134	108	61	160	128
68	95	61	150	52	87	136

4.11 An executive's telephone log showed the lengths of 65 calls initiated during the last week of July. (a) Use Excel to find the mean, median, and 10 percent trimmed mean (i.e., dropping the first seven and last seven observations). (b) Do the measures of central tendency agree? Explain. (c) Are the data symmetric or skewed? If skewed, which direction? (d) Note strengths or weaknesses of each statistic of central tendency for the data. (LO 2 & 3)   **CallLength**

1	2	10	5	3	3	2	20	1	1
6	3	13	2	2	1	26	3	1	3
1	2	1	7	1	2	3	1	2	12
1	4	2	2	29	1	1	1	8	5
1	4	2	1	1	1	1	6	1	2
3	3	6	1	3	1	1	5	1	18
2	13	13	1	6					

4.12 The number of Internet users in Latin America grew from 15.8 million in 2000 to 60.6 million in 2004. Use the geometric mean to find the mean annual growth rate. (Data are from George E. Belch and Michael A. Belch, *Advertising and Promotion* [Irwin, 2004], p. 488.) (LO 3)

4.13 Two towns in Alberta are each claiming to be the fastest-growing towns in Canada over the last four years. Town A, four years ago, had 5,000 inhabitants, and now at the end of four years, it has 12,500 inhabitants. Town B, over the last four years, has grown by 15 percent, 10 percent, 25 percent, and 35 percent annually. Assuming no other towns in Canada have grown faster over this period, which town's claim is true? (LO 3 & 5)

4.14 Every year, universities in Canada and elsewhere are rated by outside sources on various attributes and then these ratings are converted into a ranking of universities. Suppose one of these outside sources rate two universities on four attributes: reputation, class sizes, percentage of students who find jobs within six months of graduation, and research grants awarded to the university. Further suppose that when ranking the universities, reputation counts for 40 percent, class sizes counts for 5 percent, students finding jobs within 6 months of graduation counts for 35 percent, and the remaining 20 percent is scored for research grants. Which university would be ranked higher (i.e., better) if its scores (out of 100) on each of the attributes were as follows? Justify your answer. (LO 3 & 5)

Attribute	University A	University B
Reputation	30	43
Class sizes	95	5
Finding jobs	45	48
Research	28	34

4.3   Dispersion

We can use a statistic such as the mean to describe the *centre* of a distribution. But it is just as important to look at how individual data values are dispersed around the mean. For example, if two *NYSE* stocks *A* and *B* have the same mean return over the last 100 trading days, but *A* has more day-to-day variation, then the portfolio manager who wants a stable investment would prefer *B*. Consider possible sample distributions of study time spent by several university students taking an economics class:

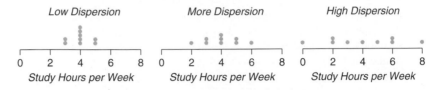

Each diagram has the same mean, but they differ in dispersion around the mean. The problem is: How do we *describe* dispersion in a sample? Because different variables have different means and different units of measurements (dollars, pounds, yen), we are looking for measures of dispersion that can be applied to many situations.

Histograms and dot plots tell us something about variation in a data set (the "spread" of data points about the centre) but formal measures of dispersion are needed. Table 4.11 lists several common measures of dispersion. All formulas shown are for sample data sets.

Range

The **range** is the difference between the largest and smallest observation:

$$Range = x_{max} - x_{min} \tag{4.8}$$

For the P/E data the range is

$$Range = 91 - 7 = 84$$

Although the range is easy to calculate and easy to understand, one of its drawbacks is that it only considers the two extreme data values. It would seem more desirable to seek a broad-based measure of dispersion that is based on *all* the data values $x_1, x_2, \ldots, x_n$. Another important drawback is that its value is biased based on the size of the sample. With all other

TABLE 4.11   Five Measures of Dispersion for a Sample

Statistic	Formula	Excel	Pro	Con
Range	$x_{max} - x_{min}$	=MAX(Data)-MIN(Data)	Easy to calculate.	Sensitive to extreme data values.
Sample variance (s^2)	$\dfrac{\sum\limits_{i=1}^{n}(x_i - \bar{x})^2}{n-1}$	=VAR(Data)	Plays a key role in mathematical statistics.	Different units of measurement.
Sample standard deviation (s)	$\sqrt{\dfrac{\sum\limits_{i=1}^{n}(x_i - \bar{x})^2}{n-1}}$	=STDEV(Data)	Most common measure. Same units as the raw data ($, £, ¥, grams, etc.).	
Coefficient of variation (cv)	$100 \times \dfrac{s}{\bar{x}}$	None	Expresses relative variation in percent so can compare data sets with different units of measurement.	Requires non-negative data.
Mean absolute deviation (MAD)	$\dfrac{\sum\limits_{i=1}^{n}|x_i - \bar{x}|}{n}$	=AVEDEV(Data)	Easy to understand.	Lacks "nice" theoretical properties.

descriptive measures the size of the data set has no bearing on their values. With the range, the larger the data set, the larger its value tends to be, making it problematic when comparing ranges for data sets of different sizes.

Variance and Standard Deviation

Another way of determining if values differ in the data set and by how much they differ is to compare each individual value with the mean of the data set. If all values are the same, each value would equal the data set's mean. If not all values are the same, some or all of the values would be different than the mean. If we calculate the differences between each data value x_i and the mean, we would have both positive and negative differences. As we observed earlier, because the mean is the balancing point of the distribution, if we just sum these differences and take the average, we will always get zero, which obviously doesn't give us a useful measure of dispersion. One way to avoid this is to *square* the differences before we find the average. Following this logic, the **population variance** (denoted σ^2, and read "sigma-squared") is defined as the sum of squared deviations from the mean divided by the population size:

$$\sigma^2 = \frac{\sum_{i=1}^{N}(x_i - \mu)^2}{N} \tag{4.9}$$

If we have a sample (i.e., most of the time), we replace μ with $\bar{x}$ to get the **sample variance** (denoted s^2):

$$s^2 = \frac{\sum_{i=1}^{n}(x_i - \bar{x})^2}{n - 1} \tag{4.10}$$

A variance is basically a mean squared deviation. But why then do we divide by $n - 1$ instead of n when using sample data? This question perplexes many students. As we will discuss in Chapter 8, the population variance σ^2 is generally unknown and needs to be estimated by taking a random sample of n observations from this population and computing a "sample variance." It can be shown mathematically that the sample variance formula (4.10) gives a "better" estimate of σ^2, on average. In particular, if we divide the sum of squared deviations by n instead of $n - 1$ this quantity would tend to underestimate the unknown population variance σ^2.

In describing dispersion, we most often use the **standard deviation** (the square root of the variance). The standard deviation is a single number that helps us understand how individual values in a data set vary from the mean. Because the square root has been taken, its units of measurement are the same as X (e.g., dollars, kilograms, kilometres). To find the standard deviation of a population we use

$$\sigma = \sqrt{\frac{\sum_{i=1}^{N}(x_i - \mu)^2}{N}} \tag{4.11}$$

and for the standard deviation of a sample

$$s = \sqrt{\frac{\sum_{i=1}^{n}(x_i - \bar{x})^2}{n - 1}} \tag{4.12}$$

Many calculators, even inexpensive ones, have built-in formulas for the standard deviation. To distinguish between the population and sample formulas, some calculators have one function key labelled σ_x and another labelled s_x. Others have one key labelled σ_n and another labelled σ_{n-1}. The only question is whether to divide the numerator by the number of data items or the number of data items minus one. Computers and calculators don't know whether your data are a sample or a population. They will use whichever formula you request. It is up to you to know which is appropriate for your data. Excel has built-in functions for these calculations:

Statistic	Excel population formula	Excel sample formula
Variance	=VARP(Data)	=VAR(Data)
Standard deviation	=STDEVP(Data)	=STDEV(Data)

Calculating a Standard Deviation

Table 4.12 illustrates the calculation of a standard deviation using Stephanie's scores on five quizzes (40, 55, 75, 95, 95). Her mean is 72. Notice that the deviations around the mean (column three) sum to zero, an important property of the mean. Because the mean is rarely a "nice" number, such calculations typically require a spreadsheet or a calculator. Stephanie's sample standard deviation is

$$s = \sqrt{\frac{\sum_{i=1}^{n}(x_i - \bar{x})^2}{n-1}} = \sqrt{\frac{2,380}{5-1}} = \sqrt{595} = 24.39$$

Characteristics of the Standard Deviation

The standard deviation is non-negative because the deviations around the mean are squared. When every observation is exactly equal to the mean, then the standard deviation is zero (i.e., there is no variation). For example, if every student received the same score on an exam, the numerators of equations 4.9 through 4.13 would be zero because every student would be at the mean. At the other extreme, the greatest dispersion would be if the data were concentrated at x_{min} and x_{max} (e.g., if half the class scored 0 and the other half scored 100).

Standard deviations can be compared *only* for data sets measured in the same units. For example, prices of hotel rooms in Tokyo (yen) cannot be compared with prices of hotel rooms in Paris (Euros). Also, standard deviations should not be compared if the means differ substantially, even when the units of measurement are the same. For instance, weights of apples (grams) have a smaller mean than weights of watermelons (grams).

Coefficient of Variation

To compare dispersion in data sets with dissimilar units of measurement (e.g., kilograms and ounces) or dissimilar means (e.g., home prices in two different cities) we define the **coefficient of variation,** which is a unit-free measure of dispersion. If we have population data, the coefficient of variation is

$$CV = 100\left(\frac{\sigma}{\mu}\right) \tag{4.13}$$

TABLE 4.12 Worksheet for Standard Deviation Stephanie

i	x_i	$x_i - \bar{x}$	$(x_i - \bar{x})^2$	x_i^2
1	40	$40 - 72 = -32$	$(-32)^2 = 1,024$	$40^2 = 1,600$
2	55	$55 - 72 = -17$	$(-17)^2 = 289$	$55^2 = 3,025$
3	75	$75 - 72 = 3$	$(3)^2 = 9$	$75^2 = 5,625$
4	95	$95 - 72 = 23$	$(23)^2 = 529$	$95^2 = 9,025$
5	95	$95 - 72 = 23$	$(23)^2 = 529$	$95^2 = 9,025$
Sum	360	0	2,380	28,300
Mean	72			

and for sample data, it is

$$cv = 100\left(\frac{s}{\bar{x}}\right)$$

(4.14)

The *CV* or *cv* is the standard deviation expressed as a percent of the mean. In some data sets, the standard deviation can actually exceed the mean, so the *CV* or *cv* can exceed 100 percent. The coefficient of variation is useful for comparing variables measured in different units. For example:

Defect rates: $s = 24.94$ $\bar{x} = 134.51$ $cv = 100 \times (24.94/134.51) = 19\%$

ABM deposits: $s = 280.80$ $\bar{x} = 233.89$ $cv = 100 \times (280.80/233.89) = 120\%$

P/E ratios: $s = 14.08$ $\bar{x} = 22.72$ $cv = 100 \times (14.08/22.72) = 62\%$

Despite the different units of measurement, we can say that ABM deposits have much greater relative dispersion (120 percent) than either defect rates (19 percent) or P/E ratios (62 percent). The chief weakness of the coefficient of variation is that it is undefined if the mean is zero or negative, so it is appropriate only for positive data.

Note: The coefficient of variation should only be used with ratio data. The meaning of the value of zero in interval data is rather arbitrary, allowing an individual to manipulate this value resulting in a mean that can also be arbitrarily altered. For example, the coefficient of variation should not be used to compare the variation in temperatures when temperature is measured in degrees Celsius in Winnipeg and degrees Fahrenheit in Chicago.

Mean Absolute Deviation

An additional measure of dispersion is the **mean absolute deviation** (*MAD*). This statistic reveals the average distance from the centre. Absolute values must be used as otherwise the deviations around the mean would sum to zero.

$$MAD = \frac{\sum_{i=1}^{n}|x_i - \bar{x}|}{n}$$

(4.15)

The *MAD* is appealing because of its simple, concrete interpretation. Using the lever analogy, the *MAD* tells us what the average distance is from an individual data point to the mean. Excel's function =AVEDEV(Data) will calculate the *MAD*.

Figure 4.19 shows that bear markets typically are short-lived (under one year) but may last nearly three years. S&P losses generally are in the 10 to 40 percent range, with one notable exception (the 1929 crash).

Mini Case   4.3

Bear Markets

Investors know that stock prices have extended cycles of downturns ("bear markets") or upturns ("bull markets"). But how long must an investor be prepared to wait for the cycle to end? Table 4.13 shows the duration of 14 bear markets since 1929 and the decline in the S&P 500 stock index.

Table 4.14 shows that both duration (months) and S&P loss (percent) are right-skewed (mean substantially exceeding median) and have similar coefficients of variation. The other measures of central tendency and dispersion cannot be compared because the units of measurement differ.

TABLE 4.13   Duration of Bear Markets   BearMarkets

Peak	Trough	Duration (months)	S&P Loss (%)
Sep 1929	Jun 1932	34	83.4
Jun 1946	Apr 1947	11	21.0
Aug 1956	Feb 1957	7	10.2
Aug 1957	Dec 1957	5	15.0
Jan 1962	Jun 1962	6	22.3
Feb 1966	Sep 1966	8	15.6
Dec 1968	Jun 1970	19	29.3
Jan 1973	Sep 1974	21	42.6
Jan 1977	Feb 1978	14	14.1
Dec 1980	Jul 1982	20	16.9
Sep 1987	Nov 1987	3	29.5
Jun 1990	Oct 1990	5	14.7
Jul 1998	Aug 1998	2	15.4
Sep 2000	Mar 2003	31	42.0

Source: TIAA/CREF, *Balance,* Summer 2004, p. 15. Downturns are defined as a loss in value of 10 percent or more. Standard & Poor's 500 stock index and S&P 500 are registered trademarks.

FIGURE 4.19

Dot Plots of Bear Market Measurements

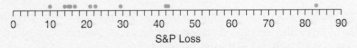

Bear Market Duration

Months

Loss of Asset Value

S&P Loss

TABLE 4.14   Statistical Summary of Bear Markets

Statistic	Duration (months)	S&P Loss (%)
Count	14	14
Mean	13.29	26.57
Median	9.5	18.95
Standard deviation	10.29	19.27
Minimum	2	10.2
Maximum	34	83.4
Range	32	73.2
Coefficient of variation	77.4%	72.5%
Mean absolute deviation	8.47	13.42

Section Exercises

4.15 Without using Excel: (a) Find the mean and standard deviation for each sample. (b) What does this exercise show? (LO 2 & 3)

Sample A: 6, 7, 8

Sample B: 61, 62, 63

Sample C: 1000, 1001, 1002

4.16 Without using Excel, for each data set: (a) Find the mean. (b) Find the standard deviation, treating the data as a sample. (c) Find the standard deviation, treating the data as a population. (d) What does this exercise show? (LO 2 & 3)

Data Set A: 6, 7, 8

Data Set B: 4, 5, 6, 7, 8, 9, 10

Data Set C: 1, 2, 3, 4, 5, 6, 7, 8, 9, 10, 11, 12, 13

4.17 Find the coefficient of variation for prices of these three stocks. (a) Which stock has the greatest relative variation? (b) To measure variability, why not just compare the standard deviations? (LO 2 & 3)

Stock A: $\bar{x} = \$24.50, s = 5.25$

Stock B: $\bar{x} = \$147.25, s = 12.25$

Stock C: $\bar{x} = \$5.75, s = 2.08$

4.18 Prof. Hardtack gave four Friday quizzes last semester in his 10-student senior tax accounting class. (a) Using Excel, find the mean, standard deviation, and coefficient of variation for each quiz. (b) How do these data sets differ in terms of central tendency and dispersion? (c) Briefly describe and compare student performance on each quiz. (LO 2 & 3) **Quizzes**

Quiz 1: 60, 60, 60, 60, 71, 73, 74, 75, 88, 99

Quiz 2: 65, 65, 65, 65, 70, 74, 79, 79, 79, 79

Quiz 3: 66, 67, 70, 71, 72, 72, 74, 74, 95, 99

Quiz 4: 10, 49, 70, 80, 85, 88, 90, 93, 97, 98

4.19 An executive's telephone log showed the lengths of 65 calls initiated during the last week of July. Use Excel to find the sample standard deviation and mean absolute deviation. (LO 3) **CallLength**

1	2	10	5	3	3	2	20	1	1
6	3	13	2	2	1	26	3	1	3
1	2	1	7	1	2	3	1	2	12
1	4	2	2	29	1	1	1	8	5
1	4	2	1	1	1	1	6	1	2
3	3	6	1	3	1	1	5	1	18
2	13	13	1	6					

4.20 Continuing with the data on Minivan sales, use Excel to calculate the population's range, standard deviation, and coefficient of variation in sales for both total minivan sales and Chrysler minivan sales. Why would it have been better for the automotive industry, for Chrysler, and for its employees to have smaller standard deviations? (LO 3)

Year	Total Minivan Sales	Chrysler Minivan
2001	1,450,940	533,573
2002	1,396,753	507,192
2003	1,299,808	451,098
2004	1,313,810	464,522
2005	1,299,102	488,287
2006	1,215,743	456,894
2007	955,282	380,591
2008	735,750	296,957

Mini Case 4.4

What Is the DJIA? DJIA

The Dow Jones Industrial Average (commonly called the DJIA) is the oldest U.S. stock market price index, based on the prices of 30 large, widely held, and actively traded "blue chip" public companies in the United States (e.g., Coca-Cola, Microsoft, Walmart, Walt Disney). Actually, only a few of its 30 component companies are "industrial." The DJIA is measured in "points" rather than dollars. Originally, a simple mean of stock prices, the DJIA now is the sum of the 30 stock prices divided by a "divisor" to compensate for stock splits and other changes over time. The divisor is revised as often as necessary (see www.djindexes.com or www.cbot.com for the latest value). Because high-priced stocks comprise a larger proportion of the sum, the DJIA is more strongly affected by changes in high-priced stocks. That is, a 10 percent price increase in a $10 stock would have less effect than a 10 percent price increase in a $50 stock, even if both companies have the same total market capitalization (the total number of shares times the price per share; often referred to as "market cap"). Broad-based market price indexes (e.g., TSX, NSDQ, AMEX, NYSE, S&P 500, Russ 2K) are widely used by fund managers, but the venerable "Dow" is still the one you see first on CNN or MSNBC.

Central Tendency versus Dispersion

Figure 4.20 shows histograms of hole diameters drilled in a steel plate during a manufacturing process. The desired distribution is shown in red. The samples from Machine *A* have the desired *mean* diameter (5 mm) but too much *variation* around the mean. It might be an older machine whose moving parts have become loose through normal wear, so there is greater variation in the holes drilled. Samples from Machine *B* have acceptable *variation* in hole diameter, but the *mean* is incorrectly adjusted (less than the desired 5 mm). To monitor quality, we would take frequent samples from the output of each machine, so that the process can be stopped and adjusted if the sample statistics indicate a problem.

Similarly, Table 4.15 shows how four professors were rated by students on eight teaching attributes (on a 10-point scale). Jones and Wu have identical means but different standard deviations. Smith and Gopal have different means but identical standard deviations. In teaching, a high mean (better rating) and a low standard deviation (more consistency) would presumably be preferred. How would *you* describe these professors?

FIGURE 4.20 **Central Tendency versus Dispersion**

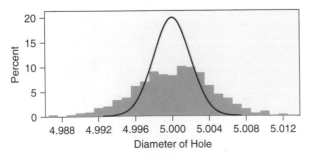
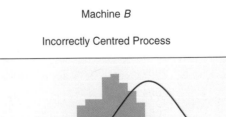
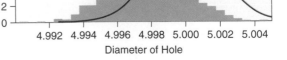

TABLE 4.15 **Average Teaching Ratings for Four Professors** ⊚ **FourProfs**

Attribute	Same Mean, Different Variance		Different Mean, Same Variance	
	Prof. Wu	Prof. Jones	Prof. Smith	Prof. Gopal
1. Challenging	8.4	5.1	6.5	8.8
2. Approachable	6.7	9.4	5.4	9.8
3. Enthusiastic	7.5	5.9	7.3	8.1
4. Helps students	7.0	9.2	5.8	8.3
5. Fair exams	7.4	7.8	6.3	8.8
6. Knowledge	6.9	8.3	6.3	7.9
7. Lecture ability	7.6	6.4	5.6	9.0
8. Organized	6.1	5.5	4.8	7.3
Mean	7.20	7.20	6.00	8.50
Std Dev	0.69	1.69	0.77	0.77
CV	9.6%	23.5%	12.8%	9.0%

4.4 Standardized Data

The standard deviation is an important measure of dispersion because of its many roles in statistics. One of its main uses is to gauge the position of items within a data array.

Chebyshev's Theorem

The French mathematician Jules Bienaymé (1796–1878) and the Russian mathematician Pafnuty Chebyshev (1821–1894) proved that for any data set, no matter how it is distributed, the percentage of observations that lie within k standard deviations of the mean (i.e., within $\mu \pm k\sigma$) must be at least $100[1 - 1/k^2]$. Commonly called **Chebyshev's Theorem,** it says that for *any population* with mean μ and standard deviation σ:

  $k = 2$: at least 75.0% will lie within $\mu \pm 2\sigma$.

  $k = 3$: at least 88.9% will lie within $\mu \pm 3\sigma$.

Although applicable to any data set, these limits tend to be rather wide, and this theorem has very limited useful applications.

The Empirical Rule

More precise statements can be made about data from a normal or Gaussian distribution, named for its discoverer Karl Gauss (1777–1855). The Gaussian distribution is the well-known bell-shaped curve. Commonly called the **Empirical Rule,** it says that for data from a *normal distribution* we expect the interval $\mu \pm k\sigma$ to contain a known percentage of the data:

  $k = 1$: about 68.26% will lie within $\mu \pm 1\sigma$.

  $k = 2$: about 95.44% will lie within $\mu \pm 2\sigma$.

  $k = 3$: about 99.73% will lie within $\mu \pm 3\sigma$.

The Empirical Rule is illustrated in Figure 4.21. The Empirical Rule does *not* give an upper bound, but merely describes what is *expected.* Rounding off a bit, we say that in samples from a normal distribution we expect 68 percent of the data within 1 standard deviation, 95 percent within 2 standard deviations, and virtually all of the data within 3 standard deviations. The last statement is imprecise, as 0.27 percent of the observations are expected outside 3 standard deviations, but it correctly conveys the idea that data values outside $\mu \pm 3\sigma$ are rare in a normal distribution.

FIGURE 4.21

FIGURE 4.21

The Empirical Rule for a Normal Population

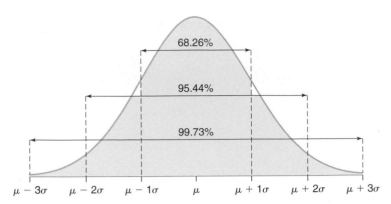

EXAMPLE 4

Exam Scores

Suppose 80 students take an exam. How many students will score within 2 standard deviations of the mean? Assuming that exam scores follow a normal or bell-shaped curve, we might be willing to rely on the Empirical Rule, which predicts that 95.44% × 80, or approximately 76 students, will score within 2 standard deviations from the mean. Because a normal distribution is symmetric about the mean, we further expect that about 2 students will score more than 2 standard deviations above the mean, and 2 below the mean. Using the Empirical Rule, we can further say that it is unlikely that any student will score more than 3 standard deviations from the mean (99.73% × 80 = 79.78 ≈ 80).

Unusual Observations

The Empirical Rule suggests criteria for detecting *unusual* observations (beyond $\mu \pm 2\sigma$) or **outliers** (beyond $\mu \pm 3\sigma$). Many variations on the criteria in Table 4.16 are possible.

TABLE 4.16   Detecting Unusual Observations

Term	Criterion
Unusual	2 or more standard deviations from the mean
Outlier	3 or more standard deviations from the mean

Note: For a large sample like $n = 1,000$ it would not be surprising to see a few data values outside the 3 standard deviation range, as 99.73% of 1,000 is only 997.

EXAMPLE 5

Unusual Observations

The P/E data set contains several large data values. Would we classify them as unusual or as outliers?

7	8	8	10	10	10	10	12	13	13	13	13
13	13	13	14	14	14	15	15	15	15	15	16
16	16	17	18	18	18	18	19	19	19	19	19
20	20	20	21	21	21	22	22	23	23	23	24
25	26	26	26	26	27	29	29	30	31	34	36
37	40	41	45	48	55	68	91				

For the P/E data, $\bar{x} = 22.72$ and $s = 14.08$. From these sample statistics, the Empirical Rule says that *if the sample came from a normal distribution:*

$\bar{x} \pm 1s$: $22.72 \pm 1(14.08)$ 68.26% of the P/E ratios would be within the interval 8.6 to 36.8.

$\bar{x} \pm 2s$: $22.72 \pm 2(14.08)$ 95.44% of the P/E ratios would be within the interval −5.4 to 50.9.

$\bar{x} \pm 3s$: $22.72 \pm 3(14.08)$ 99.73% of the P/E ratios would be within the interval −19.5 to 65.0.

We can ignore the negative lower limits, because negative P/E ratios are impossible. By these criteria, we have one *unusual* data value (55) and two *outliers* (68 and 91). In fact, our calculations suggest that the sample probably *isn't* from a normal population, because it does not match the Empirical Rule very well, as shown in Table 4.17. However, unless the sample is fairly large (say, 50 or more), comparing the tabulated sample frequencies with a normal distribution would not be very informative.

TABLE 4.17   P/E Sample versus Normal (*n* = 68)   **PERatios2**

Data Range	Sample	If Normal
Within $\bar{x} \pm 1s$	57/68, or 83.82%	68.26%
Within $\bar{x} \pm 2s$	65/68, or 95.59%	95.44%
Within $\bar{x} \pm 3s$	66/68, or 97.06%	99.73%

Chapter 5

Defining a Standardized Variable

Another approach is to redefine each observation in terms of its distance from the mean in standard deviations. We call this a **standardized variable** and denote it by the letter *Z*. We get the standardized variable *Z* by transforming each value of the random variable *X*:

$$z_i = \frac{x_i - \mu}{\sigma} \text{ for a population} \tag{4.16}$$

$$z_i = \frac{x_i - \bar{x}}{s} \text{ for a sample} \tag{4.17}$$

By looking at z_i we can tell at a glance how far away from the mean each observation lies. For the P/E data the standardized values are

−1.12	−1.05	−1.05	−0.90	−0.90	−0.90	−0.90	−0.76	−0.69	−0.69	−0.69	−0.69
−0.69	−0.69	−0.69	−0.62	−0.62	−0.62	−0.55	−0.55	−0.55	−0.55	−0.55	−0.48
−0.48	−0.48	−0.41	−0.34	−0.34	−0.34	−0.34	−0.26	−0.26	−0.26	−0.26	−0.26
−0.19	−0.19	−0.19	−0.12	−0.12	−0.12	−0.05	−0.05	0.02	0.02	0.02	0.09
0.16	0.23	0.23	0.23	0.23	0.30	0.45	0.45	0.52	0.59	0.80	0.94
1.01	1.23	1.30	1.58	1.80	2.29	3.22	4.85				

The standardizing calculations for the four largest data points (48, 55, 68, 91) are shown:

$$z_i = \frac{x_i - \bar{x}}{s} = \frac{48 - 22.72}{14.08} = 1.80 \quad \text{Within 2 standard deviations (not unusual)}$$

$$z_i = \frac{x_i - \bar{x}}{s} = \frac{55 - 22.72}{14.08} = 2.29 \quad \text{Beyond 2 standard deviations (unusual)}$$

$$z_i = \frac{x_i - \bar{x}}{s} = \frac{68 - 22.72}{14.08} = 3.22 \quad \text{Beyond 3 standard deviations (outlier)}$$

$$z_i = \frac{x_i - \bar{x}}{s} = \frac{91 - 22.72}{14.08} = 4.85 \quad \text{Beyond 4 standard deviations (extreme outlier)}$$

Visual Statistics calculates standardized values, sorts the data, checks for outliers, and tabulates the sample frequencies so that you can apply the Empirical Rule. MegaStat does the same thing, as seen in Figure 4.22 for the J.D. Powers data.

FIGURE 4.22 Empirical Rule Using MegaStat (*n* = 37 cars)

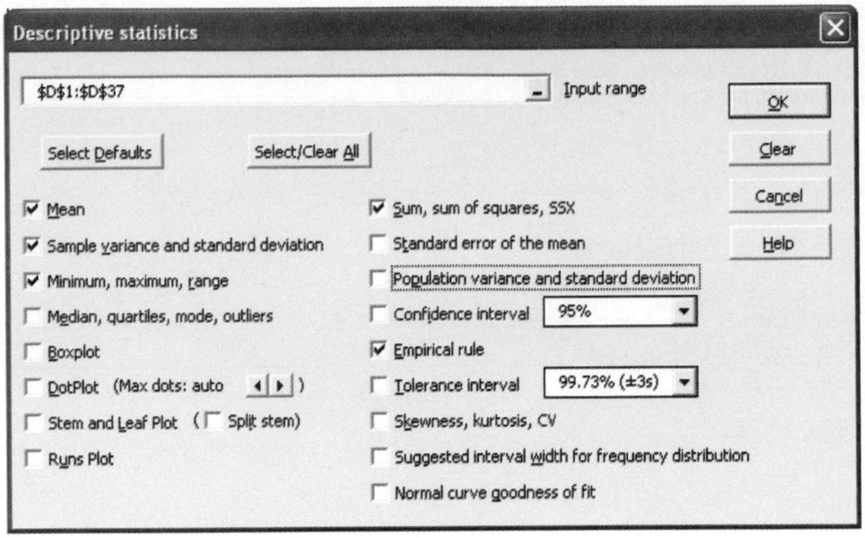

Descriptive statistics   ☒

$D$1:$D$37   — Input range   OK

Select Defaults   Select/Clear All   Clear

☑ Mean   ☑ Sum, sum of squares, SSX   Cancel

☑ Sample variance and standard deviation   ☐ Standard error of the mean   Help

☑ Minimum, maximum, range   ☐ Population variance and standard deviation

☐ Median, quartiles, mode, outliers   ☐ Confidence interval 95% ▼

☐ Boxplot   ☑ Empirical rule

☐ DotPlot (Max dots: auto ◄ ►)   ☐ Tolerance interval 99.73% (±3s) ▼

☐ Stem and Leaf Plot (☐ Split stem)   ☐ Skewness, kurtosis, CV

☐ Runs Plot   ☐ Suggested interval width for frequency distribution

                         ☐ Normal curve goodness of fit

Defects per 100 Vehicles	
count	37
mean	134.51
sample variance	621.76
sample standard deviation	24.94
minimum	91
maximum	204
range	113
sum	4,977.00
sum of squares	691,857.00
deviation sum of squares (SSX)	22,383.24
empirical rule	
mean − 1s	109.58
mean + 1s	159.45
percent in interval (68.26%)	70.3%
mean − 2s	84.64
mean + 2s	184.38
percent in interval (95.44%)	94.6%
mean − 3s	59.71
mean + 3s	209.32
percent in interval (99.73%)	100.0%

Outliers

Extreme values of a variable are annoying, but what do we do about them? It is tempting to discard unusual data points. Discarding an outlier would be reasonable if we had reason to suppose it is erroneous data. For example, a blood pressure reading of 1200/80 seems impossible (probably was supposed to be 120/80). Perhaps the lab technician was distracted by a conversation while marking down the reading. An outrageous observation is almost certainly invalid. But how do we guard against self-deception? More than one scientist has been convinced to disregard data that didn't fit the pattern, when in fact the weird observation was trying to say something important. At this stage of your statistical training, it suffices to *recognize* unusual data points and outliers and their potential impact, and to know that there are entire books that cover the topic of outliers.

Estimating Sigma

Because for a normal distribution essentially all the observations lie within $\mu \pm 3\sigma$, the range is approximately 6σ (from $\mu - 3\sigma$ to $\mu + 3\sigma$). Therefore, if you know the range R, you can estimate the standard deviation as $\sigma = R/6$. This rule can come in handy for approximating the standard deviation when all you know is the range. For example, the caffeine content of a cup of tea depends on the type of tea and length of time the tea steeps, with a range of 20 to 90 mg. Knowing only the range, we could estimate the standard deviation as $s = (90 - 20)/6$, or about 12 mg. This estimate assumes that the caffeine content of a cup of tea is normally distributed.

Section Exercises

4.21 (a) By Chebychev's Theorem, at least how many students in a class of 200 would score within the range $\mu \pm 2\sigma$? (b) By the Empirical Rule, how many students in a class of 200 would score within the range $\mu \pm 2\sigma$? (c) What assumption is required in order to apply the Empirical Rule? (LO 3)

4.22 Convert each individual X data value to a standardized Z value and interpret it. (LO 3)
   a. Class exam: $\mu = 79$, $\sigma = 5$, John's score is 91.
   b. Student GPA: $\mu = 2.87$, $\sigma = 0.31$, Mary's GPA is 3.18.
   c. Weekly study hours: $\mu = 15.0$, $\sigma = 5.0$, Jaime studies 18 hours

4.23 CIBC recorded the number of customers to use a downtown ABM during the noon hour on 32 consecutive workdays. (a) Use Excel or MegaStat to sort and standardize the data. (b) Based on the Empirical Rule, are there outliers? Unusual data values? (c) Compare the percent of observations that lie within 1 and 2 standard deviations of the mean with a normal distribution. What is your conclusion? (d) Do you feel the sample size is sufficient to assess normality? (LO 3)   **CIBC**

25	37	23	26	30	40	25	26
39	32	21	26	19	27	32	25
18	26	34	18	31	35	21	33
33	9	16	32	35	42	15	24

4.24 An executive's telephone log showed the lengths of 65 calls initiated during the last week of July. (a) Use Excel or MegaStat to sort and standardize the data. (b) Based on the Empirical Rule, are there outliers? Unusual data values? (c) Compare the percent of observations that lie within 1 and 2 standard deviations of the mean with a normal distribution. What is your conclusion? (d) Do you feel the sample size is sufficient to assess normality? (LO 3) 💿 **Length**

1	2	10	5	3	3	2	20	1	1
6	3	13	2	2	1	26	3	1	3
1	2	1	7	1	2	3	1	2	12
1	4	2	2	29	1	1	1	8	5
1	4	2	1	1	1	1	6	1	2
3	3	6	1	3	1	1	5	1	18
2	13	13	1	6					

4.5   Percentiles, Quartiles, and Box Plots

Percentiles

You may remember your elementary school days when you were subjected to various tests conducted at either the provincial or federal levels. Although these tests were mainly used to see how well your school or school board was meeting various standards, you and your parents received reports on your own personal results. Part of the report told you how well you did compared to other students writing the same tests. This comparison was reported by means of percentile scores. For example, if you are in the 83rd percentile, then 83 percent of the test-takers scored below you, and you are in the top 17 percent of all test-takers. However, only when the sample is large can we meaningfully divide the data into 100 groups (*percentiles*). Alternatively, we can divide the data into 10 groups (*deciles*) or 4 groups (*quartiles*).

In health care, manufacturing, and banking, selected percentiles (e.g., 5, 25, 50, 75, and 95 percent) are calculated to establish *benchmarks* so that any firm can compare itself with similar firms (i.e., other firms in the same industry) in terms of profit margin, debt ratio, defect rate, or any other relevant performance measure. In finance, quartiles (25, 50, and 75 percent) are commonly used to assess financial performance of companies and stock portfolio performances. In human resources, percentiles are used in employee merit evaluations and salary benchmarking. The number of groups depends on the task at hand and the sample size, but quartiles deserve special attention because they are meaningful even for fairly small samples.

Quartiles

The **quartiles** (denoted Q_1, Q_2, Q_3) are scale points that divide the sorted data into four groups of approximately equal size, that is, the 25th, 50th, and 75th percentiles, respectively.

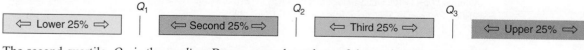

The second quartile, Q_2, is the *median*. Because equal numbers of data values lie below and above the median, it is an important indicator of *central tendency*.

FIGURE 4.23

Possible Quartile Positions

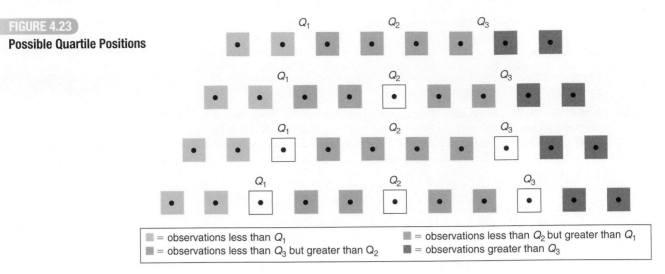

The first and third quartiles, Q_1 and Q_3, indicate *central tendency* because they define the boundaries for the middle 50 percent of the data. But Q_1 and Q_3 also indicate *dispersion,* as the *interquartile range* $Q_3 - Q_1$ measures the degree of spread for the middle 50 percent of the data.

Conceptually, the first quartile Q_1 is the median of the data values below Q_2, and the third quartile Q_3 is the median of the data values above Q_2. Depending on n, the quartiles Q_1, Q_2, Q_3 may be members of the data set or may lie *between* two of the sorted data values. Figure 4.23 shows four possible situations.

Method of Medians

For small data sets, you can find the quartiles using the **method of medians,** as illustrated in Figure 4.24.

- Step 1: Sort the observations.
- Step 2: Find the median Q_2.
- Step 3: Find the median of the data values that lie below Q_2.
- Step 4: Find the median of the data values that lie above Q_2.

This method is attractive because it is quick and logical. However, Excel uses a different method.

Formula Method

Statistical software (e.g., Excel, MegaStat, MINITAB) will not use the method of medians, but instead will use a formula to calculate the quartile positions.* There are several

*The quartiles (25th, 50th, and 75th percentiles) are a special case of percentiles. *Method A* defines the Pth percentile position as $P(n + 1)/100$ while *Method B* defines it as $1 + P(n - 1)/100$. See Eric Langford, "Quartiles in Elementary Statistics," *Journal of Statistics Education* 14, no. 3, Nov. 2006.

EXAMPLE 6

Method of Medians

A financial analyst has a portfolio of 12 energy equipment stocks. She has data on their recent price/earnings (P/E) ratios. To find the quartiles, she sorts the data, finds Q_2 (the median) halfway between the middle two data values, and then finds Q_1 and Q_3 (medians of the lower and upper halves, respectively) as illustrated in Figure 4.24.

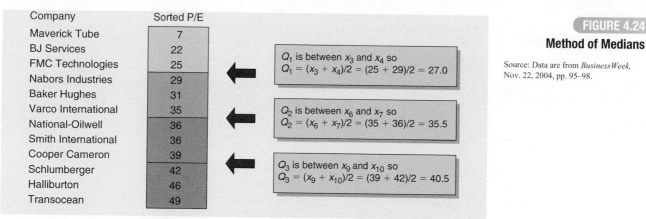

FIGURE 4.24

Method of Medians

Source: Data are from *BusinessWeek*, Nov. 22, 2004, pp. 95–98.

possible ways of calculating the quartile positions. The two that you are most likely to use are:

	Method A (MINITAB)	Method B (Excel or MegaStat)
Position of Q_1	$0.25n + 0.25$	$0.25n + 0.75$
Position of Q_2	$0.50n + 0.50$	$0.50n + 0.50$
Position of Q_3	$0.75n + 0.75$	$0.75n + 0.25$

Q_2 is the same using either method, but Q_1 and Q_3 generally are not. It depends on the gap between data values when interpolation is necessary. Most textbooks prefer MINITAB's method, so it will be illustrated here.

Excel Quartiles

Excel's function =QUARTILE(Data, k) returns the *k*th quartile, so =QUARTILE(Data, 1) would return Q_1 and =QUARTILE(Data, 3) would return Q_3. Excel treats quartiles as a special case of percentiles, so you could get the same results by using the function =PERCENTILE (Data, Percent). For example, =PERCENTILE(Data, 0.75) would return the 75th percentile or Q_3.

EXAMPLE 7

Formula Method

Figure 4.25 illustrates the quartile calculations for the same sample of P/E ratios using *Method A*. The resulting quartiles are similar to those using the method of medians.

FIGURE 4.25

Formula Interpolation Method

Source: Data are from *BusinessWeek*, Nov, 22, 2004, pp. 95–98.

Company	Sorted P/E
Maverick Tube	7
BJ Services	22
FMC Technologies	25
Nabors Industries	29
Baker Hughes	31
Varco International	35
National-Oilwell	36
Smith International	36
Cooper Cameron	39
Schlumberger	42
Halliburton	46
Transocean	49

Q_1 is at observation $0.25n + 0.25 = (0.25)(12) + 0.25 = 3.25$, so we interpolate between x_3 and x_4 to get
$Q_1 = x_3 + (0.25)(x_4 - x_3) = 25 + (0.25)(29 - 25) = 26.00$

Q_2 is at observation $0.50n + 0.50 = (0.50)(12) + 0.50 = 6.50$, so we interpolate between x_6 and x_7 to get
$Q_2 = x_6 + (0.50)(x_7 - x_6) = 35 + (0.50)(36 - 35) = 35.50$

Q_3 is at observation $0.75n + 0.75 = (0.75)(12) + 0.75 = 9.75$, so we interpolate between x_9 and x_{10} to get
$Q_3 = x_9 + (0.75)(x_{10} - x_9) = 39 + (0.75)(42 - 39) = 41.25$

EXAMPLE 8

P/E Ratios and Quartiles

A financial analyst has a diversified portfolio of 68 stocks. Their recent P/E ratios are shown. She wants to use the quartiles to define benchmarks for stocks that are low-priced (bottom quartile) or high-priced (top quartile).   **PERatios2**

7	8	8	10	10	10	10	12	13	13	13	13	13	13	13	14	14
14	15	15	15	15	15	16	16	16	17	18	18	18	18	19	19	19
19	19	20	20	20	21	21	21	22	22	23	23	23	24	25	26	26
26	26	27	29	29	30	31	34	36	37	40	41	45	48	55	68	91

Using Excel's method of interpolation (*Method B*), the quartile *positions* are:
Q_1 position: $0.25(68) + 0.75 = 17.75$ (interpolate between x_{17} and x_{18})
Q_2 position: $0.50(68) + 0.50 = 34.50$ (interpolate between x_{34} and x_{35})
Q_3 position: $0.75(68) + 0.25 = 51.25$ (interpolate between x_{51} and x_{52})

The quartiles are:
First quartile: $Q_1 = x_{17} + 0.75(x_{18} - x_{17}) = 14 + 0.75(14 - 14) = 14$
Second quartile: $Q_2 = x_{34} + 0.50(x_{35} - x_{34}) = 19 + 0.50(19 - 19) = 19$
Third quartile: $Q_3 = x_{51} + 0.25(x_{52} - x_{51}) = 26 + 0.25(26 - 26) = 26$

The median stock has a P/E ratio of 19. A stock with a P/E ratio below 14 is in the bottom quartile, while a stock with a P/E ratio above 26 is in the upper quartile. These statements are easy to understand, and convey an impression both of central tendency *and* dispersion in the sample. But notice that the quartiles do not provide clean cut-points between groups of observations because of clustering of identical data values on either side of the quartiles (a common occurrence). Because stock prices vary with the stage of the economic cycle, portfolio analysts must revise their P/E benchmarks continually and would actually use a larger sample (perhaps even *all* publicly traded stocks).

Tip

Whether you use the method of medians or Excel, your quartiles will be about the same. Small differences in calculation techniques typically do not lead to different conclusions in business applications.

Quartiles are robust statistics that generally resist outliers. However, quartiles do not always provide clean cut-points in the sorted data, particularly in small samples or when there are repeating data values. For example:

Data Set A: 1, 2, 4, 4, 8, 8, 8, 8 $Q_1 = 3, Q_2 = 6, Q_3 = 8$
Data Set B: 0, 3, 3, 6, 6, 6, 10, 15 $Q_1 = 3, Q_2 = 6, Q_3 = 8$

These two data sets have identical quartiles, but are not really similar. Because of the small sample size and "gaps" in the data, the quartiles do not represent either data set well.

Box Plots

A useful tool of *exploratory data analysis* (EDA) is the **box plot** (also called a *box-and-whisker plot*) based on the **five-number summary:**

$$x_{min}, Q_1, Q_2, Q_3, x_{max}$$

The box plot is displayed visually, like this.

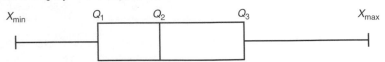

Below the box plot there is a well-labelled scale showing the values of *X*. A box plot shows *central tendency* (position of the median Q_2). A box plot shows *dispersion* (width of the

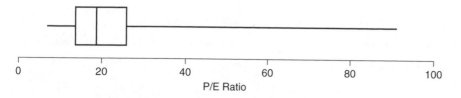

**Simple Box Plot of P/E
Ratios (*n* = 68 stocks)
(Visual Statistics)**
PERatios2

"box" defined by Q_1 and Q_3 and the range between x_{min} and x_{max}). A box plot shows *shape* (skewness if the whiskers are of unequal length and/or if the median is not in the centre of the box). For example, the five-number summary for the 68 P/E ratios is

$$7, 14, 19, 26, 91$$

Figure 4.26 shows a box plot of the P/E data. The vertical lines that define the ends of the box are located at Q_1 and Q_3 on the *X*-axis. The vertical line within the box is the median (Q_2). The "whiskers" are the horizontal lines that connect each side of the box to x_{min} and x_{max} and their length suggests the length of each tail of the distribution. The long right whisker suggests right-skewness in the P/E data, a conclusion also suggested by the fact that the median is to the left of the centre of the box (the centre of the box is the average of Q_1 and Q_3).

Fences and Unusual Data Values

We can use the quartiles to identify unusual data points. The idea is to detect data values that are far below Q_1 or far above Q_3. The *fences* are based on the **interquartile range $Q_3 - Q_1$**:

	Inner fences	*Outer fences*	
Lower fence:	$Q_1 - 1.5(Q_3 - Q_1)$	$Q_1 - 3.0(Q_3 - Q_1)$	**(4.18)**
Upper fence:	$Q_3 + 1.5(Q_3 - Q_1)$	$Q_1 + 3.0(Q_3 - Q_1)$	**(4.19)**

Observations outside the inner fences but inside the outer fences are *unusual* while those outside the outer fences are *outliers*. For the P/E data:

	Inner fences	*Outer fences*
Lower fence:	$14 - 1.5(26 - 14) = -4$	$14 - 3.0(26 - 14) = -22$
Upper fence:	$26 + 1.5(26 - 14) = +44$	$26 + 3.0(26 - 14) = +62$

In this example, we can ignore the lower fences (because P/E ratios can't be negative), but in the right tail there are three unusual P/E values (45, 48, 55) that lie above the *inner* fence and two P/E values (68, 91) that are outliers because they exceed the *outer* fence. Unusual data points are shown on a box plot by truncating the whisker or whiskers at the smallest and largest points that are within the inner fences and displaying the unusual data points as dots or asterisks, as in Figure 4.27.

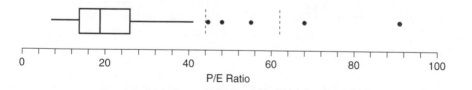

**Box Plot with Fences
(MegaStat)**
PERatios2

Section Exercises

4.25   CIBC recorded the number of customers to use a downtown ABM during the noon hour on 32 consecutive workdays. (a) Use Excel to find the quartiles. What do they tell you? (b) Make a box plot and interpret it. (LO 3)   **CIBC**

25	37	23	26	30	40	25	26
39	32	21	26	19	27	32	25
18	26	34	18	31	35	21	33
33	9	16	32	35	42	15	24

4.26 An executive's telephone log showed the lengths of 65 calls initiated during the last week of July.

(a) Use Excel to find the quartiles. What do they tell you? (b) Make a box plot and interpret it. (LO 3)   **CallLength**

1	2	10	5	3	3	2	20	1	1
6	3	13	2	2	1	26	3	1	3
1	2	1	7	1	2	3	1	2	12
1	4	2	2	29	1	1	1	8	5
1	4	2	1	1	1	1	6	1	2
3	3	6	1	3	1	1	5	1	18
2	13	13	1	6					

Mini Case   4.5

Airline Delays   **UnitedAir**

In 2005, United Airlines announced that it would award 500 frequent flier miles to every traveller on flights that arrived more than 30 minutes late on all flights departing from Chicago O'Hare to seven other hub airports (see *The Wall Street Journal,* June 14, 2005). What is the likelihood of such a delay? On a randomly chosen day (Tuesday, Apr. 26, 2005), the U.S. Bureau of Transportation Statistics Web site (www.bts.gov) showed 278 United Airlines departures from O'Hare. The mean arrival delay was -7.45 minutes (i.e., flights arrived early, on average). The quartiles were $Q_1 = -19$ minutes, $Q_2 = -10$ minutes, and $Q_3 = -3$ minutes. While these statistics show that most of the flights arrive early, we must look further to estimate the probability of a frequent flier bonus.

In the box plot with fences (Figure 4.28) the "box" is entirely below zero. In the right tail, one flight was slightly above the inner fence (unusual) and eight flights were above the outer fence (outliers). An empirical estimate of the probability of a frequent flier award is 8/278 or about a 3 percent chance. A longer period of study might alter this estimate (e.g., if there were days of bad winter weather or traffic congestion).

The dot plot (Figure 4.29) shows that the distribution of arrival delays is rather bell-shaped, except for the unusual values in the right tail. This is consistent with the view that "normal" flight operations are predictable, with only random variation around the mean. While it is impossible for flights to arrive much earlier than planned, unusual factors could delay them by a lot.

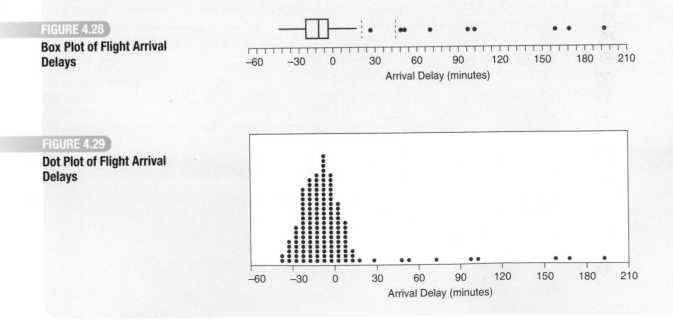

FIGURE 4.28

Box Plot of Flight Arrival Delays

FIGURE 4.29

Dot Plot of Flight Arrival Delays

4.6 Correlation

You often hear the term "significant correlation" in casual use, often imprecisely or incorrectly. Actually, the **sample correlation coefficient** is a well-known statistic that describes the degree of linearity between *paired* observations on two quantitative variables X and Y. The data set consists of n pairs (x_i, y_i) that are usually displayed on a *scatter plot* (review Chapter 3 if you need to refresh your memory about making scatter plots). The formula for the sample correlation coefficient is

$$r = \frac{\sum_{i=1}^{n}(x_i - \bar{x})(y_i - \bar{y})}{\sqrt{\sum_{i=1}^{n}(x_i - \bar{x})^2}\sqrt{\sum_{i=1}^{n}(y_i - \bar{y})^2}} \tag{4.20}$$

Its range is $-1 \leq r \leq +1$. When r is near 0 there is little or no linear relationship between X and Y in the sample data set. An r value near $+1$ indicates a strong positive relationship, while an r value near -1 indicates a strong negative relationship.

Note: In Chapter 13, the sample correlation coefficient will be used to make inferences concerning the population correlation coefficient symbolized by ρ. The formula for ρ could be stated as

$$\rho = \frac{\sum_{i=1}^{N}(x_i - \mu_X)(y_i - \mu_Y)}{\sqrt{\sum_{i=1}^{N}(x_i - \mu_X)^2}\sqrt{\sum_{i=1}^{N}(y_i - \mu_Y)^2}}$$

The values of ρ also range between -1 and $+1$ and its values have the same interpretation as r's values, except that they apply to the population data set.

Strong Negative Correlation	No Correlation	Strong Positive Correlation
-1.00	0.00	$+1.00$

Excel's formula =CORREL(XData,YData) will return the sample correlation coefficient for two columns (or rows) of paired data. In fact, many cheap scientific pocket calculators will calculate r. The diagrams in Figure 4.30 will give you some idea of what various correlations look like. The correlation coefficient is a measure of the *linear relationship,* so take special note of the last scatter plot, which shows a relationship but not a *linear* one.

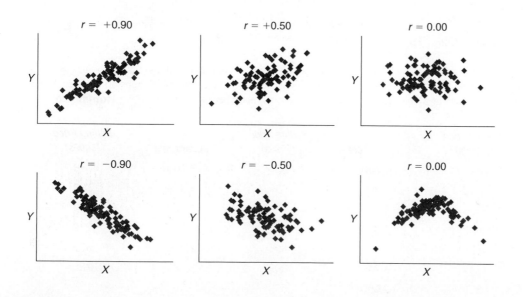

FIGURE 4.30

Illustration of Correlation Coefficients

FIGURE 4.31

Mall Area and Sales Correlation

🔘 **RetailSales**

Source: U.S. Census Bureau,
Statistical Abstract of the United States,
2007, p. 660.

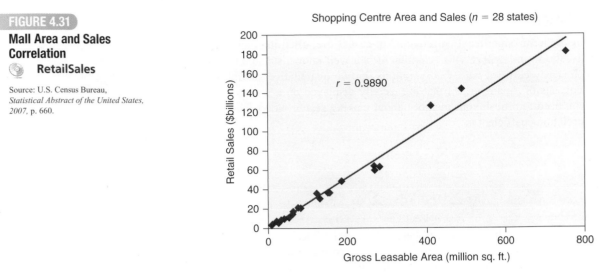
Shopping Centre Area and Sales ($n = 28$ states)

Figure 4.31 shows a scatter plot and correlation coefficient ($r = 0.9890$) for $X =$ gross leasable area (millions of square feet) and $Y =$ total retail sales (billions of dollars) for retail shopping malls in 28 states. Clearly, this is a very strong linear relationship, as you would expect (more square feet of shopping area would imply more sales). In Chapter 12, you will learn how to determine when a correlation is "significant" in a statistical sense (i.e., significantly different than zero) but for now it is enough to recognize the correlation coefficient as a *descriptive statistic*.

Section Exercises

4.27 For each X-Y data set ($n = 12$) make a scatter plot and find the sample correlation coefficient. Is there a linear relationship between X and Y? If so, describe it. *Note:* Use Excel or MegaStat or MINITAB if your instructor permits. (LO 3)

🔘 **XYDataSets**

Data Set (a)

X	64.7	25.9	65.6	49.6	50.3	26.7	39.5	56.0	90.8	35.9	39.9	64.1
Y	5.8	18.1	10.6	11.9	11.4	14.6	15.7	4.4	2.2	15.4	14.7	9.9

Data Set (b)

X	55.1	59.8	72.3	86.4	31.1	41.8	40.7	36.8	42.7	28.9	24.8	16.2
Y	15.7	17.5	15.2	20.6	7.3	8.2	9.8	8.2	13.7	11.2	7.5	4.5

Data Set (c)

X	53.3	18.1	49.8	43.8	68.3	30.4	18.6	45.8	34.0	56.7	60.3	29.3
Y	10.2	6.9	14.8	13.4	16.8	9.5	16.3	16.4	1.5	11.4	10.9	19.7

4.28 Make a scatter plot of the following data on $X =$ home size and $Y =$ selling price (thousands of dollars) for new homes ($n = 20$) in a suburb of an eastern Canadian city. Find the sample correlation coefficient. Is there a linear relationship between X and Y? If so, describe it. *Note:* Use Excel or Mega-Stat or MINITAB if your instructor permits. (LO 3) 🔘 **HomePrice**

Square Feet	Selling Price ($000s)	Square Feet	Selling Price ($000s)	Square Feet	Selling Price ($000s)
3,570	861	3,240	809	3,160	778
3,410	740	2,660	639	3,310	760
2,690	563	3,160	778	2,930	729
3,260	698	3,460	737	3,020	720
3,130	624	3,340	806	2,320	575
3,460	737	3,240	809	3,130	785
3,340	806	2,660	639		

4.7   Grouped Data

Nature of Grouped Data

Sometimes we must work with observations that have been grouped. When a data set is tabulated into bins, we lose information but gain clarity of presentation, because grouped data are often easier to display than raw data. As long as the bin limits are given, we can estimate the mean and standard deviation. The accuracy of the grouped estimates will depend on the number of bins, distribution of data within bins, and bin frequencies.

Grouped Mean and Standard Deviation

Table 4.18 shows a frequency distribution for prices of Lipitor®, a cholesterol-lowering prescription drug, for three cities (see Mini Case 4.2). The observations are classified into bins of equal width 5. When calculating a mean or standard deviation from grouped data, we treat all observations within a bin *as if they were located at the midpoint.* For example, in the third class (70 but less than 75) we pretend that all 11 prices were equal to $72.50 (the interval midpoint). In reality, observations may be scattered within each interval, but we hope that *on average* they are located at the class midpoint.

Each interval j has a midpoint m_j and a frequency f_j. We calculate the estimated mean by multiplying the midpoint of each class by its class frequency, taking the sum over all k classes, and dividing by sample size n.

$$\bar{x} = \sum_{j=1}^{k} \frac{f_j m_j}{n} = \frac{3{,}427.5}{47} = 72.925532 \qquad (4.21)$$

We then estimate the standard deviation by subtracting the estimated mean from each class midpoint, squaring the difference, multiplying by the class frequency, taking the sum over all classes to obtain the sum of squared deviations about the mean, dividing by $n - 1$, and taking the square root. *Avoid the common mistake of "rounding off" the mean before subtracting it from each midpoint.*

$$s = \sqrt{\sum_{j=1}^{k} \frac{f_j (m_j - \bar{x})^2}{n-1}} = \sqrt{\frac{2{,}091.48936}{47 - 1}} = 6.74293 \qquad (4.22)$$

Once we have the mean and standard deviation, we can estimate the coefficient of variation in the usual way:

$$cv = 100(s/\bar{x}) = 100\,(6.74293/72.925532) = 9.2\%$$

TABLE 4.18   Worksheet for Grouped Lipitor® Data ($n = 47$)   LipitorGrp

From	To	f_j	m_j	$f_j m_j$	$m_j - \bar{x}$	$(m_j - \bar{x})^2$	$f_j(m_j - \bar{x})^2$
60	65	6	62.5	375.0	−10.42553	108.69172	652.15029
65	70	11	67.5	742.5	−5.42553	29.43640	323.80036
70	75	11	72.5	797.5	−0.42553	0.18108	1.99185
75	80	13	77.5	1,007.5	4.57447	20.92576	272.03486
80	85	5	82.5	412.5	9.57447	91.67044	458.35220
85	90	0	87.5	0.0	14.57447	212.41512	0.00000
90	95	1	92.5	92.5	19.57447	383.15980	383.15980
	Sum	47	Sum	3,427.5		Sum	2,091.48936
			Mean ($\bar{x}$)	72.925532		Std Dev (s)	6.74293408

Accuracy Issues

How accurate are grouped estimates of $\bar{x}$ and s? Typically, we would have no way of knowing how much information was lost due to grouping. To the extent that observations are *not* evenly spaced within the bins, accuracy would be lost but, in terms of estimating $\bar{x}$, the most that we can err is by half of the bin widths. (For example, if the bin widths are 10 and all the actual values of X happen to be at the lower limits of their respective bins, using the midpoints of each bin would result in an estimate that is 5 higher than the actual mean.) In any case, unless there is systematic skewness (say, clustering at the low end of each class) the effects of uneven distributions within bins will tend to average out.

Accuracy tends to improve as the number of bins increases. If the first or last class is open-ended, there will be no class midpoint, and therefore no way to estimate the mean. For non-negative data (e.g., GPA) we can assume a lower limit of zero when the first class is open-ended, although this assumption may make the first class too wide. Such an assumption may occasionally be possible for an open-ended top class (e.g., the upper limit of people's ages could be assumed to be 100), but many variables have no obvious upper limit (e.g., income). It is usually possible to estimate the median and quartiles from grouped data even with open-ended classes (see *LearningStats* Unit 04, which gives the formulas and illustrates grouped quartile calculations).

Other Measures from Grouped Data

Although formulas were used to estimate the mean and the standard deviation or variance, we can also estimate other measures from grouped data. For example, we can estimate the median using an ogive by drawing a horizontal line at the cumulative frequency of 0.5 until it touches the ogive and then draw a vertical line at that point. An approximation of the median is the value of X where that line intersects the horizontal axis. We can also estimate percentiles and quartiles using a similar strategy. Instead of defining the mode as that value which occurs most often, we can redefine it as the midpoint of the bin with the greatest frequency. To estimate the range, we can be conservative and define the range as the distance between the upper boundary of the highest bin and the lower boundary of the lowest bin. To be less conservative, we can define the range as the distance between the midpoints of the two extreme bins.

Section Exercises

4.29 Consider the following table concerning the amount of gasoline (in litres) that a random sample of 50 motorists used in the last week:

Number of Litres	Number of Motorists
0 to 10	3
10 to 20	12
20 to 30	18
30 to 40	15
40 to 50	2

(a) Draw a histogram and ogive for this data set.
(b) Estimate the mean, median, mode, range, variance, and standard deviation of this data set.
(c) Estimate the first and third quartiles and draw a box plot for this data set.
(d) Estimate what proportion of motorists used more than 27 litres last week.
(e) Interpret your findings. (LO 4)

CHAPTER SUMMARY

The **mean** and **median** describe a sample's **central tendency** and also indicate **skewness.** The **mode** is useful for discrete data with a small range. The **trimmed mean** eliminates extreme values. The **geometric mean** mitigates high extremes but fails when zeros or negative values are present. Dispersion is typically measured by the **standard deviation** while **relative dispersion** is given by the **coefficient of variation** for non-negative data. **Standardized data** reveal **outliers** or unusual data values, and the **Empirical Rule** offers a comparison with a normal distribution. In measuring dispersion, the **mean absolute deviation** (*MAD*) is easy to understand, but lacks nice mathematical properties. **Quartiles** are meaningful even for fairly small data sets, while **percentiles** are used only for large data sets. **Box plots** show the quartiles and data range. The **correlation coefficient** measures the degree of linearity between two variables. We can estimate many common descriptive statistics from **grouped data.**

KEY TERMS

bimodal distribution, *114*	method of medians, *140*	sample variance, *129*
box plot, *142*	mode, *112*	skewed left, *114*
Chebyshev's Theorem, *135*	multimodal distribution, *114*	skewed right, *114*
coefficient of variation, *130*	negatively skewed, *114*	standard deviation, *129*
Empirical Rule, *135*	outliers, *136*	standardized variable, *137*
five-number summary, *142*	population variance, *129*	symmetric data, *114*
geometric mean, *122*	positively skewed, *114*	trimmed mean, *125*
interquartile range, *143*	quartiles, *139*	weighted mean, *121*
mean, *110*	range, *128*	
mean absolute deviation, *131*	sample correlation	
median, *111*	coefficient, *145*	

Commonly Used Formulas in Descriptive Statistics

Sample mean: $\bar{x} = \dfrac{1}{n}\sum_{i=1}^{n} x_i$

Geometric mean (growth rate): $GR = \sqrt[n]{(1 + x_1)(1 + x_2)\cdots(1 + x_n)} - 1$

Range: $\text{Range} = x_{\max} - x_{\min}$

Sample standard deviation: $s = \sqrt{\dfrac{\sum_{i=1}^{n}(x_i - \bar{x})^2}{n - 1}}$

Coefficient of variation: $CV = 100 \times \dfrac{s}{\bar{x}}$

Standardized variable: $z_i = \dfrac{x_i - \mu}{\sigma}$

Sample correlation coefficient: $r = \dfrac{\sum_{i=1}^{n}(x_i - \bar{x})(y_i - \bar{y})}{\sqrt{\sum_{i=1}^{n}(x_i - \bar{x})^2}\sqrt{\sum_{i=1}^{n}(y_i - \bar{y})^2}}$

Grouped mean: $\bar{x} = \sum_{j=1}^{k} \dfrac{f_j m_j}{n}$

CHAPTER REVIEW

1. What are descriptive statistics? How do they differ from visual displays of data? (LO 1)

2. Explain each concept: (a) central tendency, (b) dispersion, and (c) shape. (LO 1)

3. (a) Why is sorting usually the first step in data analysis? (b) Why is it useful to begin a data analysis by thinking about how the data were collected? (LO 3)

4. What descriptive measure is associated with each of the following symbols? (Where appropriate, state whether the symbol refers to a population or to a sample.) (a) r, (b) μ, (c) s, (d) CV, (e) σ^2, (f) $\bar{x}$ (g) GR, (h) ρ, (i) s^2 (j) cv (k) z, (l) MAD, (m) σ, (n) first quartile. (LO 1)

5. List strengths and weaknesses of each measure of central tendency and write its Excel function: (a) mean, (b) median, and (c) mode. (LO 2)

6. (a) Why must the deviations around the mean sum to zero? (b) What is the position of the median in the data array when n is even? When n is odd? (c) Why is the mode of little use in continuous data? For what type of data is the mode most useful? (LO 2)

7. (a) What is a bimodal distribution? (b) Explain two ways to detect skewness. (LO 2)

8. List strengths and weaknesses of each measure of central tendency and give its Excel function (if any): (a) geometric mean, and (b) 10 percent trimmed mean. (LO 2)

9. (a) What is dispersion? (b) Name five measures of dispersion. List the main characteristics (strengths, weaknesses) of each measure. (LO 2)

10. (a) Which standard deviation formula (population, sample) is used most often? Why? (b) When is the coefficient of variation useful? When is it useless? (LO 2)

11. (a) To what kind of data does Chebyshev's Theorem apply? (b) To what kind of data does the Empirical Rule apply? (c) What is an outlier? An unusual data value? (LO 2)

12. (a) In a normal distribution, approximately what percent of observations are within 1, 2, and 3 standard deviations of the mean? (b) In a sample of 10,000 observations, about how many observations would you expect beyond 3 standard deviations from the mean? (LO 2)

13. (a) Write the mathematical formula for a standardized variable. (b) Write the Excel formula for standardizing a data value in cell F17 from an array with mean Mu and standard deviation Sigma. (LO 3)

14. (a) Why is it dangerous to delete an outlier? (b) When might it be acceptable to delete an outlier? (LO 2)

15. (a) Explain how quartiles can measure both centrality and dispersion. (b) Why don't we calculate percentiles for small samples? (LO 2)

16. (a) Explain the method of medians for calculating quartiles. (b) Write the Excel formula for the first quartile of an array named XData. (LO 2)

17. (a) What is a box plot? What does it tell us? (b) What is the role of fences in a box plot? (c) Define the interquartile range. (LO 1)

18. What does a correlation coefficient measure? What is its range? (LO 2)

19. (a) Why is some accuracy lost when we estimate the mean or standard deviation from grouped data? (b) Why do open-ended classes in a frequency distribution make it impossible to estimate the mean and standard deviation? (c) When would grouped data be presented instead of the entire sample of raw data? (LO 2)

20. What symbols represent the following descriptive measures? (a) population variance, (b) sample correlation coefficient, (c) population mean, (d) geometric mean (growth rate), (e) weighted mean, (f) population correlation coefficient, (g) sample standard deviation, (h) mean absolute deviation, (i) sample coefficient of variation, (j) population standard deviation, (k) third quartile, (l) population coefficient of variation (m) sample variance, and (n) sample mean. (LO 1)

21. Draw a box plot which may describe each of the following distributions: (a) left-skewed unimodal distribution, (b) uniform or flat distribution, (c) bimodal symmetrical distribution, (d) mound or bell-shaped distribution, and (e) right-skewed unimodal distribution. (LO 2)

CHAPTER EXERCISES

Note: Unless otherwise instructed, you may use any desired statistical software for calculations and graphs in the following problems.

Describing Data

4.30 Below are monthly rents paid by 30 students who live off campus. (a) Find the mean, median, mode, standard deviation, and quartiles. (b) Describe the "typical" rent paid by a student. (c) Do the measures of central tendency agree? Explain. (d) Sort and standardize the data. (e) Are there outliers or unusual data values? (f) Using the Empirical Rule, do you think the data could be from a normal population? (LO 3) **Rents**

730	730	730	930	700	570
690	1,030	740	620	720	670
560	740	650	660	850	930
600	620	760	690	710	500
730	800	820	840	720	700

4.31 How many days in advance do travellers purchase their airline tickets? Below are data showing the advance days for a sample of 28 passengers on United Airlines flight 815 from Chicago to Los Angeles. (a) Prepare a dot plot and discuss it. (b) Calculate the mean, median, and mode. (c) Calculate the quartiles and coefficient of quartile variation. (d) Why can't you use the geometric mean for this data set? (e) Which is the best measure of central tendency? Why? (Data are from *The New York Times,* Apr. 12, 1998.) (LO 3 & 5) **Days**

| 11 | 7 | 11 | 4 | 15 | 14 | 71 | 29 | 8 | 7 | 16 | 28 | 17 | 249 |
| 0 | 20 | 77 | 18 | 14 | 3 | 15 | 52 | 20 | 0 | 9 | 9 | 21 | 3 |

4.32 In a particular week, the cable channel TCM (Turner Classic Movies) showed seven movies rated ****, nine movies rated ***, three movies rated **, and one movie rated *. Which measure of central tendency would you use to describe the "average" movie rating on TCM (assuming that week was typical)? (Data are from *TV Guide.*) (LO 5)

4.33 The "expense ratio" is a measure of the cost of managing the portfolio. Investors prefer a low expense ratio, all else equal. Below are expense ratios for 23 randomly chosen stock funds and 21 randomly chosen bond funds. (a) Calculate the mean, median, and mode for each sample. (b) Succinctly compare central tendency in expense ratios for stock funds and bond funds. (c) Calculate the standard deviation and coefficient of variation for each sample. Which type of fund has more variability? Explain. (d) Calculate the quartiles. What do they tell you? (Data are from *Money* 32, no. 2 [Feb. 2003]. Stock funds were selected from 1,699 funds by taking the 10th fund on each page in the list. Bond funds were selected from 499 funds by taking the 10th, 20th, and 30th fund on each page in the list.) (LO 3) **Funds**

23 Stock Funds

| 1.12 | 1.44 | 1.27 | 1.75 | 0.99 | 1.45 | 1.19 | 1.22 | 0.99 | 3.18 | 1.21 | 1.89 |
| 0.60 | 2.10 | 0.73 | 0.90 | 1.79 | 1.35 | 1.08 | 1.28 | 1.20 | 1.68 | 0.15 | |

21 Bond Funds

| 1.96 | 0.51 | 1.12 | 0.64 | 0.69 | 0.20 | 1.44 | 0.68 | 0.40 | 0.94 | 0.75 | 1.77 |
| 0.93 | 1.25 | 0.85 | 0.99 | 0.95 | 0.35 | 0.64 | 0.41 | 0.90 | | | |

4.34 Statistics students were asked to fill a one-cup measure with raisin bran, tap the cup lightly on the counter three times to settle the contents, if necessary add more raisin bran to bring the contents exactly to the one-cup line, spread the contents on a large plate, and count the raisins. The 13 students who chose Kellogg's Raisin Bran obtained the results shown below. (a) Use Excel to calculate the mean, median, and mode. (b) Which is the best measure of central tendency, and why? (c) Calculate the standard deviation and coefficient of variation. (d) Why is there variation in the number of raisins in a cup of raisin bran? Why might it be difficult for Kellogg to reduce variation? (LO 2, 3 & 5) **Raisins**

| 23 | 33 | 44 | 36 | 29 | 42 | 31 | 33 | 61 | 36 | 34 | 23 | 24 |

4.35 The table below shows estimates of the total cost of repairs in four bumper tests (full frontal, front corner, full rear, and rear corner) on 17 cars. (a) Make a dot plot for the data. (b) Calculate the mean and median. (c) Would you say the data are skewed? (d) Why is the mode not useful for these data? (Data are from Insurance Institute for Highway Safety, *Detroit Free Press,* Mar. 1, 2007, p. 2E). (LO 2, 3 & 5) **CrashDamage**

Car Tested	Damage	Car Tested	Damage	Car Tested	Damage
Chevrolet Malibu	6,646	Mazda 6	4,961	Subaru Legacy	7,448
Chrysler Sebring	7,454	Mitsubishi Galant	4,277	Toyota Camry	4,911
Ford Fusion	5,030	Nissan Altima	6,459	Volkswagen Jetta	9,020
Honda Accord	8,010	Nissan Maxima	9,051	Volkswagen Passat	8,259
Hyundai Sonata	7,565	Pontiac G6	8,919	Volvo S40	5,600
Kia Optima	5,735	Saturn Aura	6,374		

4.36 Salt-sensitive people must be careful of sodium content in foods. The sodium content (milligrams) in a 3-tablespoon serving of 33 brands of peanut butter is shown below. (a) Prepare a dot plot and discuss it. (b) Calculate the mean, median, and mode. (c) Which is the best measure of central tendency? The worst? Why? (d) Why would the geometric mean not work here? (e) Sort and standardize the data. (f) Are there outliers? Unusual data values? (Data are from *Consumer Reports* 67, no. 5.) (LO 2, 3 & 5) 🔘 **Sodium**

98	225	225	225	23	0	210	0	210	225	210	165	180	240
225	8	375	225	270	285	180	210	180	195	195	188	173	
165	165	180	180	0	300								

4.37 Below are the lengths (in yards) of 27 18-hole golf courses. (a) Prepare a dot plot and discuss it. (b) Calculate the mean, median, and mode. (c) Which is the best measure of central tendency? The worst? Why? (d) Why would the geometric mean pose a problem for this data set? (LO 2, 3 & 5)
🔘 **Golf**

5,646	5,767	5,800	5,820	6,005	6,078	6,100	6,110	6,179
6,186	6,306	6,366	6,378	6,400	6,470	6,474	6,494	6,500
6,500	6,554	6,555	6,572	6,610	6,620	6,647	6,845	7,077

4.38 The table below shows percentiles of height (in centimetres) for 20-year-old males and females. (a) Calculate the interquartile range. Why is this statistic appropriate to measure dispersion in this situation? (b) Choose a 20-year-old whose height you know and describe that person's height in comparison with these percentiles. (c) Do you suppose that height percentiles change over time for the population of a specified nation? Explain. (Data are from the National Center for Health Statistics, www.fedstats.gov.) (LO 2, 3 & 5)

Selected Percentiles for Heights of 20-Year-Olds (cm)

Gender	5%	25%	50%	75%	95%
Male	165	172	177	182	188
Female	153	159	163	168	174

4.39 Grace took a random sample of the number of steps per minute from the electronic readout of her aerobic climbing machine during a one-hour workout. (a) Calculate the mean, median, and mode. (b) Which is the best measure of central tendency? The worst? Why? (Data are from a project by Grace Obringer, MBA student.) (LO 2, 3 & 5) 🔘 **Steps**

90	110	97	144	54	60	156	86	82	64	100	47	80	164	93

4.40 How much revenue does it take to maintain a cricket club? The following table shows annual income for 18 first-class clubs that engage in league play. (a) Calculate the mean, median, and mode. Show your work carefully. (b) Describe a "typical" cricket club's income. (Data are from *The Economist* 367, no. 8329 [June 21, 2003], p. 47.) (LO 2, 3 & 5)

Annual Income of First-Class Cricket Clubs in England 🔘 **Cricket**

Club	Income (£000)	Club	Income (£000)
Lancashire	5,366	Durham	3,009
Surrey	6,386	Worcestershire	2,446
Derbyshire	2,088	Gloucestershire	2,688
Middlesex	2,280	Northamptonshire	2,416
Somerset	2,544	Glamorgan	2,133
Nottinghamshire	3,669	Essex	2,417
Kent	2,894	Warwickshire	4,272
Leicestershire	2,000	Yorkshire	2,582
Sussex	2,477	Hampshire	2,557

4.41 A plumbing supplier's mean monthly demand for vinyl washers is 24,212 with a standard deviation of 6,053. The mean monthly demand for steam boilers is 6.8 with a standard deviation of 1.7. Compare the dispersion of these distributions. Which demand pattern has more relative variation? Explain. (LO 2, 3 & 5)

4.42 The table below shows average daily sales of Rice Krispies in the month of June in 74 Noodles & Company restaurants. (a) Make a histogram for the data. Would you say the distribution is skewed? (b) Calculate the mean, median, and mode. Which best describes central tendency, and why? (c) Find the standard deviation. (d) Are there any outliers? (LO 2, 3 & 5) **RiceKrispies**

32	8	14	20	28	19	37	31	16	16
16	29	11	34	31	18	22	17	27	16
24	49	25	18	25	21	15	16	20	11
21	29	14	25	10	15	8	12	12	19
21	28	27	26	12	24	18	19	24	16
17	20	23	13	17	17	19	36	16	34
25	15	16	13	20	13	13	23	17	22
11	17	17	9						

4.43 Analysis of portfolio returns over the period 1981 to 2000 showed the statistics below. (a) Calculate and compare the coefficients of variation. (b) Why would we use a coefficient of variation? Why not just compare the standard deviations? (c) What do the data tell you about risk and return at that time period? (LO 2, 3 & 5) **Returns**

Comparative Returns on Four Types of Investments

Investment	Mean Return	Standard Deviation	Coefficient of Variation
Venture funds (adjusted)	19.2	14.0	
All common stocks	15.6	14.0	
Real estate	11.5	16.8	
Federal short-term paper	6.7	1.9	

Source: Dennis D. Spice and Stephen D. Hogan, "Venture Investing and the Role of Financial Advisors," *Journal of Financial Planning* 15, no. 3 (Mar. 2002), p. 69. These statistics are for educational use only and should not be viewed as a guide to investing.

4.44 Analysis of annualized returns over the period 1991 to 2001 showed that prepaid tuition plans had a mean return of 6.3 percent with a standard deviation of 2.7 percent, while the Standard & Poor's 500 stock index had a mean return of 12.9 percent with a standard deviation of 15.8 percent. (a) Calculate and compare the coefficients of variation. (b) Why would we use a coefficient of variation? Why not just compare the standard deviations? (c) What do the data say about risk and return of these investments at that time? (Data are from Mark C. Neath, "Section 529 Prepaid Tuition Plans: A Low Risk Investment with Surprising Applications," *Journal of Financial Planning* 15, no. 4 [Apr. 2002], p. 94.) (LO 2, 3 & 5)

4.45 The transit system in a medium-size Ontario city is considering extending its bus service into five surrounding towns. Before it does so, it wants to determine what proportion of the citizens in these towns would seriously consider using this mode of transportation. To estimate this proportion, the transit system used stratified random sampling, using each of the towns as a stratum, and summarized its findings as follows:

Town	Sample Size	Sample Proportion	Population Size
A	150	0.35	15,000
B	300	0.50	35,000
C	500	0.20	10,000
D	100	0.90	3,000
E	200	0.40	8,000

Based on the above table, use the best descriptive measure to estimate the true proportion of the citizens in these towns who would seriously consider using this mode of transportation. Explain why you chose this measure. (LO 2, 3 & 5)

4.46 A small regional airline in the Yukon has five routes that its airplanes cover. Because of the high cost of fuel and because the weight of its passengers (including luggage) affects the amount of fuel its airplanes use, it is interested in determining the average total weight of its passengers per flight so that it can have a better sense of how much it is spending on fuel per month. It randomly sampled several of its flights using stratified random sampling and summarized its findings as follows:

Route	No. of Flights Sampled	Average Total Weight of Passengers	Actual Number of Flights per Month
A	4	2,300 kg	15
B	3	3,700 kg	8
C	6	5,500 kg	6
D	2	1,500 kg	12
E	7	7,500 kg	10

Estimate the average total passenger weight per flight and estimate the total passenger weight of this airline per month. Explain why you used the measures that you did. (LO 2, 3 & 5)

4.47 The increase in the amount of break-ins in a Manitoba community has alarmed its citizens. Five years ago there were 27 break-ins. This year, there were 137 break-ins. What has been the average annual growth rate in crimes over this five-year period? (LO 2, 3 & 5)

4.48 In Ontario there are approximately 100 gymnastics clubs that are affiliated with Gymnastics Ontario, the body that governs the sport of gymnastics in Ontario. Although most clubs have athletes that compete in competitions across Ontario and beyond, the majority of their athletes and the majority of their revenues come from their recreational programs. One club boasts that their recreation program has grown from 350 athletes four years ago to over 600 athletes today. Another club in the same city has had a rate of growth in each of the last four years of 15 percent, 20 percent, 10 percent, and 30 percent. Which club has had the larger average annual growth rate over this four-year period? What are their respective annual growth rates? Justify the measure that you used in arriving at your answers. (LO 2, 3 & 5)

4.49 To try to eliminate discrepancies in grades assigned to students taking an introductory business statistics course at an Ontario university, the business school has instituted a grading scheme to eliminate the discrepancies based on the marking philosophies of different professors teaching that course. In one section of this course where the average mark was 85 and the standard deviation in marks was 6, student A received a mark of 80. In another section where the average mark was 60 and the standard deviation was 4, student B received a mark of 75. In the third section of the course where the average mark was 55 and the standard deviation was 20, student C received a mark of 82. Which of these students should get the highest grade and which should get the lowest grade? Which measure did you use to arrive at your conclusions and why? (LO 2, 3 & 5)

4.50 There are many reasons why some professional golfers are more successful than other professional golfers. One reason is that they can drive the ball further, and another reason is that they are more consistent in their driving distances. Two golfers, one more successful than the other, each were asked to hit their driver as far as they could eight times. Their driving distances were recorded as follows:

More Successful: 325, 315, 318, 322, 328, 324, 323, 319

Less Successful: 295, 287, 305, 280, 310, 274, 300, 293

For each golfer, determine the mean, median, trimmed mean (leaving off the shortest and longest drive), range, standard deviation, and coefficient of variation. For each driver, sketch a box plot of their driving distances. Which of the above measures supports the above reasons for why some professional golfers are more successful than others? Which don't support the above reasons? Explain. (LO 2, 3 & 5)

Thinking About Distributions

4.51 At the Midlothian Independent Bank, a study shows that the mean ABM transaction takes 74 seconds, the median 63 seconds, and the mode 51 seconds. (a) Sketch the distribution, based on these statistics. (b) What factors might cause the distribution to be like this? (LO 2)

4.52 At the Eureka library, the mean time a book is checked out is 13 days, the median is 10 days, and the mode is 7 days. (a) Sketch the distribution, based on these statistics. (b) What factors might cause the distribution to be like this? (LO 2)

4.53 On Prof. Hardtack's last cost accounting exam, the mean score was 71, the median was 77, and the mode was 81. (a) Sketch the distribution, based on these statistics. (b) What factors might cause the distribution to be like this? (LO 2)

4.54 (a) Sketch the histogram you would expect for the number of DVDs owned by *n* randomly chosen families. (b) Describe the expected relationship between the mean, median, and mode. How could you test your ideas about these data? (LO 2)

4.55 (a) Sketch the histogram you would expect for the price of regular gasoline yesterday at *n* service stations in your area. (b) Guess the range and median. (c) How could you test your ideas about these data? (LO 2)

4.56 The median lifespan of a mouse is 118 weeks. (a) Would you expect the mean to be higher or lower than 118? (b) Would you expect the lifespans of mice to be normally distributed? Explain. (Data are from *Science News* 161, no. 3 [Jan. 19, 2002].) (LO 2)

4.57 The median waiting time for a liver transplant in the U.S. is 1,154 days for patients with type O blood (the most common blood type). (a) Would you expect the mean to be higher or lower than 1,154 days? Explain. (b) If someone dies while waiting for a transplant, how should that be counted in the average? (Data are from *The New York Times,* Sept. 21, 2003.) (LO 2)

4.58 A company's contractual "trigger" point for a union absenteeism penalty is a certain distance above the *mean* days missed by all workers. Now the company wants to switch the trigger to a certain distance above the *median* days missed for all workers. (a) Visualize the distribution of missed days for all workers (symmetric, skewed left, skewed right). (b) Discuss the probable effect on the trigger point of switching from the mean to the median. (c) What position would the union be likely to take on the company's proposed switch? (LO 2)

Excel Projects

4.59 (a) Use Excel functions to calculate the mean and standard deviation for weekend occupancy rates (percent) in nine resort hotels during the off-season. (b) What conclusion would a casual observer draw about centrality and dispersion, based on your statistics? (c) Now calculate the median for each sample. (d) Make a dot plot for each sample. (e) What did you learn from the medians and dot plots that was not apparent from the means and standard deviations? (LO 3)

 Occupancy

Observation	Week 1	Week 2	Week 3	Week 4
1	32	33	38	37
2	41	35	39	42
3	44	45	39	45
4	47	50	40	46
5	50	52	56	47
6	53	54	57	48
7	56	58	58	50
8	59	59	61	67
9	68	64	62	68

4.60 (a) Enter the Excel function =ROUND(NORMINV(RAND(),70,10),0) in cells B1:B100. This will create 100 random data points from a normal distribution using parameters $\mu = 70$ and $\sigma = 10$. Think of these numbers as exam scores for 100 students. (b) Use the Excel functions =AVERAGE(B1:B100) and =STDEV(B1:B100) to calculate the sample mean and standard deviation for your data array. (c) Every time you press F9 you will get a new sample. Watch the sample statistics and compare them with the desired parameters $\mu = 70$ and $\sigma = 10$. Do Excel's random samples have approximately the desired characteristics? (d) Use Excel's =MIN(B1:B100) and =MAX(B1:B100) to find the range of your samples. Do the sample ranges look as you would expect from the Empirical Rule? (LO 3)

Grouped Data

Note: In each of the following tables, the upper bin limit is excluded from that bin, but is included as the lower limit of the next bin.

4.61 This table shows the fertility rate (children born per woman) in 191 world nations. (a) From the grouped data, calculate the mean, standard deviation, and coefficient of variation for each year. Show your calculations clearly in a worksheet. (b) Write a concise comparison of central tendency and dispersion for fertility rates in the two years. (c) What additional information would you have gained by having the raw data? (d) What benefit arises from having only a summary table? (e) Estimate the median, mode, and first quartile for each of the two years. (LO 4)

Fertility Rates in World Nations 🔵 **Fertile**

From	To	1990	2000
1.00	2.00	39	54
2.00	3.00	35	44
3.00	4.00	27	23
4.00	5.00	26	22
5.00	6.00	24	26
6.00	7.00	30	16
7.00	8.00	9	5
8.00	9.00	1	1
	Total	191	191

Source: World Health Organization.

4.62 This table shows the distribution of winning times in the Kentucky Derby over 74 years. Times are recorded to the nearest 1/5 second (e.g., 121.4). (a) From the grouped data, calculate the mean. Show your calculations clearly in a worksheet. (b) Estimate the median, mode, and third quartile. (c) What additional information would you have gained by having the raw data? (c) Do you think it likely that the distribution of times within each interval might not be uniform? Why would that matter? (LO 4)

Kentucky Derby Winning Times (seconds) 🔵 **Derby**

From	To	f
119	120	1
120	121	5
121	122	16
122	123	22
123	124	12
124	125	8
125	126	5
126	127	3
127	128	2
	Total	74

Source: *Sports Illustrated 2004 Sports Almanac.*

4.63 This table shows the life expectancy at birth (in years) in 153 world nations. (a) From the grouped data, calculate the mean, standard deviation, and coefficient of variation. Show your calculations clearly in a worksheet. (b) Write a concise summary of central tendency and dispersion for population increase in world nations. (c) What additional information would you have gained by having the raw data? (d) What is the advantage of having only a summary table? (LO 4)

Life Expectancy at Birth in Large Nations 🔵 **Life**

From	To	f
20	30	1
30	40	9
40	50	20
50	60	17
60	70	36
70	80	67
80	90	3
	Total	153

Source: U.S. Central Intelligence Agency, *The World Factbook, 2003.* Omits nations with population under 1 million.

4.64 The self-reported number of hours worked per week by 204 top executives is given below. (a) Estimate the mean, standard deviation, and coefficient of variation, using an Excel worksheet to organize your calculations. (b) Do the unequal class sizes hamper your calculations? Why do you suppose that was done? (LO 4)

Weekly Hours of Work by Top Executives	Work	
From	*To*	*f*
40	50	12
50	60	116
60	80	74
80	100	2
	Total	204

Source: Lamalie Associates, *Lamalie Report on Top Executives of the 1990s,* p. 11.

4.65 The table below shows the self-reported number of books read annually by 204 top executives. (a) Estimate the mean, standard deviation, and coefficient of variation, using an Excel worksheet to organize your calculations. (b) Do the unequal class sizes hamper your calculations? Why do you suppose that was done? (LO 4)

Books Read Annually by Top Executives	Books	
From	*To*	*f*
0	3	23
3	6	46
6	10	37
10	20	44
20	30	31
30	50	23
	Total	204

Source: Lamalie Associates, *Lamalie Report on Top Executives of the 1990s,* p. 12.

4.66 (a) Which sample statistics, if any, can you obtain from the following data on farm size? Explain. (b) Why were unequal class intervals and open-end classes used? (LO 4)

Distribution of U.S. Farms by Size (acres)	FarmSize	
From	*To*	*Number of Farms (000)*
0	10	154
10	50	411
50	100	295
100	180	298
180	260	165
260	500	238
500	1,000	176
1,000	2,000	101
2,000 and over		75
	Total	1,913

Source: U.S. Bureau of the Census, *Statistical Abstract of the United States,* 2002.

4.67 How long does it take to fly from Denver to Atlanta on Delta Airlines? The table below shows 56 observations on flight times (in minutes) for the first week of March 2005. (a) Use the grouped data formula to estimate the mean and standard deviation. (b) Using the ungrouped data (not shown) the *ungrouped* sample mean is 161.63 minutes and the ungrouped standard deviation is 8.07 minutes. How close did your *grouped* estimates come? (c) Why might flight times *not* be uniformly distributed within the second and third class intervals? (*Source:* www.bts.gov.) (LO 4)

Flight Times DEN to ATL (minutes)	DeltaAir	
From	*To*	*Frequency*
140	< 150	1
150	< 160	25
160	< 170	24
170	< 180	4
180	< 190	2
	Total	56

Do-It-Yourself Sampling

4.68 (a) Record the length (in minutes) of 50 movies chosen at random from a movie guide (e.g., Leonard Maltin's *Movie and Video Guide*). Include the name of each movie. (b) Make a dot plot. What does it tell you? (c) Make a frequency distribution and histogram. Describe the histogram. (d) Calculate the mean, median, and mode using the raw data and using the grouped data. Which is the best measure of central tendency? Why? (e) Calculate the standard deviation and coefficient of variation using the raw data and using the grouped data. (f) Standardize the data. Are there any outliers? (g) Find the quartiles and interquartile range using the raw data and using the grouped data. What do they tell you? (h) Make a box plot. What does it tell you? (LO 2, 3, 4 and 5)

Scatter Plots and Correlation

Note: Exercise 4.69 refers to data sets on the CD.

4.69 (a) Make an Excel scatter plot of $X =$ airspeed (nautical miles per hour) and $Y =$ cockpit noise level (decibels) for 61 aircraft flights. (b) Use Excel's =CORREL function to find the correlation coefficient. (c) What do the graph and correlation coefficient say about the relationship between airspeed and cockpit noise? Why might such a relationship exist? *Optional:* Fit an Excel trend line to the scatter plot and interpret it. (LO 3) **CockpitNoise**

Mini-Projects

4.70 (a) Choose a data set and prepare a brief, descriptive report. You may use any computer software you wish (e.g., Excel, MegaStat, Visual Statistics, MINITAB). Include relevant worksheets or graphs in your report. If some questions do not apply to your data set, explain why not. (b) Discuss any possible weaknesses in the data. (c) Sort the data. (d) Make a dot plot. What does it tell you? (e) Make a histogram. Describe its shape. (f) Calculate the mean, median, and mode(s) using raw data and using your grouped data and use them to describe central tendency for this data set. (g) Calculate the standard deviation and coefficient of variation using raw data and using your grouped data. (h) Standardize the data and check for outliers. (i) Compare the data with the Empirical Rule. Discuss. (j) Calculate the quartiles using raw data and using your grouped data and interpret them. (k) Make a box plot. Describe its appearance. (LO 3 & 4)

DATA SET A Advertising Dollars as Percent of Sales in Selected Industries (*n* = 30)		Ads	
Industry	*Percent*	*Industry*	*Percent*
Accident and health insurance	0.9	Jewellery stores	4.6
Apparel and other finished products	5.5	Management services	1.0
Beverages	7.4	Millwork, veneer, and plywood	3.5
Cable and pay TV services	1.3	Misc. furniture and fixtures	2.3
Computer data processing	1.1	Mortgage bankers and loans	4.9

Industry	Percent	Industry	Percent
Computer storage devices	1.8	Motorcycles, bicycles, and parts	1.7
Cookies and crackers	3.5	Paints, varnishes, lacquers	3.1
Drug and proprietary stores	0.9	Perfume and cosmetics	11.9
Electric housewares and fans	6.4	Photographic equipment	4.3
Equipment rental and leasing	2.0	Racing and track operations	2.5
Footwear except rubber	4.5	Real estate investment trusts	3.8
Greeting cards	3.5	Shoe stores	3.0
Grocery stores	1.1	Steel works and blast furnaces	1.9
Hobby, toy, and games shops	3.0	Tires and inner tubes	1.8
Ice cream and frozen desserts	2.0	Wine, brandy, and spirits	11.3

Source: George E. Belch and Michael A. Belch, *Advertising and Promotion*, pp. 219–220. Copyright © 2004 Richard D. Irwin. Used with permission of McGraw-Hill Companies, Inc.

DATA SET B Maximum Rate of Climb for Selected Piston Aircraft (*n* = 54) ClimbRate

Manufacturer/Model	Year	Climb (ft./min.)	Manufacturer/Model	Year	Climb (ft./min.)
AMD CH 2000	2000	820	Diamond C1 Eclipse	2002	1,000
Beech Baron 58	1984	1,750	Extra Extra 400	2000	1,400
Beech Baron 58P	1984	1,475	Lancair Columbia 300	1998	1,340
Beech Baron D55	1968	1,670	Liberty XL-2	2003	1,150
Beech Bonanza B36 TC	1982	1,030	Maule Comet	1996	920
Beech Duchess	1982	1,248	Mooney 231	1982	1,080
Beech Sierra	1972	862	Mooney Eagle M205	1999	1,050
Bellanca Super Viking	1973	1,840	Mooney M20C	1965	800
Cessna 152	1978	715	Mooney Ovation 2 M20R	2000	1,150
Cessna 170B	1953	690	OMF Aircraft Symphony	2002	850
Cessna 172 R Skyhawk	1997	720	Piper 125 Tri Pacer	1951	810
Cessna 172 RG Cutlass	1982	800	Piper Archer III	1997	667
Cessna 1825 Skylane	1997	865	Piper Aztec F	1980	1,480
Cessna 182Q Skylane	1977	1,010	Piper Dakota	1979	965
Cessna 310 R	1975	1,662	Piper Malibu Mirage	1998	1,218
Cessna 337G Skymotor II	1975	1,100	Piper Malibu Mirage	1989	1,218
Cessna 414A	1985	1,520	Piper Saratoga II TC	1998	818
Cessna 421B	1974	1,850	Piper Saratoga SP	1980	1,010
Cessna Cardinal	1970	840	Piper Seneca III	1982	1,400
Cessna P210	1982	945	Piper Seneca V	1997	1,455
Cessna T210K	1970	930	Piper Seneca V	2002	1,455
Cessna T303 Crusader	1983	1,480	Piper Super Cab	1975	960
Cessna Turbo Skylane RG	1979	1,040	Piper Turbo Lance	1979	1,000
Cessna Turbo Skylane T182T	2001	1,060	Rockwell Commander 114	1976	1,054
Cessna Turbo Stationair TU206	1981	1,010	Sky Arrow 650 TC	1998	750
Cessna U206H	1998	1,010	Socata TB20 Trinidad	1999	1,200
Cirrus SR20	1999	946	Tiger AG-5B	2002	850

Source: *Flying Magazine* (various issues from 1997 to 2002).

DATA SET C Caffeine Content of Randomly Selected Beverages ($n = 32$) 🔘 **Caffeine**

Company/Brand	mg/oz.	Company/Brand	mg/oz.
Barq's Root Beer	1.83	Mountain Dew	4.58
Coca-Cola Classic	2.83	Mr. Pibb	3.33
Cool from Nestea	1.33	Nestea Earl Grey	4.17
Cool from Nestea Raspberry Cooler	0.50	Nestea Peach	1.33
Diet A&W Cream Soda	1.83	Nestea Raspberry	1.33
Diet Ale 8	3.67	Nestea Sweet	2.17
Diet Code Red	4.42	Pepsi One	4.58
Diet Dr. Pepper	3.42	RC Edge	5.85
Diet Inca Kola	3.08	Royal Crown Cola	3.60
Diet Mountain Dew	4.58	Snapple Diet Peach Tea	2.63
Diet Mr. Pibb	3.33	Snapple Lemon Tea	2.63
Diet Pepsi-Cola	3.00	Snapple Lightning (Black Tea)	1.75
Inca Kola	3.08	Snapple Sun Tea	0.63
KMX (Blue)	0.00	Snapple Sweet Tea	1.00
Mello Yello Cherry	4.25	Sunkist Orange Soda	3.42
Mello Yello Melon	4.25	Vanilla Coke	2.83

Source: National Soft Drink Association (www.nsda.org).

DATA SET D Super Bowl Scores 1967–2007 ($n = 41$ games) 🔘 **SuperBowl**

Year	Teams and Scores	Year	Teams and Scores
1967	Green Bay 35, Kansas City 10	1988	Washington 42, Denver 10
1968	Green Bay 33, Oakland 14	1989	San Francisco 20, Cincinnati 16
1969	NY Jets 16, Baltimore 7	1990	San Francisco 55, Denver 10
1970	Kansas City 23, Minnesota 7	1991	NY Giants 20, Buffalo 19
1971	Baltimore 16, Dallas 13	1992	Washington 37, Buffalo 24
1972	Dallas 24, Miami 3	1993	Dallas 52, Buffalo 17
1973	Miami 14, Washington 7	1994	Dallas 30, Buffalo 13
1974	Miami 24, Minnesota 7	1995	San Francisco 49, San Diego 26
1975	Pittsburgh 16, Minnesota 6	1996	Dallas 27, Pittsburgh 17
1976	Pittsburgh 21, Dallas 17	1997	Green Bay 35, New England 21
1977	Oakland 32, Minnesota 14	1998	Denver 31, Green Bay 24
1978	Dallas 27, Denver 10	1999	Denver 34, Atlanta 19
1979	Pittsburgh 35, Dallas 31	2000	St. Louis 23, Tennessee 16
1980	Pittsburgh 31, LA Rams 19	2001	Baltimore 34, New York 7
1981	Oakland 27, Philadelphia 10	2002	New England 20, St. Louis 17
1982	San Francisco 26, Cincinnati 21	2003	Tampa Bay 48, Oakland 21
1983	Washington 27, Miami 17	2004	New England 32, Carolina 29
1984	LA Raiders 38, Washington 9	2005	New England 24, Philadelphia 21
1985	San Francisco 38, Miami 16	2006	Pittsburgh 21, Seattle 10
1986	Chicago 46, New England 10	2007	Indianapolis 29, Chicago 17
1987	NY Giants 39, Denver 20		

Source: *Sports Illustrated 2004 Sports Almanac, Detroit Free Press,* and www.cbs.sportsline.com.

LearningStats Unit 04   Describing Data   LS

LearningStats Unit 04 uses interesting data sets, samples, and simulations to illustrate the tools of data analysis. Your instructor may assign a specific project, but you can work on the others if they sound interesting.

Topic	*LearningStats Modules*
Overview	Describing Data
	Using MegaStat
	Using Visual Statistics
	Using MINITAB
Descriptive statistics	Basic Statistics
	Quartiles
	Box Plots
	Coefficient of Variation
	Grouped Data
	Stacked Data
	Skewness
Case studies	Brad's Bowling Scores
	Aircraft Cockpit Noise
	Batting Averages
	Bridget Jones's Diary
	Sample Variation
	Sampling NYSE Stocks
Sampling methods	Simple Random Sampling
	Systematic Sampling
	Cluster Sampling
Student projects	College Tuition
	Per Capita Income
Formulas	Table of Formulas
	Significant Digits

Key: = PowerPoint   = Word   = Excel

Visual Statistics   VS

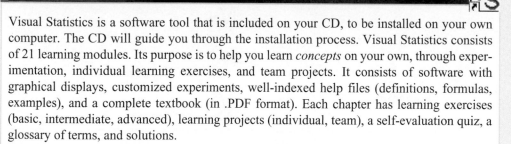

Visual Statistics is a software tool that is included on your CD, to be installed on your own computer. The CD will guide you through the installation process. Visual Statistics consists of 21 learning modules. Its purpose is to help you learn *concepts* on your own, through experimentation, individual learning exercises, and team projects. It consists of software with graphical displays, customized experiments, well-indexed help files (definitions, formulas, examples), and a complete textbook (in .PDF format). Each chapter has learning exercises (basic, intermediate, advanced), learning projects (individual, team), a self-evaluation quiz, a glossary of terms, and solutions.

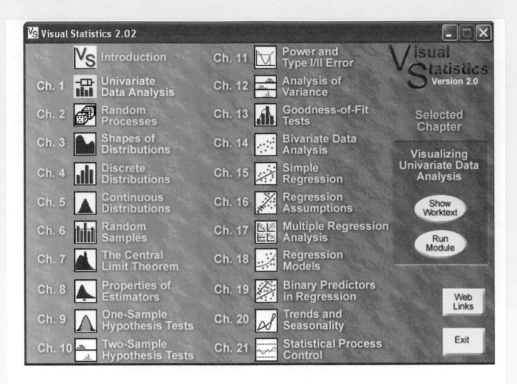

Visual Statistics modules 1, 3, and 6 are designed to help you

- Recognize and interpret different types of histograms (frequency, cumulative, relative).
- Realize how histogram setup can affect one's perception of the data.
- Be able to visualize common shape measures (centrality, dispersion, skewness).
- Recognize discrete and continuous random variables.
- Learn to infer a population's shape, mean, and standard deviation from a sample.
- See how outliers affect histograms.

Visual Statistics Modules on Describing Data

Module	Module Name
1	**Vs** Univariate Data Analysis
3	**Vs** Shapes of Distributions
6	**Vs** Random Samples

MegaStat for Excel by J. B. Orris of Butler University is an Excel add-in that is included on the CD, to be installed on your own computer. The CD will guide you through the installation process. MegaStat goes beyond Excel's built-in statistical functions to offer a full range of statistical tools to help you analyze data, create graphs, and perform calculations. MegaStat examples are shown throughout this textbook.

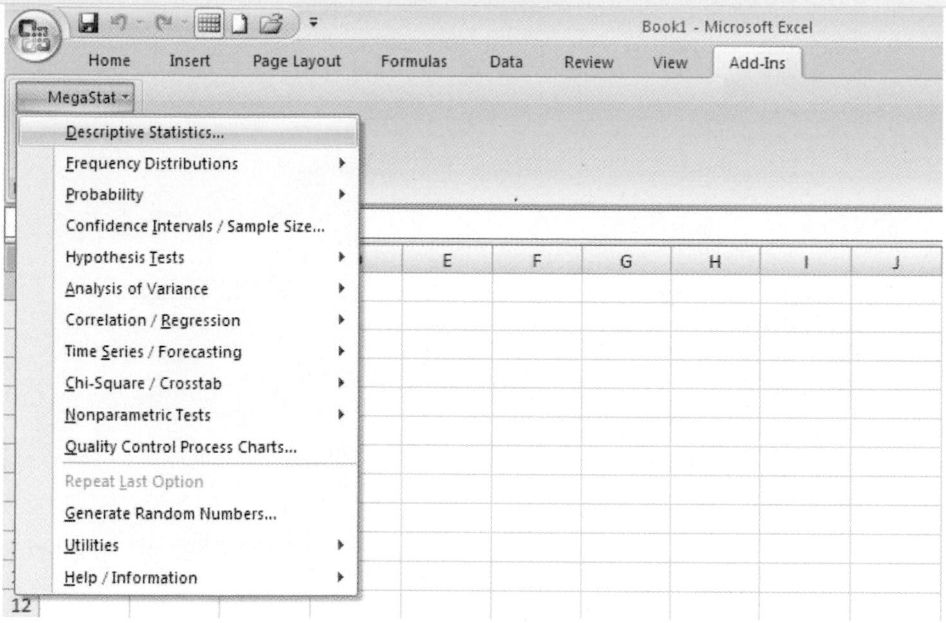

After installing MegaStat, you should see MegaStat appear on the left when you click the Add-Ins tab on the top menu bar (right side in the illustration above). If not, click the Office icon in the upper left and then click the Excel Options button (yellow highlight in the illustration below). At the bottom, find **Manage Excel Add-Ins**, click the Go button, and check the MegaStat add-in box. The CD includes further instructions.

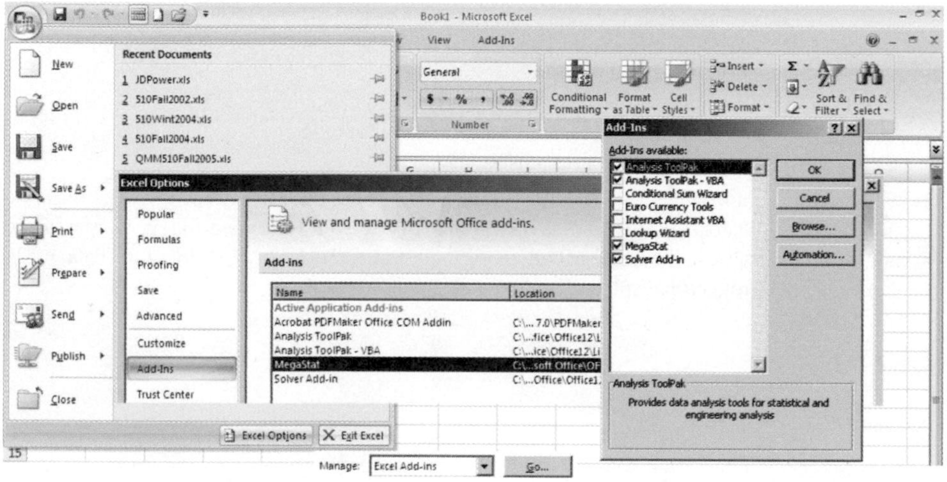

1. Which type of statistic (descriptive, inferential) is each of the following?
   a. Estimating the default rate on all Canadian mortgages from a random sample of 500 loans.
   b. Reporting the percent of students in your statistics class who use TELUS.
   c. Using a sample of 50 iPhones to predict the average battery life in typical usage.

2. Which is *not* an ethical obligation of a statistician? Explain.
   a. To know and follow accepted procedures.
   b. To ensure data integrity and accurate calculations.
   c. To support client wishes in drawing conclusions from the data.

EXAM REVIEW QUESTIONS FOR CHAPTERS 1–4

3. "Driving without a seat belt is not risky. I've done it for 25 years without an accident." This *best* illustrates which fallacy?
   a. Unconscious bias.
   b. Conclusion from a small sample.
   c. *Post hoc* reasoning.

4. Which data type (categorical, numerical) is each of the following?
   a. Your current credit card balance.
   b. Your university major.
   c. Your car's odometer reading today.

5. Give the type of measurement (nominal, ordinal, interval, ratio) for each variable.
   a. Length of time required for a randomly chosen vehicle to cross a toll bridge.
   b. Student's ranking of five cellphone service providers.
   c. The type of charge card used by a customer (Visa, MasterCard, American Express, other).

6. Tell if each variable is continuous or discrete.
   a. Tonnage carried by an oil tanker at sea.
   b. Wind velocity at 7 o'clock this morning.
   c. Number of text messages you received yesterday.

7. To choose a sample of 12 students from a statistics class of 36 students, which type of sample (simple random, systematic, cluster, convenience) is each of these?
   a. Picking every student who was wearing blue that day.
   b. Using Excel's =RANDBETWEEN(1,36) to choose students from the class list.
   c. Selecting every third student starting from a randomly chosen position.

8. Which of the following is *not* a reason for sampling? Explain.
   a. The destructive nature of some tests.
   b. High cost of studying the entire population.
   c. Bias inherent in Excel's random numbers.

9. Which statement is *correct?* Why not the others?
   a. Likert scales are interval if scale distances are meaningful.
   b. Cross-sectional data are measured over time.
   c. A census is always preferable to a sample.

10. Which statement is *false?* Explain.
    a. Sampling error can be reduced by using appropriate data coding.
    b. Selection bias means that respondents are not typical of the target population.
    c. Simple random sampling requires a list of the population.

11. The management of a theme park obtained a random sample of the ages of 36 riders of its Space Adventure Simulator. (a) Make a nice histogram. (b) Did your histogram follow Sturges' Rule? If not, why not? (c) Describe the distribution of sample data. (d) Make a dot plot of the data. (e) What can be learned from each display (dot plot and histogram)?

39	46	15	38	39	47	50	61	17
40	54	36	16	18	34	42	10	16
16	13	38	14	16	56	17	18	53
24	17	12	21	8	18	13	13	10

12. Which one of the following is *true?* Why not the others?
    a. Histograms are useful for visualizing correlations.
    b. Pyramid charts are generally preferred to bar charts.
    c. A correlation coefficient can be negative.

13. Which data would be most suitable for a pie chart? Why not the others?
    a. Leader vote in the last election by party (Liberal, Conservative, NDP, Green Party, other).
    b. Retail prices of six major brands of colour laser printers.
    c. Labour cost per vehicle for 10 major world automakers.

14. Find the mean, standard deviation, and coefficient of variation for $X = 5, 10, 20, 10, 15$.

15. Here are the ages of a random sample of 20 CEOs of Fortune 500 U.S. corporations. (a) Find the mean, median, and mode. (b) Discuss advantages and disadvantages of each of these measures of central tendency for this data set. (c) Find the quartiles and interpret them. (d) Sketch a box plot and describe it. (Source: http://www.forbes.com.)

57	56	58	46	70	62	55	60	59	64
62	67	61	55	53	58	63	51	52	77

16. A consulting firm used a random sample of 12 CIOs (Chief Information Officers) of large businesses to examine the relationship (if any) between salary and years service in the firm. (a) Make a scatter plot and describe it. (b) Calculate a correlation coefficient and interpret it.

Years (X)	4	15	15	8	11	5	5	8	10	1	6	17
Salary (Y)	133	129	143	132	144	61	128	79	140	116	88	170

17. Which statement is *true?* Why not the other?
  a. We expect the median to exceed the mean in positively skewed data.
  b. The geometric mean is not helpful when there are negative data values.

18. Which statement is *false?* Explain.
  a. If $\mu = 52$ and $\sigma = 15$, then $X = 81$ would be an outlier.
  b. If the data are from a normal population, about 68 percent of the values will be within $\mu \pm \sigma$.
  c. If $\mu = 640$ and $\sigma = 128$ then the coefficient of variation is 20 percent.

19. Which is a *not* characteristic of using a log scale to display time series data? Explain.
  a. A log scale helps if we are comparing changes in two time series of dissimilar magnitude.
  b. General business audiences find it easier to interpret a log scale.
  c. If you display data on a log scale, equal distances represent equal ratios.

McGraw Hill connect™   For solutions to odd-numbered exercises, Exam Review questions, and additional study tools to help you succeed in this course, visit *Connect* at www.mcgrawhillconnect.ca.

Chapter

5

Probability

Chapter Learning Objectives

When you finish this chapter you should be able to

1. Construct sample spaces.

2. Distinguish among the three views of probability.

3. Apply counting rules to calculate possible event arrangements and probabilities.

4. Know when and how to apply the definitions and rules of probability and odds in a problem context.

5. Distinguish between independent, mutually exclusive, or other dependent events.

6. Know when and how to apply Venn diagrams, contingency tables, and probability trees to determine probabilities.

7. Use Bayes' Theorem to calculate revised probabilities.

You've learned that a statistic is a measurement that describes a sample data set of observations. Descriptive statistics allow us to describe a business process that we have already observed. But how will that process behave in the future? Nothing makes a business person more nervous than not being able to anticipate customer demand, supplier delivery dates, or their employees' output. Businesses want to be able to quantify the *uncertainty* of future events. What are the chances that revenue next month will exceed last year's average? How likely is it that our new production system will help us decrease our product defect rate? Businesses also want to understand how they can increase the chance of positive future events (increasing market share) and decrease the chance of negative future events (failing to meet forecasted sales). The field of study called *probability* allows us to understand and quantify the uncertainty about the future. We use the rules of probability to bridge the gap between what we know now and what is unknown about the future.

5.1   Random Experiments

Sample Space

A **random experiment** is an observational process whose results cannot be known in advance. For example, when a customer enters a Lexus dealership, will the customer buy a car or not? How much will the customer spend? The set of all possible *outcomes* (denoted S) is the **sample space** for the experiment. A sample space with a countable number of outcomes is *discrete*. Some discrete sample spaces can be enumerated easily, while others may be immense or impossible to enumerate. For example, when the Bank of Montreal makes a consumer loan, we might define a sample space with only two outcomes:

$$S = \{\text{default, no default}\}$$

The sample space describing a Walmart customer's payment method might have four outcomes:

$$S = \{\text{cash, debit card, credit card, cheque}\}$$

The sample spaces of some random experiments may be described in more than one possible way. For example, the sample space for randomly selecting one card from a deck of 52 playing cards could be described as

$$S = \{\text{Ace, 2, 3, 4, 5, 6, 7, 8, 9, 10, Jack, Queen, King}\}$$

or

$$S = \{\text{spade, heart, diamond, club}\}$$

or

$$S = \{\text{A}\spadesuit, 2\spadesuit, \ldots, \text{Q}\clubsuit, \text{K}\clubsuit\}$$

Choice of the sample space depends on what probabilities concern you. If you are only interested in probabilities concerning the denomination of the selected card, the initial sample space is all you need. If you are only interesting in probabilities concerning the suit of the selected card, the second sample space is all you need. The third sample space can be used no matter which probabilities concern you and, thus, may be the preferred sample space.

No matter which sample space you use to determine the relevant probabilities, the sample space must consist of mutually exclusive (i.e., no more than one of the outcomes can occur in the same random experiment) and collectively exhaustive (i.e., the sample space must consist of all possible outcomes). As we will shortly see, if each of the outcomes in the sample space has the same likelihood or *probability* of occurring, it is often easier to determine the probability of a subset of these outcomes occurring by simply counting how many outcomes are in the subset and how many outcomes are in the sample space.

The sample space to describe rolling a die has six outcomes:

When two dice are rolled, the sample space consists of 36 outcomes, each of which is an ordered pair:

Second Die

	(1,1)	(1,2)	(1,3)	(1,4)	(1,5)	(1,6)
	(2,1)	(2,2)	(2,3)	(2,4)	(2,5)	(2,6)
First Die	(3,1)	(3,2)	(3,3)	(3,4)	(3,5)	(3,6)
	(4,1)	(4,2)	(4,3)	(4,4)	(4,5)	(4,6)
	(5,1)	(5,2)	(5,3)	(5,4)	(5,5)	(5,6)
	(6,1)	(6,2)	(6,3)	(6,4)	(6,5)	(6,6)

A sample space could be so large that it is impractical to enumerate all possibilities (e.g., the 12-digit UPC bar code on a product in your local Walmart could have 1 trillion values). If the outcome of the experiment is a *continuous* measurement, the sample space cannot be listed, but can be described by a rule. For example, the sample space for the length of a randomly chosen cellphone call would be

$$S = \{\text{all } X \text{ such that } X \geq 0\}$$

and the sample space to describe a randomly chosen student's GPA would be

$$S = \{\text{all } X \text{ such that } 0.00 \leq X \leq 4.00\}$$

Similarly, some discrete measurements are best described by a rule. For example, the sample space for the number of hits on a YouTube Web site on a given day is

$$S = \{X = 0, 1, 2, \ldots\}$$

Event

An **event** is any subset of outcomes in the sample space. A **simple event,** or *elementary event,* is a single outcome. A discrete sample space S consists of all the simple events, denoted $E_1, E_2, \ldots, E_n$.

$$S = \{E_1, E_2, \ldots, E_n\} \tag{5.1}$$

Consider the random experiment of tossing a balanced coin. The sample space for this experiment would be $S = \{\text{head, tail}\}$. The chance of observing a head is the same as the chance of observing a tail. We say that these two elementary events are *equally likely*. When you buy a lottery ticket, the sample space $S = \{\text{win, lose}\}$ also has two elementary events; however, these events are not equally likely.

Simple events are the building blocks from which we can define a **compound event** consisting of two or more simple events. For example, Amazon's Web site for "Books & Music" has seven categories that a shopper might choose: $S = \{\text{Books, DVD, VHS, Magazines, Newspapers, Music, Textbooks}\}$. Within this sample space, we could define compound events "electronic media" as $A = \{\text{Music, DVD, VHS}\}$ and "print periodicals" as $B = \{\text{Newspapers, Magazines}\}$. This can be shown in a **Venn diagram** like Figure 5.1.

Note: For those unfamiliar with Venn diagrams, Venn diagrams depict the sample space. The rectangle encloses all simple events in the sample space while the various shapes within this rectangle enclose all simple events that are part of the various compound events. If you visualize the sizes of the rectangle and the various shapes as representing the appropriate probabilities, it may be easier for you to understand some of the probability rules that will be discussed and used in this chapter.

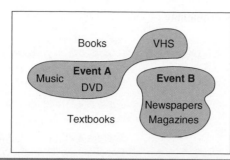

FIGURE 5.1

**Venn Diagram for Two
Compound Events**

Section Exercises

5.1   A credit card customer at Chapters can use Visa (*V*), MasterCard (*M*), or American Express (*A*). The merchandise may be books (*B*), electronic media (*E*), or other (*O*). (a) Enumerate the elementary events in the sample space describing a customer's purchase. (b) Would each elementary event be equally likely? Explain. (LO 1)

5.2   A survey asked tax accounting firms their business form (*S* = sole proprietorship, *P* = partnership, *C* = corporation) and the type of risk insurance they carry (*L* = liability only, *T* = property loss only, *B* = both liability and property). (a) Enumerate the elementary events in the sample space. (b) Would each elementary event be equally likely? Explain. (LO 1)

5.3   A baseball player bats either left-handed (*L*) or right-handed (*R*). The player either gets on base (*B*) or does not get on base (*B'*). (a) Enumerate the elementary events in the sample space. (b) Would these elementary events be equally likely? Explain. (LO 1)

5.4   A die is thrown (1, 2, 3, 4, 5, 6) and a coin is tossed (*H, T*). (a) Enumerate the elementary events in the sample space for the die/coin combination. (b) Are the elementary events equally likely? Explain. (LO 1)

5.5   A card is randomly selected from a deck of 52 playing cards. Determine if the elementary events are equally likely if we describe the sample space as

(a) S = {Ace, 2, 3, 4, 5, 6, 7, 8, 9, 10, Jack, Queen, King}
(b) S = {spade, heart, diamond, club}
(c) S = {A♠, 2♠, . . . , Q♣, K♣}

Explain. (LO 1)

5.2   Probability

The concept of probability is so familiar to most people that it can easily be misused. Therefore, we begin with some precise definitions and a few rules.

Definitions

The **probability** of an event is a number that measures the relative likelihood that the event will occur. The probability of an event *A,* denoted $P(A)$, must lie within the interval from 0 to 1:

$$0 \leq P(A) \leq 1 \tag{5.2}$$

$P(A) = 0$ means the event cannot occur while $P(A) = 1$ means the event is certain to occur. In a discrete sample space, the probabilities of all simple events must sum to 1, because it is certain that one of them will occur:

$$P(S) = P(E_1) + P(E_2) + \ldots + P(E_n) = 1 \tag{5.3}$$

For example, for a Walmart customer's payment method, if 32 percent of purchases are made by credit card, 15 percent by debit card, 35 percent by cash, and 18 percent by cheque, then

$$P(\text{credit card}) + P(\text{debit card}) + P(\text{cash}) + P(\text{cheque}) = 0.32 + 0.15 + 0.35 + 0.18 = 1$$

What Is "Probability"?

There are three distinct ways of assigning probability, listed in Table 5.1. Many people mix them up or use them interchangeably; however, each approach must be considered separately.

TABLE 5.1 **Three Views of Probability**

Approach	Example
Empirical	There is a 2 percent chance of twins in a randomly chosen birth.
Classical	There is a 50 percent chance of heads on a fair coin flip.
Subjective	There is a 20 percent chance that the Montreal Canadians will win the Stanley Cup in 2010.

Researchers at MIT prove that rolling shopping carts will almost invariably hit the most expensive car in their vicinity.

© 2005 John McPherson/Dist. by Universal Press Syndicate.

Empirical Approach

Sometimes we can collect empirical data through observations or experiments. We can use the **empirical** or **relative frequency approach** to assign probabilities by counting the frequency of observed outcomes (*f*) defined in our experimental sample space and dividing by the number of observations (*n*). For example, we could estimate the reliability of a bar code scanner:

$$P(\text{a missed scan}) = \frac{\text{number of missed scans}}{\text{number of items scanned}}$$

or the default rate on student loans:

$$P(\text{a student defaults}) = \frac{\text{number of defaults}}{\text{number of loans}}$$

Empirical estimation is necessary when we have no prior knowledge of how the random experiment works. As we increase the number of observations (*n*) or the number of times we perform the experiment, our estimate will become more and more accurate. We use the ratio *f/n*, where *f* is the frequency (the number of times the event occurs), to represent the probability. Here are some examples of empirical probabilities:

- An industrial components manufacturer interviewed 280 production workers before hiring 70 of them. (See the *Wall Street Journal,* Sept. 25, 2006.)

A = event that a randomly chosen interviewee is hired

$$P(A) = \frac{70}{280} = 0.25$$

- Over 20 years, a medical malpractice insurer saw only one claim for "wrong-site" surgery (e.g., amputating the wrong limb) in 112,994 malpractice claims. (*Source:* AHRQ, *Research Activities,* no. 308, Apr. 2006, p. 1.)

B = event that malpractice claim is for wrong-site surgery

$$P(B) = \frac{1}{112,994} = 0.00000885$$

- On average, 2,118 out of 100,000 Americans live to age 100 or older. (*Source:* www.cdc.gov/nchs/data/)

C = event that a randomly chosen American lives to 100 or older

$$P(C) = \frac{2,118}{100,000} = 0.02118$$

A Closer Look

Suppose we give you a coin and ask you what the chances are of heads on the coin flip. Is it 50 percent? Most of you would think so. But think again! You just assumed that the coin was fair or balanced. But how do you verify that? You have to use an empirical approach to verify the fairness of this coin. If, after a large number of replications of the experiment of flipping a coin, the relative frequency of heads is somewhat close to 0.5 (e.g., 0.515), we can assume that the coin is balanced or fair and that P(head) = 0.5. If, after these replications, the relative frequency of heads is quite different than 0.5 (e.g., 0.375), we would question the coin's fairness and use the relative frequency of heads as an estimate of P(head) (e.g., P(head) = 0.375).

Classical Approach

When flipping a balanced coin or rolling a pair of fair dice, we do not actually have to perform an experiment, because the nature of the process allows us to envision the entire sample space as a collection of equally likely outcomes. We can use deduction to determine $P(A)$. Statisticians use the term *a priori* to refer to the process of assigning probabilities *before* we actually observe the event. For example, the two-dice experiment shown in Figure 5.2 has 36 equally likely simple events, so the probability of rolling a seven is

$$P(A) = \frac{\text{number of outcomes with 7 dots}}{\text{number of outcomes in sample space}} = \frac{6}{36} = 0.1667$$

The probability is obtained *a priori* without actually doing an experiment. This is the **classical approach** to probability. Such calculations are rarely possible in business situations although the ever-growing business of casino gaming is one of those rare exceptions. Every bet that one makes at a casino has an outcome: a win or loss for the gambler and, equivalently,

(1,1)	(1,2)	(1,3)	(1,4)	(1,5)	(1,6)
(2,1)	(2,2)	(2,3)	(2,4)	(2,5)	(2,6)
(3,1)	(3,2)	(3,3)	(3,4)	(3,5)	(3,6)
(4,1)	(4,2)	(4,3)	(4,4)	(4,5)	(4,6)
(5,1)	(5,2)	(5,3)	(5,4)	(5,5)	(5,6)
(6,1)	(6,2)	(6,3)	(6,4)	(6,5)	(6,6)

FIGURE 5.2

Venn Diagram for Two Dice   DiceRolls

a loss or win for the casino. For most games of chance, the probability of a win or loss is known, at least by the casino, a priori, because it has knowledge of the game. And because it has this knowledge, it can determine, as will be illustrated in the next chapter, how much money the gambler will win if he/she indeed is fortunate to win the bet.

Subjective Approach

A *subjective* probability reflects someone's personal judgment about the likelihood of an event. The **subjective approach** to probability is needed when there is no repeatable random experiment. For example:

- What is the probability that Toyota's new supplier of plastic fasteners will be able to meet the September 23 shipment deadline?
- What is the probability that a new truck product program will show a return on investment of at least 10 percent?
- What is the probability that the price of Toyota stock will rise within the next 30 days?

In such cases, we rely on personal judgment or expert opinion. However, such a judgment is not random, because it is typically based on experience with similar events and knowledge of the underlying causal processes. Assessing the Toronto Maple Leafs' chances of winning the Stanley Cup next year would be an example. Thus, subjective probabilities have something in common with empirical probabilities, although their empirical basis is informal and not quantified.

Section Exercises

Instructions for Exercises 5.6–5.11: (a) Which kind of probability is it (empirical, classical, subjective)? (b) How do you think it would have been derived?

5.6 "There is a 20 percent chance that a new stock offered in an initial public offering (IPO) will reach or exceed its target price on the first day." (LO 2)

5.7 "There is a 50 percent chance that Rogers and Fido will merge." (LO 2)

5.8 "Commercial rocket launches have a 95 percent success rate." (LO 2)

5.9 "The probability of rolling three sevens in a row with two dice is 0.0046." (LO 2)

5.10 "On a given day, there is about 1 chance in 100,000 that the International Space Station will be critically damaged by a piece of orbiting debris." (See *The New York Times,* May 9, 2007, p. A15.) (LO 2)

5.11 "More than 30 percent of the results from major search engines for the keyword phrase 'ring tone' are fake pages created by spammers." (See *The New York Times,* Mar. 19, 2007, p. C4.) (LO 2)

5.3   Probability and Counting Rules

Before looking at the various probability rules for determining the probabilities of specific events occurring, let's see whether you can intuitively determine the probabilities of various events.

EXAMPLE 1

Potential Lexus Buyers

Suppose a Lexus dealership kept information on the last 250 customers who entered its dealership with the intent of purchasing of one of its vehicles. It characterized each customer by whether or not he/she bought a vehicle and by their demographics (younger male, older male, younger female, older female). It then summarized the results in the following table (which will be referred to as a contingency table later in this chapter).

	Younger Male	Older Male	Younger Female	Older Female	Totals
Bought	19	43	7	14	83
Did Not Buy	51	52	28	36	167
Totals	70	95	35	50	250

If one of these 250 customers were randomly chosen for some marketing study, what is the probability that this chosen customer

a. Is a younger male?
b. Bought a Lexus?
c. Is a younger male and bought a Lexus?
d. Is a younger male or bought a Lexus?
e. Is a female (i.e., a younger female or an older female)?
f. Is a younger female and an older female?
g. Bought a Lexus knowing that this person is a younger female?
h. Is a younger female knowing that this person bought a Lexus?

Solutions

Intuition should tell you that if a customer is randomly chosen, each customer has one chance in 250 of being chosen for this study (unless we have some previous information about that customer such as that the customer is a female), and

a. Because there are 70 (i.e., $19 + 51$) younger males out of a total of 250 individuals, the probability of that person being a younger male is 70/250 or 0.28.
b. Because there are 83 (i.e., $19 + 43 + 7 + 14$) out of 250 who bought a Lexus, the probability of that person having bought a Lexus is 83/250 or 0.332.
c. Because there are only 19 individuals who are younger males and who bought a Lexus, the probability of that individual being a younger male and buying a Lexus is 19/250 or 0.076.
d. Because there are 134 individuals (i.e., $19 + 43 + 7 + 14 + 51$) who are either younger males or who bought a Lexus, the probability of that individual being a younger male or buying a Lexus is 134/250 or 0.536.
e. Because there are 85 females (i.e., $35 + 50$), the probability of that person being a female is 85/250 or 0.34.
f. Because there is no individual who is a younger female and an older female, the probability of that individual being a younger female and an older female is zero.
g. Here we have additional information about this individual. We know that this person is a younger female, so we now only have to look at the 35 younger females, of which only 7 have bought a Lexus. Using this information, the probability that the selected individual had bought a Lexus knowing (or given that) that she is a female is 7/35 or 0.20.
h. As with our previous answer, we have additional information that this individual had bought a Lexus. There are 83 of these individuals in our database of which 7 are younger females. Using this information, the probability that the individual is a younger female knowing (or given that) this person will buy a Lexus is 7/83 or 0.0843.

A Closer Look

When trying to determine the probability of some event occurring, it is very important to understand what that particular event is. For example, the event that a person is a young male and bought a Lexus is much different than the event that a person is a young male or bought a Lexus. Although you are familiar with the words "and" and "or," you may forget what these words mean when determining the appropriate event. To be a young male and to have bought a Lexus means that this person has to be both a young male and has to have bought a Lexus. To be a young male or bought a Lexus means that this person only has to be a young male or only has to have bought a Lexus, or both, but not necessarily both.

For each of the above questions, we determined their probabilities by counting and applying the following simple probability rule:

If there are n equally likely outcomes in the sample space of some random experiment and if an event A consists of k of these outcomes,

$$P(A) = \frac{k}{n}$$

While in some cases, k and n may be obvious, in many situations they are not. Therefore, in order to determine the required probabilities, we may need to be able to count how many outcomes there are in the sample space and in the event of interest, A. In other situations, we may want to be able to count for some other reasons.

Counting Rules

Fundamental Rule of Counting If some event A consists of m characteristics with each characteristic i having n_i possible categories, and if we choose one category from each of the characteristics, the number of ways that event A can occur is

$$n_1 \cdot n_2 \cdot \cdots \cdot n_m$$

And if each characteristic has the same number of possible categories, n, the number of ways that event A can occur is n multiplied with itself m times:

$$\underbrace{n \cdot n \cdot \cdots \cdot n = n^m}_{m \text{ times}}$$

EXAMPLE 2

Do-It-Yourselfer Products

There are many stores in Canada today that sell everything-included kits that allow do-it-yourselfers to build their own projects, giving them both satisfaction and cost savings. A new type of store, also for do-it-yourselfers, has expanded on this idea by allowing the customer a variety of choices for each component that make up these kits without having to stock each possible combination of choices. It does so by selling the individual components and allowing the customer to customize his or her kit. One such kit consists of six components when completed. The first component has five possible choices, the second has three possible choices, the third has four possible choices, the fourth has seven possible choices, the fifth has three possible choices and the sixth has nine possible choices. How many different possible unique kits could be created out of these component choices? What is the probability that a customer would want one specific combination?

Here, the $(n_1)(n_2) \cdots (n_m)$ rule applies where $m = 6$ (the number of components), with the n_i's being the number of choices within each of the various components. Using this rule,

$$(n_1)(n_2) \cdots (n_m) = (5)(3)(4)(7)(3)(9) = 11{,}340$$

Obviously, there is an advantage to using this store's strategy. Instead of having to stock 11,340 different kits to satisfy any customer's wants if the kits were pre-packaged, the store only has to stock 31 different component types.

To answer the probability that the customer would want one specific combination using this counting rule, we would have to assume each combination is equally preferred. If that is the case,

$$P(A) = \frac{k}{n} = \frac{1}{11{,}340} \approx 0.0000818$$

EXAMPLE 3

Harvey's Variety

Years ago, Harvey's put a placemat on its trays that said that there were 1,024 ways to eat a Harvey's hamburger based on the toppings a customer wanted. At that time Harvey's had 10 different toppings. Today, if Harvey's offers 15 different toppings, how many ways can a customer eat one of its hamburgers?

In this example it may not be that obvious what the characteristics are or what the categories are within each characteristic. Here the characteristics are each topping (e.g., mustard) or $m = 15$, and the categories within each characteristic are "yes" and "no" (e.g., yes, I want mustard; no, I don't want mustard) or $n = 2$. Because the number of categories are the same, the n^m version of the rule applies and

$$n^m = 2^{15} = 32{,}768$$

(Obviously, with so many possibilities, Harvey's wouldn't want to "pre-package" their hamburgers ahead of time. A customer can eat a Harvey's hamburger each and every day for approximately 90 years and not duplicate the taste sensations!)

Concept Check

Suppose only 10 different toppings were available, but there were three possibilities for each topping—none, regular amount, extra amount. How many ways can a customer order a Harvey's hamburger? What would be the probability of an individual ordering a hamburger with one specific set of toppings?

FIGURE 5.3
Choosing *n* Items

Factorials

The number of unique ways that *n* items can be arranged in a particular order is *n* **factorial,** the product of all integers from 1 to *n*:

$$n! = n(n - 1)(n - 2) \cdots 1$$

This rule is useful for counting the possible arrangements of any *n* items. There are *n* ways to choose the first item, *n* − 1 ways to choose the second item, and so on until we reach the last item, as illustrated in Figure 5.3. By definition, $0! = 1$.

EXAMPLE 4
Truck Routing

In very small problems we can actually count the possibilities. For example, a home appliance service truck must make three stops (*A, B, C*). In how many ways could the three stops be arranged? There are six possible arrangements: *ABC, ACB, BAC, BCA, CAB, CBA*. But if all we want is the *number of possibilities* without listing them all, then we can use factorials:

$$3! = 3 \times 2 \times 1 = 6$$

Even in moderate-sized problems, listing all the possibilities is not feasible. For example, the number of possible arrangements of nine baseball players in a batting-order rotation is

$$9! = 9 \times 8 \times 7 \times 6 \times 5 \times 4 \times 3 \times 2 \times 1 = 362{,}880$$

Permutations

Suppose we want to choose and arrange *r* items at random without replacement from a group of *n* items. In how many ways can this be done, treating each arrangement as a different event (i.e., treating the three-letter sequence *XYZ* as different from the three-letter sequence *ZYX*)? A **permutation** is an arrangement of the *r* sample items *in a particular order.* How many such arrangements are possible? Because we have *n* items to choose from, there are *n* different ways to choose the first item. For every one of these *n* choices for the first item, there are (*n* − 1) choices for the second item, and so on. Hence the number of possible permutations of *n* items taken *r* at a time, denoted as $_nP_r$, is

$$_nP_r = n(n - 1) \cdots (n - r + 1) = \frac{n!}{(n - r)!} \tag{5.4}$$

Permutations are used when we are interested in finding how many possible arrangements there are when we select *r* items from *n* items, when each possible arrangement of items is considered different.

EXAMPLE 5
Appliance Service Calls

Five home appliance customers (*A, B, C, D, E*) need service calls, but the field technician can service only three of them before noon. The order in which they are serviced is important (to the customers, anyway) so each possible arrangement of three service calls is different. The dispatcher must assign the sequence. The number of possible permutations is

$$_nP_r = \frac{n!}{(n - r)!} = \frac{5!}{(5 - 3)!} = \frac{5 \cdot 4 \cdot 3 \cdot 2 \cdot 1}{2!} = \frac{120}{2} = 60$$

Concept Check

This may seem a surprisingly large number, but it can be enumerated. There are 10 distinct groups of three customers (two customers must be omitted):

ABC ABD ABE ACD ACE ADE BCD BCE BDE CDE

Within each group of three customers, there are six different ways to arrange the three customers. For example, the first distinct set of customers {*A, B, C*} could be arranged in six distinct ways:

ABC ACB CAB CBA BAC BCA

We could do the same for each of the other nine groups of three customers. Because there are 10 distinct groups of three customers and six possible arrangements per group, there are $10 \times 6 = 60$ permutations. Clearly, we would prefer not to enumerate sequences like this very often.

Combinations

A **combination** is a collection of *r* items chosen at random without replacement from *n* items where the order of the selected items is *not* important (i.e., treating the three-letter sequence *XYZ* as being the same as the three-letter sequence *ZYX*). Because in combinations the order does not matter, each combination of *r* items results in *r*! different arrangements. Hence the total number of combinations is the total number of permutations divided by *r*!. The number of possible combinations of *r* items chosen from *n* items is denoted $_nC_r$ and read as "*n* choose *r*":

$$_nC_r = {_nP_r}/r! = \frac{n!}{r!(n-r)!} \qquad (5.5)$$

We use combinations when the only thing that matters is which *r* items are chosen, regardless of how they are arranged.

EXAMPLE 6

Appliance Service Calls Revisited

Suppose that five customers (*A, B, C, D, E*) need service calls, and the maintenance worker can only service three of them this morning. The customers don't care when they are serviced as long as it's before noon, so the dispatcher does not care who is serviced first, second, or third. In other words, the dispatcher regards *ABC, ACB, BAC, BCA, CAB,* or *CBA* as being the same event because the same three customers (*A, B, C*) get serviced. The number of combinations is

$$_nC_r = \frac{n!}{r!(n-r)!} = \frac{5!}{3!(5-3)!} = \frac{5 \cdot 4 \cdot 3 \cdot 2 \cdot 1}{(3 \cdot 2 \cdot 1)(2 \cdot 1)} = \frac{120}{12} = 10$$

This is much smaller than the number of permutations in the previous example where order was important. In fact, the possible combinations can be enumerated easily because there are only 10 distinct groups of three customers:

ABC ABD ABE ACD ACE ADE BCD BCE BDE CDE

Permutations or Combinations?

Permutations and combinations both calculate the number of ways we could choose *r* items from *n* items. But in permutations *order is important* while in combinations *order does not matter*. The number of permutations, $_nP_r$, equals *r*! times $_nC_r$, the number of combinations.

EXAMPLE 7

Stir-Fry Combos

A Thai restaurant in Tecumseh, Ontario, offers a stir-fry in which a customer can choose 1 of 10 different meats, 4 of 25 different vegetables, 1 of 6 different noodles, 1 of 10 different sauces, and 4 different levels of spiciness. How many times can a customer eat at this restaurant without duplicating his or her meal?

Here we will need to use the $(n_1)(n_2)\cdots(n_m)$ where $m = 5$, but one of the n_i's (for the number of different vegetables) must first be determined using the combinations rule. Using the combination rule, the number of ways that a customer can select 4 vegetables out of 25 is

$$_nC_r = \frac{n!}{r!(n-r)!} = \frac{25!}{4!21!} = 12{,}650$$

Now, applying the $(n_1)(n_2)\cdots(n_m)$ rule, the number of times is

$$(10)(12650)(6)(10)(4) = 30{,}360{,}000$$

Obviously, no customer would be able to accomplish this feat!

MegaStat offers computational assistance with factorials, permutations, and combinations. It is exceptionally fast and accurate, even for very large factorials. But if you don't have access to a computer or if your calculator doesn't have a factorial key or a combinations or permutations key, a simple strategy can be used. As an example, suppose you want to calculate the number of ways that you can choose 4 vegetables from a list of 25 possible vegetables, or you want to determine

$$\frac{25!}{4!21!}$$

Using a computer or a "combination-key" on a calculator, your answer would be 12,650 as determined above. Using your calculator without such a key, your strategy should be to take 25! and convert it to $(25)(24)(23)(22)(21!)$ and then cancel out the 21! in the numerator with the 21! in the denominator, resulting in

$$\frac{(25)(24)(23)(22)(21!)}{(4)(3)(2)(1)(21!)} = \frac{(25)(24)(23)(22)}{(4)(3)(2)(1)} = \frac{303{,}600}{24} = 12{,}650$$

Section Exercises

5.12 In the 6/49 lottery you pick six different numbers between 1 and 49 and 6 numbers are randomly selected. What is the probability that you picked all six winning numbers? (LO 3)

5.13 An employee was asked to make a 7-layer bean dip for his company picnic. Not only is it important to know what ingredients make up each layer of the bean dip, it is also important to know the order in which the layers are to be arranged. (There is only one traditional way of arranging the layers!) Although he knew which ingredients comprised each layer of this dip, he didn't know how to arrange the layers. What is the probability that he will arrange the layers the traditional way if he simple guesses the correct arrangement? (LO 3)

5.14 In the United States, most zip codes consist of a sequence of five numbers. In Canada, our postal codes consist of 3 letters and 3 numbers alternating back and forth (e.g., N9X 3Q4). How many possible 5-number zip codes could exist in the United States, and how many possible postal codes can exist in Canada, assuming all numbers and letters could be used, if necessary? Do these results seem strange to you? Explain. (LO 3)

5.15 If customers order three-scoop cones at an ice cream parlour that has 31 flavours of ice cream, how many different cones could be created if the ordering of flavours on the cone is important to the customer? If the ordering of flavours on the cone is not important to the customer? (LO 3)

5.16 A not-for-profit gymnastics club is trying to set up a committee to organize a gymnastics meet. It needs six parents to sit on this committee. It has 20 parents from which to choose these six. How many different possibilities could there be for the make-up of this committee if (a) each individual will have the same responsibilities, and (b) each individual will have different responsibilities. (LO 3)

5.17 Today, when visitors spend the day at Disneyland or Disney World, one admission ticket allows them to go on any rides they wish any number of times. Years ago, there were different admission tickets that allowed a visitor to go on so many A rides, so many B rides, and so on. Suppose Disneyland at that time (there was no Disney World) had 8 A rides, 6 B rides, 4 C rides,

10 D rides, and 7 E rides, and suppose the best admission ticket allowed the visitor to go on 4 A rides, 3 B rides, 2 C rides, 6 D rides, and 3 E rides. If a visitor did not want to go on any ride more than once, in how many ways can the visitor choose the rides to go on. Assume ordering is not important. (LO 3)

5.18 American Express Business Travel uses a six-letter record locator number (RLN) for each client's trip (e.g., KEZLFS). (a) How many different RLNs can be created using capital letters (A–Z)? (b) What if they allow any mixture of capital letters (A–Z) and digits (0–9)? (c) What if they allow capital letters and digits but exclude the digits 0 and 1 and the letters O and I because they look too much alike? (LO 3)

5.19 At Oxnard University, a student ID consists of two letters (26 possibilities) followed by four digits (10 possibilities). (a) How many unique student IDs can be created? (b) Would one letter followed by three digits suffice for a university with 40,000 students? (c) Why is extra capacity in student IDs a good idea? (LO 3)

5.20 Until 2005, the UPC bar code had 12 digits (0–9). The first six digits represent the manufacturer, the next five represent the product, and the last is a check digit. (a) How many different manufacturers could be encoded? (b) How many different products could be encoded? (c) In 2005, the EAN bar code replaced the UPC bar code, adding a 13th digit. If this new digit is used for product identification, how many different products could now be encoded? (LO 3)

5.21 Bob has to study for four final exams: accounting (A), biology (B), communications (C), and drama (D). (a) If he studies one subject at a time, in how many different ways could he arrange is study schedule? (b) List the possible arrangements in the sample space. (LO 1 & 3)

5.22 In how many ways could you arrange seven books on a shelf? (b) Would it be feasible to list the possible arrangements? (LO 3)

5.23 Find the following permutations $_nP_r$:
a. $n = 8$ and $r = 3$.
b. $n = 8$ and $r = 5$.
c. $n = 8$ and $r = 1$.
d. $n = 8$ and $r = 8$. (LO 3)

5.24 Find the following combinations $_nC_r$:
a. $n = 8$ and $r = 3$.
b. $n = 8$ and $r = 5$.
b. $n = 8$ and $r = 1$.
c. $n = 8$ and $r = 8$. (LO 3)

5.25 A real estate office has 10 sales agents. Each of four new customers must be assigned an agent. (a) Find the number of agent arrangements where order *is* important. (b) Find the number of agent arrangements where order is *not* important. (c) Why is the number of combinations smaller than the number of permutations? (LO 3)

5.4   Rules of Probability

In our initial Lexus dealership example, we determined probabilities without formally discussing probability to any extent. The field of probability does have a distinct vocabulary that is important to understand and it does have rules that allow us to determine probabilities without necessarily having to count the number of possible outcomes and/or when each outcome is not necessarily equally likely to occur. This section reviews probability terms and probability rules and how to use them.

Complement of an Event

The **complement** of an event A is denoted A' and consists of all outcomes in the sample space S except those outcomes in event A, as illustrated in the Venn diagram in Figure 5.4. As previously mentioned, if we consider the sizes of the various areas to represent the probabilities of various events occurring, the area for the sample space, S, equals 1 or $P(S) = 1$, and $P(A)$ and $P(A')$ are represented by their respective areas.

FIGURE 5.4

Complement of Event *A*

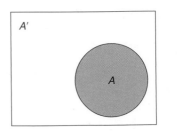

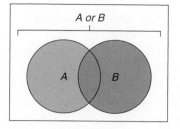

FIGURE 5.5
Union of Two Events

Because A and A' together make up the sample space, their probabilities sum to 1:

$$P(A) + P(A') = 1 \qquad (5.6)$$

The probability of the complement of A is found by subtracting the probability of A from 1:

$$P(A') = 1 - P(A) \qquad (5.7)$$

or the probability of A is found by subtracting the probability of A' from 1:

$$P(A) = 1 - P(A') \qquad (5.8)$$

For example, the *Wall Street Journal* reports that about 33 percent of all new small businesses fail within the first two years (July 12, 2004). From this we can determine that the probability that a new small business will survive at least two years is

$$P(\text{survival}) = 1 - P(\text{failure}) = 1 - 0.33 = 0.67, \text{ or } 67\%$$

Note: We use this rule, as we will use any other rule, when it will give us the answer that we seek. We don't use these rules simply because they exist. As we will illustrate later, a classic use of this rule allows us to answer the following question: "If we have 50 people in a room, what is the probability that at least two of them will have the same birthday?" When we discuss this question, we will see that it is much easier to answer the question: "If we have 50 people in a room, what is the probability that no one will have the same birthday?" If we can answer this question, which is the complement of the original question, we will be able to answer the original question by using the complement rule.

Union of Two Events

The **union** of two events consists of all outcomes in the sample space S that are contained either in event A or in event B or in both. The union of A and B is sometimes denoted $A \cup B$ or "A or B" as illustrated in the Venn diagram in Figure 5.5. The symbol $\cup$ may be read "or" because it means that either or both events occur. For example, when we choose a card at random from a deck of playing cards, if Q is the event that we draw a queen and R is the event that we draw a red card, $Q \cup R$ consists of getting *either* a queen (4 possibilities in 52) *or* a red card (26 possibilities in 52) or *both* a queen and a red card (2 possibilities in 52). After discussing intersections, we will use the Venn diagram to visualize the probability of either A or B or both occurring.

Intersection of Two Events

The **intersection** of two events A and B is the event consisting of all outcomes in the sample space S that are contained in both event A and event B. The intersection of A and B is denoted $A \cap B$ or "A and B" or simply as AB as illustrated in the Venn diagram in Figure 5.6. The probability of $A \cap B$ is called the **joint probability** and is denoted $P(A \cap B)$.

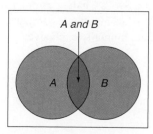

FIGURE 5.6
Intersection of Two Events

The symbol ∩ may be read "and" because the intersection means that both events occur. For example, if Q is the event that we draw a queen and R is the event that we draw a red card, then $Q \cap R$ is the event that we get a card that is both a queen and red. That is, the intersection of sets Q and R consists of two cards (Q♥ *and* Q♦).

General Law of Addition

What is $P(Q \cup R)$? That is, what is the probability that you draw a queen or a red card? We can answer that question by determining how many cards are either a queen or red. Well, there are 4 queens and 26 red cards in our deck. So do we have $4 + 26 = 30$ cards that are either a queen or a red card? NO! We did some double counting. There are two queens that are red. So the actual number is $4 + 26 - 2 = 28$. So the desired probability is 28/52. This is the logic used in the general law of addition for probabilities of compound events. Using the Venn diagram to arrive at the same answer, $P(A \cup B)$ is represented by the shaded area enclosed by the two circles in Figure 5.6. This shaded area consists of $P(A)$ plus $P(B)$, but by summing those two probabilities or areas, we notice that $P(A \cap B)$ is counted twice thus requiring us to subtract it once. So P (queen) = 4/52, P (red) = 26/52, and P (red and queen) = 2/52. Therefore, P(queen or red) = 4/52 + 26/52 − 2/52 = 28/52. This result can be expressed by the general law of addition.

The **general law of addition** says that the probability of the union of two events A and B is the sum of their probabilities less the probability of their intersection:

$$P(A \cup B) = P(A) + P(B) - P(A \cap B) \qquad (5.9)$$

This result, while simple to calculate, may not necessarily be obvious without visualizing it using a Venn diagram.

Note: How did we determine that P(queen) = 4/52 although the result appears to be intuitive? The answer would be 4/52 only if each of the 52 cards in the deck or if each outcome in the sample space were equally likely to occur.

As previously mentioned, if a sample space consists of n *equally likely* outcomes and if event A consists of k of these outcomes,

$$P(A) = \frac{k}{n}$$

For example, this rule would not apply when a magician is selecting a card if the magician can make any card appear that he wishes to be chosen.

EXAMPLE 8

Cellphones and Credit Cards ☁ **WebSurvey**

A survey of introductory statistics students showed that 29.7 percent have Rogers wireless service (event A), 73.4 percent have a Visa card (event B), and 20.3 percent have both (event $A \cap B$). The probability that a student uses Rogers *or* has a Visa card is:

$$P(A \cup B) = P(A) + P(B) - P(A \cap B) = 0.297 + 0.734 - 0.203 = 0.828$$

Mutually Exclusive Events

Events A and B are **mutually exclusive** (or **disjoint**) if their intersection is the **null set** (a set that contains no elements). In other words, the occurrence of one event precludes the other from occurring. The null set is denoted ϕ.

$$\text{If } A \cap B = \phi, \text{ then } P(A \cap B) = 0 \qquad (5.10)$$

As illustrated in Figure 5.7, the probability of $A \cap B$ is zero when the events do not overlap. For example, if A is the event that a Swiss Chalet customer finishes her lunch in less than 30 minutes and B is the event that she takes 30 minutes or more, then $P(A \cap B) = P(\phi) = 0$. Here are examples of other events that are mutually exclusive:

- *Customer age:* A = under 21, B = over 65
- *Purebred dog breed:* A = border collie, B = golden retriever
- *Business form:* A = corporation, B = sole proprietorship

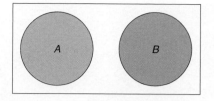

FIGURE 5.7
Mutually Exclusive Events

These events may not cover all of the possibilities (e.g., a business could also be a partnership) and, thus, may not be *collectively exhaustive.* The only issue here is whether the categories overlap. Here are examples of events that are *not* mutually exclusive (can be in both categories):

- *Student's profile:* A = attends the University of Toronto, B = economics major
- *Bank information:* A = banks at Toronto Dominion Bank, B = banks at Edmonton branch
- *Credit card information:* A = MasterCard, B = \$2,000 limit

Special Law of Addition for Mutually Exclusive Events

If A and B are mutually exclusive events, then $P(A \cap B) = 0$ and the addition law reduces to

$$P(A \cup B) = P(A) + P(B) \text{ (addition law for mutually exclusive events)}$$

This result can easily be visualized by means of a Venn diagram.

For example, if we look at a person's age, then $P(\text{under } 21) = 0.28$ and $P(\text{over } 65) = 0.12$, so $P(\text{under } 21 \text{ } or \text{ over } 65) = 0.28 + 0.12 = 0.40$ because these events do not overlap.

This law can also be extended if there are several mutually exclusive events. This law then becomes

$$P(A_1 \cup A_2 \cup \cdots \cup A_n) = P(A_1) + P(A_2) + \cdots + P(A_n)$$

Collectively Exhaustive Events

Events are **collectively exhaustive** if their union is the entire sample space S (i.e., all the events that can possibly occur). Two mutually exclusive and collectively exhaustive events are illustrated in Figure 5.8. For example, a car repair is either covered by the warranty (A) or is not covered by the warranty (A'): There can be more than two mutually exclusive, collectively exhaustive events, as illustrated in Figure 5.9. For example, a Walmart customer can pay by credit card (A), debit card (B), cash (C), or cheque (D).

Using the law of addition for mutually exclusive and collectively exhaustive events, we can easily see, using the Venn diagram, that

$$P(A_1 \cup A_2 \cup \cdots \cup A_n) = P(A_1) + P(A_2) + \cdots + P(A_n) = 1$$

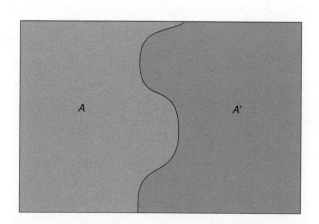

FIGURE 5.8
Two Mutually and Collectively Exhaustive Events

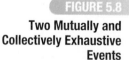

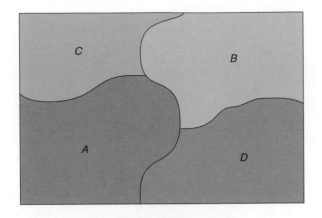

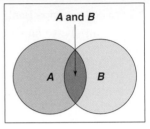

Conditional Probability

The probability of event *A given* that event *B* has occurred is a **conditional probability,** denoted *P(A|B)*, which is read "the probability of *A* given *B*." The vertical line is read as "given." The conditional probability is the joint probability of *A* and *B* divided by the probability of *B*.

$$P(A|B) = \frac{P(A \cap B)}{P(B)} \text{ for } P(B) > 0 \qquad (5.11)$$

The logic of Equation 5.11 is apparent by looking at the Venn diagram in Figure 5.10. The sample space is restricted to *B,* an event that we know has occurred (the lightly shaded green circle). The intersection, *A ∩ B,* is the part of *B* that is also in *A* (the heavily shaded area). The ratio of the relative size, in terms of probabilities, of set *A ∩ B* to set *B* is the conditional probability *P(A|B)*.

Of the population aged 16 to 21 and not in college or university, 13.50 percent are unemployed, 29.05 percent are high school dropouts, and 5.32 percent are unemployed high school dropouts. What is the conditional probability that a member of this population is unemployed, given that the person is a high school dropout? To answer this question, define

> *U* = the event that the person is unemployed
> *D* = the event that the person is a high school dropout

To get a feel for the conditional probability formula, let us first answer this question without using the conditional probability formula, and just using only our intuition. Let us imagine that there are exactly 10,000 persons aged 16 to 21 and not in college or university. Thus, based on the problem information, 1,350 of these are unemployed, 2,905 are high school dropouts, and 532 are unemployed high school dropouts.

Let us define complements of events *U* and *D.* Thus,

> *U'* = the event that the person is *not* unemployed (i.e., person is employed)
> *D'* = the event that the person is *not* a high school dropout.

We could put all the given information in a 2 × 2 table.

	D	*D'*	Total
U	532		1,350
U'			
Total	2,905		10,000

Further, because 1,350 of 10,000 are unemployed, $10,000 - 1,350 = 8,650$ are employed. Similarly, $10,000 - 2,905 = 7,095$ are not high school dropouts. Thus, we can fill-in the rest of the table as below.

	D	D′	Total
U	532	818	1,350
U″	2,373	6,277	8,650
Total	2,905	7,095	10,000

From the table, we can calculate three important facts:

$$P(U) = 1,350/10,000 = 0.1350$$
$$P(D) = 2,905/10,000 = 0.2905$$
$$P(U \cap D) = 532/10,000 = 0.0532$$

Now let us find the conditional probability that a person is unemployed, given that the person is a high school dropout. That is, we need to find $P(U|D)$. Because we are given that the person is a dropout, we should focus only on dropouts. That is, focus on the column with the heading D. Out of 2,905 dropouts, 532 are unemployed; this conditional probability should be equal to $532/2905 = 0.1831$, or 18.31%.

We get exactly the same answer by applying the conditional probability Equation 5.11 below:

$$P(U|D) = \frac{P(U \cap D)}{P(D)} = \frac{0.0532}{0.2905} = 0.1831, \text{ or } 18.31$$

The *conditional probability* of being unemployed is $P(U|D) = 0.1831$ (18.31%), which is greater than the *unconditional probability* of being unemployed $P(U) = 0.1350$ (13.50%). In other words, knowing that someone is a high school dropout alters the probability that the person is unemployed.

Concept Check

What is $P(A|B)$ if A and B are mutually exclusive events?

Independent Events

If two events are mutually exclusive, the occurrence of one of these events precludes the occurrence of the other event. In contrast to mutually exclusive events, there are other events that are **independent** of one another. Event A is independent of event B if the occurrence of one of these events does not affect the occurrence of the other event. That is, A and B are independent if, by definition, the conditional probability $P(A|B)$ is the same as the unconditional probability $P(A)$. For example, if text messaging among high school students is *independent* of gender, this means that knowing whether a student is a male or female does not *change* the probability that the student uses text messaging. To check for independence, we apply this test:

Event A is *independent* of event B if and only if $P(A|B) = P(A)$.   **(5.12)**

Another way to check for independence is to ask whether the product of the event probabilities equals the probability of their intersection:

Event A is *independent* of event B if and only if $P(A \cap B) = P(A)P(B)$.   **(5.13)**

A Closer Look

Why does this second way of checking for independence, $P(A \cap B) = P(A)P(B)$, tell us that A and B are independent? Using the fact that, by definition, $P(A|B) = P(A)$ if A and B are independent, and manipulating the conditional rule, we arrive at this conclusion as follows:

$$P(A|B) = \frac{P(A \cap B)}{P(B)} \rightarrow P(A) = \frac{P(A \cap B)}{P(B)} \rightarrow P(A \cap B) = P(A)P(B)$$

EXAMPLE 10

Television Ads

The target audience is 2,000,000 viewers. Ad A reaches 500,000 viewers, ad B reaches 300,000 viewers, and both ads reach 100,000 viewers. That is:

$$P(A) = \frac{500,000}{2,000,000} = 0.25 \quad P(B) = \frac{300,000}{2,000,000} = 0.15 \quad P(A \cap B) = \frac{100,000}{2,000,000} = 0.05$$

Applying the definition of conditional probability from Equation 5.11, the conditional probability that ad A reaches a viewer *given* that ad B reaches the viewer is:

$$P(A|B) = \frac{P(A \cap B)}{P(B)} = \frac{0.05}{0.15} = 0.3333$$

We see that A and B are not independent because $P(A) = 0.25$ is not equal to $P(A|B) = 0.3333$. That is, knowing that ad B reached the viewer raises the probability that ad A reached the viewer from $P(A) = 0.25$ to $P(A|B) = 0.3333$. Alternatively, because $P(A)P(B) = (0.25)(0.15) = 0.0375$ is not equal to $P(A \cap B) = 0.05$, we know that events A and B are not independent.

Caution: Having defined mutually exclusive events and independent events, you should realize that these two types of events are as different as any two types of events could possibly be. If A and B are mutually exclusive, A occurring does not allow B to occur. If A and B are independent events, A occurring has no effect on B occurring.

Special Law of Addition for Independent Events

The general law of addition, $P(A \cup B) = P(A) + P(B) - P(A \cap B)$, becomes

$$P(A \cup B) = P(A) + P(B) - P(A)P(B)$$

if A and B are independent events.

Dependent Events

When $P(A)$ differs from $P(A|B)$ the events are dependent (and mutually exclusive if $P(A|B) = 0$). You can easily think of examples of dependence. For example, cellphone text messaging is more common among younger people than older people, while arteriosclerosis is more common among older people than younger people. Therefore, knowing a person's age would affect the *probability* that the individual uses text messaging or has arteriosclerosis.

Using Actuarial Data

Banks and credit unions know that the probability that a customer will default on a car loan is dependent on his/her past record of unpaid credit obligations. That is why lenders consult credit bureaus before they make a loan. Your credit score is based on factors such as the ratio of your credit card balance to your credit limit, length of your credit history, number of accounts with balances, and frequency of requests for credit. Your score can be compared with actuarial data and national averages to see what percentile you are in. The lender can then decide whether your loan is worth the risk.

Automobile insurance companies (e.g., CAA, ING, State Farm) know that the probability that a driver will be involved in an accident depends on the driver's age, past traffic convictions, the city where the driver lives, and similar factors. This actuarial information is used in deciding whether to accept you as a new customer and how to set your insurance premium. The situation is similar for life insurance. Can you think of factors that might affect a person's life insurance premium?

In each of these loan and insurance examples, knowing B will affect our estimate of the likelihood of A. Obviously, bankers and insurance companies need to quantify these conditional probabilities precisely. An *actuary* studies conditional probabilities empirically, using accident statistics, mortality tables, and insurance claims records. Although few people undergo the extensive training to become actuaries, many businesses rely on actuarial services, so a business student needs to understand the concepts of conditional probability and statistical independence.

Based on past data, the probability that a customer at a certain Noodles & Company restaurant will order a dessert (event D) with the meal is approximately 0.08. The probability that a customer will order a bottled beverage (event B) is approximately 0.14. The joint probability that a customer will order both a dessert *and* a bottled beverage is approximately 0.0112. Is ordering a dessert independent of ordering a bottled beverage? Because $P(D) \times P(B) = 0.08 \times 0.14 = 0.0112 = P(D \cap B)$, we can assume that D and B are independent of one another. If we know that a customer has ordered a bottled beverage, does this information change the probability that he or she will also order a dessert? No, because the events are independent.

EXAMPLE 11

Restaurant Orders

Multiplication Law

The conditional probability law states that $P(A|B) = \dfrac{P(A \cap B)}{P(B)}$ or $P(B|A) = \dfrac{P(A \cap B)}{P(A)}$

But suppose we know $P(A|B)$ and $P(B)$ or we know $P(B|A)$ and $P(A)$ and we want to determine $P(A \cap B)$. To calculate this probability, we simply manipulate the conditional probability law to isolate $P(A \cap B)$, resulting in the multiplication law:

$$P(A \cap B) = P(B)P(A|B) \text{ or } P(A \cap B) = P(A)P(B|A)$$

For example, suppose we want to determine the probability that the top two cards in a deck of playing cards are both aces. Assuming that the deck of cards was not shuffled by a magician, using the classical approach we know that the probability that the first card is an ace, $P(A_1)$, is 4/52, and the probability that the second card is an ace given that the first card is an ace, $P(A_2|A_1)$, is 3/51 (there are only 3 aces left in the 51 remaining cards). Using the multiplication law,

$$P(A \cap B) = P(A_1 \cap A_2) = P(A_1)P(A_2|A_1) = (4/52)(3/51) = 0.00452$$

A Closer Look

Suppose the top two cards were actually aces. Would you be suspicious that the deck of cards was shuffled by a magician? You could argue that, because the probability of this happening is quite rare if the deck was shuffled by a "normal" person (approximately 0.45 percent of the time), you could be suspicious about who shuffled the deck. In general, if we make assumptions and based on these assumptions an event occurs that is highly unlikely to occur (i.e., its probability of occurrence is small if these assumptions are true), we should question these assumptions. This type of critical analysis will be dealt with more formally when we discuss hypothesis testing in later chapters.

Obviously, if A and B are mutually exclusive events, $P(A \cap B) = 0$. If A and B are independent events, $P(A \cap B) = P(A)P(B)$.

We can extend the multiplication law to more than simply A and B if all the events are independent of one another. The probability of several independent events occurring simultaneously is the product of their separate probabilities, as shown in Equation 5.12 for n independent events $A_1, A_2, \ldots, A_n$.

$$P(A_1 \cap A_2 \cap \cdots \cap A_n) = P(A_1)P(A_2) \cdots P(A_n) \text{ if the events are independent} \qquad \textbf{(5.12)}$$

If the events are not independent, we can still extend this law, which now becomes:

$$P(A_1 \cap A_2 \cap \cdots \cap A_n) = P(A_1)P(A_2|A_1)P(A_3|A_1, A_2) \cdots P(A_n|A_1, A_2, \ldots, A_{n-1})$$

Previously, the question was asked: "What is the probability that, in a room of 50 people, at least two of them will have the same birthday?" It was suggested that the complement rule should be used and the formula would then become:

$$P(\text{at least two people having the same birthday}) = 1 - P(\text{no one has the same birthday})$$

To find P(no one has the same birthday), we would use the formula

$$P(A_1 \cap A_2 \cap \cdots \cap A_n) = P(A_1)P(A_2|A_1)P(A_3|A_1, A_2) \cdots P(A_n|A_1, A_2, \ldots, A_{n-1})$$

where A_1 is the event that the first person doesn't have the same birthday as previous individuals (obviously, that probability is 1), $A_2|A_1$ is the event that the second person doesn't have the same birthday as the first person (this probability is 364/365 ignoring leap years), and so on. Ignoring leap years,

$$P(A_1 \cap A_2 \cap \cdots \cap A_{50}) = (1)\left(\frac{364}{365}\right)\left(\frac{363}{365}\right) \cdots \left(\frac{316}{365}\right) \approx 0.0296$$

or using the complement rule,

$$P(\text{at least two people having the same birthday}) = 1 - 0.0296 = 0.9704$$

This result should be somewhat surprising to most people. So although intuition was used initially in this chapter, it may fail us and rules should be relied on whenever possible.

The **multiplication law** for independent events can be applied to system reliability. To illustrate, suppose a Web site has two independent file servers (i.e., no shared power or other components). Each server has 99 percent reliability (i.e., is "up" 99 percent of the time). What is the total system reliability? Let F_1 be the event that server 1 fails, and F_2 be the event that server 2 fails. Then

$$P(F_1) = 1 - 0.99 = 0.01$$

$$P(F_2) = 1 - 0.99 = 0.01$$

Applying the rule of independence:

$$P(F_1 \cap F_2) = P(F_1)P(F_2) = (0.01)(0.01) = 0.0001$$

The probability that at least one server is up is 1 minus the probability that both servers are down, or $1 - 0.0001 = 0.9999$. Dual file servers dramatically improve reliability to 99.99 percent.

When individual components have a low reliability, high reliability can still be achieved with massive redundancy. For example, a Teramac supercomputer has over 7 million components. About 3 percent are defective (nanodevices are extremely difficult to manufacture). Yet programs can run reliably because there is significant redundancy in the interconnect circuitry so that a valid path can almost always be found (see *Scientific American* 293, no. 5 [Nov. 2005], p. 75).

EXAMPLE 12

Space Shuttle

Redundancy can increase system reliability even when individual component reliability is low. For example, the NASA space shuttle has three flight computers. Suppose that they function independently but that each has an unacceptable 0.03 chance of failure (3 failures in 100 missions). Let F_j = event that computer j fails. Then

$$
\begin{aligned}
P(\text{all 3 fail}) &= P(F_1 \cap F_2 \cap F_3) \\
&= P(F_1)P(F_2)P(F_3) \quad (\text{presuming that failures are independent}) \\
&= (0.03)(0.03)(0.03) \\
&= 0.000027, \text{ or 27 in 1,000,000 missions}
\end{aligned}
$$

Triple redundancy can reduce the probability of computer failure to 0.000027 (27 failures in 1,000,000 missions). Of course, in practice, it is very difficult to have truly independent computers, because they may share electrical buses or cables. On one shuttle mission, two of the three computers actually did fail, which proved the value of redundancy. Another example of space shuttle redundancy is the four independent fuel gauges that prevent the shuttle's main engines from shutting down too soon. Initial launch rules allowed the shuttle to fly as long as two of them were functional, but after the *Challenger* launch explosion, the rules were modified to require that three of four be functional, and were modified again after the *Columbia* accident to require that all four be functional (see http://aolsvc.news.aol.com).

TABLE 5.2   Typical System Reliabilities in Various Applications

Type of System	Typical Reliability (%)
Commercial fibre-optic cable systems	99.999
Cellular-radio base stations with mobile switches connected to public-switched telephone networks	99.99
Private-enterprise networking (e.g., connecting two company offices)	99.9
Airline luggage systems	99
Excellent student exam-taking	90

See *Scientific American* 287, no. 1 (July 2002), p. 52 and 288; no. 6, p. 56.

The Five Nines Rule

How high must reliability be? Prime business customers expect public carrier–class telecommunications data links to be available 99.999 percent of the time. This so-called five nines rule implies only five minutes of downtime per year. Such high reliability is needed not only in telecommunications but also for mission-critical systems such as airline reservation systems or banking funds transfers. Table 5.2 shows some expected system reliabilities in contemporary applications.

How Much Redundancy Is Needed?

Suppose a certain network Web server is up only 94 percent of the time (i.e., its probability of being down is 0.06). How many independent servers are needed to ensure that the system is up at least 99.99 percent of the time? This is equivalent to requiring that the probability of all the servers being down is 0.0001 (i.e., $1 - 0.9999$), or less. Four servers will accomplish the goal:

$$2 \text{ servers: } P(F_1 \cap F_2) = (0.06)(0.06) = 0.0036$$

$$3 \text{ servers: } P(F_1 \cap F_2 \cap F_3) = (0.06)(0.06)(0.06) = 0.000216$$

$$4 \text{ servers: } P(F_1 \cap F_2 \cap F_3 \cap F_4) = (0.06)(0.06)(0.06)(0.06) = 0.00001296$$

Applications of Redundancy

The principle of redundancy is found in many places. Hockey teams have more than six players, even though only six can play at once. You set two alarm clocks in case the first doesn't wake you up. The Embraer Legacy 13-passenger jet ($21.2 million) has two identical generators on each of its two engines to allow the plane to be used as a commercial regional jet (requiring 99.5 percent dispatch reliability) as well as for private corporate travel. With four generators, plus an auxiliary power unit that can be started and run in flight, the Legacy can fly even after the failure of a generator or two (*Flying* 131, no. 9 [Sept. 2004], p. 50).

Older airliners (e.g., Boeing 747) had four engines, not only because older engine designs were less powerful but also because they were less reliable. Particularly for transoceanic flights, four-engine planes could fly even if one engine failed (or maybe even two). Modern airliners (e.g., Boeing 777) have only two engines because newer engines are more powerful and more reliable. At first, two-engine airliners were not certified for lengthy over-water operations under the international rules for ETOPS (Extended Twin-engine operations). Improved engine reliability has led to relaxation of ETOPS rules to allow twin-engine commercial transport to fly routes further than 60 minutes' flying time from any diversion airports. This new definition allows twin-engine airliners like Boeing 757, 767, and 777, and Airbus A300, A320, and A330 series to fly routes that were previously off-limits to twin-engine airliners.

It is not just a matter of individual component reliability but also of cost and consequence. Cars have only one battery because the consequence of battery failure (walking home or calling CAA) does not justify the expense of having a backup battery. But spare tires are cheap enough that all cars carry one (maybe two, if you are driving in the Yukon).

Redundancy is not required when components are highly reliable, cost per component is high, and consequences of system failure are tolerable (e.g., cellphone, alarm clock). Unfortunately, true component independence is difficult to achieve. The same catastrophe (fire, flood, etc.) that damages one component may well damage the backup system. On August 24, 2001, a twin-engine Air Transat Airbus A330 transiting the Atlantic Ocean did have a double-engine shutdown with 293 passengers aboard. Fortunately, the pilot was able to glide 85 miles to a landing in the Azores, resulting in only minor injuries (*Aviation Week and Space Technology,* Sept. 3, 2001, p. 34).

Odds of an Event

Statisticians usually speak of probabilities rather than odds, but in sports and games of chance, we often hear **odds** quoted. We define the *odds in favour* of an event A as the ratio of the probability that event A will occur to the probability that event A will not occur. Its reciprocal is the *odds against* event A.

Odds in favour of A:

$$\frac{P(A)}{P(A')} = \frac{P(A)}{1 - P(A)}$$

Odds against A ($=$ odds in favour of A'):

$$\frac{P(A')}{P(A)} = \frac{1 - P(A)}{P(A)}$$

For a pair of fair dice, the probability of rolling a seven is 6/36 or 1/6, and the probability of not rolling a seven is $1 - 1/6 = 5/6$. So the odds in favour of rolling a seven are

$$\text{Odds} = \frac{P(\text{rolling seven})}{P(\text{not rolling seven})} = \frac{P(\text{rolling seven})}{1 - P(\text{rolling seven})} = \frac{1/6}{1 - 1/6} = \frac{1/6}{5/6} = \frac{1}{5}$$

This means that on the average for every time we roll seven there will be five times that we do not roll seven. The odds are 1 to 5 *in favour* of rolling a seven (or 5 to 1 *against* rolling a seven).

For those familiar with the game of roulette as played in Canadian casinos, there are 38 slots on a roulette wheel, numbered 0, 00, 1, 2, 3, . . . , 36. Eighteen of these numbers are black, 18 are red, and 0 and 00 are green. There are numerous bets you can make. With a single wager, you can bet on a single number, certain combinations of 2 numbers, 3 numbers, 4 numbers, 5 numbers, 6 numbers, 8 numbers, 12 numbers, and 18 numbers. The wheel is spun, a ball is rolled, and the winners are determined depending upon where the ball comes to rest within the roulette wheel. If a wager is bet on a specific number, the probability that the wager wins is 1/38, assuming that the roulette wheel is an unbiased (honest) wheel. Converting this probability into odds, we have:

$$\text{Odds of winning} = \frac{P(A)}{1 - P(A)} = \frac{1/38}{37/38} = 1 \text{ to } 37$$

$$\text{Odds of losing} = \frac{P(A')}{1 - P(A')} = \frac{37/38}{1/38} = 37 \text{ to } 1$$

Usually the odds would be stated as 37 to 1 (against winning).

Similarly, if a wager was made on a combination of six numbers, the probability of winning would be 6/38 or 3/19 and

$$\text{Odds of winning} = \frac{P(A)}{1 - P(A)} = \frac{6/38}{32/38} = 3 \text{ to } 16$$

$$\text{Odds of losing} = \frac{P(A')}{1 - P(A')} = \frac{32/38}{6/38} = 16 \text{ to } 3$$

Conversely, if we were told the odds of losing, we could convert the odds to probabilities of winning.

If the odds against event A are quoted as b to a, then the implied probability of event A is:

$$P(A) = \frac{a}{a + b}$$

For example, the implied probability that a six-number combination bet will win is:

$$P(A) = \frac{a}{a + b} = \frac{3}{3 + 16} = \frac{3}{19} \text{ or } \frac{6}{38}$$

Caution: In some games of chance, such as horse racing, the quoted odds cannot be converted into the probability of winning or losing because the quoted odds are not really odds, they are payouts. For example, if the quoted odds are 2 to 1, the better will win $2 for each $1 bet although the odds of the horse losing may be 2.2 to 1 depending upon how much of the total wagering goes toward taxes and winnings paid to the owners of the horses. In the game of roulette, the odds of losing when betting on a single number is 37 to 1, but the payout is 35 to 1, or $35 for each $1 bet.

If a probability is expressed as a percentage, you can easily convert it to odds. For example, the IRS tax audit rate is 1.41 percent among taxpayers earning between $100,000 and $199,999 (*The Wall Street Journal,* Apr. 15, 2006, p. A5). Let A = the event that the taxpayer is audited and set $P(A) = 0.0141$. The odds against an audit are:

$$\frac{P(\text{no audit})}{P(\text{audit})} = \frac{1 - P(A)}{P(A)} = \frac{1 - 0.0141}{0.0141} = 70 \text{ to } 1 \text{ } against \text{ being audited}$$

The following summarizes the probabilities rules covered in this section:

Conditional Probability Law:

In general: $P(A|B) = \dfrac{P(A \cap B)}{P(B)}$

If A and B are **mutually exclusive:** $P(A|B) = 0$

If A and B are **independent:** $P(A|B) = P(A)$

Multiplication Law:

In general: $P(A \cap B) = P(B)P(A|B) = P(A)P(B|A)$

If A and B are **mutually exclusive:** $P(A \cap B) = 0$

If A and B are **independent:** $P(A \cap B) = P(A)P(B)$

Addition Law:

In general: $P(A \cup B) = P(A) + P(B) - P(A \cap B)$

If A and B are **mutually exclusive:** $P(A \cup B) = P(A) + P(B)$

If A and B are **independent:** $P(A \cup B) = P(A) + P(B) - P(A)P(B)$

A Closer Look

When approaching scenarios in which determining probabilities is necessary, you should put in symbols what probabilities you are given (e.g., $P(A) = 0.3$, $P(B) = 0.7$) and what probabilities you are trying to determine (e.g., $P(A \cap B) = ?$), and you should note any other pertinent information (e.g., A and B are independent). With this information, you should then look for a rule that links what you are given with what you want to know (e.g., $P(A \cap B) = P(A)P(B)$). If such a rule exists, apply that rule (e.g., $P(A \cap B) = P(A)P(B) = (0.3)(0.7) = 0.21$. If such a rule does not exist or if other calculations may be necessary before a rule can be used, you may have to rely on material covered in subsequent sections of this chapter to help you find the answer that you are seeking. In addition, instead of using symbols A and B, try to use symbols that allow you to remember what these symbols represent. As an example, we will use the following information.

An Application: Body Mass Index of Canadians   Based on a study reported by Statistics Canada (www40.statcan.gc.ca/l01/cst01/hlth68-eng.htm) concerning the change in body mass index (BMI) of Canadians between 1994/1995 and 2006/2007, it was determined that 29.4 percent of females had increased BMI, 63.9 percent had the same BMI, and 6.7 percent had lower BMI. Of the males, 31.6 percent had increased BMI, 63.4 percent had the same BMI, and 5.0 percent had lower BMI. In the study, 51.9 percent were males and

48.1 percent were females. If an individual participating in this study was randomly selected for further analysis, what would be the probability that:

(a) The individual selected is a male?

(b) The individual selected had an increase in BMI given that the individual is a male?

(c) The individual selected had an increase in BMI given that the individual is a female?

(d) The individual is a male and had an increase in BMI?

(e) The individual is a male or had an increase in BMI?

(f) The individual had an increase in BMI?

(g) The individual is a male given that he had an increase in BMI?

and

(h) If two individuals are selected, what is the probability that both are males?

In order to answer any of the above questions, we first must realize that percentages or proportions can be converted into probabilities. For example, if 51.9 percent in the study are males, the probability that a randomly selected individual is a male is 0.519. And, instead of using As and Bs to represent outcomes, we should use letters that are easy to relate to the information that we is given. So we will use

* M to represent the person being a male

* F to represent the person being a female

* I to represent an increase in BMI

* N to represent the same or no change in BMI (we don't want to use S because S symbolizes the sample space)

* D to represent a decrease in BMI

Having defined our symbols, what information are we given? We are given:

* $P(M) = 0.519$

* $P(F) = 0.481$

* $P(I|F) = 0.294$

* $P(N|F) = 0.639$

* $P(D|F) = 0.067$

* $P(I|M) = 0.316$

* $P(N|M) = 0.634$

* $P(D|M) = 0.050$

And looking at parts (a) through (g) we want to determine $P(M)$, $P(I|M)$, $P(I|F)$, $P(I \cap M)$, $P(I \cup M)$, $P(I)$, and $P(I|M)$ in that order. Based on what information we are given, what information we want to know, and the rules available to us, we can determine

(a) The individual selected is a male $= P(M) = 0.519$ (already given)

(b) The individual selected had an increase in BMI given that the individual is a male $= P(I|M) = 0.316$ (already given)

(c) The individual selected had an increase in BMI given that the individual is a female $= P(I|F) = 0.294$ (already given)

(d) The individual is a male and had an increase in BMI $= P(I \cap M) = P(M)P(I|M) = (0.519)(0.316) \approx 0.164$

(e) The individual is a male or had an increase in BMI $= P(I \cup M) = P(I) + P(M) - P(I \cap M)$. But because we are not given $P(I)$, we cannot use this formula until we have a way to determine this probability.

(f) The individual had an increase in BMI $= P(I)$. We were given no rule that allows us to determine this probability based on the information we were given.

(g) The individual is a male given that he had an increase in BMI = $P(M|I) = \dfrac{P(I \cap M)}{P(I)}$ $= \dfrac{0.164}{P(I)} = ?$. As with the previous two questions, we don't know $P(I)$.

(h) If two individuals are selected, what is the probability that both are males? Here, we will assume the probability of the second person being a male is the same as the first person being a male because the study consists of over 14 million individuals and who was selected first would have virtually no effect on who was selected second. Therefore,

$$P(M_1 \cap M_2) = P(M_1)P(M_2) \approx (0.519)(0.519) \approx 0.269$$

Concept Check

Although we stated that we don't know $P(I)$, draw a Venn diagram and determine a formula that we can use based on the information we have, or can easily determine, for calculating $P(I)$.

Section Exercises

5.26 Are these characteristics of a student at your university mutually exclusive or not? Explain. (LO 5)
  a. A = works 20 hours or more, B = majors in accounting
  b. A = born in the United States, B = born in Canada
  c. A = owns a Toyota, B = owns a Honda

5.27 Are these events collectively exhaustive or not? Explain. (LO 5)
  a. A = university grad, B = some university, C = no university
  b. A = born in the United States, B = born in Canada, C = born in Mexico
  c. A = full-time student, B = part-time student, C = not enrolled as a student

5.28 Given $P(A) = 0.40$, $P(B) = 0.50$, and $P(A \cap B) = 0.05$, find (a) $P(A \cup B)$, (b) $P(A|B)$, and (c) $P(B|A)$. (d) Sketch a Venn diagram. (LO 4, 5 & 6)

5.29 Given $P(A) = 0.70$, $P(B) = 0.30$, and $P(A \cap B) = 0.00$, find (a) $P(A \cup B)$ and (b) $P(A|B)$. (c) Sketch a Venn diagram and describe it in words. (LO 4, 5 & 6)

5.30 Samsung ships 21.7 percent of the liquid crystal displays (LCDs) in the world. Let S be the event that a randomly selected LCD was made by Samsung. Find (a) $P(S)$, (b) $P(S')$, (c) the odds *in favour* of event S, and (d) the odds *against* event S. (Data are from *The Economist* 372, no. 8385 [July 24, 2004], p. 59.) (LO 4 & 5)

5.31 List *two* binary events that describe the possible outcomes of each situation. (LO 4)
  a. A pharmaceutical firm seeks Health Canada approval for a new drug.
  b. A baseball batter goes to bat.
  c. A woman has a mammogram test.

5.32 List *more than two* events (i.e., categorical events) that might describe the outcome of each situation. (LO 4)
  a. A student applies for admission to Queen's University.
  b. A football quarterback throws a pass.
  c. A bank customer makes an ABM transaction.

5.33 Let S be the event that a randomly chosen female aged 18 to 24 is a smoker. Let C be the event that a randomly chosen female aged 18 to 24 is a Caucasian. Given $P(S) = 0.246$, $P(C) = 0.830$, and $P(S \cap C) = 0.232$, find each probability and express the event in words. (Data are from *Statistical Abstract of the United States, 2001*.) (LO 4 & 5)
  a. $P(S')$
  b. $P(S \cup C)$
  c. $P(S|C)$
  d. $P(S|C')$

5.34 Given $P(A) = 0.40$ and $P(B) = 0.50$, if A and B are independent, find $P(A \cap B)$. (LO 4)

5.35 Given $P(A) = 0.40$, $P(B) = 0.50$, and $P(A \cap B) = 0.05$. (a) Find $P(A|B)$. (b) In this problem, are A and B independent? Explain. (LO 4 & 5)

5.36 Which pairs of events are independent? (LO 5)
  a. $P(A) = 0.60$, $P(B) = 0.40$, $P(A \cap B) = 0.24$.
  b. $P(A) = 0.90$, $P(B) = 0.20$, $P(A \cap B) = 0.18$.
  c. $P(A) = 0.50$, $P(B) = 0.70$, $P(A \cap B) = 0.25$.

5.37 The probability that a student has a Visa card (event V) is 0.73. The probability that a student has a MasterCard (event M) is 0.18. The probability that a student has both cards is 0.03. (a) Find the probability that a student has either a Visa card or a MasterCard. (b) In this problem, are V and M independent? Explain. (LO 4 & 5)

5.38 Bob sets two alarm clocks (battery-powered) to be sure he arises for his Monday 8:00 A.M. accounting exam. There is a 75 percent chance that each specific clock will wake Bob. (a) What is the probability that Bob will oversleep? (b) If Bob had three clocks, would he have a 99 percent chance of waking up? (LO 4)

5.39 A hospital's backup power system has three independent emergency electrical generators, each with uptime averaging 95 percent (some downtime is necessary for maintenance). Any of the generators can handle the hospital's power needs. Does the overall reliability of the backup power system meet the five nines test? (LO 4)

5.5 Contingency Tables

At the beginning of this chapter, we used a table, more precisely a contingency table, to test your intuition about probabilities. Now we will look at contingency tables more formally. In Chapter 4, you saw how Excel's pivot tables can be used to display the frequency of occurrence of data values (e.g., how many taxpayers in a sample are filing as "single" and also have at least one child). Because a probability usually is estimated as a *relative frequency,* we can use tables of relative frequencies to learn about relationships (e.g., dependent events or conditional probabilities) that are extremely useful in business planning. Data for the table may be from a survey or from actuarial records.

What Is a Contingency Table?

To better understand dependent events and conditional probability, let's look at some real data. A **contingency table** is a cross-tabulation of frequencies into rows and columns. The intersection of each row and column is a *cell* that shows a frequency. A contingency table is like a frequency distribution for a single variable, except it has *two* variables (rows and columns). A contingency table with r rows and c columns has rc cells and is called an $r \times c$ table. Contingency tables are often used to report the results of a survey.

Table 5.3 shows a cross-tabulation of tuition cost versus five-year net salary gains for MBA degree recipients at 67 top-tier graduate schools of business in the U.S. Here, salary gain is compensation after graduation, minus the sum of tuition and forgone compensation. Are large salary gains more likely for graduates of high-tuition MBA programs?

TABLE 5.3 Contingency Table of Frequencies (n = 67 MBA programs)   MBASalary

| Tuition | Salary Gain | | | |
	Small (S_1) Under $50K	Medium (S_2) $50K–$100K	Large (S_3) $100K +	Row Total
Low (T_1) Under $40K	5	10	1	16
Medium (T_2) $40K–$50K	7	11	1	19
High (T_3) $50K +	5	12	15	32
Column Total	17	33	17	67

Source: Data are from *Forbes* 172, no. 8 (Oct. 13, 2003), p. 78. Copyright © 2005 Forbes, Inc. Reprinted with permission.

TABLE 5.4   Marginal Probability of Event S_2

Tuition	Salary Gain Small (S_1)	Medium (S_2)	Large (S_3)	Row Total
Low (T_1)	5	10	1	16
Medium (T_2)	7	11	1	19
High (T_3)	5	12	15	32
Column Total	17	33/67 = 0.4925	17	67

Inspection of this table reveals that MBA graduates of the high-tuition schools do tend to have large salary gains (15 of the 67 schools) and that about half of the top-tier schools charge high tuition (32 of 67 schools). We can make more precise interpretations of this data by applying the concepts of probability.

Marginal Probabilities

The **marginal probability** of an event is found by dividing a row or column total by the total sample size. For example, using the column totals, 33 out of 67 schools had medium salary gains, so the marginal probability of a medium salary gain is $P(S_2) = 33/67 = 0.4925$. In other words, salary gains at about 49 percent of the top-tier schools were between $50,000 and $100,000. This calculation is shown in Table 5.4.

Using the row totals, for example, we see that 16 of the 67 schools had low tuition, so the marginal probability of low tuition is $P(T_1) = 16/67 = 0.2388$. In other words, there is a 24 percent chance that a top-tier school's MBA tuition is under $40,000. This calculation is illustrated in Table 5.5.

Joint Probabilities

Each of the nine main cells is used to calculate a *joint probability* representing the intersection of *two* events. For example, the upper right-hand cell is the joint event that the school has low tuition (T_1) *and* has large salary gains (S_3). We can write this event either as $P(T_1 \text{ and } S_3)$ or as $P(T_1 \cap S_3)$. Because only 1 out of 67 schools is in this category, the joint probability is $P(T_1 \text{ and } S_3) = 1/67 = 0.149$. In other words, there is less than a 2 percent chance that a top-tier school has *both* low tuition *and* high salary gains. This calculation is illustrated in Table 5.6.

Conditional Probabilities

Conditional probabilities may be found by *restricting* ourselves to a single row or column (the *condition*). For example, suppose we know that a school's MBA tuition is high (T_3). When we restrict ourselves to the 32 schools in the third row (those with high tuition), the conditional

TABLE 5.5   Marginal Probability of Event T_1

Tuition	Salary Gain Small (S_1)	Medium (S_2)	Large (S_3)	Row Total
Low (T_1)	5	10	1	16/67=0.2388
Medium (T_2)	7	11	1	19
High (T_3)	5	12	15	32
Column Total	17	33	17	67

TABLE 5.6 **Joint Probability of Event** $T_1 \cap S_3$

Tuition	Salary Gain Small (S_1)	Medium (S_2)	Large (S_3)	Row Total
Low (T_1)	5	10	1/67=0.0149	16
Medium (T_2)	7	11	1	19
High (T_3)	5	12	15	32
Column Total	17	33	17	67

TABLE 5.7 **Conditional Probability** $P(S_1 \mid T_3)$

Tuition	Salary Gain Small (S_1)	Medium (S_2)	Large (S_3)	Row Total
Low (T_1)	5	10	1	16
Medium (T_2)	7	11	1	19
High (T_3)	5/32=0.1563	12	15	32
Column Total	17	33	17	67

probabilities of any event may be calculated. For example, Table 5.7 illustrates the calculation of the conditional probability that salary gains are small (S_1) *given* that the MBA tuition is large (T_3). This conditional probability may be written $P(S_1 \mid T_3)$. We see that $P(S_1 \mid T_3) = 5/32 = 0.1563$, so there is about a 16 percent chance that a top-tier school's salary gains will be small despite its high tuition because there were 5 small-gain schools out of the 32 high-tuition schools.

Here are some other conditional probabilities and their interpretations:

Low Tuition MBA Program

$P(S_1 \mid T_1) = 5/16 = 0.3125$ There is a 31 percent probability that schools with low tuition will have small MBA salary gains.

$P(S_2 \mid T_1) = 10/16 = 0.6250$ There is a 63 percent probability that schools with low tuition will have medium MBA salary gains.

$P(S_3 \mid T_1) = 1/16 = 0.0625$ There is a 6 percent probability that schools with low tuition will have large MBA salary gains.

High Tuition MBA Program

$P(S_1 \mid T_3) = 5/32 = 0.1563$ There is a 16 percent probability that schools with high tuition will have small MBA salary gains.

$P(S_2 \mid T_3) = 12/32 = 0.3750$ There is a 38 percent probability that schools with high tuition will have medium MBA salary gains.

$P(S_3 \mid T_3) = 15/32 = 0.4688$ There is a 47 percent probability that schools with high tuition will have large MBA salary gains.

Caution: Conditional probabilities show, as we would expect, that higher tuition is associated with higher MBA salary gains (and conversely). But these results pertain only to a set of elite universities at a particular point in time, and few MBA students actually have access to such schools. Data from different universities or at a different point in time might show a different pattern.

Independence

To check whether events in a contingency table are independent, we can look at *conditional probabilities*. For example, if large salary gains (S_3) were independent of low tuition (T_1), then the conditional probability $P(S_3|T_1)$ would be the same as the marginal probability $P(S_3)$. But this is not the case:

Conditional	Marginal
$P(S_3|T_1) = 1/16 = 0.0625$	$P(S_3) = 17/67 = 0.2537$

Thus, large salary gains (S_3) are *not* independent of low tuition (T_1). Alternatively, we could ask whether $P(S_3 \text{ and } T_1) = P(S_3) P(T_1)$ is a necessary condition for independence. But

$$P(S_3)P(T_1) = (17/67)(16/67) = 0.0606$$

which is *not* equal to the observed joint probability

$$P(S_3 \text{ and } T_1) = 1/67 = 0.0149$$

Therefore, large salary gains (S_3) are *not* independent of low tuition (T_1).

Relative Frequencies

To facilitate probability calculations, we can divide each cell frequency f_{ij} by the total sample size ($n = 67$) to get the *relative frequencies* f_{ij}/n shown in Table 5.8. For example, the upper left-hand cell becomes $5/67 = 0.0746$.

The nine joint probabilities sum to 1.0000 because these are all the possible intersections:

$$0.0746 + 0.1045 + 0.0746 + 0.1493 + 0.1642 + 0.1791 + 0.0149 + 0.0149 + 0.2239 = 1.0000$$

Except for rounding, summing the joint probabilities across a row or down a column gives *marginal* (or *unconditional*) probabilities for the respective row or column:

Adding across rows
$0.0746 + 0.1493 + 0.0149 = 0.2388$
$0.1045 + 0.1642 + 0.0149 = 0.2836$
$0.0746 + 0.1791 + 0.2239 = 0.4776$

Adding down columns		
0.0746	0.1493	0.0149
+ 0.1045	+ 0.1642	+ 0.0149
+ 0.0746	+ 0.1791	+ 0.2239
= 0.2537	= 0.4926	= 0.2537

The marginal row and column probabilities sum to 1.0000 (except for rounding):

Columns (Salary): $P(S_1) + P(S_2) + P(S_3) = 0.2537 + 0.4926 + 0.2537 = 1.0000$
Rows (Tuition): $P(T_1) + P(T_2) + P(T_3) = 0.2388 + 0.2836 + 0.4776 = 1.0000$

Table 5.8 may be written in symbolic form as shown in Table 5.9.

TABLE 5.8   Relative Frequency Table: Each Cell Is f_{ij}/n

	Salary Gain			
Tuition	*Small (S_1)*	*Medium (S_2)*	*Large (S_3)*	*Row Total*
Low (T_1)	0.0746	0.1493	0.0149	0.2388
Medium (T_2)	0.1045	0.1642	0.0149	0.2836
High (T_3)	0.0746	0.1791	0.2239	0.4776
Column Total	0.2537	0.4926	0.2537	1.0000

TABLE 5.9   **Symbolic Notation for Relative Frequencies**

Tuition	Salary Gain Small (S_1)	Medium (S_2)	Large (S_3)	Row Total
Low (T_1)	$P(T_1 \text{ and } S_1)$	$P(T_1 \text{ and } S_2)$	$P(T_1 \text{ and } S_3)$	$P(T_1)$
Medium (T_2)	$P(T_2 \text{ and } S_1)$	$P(T_2 \text{ and } S_2)$	$P(T_2 \text{ and } S_3)$	$P(T_2)$
High (T_3)	$P(T_3 \text{ and } S_1)$	$P(T_3 \text{ and } S_2)$	$P(T_3 \text{ and } S_3)$	$P(T_3)$
Column Total	$P(S_1)$	$P(S_2)$	$P(S_3)$	1.0000

EXAMPLE 13

Payment Method and Purchase Quantity

Payment

A small grocery store would like to know if the number of items purchased by a customer is independent of the type of payment method the customer chooses to use. Having this information can help the store manager determine how to set up his/her various checkout lanes. The manager collected a random sample of 368 customer transactions. The results are shown in Table 5.10.

Looking at the frequency data presented in the table we can calculate the marginal probability that a customer will use cash to make the payment. Let C be the event that the customer chose cash as the payment method.

$$P(C) = \frac{126}{368} = 0.3424$$

Is $P(C)$ the same if we condition on number of items purchased?

$$P(C \mid 1 \text{ to } 5) = \frac{30}{88} = 0.3409 \quad P(C \mid 6 \text{ to } 9) = \frac{46}{135} = 0.3407$$

$$P(C \mid 10 \text{ to } 19) = \frac{31}{89} = 0.3483 \quad P(C \mid 20 +) = \frac{19}{56} = 0.3393$$

Notice that there is little difference in these probabilities. If we perform the same type of analysis for the next two payment methods we find that *payment method* and *number of items purchased* are essentially independent. Based on this study, the manager might decide to offer a cash-only checkout lane that is *not* restricted to the number of items purchased.

How Do We Get a Contingency Table?

Contingency tables do not just "happen" but require careful data organization and forethought. They are created from raw data. In the MBA salary example, numerical values were mapped into discrete codes, as shown in Table 5.11. If the data were already categorical (e.g., a survey with discrete responses) this step would have been unnecessary. Once the data are coded, we tabulate the frequency in each cell of the contingency table. The tabulation would be done using Excel's Pivot Table or another software package (e.g., MINITAB's Stat > Tables > Cross Tabulation).

TABLE 5.10   **Contingency Table for Payment Method by Number of Items Purchased**

Number of Items Purchased	Payment Method Cash	Cheque	Credit/Debit Card	Row Total
1 to 5	30	15	43	88
6 to 9	46	23	66	135
10 to 19	31	15	43	89
20 +	19	10	27	56
Column Total	126	63	179	368

TABLE 5.11 **Data Coding for MBA Data**  **MBA Salary**

| School | Original Data ($000) | | Coded Data | |
	Tuition	Gain	Tuition	Gain
Alabama (Manderson)	67	21	T_3	S_1
Arizona (Eller)	69	42	T_3	S_1
Arizona State (Carey)	70	41	T_3	S_1
Auburn	46	18	T_2	S_1
Babson (Olin)	22	53	T_1	S_2
⋮	⋮	⋮	⋮	⋮
Wake Forest (Babcock)	91	50	T_3	S_2
Washington U.—St. Louis (Olin)	120	61	T_3	S_2
William & Mary	94	45	T_3	S_1
Wisconsin—Madison	81	48	T_3	S_1
Yale	137	65	T_3	S_2

Note: S_1 is salary gain under $50K$, S_2 = salary gain $50K-$100K$, and S_3 is salary gain $100K+$. T_1 is tuition under $40K$, T_2 is tuition from $40K-$50K$, and T_3 is tuition of $50K+$. Data are provided for educational purposes and not as a guide to financial gains.

Source: *Forbes* 172, no. 8 (Oct. 13, 2003), p. 78. Copyright © 2005 Forbes, Inc. Reprinted by permission of Forbes magazine.

Mini Case 5.1

Smoking and Gender

Table 5.12 shows that the proportion of women over age 65 who have never smoked is much higher than for men, that a higher proportion of men than women used to smoke but have quit, and that the proportion of current smokers over 65 is about the same for men and women.

Conditional probabilities may be found from Table 5.12 by restricting ourselves to a single row or column (the *condition*). For example, for males we get:

$P(N|M) = 3,160/10,567 = 0.2990$ — There is a 29.9 percent probability that an individual never smoked *given* that the person is male.

$P(R|M) = 5,087/10,567 = 0.4814$ — There is a 48.1 percent probability that an individual is a former smoker *given* that the person is male.

$P(S|M) = 2,320/10,567 = 0.2196$ — There is a 22.0 percent probability that an individual currently smokes *given* that the person is male.

On the other hand, for females we get:

$P(N|F) = 10,437/15,305 = 0.6819$ — There is a 68.2 percent probability that an individual never smoked *given* that the person is female.

$P(R|F) = 2,861/15,305 = 0.1869$ — There is an 18.7 percent probability that an individual is a former smoker *given* that the person is female.

$P(S|F) = 2,007/15,305 = 0.1311$ — There is a 13.1 percent probability that an individual currently smokes *given* that the person is female.

These conditional probabilities show that a female is over twice as likely as a male never to have smoked. However, the number of *former* smokers is higher among males (you can't be a former smoker unless you once smoked).

Table 5.13 shows the *relative frequencies* obtained by dividing each table frequency by the sample size ($n = 25,872$).

For example, the joint probability $P(M \cap N)$ is 0.1221 (i.e., about 12.2 percent of the sample were males who had never smoked). The six joint probabilities sum to 1.0000, as they should, assuming no round-off errors.

TABLE 5.12   **Smoking and Gender for Persons Age 65 and Over (Thousands)**   💿   **Smoking**

Gender	Never Smoked (N)	Former Smoker (R)	Current Smoker (S)	Total
Male (M)	3,160	5,087	2,320	10,567
Female (F)	10,437	2,861	2,007	15,305
Total	13,597	7,948	4,327	25,872

Source: U.S. Department of Commerce, *Statistical Abstract of the United States, 1986*, p. 119.

TABLE 5.13   **Relative Frequency for Smoking and Gender for Persons Age 65 and Over**

Gender	Never Smoked (N)	Former Smoker (R)	Current Smoker (S)	Total
Male (M)	0.1221	0.1966	0.0897	0.4084
Female (F)	0.4034	0.1106	0.0776	0.5916
Total	0.5255	0.3072	0.1673	1.0000

Section Exercises

5.40   A survey of 158 introductory statistics students showed the following contingency table. Find each event probability. (LO 6)
   💿   **WebSurvey**

a. $P(V)$ b. $P(A)$ c. $P(A \cap V)$
d. $P(A \cup V)$ e. $P(A|V)$ f. $P(V|A)$

Cellphone Provider	Visa Card (V)	No Visa Card (V')	Row Total
Rogers (A)	32	15	47
Other (A')	84	27	111
Column Total	116	42	158

5.41   A survey of 156 introductory statistics students showed the following contingency table. Find each event probability. (LO 6)
   💿   **WebSurvey**

a. $P(D)$ b. $P(R)$ c. $P(D \cap R)$
d. $P(D \cup R)$ e. $P(R|D)$ f. $P(R|P)$

Newspaper Read	Living Where? Dorm (D)	Parents (P)	Apt (A)	Row Total
Never (N)	13	6	6	25
Occasionally (O)	58	30	21	109
Regularly (R)	8	7	7	22
Column Total	79	43	34	156

5.42   This contingency table describes 200 business students. Find each probability and interpret it in words. (LO 6)
   💿   **GenderMajor**

a. $P(A)$ b. $P(M)$ c. $P(A \cap M)$
d. $P(F \cap S)$ e. $P(A|M)$ f. $P(A|F)$
g. $P(F|S)$ h. $P(E \cup F)$

Gender	Major Accounting (A)	Economics (E)	Statistics (S)	Row Total
Female (F)	44	30	24	98
Male (M)	56	30	16	102
Column Total	100	60	40	200

5.43 Based on the previous problem, is major independent of gender? Explain the basis for your conclusion. (LO 5 & 6)

5.44 This contingency table shows average yield (rows) and average duration (columns) for 38 bond funds. For a randomly chosen bond fund, find the probability that: (LO 5 & 6)

    a. The bond fund is long duration.
    b. The bond fund has high yield.
    c. The bond fund has high yield given that it is of short duration.
    d. The bond fund is of short duration given that it has high yield.

	Average Portfolio Duration			
Yield	Short (D_1)	Intermediate (D_2)	Long (D_3)	Row Total
Small (Y_1)	8	2	0	10
Medium (Y_2)	1	6	6	13
High (Y_3)	2	4	9	15
Column Total	11	12	15	38

Source: Data are from *Forbes* 173, no. 2 (Feb. 2, 2004). **BondFunds**

5.6 Tree Diagrams

In the previous sections of this chapter, you learned several probability laws or rules that would allow you to determine the probabilities you were looking for if you had the necessary information. For example, suppose you wanted to determine $P(A \cup B)$ and you knew $P(A)$, $P(B)$, and $P(A \cap B)$. You could easily determine this probability by using the law of addition:

$$P(A \cup B) = P(A) + P(B) - P(A \cap B)$$

But suppose some of this information is not directly available. You may be able to create a contingency table and extract that information from there, or a Venn diagram may enable you to visualize the missing information. Another important tool you may be able to use is a tree diagram or a probability tree.

What Is a Tree?

Events and probabilities can be displayed in the form of a **tree diagram** or *probability tree* to help visualize all possible outcomes. Essentially, a probability tree consists of a sequence of branches. The initial set of branches represents unconditional events, with the subsequent sets of branches representing conditional events (including independent events).

EXAMPLE 14

Town Council Election

In a small town in northern Quebec, there is an election to determine who will sit on the town council. The town has three wards, each to elect one council person. In each ward, there are candidates who favour expansion of the mining operations within the town's borders and there are candidates that don't. In Ward A, the probability of electing a candidate who favours expansion is 0.7. The probabilities of electing a candidate who favours expansion in Wards B and C are 0.6 and 0.2, respectively. What are the possible outcomes of this election and their probabilities if we define A, B, and C as candidates being elected, in their respective wards, who favour expansion of the mining operations, and A', B', and C' as candidates being elected who don't favour this expansion?

To be able to use a probability tree to determine the possible outcomes and their probabilities, we need to set up a sequence of branches so that at the very end of the tree we will have all the possible events that could occur along with their probabilities. In setting up this sequence, the first set of branches needs to represent unconditional events with subsequent sets of branches conditioned on the previous sets of branches. In this particular example, all events are unconditional events, so it doesn't matter in which order the branches are sequenced. Arbitrarily, the first set of branches has been chosen to be A (the elected candidate in Ward A is in favour of expansion) and A' (the elected candidate in Ward A is not in favour of expansion), the second set has been chosen to be B and B', and so on as indicated in the tree diagram in Figure 5.11.

Continuing with this example and having created the probability tree, we can answer such questions as, "If a majority of the council members must be in favour of expanding mining operations before it can be expanded, what is the probability that the operations will be allowed to be expanded?"

Because a majority in this case is two or more council members in favour, we simply have to sum the probabilities for the events in which two or more council members are in favour or:

$$P(\text{at least two in favour}) = P(ABC) + P(ABC') + P(AB'C) + P(A'BC)$$
$$= 0.084 + 0.336 + 0.056 + 0.036$$
$$= 0.512$$

FIGURE 5.11

Tree Diagram for Quebec Municipal Election

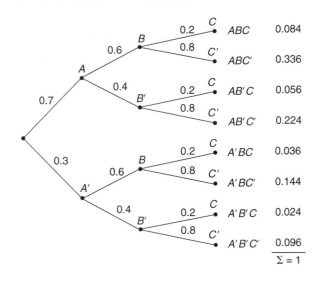

Concept Check

Some observations about Figure 5.11:
- The notation for each possible outcome has been simplified. For example, instead of stating the first outcome as $A \cap B \cap C$, we simply stated it as *ABC*, a common practice.
- The values listed along each of the branches are the probabilities of each event occurring. For example 0.6 is $P(B)$. If there were conditional events, these values would represent the conditional probabilities. For example, if the occurrence of B was dependent on the occurrence of A, the value of 0.6 along the branch connecting event A to event B would be $P(B|A)$.
- The values listed at the end of the branches are the probabilities of each outcome. For example, 0.084 is $P(ABC)$. We get these probabilities by multiplying the probabilities along the connecting branches. Why? We are simply applying the extension of the multiplication law:

$$P(A_1 \cap A_2 \cap \cdots \cap A_n) = P(A_1)P(A_2|A_1)P(A_3|A_1, A_2) \cdots P(A_n|A_1, A_2, \ldots, A_{n-1})$$

which for independent events is:

$$P(A_1 \cap A_2 \cap \cdots \cap A_n) = P(A_1)P(A_2) \cdots P(A_n)$$

Suppose a construction company in Regina, Saskatchewan, is only one of four companies around the world capable of developing sites for storing certain toxic chemicals. From past experience, it has determined that it has a 100 percent chance of winning a contract if none of the other three companies make a bid on the project, a 70 percent chance of winning a contract if there is only one other bid, a 45 percent chance if there are two other bidders, and a 15 percent chance if all other companies make a bid. Also from past experience, it knows that there is a 15 percent chance that no other companies will make a bid, a 25 percent chance that one other company will make a bid, a 40 percent chance that two companies will make a bid, and a 20 percent chance that all other companies will make a bid. Because preparing and submitting a bid could be rather expensive, the Regina company would like to know the probability of it winning a bid. For future use, it would also like to know the probabilities that if it happens to win the bid, no other company submitted a bid, one other company submitted a bid, and so on.

EXAMPLE 15

Regina Construction Company

So, this company wants to determine $P(\text{winning the contract})$ and $P(\text{no other company made a bid given that it wins the contract})$. In symbols, the company wants to determine $P(W)$ and $P(0|W)$. There is a rule to determine the conditional probabilities. For example,

$$P(0|W) = \frac{P(W \cap 0)}{P(W)}$$

Although we haven't formally stated a rule for determining $P(W)$

$$P(W) = P(W \cap 0) + P(W \cap 1) + P(W \cap 2) + P(W \cap 3)$$

Looking at either of these two formulas, we realize that the information we need to determine the probabilities we want is not directly obvious. Therefore, let us see if we can extract this information using a probability tree.

Based on the information we are given, we have four unconditional probabilities: the probabilities that no other companies make a bid, one other company makes a bid, two other companies make a bid, and all three companies make a bid. Therefore, the number of companies making a bid forms the first set of branches. The second set of branches represents the conditional events: winning given that no other companies made a bid, losing given that no other companies made a bid, winning given that one other company made a bid, and so on. This tree, with the other pertinent information, would look like Figure 5.12.

You will notice that the values included on the diagram represent probabilities. The furthest left set of probabilities are the unconditional probabilities (e.g., $P(0)$). The middle set are the conditional probabilities (e.g., $P(W|0)$) and the farthest right set of probabilities are the probabilities for the resulting intersections (e.g., $P(0 \cap W)$). These last probabilities result by simply multiplying the probabilities along the appropriate series of branches along the path (e.g., $P(1 \cap W) = (0.25)(0.70) = 0.1750$). Essentially, we are simply applying the multiplication law, because $P(1 \cap W) = P(1)P(W|1)$. On the tree diagram event "$1 \cap W$" is represented as simply "$1W$."

Looking at the eight events (terminal events) represented at the end of the branches, we notice that these events are mutually exclusive (and collectively exhaustive) and we can determine other probabilities by using this fact. From the results of this tree diagram, we can now determine the probabilities of interest.

$$P(W) = P(0 \cap W) + P(1 \cap W) + P(2 \cap W) + P(3 \cap W) = 0.150 + 0.175 + 0.180 + 0.030 = 0.535$$

$$P(0|W) = \frac{P(0 \cap W)}{P(W)} = \frac{0.150}{0.535} \approx 0.2804$$

$$P(1|W) = \frac{P(1 \cap W)}{P(W)} = \frac{0.175}{0.535} \approx 0.3271$$

$$P(2|W) = \frac{P(W \cap 2)}{P(W)} = \frac{0.180}{0.535} \approx 0.3364$$

$$P(3|W) = \frac{P(W \cap 3)}{P(W)} = \frac{0.030}{0.535} \approx 0.0561$$

FIGURE 5.12

Tree Diagram for Regina Construction Company

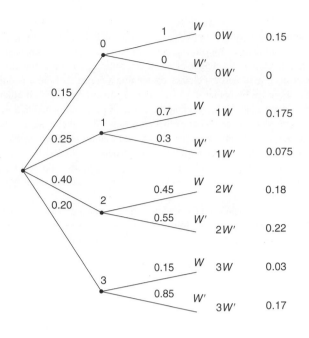

A Closer Look

Looking at the results of the probability tree, we can make the following observations:

- The prior probabilities of zero, one, two, or three of the other companies making bids were 0.15, 0.25, 0.40, and 0.20, respectively. If the Regina company did in fact win the contract, these probabilities, referred to as posterior probabilities, changed to 0.2804, 0.3271, 0.3364, and 0.0561, respectively, but they still summed to one. With the additional information of winning the contract, the original probabilities were adjusted either upward or downward, and the upward adjustments were balanced by the downward adjustments.
- The conditional probabilities sum to 1 within each set of branches; the joint probabilities also sum to 1 for all eight terminal events.
- The sum of the probabilities for each pair of terminal events equals the original unconditional probability (e.g., looking at the event that one other company makes a bid, $0.175 + 0.075 = 0.250$)

The probability tree is a powerful tool for determining probabilities when the relevant probability rules cannot directly be applied because of missing or hidden information. The one main drawback to these trees is when there are too many sets of branches that must be drawn. In the next section, we will discuss Bayes' Theorem and how to use it. The answers arrived at using this theorem could also be obtained with the proper use of a decision tree.

An Application: Passing an Exam Ben, Tom, and Jerri are students taking an introductory statistics course and are about to write their first quiz. This quiz will consist of one multiple choice (with five choices) question selected from a large test bank of multiple choice questions. Ben did not prepare for this quiz, so his only chance of passing this quiz is to just guess the correct answer. Tom studied enough so that he knows the correct answers to 40 percent of the multiple choice questions, so Tom's chance of passing depends upon knowing the correct answer to the question or purely guessing the answer if he doesn't know the correct answer. Jerri studied extensively so that she knows the correct answers to

Tree Diagrams for Multiple Choice Quiz  FIGURE 5.13

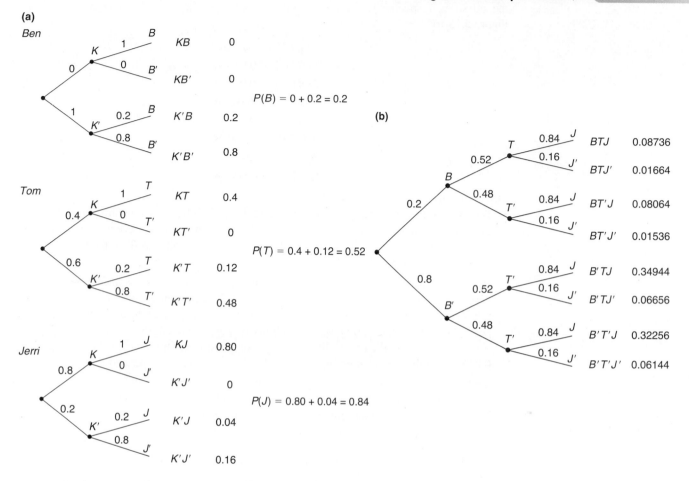

80 percent of the questions. If she doesn't know the answer, she also has the opportunity to purely guess the correct answer. What is the probability that Ben answers the question correctly? Tom answers the question correctly? Jerri answers the question correctly? If we are interested in the possible outcomes for these three students, list all the events in the sample space (e.g., $B \cap T \cap J$ [Ben and Tom and Jerri all pass the quiz]) and their respective probabilities.

Let's first determine the probability that each individual answers the question correctly using the probability trees in Figure 5.13(a) where K represents knowing the correct answer, B represents Ben answering the question correctly, T represents Tom answering the question correctly, and J represents Jerri answering the question correctly.

Consider the set of trees in Figure 5.13(a). The first set of two branches corresponds to "knowing the correct answer." Thus K represents knowing the correct answer, and K', the complement event, represents not knowing the correct answer. Thus for Ben, the probability of knowing the correct answer is 0, the number on this branch. For Tom this number is 0.4, and for Jerry it is 0.8. The second set of branches in Figure 5.13(a) corresponds to different conditional probabilities. For example, $P(T|K)$—the probability that Tom gets the right answer given that he knows the answer—equals 1. Similarly, $P(B|K) = P(J|K) = 1$. From Figure 5.13(a), we see that Ben has a probability of 0.2 of answering the question correctly, Tom has a probability of 0.52 of answering the question correctly, and Jerri has a probability 0.84 of answering the question correctly.

Using these probabilities for the sample space

$$S = \{BTJ, BTJ', BT'J, BT'J', B'TJ, B'TJ', B'T'J, B'T'J'\}$$

and using the probabilities of 0.2, 0.52, and 0.84 for Ben, Tom, and Jerri correctly answering the question, respectively, the probabilities for each of the possible outcomes are from Figure 5.13(b):

$$P(BTJ) = 0.08736$$
$$P(BTJ') = 0.01664$$
$$P(BT'J) = 0.08064$$
$$P(BT'J') = 0.01536$$
$$P(B'TJ) = 0.34944$$
$$P(B'TJ') = 0.06656$$
$$P(B'T'J) = 0.32256$$
$$P(B'T'J') = 0.06144$$

Observations:

- We can use this probability tree to determine the probability of Jerri correctly answering the question simply by summing the probabilities for those simple events in which Jerri answers correctly. If you do so, you will see that this probability is 0.84, the same probability as we determined with our previous set of probability trees.

- If this quiz was a fair quiz such that those that pass deserve to pass and those that fail deserve to fail, Ben should definitely fail and Jerri should definitely pass and it would be a travesty if Ben passed and Jerri failed. But looking at the results of the decision tree (or the previous decision trees), Ben has a probability of 0.20 of passing, Jerri has a probability of 0.16 of failing, and the probability of Ben passing and Jerri failing is 0.032 (= 0.01664 + 0.01536). In the next chapter, we will see that when the quiz is expanded to include more questions, the quiz becomes more fair the more questions that are included.

- The probability of Ben passing and Jerri failing could have been determined using the multiplication law for independent events because Ben passing does not affect the probability of Jerri failing. Using this rule:

$$P(B \cap J') = P(B)P(J') = (0.2)(0.16) = 0.032$$

- We can also use this probability tree to determine, for example, the probability that Jerri answered the question correctly knowing that only one student answered correctly. Applying the conditional probability rule and the results from the probability tree:

$$P(J|\text{only one passed}) = \frac{P(J \text{ and only one passed})}{P(\text{only one passed})}$$

$$= \frac{P(B'T'J)}{P(BT'J') + P(B'TJ') + P(B'T'J')} = \frac{0.32256}{0.01536 + 0.06656 + 0.32256} = \frac{0.32256}{0.40448} = 0.7975$$

Section Exercises

5.45 Of grocery shoppers who have a shopping cart, 70 percent pay by credit/debit card (event C_1), 20 percent pay cash (event C_2), and 10 percent pay by cheque (event C_3). Of shoppers without a shopping cart, 50 percent pay by credit/debit card (event C_1), 40 percent pay cash (event C_2), and 10 percent pay by cheque (event C_3). On Saturday morning, 80 percent of the shoppers take a shopping cart (event S_1) and 20 percent do not (event S_2). (a) Sketch a tree based on this data. (b) Calculate the probability of all joint probabilities (e.g., $S_1 \cap C_1$). (c) Verify that the joint probabilities sum to 1. (LO 6)

5.46 Suppose a study showed that 60 percent of *Globe and Mail* subscribers watch CBC every day. Of these, 70 percent watch it outside the home. Only 20 percent of those who don't watch CBC every day watch it outside the home. Let D be the event "watches CBC daily" and O be the event "watches CBC outside the home." Sketch a tree based on this data. (b) Calculate the probability of all joint probabilities (e.g., $D \cap O$). (c) Verify that the joint probabilities sum to 1. (LO 6)

5.47 Suppose the Toronto Maple Leafs have three games remaining in their season and they may need to win all three games, depending upon how other teams perform during this period. Suppose that they have a probability of 0.6 of beating Montreal, a probability of 0.7 of beating Edmonton, and a probability of 0.4 of beating Calgary. Set up a probability tree for Toronto's possible outcomes (assuming no tie games) and from this tree determine (LO 6):

(a) The probabilities that Toronto wins 0 games, 1 game, 2 games, and 3 games.
(b) The probability that Toronto beat Montreal knowing that Toronto only won 1 game.
(c) The probability that Toronto beat Montreal knowing that Toronto won 2 games.

5.48 In the application on body mass index earlier in this chapter, we were given the following information based on a study reported by Statistics Canada (www40.statcan.gc.ca/101/cst01/hlth68-eng.htm) concerning the change in body mass index (BMI) of Canadians between 1994/1995 and 2006/2007. This study determined that 29.4 percent of females had increased BMI, 63.9 percent had the same BMI, and 6.7 percent had lower BMI. Of the males, 31.6 percent had increased BMI, 63.4 percent had the same BMI, and 5.0 percent had lower BMI. In the study, 51.9 percent were males and 48.1 percent were females. We were asked to determine the following: If an individual participating in this study was randomly selected for further analysis, what would be the probability that:

(a) The individual selected is a male?
(b) The individual selected had an increase in BMI given that the individual is a male?
(c) The individual selected had an increase in BMI given that the individual is a female?
(d) The individual is a male and had an increase in BMI?
(e) The individual is a male or had an increase in BMI?
(f) The individual had an increase in BMI?
(g) The individual is a male given that he had an increase in BMI?

Using a probability tree, answer parts d) through g). (LO 6)

Mini Case 5.2

Can Amazon Read Your Mind?

You go to Amazon to purchase a copy of *Eugenie Grandet* by Honore de Balzac. Amazon offers you 714 online choices (new, used, various vendors). But Amazon also recommends that you consider buying a copy of *Hedda Gabler* by Henrik Ibsen or *Madame Bovary* by Gustave Flaubert. How did they decide on these suggestions? The answer is that Amazon has a matrix (like an Excel pivot table) that keeps track of the frequency of *co-purchased* items (e.g., books, music, DVDs) for Web shoppers. Probabilities derived from the cells in this contingency table are used to recommend products that are likely to be of interest to you, assuming that you are "like" other buyers. While such predictions of your behaviour are only probabilistic, even a modest chance of landing extra sales can make a difference in bottom-line profit. There are even more sophisticated logic engines that can track your Web clicks. Is this an invasion of your privacy? Does it bother you to think that you may be predictable? Interestingly, many consumers don't seem to mind, and actually find value in this kind of statistical information system.

5.7 Bayes' Theorem

An important theorem published by Thomas Bayes (1702–1761) provides a method of revising probabilities to reflect new information. The **prior** (unconditional) **probability** of an event B is revised after event A has been considered to yield a **posterior** (conditional) **probability.** We begin with a formula slightly different from the standard definition of conditional probability:

$$P(B|A) = \frac{P(A|B)P(B)}{P(A)} \tag{5.14}$$

Unfortunately, as was seen in our previous example, in some situations $P(A)$ is not given. $P(A)$ can be calculated as follows: $P(A) = P(AB) + P(AB') = P(A|B)P(B) + P(A|B')P(B')$. This gives us the most useful and common form of **Bayes' Theorem:**

$$P(B|A) = \frac{P(A|B)P(B)}{P(A|B)P(B) + P(A|B')P(B')} \tag{5.15}$$

FIGURE 5.14

Tree Diagram for Businesswoman

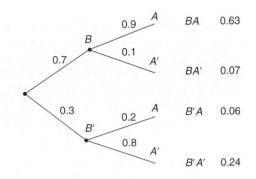

How Bayes' Theorem Works

Bayes' Theorem is best understood by an example.

Most successful business people rely on others to help them make informed decisions. One successful businesswoman has made successful decisions 70 percent of the time. When her decisions have been successful, the one person that she most confides in has correctly predicted her successes 90 percent of the time. When her decisions have been unsuccessful, this same person has incorrectly predicted success 20 percent of the time. This businesswoman has made a tentative decision. What is the probability that this person will agree or predict that her decision will be successful? If this individual has predicted that her decision will be successful, what is the probability that her decision will be successful? If this individual has predicted her decision will not be successful, what is the probability that her decision will not be successful?

If we define B as making a successful decision and A as predicting her decision will be successful, the given facts are:

$$P(B) = 0.7 \qquad P(A|B) = 0.9 \qquad P(A|B') = 0.2$$

and from these facts we can determine that:

$$P(B') = 0.3 \qquad P(A'|B) = 0.1 \qquad P(A'|B') = 0.8$$

We can use the tree in Figure 5.14 to answer these questions. Using the results from the tree,

$$P(A) = P(B \cap A) + P(B' \cap A) = 0.63 + 0.06 = 0.69$$

$$P(B|A) = \frac{P(B \cap A)}{P(A)} = \frac{0.63}{0.69} = 0.913$$

$$P(B'|A') = \frac{P(B' \cap A')}{P(A')} = \frac{0.24}{0.07 + 0.24} = \frac{0.24}{0.31} = 0.774$$

Using Bayes' Theorem formula,

$$P(B|A) = \frac{P(A|B)P(B)}{P(A|B)P(B) + P(A|B')P(B')} = \frac{(0.9)(0.7)}{(0.9)(0.7) + (0.3)(0.2)} = \frac{0.63}{0.69} = 0.913$$

and

$$P(B'|A') = \frac{P(A'|B')P(B')}{P(A'|B')P(B') + P(A'|B)P(B)} = \frac{(0.8)(0.3)}{(0.8)(0.3) + (0.1)(0.7)} = \frac{0.24}{0.31} = 0.774$$

General Form of Bayes' Theorem

A generalization of Bayes' Theorem allows event B to have as many categories as we wish $(B_1, B_2, \ldots, B_n)$ rather than just the dichotomous categories B and B', where $B_1, B_2, \ldots, B_n$ are mutually exclusive and collectively exhaustive events:

$$P(B_i|A) = \frac{P(A|B_i)P(B_i)}{P(A|B_1)P(B_1) + P(A|B_2)P(B_2) + \cdots + P(A|B_n)P(B_n)} \qquad (5.16)$$

EXAMPLE 16
Hospital Trauma Centres

Based on historical data, three hospital trauma centres have 50, 30, and 20 percent of the cases, respectively. The probabilities of a case resulting in a malpractice suit in the three hospitals are 0.001, 0.005, and 0.008, respectively. If a malpractice suit is filed, what is the probability that it originated in hospital 1? This problem is solved as follows. We define:

$$\text{Event } A = \text{a malpractice suit is filed by patient}$$

$$\text{Event } B_i = \text{patient was treated at trauma centre } i(i = 1, 2, 3)$$

The given information can be presented in a table like Table 5.14.
Applying Equation 5.16, we can find $P(B_1|A)$ as follows:

$$P(B_1|A) = \frac{P(A|B_1)P(B_1)}{P(A|B_1)P(B_1) + P(A|B_2)P(B_2) + P(A|B_3)P(B_3)}$$

$$= \frac{(0.001)(0.50)}{(0.001)(0.50) + (0.005)(0.30) + (0.008)(0.20)}$$

$$= \frac{0.0005}{0.0005 + 0.0015 + 0.0016} = \frac{0.0005}{0.0036} = 0.1389$$

The probability that the malpractice suit was filed in hospital 1 is 0.1389, or 13.89 percent. Although hospital 1 sees 50 percent of the trauma patients, it is expected to generate less than half the malpractice suits, because the other two hospitals have much higher incidence of malpractice suits.

There is nothing special about $P(B_1|A)$. In fact, it is easy to calculate *all* the posterior probabilities at once by using a worksheet, as shown in Table 5.15:

$$P(B_1|A) = 0.1389 \text{ (probability that a malpractice lawsuit originated in hospital 1)}$$

$$P(B_2|A) = 0.4167 \text{ (probability that a malpractice lawsuit originated in hospital 2)}$$

$$P(B_3|A) = 0.4444 \text{ (probability that a malpractice lawsuit originated in hospital 3)}$$

We could also approach the problem intuitively by imagining 10,000 patients, as shown in Table 5.16. First, calculate each hospital's expected number of patients (50, 30, and 20 percent of 10,000). Next, find each hospital's expected number of malpractice suits by multiplying its malpractice rate by its expected number of patients:

$$\text{Hospital 1: } 0.001 \times 5,000 = 5 \text{ (expected malpractice suits at hospital 1)}$$

$$\text{Hospital 2: } 0.005 \times 3,000 = 15 \text{ (expected malpractice suits at hospital 2)}$$

$$\text{Hospital 3: } 0.008 \times 2,000 = 16 \text{ (expected malpractice suits at hospital 3)}$$

Adding down, the total number of malpractice suits is 36. Hence, $P(B_1|A) = 5/36 = 0.1389$, $P(B_2|A) = 15/36 = 0.4167$, and $P(B_3|A) = 16/36 = 0.4444$. These three probabilities add to 1. Overall, there are 36 malpractice suits, so we can also calculate $P(A) = 36/10,000 = 0.0036$. Many people find the table method easier to understand than the formulas. Do you agree?

We could visualize this situation as shown in Figure 5.15. The initial sample space consists of three mutually exclusive and collectively exhaustive events (hospitals B_1, B_2, B_3). As indicated by their relative areas, B_1 is 50 percent of the sample space, B_2 is 30 percent of the sample space, and B_3 is 20 percent of the sample space. But *given* that a malpractice case has been filed (event A), then the relevant sample space is *reduced* to that of event A.
The revised (posterior) probabilities are the relative areas *within* event A:

$$P(B_1|A) \text{ is the proportion of } A \text{ that lies within } B_1 = 0.1389$$

$$P(B_2|A) \text{ is the proportion of } A \text{ that lies within } B_2 = 0.4167$$

$$P(B_3|A) \text{ is the proportion of } A \text{ that lies within } B_3 = 0.4444$$

These percentages were calculated in Table 5.15. A worksheet is still needed to calculate $P(A)$ for the denominator.

TABLE 5.14   Given Information for Hospital Trauma Centres ⦾ Malpractice

Hospital	Marginal	Conditional: Suit Filed
1	$P(B_1) = 0.50$	$P(A\|B_1) = 0.001$
2	$P(B_2) = 0.30$	$P(A\|B_2) = 0.005$
3	$P(B_3) = 0.20$	$P(A\|B_3) = 0.008$

TABLE 5.15   Worksheet for Bayesian Probability of Malpractice Suit ⦾ Malpractice

Hospital	Prior (Given) $P(B_i)$	Given $P(A\|B_i)$	$P(B_i \cap A = P(A\|B_i) P(B_i)$	Posterior (Revised) $P(B_i\|A) = P(B_i \cap A)/P(A)$
1	0.50	0.001	$(0.001)(0.50) = 0.0005$	$0.0005/0.0036 = 0.1389$
2	0.30	0.005	$(0.005)(0.30) = 0.0015$	$0.0015/0.0036 = 0.4167$
3	0.20	0.008	$(0.008)(0.20) = 0.0016$	$0.0016/0.0036 = 0.4444$
Total	1.00		$P(A) = 0.0036$	1.0000

TABLE 5.16   Malpractice Frequencies for 10,000 Hypothetical Patients ⦾ Malpractice

Hospital	Malpractice Suit Filed	No Malpractice Suit Filed	Total
1	5	4,995	5,000
2	15	2,985	3,000
3	16	1,984	2,000
Total	36	9,964	10,000

FIGURE 5.15

Illustration of Hospital Trauma Centre Example

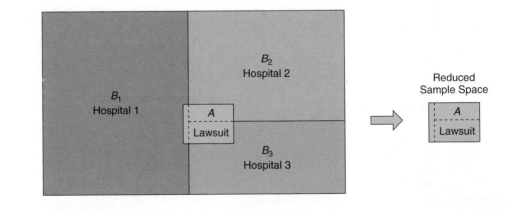

Section Exercises

5.49 A drug test for athletes has a 5 percent false positive rate and a 10 percent false negative rate. Of the athletes tested, 4 percent have actually been using the prohibited drug. If an athlete tests positive, what is the probability that the athlete has actually been using the prohibited drug? Explain your reasoning clearly. (LO 7)

5.50 Half of a set of the parts are manufactured by machine A and half by machine B. Four percent of all the parts are defective. Six percent of the parts manufactured on machine A are defective. Find the probability that a part was manufactured on machine A, given that the part is defective. Explain your reasoning clearly. (LO 7)

5.51 An airport gamma ray luggage scanner coupled with a neural net artificial intelligence program can detect a weapon in suitcases with a false positive rate of 2 percent and a false negative rate of 2 percent. Assume a 0.001 probability that a suitcase contains a weapon. If a suitcase triggers the alarm, what is the probability that the suitcase contains a weapon? Explain your reasoning. (LO 7)

5.52 When Canadians cross into the United States from Canada using the Rainbow Bridge connecting Niagara Falls, Ontario, to Niagara Falls, New York, assume that 70 percent will answer the Immigration and Customs officials truthfully, 25 percent may bend the truth slightly, and the remaining 5 percent are trying to get away with serious smuggling or other similar crimes. Based on how a Canadian answers the officials' questions, 5 percent of those answering truthfully are pulled over for further inspection, 20 percent of those bending the truth slightly are pulled over for further inspection, and 60 percent of those trying to get away with serious smuggling or other similar crimes are pulled over for further inspection. If one of these Canadians is pulled over for further inspection, what is the probability that (a) he or she answered the official's questions truthfully, (b) he or she bent the truth slightly, and (c) he or she was trying to get away with serious smuggling or other similar crimes? (LO 7)

Mini Case   5.3

Smoking and Gender Again

Table 5.17 shows that the proportion of women over age 65 who have never smoked is much higher than for men, that a higher proportion of men than women used to smoke but have quit, and that the proportion of current smokers over 65 is higher for men than for women

We see from Table 5.17 that $P(M) = 10{,}567/25{,}872 = 0.4084$ and $P(F) = 15{,}305/25{,}872 = 0.5916$. We also have these conditional probabilities:

$P(N|M) = 3{,}160/10{,}567 = 0.2990$ There is a 29.9 percent chance that an individual never smoked *given* that the person is male.

$P(R|M) = 5{,}087/10{,}567 = 0.4814$ There is a 48.1 percent chance that an individual is a former smoker *given* that the person is male.

$P(S|M) = 2{,}320/10{,}567 = 0.2196$ There is a 22.0 percent chance that an individual currently smokes *given* that the person is male.

$P(N|F) = 10{,}437/15{,}305 = 0.6819$ There is a 68.2 percent chance that an individual never smoked *given* that the person is female.

$P(R|F) = 2{,}861/15{,}305 = 0.1869$ There is an 18.7 percent chance that an individual is a former smoker *given* that the person is female.

$P(S|F) = 2{,}007/15{,}305 = 0.1311$ There is a 13.1 percent chance that an individual currently smokes *given* that the person is female.

The tree is shown in Figure 5.16.

Applying Bayes' Theorem, the probability that a 65-year-old person is male, given that a person is a smoker, is 53.62 percent (even though only 40.84 percent of 65-year-olds are males):

$$P(M|S) = \frac{P(S|M)P(M)}{P(S|M)P(M) + P(S|F)P(F)}$$

$$= \frac{(0.2196)(0.4084)}{(0.2196)(0.4084) + (0.1311)(0.5916)}$$

$$= \frac{0.0897}{0.0897 + 0.0776} = \frac{0.0897}{0.1673} = 0.5362$$

TABLE 5.17   Smoking and Gender for Persons Age 65 and Over (Thousands)   Smoking

Gender	Never Smoked (N)	Former Smoker (R)	Current Smoker (S)	Total
Male (M)	3,160	5,087	2,320	10,567
Female (F)	10,437	2,861	2,007	15,305
Total	13,597	7,948	4,327	25,872

Source: U.S. Department of Commerce, *Statistical Abstract of the United States, 1986,* p. 119.

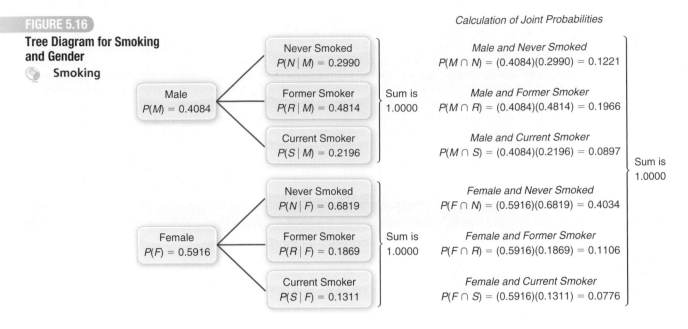

FIGURE 5.16

Tree Diagram for Smoking and Gender

Smoking

Calculation of Joint Probabilities

An Application: Game Shows A few decades ago, there was a very popular television game show called *Let's Make a Deal.* Today, there is a somewhat similar game show called *Deal or No Deal.* They are similar in the fact that both are based on contestants making a selection and then being offered the opportunity to trade their selection for some known prize. (Another similar aspect, but irrelevant here, is that both were American game shows hosted by Canadians.) The show *Deal or No Deal* consists of one basic game. A contestant chooses one of 26 available cases. Each case has a cash prize of anywhere from $0.01 to $1,000,000. The contestant then asks for certain cases to be opened and after they are opened and the contestant is allowed to see what was in those cases, he or she is offered a sum of money (based upon what cash prizes have been revealed) to trade in his or her case for that sum of money. If the contestant decides not to trade in the case, the game continues and other cases selected by the contestant are opened. The game continues in this fashion until the contestant decides to trade in his or her case or when no cases are left expect for the contestant's case. There were a variety of games on *Let's Make a Deal.* One of these games involved the contestant picking one envelope of five he or she was offered. In one of those envelopes was a key that would open the door to a car he or she would win if in fact the key worked. Once the envelope was chosen, the host would open up an envelope that he knew did not contain the sought-after key and then he would offer some prize for the chosen envelope. If the contestant refused the offer, the host would then open another envelope and a better prize than the first prize was offered. If the contestant kept on refusing the offer, the host would open up another envelope and offer an even better prize until there were only two envelopes left. At that point, if the contestant refused the offer, the contestant's envelope was opened and the key was tried.

Although these games sound quite similar in nature, there was one major difference in how the games were played. In *Deal or No Deal,* the contestant controlled which cases were opened, while in *Let's Make a Deal* the host controlled what information was revealed. But how does this difference affect the decision making of the contestant? Let's modify the two games. Suppose the *Deal or No Deal* contestant and the *Let's Make a Deal* contestant had to choose among three cases or envelopes in which there was one good prize and two prizes that were not worth winning. Using common sense, the *a priori* probability of winning the good prize in either case would be 1/3. But what would the probabilities be after the first case or first envelope was opened? To answer this question we will apply Bayes Theorem:

$$P(B|A) = \frac{P(A|B)P(B)}{P(A|B)P(B) + P(A|B')P(B')}$$

where *A* represents the event that the first case or envelope that was opened did not contain the good prize, and *B* represents the event that the original case or envelope selected by the contestant contained the good prize. Using this notation, for the *Deal or No Deal* game,

$P(B) = 1/3 \rightarrow P(B') = 2/3$

$P(A|B) = 1$ (opened case must be empty if contestant has the case with the good prize)

$P(A|B') = 1/2$ (the two unselected cases have an equally likely chance of being selected)

Applying Bayes' Theorem,

$$P(B|A) = \frac{P(A|B)P(B)}{P(A|B)P(B) + P(A|B')P(B')} = \frac{(1)(1/3)}{(1)(1/3) + (1/2)(2/3)} = \frac{1/3}{2/3} = 1/2 = 0.5$$

Most students would have guessed the correct answer if asked.

For the *Let's Make a Deal* game,

$P(B) = 1/3 \rightarrow P(B') = 2/3$

$P(A|B) = 1$ (opened case must be empty if contestant has the case with the good prize)

$P(A|B') = 1$ (the host would open up an envelope he knew was empty)

Applying Bayes' Theorem,

$$P(B|A) = \frac{P(A|B)P(B)}{P(A|B)P(B) + P(A|B')P(B')} = \frac{(1)(1/3)}{(1)(1/3) + (1)(2/3)} = \frac{1/3}{1} = 1/3 \approx 0.3333$$

Most people, let alone most students, would not have guessed the correct answer if asked. In fact if you go on the Internet and search for *Let's Make a Deal*, there are several Web sites that discuss this very same seemingly intuitively incorrect answer. Why did the probability of winning not change from the initial probability, although we saw that one of the envelopes was empty? A general rule is that if once a probability has been determined, it does not change unless there is new information. Deliberately opening an empty envelope does not give us new information because we knew that the host would be opening an empty envelope. In the *Deal or No Deal* situation, opening a case (containing a bad prize) that was selected by the contestant does give us new information because there is a greater chance of it containing a bad prize if the contestant's case contains the good prize (probability of 1) than it is of containing the bad prize if the contestant's case also contains a bad prize (probability of 0.5). Therefore, if the opened case contained the bad prize, it is more likely that the contestant's case contains the good prize.

Another variation of a game on *Let's Make a Deal* show is worth looking at as it illustrates how our intuition can lead us to making a wrong decision. A contestant is given a choice of three doors, behind one of which is a car worth $30,000. The other two doors contained essentially useless gifts. After the contestant chooses an initial door, the host then reveals an empty door among the two remaining doors and asks the contestant if he or she would like to switch to the other unopened door. The question is: Should the contestant switch? Do the odds of winning increase by switching?

The intuition of most students tells them that each of the doors, the chosen door and the unchosen doors, are equally likely to contain the prize, so there is a 50-50 chance of winning with either selection. This, however, is not true. The probability of winning by using the "switching" strategy is 2/3 while the probability of winning by not switching is 1/3. One way to explain this is as follows. The probability of picking the wrong door at the beginning of the game is 2/3. If the contestant picks the wrong door initially, the host must reveal the remaining empty door in the second stage of the game. Thus, if the contestant switches after picking the wrong door initially, the contestant will win the prize. The probability of winning by switching then is the same as the probability of picking the wrong door in the initial stage, which is clearly 2/3. Another way of explaining this is to take two contestants *A* and *B*. *A* uses the "no-switch" strategy and *B* uses the "switch" strategy. Both of them play this game a large number of times. Each time *A* makes a choice first and then *B* chooses the same door as *A*. Clearly, as before, *A*'s chances of losing are two out of three, because *A* is not switching the choice made initially. Also, if *A* wins and then *B* loses, and if *A* loses and then *B* wins, because both of them are starting with the same choice. Because *A* loses, on average, two out of three games, *B* must win, on average, two out of three games.

When students are given these explanations, they still have nagging doubts about the game. There is a "Let's Make a Deal Applet" freely available on the Web that you can play with to convince yourself. This applet (http://www.stat.sc.edu/~west/javahtml/LetsMakeaDeal.html) has been prepared by Dr. R. Webster West and Scott Street of the department of statistics at the University of South Carolina.

CHAPTER SUMMARY

The **sample space** for a **random experiment** describes all possible outcomes. **Simple events** in a **discrete** sample space can be enumerated, while outcomes of a **continuous** sample space can only be described by a rule. An **empirical** probability is based on relative frequencies, a **classical** probability can be deduced from the nature of the experiment, and a **subjective** probability is based on judgment. The number of arrangements of sampled items drawn from a population is found with the formula for **permutations** (if order is important) or **combinations** (if order does not matter). An event's **complement** is every outcome except the event. The **odds** are the ratio of an event's probability to the probability of its complement. The **union** of two events is all outcomes in either or both, while the intersection is only those events in both. **Mutually exclusive** events cannot both occur, and **collectively exhaustive** events cover all possibilities. The **conditional probability** of an event is its probability given that another event has occurred. Two events are **independent** if the conditional probability of one is the same as its **unconditional** probability. The **joint probability** of independent events is the product of their probabilities. A **contingency table** is a cross-tabulation of frequencies for two variables with categorical outcomes and can be used to calculate probabilities. A **tree** visualizes events in a sequential diagram. **Bayes' Theorem** shows how to revise a **prior probability** to obtain a **conditional** or **posterior probability** when another event's occurrence is known.

KEY TERMS

Bayes' Theorem, *205*
classical approach, *171*
collectively exhaustive, *181*
combination, *176*
complement, *178*
compound event, *168*
conditional probability, *182*
contingency table, *192*
dependent, *184*
disjoint, *180*
empirical approach, *170*
event, *168*

factorial, *175*
general law of addition, *180*
independent, *183*
intersection, *179*
joint probability, *179*
marginal probability, *193*
multiplication law, *186*
mutually exclusive, *180*
null set, *180*
odds, *188*
permutation, *175*
posterior probability, *205*

prior probability, *205*
probability, *169*
random experiment, *167*
redundancy, *186*
relative frequency
    approach, *170*
sample space, *167*
simple event, *168*
subjective approach, *172*
tree diagram, *199*
union, *179*
Venn diagram, *168*

Commonly Used Formulas in Probability

	Odds for A	Odds against A
Odds:	$\dfrac{P(A)}{1 - P(A)}$	$\dfrac{1 - P(A)}{P(A)}$

General Law of Addition: $P(A \cup B) = P(A) + P(B) - P(A \cap B)$

Permutation: $_nP_r = \dfrac{n!}{(n - r)!}$

Combination: $_nC_r = \dfrac{n!}{r!(n - r)!}$

Conditional probability: $P(A|B) = \dfrac{P(A \cap B)}{P(B)}$

Independence property: $P(A \cap B) = P(A)P(B)$

Bayes' Theorem: $P(B|A) = \dfrac{P(A|B)P(B)}{P(A|B)P(B) + P(A|B')P(B')}$

CHAPTER REVIEW

1. Define (a) random experiment, (b) sample space, (c) simple event, and (d) compound event. (LO 1)

2. Define (a) fundamental rule of counting, (b) factorial, (c) permutation, and (d) combination. (LO 3)

3. What are the three approaches to determining probability? Explain the differences among them. (LO 2)

4. Sketch a Venn diagram to illustrate (a) complement of an event, (b) union of two events, (c) intersection of two events, (d) mutually exclusive events, and (e) dichotomous events. (LO 6)

5. Use a Venn diagram to determine the rule for $P(A \cap B \cap C)$ where events *A, B,* and *C* are dependent (but not mutually exclusive) events. (LO 6)

6. Define *odds.* What does it mean to say that odds are usually quoted against an event? (LO 4)

7. (a) State the additive law. (b) Why do we subtract the intersection? (LO 4)

8. (a) Write the formula for conditional probability. (b) When are two events independent? (LO 4)

9. (a) What is a contingency table? (b) How do we convert a contingency table into a table of relative frequencies? (LO 5)

10. In a contingency table, explain the concepts of (a) marginal probability and (b) joint probability. (LO 5)

11. Why are tree diagrams useful? Why are they not always practical? (LO 6)

12. What is the main point of Bayes' Theorem? (LO 7)

Note: Explain answers and show your work clearly. Problems marked * are more difficult.

CHAPTER EXERCISES

Empirical Probability Experiments

5.53 Make your own empirical estimate of the probability that a car is parked "nose first" (as opposed to "backed in"). Choose a local parking lot, such as a grocery store. Let *A* be the event that a car is parked nose first. Out of *n* cars examined, let *f* be the number of cars parked nose first. Then $P(A) = f/n$. (b) Do you feel your sample is large enough to have a reliable empirical probability? (c) If you had chosen a different parking lot (such as a church or a police station) would you expect the estimate of $P(A)$ to be similar? That is, would $P(A|\text{church}) = P(A|\text{police station})$? Explain. (LO 2)

5.54 (a) Make your own empirical estimate of the probability that a page in this book contains a figure. For *n* pages sampled (chosen using random numbers or some other random method) let *f* be the number of pages with a figure. Then $P(A) = f/n$. (b) Do you feel your sample is large enough to have a reliable empirical probability? (c) If you had chosen a different textbook (such as a biology book or an art history book), would you expect $P(A)$ to be similar? That is, would $P(A|\text{biology}) = P(A|\text{art history})$? Explain. (LO 2)

5.55 (a) Make your own empirical estimate of the probability that a DVD movie from your collection is longer than 2 hours (120 minutes). For the *n* DVDs in your sample, let *f* be the number that exceed 2 hours. Then $P(A) = f/n$. (b) Do you feel your sample is large enough to have a reliable empirical probability? (c) If you had chosen a different DVD collection (say, your best friend's), would you expect $P(A)$ to be similar? Explain. (LO 2)

5.56 M&Ms are blended in a ratio of 13 percent brown, 14 percent yellow, 13 percent red, 24 percent blue, 20 percent orange, and 16 percent green. Suppose you choose a sample of two M&Ms at random from a large bag. (a) Show the sample space. (b) What is the probability that both are brown? (c) Both blue? (d) Both green? (e) Find the probability of one brown and one green M&M. (f) Actually take 100 samples of two M&Ms (with replacement) and record the frequency of each outcome listed in (b) and (c) above. How close did your empirical results come to your predictions? (g) Which definition of probability applies in this situation? (Data are from www.mmmars.com.) (LO 1, 2 & 3)

Problems

5.57 A survey showed that 44 percent of online Internet shoppers experience some kind of technical failure at checkout (e.g., when submitting a credit card) after loading their shopping cart. (a) What kind of probability is this? Explain. (b) What are the odds *for* a technical failure? (See J. Paul Peter and Jerry C. Olson, *Consumer Behavior and Marketing Strategy,* 7th ed. [McGraw-Hill-Irwin], p. 278.) (LO 2 & 4)

5.58 A Johnson Space Center analysis estimated a 1 in 71 chance of losing the International Space Station to space debris or a meteoroid hit. (a) What kind of probability is this? Explain. (b) What is the probability of losing the station in this way? (See *Aviation Week & Space Technology* 149, no. 16 [Oct. 19, 1998], p. 11.) (LO 2 & 4)

5.59 When watching poker tournaments on television, the commentators often mention the probabilities of a particular hand winning. What kind of probability is this? Explain. (LO 2)

5.60 Bob says he is 50 percent sure he could swim across the Thames River. (a) What kind of probability is this? (b) On what facts might Bob have based his assertion? (LO 2)

www.mcgrawhillconnect.ca

5.61 In the first year after its release, 83 percent of emergency room doctors were estimated to have tried Dermabond glue (an alternative to sutures in some situations). (a) What kind of probability is this? (b) How was it probably estimated? (c) Why might the estimate be inaccurate? (Data are from *Modern Healthcare* 29, no. 32 [Aug. 9, 1999], p. 70.) (LO 2)

5.62 The Caesarean section delivery rate in Canada in a recent year was estimated at 24 percent. (a) What kind of probability is this? (b) How was it probably estimated? (c) How accurate would you say this estimate is? (Data are from the Canadian Institute for Health Information, www.cihi.ca) (LO 2)

5.63 A recent article states that there is a 2 percent chance that an asteroid 100 meters or more in diameter will strike the earth before 2100. (a) What kind of probability is this? (b) How was it probably estimated? (c) How accurate would you say this estimate is? (Data are from *Scientific American* 289, no. 5 [Nov. 2003], p. 56.) (LO 2)

5.64 If Wiarton Willy sees his shadow on February 2, then legend says that winter will last six more weeks. In 44 years, Willy has seen his shadow 18 times. (a) What is the probability that Willy will see his shadow on a randomly chosen Groundhog Day? (b) What kind of probability is this? (Data are from www.southbrucepeninsula.org.) (LO 2)

5.65 "On Los Angeles freeways during the rush hour, there is an 18 percent probability that a driver is using a hand-held cellphone." (a) What kind of probability would you say this is? (b) How might it have been estimated? (c) How might the estimate be inaccurate? (LO 2)

5.66 Bob owns two stocks. There is an 80 percent probability that stock A will rise in price, while there is a 60 percent chance that stock B will rise in price. There is a 40 percent chance that both stocks will rise in price. Are the stock prices independent? (LO 5)

5.67 To run its network, the Ramjac Corporation wants to install a system with dual independent servers. Employee Bob grumbled, "But that will double the chance of system failure." Is Bob right? Explain your reasoning with an example. (LO 4 & 5)

5.68 A study showed that trained police officers can detect a lie 65 percent of the time, based on controlled studies of videotapes with real-life lies and truths. What are the odds that a lie will be detected? (*Source: Science News* 166, no. 5 [July 31, 2004] p. 73.) (LO 4)

5.69 During 2002, the theft probability of an Acura Integra was estimated as 1.3 percent. Find the odds against an Acura Integra being stolen. (Data are from *Popular Science* 261, no. 3 [Sept. 2002], p. 30.) (LO 4)

5.70 A person hit by lightning has a 33 percent chance of being killed (event K). (a) Find the odds that a person will be killed if struck by lightning. (b) Find the odds *against* a person being killed if struck by lightning (event K'). (Data are from Martin A. Uman, *Understanding Lightning* [Bek Technical Publications, 1971], p. 19.) (LO 4)

5.71 During the 2003 NBA playoffs, the Caesar's Palace Race and Sports Book gave the Detroit Pistons 50–1 odds against winning the NBA championship, and the New Jersey Nets 5–1 odds against winning the NBA championship. What is the implied probability of each team's victory? (Data are from *Detroit Free Press,* May 22, 2003, p. 1E.) (LO 4)

5.72 A certain model of remote-control Stanley garage door opener has nine binary (off/on) switches. The homeowner can set any code sequence. (a) How many separate codes can be programmed? (b) A newer model has 10 binary switches. How many codes can be programmed? (c) If you try to use your door opener on 1,000 other garages, how many times would you expect to succeed? What assumptions are you making in your answer? (LO 3)

5.73 (a) In a certain province, licence plates consist of three letters (A–Z) followed by three digits (0–9). How many different plates can be issued? (b) If the province allows any six-character mix (in any order) of 26 letters and 10 digits, how many unique plates are possible? (c) Why might some combinations of digits and letters be disallowed? *(d) Would the system described in (b) permit a unique licence number for every car in Canada? For every car in the world? Explain your assumptions. *(e) If the letters O and I are not used because they look too much like the numerals 0 and 1, how many different plates can be issued? (LO 3)

5.74 Bob, Mary, and Jen go to dinner. Each orders a different meal. The waiter forgets who ordered which meal, so he randomly places the meals before the three diners. Let C be the event that a diner gets the correct meal and let N be the event that a diner gets an incorrect meal. Enumerate the sample space and then find the probability that: (LO 1 & 3)

 a. No diner gets the correct meal.

 b. Exactly one diner gets the correct meal.

 c. Exactly two diners get the correct meal.

 d. All three diners get the correct meal.

5.75 An MBA program offers seven concentrations: accounting (A), finance (F), human resources (H), information systems (I), international business (B), marketing (M), and operations management (O).

Students in the capstone business policy class are assigned to teams of three. In how many different ways could a team contain exactly one student from each concentration? (LO 3)

5.76 A poker hand (5 cards) is drawn from an ordinary deck of 52 cards. Find the probability of each event, showing your reasoning carefully. (LO 3)

   a. The first four cards are the four aces.

   b. Any four cards are the four aces.

5.77 Two cards are drawn from an ordinary deck of 52 cards. Find the probability of each event, showing your reasoning carefully. (LO 3)

   a. Two aces.

   b. Two red cards.

   c. Two red aces.

   d. Two honour cards (A, K, Q, J, 10).

5.78 A certain airplane has two independent alternators to provide electrical power. The probability that a given alternator will fail on a one-hour flight is .02. What is the probability that (a) both will fail? (b) Neither will fail? (c) One or the other will fail? Show all steps carefully. (LO 4)

5.79 There is a 30 percent chance that a bidding firm will get contract *A* and a 40 percent chance it will get contract *B*. There is a 5 percent chance that the firm will get both. Are the events independent? (LO 4 & 5)

5.80 A couple has two children. What is the probability that both are boys, given that the first is a boy? (Assume that boys are equally likely to be born as girls.) (LO 4)

5.81 On July 14, 2004, a power outage in the Northwest Airlines operations centre near Minneapolis forced the airline's computer systems to shut down, leading to the cancellation of 200 flights and delays in scores of other flights. (a) Explain how the concept of statistical independence might be applicable here. (b) How would the airline decide whether, say, expenditure of $100,000 would be justified for a backup system to prevent future occurrences? (Data are from *The Wall Street Journal,* July 15, 2004.) (LO 4 & 5)

5.82 Which are likely to be independent events? For those you think are not, suggest reasons why. (LO 5)

   a. Gender of two consecutive babies born in a hospital.

   b. Car accident rates and the driver's gender.

   c. Phone call arrival rates at a university admissions office and time of day.

5.83 In child-custody cases, about 70 percent of the fathers win the case if they contest it. In the next three custody cases, what is the probability that all three win? What assumption(s) are you making? (LO 4 & 5)

5.84 RackSpace-managed hosting advertises 99.999 percent guaranteed network uptime. (a) How many independent network servers would be needed if each has 99 percent reliability? (b) If each has 90 percent reliability? (Data are from www.rackspace.com.) (LO 4 & 5)

5.85 Fifty-six percent of Canadian adults eat at a table-service restaurant at least once a week. Suppose that four Canadian adults are asked if they ate at table-service restaurants last week. What is the probability that all of them say yes? (LO 4 & 5)

5.86 The probability is 1 in 4,000,000 that a single auto trip in the United States will result in a fatality. Over a lifetime, an average U.S. driver takes 50,000 trips. (a) What is the probability of a fatal accident over a lifetime? Explain your reasoning carefully. *Hint:* Assume independent events. Why might the assumption of independence be violated? (b) Why might a driver be tempted not to use a seat belt "just on this trip"? (LO 4)

5.87 If there are two riders on a city bus, what is the probability that no two have the same birthday? What if there are 10 riders? 20 riders? 30 riders? *Hint:* Use *LearningStats.* (LO 4)

5.88 How many riders would there have to be on a bus to yield (a) a 50 percent probability that at least two will have the same birthday? (b) A 75 percent probability? Hint: Use *LearningStats.* (LO 4)

5.89 Four students divided the task of surveying the types of vehicles in parking lots of four different shopping malls. Each student examined 100 cars in each of three large suburban Detroit malls and one suburban Jamestown, New York, mall, resulting in the 5 × 4 contingency table shown below. (a) Calculate each probability (i–ix) and explain in words what it means. (b) Do you see evidence that vehicle type is not independent of mall location? Explain. (c) Do the row-total vehicle percentages correspond roughly to your experience in your own city and state? If not, discuss possible reasons for the difference. (Data are from an independent project by MBA students Steve Bennett, Alicia Morais, Steve Olson, and Greg Corda.) (LO 6)   **Malls**

   i. $P(C)$ ii. $P(G)$ iii. $P(T)$

   iv. $P(V|S)$ v. $P(C|J)$ vi. $P(J|C)$

   vii. $P(C$ and $G)$ viii. $P(T$ and $O)$ ix. $P(M$ and $J)$

Number of Vehicles of Each Type in Four Shopping Malls

Vehicle Type	Somerset (S)	Oakland (O)	Great Lakes (G)	Jamestown, NY (J)	Row Total
Car (C)	44	49	36	64	193
Minivan (M)	21	15	18	13	67
Full-size van (F)	2	3	3	2	10
SUV (V)	19	27	26	12	84
Truck (T)	14	6	17	9	46
Column Total	100	100	100	100	400

5.90 The results of the 2008 Canadian elections have been summarized in the following table according to the number of seats each party won in various regions across Canada. (LO 6)

	Prairies & Western Canada	Ontario	Quebec	Maritimes	Northern Canada
Conservatives	71	51	10	10	1
Liberals	7	38	13	17	1
NDP	14	17	1	4	1
BQ	0	0	50	0	0
Independents	0	0	1	1	0

Source: CBCnews.ca

If one of these elected Members of Parliament was randomly chosen for a television special focusing on why Canadians run for office, what is the probability that:

a. This member was from Ontario?
b. This member was an NDP member?
c. This member was either a Liberal or an NDP member?
d. This member was either a Liberal member or from Ontario?
e. This member was a BQ member and from Ontario?
f. This member was a Conservative member and from Quebec?
g. This member was a Conservative member knowing that he or she was from Ontario?
h. This member was from Quebec knowing that he or she was a BQ member?
i. This member was from Quebec knowing that he or she was a liberal member?
j. This member was a BQ member knowing that he or she was from Ontario?

If two of these elected Members were randomly chosen for this television special, what is the probability that:

k. Both were from Northern Canada?
l. At least one was from Northern Canada?
m. Exactly one was from Quebec and exactly one was from Ontario?

5.91 Analysis of forecasters' interest rate predictions over the period 1982 to 1990 was intended to see whether the predictions corresponded to what actually happened. The 2 × 2 contingency table below shows the frequencies of actual and predicted interest rate movements. (a) Calculate each probability (i–vi) and explain in words what it means. *(b) Do you think that the forecasters' predictions were accurate? Explain. (Data are from R. A. Kolb and H. O. Steckler, "How Well Do Analysts Forecast Interest Rates?" *Journal of Forecasting* 15, no. 15 [1996], pp. 385–394.) (LO 6)   **Forecasts**

i. $P(F-)$ ii. $P(A+)$ iii. $P(A-|F-)$
iv. $P(A+|F+)$ v. $P(A+ \text{ and } F+)$ vi. $P(A- \text{ and } F-)$

Interest Rate Forecast Accuracy

Forecast Change	Actual Change		Row Total
	Decline (A−)	Rise (A+)	
Decline (F−)	7	12	19
Rise (F+)	9	6	15
Column Total	16	18	34

5.92 High levels of cockpit noise in an aircraft can damage the hearing of pilots who are exposed to this hazard for many hours. Cockpit noise in a jet aircraft is mostly due to airflow at hundreds of miles per hour. This 3×3 contingency table shows 61 observations of data collected by an airline pilot using a handheld sound meter in a Boeing 727 cockpit. Noise level is defined as "low" (under 88 decibels), "medium" (88 to 91 decibels), or "high" (92 decibels or more). There are three flight phases (climb, cruise, descent). (a) Calculate each probability (i–ix) and explain in words what it means. (b) Do you see evidence that noise level depends on flight phase? Explain. (c) Where else might ambient noise be an ergonomic issue? (*Hint:* Search the Web.) (Data are from Capt. Robert E. Hartl, retired.) (LO 6)   **Cockpit**

i.	$P(B)$	ii.	$P(L)$	iii.	$P(H)$
iv.	$P(H|C)$	v.	$P(H|D)$	vi.	$P(D|L)$
vii.	$P(L \text{ and } B)$	viii.	$P(L \text{ and } C)$	ix.	$P(H \text{ and } C)$

Cockpit Noise

Noise Level	Flight Phase			Row Total
	Climb (B)	Cruise (C)	Descent (D)	
Low (L)	6	2	6	14
Medium (M)	18	3	8	29
High (H)	1	3	14	18
Column Total	25	8	28	61

5.93 A biometric security device using fingerprints erroneously refuses to admit 1 in 1,000 authorized persons from a facility containing classified information. The device will erroneously admit 1 in 1,000,000 unauthorized persons. Assume that 95 percent of those who seek access are authorized. If the alarm goes off and a person is refused admission, what is the probability that the person was really authorized? (Data are from *High Technology,* Feb. 1987, p. 54.) (LO 6)

5.94 Dolon Web Security Consultants requires all job applicants to submit to a test for illegal drugs. If the applicant has used illegal drugs, the test has a 90 percent chance of a positive result. If the applicant has not used illegal drugs, the test has an 85 percent chance of a negative result. Actually, 4 percent of the job applicants have used illegal drugs. If an applicant has a positive test, what is the probability that he or she has actually used illegal drugs? *Hint:* Make a 2×2 contingency table of frequencies, assuming 500 job applicants. (LO 6)

5.95 What separates top professional athletes from less successful professional athletes? One characteristic might be their ability to not let their past performances affect their future performances. Suppose the Toronto Maple Leafs and the Edmonton Oilers were playing a Saturday night game and a Sunday night game both in Toronto. From past experience, the Maple Leafs playing in Toronto against Edmonton should have a 60 percent chance of winning the hockey game. If this is the case, and if Saturday night's performance doesn't affect Sunday night's performance by either team, what is the probability that: (a) Toronto wins neither game; (b) Toronto wins 1 game; (c) Toronto wins both games; and (d) Toronto had won the first game knowing that Toronto won the second game? Suppose that Saturday night's performance does affect Sunday night's performance and the chances of Toronto winning the Sunday game increases to 70 percent if it wins the Saturday game and it decreases to 40 percent if it loses the Saturday game. Answer the same four questions as above. (LO 4, 6 & 7)

LearningStats Unit 05 Probability
LS

LearningStats Unit 05 reviews set notation, introduces probability concepts, illustrates decision trees and Bayes' Theorem, and explains counting rules. Modules are designed for self-study, so you can proceed at your own pace, concentrate on material that is new, and pass quickly over things that you already know. Your instructor may assign specific modules, or you may decide to check them out because the topic sounds interesting. In addition to helping you learn about statistics, they may be useful as references later on.

Topic	*LearningStats Modules*
Events and probability	🅿 Probability Basics
	🅿 Empirical Probability
Contingency tables	⊠ Contingency Tables
	⊠ Cross-Tabulations
	⊠ Independent Events
Life tables and expected value	⊠ Mortality Rates
	⊠ Using Life Tables
	⊠ Survival Curves
	⊠ Retirement Planning
Independent events	⊠ Birthday Problem
	⊠ Four-Leaf Clover
	⊠ System Reliability
	⊠ Organ Transplants
Random processes	⊠ Law of Large Numbers
	⊠ Dice Rolls
	⊠ Pick a Card
	⊠ Random Names
Bayes' Theorem	⊠ Bayes' Theorem
Life insurance	🆆 Life Insurance Terminology

Key: 🅿 = PowerPoint 🆆 = Word ⊠ = Excel

Visual Statistics
VS

Visual Statistics Modules on Continuous Distributions

Module	*Module Name*
2	Visualizing a Random Process

Visual Statistics Module 2 is designed to help you
• Recognize that outcomes of a random process exhibit regularity even though the process is random.
• Learn through experimentation how the parameters affect the outcomes of an experiment.
• Learn how a histogram can summarize the results of an experiment.
• Visualize data-generating processes that give rise to common probability distributions.
• Understand how relative frequencies can be used to estimate the probability of an event.
The work-text chapter (included on the CD as a PDF file) contains a list of concepts, objectives of the module, overview of concepts, illustration of concepts, orientation to module features, learning exercises (basic, intermediate, advanced), learning projects (individual, team), self-evaluation quiz, glossary of terms, and solutions to the self-evaluation quiz.

Chapter

6

Discrete Probability Distributions

Chapter Learning Objectives

When you finish this chapter you should be able to

1. In a problem context, identify the relevant discrete random variable and its probability distribution.

2. Calculate expected values and variances and use the concepts and rules of expected values and variances to reach conclusions, make decisions, and solve problems.

3. Recognize common discrete probability models, their parameters, and their characteristics.

4. Recognize when and how to apply the appropriate discrete model to use in a problem context.

5. Find event probabilities for discrete models by using Excel, formulas, and/or tables.

In Chapter 5, you were introduced to random experiments and how to determine their possible outcomes and their probabilities. In that chapter, the possible outcomes were, for the most part, categorical in nature (e.g., winning or losing a contract). You also learned how to determine the probability of each possible outcome (e.g., the probability of winning and the probability of losing). In this chapter and in Chapter 7, we will continue the analysis of random experiments where the outcomes will now be quantified (e.g., we can define the possible outcomes of bidding on a contract as zero [winning zero contracts] or one [winning one contract]). In this chapter we will consider random processes in which the outcomes are discrete (e.g., those that arise out of some sort of counting), while in the next chapter these outcomes will be continuous (those that result out of measuring). A random process, also called a stochastic process, is defined as a repeatable random experiment in which the outcomes are random. Almost any business process can be thought of as a stochastic process. For example, consider cars being serviced in a quick oil-change shop or a customer ordering a hamburger at Harvey's. Think of each car or customer as a random experiment and the next 10 cars or customers as a random process. The variables of interest associated with the car might be the number of litres of oil required for a particular car and the variable of interest for the next 10 cars might be the number of cars that require four litres of oil, five litres of oil, and so on. The variable of interest associated with a Harvey's customer might be the number of toppings put on the hamburger and the variable of interest for the next 10 customers might be the number of customers who request no garnishes, one garnish, and so on. To use these variables of interest to help businesses to reach conclusions, make decisions, or solve problems, we must be able to assign probabilities for each possible value of these variables. This can be accomplished through the use of probability models.

A probability model is a mathematical equation that assigns a probability to each outcome in the sample space defined by a random process. We use probability models to depict the essential characteristics of a stochastic process. How many litres of oil does the quick oil-change shop need for the next 10 cars? To answer this we need to model the process of the oil requirements of cars. Can Harvey's predict the total number of toppings being requested by the next 10 customers? To answer this question Harvey's needs to model the process of customer requests for toppings. Probability models must be reasonably realistic yet simple enough to be analyzed.

Many stochastic processes can be described by using common probability models whose properties are well known. To correctly use these probability models it is important that you understand their development. In the following sections we will explain how probability models are developed and describe several commonly used models.

6.1 Discrete Distributions

EXAMPLE 1

Selling Alarm Systems

A student in Toronto, trying to earn enough money during the summer months to pay for his tuition and textbooks for the upcoming school year, is the "front man" for a company that installs alarm systems in large private homes. Based on past experiences, he believes that his sales approach gives him a probability of 0.6 of selling such a system to any home that he approaches. Today he has three appointments. Using the tree diagram approach from the previous chapter, we can express the possible outcomes (where M represents making a sale and M' represents losing the sale) on this tree in Figure 6.1.

We can also use the results of the tree to express the outcomes in the following table:

Outcome	Probability
$M_1 M_2 M_3$	0.216
$M_1 M_2 M_3'$	0.144
$M_1 M_2' M_3$	0.144
$M_1 M_2' M_3'$	0.096
$M_1' M_2 M_3$	0.144
$M_1' M_2 M_3'$	0.096
$M_1' M_2' M_3$	0.096
$M_1' M_2' M_3'$	0.064

Note: In expressing these outcomes, we simplified the notation (e.g., $M_1 \cap M_2 \cap M_3 \rightarrow M_1 M_2 M_3$).

The student, instead of being interested in which appointments were successful and which were not, may be more interested in how many were successful. This might be the case if each of the sales earned him the same commission. If we define X as the number of sales, the possible values of X are 0, 1, 2, and 3. Simplifying the above table where the outcomes are now expressed by the number of sales, X, the table looks like this:

x	P(x)
0	0.064
1	0.288 (=0.096 + 0.096 + 0.096)
2	0.432 (=0.144 + 0.144 + 0.144)
3	0.216
Total	1

This table is one way of expressing the probability distribution of this random variable. Another way of expressing this probability distribution is by using the visual display in Figure 6.2.

In many situations there may be a third way of expressing a probability distribution—a formula that allows the calculation of $P(x)$ for any possible value x.

Random Variables

A **random variable** is a function or rule that assigns a numerical value to each outcome in the sample space of a random experiment. We use X when referring to a random variable in general, while specific values of X are shown in lowercase (e.g., x). (For example, if a particular customer requests seven toppings for his hamburger, $X =$ the number of toppings requested

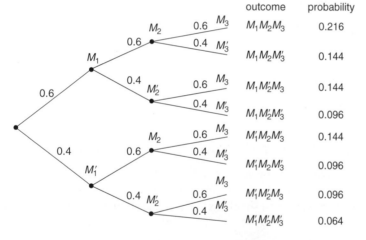

FIGURE 6.1

Tree Diagram for Alarm Systems Sales

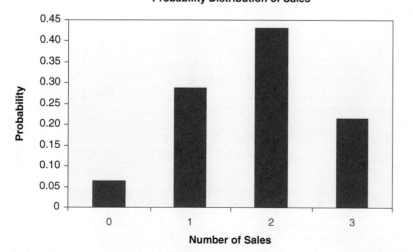

FIGURE 6.2

and $x = 7$.) A **discrete random variable** has a countable number of distinct values. Some random variables have a clear upper limit (e.g., number of toppings put on a Harvey's hamburger is limited by the number of toppings available) while others do not (e.g., number of text messages you receive in a given hour). Here are some examples of decision problems involving discrete random variables.

Decision Problem	*Discrete Random Variable*
• University of Windsor has space in its MBA program for 40 new students. In the past, 75 percent of those who are admitted actually enroll. The decision is made to admit 55 students. What is the probability that more than 40 admitted students will actually enroll?	• X = number of admitted MBA students who actually enroll ($X = 0, 1, 2, \ldots, 55$)
• During a weekday lunch hour, a particular Harvey's restaurant can fill the orders of 8 customers in a 10-minute interval. The mean arrival rate is 6 customers in a 10-minute interval. What is the probability that more than 8 customers will arrive in a given 10-minute interval?	• X = number of customers that arrive in a given 10-minute interval at this Harvey's restaurant ($X = 0, 1, 2, \ldots$)
• Rolled steel from a certain supplier averages 0.01 defects per linear metre. Toyota will reject a shipment of 500 linear metres if inspection reveals more than 10 defects. What is the probability that the order will be rejected?	• X = number of defects in 500 metres of rolled steel ($X = 0, 1, 2, \ldots$)

Probability Distributions

As indicated in the above table and graph, a **discrete probability distribution** assigns a probability to each value of a discrete random variable X. The distribution must follow the rules of probability defined in Chapter 5. If there are k distinct values of $X(x_1, x_2, \ldots, x_k)$:

$$0 \le P(x_i) \le 1 \text{ (the probability for any given value of } X, x_i\text{)} \qquad \textbf{(6.1)}$$

$$\sum_{i=1}^{k} P(x_i) = 1 \text{ (the sum of the probabilities for all values of } X\text{)} \qquad \textbf{(6.2)}$$

Each probability value must be between 0 and 1 and all the probabilities must sum to 1. Figure 6.3 illustrates the relationship between the sample space, the random variable, and the probability distribution function for a simple experiment of rolling a fair die.

FIGURE 6.3

Random Experiment: Rolling a Fair Die

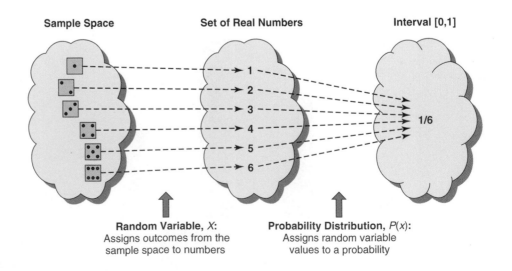

| Sample Space | Set of Real Numbers | Interval [0,1] |

Random Variable, X:
Assigns outcomes from the sample space to numbers

Probability Distribution, P(x):
Assigns random variable values to a probability

EXAMPLE 2
Town Council Election

In Chapter 5 we looked at an example concerning a small northern Quebec town where there was an election to determine who will sit on its town council. As previously stated, the town had three wards, each to elect one councillor. In each ward, there were candidates who favour expansion of the mining operations within the town's borders and there were candidates who didn't favour expansion. In Ward A, the probability of electing a candidate who favoured expansion was 0.7. The probabilities of electing a candidate who favoured expansion in Wards B and C, were 0.6 and 0.2, respectively. Using this information, we developed a probability tree that listed each of the possible election results and their probabilities. Using those results, we can express the probability distribution for X, the number of elected candidates who favour the expansion of mining operations, using the following table:

x	$P(x)$
0	0.096 (= $P(A'B'C')$ = 0.096)
1	0.392 (= $P(AB'C')$ + $P(A'BC')$ + $P(A'B'C)$ = 0.224 + 0.144 + 0.024 = 0.392)
2	0.428 (= $P(ABC')$ + $P(AB'C)$ + $P(A'BC)$ = 0.336 + 0.056 + 0.036 = 0.428)
3	0.084 (= $P(ABC)$ = 0.084)
	1

We can also use the visual display in Figure 6.4.

In each of the above two examples, we used a probability tree to create a probability distribution, which we expressed by means of a table and a visual display. If there were 10 appointments per day or 12 councillor positions, using a probability tree would be difficult because of the size of the tree. As previously mentioned, a third way of determining these probabilities could be through the use of a formula that is flexible enough so that it could be applied no matter how many appointments or positions are available and no matter what the probability of a sale or the probability of supporting the mine expansion. These types of formulas will be developed later in this chapter.

Expected Value

In the student salesperson example above, there were four possible values for the number of sales (X = 0, 1, 2, or 3). The following question may be asked: "On average, how many sales would be made per day when this student visits three potential customers each and every day, theoretically for an infinite number or days (or, equivalently, approximately what would be the average sales per day over a large number of days)?"

Because there are four possible values of X, an initial reaction may be to simply average the four values, resulting in an average number of sales of 1.5 per three potential customers. On closer look though, each time three potential customers are contacted, it is more likely that the student would make one or two sales rather than zero or three sales. Therefore, if this

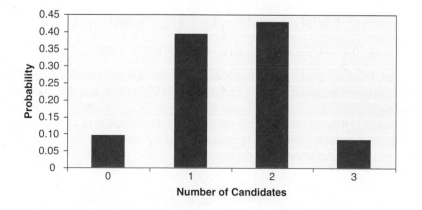

student were to visit three potential customers each day over a large number of days, he would make one or two sales more than zero or three sales. In fact, if theoretically the student would make three appointments each and every day for an infinite number of days, he should have no sales 6.4 percent of the time, one sale 28.8 percent of the time, two sales 43.2 percent of the time, and three sales 21.6 percent of the time. Thus, the values 1 and 2 should be weighted more heavily than the values 0 or 3 when calculating the average number of sales per three appointments.

In Chapter 4, we looked at calculating averages when certain values of X should be weighted more heavily than other values of X, and we developed a formula for the weighted average, where

$$\bar{x}_w = \frac{\sum x_i w_i}{\sum w_i} = \sum x_i \left(\frac{w_i}{\sum w_i} \right)$$

In this example, we will also use the weighted average but now the weights are the $P(x)$'s and, as such, the sum of the weights equals 1. This would result in a weighted average of

$$\bar{x}_w = \sum x_i P(x_i)$$

Because we are theoretically looking at the entire population of daily sales, what we should be calculating is the population mean, μ, or the expected value of X, $E(X)$.

To illustrate this important concept further, consider another example with the following frequency distribution of quiz marks in a class of 20 students.

X	Frequency	Relative Frequency
20	2	0.10
25	3	0.15
30	4	0.20
35	7	0.35
40	4	0.20
Total	20	1

What is the average mark of the class? Clearly, it is given by the following calculation:

$$\frac{20(2) + 25(3) + 30(4) + 35(7) + 40(4)}{20} = \frac{640}{20} = 32$$

Another way of looking at the same calculation is as follows:

$$20\left(\frac{2}{20}\right) + 25\left(\frac{3}{20}\right) + 30\left(\frac{4}{20}\right) + 35\left(\frac{7}{20}\right) + 40\left(\frac{4}{20}\right) = 32, \text{ or}$$
$$20(0.10) + 25(0.15) + 30(0.20) + 35(0.35) + 40(0.2) = 32$$

If we view these 20 marks as the population, and use random variable X for a student's marks, then relative frequencies can be interpreted as probabilities, and this average or mean score is called μ or $E(X)$.

The **expected value** $E(X)$ of a discrete random variable is the sum of all X values weighted by their respective probabilities. It is a measure of *central tendency*. If there are k distinct values of X $(x_1, x_2, \ldots, x_k)$, the expected value is

$$E(X) = \sum_{i=1}^{k} x_i P(x_i) \tag{6.3}$$

We often call $E(X)$ the *mean* and use the symbol μ.

In the student example, we can calculate the expected number of sales using the formula directly:

$$\mu = E(X) = \sum_{i=1}^{4} x_i P(x_i) = 0(0.064) + 1(0.288) + 2(0.432) + 3(0.216) = 1.8$$

or we can expand on the original table:

x	P(x)	xP(x)
0	0.064	0.000
1	0.288	0.288
2	0.432	0.864
3	0.216	0.648
	1.000	1.800

$$E(X) = \sum_{i=1}^{4} x_i P(x_i) = 1.800$$

How can we interpret the expected value of X? It is obvious that the student will not make 1.8 sales out of the three appointments. He will make either 0, 1, 2, or 3 sales. One way to interpret $E(X)$ is as follows: If this student has three appointments each day for, theoretically, an infinite number of days, he will make either 0, 1, 2, or 3 sales each day, but if he were to average the number of sales per day, the average number of sales would be 1.8 per day. Obviously, he will not have an infinite number of days in which he has three appointments, but the average sales per day would approach 1.8 the more days in which he has three appointments.

For the town council election example, we would calculate the expected number of council persons who would be in favour of the expansion of the mine to be:

$$E(X) = \sum_{i=1}^{4} x_i P(x_i) = 0(0.096) + 1(0.392) + 2(0.428) + 3(0.084) = 1.5$$

Note: This happens to be the same expected value if we simply averaged the four possible values: 0, 1, 2, and 3. But this is just a coincidence in this case.

Concept Check

If a discrete probability distribution is symmetrical, simply averaging the possible values of X would result in the same mean as calculated using the expected value formula. Verify that this statement is correct for the following probability distribution.

x	P(x)
1	0.1
2	0.2
3	0.4
4	0.2
5	0.1

EXAMPLE 3

Service Calls

 ServiceCalls

The distribution of Sunday emergency service calls by Ace Appliance Repair is shown in Table 6.1. The probabilities sum to 1, as must be true for any probability distribution.

The mode (most likely value of X) is 2, but the *expected* number of service calls $E(X)$ is 2.75, that is, $\mu = 2.75$. In other words, the "average" number of service calls is 2.75 on Sunday:

$$E(X)=\mu=\sum_{i=1}^{5}x_iP(x_i)=0P(0) + 1P(1) + 2P(2) + 3P(3) + 4P(4) + 5P(5)$$

$$= 0(0.05) + 1(0.10) + 2(0.30) + 3(0.25) + 4(0.20) + 5(0.10) = 2.75$$

In Figure 6.5, we see that this particular probability distribution is not symmetric around the mean $\mu = 2.75$. Note that $E(X)$ need not be an observable event. For example, you could have 2 service calls or 3 service calls, but not 2.75 service calls. This makes sense because $E(X)$ is an *average*. It is like saying that "the average Canadian family has 2.1 children" (even though families come only in integer sizes) or "Vernon Wells' batting average is .241" (even though the number of hits by Wells in a particular game must be an integer).

TABLE 6.1   Probability Distribution of Service Calls

x	P(x)	xP(x)
0	0.05	0.00
1	0.10	0.10
2	0.30	0.60
3	0.25	0.75
4	0.20	0.80
5	0.10	0.50
Total	1.00	2.75

Application: Life Insurance   Expected value is the basis of life insurance, a purchase that almost everyone makes. For example, based on mortality statistics in the U.S., the probability that a 30-year-old white American female will die within the next year is 0.00059 (see *LearningStats* Unit 05), so the probability of living another year is $1 - 0.00059 = 0.99941$. What premium should a life insurance company charge to break even on a \$500,000 one-year term insurance policy (that is, to achieve zero expected payout)? This situation is shown in Table 6.2. Let X be the amount paid by the company to settle the policy. The expected payout

TABLE 6.2   Expected Payout for a One-Year Term Life Policy

Event	x	P(x)	xP(x)
Live	0	0.99941	0.00
Die	500,000	0.00059	295.00
Total		1.00000	295.00

Source: Centers for Disease Control and Prevention, *National Vital Statistics Reports* 47, no. 28 (1999).

FIGURE 6.5

Probability Distribution for Service Calls

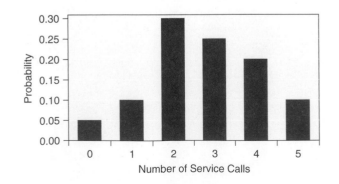

is $295, so the premium should be $295 plus whatever return the company needs to cover its administrative overhead and profit.

The mortality rate shown here is for *all* 30-year-old women. An insurance quote (e.g., from the Web) is likely to yield a lower premium, as long as you are a healthy, educated, non-smoker in a non-risky occupation. Insurance companies make money by knowing the actuarial probabilities and using them to set their premiums. The task is difficult because actuarial probabilities must be revised as life expectancies change over time.

Application: Raffle Tickets   Expected value can be applied to raffles and lotteries. If it costs $2 to buy a ticket in a raffle to win a new luxury automobile worth $55,000 and 29,346 raffle tickets are sold, the expected value of a lottery ticket is

$$E(X) = (\text{value if you win})P(\text{win})1(\text{value if you lose})P(\text{lose})$$
$$= (55{,}000)\left(\frac{1}{29{,}346}\right) + (0)\left(\frac{29{,}345}{29{,}346}\right)$$
$$= (55{,}000)(0.000034076) + (0)(0.999965924)$$
$$= \$1.87$$

The raffle ticket is actually worth $1.87. So why would you pay $2.00 for it? Partly because you hope to beat the odds, but also because you know that your ticket purchase helps the charity. Because the idea of a raffle is to raise money, the sponsor tries to sell enough tickets to push the expected value of the ticket below the price of the ticket (otherwise, the charity would lose money on the raffle). If the raffle prize is donated (or partially donated) by a well-wisher, the break-even point may be much less than the full value of the prize.

Application: Roulette   In the previous chapter you were introduced to the game of roulette. You learned that the probability of winning your bet if you bet on a single number is 1/38 and that you would win $35 for each $1 bet on a single number. You also learned that the probability of winning your bet if you bet on a six-number combination was 6/38. If you win this bet, you would win $5 for each $1 bet. The probability of you winning your bet if you bet on a red number (there are 18 red numbers) is 18/38 and you would win $1 for each dollar bet if you happen to win your bet. A couple of questions arise. Why do you win the most when you bet on a single number and the least when you bet on a red number? Why do you win $35 when you bet on a single number, $5 when you bet on a six-number combination, and $1 when you bet on a red number?

The answer to the first question should be somewhat obvious to some of you. It is more risky to bet on a single number than to bet on a red number because the likelihood of winning is less. In other courses you may have learned that people generally don't like risk and the more risk they take, the more they need to be rewarded if they are successful. To answer the second question, we will calculate the expected values of each of the three bets.

Bet on a single number:			Bet on a six-number combination:			Bet on a red number:		
x	*P(x)*	*xP(x)*	*x*	*P(x)*	*xP(x)*	*x*	*P(x)*	*xP(x)*
−1	37/38	−37/38	−1	32/38	−32/38	−1	20/38	−20/38
35	1/38	35/38	5	6/38	30/38	1	18/38	18/38
	E(X) =	−2/38		E(X) =	−2/38		E(X)	−2/38

Looking at the calculations, two observations become obvious. The first observation is that each of these three expected values is the same. These values can be interpreted as follows: If a gambler was to make any one of these bets and if he or she makes the same bet a very large number of times (theoretically, an infinite number of times), the gambler would lose an average of 2/38 dollars or approximately 5.26 cents per one dollar bet. (If you were to look at all the possible bets and their payouts that a gambler can make in the game of roulette, all but one bet would have the same expected value. The one bet that has a more negative expected value is the five-number bet. It has an expected value of −7.89 cents per one dollar bet. Based on this more negative expected value, one could argue that no one should make this particular bet.) Why are most of the payouts set up so that the gambler's expected winnings are the same for almost all the bets? The more exciting a casino game is, the more likely it is that more gamblers will play the game. Roulette becomes a more exciting game when there are a variety of bets being made. If some bets had different expected values, gamblers would tend to make the bets with the higher expected values and ignore the others.

The second observation is that these expected values are negative. The reason for this is that casinos are in the business of making a profit, and if the gamblers' expected values are negative, the casinos' expected values are positive. While one could argue that gamblers don't make an infinite number of bets, the casino is the recipient of close to an infinite number of bets and they should be able to predict quite accurately how much money they would make if they knew how many bets will be made. Why are the expected values only -5.26 cents per one dollar bet instead of, for example, -25.26 cents per one dollar bet? Although the casino would make more money per dollar bet, the gamblers wouldn't make as many bets because of this high negative expected value.

If the expected values are negative, and they are negative for all casino games (unless one can count cards at the blackjack table and get away with it), why should people consider gambling at casinos? The main reason should be that they enjoy gambling just as others may enjoy going to a movie (which would also have a negative expected value—the cost of the tickets and refreshments). The other reason is that even though the expected values are negative for all casino games, gamblers can still make money as long as they don't play the games an infinite number of times.

Actuarial Fairness   Like a lottery, an actuarially fair insurance program must collect as much in overall revenue as it pays out in claims. This is accomplished by setting the premiums to reflect empirical experience with the insured group. Individuals may gain or lose, but if the pool of insured persons is large enough, the total payout is predictable. Of course, many insurance policies have exclusionary clauses for war and natural disaster (e.g., Hurricane Katrina) to deal with cases where the events are not independent. Actuarial analysis is critical for corporate pension-fund planning. Group health insurance is another major application.

Variance and Standard Deviation

The variance $V(X)$ of a discrete random variable measures how variable the numerical outcomes are in a random process, and is the sum of the squared deviations about its expected value, weighted by the probability of each X value. If there are k distinct values of X, the variance is

$$V(X) = \sigma^2 = \sum_{i=1}^{k} (x_i - \mu)^2 P(x_i) \tag{6.4}$$

Just as the expected value $E(X)$ is a weighted average that measures *central tendency,* the variance $V(X)$ is a weighted average that measures *dispersion* about the mean. And just as we interchangeably use μ or $E(X)$ to denote the mean of a distribution, we use either σ^2 or $V(X)$ to denote its variance.

The *standard deviation* is the square root of the variance and is denoted σ:

$$\sigma = \sqrt{\sigma^2} = \sqrt{V(X)} \tag{6.5}$$

EXAMPLE 4

Bed and Breakfast
RoomRent

The Bay Street Inn is a seven-room bed-and-breakfast in Vancouver. Demand for rooms generally is strong during June, a prime month for tourists. However, experience shows that demand is quite variable. The probability distribution of room rentals during June is shown in Table 6.3 where X = the number of rooms rented (X = 0, 1, 2, 3, 4, 5, 6, 7). The worksheet shows the calculation of $E(X)$ and $V(X)$.

The formulas are:

$$E(X) = \mu = \sum_{i=1}^{7} x_i P(x_i) = 4.71$$

$$V(X) = \sigma^2 = \sum_{i=1}^{7} (x_i - \mu)^2 P(x_i) = 4.2259$$

$$\sigma = \sqrt{4.259} = 2.0557$$

This distribution is skewed to the left and bimodal. The mode (most likely value) is 7 rooms rented, but the average is only 4.71 room rentals in June. The standard deviation of 2.06 indicates that there is considerable variation around the mean, as seen in Figure 6.6.

TABLE 6.3 **Worksheet for *E(X)* and *V(X)* for June Room Rentals**

X	P(x)	xP(x)	x − μ	(x − μ)²	(x − μ)− P(x)
0	0.05	0.00	−4.71	22.1841	1.109205
1	0.05	0.05	−3.71	13.7641	0.688205
2	0.06	0.12	−2.71	7.3441	0.440646
3	0.10	0.30	−1.71	2.9241	0.292410
4	0.13	0.52	−0.71	0.5041	0.065533
5	0.20	1.00	+0.29	0.0841	0.016820
6	0.15	0.90	+1.29	1.6641	0.249615
7	0.26	1.82	+2.29	5.2441	1.363466
Total	1.00	μ = 4.71			σ² = 4.225900

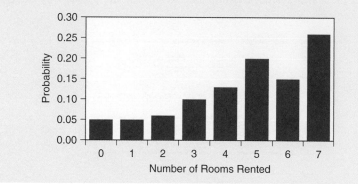

FIGURE 6.6

Probability Distribution of Rooms Rentals

In the previous roulette application, three different types of bets resulted in the same expected values. Are their standard deviations also the same? If we consider the variance or standard deviation as a measure of risk or uncertainty, we could intuitively argue that betting on a single number is more risky than betting on a 6-number combination, which should be more risky than betting on an 18-number combination. Thus, the answer to the question should be "no." Doing the calculations,

Bet on a single number:

x	P(x)	xP(x)	x − μ	(x − μ)²	(x − μ)² P(x)
−1	37/38	−37/38	−0.9474	0.8975	0.8739
35	1/38	35/38	35.0526	1228.6870	32.3339
	μ =	−2/38		σ² =	33.2078

Bet on a six-number combination:

x	P(x)	xP(x)	x − μ	(x − μ)²	(x − μ)² P(x)
−1	32/38	−32/38	−0.9474	0.8975	0.7558
5	6/38	30/38	5.0526	25.5291	4.0309
	μ =	−2/38		σ² =	4.7867

Bet on a red number:

x	P(x)	xP(x)	x − μ	(x − μ)²	(x − μ)² P(x)
−1	20/38	−37/38	−0.9474	0.8975	0.4724
1	18/38	35/38	1.0526	1.1080	0.5249
	μ =	−2/38		σ² =	0.9973

As expected, the variance for the single-number bet is greater than the variance for the 6-number bet which is greater than the variance for betting on a red number (the 18-number bet). We can now confirm that a single-number bet is the most risky of the three bets.

What Is a PDF or a CDF?

Up to now, we described probability distributions using either a table or a visual display. As previously mentioned, it may be possible in many situations to also describe a probability distribution by means of a mathematical formula. A known distribution can be described either by its **probability distribution function (PDF)** or by its **cumulative distribution function (CDF)**, both of which are mathematical formulas. A discrete PDF shows the probability of each X value, while the CDF shows the cumulative sum of probabilities, adding from the smallest to the largest X value. Figure 6.7 illustrates a discrete PDF, and Figure 6.8 illustrates the corresponding CDF. Notice that the CDF approaches 1.

Continuing with the alarm system example, we determine the probability distribution to be as follows:

x	P(x)
0	0.064
1	0.288 (= 0.096 + 0.096 + 0.096)
2	0.432 (= 0.144 + 0.144 + 0.144)
3	0.216

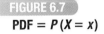

FIGURE 6.7

$$PDF = P(X = x)$$

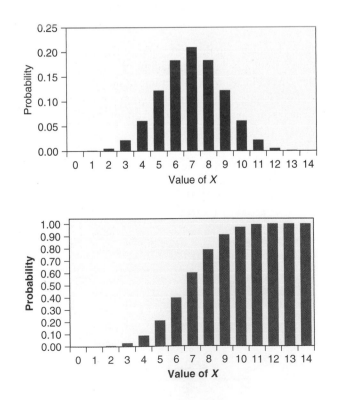

FIGURE 6.8

$$CDF = P(X < x)$$

Looking at the probability tree used to develop this distribution, we can examine how these probabilities were determined:

x	P(x)
0	$0.064 = (0.4)(0.4)(0.4) = 0.4^3 = (1)(0.6^0)(0.4^3)$
1	$0.288 = (0.6)(0.4)(0.4) + (0.4)(0.6)(0.4) + (0.4)(0.4)(0.6) = (3)(0.6^1)(0.4^2)$
2	$0.432 = (0.6)(0.6)(0.4) + (0.6)(0.4)(0.6) + (0.4)(0.6)(0.6) = (3)(0.6^2)(0.4^1)$
3	$0.216 = (0.6)(0.6)(0.6) = 0.6^3 = (1)(0.6^3)(0.4^0)$

Note: The expressions at the far right of this table are more complicated than they would need to be if we were just interested in calculating these probabilities. They were constructed in this manner to determine if we could develop an equation that could be used to calculate the probabilities no matter what the value of X, no matter how many appointments were made, and no matter the probability of making a sale at each specific appointment.

Looking at each of the expressions, we observe that the left-hand values (i.e., 1, 3, 3, 1) indicate the number of ways that the student can sell 0, 1, 2, or 3 alarm systems, respectively. The 0.6 is the probability of selling a system to each specific home, and its superscript indicates the number of homes to which a system was sold (i.e., the particular values of X). The 0.4 is the probability of not selling a system to each specific home, and its superscript indicates the number of homes to which a system was not sold (i.e., $3 - x$). The number of ways that a student can sell x alarms to three homes is $_3C_x$ or $\dfrac{3!}{x!(3 - x)!}$. So, for this example, $P(x)$, for $X = 0$, 1, 2, or 3, can be calculated using the formula:

$$P(X{=}x)=\frac{3!}{x!(3 - x)!}0.6^x 0.4^{3-x}$$

For example,

$$P(X{=}2)=\frac{3!}{2!(3 - 2)!}(0.6)^2(0.4)^{3-2}=(3)(0.36)(0.4)=0.432$$

But suppose the student has n appointments, where n can be any positive integer value, and the probability of a sale at any specific home is symbolized by π. Can this formula be applied, with the necessary modifications, to any n and any π? The answer is yes and intuition should tell us that the formula for $P(X)$ should be:

$$\text{PDF} = P(X = x) = \frac{n!}{x!(n - x)!}\pi^x (1 - \pi)^{n-x}$$

For example, suppose the student has 10 appointments and the probability of selling an alarm system to each specific home is 0.7. What is the probability that he will sell alarm systems to exactly 6 homes? In this particular case, $n = 10$, $\pi = 0.7$, $x = 6$ and

$$P(X = 6) = \frac{10!}{6!(10 - 6)!}0.7^6.(1 - 0.7)^{10-6} = (210)(0.117649)(0.0081) \approx 0.2001$$

If we wanted to determine $P(X \le 3)$,

$$\text{CDF} = P(X \le 3) = P(X = 0) + P(X = 1) + P(X = 2) + P(X = 3)$$

These particular PDF and CDF formulas will be covered again in a subsequent section in this chapter.

Recall from Chapter 2 that a parameter is a number that describes a population. A random process generates a population of outcomes. Random variables and their distributions are described by their parameters. The equations for the PDF, the CDF, and the characteristics of the distribution (such as the mean and standard deviation) will depend on the parameters of the process. The rest of this chapter explains several well-known discrete distributions and their applications. Many random business processes can be described by these common distributions.

Section Exercises

6.1 Which of the following could *not* be probability distributions? Explain. (LO 1)

Example A		Example B		Example C	
X	**P(x)**	**x**	**P(x)**	**x**	**P(x)**
0	0.80	1	0.05	50	0.30
1	0.20	2	0.15	60	0.60
		3	0.25	70	0.40
		4	0.40		
		5	0.10		

6.2 On hot, sunny, summer days, Jane rents inner tubes by the river that runs through her town. Based on her past experience, she has assigned the following probability distribution to the number of tubes she will rent on a randomly selected day. (a) Calculate the expected value and standard deviation of this random variable X by using the probability distribution table shown. (b) Describe the shape of this distribution. (LO 2)

x	25	50	75	100	Total
P(x)	0.20	0.40	0.30	0.10	1.00

6.3 On the midnight shift, the number of patients with head trauma in an emergency room has the probability distribution shown below. (a) Calculate the mean and standard deviation. (b) Describe the shape of this distribution. (LO 2)

x	0	1	2	3	4	5	Total
P(x)	0.05	0.30	0.25	0.20	0.15	0.05	1.00

6.4 Pepsi and Mountain Dew products sponsored a contest giving away a Lamborghini sports car worth $215,000. The probability of winning from a single bottle purchase was 0.00000884. Find the expected value. Show your calculations clearly. (Data are from J. Paul Peter and Jerry C. Olson, *Consumer Behavior and Marketing Strategy,* 7th ed. [McGraw-Hill/Irwin, 2005], p. 226.) (LO 2)

6.5 Student Life Insurance Company wants to offer a $1,000 student personal property plan for residence students to cover theft of certain items. Past experience suggests that the probability of a total loss claim is 0.01. What premium should be charged if the company wants to make a profit of $25 per policy (assume total loss with no deductible)? Show your calculations clearly. (LO 2)

6.6 A lottery ticket has a grand prize of $28 million. The probability of winning the grand prize is 0.000000023. Based on the expected value of the lottery ticket, would you pay $1 for a ticket? Show your calculations and reasoning clearly. (LO 2)

6.7 Oxnard Petro Ltd. is buying hurricane insurance for its off-coast oil drilling platform. During the next five years, the probability of total loss of only the above-water superstructure ($250 million) is 0.30, the probability of total loss of the facility ($950 million) is 0.30, and the probability of no loss is 0.40. Find the expected loss. (LO 2)

6.8 In 2005, approximately 28 percent of adult Canadians regularly participated in sports. If this percentage is the same today, use the PDF formula

$$\text{PDF} = P(X = x) = \frac{n!}{x!(n-x)!}\pi^x(1-\pi)^{n-x}$$

to create a table for the probability distribution for X, the number of Canadian adults in a sample of four randomly selected Canadian adults who regularly participate in sports. (Data from www.statcan.ca/Daily/English/080207/db08020207b.htm.) (LO 1)

6.9* An example in the previous chapter discussed three students, Ben, Tom, and Jerri, each with different studying habits. Ben didn't study and had to guess the answer to every five-choice multiple choice question. Tom studied enough so that he had a 40 percent chance of knowing the correct answer (and he would guess if he didn't know the answer). Jerri was a good student and studied enough so that she had an 80 percent chance of knowing the correct answer (and she would guess if she didn't know the answer). By either knowing the correct answer or by guessing, it was determined that Ben had a 20 percent chance, Tom had a 52 percent chance, and Jerri had an 84 percent chance of correctly answering the question. (a) In a one-question multiple-choice quiz, what is the expected number of correct answers for each of these students? (Remember, expected values do not have to be integers and should not be rounded to appear to be integers.) (b) In a 100-question multiple-choice exam, what is the expected number of correct answers for each of these students? (c) Many professors will give 1 point for a correct answer but subtract 0.25 points for an incorrect answer (e.g., in a two-question quiz, if a student answered one question correctly and one question incorrectly, the student would receive a mark of 0.75). In a 100-question exam when each question consists of 5 choices, what would be each student's expected final mark if this marking scheme was applied? Explain your answer. Why do you believe that this marking scheme is a good way to grade this exam or a bad way to grade this exam? (LO 2)

6.2 Transformation of Random Variables: Rules of Expected Values and Variances

In the roulette example, we made a $1 bet on three different types of bets and we calculated our expected winnings and variance in winnings. But what if we made 20 "six-numbers bets" of $50 each instead, and after we finished making these bets, the casino gave us a $5 rebate. What would be our expected winnings and variance or standard deviation in winnings? To answer this question the long way, we would have to determine all our possible winnings and each of their probabilities and then proceed to calculate the expected value and variances using their formulas. This would be a rather tedious process! Because we are getting a $5 rebate, our winnings would range between −$995 (if we lost all bets) and $5,005 (if we won all bets) in increments of $300 (by winning an additional bet, we win an additional $250 plus we get back the $50 bet). In addition to determining all the possible winnings, we would have to determine each of their probabilities (each outcome is not equally likely to occur) and then apply the formulas to the 21 possible values and their probabilities.

Let us try to use intuition to figure out our expected winnings. First of all, if our expected winnings on a $1 bet is −$0.05263, our expected winnings on a $50 bet should logically be −$2.6315 (−$0.05263 × 50). If we make 20 such bets, our total expected winnings should be −$52.63 (−$2.6315 × 20). With the $5 rebate, our expected winnings would be −$47.63.

If our intuition is correct, our answer should also be correct. To take into account situations in which intuitions may be faulty, we should rely on proven rules when they exist. The following rules apply to expected values and variances.

Using the symbols a and b to represent constants, and X to represent random variables, we will write the expected value of X as $E(X)$ or μ_X, the variance of X as $V(X)$ or σ_X^2, and standard deviation of X as σ_X.

1. $E(a) = a$ (i.e., the expected value of a constant is the constant itself).
2. $E(bX) = bE(X)$, or $\mu_{bX} = b\mu_X$.
3. $E(a + bX) = a + E(bX)$, or $\mu_{a+bX} = a + b\mu_X$.
4. $E(X_1 + X_2 + \cdots + X_k) = E(X_1) + E(X_2) + \cdots + E(X_k)$, or $\mu_{X_1 + X_2 \cdots + X_k} = \mu_{X_1} + \mu_{X_2} + \cdots \mu_{X_k}$ (i.e., for several random variables, the expected value of their sum equals the sum of their expected values).
5. If random variables $X_1, X_2, \cdots, X_k$ are independent of one another, then $E(X_1 X_2 \cdots X_k) = E(X_1)E(X_2) \cdots E(X_k)$, or $\mu_{X_1X_2 \cdots X_k} = \mu_{X_1}\mu_{X_2} \cdots \mu_{X_k}$ (i.e., if several random variables are independent, the expected value of their product equals the product of their expected values).
6. $V(a) = 0$ (i.e., because a constant does not vary, the variance of a constant is zero).
7. $V(bX) = b^2 V(X)$, or $\sigma_{bX}^2 = b^2 \sigma_X^2$. Taking the square root on both sides, we get $\sigma_{bX} = b\sigma_X$.
8. $V(a + X) = V(X)$, or equivalently, $\sigma_{a+X} = \sigma_X$ (i.e., adding a constant to a random variable does not change its variability).

9. If random variables $X_1, X_2, \cdots, X_k$ are independent of one another, then $V(X_1 \pm X_2 \pm \cdots \pm X_k) = V(X_1) + V(X_2) + \cdots + V(X_k)$, or $\sigma^2_{X_1 \pm X_2 \pm \cdots \pm X_k} = \sigma^2_{X_1} + \sigma^2_{X_2} + \cdots + \sigma^2_{X_k}$. Taking the square root on both sides, we get $\sigma_{X_1 \pm X_2 \pm \cdots \pm X_k} = \sqrt{\sigma^2_{X_1} + \sigma^2_{X_2} + \cdots + \sigma^2_{X_k}}$.

Let us explain this important last rule further by taking only two independent random variables X and Y. It says that $V(X + Y) = V(X - Y) = V(X) + V(Y)$. To find the standard deviation of $X + Y$, we have to take the square root on both sides to get $\sigma_{X+Y} = \sqrt{V(X) + V(Y)} = \sqrt{\sigma^2_X + \sigma^2_Y}$. Some authors refer to this rule as the Pythagorean Law of Statistics. So if we take a right-angle triangle with two perpendicular sides of length σ_X and σ_Y, then σ_{X+Y} is given by the length of the hypotenuse.

Note: If $X_1, X_2, \ldots,$ and X_k are not independent of one another, $V(X_1 \pm X_2 \pm \ldots \pm X_k)$ would involve not only individual instances of $V(X_i)$ but also covariances, which will be discussed in a subsequent chapter.

To answer the previous question concerning the expected value and variance for our roulette example using the above rules, we would have to use more than one of these rules for the expected value and more than one of the above rules for variances.

Expected value:

Currently, $X =$ winnings on a \$1 bet and $E(X) = -\$0.05263$.

For a \$50 bet, we need $E(50X)$ which, using rule 2, is $E(50X) = 50E(X) = 50(-\$0.05263) = -\$2.6315$.

Using rule 4 with X now being winnings on a \$50 bet, $E(X_1 + X_2 + \ldots + X_k)$ $= E(X_1) + E(X_2) + \ldots + E(X_{20}) = -\$2.6315 + -\$2.6315 + \ldots + -\$2.6315 = 20(-\$2.6315) = -\$52.63$.

Finally, when $X =$ total winnings on 20 \$50 bets and $a =$ the \$5 rebate, $E(a + X) = a + E(X) = 5 + (-\$52.63) = -\$47.63$.

Variance and standard deviation:

Currently, $X =$ winnings on a \$1 bet and $V(X) = 4.7867$ (\$²)

For a \$50 bet, we need $V(50X)$, which, using rule 7, is $50^2 V(X) = 2,500(4.7867) = 11,966.75$ (\$²)

Using rule 9 with X being winnings on a \$50 bet, $V(X_1 + X_2 + \ldots + X_k) = V(X_1) + V(X_2) + \ldots + V(X_k) = 11,966.75 + 11,966.75 + \ldots + 11,966.75 = 20(11,966.75) = 239,335(\$^2)$

Finally, using rule 8 where $X =$ total winnings on 20 \$50 bets and $a =$ \$5 rebate, $V(a + X) = V(X) = 239,335(\$^2)$, or the standard deviation in winnings is \$489.21877.

Concept Check

In Example 1 earlier in this chapter, we developed the following probability distribution for the number of sales of alarm systems a student would make per day. If this student earns \$100 per system sold and if it cost him \$50 in transportation costs per day, create a table for the probability distribution for profit earned per day. Using this table, calculate the student's expected profit per day and the standard deviation in profit per day. Then using the appropriate rules of expected value and variance, verify that the rules would result in the same expected profit and standard deviation in profits.

x	P(x)
0	0.064
1	0.288
2	0.432
3	0.216

EXAMPLE 5

Buffet Restaurant

A buffet restaurant is considering raising its current price of $13.50 per customer because it would like its expected profit to be 20 percent of its costs. To operate the restaurant, excluding the cost of food, it costs $1,500 per day. Based on past experience, the number of customers it expects per day is 250 (as long as it doesn't increase its price that much) and the expected food cost per customer is $6.25. How much should the restaurant charge for its buffet?

Initially, let X_1 = number of customers and X_2 = food cost per customer, or $E(X_1)$ = 250, $E(X_2)$ = $6.25, and total cost = $X_1 X_2$. Assuming how much one eats is independent of how many customers there are, using rule 5, $E(X_1 X_2) = E(X_1)E(X_2) = (250)(\$6.25) = \$1,562.50$. Using rule 3, where X now represents total food costs and a represents the fixed cost of $1,500 per day, the expected total cost is $E(a + X) = \$1,500 + E(X) = \$1,500 + \$1,562.50 = \$3,062.50$. To make the 20 percent expected profit, total expected revenues would need to be $(1.20)(\$3,062.50)$ or $3,675. For the expected number of 250 customers, the price per customer would need to be $14.70 $(= \$3,675/250)$.

Application: Exam Scores

Prof. Hardtack gave a tough exam whose raw scores had $\mu = 40$ and $\sigma = 10$, so he decided to raise the mean by 20 points. One way to increase the mean to 60 is to shift the curve by adding 20 points to every student's score. Rule 1 says that adding a constant to all X values will *shift the mean* but rule 8 says that will leave the standard deviation unchanged, as illustrated in the left-side graph in Figure 6.9 using $a = 1$ and $b = 20$.

Alternatively, Prof. Hardtack could multiply every exam score by 1.5, which would also accomplish the goal of raising the mean from 40 to 60. However, rule 7 says that the standard deviation would rise from 10 to 15, thereby also *increasing the dispersion*. In other words, this policy would "spread out" the students' exam scores. Some scores might even exceed 100, as illustrated in the right-side graph in Figure 6.9.

Application: Total Cost

A linear transformation useful in business is the calculation of total cost as a function of quantity produced: $C = vQ + F$, where C is total cost, v is variable cost per unit, Q is the number of units produced, and F is fixed cost. Sonoro Ltd. is a small firm that manufactures kortholts. Its variable cost per unit is $v = \$35$, its fixed cost is $F = \$24,000$, and its monthly order quantity Q is a random variable with mean $\mu_Q = 500$ units and standard deviation $\sigma_Q = 40$. Total cost C is a random variable $C = vQ + F$, so we can apply our rules:

Mean of total cost: $\mu_{vQ} + F = v\mu_Q + F = (35)(500) + 24{,}000 = \$41{,}500$

Std. Dev. of total cost: $\sigma_{vQ+F} = v\sigma_Q = (35)(40) = \$1{,}400$

Effect of Adding a Constant to *X* or Multiplying *X* by a Constant **FIGURE 6.9**

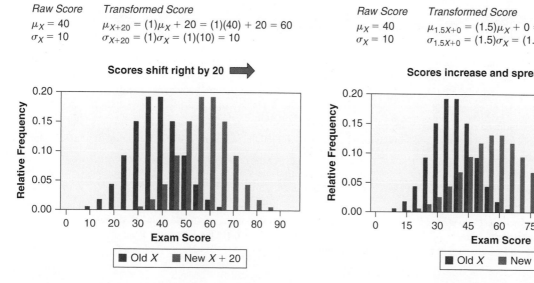

Alternative 1: Add 20

Raw Score	Transformed Score
$\mu_X = 40$	$\mu_{X+20} = (1)\mu_X + 20 = (1)(40) + 20 = 60$
$\sigma_X = 10$	$\sigma_{X+20} = (1)\sigma_X = (1)(10) = 10$

Alternative 2: Multiply by 1.5

Raw Score	Transformed Score
$\mu_X = 40$	$\mu_{1.5X+0} = (1.5)\mu_X + 0 = (1.5)(40) = 60$
$\sigma_X = 10$	$\sigma_{1.5X+0} = (1.5)\sigma_X = (1.5)(10) = 15$

Scores shift right by 20 ➡

Scores increase and spread out ➡

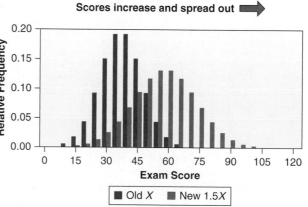

■ Old *X*　■ New *X* + 20

■ Old *X*　■ New 1.5*X*

Application: Gasoline Expenses The daily gasoline expense of Apex Movers, Inc., is a random variable with mean $\mu = \$125$ and standard deviation $\sigma = \$35$ ($\sigma^2 = 1225$). If we define Y to be the gasoline expense *per year,* and there are 250 working days per year at Apex Movers, then

$$\mu_Y = \mu + \cdots + \mu = \underbrace{\$125 + \cdots + \$125}_{250 \text{ times}} = 250(\$125) = \$31{,}250$$

$$\sigma_Y = \sqrt{\sigma^2 + \cdots + \sigma^2} = \sqrt{\underbrace{1225 + \cdots + 1225}_{250 \text{ times}}} = \sqrt{250(1225)} = \$553.40$$

This assumes that daily gasoline expenses are independent of each other.

Application: Project Scheduling The initial phase of a construction project entails three activities that must be undertaken sequentially (that is, the second activity cannot begin until the first is complete, and so on) and the time to complete each activity is a random variable with a known mean and variance:

Excavation	*Foundations*	*Structural Steel*
$\mu_1 = 25$ days	$\mu_2 = 14$ days	$\mu_3 = 58$ days
$\sigma_1^2 = 3$ days^2	$\sigma_2^2 = 2$ days^2	$\sigma_3^2 = 7$ days^2

By rule 3, the mean time to complete the whole project is the sum of the task means (even if the tasks are not independent):

$$\mu = \mu_1 + \mu_2 + \mu_3 = 25 + 14 + 58 = 97 \text{ days}$$

By rule 4, if the times to complete each activity are *independent,* the overall variance for the project is the sum of the task variances, so the standard deviation for the entire project is:

$$\sigma = \sqrt{\sigma_1^2 + \sigma_2^2 + \sigma_3^2} = \sqrt{3 + 2 + 7} = \sqrt{12} = 3.464 \text{ days}$$

From this information, we can construct $\mu \pm 1\sigma$ or $\mu \pm 2\sigma$ intervals for the entire project:

$$97 \pm (1)(3.464), \text{ or between } 93.5 \text{ and } 100.5 \text{ days}$$
$$97 \pm (2)(3.464), \text{ or between } 90.1 \text{ and } 103.9 \text{ days}$$

So the Empirical Rule implies that there is about a 95 percent chance that the project will take between 90.1 and 103.9 days. This calculation could help the construction firm estimate upper and lower bounds for the project completion time. Of course, if the distribution is not normal, the Empirical Rule may not apply.

Section Exercises

6.10 The height of a Los Angeles Lakers basketball player averages 6 feet 7.6 inches (i.e., 79.6 inches) with a standard deviation of 3.24 inches. To convert from inches to centimetres, we multiply by 2.54. (a) In centimetres, what is the mean? (b) In centimetres, what is the standard deviation? (c) Which rules did you use? (Data are from www.cnnsi.com/basketball/nba/rosters.) (LO 2)

6.11 July sales for Melodic Kortholt, Ltd., average $\mu_1 = \$9{,}500$ with $\sigma_1^2 = \$1{,}250$. August sales average $\mu_2 = \$7{,}400$ with $\sigma_2^2 = \$1{,}425$. September sales average $\mu_3 = \$8{,}600$ with $\sigma_3^2 = \$1{,}610$ (a) Find the mean and standard deviation of total sales for the third quarter. (b) What assumptions are you making? (LO 2)

6.12 The mean January temperature in Toronto is 24.4°F with a standard deviation of 4.9°F. Express these Fahrenheit parameters in degrees Celsius using the transformation C = 5/9F − 17.78. (Data are from Environment Canada, www.ec.gc.ca.) (LO 2)

6.13 There are five accounting exams. Bob's typical score on each exam is a random variable with a mean of 80 and a standard deviation of 5. His final grade is based on the sum of his exam scores. (a) Find the mean and standard deviation of Bob's point total assuming his performances on exams are independent of each other. (b) By the Empirical Rule (see Chapter 4), would you expect that Bob would earn at least 450 points (the required total for an A)? (LO 2)

6.14* Betty is considering one of two summer job opportunities at a summer resort area in southern Ontario. One job involves selling ice cream along a popular beach and the other involves selling hot dogs and sausages along that same beach. Based on previous weather patterns and demands for ice cream and hot dogs and sausages during the two-month summer, Betty developed rough probability distributions for the daily sales of ice cream and of hot dogs and sausages. Using these distributions, she calculated the expected daily sales of ice cream to be 235 with a standard deviation of 35, and she calculated the expected daily sales of hot dogs and sausages to be 185 with a standard deviation of 20. If she makes $0.30 per ice cream sold and it costs her $25 per day to rent the ice cream cart, what is Betty's expected profits per day and standard deviation in profits per day? What is Betty's expected profits and standard deviation in profits over the 62-day summer season for selling ice cream? If she makes $0.50 per hot dog or sausage sold and it costs her $50 per day to rent the hot dog cart, what is Betty's expected profits per day and standard deviation in profits per day? What is Betty's expected profits and standard deviation in profits over the 62-day summer season for selling hot dogs and sausages? Which job would Betty take if she based her decision on expected profits? Which job would Betty take if she based her decision on the standard deviation in profits? Explain. (LO 2)

TABLE 6.4 Uniform Discrete Distribution

Parameters	a = lower limit
	b = upper limit
PDF	$P(X) = \dfrac{1}{b - a + 1}$
Domain	$X = a, a + 1, a + 2, \ldots, b$
Mean	$\dfrac{a + b}{2}$
Standard deviation	$\sqrt{\dfrac{[(b - a) + 1]^2 - 1}{12}}$
Random data generation in Excel	=a+INT((b−a+1)*RAND())

6.3 Uniform Distribution

Characteristics of the Uniform Distribution

The **uniform distribution** is one of the simplest discrete probability models. It describes a random variable with a finite number of consecutive integer values from a to b with each value being equally likely. That is, the entire distribution depends only on the two parameters a (the smallest possible value) and b (the largest possible value). Table 6.4 summarizes the characteristics of the uniform discrete distribution.

EXAMPLE 6

Rolling a Die

DieRoll

When you roll a fair die, the number of dots forms a uniform discrete random variable with six equally likely integer values, 1, 2, 3, 4, 5, and 6, shown in the PDF in Figure 6.10. For this example, the PDF, mean, and standard deviation are

$$\text{PDF} = P(x) = \frac{1}{b - a + 1} = \frac{1}{6 - 1 + 1} = \frac{1}{6} \text{ for } x = 1, 2, \ldots, 6$$

$$\text{Mean} = \frac{a + b}{2} = \frac{1 + 6}{2} = 3.5$$

$$\text{Std. Dev.} = \sqrt{\frac{[(b - a) + 1]^2 - 1}{12}} = \sqrt{\frac{[(6 - 1) + 1]^2 - 1}{12}} = 1.708$$

You can see that the mean (3.5) must be halfway between 1 and 6, but there is no way you could anticipate the standard deviation without using a formula. Try rolling a die many times, or use Excel to simulate the rolling of a die by generating random integers from 1 through 6. Compare the mean and standard deviation from your random experiment to the values we calculated above.

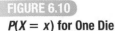

FIGURE 6.10

P(X = x) for One Die

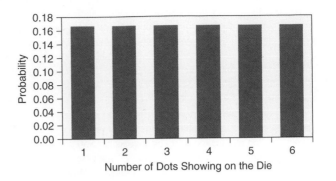

Uniform Model in *LearningStats*

Figure 6.11 shows the *uniform distribution* for one die from *LearningStats*. The distribution is visually apparent. The uniform distribution is so simple that you really don't need a spreadsheet. *LearningStats* also has demonstrations of uniform random number generation.

Section Exercises

6.15 Find the mean and standard deviation of four-digit uniformly distributed lottery numbers (0000 through 9999). (LO 4)

6.16 The ages of Java programmers at SynFlex Corp. range from 20 to 60. (a) If their ages are uniformly distributed, what would be the mean and standard deviation? (b) What is the probability that a randomly selected programmer's age is at least 40? At least 30? *Hint:* Treat employee ages as integers. (LO 4)

6.17 An auditor for a medical insurance company selects a random sample of prescription drug claims for evaluation of correct payment by company experts. The claims were selected at random from a database of 500,000 claims by using uniform random numbers between 1 and 500,000. To verify that the random numbers really were from a uniform distribution, the auditor calculated the mean and standard deviation of the random numbers. What should the mean and standard deviation be if these were uniformly distributed random integers? (LO 4)

6.18 (a) If the birthdays of students born in January are uniformly distributed, what would be their expected mean and standard deviation? (b) Do you think that birthdays in January really are uniformly distributed? (LO 4)

6.19 Use Excel to generate 100 random integers from (a) 1 through 2, inclusive; (b) 1 through 5, inclusive; and (c) 0 through 99, inclusive. (d) In each case, write the Excel formula. (e) In each case, calculate the mean and standard deviation of the sample of 100 integers you generated, and compare them with their theoretical values. *Hint:* Table 6.4 shows the Excel function. (LO 4)

FIGURE 6.11

***LearningStats* Uniform Display**

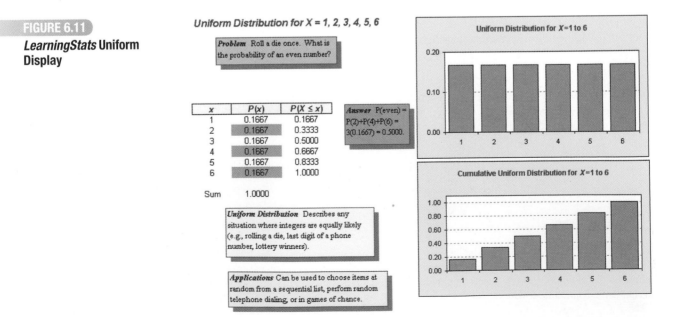

Uniform Random Integers   To generate random integers from a discrete uniform distribution we can use the Excel function =a+INT((b−a+1)*RAND()). For example, to generate a random integer from 5 through 10, the Excel function would be =5+INT((10−5+1)*RAND()). To create random integers 1 through *N*, set $a = 1$ and $b = N$ and use the Excel function =1+INT(N*RAND()). The same integer may come up more than once, so to obtain *n* distinct random integers you would have to generate a few extras and then eliminate the duplicates. This method is useful in accounting and auditing (e.g., to allow the auditor to choose numbered invoices at random).

6.4   Binomial Distribution

Characteristics of the Binomial Distribution

Chapter 4

Suppose a random experiment has only two possible outcomes. We arbitrarily call one outcome a "success" and the other a "failure." Also assume that the probability of success π (the Greek letter *pi, not* to be confused with the mathematical constant 3.14159) remains unchanged as we repeat this experiment. The **binomial distribution** arises when this experiment is repeated *n* times. In a binomial experiment, we are interested in $X =$ the number of successes in *n* trials, so the binomial random variable *X* can take any value from 0 to *n*.

The formula for calculating binomial probability is shown:

$$P(X = x) = \frac{n!}{x!(n-x)!}\pi^x(1-\pi)^{n-x}, \text{ for } X = 0, 1, 2, 3, 4, \ldots, n \qquad (6.6)$$

We applied this very same formula to the student alarm salesperson example, without formally recognizing that the binomial distribution applied, because the characteristics of that example happened to be the characteristics of a binomial distribution: There were three trials (i.e., appointments); each trial or appointment resulted in one of two possible outcomes (sale or no sale); the probability of success or sale remained the same from trial to trial (i.e., $\pi = 0.6$); and we were interested in the number of successes or sales in the three trials. You will notice that this formula was not applied to the election example. The reason for this is that the probability of success (electing a council member in favour of the mining expansion) was not the same from trial to trial (i.e., from ward to ward). For that particular example, there is no one formula that would apply to any value of *X*, the number of elected council members in favour of the mining expansion.

TABLE 6.5   Binomial Distribution

Parameters	n = number of trials
	π = probability of success
PDF	$P(X) = \dfrac{n!}{x!(n-x)!}\pi^x(1-\pi)^{n-x}$
Excel function	=BINOMDIST($x,n,\pi,0$)
Domain	$X = 0, 1, 2, \ldots, n$
Mean	$n\pi$
Standard deviation	$\sqrt{n\pi(1-\pi)}$
Random data generation in Excel	=CRITBINOM(n,π,RAND()) or use Excel's Data > Data Analysis
Comments	Skewed right if $\pi < 0.50$, skewed left if $\pi > 0.50$, and symmetric if $\pi = 0.50$.

Servicing Cars at a Quick Oil-Change Shop

Consider a shop that specializes in quick oil changes. It is important to this type of business to ensure that a car's service time is not considered "late" by the customer. Therefore, to study this process, we can define service times as being either *late* or *not late* and define the random variable X to be the number of cars that are late out of the total number of cars serviced. We further assume that cars' service times are independent of each other and the chance of a car being late stays the same for each car. Based on our knowledge of the process we know that $P(\text{car is late}) = \pi = 0.10$.

Now, think of this variable as satisfying the conditions of a binomial random variable and apply the binomial distribution. Suppose we would like to know the probability that exactly 2 of the next 12 cars serviced are late. In this case, $n = 12$, and we want to know $P(X = 2)$:

$$P(X = 2) = \frac{12!}{2!(12 - 2)!}(0.10)^2(1 - 0.10)^{12-2} = 0.2301$$

Alternatively, we could calculate this by using the Excel function =BINOMDIST(2,12,.1,0). The fourth parameter, 0, means that we want Excel to calculate $P(X = 2)$ rather than $P(X \leq 2)$.

Binomial Shape

A binomial distribution is skewed right if $\pi < 0.50$, skewed left if $\pi > 0.50$, and symmetric only if $\pi = 0.50$. However, skewness decreases as n increases, regardless of the value of π, as illustrated in Figure 6.12. Notice that $\pi = 0.20$ and $\pi = 0.80$ have the same shape, except reversed from left to right. This is true for any values of π and $1 - \pi$.

Binomial Shape

$\pi < 0.50$	skewed right
$\pi = 0.50$	symmetric
$\pi > 0.50$	skewed left

FIGURE 6.12

Binomial Distributions

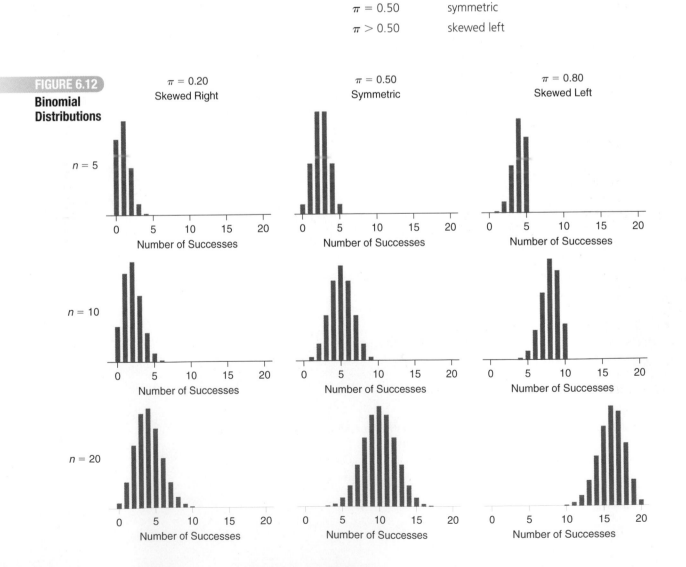

Binomial Mean, Variance, and Standard Deviation

Using the probability table for the alarm system example, we calculated the expected value of sales by extending the table. We could have also determined the variance and standard deviation in sales using the following formulas:

$$V(X) = \sigma^2 = \sum_{i=1}^{k} (x_i - \mu)^2 P(x_i) \text{ and } \sigma = \sqrt{\sigma^2} = \sqrt{V(X)}$$

x	P(x)	xP(x)	x − μ	[x − μ]²	[x − μ]² P(x)
0	0.064	0.000	−1.8	3.24	0.20736
1	0.288	0.288	0.8	0.64	0.18432
2	0.432	0.864	0.2	0.04	0.01728
3	0.216	0.648	1.2	1.44	0.31104
		1.800			0.72000

Summarizing this table,

$$E(X) = \mu = 1.8 \quad V(X) = \sigma^2 = 0.72 \quad \sigma = 0.8485$$

Obviously, if the student made 10 appointments, the calculations of the expected value, variance, and standard deviation would become more tedious using their respective formulas. Applying the relevant rules of expected values and variances, it can be shown that, if X has a binomial distribution,

$$E(X) = \mu = n\pi$$
$$V(X) = \sigma^2 = n\pi(1 - \pi)$$
$$\sigma = \sqrt{n\pi(1 - \pi)}$$

Using these formulas in this example where $n = 3$ and $\pi = 0.6$, we could easily calculate $E(X)$, $V(X)$, and σ to be:

$$E(X) = 3(0.6) = 1.8$$
$$V(X) = 3(0.6)(0.4) = 0.72$$
$$\sigma = \sqrt{0.72} = 0.8485$$

And if $n = 10$, the calculations would be just as easy!

Note: These formulas could not be applied to the mining expansion example because X, the number of council persons in favour of mine expansion, does not have a binomial distribution as π is not the same from ward to ward.

A Closer Look

If X has a binomial distribution, it was stated that $E(X) = n\pi$ and $V(X) = n\pi(1 - \pi)$. This can be verified by using the appropriate expected value and variance rules. If there is only one trial, the probability distribution for X is easily shown to be

x	P(x)
0	1 − π
1	π

Expanding the above table and using the formulas for expected values and variances,

x	P(x)	xP(x)	(x − μ)	(x − μ)² P(x)
0	1 − π	0	−π	$\pi^2(1 - \pi) = -\pi^3 + \pi^2$
1	π	π	1 − π	$(1 - \pi)^2\pi = \pi^3 - 2\pi^2 + \pi$
Total	1	π		$\pi^2 + \pi = \pi(1 - \pi)$

This gives $E(X) = \pi$ and $V(X) = \pi(1 - \pi)$.

Using Tables: Appendix A

Continuing with the alarm salesperson example, suppose this student has arranged for 25 appointments during this week, and for him to retain his job, he would need to sell at least 10 alarm systems during this period. If he still believes that he has a 60 percent chance of selling an alarm system to each specific appointment, what is the probability that he will be able to keep his job?

We already know that X, the number of sales, has a binomial distribution and we also know how to determine probabilities for the binomial distribution using the binomial formula. But here we want to determine $P(X \geq 10)$, which means that we would have to apply the binomial formula for $X = 10, 11, \ldots, 25$, or if we used the complement of $X \geq 10$, we would only have to apply the formula for $X = 0, 1, \ldots, 9$ and then use the complement rule. In either case, the calculations would be tedious. Excel allows us to calculate the CDF for a binomial distribution by allowing us to determine $P(X \geq k)$ for any k between 0 and n and for any π. Appendix A also allows us to determine these probabilities for certain n's and π's. But to use this table, whatever probabilities we are trying to determine must be able to be expressed as $P(X \leq k)$. For example, if $n = 25$ and we want to determine $P(X \geq 10)$, we would have to find the complement of $X \geq 10$ and then apply the complement rule. In this case, the complement of $X \geq 10$ is $X \leq 9$ and $P(X \geq 10) = 1 - P(X \leq 9)$.

To use Appendix A, we would find the $n = 25$ table, find the $\pi = 0.6$ column and the $k = 9$ row, and then find $P(X \leq 9)$ where that column and row intersect. From this table, we see that this probability is 0.0132 and $P(X \geq 10) = 1 - 0.0132 = 0.9868$. It appears that this student has a very high probability of keeping his job! This type of information could be very useful to someone considering taking such a job.

How would we use this table to calculate, for example, $P(X > 15)$, $P(X = 10)$, $P(X < 7)$, $P(7 < X < 12)$, or $P(7 \leq X \leq 12)$? As with the previous calculation, we would have to express each of these probabilities in terms of $P(X \leq k)$, resulting in (for $n = 25$ and $\pi = 0.6$):

$$P(X > 15) = 1 - P(X \leq 15) = 1 - 0.5754 = 0.4246$$
$$P(X = 10) = P(X < 10) - P(X \leq 9) = 0.0344 - 0.0132 = 0.0212$$
$$P(X < 7) = P(X \leq 6) = 0.0003$$
$$P(7 < X < 12) = P(X \leq 11) - P(X \leq 7) = 0.0778 - 0.0012 = 0.0766$$
$$P(7 \leq X \leq 12) = P(X \leq 12) - P(X \leq 6) = 0.1538 - 0.0003 = 0.1535$$

Using Excel and Megastat

Excel Figure 6.13 shows Excel's Insert > Function menu to calculate the probability of $x = 67$ successes in $n = 1,024$ trials with success probability $\pi = 0.048$. Alternatively, you could just enter the formula =BINOMDIST(67,1024,0.048,0) in the spreadsheet cell.

MegaStat MegaStat will compute an entire binomial PDF (not just a single point probability) for any n and π that you specify, as illustrated in Figure 6.14 for $n = 10$, $\pi = 0.50$. Optionally, you can see a graph of the PDF. This is even easier than entering your own Excel functions.

FIGURE 6.13 **Excel's Binomial Function**

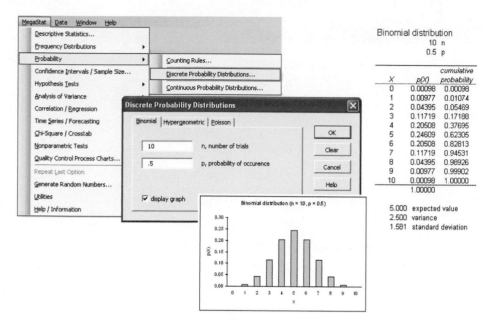

FIGURE 6.14

MegaStat's Binomial Distribution

Recognizing Binomial Applications

Can you recognize a binomial situation? The binomial distribution has four main characteristics.

- There is a fixed number of trials: n.
- There are only two outcomes for each trial: *success* or *failure.*
- There is a constant probability of success for each trial: π.
- The trials are independent of each other.

Concept Check

For each of the following situations, determine whether all the characteristics of the binomial distribution apply for determining the probability of x successes. If they don't, state which characteristics don't apply and explain why.

(a) An exclusive lottery is being conducted in which only 25 tickets will be sold. For each of the next 3 months, a ticket will be randomly drawn with a prize of $100,000 going to the winning ticket. That winning ticket will then be replaced and be eligible for any subsequent draw.

(b) An exclusive lottery is being conducted in which only 25 tickets will be sold. For each of the next 3 months, a ticket will be randomly drawn with a prize of $100,000 going to the winning ticket. That winning ticket will not be replaced and thus would not be eligible for any subsequent draw.

(c) An inspection was being conducted to determine the number of painting defects that were visible on a recently painted automobile where each defect is considered a "success."

(d) A baseball pitcher historically strikes out 20 percent of the batters he faces. Before the beginning of this pitcher's next baseball game, an analyst was interested in determining the probability of this pitcher getting at least 8 strikeouts.

A random process may follow a binomial distribution even if the value of π is not known. In these situations, π may be estimated based on past experiences.

6.20   Find the mean and standard deviation for each binomial random variable (LO 2):
   a. $n = 8$, $\pi = 0.10$
   b. $n = 10$, $\pi = 0.40$
   c. $n = 12$, $\pi = 0.50$
   d. $n = 30$, $\pi = 0.90$
   e. $n = 80$, $\pi = 0.70$
   f. $n = 20$, $\pi = 0.80$

6.21   Calculate each binomial probability (LO 4):
   a. $X = 2$, $n = 8$, $\pi = 0.10$
   b. $X = 1$, $n = 10$, $\pi = 0.40$
   c. $X = 3$, $n = 12$, $\pi = 0.70$
   d. $X = 5$, $n = 9$, $\pi = 0.90$

6.22   Calculate each compound event probability using the binomial formula and using the cumulative binomial table (LO 4):
   a. $X \leq 3$, $n = 8$, $\pi = 0.20$
   b. $X > 7$, $n = 10$, $\pi = 0.50$
   c. $X < 3$, $n = 6$, $\pi = 0.70$
   d. $X \leq 10$, $n = 14$, $\pi = 0.95$

6.23   Calculate each binomial probability using the binomial formula and using the cumulative binomial table (LO 4):
   a. Fewer than 4 successes in 12 trials with a 10 percent chance of success.
   b. At least 3 successes in 7 trials with a 40 percent chance of success.
   c. At most 9 successes in 14 trials with a 60 percent chance of success.
   d. More than 10 successes in 16 trials with an 80 percent chance of success.

6.24   In the Ardmore Hotel, 20 percent of the customers pay by American Express credit card. (a) Of the next 10 customers, what is the probability that none pay by American Express? (b) At least two? (c) Fewer than three? (d) What is the expected number who pay by American Express? (e) Find the standard deviation. (f) Construct the probability distribution (using Excel or Appendix A). (g) Make a graph of its PDF, and describe its shape. (LO 4)

6.25   Historically, 5 percent of a mail-order firm's repeat charge-account customers have an incorrect current address in the firm's computer database. (a) What is the probability that none of the next 12 repeat customers who call will have an incorrect address? (b) One customer? (c) Two customers? (d) Fewer than three? (e) Construct the probability distribution (using Excel or Appendix A), make a graph of its PDF, and describe its shape. (LO 4)

6.26   At a Noodles & Company restaurant, the probability that a customer will order a non-alcoholic beverage is 0.38. Use Excel to find the probability that in a sample of five customers (a) none of the five will order a non-alcoholic beverage, (b) at least two will, (c) fewer than four will, (d) all five will order a non-alcoholic beverage. (LO 4)

6.27   J.D. Power and Associates says that 60 percent of car buyers now use the Internet for research and price comparisons. (a) Find the probability that in a sample of eight car buyers, all eight will use the Internet; (b) at least five; (c) more than four. (d) Find the mean and standard deviation of the probability distribution. (e) Sketch the PDF (using Excel or Appendix A) and describe its appearance (e.g., skewness). (Data are from J. Paul Peter and Jerry C. Olson, *Consumer Behavior and Marketing Strategy*, 7th ed. [McGraw-Hill/Irwin, 2005], p. 188.) (LO 4)

6.28   Statistics Canada reported that 30.5 percent of Canadian adults had a higher body mass index (BMI) in 2006/2007 than in 1994/1995 (**www40.statcan.gc.ca/l01/cst01/hlth68-eng.htm**). If a sample of 20 Canadian adults was randomly chosen for further analysis, using Excel, what is the probability that (a) at least four of them had higher BMIs; (b) no more than eight had higher BMIs; (c) more than four but less than eight had higher BMIs; (d) at least five and less than ten had higher BMIs. (LO 4)

6.5   Hypergeometric Distribution

Characteristics of the Hypergeometric Distribution

One of the uses of the binomial distribution is determining probabilities of so many successes in a sample of size n when we sample from an infinite population or when we sample with replacement from a population where the proportion of successes is some known value, π. In either case, π remains constant and the binomial distribution would apply. But what if we sample without replacement from a finite population? The proportion of successes changes as we select our sample and thus the binomial distribution can no longer be used. Fortunately, there is another probability distribution that does apply. The distribution is called the hypergeometric distribution.

FIGURE 6.15

Hypergeometric Distribution

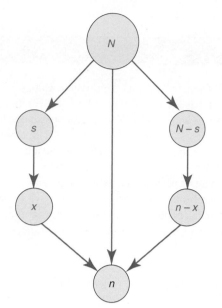

The **hypergeometric distribution** is similar to the binomial except that sampling is *without replacement* from a finite population of N items. The hypergeometric distribution has three parameters: N (the number of items in the population), n (the number of items in the sample), and s (the number of successes in the population). The distribution of X (the number of successes in the sample) is hypergeometric, with the characteristics shown in Figure 6.15. The hypergeometric distribution may be skewed right or left, and is symmetric only if $s/N = 0.50$ (i.e., if the proportion of successes in the population is 50 percent).

The hypergeometric PDF, shown in Equation 6.7, uses the formula for combinations:

$$P(x) = \frac{{_sC_x}\,{_{N-s}C_{n-x}}}{{_NC_n}} \qquad (6.7)$$

where ${_sC_x}$ = the number of ways to choose x successes from s successes in the population. Figure 6.7 illustrates this formula. The total number of ways of choosing n things out of N is ${_NC_n}$. To get x successes, they have to come out of s successes in the population. The remaining $n - x$ observations of the sample have to come out of the remaining population of size $N - s$. The total number of ways this can happen is ${_sC_x}\,{_{N-s}C_{n-x}}$, which results in the probability formula in Equation 6.7.

Parameters	N = number of items in the population
	n = sample size
	s = number of successes in population
PDF	$P(x) = \dfrac{{_sC_x}\,{_{N-s}C_{n-x}}}{{_NC_n}}$
Excel function	=HYPGEOMDIST(x,n,s,N)
Domain	$\max(0, n - N + s) \le X \le \min(s, n)$
Mean	$n\pi$ where $\pi = s/N$
Standard deviation	$\sqrt{n\pi(1 - \pi)}\,\sqrt{\dfrac{N - n}{N - 1}}$
Comments	Similar to binomial, but sampling is without replacement from a finite population. It can be approximated by a binomial with $\pi = s/N$ if $n/N < 0.05$, and is symmetric if $s/N = 0.50$.

${_{N-s}C_{n-x}}$ = the number of ways to choose $n - x$ failures from $N - s$ failures in the population; ${_NC_n}$ = the number of ways to choose n items from N items in the population; and $N - s$ = the number of failures in the population, x = the number of successes in the sample, and $n - x$ = the number of failures in the sample. For a review of combinations see Chapter 5.

A Closer Look

The above table, under "Domain," tells us the possible values of X, or it tells us that the smallest possible value of X is the larger of 0 and $n - N + s$ and that the largest possible value of X is the smaller of s and n. Why? The largest possible value of X should be intuitively obvious. X cannot be any larger than the number of successes in the population and it cannot be any larger than the sample size. Therefore, it must be smaller than both of them. Why it must be at least as large as "the maximum of 0 and $n - N + s$" requires a little more thought. Obviously X cannot be negative, but why also at least as large as $n - N + s$? If we rearrange this term, it can also be expressed as $n - (N - s)$. Because $N - s$ is the maximum number of failures in the population, we can never have more than $N - s$ failures in a sample. This means that we must have at least $n - (N - s)$ successes in a sample.

EXAMPLE 8

Damaged iPods

In a shipment of 10 iPods, 2 are damaged and 8 are good. The receiving department at Best Buy tests a sample of 3 iPods at random to see if they are defective. The number of damaged iPods in the sample is a random variable X. The problem description is as follows:

$N = 10$	(number of iPods in the shipment)
$n = 3$	(sample size drawn from the shipment)
$s = 2$	(number of damaged iPods in the shipment, i.e., successes in population)
$N - s = 8$	(number of non-damaged iPods in the shipment)
$x = ?$	(number of damaged iPods in the sample, i.e., successes in sample)
$n - x = ?$	(number of non-damaged iPods in the sample)

It is tempting to think of this as a binomial problem with $n = 3$ and $\pi = s/N = 2/10 = 0.20$. But π is not constant. On the first draw, the probability of a damaged iPod is indeed $\pi_1 = 2/10$. But on the second draw, the probability of a damaged iPod could be $\pi_2 = 1/9$ (if the first draw contained a damaged iPod) or $\pi_2 = 2/9$ (if the first draw did not contain a damaged iPod). On the third draw, the probability of a damaged iPod could be $\pi_3 = 0/8$, $\pi_3 = 1/8$, or $\pi_3 = 2/8$, depending on what happened in the first two draws.

Using the Hypergeometric Formula

For the iPod example, the only possible values of x are 0, 1, and 2 as there are only two damaged iPods in the population. The probabilities are as shown:

PDF Formula   *Excel Function*

$$P(0) = \frac{(_2C_0)(_8C_3)}{_{10}C_3} = \frac{\left(\dfrac{2!}{0!2!}\right)\left(\dfrac{8!}{3!5!}\right)}{\left(\dfrac{10!}{3!7!}\right)} = \frac{56}{120} = \frac{7}{15} = \text{HYPGEOMDIST}(0,3,2,10)$$

$$P(1) = \frac{(_2C_1)(_8C_2)}{_{10}C_3} = \frac{\left(\dfrac{2!}{1!1!}\right)\left(\dfrac{8!}{2!6!}\right)}{\left(\dfrac{10!}{3!7!}\right)} = \frac{56}{120} = \frac{7}{15} = \text{HYPGEOMDIST}(1,3,2,10)$$

$$P(2) = \frac{(_2C_2)(_8C_1)}{_{10}C_3} = \frac{\left(\dfrac{2!}{2!0!}\right)\left(\dfrac{8!}{1!7!}\right)}{\left(\dfrac{10!}{3!7!}\right)} = \frac{8}{120} = \frac{1}{15} = \text{HYPGEOMDIST}(2,3,2,10)$$

Excel's Hypergeometric Function (where $N = 194$, $n = 10$, $s = 82$) **FIGURE 6.16**

The values of $P(X)$ sum to 1, as they should: $P(0) + P(1) + P(2) = 7/15 + 7/15 + 1/15 = 1$. We can also find the probability of compound events. For example, the probability of at least one damaged iPod is $P(X \geq 1) = P(1) + P(2) = 7/15 + 1/15 = 8/15 = 0.533$, or 53.3 percent.

LS
Chapter 4

Excel   The hypergeometric formula is tedious and tables are impractical because there are three parameters, so we prefer Excel's hypergeometric function $=$HYPGEOMDIST(x,n,s,N). For example, using $X = 5$, $n = 10$, $s = 82$, $n = 194$ the formula $=$HYPGEOMDIST(5,10,82,194) gives 0.222690589, as illustrated in Figure 6.16. You can also get hypergeometric probabilities from MegaStat (menus not shown).

Recognizing Hypergeometric Applications

Look for a finite population (N) containing a known number of successes (s) and *sampling without replacement* (n items in the sample) where the probability of success is not constant for each sample item drawn. For example:

- Forty automobiles are to be inspected for emissions compliance. Thirty-two are compliant but eight are not. A sample of seven cars is chosen at random. What is the probability that all are compliant? At least five?

- An Alberta law enforcement agency must process 500 background checks for firearms purchasers. Fifty applicants are convicted felons. Through a computer error, 10 applicants are approved without a background check. What is the probability that none is a felon? At least two are?

- A medical laboratory receives 40 blood specimens to check for HIV. Eight actually contain HIV. A worker is accidentally exposed to five specimens. What is the probability that none contained HIV?

Section Exercises

6.29 (a) State the values that X can assume in each hypergeometric scenario. (b) Use the hypergeometric PDF formula to find the probability requested. (c) Check your answer by using Excel. (LO 4 & 5)

   i. $N = 10$, $n = 3$, $s = 4$, $P(X = 3)$
   ii. $N = 20$, $n = 5$, $s = 3$, $P(X = 2)$
   iii. $N = 36$, $n = 4$, $s = 9$, $P(X = 1)$
   iv. $N = 50$, $n = 7$, $s = 10$, $P(X = 3)$

6.30 Future Shop has eight refrigerators in stock. Two are side-by-side models and six are top-freezer models. (a) Using Excel, calculate the entire hypergeometric probability distribution for the number of top-freezer models in a sample of four refrigerators chosen at random. (b) Make an Excel graph of the PDF for this probability distribution and describe its appearance. (LO 4 & 5)

6.31 A statistics textbook chapter contains 60 exercises, 6 of which contain incorrect answers. A student is assigned 10 problems. (a) Use Excel to calculate the entire hypergeometric probability distribution. (b) What is the probability that all the answers are correct? (c) That at least one is incorrect? (d) That two or more are incorrect? (e) Make an Excel graph of the PDF of the hypergeometric distribution and describe its appearance. (LO 4 & 5)

6.32 Fifty employee travel expense reimbursement vouchers were filed last quarter in the finance department at Ramjac Corporation. Of these, 20 contained errors. A corporate auditor inspects five vouchers at random. Let X be the number of incorrect vouchers in the sample. (a) Use Excel to calculate the entire hypergeometric probability distribution. (b) Find $P(X = 0)$. (c) Find $P(X = 1)$. (d) Find $P(X \geq 3)$. (e) Make an Excel graph of the PDF of the hypergeometric distribution and describe its appearance. (LO 4 & 5)

6.33 A medical laboratory receives 40 blood specimens to check for HIV. Eight actually contain HIV. A worker is accidentally exposed to five specimens. (a) Use Excel to calculate the entire hypergeometric probability distribution. (b) What is the probability that none contained HIV? (c) Fewer than three? (d) At least two? (e) Make an Excel graph of the PDF of the hypergeometric distribution and describe its appearance. (LO 4 & 5)

6.34* In the popular game show *Deal or No Deal* there are 26 cases containing money ranging from $0.01 to $1,000.000. The contestant chooses one of the cases that he or she hopes contains the $1,000,000 or at least one of the seven cases that contain $100,000 or more. The contestant then picks six cases that are to be opened (excluding the one that he or she has chosen). Use the hypergeometric formula. (a) What is the probability that none of the six cases contain at least $100,000? (b) What is the probability that each of the six cases contain at least $100,000? (c) What is the probability that exactly two cases will contain at least $100,000? (d) How many of these cases would you expect to contain at least $100,000? Answer these questions under two different assumptions—you have chosen a case that contains at least $100,000, and you have chosen a case that does not contain at least $100,000. (LO 4 & 5)

Rule of Thumb for Binomial Approximation to the Hypergeometric

As the population size, N, gets larger, using the hypergeometric formula becomes more problematic if calculations are performed on commonly used calculators. If the population is quite larger than the sample, the binomial distribution may be used to approximate the true probabilities. In fact, if $n/N < 0.05$ it is safe to use the binomial approximation to the hypergeometric, with the sample size being n and the probability of success being $\pi = s/N$.

EXAMPLE 9

Lottery Tickets

Suppose you bought 4 tickets in a lottery in which only 200 tickets were sold and in which 10 winning tickets would be drawn without replacement. What would be the probability of you winning at least one of the prizes? Using the hypergeometric distribution, $N = 200$, $n = 10$, and $s = 4$, and

$$P(X \geq 1) = 1 - P(X = 0) = 1 - \frac{(_4C_0)(_{196}C_{10})}{(_{200}C_{10})} = 1 - 0.8132 = 0.1868$$

Using the binomial formula where $n = 10$ and $\pi = 4/200 = 0.02$

$$P(X \geq 1) = 1 - P(X = 0) = 1 - 0.8171 = 0.1829$$

Here $n/N = 0.05$, a borderline case for using the binomial approximation, and yet the approximated probability is quite accurate.

6.6 Poisson Distribution

Poisson Processes

Named for the French mathematician Siméon-Denis Poisson (1781–1840), the **Poisson distribution** describes the number of occurrences within a randomly chosen unit of time (e.g., minute, hour) or space (e.g., square foot, linear mile). For the Poisson distribution to apply, the events must occur randomly and independently over a continuum of time or space, as illustrated in Figure 6.17. We will call the continuum "time" because the most common Poisson application is modelling **arrivals** *per unit of time*. Each dot (•) is an occurrence of the event of interest.

One Unit of Time ⊢------→| One Unit of Time ⊢------→| One Unit of Time ⊢------→|

Flow of Time ⟶

FIGURE 6.17

Poisson Events Distributed over Time

Let X = the number of events per unit of time. The value of X is a random variable that depends on when the unit of time is observed. Figure 6.17 shows that we could get $X = 3$ or $X = 1$ or $X = 5$ events, depending on where the randomly chosen unit of time happens to fall.

We often call the Poisson distribution the *model of arrivals* (customers, defects, accidents). Arrivals can reasonably be regarded as Poisson events if each event is **independent** (i.e., each event's occurrence has no effect on the probability of other events occurring). Some situations lack this characteristic. For example, computer users know that a power interruption often presages another within seconds or minutes. But, as a practical matter, the Poisson assumptions often are met sufficiently to make it a useful model of reality. For example:

- X = number of customers arriving at a bank ABM in a given minute.
- X = number of file server virus infections at a data centre during a 24-hour period.
- X = number of asthma patient arrivals in a given hour at a walk-in clinic.
- X = number of Airbus 330 aircraft engine shutdowns per 100,000 flight hours.
- X = number of blemishes per sheet of white bond paper.

The Poisson model has only one parameter denoted λ (the Greek letter "lambda") representing the *mean number of events per unit of time or space.* The unit of time should be short enough that the mean arrival rate is not large (typically $\lambda < 20$). For this reason, the Poisson distribution is sometimes called the *model of* **rare events.** If the mean is large, we can reformulate the time units to yield a smaller mean. For example, $\lambda = 90$ events per hour is the same as $\lambda = 1.5$ events per minute.

Characteristics of the Poisson Distribution

All characteristics of the Poisson model are determined by its mean λ, as shown in Table 6.6. The constant e (the base of the natural logarithm system) is approximately 2.71828 (to see a more precise value of e, use your calculator's e^x function with $x = 1$). The mean of the Poisson distribution is λ, and its standard deviation is the square root of the mean. The simplicity of the Poisson formulas makes it an attractive model (easier than the binomial, for example). Unlike the binomial, X has no obvious upper limit, that is, the number of events that can occur in a given unit of time can theoretically be infinite. However, Poisson probabilities taper off toward zero as X increases, so the effective range is usually small.

Chapter 4

TABLE 6.6   Poisson Distribution

Parameters	λ = mean arrivals per unit of time or space
PDF	$P(x) = \dfrac{\lambda^x e^{-\lambda}}{x!}$
Excel function	=POISSON(X,λ,0)
Domain	$X = 0, 1, 2,\ldots$(no obvious upper limit)
Mean	λ
Standard deviation	$\sqrt{\lambda}$
Comments	Always right-skewed, but less so for larger λ.

TABLE 6.7   **Poisson Probabilities for Various Values of** λ

x	$\lambda = 0.1$	$\lambda = 0.5$	$\lambda = 0.8$	$\lambda = 1.6$	$\lambda = 2.0$
0	0.9048	0.6065	0.4493	0.2019	0.1353
1	0.0905	0.3033	0.3595	0.3230	0.2707
2	0.0045	0.0758	0.1438	0.2584	0.2707
3	0.0002	0.0126	0.0383	0.1378	0.1804
4	—	0.0016	0.0077	0.0551	0.0902
5	—	0.0002	0.0012	0.0176	0.0361
6	—	—	0.0002	0.0047	0.0120
7	—	—	—	0.0011	0.0034
8	—	—	—	0.0002	0.0009
9	—	—	—	—	0.0002
Sum	1.0000	1.0000	1.0000	1.0000	1.0000

Note: Probabilities less than 0.0001 have been omitted. Columns may not sum to 1 due to rounding.

FIGURE 6.18   **Poisson Becomes Less Skewed for Larger** λ

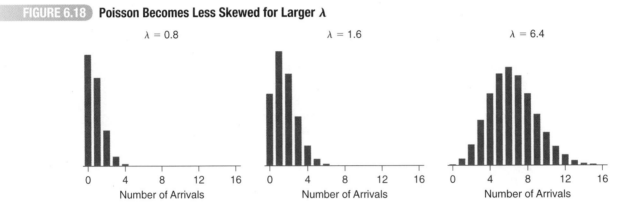

Table 6.7 shows some Poisson PDFs (i.e., P(X ≤ k)). Going down each column (one column for each stated λ), the cumulative probabilities approach 1 and they approach 1 more quickly for smaller values of λ.

The Poisson probability function is:

$$P(X = x) = \frac{\lambda^x e^{-\lambda}}{x!}, \text{ for } X = 0, 1, 2, 3, 4, \ldots \tag{6.8}$$

Poisson distributions are always right-skewed (long right tail) but become less skewed and more bell-shaped as λ increases, as illustrated in Figure 6.18.

EXAMPLE 10

Credit Union Customers
CreditUnion

On Thursday morning between 9 and 10 a.m. customers arrive at a mean rate of 1.7 customers per minute at the Hamilton Credit Union and enter the queue (if any) for the teller windows. Using the Poisson formulas with $\lambda = 1.7$, the equations for the PDF, mean, and standard deviation are:

$$\text{PDF: } P(x) = \frac{\lambda^x e^{-\lambda}}{x!} = \frac{(1.7)^x e^{-1.7}}{x!}$$

$$\text{Mean: } \lambda = 1.7$$

$$\text{Standard deviation: } \sigma = \sqrt{\lambda} = \sqrt{1.7} = 1.304$$

TABLE 6.8   Probability Distribution for $\lambda = 1.7$

x	P(X = x)	P(X ≤ x)
0	0.1827	0.1827
1	0.3106	0.4932
2	0.2640	0.7572
3	0.1496	0.9068
4	0.0636	0.9704
5	0.0216	0.9920
6	0.0061	0.9981
7	0.0015	0.9996
8	0.0003	0.9999
9	0.0001	1.0000

Using the Poisson Formula

Table 6.8 shows the probabilities for each value of X. The probabilities for individual X values can be calculated by inserting $\lambda = 1.7$ into the Poisson PDF or by using Excel's Poisson function =POISSON(x,λ,cumulative) where cumulative is 0 (if you want a PDF) or 1 (if you want a CDF).

PDF Formula   *Excel Function*

$$P(0) = \frac{1.7^0 e^{-1.7}}{0!} = 0.1827 \quad =\text{POISSON}(0,1.7,0)$$

$$P(1) = \frac{1.7^1 e^{-1.7}}{1!} = 0.3106 \quad =\text{POISSON}(1,1.7,0)$$

$$P(2) = \frac{1.7^2 e^{-1.7}}{2!} = 0.2640 \quad =\text{POISSON}(2,1.7,0)$$

$$P(3) = \frac{1.7^3 e^{-1.7}}{3!} = 0.1496 \quad =\text{POISSON}(3,1.7,0)$$

$$P(4) = \frac{1.7^4 e^{-1.7}}{4!} = 0.0636 \quad =\text{POISSON}(4,1.7,0)$$

$$P(5) = \frac{1.7^5 e^{-1.7}}{5!} = 0.0216 \quad =\text{POISSON}(5,1.7,0)$$

$$P(6) = \frac{1.7^6 e^{-1.7}}{6!} = 0.0061 \quad =\text{POISSON}(6,1.7,0)$$

$$P(7) = \frac{1.7^7 e^{-1.7}}{7!} = 0.0015 \quad =\text{POISSON}(7,1.7,0)$$

$$P(8) = \frac{1.7^8 e^{-1.7}}{8!} = 0.0003 \quad =\text{POISSON}(8,1.7,0)$$

$$P(9) = \frac{1.7^9 e^{-1.7}}{9!} = 0.0001 \quad =\text{POISSON}(9,1.7,0)$$

Poisson probabilities must sum to 1 (except due to rounding) as with any discrete probability distribution. Beyond $X = 9$, the probabilities are below 0.0001. Graphs of the PDF and CDF are shown in Figures 6.19 and 6.20. The most likely event is one arrival (probability 0.3106, or a 31.1 percent chance), although two arrivals is almost as likely (probability 0.2640,

FIGURE 6.19
Poisson PDF for $\lambda = 1.7$

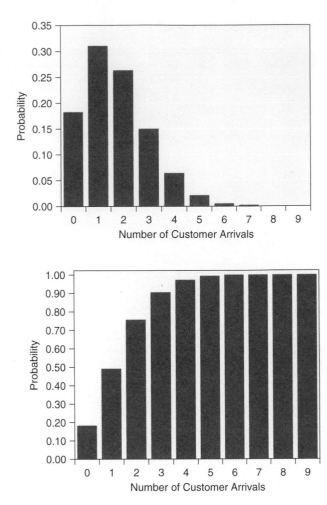

FIGURE 6.20
Poisson CDF for $\lambda = 1.7$

or a 26.4 percent chance). This PDF would help the credit union schedule its tellers for the Thursday morning work shift.

Compound Events

Cumulative probabilities can be evaluated by summing individual X probabilities. For example, the probability that two or fewer customers will arrive in a given minute is the sum of probabilities for several events:

$$P(X \leq 2) = P(0) + P(1) + P(2)$$
$$= 0.1827 + 0.3106 + 0.2640 = 0.7573$$

We could then calculate the probability of at least three customers (the complementary event):

$$P(X \geq 3) = 1 - P(X \leq 2) = 1 - 0.7573 = 0.2427$$

The cumulative probability $P(X \leq 2)$ can also be obtained by using the Excel function =POISSON(2,1.7,1).

Using Tables (Appendix B)

As with the binomial distribution, if there are several applications of the Poisson formula that would have to be used to arrive at the appropriate answer, a table that gives us cumulative probabilities instead of individual probabilities would be most practical. Appendix B provides a table for calculating cumulative Poisson probabilities for various values of λ, a portion of which is included in Figure 6.21. The following example illustrates the use of this table.

FIGURE 6.21

Poisson Probabilities for λ from Appendix B

| | λ | | | | | | | | | | | |
k	0.1	0.2	0.3	0.4	0.5	0.6	0.7	0.8	0.9	1	1.1	1.2
0	0.9048	0.8187	0.7408	0.6703	0.6065	0.5488	0.4966	0.4493	0.4066	0.3679	0.3329	0.3012
1	0.9953	0.9825	0.9631	0.9384	0.9098	0.8781	0.8442	0.8088	0.7725	0.7358	0.6990	0.6626
2	0.9998	0.9989	0.9964	0.9921	0.9856	0.9769	0.9659	0.9526	0.9371	0.9197	0.9004	0.8795
3	1.0000	0.9999	0.9997	0.9992	0.9982	0.9966	0.9942	0.9909	0.9865	0.9810	0.9743	0.9662
4		1.0000	1.0000	0.9999	0.9998	0.9996	0.9992	0.9986	0.9977	0.9963	0.9946	0.9923
5				1.0000	1.0000	1.0000	0.9999	0.9998	0.9997	0.9994	0.9990	0.9985
6							1.0000	1.0000	1.0000	0.9999	0.9999	0.9997
7										1.0000	1.0000	1.0000
⋮	⋮	⋮	⋮	⋮	⋮	⋮	⋮	⋮	⋮	⋮	⋮	⋮

EXAMPLE 11
Bus Schedules

In some cities in Canada, bus systems try to follow fixed schedules, while in other cities, buses arrive at the various stops along routes somewhat randomly and independently of one another (i.e., they arrive whenever they get there). Theoretically, for those systems that succeed in following a fixed schedule, the probability that a bus arrives at a particular stop within a certain period of time is either 1 (if the bus is scheduled to arrive within that time) or 0 (if the bus is not scheduled to arrive within that time). For these other systems in which buses arrive randomly and independently of one another at any specific stop, the Poisson distribution can be used to determine the probabilities for X, the number of buses arriving at a particular stop. One particular stop along one particular route in Montreal has buses arriving randomly and independently of one another with an average of 0.5 buses arriving within 10-minute intervals. Find the probabilities (using the above cumulative Poisson distribution) that

(a) No buses will arrive within a 10-minute interval.
(b) Exactly one bus will arrive within a 10-minute interval.
(c) At least two buses will arrive within a 10-minute interval.
(d) At least three buses will arrive within a 60-minute interval.
(e) At least two buses but no more than four buses will arrive within a 60-minute interval.

To use the cumulative Poisson probability table, as with using the cumulative binomial probability table, we have to express all probabilities in terms of $P(X \leq k)$. To answer questions (a) through (c), we look under the column where $\lambda = 0.5$ and we find:

(a) $P(X = 0) = P(X \leq 0) = 0.6065$
(b) $P(X = 1) = P(X \leq 1) - P(X \leq 0) = 0.9098 - 0.6065 = 0.3033$
(c) $P(X \geq 2) = 1 - P(X \leq 1) = 1 - 0.9098 = 0.0902$

For questions (d) and (e), we are now looking at a 60-minute interval and not a 10-minute interval. Obviously, the average number of arrivals within a 60-minute interval should be greater than the average number of arrivals within a 10-minute interval. Intuitively, the average number of arrivals within a 60-minute interval should be six times the average number of arrivals within a 10-minute interval, or λ should equal 3.0. Using this value of λ,

(d) $P(X \geq 3) = 1 - P(X \leq 2) = 1 - 0.4232 = 0.5768$
(e) $P(2 \leq X \leq 4) = P(X \leq 4) - P(X \leq 1) = 0.8153 - 0.1991 = 0.6162$

Chapter 4

Recognizing Poisson Applications

Can you recognize a Poisson situation? The Poisson distribution has three main characteristics.

- Potentially, there is an unlimited number of arrivals in a fixed time period.
- The arrivals occur randomly.
- The arrivals are independent of each other.

Ask yourself if the three characteristics above make sense in the following examples.

- In the last week, how many credit card applications did you receive by mail?
- In the last week, how many cheques did you write?
- In the last week, how many e-mail viruses did your firewall detect?

It may be a Poisson process, even if you don't know the mean (λ). In business applications, the value of λ would have to be estimated from experience, but in this chapter λ will be given.

Section Exercises

6.35 Find the mean and standard deviation for each Poisson: (LO 4)
  a. $\lambda = 1.0$
  b. $\lambda = 2.0$
  c. $\lambda = 4.0$
  d. $\lambda = 9.0$
  e. $\lambda = 12.0$

6.36 Calculate each Poisson probability: (LO 4)
  a. $X = 2, \lambda = 0.1$
  b. $X = 1, \lambda = 2.2$
  c. $X = 3, \lambda = 1.6$
  d. $X = 6, \lambda = 4.0$
  e. $X = 10, \lambda = 12.0$

6.37 Calculate each compound event probability: (LO 4)
  a. $X \leq 3, \lambda = 4.3$
  b. $X > 7, \lambda = 5.2$
  c. $X < 3, \lambda = 2.7$
  d. $X \leq 10, \lambda = 11.0$

6.38 Calculate each Poisson probability: (LO 4)
  a. Fewer than four arrivals with $\lambda = 5.8$.
  b. At least three arrivals with $\lambda = 4.8$.
  c. At most nine arrivals with $\lambda = 7.0$.
  d. More than 10 arrivals with $\lambda = 8.0$.

6.39 According to J.D. Power and Associates' 2006 Initial Quality Study, consumers reported on average 1.7 problems per vehicle with new 2006 Volkswagens. In a randomly selected new Volkswagen, find the probability of (a) at least one problem; (b) no problems; (c) more than three problems. (d) Construct the probability distribution using Excel or Appendix B, make a graph of its PDF, and describe its shape. (Data are from J.D. Power and Associates 2006 Initial Quality Study[SM].) (LO 4)

6.40 At an outpatient mental health clinic, appointment cancellations occur at a mean rate of 1.5 per day on a typical Wednesday. Let X be the number of cancellations on a particular Wednesday. (a) Justify the use of the Poisson model. (b) What is the probability that no cancellations will occur on a particular Wednesday? (c) One? (d) More than two? (e) Five or more? (LO 4)

6.41 The average number of items (such as a drink or dessert) ordered by a Noodles & Company customer in addition to the meal is 1.4. These items are called *add-ons*. Define X to be the number of add-ons ordered by a randomly selected customer. (a) Justify the use of the Poisson model. (b) What is the probability that a randomly selected customer orders at least two add-ons? (c) No add-ons? (d) Construct the probability distribution using Excel or Appendix B, make a graph of its PDF, and describe its shape. (LO 4) **noodles**

6.42 (a) Why might the number of yawns per minute by students in a warm classroom not be a Poisson event? (b) Give two additional examples of events per unit of time that might violate the assumptions of the Poisson model, and explain why. (LO 4)

6.43* On average, 2.5 cars per day crossing into Canada from the United States are smuggling firearms into the country. If the number of cars smuggling firearms into Canada follows a Poisson distribution, (a) what is the probability that no cars are smuggling firearms into Canada on a particular day? (b) What is the probability that at least four cars are smugging firearms into Canada on a particular day? (c) What is the probability that no more than five cars are smuggling firearms into Canada over a particular two-day period? (d) what is the probability that at least 10 cars are smuggling firearms into Canada during a particular week? (e) What is the probability that exactly 15 cars are smuggling firearms into Canada during a particular week? Use the Poisson formula, the cumulative Poisson probability table and Excel at least once each when answering these questions. (LO 4 & 5)

A Closer Look

The binomial, hypergeometric, and Poisson distributions all look at the number of successes in some random process. To determine which is the appropriate distribution to apply, you have to ask yourself the following questions to determine which distribution actually does apply:

* Is there a fixed sample size, *n?* If the answer is "yes," the distribution is either binomial or hypergeometric. If the answer is "no," the distribution is Poisson.
* Is there a fixed sample size and the population is either large or we sample with replacement? If these conditions apply, the distribution is binomial.
* Is there is a fixed sample size, is the population small, and is sampling done with replacement? If these conditions apply, the distribution is hypergeometric.

Having asked and answered the following questions, it is possible that none of these distributions apply in a particular situation. For example, there may be a fixed sample size and the population may be large or we may be sampling with replacement and, yet, the random process may not follow a binomial distribution because the probability of success, π, may not be constant throughout the process. As an example, suppose the random process involves rolling a die 1,000 times. The population size is infinity because the die can be theoretically rolled an infinite number of times. Yet the probability of the top face being a 1, for example, may change through wear and tear as the process of rolling the die continues. This would negate the use of the binomial distribution. And the Poisson distribution would not apply even though there is no fixed sample size if the successes are not rare or are not independent of one another.

CHAPTER SUMMARY

A **random variable** assigns a numerical value to each outcome in the sample space of a **stochastic process**. A **discrete random variable** has a countable number of distinct values. Probabilities in a **discrete probability distribution** must be between zero and one, and must sum to one. The **expected value** is the mean of the distribution, measuring central tendency, and its **variance** is a measure of dispersion. A known distribution is described by its **parameters,** which imply its **probability distribution function** (PDF) and its **cumulative distribution function** (CDF).

As summarized in Table 6.9 the **uniform distribution** has two parameters (a, b) that define its range $a \le X \le b$. The **binomial distribution** has two parameters (n, π). It describes the sum of n independent random experiments, each with two possible outcomes and each with the same probability of success. It may be skewed left $(\pi > 0.50)$ or right $(\pi < 0.50)$ or symmetric $(\pi = 0.50)$ but becomes less skewed as n increases. The **Poisson distribution** has one parameter $(\lambda$, the mean arrival rate). It describes arrivals of independent events per unit of time or space. It is always right-skewed, becoming less so as λ increases. Rules for **linear transformations** of random variables say that adding a constant to a random variable shifts the distribution, but does not change its variance, while multiplying a random variable by a constant changes both its mean and its variance. Rules for summing random variables permit adding of their means, but their variances can be summed only if the random variables are independent.

TABLE 6.9   Comparison of Models

Model	Parameters	Mean E(X)	Variance V(X)	Characteristics
Binomial	n, π	$n\pi$	$n\pi(1 - \pi)$	Skewed right if $\pi < 0.50$, left if $\pi > 0.50$.
Hypergeometric	N, n, s	$n\pi$ where $\pi = s/N$	$n\pi(1 - \pi)[(N - n)/(N - 1)]$	Like binomial except sampling without replacement from a finite population
Poisson	λ	λ	λ	Always skewed right
Uniform	a, b	$(a + b)/2$	$[(b - a + 1)^2 - 1]/12$	

KEY TERMS

actuarially fair, *228*
arrivals (Poisson), *248*
binomial distribution, *239*
cumulative distribution function (CDF), *230*
discrete probability distribution, *222*
discrete random variable, *222*

expected value, *224*
hypergeometric distribution, *245*
independent (Poisson), *249*
Poisson distribution, *248*
probability distribution function (PDF), *230*
probability model, *220*

random variable, *221*
rare events (Poisson), *249*
stochastic process, *220*
uniform distribution, *237*
variance, *228*

Commonly Used Formulas in Discrete Distributions

Total probability:

$$\sum_{i=1}^{k} P(x_i) = 1$$

Expected value:

$$E(X) = \mu = \sum_{i=1}^{k} x_i P(x_i)$$

if there are k distinct values $x_1, x_2, \ldots, x_k$

Variance:

$$V(X) = \sigma^2 = \sum_{i=1}^{k} (x_i - \mu)^2$$

Uniform PDF:

$$P(x) = \frac{1}{b - a + 1} \quad X = a, a+1, \ldots, b$$

Binomial PDF:

$$P(x) = \frac{n!}{x!(n - x)!} \pi^x (1 - \pi)^{n-x} \quad X = 0, 1, 2, \ldots, n$$

Poisson PDF:

$$P(x) = \frac{\lambda^x e^{-\lambda}}{x!} \quad X = 0, 1, 2, \ldots$$

Hypergeometric PDF:

$$P(x) = \frac{{}_s C_{x} \, {}_{N-s} C_{n-x}}{{}_N C_n} \quad \max(0, n - N + s) \le X \le \min(s, n)$$

Geometric PDF:

$$P(x) = \pi(1 - \pi)^{x-1} \quad X = 1, 2, \ldots$$

CHAPTER REVIEW

1. Define (a) stochastic process; (b) random variable; (c) discrete random variable; and (d) probability distribution. (LO 1)

2. Without using formulas, explain the meaning of (a) expected value of a random variable; (b) actuarial fairness; and (c) variance of a random variable. (LO 2)

3. What is the difference between a PDF and a CDF? Sketch a picture of each. (LO 1)

4. (a) What are the two parameters of a uniform distribution? (b) Why is the uniform distribution the first one considered in this chapter? (LO 3)

5. (a) What are the parameters of a binomial distribution? (b) What is the mean of a binomial distribution? The standard deviation? (c) When is a binomial skewed right? Skewed left? Symmetric? (d) Suggest a data-generating situation that might be binomial. (LO 3)

6. (a) What are the parameters of a Poisson distribution? (b) What is the mean of a Poisson distribution? The standard deviation? (c) Is a Poisson ever symmetric? (d) Suggest a data-generating situation that might be Poisson. (LO 3)

7. In the binomial and Poisson models, why is the assumption of independent events important? (LO 3)

8. (a) Explain a situation when we would need the hypergeometric distribution. (b) What are the three parameters of the hypergeometric distribution? (c) How does it differ from a binomial distribution? (LO 3)

9.*When are we justified in using the binomial approximation to the hypergeometric? (LO 4)

10. (a) Name a situation when we would need the (a) hypergeometric distribution; (b) uniform distribution. (LO 4)

Visual Statistics   Figure 6.22 shows a binomial distribution for $n = 10$, $\pi = 0.50$ from *Visual Statistics Module 4*. Numerical probabilities are shown in a table in the lower left (both PDF and CDF). The graph can be copied and pasted as a bitmap, and the tab-delimited table probabilities can be copied and pasted into Excel. An attractive feature of Visual Statistics is that you can "spin" both n and π and can superimpose a normal curve on your binomial distribution to see if it is bell-shaped.

LearningStats   Figure 6.23 shows a *LearningStats* binomial screen using $n = 100$ and $\pi = 0.5$ with graphs and a table of probabilities. The spin buttons let you vary n and π.

Binomial Random Data   Use Excel's Data > Data Analysis to generate binomial random data. Figure 6.24 shows how to use the Excel menu to generate 20 binomial random data values using $n = 4$ and $\pi = 0.20$.

USING SOFTWARE

Chapter 4

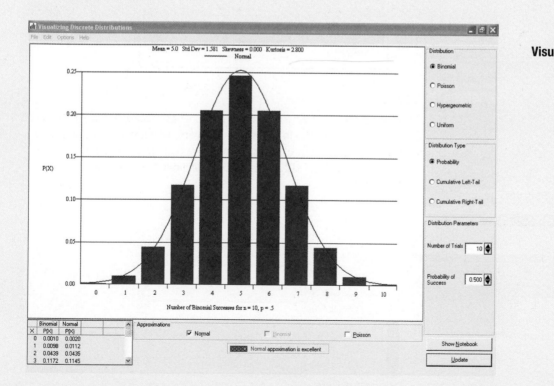

FIGURE 6.22

Visual Statistics Binomial Display

FIGURE 6.23

LearningStats Binomial Display

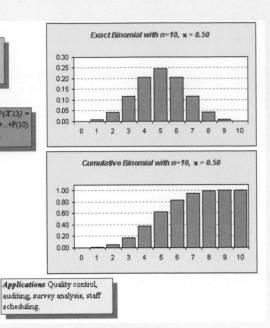

Binomial Distribution for n = 10, π = 0.50

Problem Ten patients are scheduled for appointments on Wednesday morning. The probability is 0.5 that a given patient will be late. Find the probability that at least 3 patients will be late.

x	P(x)	P(X ≤ x)	P(X > x)
0	0.00098	0.00098	0.99902
1	0.00977	0.01074	0.98926
2	0.04395	0.05469	0.94531
3	0.11719	0.17188	0.82813
4	0.20508	0.37695	0.62305
5	0.24609	0.62305	0.37695
6	0.20508	0.82813	0.17188
7	0.11719	0.94531	0.05469
8	0.04395	0.98926	0.01074
9	0.00977	0.99902	0.00098
10	0.00098	1.00000	0.00000

Sum   1.00000

Answer P(X ≥ 3) = P(3)+P(4)+...+P(10) = 0.94531.

Binomial Distribution Describes the number of successes in *n* independent trials with a constant probability *π* of success on each trial. A "success" refers to the outcome of interest (it may not be a desirable outcome, and often is an undesirable or anomalous event).

Applications Quality control, auditing, survey analysis, staff scheduling.

FIGURE 6.24

Excel's Binomial Random Number Menu

Random Number Generation

Number of Variables:	1
Number of Random Numbers:	20
Distribution:	Binomial

Parameters

p Value = 0.2
Number of trials = 4

Random Seed:

Output options
- Output Range: c3
- New Worksheet Ply:
- New Workbook

OK | Cancel | Help

Poisson Distribution

Chapter 4

Tables are helpful for taking statistics exams (when you may not have access to Excel). However, tables contain only selected λ values, and in real-world problems, we cannot expect λ always to be a nice round number. Excel's menus are illustrated in Figure 6.25. In this example, Excel calculates =POISSON(11,17,0) as 0.035544812, which is more accurate than Appendix B.

FIGURE 6.25 Excel's Poisson Function

Paste Function

Function category:
Most Recently Used
All
Financial
Date & Time
Math & Trig
Statistical
Lookup & Reference
Database
Text
Logical
Information

Function name:
PERMUT
POISSON
PROB
QUARTILE
RANK
RSQ
SKEW
SLOPE
SMALL
STANDARDIZE
STDEV

POISSON(x,mean,cumulative)

Returns the Poisson distribution.

OK | Cancel

POISSON

X 11 = 11
Mean 17 = 17
Cumulative 0 = FALSE

= 0.035544812

Returns the Poisson distribution.

Cumulative is a logical value: for the cumulative Poisson probability, use TRUE; for the Poisson probability mass function, use FALSE.

Formula result = 0.035544812

OK | Cancel

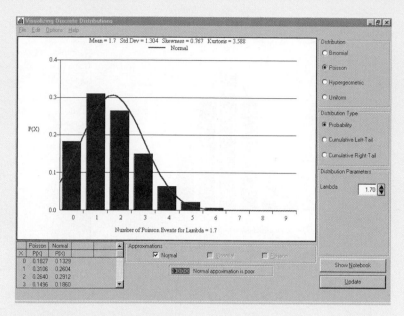

FIGURE 6.26

Visual Statistics Poisson Display

Visual Statistics   Figure 6.26 shows *Visual Statistics Module 4* using $\lambda = 1.7$. A table of probabilities is in the lower left. You can also display cumulative probabilities from either tail. The Visual Statistics graph can be copied and pasted into a report, and its table probabilities can be copied and pasted into Excel (they are tab-delimited, so they will paste nicely into Excel columns). An advantage of Visual Statistics is that you can "spin" λ and can display a normal overlay. In this example, the Poisson distribution does not resemble a normal distribution because λ is too small.

Hypergeometric Distribution

Excel   The hypergeometric formula is tedious and tables are impractical because there are three parameters, so we prefer Excel's hypergeometric function =HYPGEOMDIST(x,n,s,N). For example, using $X = 5$, $n = 10$, $s = 82$, and $n = 194$, the Excel function =HYPGEOMDIST(5,10, 82,194) gives 0.222690589, as illustrated in Figure 6.27. You can also get hypergeometric probabilities from MegaStat (menus not shown).

Visual Statistics   Figure 6.28 shows a screen from *Visual Statistics Module 4*. Numerical probabilities are shown in a table in the lower left. The graph can be copied and pasted as a bitmap and the table probabilities can be copied and pasted into Excel columns. An advantage of Visual Statistics is that you can spin N, n, and s and superimpose either a normal or binomial approximation on the hypergeometric distribution.

Excel's Hypergeometric Function (where $N = 194$, $n = 10$, $s = 82$)   **FIGURE 6.27**

Paste Function	? X
Function category:	Function name:
Most Recently Used	GROWTH
All	HARMEAN
Financial	HYPGEOMDIST
Date & Time	INTERCEPT
Math & Trig	KURT
Statistical	LARGE
Lookup & Reference	LINEST
Database	LOGEST
Text	LOGINV
Logical	LOGNORMDIST
Information	MAX

HYPGEOMDIST(sample_s,number_sample,population_s,...)

Returns the hypergeometric distribution.

[?]   OK   Cancel

HYPGEOMDIST

Sample_s	5	= 5
Number_sample	10	= 10
Population_s	82	= 82
Number_pop	194	= 194

= 0.222690589

Returns the hypergeometric distribution.

Number_pop is the population size.

[?]   Formula result =0.222690589   OK   Cancel

www.mcgrawhillconnect.ca

FIGURE 6.28

Visual Statistics Hypergeometric Display (where $N = 50$, $n = 10$, $s = 25$)

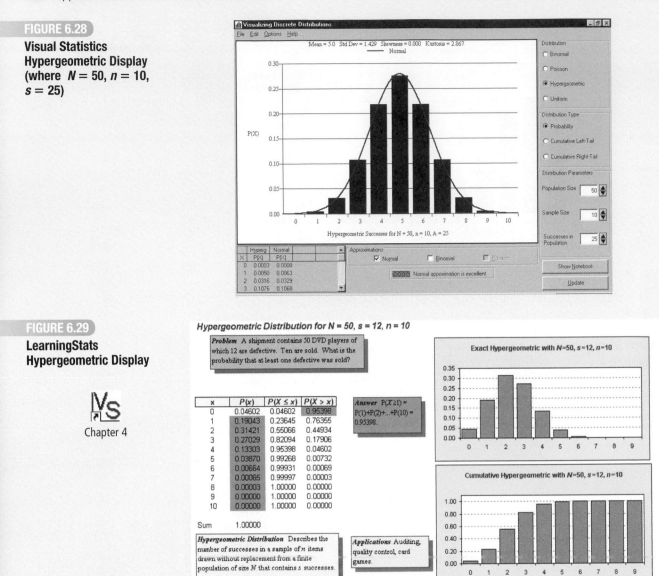

FIGURE 6.29

LearningStats Hypergeometric Display

Chapter 4

LearningStats   Figure 6.29 shows a sample screen from *LearningStats*. You can spin the values of *N, n,* and *s* to get the probability you want.

CHAPTER EXERCISES

Note: Show your work clearly. Problems marked * are harder or rely on optional material from this chapter.

6.44   The probability that a 30-year-old white male will live another year is 0.99842. What premium would an insurance company charge to break even on a one-year $1 million term life insurance policy? (Data are from National Center for Health Statistics, *National Vital Statistics Reports* 47, no. 28 [Dec. 13, 1999], p. 8.) (LO 2)

6.45   If a fair die rolled once comes up 6, you win $100. Otherwise, you lose $15. Would a rational person play this game? Justify your answer, using the definition of $E(X)$. (LO 2)

6.46   As a birthday gift, you are mailing a new personal digital assistant (PDA) to your cousin in Winnipeg. The PDA cost $250. There is a 2 percent chance it will be lost or damaged in the mail. Is it worth $4 to insure the mailing? Explain, using the concept of expected value. (LO 2)

6.47   A large sample of two-digit lottery numbers between 01 and 44 shows a mean of 29.22 and a standard deviation of 18.71. (a) To what extent do these results differ from a uniform distribution? (b) What else would you want to know to decide whether the random number generator was working correctly? (LO 3)

6.48 Use Excel to generate 1,000 random integers in the range 1 through 5. (a) What is the expected mean and standard deviation? (b) What is your sample mean and standard deviation? (c) Is your sample consistent with the uniform model? Discuss. (d) Show the Excel formula you used. (LO 2 & 3)

6.49 There is a 14 percent chance that a Noodles & Company customer will order bread with a meal. Use Excel to find the probability that in a sample of 10 customers: (a) more than 5 will order bread; (b) no more than 2 will order bread; and (c) none of the 10 will order bread. (d) Is the distribution skewed left or right? (LO 4 & 5)

6.50 In a certain year, on average 10 percent of the vehicles tested for emissions failed the test. Suppose that five vehicles are tested. (a) What is the probability that all pass? (b) All but one pass? (c) Sketch the probability distribution and discuss its shape. Use both the appropriate table and formula to answer these questions. (LO 4)

6.51 The probability that an American CEO can transact business in a foreign language is 0.20. Ten American CEOs are chosen at random. (a) What is the probability that none can transact business in a foreign language? (b) That at least two can? (c) That all 10 can? (d) Sketch the probability distribution and discuss its appearance. (See Lamalie Associates, *The Lamalie Report on Top Executives of the 1990's,* p. 11.) (LO 4 & 5)

6.52 In a certain KFC franchise, half of the customers typically request "crispy" instead of "original" chicken. (a) What is the probability that none of the next four customers will request "crispy"? (b) At least two? (c) At most two? (d) Construct the probability distribution (Excel or Appendix A), make a graph of its PDF, and describe its shape. Use the appropriate formula to answer these questions. (LO 4 & 5)

6.53 On average, 40 percent of beer drinkers order light beer. (a) What is the probability that none of the next eight customers who order beer will order light beer? (b) That one customer will? (c) Two customers? (d) Fewer than three? (e) Construct the probability distribution (Excel or Appendix A), make a graph of its PDF, and describe its shape. (See George E. Belch and Michael A. Belch, *Advertising & Promotion,* 6th ed. [McGraw-Hill, 2004], p. 43.) (LO 4 & 5)

6.54 Write the Excel binomial formula for each probability. (LO 5)

a. Three successes in 20 trials with a 30 percent chance of success.
b. Seven successes in 50 trials with a 10 percent chance of success.
c. Six or fewer successes in 80 trials with a 5 percent chance of success.
d. At least 30 successes in 120 trials with a 20 percent chance of success.

6.55 The default rate on certain student loans at a university in British Columbia is 7 percent. The university extends 10 such loans. (a) What is the probability that none of them will default? (b) That at least three will default? (c) What is the expected number of defaults? (LO 4 & 5)

6.56 Experience indicates that 8 percent of the pairs of men's trousers dropped off for dry cleaning will have an object in the pocket that should be removed before cleaning. Suppose that 14 pairs of pants are dropped off and the cleaner forgets to check the pockets. What is the probability that none have an object in the pocket? (LO 4 & 5)

6.57 A study by the Parents' Television Council showed that 80 percent of movie commercials aired on network television between 8 and 9 p.m. (the prime family viewing hour) were for restricted films. (a) Find the probability that in 16 commercials during this time slot at least 10 will be for restricted films. (b) Find the probability of fewer than 8 restricted films. (LO 4 & 5)

6.58 Write the Excel formula for each Poisson probability, using a mean arrival rate of 10 arrivals per hour. (a) Seven arrivals. (b) Three arrivals. (c) Fewer than five arrivals. (d) At least 11 arrivals. (LO 5)

6.59 A small feeder airline knows that the probability is 0.10 that a reservation holder will not show up for its daily 7:15 a.m. flight into a hub airport. The flight carries 10 passengers. (a) If the flight is fully booked, what is the probability that all those with reservations will show up? (b) If the airline overbooks by selling 11 seats, what is the probability that no one will have to be bumped? (c) That more than one passenger will be bumped? *(d) The airline wants to overbook the flight by enough seats to ensure a 95 percent chance that the flight will be full, even if some passengers may be bumped. How many seats would it sell? (LO 4 & 5)

6.60 Although television HDTV converters are tested before they are placed in the installer's truck, the installer knows that 20 percent of them still won't work properly. The driver must install eight converters today in an apartment building. (a) Ten converters are placed in the truck. What is the probability that the driver will have enough working converters? *(b) How many boxes should the driver load to ensure a 95 percent probability of having enough working converters? (LO 4 & 5)

6.61* In an example in Chapter 5, Ben, Tom, and Jerri had probabilities of 0.20, 0.52, and 0.84, respectively, of correctly answering a five-choice multiple choice question, which meant that, if a one-question multiple choice quiz was given, Ben, Tom, and Jerri would have probabilities of 0.20, 0.52, and 0.84 of passing the quiz. What is each student's probability of passing the quiz (at least 50 percent of the questions answered correctly) and what is each student's probability of getting at least an A (at least 80 percent of the questions answered correctly) if the quiz (a) consisted of 5 questions, (b) the quiz consisted of 15 questions, and, (c) the quiz consisted of 25 questions? Which of the three quizzes is the most fair? Explain your conclusion? (Remember that based on the amount of time spent studying, Ben didn't know the correct answers to any of the questions, Tom knew the correct answers to 40 percent of the questions, and Jerri knew the correct answers to 80 percent of the questions.) (LO 4 & 5)

6.62* The Calgary Flames had seven games remaining in its regular season and the more games it won, the greater the chance of it making it to the Stanley Cup Playoffs. If it has a 60 percent chance of winning each specific game, what is the probability that (a) it wins exactly one game, (b) its first win occurs in its third game, (c) it wins four of the last seven games, (d) it wins its fourth game in the seventh game that it plays? (LO 4 & 5)

6.63 (a) Why might the number of calls received per minute at a fire station not be a Poisson event? (b) Name two other events per unit of time that might violate the assumptions of the Poisson model. (LO 3)

6.64 The U.S. Mint, which produces billions of coins annually, has a mean daily defect rate of 5.2 coins. Let X be the number of defective coins produced on a given day. (a) Justify the use of the Poisson model. (b) On a given day, what is the probability of exactly five defective coins? (c) More than 10? (d) Construct the probability distribution (Excel or Appendix B) and make a graph of its PDF. (Data are from *Scientific American* 271, no. 3 [Sept. 1994], pp. 48–53.) (LO 3 & 5)

6.65 Lunch customers arrive at a Noodles & Company restaurant at an average rate of 2.8 per minute. Define X to be the number of customers to arrive during a randomly selected minute during the lunch hour and assume X has a Poisson distribution. (a) Calculate the probability that exactly five customers will arrive in a minute during the lunch hour. (b) Calculate the probability that no more than five customers will arrive in a minute. (c) What is the average customer arrival rate for a 5 minute interval? (d) What property of the Poisson distribution did you use to find this arrival rate? (LO 3 & 5)

6.66 In the U.K. in a recent year, potentially dangerous commercial aircraft incidents (e.g., near collisions) averaged 1.2 per 100,000 flying hours. Let X be the number of incidents in a 100,000-hour period. (a) Justify the use of the Poisson model. (b) What is the probability of at least one incident? (c) More than three incidents? (d) Construct the probability distribution (Excel or Appendix B) and make a graph of its PDF. (Data are from *Aviation Week and Space Technology* 151, no. 13 [Sept. 27, 1999], p. 17.) (LO 3 & 5)

6.67 Car security alarms go off at a mean rate of 3.8 per hour in a large Costco parking lot. Find the probability that in an hour there will be (a) no alarms; (b) fewer than four alarms; and (c) more than five alarms (LO 3 & 5).

6.68 In a certain automobile manufacturing paint shop, paint defects on the hood occur at a mean rate of 0.8 defects per square metre. A hood on a certain car has an area of 3 square metres. (a) Justify the use of the Poisson model. (b) If a customer inspects a hood at random, what is the probability that there will be no defects? (c) One defect? (d) Fewer than two defects? (LO 3 & 5)

6.69 In the manufacture of gallium arsenide wafers for computer chips, defects average 10 per square centimetre. Let X be the number of defects on a given square centimetre. (a) Justify the use of the Poisson model. (b) What is the probability of fewer than five defects? (c) More than 15 defects? (d) Construct the probability distribution (Excel or Appendix B) and make a graph of its PDF. (Data are from *Scientific American* 266, no. 2 [Feb. 1992], p. 102.) (LO 3 & 5)

6.70* A "rogue wave" (one far larger than others surrounding a ship) can be a threat to ocean-going vessels (e.g., naval vessels, container ships, oil tankers). The European Centre for Medium-Range Weather Forecasts issues a warning when such waves are likely. The average for this rare event is estimated to be 0.0377 rogue waves per hour in the South Atlantic. Find the probability that a ship will encounter at least one rogue wave in a five-day South Atlantic voyage (120 hours). (See *Science News,* Nov. 18, 2006, pp. 328–329)

6.71 On New York's Verrazano Narrows bridge, traffic accidents occur at a mean rate of 2.0 crashes per day. Let X be the number of crashes in a given day. (a) Justify the use of the Poisson model. (b) What is the probability of at least one crash? (c) Fewer than five crashes? (d) Construct the probability distribution (Excel or Appendix B), make a graph of its PDF, and describe its shape. (Data are from *New Yorker,* Dec. 2, 2002, p. 64.) (LO 3 & 5)

6.72* Before installing a device that would detect whether or not customers have tried to leave a particular store without paying for the items it selected (shoplifting), an average of 4.5 customers per day have tried to shoplift. With the device installed, an average of only 1.5 per day have tried to shoplift. Prior to this device and after the device was installed, what are the probabilities that (a) no customers tried to shoplift on a particular day, (b) exactly two have tried to shoplift on a particular day, (c) at least 3 have tried to shoplift on a particular day, (d) no customers have tried to shoplift during a particular 7-day week, (e) exactly 14 have tried to shoplift during a particular 7-day week, and (f) at least 21 have tried to shoplift during a particular week? Using Excel, construct the graphs of the one-week PDFs without the device and with the device and comment on your findings. (LO 4 & 5)

6.73* Twenty equally qualified individuals applied for the five available positions being created for a new committee to study how to best attract tourists into a southern Manitoba community. Of the 20, 14 had families with young children and were more likely in favour of attractions that catered toward families while the other six were unmarried individuals. If the members of this committee were randomly selected as stated by the mayor of this community, what is the probability that this committee consisted of (a) only unmarried individuals; (b) three individuals with families and two unmarried individuals; and (c) only individuals with families? If this committee actually consisted of only unmarried individuals, could you question the randomness of the selection procedure? Explain your conclusion. (LO 4 & 5)

6.74* Two very similar exclusive raffles are currently being run in an attempt to raise money for new recreational centres in two different communities in southern Quebec. Both raffles sold only 25 tickets (at $25,000 per ticket) and one ticket each month for the next 3 months will be drawn, with the value of each prize being $100,000. But in one of the raffles, the tickets will be drawn with replacement (i.e., one ticket can be selected more than once), while in the other raffle, the tickets will be drawn without replacement. A particular individual bought two tickets in each of the two raffles, Calculate the following for each individual raffle: (a) the expected number of prizes this individual should win; (b) the expected value of this individual's profits (i. e., winnings minus cost of the tickets); (c) the probability of this individual not winning any prizes; (d) the probability of this individual winning exactly one prize; (e) the probability of this individual winning three prizes. What is this individual's expected total profit (i.e., the profit from both raffles combined)? (LO 4 & 5)

APPROXIMATIONS

6.75 From a deck of 52 cards, 5 cards are dealt at random. Let X be the number of hearts in the sample. (a) Use the hypergeometric formula to find the probability that all five cards are hearts. (b) Would a binomial approximation be appropriate here? Discuss. (LO 4 & 5)

6.76* A turbine has 60 blades of which 3 have microscopic cracks. An inspector examines five blades at random. Define X to be the number of cracked blades the inspector finds in the sample. Calculate the probabilities of $X = 0$, 1, 2, and 3 using both the binomial approximation to the hypergeometric distribution and the hypergeometric distribution formulas. Were the binomial probabilities close to the hypergeometric probabilities? Why or why not? (LO 4 & 5)

RULES OF EXPECTED VALUE, VARIANCES, AND TRANSFORMATIONS

6.77 The weight of a Los Angeles Lakers basketball player averages 233.1 pounds with a standard deviation of 34.95 pounds. To express these measurements in terms a European would understand, we could convert from pounds to kilograms by multiplying by 0.4536. (a) In kilograms, what is the mean? (b) In kilograms, what is the standard deviation? (Data are from www.cnnsi.com/basketball/nba/rosters.) (LO 2)

6.78 The Rejuvo Corp. manufactures granite countertop cleaner and polish. Quarterly sales Q is a random variable with a mean of 25,000 bottles and a standard deviation of 2,000 bottles. Variable cost is $8 per unit and fixed cost is $150,000. (a) Find the mean and standard deviation of Rejuvo's total cost. (b) Based on average quarterly sales, what would the selling price have to be to break even, on average? To make a profit of $20,000? (LO 2)

6.79 The scores on Prof. Lazare's first exam have a mean of 70 with a standard deviation of 8. On the second exam, the mean is 80 with a standard deviation of 6. Each student's scores are summed. (a) What is the expected value (mean) of the sum of a student's scores on both exams? (b) What is the standard deviation of the sum? (c) What assumption was made in your answer to the previous question? Do you think it is valid? (LO 2)

6.80 A manufacturing project has five independent phases whose completion must be sequential. The time to complete each phase is a random variable. The mean and standard deviation of the time for each phase is shown below. Find the expected completion time and make a 2-sigma interval around the mean ($\mu \pm 2\sigma$). State your assumptions. (LO 2)

Phase	Mean (hours)	Std. Dev. (hours)
Set up dies and other tools	20	4
Milling and machining	10	2
Finishing and painting	14	3
Packing and crating	6	2
Shipping	48	6

6.81 In September, demand for industrial furnace boilers at a large plumbing supply warehouse has a mean of 7 boilers with a standard deviation of 2 boilers. The warehouse pays a unit cost of $2,225 per boiler plus a fee of $500 per month to act as dealer for these boilers. Boilers are sold for $2,850 each. Find the mean and standard deviation of September profit (revenue minus cost). (LO 2)

6.82 Prof. Hardtack gave an exam with a mean score of 25 and a standard deviation of 6. After looking at the distribution, he felt the scores were too low and asked two colleagues for advice on how to raise the mean to 75. Prof. Senex suggested adding 50 to everyone's score, while Prof. Juven suggested tripling everyone's score. Explain carefully the effects of these alternatives on the distribution of scores. (LO 2)

6.83 A commuter passes a certain traffic light every day on her way to work. On a randomly chosen day there is a 25 percent chance that the light will be red. (a) If she commutes to work 240 days a year, what is the expected number of times the light will be red? (b) What is the variance? (c) Construct $\mu \pm 1\sigma$ and $\mu \pm 2\sigma$ intervals about the mean and interpret them. Under what circumstances would the Empirical Rule apply? (LO 2)

6.84 A company recently bid on three contracts. It has a probability of 0.4 of winning each specific contract. For each contract that it wins, it has a probability of 0.2 of making a profit of $50,000 on the contract, a probability of 0.5 of making a profit of $100,000, and a probability of 0.3 of making a profit of $200,000. What is the expected number of contracts that it will win? What is the expected profit for each contract? What is the company's expected total profit on these three bids? (LO 2)

LearningStats Unit 06 Discrete Distribution   LS

LearningStats Unit 06 covers expected value and discrete distributions. Modules are designed for self-study, so you can proceed at your own pace, concentrate on material that is new, and pass quickly over things that you already know. Your instructor may assign specific modules, or you may decide to check them out because the topic sounds interesting.

Topic	*LearningStats Modules*
Discrete distributions	Distributions: An Overview
	Discrete Distributions
	Discrete Distributions: Examples
	Probability Calculator
	Random Discrete Data
Expected value	Life Insurance
Approximations	Binomial/Poisson Approximation
Equations	Discrete Models: Characteristics
Tables	Table A—Binomial Probabilities
	Table B—Poisson Probabilities
Applications	Hypergeometric Probabilities
	Covariance Explained
	Covariance in Asset Portfolios: A Simulation

Key: ⬛ = PowerPoint ⬛ = Word ⬛ = Excel

Visual Statistics

Visual Statistics Modules on Discrete Distr.ibutions

Module	Module Name
2	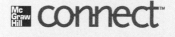 Visualizing a Random Process
4	Visualizing Discrete Distributions

Visual Statistics Modules 2 and 4 (included on your CD) are designed to help you

- Recognize that outcomes of a stochastic process may exhibit regularity even though the process is random.
- Learn through experimentation how changing the parameters can affect the outcomes of an experiment.
- Visualize data-generating situations that give rise to common probability distributions.
- Recognize common discrete distributions and their cumulative distribution functions.
- Identify the parameters of common discrete distributions and how they affect their shape.
- Understand when to apply approximations and learn to assess their accuracy.

The work-text chapter (included on the CD in PDF format) contains a list of concepts covered, objectives of the module, overview of concepts, illustration of concepts, orientation to module features, learning exercises (basic, intermediate, advanced), learning projects (individual, team), self-evaluation quiz, glossary of terms, and solutions to the self-evaluation quiz.

McGraw Hill connect™

For solutions to odd-numbered exercises, Exam Review questions, and additional study tools to help you succeed in this course, visit *Connect* at www.mcgrawhillconnect.ca.

Chapter

7

Continuous Probability Distributions

Chapter Learning Objectives

When you finish this chapter you should be able to

1. Distinguish between discrete and continuous random variables and their characteristics.

2. Display an understanding of the characteristics of the uniform and normal distributions.

3. Select and apply, in a problem context, the appropriate continuous distribution.

4. Sketch uniform and normal probability density functions and areas.

5. Use a table or spreadsheet to find uniform and normal probabilities for any given values of *X*.

6. Solve for values of *X* for given probabilities of a normal distribution.

7. Know when and how to apply the normal distribution to approximate a binomial distribution.

In Chapter 6, you learned about probability models and discrete random variables. We will now expand our discussion of probability models to include models that describe **continuous random variables.** Recall that a discrete random variable usually arises from *counting* something, such as the number of customer arrivals in the next minute, and as such, has a finite (or infinitely countable) number of possible values. In contrast, a continuous random variable usually arises from *measuring* something, such as the waiting time until the next customer arrives, and by definition, would have an infinite and uncountable number of possible values.

Probability for a discrete variable is defined at a point such as $P(X = 3)$ or as a sum over a series of points such as $P(X \leq 2) = P(0) + P(1) + P(2)$. But when X is a continuous variable

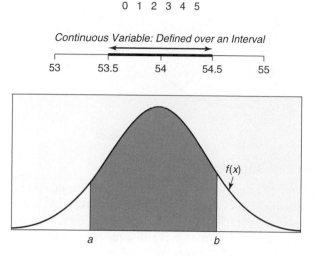

Discrete and Continuous Events

Probability as an Area

(e.g., waiting time), probabilities are defined as *areas under a curve* called the *probability density function (PDF)*, symbolized by *f(x)*. Probabilities for a continuous random variable are defined on intervals such as $P(53.5 \leq X \leq 54.5)$ or $P(X < 54)$ or $P(X \geq 53)$. Figure 7.1 illustrates the differences between discrete and continuous random variables. In Figure 7.2, the probability that a random variable X value falls between a and b, written as $P(a \leq X \leq b)$, is the shaded area between a and b under the PDF "roof." So the probability that X takes an exact value, say c, could be written as $P(c \leq X \leq c)$. The area from c to c under this PDF obviously equals 0. Thus the probability that a continuous random variable takes a specific value is always 0. This chapter explains how to recognize data-generating situations that produce continuous random variables, how to calculate event probabilities, and how to interpret the results.

7.1   Describing a Continuous Distribution

PDFs and CDFs

A probability distribution can be described either by its **probability density function (PDF)** or by its **cumulative distribution function (CDF)**. For a continuous random variable, the PDF is an equation that shows the height of the curve *f(x)* at each possible value of X. Any continuous PDF must be non-negative, and the area under the entire PDF must be 1. The mean, variance, and shape of the distribution depend on the PDF and its *parameters*. The CDF is denoted $F(x)$ and shows $P(X \leq x)$, the cumulative *area under the f(x) curve* to the left of a given value of X. There are Excel functions for most common PDFs or CDFs.

For example, Figure 7.3 shows a hypothetical PDF for a distribution of highway speeds. It is a smooth curve showing the probability density at points along the X-axis. The CDF in Figure 7.4 shows the *cumulative* proportion of speeds, gradually approaching 1 as X approaches 130. In this illustration, the distribution is symmetric and bell-shaped (Normal or Gaussian) with a mean of 115 and a standard deviation of 8.

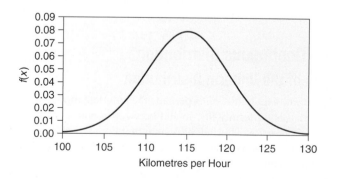

Normal PDF (kilometres per hour)

FIGURE 7.4

Normal CDF (kilometres per hour)

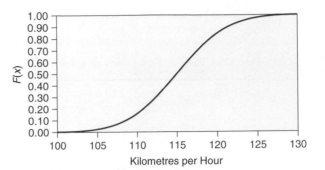

Expected Value and Variance

The mean and variance of a continuous random variable are analogous to $E(X)$ and $V(X)$ for a discrete random variable, except that the integral sign $\int$ replaces the summation sign Σ. Integrals are taken over all possible X values. The mean is still the balancing point or fulcrum for the entire distribution, and the variance is still a measure of dispersion about the mean. The mean is still the average of all X values weighted by their probabilities, and the variance is still the weighted average of all squared deviations around the mean. The standard deviation is still the square root of the variance.

	Continuous Random Variable	Discrete Random Variable	
Mean	$E(X) = \mu = \displaystyle\int_{-\infty}^{+\infty} x\,f(x)\,dx$	$E(X) = \mu = \displaystyle\sum_{\text{all }x} x\,P(x)$	**(7.1)**
Variance	$V(X) = \sigma^2 = \displaystyle\int_{-\infty}^{+\infty} (x - \mu)^2\,f(x)\,dx$	$V(X) = \sigma^2 = \displaystyle\sum_{\text{all }x}[x - \mu]^2\,P(x)$	**(7.2)**

Section Exercises

7.1 Flight 202 is departing Edmonton. Is each random variable discrete (D) or continuous (C)? (LO 1)
a. Number of airline passengers travelling with children under age 3.
b. The exact proportion of passengers travelling without checked luggage.
c. The exact weight of a randomly chosen passenger on Flight 202.

7.2 It is Saturday morning at a Tim Hortons. Is each random variable discrete (D) or continuous (C)? (LO 1)
a. The exact temperature of the coffee served to a randomly chosen customer.
b. Number of customers who order only coffee with no food.
c. The exact waiting time before a randomly chosen customer is handed the order.

7.3 Which of the following could *not* be probability density functions for a continuous random variable? Explain. *Hint:* Find the area under the function $f(x)$. (LO 1)
a. $f(x) = 0.25$ for $0 \le X \le 1$
b. $f(x) = 0.25$ for $0 \le X \le 4$
c. $f(x) = x$ for $0 \le X \le 2$

7.4 For a continuous PDF, why can't we sum the probabilities of all X values to get the total area under the curve? (LO 1)

7.2 Uniform Continuous Distribution

Characteristics of the Uniform Distribution

The **uniform continuous distribution** is perhaps the simplest model one can imagine. If X is a random variable that is uniformly distributed between a and b, its PDF, $f(x)$, has constant height, as shown in Figure 7.5. This height is such that the total area under $f(x)$ equals 1. The uniform continuous distribution is sometimes denoted $U(a, b)$ for short. Its mean and standard deviation are shown in Table 7.1.

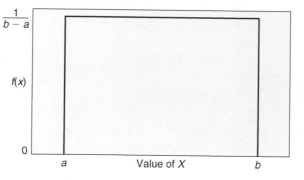

FIGURE 7.5
Uniform PDF

TABLE 7.1 **Uniform Continuous Distribution**

Parameters	a = lower limit
	b = upper limit
PDF	$f(x) = \dfrac{1}{b - a}$
CDF	$P(X \le x) = \dfrac{x - a}{b - a}$
Domain	$a \le X \le b$
Mean	$\dfrac{a + b}{2}$
Standard deviation	$\sqrt{\dfrac{(b - a)^2}{12}}$
Shape	Symmetric with no mode.
Random data in Excel	$=a+(b-a)*RAND()$

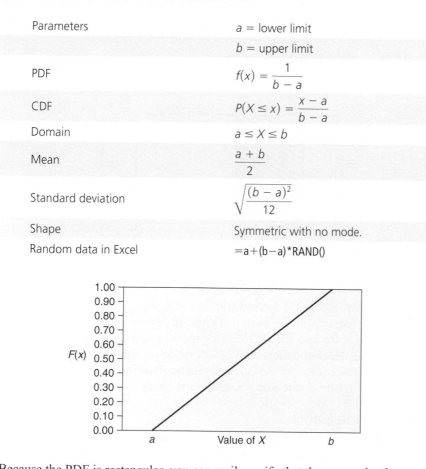

FIGURE 7.6
Uniform CDF

Because the PDF is rectangular, you can easily verify that the area under the curve is 1 by multiplying its base $(b - a)$ by its height $1/(b - a)$. Its CDF increases linearly to 1, as shown in Figure 7.6. Because probabilities of events can easily be shown as rectangular areas, we rarely need to refer to the CDF, whose formula is just $P(X \le x) = (x - a)/(b - a)$.

The continuous uniform distribution is similar to the discrete uniform distribution if the x values cover a wide range. For example, three-digit lottery numbers ranging from 000 to 999 would closely resemble a continuous uniform distribution with $a = 0$ and $b = 999$.

EXAMPLE 1

Waiting Time for the Subway Train

Suppose the TTC (Toronto Transit Commission) claims that its subways arrive three minutes apart at each station during rush hour. A businessman arrives at the Eglinton Station and must wait for a subway to arrive. Assuming that the TTC's claim is true, he knows that the next subway will arrive at any time within the next three minutes. Not knowing when the last subway left the station, he must assume that any arrival time within the next three minutes is equally likely, or that the arrival time is a uniform random variable that can take on any value between zero minutes and three minutes. In short notation, we could say that X is $U(0, 3)$. Setting $a = 0$ and $b = 3$, we obtain the mean and standard deviation:

$$\mu = \frac{a + b}{2} = \frac{0 + 3}{2} = 1.5 \text{ minutes}$$

$$\sigma = \sqrt{\frac{(b - a)^2}{12}} = \sqrt{\frac{(3 - 0)^2}{12}} = 0.87 \text{ minutes}$$

The probability of an event is simply the width of the interval corresponding to that event expressed as a proportion of the total width. Thus, the probability of taking between c and d minutes is

$$P(c < X < d) = (d - c)/(b - a) \quad \text{(area between } c \text{ and } d \text{ in a uniform model)} \qquad \textbf{(7.3)}$$

For example, the probability that the time for the subway to arrive is between 0.5 and 1.5 minutes is

$$P(0.5 < X < 1.5) = (1.5 - 0.5)/(3 - 0) = 1/3, \text{ or } 33.3\%$$

This situation is illustrated in Figure 7.7.

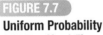

FIGURE 7.7

Uniform Probability
$P(0.5 < X < 1.5)$

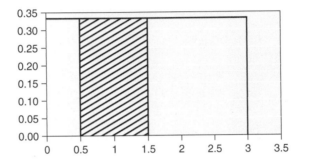

Special Case: Unit Rectangular Distribution

The **unit rectangular distribution,** denoted $U(0, 1)$, has limits $a = 0$ and $b = 1$, as shown in Figure 7.8. Using the formulas for the mean and standard deviation, you can easily show that this distribution has $\mu = 0.5$ and $\sigma = 0.2887$. This special case is important because Excel's function =RAND() uses this distribution. If you create random numbers by using =RAND() you know what their mean and standard deviation should be. This important distribution is discussed in more detail in later chapters on simulation and goodness-of-fit tests.

Uses of the Uniform Model

The uniform model $U(a, b)$ is used only when you have no reason to imagine that, within a certain range of values, any X values are more likely than others. In reality, this would be a rare situation. However, the uniform distribution can be useful in business for what-if analysis, that is, in situations where you know the "worst" and "best" range but don't want to make any assumptions about the distribution in between.

FIGURE 7.8

Unit Rectangular Distribution

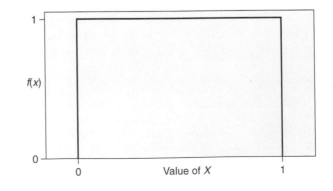

Section Exercises

7.5 Find the mean and standard deviation for each uniform continuous model. (LO 2)
a. $U(0, 10)$
b. $U(100, 200)$
c. $U(1, 99)$

7.6 Find each uniform continuous probability and sketch a graph showing it as a shaded area. (LO 4)
a. $P(X < 10)$ for $U(0, 50)$
b. $P(X > 500)$ for $U(0, 1,000)$
c. $P(25 < X < 45)$ for $U(15, 65)$

7.7 For a continuous uniform distribution, why is $P(25 < X < 45)$ the same as $P(25 \leq X \leq 45)$? (LO 1)

7.8 Assume the weight of a randomly chosen Canadian passenger car is a uniformly distributed random variable ranging from 1,200 kg to 2,000 kg. (a) What is the mean weight of a randomly chosen vehicle? (b) The standard deviation? (c) The quartiles? (d) What is the probability that a vehicle will weigh less than 1,400 kg? (e) More than 1,800 kg? (f) Between 1,400 and 1,800 kg? (LO 3)

7.3 Normal Distribution

Characteristics of the Normal Distribution

Chapter 5

The **normal** or **Gaussian distribution,** named for German mathematician Karl Gauss (1777–1855), has already been mentioned several times. Its importance gives it a major role in our discussion of continuous models. A normal probability distribution is defined by two parameters, μ and σ. The domain of a normal random variable is $-\infty < X < +\infty$; however, as a practical matter, $\mu - 3\sigma < X < \mu + 3\sigma$ includes almost all the area (as you know from the Empirical Rule in Chapter 4). Besides μ and σ, the normal probability density function $f(x)$ depends on the constants e (approximately 2.71828) and π (approximately 3.14159). It may be shown that the expected value of a normal random variable is μ and that its variance is σ^2. The normal distribution is always symmetric and bell-shaped. Table 7.2 summarizes its main characteristics.

TABLE 7.2   Normal Distribution

Parameters	μ = population mean
	σ = population standard deviation
PDF	$f(x) = \dfrac{1}{\sigma\sqrt{2\pi}} e^{-\frac{1}{2}\left(\frac{x-\mu}{\sigma}\right)^2}$
Domain	$-\infty < X < +\infty$
Mean	μ
Std. Dev.	σ
Shape	Symmetric and bell-shaped
Random data in Excel	=NORMINV(RAND(),μ,σ)

Normal PDF and CDF   FIGURE 7.9

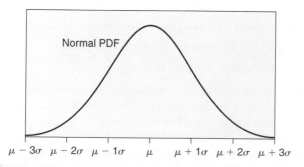

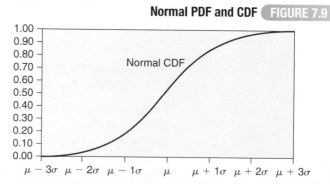

FIGURE 7.10 All Normal Distributions Look Alike Except for Scaling

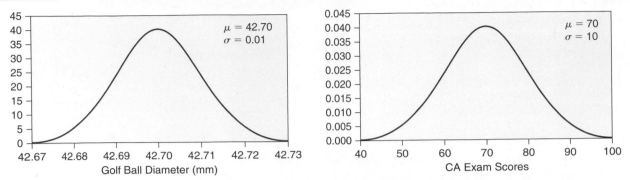

A normal distribution with mean μ and standard deviation σ is sometimes denoted $N(\mu, \sigma)$ for short. All normal distributions have the same shape, differing only in the axis scales. For example, the left chart in Figure 7.10 shows the distribution of diameters of golf balls from a manufacturing process that produces normally distributed diameters with a mean diameter of $\mu = 42.70$ mm and a standard deviation of $\sigma = 0.01$ mm, or $N(42.70, 0.01)$ in short notation. The right chart in Figure 7.10 shows the distribution of scores on the CA theory exam, assumed to be normal with a mean of $\mu = 70$ and a standard deviation of $\sigma = 10$, or $N(70, 10)$ in short notation. Although the shape of each PDF is the same, notice that the horizontal and vertical axis scales differ. If we had used the same scale for both charts, the left bell would be much steeper than the right bell.

It is a common myth that $f(x)$ must be smaller than 1, but in the left chart in Figure 7.10 you can see that this is not the case. Because the area under the entire curve must be 1, when X has a small range (e.g., the golf ball diameter range is about 0.06 mm), the height of $f(x)$ is large (about 40 for the golf ball diameters). Conversely, the right chart in Figure 7.10, when X has a large range (e.g., the CA exam range is about 60 points), the height of $f(x)$ is small (about 0.040 for the exam scores).

What Is Normal?

Many physical measurements in engineering and the sciences resemble normal distributions. Normal random variables can also be found in economic and financial data, marketing research, and operations analysis. The normal distribution is especially important as a sampling distribution for estimation and hypothesis testing. To be regarded as a candidate for normality, a random variable should:

- Be measured on a continuous scale.
- Have only one peak (unimodal).
- Exhibit tapering tails.
- Be symmetric about the mean (equal tails).

Roughly speaking, the distribution should resemble a symmetric bell.

When the range is large, we often treat a discrete variable as continuous. For example, exam scores are discrete (range from 0 to 100) but are often treated as continuous data. Here are some variables that *might* be expected to be approximately normally distributed:

- $X =$ quantity of beverage in a 2-litre bottle of Diet Pepsi.
- $X =$ absentee percentage for skilled nursing staff at a large urban hospital on Tuesday.
- $X =$ cockpit noise level in a Boeing 777 at the captain's left ear during cruise.
- $X =$ diameter in millimetres of a manufactured steel ball bearing.

Each of these variables would tend toward a certain mean but would exhibit random variation. For example, even with excellent quality control, not every bottle of a soft drink will have exactly the same fill (even if the variation is only a few millilitres).

There are statistical tests to see whether a sample came from a normal population. In Chapter 4, for example, you saw that a histogram can be used to assess normality. Visual tests suffice to detect gross departures from normality. More precise tests will be discussed later. For now, our task is to learn more about the normal distribution and its applications.

Section Exercises

7.9 If all normal distributions have the same shape, how do they differ? (LO 2)

7.10 (a) Where is the maximum of X if X has the normal distribution $N(75, 5)$? (b) Does $f(x)$ touch the X-axis at $\mu \pm 3\sigma$? (LO 2)

7.11 State the Empirical Rule for a normal distribution (see Chapter 4). (LO 2)

7.12 Discuss why you would or would not expect each of the following variables to be normally distributed. *Hint:* Would you expect a single central mode and tapering tails? Would the distribution be roughly symmetric? Would one tail be longer than the other? (LO 2)

    a. Shoe size of adult males.

    b. Years of education of 30-year-old employed women.

    c. Days from mailing home utility bills to receipt of payment.

    d. Time to clear customs and immigration at a border crossing between Canada and the United States.

7.4 Standard Normal Distribution

Characteristics of the Standard Normal

Chapter 5

To motivate the need for a special normal distribution, consider the following example. Suppose X, the amount of time a university student spends sleeping daily, follows a normal distribution with mean $\mu = 8$ hours and standard deviation $\sigma = 1.5$ hours. That is, $X \sim N(8, 1.5)$. Suppose Linda spends 9.5 hours sleeping one night. That is, $x = 9.5$. Clearly Linda slept for 1.5 hours more than the average. Did she sleep a "lot more" than the average? One way of answering this question is to ask how much more is 9.5 hours than the average of 8 hours, *relatively speaking.* As you can see, 1.5 hours equals 1 standard deviation. So we could say that Linda's sleep-time was 1 standard deviation more than the average. This "relative distance" is called the *z* value of the corresponding *x* value. If we observe John's sleep and find that he slept for 11 hours one night, then the *z* value for his sleep-time will be $(11 - 8)/1.5 = 2$. Such *z* values give rise to a standard normal distribution. Apart from the intuitive appeal of these *z* values, there is another important and practical reason for looking at this transformation from X to Z.

Because there is a different normal distribution for every pair of values of μ and σ, we often transform the variable by subtracting the mean and dividing by the standard deviation to produce a *standardized normal variable,* just as in Chapter 4, except that now we are talking about a population distribution instead of sample data. This important transformation is shown in Equation 7.4.

$$z = \frac{x - \mu}{\sigma} \quad \text{(transformation of each } x \text{ value to a } z \text{ value)} \qquad (7.4)$$

If X is normally distributed $N(\mu, \sigma)$, the standardized variable Z has a **standard normal distribution** with mean 0 and standard deviation 1, denoted $N(0, 1)$. The maximum height of PDF $f(z)$ is at 0 (the mean). The shape of the distribution is unaffected by the *z* transformation. Table 7.3 summarizes the main characteristics of the standard normal distribution.

Notation

Use an uppercase variable name like Z or X when speaking in general, and a lowercase variable name like z or x to denote a particular value of Z or X.

Because every transformed normal distribution will look the same, we can use a common scale, usually labelled from -3 to $+3$, as shown in Figure 7.11. Because $f(z)$ is a probability density function, the entire area under the curve is 1. As a rule, we are not interested in the height of the function $f(z)$ but rather in areas under the $f(z)$ curve (although Excel will provide either). The probability of an event $P(z_1 < Z < z_2)$ can be determined by using Appendix C as we describe below.

TABLE 7.3 **Standard Normal Distribution**

Parameters	μ = population mean
	σ = population standard deviation
PDF	$f(z) = \dfrac{1}{\sqrt{2\pi}} e^{-z^2/2}$ where $z = \dfrac{x - \mu}{\sigma}$
Domain	$-\infty < Z < +\infty$
Mean	0
Std. Dev.	1
Shape	Symmetric and bell-shaped
Random data in Excel	=NORMSINV(RAND())
Comment	There is no simple formula for a normal CDF, so we need normal tables or Excel to find areas.

FIGURE 7.11 **Standard Normal PDF and CDF**

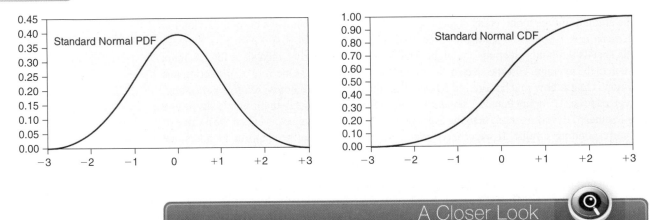

A Closer Look

If any random variable is normal, we can add or subtract a constant from that variable and/or multiply that variable by a constant and the resulting random variable would still be normal. For example, if X is normal, then $Z = \dfrac{X - \mu}{\sigma}$ is normal because we multiplied X by a constant and then subtracted a constant from the result because Z can be rewritten as $Z = \dfrac{1}{\sigma}X - \dfrac{\mu}{\sigma}$, where the two constants are $\dfrac{1}{\sigma}$ and $\dfrac{\mu}{\sigma}$.

Concept Check

Using the appropriate expected value and variance rules from Chapter 6, show why, if X has a mean, μ, and a standard deviation, σ, then Z has a mean of 0 and a standard deviation of 1.

Normal Areas from Appendix C

Tables of normal probabilities have been prepared so that you can look up any desired normal area. Such tables have many forms. Table 7.4 illustrates Appendix C, which shows areas from 0 to z using increments of 0.01 from $Z = 0$ to $Z = 3.79$. (Beyond this range, areas are very small, i.e., the probability that $Z > 3.79$ is approximately zero.) For example, to calculate

TABLE 7.4   Normal Area from 0 to z_0 (from Appendix C)

z_0	0.00	0.01	0.02	0.03	0.04	0.05	**0.06**	0.07	0.08	0.09
0.0	0.0000	0.0040	0.0080	0.0120	0.0160	0.0199	0.0239	0.0279	0.0319	0.0359
0.1	0.0398	0.0438	0.0478	0.0517	0.0557	0.0596	0.0636	0.0675	0.0714	0.0753
0.2	0.0793	0.0832	0.0871	0.0910	0.0948	0.0987	0.1026	0.1064	0.1103	0.1141
⋮	⋮	⋮	⋮	⋮	⋮	⋮	⋮	⋮	⋮	⋮
1.6	0.4452	0.4463	0.4474	0.4484	0.4495	0.4505	0.4515	0.4525	0.4535	0.4545
1.7	0.4554	0.4564	0.4573	0.4582	0.4591	0.4599	0.4608	0.4616	0.4625	0.4633
1.8	0.4641	0.4649	0.4656	0.4664	0.4671	0.4678	0.4686	0.4693	0.4699	0.4706
1.9	0.4713	0.4719	0.4726	0.4732	0.4738	0.4744	0.4750	0.4756	0.4761	0.4767
2.0	0.4772	0.4778	0.4783	0.4788	0.4793	0.4798	0.4803	0.4808	0.4812	0.4817
2.1	0.4821	0.4826	0.4830	0.4834	0.4838	0.4842	0.4846	0.4850	0.4854	0.4857
2.2	0.4861	0.4864	0.4868	0.4871	0.4875	0.4878	0.4881	0.4884	0.4887	0.4890
2.3	0.4893	0.4896	0.4898	0.4901	0.4904	0.4906	0.4909	0.4911	0.4913	0.4916
⋮	⋮	⋮	⋮	⋮	⋮	⋮	⋮	⋮	⋮	⋮
2.9	0.4981	0.4982	0.4982	0.4983	0.4984	0.4984	0.4985	0.4985	0.4986	0.4986
3.0	0.4987	0.4987	0.4987	0.4988	0.4988	0.4989	0.4989	0.4989	0.4990	0.4990

$P(0 < Z < 1.96)$, you select the row for $z = 1.9$ and the column for 0.06 (because $1.96 = 1.90 + 0.06$). This row and column are shaded in Table 7.4. At the intersection of the shaded row and column, we see $P(0 < Z < 1.96) = 0.4750$. This area is illustrated in Figure 7.12. Because the normal distribution is symmetrical, half the area lies to the right of the mean and thus we can find a right-tail area by subtraction. For example, $P(Z > 1.96) = 0.5000 - P(0 < Z < 1.96) = 0.5000 - 0.4750 = 0.0250$, as illustrated in Figure 7.12.

Suppose we want a middle area such as $P(-1.96 < Z < +1.96)$. Because the normal distribution is symmetric, we also know that $P(-1.96 < Z < 0) = 0.4750$. Adding these areas, we get

$$P(-1.96 < Z < +1.96) = P(-1.96 < Z < 0) + P(0 < Z < 1.96)$$
$$= 0.4750 + 0.4750 = 0.9500$$

So the interval $-1.96 < Z < 1.96$ encloses 95 percent of the area under the normal curve. Figure 7.13 illustrates this calculation. Because a point has no area in a continuous distribution,

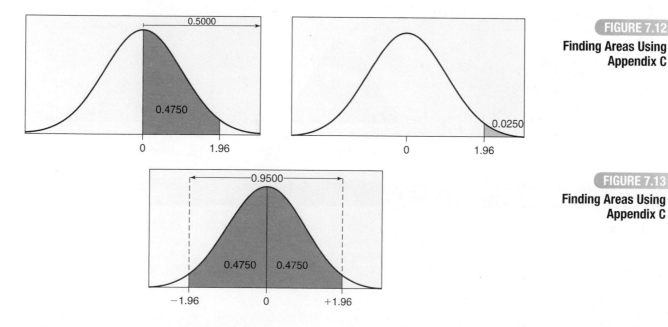

FIGURE 7.12

Finding Areas Using Appendix C

FIGURE 7.13

Finding Areas Using Appendix C

the probability $P(-1.96 \leq Z \leq +1.96)$ is the same as $P(-1.96 < Z < +1.96)$, so, for simplicity, we omit the equality.

Concept Check

You may have noticed that when determining the above probabilities, diagrams were used to illustrate what these probabilities looked like. This is a good practice to follow until you become very comfortable using the z-table.

Without actually determining the probabilities, for each of the following, draw a normal distribution indicating which area represents the probability that you are trying to determine and state whether that probability can be directly read from the table, requires you to add 0.5 to the value that appears in the table, requires you to subtract the value that appears in the table from 0.5, requires you to add together two values that appear in the table, or requires you to subtract one value that appears in the table from another value that appears in the table.

* $P(0 < Z < 1.32)$
* $P(Z > 1.32)$
* $P(Z > -1.32)$
* $P(1.32 < Z < 1.47)$
* $P(-1.32 < Z < 1.47)$

Basis for the Empirical Rule

From Appendix C we can see the basis for the Empirical Rule, illustrated in Figure 7.14. These are the "k-sigma" intervals mentioned in Chapter 4 and used by statisticians for quick reference to the normal distribution. Thus, it is *approximately* correct to say that a "2-sigma interval" contains 95 percent of the area (actually $z = 1.96$ would yield a 95 percent area):

$$P(-1.00 < Z < +1.00) = 2 \times P(0 < Z < 1.00) = 2 \times 0.3413 = 0.6826, \text{ or } 68.26\%$$
$$P(-2.00 < Z < +2.00) = 2 \times P(0 < Z < 2.00) = 2 \times 0.4772 = 0.9544, \text{ or } 95.44\%$$
$$P(-3.00 < Z < +3.00) = 2 \times P(0 < Z < 3.00) = 2 \times 0.49865 = 0.9973, \text{ or } 99.73\%$$

FIGURE 7.14 **Normal Areas within $\mu \pm k\sigma$**

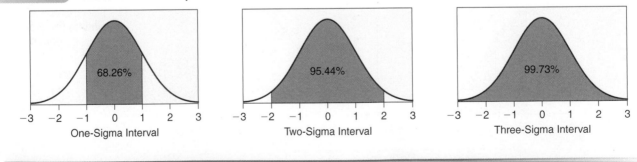

Section Exercises

7.13 Find the standard normal area for each of the following, drawing the appropriate diagram. (LO 4 & 5)

    a. $P(0 < Z < 0.50)$
    b. $P(-0.50 < Z < 0)$
    c. $P(Z > 0)$
    d. $P(Z = 0)$
    e. $P(Z > -0.50)$

7.14 Find the standard normal area for each of the following, drawing the appropriate diagram. (LO 4 & 5)

    a. $P(1.22 < Z < 2.15)$
    b. $P(2.00 < Z < 3.00)$
    c. $P(-2.00 < Z < 2.00)$
    d. $P(Z > 0.50)$

7.15 Find the standard normal area for each of the following, drawing the appropriate diagram. (LO 4 & 5)

    a. $P(-0.22 < Z < 2.15)$
    b. $P(-3.00 < Z < -2.00)$
    c. $P(Z < 2.00)$
    d. $P(Z < -2.00)$

Finding *z* for a Given Upper Tail Area

We can also use the tables to find the z value that corresponds to a given area. For example, what z value defines the top 1 percent of a normal distribution? Because we will be dealing with such questions quite frequently, we use the notation $z_{0.01}$ for this z value, or in general, z_A, where A represents the area in the upper tail. Because half the area lies above the mean, an upper area of 1 percent implies that 49 percent of the area must lie between 0 and z. Searching Appendix C for an area of 0.4900, we see that $z_{0.01} = 2.33$ yields an area of 0.4901. Without interpolation, that is as close as we can get to 49 percent. This is illustrated in Table 7.5 and Figure 7.15.

TABLE 7.5 **Normal Area from 0 to z_0 (from Appendix C)**

z_0	0.00	0.01	0.02	0.03	0.04	0.05	0.06	0.07	0.08	0.09
0.0	0.0000	0.0040	0.0080	0.0120	0.0160	0.0199	0.0239	0.0279	0.0319	0.0359
0.1	0.0398	0.0438	0.0478	0.0517	0.0557	0.0596	0.0636	0.0675	0.0714	0.0753
0.2	0.0793	0.0832	0.0871	0.0910	0.0948	0.0987	0.1026	0.1064	0.1103	0.1141
⋮	⋮	⋮	⋮	⋮	⋮	⋮	⋮	⋮	⋮	⋮
1.6	0.4452	0.4463	0.4474	0.4484	0.4495	0.4505	0.4515	0.4525	0.4535	0.4545
1.7	0.4554	0.4564	0.4573	0.4582	0.4591	0.4599	0.4608	0.4616	0.4625	0.4633
1.8	0.4641	0.4649	0.4656	0.4664	0.4671	0.4678	0.4686	0.4693	0.4699	0.4706
1.9	0.4713	0.4719	0.4726	0.4732	0.4738	0.4744	0.4750	0.4756	0.4761	0.4767
2.0	0.4772	0.4778	0.4783	0.4788	0.4793	0.4798	0.4803	0.4808	0.4812	0.4817
2.1	0.4821	0.4826	0.4830	0.4834	0.4838	0.4842	0.4846	0.4850	0.4854	0.4857
2.2	0.4861	0.4864	0.4868	0.4871	0.4875	0.4878	0.4881	0.4884	0.4887	0.4890
2.3	0.4893	0.4896	0.4898	0.4901	0.4904	0.4906	0.4909	0.4911	0.4913	0.4916
⋮	⋮	⋮	⋮	⋮	⋮	⋮	⋮	⋮	⋮	⋮
2.9	0.4981	0.4982	0.4982	0.4983	0.4984	0.4984	0.4985	0.4985	0.4986	0.4986
3.0	0.4987	0.4987	0.4987	0.4988	0.4988	0.4989	0.4989	0.4989	0.4990	0.4990

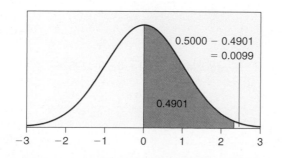

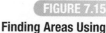

FIGURE 7.15

Finding Areas Using Appendix C

Section Exercises

7.16 Find z for each of the following probabilities. (LO 4 & 5)
    a. $P(0 < Z < z) = 0.0359$
    b. $P(Z > z) = 0.2236$
    c. $P(Z > z) = 0.8764$
    d. $P(Z < z) = 0.9750$
    e. $P(-z < Z < z) = 0.95$
    f. $P(Z > z) = 0.95.$

Finding Normal Areas with Excel

Table 7.6 and Figure 7.16 show four Excel functions that provide normal areas or z values. Excel is more accurate than a table; however, you still have to be careful of syntax. It is a good idea to *visualize* the answer you expect, so that you will recognize if you are getting the wrong answer from Excel.

Finding Areas by Using Standardized Variables

Up to now we have used the z table either for finding probabilities for given z values or for finding z values for given probabilities. Now, we will use the same table to find probabilities for given x values or for finding x values for given probabilities, where X is a normal random variable with given mean μ and given standard deviation σ. We can accomplish this by transforming x values to z values where

$$z = \frac{x - \mu}{\sigma}$$

and then using the z table to find the appropriate probabilities.

TABLE 7.6   **Four Excel Functions for Normal Areas**

Syntax of Function	Example	What It Does
$=$NORMDIST(x,μ,σ,cumulative)	$=$NORMDIST(80,70,10,1) $=$ 0.84134475	Area to the left of x for given μ and σ. Here, 84.13% of the CA exam-takers score 80 or less if $\mu = 70$ and $\sigma = 10$.
$=$NORMINV(area,μ,σ)	$=$NORMINV(0.99,70,10) $=$ 93.2634699	Value of x corresponding to a given left-tail area. Here, the 99th percentile for CPA exam-takers is a score of 93.26 or 93 to the nearest integer.
$=$NORMSDIST(z)	$=$NORMSDIST(1.96) $=$ 0.975002175	Area to the left of z in a standard normal distribution. Here, we see that 97.50% of the area is to the left of $z = 1.96$.
$=$NORMSINV(area)	$=$NORMSINV(0.75) $=$ 0.674489526	Value of z corresponding to a given left-tail area. Here, the 75th percentile (third quartile) of a standard normal is at $z = 0.675$.

Four Useful Normal Functions in Excel FIGURE 7.16

NORMDIST
X 80 = 80
Mean 70 = 70
Standard_dev 10 = 10
Cumulative 1 = TRUE

= 0.84134474
Returns the normal cumulative distribution for the specified mean and standard deviation.

X is the value for which you want the distribution.

Formula result = 0.84134474
OK   Cancel

NORMINV
Probability .99 = 0.99
Mean 70 = 70
Standard_dev 10 = 10

= 93.26341928
Returns the inverse of the normal cumulative distribution for the specified mean and standard deviation.

Probability is a probability corresponding to the normal distribution, a number between 0 and 1 inclusive.

Formula result = 93.26341928
OK   Cancel

NORMSDIST
Z 1.96 = 1.96

= 0.975002175
Returns the standard normal cumulative distribution (has a mean of zero and a standard deviation of one).

Z is the value for which you want the distribution.

Formula result = 0.975002175
OK   Cancel

NORMSINV
Probability .75 = 0.75

= 0.674490366
Returns the inverse of the standard normal cumulative distribution (has a mean of zero and a standard deviation of one).

Probability is a probability corresponding to the normal distribution, a number between 0 and 1 inclusive.

Formula result = 0.674490366
OK   Cancel

A Closer Look

Why does transforming values of X to values of Z allow us to use these values of Z to determine probabilities for X? Note that $P(\mu < X < \mu + k\sigma)$ does not depend upon the values of μ or σ, but only upon the value of k, as it is equivalent to finding $P(0 < Z < k)$. Saying that X is less than k standard deviations away from the mean is the same as saying that Z is less than k. Because $Z = 0$ is the same number of standard deviations from its mean as $X = \mu$ (both are zero standard deviations from their respective means), and because $Z = z$ is the same number of standard deviations from its mean as $X = \mu + z\sigma$ (both are z standard deviations from their respective means), $P(\mu < X < \mu + z\sigma) = P(0 < Z < z)$.

EXAMPLE 2
Economics Marks

John took an economics exam and scored 86 points. The class mean was 75 with a standard deviation of 7 and the marks in the class approximated a normal distribution. What percentile is John in? That is, what is $P(X < 86)$? We need first to calculate John's standardized z-score:

$$z_{John} = \frac{x_{John} - \mu}{\sigma} = \frac{86 - 75}{7} = \frac{11}{7} = 1.57$$

This says that John's score is 1.57 standard deviations above the mean. From Appendix C we get $P(X < 86) = P(Z < 1.57) = 0.5 + P(0 < Z < 1.57) = 0.5 + 0.4418 = 0.9418$, so John is approximately in the 94th percentile. That means that his score was better than 94 percent of the class, as illustrated in Figures 7.17 and 7.18. The table gives a slightly different value from Excel due to rounding.

On this exam, what is the probability that a randomly chosen test-taker would have a score of at least 65? We begin by standardizing:

$$z = \frac{x - \mu}{\sigma} = \frac{65 - 75}{7} = \frac{-10}{7} = -1.43$$

Using Appendix C we can calculate $P(X \geq 65) = P(Z \geq -1.43)$ as

$$P(Z \geq -1.43) = P(-1.43 < Z < 0) + 0.5000$$
$$= P(0 < Z < 1.43) + 0.5000$$
$$= 0.4236 + 0.5000 = 0.9236, \text{ or } 92.4\%$$

Thus, there is a 92.4 percent chance that a student scores 65 or above on this exam. These calculations are illustrated in Figure 7.19.

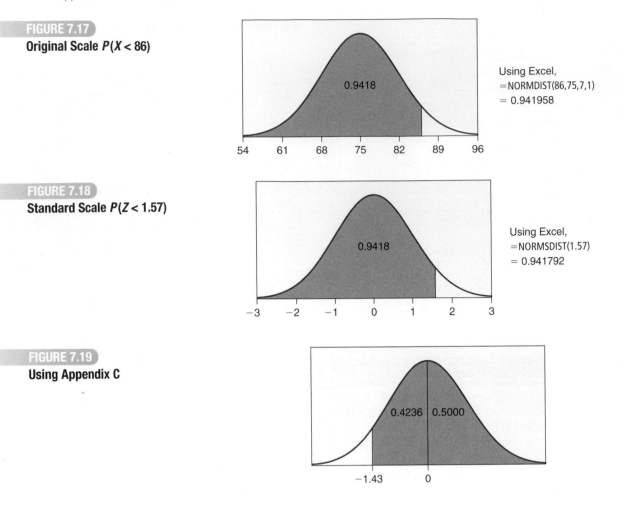

FIGURE 7.17
Original Scale $P(X < 86)$

Using Excel,
=NORMDIST(86,75,7,1)
= 0.941958

FIGURE 7.18
Standard Scale $P(Z < 1.57)$

Using Excel,
=NORMSDIST(1.57)
= 0.941792

FIGURE 7.19
Using Appendix C

Inverse Normal—Finding *X* Values for a Given Upper Tail Area

How can we find the various normal percentiles (5th, 10th, 25th, 75th, 90th, 95th, etc.)? That is, how can we find *X* for a given area? We use simple mathematical manipulations to turn the standardizing transformation around:

$$z = \frac{x - \mu}{\sigma} \Rightarrow x = \mu + z\sigma \tag{7.5}$$

EXAMPLE 3

Timing Lunch Service

A restaurant in downtown Calgary serves a lunchtime business crowd that has a limited amount of time for lunch. The restaurant wants to make the offer that if a customer does not receive one of its meals within a certain guaranteed amount of time, the customer does not have to pay for the meal. The time it takes to prepare and serve one of these meals is normally distributed with a mean time of 15 minutes and a standard deviation of 1.5 minutes. What would the guaranteed time be set at such that 95 percent of the meals would arrive at the table within that time period?

Our solution requires us to find an *x* value such that $P(X \le x) = 0.95$. Previously, when we knew *x*, we transformed *x* to *z* and we used the *z*-table or Excel to find the probability. Now we will find the answer by working in the reverse order. We know the probability. We now find *z* that corresponds to that probability. We then find *x* based on this value of *z*.

From the given probability, we see that *z* = 1.645. Applying the above transformation,

$$x = \mu + z\sigma = 15 + 1.645(1.5) = 17.4675 \approx 17.5$$

This restaurant should thus tell its customers that if they are not served one of these special meals within 17.5 minutes, they will not have to pay for their meal.

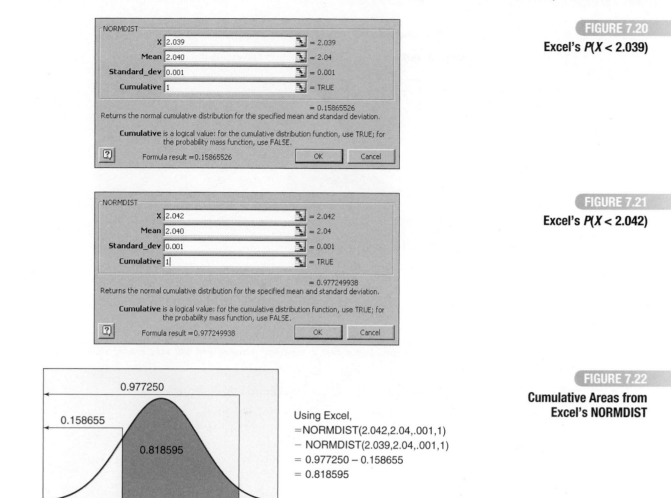

FIGURE 7.20

Excel's P(X < 2.039)

FIGURE 7.21

Excel's P(X < 2.042)

FIGURE 7.22

Cumulative Areas from Excel's NORMDIST

Using Excel without Standardizing

Excel's NORMDIST and NORMINV functions let us evaluate areas and inverse areas *without* standardizing. For example, let X be the diameter of a manufactured steel ball bearing whose mean diameter is $\mu = 2.040$ cm and whose standard deviation is $\sigma = 0.001$ cm. What is the probability that a given steel bearing will have a diameter between 2.039 and 2.042 cm? We use Excel's function =NORMDIST(x,μ,σ,cumulative) where cumulative is TRUE.

Because Excel gives left-tail areas, we first calculate $P(X < 2.039)$ and $P(X < 2.042)$ as in Figures 7.20 and 7.21. We then obtain the area between by subtraction, as illustrated in Figure 7.22. The desired area is approximately 81.9 percent. Of course, we could do exactly the same thing by using Appendix C:

$$P(2.039 < X < 2.042) = P(X < 2.042) - P(X < 2.039)$$
$$= 0.9773 - 0.1587 = 0.8186, \text{ or } 81.9\%$$

EXAMPLE 4

Service Times in a Quick Oil Change Shop

After studying the process of changing oil, the shop's manager has found that the distribution of service times, X, is normal with a mean of $\mu = 28$ minutes and a standard deviation of $\sigma = 5$ minutes, that is, $X \sim N(28, 5)$. This information can now be used to answer questions such as "What proportion of cars will be finished in less than half an hour?" "What is the chance that a randomly selected car will take longer than 40 minutes to service?" or "What service time corresponds to the 90th percentile?"

To answer these types of questions it is helpful to follow a few basic steps. (1) Draw a picture and label the picture with the information you know. (2) Shade in the area that will answer your question. (3) Standardize the random variable. (4) Find the area by using the z table or Excel.

Q1. What proportion of cars will be finished in less than half an hour?

- **Steps 1 and 2:**   Draw a picture and shade the desired area.

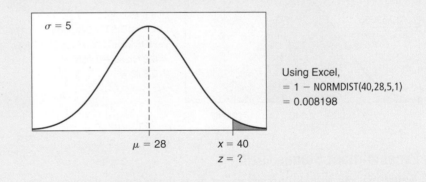

Using Excel,
=NORMDIST(30,28,5,1)
= 0.655422

$\mu = 28$ $x = 30$
$z = ?$

- **Step 3:** $z = \dfrac{30 - 28}{5} = 0.40$

- **Step 4:**   Using Appendix C or Excel we find that $P(Z < 0.40) = 0.5 + 0.1554 = 0.6554$.

Approximately 66 percent of the cars will be finished in less than half an hour.

Q2. What is the chance that a randomly selected car will take longer than 40 minutes to complete?

- **Steps 1 and 2:**   Draw a picture and shade the desired area.

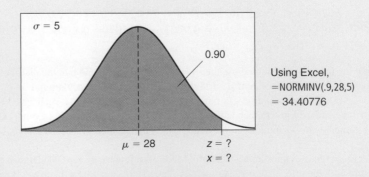

Using Excel,
= 1 − NORMDIST(40,28,5,1)
= 0.008198

$\mu = 28$ $x = 40$
$z = ?$

- **Step 3:** $z = \dfrac{40 - 28}{5} = 2.4$

- **Step 4:**   Using Appendix C or Excel we find that $P(Z > 2.4) = 1 - P(Z \leq 2.4) = 0.5 - 0.4418 = 0.0082$.

There is less than a 1 percent chance that a car will take longer than 40 minutes to complete.

Q3. What service time corresponds to the 90th percentile?

- **Steps 1 and 2:**   Draw a picture and shade the desired area.

$\sigma = 5$

0.90

Using Excel,
=NORMINV(.9,28,5)
= 34.40776

$\mu = 28$ $z = ?$
$x = ?$

In this case, steps 3 and 4 need to be reversed.

- **Step 3:** 90th percentile corresponds to the right-tail area of 0.1. So we are looking for the z value that corresponds to this right-tail area. That is, we want to find $z_{0.1}$. To find this value we first must determine the area between $Z = 0$ and $Z = z_{0.1}$ ($= 0.5 - 0.1 = 0.4$). Looking inside the table in Appendix C for an area as close to 0.4 as possible, we see that this area is 0.3997 and corresponds to a z value of 1.28. So we will use $z_{0.1} = 1.28$.

- **Step 4:** Now there two ways to find the desired x value: the intuitive way and the algebraic way. First, because $z = 1.28$, we know that our x value is 1.28 standard deviations to the right of the mean μ. So to get the desired x value, we start from the mean of 28 and go forward 1.28 standard deviations. That is, $x = 28 + 1.28(5) = 34.4$ minutes. The algebraic way is to simply use this z value in Equation 7.5, which relates z to x. So, $1.28 = \dfrac{x - 28}{5}$, or $x = 28 + 5(1.28) = 34.4$ minutes, as before. So, 90 percent of the cars will be finished in 34.4 minutes or less.

Application: Buying an Extended Warranty You bought a particular model of HD LCD television that has a warranty period of 12 months and a lifetime (before repairs are needed or before it has to be replaced) that is normally distributed with a mean of 26 months and a standard deviation of 8 months.

a. What is the probability that this brand of television will not need repairs during the warranty period?

b. What is the probability that this television will not need repairs during the first 24 months?

c. If a one-year extended warranty was offered at the time of purchase (i.e., the warranty period is extended to 24 months) and you purchased it, what is the probability that you made a wise decision (assuming the cost of repairs or replacement exceeded the cost of the additional warranty)?

d. If you did not purchase the extended warranty initially but could purchase it and did purchase it when your initial warranty expired, what is the probability that you made a wise decision (again assuming the cost of repairs or replacement exceeded the cost of the additional warranty)? Should this warranty cost more than if you had purchased it initially? Explain.

e. What would the length of the initial warranty period have to be so that only 1 percent of the televisions would have to be repaired or replaced under warranty?

f. If the warranty period remains at 12 months and if the mean lifetime can be changed by using better quality components, what would the mean lifetime have to change to so that only 1 percent of the televisions would have to be repaired or replaced under warranty?

g. If the standard deviation in lifetimes can be changed by using better quality controls, what would the standard deviation in lifetimes have to change to so that only 1 percent of the televisions would have to be repaired or replaced under warranty?

h. What are the pros and cons of changing the warranty period? Changing the mean lifetime? Changing the standard deviation in lifetimes?

   Although this application is somewhat lengthy, it does cover all aspects of the normal distribution that you should know how to analyze and manipulate. Let random variable X represent the lifetime of this television.

a. $P(X > 12) = P\left(Z > \dfrac{12 - 26}{8}\right) = P(Z > -1.75) = 0.5 + 0.4599 = 0.9599$

b. $P(X > 24) = P\left(Z > \dfrac{24 - 26}{8}\right) = P(Z > -0.25) = 0.5 - 0.0987 = 0.5987$

c. Here, you have made a wise decision if the television needs repairs after 12 months and before the end of the 24th month. The probability of this happening is

$$P(12 < X < 24) = P\left(\frac{12 - 26}{8} < Z < \frac{24 - 26}{8}\right) = P(-1.75 < Z < -0.25)$$
$$= 0.4599 - 0.0987 = 0.3612$$

d. To answer this question, we need to use conditional probabilities. That is, we have to determine the probability that the television would need repairs or replacement between the 13th and 24th months given that it didn't need repairs before that, or

$$P(12 < X < 24 \,|\, X > 12) = \frac{P(12 < X < 24)}{P(X > 12)} = \frac{0.3612}{0.9599} = 0.3763$$

Because there is a greater probability that it will need repairs after the end of the first year but before the end of the second year, given that the television lasted the first 12 months, you should expect to pay more for the extended warranty if you didn't purchase it until the initial warranty period expired.

e. Here we want to determine x, the length of the warranty period so that only 1 percent of these televisions need to be repaired or replaced within the warranty period, or

$$P(X < x) = 0.01 \quad \Rightarrow \quad P(Z < z) = 0.01 \quad \Rightarrow \quad z = -2.33$$
$$z = \frac{x - \mu}{\sigma} \quad \Rightarrow \quad -2.33 = \frac{x - 26}{8} \quad \Rightarrow \quad x = 26 - 2.33(8) = 7.36$$

The warranty period would have to be only 7.36 months if only 1 percent of these televisions are to be replaced under warranty.

f. To answer this question, we use the same manipulations as above, except now we need to solve for μ, or

$$P(X < 12) = 0.01 \quad \Rightarrow \quad P(Z < z) = 0.01 \quad \Rightarrow \quad z = -2.33$$
$$z = \frac{x - \mu}{\sigma} \quad \Rightarrow \quad -2.33 = \frac{12 - \mu}{8} \quad \Rightarrow \quad \mu = 12 + 2.33(8) = 30.64$$

The average lifetime would have to be increased to 30.64 months if only 1 percent of these televisions are to be replaced under warranty.

g. Using the same manipulations as above, except that we need to solve for σ, or

$$P(X < 12) = 0.01 \quad \Rightarrow \quad P(Z < z) = 0.01 \quad \Rightarrow \quad z = -2.33$$
$$z = \frac{x - \mu}{\sigma} \quad \Rightarrow \quad -2.33 = \frac{12 - 26}{\sigma} \quad \Rightarrow \quad \sigma = \frac{-14}{-2.33} = 6.01$$

The standard deviation in lifetimes would have to be decreased to 6.01 months if only 1 percent of these televisions are to be replaced under warranty.

h. What are the pros and cons of reducing the warranty period to 7.36 months, other than the pro that only 1 percent would now need repairs under warranty? The pro would be that it would not add additional costs to the manufacturer for producing these televisions. The con is, and it could be a major con, that the manufacturer would probably lose sales, especially if other manufacturers offer a 12-month warranty. What are the pros and cons of increasing the average lifetime to 30.64 months, other than the pro that only 1 percent would now need repairs under warranty? The pro would be that more people may purchase this television because it is more likely to last longer. The cons are that it would probably cost more to produce a longer-lasting television, and there may be fewer repeat sales because individuals would not have to replace their televisions as often. What are the pros and cons of reducing the standard deviation in lifetimes to 6.01 months, other than the pro that only 1 percent would now need repairs under warranty? The pros are that sales may increase when consumers realize that the manufacturer can produce a consistently good product, and repeat sales would not decrease. The only con might be that it may cost more to produce a consistently good product. Comparing the pros and cons of each and assuming the costs of either producing a television with a longer average life or a more consistent life, reducing the standard deviation in lifetime is the preferred strategy.

Section Exercises

Note: Problems marked * are harder or rely on optional material from this chapter.

7.17 Daily output of Irving's Saint John, New Brunswick, refinery is normally distributed with a mean of 232,000 barrels of crude oil per day with a standard deviation of 7,000 barrels. (a) What is the probability of producing at least 232,000 barrels? (b) Between 232,000 and 239,000 barrels? (c) Fewer than 239,000 barrels? (d) Fewer than 245,000 barrels? (e) More than 225,000 barrels? (LO 5)

7.18 Assume that the number of calories in a McDonald's Egg McMuffin is a normally distributed random variable with a mean of 290 calories and a standard deviation of 14 calories. (a) What is the probability that a particular serving contains fewer than 300 calories? (b) More than 250 calories? (c) Between 275 and 310 calories? Show all work clearly. (Data are from McDonalds.com) (LO 5)

7.19 The weight of a miniature Tootsie Roll is normally distributed with a mean of 3.30 grams and a standard deviation of 0.13 grams. (a) Within what weight range will the middle 95 percent of all miniature Tootsie Rolls fall? (b) What is the probability that a randomly chosen miniature Tootsie Roll will weigh more than 3.50 grams? (Data are from a project by MBA student Henry Scussel.) (LO 5)

7.20 The pediatrics unit at Carver Hospital has 24 beds. The number of patients needing a bed at any point in time is $N(19.2, 2.5)$. What is the probability that the number of patients needing a bed will exceed the pediatric unit's bed capacity? (LO 5)

7.21 The cabin of the Hawker 850XP business jet has a height of 175 cm. If the height of business travellers is $N(154cm, 7cm)$, what percentage of the business travellers will have to stoop? (See *Flying* 133, no. 11, 2006, p. 83.) (LO 5)

7.22 The time required to verify and fill a common prescription at a neighbourhood pharmacy is normally distributed with a mean of 10 minutes and a standard deviation of 3 minutes. Find the time for each event. Show your work. (LO 6)
a. Highest 10 percent
b. Highest 50 percent
c. Highest 5 percent
d. Highest 80 percent
e. Lowest 10 percent
f. Middle 50 percent
g. Lowest 93 percent
h. Middle 95 percent
i. Lowest 7 percent

7.23 The weight of a small Starbucks coffee is a normally distributed random variable with a mean of 360 grams and a standard deviation of 9 grams. Find the weight that corresponds to each event. Show your work. (LO 6)
a. Highest 10 percent
b. Highest 50 percent
c. Highest 5 percent
d. Highest 80 percent
e. Lowest 10 percent
f. Middle 50 percent
g. Lowest 90 percent
h. Middle 95 percent
i. Highest 4 percent

7.24 The weight of newborn babies in British Columbia hospitals is normally distributed with a mean of 3.2 kg and a standard deviation of 0.55 kg. (a) How unusual is if for a baby to weigh 4.0 kg or more? (b) What would be the 90th percentile for birth weight? (c) Within what range would the middle 95 percent of birth weights lie? (LO 6)

7.25 The credit score of a 35-year-old applying for a mortgage at Ulysses Mortgage Associates is normally distributed with a mean of 600 and a standard deviation of 100. (a) Find the credit score that defines the upper 5 percent. (b) Seventy-five percent of the customers will have a credit score higher than what value? (c) Within what range would the middle 80 percent of credit scores lie? (LO 6)

7.26 The number of patients needing a bed at any point in time in the pediatrics unit at Carver Hospital is $N(19.2, 2.5)$. Find the middle 50 percent of the number of beds needed (round to the next higher integer as a "bed" is indivisible). (LO 6)

7.27 High-strength concrete is supposed to have a compressive strength greater than 40,000 kilopascals (kPa). A certain type of concrete has a mean compressive strength of 50,000 kPa, but due to variability in the mixing process it has a standard deviation of 3,500 kPa, assuming a normal distribution. What is the probability that a given pour of concrete from this mixture will fail to meet the high-strength criterion? In your judgment, does this mixture provide an adequate margin of safety? (LO 5)

7.28* A Canadian importer of MP3 players is concerned about the quality of the players that it is purchasing from Asia. Its Asian supplier claims that its MP3 players have lifetimes that are normally distributed with an average life of 1.6 years and a standard deviation of 0.35 years. The Canadian importer offers a one-year warranty to its customers. If the claims of its supplier are true: (a) What is the probability that one of these MP3 players will last for more than two years? (b) What proportion of these MP3 players will need repairs or replacements under warranty? (c) What would the warranty period need to be so that only 3 percent of these MP3 players would need repairs or replacements under warranty? If the warranty period was kept at one year, what other parameter changes could be made so that only 3 percent of these MP3 players would need repairs or replacements under warranty? Precisely, what would those changes be if only one change would be made? (LO 5 & 6)

7.29* The owner of a local brew pub in northern Saskatchewan is considering bottling its beer for sale to its customers. It plans to sell beer in one-litre sizes in bottles that can hold up to 1.05 litres of liquid. The bottling machine that it is considering can be adjusted to dispense any average amount of beer but its standard deviation in amounts dispensed is 0.025 litres. Assuming that the amount dispensed is normally distributed, answer the following: (LO 5 & 6)
a. If the average amount is set to 1.0 litres, what proportion of bottles will contain at least 1.0 litres? What proportion of bottles will overflow?

  b. If the average amount is set to 1.02 litres, what proportion of bottles will contain at least 1.0 litres? What proportion of bottles will overflow?
  c. What would the average amount have to be adjusted to so that only 1 percent of the bottles will contain less than 1.0 litres of beer?
  d. If the owner can obtain a different bottling machine that has a standard deviation in amounts dispensed of only 0.01, what would the average amount have to be adjusted to so that only 1 percent of the bottles will contain less than 1.0 litres of beer?

7.30* A large number of Canadian youth and young adults can most often be seen with earphones sticking out of their ears, listening to their favourite tunes on their MP3 players, fearful, at any moment, that the batteries will die. Suppose the play time of a fully charged battery used in a particular brand of MP3 player is normally distributed with an average play time of 12.5 hours and a standard deviation of 1.7 hours. (LO 5 & 6)
  a. What is the probability that the play time on a fully charged battery will be less than 9 hours?
  b. What is the probability that the play time on a fully charged battery will be between 10 and 14 hours?
  c. What is the probability that the play time will be between 10 and 14 hours knowing that the play time has already reached 9 hours?
  d. What play time would be exceeded 5 percent of the time?

7.5   Normal Approximation to the Binomial

When Is an Approximation Needed?

In the previous chapter, we needed to rely on tables or Excel when finding answers to problems that would have required many applications of the binomial formula. When the value of n is larger than what would normally be found on a binomial table (or the value of π would not normally be found on such a table) and Excel or similar programs are not available, we need an alternative when seeking a solution. Under certain conditions, we can use a normal approximation. The logic of this approximation is that as n becomes large, the discrete binomial bars become more like a smooth, continuous, normal curve. Figure 7.23 illustrates this idea for 4, 8, and 16 flips of a fair coin with X defined as the number of heads in n tries. As sample size increases it becomes easier to visualize a smooth, bell-shaped curve overlaid on the bars in Figure 7.23.

As a rule of thumb, when $n \geq 9\pi/(1 - \pi)$ and $n \geq 9(1 - \pi)/\pi$, it is appropriate to use the normal approximation to the binomial, setting the normal μ and σ equal to the binomial mean and standard deviation:

$$\mu = n\pi \tag{7.6}$$

$$\sigma = \sqrt{n\pi(1 - \pi)} \tag{7.7}$$

Chapter 4

FIGURE 7.23   **Binomial with $n = 4$, $n = 8$, and $n = 16$**

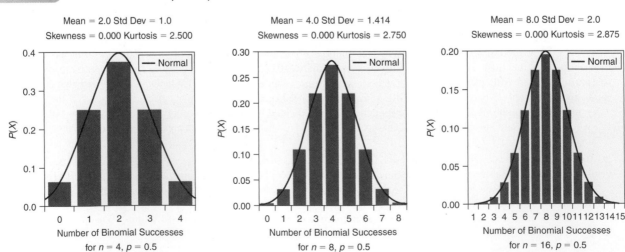

This rule of thumb is used to ensure that, by using the approximation, $P(X < 0)$ is close to zero and $P(X > n)$ is also close to zero.

A Closer Look

Why does using the above rule of thumb ensure that by using the normal approximation to the binomial that $P(X < 0)$ is close to zero and that $P(X > n)$ is also close to zero? This is based on a previous observation that the probability that a normal random variable is more than 3 standard deviations from its mean in either direction is approximately zero. Why do we want to ensure that, when using the normal approximation to the binomial, $P(X < 0)$ and $P(X > n)$ are close to zero? They should be close to zero because a binomial random variable cannot be less than zero or greater than n. How do these rules of thumb ensure that these probabilities are close to zero? These rules of thumb were developed so that the average number of successes are at least 3 standard deviations above $X = 0$ and at least 3 standard deviations below n. Mathematically, we want

$$n\pi \geq 0 + 3\sqrt{n\pi(1 - \pi)} \text{ and } n\pi \leq n - 3\sqrt{n\pi(1 - \pi)}$$

Using these expressions,

$$n\pi \geq 0 + 3\sqrt{n\pi(1 - \pi)} \Rightarrow n^2\pi^2 \geq 9n\pi(1 - \pi) \Rightarrow n\pi \geq 9(1 - \pi)$$
$$\Rightarrow n \geq 9(1 - \pi)/\pi$$

and

$$n\pi \leq n - 3\sqrt{n\pi(1 - \pi)} \Rightarrow n\pi - n \leq -3\sqrt{n\pi(1 - \pi)} \Rightarrow n(1 - \pi) \geq 3\sqrt{n\pi(1 - \pi)}$$
$$\Rightarrow n^2(1 - \pi)^2 \geq 9n\pi(1 - \pi) \Rightarrow n(1 - \pi) \geq 9\pi \Rightarrow n \geq 9\pi/(1 - \pi)$$

EXAMPLE 5

Coin Flips

What is the probability of more than 17 heads in 32 flips of a fair coin? In binomial terms, this would be $P(X \geq 18) = P(18) + P(19) + \cdots + P(32)$, which would be a tedious sum even if we had a table. Could the normal approximation be used? With $n = 32$ and $\pi = 0.50$ we clearly meet the requirement that $n \geq 9\pi/(1 - \pi)$ and $n \geq 9(1 - \pi)/\pi$. However, when translating a discrete scale into a continuous scale we must first convert individual points into intervals so that the gaps between the individual points disappear. Logically, the best way to accomplish this is to take each individual point, x (except the points 0 and n), and create intervals $x \pm 0.5$. For example, 18 would become the interval (17.5, 18.5), 19 would become the interval (18.5, 19.5), and so on. The event "more than 17" would then become the interval $(17.5, \infty)$ as seen in Figure 7.24. For this interval to stretch to ∞, the point n would need to become the interval $(n - 0.5, \infty)$. Similarly the point 0 would become the interval $(-\infty, 0 + 0.5)$. We need to do this because the normal distribution, which we are using to approximate the binomial distribution, ranges between $-\infty$ and $+\infty$ and we must ensure that the intervals we create also cover the range between $-\infty$ and $+\infty$. If not, the sum of the probabilities for $X = 0$ to $X = n$ using the normal approximation would be less than 1.

You don't need to draw the entire distribution. All you need is a little diagram (ignoring the low and high ends of the scale as they are not relevant) to show the event "more than 17" visually:

$$\ldots 14 \quad 15 \quad 16 \quad 17 \quad \mathbf{\mathit{18}} \quad \mathbf{\mathit{19}} \quad \mathbf{\mathit{20}} \quad \mathbf{\mathit{21}} \quad \mathbf{\mathit{22}} \quad \mathbf{\mathit{23}} \ldots$$

If you make a diagram like this, you can *see* the correct cutoff point. Because the cutoff point for "more than 17" is halfway between 17 and 18, the normal approximation is $P(X > 17.5)$. The 0.5 that has been added to X is called the **continuity correction.** The normal parameters are

$$\mu = n\pi = (32)(0.5) = 16$$

$$\sigma = \sqrt{n\pi(1 - \pi)} = \sqrt{(32)(0.5)(1 - 0.5)} = 2.82843$$

We then perform the usual standardizing transformation with the continuity-corrected X value:

$$z = \frac{x - \mu}{\sigma} = \frac{17.5 - 16}{2.82843} = 0.53$$

From Appendix C we find $P(Z > 0.53) = 0.5000 - P(0 < Z < 0.53) = 0.5000 - 0.2019 = 0.2981$. The calculations are illustrated in Figure 7.25.

FIGURE 7.24

Normal Approximation to $P(X \geq 18)$

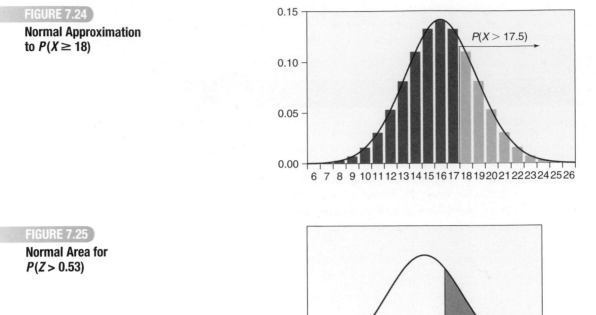

$P(X > 17.5)$

FIGURE 7.25

Normal Area for $P(Z > 0.53)$

0.2981

0.53

How accurate is this normal approximation to the binomial $P(X \geq 18)$ in our coin flip example? We can check it by using Excel. Because Excel's function is cumulative to the left, we find $P(X \leq 17)$ with the Excel function =BINOMDIST(17,32,0.5,1) and then subtract from 1:

$$P(X \geq 18) = 1 - P(X \leq 17) = 1 - 0.7017 = 0.2983$$

In this case, the normal approximation (.2981) is very close to the binomial probability, partly because this binomial is roughly symmetric (π is near 0.50).

What about when a binomial distribution is badly skewed (π near 0 or 1)? When n is large, the normal approximation improves, regardless of π. But sample size alone does not guarantee a good approximation. For example, if $n = 80$ and $\pi = 0.03$, we have a severely *right-skewed* binomial distribution even though n is fairly large, as shown in Figure 7.26. The normal approximation is inadvisable in this example as $n < 9(1 - \pi)/\pi = 9(0.97)/0.03 = 291$, which violates our rule of thumb.

To be sure you understand the continuity correction, consider the events in the table below. We sketch a diagram to find the correct cutoff point to approximate a discrete model with a continuous one.

FIGURE 7.26

Poor Normal Approximation

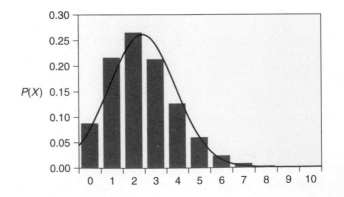

$P(X)$

Event	Relevent Range of X	Normal Cutoff
At least 17	. . . 14 15 16 **17 18 19 20** . . .	Use x = 16.5
More than 15	. . . 14 15 **16 17 18 19 20** . . .	Use x = 15.5
Fewer than 19	. . . **14 15 16 17 18** 19 20 . . .	Use x = 18.5
At least 16 and at most 18	. . . 14 15 **16 17 18** 19 20 . . .	Use x = 15.5 and x = 18.5

Concept Check

Without determining the probabilities for X, convert each of the following to intervals that can then be used to approximate probabilities using the normal distribution.

a. $P(X > 15)$

b. $P(X \geq 15)$

c. $P(X = 15)$

d. $P(X < 18)$

e. $P(X \leq 18)$

f. $P(15 < X < 18)$

g. $P(15 \leq X \leq 18)$

Section Exercises

Note: Use Appendix C for these exercises.

7.31 If $n = 50$ and $\pi = 0.4$, determine the appropriate normal cutoffs and then estimate the following probabilities for: (LO 7)
   a. $P(X > 15)$
   b. $P(X \geq 15)$
   c. $P(X = 15)$
   d. $P(X < 18)$
   e. $P(X \leq 18)$
   f. $P(15 < X < 18)$
   g. $P(15 \leq X \leq 18)$

7.32 In a previous example in an earlier chapter we learned that Jeri, a serious student, had a probability of 0.85, either through her knowledge or guessing, of correctly answering any individual multiple choice question. If Jeri wrote a 100-question multiple-choice exam, estimate the probability that she would (LO 7)
   a. Score at least 80 on this exam (for a grade of A).
   b. Score at least 70 but less than 80 on this exam (for a grade of B).

7.33 The default rate on government-guaranteed student loans at a certain university is 7 percent. (a) If 1,000 student loans are made, what is the probability of fewer than 50 defaults? (b) More than 100? Show your work carefully. (LO 7)

7.34 In a certain store, there is a 0.03 probability that the scanned price in the bar code scanner will not match the advertised price. The cashier scans 800 items. (a) What is the expected number of mismatches? The standard deviation? (b) What is the probability of at least 20 mismatches? (c) What is the probability of more than 30 mismatches? Show your calculations clearly. (LO 7)

7.35 The probability that a vending machine in the University of Windsor Student Centre will dispense the desired item when correct change is inserted is 0.90. If 200 customers try the machine, find the probability that (a) at least 175 will receive the desired item and (b) fewer than 190 will receive the desired item. Explain. (LO 7)

7.36 When confronted with an in-flight medical emergency, pilots and crew can consult staff physicians at MedAire, an emergency facility in Tempe, Arizona. If MedAire is called, there is a 4.8 percent chance that the flight will be diverted for an immediate landing. (a) If MedAire is called 8,465 times (as it was in 2002), what is the expected number of diversions? (b) What is the probability of at least 400 diversions? (c) Fewer than 450 diversions? Show your work carefully. (Data are from *Popular Science* 263, no. 5 [Nov. 2003], p. 70.) (LO 7)

CHAPTER SUMMARY

The **probability density function (PDF)** of a **continuous random variable** is a smooth curve, and probabilities are determined by **areas** under the curve. The area under the entire PDF is 1. The **cumulative distribution function (CDF)** shows the area under the PDF to the left of X, approaching 1 as X approaches its maximum value. The mean $E(X)$ and variance $V(X)$ are integrals, rather than sums, as for a discrete random variable. The **uniform continuous distribution,** denoted $U(a, b)$, has two parameters a and b that enclose the range. The symmetric, bell-shaped **normal (or Gaussian) distribution,** denoted $N(\mu, \sigma)$, has two parameters, the mean μ and standard deviation σ. Because there is a different normal distribution for every possible μ and σ, we apply the transformation $z = (x - \mu)/\sigma$ to get a new random variable that follows a **standard normal distribution,** denoted $N(0, 1)$, with mean 0 and standard deviation 1. There is no simple formula for normal areas, but tables or Excel functions are available to find an area under the curve for given z values or to find z values that give a specified area (the "inverse normal").

KEY TERMS

cumulative distribution function (CDF), *267*

continuity correction, *287*

continuous random variable, *266*

normal (or Gaussian) distribution, *271*

probability density function (PDF), *267*

standard normal distribution, *273*

uniform continuous distribution, *268*

unit rectangular distribution, *270*

Commonly Used Formulas in Continuous Distributions

Uniform CDF: $P(X \leq x) = \dfrac{x - a}{b - a}$ for $a \leq X \leq b$

Standard Normal Random Variable: $z = \dfrac{x - \mu}{\sigma}$ for $-\infty < X < +\infty$

Normal Approximation to Binomial:

$\mu = n\pi$ and $\sigma = \sqrt{n\pi(1 - \pi)}$ for $n \geq 9\pi/(1 - \pi)$ and $n \geq 9(1 - \pi)/\pi$

CHAPTER REVIEW

1. (a) Why does a point have no probability in a continuous distribution? (b) Why are probabilities areas under curves in a continuous distribution? (LO 1)

2. Define (a) parameter, (b) PDF, and (c) CDF. (LO 1)

3. For the uniform distribution: (a) tell how many parameters it has; (b) indicate what the parameters represent; (c) describe its shape; and (d) explain when it would be used. (LO 2)

4. For the normal distribution: (a) tell how many parameters it has; (b) indicate what the parameters represent; (c) describe its shape; and (d) explain why all normal distributions are alike despite having different μ and σ. (LO 2)

5. (a) What features of a stochastic process might lead you to anticipate a normal distribution? (LO 2) (b) Give two examples of random variables that might be considered normal. (LO 2)

6. (a) What is the transformation to standardize a normal random variable? (b) Why do we standardize a variable to find normal areas? (c) How does a standard normal distribution differ from any other normal distribution, and how is it similar? (LO 2)

7. When does the normal give an acceptable approximation (a) to a binomial (b) Why might you never need these approximations? (c) When might you need them? (LO 7)

8. Why is calculus needed to find probabilities for continuous distributions, but not for discrete distributions? (LO 1)

CHAPTER EXERCISES

Note: Show your work clearly. Problems marked * are harder or rely on optional material from this chapter.

7.37   Which of the following is a continuous random variable? (LO 1)
   a. Number of Honda Civics sold in a given day at a car dealership.
   b. Litres of gasoline used for a 200-km trip in a Honda Civic.
   c. Distance driven on a particular Thursday by the owner of a Honda Civic.

7.38 Which of the following could be probability density functions for a continuous random variable? Explain. (LO 1)

 a. $f(x) = 0.50$ for $0 \leq X \leq 2$

 b. $f(x) = 2 - x$ for $0 \leq X \leq 2$

 c. $f(x) = 0.5x$ for $0 \leq X \leq 2$

7.39 Applicants for a night caretaker position are uniformly distributed in age between 25 and 65. (a) What is the mean age of an applicant? (b) The standard deviation? (c) What is the probability that an applicant will be over 45? (d) Over 55? (e) Between 30 and 60? (LO 3)

7.40 Discuss why you would or would not expect each of the following variables to be normally distributed. *Hint:* Would you expect a single central mode and tapering tails? Would the distribution be roughly symmetric? Would one tail be longer than the other? (LO 2)

 a. Amount of automobile collision damage claims.

 b. Diameters of randomly chosen circulated quarters.

 c. Volume of contents of 1.89-litre carton of Tropicana Orange Juice.

7.41 Scores on a certain accounting exam were normally distributed with a mean of 75 and a standard deviation of 7. Find the percentile for each individual using Excel's =NORMSDIST function. (a) Bob's score was 82. (b) Phyllis's score was 93. (c) Tom's score was 63. (LO 5)

7.42 Chlorine concentration in a municipal water supply is a uniformly distributed random variable that ranges between 0.74 ppm and 0.98 ppm. (a) What is the mean chlorine concentration? (b) The standard deviation? (c) What is the probability that the chlorine concentration will exceed 0.80 ppm on a given day? (d) Will be under 0.85 ppm? (e) Will be between 0.80 ppm and 0.90 ppm? (f) Why is chlorine added to municipal water? What if there is too much? Too little? *Hint:* Use the Internet. (LO 3)

7.43 The weekly demand, *X*, for Baked Lay's potato chips at a certain Subway sandwich shop is a normal random variable with a mean of 450 bags and a standard deviation 80 bags. Find the value of *X* for each event. Show your work. (LO 6)

 a. Highest 50 percent   b. Lowest 25 percent   c. 90th percentile

 d. Highest 80 percent   e. Highest 5 percent   f. Middle 50 percent

 g. 20th percentile   h. Middle 95 percent   i. Highest 1 percent

7.44 The length of an Ontario brook trout is normally distributed. (a) What is the probability that a brook trout's length exceeds the mean? (b) Exceeds the mean by at least 1 standard deviation? (c) Exceeds the mean by at least 2 standard deviations? (d) Is within 2 standard deviations? (LO 5)

7.45 The caffeine content of a cup of home-brewed coffee is a normally distributed random variable with a mean of 115 mg with a standard deviation of 20 mg. (a) What is the probability that a randomly chosen cup of home-brewed coffee will have more than 130 mg of caffeine? (b) Less than 100 mg? (c) A very strong cup of tea has a caffeine content of 91 mg. What is the probability that a cup of coffee will have less caffeine than a very strong cup of tea? (Data are from *Popular Science* 254, no. 5 [May 1999], p. 95.) (LO 5)

7.46 The fracture strength of a certain type of manufactured glass is normally distributed with a mean of 579 MPa with a standard deviation of 14 MPa. (a) What is the probability that a randomly chosen sample of glass will break at less than 579 MPa? (b) More than 590 MPa? (c) Less than 600 MPa? (Data are from *Science* 283 [Feb. 26, 1999], p. 1296.) (LO 5)

7.47 Tire pressure in a certain car is a normally distributed random variable with mean 210 kPa (kilopascals) and standard deviation 15 kPa. The manufacturer's recommended correct inflation range is 195 kPa to 225 kPa. A motorist's tire is inspected at random. (a) What is the probability that the tire's inflation is within the recommended range? (b) What is the probability that the tire is underinflated? *(c) The Alliance of Automotive Manufacturers has developed a microchip that will warn when a tire is 25 percent below the recommended mean, to warn of dangerously low tire pressure. How often would such an alarm be triggered? (See *The Wall Street Journal,* July 14, 2004.) (LO 5 & 6)

7.48 In a certain microwave oven on the high power setting, the time it takes a randomly chosen kernel of popcorn to pop is normally distributed with a mean of 140 seconds and a standard deviation of 25 seconds. (a) What percentage of the kernels will fail to pop if the popcorn is cooked for (i) 2 minutes? (ii) Three minutes? (b) If you wanted 95 percent of the kernels to pop, what time would you allow? (c) If you wanted 99 percent to pop, what time would you allow? (LO 5 & 6)

7.49 Procyon Manufacturing produces tennis balls. Their manufacturing process has a mean ball weight of 2.035 ounces with a standard deviation of 0.03 ounces. Regulation tennis balls are required to have a weight between 1.975 ounces and 2.095 ounces. What proportion of Procyon's production will fail to meet these specifications? (See *Scientific American* 292, no. 4 [Apr. 2005], p. 95.) (LO 5)

7.50 Manufacturers of HRT (hormone replacement therapy) drugs need to know the potential market for their products that relieve side effects of menopause. For women without hysterectomy, the average age at menopause is 51.4 years. Assume a standard deviation of 3.8 years. (a) What is the probability that menopause will occur before age 40? (b) After age 55? (c) What assumptions did you make? *(d) Among the 73.1 million American women between ages 30 and 75, how many would be potential users of HRT? *Hint:* Assume equal numbers of women in all ages from 30 to 75, and compute the $\mu \pm 3\sigma$ range for menopause age. (Data are from *Statistical Abstract of the United States, 2001*.) (LO 5)

7.51 In a study of e-mail consultations with physicians at the University of Virginia Children's Medical Center, the monthly average was 37.6 requests with a standard deviation of 15.9 requests. (a) What is the probability of (i) more than 50 requests in a given month? (ii) Fewer than 29? (iii) Between 40 and 50 requests? (b) What assumptions did you make?

7.52 The time it takes to give a man a shampoo and haircut is normally distributed with mean 22 minutes and standard deviation 3 minutes. Customers are scheduled every 30 minutes. (a) What is the probability that a male customer will take longer than the allotted time? *(b) If three male customers are scheduled sequentially on the half-hour, what is the probability that all three will be finished within their allotted half-hour times? (LO 5)

7.53 The length of a time-out during a televised professional football game is normally distributed with a mean of 84 seconds and a standard deviation of 10 seconds. If the network runs consecutive commercials totalling 90 seconds, what is the probability that play will resume before the commercials are over? What assumption(s) did you make in answering this question? (LO 5)

7.54* In Rivendell Memorial Hospital the time to complete surgery in a routine tubal ligation without complications is normally distributed with a mean of 30 minutes and a standard deviation of 8 minutes. The next procedure has been scheduled in the same operating room 60 minutes after the beginning of a tubal ligation procedure. Allowing 20 minutes to vacate and prepare the operating room between procedures, what is the probability that the next procedure will have to be delayed? Explain carefully. (LO 5)

7.55 Demand for residential electricity at 6 p.m. on the first Monday in October in Essex County is normally distributed with a mean of 4,905 MW (megawatts) and a standard deviation of 355 MW. Due to scheduled maintenance and unexpected system failures in a generating station the utility can supply a maximum of 5,200 MW at that time. What is the probability that the utility will have to purchase electricity from other utilities or allow brownouts? (LO 5)

7.56 Jim's systolic blood pressure is a random variable with a mean of 145 mmHg and a standard deviation of 20 mmHg. For Jim's age group, 140 is the cutoff for high blood pressure. (a) If Jim's systolic blood pressure is taken at a randomly chosen moment, what is the probability that it will be (i) 135 or less? (ii) 175 or more? (iii) Between 125 and 165? (b) Discuss the implications of variability for physicians who are trying to identify patients with high blood pressure. (LO 5)

7.57 A statistics exam was given. Explain the meaning of each z value. (LO 2)
   a. John's z-score was -1.62.
   b. Mary's z-score was 0.50.
   c. Zak's z-score was 1.79.
   d. Frieda's z-score was 2.48.

7.58 Are the following statements true or false? Explain your reasoning. (LO 2)
   a. "If we see a standardized z value beyond ± 3, the variable cannot be normally distributed."
   b. "If X and Y are two normally distributed random variables measured in different units (e.g., X is in pounds and Y is in kilograms), then it is not meaningful to compare the standardized z values."
   c. "Two machines fill 2-litre soft drink bottles by using a similar process. Machine A has $\mu = 1,990$ ml and $\sigma = 5$ ml while Machine B has $\mu = 1,995$ ml and $\sigma = 3$ ml. The variables cannot both be normally distributed since they have different standard deviations."

7.59 John can take either of two routes (*A* or *B*) to Montreal's Trudeau Airport. At midday on a typical Wednesday the travel time on either route is normally distributed with parameters $\mu_A = 54$ minutes, $\sigma_A = 6$ minutes, $\mu_B = 60$ minutes, and $\sigma_B = 3$ minutes. (a) Which route should he choose if he wants to be at the airport in 54 minutes to pick up his spouse? (b) Sixty minutes? (c) Sixty-six minutes? Explain carefully. (LO 3)

7.60* The amount of fill in a half-litre (500-ml) soft drink bottle is normally distributed. The process has a standard deviation of 5 ml. The mean is adjustable. (a) Where should the mean be set to ensure a 95 percent probability that a half-litre bottle will not be underfilled? (b) A 99 percent probability? (c) A 99.9 percent probability? Explain. (LO 3)

7.61 The length of a certain kind of an Ontario brook trout is normally distributed with a mean of 30 cm and a standard deviation of 5 cm. What minimum size limit should be set by the appropriate government agency if it wishes to allow people to keep 80 percent of the trout they catch? (LO 6)

7.62 Times for a surgical procedure are normally distributed. There are two methods. Method *A* has a mean of 28 minutes and a standard deviation of 4 minutes, while method *B* has a mean of 32 minutes and a standard deviation of 2 minutes. (a) Which procedure is preferred if the procedure must be completed within 28 minutes? (b) Thirty-eight minutes? (c) Thirty-six minutes? Explain your reasoning fully. (LO 3)

7.63 The length of a brook trout is normally distributed. Two brook trout are caught. (a) What is the probability that both exceed the mean? (b) Neither exceeds the mean? (c) One is above the mean and one is below? (d) Both are equal to the mean? (LO 3)

7.64* Currently the batteries used in an MP3 player allow an average of 12 hours of play time with a standard deviation of 0.7 hours when fully charged (and play time is normally distributed). (a) What is the probability that an MP3 player will play for at least 11 hours on a fully charged battery? (b) Less than 10 hours on a fully charged battery? (c) Play between 11 and 13 hours on a fully charged battery? (d) What play time would be exceeded 90 percent of the time? (e) If a new brand of battery was available with a standard deviation in play time of 0.4 hours (at the same average play time of 12 hours) when fully charged, answer parts (a) through (d). (f) From the perspective of an MP3 user, which is the better battery? Explain. (LO 5 & 6)

7.65* A Canadian importer of GPSs has a one-year warranty on its products. The life expectancy of these products are normally distributed with an average of 1.7 years and a standard deviation of 0.4 years. What proportion of these GPSs would need repairs or replacement under warranty? Suppose the percentage of these GPSs that needed repairs or replacement under warranty had to be no greater than 2 percent for it to be financially viable to import these GPSs. (a) What would the warranty period need to be changed to? (b) What would the average life expectancy need to be? (c) What would the standard deviation in life expectancy need to be in order to satisfy this requirement? (LO 5 & 6)

7.66* Denise, the manager of a store in Devonshire Mall, is supposed to open the store in 30 minutes but has yet to leave her house. There are two routes that she could take. Based on her past experience, one of the routes would take her between 15 and 35 minutes to get to her store, and because of construction along that route, there is no reason to believe that any times are more likely than any other times. The time it would take along the other route is normally distributed with a mean of 20 minutes with a standard deviation of 5 minutes. Which route should she take? Explain. Suppose she needed to open the store in 35 minutes, which route should she take? (LO 3)

7.67 Among live deliveries, the probability of a twin birth is 0.02. (a) In 2,000 live deliveries what is the probability of at least 50 twin births? (b) Fewer than 35? Explain carefully. (LO 7)

7.68 Nationwide, the probability that a rental car is from Hertz is 25 percent. In a sample of 100 rental cars, what is the probability that fewer than 20 are from Hertz? Explain. (LO 7)

7.69 The probability that a certain kind of flower seed will germinate is 0.80. (a) If 200 seeds are planted, what is the probability that fewer than 150 will germinate? (b) That at least 150 will germinate? (LO 7)

7.70 On a cold morning the probability is 0.02 that a given car will not start. In the small town of Eureka, 1,500 cars are started each cold morning. (a) What is the probability that at least 25 cars will not start? (b) More than 40? (LO 7)

APPROXIMATIONS

DISCUSSION QUESTION   **7.71**   On a police sergeant's examination, the historical mean score was 80 with a standard deviation of 20. Four officers who were alleged to be cronies of the police chief scored 195, 171, 191, and 189, respectively, on the test. This led to allegations of irregularity in the exam. (a) Convert these four officers' scores to standardized *z* values. (b) Do you think there was sufficient reason to question these four exam scores? What assumptions are you making? (Data are from *Detroit Free Press*, Mar. 19, 1999, p. 10A.) (LO 3)

LearningStats Unit 07 Continuous Distributions ⎹ LS ⎸

LearningStats Unit 07 lets you work with continuous distributions, particularly the normal distribution, demonstrating how to calculate areas and showing the shapes of the distributions. Modules are designed for self-study, so you can proceed at your own pace.

Topic	*LearningStats Modules*
Overview	▣ Continuous Distributions
Calculations	▩ Continuous Distributions: Examples
	▩ Normal Areas
	▩ Probability Calculator
Normal approximations	▩ Evaluating Rules of Thumb
Random data	▩ Random Continuous Data
Tables	▩ Table C—Normal Probabilities
Applications	▤ Formulas for Continuous PDFs
	▤ Exponential Model and Problems
	▤ Random Normal Data

Key: ▣ = PowerPoint ▤ = Word ▩ = Excel

Visual Statistics ⎹ Vs ⎸

Visual Statistics Modules on Continuous Distributions

Module	*Module Name*
5	Visualizing Continuous Distributions

Visual Statistics Module 5 (included on your CD) is designed to help you

- Recognize common continuous distributions and their distribution functions.
- Identify the parameters of common continuous distributions and how they affect shape.
- Recognize shape measures for common distributions.
- Understand when common continuous distributions can be approximated by a normal.
- Understand the relation between a value of a distribution and its tail area.

The worktext chapter (included on the CD in PDF format) contains a list of concepts covered, objectives of the module, overview of concepts, illustration of concepts, orientation to module features, learning exercises (basic, intermediate, advanced), learning projects (individual, team), self-evaluation quiz, glossary of terms, and solutions to a self-evaluation quiz.

1. Which type of probability (empirical, classical, subjective) is each of the following?
   a. On a given Friday, the probability that Flight 277 to Halifax is on time is 23.7 percent.
   b. Your chance of going to Disney World next year is 10 percent.
   c. The chance of rolling a 3 on two dice is 1/18.

2. For the following contingency table, find (a) $P(H \cap T)$; (b) $P(S|G)$; (c) $P(S)$

	R	S	T	Row Total
G	10	50	30	90
H	20	50	40	110
Column Total	30	100	70	200

3. If $P(A) = 0.30$, $P(B) = 0.70$, and $P(A \cap B) = 0.25$ are A and B independent events? Explain.
4. Which statement is *false?* Explain.
   a. If $P(A) = 0.05$ then the odds against event A's occurrence are 19 to 1.
   b. If A and B are mutually exclusive events, then $P(A \cup B) = 0$.
   c. The number of permutations of 5 things taken 2 at a time is 20.

5. Which statement is *true?* Why not the others?
   a. The Poisson distribution has two parameters.
   b. The binomial distribution assumes dependent random trials.
   c. The uniform distribution has two parameters.

6. If the payoff of a risky investment has three possible outcomes ($1,000, $2,000, $5,000) with probabilities 0.60, 0.30, and 0.10, respectively, find the expected value.
   a. $1,500
   b. $2,300
   c. $1,700

7. Assuming independent arrivals with a mean of 2.5 arrivals per minute, find the probability that in a given minute there will be (a) exactly 2 arrivals; (b) at least 3 arrivals; (c) fewer than 4 arrivals. Which probability distribution did you use and why?

8. If a random experiment whose success probability is 0.20 is repeated 8 times, find the probability of (a) exactly 3 successes; (b) more than 3 successes; (c) at most 2 successes. Which probability distribution did you use and why?

9. In a random experiment with 50 independent trials with constant probability of success 0.30, find the mean and standard deviation of the number of successes.

10. Which probability distribution (uniform, binomial, Poisson) is most nearly appropriate to describe each situation (assuming you knew the relevant parameters)?
    a. The number of dimes older than 10 years in a random sample of 8 dimes.
    b. The number of hospital patients admitted during a given minute on Tuesday morning.
    c. The last digit of a randomly chosen student's Social Insurance Number.

11. Which statement is *false?* Explain.
    a. In the hypergeometric distribution, sampling is done without replacement.
    b. The mean of the uniform distribution is always $(a + b)/2$.

12. Which statement is *false?* Explain.
    a. To find probabilities in a continuous distribution we add up the probabilities at each point.
    b. A uniform continuous model $U(5, 21)$ has mean 13 and standard deviation 4.619.
    c. A uniform PDF is constant for all values within the interval $a \leq X \leq b$.

13. Which statement is *true* for a normal distribution? Why not the others?
    a. The shape of the PDF is always symmetric regardless of μ and σ.
    b. The shape of the CDF resembles a bell-shaped curve.
    c. When no tables are available, areas may be found by a simple formula.

14. If highway speeds are normally distributed with a mean of $\mu = 100$ km/h and $\sigma = 10$ km/h, find the probability that the speed of a randomly chosen vehicle (a) exceeds 78 km/h; (b) is between 95 and 105 km/h; (c) is less than 105 km/h.

15. In the previous problem, calculate (a) the 95th percentile of vehicle speeds (i.e., 95 percent below); (b) the lowest 10 percent of speeds; (c) the highest 25 percent of speeds (3rd quartile).

16. Which of the following Excel formulas would be a correct way to calculate $P(X < 450)$ given that X is $N(500, 60)$?
    a. =NORMDIST(450,500,60,1)
    b. =NORMSDIST(450,60)
    c. =1–NORMDIST(450,500,60,0)

17. Which statement is *correct* concerning the normal approximation? Why not the others?
    a. The normal binomial approximation is better when n is small and π is large.
    b. Normal approximations are needed because Excel lacks discrete probability functions.

Appendix: Exponential Distribution

Characteristics of the Exponential Distribution

In Chapter 6 we introduced the idea of a *random process*. For example, consider the process of customers arriving at a Noodles & Company restaurant, illustrated in Figure 7.27. There are two different variables that could be used to describe this process. We could count the number of customers who arrive in a randomly selected minute, or we could measure the time between two customer arrivals. As you learned in Chapter 6, the *count* of customer arrivals is a discrete random variable and typically has a Poisson distribution. When the count of customer arrivals has a Poisson distribution, the distribution of the time between two customer arrivals, will have an **exponential distribution**, detailed in Table 7.7. In the exponential model, the focus is on the waiting time until the next event, a continuous variable. The exponential probability function approaches zero as x increases, and is very skewed, as shown in Figures 7.28 and 7.29.

We are usually not interested in the height of the function $f(x)$ but rather in areas under the curve. Fortunately, the CDF is simple; no tables are needed, just a calculator that has the e^x function key. The probability of waiting more than x units of time until the next arrival is $e^{-\lambda x}$, while the probability of waiting x units of time or less is $1 - e^{-\lambda x}$.

$$\text{Right-tail area: } P(X > x) = e^{-\lambda x} \quad \text{(probability of waiting \textit{more} than } x) \tag{7.8}$$

$$\text{Left-tail area: } P(X \le x) = 1 - e^{-\lambda x} \quad \text{(probability of waiting } x \text{ or less)} \tag{7.9}$$

FIGURE 7.27

Customer Arrival Process at a Noodles & Company Restaurant

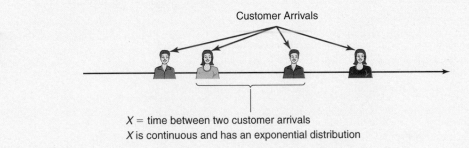

X = time between two customer arrivals
X is continuous and has an exponential distribution

TABLE 7.7   Exponential Distribution

Parameters	λ = mean arrival rate per unit of time or space (same as Poisson mean)
PDF	$f(x) = \lambda e^{-\lambda x}$
CDF	$P(X \le x) = 1 - e^{-\lambda x}$
Domain	$X \ge 0$
Mean	$1/\lambda$
Standard deviation	$1/\lambda$
Shape	Always right-skewed
Comments	Waiting time is exponential when arrivals follow a Poisson model. Often $1/\lambda$ is given (mean time between events) rather than λ.

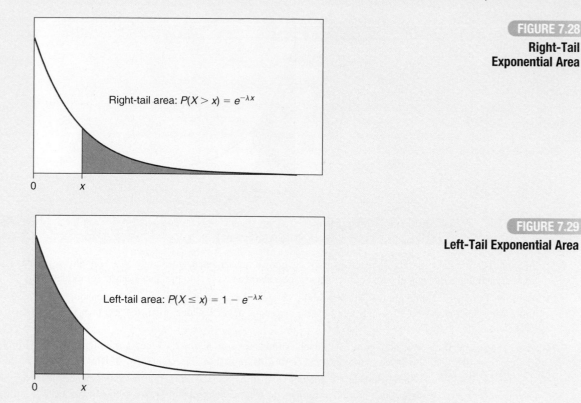

FIGURE 7.28

**Right-Tail
Exponential Area**

Right-tail area: $P(X > x) = e^{-\lambda x}$

FIGURE 7.29

Left-Tail Exponential Area

Left-tail area: $P(X \leq x) = 1 - e^{-\lambda x}$

Recall that $P(X \leq x)$ is the same as $P(X < x)$ as the point x has no area. For this reason, we could use either $<$ or $\leq$ in Equation 7.9.

EXAMPLE 6

Customer Waiting Time

Between 2 p.m. and 4 p.m. on Wednesday, patient insurance inquiries arrive at Greenshield Canada at a mean rate of 2.2 calls per minute. What is the probability of waiting more than 30 seconds for the next call? We set $\lambda = 2.2$ events per minute and $x = 0.50$ minutes. Note that we must convert 30 seconds to 0.50 minutes as λ is expressed in minutes, and the units of measurement must be the same. We have

$$P(X > 0.50) = e^{-\lambda x} = e^{-(2.2)(0.50)} = 0.3329, \text{ or } 33.29\%$$

There is about a 33 percent chance of waiting more than 30 seconds before the next call arrives. Because $x = 0.50$ is a *point* that has no area in a continuous model, $P(X \geq 0.50)$ and $P(X > 0.50)$ refer to the same event (unlike, say, a binomial model, in which a point *does* have a probability). The probability that 30 seconds or less (0.50 minutes) will be needed before the next call arrives is

$$P(X \leq 0.50) = 1 - e^{-(2.2)(0.50)} = 1 - 0.3329 = 0.6671$$

These calculations are illustrated in Figures 7.30 and 7.31.

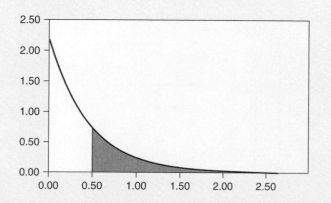

FIGURE 7.30

$P(X > 0.50)$ for $\lambda = 2.2$

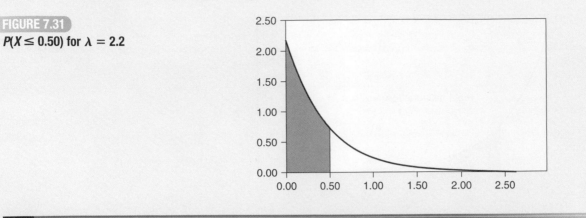

FIGURE 7.31

$P(X \le 0.50)$ for $\lambda = 2.2$

Section Exercises

7.72 In Santa Theresa, false alarms are received at the downtown fire station at a mean rate of 0.3 per day. (a) What is the probability that more than 7 days will pass before the next false alarm arrives? (b) Less than 2 days? (c) Explain fully.

7.73 Between 11 p.m. and midnight on Thursday night, Mystery Pizza gets an average of 4.2 telephone orders per hour. Find the probability that (a) at least 30 minutes will elapse before the next telephone order; (b) less than 15 minutes will elapse; and (c) between 15 and 30 minutes will elapse.

7.74 A passenger metal detector at Toronto's Pearson Airport gives an alarm 2.1 times a minute. What is the probability that (a) less than 60 seconds will pass before the next alarm? (b) More than 30 seconds? (c) At least 45 seconds?

7.75 The Johnson family uses a propane tank for cooking on their barbecue. During the summer they need to replace their tank on average every 30 days. At a randomly chosen moment, what is the probability that they can barbecue (a) at least 40 days before they need to replace their tank? (b) No more than 20 days?

7.76 At a certain Noodles & Company restaurant, customers arrive during the lunch hour at a rate of 2.8 per minute. What is the probability that (a) at least 30 seconds will pass before the next customer walks in? (b) No more than 15 seconds? (c) More than 1 minute?

Inverse Exponential

We can use the exponential area formula in reverse. Looking back to Example 6 above, if the mean arrival rate is 2.2 calls per minute, we want the 90th percentile for waiting time (the top 10 percent of waiting time) as illustrated in Figure 7.32. We want to find the x value that defines the upper 10 percent.

Call the unknown time x. Because $P(X \le x) = 0.90$ implies $P(X > x) = 0.10$, we set the right-tail area to 0.10, take the natural logarithm of both sides, and solve for x:

$$e^{-\lambda x} = 0.10$$
$$-\lambda x = ln(0.10)$$
$$-\lambda x = -2.302585$$
$$x = 2.302585/\lambda$$

FIGURE 7.32

Finding x for the Upper 10 Percent

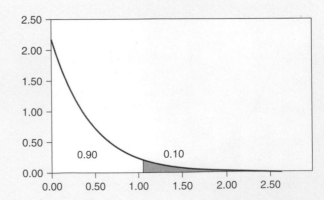

TABLE 7.8   Quartiles for Exponential with $\lambda = 2.2$

First Quartile Q_1	Second Quartile Q_2 (median)	Third Quartile Q_3
$e^{-\lambda x} = 0.75$	$e^{-\lambda x} = 0.50$	$e^{-\lambda x} = 0.25$
$-\lambda x = ln(0.75)$	$-\lambda x = ln(0.50)$	$-\lambda x = ln(0.25)$
$-\lambda x = -0.2876821$	$-\lambda x = -0.6931472$	$-\lambda x = -1.386294$
$x = 0.2876821/\lambda$	$x = 0.6931472/\lambda$	$x = 1.386294/\lambda$
$x = 0.2876821/2.2$	$x = 0.6931472/2.2$	$x = 1.386294/2.2$
$x = 0.1308$ minutes, or 7.8 seconds	$x = 0.3151$ minutes, or 18.9 seconds	$x = 0.6301$ minutes, or 37.8 seconds

$$x = 2.302585/2.2$$
$$x = 1.0466 \text{ minutes}$$

So 90 percent of the calls will arrive within 1.0466 minutes (or 62.8 seconds). We can find any percentile in the same way. For example, Table 7.8 illustrates similar calculations to find the quartiles (25 percent, 50 percent, 75 percent) of waiting time.

In Example 6, we assume that the mean arrival rate is 2.2 calls per minute; that is, $\lambda = 2.2$ calls per minutes, or equivalently, the mean waiting time is $1/\lambda = 1/2.2 = 0.4545$ minutes, or approximately 27 seconds. It is instructive to note that the median waiting time (18.9 seconds) is less than the mean. Because the exponential distribution is highly right-skewed, we would expect the mean waiting time to be above the median, which it is.

Mean Time between Events

Exponential waiting times are often described in terms of the *mean time between events (MTBE)* rather than in terms of Poisson arrivals per unit of time. In other words, we might be given $1/\lambda$ instead of λ.

$$\text{MTBE} = 1/\lambda = mean\ time\ between\ events\ (\text{units of time per event})$$
$$1/\text{MTBE} = \lambda = mean\ events\ per\ unit\ of\ time\ (\text{events per unit of time})$$

For example, if the mean time between patient arrivals in an emergency room is 20 minutes, then $\lambda = 1/20 = 0.05$ arrivals per minute (or $\lambda = 3.0$ arrivals per hour). We could work a problem using either hours or minutes, as long as we are careful to make sure that x and λ are expressed in the same units when we calculate $e^{-\lambda x}$. For example, $P(X > 12 \text{ minutes}) = e^{-(0.05)(12)} = e^{-0.60}$ is the same as $P(X > 0.20 \text{ hour}) = e^{-(3)(0.20)} = e^{-0.60}$.

EXAMPLE 7
Flat-Panel Displays

The NexGenCo colour flat-panel display in an aircraft cockpit has a mean time between failures (MTBF) of 22,500 flight hours. What is the probability of a failure within the next 10,000 flight hours? Because 22,500 hours per failure implies $\lambda = 1/22,500$ failures per hour, we calculate

$$P(X < 10,000) = 1 - e^{-\lambda x} = 1 - e^{-(1/22,500)(10,000)} = 1 - e^{-0.4444} = 1 - 0.6412 = 0.3588$$

There is a 35.88 percent chance of failure within the next 10,000 hours of flight. This assumes that failures follow the Poisson model.

EXAMPLE 8
Warranty Period

A manufacturer of GPS navigation receivers for boats knows that their mean life under typical maritime conditions is seven years. What warranty should be offered in order that not more than 30 percent of the GPS units will fail before the warranty expires? The situation is illustrated in Figure 7.33.

Let x be the length of the warranty. To solve this problem, we note that if 30 percent fail before the warranty expires, 70 percent will fail afterward. That is, $P(X > x) = 1 - P(X \le x) = 1 - 0.30 = 0.70$.

We set $P(X > x) = e^{-\lambda x} = 0.70$ and solve for x by taking the natural log of both sides of the equation:

$$e^{-\lambda x} = 0.70$$
$$-\lambda x = ln(0.70)$$
$$-\lambda x = -0.356675$$
$$x = (0.356675)/\lambda$$

But in this case, we are not given λ but rather its reciprocal MTBF = $1/\lambda$. Seven years *mean time between failures* is the same as saying $\lambda = 1/7$ *failures per year*. So we plug in $\lambda = 1/7 = 0.1428571$ to finish solving for x:

$$x = (0.356675)/(0.142857) = 2.497 \text{ years}$$

Thus, the firm would offer a 30-month warranty.

It may seem paradoxical that such a short warranty would be offered for something that lasts seven years. However, the right tail is very long. A few long-lived GPS units will pull up the mean. This is typical of electronic equipment, which helps explain why your laptop computer may have only a one-year warranty when we know that laptops often last for many years. Similarly, automobiles typically outlast their warranty period (although competitive pressures have recently led to warranties of five years or more, even though it may result in a loss on the warranty). In general, warranty periods are a policy tool used by business to balance costs of expected claims against the competitive need to offer contract protection to consumers.

FIGURE 7.33

Finding *x* for the Lower 30 Percent

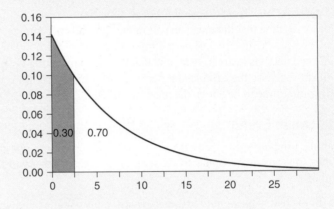

Using Excel

The Excel function =EXPONDIST(x,λ,1) will return the left-tail area $P(X \le x)$. The "1" indicates a cumulative area. If you enter 0 instead of 1, you will get the height of the PDF instead of the left-tail area for the CDF.

Every situation with Poisson arrivals over time is associated with an exponential waiting time. Both models depend solely on the parameter λ = mean arrival rate per unit of time. These two closely related distributions are summarized in Table 7.9.

The exponential model may also remind you of the geometric model, which describes the number of items that must be sampled until the first success. In spirit, they are similar. However, the models are different because the geometric model tells us the number of *discrete* events until the next success, while the exponential model tells the *continuous* waiting time until the next arrival of an event.

TABLE 7.9   Relation between Exponential and Poisson Models

Model	Random Variable	Parameter	Domain	Variable Type
Poisson	X = number of arrivals per unit of time	$\lambda = \dfrac{(\text{mean arrivals})}{(\text{unit of time})}$	$X = 0, 1, 2, \ldots$	Discrete
Exponential	X = waiting time until next arrival	$\lambda = \dfrac{(\text{mean arrivals})}{(\text{unit of time})}$	$X \ge 0$	Continuous

Section Exercises

7.77   The time it takes a ski patroller to respond to an accident call has an exponential distribution with an average equal to five minutes. (a) In what time will 90 percent of all ski accident calls be responded to? (b) If the ski patrol would like to be able to respond to 90 percent of the accident calls within 10 minutes, what does the average response time need to be?

7.78   Between 11 p.m. and midnight on Thursday night, Mystery Pizza gets an average of 4.2 telephone orders per hour. (a) Find the median waiting time until the next telephone order. (b) Find the upper quartile of waiting time before the next telephone order. (c) What is the upper 10 percent of waiting time until the next telephone order? Show all calculations clearly.

7.79   A passenger metal detector at Montreal's Trudeau Airport gives an alarm 0.5 times a minute. (a) Find the median waiting time until the next alarm. (b) Find the first quartile of waiting time before the next alarm. (c) Find the 30th percentile waiting time until the next alarm. Show all calculations clearly.

7.80   Between 2 a.m. and 4 a.m. at an all-night pizza parlour, the mean time between arrival of telephone pizza orders is 20 minutes. (a) Find the median wait for pizza order arrivals. (b) Explain why the median is not equal to the mean. (c) Find the upper quartile.

7.81   The mean life of a certain computer hard drive in continual use is eight years. (a) How long a warranty should be offered if the vendor wants to ensure that not more than 10 percent of the hard drives will fail within the warranty period? (b) Not more than 20 percent?

7.82   The HP dvd1040i 20X Multiformat DVD Writer has an MTBF of 70,000 hours. (a) Assuming continuous operation, what is the probability that the DVD writer will last more than 100,000 hours? (b) Less than 50,000 hours? (c) At least 50,000 hours but not more than 80,000 hours? (Product specifications are from www.hp.com.)

7.83   Automobile warranty claims for engine mount failure in a Troppo Malo 2000 SE are rare at a certain dealership, occurring at a mean rate of 0.1 claims per month. (a) What is the probability that the dealership will wait at least six months until the next claim? (b) At least a year? (c) At least two years? (d) At least six months but not more than one year?

7.84   Suppose the average time to service a Noodles & Company customer at a certain restaurant is three minutes and the service time follows an exponential distribution. (a) What is the probability that a customer will be serviced in less than three minutes? (b) Why is your answer more than 50 percent? Shouldn't exactly half the area be below the mean?

7.85   Systron Donner Inertial manufactures inertial subsystems for automotive, commercial/industrial, and aerospace and defence applications. The sensors use a one-piece, micro-machined inertial sensing element to measure angular rotational velocity or linear acceleration. The MTBF for a single axis sensor is 400,000 hours. (a) Find the probability that a sensor lasts at least 30 years, assuming continuous operation. (b)Would you be surprised to learn that a sensor has failed within the first three years? Explain. (Product specifications are from www.systron.com/techsupp_A.asp.)

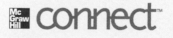   For solutions to odd-numbered exercises, Exam Review questions, and additional study tools to help you succeed in this course, visit *Connect* at www.mcgrawhillconnect.ca.

Chapter

8

Sampling Distributions and Estimation

Chapter Learning Objectives

When you finish this chapter you should be able to

1. Define and understand sampling variation, sampling error, parameter, estimator, and other statistical terms.

2. Explain what sampling distributions are and why it is desirable that we create sampling distributions for unbiased, consistent, and efficient estimators.

3. Use the appropriate sampling distributions to determine probabilities for $\overline{X}$ and P and to construct confidence intervals for a single population mean, a single population proportion, and a single population variance.

4. Describe similarities and differences between z, Student's t, and χ^2 distributions.

5. Find t values and χ^2 in tables or Excel for a desired confidence level.

6. Calculate sample size for a given precision and confidence level to estimate μ or π.

In Chapter 1, you were introduced to the field of statistics and the fact that it can be separated into two components—*descriptive statistics* that deals with the collection and summarization of data, and *inferential statistics* that involves making inferences about the unknown values of population parameters (the values of μ, σ, π, etc.) based on sampling and the values of the appropriate statistics (the values of $\overline{X}$, S, P, etc.) obtained from these samples. In Chapter 2, you were exposed to types of data and basic sampling concepts and methods. In Chapters 3 and 4, you learned how to take the data that were collected and, depending on the type of data and the purpose of the study, convert them into relevant statistics. In this and subsequent chapters, you will learn how to use these statistics to make inferences concerning certain aspects, or *parameters,* of the population. But to be able to make these inferences, you will need to know the relationship between the relevant statistic and the parameter of interest. Unlike, for example, the relationship between degrees Celsius and degrees Fahrenheit, the relationship between statistics and parameters, if they exist, are stochastic or probabilistic, requiring you to have some exposure to probability and its basic rules, expected values and variance and their rules, and important probability distributions. This exposure was obtained in Chapters 5, 6, and 7. But for these relationships to exist and for you to know what these relationships are, you need to know how the data were collected and you need to know that the data were somehow obtained randomly. For example, if you use the sample mean, $\overline{X}$, to make inferences concerning the population mean, μ, the relationship between the two would be different if you used stratified random sampling as opposed to having used simple random sampling. If you used a sampling scheme that did not involve some randomness in the selection of the sample (e.g., convenience sampling), one could seriously question if any known relationship actually existed. You will also learn that the relationship between $\overline{X}$ and μ, for example, would be different if you knew the population variance as opposed to not knowing its value, or if the population was relatively small or large. In this chapter and subsequent chapters, we will assume, unless otherwise stated, that simple random sampling is used and that the population is relatively large compared to the sample. We will look at relationships when the population variance is known and when it is unknown.

In summary, we will be collecting data, converting that data into relevant statistics, and making inferences concerning a population parameter based on the value of the statistic and its probability distribution, which we will now refer to as a *sampling distribution.* The question that now arises is: "What is the best statistic that we can use to make our inference?" Stated another way, what characteristics should this statistic have that will improve our chances of us making a good inference?

To elaborate further, suppose we are going to estimate the mean of a large population, as we normally do, by taking a simple random sample from this population and using the sample mean as an estimate of the population mean, certain natural questions arise. For example, how close would this sample mean be to the unknown population mean? Further, because every time we take such a sample, we will perhaps end up with a different sample mean. We might ask how frequently would these sample means be close to the population mean? In other words, what are the chances that our sample mean will be close to the population mean? Intuition tells us that a larger random sample would perhaps be more representative of the population and its resulting sample mean may provide a better estimate of the population mean. But, how much better? Because the sample mean values will change from sample to sample, a sample mean (in fact, any sample statistic) is considered a random variable and has a probability distribution. Study of such probability distributions (i.e., sampling distributions) will enable us to answer the questions posed above and be useful for different kinds of inferences. The following two sections discuss what characteristics make the best statistic.

8.1 Sampling Variation

A sample statistic is a *random variable* whose value depends on which population items happen to be included in the *random sample.* Some samples may represent the population well, while other samples could differ greatly from the population (particularly if the sample size is small). To illustrate sampling variation, let's draw some simple random samples from a large population of GMAT scores for MBA applicants. Assume the population *parameters* are $\mu = 520.78$ and $\sigma = 86.80$. Figure 8.1 shows a dot plot of the entire population ($N = 2,637$), which resembles a normal distribution.

FIGURE 8.1

Dot Plot of GMAT Population **GMAT**

Source: Data for 2,637 MBA applicants at a medium-sized public university located in the midwestern United States.

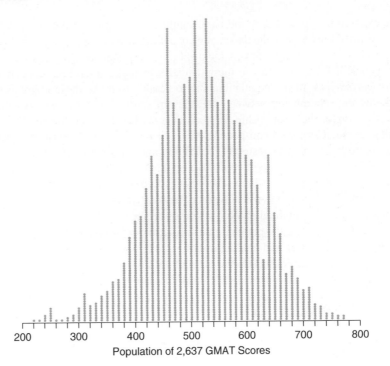

Population of 2,637 GMAT Scores

The table below shows eight random samples of $n = 5$ from this population. The samples vary because of the variability of GMAT scores in the population. Sampling variation is inevitable, yet there is a tendency for the sample means to be close to the population mean ($\mu = 520.78$), as shown in Figure 8.2. In larger samples, the sample means would tend to be even closer to μ. This phenomenon is the basis for **statistical estimation.**

Random Samples ($n = 5$) from the GMAT Score Population

Sample 1	Sample 2	Sample 3	Sample 4	Sample 5	Sample 6	Sample 7	Sample 8
490	310	500	450	420	450	490	670
580	590	450	590	640	670	450	610
440	730	510	710	470	390	590	550
580	710	570	240	530	500	640	540
430	540	610	510	640	470	650	540

$\bar{x}_1 = 504.0$ $\bar{x}_2 = 576.0$ $\bar{x}_3 = 528.0$ $\bar{x}_4 = 500.0$ $\bar{x}_5 = 540.0$ $\bar{x}_6 = 496.0$ $\bar{x}_7 = 564.0$ $\bar{x}_8 = 582.0$

From Figure 8.2 we see that the sample *means* (red markers) have much less variation than the *individual* sample items. This is because the mean is an *average*. This chapter describes

FIGURE 8.2

Dot Plots of Eight Sample Means

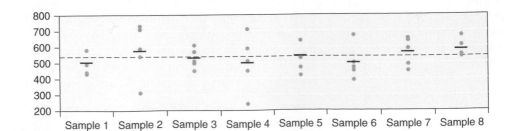

the behaviour of the sample mean and other statistical estimators of population parameters, and explains how to make *inferences* about a population that take into account four factors:

- Sampling variation (uncontrollable)
- Population variation (uncontrollable)
- Sample size (controllable)
- Desired *confidence* in the estimate (controllable)

SHOE By Jeff MacNelly

Distributed by Tribune Media Services. Used with permission.

8.2   Estimators and Sampling Distributions

Some Terminology

An **estimator** is a statistic derived from a sample in order to infer the value of a population **parameter**. For example, $\overline{X}$ is an estimator. An **estimate** is the value of the estimator in a particular sample. Table 8.1 and Figure 8.3 show some common estimators. We usually

TABLE 8.1   Examples of Estimators

Estimator	Formula	Parameter
Sample mean	$\overline{x} = \dfrac{1}{n}\sum_{i=1}^{n} x_i$, where x_i is the ith data value and n is the sample size.	μ
Sample proportion	$p = x/n$, where x is the number of successes in the sample and n is the sample size.	π
Sample standard deviation	$s = \sqrt{\dfrac{\sum_{i=1}^{n}(x_i - \overline{x})^2}{n-1}}$, where x_i is the ith data value and n is the sample size.	σ

Sampling

Population
Parameters
μ
σ
π

Sample
Estimators
$\overline{x}$
s
p

Inference

FIGURE 8.3

Sample Estimators of Population Parameters

denote a population parameter by a Greek letter (e.g., μ, σ, or π). The corresponding sample estimator is usually a capital Roman letter (e.g., $\overline{X}$, S, or P) or a Greek letter with a "hat" (e.g., $\hat{\mu}$, $\hat{\sigma}$, or $\hat{\pi}$). Statistics books may use different symbols for these measures. That's because the science of statistics developed over many decades and its founders had various ways of expressing their ideas.

Sampling Distributions and Sampling Error

Random samples vary, so an estimator is a *random variable*. The **sampling distribution** of an estimator is the probability distribution of all possible values the statistic may assume when a random sample of size n is taken. It has a probability distribution, a mean, and a variance. Statisticians derive sampling distributions by using laws of probability and high-level mathematics. But we can get a feel of a sampling distribution by drawing a large number of samples of the same size from the population, calculating the value of the desired statistic each time, and using methods from Chapters 3 and 4 to get frequency distributions and histograms. Excel is a powerful tool to do such simulations and illustrate many theoretical concepts for estimators.

Using Excel to Simulate a Sampling Distribution

We illustrate these concepts with the following Excel example when we randomly draw 500 samples, each of size 6, from a unit rectangular distribution, discussed in Section 7.2. Recall that if X follows a unit rectangular distribution, $U(0, 1)$, it can have any values from 0 to 1. That is $a = 0$, $b = 1$, and $P(c \leq X \leq d) = d - c$, where d and c lie between 0 and 1, and

$$\mu = E(X) = 0.5, \sigma = \frac{1}{\sqrt{12}} = 0.289$$

You should open your Excel program with a blank worksheet and follow these steps. Once you have completed all these steps, we will make several observations. A completed Excel worksheet is shown below.

1. Label the first row with column headings as shown in the Excel worksheet below.

2. Put numbers 1 to 500 in the first column.

3. Hide rows from row 21 to row 490. This can be done by selecting these rows, right-clicking, and selecting **HIDE**.

4. In cell B2, enter the formula =RAND(). This generates a random number between 0 and 1.

5. Copy this formula, and paste it to range B2:G501. We have, through these steps, generated 500 random samples, each of size 6. Row 2 has the first sample of 6 observations, row 3 has the second sample, and so on.

6. In cell H2, enter the formula AVERAGE(A2:G2). This creates an average (sample mean) of the first sample.

7. Copy this formula and paste it to range H2:H501. Thus column H contains 500 sample means. We first want to create a frequency distribution (histogram) of these 500 sample means in the table in range J1:L12.

8. First, fill in columns J and K of this table with numbers given in the Excel worksheet below. Now select the range L2:L11, enter the "array" formula =FREQUENCY (H2:H501, K2:K11), and press Ctrl + Shift + Enter. This means while keeping Ctrl and Shift keys pressed, press the Enter key.

9. You should now see in the column labelled "Frequency" frequencies of these 500 sample means.

10. Each time you press the F9 (Refresh) key, you will have 500 new random samples, and new frequencies.

11. You can use the Chart Wizard to create both the histogram and X-Y scatter plot of this frequency distribution. As you press the F9 key again and again, the figures will change to reflect a new frequency distribution.

	A	B	C	D	E	F	G	H	I	J	K	L	M	N	O
1	Sample #	Obs. 1	Obs. 2	Obs. 3	Obs. 4	Obs. 5	Obs. 6	Sample mean		From	To	Frequency			
2	1	0.464	0.382	0.779	0.630	0.146	0.881	0.547		0	0.1	0			
3	2	0.570	0.947	0.218	0.407	0.515	0.145	0.467		0.1	0.2	3			
4	3	0.842	0.463	0.678	0.508	0.110	0.666	0.545		0.2	0.3	15			
5	4	0.306	0.012	0.314	0.029	0.760	0.175	0.266		0.3	0.4	97			
6	5	0.960	0.836	0.726	0.326	0.349	0.926	0.687		0.4	0.5	145			
7	6	0.468	0.270	0.486	0.618	0.198	0.407	0.408		0.5	0.6	131			
8	7	0.998	0.691	0.224	0.460	0.089	0.064	0.421		0.6	0.7	82			
9	8	0.232	0.468	0.578	0.277	0.830	0.758	0.524		0.7	0.8	24			
10	9	0.365	0.494	0.574	0.343	0.093	0.885	0.459		0.8	0.9	3			
11	10	0.216	0.629	0.027	0.471	0.827	0.399	0.428		0.9	1	0			
12	11	0.284	0.706	0.605	0.056	0.207	0.315	0.362		Total		500			
13	12	0.852	0.498	0.109	0.292	0.010	0.993	0.459							
14	13	0.765	0.051	0.968	0.751	0.880	0.553	0.661							
15	14	0.198	0.853	0.969	0.199	0.901	0.382	0.584							
16	15	0.386	0.009	0.474	0.051	0.848	0.169	0.323							
17	16	0.902	0.541	0.693	0.535	0.467	0.823	0.660							
18	17	0.364	0.735	0.135	0.473	0.285	0.909	0.484							
19	18	0.124	0.855	0.989	0.824	0.121	0.943	0.643							
20	19	0.697	0.656	0.648	0.060	0.381	0.455	0.483							
491	490	0.044	0.500	0.994	0.694	0.998	0.509	0.623							
492	491	0.936	0.465	0.106	0.299	0.866	0.174	0.474							
493	492	0.792	0.990	0.868	0.825	0.444	0.202	0.687							
494	493	0.461	0.740	0.000	0.464	0.707	0.244	0.436							
495	494	0.318	0.951	0.311	0.237	0.876	0.302	0.499							
496	495	0.311	0.248	0.367	0.395	0.671	0.220	0.369							
497	496	0.151	0.608	0.250	0.747	0.033	0.912	0.450							
498	497	0.749	0.839	0.272	0.210	0.137	0.260	0.411							
499	498	0.208	0.402	0.539	0.692	0.462	0.533	0.473							
500	499	0.932	0.617	0.878	0.964	0.118	0.157	0.611							
501	500	0.353	0.126	0.213	0.214	0.474	0.255	0.272							
502	Mean	0.513	0.484	0.495	0.495	0.483	0.516	0.498							
503	StdDev	0.288	0.284	0.283	0.293	0.290	0.292	0.121							
504															
505															
506															
507															
508															

Frequency

We can now make several observations based on this Excel worksheet.

1. This frequency distribution gives an approximate sampling distribution of the sample mean $\overline{X}$, an estimator of the population mean $\mu\ (= 0.5)$. Note that $\overline{X}$ is a random variable as its value (called an estimate) varies from sample to sample.

2. The average of these 500 sample means is 0.498 (in cell H502) for these 500 samples. Note that it is quite close to the population mean μ. Theory says that $E(\overline{X}) = \mu (= 0.5)$.

3. The standard deviation of these 500 sample means is 0.121 (in cell H502). Theory says that

$$\sigma_{\overline{X}} = \frac{\sigma}{\sqrt{n}} = \frac{0.289}{\sqrt{6}} = 0.118$$

4. We can make approximate probability statements about $\overline{X}$. For example, what is the probability that $\overline{X}$ is between 0.2 and 0.4? Looking at the frequency distribution, we see out of 500 sample means, 112 $(= 15 + 97)$ fall in this range. The relative frequency 0.224 $(= 112/500)$ is the approximate probability.

A Closer Look

Although theory says that $E(\overline{X}) = \mu$ and $\sigma_x = \dfrac{\sigma}{\sqrt{n}}$ where μ and σ are the mean and standard deviation of the population, respectively, using the rules of expected values and variances would allow us to reach the same conclusions. In Chapter 6, four of these rules were:

$$E(aX + b) = aE(X) + b$$
$$E(X_1 + X_2 + \ldots + X_n) = E(X_1) + E(X_2) + \ldots + E(X_n)$$

$$V(aX + b) = a^2 V(X)$$
$$V(X_1 + X_2 + \ldots + X_n) = V(X_1) + V(X_2) + \ldots + V(X_n)$$

if $X_1, X_2, \ldots, X_n$ are independent

Using the combination of the first two rules:

$$E(\overline{X}) = E\left(\frac{1}{n}\sum_{i=1}^{n}x_i\right) = \frac{1}{n}E\left(\sum_{i=1}^{n}X_i\right) = \frac{1}{n}[E(X_1) + E(X_2) + \ldots + E(X_n)]$$
$$= \frac{1}{n}(\mu_1 + \mu_2 + \ldots + \mu_n) = \frac{1}{n}(\mu + \mu + \ldots + \mu) = \frac{1}{n}(n\mu)$$
$$= \mu$$

And using a combination of the latter two rules and the fact that the X_i's are independent of one another:

$$V(\overline{X}) = V\left(\frac{1}{n}\sum_{i=1}^{n}x_i\right) = \left(\frac{1}{n}\right)^2 V\left(\sum_{i=1}^{n}X_i\right) = \frac{1}{n^2}[V(X_1) + V(X_2) + \ldots + V(X_n)]$$
$$= \frac{1}{n^2}(\sigma_1^2 + \sigma_2^2 + \ldots + \sigma_n^2) = \frac{1}{n^2}(\sigma^2 + \sigma^2 + \ldots + \sigma^2) = \frac{1}{n^2}(n\sigma^2)$$
$$= \frac{\sigma^2}{n}$$

and

$$\sigma_{\overline{X}} = \sqrt{V(\overline{X})} = \sqrt{\frac{\sigma^2}{n}} = \frac{\sigma}{\sqrt{n}}$$

Bias

The **bias** is the difference between the expected value (i.e., the average value) of the estimator and the true parameter value:

$$\text{bias} = E(\hat{\theta}) - \theta \tag{8.1}$$

An estimator is *unbiased* if $E(\hat{\theta}) = \theta$. Thus, an **unbiased estimator** neither overstates nor understates the true parameter *on average*. That is, $\hat{\theta} = \theta$, on average. *The key words are "on average."* If you look again at the Excel worksheet developed above, $\overline{x}$ values change from sample to sample; some of them are below μ and some of them are above μ, but the average of these 500 sample means gets quite close to 0.5.

To illustrate the concept of unbiasedness, consider an analogy with target shooting, illustrated in Figure 8.4. An expert whose rifle sights are correctly aligned will produce a target pattern like one on the left. The same expert shooting a rifle with misaligned sights might produce the pattern on the right. There is sample variation, but the unbiased estimator is correctly

FIGURE 8.4

Illustration of Bias

Chapter 8

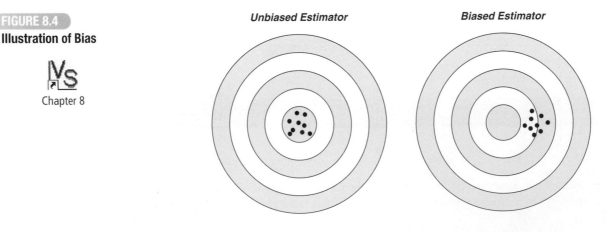

Unbiased Estimator　　　　*Biased Estimator*

aimed. Thus, the shooting pattern in the left figure corresponds to different estimates of an unbiased estimator, whereas the one of the right corresponds to different estimates of a biased estimator.

Some samples may happen to hit closer to the bull's eye than others, but at least an unbiased estimator on average gets to the bull's eye.

You cannot observe bias in a sample because you do not know the true population parameter, but bias can be studied mathematically or by simulation experiments (e.g., the Excel worksheet above, and Visual Statistics). Statisticians have shown (and previously discussed rules of expected values can easily show) that the sample mean $\overline{X}$ and the sample proportion P are unbiased estimators for μ and π, respectively. Similarly, S^2 is an unbiased estimate of σ^2. That is,

$$E(\overline{X}) = \mu, \ E(P) = \pi, \ E(S^2) = \sigma^2$$

Note that we generally represent random variables with capital letters, and particular values of these random variables with small letters. Because estimators are random variables, they are named with capital letters (e.g. $\overline{X}$, S^2, and P), and estimates, being values of these estimators, are designated with small letters (e.g. $\overline{x}$, s^2, and, p, respectively).

Efficiency

Efficiency refers to the variance of the estimator's sampling distribution. Smaller variance means a more efficient estimator. Figure 8.5 shows two unbiased estimators. Both patterns are centred on the bull's eye, but the estimator on the left has less variation. You cannot assess efficiency from one sample, but it can be studied either mathematically or by simulation (e.g., Visual Statistics). Statisticians have proved that, for a normal distribution, $\overline{X}$ and S^2 are the most efficient estimators of μ and σ^2, respectively (i.e., no other estimators can have smaller variance for the same sample size). Similarly, the sample proportion P, is the most efficient estimator of the population proportion, π. That is one reason these statistics are widely used.

Consistency

A **consistent estimator** converges toward the parameter being estimated as the sample size increases. That is, the sample distribution collapses on the true parameter, as illustrated in Figure 8.6. It seems logical that in larger samples $\overline{x}$ ought to be closer to μ, p ought to be closer to π, and s ought to be closer to σ. In fact, it can be shown that the variances of these three estimators diminish as n increases, so all are consistent estimators. Figure 8.6 illustrates the importance of a large sample, because in a large sample your estimate is likely to be closer to θ.

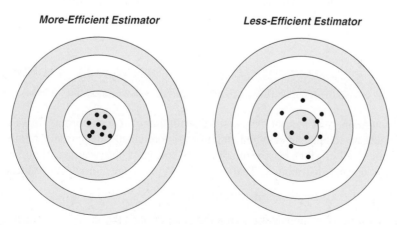

More-Efficient Estimator *Less-Efficient Estimator*

FIGURE 8.5

Illustration of Efficiency

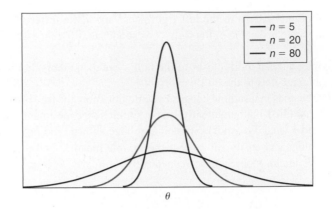

8.3 Sample Mean and the Central Limit Theorem

Chapter 7

Consider the sample mean $\overline{X}$ used to estimate the population mean μ. Our ultimate objective is to use the sampling distribution of $\overline{X}$ to say something about the mean of the population that we are studying. To describe the sampling distribution we need to know the mean, variance, and shape of the distribution. As we've already learned, the sample mean is an unbiased estimator for μ; therefore,

$$E(\overline{X}) = \mu \text{ (expected value of the mean)} \tag{8.2}$$

We've also learned that the value of $\overline{X}$ will change whenever we take a different sample. And as long as our samples are *random samples,* we should feel confident that the only type of error we will have in our estimating process is **sampling error,** which is the difference between the values of $\overline{X}$ and μ. The sampling error of the sample mean is described by its standard deviation. This value has a special name, the **standard error of the mean.** Using some of the previously discussed rules for variances (and standard deviations), you will notice that the standard error of the mean decreases as the sample size increases:

$$\sigma_{\overline{X}} = \frac{\sigma}{\sqrt{n}} \text{ (standard error of the mean)} \tag{8.3}$$

Suppose the average price, μ, of a 2 GB MP3 player is $80.00 with a standard deviation, σ, equal to $10.00. What will be the mean and standard error of $\overline{X}$ from a sample of 20 MP3 players?

$$\mu_{\overline{X}} = \$80.00, \quad \sigma_{\overline{X}} = \frac{\$10.00}{\sqrt{20}} = \$2.24$$

Furthermore, if we know that the population is normal, then the sample mean $\overline{X}$ also follows a normal distribution for any sample size, but the distribution of $\overline{X}$ has a smaller standard deviation, namely $2.24 as compared to $10 for the original population.

A Closer Look

If the population, X, is normal, why is the distribution of $\overline{X}$ also normal? If we create a new variable by adding and/or subtracting two or more independent normal random variables, some or all of which may be multiplied by constants, the resulting random variable also has a normal distribution. That is, if $X_1, X_2, \ldots$ are normal and independent, $Y = aX_1 + bX_2 + \ldots$ is also normal. Because $\overline{X} = \frac{1}{n}\sum_{i-1}^{n}X_i = \frac{1}{n}X_1 + \frac{1}{n}X_2 + \cdots + \frac{1}{n}X_n$ is such a variable if the population size is much larger than the sample size, then $\overline{X}$ has a normal distribution.

Our Excel worksheet in Section 8.2, above, developed for simulating a sampling distribution of $\overline{X}$, illustrates this point. This random variable, X, follows a uniform distribution with mean $\mu = 0.5$ and standard deviation $\sigma = 0.289$. Each of the six columns B through G could be thought of as a sample of 500 observations of X. The sample standard deviation, s, for these six samples is given in cells B503 though G503, and all are close to 0.289. Now column H could be viewed as a sample of 500 observations of $\overline{X}$. The standard deviation of these 500 observations is 0.121, given in cell H503. This value is much smaller than 0.289, and very close to $\sigma_{\overline{X}}$, which was calculated to be 0.118.

For you to better understand the implications of this discussion, it is very important that we explain it further with the following example.

EXAMPLE 1

Morning Coffee Rush

During the morning rush hour at a local Tim Hortons, assume that X, the time between placing and picking up the order, is normally distributed with a mean μ of 3 minutes and a standard deviation σ of 0.8 minutes; that is, $X \sim N(3, 0.8)$ or $Z = \dfrac{X - \mu}{\sigma} = \dfrac{X - 3}{0.8} \sim N(0, 1)$.

1. What is the probability that the time that elapsed between placing an order and picking up the order would lie somewhere between 2 and 4 minutes?

$$P(2 < X < 4) = P\left(\frac{2 - 3}{0.8} < \frac{X - \mu}{\sigma} < \frac{4 - 3}{0.8}\right) = P(-1.25 < Z < 1.25) = 0.7887.$$

So there is about a 79 percent chance that the customer will be served in between 2 and 4 minutes.

2. What is the probability that the *average time* between placing orders and picking up orders for four randomly selected customers lies somewhere between 2 and 4 minutes?

Now we have to find the probability that the sample mean $\overline{X}$ is between 2 and 4. Because the population is normal, $\overline{X}$ also follows a normal distribution. Because $\overline{X}$ is an unbiased estimator of μ, $E(\overline{X}) = \mu = 3$. According to Equation 8.3, we calculate the standard deviation of $\overline{X}$ as $\sigma_{\overline{X}} = \dfrac{\sigma}{\sqrt{n}} = \dfrac{0.8}{\sqrt{4}} = 0.4$. Thus, $\overline{X}$ follows a normal distribution with a mean of 3 and a standard deviation of 0.4, and we could write this as $N \sim (3, 0.4)$ or $Z = \dfrac{\overline{X} - \mu}{\sigma_{\overline{X}}} = \dfrac{\overline{X} - \mu}{\sigma/\sqrt{n}} = \dfrac{\overline{X} - 3}{0.8/\sqrt{4}} = \dfrac{\overline{X} - 3}{0.4}$. Now,

$$P(2 < \overline{X} < 4) = P\left(\frac{2 - 3}{0.4} < \frac{\overline{X} - \mu}{\sigma_{\overline{X}}} < \frac{4 - 3}{0.4}\right) = P(-2.5 < Z < 2.5) = 0.9876$$

Thus, there is about a 99 percent chance that the average service time of these four customers will be between 2 and 4 minutes.

3. What is the probability that the average time between placing orders and picking up orders for 16 randomly selected customers lies somewhere between 2 and 4 minutes?

Now $n = 16$. Thus, $\overline{X} \sim N\left(\mu, \dfrac{\sigma}{\sqrt{n}}\right) = N\left(3, \dfrac{0.8}{\sqrt{16}}\right) = N(3, 0.2)$ or $Z = \dfrac{\overline{X} - 3}{0.2}$ and

$$P(2 < \overline{X} < 4) = P\left(\frac{2 - 3}{0.2} < \frac{\overline{X} - \mu}{\sigma_{\overline{X}}} < \frac{4 - 3}{0.2}\right) = P(-5 < Z < 5) \approx 1$$

Thus, we are practically 100 percent certain that the average service time of these 16 customers will be between 2 and 4 minutes.

Note: Instead of using "<" to answer both questions, we could have used "≤" and, because X and $\overline{X}$ are continuous random variables, we would have arrived at the same probabilities.

Three normal bells in the figure below show the areas from 2 to 4 minutes under each of the three normal "roofs." Let us make some observations about these three normal distributions. If we take a single customer and measure his/her service time ($n = 1$), the sample mean is just X, and the standard deviation of the sample mean is the same as the standard deviation of the population, which is 0.8 or $Z = \dfrac{\overline{X} - \mu}{\sigma/\sqrt{n}} = \dfrac{\overline{X} - 3}{0.8/\sqrt{1}} = \dfrac{X - 3}{0.8}$. For a sample of size 4, the standard deviation of the sample mean (standard error) is 0.4; for a sample of size 16, the standard error is 0.2 (half of what it was before). That is, to halve the standard error, we have to quadruple the sample size. The normal-bell will keep collapsing at the true population mean μ as the sample size keeps increasing.

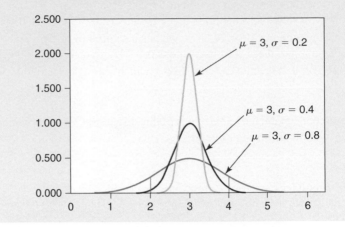

Section Exercises

Note: Problems marked * are harder or rely on optional material from this chapter.

8.1 Find the standard error of the mean for each sampling situation. What happens to the standard error each time you quadruple the sample size? (LO 1)
   a. $\sigma = 32, n = 4$
   b. $\sigma = 32, n = 16$
   c. $\sigma = 32, n = 64$

8.2 Find the 95 percent range for the sample mean, assuming that each sample is from a normal population. (LO 3)
   a. $\mu = 200, \sigma = 12, n = 36$
   b. $\mu = 1{,}000, \sigma = 15, n = 9$
   c. $\mu = 50, \sigma = 1, n = 25$

8.3* The diameter of bushings turned out by a manufacturing process is a normally distributed random variable with a mean of 4.035 mm and a standard deviation of 0.005 mm. The inspection procedure requires a sample of 25 bushings once an hour. (a) Within what range should 95 percent of the bushing diameters fall? (b) Within what range should 95 percent of the sample *means* fall? (c) What conclusion would you reach if you saw a sample mean of 4.020? A sample mean of 4.055? (LO 3)

8.4* A manufacturer of batteries for a particular MP3 player claims that its batteries, when fully charged, will last for 16 hours of play time before they need recharging. If this claim is true, if the standard deviation of play time is 1.5 hours, and if play time has a normal distribution, what is the probability that (a) a randomly selected, fully charged battery will last less than 15 hours? (b) Four randomly selected, fully charged batteries will last less than 15 hours on average? (c) Sixteen randomly selected, fully charged batteries will last less than 15 hours on average? If each of the above results occurred, which result could best be used to question the claim of this manufacturer? Explain. (LO 3)

Central Limit Theorem for a Mean

In the above discussion of the sampling distribution of $\overline{X}$, it was assumed that the population, X, had a normal distribution. Unfortunately, the population may not have a normal distribution, or we may simply not know what the population distribution looks like. What can we do

Central Limit Theorem for a Mean

If a random sample of size n is drawn from a population with mean μ and standard deviation σ, the distribution of the sample mean $\overline{X}$ approaches a normal distribution with mean μ and standard deviation $\sigma_{\overline{X}} = \sigma/\sqrt{n}$ as the sample size increases.

in these circumstances? We can use one of the most fundamental theorems of statistics: the Central Limit Theorem.

The **Central Limit Theorem (CLT)** is a powerful result that allows us to approximate the shape of the sampling distribution of $\overline{X}$ even when we don't know what the population looks like.

Let us first give an intuitive explanation of the CLT. Consider an experiment of drawing a random sample of n observations from some given population (not necessarily normal) and calculating the sample mean. Suppose you repeat this experiment by drawing another random sample from the population and calculating the new sample mean. If you repeat this experiment a large number of times, the average of all the sample means computed will be close to the population mean μ. Further, if the sample size n is sufficiently large, and if you made a histogram of these different sample means, this histogram would form the shape of a normal distribution. Thus, even if the population is not normal, we can make probability statements about $\overline{X}$ by using a normal distribution, provided our sample size is sufficiently large. You can do such experiments using Excel but a better approach is to use Visual Statistics, an e-book that comes on the CD accompanying your textbook.

Here are three important facts about the sample mean.

1. If the population is exactly normal, the sample mean follows a normal distribution centred at μ regardless of sample size, with a standard error equal to $\sigma/\sqrt{n}$.

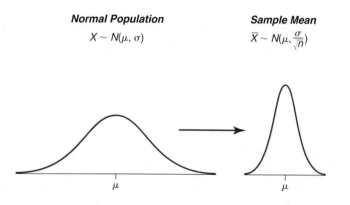

Normal Population

$X \sim N(\mu, \sigma)$

Sample Mean

$\overline{X} \sim N(\mu, \frac{\sigma}{\sqrt{n}})$

2. As sample size n increases, the distribution of sample means narrows in on the population mean μ (i.e., the *standard error of the mean* $\sigma_{\overline{X}} = \sigma/\sqrt{n}$ approaches zero).

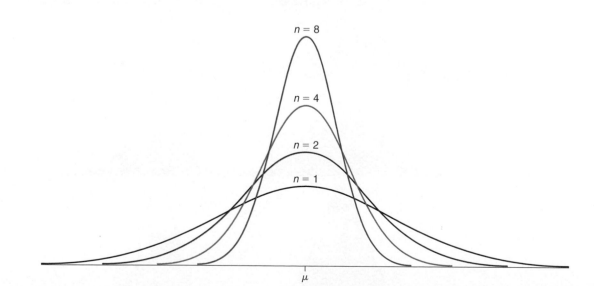

3. By the Central Limit Theorem, if the sample size is large enough, the sample means will have approximately a normal distribution even if the population is *not* normal.

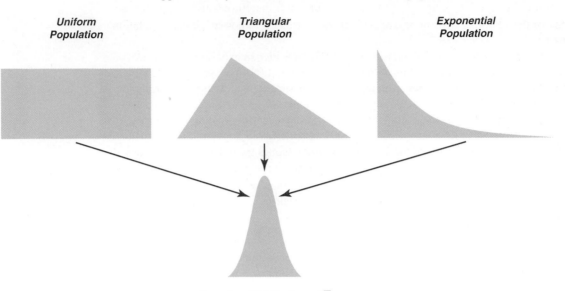

Sampling Distribution of $\overline{X}$

The left part of Figure 8.7 shows histograms of the actual means of many samples drawn from a uniform population, whereas the right part of this figure shows histograms of the actual means of many samples drawn from a skewed population. For symmetric populations,

FIGURE 8.7

Illustrations of Central Limit Theorem

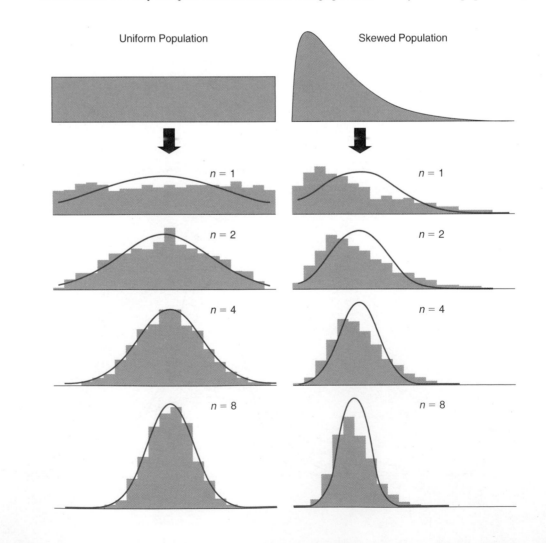

the histogram approaches a normal distribution for much smaller n in comparison to skewed population. More skewed the population, the larger the n needed to make $\overline{X}$ behave like a normal random variable. Generally, $n \geq 30$ is enough to ensure normality, but for highly skewed populations, even $n \geq 30$ may not ensure normality. As a rule of thumb if $n \geq 30$, we can assume that $\overline{X}$ behaves like a normal random variable.

Figure 8.7 shows histograms of the actual means of many samples drawn from this skewed population.

Our Excel worksheet, developed in Section 8.2 above, illustrates that if the original population is symmetric, then even a small sample provides an approximate normal distribution. In that example, $n = 6$, and still the scatter diagram there suggests that we get an approximate normal distribution for $\overline{X}$.

Let us illustrate use of the Central Limit Theorem with an example.

EXAMPLE 2
Border Crossings

Suppose we change the scenario of Example 1 and observe X, the time taken for a Canadian car to clear U.S. customs at the Canada–U.S. border at the Peace Arch Bridge in Surrey, British Columbia. Assume the average time taken is $\mu = 15$ minutes, and the standard deviation is $\sigma = 18$ minutes. We again ask three questions similar to the ones we asked in Example 1.

1. Suppose we observe a random car crossing the border. What is the probability that the time to clear customs will be between 12 and 18 minutes?
2. Suppose we observe six random cars crossing the border. What is the probability that the average time to clear customs will be between 12 and 18 minutes?
3. Suppose we observe 36 random cars crossing the border. What is the probability that the average time to clear customs will be between 12 and 18 minutes?

We cannot answer Questions 1 and 2 because we do not know the distribution of the population of customs-clearance times and our sample is quite small. In fact, we know the distribution of customs-clearance times is right-skewed as some cars can take a large amount of time to clear customs. This observation is also supported by the fact that σ is large compared to the value of μ. However, we can use the Central Limit Theorem to answer Question 3 because $n = 36$, and we assume that $\overline{X}$ follows approximately a normal distribution with $E(\overline{X}) = \mu = 15$, and $\sigma_{\overline{X}} = \dfrac{\sigma}{\sqrt{n}} = \dfrac{18}{\sqrt{36}} = 3$. Hence,

$$P(12 < \overline{X} < 18) = P\left(\frac{12 - 15}{3} < \frac{\overline{X} - \mu}{\sigma_{\overline{X}}} < \frac{18 - 15}{3}\right) \approx P(-1 < Z < 1) = 0.6826$$

8.4 Confidence Interval for a Mean (μ) with Known σ

What Is a Confidence Interval?

Chapter 9

A sample mean $\overline{x}$ calculated from a random sample $x_1, x_2, \ldots, x_n$ is a **point estimate** of the population mean μ. Because samples vary, we need to indicate our uncertainty about the true value of μ. Based on our knowledge of the sampling distribution (using the Central Limit Theorem) we create an *interval estimate* by specifying the *probability* that the interval will contain μ. The probability that the interval contains the true mean is usually expressed as a percentage, called the **confidence level** (commonly 90, 95, or 99 percent). The interval estimate is then called the **confidence interval.**

A confidence interval is constructed around the point estimate $\overline{x}$ by adding and subtracting a **margin of error.** The margin of error depends on the sample size n, the standard deviation σ of the population, and the confidence level (generally assumed to be 95%) that we seek.

Let us explain how to calculate this margin of error and how this allows us to associate a confidence level with the interval obtained.

Consider Example 2, above, where we assumed that μ, the average time to clear customs, was 15 minutes. Suppose this μ is unknown and we plan to take a random sample of

36 ($n = 36$) custom-clearance times and use the sample mean $\overline{X}$ to estimate this unknown μ. As we saw before,

$$E(\overline{X}) = \mu, \sigma_{\overline{X}} = \frac{\sigma}{\sqrt{n}} = \frac{18}{\sqrt{36}} = 3$$

Thus, $\overline{X}$ follows a normal distribution with mean μ and standard deviation 3. The figure below shows the distribution. The normal bell is centred at μ (unknown) with a standard deviation $\sigma = 3$.

Now from Appendix C, we know that $z = 1.96$ corresponds to an area of 0.4750. That is, $P(0 < Z < 1.96) = 0.4750$. By symmetry, we have $P(-1.96 < Z < 1.96) = 2(0.4750) = 0.95$. That is, we cover an area of 95 percent within ± 1.96 standard deviations of the mean. So, for $\overline{X}$, 95 percent of its values must be within $\pm 1.96\sigma_{\overline{X}} = \pm 1.96(3) = \pm 5.88$ of the population mean. Mathematically, we can write this as

$$P(\mu - 5.88 < \overline{X} < \mu + 5.88) = 0.95$$

The following figure illustrates this point.

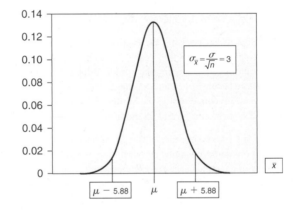

By rearranging, the above can also be written as

$$P(\overline{X} - 5.88 < \mu < \overline{X} + 5.88) = 0.95$$

Thus, our 95 percent confidence interval for μ is $\overline{X} \pm 5.88$, and 5.88 is the margin of error. A 95 percent confidence interval is also sometimes stated as a confidence interval with a *confidence coefficient of 0.95*. How do we interpret this interval? Suppose we take a random sample of 36 customs-clearance times and find that $\overline{X} = 19.6$ minutes. Then our confidence interval for μ will be 19.60 ± 5.88. That is, we claim that we are 95 percent confident that the unknown population mean μ is somewhere between 13.72 and 25.48 minutes. Suppose now we take another random sample of 36 customs-clearance times, and this time our sample mean turns out to be 15.9 minutes. Then our 95 percent confidence interval will now be from 10.02 minutes to 21.78 minutes, and again we will claim to be 95 percent confident that population mean μ is somewhere between 10.02 and 21.78 minutes. Is μ between 13.72 and 25.48, or between 10.02 and 21.78? We don't know. The answer to each question could be either yes or no! By stating a confidence level of less than 100 percent, we are admitting that μ may lie outside this interval. So how do we interpret and justify 95 percent confidence with any interval obtained in this manner?

From the probability statement above, we can say that if we repeated this sampling process a large number of times, then about 95 percent of the intervals so obtained would contain μ. Thus, if we pick one of these large number of intervals at random, there is a 95 percent chance that the picked interval is the "right one" (i.e., μ falls in the obtained interval).

The following figure illustrates this point. Out of the four repeated samples, three (first, third, and fourth) resulted in correct intervals, as the intervals obtained crossed the μ-line. Approximately 95 percent of such intervals would cross the μ-line.

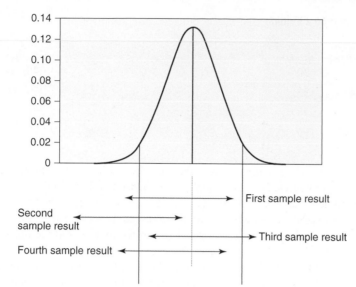

What if we wanted a 99 percent confidence interval for μ, still working with a sample size $n = 36$? We used $\overline{X} \pm 1.96\sigma_{\overline{X}}$ to obtain a 95 percent confidence interval. So we want to capture an area of 99 percent, as opposed to 95 percent, around μ. If we use Appendix C for an area of $0.99/2 = 0.4950$, the closest z value that corresponds to this area is either 2.57 or 2.58. With $z = 2.57$, we get an area of from 0 to z of 0.4949, and when we use $z = 2.58$, we get an area of 0.4951. So we take the average of 2.57 and 2.58, and use 2.575 to find our margin of error, and the formula for 99 percent confidence interval becomes

$$\overline{X} \pm 2.575\sigma_{\overline{X}} = \overline{X} \pm 2.575\frac{\sigma}{\sqrt{n}} = \overline{X} \pm 2.575(3) = \overline{X} \pm 7.725$$

To develop a general formula for a confidence interval for μ, recall the notation z_A that we introduced in Chapter 7. It corresponds to the z value corresponding to right-tail area A. Thus

$$z_{0.025} = 1.96, z_{0.005} = 2.575$$

So, let us assume that we want a confidence interval for μ with a confidence coefficient of $(1 - \alpha)$, or equivalently a $100(1 - \alpha)$ percent confidence interval for μ. That is, we want to capture an area of $(1 - \alpha)$ around μ. The remaining area is α, half of which $(\alpha/2)$ is the right-tail area, and the other half of which is the left-tail area. According to our definition, the z value for this right-tail area of $\alpha/2$ is $z_{\alpha/2}$. So our general formula becomes

$$\overline{X} \pm z_{\alpha/2}\sigma_{\overline{X}} = \overline{X} \pm z_{\alpha/2}\frac{\sigma}{\sqrt{n}}$$

Let us apply this formula to find a 90 percent confidence interval for unknown μ—the average time to cross the border. Then $1 - \alpha = 0.9$. So $\alpha = 0.10$, and $\alpha/2 = 0.05$. The z value for the right-tail (upper-tail) area of 0.05 is 1.645. So $z_{0.05} = 1.645$. Hence, our 90 percent confidence interval for μ is

$$\overline{X} \pm z_{\alpha/2}\frac{\sigma}{\sqrt{n}} = \overline{X} \pm 1.645\frac{18}{36} = \overline{X} \pm 1.645(3) = \overline{X} \pm 4.935$$

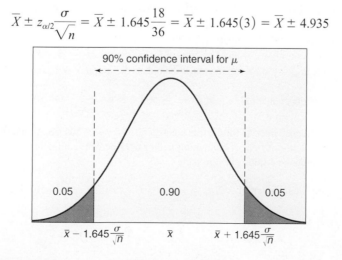

TABLE 8.2 Common z Values

Confidence Level	z
90	$z_{0.05} = 1.645$
95	$z_{0.025} = 1.960$
98	$z_{0.01} = 2.330$
99	$z_{0.005} = 2.575$

The middle area of the curve corresponds to the confidence level, 0.90. The remaining area is divided into two symmetrical tails each equal to $(1 - 0.90)/2$ or 0.05. Table 8.2 shows z values for common confidence levels.

You might also see the confidence interval expressed as a range $\mu_{\text{lower}} < \mu < \mu_{\text{upper}}$. The lower confidence limit is the smallest value of μ that we expect, and the upper confidence limit is the largest value of μ that we expect.

The rule of thumb that $n \geq 30$ to assume normality is sufficient for a symmetric or slightly skewed population without outliers. However, a larger n may be needed if you are sampling from a strongly skewed population or one with outliers.

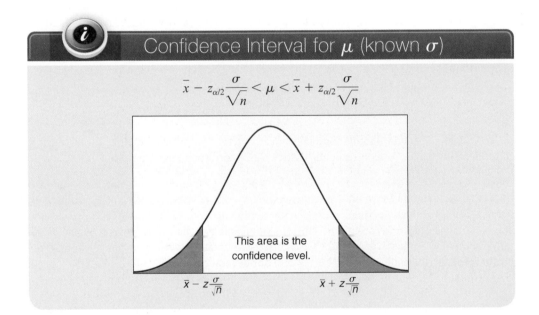

Confidence Interval for μ (known σ)

$$\bar{x} - z_{\alpha/2}\frac{\sigma}{\sqrt{n}} < \mu < \bar{x} + z_{\alpha/2}\frac{\sigma}{\sqrt{n}}$$

This area is the confidence level.

$$\bar{x} - z\frac{\sigma}{\sqrt{n}} \qquad \bar{x} + z\frac{\sigma}{\sqrt{n}}$$

EXAMPLE 3

Bottle Filling: Confidence Intervals for μ

The amount of fill in a half-litre bottle of Diet Coke is normally distributed. From past experience, the process standard deviation is known to be $\sigma = 1.20$ ml. The mean amount of fill can be adjusted. A sample of 10 bottles gives a sample mean of $\bar{X} = 503.4$ ml. Because the population is normal, the sample mean is a normally distributed random variable for any sample size, so we can use the z distribution to construct a confidence interval.

For a 90 percent confidence interval estimate for μ, we insert $z = 1.645$ in the formula along with the sample mean $\bar{X} = 503.4$ and the known standard deviation $\sigma = 1.20$:

$$90\% \text{ confidence interval: } \bar{x} \pm z_{0.05}\frac{\sigma}{\sqrt{n}} = 503.4 \pm 1.645\frac{1.20}{\sqrt{10}} = 503.4 \pm 0.62$$

The 90 percent confidence interval for the true mean is $502.78 < \mu < 504.02$. An interval constructed this way has a probability of 0.90 of containing μ. For a 95 percent confidence interval, we would use $z = 1.960$, keeping everything else the same:

$$95\% \text{ confidence interval: } \bar{x} \pm z_{0.025}\frac{\sigma}{\sqrt{n}} = 503.4 \pm 1.96\frac{1.20}{\sqrt{10}} = 503.4 \pm 0.74$$

The 95 percent confidence interval for μ is $502.66 < \mu < 504.14$. There is a probability of 0.95 that an interval constructed this way will contain μ. For a 99 percent confidence interval, we would use $z = 2.576$ in the formula, keeping everything else the same:

$$99\% \text{ confidence interval: } \bar{x} \pm z_{0.005}\frac{\sigma}{\sqrt{n}} = 503.4 \pm 2.576\frac{1.2}{\sqrt{10}} = 503.4 \pm 0.98$$

The 99 percent confidence interval for μ is $502.42 < \mu < 504.38$. There is a probability of 0.99 that an interval created in this manner will enclose μ.

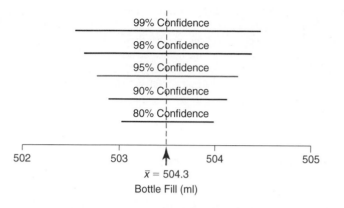

FIGURE 8.8

Confidence Intervals for True Mean μ

Choosing a Confidence Level

You might be tempted to assume that a higher confidence level gives a "better" estimate. However, *a higher confidence level leads to a wider confidence interval* (as shown in the preceding calculations). Thus, greater confidence implies *loss of precision* as shown in Figure 8.8. A 95 percent confidence level is often used because it is a reasonable compromise between confidence and precision. It is clear that for a fixed sample size, a larger confidence means less precision (resulting in a wider confidence interval). A well-known adage says "There's No Such Thing as a Free Lunch." For the same effort, to get more of one thing that we like, we usually have to live with less of another thing that we also like. Making decisions requires trading off one desirable against another.

Interpretation   A confidence interval either *does* or *does not* contain μ. But the confidence level quantifies the *risk*. If 100 statisticians were to use exactly this procedure to create 95 percent confidence intervals, approximately 95 of their intervals *would* contain μ, while approximately 5 unlucky ones *would not* contain μ. Because you only do it once, you don't know if you captured the true mean or not. For the bottle-filling example, lower bounds for all five of the confidence intervals shown in Figure 8.8 are well above 500, indicating that the mean of the bottle-filling process is safely above the required minimum half-litre (500 ml).

Is σ Ever Known?

Yes, but not very often. In quality control applications with ongoing manufacturing processes, it may be reasonable to assume that σ stays the same over time. The type of confidence interval just seen is therefore important because it is used to construct *control charts* to track the mean of a process (such as bottle filling) over time. However, the case of unknown σ is more typical, and will be examined in the next section.

Section Exercises

8.5   Find a confidence interval for μ assuming that each sample is from a normal population. (LO 3)
   a. $\bar{x} = 14, \sigma = 4, n = 5$, 90 percent confidence
   b. $\bar{x} = 37, \sigma = 5, n = 15$, 99 percent confidence
   c. $\bar{x} = 121, \sigma = 15, n = 25$, 95 percent confidence

8.6   Prof. Hardtack gave three exams last semester in a large lecture class. The standard deviation $\sigma = 7$ was the same on all three exams, and scores were normally distributed. Below are scores for 10 randomly chosen students on each exam. Find the 95 percent confidence interval for the mean score on each exam. Do the confidence intervals overlap? If so, what does this suggest? (LO 3)   **Exams1**

   Exam 1: 71, 69, 78, 80, 72, 76, 70, 82, 76, 76
   Exam 2: 77, 66, 71, 73, 94, 85, 83, 72, 89, 80
   Exam 3: 67, 69, 64, 65, 72, 59, 64, 70, 64, 56

8.7   Bob said, "About 95 percent of the individual X values will lie within the 95 percent confidence interval for the mean." Explain why his statement is *incorrect*. (LO 3)

8.8   Most North American dealerships charge customers a fixed number of hours for specific servicing packages, whether or not the actual service time is quicker or slower than that fixed number of hours. One particular dealership charges its customers for three hours of labour for its maintenance #4 service package. To check whether these hours were reasonable hours to charge for this package, a consumer advocacy group monitored the labour time it took the dealership to service 30 randomly selected automobiles having this type of maintenance. The average time for this sample was 2.75 hours. Assuming that the population standard deviation in service times is 0.47 hours, calculate the 95 percent confidence interval for the true average service time for this package. Based on your results, is the three-hour charge a reasonable charge for this package? Explain. (LO 3)

8.5   Confidence Interval for a Mean (μ) with Unknown σ

Student's *t* Distribution

In situations where the population is normal but its standard deviation σ is unknown, the Student's *t* distribution should be used instead of the normal *z* distribution.

The Student's *t* distributions were proposed by a Dublin brewer named W. S. Gossett (1876–1937), who published his research under the name "Student" because his employer did not approve of publishing research based on company data. The *t* distributions are symmetric and shaped very much like the standard normal distribution, except they are somewhat less peaked and have thicker tails. *Note that the t distributions are a class of distributions, each of which is dependent on the size of the sample we are using.* Figure 8.9 shows how the tails of the distributions change as the sample size increases. A closer look reveals that the *t* distribution's tails lie *above* the normal (i.e., the *t* distribution always has heavier tails).

Degrees of Freedom

Knowing the sample size allows us to calculate a parameter called **degrees of freedom** (sometimes abbreviated d.f.). This parameter is used to determine the value of the *t* statistic used in the confidence interval formula. The degrees of freedom tell us how many observations we used to calculate *s,* the sample standard deviation, less the number of intermediate estimates we used in our calculation. Recall that the formula for *s* uses all *n* individual values from the sample and also $\overline{X}$, the sample mean, as an estimate of μ. Therefore, the degrees of freedom

FIGURE 8.9 ▶ **Comparison of Normal and Student's *t***

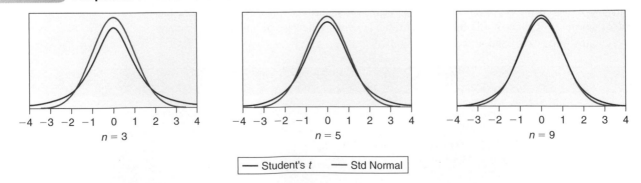

are equal to the sample size minus 1 (the minus 1 for estimating μ with $\bar{x}$). We will use the symbol ν (the Greek letter "nu"), to represent degrees of freedom.

$$\text{d.f.} = \nu = n - 1 \quad \text{(degrees of freedom for a confidence interval for } \mu) \quad \textbf{(8.4)}$$

For large degrees of freedom, the t distribution approaches the shape of the normal distribution, as illustrated in Figure 8.9. However, in small samples, the difference is important. For example, in Figure 8.9 the lower axis scale range extends out to ± 4, while a range of ± 3 would cover most of the area for a standard normal distribution. We have to go out further into the tails of the t distribution to enclose a given area, so for a given confidence level, t *is always larger than* z so the confidence interval is always *wider* than if z were used.

Because the t-distribution depends on the degrees of freedom, each sample size gives a different t table. So the t table in Appendix D provides t values for certain commonly used tail areas and different degrees of freedom.

To illustrate the use of the t table, we print below part of the t table in Appendix D.

			Right-Tail Area α								
ν	0.1	0.05	0.025	0.01	0.005	ν	0.1	0.05	0.025	0.01	0.005
1	3.078	6.314	12.706	31.821	63.657	36	1.306	1.688	2.028	2.434	2.719
2	1.886	2.920	4.303	6.965	9.925	37	1.305	1.687	2.026	2.431	2.715
3	1.638	2.353	3.182	4.541	5.841	38	1.304	1.686	2.024	2.429	2.712
4	1.533	2.132	2.776	3.747	4.604	39	1.304	1.685	2.023	2.426	2.708
5	1.476	2.015	2.571	3.365	4.032	40	1.303	1.684	2.021	2.423	2.704
⋮	⋮	⋮	⋮	⋮	⋮	⋮	⋮	⋮	⋮	⋮	⋮
26	1.315	1.706	2.056	2.479	2.779	110	1.289	1.659	1.982	2.361	2.621
27	1.314	1.703	2.052	2.473	2.771	120	1.289	1.658	1.980	2.358	2.617
28	1.313	1.701	2.048	2.467	2.763	130	1.288	1.657	1.978	2.355	2.614
29	1.311	1.699	2.045	2.462	2.756	140	1.288	1.656	1.977	2.353	2.611
30	1.310	1.697	2.042	2.457	2.750	150	1.287	1.655	1.976	2.351	2.609
31	1.309	1.696	2.040	2.453	2.744	inf.	1.280	1.645	1.96	2.33	2.575
32	1.309	1.694	2.037	2.449	2.738						
33	1.308	1.692	2.035	2.445	2.733						
34	1.307	1.691	2.032	2.441	2.728				z **values**		
35	1.306	1.690	2.030	2.438	2.724						

Suppose we take a random sample of 27 observations. Then degrees of freedom $\nu = 27 - 1 = 26$. Looking under the column for a right-tail area of 0.025, we see that the t value (in the highlighted box) = 2.056. We write this as $t_{26,0.025} = 2.056$. If t_{26} represents the random variable corresponding to the t-distribution with 26 degrees of freedom, then we can equivalently make a probability statement $P(t_{26} > 2.056) = 0.025$.

Now if we had taken a sample of 41 observations instead, we have $t_{40,0.025} = 2.021$. If we had taken even a larger sample of 151 observations, we have $t_{150,0.025} = 1.976$. As the sample size increases, the t value approaches 1.96 ($z_{0.025} = 1.96$), which is the z value for a right-tail area of 0.025.

Comparison of z and t

The above partial t table shows that for very small samples the t values differ substantially from their respective z values. As degrees of freedom increase, the t values approach the familiar normal z values (shown at the bottom of each column corresponding to an infinitely large sample). For example, for $n = 31$, we would have degrees of freedom $\nu = 31 - 1 = 30$, so for a 90 percent confidence interval ($\alpha = 0.10$), we would use $t_{\alpha/2,n-1} = t_{0.05,30} = 1.697$, which is only slightly larger than $z_{\alpha/2} = z_{0.05} = 1.645$ in the formula developed below.

A Closer Look

Why is the t-distribution "wider" than the z-distribution but approaches the z-distribution as the sample size gets larger? An intuitive answer could be proposed as follows. A perfect relationship between an estimator and a parameter would be described by a probability distribution with a zero width (i.e., by a vertical line). The less perfect the relationship, the "wider" the distribution would be. Using S as an estimate of σ instead of using σ adds additional uncertainty into the relationship between $\overline{X}$ and μ, resulting in a wider distribution than the z-distribution. As the sample size increases, the better the estimate of σ and the less uncertainty the relationship between $\overline{X}$ and μ should be. As a result, the probability distribution narrows as the sample size increases. Because the z-distribution always has less uncertainty than the t-distribution, at best the t-distribution can only approach the z-distribution as the sample size gets very large.

We now develop a general formula for the confidence interval. It can be shown that

$$t_{n-1} = \frac{\overline{X} - \mu}{\left(S/\sqrt{n} \right)}$$

follows the t-distribution with $(n-1)$ degrees of freedom.

To cover an area of $(1 - \alpha)$ symmetrically around the mean of the t-distribution (which equals 0), we can make the following probability statement:

$$P\left(-t_{\alpha/2,n-1} < \frac{\overline{X} - \mu}{\left(S/\sqrt{n} \right)} < t_{\alpha/2,n-1} \right) = 1 - \alpha$$

By rearranging we can write the above as

$$P\left(\overline{X} - t_{\alpha/2,n-1} \frac{S}{\sqrt{n}} < \mu < \overline{X} + t_{\alpha/2,n-1} \frac{S}{\sqrt{n}} \right) = 1 - \alpha$$

and we have the formula in the box below:

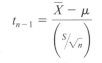

Confidence Interval for μ (unknown σ)

$$\overline{x} - t_{\alpha/2} \frac{S}{\sqrt{n}} \leq \mu \leq \overline{x} + t_{\alpha/2} \frac{S}{\sqrt{n}}$$

When σ is unknown, the formula for a confidence interval resembles the formula for known σ except that t replaces z and S replaces σ. To calculate this confidence interval we first calculate $\overline{x}$ and s from the sample and the actual interval becomes:

$$\overline{x} - t_{\alpha/2} \frac{S}{\sqrt{n}} \leq \mu \leq \overline{x} + t_{\alpha/2} \frac{S}{\sqrt{n}} \quad \text{(confidence interval for } \mu \text{ with unknown } \sigma) \quad \textbf{(8.5)}$$

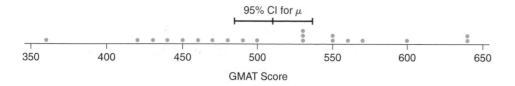

FIGURE 8.10

Dot Plot and Confidence Interval (*n* = 20 Scores)
GMATScores

EXAMPLE 4

GMAT Scores, Again
GMATScores

Let's look at the random sample of GMAT scores submitted by 20 applicants to an MBA program. A dot plot of this sample is shown in Figure 8.10.

530	450	600	570	360
550	640	490	460	550
480	440	530	470	560
500	430	640	420	530

We will construct a 90 percent confidence interval for the mean GMAT score of all MBA applicants. The sample mean is $\bar{X} = 510$ and the sample standard deviation is $s = 73.77$. Because the population standard deviation σ is unknown, we will use the Student's t for our confidence interval with 19 degrees of freedom:

$$\nu = n - 1 = 20 - 1 = 19 \quad (\text{degrees of freedom for } n = 20)$$

For a 90 percent confidence interval, we consult Appendix D and find $t_{0.05,19} = 1.729$. The 90 percent confidence interval is

$$\bar{x} \pm t_{0.05,19}\frac{s}{\sqrt{n}} = 510 \pm (1.729)\frac{73.77}{\sqrt{20}} = 510 \pm 28.52$$

We are 90 percent confident that the true mean GMAT score is within the interval $481.48 < \mu < 538.52$ (see Figure 8.10). There is a 90 percent chance that an interval constructed in this manner contains μ (and a 10 percent chance that it does not). If we wanted a narrower confidence interval with the same level of confidence, we would need a larger sample size because the width, according to the formula for this confidence interval, varies inversely with n; width $= 2t_{\alpha/2,n-1}\dfrac{s}{\sqrt{n}}$ or 2(28.52).

EXAMPLE 5

Hospital Stays
Maternity

During a certain period of time, Balzac Hospital had 8,261 maternity cases. Each case is assigned a code called a DRG (which stands for *Diagnostic Related Group*). The most common DRG was 373 (simple delivery without complicating diagnoses), accounting for 4,409 cases during the study period. Hospital management needs to know the mean length of stay (LOS) so that they can plan the maternity unit bed capacity and schedule the nursing staff. For DRG 373, a random sample of hospital records for $n = 25$ births, the mean length of stay was $\bar{X} = 39.144$ hours with a standard deviation of $s = 16.204$ hours. What is the 95 percent confidence interval for the true mean?

To justify using the Student's t distribution we will assume that the population is normal (we will examine this assumption later). Because the population standard deviation is unknown, we use the Student's t for our confidence interval with 24 degrees of freedom:

$$\nu = n - 1 = 25 - 1 = 24 \quad (\text{degrees of freedom for } n = 25)$$

For a 95 percent confidence interval, we consult Appendix D and find $t_{0.025,24} = 2.064$. The 95 percent confidence interval is

$$\bar{x} \pm t_{0.025,24}\frac{s}{\sqrt{n}} = 39.144 \pm (2.064)\frac{16.204}{\sqrt{25}} = 39.144 \pm 6.689$$

With 95 percent confidence, the true mean LOS is within the interval $32.455 < \mu < 45.833$, so our best guess is that a simple maternity stay averages between 32.5 hours and 45.8 hours. A dot plot of this sample and confidence interval are shown in Figure 8.11.

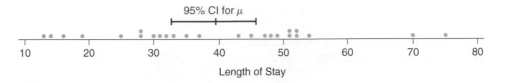

FIGURE 8.11

Dot Plot and Confidence Interval ($n = 25$ Births)
Maternity

Confidence Interval Width

As mentioned above, the width for the confidence interval for μ when σ is unknown is

$$2t_{\alpha/2,\,n-1}\frac{s}{\sqrt{n}}$$

From this formula, we see this width reflects the sample size, the confidence level, and the standard deviation. If we wanted a narrower interval (i.e., more precision) we could either increase the sample size or lower the confidence level (e.g., to 90 percent or even 80 percent). But we cannot do anything about the standard deviation, because it is an aspect of the sample. In fact, some samples could have larger standard deviations than this one. You will be introduced to formulas for determining sample sizes in Section 8.7.

Concept Check

Increasing the sample size decreases the width of the confidence interval for μ when σ is known or when it is unknown. When σ is known, the sample size affects the width because the width varies inversely with the square root of n. When σ is unknown, the sample size also affects the width in another way. How?

A "Good" Sample?

Was our sample of 25 births typical? If we took a different sample, would we get a different confidence interval? Let's take a few new samples and see what happens. Figure 8.12 shows 95 percent confidence intervals using five *different* random samples of 25 births (the samples are from a very large population of $N = 4,409$ births). Samples 1 through 4 give similar results. However, sample 5 has a much higher mean and standard deviation, and a very wide confidence interval.

Sample 5 included one patient who stayed in the hospital for 254 hours (more than 10 days), skewing the sample severely (see Figure 8.13). Yet an observer might still conclude that a "typical" length of maternity stay is around 40 hours. It is just a matter of luck which sample you get. However, the statistician who obtains sample 5 is not helpless. He/she would know that the sample contained a severe outlier, and might suggest taking a larger sample. It would

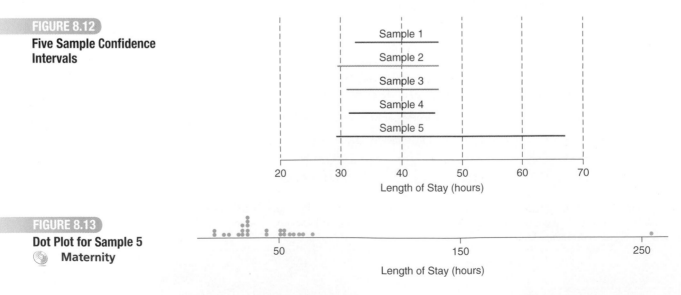

FIGURE 8.12

Five Sample Confidence Intervals

FIGURE 8.13

Dot Plot for Sample 5
Maternity

certainly be a warning that the confidence interval from sample 5 cannot be trusted. We might consider constructing a confidence interval without the outlier to see how much it is affecting our results. More importantly, the existence of an outlier reminds us that the mean is not always a good measure of the "typical" value of X.

Must the Population Be Normal?

The t distribution assumes a normal population, but in practice, this assumption can be relaxed, as long as the population is not badly skewed. Large sample size offers further protection if the normality assumption is questionable. The appendix at the end of this chapter shows you how to check for this normality assumption.

Using Appendix D

Beyond $\nu = 50$, Appendix D shows ν in steps of 5 or 10. *If Appendix D does not show the exact degrees of freedom that you want, use the t value for the next lower ν.* For example, if $\nu = 54$, you would use $\nu = 50$. Using the next lower degrees of freedom is a conservative procedure because it overestimates the margin of error. Because t values change very slowly as ν rises beyond $\nu = 50$, rounding down will make little difference.

Can I Ever Use *z* Instead of *t*?

In large samples, z and t give similar results. But a conservative statistician always uses the t distribution for confidence intervals when σ is unknown because using z would underestimate the margin of error. Because t tables are easy to use (or we can get t values from Excel) there isn't much justification for using z when σ is unknown.

Using Excel for the Confidence Interval for μ with σ Unknown

If you have access to Excel, you don't need tables. Excel's function =TINV(probability, degrees of freedom) gives a two-tailed value of t, where probability is 1 minus the confidence level. For example, for a 95 percent confidence interval with 60 degrees of freedom, the function = TINV(0.05,60) yields $t = 2.000298$. Because Excel wants the *two-tailed area* outside the confidence interval, we would use 0.05 for 95 percent, 0.01 for 99 percent, etc. The output from Excel's Data > Data Analysis > Descriptive Statistics does not give the confidence interval limits, but it does give the standard error and the margin of error, $t_{\alpha/2, n-1}s/\sqrt{n}$, (the oddly labelled last line in the table), which can then be converted to the width of the confidence interval by multiplying it by two. Figure 8.14 shows Excel's results for sample 1 (maternity LOS).

Using MegaStat for the Confidence Interval for μ with σ Unknown

If you really want to make the calculations easy, MegaStat gives you a choice of z or t, and does all the calculations for you, as illustrated in Figure 8.15 for sample 1 (maternity LOS). Notice the Preview button. If you click OK you will also see the t value and other details.

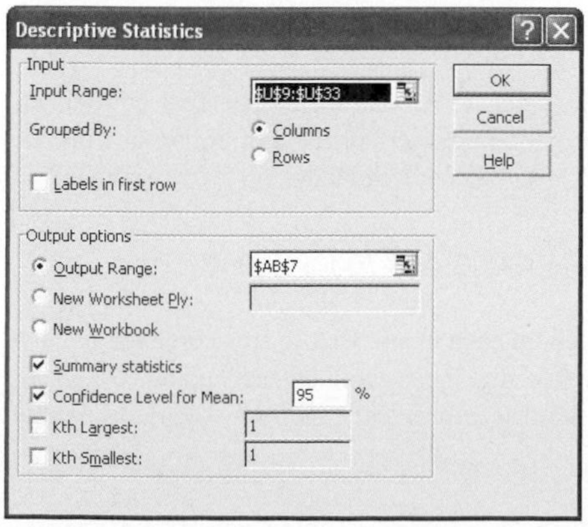

Mean	39.144
Standard Error	3.240769405
Median	37.37
Mode	#N/A
Standard Deviation	16.20384702
Sample Variance	262.5646583
Kurtosis	−0.28780002
Skewness	0.263313568
Range	61.92
Minimum	12.59
Maximum	74.51
Sum	978.6
Count	25
Confidence Level(95.0%)	6.688617936

FIGURE 8.14

Excel's Confidence Interval

Section Exercises

8.9 Find a confidence interval for μ assuming that each sample is from a normal population. (LO 3)
    a. $\bar{x} = 24$, $s = 3$, $n = 7$, 90 percent confidence
    b. $\bar{x} = 42$, $s = 6$, $n = 18$, 99 percent confidence
    c. $\bar{x} = 119$, $s = 14$, $n = 28$, 95 percent confidence

8.10 For each value of v (degrees of freedom) look up the value of Student's t in Appendix D for the stated level of confidence. Then use Excel to find the value of Student's t to four decimal places. Which method (Appendix D or Excel) do you prefer, and why? (LO 5)
    a. $v = 9$, 95 percent confidence
    b. $v = 15$, 98 percent confidence
    c. $v = 47$, 90 percent confidence

8.11 For each value of v look up the value of Student's t in Appendix D for the stated level of confidence. How close is the t value to the corresponding z value (at the bottom of the column for $v = \infty$)? (LO 5)
    a. $v = 40$, 95 percent confidence
    b. $v = 80$, 95 percent confidence
    c. $v = 100$, 95 percent confidence

8.12 A sample of 21 minivan electrical warranty repairs for "loose, not attached" wires (one of several electrical failure categories the dealership mechanic can select) showed a mean repair cost of $45.66 with a standard deviation of $27.79. (a) Construct a 95 percent confidence interval for the true mean repair cost. (b) How could the confidence interval be made narrower? (Data are from a project by MBA student Tim Polulak.) (LO 3)

8.13 A random sample of 16 pharmacy customers showed the waiting times below (in minutes). Find a 90 percent confidence interval for μ, assuming that the sample is from a normal population. (LO 3)   **Pharmacy**

21	22	22	17	21	17	23	20
20	24	9	22	16	21	22	21

8.14 A random sample of monthly rent paid by 12 fourth-year university students living off campus gave the results below (in dollars). Find a 99 percent confidence interval for μ, assuming that the sample is from a normal population. (LO 3)
   Rent1

900	810	770	860	850	790
810	800	890	720	910	640

8.15 A random sample of 10 shipments of stick-on labels showed the following order sizes. (a) Construct a 95 percent confidence interval for the true mean order size. (b) How could the confidence interval be made narrower? (c) Do you think the population is normal? (Data are from a project by MBA student Henry Olthof, Jr.) (LO 3)   **OrderSize**

12,000	18,000	30,000	60,000	14,000	10,500	52,000	14,000	15,700	19,000

8.16 Prof. Softtouch gave three exams last semester. Scores were normally distributed on each exam. Below are scores for 10 randomly chosen students on each exam. (a) Find the 95 percent confidence interval for the mean score on each exam. (b) Do the confidence intervals overlap? What inference might you draw by comparing the three confidence intervals? (c) How is this problem different from Exercise 8.6? (LO 3)   **Exams2**

Exam 1: 81, 79, 88, 90, 82, 86, 80, 92, 86, 86
Exam 2: 87, 76, 81, 83, 100, 95, 93, 82, 99, 90
Exam 3: 77, 79, 74, 75, 82, 69, 74, 80, 74, 76

8.17* The local diner in a small New Brunswick community is up for sale and there is a potential buyer. Before this individual will commit to making an offer to purchase the restaurant, she wants to have some idea of the average number of customers that this diner attracts per day. To estimate this average, she randomly chose eight days during the last month and observed the following number of customers:

85, 103, 78, 58, 97, 82, 91, 89

Assuming that the number of customers approximately follows a normal distribution, estimate with 95% confidence, the actual daily average number of customers this diner attracts. Why could the number of customers not have a normal distribution? Instead of estimating the average number of customers per day, what would be a better parameter to estimate? Explain. Instead of randomly selecting eight days during the last month, what might be a better sampling scheme to use? Explain. (LO 3)

8.18* What separates the more successful professional golfers from the less successful? One could argue that one of the determining factors is how far the golfer can hit his driver during a tournament. A more successful and a less successful professional were randomly chosen and how far (in yards) they hit their drivers on seven randomly selected holes over the past six months were recorded as follows:

More successful: 312, 300, 298, 308, 312, 306, 302
Less successful: 285, 295, 305, 275, 284, 276, 295

Estimate, with 95% confidence, the true average distance each golfer can hit his driver. By comparing these two confidence intervals, could you argue that the more successful golfers do outhit the less successful golfers, on average? Explain. (LO 3)

8.6 Confidence Interval for a Proportion (π)

The Central Limit Theorem (CLT) also applies to a sample proportion, because a proportion is just a mean of data whose only values are 0 or 1. For a proportion, the CLT says that the distribution of a sample proportion $P = X/n$ tends toward normality as n increases. Here X represents the number of successes in the sample of size n. The distribution is centred at the population proportion π. Its standard error σ_P will decrease as n increases just as in the case of the standard error for $\overline{X}$. It can be shown that $P = X/n$ is an unbiased, *consistent, and efficient* estimator of π.

Central Limit Theorem for a Proportion

As sample size increases, the distribution of the sample proportion $P = X/n$ approaches a normal distribution with mean π and standard deviation $\sigma_P = \sqrt{\dfrac{\pi(1 - \pi)}{n}}$.

Concept Check

In Chapter 6, you were introduced to the binomial distribution in which the binomial random variable, X, had a mean of $n\pi$ and a standard deviation of $\sqrt{n\pi(1 - \pi)}$. Using the appropriate expected value and variance rules, verify that P has a mean of π and a standard deviation of $\sqrt{\dfrac{\pi(1 - \pi)}{n}}$.

Illustration: Internet Hotel Reservations   **Hotel**

Management of the Pan-Asian Hotel System tracks the percent of hotel reservations made over the Internet to adjust its advertising and Web reservation system. Such data are binary: either a reservation is made on the Internet (x) or not (o). Last week (2,000 reservations) the proportion of Internet reservations was 20 percent ($\pi = 0.20$) as you can verify if you have the time. We can visualize the week's data like this:

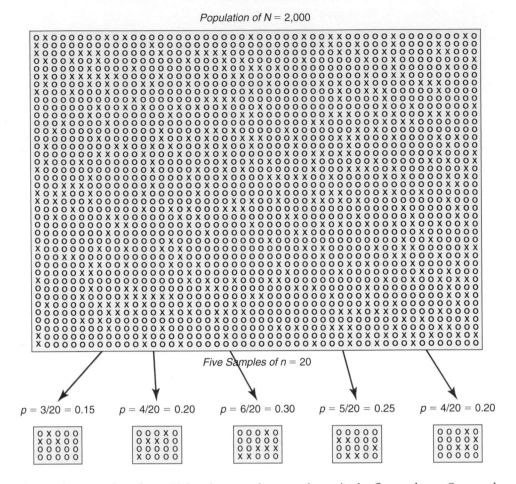

Population of N = 2,000

Five Samples of n = 20

| $p = 3/20 = 0.15$ | $p = 4/20 = 0.20$ | $p = 6/20 = 0.30$ | $p = 5/20 = 0.25$ | $p = 4/20 = 0.20$ |

Five random samples of $n = 20$ hotel reservations are shown in the figure above. Some values of sample proportions (P) are close to $\pi = 0.20$ while others are not, due to sampling variation. But each value of the sample proportion P is a valid *point estimate value* of the population proportion π:

$$P = \frac{X}{n} = \frac{\text{number of Internet reservations}}{\text{number of items in the sample}}$$

If we took many such samples, we could empirically study the *sampling distribution* of P by looking at the histogram of these proportions. But even for a single sample, we can apply the CLT to *predict* the behaviour of P. In Chapter 6, you learned that the binomial model describes the number of successes in a sample of n items from a population with constant probability of success π. A binomial distribution is symmetric if $\pi = 0.50$, and as n increases, the distribution becomes more and more symmetric, even if $\pi \neq 0.50$. The same is true for the distribution of the sample proportion $P = X/n$. Figure 8.16 shows histograms of $P = X/n$ for 1,000 samples of various sizes with $\pi = 0.20$. For small n, the distribution is quite discrete. For example:

Sample Size	Possible Values of $P = X/n$
$n = 5$	0/5, 1/5, 2/5, 3/5, 4/5, 5/5
$n = 10$	0/10, 1/10, 2/10, 3/10, 4/10, 5/10, 6/10, 7/10, 8/10, 9/10, 10/10

Histograms of $p = x/n$ When $\pi = 0.20$ **Hotel**   FIGURE 8.16

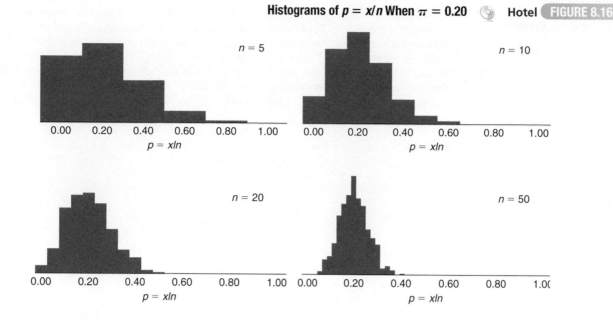

As n increases, the statistic $P = X/n$ more closely resembles a continuous random variable and its distribution becomes more symmetric and bell-shaped.

As n increases, the range of the sample proportion $P = X/n$ narrows, because n appears in the denominator of the *standard error:*

$$\sigma_p = \sqrt{\frac{\pi(1-\pi)}{n}} \quad \text{(standard error of the sample proportion)} \tag{8.6}$$

Therefore, the sampling variation can be reduced by increasing the sample size. Larger samples also help justify the use of the normal distribution.

When Is It Safe to Assume Normality?

The statistic $P = X/n$ may be assumed normally distributed when the sample is "large." How large must n be? As discussed in Chapter 7, normality may be assumed whenever $n \geq 9\left(\dfrac{\pi}{1-\pi}\right)$ and $n \geq 9\left(\dfrac{1-\pi}{\pi}\right)$.

Rule of Thumb

The sample proportion $P = X/n$ may be assumed normal if both $n \geq 9\left(\dfrac{\pi}{1-\pi}\right)$ and $n \geq 9\left(\dfrac{1-\pi}{\pi}\right)$.

Assuming P is normal, we can express the distribution of P as $P \sim N\left(\pi, \sqrt{\dfrac{\pi(1-\pi)}{n}}\right)$ or $Z = \dfrac{P - \pi}{\sqrt{\dfrac{\pi(1-\pi)}{n}}}$. Using this relationship, $Z = \dfrac{P - \pi}{\sqrt{\dfrac{\pi(1-\pi)}{n}}}$, between P and π, we can either determine probabilities for P knowing the value of π, or we can make inferences concerning π knowing the value of P. While estimation is the focus of this chapter, the following example illustrates the use of this sampling distribution to determine probabilities for P.

EXAMPLE 6

Brand Name Preferences

The manager of a Zehrs store in southern Ontario claims that 70 percent of its customers prefer to purchase the President's Choice brands of sauces and condiments (e.g., mustard, salad dressing) than the national brand name sauces and condiments. If that claim is true, what is the probability that, in a random sample of 150 of its customers, (a) at least 65 percent preferred the President's Choice brand, (b) between 75 percent and 80 percent preferred the President's Choice brand, and (c) less than 60 percent preferred the President's Choice brand? If, in fact, less than 60 percent in the sample actually preferred the President's Choice brand, what can we say about this manager's claim?

(a) $\quad P(P \geq 0.65) = P\left(Z \geq \dfrac{0.65 - 0.70}{\sqrt{\dfrac{0.70(1 - 0.70)}{150}}} \right) = P(Z \geq -1.34) = 0.5 + 0.4099 = 0.9099$

(b) $\quad P(0.75 \leq P \leq 0.80) = P\left(\dfrac{0.75 - 0.70}{\sqrt{\dfrac{0.70(1 - 0.70)}{150}}} \leq Z \leq \dfrac{0.80 - 0.70}{\sqrt{\dfrac{0.70(1 - 0.70)}{150}}} \right)$

$$= P(1.34 \leq Z \leq 2.67) = 0.4962 - 0.4099 = 0.0863$$

(c) $\quad P(P < 0.60) = P\left(Z < \dfrac{0.60 - 0.70}{\sqrt{\dfrac{0.70(1 - 0.70)}{150}}} \right) = P(Z < -2.67) = 0.5 - 0.4962 = 0.0038$

If less than 60 percent actually preferred the President's Choice brand, we could argue that because this outcome is quite unlikely to occur (a probability of only 0.0038) if the manager's claim was true, the manager's claim is not true.

Confidence Interval for π

By the Central Limit Theorem, we can state the probability that a sample proportion will fall within a given interval. For example, there is a 95 percent chance that P will fall within the range $\pi \pm z_{0.025}\sigma_P = \pi \pm z_{0.025}\sqrt{\dfrac{\pi(1 - \pi)}{n}}$ where $z_{0.025} = 1.96$. Thus, we can make the following probability statement:

$$P(\pi - z_{0.025}\sigma_P < P < \pi + z_{0.025}\sigma_P) = 0.95$$

As before, rearranging P and π, we can equivalently write as follows:

$$P(P - z_{0.025}\sigma_P < \pi < P + z_{0.025}\sigma_P) = 0.95$$

This is the basis for a confidence interval estimate of π:

$$p \pm z_{0.025}\sigma_P = p \pm z_{0.025}\sqrt{\dfrac{\pi(1 - \pi)}{n}}$$

Replacing π with $P = X/n$ (since π is unknown) and assuming a large sample (to justify the assumption of normality), the confidence interval for π is

$$p \pm z_{\alpha/2}\sqrt{\dfrac{p(1 - p)}{n}} \qquad \text{(confidence interval for } \pi\text{)} \qquad \textbf{(8.7)}$$

We can choose z for any confidence level we want. For example

$z_{0.05} = 1.645$, for 90 percent confidence

$z_{0.025} = 1.960$, for 95 percent confidence

$z_{0.01} = 2.330$, for 98 percent confidence

$z_{0.005} = 2.575$, for 99 percent confidence

EXAMPLE 7
Auditing

A sample of 75 retail in-store purchases showed that 24 were paid in cash. We will construct a 95 percent confidence interval for the proportion of all retail in-store purchases that are paid in cash. The sample proportion is $p = x/n = 24/75 = 0.32$ (proportion of in-store cash transactions).

We can assume that p is normally distributed because

$$n \geq 9\left(\frac{\pi}{1 - \pi}\right) \approx 9\left(\frac{0.32}{1 - 0.32}\right) = 4.24, \quad n \geq 9\left(\frac{1 - \pi}{\pi}\right) \approx 9\left(\frac{0.68}{0.32}\right) = 19.13$$

The 95 percent confidence interval ($\alpha = 0.05$) is

$$p \pm z_{\alpha/2}\sqrt{\frac{p(1 - p)}{n}} = p \pm z_{0.025}\sqrt{\frac{p(1 - p)}{n}} = 0.32 \pm 1.960\sqrt{\frac{0.32(1 - 0.32)}{75}}$$

$$= 0.32 \pm 0.106 \rightarrow 0.214 < \pi < 0.426$$

There is a 95 percent probability that an interval constructed in this way contains the true population proportion π. We think that the true proportion π is between 21.4 percent and 42.6 percent, and our best guess (point estimate) is 32 percent. Different samples could yield different estimates. *We cannot know whether the true proportion lies within the interval we have constructed.* Either it does, or it does not. What we *do* know is that the odds are very good (95 to 5 or 19 to 1) that our 95 percent confidence interval will contain the true proportion π.

Narrowing the Interval?

In this example, the confidence interval is fairly wide. The width of the confidence interval for π depends on

- Sample size
- Confidence level
- Sample proportion p

More precisely, the width is $2z_{\alpha/2}\sqrt{\frac{p(1 - p)}{n}}$, where p is the value of P calculated from the sample.

We cannot do anything about p because it is an aspect of the sample. If we want a narrower interval (i.e., more precision), we could either increase the sample size or reduce the confidence level (e.g., from 95 percent to 90 percent). If the confidence level is sacrosanct, our only choice is to increase n. Of course, larger samples are more costly (or even impossible).

EXAMPLE 8
Display Ads

A random sample of 200 pages from the *Toronto Yellow Pages* telephone directory revealed that 30 of the selected pages contained at least one multicoloured display ad (large blocks with illustrations, maps, and text). What is the 90 percent confidence interval for the proportion of all pages with at least one such display ad? The sample proportion value is $p = x/n = 30/200 = 0.15$ (proportion of pages with at least one display ad).

The normality test is easily verified. The 90 percent confidence interval ($\alpha = 0.10$) requires us to use $z_{\alpha/2} = z_{0.05} = 1.645$, and

$$p \pm z_{\alpha/2}\sqrt{\frac{p(1 - p)}{n}} = p \pm z_{0.05}\sqrt{\frac{p(1 - p)}{n}} = 0.15 \pm 1.645\sqrt{\frac{0.15(1 - 0.15)}{200}}$$

$$= 0.15 \pm 0.042 \rightarrow 0.108 < \pi < 0.192$$

With 90 percent confidence, between 10.8 percent and 19.2 percent of the pages have multicolour display ads. This confidence interval is narrower than the previous example because the sample size is larger, this sample proportion is farther from 0.5, and the confidence level is lower.

Using Excel and MegaStat

Excel's Data > Data Analysis does not offer a confidence interval for a proportion, presumably because the calculations are easy. For example:

=0.15−NORMSINV(.95)*SQRT(0.15*(1−0.15)/200) for the lower 95 confidence limit
=0.15+NORMSINV(.95)*SQRT(0.15*(1−0.15)/200) for the upper 95 confidence limit

FIGURE 8.17

MegaStat's Confidence Interval

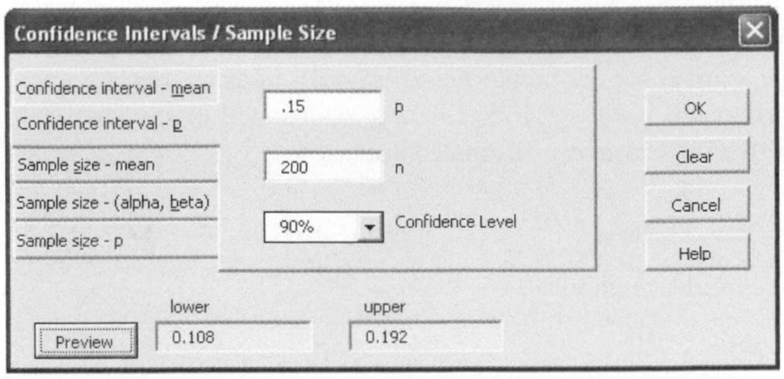

TABLE 8.3 Margin of Error for 95 Percent Confidence Interval Assuming $\pi = 0.50$

n = 100	n = 200	n = 400	n = 800	n = 1,200	n = 1,600
±9.8%	±6.9%	±4.9%	±3.5%	±2.8%	±2.5%

However, MegaStat makes it even easier, as shown in Figure 8.17. You only need to enter p and n. A convenient feature is that if you enter p greater than 1, MegaStat assumes that it is the x value in $p = x/n$ so you don't even have to calculate p. Click the Preview button to see the confidence interval. This example verifies the calculations shown in Example 8 above (click OK for additional details). MegaStat always assumes normality, even when it is not justified, so you need to check this assumption for yourself.

Polls and Margin of Error

In polls and survey research, the margin of error is typically based on a 95 percent confidence level and the initial assumption that $\pi = 0.50$. This is a conservative assumption as σ_P is at its maximum when $\pi = 0.50$. (This can be verified by plotting values of σ_P for various values of π.) Table 8.3 shows the margin of error for various sample sizes. The law of diminishing returns is apparent. Greater accuracy is possible, but each reduction in the margin of error requires a disproportionately larger sample size.

Proportions Are Important in Business

Proportions are easy to work with, and they occur frequently in business (most often expressed as percents). In many ways, estimating π is simpler than estimating μ because you are just counting things.

Section Exercises

8.19 Calculate the standard error for P. May normality be assumed? (LO 3)

    a. $n = 30, \pi = 0.50$
    b. $n = 50, \pi = 0.20$
    c. $n = 100, \pi = 0.10$
    d. $n = 500, \pi = 0.005$

8.20 A leading expert on the game of golf claims that a successful professional golfer's tee shots should land in the fairway 85 percent of the time. If this claim is true, what is the probability that a successful golfer would land at least 64 of 80 tee shots in the fairway? (LO 3)

8.21 After purchasing an HD flat-panel television set at a large electronics store chain, customers are always encouraged by the salespeople to purchase an extended warranty. One of the selling points made by a particular salesperson is that 75 percent of the store's customers purchase this warranty. If this selling point is true, (a) what is the probability that in a sample of 50 customers, between 70 percent and 80 percent purchased this warranty? (b) What is the probability that, in a sample of 50 customers, less than 57 percent purchased this warranty? If less than 57 percent actually purchased the extended warranty, could you question the selling point's claim? Explain. (LO 3)

8.22 A car dealer is taking a customer satisfaction survey. Find the margin of error (i.e., assuming 95 percent confidence and $\pi = 0.50$) for (a) 250 respondents, (b) 125 respondents, and (c) 65 respondents. (LO 3)

8.23 In a sample of 500 new Web sites registered on the Internet, 24 were anonymous (i.e., they shielded their name and contact information). (a) Construct a 95 percent confidence interval for the proportion of all new Web sites that were anonymous. (b) May normality be assumed? Explain. (Data are from "New Services Are Making It Easier to Hide Who Is Behind Web Sites," *The Wall Street Journal,* Sept. 30, 2004.) (LO 3)

8.24 From a list of stock mutual funds, 52 funds were selected at random. Of the funds chosen, it was found that 19 required a minimum initial investment under $1,000. (a) Construct a 90 percent confidence interval for the true proportion requiring an initial investment under $1,000. (b) May normality be assumed? Explain. (LO 3)

8.25 Of 43 bank customers depositing a cheque, 18 received some cash back. (a) Construct a 90 percent confidence interval for the proportion of all depositors who ask for cash back. (b) Check the normality assumption. (LO 3)

8.26 A 2003 survey showed that 4.8 percent of the 250 Americans surveyed had suffered some kind of identity theft in the past 12 months. (a) Construct a 98 percent confidence interval for the true proportion of Americans who had suffered identity theft in the past 12 months. (b) May normality be assumed? Explain. (Data are from *Scientific American* 291, no. 6, p. 33.) (LO 3)

8.27 A sample of 50 homes in a subdivision revealed that 24 were ranch style (as opposed to colonial, tri-level, or Cape Cod). (a) Construct a 98 percent confidence interval for the true proportion of ranch-style homes. (b) Check the normality assumption. (LO 3)

8.28 What separates the more successful professional golfers from the less successful? One could argue that one of the determining factors is the proportion of times that he can land his tee shots in the fairway. A more successful and a less successful professional was randomly chosen. Each hit 100 tee shots using their drivers on a typical par four layout. The more successful golfer landed 82 of his shots on the fairway while the less successful golfer landed 63 of his tee shots on the same fairway. Estimate, with 99 percent confidence, the true proportion of times that more successful and less successful professional golfers can land his tee shots on a typical par four layout using their drivers. By comparing these two confidence intervals, could you argue that the more successful golfers land a greater percentage of their tee shots in the fairway than less successful golfers. Explain. (LO 3)

Mini Case 8.1

Airline Water Quality

Is the water on your airline flight safe to drink? It isn't feasible to analyze the water on every flight, so sampling is necessary. In August and September 2004, the U.S. Environmental Protection Agency (EPA) found bacterial contamination in water samples from the lavatories and galley water taps on 20 of 158 randomly selected U.S. flights (12.7 percent of the flights). Alarmed by the data, the EPA ordered sanitation improvements and then tested water samples again in November and December 2004. In the second sample, bacterial contamination was found in 29 of 169 randomly sampled flights (17.2 percent of the flights).

Aug./Sep. sample: $p = 20/158 = 0.12658$, or 12.7% contaminated
Nov./Dec. sample: $p = 29/169 = 0.17160$, or 17.2% contaminated

Is the problem getting worse instead of better? From these samples, we can construct confidence intervals for the true proportion of flights with contaminated water. We begin with the 95 percent confidence interval for π based on the August/September water sample:

$$p \pm z_{0.025}\sqrt{\frac{p(1-p)}{n}} = 0.12658 \pm 1.96\sqrt{\frac{0.12658(1-0.12658)}{158}}$$
$$= 0.12658 \pm 0.05185, \text{ or } 7.5 \text{ to } 17.8\%$$

Next we determine the 95 percent confidence interval for π based on the November/December water sample:

$$p \pm z_{0.025}\sqrt{\frac{p(1-p)}{n}} = 0.17160 \pm 1.96\sqrt{\frac{0.17160(1-0.17160)}{169}}$$
$$= 0.17160 \pm 0.05684, \text{ or } 11.5 \text{ to } 22.8\%$$

Although the sample percentage (a point estimate of π) did rise, the margin of error is a little over 5 percent in each sample. Because the confidence intervals overlap, we cannot rule out the possibility that there has been no change in water contamination on airline flights; that is, the difference could be due to sampling variation. Nonetheless, the EPA is taking further steps to encourage airlines to improve water quality.

Source: *The Wall Street Journal,* Nov. 10, 2004, and Jan. 20, 2005.

8.7   Sample Size Determination for a Mean

A Myth

Many people feel that when the population is large, you need a larger sample to obtain a given level of precision in the estimate. This is incorrect. For a given level of precision, it is the sample size that matters, even if the population is a million or a billion. This is apparent from the confidence interval formula, which includes n but not N.*

Sample Size to Estimate μ

Suppose we wish to estimate a population mean with an allowable margin of error of $\pm E$. What sample size is required? We start with the general form of the confidence interval:

General Form	What We Want
$\bar{X} \pm z_{\alpha/2}\dfrac{\sigma}{\sqrt{n}}$	$\bar{X} \pm E$

In this confidence interval, we use z instead of t because we are going to solve for n, and degrees of freedom cannot be determined unless we know n. Equating the allowable error E to half of the confidence interval width and solving for n,

$$E = z_{\alpha/2}\frac{\sigma}{\sqrt{n}} \rightarrow E^2 = z_{\alpha/2}^2\frac{\sigma^2}{n} \rightarrow n = z_{\alpha/2}^2\frac{\sigma^2}{E^2}$$

Thus, the formula for the sample size can also be written

$$n = \left(\frac{z_{\alpha/2}\sigma}{E}\right)^2 \quad \text{(sample size to estimate } \mu) \tag{8.8}$$

Once n is calculated, always round n to the next higher integer to be conservative.

Concept Check

Looking at the formula for the sample size, for a given level of confidence, when would you take a larger sample? When getting blood tests at a medical laboratory or a hospital, the medical technician or nurse inserts a needle in only one spot on your body (i.e., only takes a sample of size 1). Why?

How to Estimate σ

Into this formula, we can plug our desired precision E and the appropriate z for the desired confidence level. However, σ poses a problem because it is usually unknown. Table 8.4

TABLE 8.4   Two Ways to Estimate σ

Method 1: Take a Preliminary Sample
Take a small preliminary sample and use the sample estimate s in place of σ. This method is the most common, though its logic is somewhat circular (i.e., take a sample to plan a sample).

Method 2: Assume Normal Population
Estimate rough upper and lower bounds a and b, and set $\sigma = (b - a)/4$. This assumes normality with most of the data within $\mu + 2\sigma$ and $\mu - 2\sigma$ so the range is 4σ. For example, we might guess the weight of a light truck to range from 1,500 pounds to 3,500 pounds, implying $\sigma = (3,500 - 1,500)/4 = 500$ pounds. Some books suggest $\sigma = R/6$ based on the Empirical Rule, but recent research shows that rule is not conservative enough.

* The special case of sampling finite populations is discussed in *LearningStats*.

shows a couple of ways to approximate the value of σ. You can always try both methods and see how much difference it makes. But until you take the sample, you will not know for sure if you have achieved your goal (i.e., the desired precision E).

<table>
<tr><td>

A produce manager wants to estimate the mean weight of Spanish onions being delivered by a supplier, with 95 percent confidence and an error of ± 1 ounce. A preliminary sample of 12 onions shows a sample standard deviation of 3.60 ounces. For a 95 percent confidence interval, we will set $z = 1.96$. We use $s = 3.60$ in place of σ and set the desired error $E = 1$ to obtain the required sample size:

$$n = [(1.96)(3.60)/(1)]^2 = 49.79, \text{ or } 50 \text{ onions}$$

We would round to the next higher integer and take a sample of 50 Spanish onions. This should ensure an estimate of the true mean weight with an error not exceeding ± 1 ounce.

A seemingly modest change in E can have a major effect on the sample size because it is squared. Suppose we reduce the allowable error to $E = 0.5$ ounce to obtain a more precise estimate. The required sample size would then be

$$n = [(1.96)(3.60)/(0.5)]^2 = 199.1, \text{ or } 200 \text{ onions}$$

</td><td>

EXAMPLE 9
Onion Weight

</td></tr>
</table>

Using MegaStat for Sample Size Determination for μ

There is also a sample size calculator in MegaStat, as illustrated in Figure 8.18. The Preview button lets you change the setup and see the result immediately.

Caution 1: Units of Measure

When estimating a mean, the allowable error E is expressed in the same units as X and σ. For example, E would be expressed in dollars when estimating the mean order size for mail-order customers (e.g., $E = \$2$) or in minutes to estimate the mean wait time for patients at a clinic (e.g., $E = 10$ minutes). To estimate last year's starting salaries for MBA graduates from a university, the allowable error could be large (e.g., $E = \$2,000$) because a $2,000 error in estimating μ might still be a reasonably accurate estimate.

Caution 2: Using z

Using z in the sample size formula for a mean is necessary but not conservative. Because t always exceeds z for a given confidence level, your actual interval may be wider than $\pm E$ as intended. As long as the required sample size is large (say 30 or more), the difference will be acceptable.

Caution 3: Larger n Is Better

The sample size formulas for a mean are not conservative, that is, they tend to underestimate the required sample size. Therefore, the sample size formulas for a mean should be regarded only as a minimum guideline. Whenever possible, samples should exceed this minimum, although the cost of taking a larger sample should be taken into consideration.

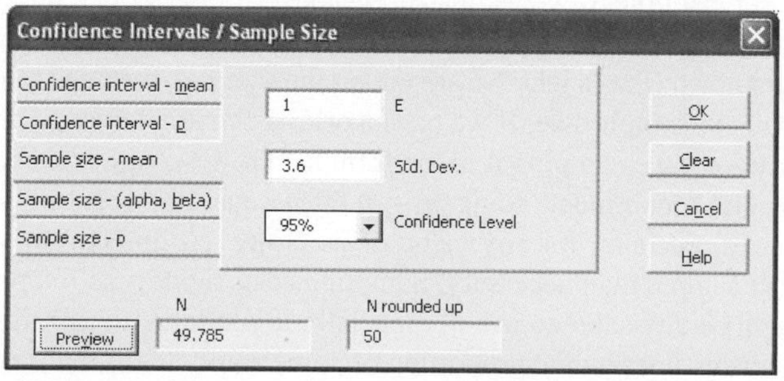

FIGURE 8.18

MegaStat's Sample Size
for a Mean

8.29 For each level of precision, find the required sample size to estimate the mean starting salary for a new Chartered Accountant with 95 percent confidence, assuming a population standard deviation of $7,500 (same as last year). (LO 6)
   a. $E = \$2,000$
   b. $E = \$1,000$
   c. $E = \$500$

8.30 Last year, a study showed that the average ABM cash withdrawal took 65 seconds with a standard deviation of 10 seconds. The study is to be repeated this year. How large a sample would be needed to estimate this year's mean with 95 percent confidence and an error of ± 4 seconds? (LO 6)

8.31 The city/highway fuel efficiency range for a Saturn Vue FWD automatic 5-speed transmission is 8.2 to 11.8 km/L. If you owned this vehicle, how large a sample (e.g., how many tanks of gas) would be required to estimate your mean fuel efficiency (km/L) with an error of ± 0.3 km/L and 99 percent confidence? Explain your assumption about σ. (LO 6)

8.32 Popcorn kernels are believed to take between 100 and 200 seconds to pop in a certain microwave. What sample size (number of kernels) would be needed to estimate the true mean seconds to pop with an error of ± 5 seconds and 95 percent confidence? Explain your assumption about σ. (LO 6)

8.33 How large would the samples have to be if we wished to estimate, with 95 percent confidence, the true average driving distance to within 5 yards for a more successful professional golfer and a less successful professional golfer. Assume that the standard deviation in driving distance for a more successful golfer is 7 yards and is 14 yards for a less successful golfer. (LO 6)

8.34 Noodles & Company wants to estimate the mean spending per customer at a certain restaurant with 95 percent confidence and an error of $\pm\$0.25$. What is the required sample size, assuming a standard deviation of $2.50 (based on similar restaurants elsewhere)? (LO 6) noodles & company

8.8   Sample Size Determination for a Proportion

Suppose we wish to estimate a population proportion with a precision (allowable error) of $\pm E$. What sample size is required? We start with the general form of the confidence interval:

General Form	*What We Want*
$p \pm z_{\alpha/2} \sqrt{\dfrac{\pi(1-\pi)}{n}}$	$p \pm E$

We equate the allowable error E to half of the confidence interval width and solve for n:

$$E = z_{\alpha/2}\sqrt{\frac{\pi(1-\pi)}{n}} \quad\rightarrow\quad E^2 = z_{\alpha/2}^2 \frac{\pi(1-\pi)}{n} \rightarrow n = z_{\alpha/2}^2 \frac{\pi(1-\pi)}{E^2}$$

Thus, the formula for the sample size for a proportion can be written as follows:

$$n = \left(\frac{z_{\alpha/2}}{E}\right)^2 \pi(1-\pi) \quad \text{(sample size to estimate } \pi) \tag{8.9}$$

As before, always round n to the next higher integer.

Because a proportion is a number between 0 and 1, the precision allowable error E is also between 0 and 1. For example, if we want an allowable error of ± 7 percent we would specify $E = 0.07$.

Because π is unknown (that's why we are taking the sample), we need to make an assumption about π to plan our sample size. If we have a prior estimate of π (e.g., from last year or a comparable application), we can plug it in the formula. Or we could take a small preliminary sample. Some experts recommend using $\pi = 0.50$ because the resulting sample size will guarantee the desired precision for any value of π. However, this conservative assumption may lead to a larger sample than necessary. Sampling costs money, so if a prior estimate of π is available, it might be advisable to use it, especially if you think that π differs greatly from 0.50. For example, in estimating the proportion of home equity loans that result in default, we

TABLE 8.5   Three Ways to Estimate π

Method 1: Take a Preliminary Sample

Take a small preliminary sample and insert p into the sample size formula in place of π. This method is appropriate if π is believed to differ greatly from 0.50, as is often the case, though its logic is somewhat circular (i.e., we must take a sample to plan our sample).

Method 2: Use a Prior Sample or Historical Data

A reasonable approach, but how often are such data available? And might π have changed enough to make it a questionable assumption?

Method 3: Assume That $\pi = 0.50$

This method is conservative and ensures the desired precision. It is therefore a sound choice. However, the sample may end up being larger than necessary.

would expect π to be much smaller than 0.50, while in estimating the proportion of motorists who use seat belts, we would hope that π would be much greater than 0.50. Table 8.5 details three ways to estimate π.

EXAMPLE 10
ABM Withdrawals

A university credit union wants to know the proportion of cash withdrawals that exceed $50 at its ABM located in the student union building. With an error of ± 2 percent and a confidence level of 95 percent, how large a sample is needed to estimate the proportion of withdrawals exceeding $50? The z value for 95 percent confidence is $z = 1.960$. Using $E = 0.02$ and assuming conservatively that $\pi = 0.50$, the required sample size is

$$n = \left(\frac{z_{0.025}}{E}\right)^2 \pi(1 - \pi) = \left(\frac{1.960}{0.02}\right)^2 (0.50)(1 - 0.50) = 2{,}401$$

We would need to examine $n = 2{,}401$ withdrawals to estimate π within ± 2 percent and with 95 percent confidence. In this case, last year's proportion of ABM withdrawals over $50 was 27 percent. If we had used this estimate in our calculation, the required sample size would be

$$n = \left(\frac{z_{0.025}}{E}\right)^2 p(1 - p) = \left(\frac{1.960}{0.02}\right)^2 (0.27)(1 - 0.27) = 1{,}893 \quad \text{(rounded to next higher integer)}$$

We would need to examine $n = 1{,}893$ withdrawals to estimate π within ± 0.02. The required sample size is smaller than when we make the conservative assumption $\pi = 0.50$.

Caution: Units of Measure

A common error is to insert $E = 2$ in the formula when you want an error of ± 2 percent. Because we are dealing with a *proportion,* a 2% error is $E = 0.02$. In other words, when estimating a proportion, E is always between 0 and 1.

Section Exercises

8.35 In a grocery store parking lot, 32 of 136 cars selected at random were white. (a) Construct a 98 percent confidence interval for the true proportion of white cars. (b) May normality be assumed? Explain. (c) What sample size would be needed to estimate the true proportion of white cars with an error of ± 0.06 and 90 percent confidence? With an error of ± 0.03 and 95 percent confidence? (d) Why are the sample sizes in (c) so different? (LO 6)

8.36 (a) What sample size would be required to estimate the true proportion of Canadian female business executives who prefer the title "Ms.," with an error of ± 0.025 and 98 percent confidence? (b) What method would you recommend for estimating π? Explain. (LO 6)

8.37 (a) What sample size would be needed to estimate the true proportion of Canadian households that own more than one DVD player, with 90 percent confidence and an error of ± 0.02? (b) What sampling method would you recommend? Why? (LO 6)

8.38 (a) What sample size would be needed to estimate the true proportion of students at your university (if you are a student) who are wearing backpacks, with 95 percent confidence and an error of ± 0.04? (b) What sampling method would you recommend? Why? (LO 6)

8.39 (a) What sample size would be needed to estimate the true proportion of European adults who know their cholesterol level, using 95 percent confidence and an error of ± 0.02? (b) What sampling method would you recommend, and why? (LO 6)

8.40* A manufacturer of light bulbs was interested in estimating what proportion of Canadian households would use and like their new energy-efficient—but rather ugly—light bulb. It initially handed out a dozen of these light bulbs to each of 100 randomly selected households across Canada and contacted these households three weeks later to see if they had used them and if they had liked them. Twenty of these households had used them and liked them. Estimate, with 95 percent confidence, the proportion of all Canadian households that would use them and like them. Suppose a more extensive study was necessary, how large a sample would have to be taken such that the margin of error would be no greater than 0.02? Calculate this sample size using the results from the initial study and calculate the sample size using the conservative method. Instead of using random sampling to conduct this study, what might be a better sampling scheme to use? Explain why. (LO 6)

8.41 It is claimed that the more successful professional golfers are more likely to hit the fairway with their tee shots than the less professional golfers. Relative small samples of tee shots from both the more successful golfers and less successful golfers were taken. The sample results indicated that 85 percent of the more successful golfers hit the fairway with their tee shots while the less successful golfers hit the fairways only 60 percent of the time. Using these sample estimates, how large would the samples have to be in order to estimate to within 5 percent of the true percentage of times the more successful golfers hit the fairway and the less successful golfers hit the fairway? How large would the samples have to be using the conservative method? Use a 90 percent level of confidence in all cases. Why is the difference in sample sizes calculated using the sample estimate of π and the conservative estimate of π greater for the more successful golfer than for the less successful golfer? (LO 6)

8.9 Confidence Interval for a Population Variance, σ^2

Chi-Square Distribution

In our previous discussions of means and differences in means, we have indicated that many times we do not know the population variance, σ^2. A variance estimate can be useful information for many business applications. For us to be able to estimate σ^2, we use its best estimator, S^2, and its relationship with σ^2. If the population is normal, the relationship takes the form of a **chi-square distribution** where $\chi^2 = \dfrac{(n-1)S^2}{\sigma^2}$ has a χ^2 distribution with degrees of freedom, $\nu = n - 1$.

Using similar mathematical manipulations as with all of our confidence interval formulas, our confidence interval becomes.

$$\frac{(n-1)s^2}{\chi^2_{\alpha/2,n-1}} < \sigma^2 < \frac{(n-1)s^2}{\chi^2_{1-\alpha/2,n-1}} \tag{8.10}$$

Note: χ^2 distributions, unlike the Z and t distributions, are not symmetrical, and their smallest possible χ^2 value is zero. One change that this causes is that the lower-tail value of χ^2 is not the negative of the upper-tail value of χ^2. Therefore, we need a table that reflects this fact and we need to subscript in such a way so we know what value of χ^2 we need to determine. In addition to including $(n-1)$ in the subscripts for χ^2, we have included either $\alpha/2$ or $1 - \alpha/2$. Both these subscripts refer to the area to the right of the value of χ^2 of interest or to the area in the upper tail (which could, theoretically, be as large as 1). So, if we want to find the 95 percent confidence interval for σ^2, we would go to Appendix E and, in addition to locating the appropriate degrees of freedom, we would locate the columns $\chi^2_{0.025}$ and $\chi^2_{0.975}$. Reading across the appropriate row and down the appropriate columns, we would find the appropriate values of $\chi^2_{0.025}$ and $\chi^2_{0.975}$.

EXAMPLE 11
DVD Prices DVD

In a particular week, the prices of the top 40 DVD movies at Blockbuster showed a mean of $\bar{X} = 24.76$ with a sample variance of $s^2 = 12.77$.

29.51	21.09	29.98	29.95	21.07	29.52	21.07	24.95	21.07	24.95
24.98	29.95	24.95	21.07	25.30	25.30	29.95	29.99	29.95	24.95
24.95	21.07	24.98	21.09	21.07	24.98	21.07	25.30	29.95	25.30
25.30	24.98	16.86	25.30	25.30	16.86	24.95	24.98	25.30	21.07

Source: From a project by statistics students Robyn Freeman, Sarah Jespersen, and Jennifer Pritchett.

The sample data were nearly symmetric (median $24.98) with no outliers. Normality of the prices will be assumed. From Appendix E, using 39 degrees of freedom ($\nu = n - 1 = 40 - 1 = 39$) we obtain bounds for the 95 percent middle area, as illustrated in the figure below.

CHI-SQUARE CRITICAL VALUES

Left   Right

					Upper Tail Area					
ν	0.995	0.99	0.975	0.95	0.9	0.1	0.05	0.025	0.01	0.005
1	0.000	0.000	0.001	0.004	0.016	2.706	3.841	5.024	6.635	7.879
2	0.010	0.020	0.051	0.103	0.211	4.605	5.991	7.378	9.210	10.597
3	0.072	0.115	0.216	0.352	0.584	6.251	7.815	9.348	11.345	12.838
4	0.207	0.297	0.484	0.711	1.064	7.779	9.488	11.143	13.277	14.860
5	0.412	0.554	0.831	1.145	1.610	9.236	11.070	12.833	15.086	16.750
36	17.887	19.233	21.336	23.269	25.643	47.212	50.998	54.437	58.619	61.581
37	18.586	19.960	22.106	24.075	26.492	48.363	52.192	55.668	59.893	62.883
38	19.289	20.691	22.878	24.884	27.343	49.513	53.384	56.896	61.162	64.181
39	19.996	21.426	23.654	25.695	28.196	50.660	54.572	58.120	62.428	65.476
40	20.707	22.164	24.433	26.509	29.051	51.805	55.758	59.342	63.691	66.766
...	...	...	...	...	...	...	...	...	...	...
50	27.991	29.707	32.357	34.764	37.689	63.167	67.505	71.420	76.154	79.490
60	35.534	37.485	40.482	43.188	46.459	74.397	79.082	83.298	88.379	91.952
70	43.275	45.442	48.758	51.739	55.329	85.527	90.531	95.023	100.425	104.215
80	51.172	53.540	57.153	60.391	64.278	96.578	101.879	106.629	112.329	116.321
90	59.196	61.754	65.647	69.126	73.291	107.565	113.145	118.136	124.116	128.299
100	67.328	70.065	74.222	77.929	82.358	118.498	124.342	129.561	135.807	140.169

$$\chi^2_{0.975,39} = 23.654 \text{ (upper 97.5 percent is the same as lower 2.5 percent)}$$

$$\chi^2_{0.025,39} = 58.12 \text{ (upper 2.5 percent)}$$

The 95 percent confidence interval for the population variance σ^2 is

$$\text{Lower bound: } \frac{(n-1)s^2}{\chi^2_{0.025,39}} = \frac{(40-1)(12.77)}{58.12} = 8.569$$

$$\text{Upper bound: } \frac{(n-1)s^2}{\chi^2_{0.975,39}} = \frac{(40-1)(12.77)}{23.654} = 21.055$$

With 95 percent confidence, we believe that $8.569 < \sigma^2 < 21.058$.

If you want a confidence interval for the standard deviation σ, just take the square root of the interval bounds. In the DVD example, we get $2.93 < \sigma < 4.59$.

Section Exercises

8.42 Find the 95 percent confidence interval for the population variance from these samples. (LO 3)
   a. $n = 15$ commuters, $s = 10$ kilometres driven
   b. $n = 18$ students, $s = 12$ study hours

8.43 The weights of 20 oranges (in ounces) are shown below. Construct a 95 percent confidence interval for the population standard deviation. *Note:* Scale was only accurate to the nearest 1/4 ounce. (Data are from a project by statistics student Julie Gillman.) (LO 3) **Oranges**

5.50	6.25	6.25	6.50	6.50	7.00	7.00	7.00	7.50	7.50
7.75	8.00	8.00	8.50	8.50	9.00	9.00	9.25	10.00	10.50

8.44 A pediatrician's records showed the mean height of a random sample of 25 girls at age 12 months to be 75 cm with a standard deviation of 2.75 cm. Construct a 95 percent confidence interval for the population variance. (LO 3)

8.45 Find the 90 percent confidence interval for the population standard deviation of gasoline mileage based on mileage recorded for a random sample of these 16 commuters driving hybrid gas-electric vehicles. (LO 3) **Hybrid**

38.8	48.9	28.5	40.0	38.8	29.2	29.1	38.5
34.4	46.1	51.8	30.7	36.9	25.6	42.7	38.3

8.46 For many years there has been an ongoing discussion about raising the speed limit along Highway 401, connecting Windsor, Ontario, with the western border of Quebec. Those not wanting the speed limit raised argue that higher speeds would create more accidents, while those arguing for the increased limit say that the variability in speeds among drivers would decrease causing fewer accidents. Currently, the variability in speeds along the 401 is 18 km/h. Suppose the speed limit along the 401 was raised to 125 km/h for a brief period of time and a random sample of 15 cars driving along a randomly selecting portion of the 401 with no traffic congestion revealed a standard deviation in speeds of 8 km/h. Estimate, with 95 percent confidence, the standard deviation in speeds along the 401 is the speed limit was raised to 125 km/h. Why might this estimate not apply in heavy traffic? Explain. (LO 3)

8.47 What separates the more successful professional golfers from the less successful? One could argue that one of the determining factors is how consistent (i.e., how similar the driving distances are) a golfer can hit his driver during a tournament. A more successful and a less successful professional were randomly chosen and how far (in yards) they hit their drivers on seven randomly selected holes over the past six months were recorded as follows:

More successful: 312, 300, 298, 308, 312, 306, 302

Less successful: 285, 295, 305, 275, 284, 276, 295

Estimate, with 95 percent confidence, the true standard deviation in distance each golfer can hit his driver. By comparing these two confidence intervals, could you argue that the more successful golfers are more consistent than the less successful golfers? Explain. (LO 3)

CHAPTER SUMMARY

An **estimator** is a sample statistic ($\bar{X}$, S, P) that is used to estimate an unknown population **parameter** (μ, σ, π). A desirable estimator is **unbiased** (correctly centred), **efficient** (minimum variance), and **consistent** (variance goes to zero as n increases). **Sampling error** (the difference between an estimator and its parameter) is inevitable, but a larger sample size yields estimates that are generally closer to the unknown parameter. The **Central Limit Theorem (CLT)** states that the sample mean $\bar{X}$ follows a normal distribution if n is large, regardless of the population shape. A **confidence interval** for μ consists of lower and upper bounds that have a specified probability (called the **confidence level**) of enclosing μ. Any confidence level may be used, but 90, 95, and 99 percent are common. If the population variance is unknown, we replace z in the confidence interval formula for μ with **Student's t** using $n - 1$ degrees of freedom. The CLT also applies to the sample proportion (P) as an estimator of π, using a rule of thumb to decide if normality may be assumed. The **margin of error** is the half-width of the confidence interval. Formulas exist for the required **sample size** for a given level of precision in a confidence interval for μ or π, although they entail assumptions and are only approximate. Confidence intervals and sample sizes may be adjusted for finite populations, but often the adjustments are not material. Confidence intervals may be created for differences of means or proportions, or for a variance.

KEY TERMS

bias, *308*	efficiency (efficient estimator), *309*	sampling distribution, *306*
Central Limit Theorem (CLT), *313*	estimate, *305*	sampling error, *310*
chi-square distribution, *338*	estimator, *305*	sampling variation, *303*
confidence interval, *315*	interval estimate, *318*	standard error of the mean, *310*
confidence level, *315*	margin of error, *315*	statistical estimation, *304*
consistent estimator, *309*	parameter, *305*	Student's *t* distribution, *320*
degrees of freedom, *320*	point estimate, *315*	unbiased estimator, *308*

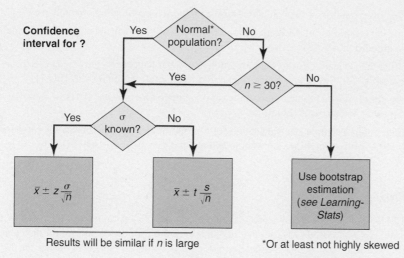

Commonly Used Formulas in Sampling Distributions and Estimation

Sample Proportion: $p = \dfrac{x}{n}$

Standard Error of the Sample Mean: $\sigma_{\bar{X}} = \dfrac{\sigma}{\sqrt{n}}$

Confidence Interval for μ, known σ: $\bar{x} \pm z_{\alpha/2}\dfrac{\sigma}{\sqrt{n}}$

Confidence Interval for μ, unknown σ: $\bar{x} \pm t_{\alpha/2,\,n-1}\dfrac{s}{\sqrt{n}}$

Degrees of Freedom: $\nu = n-1$

Standard Error of the Sample Proportion: $\sigma_p = \sqrt{\dfrac{\pi(1-\pi)}{n}}$

Confidence Interval for π: $p \pm z_{\alpha/2}\sqrt{\dfrac{p(1-p)}{n}}$

Sample Size to Estimate μ: $n = \left(\dfrac{z\sigma}{E}\right)^2$

Sample Size to Estimate π: $n = \left(\dfrac{z}{E}\right)^2 \pi(1-\pi)$

1. Define (a) parameter, (b) estimator, (c) sampling error, and (d) sampling distribution. (LO 1)

2. Explain the difference between sampling error and bias. Can they be controlled? (LO 1)

3. Name three estimators. Which ones are unbiased? (LO 1)

4. Explain what it means to say an estimator is (a) unbiased, (b) efficient, and (c) consistent. (LO 2)

5. State the main points of the Central Limit Theorem for a mean. (LO 3)

6. Why is population shape of concern when estimating a mean? What does sample size have to do with it? (LO 3)

7. (a) Define the standard error of the mean. (b) What happens to the standard error as sample size increases? (c) How does the law of diminishing returns apply to the standard error? (LO 1)

8. Define (a) point estimate, (b) margin of error, (c) confidence interval, and (d) confidence level. (LO 1)

9. List some common confidence levels. Why not use other confidence levels? (LO 2)

10. List differences and similarities between Student's *t* and the standard normal distribution. (LO 4)

11. Give an example to show that (a) for a given confidence level, the Student's *t* confidence interval for the mean is wider than if we use a *z* value; and (b) it makes little difference in a large sample whether we use Student's *t* or *z*. (LO 4)

CHAPTER REVIEW

12. Why do outliers and skewed populations pose a problem for estimating a sample mean? (LO 1)

13. (a) State the Central Limit Theorem for a proportion. (b) When is it safe to assume normality for a sample proportion? (LO 3)

14. (a) Define the standard error of the proportion. (b) What happens to the standard error as sample size increases? (c) Why does a larger sample improve a confidence interval? (LO 1)

15. (a) Why does σ pose a problem for sample size calculation for a mean? (b) How can σ be approximated when it is unknown? (LO 6)

16. (a) When doing a sample size calculation for a proportion, why is it conservative to assume that $\pi = 0.50$? (b) When might we not want to assume that $\pi = 0.50$, and why? (LO 6)

USING SOFTWARE

Using MINITAB

Use MINITAB's Stat > Basic Statistics *Stat* > Graphical Summary to get confidence intervals, as well as a histogram and box plot. MINITAB uses the Student's *t* for the confidence interval for the mean. It also gives confidence intervals for the median and standard deviation. Figure 8.20 shows the MINITAB Graphical Summary for sample 1 (maternity LOS).

FIGURE 8.20

MINITAB's Confidence Interval

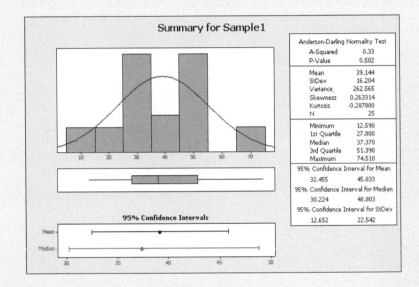

Small Samples: MINITAB

If the sample is small (i.e., if we cannot meet the normality), the distribution of *P* may not be well approximated by the normal. Instead of assuming a continuous normal model, confidence limits around *P* can be constructed by using the binomial distribution. MINITAB uses this method by default, as it works for any *n* (you have to press the Options button to assume normality). Although the underlying calculations are a bit complex, MINITAB does all the work and the resulting interval is correct for any *n* and *p*.

For example, *The New York Times Magazine* reported that in a sample of 14 purchasers of the *Spider-Man 2* DVD, 11 watched only the film and never even looked at the "extras" (Nov. 14, 2004, p. 107). The sample proportion is $p = 11/14$. What is the 95 percent confidence interval for the proportion of purchasers who never viewed the "extras"? Because $n < 9p/(1 - p)$ ($n = 14$ and $9p(1 - p)$ = 33), we should not assume normality. Figure 8.21 shows a sample of MINITAB's confidence interval using the binomial distribution with Stat > Basic Statistics > One Proportion. MINITAB's binomial confidence interval (0.492, 0.953) is quite different from the normal confidence interval (0.571, 1.000). MINITAB includes a warning about the normal confidence interval.

MINITAB's Confidence Interval FIGURE 8.21

1 Proportion (Test and Confidence Interval)   ☒

    ○ Samples in columns:

    ● Summarized data
       Number of trials: `14`
       Number of events: `11`

    Select   Options...

    Help   OK   Cancel

```
CI for One Proportion (Using Binomial)
Sample   X    N   Sample p          95% CI
1       11   14   0.785714   (0.492024, 0.953421)

CI for One Proportion (Assuming Normality)
Sample   X    N   Sample p          95% CI
1       11   14   0.785714   (0.570776, 1.000000)
* NOTE * The normal approximation may be inaccurate for small samples.
```

Using LearningStats for Sample Size Determination for μ

There is a sample size calculator in *LearningStats* that makes these calculations easy, as illustrated in Figure 8.22 for $E = 1$ and $E = 0.5$.

Assuming $E = \pm 1$ and $\sigma = 1$

	Desired Confidence Level				
	90%	95%	98%	99%	99.9%
z	1.645	1.960	2.330	2.575	3.291
n	36	50	71	86	141

Assuming $E = \pm 1$ and $\sigma = 0.5$

	Desired Confidence Level				
	90%	95%	98%	99%	99.9%
z	1.645	1.960	2.330	2.575	3.291
n	141	200	281	344	562

FIGURE 8.22

LearningStats Sample Size for a Mean

Using LearningStats for Sample Size Determination for π

The sample size calculator in *LearningStats* makes these calculations easy, as illustrated in Figure 8.23 for $\pi = 0.50$ and $E = 0.02$.

FIGURE 8.23

LearningStats Sample Size for a Proportion

	Desired Confidence Level				
	90%	95%	98%	99%	99.9%
z	1.645	1.960	2.330	2.575	3.291
n	1691	2401	3383	4147	6768

Using MINITAB for Confidence Intervals

If you have raw data, MINITAB's Stats > Basic Statistics > Graphical Summary gives nice confidence intervals for the mean, median, and standard deviation for a column of raw data, as well as a histogram and box plot. MINITAB uses Student's *t* for the confidence interval for the mean and calculates the confidence interval for σ, as illustrated in Figure 8.24.

FIGURE 8.24

MINITAB's Confidence Intervals

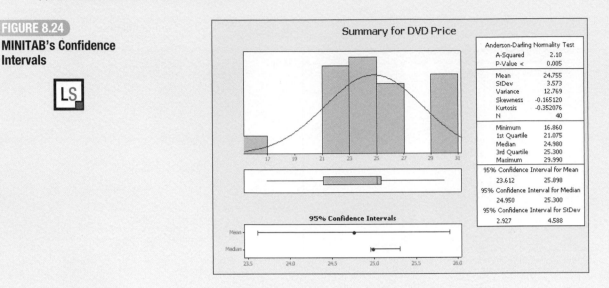

Using LearningStats for Chi-Square Distribution

Figure 8.25 shows the chi-square distribution for $\nu = 39$. The sample screen is from *LearningStats*. Although the chi-square distribution is always right-skewed, this one is somewhat bell-shaped because the sample size is large (i.e., large degrees of freedom). In smaller samples, its skewness would be more apparent.

FIGURE 8.25 *LearningStats'* **Chi-Square Distribution**

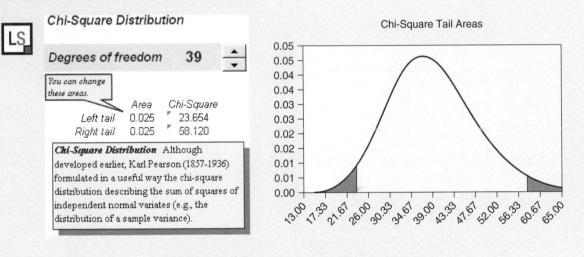

CHAPTER EXERCISES

Note: Explain answers and show your work clearly.

8.48 This is an exercise using Excel. (a) Use =RANDBETWEEN(0,99) to create 20 samples of size $n = 4$ by choosing two-digit random numbers between 00 and 99. (b) For each sample, calculate the mean. (c) Make a histogram of the 80 *individual X values* using bins 10 units wide (i.e., 0, 10, 20, ..., 100). Describe the shape of the histogram. (d) Make a histogram of your 20 *sample means* using bins 10 units wide. (e) Discuss the histogram shape. Does the Central Limit Theorem seem to be working? (f) Find the mean of the sample means. Was it what you would expect by the CLT? Explain. (g) Find the average standard deviation of the sample means. Was it what you would expect by the CLT? (LO 5)

8.49 A random sample of 21 nickels measured with a very accurate micrometer showed a mean diameter of 21.19 mm with a standard deviation of 0.048 mm. (a) Why would nickel diameters vary? (b) Construct a 99 percent confidence interval for the true mean diameter of a nickel. (c) Discuss any assumptions that are needed. (d) What sample size would ensure an error of ±0.01 mm with 99 percent confidence? (LO 3)

8.50 A random sample of 10 miniature Tootsie Rolls was taken from a bag. Each piece was weighed on a very accurate scale. The results in grams were

3.087 3.131 3.241 3.241 3.270 3.353 3.400 3.411 3.437 3.477

(a) Construct a 90 percent confidence interval for the true mean weight. (b) What sample size would be necessary to estimate the true weight with an error of ±0.03 grams with 90 percent confidence? (c) Discuss the factors which might cause variation in the weight of Tootsie Rolls during manufacture. (LO 3) **Tootsie**

8.51 Statistics students were asked to go home and fill a 1-cup measure with raisin bran, tap the cup lightly on the counter three times to settle the contents, if necessary add more raisin bran to bring the contents exactly up to the 1-cup line, spread the contents on a large plate, and count the raisins. For the 13 students who chose Kellogg's brand the reported results were

23 33 44 36 29 42 31 33 61 36 34 23 24

(a) Construct a 90 percent confidence interval for the mean number of raisins per cup. Show your work clearly. (b) Can you think of features of the sample or data-gathering method that might create problems? If so, how could they be improved? (c) Identify factors that might prevent Kellogg's from achieving uniformity in the number of raisins per cup of raisin bran. (d) How might a quality control system work to produce more uniform quantities of raisins, assuming that improvement is desired? (LO 3) **Raisins**

8.52 A sample of 20 pages was taken without replacement from a 1,591-page *Yellow Pages* phone directory. On each page, the mean area devoted to display ads was measured (a display ad is a large block of multicoloured illustrations, maps, and text). The data (in square millimetres) are shown below:

| 0 | 260 | 356 | 403 | 536 | 0 | 268 | 369 | 428 | 536 |
| 268 | 396 | 469 | 536 | 162 | 338 | 403 | 536 | 536 | 130 |

(a) Construct a 95 percent confidence interval for the true mean. (b) Why might normality be an issue here? (c) What sample size would be needed to obtain an error of ±10 square millimetres with 99 percent confidence? (d) If this is not a reasonable requirement, suggest one that is. (LO 3) **DisplayAds**

8.53 Sixteen owners of 2005 Chrysler Pacifica 2WD vehicles kept track of their average fuel economy for a month. The results are shown below. (a) Construct a 95 percent confidence interval for the mean. (b) What factor(s) limit the conclusions that can be drawn about the true mean? (LO 3) **MPG**

| 20.8 | 20.0 | 19.4 | 19.7 | 21.1 | 22.6 | 18.3 | 20.1 |
| 20.5 | 19.5 | 17.4 | 22.4 | 18.9 | 20.2 | 19.6 | 19.0 |

8.54 Twenty-five blood samples were selected by taking every seventh blood sample from racks holding 187 blood samples from the morning draw at a medical centre. The white blood count (WBC) was measured using a Coulter Counter Model S. The mean WBC was 8.636 with a standard deviation of 3.9265. (a) Construct a 90 percent confidence interval for the true mean. (b) Why might normality be an issue here? (c) What sample size would be needed for an error of ±1.5 with 98 percent confidence? (LO 3 & 6)

8.55 Dave the jogger runs the same route every day (about 3.5 kilometres). On 18 consecutive days, he recorded the number of steps using a pedometer. The results were

| 3,450 | 3,363 | 3,228 | 3,360 | 3,304 | 3,407 | 3,324 | 3,365 | 3,290 |
| 3,289 | 3,346 | 3,252 | 3,237 | 3,210 | 3,140 | 3,220 | 3,103 | 3,129 |

(a) Construct a 95 percent confidence interval for the true mean number of steps Dave takes on his run. (b) What sample size would be needed to obtain an error of ±20 steps with 95 percent confidence? (c) Using Excel, plot a line chart of the data. What does the data suggest about the pattern over time? (LO 3 & 6) **DaveSteps**

8.56 A pediatrician's records showed the mean height of a random sample of 25 girls at age 12 months to be 75 centimetres with a standard deviation of 3 centimetres. (a) Construct a 95 percent confidence interval for the true mean height. (b) Could normality reasonably be assumed for this population? (c) What sample size would be needed for 95 percent confidence and an error of ± 0.5 centimetres? (LO 3 & 6)

8.57 A sample of 40 CDs from a student's collection showed a mean length of 52.74 minutes with a standard deviation of 13.21 minutes. (a) Construct a 95 percent confidence interval for the mean. (b) Why might the normality assumption be an issue here? (c) What sample size would be needed for 95 percent confidence and an error of ± 3 minutes? (LO 3 & 6)

8.58 The U.S. Environmental Protection Agency (EPA) requires that cities monitor over 80 contaminants in their drinking water. Samples from the Lake Huron Water Treatment Plant gave the results shown here. Only the range is reported, not the mean (presumably the mean would be the midrange). (a) For each substance, estimate the *standard deviation* σ by using one of the methods shown in Table 8.4 in Section 8.7. (b) Why might an estimate of σ be helpful in planning future water sample testing? (LO 3)

Substance	MCLG Range Detected	Allowable MCLG	Origin of Substance
Chromium	0.47 to 0.69	100	Discharge for steel and pulp mills, natural erosion
Selenium	0 to 0.0014	50	Corrosion of household plumbing, leaching from wood preservatives, natural erosion
Barium	0.004 to 0.019	2	Discharge from drilling wastes, metal refineries, natural erosion
Fluoride	1.07 to 1.17	4.0	Natural erosion, water additive, discharge from fertilizer and aluminum factories

MCLG = Maximum contaminant level goal

8.59 In a sample of 100 Planter's Mixed Nuts, 19 were found to be almonds. (a) Construct a 90 percent confidence interval for the true proportion of almonds. (b) May normality be assumed? Explain. (c) What sample size would be needed for 90 percent confidence and an error of ± 0.03? (d) Why would a quality control manager at Planter's need to understand sampling? (LO 3 & 6)

8.60 Fourteen of 180 publicly traded business services companies in the U.S. failed a test for compliance with Sarbanes-Oxley requirements for financial records and fraud protection. (a) Assuming that these are a random sample of all publicly traded companies, construct a 95 percent confidence interval for the overall non-compliance proportion. (b) Why might this statistic not apply to all sectors of publicly traded companies (e.g., aerospace and defence)? See *The New York Times,* Apr. 27, 2005, p. BU5. (LO 3)

8.61 How "decaffeinated" is decaffeinated coffee? If a researcher wants to estimate the mean caffeine content of a cup of Starbucks decaffeinated espresso with 98 percent confidence and an error of ± 0.1 mg, what is the required number of cups that must be tested? Assume a standard deviation of 0.5 mg, based on a small preliminary sample of 12 cups. (See R. R. McCusker, B. A. Goldberger, and E. J. Cone, "Caffeine Content of Decaffeinated Coffee," *Journal of Analytical Toxicology* 30, no. 7 [Oct. 2006], pp. 611–613.) (LO 6)

8.62 Noodles & Company wants to estimate the percent of customers who order dessert, with 95 percent confidence and an error of ± 10 percent. What is the required sample size? (LO 6)

8.63 Junior Achievement and Deloitte commissioned a "teen ethics poll" of 787 students aged 13 to 18, finding that 29 percent felt inadequately prepared to make ethical judgments. (a) Assuming that this was a random sample, find the 95 percent confidence interval for the true proportion of U.S. teens who feel inadequately prepared to make ethical judgments. (b) Is the sample size large enough to assume normality? (See ja.org/about_newsitem.asp?StoryID=376.) (LO 3)

8.64 NBC asked a sample of VCR owners to record *Late Night with David Letterman* on their VCRs. Of the 125 VCR owners surveyed, 83 either "gave up or screwed up" because they did not understand how to program the VCR. (a) Construct a 90 percent confidence interval for the true proportion of VCR owners who cannot program their VCRs. (b) Would viewers of this program be typical of all television viewers? Explain. (Data are from *Popular Science* 237, no. 5, p. 63.) (LO 3)

8.65 A "teen ethics poll" was commissioned by Junior Achievement and Deloitte. The survey by Harris Interactive surveyed 787 students aged 13 to 18. (a) Assuming that this was a random sample of all students in this age group, find the margin of error of the poll. (b) Would the margin of error be greater or smaller for the subgroup consisting only of male students? Explain. (See ja.org/about_newsitem.asp?StoryID=376.) (LO 3)

8.66 Biting an unpopped kernel of popcorn hurts! As an experiment, a self-confessed connoisseur of cheap popcorn carefully counted 773 kernels and put them in a popper. After popping, the unpopped kernels were counted. There were 86. (a) Construct a 90 percent confidence interval for the proportion of all kernels that would not pop. (b) Check the normality assumption. (c) Why might this sample not be typical? (LO 3)

8.67 A sample of 213 newspaper tire ads from several Sunday papers showed that 98 contained a low-price guarantee (offer to "meet or beat any price"). (a) Assuming that this was a random sample, construct a 95 percent confidence interval for the proportion of all Sunday newspaper tire ads that contain a low-price guarantee. (b) Is the criterion for normality met? (See *The New York Times,* Jan. 11, 2007, p. C3.) (LO 3)

8.68 Of 250 university students taking a statistics class, four reported an allergy to peanuts. (a) Is the criterion for normality met? (b) Assuming that this was a random sample, use MINITAB to construct a 95 percent confidence interval for the proportion of all university statistics students with a peanut allergy. (LO 3)

8.69 Acoustomagnetic surveillance antitheft portals (the kind used to prevent shoplifting) temporarily affected the pacemakers in 48 out of 50 subjects tested. (a) Construct a 90 percent confidence interval for the proportion of all subjects whose pacemakers would be affected. (b) What problems of interpretation arise? (c) Check the normality assumption. If not met, what could we do? (d) Use MINITAB to estimate a confidence interval without assuming normality. (Data are from *Science News* 154, no. 19, p. 294.) (LO 3)

8.70 (a) A poll of 2,277 voters throughout Britain on the proposed EU constitution would have approximately what margin of error? (b) The poll showed that 44 percent opposed Britain's signing the proposed constitution. Construct a 90 percent confidence interval for the true proportion opposed to signing it. (c) Would you say that the percentage of all voters opposed could be 50 percent? Explain. (Data are from *The Economist* 268, no. 8331 [July 5, 2003], p. 30.) (LO 3)

8.71 To determine the proportion of taxpayers who prefer filing tax returns electronically, a survey of 600 taxpayers was conducted. Calculate the margin of error used to estimate this proportion. What assumptions are required to find the margin of error? (LO 3)

8.72 A sample of 40 CDs from a student's collection showed a mean length of 52.74 minutes with a standard deviation of 13.21 minutes. Construct a 95 percent confidence interval for the population standard deviation. (Data are from a project by statistics students Michael Evatz, Nancy Petack, and Jennifer Skladanowski.) (LO 3)

OVERALL CHAPTER QUESTIONS

8.73* The manufacturer of a "long-lasting" light bulb claims that its bulbs last an average of 2,500 hours. A consumer testing organization purchased 25 of these light bulbs at different stores across Canada. If the standard deviation in lifetime is known to be 50 hours, calculate the probability that (a) one specifically chosen light bulb lasts less than 1,950 hours; (b) that each of three specifically chosen light bulbs each lasts less than 1,950 hours; and (c) that the average life of the 25 light bulbs is less than 1,950 hours. Suppose each of the above outcomes actually occurred. Which outcome would cause you to question the claim the most? Explain. Suppose the average life of these 25 light bulbs was 1,980 hours. Estimate, with 95 percent confidence, the true average life of this manufacturer's "long-lasting" light bulbs. How large a sample would have had to be taken in order to estimate, with 95 percent confidence, the true average life to within three hours? (LO 3 & 6)

8.74 Suppose a Canadian magazine article written about the Canadian restaurant industry claims that 70 percent of customers in higher-end restaurants leave tips of 20 percent or higher. If this claim is true, what is the probability that, in a random sample of 250 customers in these restaurants, no more than 150 left a tip of 20 percent or higher? In a sample of 100 customers, what is the probability that no more than 60 left a tip of 20 percent or higher if this claim is true? If in a sample of 250 customers, 145 left a tip of 20 percent or higher, estimate with 99 percent confidence the true proportion of customers in higher-end restaurants that leave a tip of 20 percent or higher. Using this sample estimate, how large a sample would have had to be taken to estimate the true proportion within 0.01 with 99 percent confidence. (LO 3 & 6)

8.75* To answer questions about their products, many manufacturers rely on call centres when responding to their customers. Some of these call centres use a strategy of allowing the customer to access a customer service representative directly while others use a strategy that requires the customers to respond to questions using the touch pads of their telephones before they finally reach a person to whom they can actually talk. A manufacturer who is about to sign a contract with one of two call centres (one using the strategy of direct access, the other using the strategy of indirect access), wanted to conduct a study to estimate the average time that a customer would spend with a customer representative under each of the two strategies. Suppose the manufacturer was allowed to use each call centre and monitor a limited amount of calls from its customers. The 15 calls where direct access was allowed averaged 7.3 minutes with a customer service representative with a standard deviation of 2.1 minutes. The 12 calls where indirect access was used averaged 6.0 minutes with a standard deviation of 1.8 minutes. Assuming that the amounts of time spent with customer service representatives are normally distributed, estimate, with 95 percent confidence, the true average time its customers would spend with a customer service representative under each strategy. (LO 3)

8.76 To save costs, most call centres are located outside of North America where labour costs are much cheaper. But, are customers as satisfied with these "off-shore" call centres? A random sample of 100 who used a North American call centre was contacted and 67 percent indicated that they were satisfied with the service. A random sample of 75 customers who used an off-shore call centre revealed that only 58 percent were satisfied with the service. Assuming that the normal distribution can be used, estimate with 95 percent confidence the true proportion of customers that are satisfied with each individual call centre. Comment on your findings. (LO 3)

8.77* Two students just completed a 100-question multiple-choice exam where the questions were randomly selected from a very large test bank of questions. Because answering incorrectly was severely punished, the two students only answered the questions for which they knew the answers. Ted answered 47 percent of the questions correctly and thus failed the exam, while Nora answered 54 percent of the questions correctly and thus passed the exam. Assuming that the normal distribution can be used, estimate with 98 percent confidence the true proportion of test bank questions that each student knows. (LO 3)

EXPERIMENTS

8.78 For 10 tanks of gas for your car, calculate the fuel efficiency in kilometres per litre (km/L). (a) Construct a 95 percent confidence interval for the true mean fuel efficiency for your car. (b) Discuss the normality assumption. (c) How many tanks of gas would you need to obtain an error of ± 0.2 km/L with 95 percent confidence? (LO 3 & 6)

8.79 (a) Look at 50 vehicles in a parking lot near you. Count the number that are SUVs (state your definition of SUV). Use any sampling method you like (e.g., the first 50 you see). (b) Construct a 95 percent confidence interval for the true population proportion of SUVs. (c) What sample size would be needed to ensure an error of ± 0.025 with 98 percent confidence? (d) Would the proportion be the same if this experiment were repeated in a university parking lot? (LO 3 & 6)

8.80 (a) From a sports almanac or Web site, take a random sample of 50 NBA players and calculate the proportion who are at least 7 feet in height. (b) Make a 90 percent confidence interval for the population proportion of all NBA players who are at least 7 feet tall. (LO 3)

8.81 (a) Look at 50 vehicles from a college or university student parking lot. Count the number of two-door vehicles. Use any sampling method you like (e.g., the first 50 you see). (b) Do the same for a grocery store that is not very close to the college or university. (c) Construct a 95 percent confidence interval for the difference in population proportions. Is there a significant difference? Discuss. (LO 3)

APPENDIX: TESTING FOR NORMALITY ASSUMPTION

Throughout the text we will see many situations where we need to assume that the population being sampled is normal. If we have a histogram of the sampled data, it might suggest if it is safe to assume that the population is normal. However, using Excel or Appendix C to find normal probabilities, we can fairly easily create a plot called "The Normal Probability Plot" that enables us to check if it is safe to assume normal population. Following are the steps for creating this plot.

1. Order the data from smallest to largest, calling them "ordered values."

2. Number the "ordered values" $i = 1, \ldots, n$, where the smallest value is numbered 1 and the largest value is numbered n.

3. Compute the quantile (cumulative probability) $\dfrac{i - 0.5}{n}$ for $i = 1, \ldots, n$.

4. Use Appendix C or Excel formula =NORMSINV(quantile) to find the z values corresponding to the quantiles computed in step 3. For example, if $n = 10$, then our first quantile is $\dfrac{1 - 0.5}{10} = 0.05$.

   Corresponding to this quantile (left-tail area $= 0.05$), our z value can be read from Appendix C or by using the formula =NORMSINV(0.05). The z value is -1.645. That is, for the standard normal distribution, left-tail area of 0.05 corresponds to a z value of -1.645. These z-scores are also called the "Normal Scores."

5. Create the Normal Probability Plot by plotting the n pairs, (z value, ordered value). If the plotted points more or less fall on a straight line, then it is safe to assume a normal distribution.

We illustrate this with the example "GMAT Score, Again." The Excel worksheet with the plot is shown below:

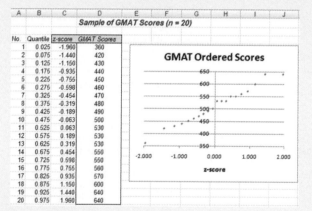

As you can see above, the points more or less lie on a straight line. So it is safe to assume that the population being sampled is normal.

LearningStats Unit 08 Estimation

LearningStats Unit 08 illustrates the idea of sample variation, the Central Limit Theorem, and confidence intervals. Your instructor may assign specific units, or you may decide to check them out because the topic sounds interesting.

Topic	LearningStats Modules
Overview	Survey Guidelines
	Sampling Methods
	Confidence Intervals
	Sample Size
Central Limit Theorem	CLT Demonstration: Simulation
	CLT Demonstration: Finite Population
Sampling distributions	Sampling Distributions
	Critical Values (z, t, χ^2)
	Sample Proportion Demonstration
Confidence intervals	Confidence Interval: Means
	Confidence Interval: Proportions
	Confidence Interval: Variances
	Confidence Interval: Simulation
	Confidence Interval: Bootstrap
Sample size	Sample Size Calculator
Student projects	Coffee Drinking Habits
	Office Chairs with Wheels
Applications and case studies	Sample Variation
	Finite Populations
	Bootstrap Explained
Tables	Appendix C—Normal
	Appendix D—Student's t
	Appendix E—Chi-Square
Equations	Equations: Confidence Intervals
	Equations: PDFs

Key: = PowerPoint   = Word   = Excel

Visual Statistics

Visual Statistics Modules on Estimation

Module	Module Name
6	Visualizing Random Samples
7	Visualizing the Central Limit Theorem
8	Visualizing Properties of Estimators
9	Visualizing One-Sample Hypothesis Tests

Visual Statistics Modules 6, 7, 8, and 9 (included on your CD) are designed to help you

- Understand variability in samples.
- Learn to infer a population's shape from samples.
- Recognize outliers and their effects.
- Distinguish between the population sampled and the sampling distribution of the mean.
- Understand how sample size affects the standard error.
- Understand unbiasedness, efficiency, and consistency.
- Learn what a confidence interval represents.

The worktext contains lists of concepts covered, objectives of the modules, overviews of concepts, illustrations of concepts, orientations to module features, learning exercises (basic, intermediate, advanced), learning projects (individual, team), self-evaluation quizzes, glossaries of terms, and solutions to self-evaluation quizzes.

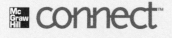

For solutions to odd-numbered exercises, Exam Review questions, and additional study tools to help you succeed in this course, visit *Connect* at www.mcgrawhillconnect.ca.

Chapter

9

One-Sample Hypothesis Tests

Chapter Learning Objectives

When you finish this chapter you should be able to

1.   Understand how hypothesis testing works.

2.   Recognize the key terms used in hypothesis testing.

3.   Apply the steps involved in hypothesis testing.

4.   In a problem context, formulate the null and alternative hypotheses, use the appropriate test statistic, determine the decision rule or rejection region, and reach the appropriate conclusion for testing a population mean and proportion.

5.   In a problem context, determine the p value by using z, t tables, and Excel, and use the p value to reach the appropriate conclusion.

6.   In a problem context, conduct hypothesis testing for a population variance (optional).

Data are used in business every day to support marketing claims, to help managers make decisions, and to show business improvement. Whether the business is small or large, profit or non-profit, the use of data allows businesses to find better answers to their questions. Such questions might be:

• Does a new airline mishandle fewer bags than the industry benchmark?

• Did the proportion of defective products decrease after a new manufacturing process was introduced?

- Has the average service time at a Noodles & Company restaurant decreased since last year?

- Has a ski resort decreased its average response time to accidents?

- Has a dealership's proportion of satisfied car repair customers increased after providing more training to its employees?

Savvy business people use data and many of the statistical tools that you've already learned to answer these types of questions. We will build on these tools in this chapter and learn about one of the most widely used statistical tools—*hypothesis testing*. Hypothesis testing is used in both science and business to test assumptions and theories and ultimately guide managers when facing decisions. First we will explain the logic behind hypothesis testing and then show how *statistical hypothesis testing* helps businesses make better decisions.

Perhaps the best way to introduce the concept of hypothesis testing is to consider a criminal trial that is detailed further in the chapter. Our legal system assumes a defendant is innocent *unless the evidence gathered by the prosecutor allows the jury to reject this assumption*. Our initial assumption is stated as a **null hypothesis** (H_0, pronounced "H-naught"). The opposite of the null hypothesis is called the **alternative hypothesis** (H_1). The alternative hypothesis is also called the research hypothesis. Thus the two hypotheses are:

H_0: The defendant is innocent.

H_1: The defendant is guilty.

For the jury to declare the defendant guilty, the evidence presented by the prosecutor must convince a jury "beyond a reasonable doubt" that the defendant is guilty. The defence might produce enough evidence to cast doubt about the defendant's guilt. The jury has to reach one of two conclusions (assume there is no hung jury allowed): either declare the defendant guilty (reject the null hypothesis in favour of the alternative hypothesis), or declare the defendant not guilty because there is not enough evidence for a guilty verdict. Note that in this case the jury is not saying the defendant is innocent.

No matter which decision the jury takes, it is possible that it makes an error. And there are two types of errors that it can make. A *Type I error* would occur if the defendant was declared guilty when in fact he/she was innocent. That is, the null hypothesis is rejected when the null hypothesis is true, or equivalently the null hypothesis is wrongly rejected. On the other hand, a *Type II error* would be made if the guilty defendant was declared not guilty by the jury. That is, the null hypothesis is not rejected when it should have been rejected.

9.1   Logic of Hypothesis Testing

Logical inquiry occurs when we ask questions, propose theories, make conjectures, and assume truths about the world around us. The process of inquiry requires that these theories, conjectures, and assumptions be tested rigorously and under various conditions. A theory or assumption that has not been disproved, in spite of repeated efforts to do so by testing, is a strong theory. The scientific community will often operate under the assumption that a strong theory is true, as long as they have no evidence that says otherwise. When testing a theory, a scientist states a clear assumption, called a **hypothesis,** which is then tested using a well-defined procedure that requires data collection. **Hypothesis testing** is the name of the statistical tool that compares the collected data against the assumption to determine if the data are consistent or inconsistent with the assumption. When the data are found to be inconsistent (i.e., in conflict) with the assumption, the assumption is either discarded or the hypothesis is reformulated. As you might imagine, the process of hypothesis testing can be an iterative process.

Who Uses Hypothesis Testing?

Anyone who does research in science, engineering, social science, education, or medicine needs strong training in hypothesis testing. Furthermore, all business managers need at least a basic understanding of hypothesis testing because managers often interact with specialists and deal with technical reports. Managers in accounting, finance, and human resources must know enough not to be intimidated. Those involved in marketing, operations analysis, or quality management need somewhat stronger skills.

Why? Because the innovative vigour of our economy is largely based on technology: new materials, new manufacturing methods, new distribution systems, new information strategies. A manager must understand especially the meaning of concepts such as *significance* and *power,* because financial or strategic decisions often are required. For example, if a redesigned process could improve a truck engine's mpg rating *significantly,* but requires spending $250 million, is it worth doing? Such a decision requires clear understanding not only of significance, but also of the importance of the potential improvement: the magnitude of the effect, and its implications for product durability, customer satisfaction, budgets, cash flow, and staffing. Sound business decisions cannot be made without understanding the basic ideas of hypothesis tests.

Steps in Hypothesis Testing

Step 1: State the two hypotheses involved in the test: the hypothesis we initially assume to be true and the alternative to this hypothesis.

Step 2: Specify what evidence is required that will allow us to reject the initial hypothesis. This is called a decision rule, or is referred to as the rejection region.

Step 3: Collect data and calculate the necessary evidence or statistics to test the initial hypothesis.

Step 4: Make a decision based on comparing the evidence that is calculated with what is required to reject the initial hypothesis. Should the initial hypothesis be rejected or not?

Step 5: Take action based on the decision. (This could include conducting a new test with a reformulated pair of hypotheses.)

Step 1: State the Null and Alternative Hypotheses We formulate a pair of mutually exclusive, collectively exhaustive statements about the world. One statement or the other must be true, but they cannot both be true. The null hypothesis is the hypothesis we initially *assume* to be true while the other hypothesis is referred to as the alternative hypothesis (or the research hypothesis) and it is this hypothesis that we are attempting to *conclude* to be true by conducting our test. (For example, although we initially assume that the defendant is innocent, we conduct trials because we are attempting to conclude that the defendant is guilty. We do not conduct trials in an attempt to support the defendant's innocence.)

H_0: Null hypothesis

H_1: Alternative hypothesis

The two statements are called *hypotheses* because the truth is unknown. Efforts will be made to reject the *null hypothesis.* If H_0 happens to be a favourite theory, we might not really wish to reject it, but we try anyway. If we reject H_0, we conclude that the *alternative hypothesis H_1* is true.

Sometimes it is not clear which one should be null hypothesis and which one should be alternative hypothesis. As a general rule, whatever we are trying to prove, conclude to be true, find sufficient evidence for, or test should be stated as H_1 so that the rejection of H_0 supports our claim or research conclusion, beyond any reasonable doubt. Another approach is to set up our hypotheses so that the more serious of the two possible errors is the Type I error. In the criminal trial scenario that we started with, the Type I error occurs when the jury convicts an innocent defendant. In our justice system, this error is more serious than the error of letting a guilty person be declared not guilty. This is consistent with the statement attributed to English jurist William Blackstone: "Better that ten guilty escape than one innocent suffer."

We give below several examples of hypothesis testing in non-statistical scenarios.

Criminal Trial As discussed above, in a criminal trial, the hypotheses are

H_0: The defendant is innocent.

H_1: The defendant is guilty.

Our legal system assumes a defendant is innocent unless the evidence gathered by the prosecutor allows us to reject this assumption.

Drug Testing When an Olympic athlete is tested for performance-enhancing drugs like steroids, the presumption is that the athlete is in compliance with the rules. The hypotheses are

H_0: No illegal steroid use

H_1: Illegal steroid use

Samples of urine or blood are taken as evidence and used only to disprove the null hypothesis because we assume the athlete is free of illegal steroids.

Instant Replays Many sports leagues (CFL, NFL, NHL, MLB) use instant replays to verify whether the initial ruling, by individuals officiating a game, is the correct ruling. Here, the initial assumption is that the ruling is correct and this ruling would only be overruled if there is sufficient evidence (in these situations, the claim is that there must be irrefutable evidence) to indicate that the ruling was wrong. The hypotheses in these cases are

H_0: The ruling is correct.

H_1: The ruling is incorrect.

Here, the evidence relied on are the instant replays of the play in question.

Step 2: Specify the Decision Rule Before collecting data to test the hypotheses, the researcher must specify *how strong* the evidence must be or *how sufficient* the evidence must be against the null hypothesis before the null hypothesis can be rejected. This amount of evidence, to a large extent, depends on how willing the researcher is to reject the null hypothesis when the null hypothesis is true. In our legal system, the evidence presented by the prosecutor must convince a jury "beyond a reasonable doubt" that the defendant is not innocent. In this case, the willingness of the jury to find an innocent person guilty determines its decision rule. In steroid testing, the lab that analyzes the urine or blood sample must conduct duplicate tests to decide whether the sample exceeds the agreed-upon benchmark. With biometric screening, the designer of the security system determines how many consistencies on a fingerprint would indicate an authorized user. With instant replays in sporting events, theoretically, the decision rule is that the null hypothesis would only be rejected if the instant replays show with absolute certainty that the call was incorrect.

A Closer Look

In determining how willing a researcher should be to reject the null hypothesis when it is true, the cost to that researcher of making a Type I error is most often the determining factor. The higher the cost of making the Type I error, the less willing that researcher should be to make this error. Thus, that researcher would need more evidence against the null hypothesis before rejecting it.

Steps 3 and 4: Data Collection and Decision Making Much of the critical work in hypothesis testing takes place during steps 1 and 2. Once the hypotheses and decision rule have been clearly articulated, the process of data collection, while time-consuming, is often straightforward. If the decision rule can be quantified, and if we convert that data into a similar quantifiable measure, often referred to as a *test statistic,* we then compare the value of the test statistic against the decision rule and decide to reject or not reject the null hypothesis. In some of the above examples, for example the jury trial, we really can't quantify either the decision rule or the evidence gathered, and whatever the decision the jury reaches can often be questioned.

Step 5: Take Action Based on Decision This last step—taking action—requires experience and expertise on the part of the decision maker. Suppose the evidence presented at a trial convinces a jury that the defendant is guilty. What punishment should the judge impose? Or suppose the blood sample of an athlete shows steroid use. What fine should the athletic commission impose? Should the athlete be banned from competing? If the fingerprint presented for authentication has been rejected, should an alarm go off? Should a security breach be recorded in the system? Appropriate action for the decision should relate back to the purpose of conducting the hypothesis test in the first place.

Can a Null Hypothesis Be Proved?

No, we cannot prove a null hypothesis—we can only *fail to reject* it. A null hypothesis that survives repeated tests without rejection is "true" only in the limited sense that it has been thoroughly scrutinized. Today's "true" hypothesis could be "false" tomorrow. If we fail to reject H_0, we provisionally accept H_0. However, an "accepted" hypothesis may be retested. That is how scientific inquiry works. Einstein's theories, for example, are over 100 years old but are still being subjected to rigorous tests. Yet few scientists really think that Einstein's theories are "wrong." It's in the nature of science to keep trying to refute accepted theories, especially when a new test is possible or when new data become available. Similarly, the safety of commonly used prescription drugs is continually being studied. Sometimes, "safe" drugs are revealed to have serious side effects only after large-scale, long-term use by consumers (e.g., the Vioxx arthritis drug that was shown to be safe in clinical trials, but later showed a dangerous association with heart attacks after years of use by millions of people).

A Closer Look

As mentioned above, if we fail to reject H_0, we can provisionally accept H_0 or we can continue to assume that it is true. Failing to reject H_0 does not mean that we can conclude H_0 is true. Based on the results of hypothesis testing, the only hypothesis that we can conclude to be true (even though our conclusion may be incorrect) is H_1. The reason being that the test measures the evidence against H_0 and in favour of H_1; it does not measure the evidence in favour of H_0. Thus, in a criminal trial, the jury never finds the defendant "innocent," it only finds the defendant "not guilty," which is short for stating that "there is not enough evidence to find the defendant guilty." One of the most watched murder trials ever was the O.J Simpson trial in which the defendant was found "not guilty." Although many jurors, on being interviewed after the trial, thought that the evidence indicated that he was guilty, they didn't believe that the evidence was strong enough to vote for a guilty verdict.

Types of Error

In the initial criminal trial example, the two possible types of mistakes that can be made in hypothesis testing were introduced—the Type I and Type II error. While there is the possibility of making either type of mistake, the possibilities of reaching correct decisions should be much greater if hypothesis testing is carried out effectively. Table 9.1 summarizes the possible results of hypothesis testing.

TABLE 9.1 Type I and II Error

Decision	True Situation	
	H_0 is true.	H_0 is false.
Reject H_0	Type I error	Correct decision
Fail to reject H_0	Correct decision	Type II error

The true situation determines whether our decision was correct. If the decision about the null hypothesis matches the true situation, there is no error. Rejecting the null hypothesis when it is true is a Type I error. Failure to reject the null hypothesis when it is false is a Type II error.

Will We Ever Know If We Made an Error?   In some situations, yes. But, in these situations, we will only know if we made an error when it is too late to alter our conclusion and our subsequent decision. For example, if we concluded that our business would be successful and it eventually failed, we know that we made a mistake but not until we had already committed our resources to that endeavour. But because we rarely have perfect information about the true situation when we actually test the hypotheses and make our decisions, we can't know immediately if we have committed Type I or Type II errors, and we may never know. When constructing the decision rule we try to minimize the chance of either of these errors by collecting as much evidence as our resources allow. We also try to understand the consequences of making an error in order to be as informed as possible before taking action. Statistics lets us determine the risks of Type I or II errors so that we can assess the *probability* of making an incorrect decision.

Consequences of Type I and Type II Errors

The consequences of these two errors are quite different, and the costs are borne by different parties. Depending on the situation, decision makers may fear one error more than the other. It would be nice if both types of error could be avoided. Unfortunately, when making a decision based on a fixed body of sample evidence, reducing the risk of one type of error often increases the risk of the other. Consider our examples of a criminal trial, drug testing, and instant replays.

Criminal Trial   As we saw before, a Type I error is convicting an innocent defendant, so the costs are borne by the defendant. The Type II error is failing to convict a guilty defendant, so the costs are borne by society if the guilty person returns to the streets. Concern for the rights of the accused and stricter rules of evidence during the 1960s and 1970s led American courts to try to reduce the risk of a Type I error, which probably increased the risk of a Type II error. But during the 1980s and 1990s, amid growing concern over the social costs of crime and victims' rights, courts began closing loopholes to reduce the Type II error, presumably at the expense of the Type I error. Both risks can be reduced only by devoting more effort to gathering evidence and strengthening the legal process (expediting trials, improving jury quality, increasing investigative work).

H_0: Defendant is innocent.

H_1: Defendant is guilty.

Concept Check

The topic of reinstating the death penalty in Canada is brought up occasionally with the argument that the prospect of a death penalty should deter people from committing violent acts. If the death penalty was an option in a criminal case in Canada, the cost of a Type I error to the defendant would be severe. But what would the cost to the jury be? Would a jury deliberating that case be more or less willing to find an innocent person guilty if that person may face the death penalty? Based on your answer, would a jury need weaker or stronger evidence against a defendant's innocence before finding that person guilty? Based on your answer to this last question, can you argue either that the death penalty would be a deterrent or that it would not be a deterrent? Explain.

Drug Testing   Here, the Type I error is unfairly disqualifying an athlete who is "clean" and the Type II error is letting the drug user get away with it and have an unfair competitive advantage. The costs of Type I error are hard feelings and unnecessary embarrassment. The costs of Type II error are tarnishing the Olympic image and rewarding those who break the rules. Over time, improved tests have reduced the risk of both types of error. However, for a given technology, the threshold can be set lower or higher, balancing Type I and Type II error. Which error is more to be feared?

H_0: No illegal steroid use

H_1: Illegal steroid use

Instant Replays   The Type I error means overturning the official's initial correct ruling. The Type II error is not overturning the official's ruling when it is incorrect. As previously mentioned, theoretically, a Type I error will never be made. Which error is more costly? Obviously, when the rules for using instant replays were set up, the Type I error in this case was thought to be extremely costly or else the rules would have allowed for a Type I error.

In many hypothesis testing situations it is not clear how the null and the alternative hypothesis should be stated. As previously mentioned, *when setting up the two hypotheses, the null and alternative hypotheses should be set up such that the more serious or higher cost mistake is the Type I error.* (This is consistent with the null hypothesis often representing the status quo, since more often than not, people do not like change and the higher-cost mistake would be rejecting the status quo when the status quo is best.) But, when analyzing costs, one individual's higher-cost mistake may not necessarily be another individual's higher-cost mistake. If this situation occurs, some third party may need to be involved when determining the two hypotheses. For example, Pharmaceutical Company A has a pill in the market that reduces blood pressure. Pharmaceutical Company B claims that its pill is better than Company A's pill and wants the government to allow its pill on the market. For this pill to be allowed on the market, Company B's claim must be tested. Here, the two possible pairs of hypotheses are

H_0: Company B's pill is better.

H_1: Company B's pill is not better.

Or

H_0: Company B's pill is not better.

H_1: Company B's pill is better.

Obviously, Company A would not want Company B's pill to be marketed, so the higher-cost mistake as far as it is concerned is finding Company B's pill to be better when it isn't, and thus, it would want that mistake to be the Type I error as it would be with the second pair of hypotheses. Conversely, Company B's higher-cost mistake would be finding Company B's pill to be not better when it actually is better, and it would thus like it to be the Type I error, which it would be using the first pair of hypothesis. In this situation, the government may specify which pair of hypotheses to use because it is its ultimate decision whether to allow the pill to be marketed. In most cases, it would want Company B to have to prove that its pill is better as it claims and, therefore, would choose the second pair of hypotheses.

Concept Check

Prof. Plum and Prof. Wine both teach introductory statistics courses. Because exams don't measure precisely how much a student knows and what grade he/she actually deserves, Prof. Plum thinks it is more costly to fail a student who deserves to pass and, thus, will only fail students if there is enough evidence on their exams that they deserve to fail. In contrast, Prof. Wine thinks it more costly to pass a student who deserves to fail and, thus, will only pass students if there is enough evidence on their exams that they deserve to pass. If the two hypotheses are "deserves to pass" and "deserves to fail," what would be Prof. Plum's H_0 and H_1 be? What would Prof. Wine's H_0 and H_1 be? Which mistake is more costly to a student, and thus, what H_0 and H_1 would a student prefer?

9.2   Statistical Hypothesis Testing

You are already halfway there, if you understand the previous chapter. A confidence interval often gives enough information to make a decision. Knowing the 95 percent range of likely values for a key decision parameter (e.g., the proportion of repeat customers under age 30) may be all that an experienced statistician needs. But the inexperienced individual is more likely to make mistakes using the confidence interval method than by using hypothesis testing. Therefore, this and subsequent chapters will structure hypothesis testing more formally. This structure will include the two hypotheses, the test statistic, the decision rule (or rejection region), and the conclusions (and any subsequent decisions).

Before we develop a general framework for statistical hypothesis testing, let us consider a specific example.

EXAMPLE 1

Hybrid Car

A famous automobile manufacturing company has a hybrid small car that currently uses 4.5 litres per 100 kilometres, on the average. The company has been working hard on redesigning the car to further improve its fuel economy. A prototype is to be tested for its fuel economy to see whether it outperforms the current model. Let μ be the average amount of fuel needed for 100 kilometres. The company sets up the following null and alternative hypotheses:

$$H_0: \mu \geq 4.5$$
$$H_1: \mu < 4.5$$

The company plans to test-drive several copies of this prototype and determine the value of the statistic $\overline{X}$, the average amount of fuel (L/100 km) needed. If this sample mean turns out to be "sufficiently smaller" than 4.5, then the company can reject the null hypothesis in favour of the alternative hypothesis and claim that the new design outperforms the old one. If the sample mean value is greater than 4.5, we cannot reject the null hypothesis. If $\overline{X}$ is a little less than 4.5, we may or may not reject the null hypothesis depending on other factors such as the sample size, the variability in amount of fuel needed among the prototypes, and the willingness of the researcher to make a Type I error. For a given sample size, variability and the researcher's willingness to make a Type I error, the further it is to the left of 4.5 (i.e., the smaller its value), the stronger will be the evidence of the new design outperforming the old one. This test is, therefore, called a *left-tailed test*.

It is important to note that in order to make a decision we are comparing the value of $\overline{X}$ with the benchmark value 4.5. So we might as well state our null hypothesis with the equality:

$$H_0: \mu = 4.5$$
$$H_1: \mu < 4.5$$

Note that in both setups our alternative hypothesis is the same. No matter whether we write the null hypothesis in "=" form or in "≥" form, we compare our sample mean with 4.5 to make a decision. If we conclude that the alternative hypothesis ($\mu < 4.5$) is true when we assume that the mean is equal to 4.5, we will certainly arrive at the same conclusion if we assumed initially that the mean was more than 4.5. As a result, *we will always state our null hypothesis in equality form.* An important side effect of this setup is that it leads students to focus on the alternative hypothesis, as they should. Always keep in mind, however, that the theoretically correct statement of the null hypothesis is the complement (or opposite) of the statement in the alternative hypothesis.

A **statistical hypothesis** is a statement about the unknown value of a population parameter that we are interested in (call it θ). For example, the parameter θ could represent the population mean μ, the population proportion π, the population variance σ^2, or some other parameter that will be discussed in subsequent chapters. As previously discussed, a **hypothesis test** is a decision between two competing, mutually exclusive, and collectively exhaustive hypotheses about the value of θ. The hypotheses used for testing the θ's in this chapter and most of the θ's tested in subsequent chapters can be set up as follows:

Left-Tailed Test	Two-Tailed Test	Right-Tailed Test
$H_0: \theta = \theta_0$	$H_0: \theta = \theta_0$	$H_0: \theta = \theta_0$
$H_1: \theta < \theta_0$	$H_1: \theta \neq \theta_0$	$H_1: \theta > \theta_0$

FIGURE 9.1

Outcomes in a Sampling Distribution

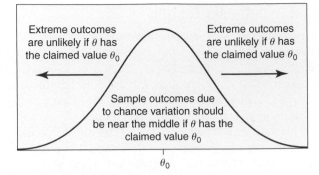

In the hybrid-car scenario above, we have $\theta = \mu$ and $\theta_0 = 4.5$. The direction of the test is indicated by the alternative hypothesis H_1:

$<$ indicates a **left-tailed test** (i.e., indicates that we are testing whether θ is less than some specified value, θ_0)

$\neq$ indicates a **two-tailed test** (i.e., indicates that we are testing whether θ is different than some specified value, θ_0)

$>$ indicates a **right-tailed test** (i.e., indicates that we are testing whether θ is greater than some specified value, θ_0)

The hypothesized value θ_0 is the centre of interest. If the true value of θ is θ_0, then a sample estimate, $\hat{\theta}$, should not differ greatly from θ_0. We rely on our knowledge of the *sampling distribution* and the *standard error (or standard deviation) of the estimate* to decide if the sample estimate is far enough away from θ_0 to contradict the assumption that $\theta = \theta_0$, as illustrated in Figure 9.1.

The parameter we test is typically a mean, μ, or a proportion, π. Stating the null hypothesis requires a benchmark value for μ or π that we denote with the subscript "0" as in μ_0 or π_0. This value does not come from a sample but is based on past performance, an industry standard, or a product specification.

Where Do We Get μ_0 (or π_0)?

The value of μ_0 (or π_0) that we are testing is a *benchmark,* such as past experience, an industry standard, or a product specification. The value of μ_0 (or π_0) does *not* come from a sample.

The application or the question we want answered will dictate which type of test we should construct. When testing a mean we can choose between three tests:

Left-Tailed Test	*Two-Tailed Test*	*Right-Tailed Test*
$H_0: \mu = \mu_0$	$H_0: \mu = \mu_0$	$H_0: \mu = \mu_0$
$H_1: \mu < \mu_0$	$H_1: \mu \neq \mu_0$	$H_1: \mu > \mu_0$

EXAMPLE 2

Testing a Mean

When deciding whether to purchase a restaurant that is currently for sale, the potential buyer wants to be fairly certain that there is enough customer traffic to make it profitable. After talking with various experts, he has determined that the average number of customers would have to be more than 216 per day to be a successful acquisition. To determine whether there is evidence to indicate that the traffic does exceed 216 customers per day, he randomly selected several days over the previous two months and counted how many customers entered the restaurant. From these data, he calculated the average and the standard deviation in the number of customers per day. Using these data he has three possible pairs of hypotheses he could test.

Left-Tailed Test	Two-Tailed Test	Right-Tailed Test
$H_0: \mu = 216$	$H_0: \mu = 216$	$H_0: \mu = 216$
$H_1: \mu < 216$	$H_1: \mu \neq 216$	$H_1: \mu > 216$

If he wants to be fairly certain that the average number of customers per day exceeds 216, his sample mean should be "sufficiently higher than 216." That is, he will logically use the right-tailed test. Once he decides to use this right-tailed test, he still has to decide what "sufficiently higher than 216" means, or, using hypothesis testing, he has to decide how willing he is to conclude that the average exceeds 216 when in fact it doesn't. Once he determines his "willingness" (to be explained in detail later), he determines what his decision rule would be to reject the null hypothesis. He then would compare the evidence he has collected (i.e., the value of his test statistic) with his decision rule. If the evidence fits his decision rule, he will reject the null hypothesis and conclude that the average exceeds 216 customers per day and buy the restaurant. If his evidence does not fit his decision rule, he will not reject the null hypothesis and not buy the restaurant.

Similarly, when testing for a proportion π we choose between three tests:

Left-Tailed Test	Two-Tailed Test	Right-Tailed Test
$H_0: \pi = \pi_0$	$H_0: \pi = \pi_0$	$H_0: \pi = \pi_0$
$H_1: \pi < \pi_0$	$H_1: \pi \neq \pi_0$	$H_1: \pi > \pi_0$

EXAMPLE 3

Testing a Proportion

In 2006, U.S. airlines mishandled 6 out of every 1,000 bags checked for air travel. One airline, FlyFast, found that 54 percent of their mishandled bag incidents were related to transferring baggage to a connecting flight. FlyFast recently installed an RFID (radio frequency identification) system with the goal of decreasing the proportion of mistakes caused during transfer and ultimately reducing the overall proportion of lost bags. After operating their new system for several months, FlyFast would like to know if the wireless system has been effective. FlyFast could use a hypothesis test to answer this question. The benchmark for the null hypothesis is their proportion of transfer mistakes using their old system ($\pi_0 = 0.54$). The possible set of statistical hypotheses would be:

Left-Tailed Test	Two-Tailed Test	Right-Tailed Test
$H_0: \pi = 0.54$	$H_0: \pi = 0.54$	$H_0: \pi = 0.54$
$H_1: \pi < 0.54$	$H_1: \pi \neq 0.54$	$H_1: \pi > 0.54$

Which set of hypotheses would be most logical for FlyFast to use? Because FlyFast believes the RFID system will reduce the proportion of transfer errors, they might use a left-tailed test. They would assume there has been no improvement, unless their evidence shows otherwise. If they can reject H_0 in favour of H_1 in a left-tailed test, FlyFast would be able to say that their data provide evidence that the proportion of transfer errors has decreased since the RFID tagging system was implemented.

Decision Rule

When performing a statistical hypothesis test, we compare a sample statistic to the hypothesized value of the population parameter stated in the null hypothesis. Extreme outcomes occurring in the left tail would cause us to reject the null hypothesis in a left-tailed test. Extreme outcomes occurring in the right tail would cause us to reject the null hypothesis in a right-tailed test. Extreme values in *either* the left or right tail would cause us to reject the null hypothesis in a two-tailed test.

We specify our decision rule by defining "extreme" outcomes. These outcomes are determined by: *our willingness to reject the null hypothesis when it is true; the sampling distribution of the test statistic; and our expectations about the value of the test statistic if the alternative hypothesis is true.* This definition of "extreme outcomes" is called the *rejection region,* or *decision rule.* For example, if we are dealing with a normal sampling distribution, and we are conducting a two-tailed test (i.e., testing that θ is different than θ_0), and we are

TABLE 9.2 Three Types of Decision Rules

Test Type	Decision Rule
Left-tailed	Reject H_0 if test statistic < left-tail critical value
Two-tailed	Reject H_0 if test statistic < left-tail critical value or if test statistic > right-tail critical value
Right-tailed	Reject H_0 if test statistic > right-tail critical value

FIGURE 9.2 Three Types of Decision Rules

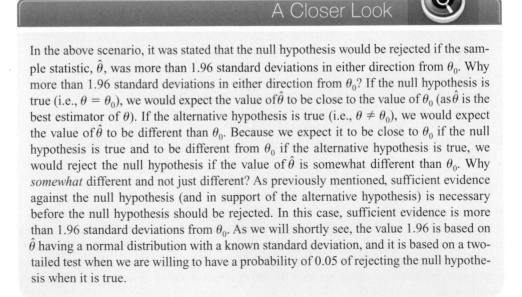

willing to have a probability of 0.05 of rejecting the null hypothesis when it is true, we will reject H_0 if the sample statistic is more than 1.96 standard deviations in either direction from θ_0. We calculate a *test statistic* to determine how far our sample statistic is from the hypothesized population parameter. Before we collect sample data, we decide what the critical value of the test statistic would have to be in order to reject H_0. Table 9.2 and Figure 9.2 illustrate the three test types, the rejection regions, and corresponding decision rules.

A Closer Look

In the above scenario, it was stated that the null hypothesis would be rejected if the sample statistic, $\hat{\theta}$, was more than 1.96 standard deviations in either direction from θ_0. Why more than 1.96 standard deviations in either direction from θ_0? If the null hypothesis is true (i.e., $\theta = \theta_0$), we would expect the value of $\hat{\theta}$ to be close to the value of θ_0 (as $\hat{\theta}$ is the best estimator of θ). If the alternative hypothesis is true (i.e., $\theta \neq \theta_0$), we would expect the value of $\hat{\theta}$ to be different than θ_0. Because we expect it to be close to θ_0 if the null hypothesis is true and to be different from θ_0 if the alternative hypothesis is true, we would reject the null hypothesis if the value of $\hat{\theta}$ is somewhat different than θ_0. Why *somewhat* different and not just different? As previously mentioned, sufficient evidence against the null hypothesis (and in support of the alternative hypothesis) is necessary before the null hypothesis should be rejected. In this case, sufficient evidence is more than 1.96 standard deviations from θ_0. As we will shortly see, the value 1.96 is based on $\hat{\theta}$ having a normal distribution with a known standard deviation, and it is based on a two-tailed test when we are willing to have a probability of 0.05 of rejecting the null hypothesis when it is true.

In quality control, any deviation from specifications (or control limits) indicates that something may be wrong with the process, so a two-tailed test is common. In a two-tailed test, the decision maker has no *a priori* reason to expect rejection in one direction. In such cases, it is reasonable to use a two-tailed test. As you'll soon see, rejection in a two-tailed test guarantees rejection in the appropriate one-tailed test, other things being equal.

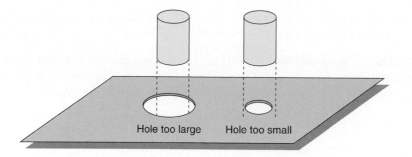

FIGURE 9.3

**Asymmetric Effects of
Nonconformance**

However, when the consequences of rejecting H_0 are asymmetric, or where one tail is of special importance to the researcher, we might prefer a one-tailed test. For example, suppose that a machine is supposed to bore holes with a 3.5-mm diameter in a piece of sheet metal. Although any deviation from 3.5 mm is a violation of the specification, the consequences of rejecting H_0 may be different. Suppose an attachment pin is to be inserted into the hole. If the hole is too small, the pin cannot be inserted, but the metal piece could probably be reworked to enlarge the hole so that the pin does fit. On the other hand, if the hole is too large, the pin will fit too loosely and may fall out. The piece may have to be discarded because an oversized hole cannot be made smaller. This is illustrated in Figure 9.3.

Probability of Type I Error and Type II Error

Type I Error   The probability of Type I error is denoted α and is commonly called the **level of significance.** It is the risk that we are willing to take to wrongly reject a true H_0. When stating the decision rule, the decision maker decides what the *level of significance* will be for the hypothesis test or he or she decides how willing they are to reject the null hypothesis when it is true. Note that α is the acceptable level of risk of making a Type I error.

$$\alpha = P(\text{reject } H_0 \mid H_0 \text{ is true}) \tag{9.1}$$

> ## Type I Error
>
> The probability of rejecting the null hypothesis when it is true is denoted α and is called the *level of significance.*

If we specify a decision rule based on a choice of $\alpha = 0.05$, we would expect to commit a Type I error about 5 times in 100 samples *if H_0 is true.* We would like α to be small, usually less than 0.10. Common choices for α are 0.10, 0.05, and 0.01. The level of significance is usually expressed as a percent, that is, 10, 5, or 1 percent.

Stated differently, α is the probability that the test statistic would happen to fall in the rejection region even though H_0 is true. Because we don't want to reject a true null hypothesis, this would be a Type I error. This α risk is the area under the tail(s) of the sampling distribution of the statistic we are using to measure the evidence. In a two-tailed test, the α risk is split, with $\alpha/2$ in each tail, as there are two ways to reject H_0 (if the test statistic is too far above or below the expected value). Thus, in a two-tailed test using $\alpha = 0.10$ we would put half the risk ($\alpha/2 = 0.05$) in each tail. Figure 9.2 illustrates these concepts.

By choosing a small α (e.g., $\alpha = 0.01$), the decision maker can make it harder to reject the null hypothesis when it is true. By choosing a larger α (e.g., $\alpha = 0.05$), it is easier to reject the null hypothesis when it is true. To make it harder to reject the null hypothesis when it is true, we would need to gather stronger evidence against the null hypothesis before it can be rejected. This raises the possibility of manipulating the decision. For this reason, the choice of α should precede the calculation of the test statistic, thereby minimizing the temptation to select α so as to favour one conclusion over the other. Why would someone want an α closer to 0.10 while someone else would want an α closer to 0.01? As stated, the smaller the α, the harder it is to reject the null hypothesis when it is true. Why would someone want it to be harder to reject the null hypothesis when it is true? When the cost of making a Type I error is higher.

Type II Error The probability of Type II error, sometimes referred to as β risk, is the probability that the test statistic does not fall in the rejection region even though the null hypothesis H_0 is actually false. It is the risk that we will wrongly accept a false H_0.

$$P(\text{fail to reject } H_0 \mid H_0 \text{ is false}) = \beta \qquad (9.2)$$

> ## Type II Error
>
> The probability of accepting the null hypothesis when it is false is denoted by β.

Unlike α, we cannot choose β in advance. The reason is that β depends on several things, including our choice for α, the size of the sample, and the value of θ, if the alternative hypothesis is true. Other things being equal, we would like β to be small. However, for a given sample, there is a trade-off between α and β. We will discuss this trade-off in more detail shortly.

Power of a Test If the null hypothesis is false, we ought to reject it. If we do so, we have done the right thing, and there is no Type II error. The **power** of a test is the probability that a false null hypothesis will be rejected, as it should be. More power is good, because power is the probability of doing the right thing. Power is the complement of beta risk $(1 - \beta)$. If we have low β risk, we have high power:

$$\text{Power} = P(\text{reject } H_0 \mid H_0 \text{ is false}) = 1 - \beta \qquad (9.3)$$

> ## Power
>
> The probability of rejecting the null hypothesis when it is false is $1 - \beta$ and is called *power*.

More powerful tests are more likely to detect false null hypotheses. For example, if a new weight-loss drug actually is effective, we would want to reject the null hypothesis that the drug has no effect. We prefer the most powerful test possible. Larger samples lead to increased power, which is why clinical trials often involve thousands of people.

Relationship between α and β

We desire tests that avoid Type II errors (small β risk), yet we also want to avoid Type I errors (small α risk). Given two acceptable tests, we will choose the more powerful one. But for a given type of test and fixed sample size, there is a trade-off between α and β. The larger critical value needed to reduce α risk makes it harder to reject H_0, thereby increasing β risk. The proper balance between α and β can be elusive. Consider these examples:

- If your household carbon monoxide detector's sensitivity threshold is increased to reduce the risk of overlooking danger (reduced β), there will be more false alarms (increased α).
- A doctor who is conservative about admitting patients with symptoms of myocardial infarction to the ICU (reduced β) will admit more patients without myocardial infarction (increased α).
- Reducing the threshold for dangerously high blood pressure from 140/90 to 130/80 will reduce the chance of missing the diagnosis of hypertension (reduced β), but some patients may incorrectly be given medication that is not needed (increased α).

Both α and β risk can be reduced simultaneously only by increasing the sample size (gathering more evidence), which is not always feasible or cost-effective.

A Closer Look

In addition to the trade-off between α and β, the value of β, as previously mentioned, is also affected by the sample size (the larger the sample, the smaller the β, all other things being equal). The value of β is also affected by how similar the two hypotheses are. The more similar they are, the larger the β. To determine how similar they are, we need to know the value of θ if the alternative hypothesis is true. Because we usually don't know that value, we usually cannot determine β. But we *can* say that the closer that value is to the value θ_0, the larger the β is. Logically, this should make sense. The more similar the two hypotheses are, the more difficult it should be to determine which one is true. Thus, it is more likely that a mistake will be made.

Firms are increasingly wary of committing a Type II error (e.g., failing to recall a product as soon as sample evidence begins to indicate potential problems):

EXAMPLE 4

Consequences of Type II Error

H_0: Product is performing safely.

H_1: Product is not performing safely.

They may even order a precautionary product recall before the statistical evidence has become convincing (e.g., Verizon's 2004 recall of 50,000 cellphone batteries after one exploded and another caused a car fire) or even *before* anything bad happens (e.g., Intel's 2004 recall of its 915 G/P and 925X chip sets from OEMs [original equipment manufacturers], before the chips actually reached any consumers). Failure to act swiftly can generate liability and adverse publicity, as with the spate of Ford Explorer rollover accidents and eventual recall of certain 15-inch Firestone radial tires. Ford and Firestone believed they had found an engineering workaround to make the tire design safe, until accumulating accident data, lawsuits, and NHTSA pressure forced recognition that there was a problem. In 2004, certain COX-2 inhibitor drugs that had previously been thought effective and safe, based on extensive clinical trials, were found to be associated with increased risk of heart attack. The makers' stock price plunged (e.g., Merck). Lawyers, of course, have an incentive to claim product defects, even when the evidence is doubtful (e.g., Dow's silicone breast implants). The courts, therefore, often must use statistical evidence to adjudicate product liability claims.

Statistical Significance versus Practical Importance

The standard error of most sample estimators approaches zero as sample size increases (if they are consistent estimators), so almost any difference between the actual value of θ and θ_0, no matter how tiny, will be significant if the sample size is large enough. Researchers who deal with large samples must expect "significant" effects, even when an effect is too slight to have any *practical importance*. Is an improvement of 0.02 L/100 km in fuel economy *important* to Toyota buyers? Is a 0.5 percent loss of market share *important* to Hertz? Is a laptop battery life increase of 15 minutes *important* to Dell customers? Such questions depend not so much on statistics as on the cost/benefit calculation. Because resources are always scarce, a dollar spent on a quality improvement always has an opportunity cost (the foregone alternative). If we spend money to make a certain product improvement, then some other project may have to be shelved. Because we can't do everything, we must ask whether the proposed product improvement is the best use of our scarce resources. These are questions that must be answered by experts in medicine, marketing, product safety, or engineering, rather than by statisticians.

Section Exercises

9.1 Sketch a diagram of the decision rule for each pair of hypotheses. (LO 1)
   a. $H_0: \mu = 80$ versus $H_1: \mu < 80$
   b. $H_0: \mu = 80$ versus $H_1: \mu \neq 80$
   c. $H_0: \mu = 80$ versus $H_1: \mu > 80$

9.2 In 1,000 samples, assuming that H_0 is true, how many times would you expect to commit a Type I error if (a) $\alpha = 0.05$, (b) $\alpha = 0.01$, and (c) $\alpha = 0.001$. (LO 1)

9.3 Define the Type I and Type II error for each scenario, and discuss the cost(s) of each type of error. (LO 1 & 2)
  a. A 25-year-old ER patient in Toronto complains of chest pain. Heart attacks in 25-year-olds are rare, and beds are scarce in the hospital. The null hypothesis is that there is no heart attack (probably muscle pain due to shovelling snow).
  b. Approaching Toronto's Pearson International airport for landing, an Air Canada flight from London has been in a holding pattern for 45 minutes due to bad weather. Landing is expected within 15 minutes. The flight crew could declare an emergency and land immediately, but an investigation would be launched. The null hypothesis is that there is enough fuel to stay aloft for 15 more minutes.
  c. You are trying to finish a lengthy statistics report and print it for your evening class. Your colour printer is very low on ink, and you just have time to get to Staples for a new cartridge. But it is snowing and you need every minute to finish the report. The null hypothesis is that you have enough ink.

9.4 Discuss the issues of *statistical significance* and *practical importance* in each scenario. (LO 1)
  a. A process for producing I-beams of oriented strand board used as main support beams in new houses has a mean breaking strength of 2,000 lbs./ft. A sample of boards from a new process has a mean breaking strength of 2,150 lbs./ft. The improvement is statistically significant, but the per-unit cost is higher.
  b. Under continuous use, the mean battery life in a certain cellphone is 45 hours. In tests of a new type of battery, the sample mean battery life is 46 hours. The improvement is statistically significant, but the new battery costs more to produce.
  c. For a wide-screen HDTV LCD unit, the mean half-life (i.e., to lose 50 percent of its brightness) is 32,000 hours. A new process is developed. In tests of the new display, the sample mean half-life is 35,000 hours. The improvement is statistically significant, though the new process is more costly.

9.5 A firm decides to test its employees for illegal drugs. (a) State the null and alternative hypotheses. (b) Define the Type I and Type II errors. (c) What are the consequences of each? Which is more to be feared, and by whom? (LO 1 & 2)

9.6 A hotel installs smoke detectors with adjustable sensitivity in all public guest rooms. (a) State the null and alternative hypotheses. (b) Define the Type I and II errors. What are the consequences of each? (c) Which is more to be feared, and by whom? (d) If the hotel decides to reduce β risk, what would be the consequences? Who would be affected? (LO 1 & 2)

9.7 In both the Canadian federal election and the U.S. presidential election, the opposition parties often accused their adversaries of lying or, more politely, telling mistruths. It would then be left up to voters or to commentators to judge whether a lie was actually told. Suppose Party A made a statement that others accused of being a lie. Suppose the voters used hypothesis testing to test the two hypotheses are "lie" and "not a lie." (LO 1 & 2)
  a. What would Party A like the voters to set as H_0 and as H_1? Explain.
  b. What would the other parties like the voters to set as H_0 and as H_1? Explain.
  c. If the voters set H_0 as "lie," would Party A like the voters to use a small or large α? Explain.
  d. If the voters set H_0 as "lie," would the other parties like the voters to use a small or large α? Explain.

9.8 Suppose that in a courthouse in Kamloops, British Columbia, two trials are starting on the same day: a murder trial in which a defendant is charged with randomly killing several individuals, and a trial in which a defendant is charged with several parking ticket violations (worth a total of $100 in fines). For each of these trials, (a) what are the consequences of the Type I and Type II errors; (b) what alpha should be set (small or large); (c) what value of beta (small or large) is desirable; and (d), how lengthy should the trial be (short or long)? Explain your answers. (LO 1 & 2)

 Mini Case 9.1

Type I and Type II Errors

In the medical field, a Type I error, rejecting a true H_0, is often referred to a "false positive" or a "false rejection," and a Type II error, failing to reject a false H_0, is often called a "false negative" or a "false acceptance." Technology is always changing, but this mini case shows some actual rates of Type I error and Type II error in real applications. In each application, ask: What is the cost of a false positive or a false negative? Who bears these costs? This way of thinking will help you decide whether a Type I or a Type II error is more to be feared, and why.

MEDICAL TESTS
Cancer-screening tests have become routine. Unfortunately, they have fairly high rates of Type I error (unnecessary alarm, risk of biopsy) and Type II error (missed cancer). The hypotheses are

H_0: No cancer exists.
H_1: Cancer exists.

Consider these examples. Up to 25 percent of men with prostate cancer have normal PSA levels, while 50 percent of those with no cancer have elevated PSA levels and 70 percent of men with high PSA levels do not have cancer. Up to 33 percent of the PAP smears for cancer of the cervix give false positives—a rate that may soon be reduced by applying computer pattern recognition to the 50 million tests done every year by human technicians. MRI scanning for breast cancer detects about 80 percent of invasive growths in women (power = $1 - \beta$) compared with only 33 percent for standard mammography. In other medical testing, of the 250,000 people treated annually for appendicitis, from 15 percent to 40 percent have a healthy appendix removed, while about 20 percent of the time the appendicitis diagnosis is missed.

Sources: *Scientific American* 284, no. 12 (Dec. 1998), p. 75; *Technology Review* 107, no. 6, p. 64; *Popular Science* 247, no. 6, p. 76; *The Wall Street Journal*, July 29, 2004; and *Science News* 153 (Jan. 31, 1998), p. 78.

OTHER APPLICATIONS

Tests for mad cow disease have a 1 in 10,000 chance of a false positive. Most computer virus-detection software packages have very low rates of false positives (e.g., McAfee and Norton Antivirus had only 1 false positive in 3,700,000 files tested). But in spam detection, the results are not as good (e.g., in one test, Zone Alarm misidentified less than 1 percent of legitimate e-mails as spam but failed to detect 4 percent of actual spam). Accuracy will improve over time in most of these applications.

Sources: www.npr.org, accessed July 3, 2004; *PC Magazine* 23, no. 10 (June 8, 2004), p. 116, and 24, no. 2 (Feb. 8, 2005), p. 40.

9.3 Testing a Mean: Known Population Variance

Chapter 9

A hypothesis test tests a claim about a population parameter such as π, μ, or σ. We will first explain how to test a population mean, μ. The sample statistic used to estimate μ is $\overline{X}$. The sampling distribution for $\overline{X}$ depends on whether the population variance σ^2 is known. We begin with the case of known σ^2. We learned in Chapter 8 that the sampling distribution of $\overline{X}$ will be a normal distribution provided that we have a normal population (or, by the Central Limit Theorem, if the sample size is large). In Section 9.4 we will turn to the more common case of when σ^2 is estimated.

Consider the hybrid-car scenario (Example 1) we discussed earlier in this chapter. We set up our hypotheses as follows:

H_0: $\mu = 4.5$ $(= \mu_0)$

H_1: $\mu < 4.5$

Although we do not know the value of μ, let us assume that the population variance σ^2 is known and equals 0.36. That is, the population standard deviation $\sigma = \sqrt{0.36} = 0.6$ litres.

For our decision rule, suppose we plan to test-drive a random sample of 36 ($n = 36$) "prototype" cars, measure fuel need (L/100 km) for each one of these cars, and compute the $\overline{X}$ value. Earlier, based on our intuition, we said that we should reject the null hypothesis in favour of the alternative hypothesis if the value of $\overline{X}$ is "sufficiently smaller" than 4.5. But what do we mean by saying "sufficiently smaller" than 4.5? We need to specify an exact *critical value*, which will be symbolized by subscripting the statistic with "*crit*." For now let us assume that this value is 4.35 litres. That is, $\overline{x}_{crit} = 4.35$ and our decision rule is to reject the null hypothesis if our $\overline{X}$ value is less than 4.35.

The first question we ask is, "What is α, the probability of making a Type I error, with this decision rule?"

Recall that α is the probability of rejecting the true null hypothesis. That is, if $\mu = 4.5$, what are the chances that $\overline{X}$ will be less than the threshold 4.35? Recall from Chapter 8 that

$$E(\overline{X}) = \mu_0 = 4.5, \; \sigma_{\overline{X}} = \frac{\sigma}{\sqrt{n}} = \frac{0.6}{\sqrt{36}} = 0.1$$

Thus, under a true null hypothesis, the statistic $\overline{X}$ follows a normal distribution with the normal bell centred at 4.5 with a standard deviation of 0.1:

$$\alpha = P(\overline{X} < 4.35 \mid \mu_0 = 4.5)$$

$$= P\left(Z < \frac{\overline{X} - \mu_0}{\sigma_{\overline{X}}}\right) = P\left(Z < \frac{4.35 - 4.5}{0.1}\right) = P(Z < -1.5) = 0.0668$$

With our decision, there is just under a 6.7 percent chance of making a Type I error. The figure below illustrates this error. The shaded area gives us the probability of making a Type I error.

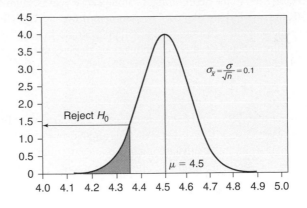

Sampling Distribution of Sample Mean under True Null Hypthesis

Because α, the probability of making a Type I error, is also called the level of significance, our decision rule with a critical value of 4.35 corresponds to a level of significance of 0.0668. Generally, we specify the level of significance and then we need to determine the critical value $\bar{x}_{crit}$ for this value of α, or we need to determine the critical value of some other statistic. Suppose $\alpha = 0.05$. The corresponding critical value is easily determined using the z-table. Because the left-tail area of 0.05 corresponds to the z value of -1.645 ($z_{0.05} = z_{crit} = 1.645$), our critical value is 1.645 standard deviations to the left of μ_0. That is,

$$\bar{x}_{crit} = \mu_0 - z_{0.05}\sigma_{\bar{x}} = 4.5 - 1.645(0.1) = 4.3355$$

Another equivalent way is to solve for $\bar{x}_{crit}$ in the equation below:

$$z_{crit} = \frac{\bar{x}_{crit} - \mu_0}{\sigma_{\bar{x}}} = \frac{\bar{x}_{crit} - 4.5}{0.1} = -1.645$$

Multiplying both sides by 0.1 and then adding 4.5 gives the same answer. Note that there are now two equivalent ways of stating our decision rule.

1. Reject the null hypothesis if the sample mean is less than 4.3355. We will call this the "absolute" method.

2. Reject the null hypothesis if the z value calculated from the sample results is less than -1.645. This method is called the "relative" method.

Just to emphasize the equivalence of these two methods, suppose our sample of 36 observations gives us $\bar{x}_{calc} = 4.27$. According to the "absolute" method, we will clearly reject H_0 because $4.27 < 4.335$. To use the "relative" method, we have $z_{calc} = \dfrac{4.27 - 4.5}{0.1} = -2.3$.

Because this z value is less than the critical z value of -1.645, we again reject the null hypothesis. Here we use the subscript "calc" to refer to the statistic's calculated value.

Test Statistic

As previously mentioned, a decision rule is specified based on our chosen level of significance, the sampling distribution of the sample statistic, and our expectations about the statistic if the alternative hypothesis is true. When testing for a population mean with the population variance known, the **test statistic** used is the z-statistic that measures the difference between $\bar{x}$ and μ_0 in terms of the standard error of the mean. Think of the test statistic as the "standardized score" of the sample statistic. When testing for μ with a known σ, the test statistic is the z score. Once we have collected our sample, we calculate a value of the test statistic using the sample mean and then compare it against the critical value of z. We will refer to the calculated value of the test statistic as z_{calc}.

TABLE 9.3   Some Common *z* Values

Level of Significance (α)	Two-Tailed Test	Right-Tailed Test	Left-Tailed Test
0.10	±1.645	1.282	−1.282
0.05	±1.960	1.645	−1.645
0.01	±2.575	2.326	−2.326

$$z_{calc} = \frac{\bar{x} - \mu_0}{\sigma_{\bar{x}}} = \frac{\bar{x} - \mu_0}{\dfrac{\sigma}{\sqrt{n}}} \text{ (test statistic for a mean with known } \sigma) \qquad (9.4)$$

The critical value of the test statistic will be referenced by the tail area of the rejection region. If the true mean of the population is μ_0, then the value of $\bar{x}$ calculated from our sample should be near μ_0 and therefore the test statistic should be near zero. But what should our expectations be if the alternative hypothesis is true? If $H_1: \mu > \mu_0$ were true, we would expect the value of $\bar{x}$ to be greater than μ_0 (as $\bar{x}$ is the best estimate of μ) and, thus, we would expect z_{calc} to be greater than zero. If $H_1: \mu < \mu_0$ were true, we would expect the value of $\bar{x}$ to be less than μ_0 and, thus, we would expect z_{calc} to be less than zero. If $H_1: \mu \neq \mu_0$ were true, we would expect the value of $\bar{x}$ to be different than μ_0 and, thus, we would expect z_{calc} to be different than zero.

Critical Value

The test statistic is compared with a **critical value** from a table. The critical value is the boundary between two regions (reject H_0, do not reject H_0) in the decision rule. The critical value separates the range of values for the test statistic that would be expected by chance if the null hypothesis were true and the range of values that would not be expected by chance if the null hypothesis were true. For a one-tailed test this critical value is determined when the entire risk of a Type I error (i.e., α) goes in the appropriate tail. In a two-tailed test, half the risk of a Type I error (i.e., $\alpha/2$) goes in each tail, as shown in Table 9.3. You can verify these z values from Excel or from Appendix C.

EXAMPLE 5

Paper Manufacturing

The Hammermill Company produces paper for laser printers. Standard paper width is supposed to be 216 mm. Suppose that the actual width is a random variable that is normally distributed with a known standard deviation of 0.023 mm. This standard deviation reflects the manufacturing technology currently in use and is known from long experience with this type of equipment. The standard deviation is small, due to the company's considerable effort to maintain precise control over paper width. However, variation still arises during manufacturing because of slight differences in the paper stock, vibration in the rollers and cutting tools, and wear and tear on the equipment. The cutters can be adjusted if the paper width drifts from the correct mean. A quality control inspector chooses 50 sheets at random and measures them with a precise instrument, showing a mean width of 216.007 mm. Using a 5 percent level of significance ($\alpha = 0.05$), does this sample show that the product mean exceeds the specification?   **Paper**

STEP 1: STATE THE HYPOTHESES

The question we want to answer indicates a right-tailed test, so the hypotheses would be

   $H_0: \mu = 216$ mm (product mean does not exceed the specification)

   $H_1: \mu > 216$ mm (product mean has risen above the specification)

From the null hypothesis we see that $\mu_0 = 216$ mm, which is the product specification.

STEP 2: SPECIFY THE DECISION RULE

We use the *level of significance* to find the *critical value* of the z statistic that determines the threshold for rejecting the null hypothesis to be $\alpha = 0.05$. The critical value of z that accomplishes this is $z_{0.05} = 1.645$. As illustrated in Figure 9.4, the decision rule is

   Reject H_0 if $z_{calc} > 1.645$.

   Otherwise do not reject H_0.

It is instructive to specify the decision rule in "absolute" terms also. That is, what kind of $\bar{x}$ values will lead us to reject the null hypothesis. Because the test is a right-tailed test now, our critical $\bar{x}$ value is 1.645 standard deviations to the right of μ_0. So

$$\bar{x}_{\text{crit}} = \mu_0 + 1.645\sigma_{\bar{x}} = \mu_0 + 1.645\frac{\sigma}{\sqrt{n}} = 216 + 1.645\frac{0.023}{\sqrt{50}} = 216.0054$$

STEP 3: COLLECT SAMPLE DATA AND CALCULATE THE TEST STATISTIC

If H_0 is true, then the test statistic should be near 0 because $\bar{x}$ should be near μ_0. The value of the test statistic is

$$z_{\text{calc}} = \frac{\bar{x} - \mu_0}{\dfrac{\sigma}{\sqrt{n}}} = \frac{216.007 - 216.000}{\dfrac{0.023}{\sqrt{50}}} = \frac{0.007}{0.00325269} = 2.152$$

STEP 4: MAKE THE DECISION

The test statistic falls in the right rejection region, so we reject the null hypothesis $H_0: \mu = 216$ and conclude the alternative hypothesis $H_1: \mu > 216$ at the 5 percent level of significance. Although the difference is slight, it is statistically significant. (Of course, we would arrive at the same decision by using the "absolute" method.)

STEP 5: TAKE ACTION

Now that we have concluded that the process is producing paper with an average width *greater* than the specification, it is time to adjust our manufacturing process to bring the average width back to specification. Our course of action could be to readjust the machine settings or it could be time to resharpen the cutting tools. At this point it is the responsibility of the process engineers to determine the best course of action.

p-Value Method

The critical value method described above requires that you specify your rejection criterion in terms of the test statistic before you take a sample. The *p-value method* is a different approach that is often preferred by researchers over the critical value method due to the ease with which a *p* value can be found using standard software like Excel. It requires that you express the strength of your evidence (i.e., your sample) against the null hypothesis in terms of a probability. The *p* value answers the following question: What is the probability that we would observe our particular sample mean (or something even farther away from μ_0) if, in fact, the null hypothesis is true? The *p* value gives us more information than a test using one particular value of α.

The *p* value is compared to the level of significance. In order to calculate the *p* value, we still need to find z_{calc}. For a right-tailed test, the decision rule using the *p* value approach is stated as follows:

Reject H_0 if $P(Z > z_{\text{calc}}) < \alpha$; otherwise fail to reject H_0.

Whether we use the critical value approach or the *p*-value approach, our decision about the null hypothesis will be the same.

FIGURE 9.4

Right-Tailed *z*-Test for $\alpha = 0.05$

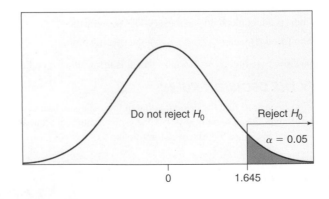

Concept Check

By sketching the appropriate diagrams for either a one-tailed or a two-tailed test, illustrate why using the *p*-value approach will result in the same decision about the null hypothesis as using the critical value approach.

---

p value

A *p* value directly measures how well the sample agrees with H_0. The smaller the *p* value, the less the sample agrees with H_0 and, thus, the stronger is the evidence for rejecting H_0.

The *p* value for the test in Example 5, above, is $P(Z > 2.152)$. Note that the direction of the inequality in the *p* value is the same as in the alternative hypothesis: $H_1: \mu > 216$ mm.

To find the *p* value, we can use Excel's function =NORMSDIST(2.152) to obtain the left-tail area for the cumulative *Z* distribution (see Figure 9.5). Because $P(Z < 2.152) = 0.9843$, the right-tail area is $P(Z > 2.152) = 1 - 0.9843 = 0.0157$. This is the *p* value for the right-tailed test, as illustrated in Figure 9.5. The *p* value diagram does not show α. The *p* value of 0.0157 says that in a right-tailed test, a test statistic of $z_{calc} = 2.152$ (or a more extreme test statistic) would happen by chance about 1.57 percent of the time if the null hypothesis were true.

We could also obtain the *p* value from Appendix C, which shows standard normal areas from 0 to *z*. Using $z = 2.15$, we see the area between 0 and 2.15 as 0.4842. So the *p* value of the test = $P(Z > 2.15) = 0.5 - 0.4842 = 0.0158$. Thus there is only 1.58 percent chance that we would see a sample mean as large as 216.007 or larger if the null hypothesis were true. Clearly we feel much more comfortable rejecting the null hypothesis in favour of the alternative hypothesis if the *p* value is very small. Another advantage of the *p* value method is that once you have calculated the *p* value of a test, it is trivial to make a decision for any level of significance α. All you need to do is to reject H_0 if the *p* value is less than the given α. So if you reject the null hypothesis for $\alpha = 0.05$, you will reject H_0 for any $\alpha > 0.05$.

Most statistical software provides *p* values for different tests.

Two-Tailed Test

What if we used a two-tailed test? This might be appropriate if the objective is to detect a deviation from the desired mean in *either* direction. To demonstrate, again we return to our scenario in Example 5, above.

***p* Value for a Right-Tailed Test with $z_{calc} = 2.152$, Using Excel**   FIGURE 9.5

FIGURE 9.6

Two-Tailed z-Test for α = 0.05

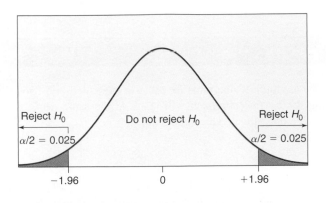

Step 1: State the Hypotheses For a two-tailed test, the hypotheses are

$H_0: \mu = 216$ mm (product mean is what it is supposed to be)

$H_1: \mu \neq 216$ mm (product mean is not what it is supposed to be)

Step 2: Specify the Decision Rule We will use the same $\alpha = 0.05$ as in the right-tailed test. But for a two-tailed test, we split the risk of Type I error by putting $\alpha/2 = 0.05/2 = 0.025$ in each tail. For $\alpha = 0.05$ in a two-tailed test, the critical value is $z_{0.025} = \pm 1.96$, so the decision rule is

Reject H_0 if $z_{calc} > 1.96$ or if $z_{calc} < -1.96$.

Otherwise do not reject H_0.

The decision rule is illustrated in Figure 9.6.

Step 3: Calculate the Test Statistic Although the test statistic is affected by the value of μ_0, it is *unaffected by the form of the hypotheses or the level of significance.* The value of the test statistic is the same as for the one-tailed test:

$$z_{calc} = \frac{\bar{x} - \mu_0}{\dfrac{\sigma}{\sqrt{n}}} = \frac{216.007 - 216.000}{\dfrac{0.023}{\sqrt{50}}} = \frac{0.007}{0.00325269} = 2.152$$

Step 4: Make the Decision Because the test statistic falls in the right tail of the rejection region, we reject the null hypothesis $H_0: \mu = 216$ and conclude $H_1: \mu \neq 216$ at the 5 percent level of significance. Another way to say this is that the sample mean *differs significantly* from the desired specification at $\alpha = 0.05$ in a two-tailed test. Note that this decision is rather a close one, as the test statistic just barely falls into the rejection region.

Using the p-Value Approach

In a two-tailed test, the decision rule using the p value is the same as in a one-tailed test.

Reject H_0 if p value $< \alpha$.

The difference between a one-tailed and a two-tailed test is how we obtain the p value. Because we allow rejection in either the left or the right tail in a two-tailed test, the level of significance, α, is divided equally between the two tails to establish the rejection region. In order to fairly evaluate the p value against α, we must now double the tail area. The p value in this two-tailed test is $2 \times P(Z > 2.152) = 2 \times 0.0157 = 0.0314$. See Figure 9.7. This says that in a two-tailed test a result as extreme as 2.152 would arise about 3.14 percent of the time by chance alone *if the null hypothesis were true.*

Interpretation Although the sample mean 216.007 might seem very close to 216, it is more than two standard deviations from the desired mean. This example shows that even a small difference can be significant. It all depends on σ and n, that is, on the standard error of the mean in the denominator of the test statistic. In this case, there is a high degree of precision

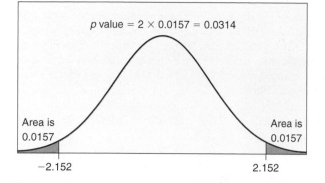

FIGURE 9.7

**Two-Tailed *p* Value for
z = 2.152**

in the manufacturing process ($\sigma = 0.023$ is very small), so the standard error (and hence the allowable variation) is extremely small. Such a tiny difference in means would not be noticeable to consumers, but stringent quality control standards are applied to ensure that no shipment goes out with any noticeable non-conformance.

Our statistical tests show that there is a statistically *significant* departure from the desired mean for paper width at $\alpha = 0.05$. But is the difference *important?* Is 216.007 so close to 216 that nobody could tell the difference? The question of whether to adjust the process is up to the engineers or business managers, not statisticians.

Analogy to Confidence Intervals

A two-tailed hypothesis test at the 5 percent level of significance ($\alpha = 0.05$) is exactly equivalent to asking whether the 95 percent confidence interval for the mean includes the hypothesized mean. If the confidence interval includes the hypothesized mean H_0: $\mu = 216$, then we cannot reject the null hypothesis. In this case the 95 percent confidence interval would be

$$\bar{x} \pm z\frac{\sigma}{\sqrt{n}} = 216.007 \pm 1.96\frac{0.023}{\sqrt{50}} = 216.001 < \mu < 216.013$$

Because this confidence interval does not include 216, we reject the null hypothesis H_0: $\mu = 216$. However, the decision is rather a close one as it was with the two-tailed hypothesis test, as the lower limit of the confidence interval almost includes 216.

Note: As previously mentioned, the null and alternative hypotheses are usually set up such that the higher-cost mistake is the Type I error. Because students are probably not familiar enough with most of the scenarios in the exercises to determine which is the higher-cost mistake, you should use the following facts about the two hypotheses when determining which hypothesis should be the null and which should be the alternative. We can only *assume* that the null hypothesis is true. We can *conclude* that the alternative hypothesis is true. We cannot determine if there is sufficient evidence for the null hypothesis. We can determine if there is sufficient evidence against the null hypothesis (and in favour of the alternative hypothesis).

Section Exercises

9.9 Calculate the z test statistic and p value for each sample. (LO 4 & 5)
   a. $H_0 : \mu = 60$ versus $H_1 : \mu \neq 60$, $\alpha = 0.025$, $\bar{x} = 63$, $\sigma = 8$, $n = 16$
   b. $H_0 : \mu \geq 60$ versus $H_1 : \mu < 60$, $\alpha = 0.05$, $\bar{x} = 58$, $\sigma = 5$, $n = 25$
   c. $H_0 : \mu \leq 60$ versus $H_1 : \mu > 60$, $\alpha = 0.05$, $\bar{x} = 65$, $\sigma = 8$, $n = 36$

9.10 Find the p value for each test statistic. (LO 5)
   a. Right-tailed test, $z = +1.34$
   b. Left-tailed test, $z = -2.07$
   c. Two-tailed test, $z = -1.69$

9.11 Procyon Manufacturing produces tennis balls. Weights are supposed to be normally distributed with a mean of 2.035 ounces and a standard deviation of 0.002 ounces. A sample of 25 tennis balls shows a mean weight of 2.036 ounces. At $\alpha = 0.025$, is there sufficient evidence that the mean weight is heavier than it is supposed to be? Calculate the p value for this test. (LO 3, 4 & 5)

9.12 Suppose the mean arrival rate of flights at Winnipeg International Airport in marginal weather is 195 flights per hour with a historical standard deviation of 13 flights. To increase arrivals, a new air traffic control procedure is implemented. In the next 30 days of marginal weather, the mean arrival rate is 200 flights per hour. (a) Set up the decision rule at $\alpha = 0.025$ to decide whether there has been a significant increase in the mean number of arrivals per hour. (b) Carry out the test and make the decision. Is it close? Would the decision be different if you used $\alpha = 0.01$? (c) Calculate the p value for this test. (d) What assumptions are you making, if any? (LO 3, 4 & 5) **Flights**

210	215	200	189	200	213	202	181	197	199
193	209	215	192	179	196	225	199	196	210
199	188	174	176	202	195	195	208	222	221

9.13 An airline serves bottles of Galena Spring Water that are supposed to contain an average of 10 ounces. The filling process follows a normal distribution with process standard deviation 0.07 ounce. Twelve randomly chosen bottles had the weights shown below (in ounces). (a) Set up a decision rule to detect quality control violations using the 5 percent level of significance. (b) Carry out the test. (c) What assumptions are you making, if any? (d) Calculate the p value of this test. (LO 3, 4 & 5) **BottleFill**

| 10.02 | 9.95 | 10.11 | 10.10 | 10.08 | 10.04 | 10.06 | 10.03 | 9.98 | 10.01 | 9.92 | 9.89 |

9.14 Suppose the Leamington, Ontario, fire department aims to respond to fire calls in 4 minutes or less, on average. Response times are normally distributed with a standard deviation of 1 minute. Would a sample of 18 fire calls with a mean response time of 4 minutes 30 seconds provide sufficient evidence to show that the goal is not being met at $\alpha = 0.01$? What is the p value? (LO 3, 4 & 5)

9.15 The lifespan of xenon metal halide arc-discharge bulbs for aircraft landing lights is normally distributed with a mean of 3,000 hours and a standard deviation of 500 hours. If a new ballast system shows a mean life of 3,515 hours in a test on a sample of 10 prototype new bulbs, would you conclude that the new lamp's mean life exceeds the current mean life at $\alpha = 0.01$? What is the p value? (For more information, see www.xevision.com.) (LO 3, 4 & 5)

9.16 The current battery used in a popular MP3 player has an average play time, when fully charged, of 12.7 hours with a standard deviation of 1.1 hours. The manufacturer of this MP3 player would switch to a new battery if there is sufficient evidence to indicate that the new battery would have an average play time greater than 14 when fully charged. The manufacturer tested this new battery in 25 of its MP3 players and calculated the average play time to be 14.8 hours. Assuming that play times are normally distributed and that the standard deviation in play times is the same as the old battery, will the manufacturer switch to the new battery? Use a 0.02 level of significance. Calculate the p value of this test. (LO 3, 4 & 5)

9.17 Over the years, the issue of grade inflation has been raised by many individuals who are worried that the grades students get today would not be the same grades that they would have received several years ago. Others argue that the grades have decreased because students have different study habits that have not been addressed by the professors teaching the course. Ten years ago, the average grade in a particular introductory statistics course was 65 percent with a standard deviation in grades of 4 percent. This year, a random sample of 35 students taking the same course revealed an average grade of 71 percent. Assuming that grades follow a normal distribution with the same standard deviation as before, at the 0.05 level of significance, can we conclude that average grades in this course have increased? Calculate the p value of this test. (LO 3, 4 & 5)

Chapter 9

9.4 Testing a Mean: Unknown Population Variance

If the population variance σ^2 must be estimated from the sample (as is generally the case), the hypothesis testing procedure must be modified. There is a loss of information when s replaces σ in the formulas, and it is no longer appropriate to use the normal distribution. However, the basic hypothesis testing steps are the same.

Using Student's t

When the population standard deviation σ is unknown and the population may be assumed normal (or generally symmetric with no outliers), the test statistic $\dfrac{\overline{X} - \mu}{S/\sqrt{n}}$ follows the Student's t

distribution with $n - 1$ degrees of freedom. Because σ is rarely known, we generally expect to use Student's t instead of z, as you saw for confidence intervals in the previous chapter. The value of the test statistic, assuming true H_0, is calculated as:

$$t_{calc} = \frac{\bar{x} - \mu_0}{\dfrac{s}{\sqrt{n}}}$$

(9.5)

EXAMPLE 6
Hot Chocolate

In addition to its core business of bagels and coffee, Bruegger's Bagels also sells hot chocolate for the non-coffee crowd. Customer research shows that the ideal temperature for hot chocolate is 142°F (or 61.1°C)—hot but not too hot. A random sample of 24 cups of hot chocolate is taken at various times, and the temperature of each cup is measured using an ordinary kitchen thermometer that is accurate to the nearest whole degree. **HotChoc**

140	140	141	145	143	144	142	140
145	143	140	140	141	141	137	142
143	141	142	142	143	141	138	139

The sample mean is 141.375 with a sample standard deviation of 1.99592. At $\alpha = 0.10$, does this sample evidence show that the true mean differs from 142?

STEP 1: STATE THE HYPOTHESES

We use a two-tailed test. The null hypothesis is in conformance with the desired standard.

H_0: $\mu = 142$ (mean temperature is correct)

H_1: $\mu \neq 142$ (mean temperature is incorrect)

STEP 2: SPECIFY THE DECISION RULE

For $\alpha = 0.10$, using Excel, the critical value for $\nu = n - 1 = 24 - 1 = 23$ degrees of freedom is =TINV(0.10,23) = 1.714 (note that Excel's inverse t assumes a two-tailed test). The same value can be obtained from Appendix D, shown here in abbreviated form:

			Upper Tail Area		
ν	0.10	0.05	0.025	0.01	0.005
1	3.078	6.314	12.706	31.821	63.657
2	1.886	2.920	4.303	6.965	9.925
3	1.638	2.353	3.182	4.541	5.841
⋮	⋮	⋮	⋮	⋮	⋮
21	1.323	1.721	2.080	2.518	2.831
22	1.321	1.717	2.074	2.508	2.819
23	1.319	**1.714**	2.069	2.500	2.807
24	1.318	1.711	2.064	2.492	2.797
25	1.316	1.708	2.060	2.485	2.787

Based on our expectations that the value of t should be different than zero if H_1 is true and that the test statistic has a t distribution with $n - 1$ degrees of freedom, we will reject H_0 if $t_{calc} > 1.714$ or if $t_{calc} < -1.714$, as illustrated in Figure 9.8.

STEP 3: CALCULATE THE VALUE OF THE TEST STATISTIC

Plugging in the sample information, the test statistic value is

$$t_{calc} = \frac{\bar{x} - \mu_0}{\dfrac{s}{\sqrt{n}}} = \frac{141.375 - 142}{\dfrac{1.99592}{\sqrt{24}}} = \frac{-0.6250}{0.40742} = -1.534$$

STEP 4: MAKE THE DECISION

Because the test statistic lies within the range of chance variation, we cannot reject the null hypothesis H_0: $\mu = 142$.

FIGURE 9.8

Two-Tailed Test for a Mean Using t for $\nu = 23$

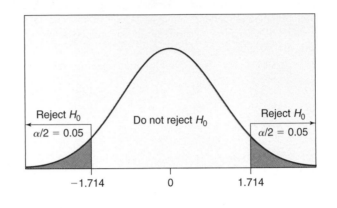

Using the p Value

A more general approach favoured by researchers is to find the p value. We want to determine the tail area less than $t = -1.534$ or greater than $t = +1.534$. However, from Appendix D we can only get a range for the p value. From Appendix D, we see that the two-tail p value must lie between 0.20 and 0.10 (it's a two-tailed test, so we double the right-tail area). It is easier and more precise to use Excel's function =TDIST(t test statistic, degrees of freedom, tails). In this case the formula=TDIST(1.534,23,2) gives the two-tailed p value of 0.13867. The area of each tail is half that, or 0.06934, as shown in Figure 9.9. A sample mean as extreme in either tail would occur by chance about 139 times in 1,000 two-tailed tests if H_0 were true. Because the p value is greater than α, we cannot reject H_0.

Confidence Interval Versus Hypothesis Test for μ

The two-tailed test at the 10 percent level of significance is equivalent to a two-tailed 90 percent confidence interval. If the confidence interval does not contain μ_0, we reject H_0. For the

FIGURE 9.9 **Two-Tailed p Value for $t = 1.534$**

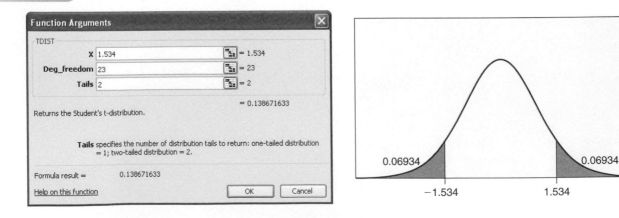

FIGURE 9.10

90 Percent Confidence Interval for μ

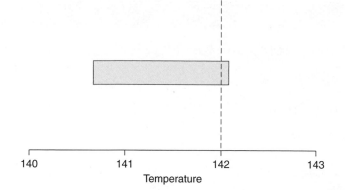

hot chocolate, the sample mean is 141.375 with a sample standard deviation of 1.99592. Using Appendix D we find $t_{0.05} = 1.714$, so the 90 percent confidence interval for μ is

$$\bar{x} \pm t_{\alpha/2, n-1}\frac{s}{\sqrt{n}} = 141.375 \pm (1.714)\frac{1.99592}{\sqrt{24}} = 141.375 \pm 0.6983$$

Because $\mu = 142$ lies within the 90 percent confidence interval $140.677 < \mu < 142.073$, we cannot reject the hypothesis H_0: $\mu = 142$ at $\alpha = 0.10$ in a two-tailed test. Many decisions can be handled either as hypothesis tests or using confidence intervals. The confidence interval has the appeal of providing a graphical feeling for the location of the hypothesized mean within the confidence interval, as shown in Figure 9.10. We can see that 142 is near the upper end of the confidence interval, nearly (but not quite) leading to a rejection of H_0: $\mu = 142$.

Using MegaStat for one Mean

You can get tests for one mean, including a confidence interval, using MegaStat. Figure 9.11 shows its setup screen and output for the test of one mean for the hot chocolate data. You enter the data range and everything else is automatic. It gives a choice of z or t, but to use z you must know σ.

Large Samples

From Appendix D you can verify that when n is large, there is little difference between critical values of t and z (the last line in Appendix D, for $\nu = \infty$). For this reason, it is unlikely that harm will result if you use z instead of t, as long as the sample size is not small. The test statistic value is

$$z_{\text{calc}} = \frac{\bar{x} - \mu_0}{\dfrac{s}{\sqrt{n}}} \quad (\text{large sample, unknown } \sigma) \qquad (9.6)$$

However, using z instead of t is not conservative, because it will increase the Type I error somewhat. Therefore, statisticians recommend that we always apply t when σ is unknown. We then can use Excel or Appendix D to get the critical value.

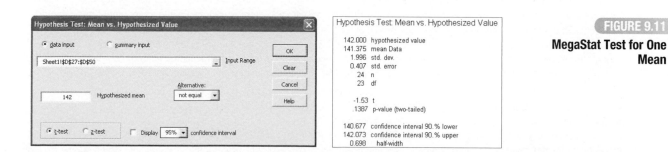

FIGURE 9.11

MegaStat Test for One Mean

Section Exercises

9.18 Estimate the *p* value *as a range* using Appendix D (*not* Excel): (LO 5)
   a. $t = 1.457, \nu = 14$, right-tailed test
   b. $t = 2.601, \nu = 8$, two-tailed test
   c. $t = -1.847, \nu = 22$, left-tailed test

9.19 Find the *p* value using Excel (*not* Appendix D): (LO 5)
   a. $t = 1.457, \nu = 14$, right-tailed test
   b. $t = 2.601, \nu = 8$, two-tailed test
   c. $t = -1.847, \nu = 22$, left-tailed test

9.20 Use Excel to find the *p* value for each test statistic. (LO 5)
   a. Right-tailed test, $t = +1.677, n = 13$
   b. Left-tailed test, $t = -2.107, n = 5$
   c. Two-tailed test, $t = -1.865, n = 34$

9.21 Calculate the test statistic and *p* value for each sample. State the conclusion for the specified α. (LO 4 & 5)
   a. $H_0: \mu = 200$ versus $H_1: \mu \neq 200, \alpha = 0.025, \bar{x} = 203, s = 8, n = 16$
   b. $H_0: \mu \geq 200$ versus $H_1: \mu < 200, \alpha = 0.05, \bar{x} = 198, s = 5, n = 25$
   c. $H_0: \mu \leq 200$ versus $H_1: \mu > 200, \alpha = 0.05, \bar{x} = 205, s = 8, n = 36$

9.22 The manufacturer of an airport baggage scanning machine claims it can handle an average of 530 bags per hour. (a) At $\alpha = 0.05$, in a left-tailed test, would a sample of 16 randomly chosen hours with a mean of 510 and a standard deviation of 50 indicate that the manufacturer's claim is overstated? (b) Why might the assumption of a normal population be doubtful? (See *Aviation Week and Space Technology* 162, no. 4 (Jan. 24, 2005), p. 42.) (LO 3 & 4)

9.23 The manufacturer of Glo-More flat white interior latex paint claims one-coat coverage of at least 10 square metres per litre on interior walls. A painter keeps careful track of 6 litres and finds coverage (in square metres) of 9.0, 10.5, 8.5, 8.0, 9.5, and 10.0. (a) At $\alpha = 0.10$ does this evidence contradict the claim? State your hypotheses and decision rule. (b) Is this conclusion sensitive to the choice of α? (c) Use Excel to find the *p* value. Interpret it. (d) Discuss the distinction between importance and significance in this example. (LO 3, 4 & 5) **Paint**

9.24 The average weight of a package of rolled oats is supposed to be at least 0.5 kg. A sample of 18 packages shows a mean of 0.47 kg with a standard deviation of 0.07 kg. (a) At the 5 percent level of significance, is the true mean smaller than the specification? Clearly state your hypotheses and decision rule. (b) Is this conclusion sensitive to the choice of α? (c) Use Excel to find the *p* value. Interpret it. (LO 3, 4 & 5)

9.25 According to J.D. Power & Associates, the mean wait for an airport rental car shuttle bus in 2004 was 19 minutes. In 2005, a random sample of 20 business travellers showed a mean wait of 15 minutes with a standard deviation of 7 minutes. (a) At $\alpha = 0.05$, has the mean wait decreased? State the hypotheses and decision rule clearly. (b) Use Excel to find the *p* value. Interpret it. (LO 3, 4 & 5)

9.26 In 2004, a small dealership leased 21 Chevrolet Impalas on 2-year leases. When the cars were returned in 2006, the mileage was recorded (see below). Is the dealer's mean significantly greater than the national average of 30,000 kilometres for 2-year leased vehicles, using the 10 percent level of significance? (LO 3 & 4) **Mileage**

40,060	24,960	14,310	17,370	44,740	44,550	20,250
33,380	24,270	41,740	58,630	35,830	25,750	28,910
25,090	43,380	23,940	43,510	53,680	31,810	36,780

9.27 At Queen's University, a sample of 18 senior accounting majors showed a mean cumulative GPA of 3.35 with a standard deviation of 0.25. At $\alpha = 0.05$, does this differ significantly from 3.25 (the mean GPA for all fourth-year business school students at the university)? (LO 3 & 4)

9.28 The more quickly a customer representative can service a customer at a call centre, the fewer the number of representatives a call centre would need to employ and the greater its profit. A particular call centre is up for sale and the potential buyer would only consider making an offer if he is fairly convinced that the average time per call is less than 4.7 minutes. This potential buyer was allowed to monitor 23 calls. The average time per call was 4.2 minutes and the standard deviation in call times was 1.1 minutes. At the 0.05 level of significance, is there sufficient evidence that the average time meets the potential buyer's criterion? Will this potential buyer make an offer to purchase? Explain. Use the *t* table to estimate the *p* value of this test. (LO 3 & 4)

9.29 Statistics Canada reported that in 2008, 5.6 percent of Canadians' total personal expenditure on consumer goods and services was spent on medical care and health services (Statistics Canada, CANSIM, table 380-0024). Suppose that during 2009, a random sample of 15 Canadians kept track of their personal expenditures and their percentage spent on medical care and health services averaged 6.3 percent, with a standard deviation of 1.8 percent. At the 0.05 level of significance, can we conclude that the average percentage that all Canadians spent on medical care and health services in 2009 is different than 5.6 percent? (LO 3 & 4)

Mini Case   9.2

Beauty Products and Small Business

Lisa has been working at a beauty counter in a department store for five years. In her spare time she's also been creating lotions and fragrances using all natural products. After receiving positive feedback from her friends and family about her beauty products, Lisa decides to open her own store. Lisa knows that convincing a bank to help fund her new business will require more than a few positive testimonials from family. Based on her experience working at the department store, Lisa believes women in her area spend more than the national average on fragrance products. This fact could help make her business successful.

Lisa would like to be able to support her belief with data to include in a business plan proposal that she would then use to obtain a small business loan. Lisa took a business statistics course while in college and decides to use the hypothesis testing tool she learned. After conducting research she learns that the national average spending by women on fragrance products is $59 every three months.

The hypothesis test is based on this survey result:

H_0: $\mu = \$59$
H_1: $\mu > \$59$

In other words, she will assume the average spending in her town is the same as the national average *unless she has strong evidence that says otherwise*. Lisa takes a random sample of 25 women and finds that the sample mean $\bar{x}$ is $68 and the sample standard deviation s is $15. Lisa uses a t statistic because she doesn't know the population standard deviation. Her calculated t statistic value is

$$t_{\text{calc}} = \frac{68 - 59}{\dfrac{15}{\sqrt{25}}} = 3.00 \quad \text{with 24 degrees of freedom}$$

Using the Excel formula =TDIST(3,24,1), Lisa finds that the one-tailed p value is 0.003103. This p value is quite small and she can safely reject her null hypothesis. Lisa now has strong evidence to conclude that over a three-month period, women in her area spend more than $59 on average.

Lisa would also like to include an estimate for the average amount women in her area *do* spend. Calculating a confidence interval would be her next step. Lisa chooses a 95 percent confidence level and finds the t value to use in her calculations by using the Excel formula =TINV(0.05,24). The result is $t = 2.0639$. Her 95 percent confidence interval for μ is

$$\$68 \pm \$2.0639 \frac{15}{\sqrt{25}} = \$68 \pm \$6.19$$

Lisa's business plan proposal can confidently claim that women in her town spend more than the national average on fragrance products and that she estimates the average spending is between $62 and $74 every three months. Hopefully, the bank will see that Lisa not only creates excellent beauty products but also is a smart businessperson!

Source: For national average spending see The NPD Group press release, "New NPD Beauty Study Identifies Key Consumer Differences and Preferences," Mar. 28, 2005.

9.5   Testing a Population Proportion

Proportions are used frequently in business situations and collecting proportion data is straightforward. It is easier for customers to say whether they like or dislike this year's new automobile colour than it is for customers to quantify their degree of satisfaction with the new colour. Also, many business performance indicators such as market share, employee retention rates, and employee accident rates are expressed as proportions.

The steps we follow for testing a hypothesis about a population proportion, π, are the same as the ones we follow for testing a mean. The difference is that we now calculate a sample proportion, P, to calculate the test statistic. We know from Chapter 8 that for a sufficiently large sample the sample proportion can be assumed to follow a normal distribution with mean π and standard deviation (standard error) $\sigma_P = \sqrt{\dfrac{\pi(1 - \pi)}{n}}$. Our rule is to assume normality if

$n \geq 9\dfrac{\pi}{1 - \pi}$ and $n \geq 9\dfrac{1 - \pi}{\pi}$. Under normality, $P \sim N(\pi, \sigma_P) = N\left(\pi, \sqrt{\dfrac{\pi(1 - \pi)}{n}}\right)$ and the test statistic would be the Z-score. Recall that the sample proportion is

$$P = \frac{X}{n} = \frac{\text{number of successes}}{\text{sample size}} \qquad (9.7)$$

The test statistic, calculated from sample data, is the difference between the sample proportion p and the hypothesized proportion π_0 divided by the *estimated standard error of the proportion P* (sometimes denoted σ_P), and is calculated as

$$z_{\text{calc}} = \frac{p - \pi_0}{\sigma_P} = \frac{p - \pi_0}{\sqrt{\dfrac{\pi_0(1 - \pi_0)}{n}}} \qquad (9.8)$$

The value of π_0 we are testing is a **benchmark,** such as past performance, an industry standard, or a product specification. The value of π_0 does *not* come from a sample.

EXAMPLE 7

Return Policy

Retailers such as Guess, Staples, Sports Authority, and Limited Brands are employing new technology to crack down on "serial exchangers"—customers who abuse their return and exchange policies (*The Wall Street Journal,* Nov. 29, 2004). For example, some customers buy an outfit, wear it once or twice, and then return it. Software called Verify-1, a product of a company called Return Exchange, tracks a shopper's record of bringing back items. The historical return rate for merchandise at department stores is 13.0 percent. At one department store, after implementing the new software, there were 22 returns in a sample of 250 purchases. At $\alpha = 0.05$, does this sample prove that the true return rate has fallen?

STEP 1: STATE THE HYPOTHESES

The hypotheses are

H_0: $\pi = 0.13$ (return rate is the same as the historical rate)

H_1: $\pi < 0.13$ (return rate has fallen below 0.13)

STEP 2: SPECIFY THE DECISION RULE

For $\alpha = 0.05$ in a left-tailed test, the critical value is $z_{0.05} = -1.645$, so the decision rule is

Reject H_0 if $z_{\text{calc}} < -1.645$.

Otherwise do not reject H_0.

This decision rule is illustrated in Figure 9.12.

How about the decision rule in "absolute" terms? The critical sample proportion value, P_{crit}, is 1.645 standard deviations to the left of π_0. That is,

$$P_{\text{crit}} = 0.13 - 1.645\sigma_P = 0.13 - 1.645\sqrt{\frac{\pi_0(1 - \pi_0)}{n}}$$

$$= 0.13 - 1.645\sqrt{\frac{0.13(1 - 0.13)}{250}} = 0.13 - 0.035 = 0.095$$

We should reject the null hypothesis if our sample proportion is less than 0.095.

Before using z we should check the normality assumption. It is easy to verify that these conditions are met:

$$n \geq 9\left(\frac{\pi_0}{1 - \pi_0}\right) = 9\left(\frac{0.13}{0.87}\right) = 1.34, \ n \geq 9\left(\frac{1 - \pi_0}{\pi_0}\right) = 9\left(\frac{0.87}{0.13}\right) = 60.23$$

and our $n = 250$.

STEP 3: CALCULATE THE TEST STATISTIC

Because $p = x/n = 22/250 = 0.088$, the sample seems to favour H_1. But we will assume that H_0 is true and see if the test statistic contradicts this assumption. We test the hypothesis at $\pi = 0.13$. If we can reject $\pi = 0.13$ in favour of $\pi < 0.13$, then we implicitly reject the class of hypotheses $\pi \geq 0.13$. The test statistic is the difference between the sample proportion $p = x/n$ and the hypothesized parameter π_0 divided by the standard error of P:

$$z_{calc} = \frac{p - \pi_0}{\sqrt{\dfrac{\pi_0(1 - \pi_0)}{n}}} = \frac{0.088 - 0.13}{\sqrt{\dfrac{0.13(1 - 0.13)}{250}}} = \frac{-0.042}{0.02127} = -1.975$$

STEP 4: MAKE THE DECISION

Because the test statistic falls in the left-tail rejection region, we reject H_0. We conclude that the return rate is less than 0.13 after implementing the new software.

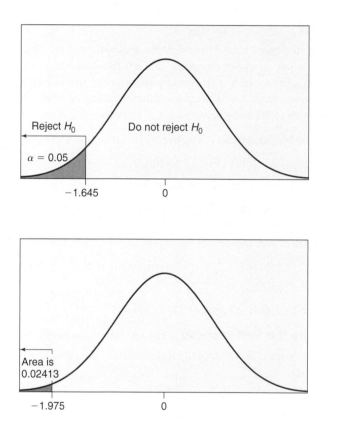

FIGURE 9.12

Left-Tailed *z* Test Using
$\alpha = 0.05$

FIGURE 9.13

p Value for a Left-Tailed Test with $z_{calc} = -1.975$

Calculating the *p* Value

For our test statistic $z_{calc} = -1.975$, the *p* value (0.02413) can be obtained from Excel's cumulative standard normal =NORMSDIST(-1.975). Alternatively, we can use Appendix C. The area to the left of $z = -1.975$ is the same as the area to the right of $z = 1.975$. For $z = 1.97$, we see this area is 0.4756, and for $z = 1.98$, this area is 0.4761. We use the average of these two values $(0.4756 + 0.4761)/2 = 0.4758$. Thus, $P(Z < -1.975) = P(Z > 1.975) = 0.5 - 0.4758 = 0.0242$. Figure 9.13 illustrates the *p* value.

The *smaller* the *p* value, the more we want to *reject* H_0. Does this seem backward? You might think a large *p* value would be "more significant" than a small one. But the *p* value is a direct measure of the level of significance at which we could reject H_0, so *a smaller p value is more convincing* for rejecting the null hypothesis in favour of the research hypothesis. For the left-tailed test, the *p* value tells us that there is a 0.02413 probability of getting a sample proportion of 0.088 or less if the true proportion is .13; that is, such a sample would arise by chance only about 24 times in 1,000 tests if the null hypothesis is true. In our left-tailed test, we would reject H_0 because the *p* value (0.02413) is smaller than α (0.05). As we said before, we would reject H_0 at *any* α greater than 0.02413.

Two-Tailed *z* Test for
$\alpha = 0.05$

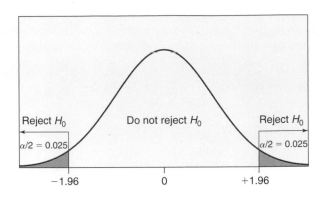

Two-Tailed Test

What if we used a two-tailed test? This might be appropriate if the objective is to detect a change in the return rate in *either* direction. In fact, two-tailed tests are used more often, because rejection in a two-tailed test always implies rejection in a one-tailed test, other things being equal. The same sample can be used for either a one-tailed or two-tailed test. The type of hypothesis test is up to the statistician. Again, we use the criteria from Example 7, above.

Step 1: State the Hypotheses   The hypotheses are

$H_0: \pi = 0.13$ (return rate is the same as the historical rate)

$H_1: \pi \neq 0.13$ (return rate is different from the historical rate)

Step 2: Specify the Decision Rule   For a two-tailed test, we split the risk of Type I error by putting $\alpha/2 = 0.05/2 = 0.025$ in each tail (as we would for a confidence interval). For $\alpha = 0.05$ in a two-tailed test, the critical value is $z_{0.025} = 1.96$, so the decision rule is

Reject H_0 if $z_{calc} > +1.96$ or if $z_{calc} < -1.96$ (or simply if $|z_{calc}| > 1.96$).
Otherwise do not reject H_0.

The decision rule is illustrated in Figure 9.14.

Step 3: Calculate the Test Statistic   The test statistic is *unaffected by the hypotheses or the level of significance.* The value of the test statistic is the same as for the one-tailed test:

$$z_{calc} = \frac{p - \pi_0}{\sqrt{\dfrac{\pi_0(1 - \pi_0)}{n}}} = \frac{0.088 - 0.13}{\sqrt{\dfrac{0.13(1 - 0.13)}{250}}} = \frac{-0.042}{0.02127} = -1.975$$

Step 4: Make the Decision   Because the test statistic falls in the left tail of the rejection region, we reject the null hypothesis $H_0: \pi = 0.13$ and conclude $H_1: \pi \neq 0.13$ at the 5 percent level of significance. Another way to say this is that the sample proportion *differs significantly* from the historical return rate at $\alpha = 0.05$ in a two-tailed test. Note that this decision is rather a close one, as the test statistic just barely falls into the rejection region.

Notice also that the rejection was stronger in a one-tailed test, that is, the test statistic is farther from the critical value. *Holding α constant, rejection in a two-tailed test always implies rejection in a one-tailed test.* This reinforces the logic of choosing a two-tailed test unless there is a specific reason to prefer a one-tailed test.

Calculating a *p* Value for a Two-Tailed Test

In a two-tailed test, we divide the risk into equal tails, one on the left and one on the right, to allow for the possibility that we will reject H_0 whenever the sample statistic is very small or very large. With the *p*-value approach in a two-tailed test, we find the tail area associated with our sample test statistic, multiply this by two, and then compare that probability to α. Our *z* statistic was calculated to be -1.975. The *p* value would then be

$$2 \times P(Z < -1.975) = 2 \times 0.02413 = 0.04826$$

We would reject the null hypothesis because the *p* value 0.04826 is less than $\alpha(0.05)$.

A Closer Look

In all hypothesis testing scenarios that we have looked at, the null hypothesis always contained the equality sign (e.g. $H_0: \pi = 0.5$ or $H_0: \pi \geq 0.5$) as it should. But, suppose we want to determine if there is sufficient evidence that the proportion is at least 0.5? Theoretically, the alternative hypothesis should be stated as $H_1: \pi \geq 0.5$, with the equality sign now being contained in H_1. How do we get around this dilemma? We can state the alternative hypothesis as being $H_1: \pi > 0.499999. . .$, which we can then round to read $H_1: \pi > 0.5$.

Concept Check

Earlier in this chapter, you were introduced to Prof. Plum and Prof. Wine. As previously mentioned, exams don't measure precisely how much a student knows and what grade he/she actually deserves. Prof. Plum's attitude is that it is more costly to fail a student who deserves to pass and, thus, will only fail students if there is enough evidence on their exams that they deserve to fail. In contrast, Prof. Wine thinks it more costly to pass a student who deserves to fail and, thus, will only pass students if there is enough evidence on their exams that they deserve to fail. Suppose each gives a 200-question true/false exam. Because both professors assign a very costly penalty for an incorrect answer, no student will attempt to answer a question unless he/she knows the answer. At the 0.05 level of significance, would a student in Prof. Plum's class pass the course (actually knows at least 50 percent of the material in the course) if he/she correctly answered 96 of the 200 questions? At the 0.05 level of significance, would a student in Prof. Wine's class pass the course if he/she correctly answered 105 of the 200 questions? What percentage on the exam would a student need to pass Prof. Plum's course? What percentage on the exam would a student need to pass Prof. Plum's course?

Effect of α

Would the return-rate decision be the same if we had used a different level of significance? Table 9.4 shows some possibilities. *The test statistic is the same regardless of α.* While we can reject the null hypothesis at $\alpha = 0.10$ or $\alpha = 0.05$, we cannot reject at $\alpha = 0.01$. Therefore, we would say that the current return rate differs from the historical return rate at the 10 percent and 5 percent levels of significance, but not at the 1 percent level of significance.

Which level of significance is the "right" one? They all are. It depends on how much Type I error we are willing to allow. Before concluding that $\alpha = 0.01$ is "better" than the others because it allows less Type I error, you should remember that smaller Type I error leads to increased Type II error. In this case, Type I error would imply that there has been a change in return rates when in reality nothing has changed, while Type II error implies that the software had no effect on the return rate, when in reality the software did decrease the return rate.

TABLE 9.4   Effect of Varying α

α	Test Statistic	Two-Tailed Critical Values	Decision
0.10	$z_{calc} = -1.975$	$z_{0.05} = \pm 1.645$	Reject H_0
0.05	$z_{calc} = -1.975$	$z_{0.025} = \pm 1.960$	Reject H_0
0.01	$z_{calc} = -1.975$	$z_{0.005} = \pm 2.576$	Don't reject H_0

A hospital is comparing its performance against an industry benchmark that no more than 50 percent of normal births should result in a hospital stay exceeding 2 days (48 hours). Thirty-one births in a sample of 50 normal births had a length of stay (LOS) greater than 48 hours. At $\alpha = 0.025$, does this sample prove that the hospital exceeds the benchmark? This question requires a right-tailed test.

STEP 1: STATE THE HYPOTHESES

The hypotheses are

H_0: $\pi = 0.50$ (the hospital is compliant with the benchmark)

H_1: $\pi > 0.50$ (the hospital is exceeding the benchmark)

STEP 2: SPECIFY THE DECISION RULE

For $\alpha = 0.025$ in a right-tailed test, the critical value is $z_{0.025} = 1.96$, so the decision rule is

Reject H_0 if $z > 1.960$.

Otherwise do not reject H_0.

This decision rule is illustrated in Figure 9.15.

Before using z we should check the normality assumption. To assume normality we require that $n \geq 9\dfrac{\pi}{1-\pi}$ and $n \geq 9\dfrac{1-\pi}{\pi}$. Inserting $\pi_0 = 0.50$ and $n = 50$ we see that the normality conditions are easily met as both conditions require that $n \geq 9$.

STEP 3: CALCULATE THE TEST STATISTIC

Because $p = x/n = 31/50 = 0.62$, the sample seems to favour H_1. But we will assume that H_0 is true and see if the test statistic contradicts this assumption. We test the hypothesis at $\pi = 0.50$. If we can reject $\pi = 0.50$ in favour of $\pi > 0.50$, then we can reject the class of hypotheses $\pi \leq 0.50$. The test statistic value is the difference between the sample proportion $p = x/n$ and the hypothesized parameter π_0 divided by the standard error of p:

$$z_{calc} = \frac{p - \pi_0}{\sqrt{\dfrac{\pi_0(1 - \pi_0)}{n}}} = \frac{0.62 - 0.50}{\sqrt{\dfrac{0.50(1 - 0.50)}{50}}} = \frac{0.12}{0.07071068} = 1.697$$

STEP 4: MAKE THE DECISION

The test statistic does not fall in the right-tail rejection region, so we cannot reject the hypothesis that $\pi \leq 0.50$ at the 2.5 percent level of significance. In other words, the test statistic is within the realm of chance at $\alpha = 0.025$.

Calculating the p Value

In this case, the p value can be obtained from Excel's cumulative standard normal function $=1-\text{NORMSDIST}(1.697) = 0.04485$, or from Appendix C (using $z = 1.70$ we get $p = 0.5 - 0.4554 = 0.0446$). Excel's accuracy is greater because $z = 1.697$ is not rounded to $z = 1.70$. Because we want a right-tail area, we must subtract the cumulative distribution function from 1. The p value is greater than 0.025, so we fail to reject the null hypothesis in a right-tailed test.

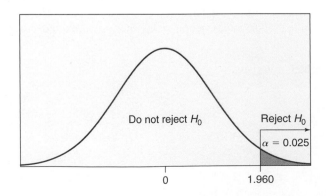

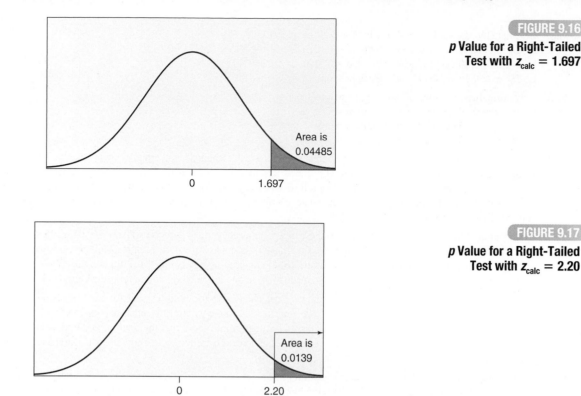

FIGURE 9.16

p Value for a Right-Tailed Test with $z_{calc} = 1.697$

Area is 0.04485

0   1.697

FIGURE 9.17

p Value for a Right-Tailed Test with $z_{calc} = 2.20$

Area is 0.0139

0   2.20

We could (barely) reject at $\alpha = 0.05$. This demonstrates that the level of significance can affect our decision. The advantage of the p value is that it tells you exactly the point of indifference between rejecting or not rejecting H_0. The p value is illustrated in Figure 9.16.

Effect of a Larger Sample

In general, a larger sample *increases power* (our ability to detect a false null hypothesis). In this case, a larger sample was possible. Fifty more births were examined, increasing the sample size to $n = 100$ births. In this new sample, 61 had an LOS exceeding 48 hours, or $p = 61/100 = 0.61$. The new test statistic value is

$$z_{calc} = \frac{p - \pi_0}{\sqrt{\dfrac{\pi_0(1 - \pi_0)}{n}}} = \frac{0.61 - 0.50}{\sqrt{\dfrac{0.50(1 - 0.50)}{100}}} = \frac{0.11}{0.05} = 2.20$$

This time we obtain a rejection as $z = 2.20$ exceeds the critical value $z_{0.025} = 1.96$. With the larger sample, the rejection is decisive. The new p value ($p = 0.0139$) shown in Figure 9.17 indicates that such a test statistic would arise only 1.39 percent of the time by chance alone, if the true proportion were 0.50.

Section Exercises

9.30   Interpret each p value in your own words: (LO 5)
   a. p value $= 0.387$, H_0: $\pi \geq 0.20$, H_1: $\pi < 0.20$, $\alpha = 0.10$
   b. p value $= 0.043$, H_0: $\pi \leq 0.90$, H_1: $\pi > 0.90$, $\alpha = 0.05$
   c. p value $= 0.0012$, H_0: $\pi = 0.50$, H_1: $\pi \neq 0.50$, $\alpha = 0.01$

9.31   Calculate the test statistic and p value for each sample. (LO 4 & 5)
   a. H_0: $\pi = 0.20$ versus H_1: $\pi \neq 0.20$, $\alpha = 0.025$, $p = 0.28$, $n = 100$
   b. H_0: $\pi \leq 0.50$ versus H_1: $\pi > 0.50$, $\alpha = 0.025$, $p = 0.60$, $n = 90$
   c. H_0: $\pi \leq 0.75$ versus H_1: $\pi > 0.75$, $\alpha = 0.10$, $p = 0.82$, $n = 50$

9.32 Calculate the test statistic and p value for each sample. (LO 4 & 5)
   a. $H_0: \pi \leq 0.60$ versus $H_1: \pi > 0.60, \alpha = 0.05, x = 56, n = 80$
   b. $H_0: \pi = 0.30$ versus $H_1: \pi \neq 0.30, \alpha = 0.05, x = 18, n = 40$
   c. $H_0: \pi \geq 0.10$ versus $H_1: \pi < 0.10, \alpha = 0.01, x = 3, n = 100$

9.33 May normality be assumed? Show your work. (LO 3)
   a. $H_0: \pi = 0.30$ versus $H_1: \pi \neq 0.30, n = 20$
   b. $H_0: \pi = 0.05$ versus $H_1: \pi \neq 0.05, n = 50$
   c. $H_0: \pi = 0.10$ versus $H_1: \pi \neq 0.10, n = 400$

9.34 In a recent survey, 10 percent of the participants rated Pepsi as being "concerned with my health." PepsiCo's response included a new "Smart Spot" symbol on its products that meet certain nutrition criteria, to help consumers who seek more healthful eating options. At $\alpha = 0.05$, would a follow-up survey showing that 18 of 100 persons now rate Pepsi as being "concerned with my health" provide sufficient evidence that the percentage has increased? (Data are from *The Wall Street Journal,* July 30, 2004.) (LO 3 & 4)

9.35 In a hospital's shipment of 3,500 insulin syringes, 14 were unusable due to defects. (a) At $\alpha = 0.05$, is this sufficient evidence to reject future shipments from this supplier if the hospital's quality standard requires 99.7 percent of the syringes to be acceptable? State the hypotheses and decision rule. (b) May normality be assumed? (c) Explain the effects of Type I error and Type II error. (d) Find the p value. (e) Would reducing α be a good idea? Explain the pros and cons. (LO 3, 4 & 5)

9.36 The Tri-Cities Tobacco Coalition sent three underage teenagers into various stores in Detroit and Highland Park, Michigan, to see if they could purchase cigarettes. Of 320 stores checked, 82 sold cigarettes to teens between 15 and 17 years old. (a) If the goal is to reduce the percent to 20 percent or less, does this sample show that the goal is *not* being achieved at $\alpha = 0.05$? (b) Construct a 95 percent confidence interval for the true percent of sellers who allow teens to purchase tobacco. (Data are from *Detroit Free Press,* Mar. 19, 2001, p. 2C.) (LO 3 & 4)

9.37 To encourage telephone efficiency, a catalogue call centre issues a guideline that at least half of all telephone orders should be completed within 2 minutes. Subsequently, a random sample of 64 telephone calls showed that 40 calls lasted over 2 minutes. (a) At $\alpha = 0.05$ is this a significant departure from the guideline? State your hypotheses and decision rule. (b) Find the p value. (c) Is the difference important (as opposed to significant)? (LO 3, 4 & 5)

9.38 The recent default rate on all student loans is 5.2 percent. In a recent random sample of 300 loans at private universities there were nine defaults. (a) Does this sample show sufficient evidence that the private university loan default rate is below the rate for all universities, at $\alpha = 0.01$? (b) Calculate the p value. (c) Verify that the assumption of normality is justified. (LO 3, 4 & 5)

9.39 The Association of Flight Attendants/Communication Workers of America and National Consumers League conducted a poll of 702 frequent and occasional fliers and found that 442 respondents favoured a ban on cellphones in flight, even if technology permits it. At $\alpha = 0.05$, can we conclude that more than half the sampled population supports a ban? (Data are from *Aviation Week and Space Technology* 182, no. 15 [Apr. 11, 2005], p. 14.) (LO 3 & 4)

9.40 A recent university graduate at an interview with a sales organization claims that he can make a sale with more than 70 percent of the customers that he contacts. To test this assertion, the organization randomly selected 75 potential customers to contact. The graduate made a sale to 57 customers. Using the 0.05 level of significance, is there sufficient evidence that the graduate's claim is true? Calculate the p value for this test. (LO 3, 4 & 5)

9.41 A study by Statistics Canada indicated that in 2005, 35.5 percent of Canadian males regularly participated in sports and that this was a drop of 6.2 percent from the year 1998. (Data are from "Study: Participation in Sports, 2005," *The Daily,* February 7, 2008.) Suppose that a random sample of 150 Canadian males taken in 2009 revealed that 45 regularly participated in sports. At the 0.05 level of significance, is there sufficient evidence that this downward trend is continuing (i.e., the participation rate in 2009 is below 35.5 percent)? Calculate the p value for this test. (LO 3, 4 & 5)

Mini Case   9.3

Every Minute Counts

As more company business is transacted by telephone or Internet, there is a considerable premium to reduce customer time spent with human operators. Rogers recently installed a new speech recognition system for its repair calls. In the old system, the user had to press keys on the numeric keypad to answer questions, which led many callers to opt to talk to an operator instead. Under the old system, 94 percent of the customers had to talk to an operator to get their needs met. Suppose that using the new system, a sample of 150 calls showed that 120 required an operator. The hypotheses are

$H_0: \pi = 0.94$ (the new system is no better than the old system)
$H_1: \pi < 0.94$ (the new system has reduced the proportion of operator calls)

These hypotheses call for a left-tailed test. Using $\alpha = 0.01$, the left-tail critical value is $z_{0.01} = -2.326$, as illustrated in Figure 9.18.

The normality conditions are met as our sample size $n = 150$, and

$$n \geq 9\left(\frac{\pi_0}{1 - \pi_0}\right) = 9\left(\frac{0.94}{0.06}\right) = 141, n \geq 9\left(\frac{0.06}{0.94}\right) = 0.57$$

The sample proportion is $p = 120/150 = 0.80$, so the value of our test statistic is

$$z_{calc} = \frac{p - \pi_0}{\sqrt{\dfrac{\pi_0(1 - \pi_0)}{n}}} = \frac{0.80 - 0.94}{\sqrt{\dfrac{0.94(1 - 0.94)}{150}}} = \frac{-0.14}{0.01939} = -7.22$$

The test statistic is far below the critical value of -2.326, so we conclude that the percentage of customers who require an operator has declined; p value $= P(Z < -7.22) \approx 0$.

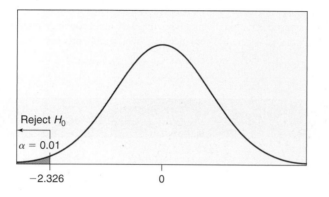

FIGURE 9.18

Decision Rule for Left-Tailed Test

9.6 Testing a Population Variance

Not all business hypothesis tests involve proportions or means. In quality control, for example, it is important to compare the variance of a process with a historical benchmark, σ_0^2, to see whether variance reduction has been achieved, or to compare a process standard deviation with an engineering specification.

EXAMPLE 9

Attachment Times

Historical statistics show that the standard deviation of attachment times for an instrument panel in an automotive assembly line is $\sigma = 7$ seconds. Observations on 20 randomly chosen attachment times are shown in Table 9.5. At $\alpha = 0.05$, does the variance in attachment times differ from the historical variance ($\sigma^2 = 7^2 = 49$)?

TABLE 9.5 Panel Attachment Times (seconds)   Attachment

120	143	136	126	122
140	133	133	131	131
129	128	131	123	119
135	137	134	115	122

The sample mean is $\bar{x} = 129.400$ with a standard deviation of $s = 7.44382$. We ignore the sample mean as it is irrelevant to this test. For a two-tailed test, the hypotheses are

$H_0: \sigma^2 = 49$
$H_1: \sigma^2 \neq 49$

For a test of one variance, assuming a normal population, the test statistic $\frac{(n-1)s^2}{\sigma^2}$ follows the **chi-square distribution** with degrees of freedom equal to $\nu = n - 1 = 20 - 1 = 19$. The test statistic value is

$$\chi^2_{\text{calc}} = \frac{(n-1)s^2}{\sigma_0^2} \quad (\text{test for one variance}) \tag{9.9}$$

For a two-tailed test, the decision rule based on the upper and lower critical values of chi-square is

Reject H_0 if $\chi^2_{\text{calc}} < \chi^2_{1-\alpha/2,\, n-1}$ or $\chi^2_{\text{calc}} > \chi^2_{\alpha/2,\, n-1}$.

Otherwise do not reject H_0
From Appendix E, we obtain the two critical values of chi-square to define the rejection region, as illustrated in Figures 9.19 and 9.20.
The critical values are $\chi^2_{1-\alpha/2,\, n-1} = 8.907$ and $\chi^2_{\alpha/2,\, n-1} = 32.852$. The value of the test statistic is

$$\chi^2_{\text{calc}} = \frac{(n-1)s^2}{\sigma_0^2} = \frac{(20-1)(7.44382)^2}{7^2} = 21.49$$

Because the test statistic is within the middle range, we cannot conclude that the population variance differs from 49; that is, we cannot conclude that the assembly process variance has changed.

FIGURE 9.19

Two-Tail Chi-Square Values for ν=19 and $\alpha = 0.05$

APPENDIX E

Critical Values of Chi-Square for area A

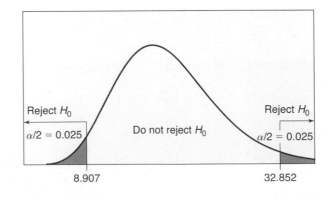

df	0.995	0.99	0.975	0.95	0.9	0.1	0.05	0.025	0.01	0.005	df
1	0.00	0.00	0.00	0.00	0.02	2.71	3.84	5.02	6.63	7.88	1
2	0.01	0.02	0.05	0.10	0.21	4.61	5.99	7.38	9.21	10.60	2
3	0.07	0.11	0.22	0.35	0.58	6.25	7.81	9.35	11.34	12.84	3
4	0.21	0.30	0.48	0.71	1.06	7.78	9.49	11.14	13.28	14.86	4
5	0.41	0.55	0.83	1.15	1.61	9.24	11.07	12.83	15.09	16.75	5
6	0.68	0.87	1.24	1.64	2.20	10.64	12.59	14.45	16.81	18.55	6
7	0.99	1.24	1.69	2.17	2.83	12.02	14.07	16.01	18.48	20.28	7
8	1.34	1.65	2.18	2.73	3.49	13.36	15.51	17.53	20.09	21.95	8

FIGURE 9.20

Decision Rule for Chi-Square Test

Reject H_0
$\alpha/2 = 0.025$

Do not reject H_0

Reject H_0
$\alpha/2 = 0.025$

8.907

32.852

Using MegaStat

MegaStat does tests for one variance, including a confidence interval. Figure 9.21 shows its setup screen and output for the variance test.

MegaStat Test for One Variance   FIGURE 9.21

Chi-square Variance Test dialog box (data input / summary input options, Input Range Sheet1!$E$9:$E$11, Select range with label, variance, n; Hypothesized variance 49; Alternative: not equal; Display 95% confidence interval)

Chi-square Variance Test

49.000000	hypothesized variance
55.410456	observed variance
20	n
19	df
21.49	chi-square
.6212	p-value (two-tailed)
32.046386	confidence interval 95% lower
118.205464	confidence interval 95% upper

When to Use Tests for One Variance

In general, we would be interested in a test of variances when it is not the *centre* of the distribution, but rather the *variability* of the process that matters. More variation implies a more erratic data-generating process. For example, variance tests are important in manufacturing processes, because increased variation around the mean can be a sign of wear and tear on equipment that would require attention.

Caution   The chi-square test for a variance is not robust to non-normality of the population. If normality cannot be assumed (e.g., if the data set has outliers or severe skewness), you might need to use a bootstrap method (see *LearningStats* Unit 08) to test the hypothesis, using specialized software. In such a situation, it is best to consult a statistician.

Section Exercises

9.42   A sample of size $n = 15$ has variance $s^2 = 35$. At $\alpha = 0.01$ in a left-tailed test, does this sample contradict the hypothesis that $\sigma^2 = 50$? (LO 3 & 6)

9.43   A sample of size $n = 10$ has variance $s^2 = 16$. At $\alpha = 0.10$ in a two-tailed test, does this sample contradict the hypothesis that $\sigma^2 = 24$? (LO 3 & 6)

9.44   A sample of size $n = 19$ has variance $s^2 = 1.96$. At $\alpha = 0.05$ in a right-tailed test, does this sample contradict the hypothesis that $\sigma^2 = 1.21$? (LO 3 & 6)

9.45   In U.S. hospitals, the average length of stay (LOS) for a diagnosis of pneumonia is 137 hours with a standard deviation of 25 hours. The LOS (in hours) for a sample of 12 pneumonia patients at Santa Theresa Memorial Hospital is shown below. At $\alpha = 0.05$, does this sample standard deviation indicate that the true standard deviation in LOS at this hospital is inconsistent with the national norms? Show all steps, including the hypotheses and critical values from Appendix E. *Hint:* Ignore the mean. (See National Center for Health Statistics, *Advance Data from Vital and Health Statistics,* no. 332 [Apr. 9, 2003], p. 13.) (LO 3 & 6)   **Pneumonia**

132	143	143	120	124	116
130	165	100	83	115	141

9.46   Should the speed limit on Highway 401 between Windsor, Ontario, and the western border of Quebec be increased? Some argue that this will increase the average speed of cars leading to more accidents. Others argue that by increasing the speed this will reduce the variability in speeds, thus reducing the number of accidents. At the current speed limit of 100 km/h, the standard deviation in speeds of cars driving along a typical stretch of the 401 without heavy traffic is 7.5 km/h. In an experiment in which the speed limit along a typical stretch was increased to 125 km/h, the standard deviation in speeds for a random sample of 23 cars was 5.1 km/h. At the 0.05 level of significance, is there sufficient evidence that increasing the speed limit will reduce the variability in speeds along the 401? (LO 3 & 6)

9.47   Owners of MP3 players would obviously prefer their batteries to have a long play time on a fully charged battery. But what may annoy these owners more than a short play time is the uncertainty as to how long they can use their players without having to recharge the batteries. The current make of battery used in a certain brand of MP3 player has a standard deviation in play times when fully charged of 1.8 hours. A new make of battery was tested in a random sample of 18 of these MP3 players, and this battery had a standard deviation in play times when fully charged of 1.6 hours. At the 0.05 level of significance, can we conclude that there is a difference in standard deviation in play times between the two makes of batteries? (LO 3 & 6)

9.7 Power Curves and OC Curves (Optional)

Recall that *power* is the probability of correctly rejecting a false null hypothesis. While we cannot always attain the power we desire in a statistical test, we can at least calculate what the power would be in various possible situations. We will show step by step how to calculate power for tests of a mean or proportion, and how to draw *power curves* that show how power depends on the true value of the parameter we are estimating.

Power Curve for a Mean: An Example

Power depends on how far the true value of the parameter is from the null hypothesis value. The further away the true population value is from the assumed value, the easier it is for your hypothesis test to detect and the more power it has. To illustrate the calculation of β risk and power, consider a utility that is installing underground PVC pipe as a cable conduit. The specifications call for a mean strength of 12,000 psi (pounds per square inch). A sample of 25 pieces of pipe is tested under laboratory conditions to ascertain the compressive pressure that causes the pipe to collapse. The standard deviation is known from past experience to be $\sigma = 500$ psi. If the pipe proves stronger than the specification, there is no problem, so the utility requires a left-tailed test:

H_0: $\mu = 12,000$ psi

H_1: $\mu < 12,000$ psi

If the true mean strength is 11,900 psi, what is the probability that the utility will not reject the null hypothesis and mistakenly conclude that $\mu = 12,000$? At $\alpha = 0.05$, what is the power of the test? Recall that β is the risk of Type II error, the probability of incorrectly not rejecting a false hypothesis. Type II error is bad, so we want β to be small.

$$\beta = P(\text{do not reject } H_0 \mid H_0 \text{ is false}) \qquad (9.10)$$

In this example, $\beta = P(\text{conclude } \mu = 12,000 | \mu = 11,900)$.

Conversely, power is the probability that we correctly reject a false hypothesis. More power is better, so we want power to be as close to 1 as possible:

$$\text{Power} = P(\text{reject } H_0 \mid H_0 \text{ is false}) = 1 - \beta \qquad (9.11)$$

The values of β and power will vary, depending on the difference between the true mean μ and the hypothesized mean μ_0, the standard deviation σ, the sample size n, and the level of significance α.

$$\text{Power} = f(\mu - \mu_0, \sigma, n, \alpha) \quad (\text{determinants of power for a mean}) \qquad (9.12)$$

Table 9.6 summarizes their effects. While we cannot change μ and σ, the sample size and level of significance often are under our control. We can get more power by increasing α, but would we really want to increase Type I error in order to reduce Type II error? Probably not, so the way we usually increase power is by choosing a larger sample size. We will discuss each of these effects in turn.

Calculating Power

To calculate β and power, we follow a simple sequence of steps for any given values of μ, σ, n, and α. We assume a normal population (or a large sample) so that the sample mean $\overline{X}$ may be assumed normally distributed.

TABLE 9.6 Determinants of Power in Testing One Mean

Parameter	If . . .	then . . .
True mean (μ)	$|\mu - \mu_0| \uparrow$	Power ↑
True standard deviation (σ)	$\sigma \uparrow$	Power ↓
Sample size (n)	$n \uparrow$	Power ↑
Level of significance (α)	$\alpha \uparrow$	Power ↑

Step 1   Find the left-tail *critical value* for the sample mean. At $\alpha = 0.05$ in a left-tailed test, we know that $z_{0.05} = -1.645$. Using the formula for a z-score,

$$z_{\text{critical}} = \frac{\bar{x}_{\text{critical}} - \mu_0}{\dfrac{\sigma}{\sqrt{n}}}$$

we can solve algebraically for $\bar{x}_{\text{critical}}$:

$$\bar{x}_{\text{critical}} = \mu_0 + z_{\text{critical}}\frac{\sigma}{\sqrt{n}} = 12{,}000 - 1.645\left(\frac{500}{\sqrt{25}}\right) = 11{,}835.5$$

In terms of the data units of measurement (pounds per square inch) the decision rule is

Reject H_0: $\mu = 12{,}000$ if $\bar{X} < 11{,}835.5$ psi.

Otherwise do not reject H_0.

Now suppose that the true mean is $\mu = 11{,}900$. Then the sampling distribution of $\bar{X}$ would be centred at 11,900 instead of 12,000 as we hypothesized. The probability of β error is the area to the right of the critical value $\bar{x}_{\text{critical}} = 11{,}835.5$ (the acceptance region) representing $P(\bar{X} > \bar{x}_{\text{critical}} \mid \mu = 11{,}900)$. Figure 9.22 illustrates this situation.

Step 2   Express the difference between the critical value $\bar{x}_{\text{critical}}$ and the true mean μ as a z value:

$$z = \frac{\bar{x}_{\text{critical}} - \mu}{\dfrac{\sigma}{\sqrt{n}}} = \frac{11{,}835.5 - 11{,}900}{\dfrac{500}{\sqrt{25}}} = -0.645$$

Step 3   Find the β risk and power as areas under the normal curve, using Appendix C or Excel:

Calculation of β

$\beta = P(\bar{X} > \bar{x}_{\text{critical}} \mid \mu = 11{,}900)$

$\quad = P(Z > -0.645)$

$\quad = 0.2406 + 0.5000$

$\quad = 0.7406$, or 74.1%

Calculation of Power

$Power = P(\bar{X} < \bar{x}_{\text{critical}} \mid \mu = 11{,}900)$

$\quad = 1 - \beta$

$\quad = 1 - 0.7406$

$\quad = 0.2594$, or 26.0%

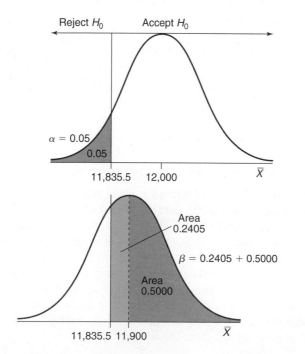

FIGURE 9.22

Finding β When $\mu = 11{,}900$

TABLE 9.7 β and Power for $\mu_0 = 12{,}000$

	n = 25			n = 50			n = 100		
True μ	z	β	Power	z	β	Power	z	β	Power
12,000	−1.645	0.9500	0.0500	−1.645	0.9500	0.0500	−1.645	0.9500	0.0500
11,950	−1.145	0.8739	0.1261	−0.938	0.8258	0.1742	−0.645	0.7405	0.2595
11,900	−0.645	0.7405	0.2595	−0.231	0.5912	0.4088	0.355	0.3612	0.6388
11,850	−0.145	0.5576	0.4424	0.476	0.3169	0.6831	1.355	0.0877	0.9123
11,800	0.355	0.3612	0.6388	1.184	0.1183	0.8817	2.355	0.0093	0.9907
11,750	0.855	0.1962	0.8038	1.891	0.0293	0.9707	3.355	0.0004	0.9996
11,700	1.355	0.0877	0.9123	2.598	0.0047	0.9953	4.355	0.0000	1.0000
11,650	1.855	0.0318	0.9682	3.305	0.0005	0.9995	5.355	0.0000	1.0000
11,600	2.355	0.0093	0.9907	4.012	0.0000	1.0000	6.355	0.0000	1.0000

This calculation shows that if the true mean is $\mu = 11{,}900$, then there is a 74.05 percent chance that we will commit β error by failing to reject $\mu = 12{,}000$. Because 11,900 is not very far from 12,000 in terms of the standard error, our test has relatively low power. Although our test may not be sensitive enough to reject the null hypothesis reliably if μ is only *slightly* less than 12,000, we would expect that if μ is *far* below 12,000, our test would be more likely to lead to rejection of H_0. Although we cannot know the true mean, we *can* repeat our power calculation for as many values of μ and n as we wish. These calculations may appear tedious, but they are straightforward in a spreadsheet. Table 9.7 shows β and power for samples of $n = 25$, 50, and 100 over a range of μ values from 12,000 down to 11,600.

Notice that β drops toward 0 and power approaches 1 when the true value μ is far from the hypothesized mean $\mu_0 = 12{,}000$. When $\mu = 12{,}000$ there can be no β error because β error can only occur if H_0 is false. Power is then equal to $\alpha = 0.05$, the lowest power possible.

Effect of Sample Size

Table 9.7 also shows that, other things being equal, if sample size were to increase, β risk would decline and power would increase because the critical value $\bar{x}_{\text{critical}}$ would be closer to the hypothesized mean μ. For example, if the sample size were increased to $n = 50$, then

$$\bar{x}_{\text{critical}} = \mu_0 + z_{\text{critical}}\frac{\sigma}{\sqrt{n}} = 12{,}000 - 1.645\left(\frac{500}{\sqrt{50}}\right) = 11{,}883.68$$

$$z = \frac{\bar{x}_{\text{critical}} - \mu}{\dfrac{\sigma}{\sqrt{n}}} = \frac{11{,}883.68 - 11{,}900}{\dfrac{500}{\sqrt{50}}} = -0.231$$

$$\text{Power} = P(\bar{X} < \bar{x}_{\text{critical}} \mid \mu = 11{,}900) = P(Z < -0.231) = 0.4088, \text{ or } 40.9\%$$

Relationship of the Power and OC Curves

Power is much easier to understand when it is made into a graph. A **power curve** is a graph whose Y-axis shows the power of the test $(1 - \beta)$ and whose X-axis shows the various possible true values of the parameter while holding the sample size constant. Figure 9.23 shows the power curve for this example, using three different sample sizes. You can see that power increases as the departure of μ from 12,000 becomes greater and that each larger sample size creates a higher power curve. In other words, larger samples have more power. Because the power curve approaches $\alpha = 0.05$ as the true mean approaches the hypothesized mean of 12,000, we can see that α also affects the power curve. If we increase α, the power curve will shift up. Although it is not illustrated here, power also rises if the standard deviation is smaller, because a small σ gives the test more precision.

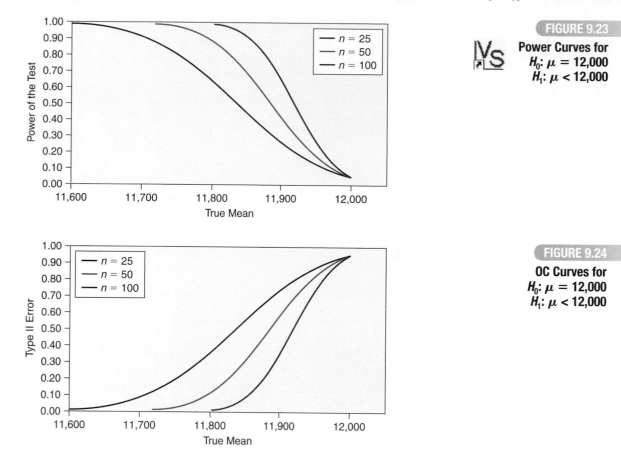

FIGURE 9.23

Power Curves for
H_0: $\mu = 12{,}000$
H_1: $\mu < 12{,}000$

FIGURE 9.24

OC Curves for
H_0: $\mu = 12{,}000$
H_1: $\mu < 12{,}000$

The graph of β risk against this same X-axis is called the **operating characteristic** or **OC curve**. Figure 9.24 shows the *OC* curve for this example. It is simply the converse of the power curve, so it is redundant if you already have the power curve.

Power Curve for Tests of a Proportion

For tests of a proportion, power depends on the true proportion π, the hypothesized proportion π_0, the sample size n, and the level of significance α. Table 9.8 summarizes their effects on power. As with a mean, enlarging the sample size is the most common method of increasing power, unless we are willing to raise the level of significance (that is, trade off Type I error against Type II error).

TABLE 9.8   Determinants of Power in Testing a Proportion

Parameter	If . . .	then . . .
True proportion π	$\lvert \pi - \pi_0 \rvert \uparrow$	Power $\uparrow$
Sample size n	$n\uparrow$	Power $\uparrow$
Level of significance α	$\alpha\uparrow$	Power $\uparrow$

EXAMPLE 10

Length of Hospital Stay: Power Curve

A sample is taken of 50 births in a major hospital. We are interested in knowing whether at least half of all mothers have a length of stay (LOS) less than 48 hours. We will do a right-tailed test using $\alpha = 0.10$. The hypotheses are

H_0: $\pi = 0.50$

H_1: $\pi > 0.50$

To find the power curve, we follow the same procedure as for a mean—actually, it is easier than a mean, because we don't have to worry about σ. For example, what would be the power of the test if the true proportion were $\pi = 0.60$ and the sample size were $n = 50$?

STEP 1

Find the right-tail *critical value* for the sample proportion. At $\alpha = 0.10$ in a right-tailed test, we would use $z_{0.10} = 1.282$ (actually, $z = 1.28155$ if we use Excel) so

$$p_{critical} = \pi_0 + 1.28155\sqrt{\frac{\pi_0(1 - \pi_0)}{n}} = 0.50 + 1.28155\sqrt{\frac{(0.50)(1 - 0.50)}{50}} = 0.590619$$

STEP 2

Express the difference between the critical value $p_{critical}$ and the true proportion π as a z value:

$$z = \frac{p_{critical} - \pi}{\sqrt{\frac{\pi(1 - \pi)}{n}}} = \frac{0.590619 - 0.600000}{\sqrt{\frac{(0.60)(1 - 0.60)}{50}}} = -0.1354$$

STEP 3

Find the β risk and power as areas under the normal curve:

Calculation of β	Calculation of Power
$\beta = P(P < p_{critical}\|\pi = 0.60)$	Power $= P(P > p_{critical}\|\pi = 0.60)$
$= P(Z < -0.1354)$	$= 1 - \beta$
$= 0.4461$, or 44.61%	$= 1 - 0.4461$
	$= 0.5539$, or 55.39%

We can repeat these calculations for any values of π and n. Table 9.9 illustrates power for values of π ranging from 0.50 to 0.70, at which point power is near its maximum, and for sample sizes of $n = 50, 100,$ and 200. As expected, power increases sharply as sample size increases, and as π differs more from $\pi_0 = 0.50$.

TABLE 9.9 β and Power for $\pi_0 = 0.50$

	$n = 50$			$n = 100$			$n = 200$		
π	z	β	Power	z	β	Power	z	β	Power
0.50	1.282	0.9000	0.1000	1.282	0.9000	0.1000	1.282	0.9000	0.1000
0.52	1.000	0.8412	0.1588	0.882	0.8112	0.1888	0.716	0.7631	0.2369
0.54	0.718	0.7637	0.2363	0.483	0.6855	0.3145	0.151	0.5599	0.4401
0.56	0.436	0.6686	0.3314	0.082	0.5327	0.4673	−0.419	0.3378	0.6622
0.58	0.152	0.5605	0.4395	−0.323	0.3735	0.6265	−0.994	0.1601	0.8399
0.60	−0.135	0.4461	0.5539	−0.733	0.2317	0.7683	−1.579	0.0572	0.9428
0.62	−0.428	0.3343	0.6657	−1.152	0.1246	0.8754	−2.176	0.0148	0.9852
0.64	−0.727	0.2335	0.7665	−1.582	0.0569	0.9431	−2.790	0.0026	0.9974
0.66	−1.036	0.1502	0.8498	−2.025	0.0214	0.9786	−3.424	0.0003	0.9997
0.68	−1.355	0.0877	0.9123	−2.485	0.0065	0.9935	−4.083	0.0000	1.0000
0.70	−1.688	0.0457	0.9543	−2.966	0.0015	0.9985	−4.774	0.0000	1.0000

Interpretation   Figure 9.25 presents the results for our LOS example visually. As would be expected, the power curves for the larger sample sizes are higher, and the power of each curve is lowest when π is near the hypothesized value of $\pi_0 = 0.50$. The lowest point on the curve has power equal to $\alpha = 0.10$. Thus, if we increase α, the power curve would shift up. Otherwise, we can only decrease β (and thereby raise power) by increasing the chance of Type I error, a trade-off we might not wish to make.

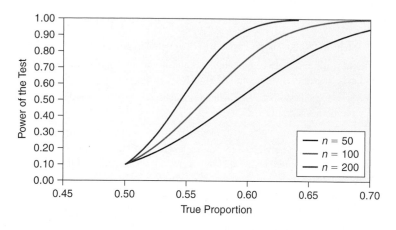

FIGURE 9.25

Power Curve Families for
$H_0: \pi \le 0.50$ $H_1: \pi > 0.50$

CHAPTER SUMMARY

The **null hypothesis (H_0)** represents the status quo or a benchmark. We test to determine whether we can reject H_0 in favour of the **alternative hypothesis (H_1)** on the basis of the sample evidence. The alternative hypothesis points to the tail of the test (< for a left-tailed test, > for a right-tailed test, ≠ for a two-tailed test). Rejecting a true H_0 is referred to as a **Type I error,** while failing to reject a false H_0 is called a **Type II error.** The **power** of the test is the probability of correctly rejecting a false H_0. The probability of Type I error is denoted α (often called the **level of significance**) and can be set by the researcher. The probability of Type II error is denoted β and is dependent on the true parameter value, sample size, and α. In general, lowering α increases β, and vice versa. The **test statistic** compares the sample statistic with the hypothesized parameter. For a mean, the **decision rule** tells us whether to reject H_0 by comparing the test statistic with the **critical value** of z (known σ) or t (unknown σ) from a table or from Excel. Tests of a proportion are based on the normal distribution (if the sample is large enough, according to a rule of thumb), although in small samples the binomial is required. In any hypothesis test, the **p value** shows the probability that the test statistic (or one more extreme) would be observed by chance, assuming that H_0 is true. If the p value is smaller than α, we reject H_0 (i.e., a small p value indicates a **significant** departure from H_0). A two-tailed test is analogous to a confidence interval seen in the last chapter. Power increases as the true parameter is further away from the null hypothesis value. A **power curve** is a graph that plots the power of the test against possible values of the true parameter. Tests of a variance use the **chi-square distribution** and suffer if the data are badly skewed.

KEY TERMS

alternative hypothesis, *353*
benchmark, *380*
chi-square distribution, *388*
critical value, *369*
decision rule, *354*
hypothesis, *353*
hypothesis test, *359*
hypothesis testing, *353*
importance, *354*

left-tailed test, *360*
level of significance, *363*
null hypothesis, *353*
operating characteristic (OC)
   curve, *393*
power, *364*
power curve, *392*
p-value method, *370*
rejection region, *354*

right-tailed test, *360*
significance, *354*
statistical hypothesis, *359*
test statistic, *368*
two-tailed test, *360*
Type I error, *357*
Type II error, *357*

Commonly Used Formulas in One-Sample Hypothesis Tests

Type I error: $\alpha = P(\text{reject } H_0 | H_0 \text{ is true})$

Type II error: $\beta = P(\text{fail to reject } H_0 | H_0 \text{ is false})$

Power: $1 - \beta = P(\text{reject } H_0 | H_0 \text{ is false})$

Test statistic value for sample mean, σ known: $z_{\text{calc}} = \dfrac{\bar{x} - \mu_0}{\dfrac{\sigma}{\sqrt{n}}}$

Test statistic value for sample mean, σ unknown: $t_{\text{calc}} = \dfrac{\bar{x} - \mu_0}{\dfrac{s}{\sqrt{n}}}$

Test statistic value for sample proportion: $z_{\text{calc}} = \dfrac{p - \pi_0}{\sqrt{\dfrac{\pi_0(1 - \pi_0)}{n}}}$

CHAPTER REVIEW

Note: Questions labelled * are based on optional material from this chapter.

1. (a) List the steps in testing a hypothesis. (b) Why can't a hypothesis ever be proven? (LO 1)

2. (a) Explain the difference between the null hypothesis and the alternative hypothesis. (b) How is the null hypothesis chosen (why is it "null")? (LO 1 & 2)

3. (a) Why do we say "fail to reject H_0" instead of "accept H_0"? (b) What does it mean to "provisionally accept a hypothesis"? (LO 1 & 2)

4. (a) Define Type I error and Type II error. (b) Give an original example to illustrate. (LO 2)

5. (a) Explain the difference between a left-tailed test, two-tailed test, and right-tailed test. (b) When would we choose a two-tailed test? (c) How can we tell the direction of the test by looking at a pair of hypotheses? (LO 2)

6. (a) Explain the meaning of the rejection region in a decision rule. (b) Why do we need to know the sampling distribution of a statistic before we can do a hypothesis test? (LO 1 & 2)

7. (a) Define level of significance. (b) Define the power of a test. (LO 2)

8. (a) Why do we prefer low values for α and β? (b) For a given sample size, why is there a trade-off between α and β? (c) How could we decrease both α and β? (LO 1)

9. (a) Why is a "statistically significant difference" not necessarily a "practically important difference"? Give an illustration. (b) Why do statisticians play only a limited role in deciding whether a significant difference requires action? (LO 1)

10. (a) In a hypothesis test for a proportion, when can normality be assumed? *(b) If the sample is too small to assume normality, what can we do? (LO 4)

11. (a) In a hypothesis test of one mean, what assumptions do we make? (b) When do we use t instead of z? (c) When is the difference between z and t immaterial? (LO 4)

12. (a) Explain what a p value means. Give an example and interpret it. (b) Why is the p value method an attractive alternative to specifying α in advance? (LO 5)

13. Why is a confidence interval similar to a two-tailed test? (LO 1)

14. (a) In testing a hypothesis about a variance, what distribution do we use? (b) When would a test of a variance be needed? (c) If the population is not normal, what can we do? (LO 6)

*15. (a) What does a power curve show? (b) What factors affect power for a test of a mean? (c) What factors affect power for a proportion? (d) What is the most commonly used method of increasing power? (LO 1)

USING SOFTWARE

Using LearningStats

There are do-it-yourself demonstrations in *LearningStats* that let you create power curves for a mean or a proportion without tedious calculations. An example is shown in Figure 9.26.

www.mcgrawhillconnect.ca

FIGURE 9.26

LearningStats Two-Tail Power Curve for a Mean

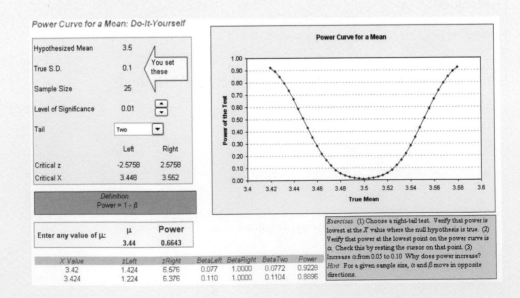

FIGURE 9.27

Visual Statistics Power Curve Families for a Proportion

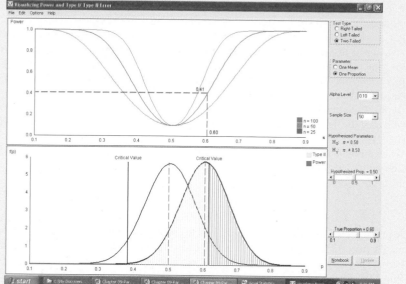

Using Visual Statistics

There is a demonstration in Visual Statistics that allows you to create power curves for a mean or a proportion, including families of curves based on sample size (e.g., *n/2, n, 2n*), without tedious calculations. An example is shown in Figure 9.27.

Section Exercises

Note: Check your answers using *LearningStats*.

9.48 A quality expert inspects 400 items to test whether the population proportion of defectives exceeds 0.03, using a right-tailed test at $\alpha = 0.10$. (a) What is the power of this test if the true proportion of defectives is $\pi = 0.04$? (b) If the true proportion is $\pi = 0.05$? (c) If the true proportion of defectives is $\pi = 0.06$?

9.49 Repeat the previous exercise, using $\alpha = 0.05$. For each true value of π, is the power higher or lower?

9.50 For a certain wine, the mean pH (a measure of acidity) is supposed to be 3.50 with a known standard deviation of $\sigma = 0.10$. The quality inspector examines 25 bottles at random to test whether the pH is too low, using a left-tailed test at $\alpha = 0.01$. (a) What is the power of this test if the true mean is $\mu = 3.48$? (b) If the true mean is $\mu = 3.46$? (c) If the true mean is $\mu = 3.44$?

9.51 Repeat the previous exercise, using $\alpha = 0.05$. For each true value of μ, is the power higher or lower?

Note: Explain answers and show your work clearly. Problems marked * rely on optional material from this chapter.

CHAPTER EXERCISES

9.52 Suppose you always reject the null hypothesis, regardless of any sample evidence. (a) What is the probability of a Type II error? (b) Why might this be a bad policy? (LO 1)

TYPE I AND II ERROR

9.53 Suppose the judge decides to acquit all defendants, regardless of the evidence. (a) What is the probability of Type I error? (b) Why might this be a bad policy? (LO 1)

9.54 High blood pressure, if untreated, can lead to increased risk of stroke and heart attack. A common definition of hypertension is diastolic blood pressure of 90 or more. (a) State the null and alternative hypotheses for a physician who checks your blood pressure. (b) Define Type I and II errors. What are the consequences of each? (c) Which type of error is more to be feared, and by whom? (LO 1)

9.55 If the true mean is 50 and we reject the hypothesis that $\mu = 50$, what is the probability of Type II error? *Hint:* This is a trick question. (LO 1)

9.56 If the null hypothesis that $\pi = 0.50$ is accepted even though the true proportion is 0.60, what is the probability of Type I error? *Hint:* This is a trick question. (LO 1)

9.57 Pap smears are a test for abnormal cancerous and precancerous cells taken from the cervix. (a) State a pair of hypotheses and then explain the meaning of a false negative and a false positive. (b) Why is the null hypothesis "null"? (c) Who bears the cost of each type of error? (LO 1)

9.58 In a commercially available fingerprint scanner (e.g., for your home or office PC), false acceptances are 1 in 25 million for high-end devices, with false rejection rates of around 3 percent. (a) Define Type I and II errors. (b) Why do you suppose the false rejection rate is so high compared with the false acceptance rate? (Data are from *Scientific American* 288, no. 3 [Mar. 2003], p. 98.) (LO 1)

9.59 When told that over a 10-year period a mammogram test has a false positive rate of 50 percent, Bob said, "That means that about half the women tested actually have no cancer." Correct Bob's mistaken interpretation. (LO 1)

TESTS OF MEANS AND PROPORTIONS

9.60 A can of peeled whole tomatoes is supposed to contain an average of 0.6 kg of tomatoes (excluding the juice). The actual weight is a normally distributed random variable whose standard deviation is known to be 0.03kg. (a) In quality control, would a one-tailed or two-tailed test be used? Why? (b) Explain the consequences of departure from the mean in either direction. (c) Which sampling distribution would you use if samples of four cans are weighed? Why? (d) Set up a two-tailed decision rule for $\alpha = 0.01$. (LO 4)

9.61 At Ajax Spring Water, a half-litre bottle of soft drink is supposed to contain a mean of 520 ml. The filling process follows a normal distribution with a known process standard deviation of 4 ml. (a) Which sampling distribution would you use if random samples of 10 bottles are to be weighed? Why? (b) Set up hypotheses and a two-tailed decision rule for the correct mean using the 5 percent level of significance. (c) If a sample of 16 bottles shows a mean fill of 515 ml, does this contradict the hypothesis that the true mean is 520 ml? (LO 3 & 4)

9.62 On eight Friday quizzes, Bob received scores of 80, 85, 95, 92, 89, 84, 90, and 92. He tells Prof. Hardtack that he is really a 90+ performer but this sample just happened to fall below his true performance level. (a) State an appropriate pair of hypotheses to see if there is sufficient evidence to show that Bob's claim is incorrect. (b) State the formula for the test statistic and show your decision rule using the 1 percent level of significance. (c) Carry out the test. Show your work. (d) What assumptions are required? (e) Use Excel to find the p value and interpret it. (LO 3, 4 & 5)   **BobQuiz**

9.63 Faced with rising fax costs, a firm issued a guideline that transmissions of ten pages or more should be sent by two-day mail instead. Exceptions are allowed, but they want the average to be ten or below. The firm examined 35 randomly chosen fax transmissions during the next year, yielding a sample mean of 14.44 with a standard deviation of 4.45 pages. (a) At the 0.01 level of significance, is the true mean greater than 10? (b) Use Excel to find the right-tail p value. (LO 3, 4 & 5)

9.64 A U.S. dime weighs 2.268 grams when minted. A random sample of 15 circulated dimes showed a mean weight of 2.256 grams with a standard deviation of 0.026 grams. (a) Using $\alpha = 0.05$, is the mean weight of all circulated dimes lower than the mint weight? State your hypotheses and decision rule. (b) Why might circulated dimes weigh less than the mint specification? (See *Science News* 157, no. 14 [Apr. 1, 2000], p. 216.) (LO 3 & 4)

9.65 A coin was flipped 60 times and came up heads 38 times. (a) At the 0.10 level of significance, is the coin biased toward heads? Show your decision rule and calculations. (b) Calculate a p value and interpret it. (LO 3, 4 & 5)

9.66 A sample of 100 U.S. one-dollar bills from a Subway cash register revealed that 16 had something written on them besides the normal printing (e.g., "Bob ♥ Mary"). (a) At $\alpha = 0.05$, is this sample evidence inconsistent with the hypothesis that 10 percent or fewer of all dollar bills have anything written on them besides the normal printing? Include a sketch of your decision rule and show all calculations. (b) Is your decision sensitive to the choice of α? (c) Find the p value. (LO 3, 4 & 5)

9.67 A sample of 100 mortgages approved during the current year showed that 31 were issued to a single-earner family or individual. The historical average is 25 percent. (a) At the 0.05 level of significance, has the percentage of single-earner or individual mortgages risen? Include a sketch of your decision rule and show all work. (b) Is this a close decision? (c) State any assumptions that are required. (LO 3 & 4)

9.68 A provincial weights-and-measures standard requires that no more than 5 percent of bags of Halloween candy be underweight. A random sample of 200 bags showed that 16 were underweight. (a) At $\alpha = 0.025$, is the standard being violated? (b) Find the p value. (LO 3, 4 & 5))

9.69 Ages for the 2005 Boston Red Sox pitchers are shown below. (a) Assuming this is a random sample of major league pitchers, at the 5 percent level of significance does this sample show that the true mean age of all American League pitchers is over 30 years? State your hypotheses and decision rule and show all work. (b) If there is a difference, is it important? (c) Find the p value and interpret it. (Data are from http://boston.redsox.mlb.com.) (LO 3, 4 & 5) 🌐 **RedSox**

Ages of Boston Red Sox Pitchers, October 2005							
Arroyo	28	Foulke	33	Mantei	32	Timlin	39
Clement	31	Gonzalez	30	Miller	29	Wakefield	39
Embree	35	Halama	33	Myers	36	Wells	42

9.70 The U.S. Environmental Protection Agency (EPA) is concerned about the quality of drinking water served on airline flights. In September 2004, a sample of 158 flights found unacceptable bacterial contamination on 20 flights. (a) At $\alpha = 0.05$, does this sample show that more than 10 percent of all flights have contaminated water? (b) Find the p value. (Data are from *The Wall Street Journal,* Nov. 10, 2004, p. D1.) (LO 3, 4 & 5)

9.71 The Web-based company *Oh Baby! Gifts* has a goal of processing 95 percent of its orders on the same day they are received. If 485 out of the next 500 orders are processed on the same day, would this prove that they are exceeding their goal, using $\alpha = 0.025$? (See story.news.yahoo.com accessed June 25, 2004.) (LO 3, 4 & 5)

9.72 In the Big Ten (an NCAA sports conference) a sample showed that only 267 out of 584 freshmen football players graduated within 6 years. (a) At $\alpha = 0.05$ does this sample contradict the claim that at least half graduate within 6 years? State your hypotheses and decision rule. (b) Calculate the p value and interpret it. (c) Do you think the difference is important, as opposed to significant? (LO 3, 4 & 5)

9.73 An auditor reviewed 25 oral surgery insurance claims from a particular surgical office, determining that the mean out-of-pocket patient billing above the reimbursed amount was $275.66 with a standard deviation of $78.11. (a) At the 5 percent level of significance, does this sample prove a violation of the guideline that the average patient should pay no more than $250 out-of-pocket? State your hypotheses and decision rule. (b) Is this a close decision? (LO 3 & 4)

9.74 The average service time at a Noodles & Company restaurant was 3.5 minutes in the previous year. Noodles implemented some time-saving measures and would like to know if they have been effective. They sample 20 service times and find the sample average is 3.2 minutes with a sample standard deviation of 0.4 minutes. Using $\alpha = 0.05$, were the measures effective? (LO 3 & 4)

9.75 A digital camcorder repair service has set a goal not to exceed an average of five working days from the time the unit is brought in to the time repairs are completed. A random sample of 12 repair records showed the following repair times (in days): 9, 2, 5, 1, 5, 4, 7, 5, 11, 3, 7, 2. At $\alpha = 0.05$ is the goal being met? (LO 3 & 4) 🌐 **Repair**

9.76 Beer shelf life is a problem for brewers and distributors, because when beer is stored at room temperature, its flavour deteriorates. When the average furfuryl ether content reaches 6 mg per litre, a typical consumer begins wto taste an unpleasant chemical flavour. At $\alpha = 0.05$, would the following sample of 12 randomly chosen bottles stored for a month convince you that the mean furfuryl ether content exceeds the taste threshold? What is the p value? (See *Science News,* Dec. 3, 2005, p. 363.) (LO 3, 4 & 5) 🌐 **BeerTaste**

6.53, 5.68, 8.10, 7.50, 6.32, 8.75, 5.98, 7.50, 5.01, 5.95, 6.40, 7.02

PROPORTIONS: LARGE SAMPLES

9.77 An automaker states that its cars equipped with electronic fuel injection and computerized engine controls will start on the first try (hot or cold) 99 percent of the time. A survey of 1,000 new car owners revealed that 30 had not started on the first try during a recent cold snap. (a) At $\alpha = 0.025$, does this demonstrate that the automaker's claim is incorrect? (b) Calculate the p value and interpret it. (LO 3, 4 & 5)

9.78 A quality standard says that no more than 2 percent of the eggs sold in a store may be cracked (not broken, just cracked). In 30 cartons (12 eggs each carton), 20 eggs are cracked. (a) At the 0.10 level of significance, does this prove that the standard is exceeded? (b) Calculate a p value for the observed sample result. (LO 3, 4 & 6)

9.79 An experimental medication is administered to 160 people who suffer from migraines. After an hour, 100 say they feel better. Is the medication effective (i.e., is the percent who feel better greater than 50 percent)? Use $\alpha = 0.10$, explain fully, and show all steps. (LO 3, 4 & 5)

9.80 (a) A statistical study reported that a drug was effective with a p value of 0.042. Explain in words what this tells you. (b) How would that compare to a drug that had a p value of 0.087? (LO 5)

9.81 Bob said, "Why is a small p value significant, when a large one isn't? That seems backwards." Try to explain it to Bob, giving an example to make your point. (LO 5)

9.82 Before instituting a new policy, a particular supermarket had on its shelves, 10 percent of its items whose expiry dates had passed. With this new policy, a check of 200 randomly selected items revealed that 15 items had expiry dates which had passed. At the 0.05 level of significance, is there sufficient evidence to indicate that the new policy is effective in reducing the percentage of items whose expiry dates had passed? Calculate the p value of this test. (LO 3, 4 & 5)

9.83 A hospital in a southern British Columbia town has been trying to reduce the percentage of emergency room patients who have to wait more than three hours before being seen by the attending physician. Previously, this percentage was 35 percent. After introducing a new policy, a random sample of 80 patients revealed that 27 had to wait more than 3 hours. At the 0.05 level of significance, can we conclude that this new policy is effective? Calculate the p value of this test. (LO 3, 4 & 5)

POWER

Hint: In the power problems, use *LearningStats* to check your answers.

9.84 A certain brand of flat white interior latex paint claims one-coat coverage of 400 square feet per gallon. The standard deviation is known to be 20. A sample of 16 gallons is tested. (a) At $\alpha = 0.05$ in a left-tailed test, find the β risk and power assuming that the true mean is really 380 square feet per gallon. (b) Construct a left-tailed power curve, using increments of 5 square feet (400, 395, 390, 385, 380).

9.85 A process is normally distributed with standard deviation 12. Samples of size 4 are taken. Suppose that you wish to test the hypothesis that $\mu = 500$ at $\alpha = 0.05$ in a left-tailed test. (a) What is the β risk if the true mean is 495? If the true mean is 490? If the true mean is 485? If the true mean is 480? (b) Calculate the power for each of the preceding values of μ and sketch a power curve. (c) Repeat the previous exercises using $n = 16$.

TESTS OF VARIANCES

Hint: Use MegaStat to check your work.

9.86 Is this sample of 25 exam scores inconsistent with the hypothesis that the true variance is 64 (i.e., $\sigma = 8$)? Use the 5 percent level of significance in a two-tailed test. Show all steps, including the hypotheses and critical values from Appendix E. (LO 4 & 6) **Exams**

80	79	69	71	74
73	77	75	65	52
81	84	84	79	70
78	62	77	68	77
88	70	75	85	84

9.87 Hammermill Premium Inkjet 24 lb. paper has a specified brightness of 106. (a) At $\alpha = 0.005$, does this sample of 24 randomly chosen test sheets from a day's production run show that the mean brightness exceeds the specification? (b) Does the sample show that $\sigma^2 < 0.0025$? State the hypotheses and critical value for the left-tailed test from Appendix E. (LO 4 & 6) **Brightness**

106.98	107.02	106.99	106.98	107.06	107.05	107.03	107.04
107.01	107.00	107.02	107.04	107.00	106.98	106.91	106.93
107.01	106.98	106.97	106.99	106.94	106.98	107.03	106.98

9.88 Read the passage below, and then consider the following scenario. A physician is trying to decide whether to prescribe medication for cholesterol reduction in a 45-year-old female patient. The null hypothesis is that the patient's cholesterol is less than the threshold of treatable hypercholesterolemia. However, a sample of readings over a two-year time period shows considerable variation, usually below but sometimes above the threshold. (a) Define the Type I and Type II errors. (b) List the costs of each type of error (in general terms). Who bears the cost of each? (c) How might the patient's point of view differ from the doctor's? (d) In what sense is this a business problem? A societal problem? An individual problem? (LO 1 & 2)

SHORT ESSAY

Hypercholesterolemia is a known risk factor for coronary artery disease. The risk of death from coronary artery disease has a continuous and graded relation to total serum cholesterol levels higher than 180 mg/dl. However, the ratio of total cholesterol to HDL cholesterol is a better predictor of coronary artery disease than the level of either fraction alone. . . . After menopause, plasma LDL cholesterol concentrations rise to equal, and then to exceed, those of men, at the same time HDL cholesterol concentrations fall slightly. . . . This puts women at equal or greater risk for cardiovascular disease. According to the results of medical trials, there is compelling evidence that a reduction in the level of cholesterol leads to a significant decrease in the rate of cardiovascular events. . . . Therefore, screening for high blood cholesterol is an important clinical intervention. The National Heart, Lung, and Blood Institute . . . recommends that all persons aged 20 and above have a cholesterol determination at least once every five years. . . . Timely identification of high-risk individuals allows consideration of various treatment alternatives. For patients who do not have coronary heart disease or peripheral vascular disease, emphasis should be placed on non-pharmacologic approaches, mainly changes in diet and exercise. Drug therapy should be reserved for those at highest risk of coronary heart disease: men above 35 years of age and postmenopausal women. (Source: www.dakotacare.com.)

LearningStats Unit 09 One-Sample Hypothesis Tests

LearningStats Unit 09 explains the logic of hypothesis testing, gives examples of the most common one-sample hypothesis tests (one mean, one proportion, one variance), and discusses Type I and II errors. Your instructor may assign specific modules, or you may decide to check them out because the topic sounds interesting.

Topic	*LearningStats Modules*
Hypothesis testing	Overview of Hypothesis Testing
	One-Sample Hypothesis Tests
Common hypothesis tests	One-Sample Tests
	Do-It-Yourself Simulation
	Sampling Distribution Examples
Type I error and power	Type I Error
	p-Value Illustration
	Power Curves: Examples
	Power Curves: Do-It-Yourself
	Power Curve Families: μ
	Power Curve Families: π
Optional topics	Probability Plots
	Finite Population Correction
Equations	One-Sample Formulas
	Sampling Distributions
Tables	Appendix C—Normal
	Appendix D—Student's t
	Appendix E—Chi-Square

Key: ◘ = PowerPoint 📄 = Word ✖ = Excel

Visual Statistics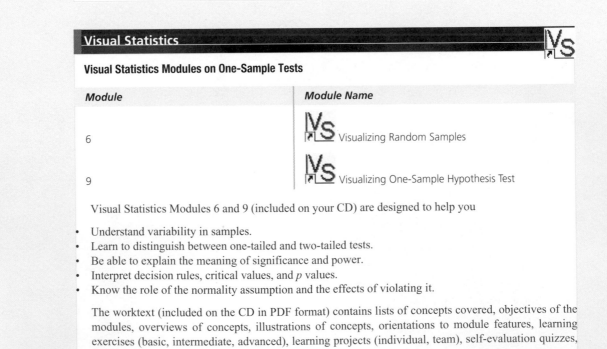

Visual Statistics Modules on One-Sample Tests

Module	Module Name
6	Visualizing Random Samples
9	Visualizing One-Sample Hypothesis Test

Visual Statistics Modules 6 and 9 (included on your CD) are designed to help you

- Understand variability in samples.
- Learn to distinguish between one-tailed and two-tailed tests.
- Be able to explain the meaning of significance and power.
- Interpret decision rules, critical values, and p values.
- Know the role of the normality assumption and the effects of violating it.

The worktext (included on the CD in PDF format) contains lists of concepts covered, objectives of the modules, overviews of concepts, illustrations of concepts, orientations to module features, learning exercises (basic, intermediate, advanced), learning projects (individual, team), self-evaluation quizzes, glossaries of terms, and solutions to self-evaluation quizzes.

Two-Sample Inference

Chapter Learning Objectives

When you finish this chapter you should be able to

1. Recognize when and what two-sample tests are required in a problem context.

2. In a problem context, carry out two-sample tests and confidence intervals for proportions and means using independent samples

3. Recognize when data sets are independent and when they are paired.

4. Perform a paired *t* test.

5. List the main characteristics of the *F* distribution and why it is used.

6. In a problem context, perform a one-tailed or two-tailed test to compare two variances.

7. Use one or more computer software packages to do two-sample tests.

10.1   Two-Sample Sampling Distributions

In Chapters 8 and 9, we used the sampling distributions of $\overline{X}$, P, and S^2 to make inferences concerning μ, π, and σ^2, respectively. In this chapter, we want to make inferences concerning $\mu_1 - \mu_2$, $\pi_1 - \pi_2$, and σ_1^2/σ_2^2 (where the subscripts refer to populations 1 and 2). To do so, we will use the sampling distributions of their best estimators, $\overline{X}_1 - \overline{X}_2$, $P_1 - P_2$, and S_1^2/S_2^2, respectively. Each sampling distribution will briefly be developed using the following basic rule where applicable.

Rule

If we create a new random variable by subtracting one normal random variable from another normal variable, and if they are independent of one another, the resulting variable will also be normally distributed with a mean equal to the difference in the means of the original random variables and a variance equal to the sum of the variances of the original random variables.

Note: In this section, we are assuming that our two samples are independent of one another. That is, the selection of one sample does not influence the selection of another sample. In Section 10.4, we will be using a sampling distribution to make inferences concerning $\mu_1 - \mu_2$ using matched or paired samples.

Sampling Distributions of $\overline{X}_1 - \overline{X}_2$

There are three sampling distributions of $\overline{X}_1 - \overline{X}_2$, depending on whether the population variances are known or unknown and, if they are unknown, whether the population variances are equal or unequal.

If the population variances are known and if $\overline{X}_1$ and $\overline{X}_2$ are normally distributed, then $\overline{X}_1 - \overline{X}_2$ is normally distributed with a mean of $\mu_1 - \mu_2$ and a standard deviation of $\sqrt{\dfrac{\sigma_1^2}{n_1} + \dfrac{\sigma_2^2}{n_2}}$. This allows us to express the sampling distribution as

$$z = \frac{(\overline{x}_1 - \overline{x}_2) - (\mu_1 - \mu_2)}{\sqrt{\dfrac{\sigma_1^2}{n_1} + \dfrac{\sigma_2^2}{n_2}}}$$

If the population variances are unknown but assumed equal, we would have to estimate these variances, and because they are equal, there should be one common estimate of σ_1^2 and σ_2^2. This common estimate is most often represented by s_p^2 (p symbolizing the fact that this estimate pools the results of both samples) where

$$s_p^2 = \frac{(n_1 - 1)s_1^2 + (n_2 - 1)s_2^2}{n_1 + n_2 - 2}$$

That is, s_p^2 is a weighted average of s_1^2 and s_2^2, weighted by their sample sizes minus 1.

Because the population variances are estimated, the sampling distribution takes the form of a t-distribution, where

$$t = \frac{(\overline{x}_1 - \overline{x}_2) - (\mu_1 - \mu_2)}{\sqrt{\dfrac{s_p^2}{n_1} + \dfrac{s_p^2}{n_2}}}$$

has a t-distribution with degrees of freedom, $\nu = n_1 + n_2 - 2$.

If the variances are unknown and not assumed equal, σ_1^2 and σ_2^2 will be estimated with the individual sample variances s_1^2 and s_2^2, and again, the sampling distribution takes the form of a t-distribution, where

$$t = \frac{(\overline{x}_1 - \overline{x}_2) - (\mu_1 - \mu_2)}{\sqrt{\dfrac{s_1^2}{n_1} + \dfrac{s_2^2}{n_2}}}$$

has a t-distribution with a complicated formula for degrees of freedom. Statisticians have shown that under the condition of unequal variances, the distribution of the random variable $\overline{X}_1 - \overline{X}_2$ is no longer certain, a difficulty known as the **Behrens-Fisher problem**. This **Welch-Satterthwaite t-distribution** uses **Welch's adjusted degrees of freedom**.

$$\nu' = \frac{[s_1^2/n_1 + s_2^2/n_2]^2}{\dfrac{(s_1^2/n_1)^2}{n_1 - 1} + \dfrac{(s_2^2/n_2)^2}{n_2 - 1}} \text{ (Welch's adjusted degrees of freedom)}$$

Sampling Distribution of $P_1 - P_2$

Using the rule mentioned above, the fact that P_1 has a mean of π_1 and a standard deviation of $\sqrt{\dfrac{\pi_1(1 - \pi_1)}{n_1}}$ and that P_2 has a mean of π_2 and a standard deviation of $\sqrt{\dfrac{\pi_2(1 - \pi_2)}{n_2}}$, and the fact that, under most situations, P_1 and P_2 are normally distributed, $P_1 - P_2$ is, under most situations, normally distributed with mean $\pi_1 - \pi_2$, and standard deviation $\sqrt{\dfrac{\pi_1(1 - \pi_1)}{n_1} + \dfrac{\pi_2(1 - \pi_2)}{n_2}}$. Therefore, we can express the sampling distribution of $P_1 - P_2$ as

$$z = \frac{(p_1 - p_2) - (\pi_1 - \pi_2)}{\sqrt{\dfrac{\pi_1(1 - \pi_1)}{n_1} + \dfrac{\pi_2(1 - \pi_2)}{n_2}}}$$

Sampling Distribution of S_1^2/S_2^2

Unlike the sampling distributions of $\overline{X}_1 - \overline{X}_2$ and $P_1 - P_2$, the sampling distribution of S_1^2/S_2^2 is not normally distributed. If the individual populations, X_1 and X_2, are normally distributed, then the sampling distribution of S_1^2/S_2^2 can be expressed as

$$F = \frac{S_1^2/S_2^2}{\sigma_1^2/\sigma_2^2}$$

where F has an F-distribution with two different degrees of freedom, $\nu_1 = n_1 - 1$ and $\nu_2 = n_2 - 1$. How to use this information to make inferences concerning σ_1^2/σ_2^2 will be discussed in a later section of this chapter.

Knowing the appropriate sampling distributions, we can then manipulate these distributions to either test hypotheses or estimate the relevant population parameters.

10.2   Two-Sample Tests

The logic and applications of hypothesis testing that you learned in Chapter 9 will continue here, but now we focus on two-sample tests. The two-sample test is used to make inferences about the two populations from which the samples were drawn. The use of these techniques is widespread in science and engineering as well as social sciences. Drug companies use sophisticated versions called clinical trials to determine the effectiveness of new drugs; agricultural science continually uses these methods to compare yields to improve productivity; political parties use them to compare their popularity from one period in time to another; and a wide variety of businesses use them to test or compare the effectiveness of advertising campaigns or to compare their performances with their competitors.

What Is a Two-Sample Test?

When using hypothesis testing to make inferences comparing the parameters of two populations, a one-sample test or a two-sample test may be conducted. Two-sample tests use estimates from each of two samples to compare two parameters whose values are both unknown, whereas one-sample tests compare a sample estimate with a known benchmark (a claim or prior belief about a population parameter). As an example, suppose we want to test whether average daily sales at some local convenience store are lower this year compared to last year. If we knew the actual daily sales last year (e.g., $\mu = \$1,250$) and all we had available to us this year was the average daily sales for a sample of days (e.g., $\bar{x} = \$1,125$), we would use a one-sample test with the alternative hypothesis being $H_1: \mu < \$1,250$ (where μ now symbolizes this year's average daily sales). If we didn't know either last year's or this year's average daily sales, we would have to take samples from each of the two years, determine each sample's average daily sales, and use a two-sample test with the alternative hypothesis being stated as $H_1: \mu_1 - \mu_2 > 0$ or $H_1: \mu_1 > \mu_2$ (if μ_1 represents last year's average daily sales and μ_2 represents this year's average daily sales). Here are some actual two-sample tests:

Automotive   A new bumper is installed on selected vehicles in a corporate fleet. During a one-year test period, 12 vehicles with the new bumper were involved in accidents, incurring mean damage of $1,101 with a standard deviation of $696. During the same year, nine vehicles with the old bumpers were involved in accidents, incurring mean damage of $1,766 with a standard deviation of $838. Did the new bumper significantly reduce damage? Did it reduce variation?

Marketing   At a matinee performance of *Spider-Man 3,* a random sample of 25 concession purchases showed a mean of $7.29 with a standard deviation of $3.02. For the evening performance a random sample of 25 concession purchases showed a mean of $7.12 with a standard deviation of $2.14. Is there sufficient evidence to indicate that there is less variation in the evenings?

Safety   In Dallas, some fire trucks were painted yellow (instead of red) to heighten their visibility. During a test period, the fleet of red fire trucks made 153,348 runs and had 20 accidents, while the fleet of yellow fire trucks made 135,035 runs and had 4 accidents. Is the difference in accident rates in the sample significant enough to conclude a true difference in accident rates?

Medicine   Half of a group of 18,882 healthy men with no sign of prostate cancer were given an experimental drug called Finasteride, while half were given a placebo, based on a random selection process. Participants underwent annual exams and blood tests. Over the next 7 years, 571 men in the placebo group developed prostate cancer, compared with only 435 in the Finasteride group. Is the difference in cancer rates in the sample significant enough to conclude a true difference in cancer rates?

Education   In a certain university class, 20 randomly chosen students were given a tutorial, while 20 others used a self-study computer simulation. On the same 20-point quiz, the tutorial students' mean score was 16.7 with a standard deviation of 2.5, compared with a mean of 14.5 and a standard deviation of 3.2 for the simulation students. Do tutorial students do better, or did these results simply occur by chance? Is there any significant difference in the degree of variation in the two groups to conclude that there is a true difference in the degree of variation?

Basis of Two-Sample Tests

Two-sample tests are especially useful because they possess a built-in point of comparison. You can think of many situations where two groups are to be compared (e.g., before and after, old and new, experimental and control). Sometimes we don't really care about the actual value of the population parameter, but only whether the parameter is the same for both populations. Usually, the null hypothesis is that both samples were drawn from populations with the same parameter value, but we can also test for a given degree of difference.

The logic of two-sample tests is based on the fact that two samples drawn from the *same population* may yield *different estimates* of a parameter due to chance. For example, exhaust emission tests could yield different results for two vehicles of the same type. Only if the two sample statistics differ by more than the amount attributable to chance can we conclude that the samples came from populations with different parameter values, as illustrated in Figure 10.1.

Test Procedure

The testing procedure is like that of one-sample tests. We state our hypotheses, set up a decision rule, insert the sample statistics, and make a decision, or we can use *p* **values.** Because the true parameters are unknown, we rely on statistical theory to help us reach a defensible

FIGURE 10.1

Same Population or Different?

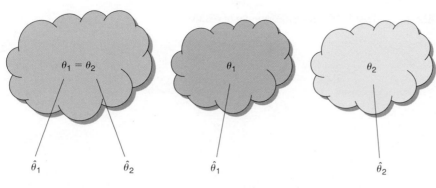

Samples came from the same population.
Any differences are due to sampling variation.

Samples came from populations
with different parameter values.

conclusion about our hypotheses. Our decision could be wrong—we could commit a **Type I** or a **Type II error**—but at least we can specify our acceptable risk levels. Larger samples are always desirable because they permit us to reduce either Type I error or Type II error (i.e., increase the power of the test) or some combination, as we choose.

Comparing two means is a common business problem. Is the average customer purchase at Starbucks the same on Saturday and Sunday morning? Is the average customer waiting time the same at two different branches of TD Canada Trust? Do male and female Walmart employees work the same average overtime hours?

10.3 Comparing Two Means: Independent Samples

Format of Hypotheses

Chapter 10

As with testing a single population mean, there are three possible pairs of hypotheses that can be tested for the difference in two population means. These possible pairs of hypotheses are

Left-Tailed Test	*Two-Tailed Test*	*Right-Tailed Test*
$H_0: \mu_1 - \mu_2 = d_0$	$H_0: \mu_1 - \mu_2 = d_0$	$H_0: \mu_1 - \mu_2 = d_0$
$H_1: \mu_1 - \mu_2 < d_0$	$H_1: \mu_1 - \mu_2 \neq d_0$	$H_1: \mu_1 - \mu_2 > d_0$

where d_0 symbolizes the hypothesized difference, which in most situations would be zero. If $d_0 = 0$, we could also express the null hypothesis as $H_0: \mu_1 = \mu_2$ and the alternative hypothesis as $H_1: \mu_1 < \mu_2$, $H_1: \mu_1 \neq \mu_2$, or $H_1: \mu_1 > \mu_2$.

Test Statistic

As with previous test statistics, the **test statistic** is based on the sampling distribution of $\overline{X}_1 - \overline{X}_2$ assuming that the null hypothesis is true. If the population variances σ_1^2 and σ_2^2 are known (a rarity), we can use the normal distribution. If the variances are estimated using s_1^2 and s_2^2, we must use Student's t (the typical situation). Because there are three sampling distributions of $\overline{X}_1 - \overline{X}_2$, there are three possible test statistics or cases as shown in Table 10.1. All of these test statistics presume independent samples and normal populations, although in practice they are robust to non-normality as long as the samples are not too small and the population is not too skewed. The Chapter 8 Appendix, "Testing for Normality Assumption," describes how, using Excel, we can easily do this test by creating a "Normal Probability Plot."

The formulas in Table 10.1 require some calculations, but most of the time you will be using a computer. As long as you have raw data (i.e., the original samples of n_1 and n_2 observations), Excel's **Data > Data Analysis** menu handles all three cases, as shown in Figure 10.2. MegaStat and MINITAB also perform these tests. *LearningStats* also provides a calculator for summarized data (i.e., when you have $\bar{x}_1$, $\bar{x}_2$, s_1, s_2 instead of the n_1 and n_2 data columns).

TABLE 10.1 **Test Statistic for Difference of Means**

Case 1 *Known Variances*	Case 2 *Unknown Variances,* *Assumed Equal*	Case 3 *Unknown Variances,* *Assumed Unequal*
$z_{calc} = \dfrac{(\bar{x}_1 - \bar{x}_2) - d_0}{\sqrt{\dfrac{\sigma_1^2}{n_1} + \dfrac{\sigma_2^2}{n_2}}}$	$t_{calc} = \dfrac{(\bar{x}_1 - \bar{x}_2) - d_0}{\sqrt{\dfrac{s_p^2}{n_1} + \dfrac{s_p^2}{n_2}}}$	$t_{calc} = \dfrac{(\bar{x}_1 - \bar{x}_2) - d_0}{\sqrt{\dfrac{s_1^2}{n_1} + \dfrac{s_2^2}{n_2}}}$

$$s_p^2 = \frac{(n_1 - 1)s_1^2 + (n_2 - 1)s_2^2}{n_1 + n_2 - 2}$$

For the critical value, use the normal distribution.	For the critical value, use Student's t with $n_1 + n_2 - 2$ degrees of freedom.	For the critical value, use Student's t with Welch's adjusted degrees of freedom (see above).

FIGURE 10.2

Excel's Data > Data Analysis Menu

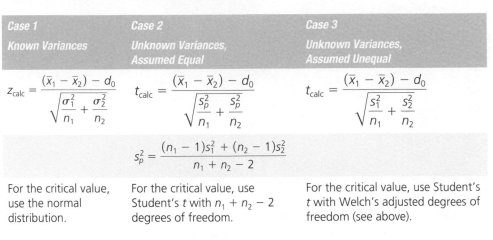

A Closer Look

If the sample sizes are equal, the value of t_{calc} will be the same in Case 3 as in Case 2, although the degrees of freedom may differ. If the variances are similar, Welch's adjusted degrees of freedom ν' (i.e., Case 3) will be almost the same as the unadjusted degrees of freedom $\nu = n_1 + n_2 - 2$ (i.e., Case 2). Finding Welch's adjusted degrees of freedom requires a tedious calculation, but this is easily handled by Excel, MegaStat, or MINITAB. Welch's adjusted degrees of freedom ν' is always between $\min(n_1 - 1, n_2 - 1)$ and $n_1 + n_2 - 2$. The formulas for Case 2 and Case 3 will usually result in the same decision unless the sample sizes and variances differ greatly.

EXAMPLE 1

Drug Prices in Two States

The price of prescription drugs is an ongoing national issue in the United States. Zocor is a common cholesterol-reducing drug prescribed for people who are at risk for heart disease. Table 10.2 shows Zocor prices from 15 randomly selected pharmacies in two states. At $\alpha = 0.05$, is there sufficient evidence to conclude that the true mean price of this drug is not the same in Colorado as it is in Texas?

As with the one-sample (or one-population) tests of Chapter 9, we use the following same procedure for two-sample tests.

STEP 1: STATE THE HYPOTHESES

To check for a difference in population means without regard for its direction, we choose a two-tailed test. The hypotheses to be tested are

$$H_0: \mu_1 = \mu_2 \text{ (or } H_0: \mu_1 - \mu_2 = 0)$$
$$H_1: \mu_1 \neq \mu_2 \text{ (or } H_1: \mu_1 - \mu_2 \neq 0)$$

TABLE 10.2   Zocor Prices (30-Day Supply) in Two States

Colorado Pharmacies		Texas Pharmacies	
City	Price ($)	City	Price ($)
Alamosa	125.05	Austin	145.32
Avon	137.56	Austin	131.19
Broomfield	142.50	Austin	151.65
Buena Vista	145.95	Austin	141.55
Colorado Springs	117.49	Austin	125.99
Colorado Springs	142.75	Dallas	126.29
Denver	121.99	Dallas	139.19
Denver	117.49	Dallas	156.00
Eaton	141.64	Dallas	137.56
Fort Collins	128.69	Houston	154.10
Gunnison	130.29	Houston	126.41
Pueblo	142.39	Houston	114.00
Pueblo	121.99	Houston	144.99
Pueblo	141.30		
Sterling	153.43		
Walsenburg	133.39		

$\bar{x}_1 = \$133.994$ $\bar{x}_2 = \$138.018$

$s_1 = \$11.015$ $s_2 = \$12.663$

$n_1 = 16$ pharmacies $n_2 = 13$ pharmacies

Source: Public Interest Research Group (www.pirg.org). Surveyed pharmacies were chosen from the telephone directory in 2004. Data used with permission.

STEP 2: SPECIFY THE DECISION RULE

We will assume equal variances. For the pooled-variance t test, degrees of freedom are $\nu = n_1 + n_2 - 2 = 16 + 13 - 2 = 27$. From Appendix D we get the two-tail critical value $t = \pm 2.052$. The decision rule is illustrated in Figure 10.3.

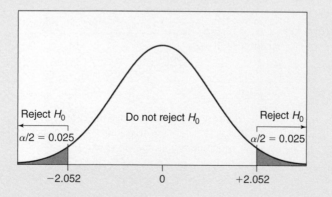

STEP 3: CALCULATE THE TEST STATISTIC

The sample statistics values are

$\bar{x}_1 = 133.994$ $\bar{x}_2 = 138.018$

$s_1 = 11.015$ $s_2 = 12.663$

$n_1 = 16$ $n_2 = 13$

The **pooled variance** s_p^2 value is

$$s_p^2 = \frac{(n_1 - 1)s_1^2 + (n_2 - 1)s_2^2}{n_1 + n_2 - 2} = \frac{(16 - 1)(11.015)^2 + (13 - 1)(12.663)^2}{16 + 13 - 2} = 138.6730$$

Using s_p^2 the test statistic value is

$$t_{calc} = \frac{\bar{x}_1 - \bar{x}_2}{\sqrt{\dfrac{s_p^2}{n_1} + \dfrac{s_p^2}{n_2}}} = \frac{133.994 - 138.018}{\sqrt{\dfrac{138.6730}{16} + \dfrac{138.6730}{13}}} = \frac{-4.024}{4.39707} = -0.915$$

The pooled standard deviation is $s_p = \sqrt{138.6730} = 11.776$. Notice that s_p always lies between s_1 and s_2 (if not, you have made an arithmetic error). This is because s_p^2 is a weighted average of s_1^2 and s_2^2.

STEP 4: MAKE THE DECISION

The test statistic $t_{calc} = -0.915$ does not fall in the rejection region, so we cannot reject the hypothesis of equal means. Excel's menu and output are shown in Figure 10.4. Both one-tailed and two-tailed tests are shown.

FIGURE 10.4

Excel's Data > Data Analysis **with Unknown but Equal Variances**

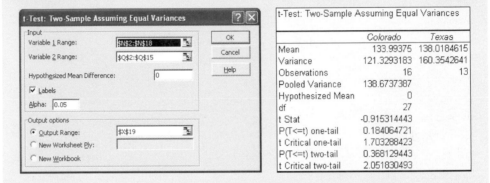

t-Test: Two-Sample Assuming Equal Variances	Colorado	Texas
Mean	133.99375	138.0184615
Variance	121.3293183	160.3542641
Observations	16	13
Pooled Variance	138.6737387	
Hypothesized Mean	0	
df	27	
t Stat	-0.915314443	
P(T<=t) one-tail	0.184064721	
t Critical one-tail	1.703288423	
P(T<=t) two-tail	0.368129443	
t Critical two-tail	2.051830493	

The p value can be calculated using Excel's two-tail function =TDIST(.915,27,2), which gives $p = 0.3681$. This large p value says that a result this extreme would happen by chance about 37 percent of the time if $\mu_1 = \mu_2$. The difference in sample means seems to be well within the realm of chance.

The sample variances in this example are similar, so the assumption of equal variances is reasonable. But if we instead use the formulas for Case 3 (assuming *unequal* variances), the test statistic value is

$$t_{calc} = \frac{\bar{x}_1 - \bar{x}_2}{\sqrt{\dfrac{s_1^2}{n_1} + \dfrac{s_2^2}{n_2}}} = \frac{133.994 - 138.018}{\sqrt{\dfrac{(11.015)^2}{16} + \dfrac{(12.663)^2}{13}}} = \frac{-4.024}{4.4629} = -0.902$$

The formula for adjusted degrees of freedom is

$$\nu' = \frac{\left[\dfrac{s_1^2}{n_1} + \dfrac{s_2^2}{n_2}\right]^2}{\dfrac{\left(\dfrac{s_1^2}{n_1}\right)^2}{n_1 - 1} + \dfrac{\left(\dfrac{s_2^2}{n_2}\right)^2}{n_2 - 1}} = \frac{\left[\dfrac{(11.015)^2}{16} + \dfrac{(12.663)^2}{13}\right]^2}{\dfrac{\left(\dfrac{(11.015)^2}{16}\right)^2}{16 - 1} + \dfrac{\left(\dfrac{(12.663)^2}{13}\right)^2}{13 - 1}} = 24$$

The adjusted degrees of freedom are rounded to the next lower integer, to be conservative.

For the unequal-variance t test with degrees of freedom $\nu' = 24$, Appendix D gives the critical value $t_{0.025,24} = \pm 2.064$. The decision rule is illustrated in Figure 10.5.

FIGURE 10.5

Two-Tail Decision Rule for Student's *t* with $\alpha = 0.05$ and d.f. = 24

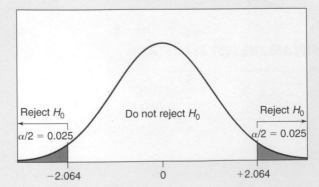

The calculations are best done by computer. Excel's menu and output are shown in Figure 10.6. Both one-tailed and two-tailed tests are shown.

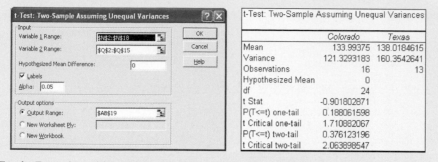

FIGURE 10.6

Excel's Data > Data Analysis **with Unknown but Equal Variances**

For the Zocor data, either assumption leads to the same conclusion:

Assumption	Test Statistic	d.f.	Critical Value	Decision
Case 2 (equal variances)	$t_{calc} = -0.915$	27	$t_{0.025} = \pm 2.052$	Don't reject
Case 3 (unequal variances)	$t_{calc} = -0.902$	24	$t_{0.025} = \pm 2.064$	Don't reject

A Closer Look

In both of the above examples (assuming equal variances and not assuming equal variances), Excel gave us both a one-tail and a two-tail *p* value. The quoted two-tail *p* value is the correct *p* value to use if we are testing that the population means are different. The quoted one-tail *p* value may not be the correct *p* value to use if we are testing that the mean of population 1 is greater than the mean of population 2, or if the mean of population 1 is less than the mean of population 2. For this quoted *p* value to be the correct *p* value, the value of the test statistic must support the alternative hypothesis. For example, if we test whether the mean of population 1 is greater than the mean of population 2, a negative value of the test statistic t_{calc} does not support the alternative hypothesis and thus the quoted *p* value is not the correct *p* value to use. In this situation, the *p* value would be $1 - 0.184$, or 0.816, when equal population variances are assumed.

Which Assumption Is Best?

If the *sample sizes are equal,* the Case 2 and Case 3 test statistics will be identical, although the degrees of freedom may differ. If the *variances are similar,* the two tests usually agree. If you have no information about the population variances, then the best choice is Case 3. The fewer assumptions you make about your populations, the less likely you are to make a mistake in your conclusions. Note that Section 10.5 discusses how to test if the two variances are equal. Case 1 (known population variances) is not explored further here because it is so uncommon in business.

Large Samples

For unknown variances, if both samples are large ($n_1 \geq 30$ and $n_2 \geq 30$) and you have reason to think the population isn't badly skewed (look at the histograms or dot plots of the samples), it is common to use Equation 10.1 with Appendix C.

$$z_{calc} = \frac{(\bar{x}_1 - \bar{x}_2) - d_0}{\sqrt{\dfrac{s_1^2}{n_1} + \dfrac{s_2^2}{n_2}}} \quad \text{(large samples, symmetric populations)} \qquad \textbf{(10.1)}$$

TABLE 10.3 **Article Length in JASA**

June 1990 JASA	June 2000 JASA
$\bar{x}_1 = 7.1333$ pages	$\bar{x}_2 = 11.8333$ pages
$s_1 = 1.9250$ pages	$s_2 = 2.5166$ pages
$n_1 = 30$ articles	$n_2 = 12$ articles

Source: Journal of the American Statistical Association 85, no. 410, and 95, no. 450.

Mini Case   10.1

Length of Statistics Articles

Are articles in leading statistics journals getting longer? It appears so, based on a comparison of the June 2000 and June 1990 issues of the *Journal of the American Statistical Association (JASA)*, shown in Table 10.3. We will do a left-tailed test at $\alpha = 0.01$. The hypotheses are

$$H_0: \mu_1 = \mu_2$$
$$H_1: \mu_1 < \mu_2$$

Because the variances are unknown, we will use a *t* test (both equal and unequal variances), checking the results with Excel. The pooled-variance test (Case 2) requires degrees of freedom $\nu = n_1 + n_2 - 2 = 30 + 12 - 2 = 40$, yielding a left-tail critical value of $t_{0.01} = -2.423$. The estimate of the pooled variance is

$$s_p^2 = \frac{(n_1 - 1)s_1^2 + (n_2 - 1)s_2^2}{n_1 + n_2 - 2} = \frac{(30 - 1)(1.9250)^2 + (12 - 1)(2.5166)^2}{30 + 12 - 2}$$

$$= 4.428229$$

The test statistic is $t_{calc} = -6.539$, indicating a very strong rejection of the hypothesis of equal means:

$$t_{calc} = \frac{\bar{x}_1 - \bar{x}_2}{\sqrt{\dfrac{s_p^2}{n_1} + \dfrac{s_p^2}{n_2}}} = \frac{7.1333 - 11.8333}{\sqrt{\dfrac{4.428229}{30} + \dfrac{4.428229}{12}}} = \frac{-4.70000}{0.718767} = -6.539$$

Using the Welch-Sattherwaite *t* test (assuming unequal variances), the test statistic is

$$t_{calc} = \frac{\bar{x}_1 - \bar{x}_2}{\sqrt{\dfrac{s_1^2}{n_1} + \dfrac{s_2^2}{n_2}}} = \frac{7.1333 - 11.8333}{\sqrt{\dfrac{(1.9250)^2}{30} + \dfrac{(2.5166)^2}{12}}} = \frac{-4.7000}{0.80703} = -5.824$$

The formula for adjusted degrees of freedom for the Welch-Satterthwaite test is

$$\nu' = \frac{\left[\dfrac{s_1^2}{n_1} + \dfrac{s_2^2}{n_2}\right]^2}{\dfrac{\left(\dfrac{s_1^2}{n_1}\right)^2}{n_1 - 1} + \dfrac{\left(\dfrac{s_2^2}{n_2}\right)^2}{n_2 - 1}} = \frac{\left[\dfrac{(1.9250)^2}{30} + \dfrac{(2.5166)^2}{12}\right]^2}{\dfrac{\left(\dfrac{(1.9250)^2}{30}\right)^2}{30 - 1} + \dfrac{\left(\dfrac{(2.5166)^2}{12}\right)^2}{12 - 1}} = 16$$

so the critical value is $t_{0.01} = -2.583$. Regardless of our assumption about variances, we conclude that articles in *JASA* are getting longer. The decision is clear-cut. Our conviction about the conclusion depends on whether these samples are truly representative of *JASA* articles. This question might be probed further, and more articles could be examined. However, this result seems reasonable *a priori,* due to the growing use of graphics and computer simulation that could lengthen the articles. Is a difference of 4.7 pages of practical importance? Well, editors must find room for articles, so if articles are getting longer, journals must contain more pages or publish fewer articles. A difference of 5 pages over 20 or 30 articles might indeed be important.

A Closer Look

When conducting two-sample tests, choosing which sample or population is given the subscript 1 and which is given the subscript 2 is arbitrary. Reversing the subscripts would not affect the conclusions reached. In the above JASA example, the pair of hypotheses were H_0: $\mu_1 = \mu_2$ and H_1: $\mu_1 < \mu_2$, the test statistic was originally $t_{calc} = -6.539$, and the rejection region or the decision rule was to reject the null hypothesis if $t_{calc} < -2.423$. Thus, we rejected the null hypothesis. If we had reversed our definitions of population 1 and population 2 such that June 2000 was given the subscript 1 and June 1990 was given the subscript 2, the two hypotheses would now be H_0: $\mu_1 = \mu_2$ and H_1: $\mu_1 > \mu_2$, t_{calc} would now equal 6.539 and our decision rule would be to reject the null hypothesis if $t_{calc} > 2.423$. As before, we would reject the null hypothesis. Conversely, if we didn't reject the null hypothesis originally, we wouldn't reject the null hypothesis if we were to switch our definitions.

Concept Check

In a previous example, pharmaceutical prices were compared between two states, but now consider the following. Many Americans come to Canada to purchase certain drugs because many drugs are perceived to be priced much lower in Canada as a result of the influence of the Canadian government. Suppose that Zocor was priced at randomly selected pharmacies in the United States (sample 1) and at randomly selected pharmacies in Canada (sample 2) with the objective of trying to conclude that American prices for Zocor are, on average, in excess of $20 more (for a 30-day supply) than they are in Canada. What would the null and alternative hypotheses be? If we redefined the two samples or populations such that Canada's sample was referred to as sample 1 and the American sample was referred to as sample 2, what would the null and alternative hypotheses be?

Should Sample Sizes Be Equal?

Many people instinctively try to choose equal sample sizes for tests of means. It is preferable to avoid unbalanced sample sizes, but it is not necessary. Unequal sample sizes are common, and the formulas still apply.

Confidence Intervals for $\mu_1 - \mu_2$

In Chapter 8, we used the sample distributions of a single sample mean to estimate (best estimate and confidence interval) a single population mean. We can also use the sampling distribution of the difference in two sample means to estimate the difference in two population means. We would accomplish this using the same reasoning and the same manipulations as before. As a review, using the sampling distribution of $\overline{X}$, knowing the population variance, the relationship was converted to a confidence interval as follows:

$$z = \frac{\overline{x} - \mu}{\sigma/\sqrt{n}} \quad \rightarrow \quad \overline{x} \pm z_{\alpha/2}\frac{\sigma}{\sqrt{n}}$$

Or, the confidence interval became the best estimate $\pm z_{\alpha/2}$ standard deviations, where $z_{\alpha/2}$ is determined from the level of confidence, $1 - \alpha$. Based on the appropriate sampling distribution of $\overline{X}_1 - \overline{X}_2$ and the same mathematical manipulations, the appropriate confidence intervals would be as follows:

Case 1 (known population variances)

$$z = \frac{(\bar{x}_1 - \bar{x}_2) - (\mu_1 - \mu_2)}{\sqrt{\dfrac{\sigma_1^2}{n_1} + \dfrac{\sigma_2^2}{n_2}}} \quad \rightarrow \quad (\bar{x}_1 - \bar{x}_2) \pm z_{\alpha/2}\sqrt{\frac{\sigma_1^2}{n_1} + \frac{\sigma_2^2}{n_2}}$$

(again the confidence interval becomes the best estimate $\pm z_{\alpha/2}$ standard deviations)

Case 2 (unknown population variances but assumed equal)

$$t = \frac{(\bar{x}_1 - \bar{x}_2) - (\mu_1 - \mu_2)}{\sqrt{\dfrac{s_p^2}{n_1} + \dfrac{s_p^2}{n_2}}} \quad \rightarrow \quad (\bar{x}_1 - \bar{x}_2) \pm t_{\alpha/2,\nu}\sqrt{\frac{s_p^2}{n_1} + \frac{s_p^2}{n_2}}$$

where

$$s_p^2 = \frac{(n_1 - 1)s_1^2 + (n_2 - 1)s_2^2}{n_1 + n_2 - 2} \text{ and } \nu = n_1 + n_2 - 2$$

(here, the confidence interval becomes the best estimate $\pm t_{\alpha/2,\nu}$ estimated standard deviation).

Case 3 (unknown population variances and assumed not equal)

$$t = \frac{(\bar{x}_1 - \bar{x}_2) - (\mu_1 - \mu_2)}{\sqrt{\dfrac{s_1^2}{n_1} + \dfrac{s_2^2}{n_2}}} \quad \rightarrow \quad (\bar{x}_1 - \bar{x}_2) \pm t_{\alpha/2,\nu}\sqrt{\frac{s_1^2}{n_1} + \frac{s_2^2}{n_2}}$$

where

$$\nu' = \frac{[s_1^2/n_1 + s_2^2/n_2]^2}{\dfrac{(s_1^2/n_1)^2}{n_1 - 1} + \dfrac{(s_2^2/n_2)^2}{n_2 - 1}}$$

(again, the confidence interval becomes the best estimate $\pm t_{\alpha/2,\nu}$ estimated standard deviation).

EXAMPLE 2

Marketing Teams

Fourth-year marketing majors were randomly assigned to a virtual team that met only electronically or to a face-to-face team that met in person. Both teams were presented with the task of analyzing eight complex marketing cases. After completing the project, they were asked to respond on a 1 to 5 Likert scale to this question: "As compared to other teams, the members got along together."

TABLE 10.4   Means and Standard Deviations for the Two Marketing Teams

Statistic	*Virtual Team*	*Face-to-Face Team*
Sample Mean	$\bar{x}_1 = 2.48$	$\bar{x}_2 = 1.83$
Sample Std. Dev.	$s_1 = 0.76$	$s_2 = 0.82$
Sample Size	$n_1 = 44$	$n_2 = 42$

Source: Roger W. Berry, "The Efficacy of Electronic Communication in the Business School: Marketing Students' Perception of Virtual Teams," *Marketing Education Review* 12, no. 2 (Summer 2002), pp. 73–78. Copyright © 2002. Reprinted with permission, CTC Press. All rights reserved.

Table 10.4 shows the means and standard deviations for the two groups. The population variances are unknown, but will be assumed equal. For a confidence level of 90 percent we use Student's t with $\nu = 44 + 42 - 2 = 84$. From Appendix D we obtain $t_{0.05} = 1.664$ (using 80 degrees of freedom, the next lower value). To determine the confidence interval

$$s_p^2 = \frac{(n_1 - 1)s_1^2 + (n_2 - 1)s_2^2}{n_1 + n_2 - 2} = \frac{(44 - 1)(0.76)^2 + (42 - 1)(0.82)^2}{44 + 42 - 2} = 0.6239$$

$$(\bar{x}_1 - \bar{x}_2) \pm t_{0.05,84}\sqrt{\frac{s_p^2}{n_1} + \frac{s_p^2}{n_2}}$$

$$= (2.48 - 1.83) \pm (1.664)\sqrt{\frac{0.6239}{44} + \frac{0.6239}{42}}$$

$$= 0.65 \pm 0.284 \quad or \quad 0.366 < \mu_1 - \mu_2 < 0.934$$

We are 90 percent confident that the true difference in average Likert scale scores between the virtual team and the face-to-face team lies between 0.366 and 0.934, with the best estimate being 0.65. Because this confidence interval does not include zero, we can say with 90 percent confidence that there is a difference between the population means μ_1 and μ_2 (i.e., the virtual team's mean differs from the face-to-face team's mean).

Section Exercises

Hint: Show all formulas and calculations, but use the calculator in *LearningStats* Unit 10 to check your work. Calculate the *p*-values using Excel, and show each Excel formula you used (note that Excel's TDIST function requires that you omit the sign if the test statistic is negative).

10.1 Do a two-sample test for equality of means assuming equal variances. Calculate the *p* value. (LO 2)

  a. Comparison of GPA for randomly chosen third- and fourth-year university students: $\bar{x}_1 = 3.05, s_1 = 0.20, n_1 = 15,$ $\bar{x}_2 = 3.25, s_2 = 0.30, n_2 = 15, \alpha = 0.025$, left-tailed test.

  b. Comparison of average commute kilometres for randomly chosen students at two universities: $\bar{x}_1 = 15, s_1 = 5, n_1 = 22, \bar{x}_2 = 18,$ $s_2 = 7, n_2 = 19, \alpha = 0.05$, two-tailed test.

  c. Comparison of credits at time of graduation for randomly chosen accounting and economics students: $\bar{x}_1 = 139, s_1 = 2.8,$ $n_1 = 12, \bar{x}_2 = 137, s_2 = 2.7, n_2 = 17, \alpha = 0.05$, right-tailed test.

10.2 Repeat the previous exercise, assuming unequal variances. Calculate the *p* value using Excel, and show the Excel formula you used. (LO 2)

10.3 When the background music was slow, the mean amount of bar purchases for a sample of 17 restaurant patrons was $30.47 with a standard deviation of $15.10. When the background music was fast, the mean amount of bar purchases for a sample of 14 patrons in the same restaurant was $21.62 with a standard deviation of $9.50. (a) Assuming unequal variances, at $\alpha = 0.01$, is the true mean higher when the music is slow? (b) Calculate the *p* value using Excel. (LO 2)

10.4 Are women's feet getting bigger? Retailers in the last 20 years have had to increase their stock of larger sizes. Walmart Stores, Inc., and Payless ShoeSource, Inc., have been aggressive in stocking larger sizes. Assuming equal variances, at $\alpha = 0.025$, do these random shoe size samples of 12 randomly chosen women in each age group show that women's shoe sizes have increased? (See *The Wall Street Journal*, July 17, 2004.) (LO 2) **ShoeSize**

Born in 1980:	8	7.5	8.5	8.5	8	7.5	9.5	7.5	8	8	8.5	9
Born in 1960:	8.5	7.5	8	8	7.5	7.5	7.5	8	7	8	7	8

10.5 Just how "decaffeinated" is decaffeinated coffee? Researchers analyzed 12 samples of two kinds of Starbucks' decaffeinated coffee. The caffeine in a cup of decaffeinated espresso had a mean of 9.4 mg with a standard deviation of 3.2 mg, while brewed decaffeinated coffee had a mean of 12.7 mg with a standard deviation of 0.35 mg. Assuming unequal population variances, is there sufficient evidence to indicate a difference in average caffeine content between these two beverages at $\alpha = 0.01$? (Based on McCusker, R. R., *Journal of Analytical Toxicology* 30 [March 2006], pp. 112–114.) (LO 2)

10.6 In an attempt to increase sales, a store in Fredericton, New Brunswick, is considering offering either a 10 percent discount or a 20 percent discount to its customers. Before making a decision, it decided to conduct a small study. On a randomly selected day, it gave a random sample of 15 customers a coupon that offered a 10 percent discount, and on the other day, it gave a random sample of 10 of its customers a coupon that offered a 20 percent discount. Those offered a 10 percent discount spent an average of $127 with a standard deviation of $23. Those offered a 20 percent discount spent an average of $152 with a standard deviation of $27. Assuming equal population variances, is there sufficient evidence, at the 0.05 level of significance, that the average sales is higher with the 20 percent discount? After analyzing the results, the store felt that for it to be worthwhile financially, the offer of a 20 percent discount would have to have average sales in excess of $10 higher than average sales with the offer of a 10 percent discount. Assuming equal population variances, can the store conclude, at the 0.05 level of significance, that the offer of a 20 percent discount is worthwhile financially? Which discount should the store offer? Explain. (LO 2)

10.7 A special bumper was installed on selected vehicles in a large fleet. The dollar cost of body repairs was recorded for all vehicles that were involved in accidents over a one-year period. Those with the special bumper are the test group and the other vehicles are the control group, shown below. Each "repair incident" is defined as an invoice (which might include more than one separate type of damage).

Statistic	Test Group	Control Group
Mean Damage	$\bar{x}_1 = \$1{,}101$	$\bar{x}_2 = \$1{,}766$
Sample Std. Dev.	$s_1 = \$696$	$s_2 = \$838$
Repair Incidents	$n_1 = 12$	$n_2 = 9$

Source: Unpublished study by Thomas W. Lauer and Floyd G. Willoughby.

(a) Construct a 90 percent confidence interval for the true difference of the means assuming equal variances. Show all work clearly. (b) Repeat, using the assumption of unequal variances. Did the assumption about variances make a major difference, in your opinion? (c) Construct separate confidence intervals for each mean. Do they overlap? (d) What conclusions can you draw? (LO 3)

10.8 In trials of an experimental Internet-based method of learning statistics, pre-tests and post-tests were given to two groups: traditional instruction (22 students) and Internet-based (17 students). Pre-test scores were not significantly different. On the post-test, the first group (traditional instruction) had a mean score of 8.64 with a standard deviation of 1.88, while the second group (experimental instruction) had a mean score of 8.82 with a standard deviation of 1.70. (a) Construct a 90 percent confidence interval for the true difference of the means assuming equal variances. Show all work clearly. (b) Repeat, using the assumption of unequal variances. Did the assumption about variances make a major difference, in your opinion? (c) Construct separate confidence intervals for each mean. Do they overlap? (d) What conclusions can you draw? (LO 3)

10.9 Construct a 95 percent confidence interval for the difference of mean monthly rent paid by undergraduates and graduate students assuming equal population variances. What do you conclude? (LO 3) ⊙ **Rent2**

Undergraduate Student Rents (n = 10)

820	780	870	670	800
790	810	680	1,000	730

Graduate Student Rents (n = 12)

1,130	920	930	880	780	910
790	840	930	910	860	850

10.4 Comparing Two Means: Paired Samples

EXAMPLE 3

Diet Plans

One advertised diet plan (Plan A) claims that individuals using its plan lose more weight, on average, than those using the best-selling diet plan (Plan B). To offer proof, it presented the following data (study 1) on the weight losses (in kg) of 12 individuals, 6 using its plan and 6 using the best-selling plan.

Weight Loss	
Plan A	Plan B
53	12
56	14
54	13
55	12
56	11
57	14

Another study (study 2) was conducted and the results were as follows:

Weight Loss	
Plan A	**Plan B**
11	10
33	32
40	38
52	50
61	60
69	67

To test the claim, the following pair of hypotheses were used:

H_0: $\mu_1 = \mu_2$ (average weight loss the same for both plans)

H_1: $\mu_1 > \mu_2$ (average weight loss greater for Plan A)

Assuming equal variances, the value of the test statistic would be

$$t_{calc} = \frac{\bar{x}_1 - \bar{x}_2}{\sqrt{\frac{s_p^2}{n_1} + \frac{s_p^2}{n_2}}}$$

and we would reject H_0 if $t_{calc} > t_{\alpha, n-1}$

Without doing any of the actual calculations, we can easily observe from the data in study 1 that the average weight loss using Plan A is much greater than the average weight loss using Plan B and the variance within each diet plan is quite small, resulting in a small s_p^2. With these observations, it can easily be concluded that t_{calc} would be quite large, resulting in us rejecting the null hypothesis and us concluding that Plan A is better. Conversely, looking at the data in study 2, the means are quite similar and the two sample variances are quite large resulting in a large s_p^2. With these observations, we can easily conclude that t_{calc} will be small, resulting in us not rejecting the null hypothesis and not concluding that diet Plan A is better.

Suppose we decided to look at those participating in the two studies. In study 1, it was determined that those individuals using Plan A were at least 75 kg overweight before the study began and those using Plan B were less than 20 kg overweight before the study began. The question that should be asked at this point is: "Did the individuals using Plan A lose more weight because of the diet plan or because they had so much more weight to lose?" With this additional information on the participants, there is no definitive answer to this question. In study 2, suppose we determined that those who lost 11 kg and 10 kg both were 15 kg overweight before the study began, those who lost 33 kg and 32 kg were 40 kg overweight, those who lost 40 kg and 38 kg were 50 kg overweight, those who lost 52 kg and 50 kg were 65 kg overweight, those who lost 61 kg and 60 kg were 75 kg overweight, and those who lost 69 kg and 67 kg were 85 kg overweight before the study began. Based on this additional information, could we argue that maybe Plan A is better? One argument that can be made is that if we compare individuals with similar amounts overweight, Plan A, in all six cases, resulted in greater weight losses and, thus, plan A may be better.

It appears that, in this example, there is a characteristic of the individuals (amount overweight) that may cause erroneous conclusions if we used independent random samples instead of matching or pairing the samples according to this characteristic. And if we did pair the samples, it appears that, intuitively, our test should be based on comparing the values of X within each pair.

Paired Data

When sample data consist of n matched pairs, a different approach is required. If the *same* individuals are observed twice but under different circumstances, or if similar individuals are paired, we have a **paired comparison.** For example:

- Fifteen retirees with diagnosed hypertension are assigned a program of diet, exercise, and meditation. A baseline measurement of blood pressure is taken *before* the program begins and again *after* two months. Was the program effective in reducing blood pressure?

- Ten cutting tools use lubricant A for ten minutes. The blade temperatures are taken. When the machine has cooled, it is run with lubricant B for ten minutes and the blade temperatures are again measured. Which lubricant makes the blades run cooler?

- Weekly sales of Snapple at 12 Walmart stores are compared *before* and *after* installing a new eye-catching display. Did the new display increase sales?

Paired data typically come from a *before-after* experiment. If we treat the data as two independent samples, ignoring the *dependence* between the data pairs, the test is less powerful.

Paired *t* Test

In the **paired *t* test** we define a new random variable $d = X_1 - X_2$ as the *difference* between X_1 and X_2. We usually present the n observed differences in column form:

Obs	X_1	X_2	$d = X_1 - X_2$
1	XXX	XXX	XXX
2	XXX	XXX	XXX
3	XXX	XXX	XXX
. . .	. . .	. . .	. . .
. . .	. . .	. . .	. . .
n	XXX	XXX	XXX

The same sample data could also be presented in row form:

Obs	1	2	3	. . .	. . .	n
X_1	XXX	XXX	XXX	. . .	. . .	XXX
X_2	XXX	XXX	XXX	. . .	. . .	XXX
$d = X_1 - X_2$	XXX	XXX	XXX	. . .	. . .	XXX

The mean $\bar{d}$ and standard deviation s_d of the sample of n differences are calculated with the usual formulas for a mean and standard deviation. We call the mean $\bar{d}$ instead of $\bar{x}$ merely to remind ourselves that we are dealing with *differences.*

Let $\mu_d = \mu_1 - \mu_2$ be the difference of the two population means. Note that μ_d also equals the mean of the *differences* of the corresponding population values. With this notation, our hypotheses are one of three kinds:

Left-tailed test: $H_0: \mu_d = d_0, H_1: \mu_d < d_0$
Right-tailed test: $H_0: \mu_d = d_0, H_1: \mu_d > d_0$
Two-tailed test: $H_0: \mu_d = d_0, H_1: \mu_d \neq d_0$

$$\bar{d} = \frac{\sum_{i=1}^{n} d_i}{n} \quad \text{(mean of } n \text{ differences)} \tag{10.2}$$

$$s_d = \sqrt{\sum_{i=1}^{n} \frac{(d_i - \bar{d})^2}{n-1}} \quad \text{(std. dev. of } n \text{ differences)} \tag{10.3}$$

Because the population variance of d is unknown, we will do a paired t test using Student's t with $n - 1$ degrees of freedom to compare the sample mean difference $\bar{d}$ with a hypothesized difference of d_0. The test statistic is really a one-sample t test, just like those in Chapter 9.

$$t_{\text{calc}} = \frac{d_0}{s_d/\sqrt{n}} \quad \text{(test statistic for \textbf{paired samples})} \tag{10.4}$$

Note that for the paired t test to be valid, we need to assume that the population of differences has a normal distribution, or equivalently, random variable $d = X_1 - X_2$ follows a normal distribution. Testing for this assumption is crucial if the sample size is small.

EXAMPLE 4

Repair Estimates
Repair

An insurance company's procedure in settling a claim under $10,000 for fire or water damage to a home owner is to require two estimates for cleanup and repair of structural damage before allowing the insured to proceed with the work. The insurance company compares estimates from two contractors who most frequently handle this type of work in this geographical area. Table 10.5 shows the 10 most recent claims for which damage estimates were provided by both contractors. At the 0.05 level of significance, is there a difference between the two contractors?

Note that when you compare two contractors, it is quite natural to compare them for the same claim. So there is a natural pairing of these claims. Hence we should treat these samples as not independent and perform a paired t test.

TABLE 10.5 Damage Repair Estimates ($) for 10 Claims Repair

Claim	X_1 Contractor A	X_2 Contractor B	$d = X_1 - X_2$ Difference
1. Jones, C.	5,500	6,000	−500
2. Smith, R.	1,000	900	100
3. Xia, Y.	2,500	2,500	0
4. Gallo, J.	7,800	8,300	−500
5. Carson, R.	6,400	6,200	200
6. Petty, M.	8,800	9,400	−600
7. Tracy, L.	600	500	100
8. Barnes, J.	3,300	3,500	−200
9. Rodriguez, J.	4,500	5,200	−700
10. Van Dyke, P.	6,500	6,800	−300

$$\overline{d} = -240.00$$
$$s_d = 327.28$$
$$n = 10$$

STEP 1: STATE THE HYPOTHESES

Because we have no reason to be interested in directionality, we will choose a two-tailed test using these hypotheses:

$$H_0: \mu_d = 0$$
$$H_1: \mu_d \neq 0$$

STEP 2: SPECIFY THE DECISION RULE

Our test statistic will follow a Student's t distribution with d.f. $= n - 1 = 10 - 1 = 9$, so from Appendix D with $\alpha = 0.05$ the two-tail critical value is $t_{0.025} = \pm 2.262$, as illustrated in Figure 10.7. The decision rule is

Reject H_0 if $t_{calc} < -2.262$ or if $t_{calc} > +2.262$.

Otherwise do not reject H_0.

STEP 3: CALCULATE THE TEST STATISTIC

The mean and standard deviation are calculated in the usual way, as shown in Table 10.4, so the test statistic is

$$t_{calc} = \frac{\overline{d}}{\frac{s_d}{\sqrt{n}}} = \frac{-240}{\left(\frac{327.28}{\sqrt{10}}\right)} = \frac{-240}{103.495} = -2.319$$

STEP 4: MAKE THE DECISION

Because $t_{calc} = -2.319$ falls in the left-tail critical region (below −2.262), we reject the null hypothesis and conclude that there is a significant difference between the two contractors. However, it is a *very* close decision.

FIGURE 10.7

Decision Rule for Two-Tailed Paired *t* Test at $\alpha = 0.05$

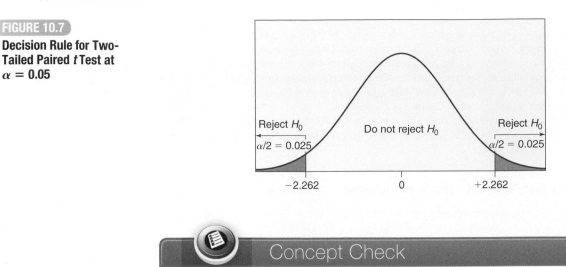

Reject H_0
$\alpha/2 = 0.025$

Do not reject H_0

Reject H_0
$\alpha/2 = 0.025$

-2.262 0 $+2.262$

Concept Check

If we had used the t_{calc} formula for independent samples, how would its numerator value compare to the above numerator value of -240? Explain. What would we expect its denominator value to be compared to the above denominator value of 103.495? Explain.

Excel's Paired Difference Test

The calculations for our repair estimates example are easy in Excel, as illustrated in Figure 10.8. Excel gives you the option of choosing either a one-tailed or two-tailed test, and also shows the p value. For a two-tailed test, the p value is $p = 0.0456$, which would barely lead to rejection of the hypothesis of zero difference of means at $\alpha = 0.05$. The borderline p value reinforces our conclusion that the decision is sensitive to our choice of α. MegaStat and MINITAB also provide a paired t test.

A Closer Look

Excel's paired difference test not only gives us statistics for testing the difference in means using paired samples but also gives us Pearson's Correlation coefficient (to be discussed in Chapter 13), which measures the strength of the linear relationship between two variables. If one variable tends to increase in value while the other decreases, the coefficient would be negative. If one variable tends to increase (or decrease) in value while the other variable also tends to increase (or decrease), the coefficient would be positive. If there is no relationship in the values of these variables, the coefficient would theoretically be zero. If plotted on a scatter diagram, the more closely the points (x, y) fit a straight line, the closer the correlation coefficient is to ± 1. The value of this coefficient tells us nothing about the difference in the population means. In other words, when the coefficient is positive, the mean of population 1 may be equal to, less than, or greater than the mean of population 2.

Concept Check

Although Pearson's Correlation coefficient tells us nothing about the difference in the population means, it tells us something about our decision to pair our samples. Explain. What values of this coefficient (positive, zero, or negative) would support our decision to pair the samples? Explain.

Results of Excel's Paired *t* Test at $\alpha = 0.05$ FIGURE 10.8

Data Analysis

Analysis Tools

Histogram
Moving Average
Random Number Generation
Rank and Percentile
Regression
Sampling
t-Test: Paired Two Sample for Means
t-Test: Two-Sample Assuming Equal Variances
t-Test: Two-Sample Assuming Unequal Variances
z-Test: Two Sample for Means

OK
Cancel
Help

t-Test: Paired Two Sample for Means

	Contractor A	Contractor B
Mean	4690	4930
Variance	7836555.556	9053444.444
Observations	10	10
Pearson Correlation	0.996247386	
Hypothesized Mean Difference	0	
df	9	
t Stat	-2.318963855	
P(T<=t) one-tail	0.022781515	
t Critical one-tail	1.833112923	
P(T<=t) two-tail	0.045563029	
t Critical two-tail	2.262157158	

Analogy to Confidence Interval

A two-tailed test for a zero difference is equivalent to asking whether the confidence interval for the true mean difference μ_d includes zero.

$$\bar{d} \pm t\frac{s_d}{\sqrt{n}} \quad \text{(confidence interval for difference of paired means)} \qquad \textbf{(10.5)}$$

It depends on the confidence level:

90% confidence ($t = 1.833$): $-429.71 < \mu_d < -50.29$

95% confidence ($t = 2.262$): $-474.10 < \mu_d < -5.8954$

99% confidence ($t = 3.250$): $-576.36 < \mu_d < +96.36$

As Figure 10.9 shows, the 99 percent confidence interval includes zero, but the 90 percent and 95 percent confidence intervals do not.

Confidence Intervals for μ_d

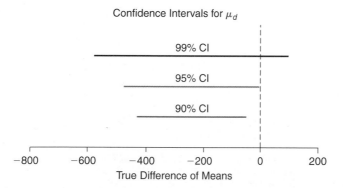

99% CI

95% CI

90% CI

-800   -600   -400   -200   0   200
True Difference of Means

FIGURE 10.9

Confidence Intervals for Difference of Means

EXAMPLE 5

The Diet Plan Example Revisited

Using the paired data of study 2 in the earlier diet plan scenario (Example 3), can we conclude, at $\alpha = 0.05$ that Plan A is better?

We use the following table to do our calculations:

Weight Loss (kg)

Pair	Plan A	Plan B	d_i	$d_i - \bar{d}$	$(d_i - \bar{d})^2$
1	11	10	1	-0.5	0.25
2	33	32	1	-0.5	0.25
3	40	38	2	0.5	0.25
4	52	50	2	0.5	0.25
5	61	60	1	-0.5	0.25
6	69	67	2	0.5	0.25
			9		1.5

$$\bar{d} = \frac{\sum_{i=1}^{n} d_i}{n} = \frac{9}{6} = 1.5 \qquad s_d = \sqrt{\frac{\sum_{i=1}^{n}(d_i - \bar{d})^2}{n-1}} = \sqrt{\frac{1.5}{5}} = 0.548$$

The test now becomes

$$H_0: \mu_d = 0$$
$$H_1: \mu_d > 0$$

TEST STATISTIC

$$t_{calc} = \frac{\bar{d}}{s_d/\sqrt{n}} = \frac{1.5 - 0}{0.548/\sqrt{6}} = 6.705$$

Decision rule: reject the null hypothesis if $t_{calc} > t_{\alpha, n-1}$ or if $t_{calc} > 2.015$ ($\alpha = 0.05$ and $n - 1 = 5$). As $6.705 > 2.015$, we reject the null hypothesis at $\alpha = 0.05$ and conclude that Plan A is better.

Why Not Treat Paired Data As Independent Samples?

When observations are matched pairs, the paired t test is more powerful, because it utilizes information that is ignored if we treat the samples separately. To show this, let's treat each data column for the damage repair example as an **independent sample.** The summary statistics are

$$\bar{x}_1 = 4{,}690.00 \qquad\qquad \bar{x}_2 = 4{,}930.00$$
$$s_1 = 2{,}799.38 \qquad\qquad s_2 = 3{,}008.89$$
$$n_1 = 10 \qquad\qquad\qquad n_2 = 10$$

Assuming equal variances, we get the results shown in Figure 10.10. The p values (one-tail or two-tail) are not even close to being significant at the usual α levels. By ignoring the dependence between the samples, we unnecessarily *sacrifice the power of the test.* Therefore, if the two data columns are paired, we should not treat them independently.

FIGURE 10.10

Excel's Independent Sample t Test

t-Test: Two-Sample Assuming Equal Variances		
	Contractor A	Contractor B
Mean	4690	4930
Variance	7836555.6	9053444.4
Observations	10	10
Pooled Variance	8445000	
Hypothesized Mean Difference	0	
df	18	
t Stat	-0.1846700	
P(T<=t) one-tail	0.4277763	
t Critical one-tail	1.7340631	
P(T<=t) two-tail	0.8555526	
t Critical two-tail	2.1009237	

Section Exercises

10.10 A new cellphone battery is being considered as a replacement for the current one. Ten university student cellphone users are selected to try each battery in their usual mix of "talk" and "standby" and to record the number of hours until recharge was needed. (a) Do these results allow us to conclude that the new battery has a longer life using $\alpha = 0.05$? State your hypotheses and show all steps clearly. (b) Is the decision close? (c) Are you convinced? (LO 4) **Battery**

	Bob	May	Deno	Sri	Pat	Alexis	Scott	Aretha	Jen	Ben
New battery	45	41	53	40	43	43	49	39	41	43
Old battery	52	34	40	38	38	44	34	45	28	33

10.11 (a) At $\alpha = 0.05$, does the following sample show that daughters are taller than their mothers? (b) Is the decision close? (c) Why might daughters tend to be taller than their mothers? Why might they not? (LO 4)   **Height**

Family	Daughter's Height (cm)	Mother's Height (cm)
1	167	172
2	166	162
3	176	157
4	171	159
5	165	157
6	181	177
7	173	174

10.12 An experimental surgical procedure is being studied as an alternative to the old method. Both methods are considered safe. Five surgeons perform the operation on two patients matched by age, sex, and other relevant factors, with the results shown. The time to complete the surgery (in minutes) is recorded. (a) At the 5 percent significance level, is the new way faster? State your hypotheses and show all steps clearly. (b) Is the decision close? (LO 4)   **Surgery**

	Surgeon 1	Surgeon 2	Surgeon 3	Surgeon 4	Surgeon 5
Old way	36	55	28	40	62
New way	29	42	30	32	56

10.13 Blockbuster is testing a new policy of waiving all late fees on DVD rentals using a sample of 10 randomly chosen customers. (a) At $\alpha = 0.10$, do the data show that the mean number of monthly rentals has increased? (b) Is the decision close? (c) Are you convinced? (LO 4)   **DVDRental**

Customer	No Late Fee	Late Fee
1	14	10
2	12	7
3	14	10
4	13	13
5	10	9
6	13	14
7	12	12
8	10	7
9	13	13
10	13	9

10.14 Below is a random sample of shoe sizes for 12 mothers and their daughters. (a) At $\alpha = 0.01$, does this sample show that women's shoe sizes have increased? State your hypotheses and show all steps clearly. (b) Is the decision close? (c) Are you convinced? (d) Why might shoe sizes change over time? (See *The Wall Street Journal*, July 17, 2004.) (LO 4)   **ShoeSize2**

	1	2	3	4	5	6	7	8	9	10	11	12
Daughter	8	8	7.5	8	9	9	8.5	9	9	8	7	8
Mother	7	7	7.5	8	8.5	8.5	7.5	7.5	6	8	7	7

10.15 A newly installed automatic gate system was being tested to see if the number of failures in 1,000 entry attempts was the same as the number of failures in 1,000 exit attempts. A random sample of eight delivery trucks was selected for data collection. Do these sample results show that there is a true difference, on average, between entry and exit gate failures? Use $\alpha = 0.01$. (LO 4) 🔵 **Gates**

	Truck 1	Truck 2	Truck 3	Truck 4	Truck 5	Truck 6	Truck 7	Truck 8
Entry failures	43	45	53	56	61	51	48	44
Exit failures	48	51	60	58	58	45	55	50

10.16 Currently, a large Canadian electronics store chain pays its salespeople an hourly wage with no commissions. In an attempt to increase sales, the chain is considering paying the same hourly wage plus a 5 percent commission on sales. It will only implement this strategy if there is sufficient evidence in a small study to indicate that average weekly sales per salesperson will increase by more than $2,000. To conduct this study, five pairs of salespeople, matched according to similar levels of sales without commissions being offered. During one selected week, five of these salespeople were paid salary only while the other five were paid salary plus sales commission. Their weekly sales (in $1,000s) were recorded as follows:

	Pair A	Pair B	Pair C	Pair D	Pair E
With commission	4.7	7.2	6.4	10.4	6.1
Salary only	2.3	4.1	4.0	7.8	4.4

At the 0.01 level of significance, is there sufficient evidence that the chain should change its wage policy to hourly wage plus commission? Justify your answer. Estimate the p value of this test using a t table. Estimate, with 99 percent confidence, the true difference in average weekly sales between those salespeople with commission and those with salary only. (LO 4)

10.5 Comparing Two Proportions

The test for two proportions is the simplest and perhaps most commonly used two-sample test, because percents are ubiquitous. Is the prime minister's approval rating greater, lower, or the same as last month? Is the proportion of satisfied Dell customers greater than Gateway's? Is the annual nursing turnover percentage at Winnipeg's Seven Oaks General Hospital higher, lower, or the same as at Victoria General Hospital? To answer such questions, we would compare two sample proportions.

Testing for Zero Difference: $\pi_1 = \pi_2$

Let the true proportions in the two populations be denoted π_1 and π_2. To compare the two population proportions, the pairs of possible hypotheses are

Left-Tailed Test	*Two-Tailed Test*	*Right-Tailed Test*
$H_0: \pi_1 = \pi_2$	$H_0: \pi_1 = \pi_2$	$H_0: \pi_1 = \pi_2$
$H_1: \pi_1 < \pi_2$	$H_1: \pi_1 \neq \pi_2$	$H_1: \pi_1 > \pi_2$

As with previous test statistics, the test statistic would simply be the relationship between the best estimator and the parameter of interest assuming the null hypothesis were true. The relationship between the best estimator $P_1 - P_2$ and the parameter $\pi_1 - \pi_2$ was developed in Section 10.1 to be

$$z = \frac{(p_1 - p_2) - (\pi_1 - \pi_2)}{\sqrt{\frac{\pi_1(1 - \pi_1)}{n_1} + \frac{\pi_2(1 - \pi_2)}{n_2}}}$$

Assuming that the null hypothesis is true (i.e., $\pi_1 = \pi_2$ or $\pi_1 - \pi_2 = 0$), this relationship becomes

$$z = \frac{(p_1 - p_2) - 0}{\sqrt{\dfrac{\pi(1 - \pi)}{n_1} + \dfrac{\pi(1 - \pi)}{n_2}}}$$

if normality can be assumed (i.e., if the samples are large).

You will notice that we dropped the subscripts for the two population proportions, because if the null hypothesis is true, the proportions are the same and there is no need to distinguish between the two. But, knowing what H_0 is does not tell us what the value of the two proportions are, requiring us to estimate their common value before being able to calculate the test statistic. A logical thing to do would be to combine both samples into one and use this sample's proportion of successes, symbolized by $\bar{p}$, where

$$\bar{p} = \frac{x_1 + x_2}{n_1 + n_2} = \frac{\text{number of successes in combined samples}}{\text{combined sample size}} \quad (\textbf{pooled proportion})$$

Alternatively, knowing the sample proportions we can use a weighted average, weighted by their sample sizes, and arrive at the same estimate, which in this case would be determined using

$$\bar{p} = \frac{n_1 p_1 + n_2 p_2}{n_1 + n_2}$$

Concept Check

Show why the two formulas for $\bar{p}$ would result in the same value.

Test Statistic

If the samples are large, using the above relationship and the pooled estimates of the proportion of successes, assuming the null hypothesis is true (no difference in proportions), the test statistic can be calculated using

$$z_{\text{calc}} = \frac{p_1 - p_2}{\sqrt{\dfrac{\bar{p}(1 - \bar{p})}{n_1} + \dfrac{\bar{p}(1 - \bar{p})}{n_2}}} \quad (\text{test statistic for equality of proportions})$$

If you find it easier for computation, the test statistic may also be written

$$z_{\text{calc}} = \frac{p_1 - p_2}{\sqrt{\bar{p}(1 - \bar{p})\left(\dfrac{1}{n_1} + \dfrac{1}{n_2}\right)}}$$

A study showed 118 instances of breast cancer among 3,033 mothers who used diethylstilbestrol (DES), an estrogen-like substance formerly used to prevent miscarriage, compared with 80 cases in 3,033 unexposed women making up a control group (see Table 10.7). At the 0.01 level of significance, was the incidence of cancer greater in the DES users?

EXAMPLE 6
DES and Cancer

TABLE 10.7   Cancer Study Results

Statistic	DES Takers	Non-DES Takers
Number of cancers	$x_1 = 118$ cancers	$x_2 = 80$ cancers
Number of mothers	$n_1 = 3{,}033$ women	$n_2 = 3{,}033$ women
Cancer rate	$p_1 = \dfrac{118}{3{,}033} = 0.03891$	$p_2 = \dfrac{80}{3{,}033} = 0.02638$

Source: *Science News* 126, no. 22 (1984), p. 343.

STEP 1: STATE THE HYPOTHESES

Because it is suspected that DES increases the cancer risk, we will do a right-tailed test for equality of proportions.

$$H_0: \pi_1 = \pi_2 \text{ or } H_0: \pi_1 - \pi_2 = 0$$
$$H_1: \pi_1 > \pi_2 \text{ or } H_1: \pi_1 - \pi_2 > 0$$

STEP 2: SPECIFY THE DECISION RULE

At $\alpha = 0.01$ the right-tail critical value is $z_{0.01} = 2.326$, which yields the decision rule

Reject H_0 if $z_{calc} > 2.326$.

Otherwise do not reject H_0.

The decision rule is illustrated in Figure 10.11. Because Excel uses cumulative left-tail areas, the right-tail critical value $z_{0.01} = 2.326$ is obtained using =NORMSINV(0.99).

STEP 3: CALCULATE THE TEST STATISTIC

The sample proportions indicate that DES-users have a higher incidence of breast cancer (0.03891) than non-DES users (0.02638). We assume that $\pi_1 = \pi_2$ and see if a contradiction stems from this assumption. Assuming that $\pi_1 = \pi_2$, we can pool the two samples to obtain a pooled estimate of the common proportion by dividing the combined number of breast cancer cases by the combined sample size:

$$\bar{p} = \frac{x_1 + x_2}{n_1 + n_2} = \frac{118 + 80}{3{,}033 + 3{,}033} = \frac{198}{6{,}066} = 0.03264, \text{ or } 3.26\%$$

Assuming normality (i.e., large samples) the test statistic is

$$z_{calc} = \frac{p_1 - p_2}{\sqrt{\bar{p}(1 - \bar{p})\left[\dfrac{1}{n_1} + \dfrac{1}{n_2}\right]}} = \frac{0.03891 - 0.02638}{\sqrt{0.03264(1 - 0.03264)\left[\dfrac{1}{3{,}033} + \dfrac{1}{3{,}033}\right]}} = 2.746$$

STEP 4: MAKE THE DECISION

If H_0 is true, the test statistic should be near zero. Because the test statistic ($z_{calc} = 2.746$) exceeds the critical value ($z_{0.01} = 2.326$), we reject the null hypothesis and conclude that $\pi_1 > \pi_2$. Because we are able to reject the hypothesis $\pi_1 = \pi_2$, we can also reject the entire class of hypotheses $\pi_1 \leq \pi_2$ at $\alpha = 0.01$, that is, DES users have a significantly higher cancer rate than non-DES users.

Using the p Value

We can find the right-tail area for $z_{calc} = 2.746$ by using the function =1−NORMSDIST(2.746) in Excel:

$$P(Z > 2.746) = 1 - 0.9970 = 0.0030 \quad \text{(from Excel)}$$

This p value of 0.003 is the level of significance that would allow us to reject H_0. The p value says that if H_0 were true, a sample result as extreme as ours would happen by chance approxi-

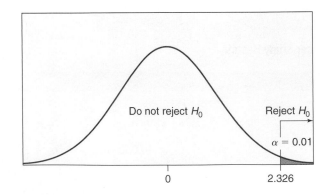

FIGURE 10.11

Right-Tailed Test for Two Proportions

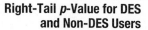

FIGURE 10.12

Right-Tail *p*-Value for DES and Non-DES Users

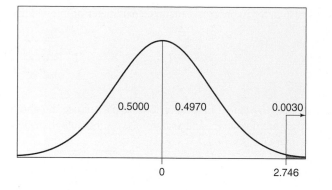

mately 3 times in 1,000 decisions. If we don't have Excel, we can obtain the same result from Appendix C even though it requires rounding the *z* value slightly to two digits:

$$P(Z > 2.75) = 0.5 - 0.4970 = 0.0030 \text{ (from Appendix C)}$$

Because the *p* value (0.0030) is less than the chosen level of significance ($\alpha = 0.01$), we would reject H_0 in a right-tailed test. The advantage of the *p* value approach is that it gives more information and lets different researchers choose their own α values. For example, Health Canada might have a different view of a Type I error than a cancer patient. The *p* value directly shows our chance of Type I error if we reject H_0. *A smaller p value indicates a more significant difference.* Figure 10.12 illustrates the *p* value.

Checking Normality

We have assumed a normal distribution for the statistic $p_1 - p_2$. This assumption can be checked. For a test of two proportions, the criterion for normality is $n \geq 9\dfrac{\pi}{1 - \pi}, n \geq 9\dfrac{1 - \pi}{\pi}$ for *each* sample, using each sample proportion in place of π. The normality requirement is comfortably fulfilled in this case.

Using Software for Calculations

Given the tedium of the calculations, it is desirable to use software. MegaStat gives you the option of entering sample proportions or the fractions. MINITAB gives you the option of non-pooled proportions, which we will discuss shortly. Figure 10.13 illustrates their data-entry screens using the DES data.

Confidence Interval for Difference of Two Population Proportions $\pi_1 - \pi_2$

We develop the confidence interval for $\pi_1 - \pi_2$ in the same way as we developed all other confidence intervals where the *z* distribution was involved. While incorporating the level of confidence, $1 - \alpha$, with the *z* distribution, we manipulate the relationship between the parameter of

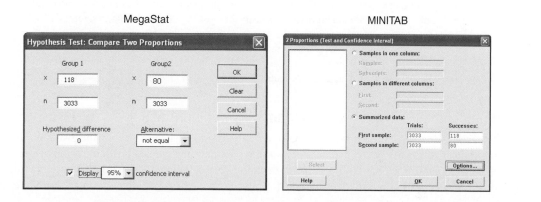

FIGURE 10.13

Two Proportion Tests Using MegaStat and MINITAB

interest and its best estimator in order to isolate the parameter of interest. Doing so in this particular case gives

$$z = \frac{(p_1 - p_2) - (\pi_1 - \pi_2)}{\sqrt{\dfrac{\pi_1(1 - \pi_1)}{n_1} + \dfrac{\pi_2(1 - \pi_2)}{n_2}}} \quad \rightarrow \quad (p_1 - p_2) \pm z_{\alpha/2}\sqrt{\frac{\pi_1(1 - \pi_1)}{n_1} + \frac{\pi_2(1 - \pi_2)}{n_2}}$$

As with estimating a single population proportion, we cannot use the above formula because the values of π_1 and π_2 are unknown, and as before, we substitute their best estimates, resulting in a confidence interval of

$$(p_1 - p_2) \pm z_{\alpha/2}\sqrt{\frac{p_1(1 - p_1)}{n_1} + \frac{p_2(1 - p_2)}{n_2}} \qquad (10.6)$$

(As before, to use the z distribution, we assume n_1 and n_2 are large enough such that

$$n \geq 9\frac{\pi}{1 - \pi} \text{ and } n \geq 9\frac{1 - \pi}{\pi} \text{ for each sample.})$$

EXAMPLE 7

Fire Truck Colour

Compared to a traditional red fire truck, does a bright yellow fire truck have a lower accident rate? Proponents of the brighter yellow colour argued that its enhanced visibility allowed other traffic to see the trucks and avoid them during fire runs. A four-year study in Dallas, Texas, produced the statistics shown in Table 10.8.

TABLE 10.8 Accident Rate for Dallas Fire Trucks

Statistic	Red Fire Trucks	Yellow Fire Trucks
Number of accidents	$x_1 = 20$ accidents	$x_2 = 4$ accidents
Number of fire runs	$n_1 = 153{,}348$ runs	$n_2 = 135{,}035$ runs
Accident rate	$p_1 = \dfrac{20}{153{,}348} = 0.000130422$	$p_2 = \dfrac{4}{135{,}035} = 0.000029622$

Source: *The Wall Street Journal*, June 26, 1995, p. B1.

Although the conditions necessary to assume normality may not be satisfied in this case, we will assume they are, in order to calculate the confidence interval. The 95 percent confidence interval for the difference between the proportions is

$$(p_1 - p_2) \pm z_{\alpha/2}\sqrt{\frac{p_1(1 - p_1)}{n_1} + \frac{p_2(1 - p_2)}{n_2}}$$

$$= (0.000130422 - 0.000029622)$$

$$\pm (1.960)\sqrt{\frac{(0.000130422)(0.999869578)}{153{,}348} + \frac{(0.000029622)(0.999970378)}{135{,}035}}$$

$$= 0.00003669 < \pi_1 - \pi_2 < 0.0001649$$

Because the confidence interval for $\pi_1 - \pi_2$ does not include zero, it appears that the accident rates are significantly different. Should all fire trucks be painted yellow? With such large samples, no one could say that this was a "small sample" fluke. However, both accident rates are quite small to begin with, an argument used by those who favour the traditional red colour. A greater problem, the critics say, is that the public has become inured to sirens and flashing lights. As often happens, statistics may play only a small part in the policy decision.

Analogy between Confidence Intervals and Hypothesis Tests

Especially for two-tailed tests, the analogy between confidence intervals and two sample hypothesis tests is very strong. The main difference that may cause conflicting conclusions in some situations is the way the standard deviations are calculated. We estimate the standard deviation using the confidence interval formula for $\pi_1 - \pi_2$ *without pooling the sample*

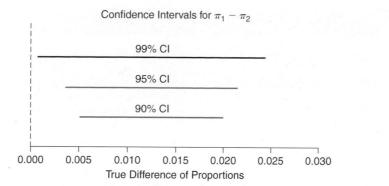

FIGURE 10.14

Confidence Intervals for Difference of Proportions

proportions, while in hypothesis testing, we pool the sample proportions when estimating the standard deviation.

In the DES and cancer example (Example 6), plugging in $p_1 = 118/3{,}033$ and $p_2 = 80/3{,}033$, we obtain confidence intervals for $\pi_1 - \pi_2$ shown below (calculations not shown).

Confidence Level	*Confidence Interval for $\pi_1 - \pi_2$*
90% ($z = \pm 1.645$)	$0.00503 < \pi_1 - \pi_2 < 0.02003$
95% ($z = \pm 1.960$)	$0.00359 < \pi_1 - \pi_2 < 0.02147$
99% ($z = \pm 2.576$)	$0.00078 < \pi_1 - \pi_2 < 0.02428$

All three confidence intervals for the difference of proportions fail to include zero, suggesting rejection of $H_0: \pi_1 - \pi_2 = 0$. These confidence intervals are more vivid if displayed graphically, as in Figure 10.14. Although none of the confidence intervals includes zero, the 99 percent confidence interval *almost* does, so our rejection of $H_0: \pi_1 - \pi_2 = 0$ would be a close call for 99 percent confidence and a two-tailed test.

To test for equal population proportions, you might wonder why we don't just construct a confidence interval for π_1 (as we did in Chapter 8) and then do the same for π_2. If the intervals overlap, would that not suggest that the population proportions are the same? Although intuitively appealing, researchers have found that this method fails to maintain the desired Type I error. So it is better to use Equation 10.6 to construct a single confidence interval for the difference $\pi_1 - \pi_2$.

Mini Case   10.2

How Does Noodles & Company Provide Value to Customers?

Value perception is an important concept for all companies, but it is especially relevant for consumer-oriented industries such as retail and restaurants. Most retailers and restaurant concepts periodically make price increases to reflect changes in inflationary items such as cost of goods and labour costs. In 2006, however, Noodles & Company took the opposite approach when it evaluated its value perception through its consumers.

Through rigorous statistical analysis Noodles recognized that a significant percentage of current customers would increase their frequency of visits if the menu items were priced slightly lower. The company evaluated the trade-offs that a price decrease would represent and determined that they would actually be able to increase revenue by reducing price. Despite not advertising this price decrease, the company did in fact see an increase in frequency of visits resulting from the change. To measure the impact, the company statistically evaluated both the increase in frequency as well as customer evaluations of Noodles & Company's value perception. Within a few months, the statistical analysis showed that not only had customer frequency increased by 2 to 3 percent, but also that the improved value perception led to an increase in average party size of 2 percent. Ultimately, the price decrease of roughly 2 percent led to a total revenue increase of 4 to 5 percent.

Hint: Show all formulas and calculations, but use the calculator in *LearningStats* Unit 10 to check your work.

10.17 Find the sample proportions and test statistic for equal proportions. Is the decision close? Find the *p* value. (LO 2)
 a. Dissatisfied workers in two companies: $x_1 = 40$, $n_1 = 100$, $x_2 = 30$, $n_2 = 100$, $\alpha = 0.05$, two-tailed test.
 b. Rooms rented at least a week in advance at two hotels: $x_1 = 24$, $n_1 = 200$, $x_2 = 12$, $n_2 = 50$, $\alpha = 0.01$, left-tailed test.
 c. Home equity loan default rates in two banks: $x_1 = 36$, $n_1 = 480$, $x_2 = 26$, $n_2 = 520$, $\alpha = 0.05$, right-tailed test.

10.18 Find the test statistic and do the two-sample test for equality of proportions. Is the decision close? (LO 2)
 a. Repeat buyers at two car dealerships: $P_1 = 0.30$, $n_1 = 50$, $P_2 = 0.54$, $n_2 = 50$, $\alpha = 0.01$, left-tailed test.
 b. Honour roll students in two sororities: $P_1 = 0.45$, $n_1 = 80$, $P_2 = 0.25$, $n_2 = 48$, $\alpha = 0.10$, two-tailed test.
 c. First-time Niagara Falls visitors at two hotels: $P_1 = 0.20$, $n_1 = 80$, $P_2 = 0.32$, $n_2 = 75$, $\alpha = 0.05$, left-tailed test.

10.19 In 1999, a sample of 200 in-store shoppers showed that 42 paid by debit card. In 2004, a sample of the same size showed that 62 paid by debit card. (a) Formulate appropriate hypotheses to test whether the percentage of debit card shoppers increased. (b) Carry out the test at $\alpha = 0.01$. (c) Find the *p* value. (d) Test whether normality may be assumed. (LO 2)

10.20 A survey of 100 mayonnaise purchasers showed that 65 were loyal to one brand. For 100 bath soap purchasers, only 53 were loyal to one brand. (a) Perform a two-tailed test comparing the proportion of brand-loyal customers at $\alpha = 0.05$. (b) Form a confidence interval for the difference of proportions, without pooling the samples. Does it include zero? (LO 2)

10.21 A 20-minute consumer survey mailed to 500 adults aged 25–34 included a $5 Starbucks gift certificate. The same survey was mailed to 500 adults aged 25–34 without the gift certificate. There were 65 responses from the first group and 45 from the second group. (a) Perform a two-tailed test comparing the response rates (proportions) at $\alpha = 0.05$. (b) Form a confidence interval for the difference of proportions, without pooling the samples. Does it include zero? (LO 2)

10.22 Is the water on your airline flight safe to drink? It is not feasible to analyze the water on every flight, so sampling is necessary. In August and September 2004, the U.S. Environmental Protection Agency (EPA) found bacterial contamination in water samples from the lavatories and galley water taps on 20 of 158 randomly selected U.S. flights. Alarmed by the data, the EPA ordered sanitation improvements, and then tested water samples again in November and December 2004. In the second sample, bacterial contamination was found in 29 of 169 randomly sampled flights. (a) At $\alpha = 0.05$, can we conclude that the percent of all flights with contaminated water was lower in the first sample? (b) Find the *p* value. (c) Discuss the question of significance versus importance in this specific application. (d) Test whether normality may be assumed. (Data are from *The Wall Street Journal,* Nov. 10, 2004, and Jan. 20, 2005.) (LO 2)

10.23 In an attempt to keep their current customers and attract new ones, companies are always coming up with "new and improved" versions of their products. But do these products improve the level of satisfaction among its customers? To see whether a new version of its leading product is accomplishing the management goal, an Ontario company conducted a study. This study looked at levels of satisfaction both with the older and the newer versions of this product. Before the new version was put on the market, a random sample of 300 users of the old version revealed that 220 were satisfied with the product and would continue purchasing it. After the new version was introduced, a random sample of 200 users of the new version revealed that 152 were satisfied and would continue purchasing it. At the 0.05 level of significance, is there sufficient evidence that the company is accomplishing what it wants to accomplish with this "new and improved" version? Calculate the *p* value of this test. (LO 2)

10.24 The American Bankers Association reports that in a sample of 120 consumer purchases in France, 60 were made with cash, compared with 26 in a sample of 50 consumer purchases in the United States. Construct a 90 percent confidence interval for the difference in proportions. (Data are from *The Wall Street Journal,* July 27, 2004.) (LO 2)

10.25 A study showed that 120 of 240 cellphone users with a headset missed their exit, compared with 30 of 240 talking to a passenger. Construct a 95 percent confidence interval for the difference in proportions. (LO 2)

10.26 A survey of 100 cigarette smokers showed that 71 were loyal to one brand, compared to 122 of 200 toothpaste users. Construct a 90 percent confidence interval for the difference in proportions. (Data are from J. Paul Peter and Jerry C. Olson, *Consumer Behavior and Marketing Strategy,* 7th ed. [McGraw-Hill, 2005], p. 97.) (LO 2)

10.27 A study comparing Canadian and American attitudes toward government-run universal health care revealed that 150 out of 200 Canadians supported this system of health care while only 25 out of 100 Americans support this system. Estimate, with 95 percent confidence, the difference in the proportions, between Canadians and Americans, who support government-run universal health care. (LO 2)

Testing for Non-Zero Difference (Optional)

While testing the null hypothesis of equal population proportions is the most common null hypothesis for testing two proportions, we may also want to test for some other specified difference, d_0. Here, the three forms of the hypotheses pair are:

Left-Tailed Test	Two-Tailed Test	Right-Tailed Test
$H_0: \pi_1 - \pi_2 = d_0$	$H_0: \pi_1 - \pi_2 = d_0$	$H_0: \pi_1 - \pi_2 = d_0$
$H_1: \pi_1 - \pi_2 < d_0$	$H_1: \pi_1 - \pi_2 \neq d_0$	$H_1: \pi_1 - \pi_2 > d_0$

When $d_0 = 0$, that is, $\pi_1 = \pi_2$, we used a common estimate of the two proportions when estimating the standard deviation of $P_1 - P_2$. If the hypothesized difference d_0 is non-zero, the two proportions are not equal and, thus, we use their individual estimates resulting in the test statistic shown in Equation 10.7.

$$z_{calc} = \frac{p_1 - p_2 - d_0}{\sqrt{\dfrac{p_1(1 - p_1)}{n_1} + \dfrac{p_2(1 - p_2)}{n_2}}} \quad \text{(test statistic for non-zero difference } d_0\text{)} \qquad \textbf{(10.7)}$$

EXAMPLE 8

Magazine Ads

A sample of 111 magazine advertisements in *Good Housekeeping* showed 70 that listed a Web site. In *Fortune*, a sample of 145 advertisements showed 131 that listed a Web site. At $\alpha = 0.025$, does the *Fortune* proportion differ from the *Good Housekeeping* proportion by more than 20 percent? Table 10.9 shows the data.

TABLE 10.9   Magazine Ads with Web Sites

Statistic	Fortune	Good Housekeeping
Number with Web sites	$x_1 = 131$ with Web site	$x_2 = 70$ with Web site
Number of ads examined	$n_1 = 145$ ads	$n_2 = 111$ ads
Proportion	$p_1 = \dfrac{131}{145} = 0.90345$	$p_2 = \dfrac{70}{111} = 0.63063$

Source: Project by MBA students Frank George, Karen Orso, and Lincy Zachariah.

TEST STATISTIC

Based on the question asked, we will do a right-tailed test where $d_0 = 0.20$. The hypotheses are

$$H_0: \pi_1 - \pi_2 = 0.20$$
$$H_1: \pi_1 - \pi_2 > 0.20$$

The test statistic is

$$z_{calc} = \frac{p_1 - p_2 - d_0}{\sqrt{\dfrac{p_1(1 - p_1)}{n_1} + \dfrac{p_2(1 - p_2)}{n_2}}}$$

$$= \frac{0.90345 - 0.63063 - 0.20}{\sqrt{\dfrac{0.90345(1 - 0.90345)}{145} + \dfrac{0.63063(1 - 0.63063)}{111}}} = 1.401$$

At $\alpha = 0.025$ the right-tail critical value is $z_{0.025} = 1.960$, so the difference of proportions is insufficient to reject the hypothesis that the difference is 0.20 or less. The decision rule is illustrated in Figure 10.15.

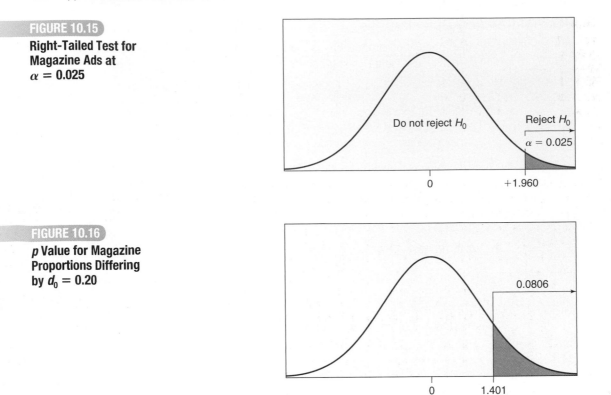

FIGURE 10.15

Right-Tailed Test for Magazine Ads at $\alpha = 0.025$

FIGURE 10.16

p Value for Magazine Proportions Differing by $d_0 = 0.20$

Calculating the p Value

Using the p value approach, we would insert the test statistic $z_{calc} = 1.401$ into Excel's cumulative normal =1–NORMSDIST(1.401) to obtain a right-tail area of 0.0806 as shown in Figure 10.16. Because the p value > 0.025, we would not reject H_0. The conclusion is that the difference in proportions is not greater than 0.20.

Section Exercises

10.28 In 1999, a sample of 200 in-store shoppers showed that 42 paid by debit card. In 2004, a sample of the same size showed that 62 paid by debit card. (a) Formulate the appropriate hypotheses and test whether the percentage of debit card shoppers increased by more than 5 percent, using $\alpha = 0.10$. (b) Find the p value. (LO 2)

10.29 From a telephone log, an executive finds that 36 of 128 incoming telephone calls last week lasted at least 5 minutes. She vows to make an effort to reduce the length of time spent on calls. The phone log for the next week shows that 14 of 96 incoming calls lasted at least 5 minutes. (a) At $\alpha = 0.05$, has the proportion of 5-minute phone calls declined by more than 10 percent? (b) Find the p value. (LO 2)

10.30 A 30-minute consumer survey mailed to 500 adults aged 25–34 included a $10 gift certificate to Chapters. The same survey was mailed to 500 adults aged 25–34 without the gift certificate. There were 185 responses from the first group and 45 from the second group. (a) At $\alpha = 0.025$, did the gift certificate increase the response rate by more than 20 percent? (b) Find the p value. (LO 2)

10.31 Unscientific evidence suggests that Canadian customers phoning a company for information don't like to listen to several automated instructions before direct conversations with a customer representative. One particular Canadian company is considering changing its automated system to a system in which customers have direct contact with representatives immediately after they answer, whether they want service in English or in French. But it will only do so if there is sufficient scientific evidence that this new personal system will increase the proportion of satisfied customers by more than 15 percent. In an attempt to gather this evidence, it randomly selected 100 recent customers who phoned its service number, and through a follow-up phone call, it found that only 43 were satisfied with the service they received. It also used direct access to representatives for 150 randomly selected phone calls. On follow-up, it was determined that 94 were satisfied with the service they received. At the 0.05 level of significance, is there sufficient evidence to suggest that this company will change to the more personal system? Calculate the p value of this test. (LO 2)

TABLE 10.10   **Proportion of Failed Gate Activations**

Statistic	Campus 1	Campus 2
Number of failed activations	$x_1 = 52$	$x_2 = 63$
Sample size (number of entry/exit attempts)	$n_1 = 1{,}000$	$n_2 = 1{,}000$
Proportion	$p_1 = \dfrac{52}{1{,}000} = 0.052$	$p_2 = \dfrac{63}{1{,}000} = 0.063$

 Mini Case   **10.3**

Automated Parking Lot Entry/Exit Gate System

Large universities have many different parking lots. Delivery trucks travel between various buildings all day long to deliver food, mail, and other items. Automated entry/exit gates make travel time much faster for the trucks and cars entering and exiting the different parking lots because the drivers do not have to stop to activate the gate manually. The gate is electronically activated as the truck or car approaches the parking lot.

One large university with two campuses recently negotiated with a company to install a new automated system. One requirement of the contract stated that the proportion of failed gate activations on one campus would be no different from the proportion of failed gate activations on the second campus. (A failed activation was one in which the driver had to manually activate the gate.) The university facilities operations manager designed and conducted a test to establish whether the gate company had violated this requirement of the contract. The university could renegotiate the contract if there was significant evidence showing that the two proportions were different.

The test was set up as a two-tailed test and the hypotheses tested were

$$H_0: \pi_1 = \pi_2$$
$$H_1: \pi_1 \neq \pi_2$$

Both the university and the gate company agreed on a 5 percent level of significance. Random samples from each campus were collected. The data are shown in Table 10.10. The pooled proportion is

$$\bar{p} = \frac{x_1 + x_2}{n_1 + n_2} = \frac{52 + 63}{1{,}000 + 1{,}000} = \frac{115}{2{,}000} = 0.0575$$

The test statistic is

$$z_{calc} = \frac{p_1 - p_2}{\sqrt{\bar{p}(1 - \bar{p})\left[\dfrac{1}{n_1} + \dfrac{1}{n_2}\right]}} = \frac{0.052 - 0.063}{\sqrt{0.0575(1 - 0.0575)\left[\dfrac{1}{1{,}000} + \dfrac{1}{1{,}000}\right]}} = -1.057$$

Using the 5 percent level of significance the critical value is $z_{0.025} = \pm 1.96$, so it is clear that there is no significant difference between these two proportions. This conclusion is reinforced by Excel's cumulative normal function =NORMSDIST(−1.057), which gives the area to the left of −1.057 as 0.1453. Because this is a two-tailed test, the p value is 0.2906.

Was it reasonable to assume normality of the test statistic? Yes, the criterion was met.

$$n_1 \geq 9\left(\frac{p_1}{1 - p_1}\right) = 9\left(\frac{0.052}{0.948}\right) = 0.49, \, n_1 \geq 9\left(\frac{1 - p_1}{p_1}\right) = 9\left(\frac{0.948}{0.052}\right) = 164.08$$

$$n_2 \geq 9\left(\frac{p_2}{1 - p_2}\right) = 9\left(\frac{0.063}{0.937}\right) = 0.61, \, n_2 \geq 9\left(\frac{1 - p_2}{p_2}\right) = 9\left(\frac{0.937}{0.063}\right) = 133.86$$

Based on this sample, the university had no evidence to refute the gate company's claim that the failed activation proportions were the same for each campus.

Source: This case was based on a real contract negotiation between a large western university and a private company. The contract was still being negotiated as of the publication of this text.

Chapter 10

10.6 Comparing Two Variances

The business statistician knows that comparing the *variances* may be as important as comparing the *means* of two populations. In manufacturing, smaller variation around the mean would indicate a more reliable product. In finance, smaller variation around the mean would indicate less volatility in asset returns. In services, smaller variation around the mean would indicate more consistency in customer treatment. For example, is the *variance* in Ford Mustang assembly times the same this month as last month? Is the *variability* in customer waiting times the same at two Tim Hortons franchises? Is the *variation* the same for customer concession purchases at a movie theatre on Friday and Saturday nights?

When comparing two population variances, we don't look at their differences as we did when comparing two population means or two population proportions. We look at σ_1^2/σ_2^2, because we know the relationship between this ratio and its sample estimator, S_1^2/S_2^2. If the two sample variances are independent of one another and the populations are normally distributed, then, as stated in Section 10.1, random variable F can be expressed as

$$F = \frac{S_1^2/S_2^2}{\sigma_1^2/\sigma_2^2}$$

where F has an **F distribution** (named for Ronald A. Fisher [1890–1962], one of the most famous statisticians of all time) with two sets of degrees of freedom, $v_1 = n_1 - 1$ and $v_2 = n_2 - 1$. When looking at the F distribution, it is somewhat similar to the x^2 distribution in that it is a right-skewed distribution with a minimum value of zero.

To be able to use this relationship to test hypotheses for σ_1^2/σ_2^2, we need to be able to equate values of F with probabilities. As with the x^2 distribution, we will equate values of F with probabilities in the right tail (or with probabilities to the right of the value of F). That is, we need to be able to determine F_A such that $P(F > F_A) = A$. Appendix F allows us to determine F_{A, v_1, v_2} for values of $A = 0.10, 0.05, 0.025,$ and 0.01 for various values of v_1 and v_2, while Excel and other statistical packages are more flexible. For, example, suppose we want to find the value of F when the area in the right tail is 0.05, $v_1 = 7$, and $v_2 = 9$. To use Appendix F, we first have to locate the pages where the area in the right tail is 0.05. We then find the $v_1 = 7$ column and the $v_2 = 9$ row, and where that row and column intersect we read the value of F, $F_{0.05,7,9} = 3.29$.

Now suppose we want to find the value of F when the area in the right tail is 0.95 (or when the area in the left tail is 0.05), $v_1 = 7$, and $v_2 = 9$. Unlike the x^2 table, 0.95 is not one of the areas listed in Appendix F. To find this value of F, we use the table for $A = 0.05$ and use the following relationship:

$$F_{1-A,v_1,v_2} = \frac{1}{F_{A,v_2,v_1}}$$

Essentially, we are taking the reciprocal of F_A after reversing the two degrees of freedom. Or, in this example,

$$F_{0.95,7,9} = \frac{1}{F_{0.05,9,7}} = \frac{1}{3.68} \approx 0.272$$

Format of Hypotheses

When comparing two population variances using hypothesis testing, the null hypothesis, as done in Chapter 9, states that the two population variances are equal. But we can test the null hypothesis against a left-tailed, two-tailed, or right-tailed alternative:

Left-Tailed Test	Two-Tailed Test	Right-Tailed Test
$H_0: \sigma_1^2 = \sigma_2^2$	$H_0: \sigma_1^2 = \sigma_2^2$	$H_0: \sigma_1^2 = \sigma_2^2$
$H_1: \sigma_1^2 < \sigma_2^2$	$H_1: \sigma_1^2 = \sigma_2^2$	$H_1: \sigma_1^2 > \sigma_2^2$

An equivalent way to state these hypotheses is to look at the *ratio* of the two variances. A ratio near 1 would indicate equal variances.

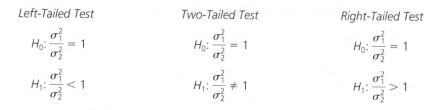

Left-Tailed Test

$$H_0: \frac{\sigma_1^2}{\sigma_2^2} = 1$$

$$H_1: \frac{\sigma_1^2}{\sigma_2^2} < 1$$

Two-Tailed Test

$$H_0: \frac{\sigma_1^2}{\sigma_2^2} = 1$$

$$H_1: \frac{\sigma_1^2}{\sigma_2^2} \neq 1$$

Right-Tailed Test

$$H_0: \frac{\sigma_1^2}{\sigma_2^2} = 1$$

$$H_1: \frac{\sigma_1^2}{\sigma_2^2} > 1$$

As with previous tests, our test statistic is the relationship between the statistic and the parameter of interest if the null hypothesis is true. In this case, the test statistic becomes

$$F = \frac{S_1^2/S_2^2}{\sigma_1^2/\sigma_2^2} = \frac{S_1^2/S_2^2}{1} = \frac{S_1^2}{S_2^2}$$

and the value of the test statistic becomes

$$F_{calc} = \frac{s_1^2}{s_2^2}$$

As before, we ask ourselves what we would expect from the test statistic if the null hypothesis is true. In this case, if the null hypothesis of equal variances is true, this ratio should be near 1 or $F_{calc} \approx 1$ (if H_0 is true). We would reject the null hypothesis depending on the form of the alternative hypothesis. If $H_1: \sigma_1^2 < \sigma_2^2$ we would reject the null hypothesis if F_{calc} is much less than 1 (because less than 1 is what we would expect if H_1 is true). If $H_1: \sigma_1^2 \neq \sigma_2^2$ we would reject the null hypothesis if F_{calc} is much less than or much greater than 1 (because different than 1 is what we would expect if H_1 is true). If $H_1: \sigma_1^2 > \sigma_2^2$ we would reject the null hypothesis if F_{calc} is much greater than 1 (because greater than 1 is what we would expect if H_1 is true). (See *LearningStats* Unit 10 for more details about the F distribution.)

Critical Values

Critical values for the **F test** are denoted by the area in the test's right tail and the two degrees of freedom. Based upon the form of the test, the α used, and the two sample sizes, the critical values of F will be

$$F_{crit} = F_{1-\alpha,\nu_1,\nu_2} \text{ if } H_1: \frac{\sigma_1^2}{\sigma_2^2} < 1$$

$$F_{crit} = F_{1-\alpha/2,\nu_1,\nu_2} \text{ and } F_{\alpha/2,\nu_1,\nu_2} \text{ if } H_1: \frac{\sigma_1^2}{\sigma_2^2} \neq 1$$

or

$$F_{crit} = F_{\alpha,\nu_1,\nu_2} \text{ if } H_1: \frac{\sigma_1^2}{\sigma_2^2} > 1$$

Figure 10.17 illustrates the rejection region for a two-tailed test.

Excel will give the appropriate critical values using the FINV function and the appropriate right-tail areas and degrees of freedom.

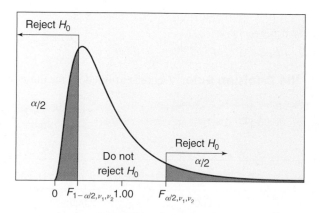

FIGURE 10.17

Critical Values for *F* Test for Variances

TABLE 10.11 Repair Cost (\$) for Accident Damage Damage

Experimental Vehicles	Control Vehicles
1,973	1,185
403	885
509	2,955
2,103	815
1,153	2,852
292	1,217
1,916	1,762
1,602	2,592
1,559	1,632
547	
801	
359	
$\bar{x}_1 = \$1,101.42$	$\bar{x}_2 = \$1,766.11$
$s_1 = \$696.20$	$s_2 = \$837.62$
$n_1 = 12$ incidents	$n_2 = 9$ incidents

Source: Unpublished study by Floyd G. Willoughby and Thomas W. Lauer, Oakland University.

Illustration: Collision Damage

An experimental bumper was designed to reduce damage in low-speed collisions. This bumper was installed on an experimental group of vans in a large fleet, but not on a control group. At the end of a trial period, accident data showed 12 repair incidents (a "repair incident" is a repair invoice) for the experimental vehicles and 9 repair incidents for the control group vehicles. Table 10.11 shows the dollar cost of the repair incidents.

The same data set could be used to compare either the means or the variances. A dot plot of the two samples, shown in Figure 10.18, suggests that the new bumper may have reduced the *mean* damage. However, the firm was also interested in whether the *variance* in damage had changed. The null hypothesis is that the variances are the same for the control group and the experimental group. We can use the F test to test the hypothesis of equal variances.

Comparison of Variances: Two-Tailed Test

Do the sample variances refute the idea of equal variances in the population? We will perform a two-tailed test.

Step 1: State the Hypotheses   For a two-tailed test for equality of variances, the hypotheses are

$$H_0: \sigma_1^2 = \sigma_2^2 \text{ or } H_0: \sigma_1^2/\sigma_2^2 = 1$$
$$H_1: \sigma_1^2 \neq \sigma_2^2 \text{ or } H_1: \sigma_1^2/\sigma_2^2 \neq 1$$

Step 2: Specify the Decision Rule   Degrees of freedom for the F test are

Numerator: $\nu_1 = n_1 - 1 = 12 - 1 = 11$
Denominator: $\nu_2 = n_2 - 1 = 9 - 1 = 8$

FIGURE 10.18

Dot Plots for Collision Repair Costs

 Damage

CRITICAL VALUES OF $F_{.025}$

This table shows the 2.5 percent right-tail critical values of F for the stated degrees of freedom (ν).

Denominator Degrees of Freedom (ν_2)	Numerator Degrees of Freedom (ν_1)										
	1	2	3	4	5	6	7	8	9	10	12
1	647.8	799.5	864.2	899.6	921.8	937.1	948.2	956.6	963.3	968.6	976.7
2	38.51	39.00	39.17	39.25	39.30	39.33	39.36	39.37	39.39	39.40	39.41
3	17.44	16.04	15.44	15.10	14.88	14.73	14.62	14.54	14.47	14.42	14.34
4	12.22	10.65	9.98	9.60	9.36	9.20	9.07	8.98	8.90	8.84	8.75
5	10.01	8.43	7.76	7.39	7.15	6.98	6.85	6.76	6.68	6.62	6.52
6	8.81	7.26	6.60	6.23	5.99	5.82	5.70	5.60	5.52	5.46	5.37
7	8.07	6.54	5.89	5.52	5.29	5.12	4.99	4.90	4.82	4.76	4.67
8	7.57	6.06	5.42	5.05	4.82	4.65	4.53	4.43	4.36	4.30	4.20
9	7.21	5.71	5.08	4.72	4.48	4.32	4.20	4.10	4.03	3.96	3.87
10	6.94	5.46	4.83	4.47	4.24	4.07	3.95	3.85	3.78	3.72	3.62
11	6.72	5.26	4.63	4.28	4.04	3.88	3.76	3.66	3.59	3.53	3.43
12	6.55	5.10	4.47	4.12	3.89	3.73	3.61	3.51	3.44	3.37	3.28
13	6.41	4.97	4.35	4.00	3.77	3.60	3.48	3.39	3.31	3.25	3.15
14	6.30	4.86	4.24	3.89	3.66	3.50	3.38	3.29	3.21	3.15	3.05
15	6.20	4.77	4.15	3.80	3.58	3.41	3.29	3.20	3.12	3.06	2.96

FIGURE 10.19

Critical Value for Right-Tail F for $\alpha/2 = 0.025$

For a two-tailed test, we split the α risk and put $\alpha/2$ in each tail. For $\alpha = 0.05$ we use Appendix F with $\alpha/2 = 0.025$. To avoid interpolating, we use the next lower degrees of freedom when the required entry is not found in Appendix F. This conservative practice will not increase the probability of Type I error. For example, because $F_{0.025,11,8}$ is not in the table, we use $F_{0.025,10,8}$, as shown in Figure 10.19.

$$F_{\text{crit}} = F_{\alpha/2,\nu_1,\nu_2} = F_{0.025,11,8} \approx F_{0.025,10,8} = 4.30 \text{ (right-tail critical value)}$$

Alternatively, we could use Excel to get $F_{\alpha/2,\nu_1,\nu_2} = $ FINV(.025,11,8) $= 4.243$ and $F_{1-\alpha/2,\nu_1,\nu_2} = $ FINV(.975,11,8) $= 0.273$. To find the left-tail critical value we reverse the numerator and denominator degrees of freedom, find the critical value from Appendix F, and take its reciprocal, as shown in Figure 10.20. (Excel's function =FINV returns a *right-tail* area.)

CRITICAL VALUES OF $F_{.025}$

This table shows the 2.5 percent right-tail critical values of F for the stated degrees of freedom (ν).

Denominator Degrees of Freedom (ν_2)	Numerator Degrees of Freedom (ν_1)										
	1	2	3	4	5	6	7	8	9	10	12
1	647.8	799.5	864.2	899.6	921.8	937.1	948.2	956.6	963.3	968.6	976.7
2	38.51	39.00	39.17	39.25	39.30	39.33	39.36	39.37	39.39	39.40	39.41
3	17.44	16.04	15.44	15.10	14.88	14.73	14.62	14.54	14.47	14.42	14.34
4	12.22	10.65	9.98	9.60	9.36	9.20	9.07	8.98	8.90	8.84	8.75
5	10.01	8.43	7.76	7.39	7.15	6.98	6.85	6.76	6.68	6.62	6.52
6	8.81	7.26	6.60	6.23	5.99	5.82	5.70	5.60	5.52	5.46	5.37
7	8.07	6.54	5.89	5.52	5.29	5.12	4.99	4.90	4.82	4.76	4.67
8	7.57	6.06	5.42	5.05	4.82	4.65	4.53	4.43	4.36	4.30	4.20
9	7.21	5.71	5.08	4.72	4.48	4.32	4.20	4.10	4.03	3.96	3.87
10	6.94	5.46	4.83	4.47	4.24	4.07	3.95	3.85	3.78	3.72	3.62
11	6.72	5.26	4.63	4.28	4.04	3.88	3.76	3.66	3.59	3.53	3.43
12	6.55	5.10	4.47	4.12	3.89	3.73	3.61	3.51	3.44	3.37	3.28
13	6.41	4.97	4.35	4.00	3.77	3.60	3.48	3.39	3.31	3.25	3.15
14	6.30	4.86	4.24	3.89	3.66	3.50	3.38	3.29	3.21	3.15	3.05
15	6.20	4.77	4.15	3.80	3.58	3.41	3.29	3.20	3.12	3.06	2.96

FIGURE 10.20

Critical Value for Left-Tail F for $\alpha/2 = 0.025$

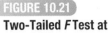

Two-Tailed _F_ Test at
$\alpha = 0.05$

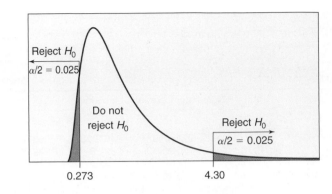

$$F_{\text{crit}} = F_{1-\alpha/2,\nu_1,\nu_2} = F_{0.975,11,8} = \frac{1}{F_{0.025,8,11}} = \frac{1}{3.66} \approx 0.273 \text{ (left-tail critical value)}$$

As shown in Figure 10.21, the two-tailed decision rule is

Reject H_0 if $F_{\text{calc}} < 0.273$ or if $F_{\text{calc}} > 4.30$.

Otherwise do not reject H_0.

Step 3: Calculate the Test Statistic   The test statistic is

$$F_{\text{calc}} = \frac{s_1^2}{s_2^2} = \frac{(696.20)^2}{(837.62)^2} = 0.691$$

Step 4: Make the Decision   Because $F_{\text{calc}} = 0.691$, we cannot reject the hypothesis of equal variances in a two-tailed test at $\alpha = 0.05$. In other words, the ratio of the sample variances does not differ significantly from 1. Because Excel's function =FDIST gives a *right-tail* area, the function you use for the p value will depend on the value of F_{calc}:

If $F_{\text{calc}} > 1$ Two-tailed p value is =2*FDIST(F_{calc}, df1, df2)

If $F_{\text{calc}} < 1$ Two-tailed p value is =2*FDIST(1/ F_{calc}, df2, df1)

For the bumper data, $F_{\text{calc}} = 0.691$ so Excel's two-tailed p value is =2*FDIST((1/0.691),8,11) = 0.5575.

Folded _F_ Test

We can make the two-tailed test for equal variances into a right-tailed test, so it is easier to look up the critical values in Appendix F. This method requires that we put the *larger observed variance* in the numerator, and then look up the critical value for $\alpha/2$ instead of the chosen α. The test statistic for the folded F test is

$$F_{\text{calc}} = \frac{s_{\text{larger}}^2}{s_{\text{smaller}}^2}$$

The larger variance goes in the numerator and the smaller variance in the denominator. *"Larger" refers to the variance (not to the sample size).* But the hypotheses are the same as for a two-tailed test:

$H_0: \sigma_1^2 = \sigma_2^2$
$H_1: \sigma_1^2 \neq \sigma_2^2$

For the bumper data, the second sample variance ($s_2^2 = 837.62$) is larger than the first sample variance ($s_1^2 = 696.20$), so the folded F test statistic is

$$F_{\text{calc}} = \frac{s_{\text{larger}}^2}{s_{\text{smaller}}^2} = \frac{s_2^2}{s_1^2} = \frac{(837.62)^2}{(696.20)^2} = 1.448$$

We must be careful that the degrees of freedom match the variances in the modified F statistic. In this case, the second sample variance is larger (it goes in the numerator), so we must reverse the degrees of freedom:

Numerator: $n_2 - 1 = 9 - 1 = 8$

Denominator: $n_1 - 1 = 12 - 1 = 11$

Now we look up the critical value for $F_{8,11}$ in Appendix F using $\alpha/2 = 0.05/2 = 0.025$:

$$F_{0.025} = 3.66$$

Because the test statistic $F_{calc} = 1.448$ does not exceed the critical value $F_{.025} = 3.66$, we cannot reject the hypothesis of equal variances. This is the same conclusion that we reached in the two-tailed test. Because $F_{calc} > 1$, Excel's two-tailed p value is $=2*$FDIST$(1.448,8,11)$ $= 0.5569$, which is the same as in the previous result except for rounding. Whenever you want a two-tailed F test, you may use the folded F test if you think it is easier.

Comparison of Variances: One-Tailed Test

In this case, the firm was interested in knowing whether the new bumper had *reduced* the variance in collision damage cost, so the consultant was asked to do a left-tailed test.

Step 1: State the Hypotheses   The hypotheses for a left-tailed test are

$H_0: \sigma_1^2 = \sigma_2^2$

$H_1: \sigma_1^2 < \sigma_2^2$

Step 2: Specify the Decision Rule   Degrees of freedom for the F test are the same as for a two-tailed test (the hypothesis doesn't affect the degrees of freedom):

Numerator: $\nu_1 = n_1 - 1 = 12 - 1 = 11$

Denominator: $\nu_2 = n_2 - 1 = 9 - 1 = 8$

However, now the entire $\alpha = 0.05$ goes in the left tail. We reverse the degrees of freedom and find the left-tail critical value from Appendix F as the reciprocal of the table value, as illustrated in Figures 10.22 and 10.23. Notice that the asymmetry of the F distribution causes the left-tail area to be compressed in the horizontal direction.

Right-Tail F_{crit} for $\alpha = 0.05$

CRITICAL VALUES OF $F_{.05}$

This table shows the 5 percent right-tail critical values of F for the stated degrees of freedom (ν).

Denominator Degrees of Freedom (ν_2)	Numerator Degrees of Freedom (ν_1)										
	1	2	3	4	5	6	7	8	9	10	12
1	161.4	199.5	215.7	224.6	230.2	234.0	236.8	238.9	240.5	241.9	243.9
2	18.51	19.00	19.16	19.25	19.30	19.33	19.35	19.37	19.38	19.40	19.41
3	10.13	9.55	9.28	9.12	9.01	8.94	8.89	8.85	8.81	8.79	8.74
4	7.71	6.94	6.59	6.39	6.26	6.16	6.09	6.04	6.00	5.96	5.91
5	6.61	5.79	5.41	5.19	5.05	4.95	4.88	4.82	4.77	4.74	4.68
6	5.99	5.14	4.76	4.53	4.39	4.28	4.21	4.15	4.10	4.06	4.00
7	5.59	4.74	4.35	4.12	3.97	3.87	3.79	3.73	3.68	3.64	3.57
8	5.32	4.46	4.07	3.84	3.69	3.58	3.50	3.44	3.39	3.35	3.28
9	5.12	4.26	3.86	3.63	3.48	3.37	3.29	3.23	3.18	3.14	3.07
10	4.96	4.10	3.71	3.48	3.33	3.22	3.14	3.07	3.02	2.98	2.91
11	4.84	3.98	3.59	3.36	3.20	3.09	3.01	2.95	2.90	2.85	2.79
12	4.75	3.89	3.49	3.26	3.11	3.00	2.91	2.85	2.80	2.75	2.69
13	4.67	3.81	3.41	3.18	3.03	2.92	2.83	2.77	2.71	2.67	2.60
14	4.60	3.74	3.34	3.11	2.96	2.85	2.76	2.70	2.65	2.60	2.53
15	4.54	3.68	3.29	3.06	2.90	2.79	2.71	2.64	2.59	2.54	2.48

FIGURE 10.23

Left-Tail F_{crit} for $\alpha = 0.05$

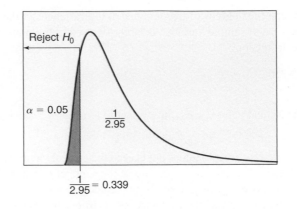

$$F_{crit} = F_{1-\alpha,\nu_1,\nu_2} = \frac{1}{F_{\alpha,\nu_2,\nu_1}} = \frac{1}{F_{0.05,8,11}} = \frac{1}{2.95} \approx 0.339 \text{ (left-tail critical value)}$$

The decision rule is

    Reject H_0 if $F_{calc} < 0.339$.

    Otherwise do not reject H_0.

Step 3: Calculate the Test Statistic The test statistic is the same as for a two-tailed test (the hypothesis doesn't affect the test statistic):

$$F_{calc} = \frac{s_1^2}{s_2^2} = \frac{(696.20)^2}{(837.62)^2} = 0.691$$

Step 4: Make the Decision Because the test statistic $F = 0.691$ is not in the critical region, we cannot reject the hypothesis of equal variances in a one-tailed test. The bumpers did not significantly decrease the variance in collision repair cost.

Excel's F Test

Excel makes it quite easy to do the F test for variances. Figure 10.24 shows Excel's left-tailed test. One advantage of using Excel is that you also get a p value. For the bumper data, the large p value of 0.279 indicates that we would face a Type I error risk of about 28 percent if we were to reject H_0. In other words, a sample variance ratio as extreme as $F = 0.691$ would occur by chance about 28 percent of the time if the population variances were in fact equal. The sample evidence does not indicate that the variances differ.

Assumptions of the F Test

The F test assumes that the populations being sampled are normal. Unfortunately, the test is rather sensitive to non-normality of the sampled populations.

FIGURE 10.24 **Excel's F Test of Variances**

F-Test Two-Sample for Variances		
	Experimental	*Control*
Mean	1101.416667	1766.111111
Variance	484700.8106	701611.1111
Observations	12	9
df	11	8
F	0.690839702	
P(F<=f) one-tail	0.278623089	
F Critical one-tail	0.33921414	

Hint: Use Excel or MegaStat.

10.32 Which samples show unequal variances? Use $\alpha = 0.05$ in all tests. Show the critical values and degrees of freedom clearly and illustrate the decision rule. (LO 6)

   a. $s_1 = 5.1$, $n_1 = 11$, $s_2 = 3.2$, $n_2 = 8$, two-tailed test
   b. $s_1 = 221$, $n_1 = 8$, $s_2 = 445$, $n_2 = 8$, left-tailed test
   c. $s_1 = 67$, $n_1 = 10$, $s_2 = 15$, $n_2 = 13$, right-tailed test

10.33 Researchers at the Mayo Clinic have studied the effect of sound levels on patient healing and have found a significant association (louder hospital ambient sound level is associated with slower post-surgical healing). Based on the Mayo Clinic's experience, Ardmore Hospital installed new vinyl flooring that is supposed to reduce the mean sound level (decibels) in the hospital corridors. The sound level is measured at five randomly selected times in the main corridor. (a) At $\alpha = 0.05$, has the mean been reduced? Show the hypotheses, decision rule, and test statistic. (b) At $\alpha = 0.05$, has the variance changed? Show the hypotheses, decision rule, and test statistic. (See *Detroit Free Press,* Feb. 2, 2004, p. 8H.) (LO 6) **Decibels**

New Flooring	Old Flooring
42	48
41	51
40	44
37	48
44	52

10.34 A manufacturing process drills holes in sheet metal that are supposed to be 0.5000 cm in diameter. Before and after a new drill press is installed, the hole diameter is carefully measured (in cm) for 12 randomly chosen parts. At $\alpha = 0.05$, do these independent random samples indicate that the new process has smaller variance? Show the hypotheses, decision rule, and test statistic. *Hint:* Use Excel $=$FINV$(1-\alpha, \nu_1, \nu_2)$ to get F_{crit}. (LO 6) **Diameter**

New drill:	0.5005	0.5010	0.5024	0.4988	0.4997	0.4995
	0.4976	0.5042	0.5014	0.4995	0.4988	0.4992
Old drill:	0.5052	0.5053	0.4947	0.4907	0.5031	0.4923
	0.5040	0.5035	0.5061	0.4956	0.5035	0.4962

10.35 Examine the data below showing the weights (in kg) of randomly selected checked bags for an airline's flights on the same day. (a) At $\alpha = 0.05$ is the mean weight of an international bag greater? Show the hypotheses, decision rule, and test statistic. (b) At $\alpha = 0.05$, is the variance greater for bags on a domestic flight? Show the hypotheses, decision rule, and test statistic. (LO 6) **Luggage**

Domestic (10 bags)		International (15 bags)		
18	21	13	17	20
24	22	16	15	19
21	13	15	13	15
18	24	15	20	16
31	28	17	18	18

10.36 Before a manufacturer of MP3 players will change the supplier that it uses to produce batteries for its players, it needs sufficient evidence that the variance in play times on a fully charged battery is less than its current battery's variance. As a test, it randomly selected eight of its MP3 players with the currently used fully charged battery and played each until the batteries died. The standard deviation in play times was 2.1 hours. It also randomly selected 10 of its players and substituted the new proposed fully charged battery and played each until these batteries died. The standard deviation in their play times was 1.3 hours. At the 0.05 level of significance, will the MP3 manufacturer change the supplier of its batteries? Explain your answer. (LO 6)

CHAPTER SUMMARY

A **two-sample test** compares samples with each other rather than comparing with a benchmark, as in a one-sample test. For **independent samples,** the comparison of means generally utilizes the Student's t distribution, because the population variances are almost always unknown. If the unknown variances are **assumed equal,** we use a **pooled variance** estimate and **add the degrees of freedom.** If the unknown variances are **assumed unequal,** we do not pool the variances and we reduce the degrees of freedom by using **Welch's formula.** The test statistic is the difference of means divided by their standard error. For tests of means or proportions, **equal sample sizes** are desirable, but not necessary. The t **test for paired samples** uses the differences of n paired observations, thereby being a **one-sample** t **test.** For two proportions, the samples may be **pooled** if the population proportions are assumed equal, and the test statistic is the difference of proportions divided by the standard error, the square root of the sum of the sample variances. For proportions, **normality** may be assumed if both samples are large, that is, if they each contain at least 10 successes and 10 failures. The **F test** for equality of **two variances** is named after Sir Ronald Fisher. Its test statistic is the **ratio** of the sample variances. We want to see if the ratio differs significantly from 1. The F table shows critical values based on both **numerator** and **denominator** degrees of freedom.

KEY TERMS

Behrens-Fisher problem, *404*
F distribution, *434*
F test, *435*
independent sample, *422*
paired comparison, *417*
paired samples, *418*
paired t test, *418*

pooled estimate, *426*
pooled proportion, *425*
pooled variance, *410*
p values, *406*
test statistic, *407*
two-sample tests, *405*
Type I error, *407*

Type II error, *407*
Welch-Satterthwaite
 t-distribution, *404*
Welch's adjusted degrees of
 freedom, *404*

Commonly Used Formulas in Two-Sample Hypothesis Tests

Test Statistic (Difference of Means, Equal Variances): $t_{calc} = \dfrac{(\bar{x}_1 - \bar{x}_2) - d_0}{\sqrt{\dfrac{s_p^2}{n_1} + \dfrac{s_p^2}{n_2}}}$

$$df = n_1 + n_2 - 2$$

$$s_p^2 = \frac{(n_1 - 1)s_1^2 + (n_2 - 1)s_2^2}{n_1 + n_2 - 2}$$

Test Statistic (Difference of Means, Unequal Variances): $t_{calc} = \dfrac{(\bar{x}_1 - \bar{x}_2) - D_0}{\sqrt{\dfrac{s_p^2}{n_1} + \dfrac{s_p^2}{n_2}}}$

$$df = \frac{[s_1^2/n_1 + s_2^2/n_2]^2}{\dfrac{(s_1^2/n_1)^2}{n_1 - 1} + \dfrac{(s_2^2/n_2)^2}{n_2 - 1}}$$

Test Statistic (Paired Differences): $t_{calc} = \dfrac{\bar{d}}{\dfrac{s_d}{\sqrt{n}}}$

$$df = n - 1$$

Test Statistic (Equality of Proportions): $z_{calc} = \dfrac{p_1 - p_2}{\sqrt{\bar{p}(1 - \bar{p})\left[\dfrac{1}{n_1} + \dfrac{1}{n_2}\right]}}$

$$\bar{p} = \frac{x_1 + x_2}{n_1 + n_2}$$

Confidence Interval for $\pi_1 - \pi_2$: $(p_1 - p_2) \pm z_{\alpha/2}\sqrt{\dfrac{p_1(1 - p_1)}{n_1} + \dfrac{p_2(1 - p_2)}{n_2}}$

Test Statistic (Two Variances): $F_{calc} = \dfrac{s_1^2}{s_2^2}$

$$df_1 = n_1 - 1, df_2 = n_2 - 1$$

1. (a) In a two-sample test of proportions, what is a pooled proportion? (b) Why is the test for normality important for a two-sample test of proportions? (c) What is the criterion for assuming normality of the test statistic? (LO 2)

2. (a) Is it necessary that sample sizes be equal for a two-sample test of proportions? Is it desirable? (b) Explain the analogy between overlapping confidence intervals and testing for equality of two proportions. (LO 2)

3. List the three cases for a test comparing two means. Explain carefully how they differ. (LO 1)

4. Consider Case 1 (known variances) in the test comparing two means. (a) Why is Case 1 unusual and not used very often? (b) What distribution is used for the test statistic? (c) Write the formula for the test statistic. (LO 1)

5. Consider Case 2 (unknown but equal variances) in the test comparing two means. (a) Why is Case 2 common? (b) What distribution is used for the test statistic? (c) State the degrees of freedom used in this test. (d) Write the formula for the pooled variance and interpret it. (e) Write the formula for the test statistic. (LO 1)

6. Consider Case 3 (unknown and unequal variances) in the test comparing two means. (a) What complication arises in degrees of freedom for Case 3? (b) What distribution is used for the test statistic? (c) Write the formula for the test statistic. (LO 1)

7. (a) Is it ever acceptable to use a normal distribution in a test of means with unknown variances? (b) If we assume normality, what is gained? What is lost? (LO 1)

8. Why is it a good idea to use a computer program like Excel to do tests of means? (LO 7)

9. (a) Explain why the paired *t* test for dependent samples is really a one-sample test. (b) State the degrees of freedom for the paired *t* test. (c) Why not treat two paired samples as if they were independent? (LO 1)

10. Explain how a difference in means could be statistically *significant* but not *important*. (LO 1)

11. (a) Why do we use an *F* test? (b) Where did it get its name? (c) When two population variances are equal, what value would you expect of the *F* test statistic? (LO 5)

12. (a) In an *F* test for two variances, explain how to obtain left- and right-tail critical values. (b) What are the assumptions underlying the *F* test? (LO 6)

Note: For tests on two proportions, two means, or two variances it is a good idea to check your work by using MINITAB, MegaStat, or the *LearningStats* two-sample calculators in Unit 10.

10.37 The top food snacks consumed by adults aged 18–54 are gum, chocolate candy, fresh fruit, potato chips, breath mints/candy, ice cream, nuts, cookies, bars, yogourt, and crackers. Out of a random sample of 25 men, 15 ranked fresh fruit in their top five snack choices. Out of a random sample of 32 women, 22 ranked fresh fruit in their top five snack choices. Is there a difference in the proportion of men and women who rank fresh fruit in their top five lists of snacks? (a) State the hypotheses and a decision rule for $\alpha = 0.10$. (b) Calculate the sample proportions. (c) Find the test statistic and its *p* value. What is your conclusion? (d) Is normality assured? (Data are from The NPD Group press release, "Fruit #1 Snack Food Consumed by Kids," June 16, 2005.) (LO 2)

10.38 In Dallas, some fire trucks were painted yellow (instead of red) to heighten their visibility. During a test period, the fleet of red fire trucks made 153,348 runs and had 20 accidents, while the fleet of yellow fire trucks made 135,035 runs and had 4 accidents. At $\alpha = 0.01$, did the yellow fire trucks have a significantly lower accident rate? (a) State the hypotheses. (b) State the decision rule and sketch it. (c) Find the sample proportions and *z* test statistic. (d) Make a decision. (e) Find the *p* value and interpret it. (f) If statistically significant, do you think the difference is large enough to be important? If so, to whom, and why? (g) Is the normality assumption fulfilled? Explain. (LO 2)

Accident Rate for Dallas Fire Trucks

Statistic	Red Fire Trucks	Yellow Fire Trucks
Number of accidents	$x_1 = 20$ accidents	$x_2 = 4$ accidents
Number of fire runs	$n_1 = 153,348$ runs	$n_2 = 135,035$ runs

Source: *The Wall Street Journal,* June 26, 1995, p. B1.

10.39 Do a larger proportion of university students than young children eat cereal? Researchers surveyed both age groups to find the answer. The results are shown in the table below. (a) State the hypotheses used to answer the question. (b) Using $\alpha = 0.05$, state the decision rule and sketch it. (c) Find the sample proportions and z statistic. (d) Make a decision. (e) Find the p value and interpret it. (f) Is the normality assumption fulfilled? Explain. (LO 2)

Statistic	University Students (ages 18–25)	Young Children (ages 6–11)
Number who eat cereal	$x_1 = 833$	$x_2 = 692$
Number surveyed	$n_1 = 850$	$n_2 = 740$

10.40 A 2005 study found that 202 women held board seats out of a total of 1,195 seats in the Fortune 100 companies. A 2003 study found that 779 women held board seats out of a total of 5,727 seats in the Fortune 500 companies. Treating these as random samples (as board seat assignments change often), can we conclude that Fortune 100 companies have a greater proportion of women board members than the Fortune 500? (a) State the hypotheses. (b) Calculate the sample proportions. (c) Find the test statistic and its p value. What is your conclusion at $\alpha = 0.05$? (d) If statistically significant, can you suggest factors that might explain the increase? (Data are from *The 2003 Catalyst Census of Women Board Directors of the Fortune 500,* and "Women and Minorities on Fortune 100 Boards," *The Alliance for Board Diversity,* May 17, 2005.) (LO 2)

10.41 A study of the Fortune 100 board of director members showed that there were 36 minority women holding board seats out of 202 total female board members. There were 142 minority men holding board seats out of 993 total male board members. (a) Treating the findings from this study as samples, calculate the sample proportions. (b) Find the test statistic and its p value. (c) At the 5 percent level of significance, is there a difference in the percentage of minority women board directors and minority men board directors? (Data are from "Women and Minorities on Fortune 100 Boards," *The Alliance for Board Diversity,* May 17, 2005.) (LO 2)

10.42 To test his hypothesis that students who finish an exam first get better grades, a Trent University professor kept track of the order in which papers were handed in. Of the first 25 papers, 10 received a B or better compared with 8 of the last 24 papers handed in. Does this evidence support this professor's hypothesis, at $\alpha = 0.10$? (a) State your hypotheses and obtain a test statistic and p value. Interpret the results. (b) Are the samples large enough to assure normality? (c) Make an argument that early-finishers should do better. Then make the opposite argument. Which is more convincing? (LO 2)

10.43 How many full-page advertisements are found in a magazine? In an October issue of *Muscle and Fitness,* there were 252 ads, of which 97 were full-page. For the same month, the magazine *Glamour* had 342 ads, of which 167 were full-page. (a) Is the difference in the proportion of ads that are full-page significant at $\alpha = 0.01$? (b) Find the p value. (c) Is normality assured? (d) Based on what you know of these magazines, why might the proportions of full-page ads differ? (Data are from a project by MBA students Amy DeGuire and Don Finney.) (LO 2)

10.44 Are individuals who appear to be overweight more likely to prefer chocolate ice cream than individuals who do not appear to be overweight? To test this theory, a random sample of 125 individuals who appear to be overweight and a random sample of 100 individuals who do not appear to be overweight were observed ordering ice cream in an ice cream store in North Bay, Ontario. Of the overweight individuals, 38 ordered chocolate ice cream. Of the other group, 20 ordered chocolate ice cream. At the 0.05 level of significance, is there sufficient evidence to indicate that overweight individuals are more likely to order chocolate ice cream than non-overweight individuals? At the 0.05 level of significance, is the proportion of overweight individuals ordering chocolate ice cream more than 0.05 greater than the proportion of non-overweight individuals ordering chocolate? In both cases, determine the p value. (LO 2)

10.45 After John F. Kennedy, Jr., was killed in an airplane crash at night, a survey was taken asking whether a non-instrument-rated pilot should be allowed to fly at night. Of 409 New York State residents, 61 said yes. Of 70 aviation experts who were asked the same question, 40 said yes. (a) At $\alpha = 0.01$, did a larger proportion of experts say yes compared with the general public, or is the difference within the realm of chance? (b) Find the p value and interpret it. (b) Is normality assured? (Data are from www.siena.edu/sri.) (LO 2)

10.46 A ski company in Whistler owns two ski shops, one on the east side and one on the west side. Sales data showed that at the eastern location there were 56 pairs of large gloves sold out of 304 total pairs sold. At the western location there were 145 pairs of large gloves sold out of

562 total pairs sold. (a) Calculate the sample proportion of large gloves for each location. (b) At $\alpha = 0.05$, is there a significant difference in the proportion of large gloves sold? (c) Can you suggest any reasons why a difference might exist? (*Note:* Problem is based on actual sales data). (LO 2)

10.47   A sample of Grade 12 high school students showed that 18 of 60 who owned PlayStation 3 spent more than an hour a day playing games, compared with 32 of 80 who owned Xbox 360. Is there a significant difference in the population proportions at $\alpha = 0.10$? (LO 2)

10.48   Does a "follow-up reminder" increase the renewal rate on a magazine subscription? A magazine sent out 760 subscription renewal notices (without a reminder) and got 703 renewals. As an experiment, they sent out 240 subscription renewal notices (with a reminder) and got 228 renewals. (a) At $\alpha = 0.05$, was the renewal rate higher in the experimental group? (b) Can normality be assumed? (LO 2)

10.49   In a marketing class, 44 student members of virtual (Internet) project teams (group 1) and 42 members of face-to-face project teams (group 2) were asked to respond on a 1–5 scale to the question: "As compared to other teams, the members helped each other." For group 1 the mean was 2.73 with a standard deviation of 0.97, while for group 2 the mean was 1.90 with a standard deviation of 0.91. At $\alpha = 0.01$, is the virtual team mean significantly higher? (Data are from Roger W. Berry, *Marketing Education Review* 12, no. 2 [2002], pp. 73–78.) (LO 2)

10.50   Does lovastatin (a cholesterol-lowering drug) reduce the risk of heart attack? In a Texas study, researchers gave lovastatin to 2,325 people and an inactive substitute to 2,081 people (average age 58). After 5 years, 57 of the lovastatin group had suffered a heart attack, compared with 97 for the inactive pill. (a) State the appropriate hypotheses. (b) Obtain a test statistic and p value. Interpret the results at $\alpha = 0.01$. (c) Is normality assured? (d) Is the difference large enough to be important? (e) What else would medical researchers need to know before prescribing this drug widely? (Data are from *Science News* 153 [May 30, 1998], p. 343.) (LO 2)

10.51   To test the hypothesis that students who finish an exam first get better grades, Prof. Hardtack kept track of the order in which papers were handed in. The first 25 papers showed a mean score of 77.1 with a standard deviation of 19.6, while the last 24 papers handed in showed a mean score of 69.3 with a standard deviation of 24.9. Is there sufficient evidence to support Prof. Hardtack's hypothesis, at $\alpha = 0.05$? (a) State the hypotheses for a right-tailed test. (b) Obtain a test statistic and p value assuming equal variances. Interpret these results. (c) Is the difference in mean scores large enough to be important? (d) Is it reasonable to assume equal variances? (e) Carry out a formal test for equal variances at $\alpha = 0.05$, showing all steps clearly. (LO 2)

10.52   Did the cost to outsource a standard employee background check changed from 2005 to 2006? A random sample of 10 companies in spring 2005 showed a sample average of $105 with a sample standard deviation equal to $32. A random sample of 10 different companies in spring 2006 resulted in a sample average of $75 with a sample standard deviation equal to $45. (a) Conduct a hypothesis test to test the difference in sample means with a level of significance equal to 0.05. Assume the population variances are not equal. (b) Discuss why a paired sample design might have made more sense in this case. (LO 2)

10.53   From her firm's computer telephone log, an executive found that the mean length of 64 telephone calls during July was 4.48 minutes with a standard deviation of 5.87 minutes. She vowed to make an effort to reduce the length of calls. The August phone log showed 48 telephone calls whose mean was 2.396 minutes with a standard deviation of 2.018 minutes. (a) State the hypotheses to test whether she was successful. (b) Obtain a test statistic and p value assuming unequal variances. Interpret these results using $\alpha = 0.01$. (c) Why might the sample data *not* follow a normal, bell-shaped curve? If not, how might this affect your conclusions? (LO 2)

10.54   An experimental bumper was designed to reduce damage in low-speed collisions. This bumper was installed on an experimental group of vans in a large fleet, but not on a control group. At the end of a trial period, accident data showed 12 repair incidents for the experimental group and 9 repair incidents for the control group. Vehicle downtime (in days per repair incident) is shown below. At $\alpha = 0.05$, did the new bumper reduce downtime? (a) Make stacked dot plots of the data (a sketch is acceptable). (b) State the hypotheses. (c) State the decision rule and sketch it. (d) Find the test statistic. (e) Make a decision. (f) Find the p value and interpret it. (g) Do you think the difference is large enough to be important? Explain. (Data are from an unpublished study by Floyd G. Willoughby and Thomas W. Lauer, Oakland University.) (LO 2)   **DownTime**

New bumper (12 repair incidents): 9, 2, 5, 12, 5, 4, 7, 5, 11, 3, 7, 1

Control group (9 repair incidents): 7, 5, 7, 4, 18, 4, 8, 14, 13

10.55 In a 15-day survey of air pollution in two European capitals, the mean particulate count (micrograms per cubic metre) in Athens was 39.5 with a standard deviation of 3.75, while in London the mean was 31.5 with a standard deviation of 2.25. (a) Assuming equal population variances, does this evidence convince you that the mean particulate count is higher in Athens, at $\alpha = 0.05$? (b) Are the variances equal or not, at $\alpha = 0.05$? (Based on *The Economist* 383, no. 8514 [Feb. 3, 2007], p. 58.) (LO 2 & 6)

10.56 One group of accounting students took a distance learning class, while another group took the same course in a traditional classroom. At $\alpha = 0.10$, is there a significant difference in the mean scores listed below? (a) State the hypotheses. (b) State the decision rule and sketch it. (c) Find the test statistic. (d) Make a decision. (e) Use Excel to find the p value and interpret it. (LO 2 & 7)

Exam Scores for Accounting Students

Statistic	Distance	Classroom
Mean scores	$\bar{x}_1 = 9.1$	$\bar{x}_2 = 10.3$
Sample std. dev.	$s_1 = 2.4$	$s_2 = 2.5$
Number of students	$n_1 = 20$	$n_2 = 20$

10.57 Do male and female school superintendents earn the same pay? Salaries for 20 males and 17 females in a certain metropolitan area are shown below. At $\alpha = 0.01$, were the mean superintendent salaries greater for men than for women? (a) Make stacked dot plots of the sample data (a sketch will do). (b) State the hypotheses. (c) State the decision rule and sketch it. (d) Find the test statistic. (e) Make a decision. (f) Estimate the p value and interpret it. (g) If statistically significant, do you think the difference is large enough to be important? Explain. (LO 2)

School Superintendent Pay

Men (n = 20)		Women (n = 17)	
114,000	121,421	94,675	96,000
115,024	112,187	123,484	112,455
115,598	110,160	99,703	120,118
108,400	128,322	86,000	124,163
109,900	128,041	108,000	76,340
120,352	125,462	94,940	89,600
118,000	113,611	83,933	91,993
108,209	123,814	102,181	
110,000	111,280	86,840	
151,008	112,280	85,000	

10.58 The average take-out order size for Ashoka Curry House restaurant is shown. Assuming equal variances, at $\alpha = 0.05$, is there a significant difference in the order sizes? (a) State the hypotheses. (b) State the decision rule and sketch it. (c) Find the test statistic. (d) Make a decision. (e) Use Excel to find the p value and interpret it. (LO 2)

Customer Order Size

Statistic	Friday Night	Saturday Night
Mean order size	$\bar{x}_1 = 22.32$	$\bar{x}_2 = 25.56$
Standard deviation	$s_1 = 4.35$	$s_2 = 6.16$
Number of orders	$n_1 = 13$	$n_2 = 18$

10.59 Cash withdrawals (in multiples of $20) at an on-campus ABM for a random sample of 30 Fridays and 30 Mondays are shown following. At $\alpha = 0.01$, is there a difference in the mean ABM withdrawal on Monday and Friday? (a) Make stacked dot plots of the data (a sketch is acceptable). (b) State the hypotheses. (c) State the decision rule and sketch it. (d) Find the test statistic. (e) Make a decision. (f) Find the p value and interpret it. (LO 2) 🖫 **ATM**

Randomly Chosen ABM Withdrawals ($)

Friday			Monday		
250	10	10	40	30	10
20	10	30	100	70	370
110	20	10	20	20	10
40	20	40	30	50	30
70	10	10	200	20	40
20	20	400	20	30	20
10	20	10	10	20	100
50	20	10	30	40	20
100	20	20	50	10	20
20	60	70	60	10	20

10.60 A sample of 25 concession stand purchases at the May 12 matinee of *Spider-Man 3* showed a mean purchase of $7.29 with a standard deviation of $3.02. For the May 18 evening showing of the same movie, for a sample of 25 purchases the mean was $7.12 with a standard deviation of $2.14. The means appear to be very close, but not the variances. At $\alpha = 0.05$, is there a difference in variances? Show all steps clearly, including an illustration of the decision rule. (LO 6)

10.61 A ski company in Whistler owns two ski shops, one on the west side and one on the east side. Is there a difference in daily average goggle sales between the two stores? Assume equal variances. (a) State the hypotheses. (b) State the decision rule for a level of significance equal to 5 percent and sketch it. (c) Find the test statistic and state your conclusion. (LO 2)

Sales Data for Ski Goggles

Statistic	East Side Shop	West Side Shop
Mean sales	$328	$435
Sample std. dev.	$104	$147
Sample size	28 days	29 days

10.62 A ski company in Mont Tremblant owns two ski shops, one on the west side and one on the east side. Ski hat sales data (in dollars) for a random sample of five Saturdays during the 2004 season showed the following results. Is there a significant difference in sales dollars of hats between the west side and east side stores at the 5 percent level of significance? (a) State the hypotheses. (b) State the decision rule and sketch it. (c) Find the test statistic and state your conclusion. (LO 4) 🖫 **Hats**

Saturday Sales Data ($) for Ski Hats

Saturday	East Side Shop	West Side Shop
1	548	523
2	493	721
3	609	695
4	567	510
5	432	532

10.63 Emergency room arrivals in a large hospital showed the statistics below for two months. At $\alpha = 0.05$, has the variance changed? Show all steps clearly, including an illustration of the decision rule. (LO 6)

Statistic	October	November
Mean arrivals	177.0323	171.7333
Standard deviation	13.48205	15.4271
Days	31	30

10.64 Here are heart rates for a sample of 30 students before and after a class break. At $\alpha = 0.05$, is there sufficient evidence to indicate that mean heart rates of students differ before and after class? (a) State the hypotheses. (b) State the decision rule and sketch it. (c) Find the test statistic. (d) Make a decision. (e) Estimate the p value and interpret it. (LO 4) **HeartRate**

Heart Rate before and after Class Break

Student	Before	After	Student	Before	After
1	60	62	16	70	64
2	70	76	17	69	66
3	77	78	18	64	69
4	80	83	19	70	73
5	82	82	20	59	58
6	82	83	21	62	65
7	41	66	22	66	68
8	65	63	23	81	77
9	58	60	24	56	57
10	50	54	25	64	62
11	82	93	26	78	79
12	56	55	27	75	74
13	71	67	28	66	67
14	67	68	29	59	63
15	66	75	30	98	82

Note: Thanks to colleague Gene Fliedner for having his evening students take their own pulses before and after the 10-minute class break.

10.65 A certain company will purchase the house of any employee who is transferred out of the province and will handle all details of reselling the house. The purchase price is based on two assessments, one assessor being chosen by the employee and one by the company. Based on the sample of eight assessments shown, is there sufficient evidence that the two assessors disagree, on average? Use the 0.01 level of significance, state hypotheses clearly, and show all steps. (LO 4) **Home Value**

Assessments of Eight Homes ($ thousands)

Assessed By	Home 1	Home 2	Home 3	Home 4	Home 5	Home 6	Home 7	Home 8
Company	328	350	455	278	290	285	535	745
Employee	318	345	470	285	310	280	525	765

10.66 Two labs produce 1280 × 1024 LCD displays. At random, records are examined for 12 independently chosen hours of production in each lab, and the number of bad pixels per thousand displays is recorded. (a) Assuming equal variances, at the 0.01 level of significance, is there a difference in the defect rate between the two labs? State your hypotheses and show all steps clearly. (b) At the 0.01 level of significance, can you reject the hypothesis of equal variances? State your hypotheses and show all steps clearly. (LO 2 & 6) **LCDDefects**

Defects in Randomly Inspected LCD Displays

Lab A	422, 319, 326, 410, 393, 368, 497, 381, 515, 472, 423, 355
Lab B	497, 421, 408, 375, 410, 489, 389, 418, 447, 429, 404, 477

10.67 A cognitive retraining clinic assists outpatient victims of head injury, anoxia, or other conditions that result in cognitive impairment. Each incoming patient is evaluated to establish an appropriate treatment program and estimated length of stay. To see if the evaluation teams are consistent, 12 randomly chosen patients are separately evaluated by two expert teams (*A* and *B*) as shown. At the 0.10 level of significance, are the evaluator teams consistent in their estimates? State your hypotheses and show all steps clearly. (LO 4) **LengthStay**

Estimated Length of Stay in Weeks

	Patient											
Team	**1**	**2**	**3**	**4**	**5**	**6**	**7**	**8**	**9**	**10**	**11**	**12**
A	24	24	52	30	40	30	18	30	18	40	24	12
B	24	20	52	36	36	36	24	36	16	52	24	16

10.68 Rates of return (annualized) in two investment portfolios are compared over the last 12 quarters. They are considered similar in safety, but portfolio *B* is advertised as being "less volatile." (a) At $\alpha = 0.025$, does the sample show that portfolio *A* has significantly greater variance in rates of return than portfolio *B*? (b) At $\alpha = 0.025$, is there a significant difference in the means? (LO 2 & 6) **Portfolio**

Portfolio A	Portfolio B	Portfolio A	Portfolio B
5.23	8.96	7.89	7.68
10.91	8.60	9.82	7.62
12.49	7.61	9.62	8.71
4.17	6.60	4.93	8.97
5.54	7.77	11.66	7.71
8.68	7.06	11.49	9.91

10.69 Do women get the same pay as men for equal work? One Canadian manufacturer claims that its female employees do get the same pay as its male employees performing similar jobs. To see if this claim is true or not, one male and one female in each of the six job categories in which this manufacturer classifies its employees were randomly selected and their hourly wages were determined as follows:

Category	Male Wage	Female Wage
A	$23.50	$22.75
B	$34.50	$31.75
C	$18.00	$18.25
D	$25.80	$23.90
E	$31.25	$29.80
F	$12.50	$10.00

(a) At the 0.05 level of significance, can we conclude that the company's claim is false and that female wages are lower, on average? (b) At the 0.05 level of significance, can we conclude that this company is paying women, on average, over $1 less than its male counterparts for performing similar jobs? If there are differences in wages, what may explain this other than a person's gender? (LO 4)

10.70 There has been an ongoing argument over whether the Canadian or American health care system is better. One argument for the Canadian system is that the costs of prescription medicines in Canada are substantially lower than the costs of the same medicines in the United States. To verify this claim, the five leading prescription medicines were priced (per pill) in both countries, with the following results:

Medicine	United States	Canada
A	$0.75	$0.50
B	$3.50	$2.75
C	$2.25	$1.75
D	$1.47	$1.03
E	$2.95	$2.85

At the 0.05 level of significance, is there sufficient evidence that, on average, prescription medicines cost less in Canada? (LO 4)

DO-IT-YOURSELF

10.71 Count the number of two-door vehicles among 50 vehicles from a university student parking lot. Use any sampling method you like (e.g., the first 50 you see). Do the same for a grocery store that is not very close to the university. At $\alpha = 0.10$, is there a significant difference in the proportion of two-door vehicles in these two locations? (a) State the hypotheses. (b) State the decision rule and sketch it. (c) Find the sample proportions and z test statistic. (d) Make a decision. (e) Find the p value and interpret it. (f) Is the normality assumption fulfilled? Explain. (LO 1 & 2)

10.72 Choose 40 words at random from this book (use a systematic sampling method, such as every fifth word on every tenth page). Then do the same for a novel of your choice. List the words and count the syllables in each. Find the mean and standard deviation. Is there a significant difference in the number of syllables at the 0.05 level? If so, is the difference important, as well as significant? To whom, and why? Show all work carefully. (LO 1 & 2)

10.73 Choose 100 words at random from this book (use a systematic sampling method, such as every tenth word on every fifth page). Then do the same for a novel of your choice. List the words and count the syllables in each. For each sample, find the proportion of words with more than three syllables. Is there a significant difference in the mean number of syllables at the 0.05 level? How does this analysis differ from the preceding exercise? (LO 1 & 2)

10.74 Use the *LearningStats* MBA database for this exercise. Choose either year (1990 or 1998) and sort the data on any variable you wish (sex, GPA, major, etc.). Then split the data into two groups based on the sorted list (e.g., male or female, high GPA or low GPA). For each group, calculate the mean and standard deviation for a quantitative variable of your choice (number of siblings, hours of work, number of traffic tickets, etc.). Test for significant difference of two means, choosing any level of significance you wish. State your hypotheses clearly and tell why you might expect a difference (or not, if none is expected). Show work and explain. (LO 1 & 2)

10.75 Use the *LearningStats* MBA database for this exercise. Choose either year (1990 or 1998) and sort the data on any variable you wish (sex, GPA, major, etc.). Then split the data into two groups based on the sorted list (e.g., male or female, high GPA or low GPA). For each group, calculate a proportion of your choice (proportion who read a daily newspaper, proportion who can conduct transactions in a foreign language, etc.). Choose any level of significance you wish. State your hypotheses clearly and tell why you might expect a difference (or not, if none is expected). Show all work and explain fully. (LO 1 & 2)

10.76 Use the *LearningStats* nations data for this exercise. Choose a database for any year (1995, 1999, or 2002). (a) Copy three data columns into a new worksheet: Nation, BirthRate, and InfMort. (b) Sort the data on BirthRate and then split the nations into two roughly equal groups (low births, high births). (c) For each group, calculate the mean and standard deviation for InfMort and carry out a test for difference of means at $\alpha = 0.05$. Explain fully. (d) Perform a test for equal variances in the two groups at $\alpha = 0.05$. Explain fully. (e) Does birth rate seem to be related to infant mortality? (f) Make a scatter plot of BirthRate and InfMort. What does it suggest? (LO 1, 2 & 6)

LearningStats Unit 10   Two-Sample Hypothesis Tests

LS

LearningStats Unit 10 gives examples of the most common two-sample hypothesis tests (two means, two proportions, two variances) and offers tables of critical values. Your instructor may assign specific modules, or you may pursue those that sound interesting.

Topic	LearningStats Modules
Hypothesis testing	Two-Sample Hypothesis Tests
Common hypothesis tests	Two-Sample Tests
	Calculator for Two Means
	Calculator for Two Proportions
Simulations	Two-Sample Generator
	Paired Data Generator
	Two-Sample Bootstrap
	Welch Correction Demo
Case studies	Case—Exam Scores
	Case—Weight-Loss Paired Data
	Case—Heart Rate Paired
	Case—Right-Handed Desks
Equations	Formulas for Two-Sample Tests
	Sampling Distribution PDFs
Tables	Appendix C—Normal
	Appendix D—Student's *t*
	Appendix F—*F* Distribution

Key: = PowerPoint   = Word   = Excel

Visual Statistics

VS

Visual Statistics Modules on Two-Sample Tests

Module	Module Name
10	**VS** Visualizing Two-Sample Hypothesis Tests

Visual Statistics Module 10 (included on your CD) is designed to help you

- Become familiar with the sampling distributions used in tests of two means or two variances.
- Understand the relationship between a confidence interval and a two-sample test.
- Be able to explain Type I error, Type II error, and power for two-sample tests.
- Know the assumptions underlying two-sample tests and the effects of violating them.

The worktext (included on the CD in PDF format) contains lists of concepts covered, objectives of the modules, overviews of concepts, illustrations of concepts, orientations to module features, learning exercises (basic, intermediate, advanced), learning projects (individual, team), self-evaluation quizzes, glossaries of terms, and solutions to self-evaluation quizzes.

EXAM REVIEW QUESTIONS FOR CHAPTERS 8–10

1. Which statement is *not* correct? Explain.
    a. The sample data $x_1, x_2, \ldots, x_n$ will be approximately normal if the sample size n is large.
    b. For a skewed population, the distribution of $\overline{X}$ is approximately normal if n is large.
    c. The expected value of $\overline{X}$ is equal to the true mean μ even if the population is skewed.

2. Match each statement to the correct property of an estimator (unbiased, consistent, efficient):
    a. The estimator "collapses" on the true parameter as n increases.
    b. The estimator has a relatively small variance.
    c. The expected value of the estimator is the true parameter.

3. Concerning confidence intervals, which statement is *most nearly* correct? Why not the others?
    a. We should use z instead of t when n is large.
    b. We use the Student's t distribution when σ is unknown.
    c. Using the Student's t distribution instead of z narrows the confidence interval.

4. A sample of 9 customers in the "quick" lane in a supermarket showed a mean purchase of $14.75 with a standard deviation of $2.10. (a) Find the 95 percent confidence interval for the true mean. (b) Why should you use t instead of z in this case?

5. A sample of 200 customers at a supermarket showed that 28 used a debit card to pay for their purchases. (a) Find the 95 percent confidence interval for the population proportion. (b) Why is it OK to assume normality in this case? (c) What sample size would be needed to estimate the population proportion with 90 percent confidence and an error of ± 0.03?

6. Which statement is *incorrect?* Explain.
    a. If $p = 0.50$ and $n = 100$ the estimated standard error of the sample proportion is 0.05.
    b. In a sample size calculation for estimating π it is conservative to assume $\pi = 0.50$.
    c. If $n = 250$ and $p = 0.07$ it is not safe to assume normality in a confidence interval for π.

7. Given $H_0\colon \mu \geq 18$ and $H_1\colon \mu < 18$, we would commit Type I error if we
    a. conclude that $\mu \geq 18$ when the truth is that $\mu < 18$.
    b. conclude that $\mu < 18$ when the truth is that $\mu \geq 18$.
    c. fail to reject $\mu \geq 18$ when the truth is that $\mu < 18$.

8. Which is the correct z value for a two-tailed test at $\alpha = 0.05$?
    a. $z = \pm 1.645$
    b. $z = \pm 1.960$
    c. $z = \pm 2.326$

9. The process that produces Sonora Bars (a type of candy) is intended to produce bars with a mean weight of 56 g. The process standard deviation is known to be 0.77 g. A random sample of 49 Sonora bars yields a mean weight of 55.82 g. (a) State the hypotheses to test whether the mean is smaller than it is supposed to be. (b) What is the test statistic? (c) At $\alpha = 0.05$, what is the critical value for this test? (d) What is your conclusion?

10. A sample of 16 ABM transactions shows a mean transaction time of 67 seconds with a standard deviation of 12 seconds. (a) State the hypotheses to test whether the mean transaction time exceeds 60 seconds. (b) Find the test statistic. (c) At $\alpha = 0.025$, what is the critical value for this test? (d) What is your conclusion?

11. Which statement is *correct?* Why not the others?
    a. The level of significance α is the probability of committing Type I error.
    b. As the sample size increases, critical values of $t_{0.05}$ increase, gradually approaching $z_{0.05}$.
    c. When σ is unknown, it is conservative to use $z_{0.05}$ instead of $t_{0.05}$ in a hypothesis test for μ.

12. Last month, 85 percent of the visitors to the Sonora Candy Factory made a purchase in the on-site candy shop after taking the factory tour. This month, a random sample of 500 such visitors showed that 435 purchased candy after the tour. The manager said "Good, the percentage of candy-buyers has risen significantly." (a) At $\alpha = 0.05$, do you agree? (b) Why is it acceptable to assume normality in this test?

13. Weights of 12 randomly-chosen Sonora Bars (a type of candy) from assembly line 1 had a mean weight of 56.25 g with a standard deviation of 0.65 g, while the weights of 12 randomly chosen Sonora Bars from assembly line 2 had a mean weight of 56.75 g with a standard deviation of 0.55 g. (a) Find the test statistic to test whether or not the mean population weights are the same for both assembly lines (i.e., that the difference is due to random variation). (b) State the critical value for $\alpha = 0.05$ and degrees of freedom that you are using. (c) State your conclusion.

14. In a random sample of 200 British Columbia residents, 150 had skied at least once last winter. A similar sample of 200 Quebec residents revealed that 140 had skied at least once last winter. At $\alpha = 0.025$, is the percentage significantly greater in British Columbia? Explain fully and show calculations.

15. Five students in a large lecture class compared their scores on two exams. "Looks like the class mean was higher on the second exam," Bob said. (a) What kind of test would you use? (b) At $\alpha = 0.10$, what is the critical value? (c) Do you agree with Bob? Explain.

	Bill	**Mary**	**Sam**	**Sarah**	**Megan**
Exam 1	75	85	90	65	86
Exam 2	86	81	90	71	89

16. Which statement is *not* correct concerning a *p*-value? Explain.
    a. All else being equal, a larger *p* value makes it more likely that H_0 will be rejected.
    b. The *p* value shows the risk of Type I error if we reject H_0 when H_0 is true.
    c. In making a decision, we compare the *p* value with the desired level of significance α.

17. Suppose $n_1 = 8$, $s_1 = 14$, $n_2 = 12$, and $s_2 = 7$. (a) Find the test statistic for a test for equal population variances. (b) At $\alpha = 0.05$ in a two-tailed test, state the critical value and degrees of freedom.

For solutions to odd-numbered exercises, Exam Review questions, and additional study tools to help you succeed in this course, visit *Connect* at www.mcgrawhillconnect.ca.

Chapter

11

Analysis of Variance

Chapter Learning Objectives

When you finish this chapter you should be able to

1. Understand how ANOVA works and how to use basic ANOVA terminology correctly (e.g., response variable, factors, treatments).

2. Recognize from the data format which type of ANOVA is appropriate.

3. Use Excel or other software package to perform the appropriate ANOVA.

4. Explain the assumptions of ANOVA and why they are important.

5. Interpret main effects and interaction effects in two-factor ANOVA.

11.1 Overview of ANOVA

In Chapter 10, you learned how to test the means of two populations by taking samples within each population. In this chapter, you will learn how to test more than two means *simultaneously* and how to trace sources of variation to potential explanatory factors by using **analysis of variance** (commonly referred to as **ANOVA**). Although ANOVA will be used to test the means of more than two populations, it can be used to analyze far more complex issues. Through the use of proper *experimental design,* ANOVA can be used to make efficient use of limited data to draw the strongest possible inferences concerning

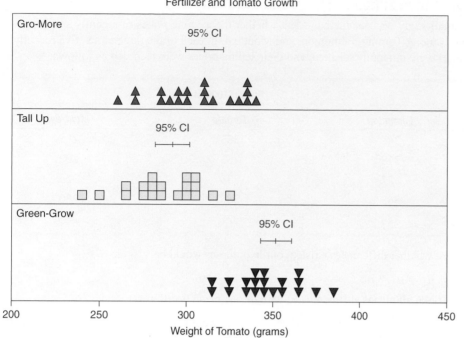

FIGURE 11.1

Fertilizer and Tomato Growth

these issues. Although analysis of variance has a relatively short history, it is one of the richest and most thoroughly explored fields of statistics. Originally developed by the English statistician Ronald A. Fisher (1890–1962) in connection with agricultural research (factors affecting crop growth), it was quickly applied in biology and medicine. Because of its versatility, it is now used in engineering, psychology, marketing, and many other areas. In this chapter, we will only illustrate a few kinds of problems where ANOVA may be utilized.

Illustration 1: Fertilizer and Tomato Growth

A field of hybrid tomatoes is subdivided into three plots, and a different fertilizer is applied to each plot. The three different fertilizers being considered are Gro-More, Tall-Up, and Green-Grow. Assume plots are similar in terms of soil, drainage, and planting depth. After 10 weeks, 20 tomatoes are sampled at random from each plot and their weights measured. Can we claim that there is a difference in these three fertilizers? Let $\mu_1, \mu_2,$ and μ_3 be the mean tomato weight using "treatments" Gro-More, Tall-Up, and Green-Grow, respectively. So we can set up our hypotheses:

$H_0: \mu_1 = \mu_2 = \mu_3$
$H_1:$ Not all the μ's are equal

If we reject the null hypothesis, then we are claiming that at least one of three population means is different. If we cannot reject H_0, then we assume that there is no difference in these three fertilizers or treatments. Assuming tomato weights follow a normal distribution, we obtain a confidence interval for each of the population means. Dot plots and 95 percent confidence intervals are graphed in Figure 11.1 using Visual Statistics (software on the accompanying CD).

The three confidence intervals seem to suggest that we may be able to reject the null hypothesis and conclude that the population means $\mu_1, \mu_2,$ and μ_3 are not all the same.

Illustration 2: House Prices and Location

A small study was conducted to test whether the average prices of recently sold homes differed among Toronto, Edmonton, and Montreal. In each of the three cities, five recently sold homes were randomly selected, and their selling prices were recorded as follows:

Price ($1000s)		
Edmonton	*Toronto*	*Montreal*
347	385	285
318	368	295
327	335	325
363	385	280
345	327	265

To test whether differences existed, our hypotheses would be

$H_0: \mu_1 = \mu_2 = \mu_3$
H_1: Not all means are equal (i.e., at least one mean is different)

If we were to reject the null hypothesis, then we would conclude that at least one of the three population means is different. (We would not be able to conclude that all means are different without additional testing.) If we cannot reject H_0, then we may assume that there is no difference in average selling prices among the three cities. Intuitively, what might this test look like? If we constructed confidence intervals for each of the cities and used these confidence intervals to test these hypotheses, we may decide to reject the null hypothesis if at least one of the confidence intervals did not overlap with the others, and not reject the null hypothesis if all three confidence intervals overlapped. If we were only interested in comparing the average selling prices of two cities, we could have used a t test from Chapter 10 and reached a conclusion. But we have three means that we are testing. How can we visualize extending this test to include three or even more than three populations? Looking at the test statistic from the previous chapter (Section 10.3, assuming equal variances),

$$t_{calc} = \frac{\bar{x}_1 - \bar{x}_2}{\sqrt{\dfrac{s_p^2}{n_1} + \dfrac{s_p^2}{n_2}}}$$

we observe that the numerator of this test statistic looks at how different the two sample means are and the denominator looks at how different the values are within the two samples. Looking at the means and variances of each of our three sample cities,

Location	Mean	Variance
Edmonton	340	314
Toronto	360	757
Montreal	290	500
Average	330	523.67

ANOVA (*AN*alysis *Of VA*riance) procedures to be described in this chapter will enable us to test these hypotheses by developing a test statistic with a numerator that also measures how different the sample means are among the samples and with a denominator that also measures how different the values are within the samples.

The Goal: Explaining Variation

By examining the above data, it is obvious that not all 15 selling prices are equal or that the selling prices differ. It is also obvious that the selling prices in Montreal tend to be less than the selling prices in the other two cities, as substantiated by their respective sample means. So we could argue that some of the variability in house prices (lower prices in Montreal vs. higher prices in Toronto and Edmonton) could be attributed to where these houses were sold. Analysis of variance seeks to identify the *sources of variation,* and their magnitudes, in a numerical *dependent* variable Y (the **response variable**). Variation in the response variable about its mean either is **explained** by one or more categorical *independent* variables (the **factors**) or is **unexplained** (random error):

$$\frac{\text{Variation in } Y}{(\text{around its mean})} = \frac{\text{Explained Variation}}{(\text{due to factors})} + \frac{\text{Unexplained Variation}}{(\text{random error})}$$

In the above example, the response variable is the selling price and the factor is the location of the home, or,

$$\text{Variation in Prices} = \frac{\text{Variation in Prices Explained}}{\text{by Location}} + \frac{\text{Unexplained Variation}}{\text{in Prices}}$$

As mentioned above, ANOVA is essentially a *comparison of* means. A factor may have several levels or forms. In our illustration, our factor "Location" has three levels: Edmonton, Toronto, and Montreal. When our study involves only one factor, each treatment corresponds to a different factor level. Thus we could equivalently say that factor Location has three treatments. Sample observations within different factor levels or **treatments** are viewed as coming from populations with possibly different means. We test whether each factor has a significant effect on Y by testing whether its level means differ and sometimes we test for interaction between factors if there is more than one factor. The test uses the F distribution for the same reasons that the F distribution was used in Chapter 10. Although ANOVA can handle any number of factors, the researcher often is interested only in a few. Also, data collection costs may impose practical limits on the number of factors or treatments we can choose. This chapter concentrates on ANOVA models with one or two factors, although more complex models are briefly mentioned at the end of the chapter.

Illustration 3: Manufacturing Defect Rates

Figure 11.2 shows a dot plot of daily defect rates for automotive computer chips manufactured at four plant locations. Samples of 10 days' production were taken at each plant. Are the observed differences in the plants' sample mean defect rates merely due to random variation? Or are the observed differences between the plants' defect rates too great to be attributed to chance? This is the kind of question that ANOVA is designed to answer by partitioning the variation in Y (defect rates) into its various components (the factor "plant location," and the unexplained). As with the previous example, a simple way to state the ANOVA hypothesis is

$H_0: \mu_1 = \mu_2 = \mu_3 = \mu_4$ (mean defect rates are the same at all four plants)

$H_1:$ Not all the means are equal (at least one mean differs from the others)

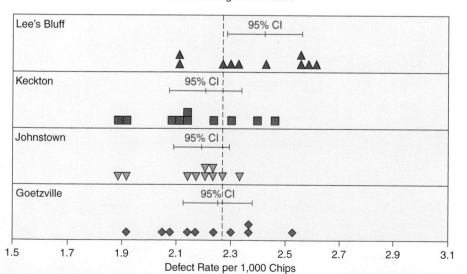

FIGURE 11.2

Chip Defect Rates at Four Plants

The treatment (plant) means are significantly different (p value = 0.02). Note that the confidence interval for Lee's Bluff falls to the right of the dotted vertical line, which represents the overall mean.

FIGURE 11.3

ANOVA Model for Chip Defect Rate

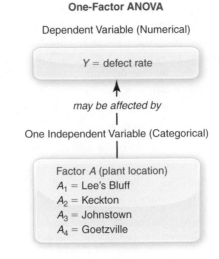

One-Factor ANOVA

Dependent Variable (Numerical)

Y = defect rate

may be affected by

One Independent Variable (Categorical)

Factor A (plant location)
A_1 = Lee's Bluff
A_2 = Keckton
A_3 = Johnstown
A_4 = Goetzville

If we cannot reject H_0, then we may assume that the observations within each treatment or group actually have a common mean μ (represented by a dashed line in Figure 11.2). This one-factor ANOVA model may be visualized as in Figure 11.3.

Illustration 4: Hospital Length of Stay

To allocate resources and fixed costs correctly, hospital management needs to test whether a patient's length of a stay (LOS) depends on the diagnostic-related group (DRG) code and the patient's age group. Consider the case of a bone fracture. LOS is a *numerical* response variable (measured in hours). The hospital organizes the data by using five diagnostic codes for type of fracture (facial, radius or ulna, hip or femur, other lower extremity, all other) and three age groups (under 18, 18 to 64, 65 and over). Although patient age is a numerical variable, it is coded into three categories based on stages of bone growth. Figure 11.4 illustrates two possible ANOVA models (one-factor or two-factor). We could also test for **interaction** between factors, as you will see later on.

> One factor: *Length of stay = f(Type of Fracture)*
>
> Two factors: *Length of stay = f(Type of Fracture, Age Group)*

Illustration 5: Automobile Painting

Paint quality is a major concern of car makers. A key characteristic of paint is its viscosity, a continuous *numerical* variable. Viscosity is to be tested for dependence on application temperature

FIGURE 11.4 **ANOVA Models for Hospital Length of Stay**

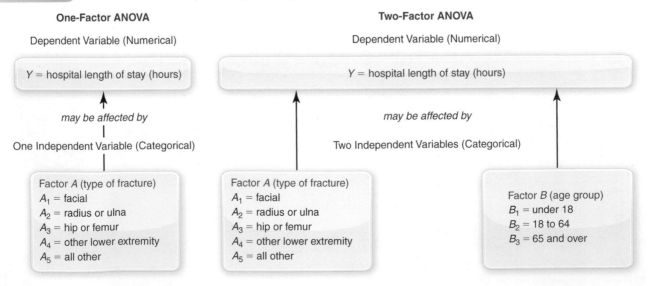

One-Factor ANOVA

Dependent Variable (Numerical)

Y = hospital length of stay (hours)

may be affected by

One Independent Variable (Categorical)

Factor A (type of fracture)
A_1 = facial
A_2 = radius or ulna
A_3 = hip or femur
A_4 = other lower extremity
A_5 = all other

Two-Factor ANOVA

Dependent Variable (Numerical)

Y = hospital length of stay (hours)

may be affected by

Two Independent Variables (Categorical)

Factor A (type of fracture)
A_1 = facial
A_2 = radius or ulna
A_3 = hip or femur
A_4 = other lower extremity
A_5 = all other

Factor B (age group)
B_1 = under 18
B_2 = 18 to 64
B_3 = 65 and over

Several ANOVA Models for Paint Viscosity **FIGURE 11.5**

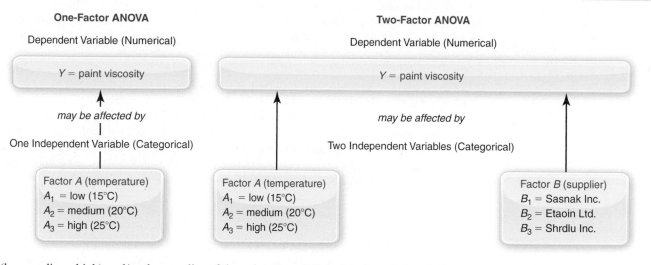

(low, medium, high) and/or the supplier of the paint (Sasnak Inc., Etaoin Ltd., or Shrdlu Inc.). Although temperature is a numerical variable, it has been coded into *categories* that represent the test conditions of the experiment. Figure 11.5 illustrates two potential ANOVA models:

One factor: *Viscosity = f(temperature)*

Two factors: *Viscosity = f(temperature, supplier)*

ANOVA Assumptions

Analysis of variance assumes that the

- Observations on *Y* are independent.
- Populations being sampled are normal.
- Populations being sampled have the same unknown variance, σ^2.

Fortunately, ANOVA is somewhat robust to departures from the normality and equal variance assumptions. Later in this chapter, you will see tests for equal variances and normality.

ANOVA Calculations

ANOVA calculations usually are too tedious to do by calculator, so after we choose an ANOVA model and collect the data, we rely on software (e.g., Excel, MegaStat, MINITAB, SPSS) to do the calculations. In some applications (accounting, finance, human resources, marketing), large samples can easily be taken from existing records, while in others (engineering, manufacturing, computer systems), experimental data collection is so expensive that small samples are used. Large samples increase the power of the test, but power also depends on the degree of variation in *Y*. Lowest power would be in small samples with high variation in *Y*. Specialized software is needed to calculate power for ANOVA experiments.

11.2   One-Factor ANOVA (Completely Randomized Model)

An Intuitive Explanation

Before we describe the formal details of the model, let us attempt to present an intuitive explanation and motivation for the model and its method. The first question that comes to mind is: Why are we analyzing variances when all we are trying to do is to compare population means?

Consider Illustration 2 where we presented data about the selling prices of 15 houses recently sold: five in Edmonton, five in Toronto, and five in Montreal. Sample statistics obtained were as follows:

$$\bar{x}_1 = 340,\ s_1^2 = 314$$

$$\bar{x}_2 = 360,\ s_2^2 = 757$$

$$\bar{x}_3 = 290,\ s_3^2 = 500$$

Note that the ANOVA model assumes that all three populations (house prices in Edmonton, Toronto, and Montreal) have the same variance. That is, $\sigma_1^2 = \sigma_2^2 = \sigma_3^2 = \sigma^2$ (unknown). So, the best estimate of this unknown common variance, σ^2, is the "pooled" sample variance, obtained by taking the average of these sample variances: $(314 + 757 + 500)/3 = 523.67$. (In this case, we can pool the sample variances by simply taking their arithmetic average because their sample sizes are the same. Otherwise, we would have to use a formula similar to the formula for s_p^2 in Chapter 10.) Because this estimate of σ^2 is obtained by looking at the variability within each sample, let us call 523.67 the *within groups* estimate of σ^2.

Now let us assume that the null hypothesis ($H_0: \mu_1 = \mu_2 = \mu_3 = \mu$) is true. This means that average house selling price is the same for all three cities, and we could think of these three sample means as three observations from the sampling distribution of the sample mean $\bar{X}$, the average selling price of houses in the three cities combined. Recall from Chapter 7 that the variance of $\bar{X}$, $\sigma_{\bar{X}}^2$, is given by the formula

$$\sigma_{\bar{X}}^2 = \frac{\sigma^2}{n}$$

where $n = 5$. Note that each sample mean is obtained by taking an average of five observations. To estimate $\sigma_{\bar{X}}^2$, call it $s_{\bar{X}}^2$, we simply find the sample variance of the three sample means: 340, 360, and 290. That is,

$$s_{\bar{X}}^2 = \frac{(340 - 330)^2 + (360 - 330)^2 + (290 - 330)^2}{3 - 1} = \frac{2,600}{2} = 1,300$$

Thus, 1,300 is an estimate of σ^2/n, or $\sigma^2/5$. This, of course, is under the assumption that the null hypothesis is true. Thus, an estimate of σ^2, assuming that H_0 is true, is 6,500 ($= 1,300 \times 5$). Let us call this quantity the *between groups* estimate of σ^2. If the null hypothesis is actually true, we would expect that these two estimates of σ^2, the between groups estimate and the within groups estimate, to be close to each other. If, however, the null hypothesis is actually false, and all the three population means are quite different from each other, we would expect the three sample means to be quite different from each other, and hence expect the between groups estimate of σ^2 to be much larger than the within groups estimate of σ^2. In our example, these two estimates are 6,500 and 523.67, respectively, and most likely would imply that the null hypothesis is not true.

Data Format

If we are only interested in comparing the means of c groups (*treatments* or *factor levels*), we have a **one-factor ANOVA.*** This is by far the most common ANOVA model that covers many business problems. The one-factor ANOVA is usually viewed as a comparison between several columns of data (e.g., the house price example), although the data could also be presented in rows. Table 11.1 illustrates the data format for a one-factor ANOVA with c treatments, denoted $A_1, A_2, \ldots, A_c$. The group means are $\bar{y}_1, \bar{y}_2, \ldots, \bar{y}_c$.

TABLE 11.1 Format of One-Factor ANOVA Data

One-Factor ANOVA: Data in Columns				One-Factor ANOVA: Data in Rows						
A_1	A_2	...	A_c							
y_{11}	y_{12}	...	y_{1c}	A_1	y_{11}	y_{21}	y_{31}	...	etc.	n_1 obs.	$\bar{y}_1$
y_{21}	y_{22}	...	y_{2c}	A_2	y_{12}	y_{22}	y_{32}	...	etc.	n_2 obs.	$\bar{y}_2$
y_{31}	y_{32}	...	y_{3c}	...							
...	...	...	...	A_c	y_{1c}	y_{2c}	y_{3c}	...	etc.	n_c obs.	$\bar{y}_c$
etc.	etc.	...	etc.							
n_1 obs.	n_2 obs.	...	n_c obs.							
$\bar{y}_1$	$\bar{y}_2$	...	$\bar{y}_c$							

*If subjects (or individuals) are assigned randomly to treatments, then we call this the *completely randomized model.*

Within treatment j, we have n_j observations on Y. The total number of observations is the sum of the sample sizes for each treatment:

$$n = n_1 + n_2 + \cdots + n_c \qquad (11.1)$$

Hypotheses to Be Tested

The question of interest is whether the mean of Y varies from treatment to treatment. The hypotheses to be tested are

H_0: $\mu_1 = \mu_2 = \cdots = \mu_c$ (all the treatment means are equal)

H_1: Not all the means are equal (at least one treatment mean is different)

Because one-factor ANOVA is a generalization of the test for equality of two means, why not just compare all possible pairs of means by using repeated two-sample t tests (as in Chapter 10)? Consider our experiment comparing the four manufacturing plant average defect rates (Illustration 3, earlier in this chapter). To compare pairs of plant averages, we would have to perform six (i.e., $_4C_2$) different t tests. If each t test has a Type I error probability equal to 0.05, then, based on previously discussed probability rules, the probability that at least one of those tests results in a Type I error is $1 - (0.95)^6 = 0.2649$. ANOVA tests all the means *simultaneously* (i.e., only one test is conducted) and therefore does not inflate our Type I error.

One-Factor ANOVA as a Linear Model

An equivalent way to express the one-factor model is to say that observations in treatment j came from a population with a common mean (μ) plus a treatment effect (A_j) plus random error (ε_{ij}):

$$y_{ij} = \mu + A_j + \varepsilon_{ij}, \quad j = 1, 2, \ldots, c, \text{ and } i = 1, 2, \ldots, n_j \qquad (11.2)$$

The random error is assumed to be normally distributed with zero mean and the same variance for all treatments. If we are interested only in what happens to the response for the particular *levels* of the factor that were selected (a **fixed-effects model**), then the hypotheses to be tested are

H_0: $A_1 = A_2 = \cdots = A_c = 0$ (all treatment effects are zero)

H_1: Not all A_j are zero (some treatment effects are non-zero)

If the null hypothesis is true ($A_j = 0$ for all j), then knowing that an observation x came from treatment j does not help explain the variation in Y and the ANOVA model collapses to

$$y_{ij} = \mu + \varepsilon_{ij} \qquad (11.3)$$

Group Means

The *mean of each group* is calculated in the usual way by summing the observations in the treatment and dividing by the sample size:

$$\bar{y}_j = \frac{1}{n_j} \sum_{i=1}^{n_j} y_{ij} \qquad (11.4)$$

The *overall sample mean* or *grand mean* $\bar{y}$ can be calculated either by summing *all* the observations and dividing by n or by taking a weighted average of the c sample means:

$$\bar{y} = \frac{1}{n} \sum_{j=1}^{c} \sum_{i=1}^{n_j} y_{ij} = \frac{1}{n} \sum_{j=1}^{c} n_j \bar{y}_j \qquad (11.5)$$

Partitioned Sum of Squares

To understand the logic of ANOVA, consider that for a given observation y_{ij} the following relationship must hold (on the right-hand side we just add and subtract $\bar{y}_j$):

$$(y_{ij} - \bar{y}) = (\bar{y}_j - \bar{y}) + (y_{ij} - \bar{y}_j) \qquad (11.6)$$

This says that any deviation of an observation from the grand mean $\bar{y}$ may be expressed in two parts: the deviation of the column mean $(\bar{y}_j)$ from the grand mean $(\bar{y})$, or *between* treatments, and the deviation of the observation (y_{ij}) from its own column mean $(\bar{y}_j)$, or *within* treatments. We can show that this relationship also holds for *sums* of squared deviations, yielding the **partitioned sum of squares:**

$$\sum_{j=1}^{c}\sum_{i=1}^{n_j}(y_{ij} - \bar{y})^2 = \sum_{j=1}^{c} n_j(\bar{y}_j - \bar{y})^2 + \sum_{j=1}^{c}\sum_{i=1}^{n_j}(y_{ij} - \bar{y}_j)^2 \tag{11.7}$$

This important relationship may be expressed simply as

$$SST = SSA + SSE \text{ (partitioned sum of squares)} \tag{11.8}$$

Partitioned Sum of Squares

Sum of Squares Total (SST)	=	Sum of Squares between Treatments (SSA)	+	Sum of Squares within Treatments (SSE)
		↑		↑
		Explained by Factor A		Unexplained Random Error

If the treatment means do not differ greatly from the grand mean, SSA will be small. The sums SSA and SSE may be used to test the hypothesis that the treatment means differ from the grand mean. However, we first divide each sum of squares by its *degrees of freedom* (to adjust for group sizes). The *F test statistic* is the ratio of the resulting **mean squares.** These calculations can be arranged in a worksheet like Table 11.2.

The ANOVA calculations are mathematically simple but involve tedious sums. These calculations are almost always done on a computer.* For example, Excel's one-factor ANOVA menu using Data > Data Analysis is shown in Figure 11.6. MegaStat uses a similar menu.

Concept Check

For each of the following scenarios concerning a study of house prices in Toronto, Edmonton, and Montreal, state which of *SST, SSA,* and *SSE* will have positive values and which will have a value of zero, and explain why.

(a) All houses in the study sold at exactly the same price.

(b) Not all houses in the study sold at exactly the same price, but the houses within each city sold at the same price.

(c) Not all houses within one or more of the cities sold at exactly the same price, and house prices in Montreal tended to be lower than the house prices in either Toronto or Edmonton.

(d) Not all houses within one or more of the cities sold at exactly the same price although the average selling prices were the same for the three cities.

---

*Detailed step-by-step examples of all ANOVA calculations can be found in the case studies in *LearningStats* Unit 11.

TABLE 11.2 **One-Factor ANOVA Table**

Source of Variation	Sum of Squares	Degrees of Freedom	Mean Square	F Statistic
Treatment (between groups)	$SSA = \sum_{j=1}^{c} n_j(\bar{y}_j - \bar{y})^2$	$c - 1$	$MSA = \dfrac{SSA}{c-1}$	$F = \dfrac{MSA}{MSE}$
Error (within groups)	$SSE = \sum_{j=1}^{c}\sum_{i=1}^{n_j} (y_{ij} - \bar{y}_j)^2$	$n - c$	$MSE = \dfrac{SSE}{n-c}$	
Total	$SST = \sum_{j=1}^{c}\sum_{i=1}^{n_j} (y_{ij} - \bar{y})^2$	$n - 1$		

FIGURE 11.6

Excel's ANOVA Menu

Test Statistic

At the beginning of this chapter we described the variation in Y as consisting of explained variation and unexplained variation. To test whether the independent variable explains a significant proportion of the variation in Y, we need to compare the explained (due to treatments) and unexplained (due to error) variation. Recall that the F distribution describes the *ratio of two variances*. Therefore it makes sense that the ANOVA test statistic is the F *test statistic*. The F statistic is the ratio of the variance due to treatments to the variance due to error. MSA is the mean square due to treatments, and MSE is the mean square within treatments. Equation 11.9 shows the F statistic and its degrees of freedom.

$$F = \frac{MSA}{MSE} = \frac{\left(\dfrac{SSA}{c-1}\right)}{\left(\dfrac{SSE}{n-c}\right)} \quad \begin{array}{l} \nwarrow \nu_1 = c - 1 \text{ (numerator)} \\ \swarrow \nu_2 = n - c \text{ (denominator)} \end{array} \tag{11.9}$$

The test statistic $F = MSA/MSE$ cannot be negative (it's based on sums of squares—see Table 11.2). The F test for equal treatment means is always a right-tailed test. If there is little difference among treatments, we would expect MSA to be small because the treatment means $\bar{y}_j$ would be near the overall mean $\bar{y}$. Thus, when F is small we would not expect to reject the hypothesis of equal group means. The larger the F statistic, the more we are inclined to reject the hypothesis of equal means. But how large must F be to convince us that the means differ? Just as with a z test or a t test, we need a *decision rule*.

Decision Rule

If the null hypothesis is true, then it can be shown that $E(MSA) = E(MSE) = \sigma^2$, the unknown common population variance, and thus, the test statistic F should be close to one. If the null hypothesis is not true, then $E(MSA) > E(MSE)$, and thus, the F test statistic is expected to be greater than one. If the population means differ a lot from each other, then F is expected to be much larger than 1. Thus, under the null hypothesis, the test statistic $F = \dfrac{MSA}{MSE}$ follows the F distribution $F_{c-1,n-c}$. As discussed in Chapter 10, the F distribution is a right-skewed distribution that starts at zero (F cannot be negative as SSA and SSE are sums of squares) and has no upper limit (as the variances could be of any magnitude). The higher the F value, the stronger is the evidence toward rejecting the null hypothesis. Thus for ANOVA, the F test is

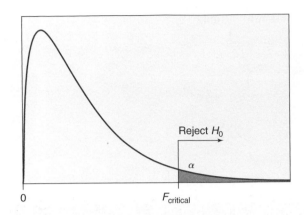

a right-tailed test. For a given level of significance α, we can use Appendix F to obtain the right-tail critical value of F. Alternatively, we can use Excel's function $=\text{FINV}(\alpha, \nu_1, \nu_2)$. The decision rule is illustrated in Figure 11.7. This critical value is denoted F_{α, ν_1, ν_2} or $F_{\alpha, c-1, n-1}$.

Concept Check

Based on the discussion of degrees of freedom in Chapter 8, why is the degrees of freedom for the treatments equal to $c - 1$? Why is the degrees of freedom for the error equal to $n - c$? Why is the degrees of freedom for the total variation equal to $n - 1$? Explain your answers.

EXAMPLE 1

Carton Packing

A cosmetics manufacturer's regional distribution centre has four workstations that are responsible for packing cartons for shipment to small retailers. Each workstation is staffed by two workers. The task involves assembling each order, placing it in a shipping carton, inserting packing material, taping the carton, and placing a computer-generated shipping label on each carton. Generally, each station can pack 200 cartons a day, and often more. However, there is variability, due to differences in orders, labels, and cartons. Table 11.3 shows the number of cartons packed per day during a recent week. Is the variation among stations within the range attributable to chance, or do these samples indicate actual differences in the means?

TABLE 11.3   Number of Cartons Packed   Cartons

	Station 1	Station 2	Station 3	Station 4
	236	238	220	241
	250	239	236	233
	252	262	232	212
	233	247	243	231
	239	246	213	213
Sum	1,210	1,232	1,144	1,130
Mean	242.0	246.4	228.8	226.0
St. Dev.	8.515	9.607	12.153	12.884
n	5	5	5	5

As a preliminary step, we plot the data (Figure 11.8) to check for any time pattern and just to visualize the data. We see some potential differences in means, but no obvious time pattern (otherwise we would have to consider observation order as a second factor). We proceed with the hypothesis test.

STEP 1: STATE THE HYPOTHESES

The hypotheses to be tested are

H_0: $\mu_1 = \mu_2 = \mu_3 = \mu_4$ (the means are equal)

H_1: Not all the means are equal (at least one mean is different)

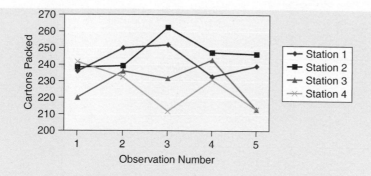

FIGURE 11.8

Plot of the Data

STEP 2: STATE THE DECISION RULE

There are $c = 4$ groups and $n = 20$ observations, so degrees of freedom for the F test are

Numerator: $\nu_1 = c - 1 = 4 - 1 = 3$ (between treatments, factor)

Denominator: $\nu_2 = n - c = 20 - 4 = 16$ (within treatments, error)

We will use $\alpha = 0.05$ for the test. The 5 percent right-tail critical value from Appendix F is $F_{3,16}$ = 3.24. Instead of Appendix F we could use Excel's function =FINV(0.05,3,16), which yields $F_{0.05,3,16}$ = 3.238872. This decision rule is illustrated in Figure 11.9.

STEP 3: PERFORM THE CALCULATIONS

Using Excel for the calculations, we obtain the results shown in Figure 11.10. You can specify the desired level of significance (Excel's default is $\alpha = 0.05$). Note that Excel labels *SSA* "between groups" and *SSE* "within groups." This is an intuitive and attractive way to describe the variation.

STEP 4: MAKE THE DECISION

Because the test statistic $F = 4.12$ exceeds the critical value $F_{0.05,3,16} = 3.24$, we can reject the hypothesis of equal means. Because Excel gives the p value, you don't actually need Excel's critical value.

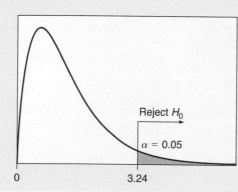

FIGURE 11.9

F Test Using
$\alpha = 0.05$ with $F_{3,16}$

Critical Values of $F_{0.01}$

									Top d.f. = ν_1											
	1	*2*	*3*	*4*	*5*	*6*	*7*	*8*	*9*	*10*	*11*	*12*	*13*	*14*	*15*	*16*	*17*	*18*	*19*	*20*
1	4052.18	4999.50	5403.35	5624.58	5763.65	5858.99	5928.36	5981.07	6022.47	6055.85	6083.32	6106.32	6125.86	6142.67	6157.28	6170.10	6181.43	6191.53	6200.58	6208.73
2	98.50	99.00	99.17	99.25	99.30	99.33	99.36	99.37	99.39	99.40	99.41	99.42	99.42	99.43	99.43	99.44	99.44	99.44	99.45	99.45
3	34.12	30.82	29.46	28.71	28.24	27.91	27.67	27.49	27.35	27.23	27.13	27.05	26.98	26.92	26.87	26.83	26.79	26.75	26.72	26.69
4	21.20	18.00	16.69	15.98	15.52	15.21	14.98	14.80	14.66	14.55	14.45	14.37	14.31	14.25	14.20	14.15	14.11	14.08	14.05	14.02
5	16.26	13.27	12.06	11.39	10.97	10.67	10.46	10.29	10.16	10.05	9.96	9.89	9.82	9.77	9.72	9.68	9.64	9.61	9.58	9.55
6	13.75	10.92	9.78	9.15	8.75	8.47	8.26	8.10	7.98	7.87	7.79	7.72	7.66	7.60	7.56	7.52	7.48	7.45	7.42	7.40
7	12.25	9.55	8.45	7.85	7.46	7.19	6.99	6.84	6.72	6.62	6.54	6.47	6.41	6.36	6.31	6.28	6.24	6.21	6.18	6.16
8	11.26	8.65	7.59	7.01	6.63	6.37	6.18	6.03	5.91	5.81	5.73	5.67	5.61	5.56	5.52	5.48	5.44	5.41	5.38	5.36
9	10.56	8.02	6.99	6.42	6.06	5.80	5.61	5.47	5.35	5.26	5.18	5.11	5.05	5.01	4.96	4.92	4.89	4.86	4.83	4.81
10	10.04	7.56	6.55	5.99	5.64	5.39	5.20	5.06	4.94	4.85	4.77	4.71	4.65	4.60	4.56	4.52	4.49	4.46	4.43	4.41
Bottom 11	9.65	7.21	6.22	5.67	5.32	5.07	4.89	4.74	4.63	4.54	4.46	4.40	4.34	4.29	4.25	4.21	4.18	4.15	4.12	4.10
d.f. = ν_2 12	9.33	6.93	5.95	5.41	5.06	4.82	4.64	4.50	4.39	4.30	4.22	4.16	4.10	4.05	4.01	3.97	3.94	3.91	3.88	3.86
13	9.07	6.70	5.74	5.21	4.86	4.62	4.44	4.30	4.19	4.10	4.02	3.96	3.91	3.86	3.82	3.78	3.75	3.72	3.69	3.66
14	8.86	6.51	5.56	5.04	4.69	4.46	4.28	4.14	4.03	3.94	3.86	3.80	3.75	3.70	3.66	3.62	3.59	3.56	3.53	3.51
15	8.68	6.36	5.42	4.89	4.56	4.32	4.14	4.00	3.89	3.80	3.73	3.67	3.61	3.56	3.52	3.49	3.45	3.42	3.40	3.37
16	8.53	6.23	5.29	4.77	4.44	4.20	4.03	3.89	3.78	3.69	3.62	3.55	3.50	3.45	3.41	3.37	3.34	3.31	3.28	3.26
17	8.40	6.11	5.18	4.67	4.34	4.10	3.93	3.79	3.68	3.59	3.52	3.46	3.40	3.35	3.31	3.27	3.24	3.21	3.19	3.16
18	8.29	6.01	5.09	4.58	4.25	4.01	3.84	3.71	3.60	3.51	3.43	3.37	3.32	3.27	3.23	3.19	3.16	3.13	3.10	3.08
19	8.18	5.93	5.01	4.50	4.17	3.94	3.77	3.63	3.52	3.43	3.36	3.30	3.24	3.19	3.15	3.12	3.08	3.05	3.03	3.00
20	8.10	5.85	4.94	4.43	4.10	3.87	3.70	3.56	3.46	3.37	3.29	3.23	3.18	3.13	3.09	3.05	3.02	2.99	2.96	2.94
21	8.02	5.78	4.87	4.37	4.04	3.81	3.64	3.51	3.40	3.31	3.24	3.17	3.12	3.07	3.03	2.99	2.96	2.93	2.90	2.88
22	7.95	5.72	4.82	4.31	3.99	3.76	3.59	3.45	3.35	3.26	3.18	3.12	3.07	3.02	2.98	2.94	2.91	2.88	2.85	2.83
23	7.88	5.66	4.76	4.26	3.94	3.71	3.54	3.41	3.30	3.21	3.14	3.07	3.02	2.97	2.93	2.89	2.86	2.83	2.80	2.78
24	7.82	5.61	4.72	4.22	3.90	3.67	3.50	3.36	3.26	3.17	3.09	3.03	2.98	2.93	2.89	2.85	2.82	2.79	2.76	2.74
25	7.77	5.57	4.68	4.18	3.85	3.63	3.46	3.32	3.22	3.13	3.06	2.99	2.94	2.89	2.85	2.81	2.78	2.75	2.72	2.70

FIGURE 11.10

Excel's One-Factor ANOVA Results

Cartons

Anova: Single Factor

SUMMARY

Groups	Count	Sum	Average	Variance
Station 1	5	1210	242	72.5
Station 2	5	1232	246.4	92.3
Station 3	5	1144	228.8	147.7
Station 4	5	1130	226	166

ANOVA

Source of Variation	SS	df	MS	F	P-value	F crit
Between Groups	1479.2	3	493.0667	4.121769	0.024124	3.238872
Within Groups	1914	16	119.625			
Total	3393.2	19				

FIGURE 11.11

MegaStat's One-Factor ANOVA Results

Cartons

One factor ANOVA

Mean	n	Std. Dev	
242.0	5	8.51	Station 1
246.4	5	9.61	Station 2
228.8	5	12.15	Station 3
226.0	5	12.88	Station 4
235.8	20	13.36	Total

ANOVA table

Source	SS	df	MS	F	p-value
Treatment	1,479.20	3	493.067	4.12	.0241
Error	1,914.00	16	119.625		
Total	3,393.20	19			

The p value ($p = 0.024124$) is less than the level of significance ($\alpha = 0.05$), which confirms that we should reject the hypothesis of equal treatment means. For comparison, Figure 11.11 shows MegaStat's ANOVA table for the same data. The results are the same, although MegaStat rounds things off, highlights significant p values, and gives standard deviations instead of variances for each treatment.

MegaStat provides additional insights by showing a dot plot of observations by group, shown in Figure 11.12. The display includes group means (shown as short horizontal tick marks) and the overall mean (shown as a dashed line). The dot plot suggests that workstations 3 and 4 have means below the overall mean, while workstations 1 and 2 are above the overall mean.

FIGURE 11.12

Dot Plot of Four Samples

Cartons

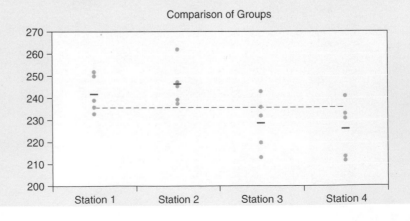

Comparison of Groups

MINITAB's One-Factor ANOVA FIGURE 11.13

Using MINITAB

MINITAB's output, shown in Figure 11.13, is the same as Excel's except that MINITAB rounds off the results and displays a confidence interval for each group mean, an attractive feature.* In our carton example, the confidence intervals overlap, except possibly workstations 2 and 4. But comparing pairs of confidence intervals is not quite the same as what an ANOVA test does, as ANOVA seeks to compare *all* the group means *simultaneously*.

EXAMPLE 2

House Prices and Location

Let us consider the example in Illustration 2, earlier in this chapter, and use Excel for our ANOVA calculations, and follow the steps of our hypothesis testing procedure.

STEP 1: STATE THE HYPOTHESES

The hypotheses to be tested are

$H_0: \mu_1 = \mu_2 = \mu_3$ (the means are equal)

H_1: Not all the means are equal (at least one mean is different)

STEP 2: STATE THE DECISION RULE

There are $c = 3$ groups and $n = 15$ observations, so the degrees of freedom for the F test are

Numerator: $\nu_1 = c - 1 = 3 - 1 = 2$ (between treatments, factor)

Denominator: $\nu_2 = n - c = 15 - 3 = 12$ (within treatments, error)

STEP 3: PERFORM THE CALCULATIONS

Figure 11.14 shows the data and Excel output.

STEP 4: MAKE THE DECISION

Compare the numbers under the column "MS": 6500.00 and 523.67. These are the same numbers that we obtained under intuitive explanation of the ANOVA procedure. We used this test using $\alpha = 0.05$. The critical F value $= F_{\alpha, \nu_1, \nu_2} = F_{0.05, 2, 12} = 3.89$, and $F_{calc} = 12.41$, which happens to fall in the rejection region. So we reject the null hypothesis and claim that at least one of the population means is different. Note that the computer output also gives us p value $= 0.001$. Any α, or level of significance, greater than this p value would lead us to reject the null hypothesis.

---

*MINITAB and most other statistical packages prefer the data in *stacked* format. Each variable has its own column (e.g., column one contains all the Y values, while column two contains group labels like "Station 1"). MINITAB will convert *unstacked* data to *stacked* data for one-factor ANOVA, but not for other ANOVA models. See *LearningStats* Unit 11 for examples of *stacked* versus *unstacked* data.

FIGURE 11.14 **House Prices and Locations**

	A	B	C	D	E	F	G	H
1		**Edmonton**	**Toronto**	**Montreal**				
2		347	385	285				
3		318	368	295				
4		327	335	325				
5		363	385	280				
6		345	327	265				
7								
8		**Anova: Single Factor output**						
9								
10		**SUMMARY**						
11		*Groups*	*Count*	*Sum*	*Average*	*Variance*		
12		Edmonton	5	1700	340	314		
13		Toronto	5	1800	360	757		
14		Montreal	5	1450	290	500		
15								
16		**ANOVA**						
17		*Source of Variation*	*SS*	*df*	*MS*	*F*	*P-value*	*F crit*
18		Between Groups	13000	2	6500.00	12.41	0.001	3.89
19		Within Groups	6284	12	523.67			
20								
21		Total	19284	14				

A Closer Look

1. Using ANOVA to test means is equivalent to testing for a relationship between a quantitative response variable (e.g., house prices) and a qualitative variable (e.g., location of house). Concluding that the means are not the same for the various treatments is equivalent to concluding that there is a relationship between Y and the factor being tested. (For example, concluding that mean house prices are not all the same for Toronto, Edmonton, and Montreal is equivalent to stating that there is a relationship between house prices and where the house is located.)

2. We can also use ANOVA to test the difference in the means of only two populations. This test is equivalent to the t test for independent samples assuming equal population variances. If you conduct these two tests on the same set of data, you would find that F_{calc} using ANOVA equals $(t_{calc})^2$ using the t test. You would also find that $F_{crit} = (t_{crit})^2$, which means that if we were to reject the null hypothesis using ANOVA, you would also reject the null hypothesis using the t test.

3. Interpretation of the results of our tests depends upon how we select treatments within a factor. For example, because we had specifically chosen Toronto, Edmonton, and Montreal, our results apply to only these three cities, and because we rejected the null hypothesis, our conclusion is that mean house prices are not all the same for Toronto, Edmonton, and Montreal, or that there is a relationship, for Toronto, Edmonton, and Montreal, between house prices and their location. If we had randomly selected these three cities from among all cities in Canada, our results would apply to all cities in

Canada, our conclusion then would be that mean house prices are not all the same for cities across Canada, or that there is a relationship between house prices in Canadian cities and where the house is located. If the treatments are arbitrarily selected, the model used is referred to as a fixed-effects model. If the treatments are randomly selected, the model is called a **random-effects model.** Where there is more than one factor, with some having their treatments randomly selected and others having their treatments arbitrarily selected, the model is referred to as a **mixed-effects model.** With a one-factor model, the test statistic and decision rule, and thus your conclusions, are the same for both fixed-effects and random-effects models. For models with more than one factor, the test statistics and decision rules are not necessarily the same for the three types of models and may affect your conclusions.

Section Exercises

Instructions: For each data set: (a) State the hypotheses. (b) Use Excel's Data > Data Analysis (or MegaStat or MINITAB) to perform the one-factor ANOVA, using $\alpha = 0.05$. (c) State your conclusion about the population means. Was the decision close? (d) Interpret the *p* value carefully. (e) Include a plot of the data for each group if you are using MegaStat, and confidence intervals for the group means if you are using MINITAB. What do the plots show?

11.1 Scrap rates per thousand (parts whose defects cannot be reworked) are compared for five randomly selected days at three plants. Does the data prove a significant difference in mean scrap rates? (LO 3) **ScrapRate**

Scrap Rate (per Thousand Units)

Plant A	Plant B	Plant C
11.4	11.1	10.2
12.5	14.1	9.5
10.1	16.8	9.0
13.8	13.2	13.3
13.7	14.6	5.9

11.2 One particular morning, the length of time spent in the examination rooms is recorded for each patient seen by each physician at an orthopedic clinic. Does the data prove a significant difference in mean times? (LO 3) **Physicians**

Time in Examination Rooms

Physician 1	Physician 2	Physician 3	Physician 4
34	33	17	28
25	35	30	33
27	31	30	31
31	31	26	27
26	42	32	32
34	33	28	33
21		26	40
		29	

11.3 Semester GPAs are compared for seven randomly chosen students in each class level at Queen's University. Does the data prove a significant difference in mean GPAs? (LO 3) **GPA1**

GPA for Randomly Selected Students in Four Business Majors

Accounting	Finance	Human Resources	Marketing
2.48	3.16	2.93	3.54
2.19	3.01	2.89	3.71
2.62	3.07	3.48	2.94
3.15	2.88	3.33	3.46
3.56	3.33	3.53	3.50
2.53	2.87	2.95	3.25
3.31	2.85	3.58	3.20

11.4 Sales of *People* magazine are compared over a five-week period at four Chapters stores in Toronto. Does the data prove a significant difference in mean weekly sales? (LO 3) **Magazines**

Weekly Sales

Store 1	Store 2	Store 3	Store 4
102	97	89	100
106	77	91	116
105	82	75	87
115	80	106	102
112	101	94	100

11.5 Getting to work each day is not much fun if you happen to live in Mississauga and work in Pickering. One such individual who has recently assumed that role has analyzed the traffic situation and has determined that there are three possible routes that he would consider taking from home to work. To help him decide which route would be his route of choice, he randomly selected his routes over a month-long period and measured his travelling times (in minutes) as follows (not counting any days in which accidents affected his commuting time):

Route A	Route B	Route C
73	65	75
77	64	78
69	68	73
79	69	72
74	67	77
76	63	71
75		75

At the 0.05 level of significance, can this commuter conclude that the average commuting times are not all the same? (LO 3)

11.3 Two-Factor ANOVA without Replication (Randomized Block Model)

Data Format

Suppose that two factors A and B (e.g., type of home and location of home) may affect Y (e.g., selling price). One way to visualize this is to imagine a data matrix with r rows (e.g., five rows, each representing a type of home) and c columns (e.g., three columns, each representing a different Canadian city). Each row is a level of factor A (type of home), while each column is a level of factor B (location). Initially, we will consider the case where all levels of both factors

TABLE 11.4 **Format of Two-Factor ANOVA Data Set without Replication**

Levels of Factor A	Levels of Factor B B_1	B_2		B_c	Row Mean
A_1	y_{11}	y_{12}	$\cdots$	y_{1c}	$\bar{y}_{1\cdot}$
A_2	y_{21}	y_{22}	$\cdots$	y_{2c}	$\bar{y}_{2\cdot}$
$\cdots$	$\cdots$	$\cdots$	$\cdots$	$\cdots$	$\cdots$
A_r	y_{r1}	y_{r2}	$\cdots$	y_{rc}	$\bar{y}_{r\cdot}$
Col Mean	$\bar{y}_{\cdot 1}$	$\bar{y}_{\cdot 2}$	$\cdots$	$\bar{y}_{\cdot c}$	$\bar{y}$

occur, and each cell contains only one observation. In this **two-factor ANOVA without replication** (or *non-repeated measures design*) each factor combination is observed exactly once. The mean of Y can be computed either across the rows or down the columns, as shown in Table 11.4. The grand mean $\bar{y}$ is the sum of all data values divided by the sample size rc.

Two-Factor ANOVA Model

Expressed in linear form, the two-factor ANOVA model is

$$y_{jk} = \mu + A_j + B_k + \varepsilon_{jk} \tag{11.10}$$

where

y_{jk} = observed data value in row j and column k

μ = common mean for all treatments

A_j = effect of row factor A ($j = 1, 2, \ldots, r$)

B_k = effect of column factor B ($k = 1, 2, \ldots, c$)

ε_{jk} = random error

The random error within each row-column combination of factors is assumed to be normally distributed with zero mean and the same variance for all row-column combinations. In addition, there is assumed to be no interaction effect of row and column factors on Y. More will be said about interaction effects later in this chapter.

Hypotheses to Be Tested

If we are interested only in what happens to the response for the particular levels of the factors that were selected (a *fixed-effects model*), then the hypotheses to be tested are

Factor A

H_0: $A_1 = A_2 = \cdots = A_r = 0$ (row means are the same)

H_1: Not all the A_j are equal to zero (row means are not all the same)

Factor B

H_0: $B_1 = B_2 = \cdots = B_c = 0$ (column means are the same)

H_1: Not all the B_k are equal to zero (column means are not all the same)

If we are unable to reject either null hypothesis, all variation in Y is just a random disturbance around the mean μ:

$$Y_{jk} = \mu + \varepsilon_{jk} \tag{11.11}$$

Randomized Block Design Model (Extension of Paired t Test)

A special terminology is used when only one factor A is of research interest and the other factor B is merely used to control for potential confounding influences. In this case, the two-factor ANOVA model with one observation per cell is sometimes called the **randomized block design model.** In this design, the experimental units or subjects are first sorted into homogeneous

TABLE 11.5 Format of Randomized Block Experiment: Two Factors

Block (Soil Type)	Treatment (Fertilizer) F_1	F_2	F_3	F_4
S_1				
S_2				
S_3				

groups, called blocks, and the treatments are then assigned at random within the blocks. In the randomized block design model, it is customary to call the column effects *treatments* (as in one-factor ANOVA to signify that they are the effect of interest) while the row effects are called *blocks*.* For example, an Alberta agribusiness might want to study the effect of four kinds of fertilizer (F_1, F_2, F_3, F_4) in promoting wheat growth (Y) on three soil types (S_1, S_2, S_3). To control for the effects of soil type, we could define three blocks (rows), each containing one soil type, as shown in Table 11.5. Subjects within each block (soil type) would be randomly assigned to the treatments (fertilizer).

A randomized block model looks like a two-factor ANOVA and is computed exactly like a two-factor ANOVA. However, its interpretation by the researcher may resemble a one-factor ANOVA as only the column effects (treatments) are of interest when a randomized block design model is used to test means of three or more populations (or two) using matched samples. As with the paired *t* test, we match our samples when we believe that there is some characteristic that may adversely affect our conclusions if our samples were not matched. For example, if we wish to compare the effectiveness of three diet plans, we may want to match our samples based on how much overweight the individuals were before being exposed to the diets if we believe that the amount of overweight will affect how much weight they lose no matter what the diet plan. Similarly, if we wish to compare the house prices in Toronto, Edmonton, and Montreal, we may want to match our samples according to type of homes sold if we believe that different types of homes tend to sell for different prices. The blocks exist not only to reduce the possibility of erroneous conclusions but also to reduce the unexplained variation. In these situations, although the effect of the blocks will show up in the hypothesis test, the blocks are of no interest to the researcher as a separate factor.

Calculation of Non-Replicated Two-Factor ANOVA

Calculations for the non-replicated two-factor ANOVA may be arranged as in Table 11.6. Degrees of freedom sum to $n - 1$. For a data set with r rows and c columns, notice that $n = rc$. The total sum of squares shown in Table 11.6 has three components:

$$SST = SSA + SSB + SSE \qquad \text{(11.12)}$$

where

> SST = total sum of squared deviations about the mean
>
> SSA = between rows sum of squares (effect of factor A)
>
> SSB = between columns sum of squares (effect of factor B)
>
> SSE = error sum of squares (residual variation)

SST measures the total variation in the data. *SSA* measures the variation in the treatment means of factor A or the effect that factor A has on the response variable. *SSB* measures the variation in the means of factor B levels, or the effect that factor B has on the response variable. *SSE* is a measure of unexplained variation. If *SSE* is relatively high compared to *SSA* and *SSB*, we would fail to reject the null hypotheses that either of the factor effects do not differ significantly from zero. Conversely, if *SSE* is relatively small compared to *SSA* and/or *SSB*, it is a sign that at least one factor is a relevant predictor of *Y*. Before doing the *F* test, each sum of squares must be divided by its degrees of freedom to obtain the *mean square*. Calculations

*In principle, either rows or columns could be the blocking factor, but it is customary to put the blocking factor in rows.

TABLE 11.6   Format of Two-Factor ANOVA with One Observation per Cell

Source of Variation	Sum of Squares	Degrees of Freedom	Mean Square	F Ratio
Factor A (row effect)	$SSA = c\sum_{j=1}^{r}(\bar{y}_j - \bar{y})^2$	$r - 1$	$MSA = \dfrac{SSA}{r-1}$	$F_A = \dfrac{MSA}{MSE}$
Factor B (column effect)	$SSB = r\sum_{k=1}^{c}(\bar{y}_k - \bar{y})^2$	$c - 1$	$MSB = \dfrac{SSB}{c-1}$	$F_B = \dfrac{MSB}{MSE}$
Error	$SSE = \sum_{j=1}^{r}\sum_{k=1}^{c}(y_{jk} - \bar{y}_j - \bar{y}_k + \bar{y})^2$	$(r-1)(c-1)$	$MSE = \dfrac{SSE}{(c-1)(r-1)}$	
Total	$SST = \sum_{j=1}^{c}\sum_{k=1}^{r}(y_{jk} - \bar{y})^2$	$rc - 1$		

are almost always done by a computer. For details of two-factor calculation methods, see *LearningStats* Unit 11. There are case studies for each ANOVA.

EXAMPLE 3

Types of Housing

When comparing house prices in Toronto, Edmonton, and Montreal, suppose we believed that the type of housing unit affects the selling price of that unit. Therefore, in conducting our study, we decided to define housing types as high-rise condominiums, townhouses, ranch-style houses, and multi-level single-unit houses. In each of these three cities we randomly selected one recently sold home in each of these categories and recorded their selling prices (in $1000s) as follows:

House Prices ($1000's)

	Toronto	Edmonton	Montreal
High-rise Condos	250	255	220
Townhouses	275	285	240
Ranch-style Houses	335	360	305
Multi-level Houses	425	450	395

Let us follow the steps of hypothesis testing with the above example using Excel for ANOVA output. Figure 11.15 shows the Excel worksheet with this basic data.

STEP 1: STATE THE HYPOTHESES

It is helpful to assign short, descriptive variable names to each factor. The general form of the model is

$$House\ price = f(location,\ house\ type)$$

Stated as a linear model:

$$y_{jk} = \mu + A_j + B_k + \varepsilon_{jk}$$

The hypotheses are

Factor A (house type)

$H_0: A_1 = A_2 = A_3 = A_4$ (house type has no effect on prices)

$H_1:$ Not all the A_j are equal to zero (house type has an effect on prices)

	A	B	C	D
1		Housing Prices ($1000s)		
2		Toronto	Edmonton	Montreal
3	High-rise Condos	250	255	220
4	Townhouses	275	285	240
5	Ranch-style Houses	335	360	305
6	Multi-level Houses	425	450	395

FIGURE 11.15

Excel Worksheet for ANOVA Output

Factor *B* (location)

H_0: $B_1 = B_2 = B_3 = 0$ (house location has no effect on prices)

H_1: Not all the B_k are equal to zero (house location has an effect on prices)

STEP 2: STATE THE DECISION RULE

Each *F* test may require a different right-tail critical value because the numerator degrees of freedom depend on the number of factor levels, while denominator degrees of freedom (error *SSE*) are the same for all three tests:

Factor A: $\nu_1 = r - 1 = 4 - 1 = 3$ ($r = 4$ house types)

Factor B: $\nu_1 = c - 1 = 3 - 1 = 2$ ($c = 3$ locations)

Error: $\nu_2 = (r - 1)(c - 1) = (4 - 1)(3 - 1) = 6$

From Appendix F, the 5 percent critical values in a right-tailed test (all ANOVA tests are right-tailed tests) are

$F_{0.05,3,6} = 4.76$ for factor *A*

$F_{0.05,2,6} = 5.14$ for factor *B*

We will reject the appropriate null hypothesis (no factor effect) if its *F* test statistic exceeds the critical value.

STEP 3: PERFORM THE CALCULATIONS

In the Excel worksheet, select the data A2:D6. Follow the menu path Data > Data Analysis. You see the window in Figure 11.16. Select Anova: Two-Factor Without Replication and then OK.

FIGURE 11.16

Excel's ANOVA Menu: Two Factor without Replication

In the window that appears, fill in the information as displayed in the image in Figure 11.17.

FIGURE 11.17

Inputting for ANOVA: Two Factor without Replication

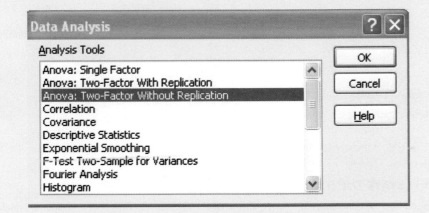

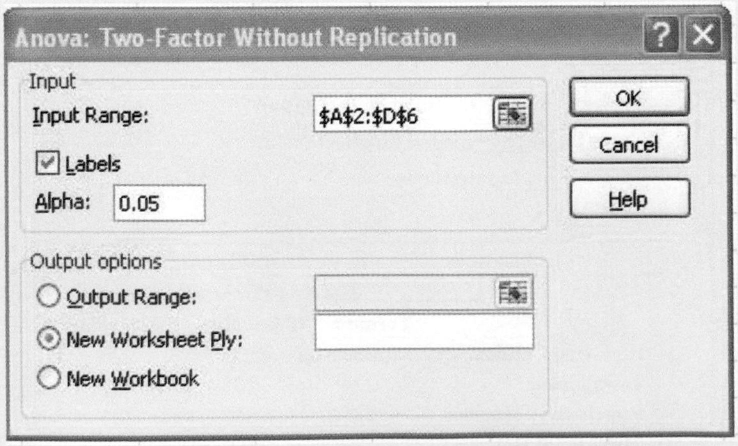

The results are shown in a new worksheet. There is a table of means and variances, followed by the ANOVA table, displayed in Figure 11.18.

	A	B	C	D	E	F	G
1	Anova: Two-Factor Without Replication						
2							
3	*SUMMARY*	*Count*	*Sum*	*Average*	*Variance*		
4	High-rise Condos	3	725	241.667	358.333		
5	Townhouses	3	800	266.667	558.333		
6	Ranch-style Houses	3	1000	333.333	758.333		
7	Multi-level Houses	3	1270	423.333	758.333		
8							
9	Toronto	4	1285	321.25	6056.25		
10	Edmonton	4	1350	337.5	7575		
11	Montreal	4	1160	290	6216.67		
12							
13							
14	ANOVA						
15	*Source of Variation*	*SS*	*df*	*MS*	*F*	*P-value*	*F crit*
16	Rows	59339.58	3	19779.86	581.286	0.000	4.757
17	Columns	4662.5	2	2331.25	68.510	0.000	5.143
18	Error	204.1667	6	34.02778			
19							
20	Total	64206.25	11				

FIGURE 11.18
ANOVA Worksheet: Two Factor without Replication

STEP 4: MAKE THE DECISION

Because $F_A = 581.286$ (rows) exceeds $F_{0.05,3,6} = 4.757$, we see that factor A (house type) has a significant effect on the selling price. The p value for house type is practically 0, which says that the F statistic is not due to chance. Similarly, $F_B = 68.51$ exceeds $F_{0.05,2,6} = 5.143$, so we see that factor B (location) also has a significant effect on the selling price. Again p value is practically 0, implying that it is extremely unlikely to be a chance result. In short, we conclude that

- House price is significantly affected by house type ($p = 0$).
- House price is significantly affected by location of house ($p = 0$).

Always remember the dictum: The smaller the p value, the stronger is the evidence for rejecting the null hypothesis.

A Closer Look

As previously mentioned, this model assumes no interaction effect on Y. Essentially, what this means is that the effect of the levels that one factor has on Y is the same no matter what the level of the other factor. For example, if multi-level houses cost, on average, $50,000 more than ranch-style houses in Toronto, they also cost $50,000 more, on average, in Edmonton and in Montreal. Figures 11.19 and 11.20 show the true average prices of different types of homes in each of the three cities: Figure 11.19 indicates no interaction effect while Figure 11.20 indicates such an effect.

FIGURE 11.19

True Average Home Prices without Interaction Effect

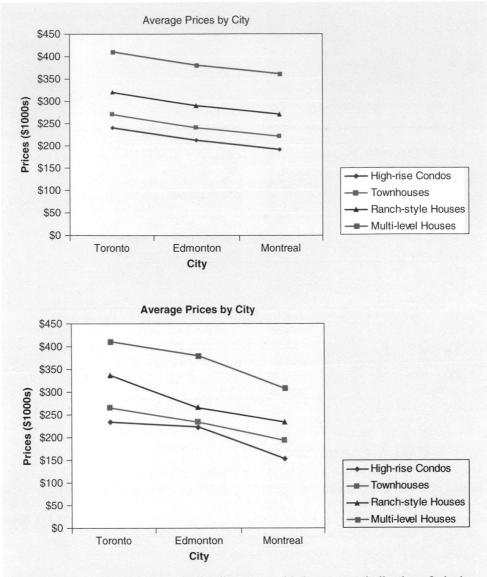

Plotting the sample prices on a similar diagram would give us some indication of whether an interaction effect is present. The resulting diagram (Figure 11.21) does not deviate significantly from a "no interaction effect" diagram and thus we can continue to assume that there is no interaction effect.

FIGURE 11.20

True Average Home Prices with Interaction Effect

FIGURE 11.21

Plotting Sample Home Prices: No Interaction Effect

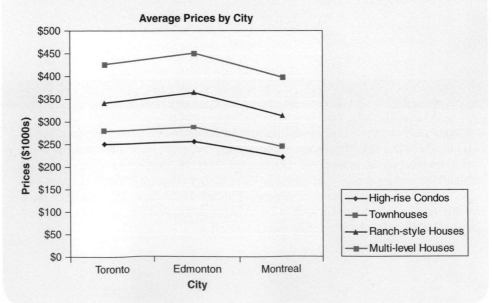

Concept Check

If we had exactly the same set of data without recognizing that the samples were matched by type of housing unit and without doing any calculations, how would that change the values of *SST, SSA,* and *SSE?* Explain. How would that change the value of the test statistic for testing factor *A?* Explain. How would the critical value, F_{crit}, for testing factor *A* change? Explain. How would that affect whether the null hypothesis would be rejected? Explain.

Limitations of Two-Factor ANOVA without Replication

When replication is impossible or extremely expensive, two-factor ANOVA without replication must suffice. For example, crash-testing of automobiles to estimate collision damage is very costly. However, whenever possible, there is a strong incentive to replicate the experiment to add power to the tests. Would different results have been obtained if the car had been tested not once but several times at each speed? Or if several different cars had been tested? For testing acceleration, there would seem to be no major cost impediment to replication except the time and effort required to take the measurements. Of course, it could be argued that if the measurements of acceleration were careful and precise the first time, replication would be a waste of time. And yet some random variation is found in any experiment. These are matters to ponder. But two-factor ANOVA *with replication* does offer advantages, as you will see.

   Note: When the ANOVA model in the next section of this chapter is discussed, interaction effects will be mentioned. To conduct the above tests using the above model, we assume that there are no interaction effects.

Section Exercises

Instructions: For each data set: (a) State the hypotheses. If you are viewing this data set as a randomized block, which is the blocking factor and why? (b) Use Excel's **Data > Data Analysis** (or MegaStat or MINITAB) to perform the two-factor ANOVA without replication, using $\alpha = 0.05$. (c) State your conclusions about the treatment means. (d) Interpret the *p* values carefully. (e) Include a plot of the data for each group if you are using MegaStat, or individual value plots if you are using MINITAB. What do the plots show?

11.6   Concerned about Friday absenteeism, management examined absenteeism rates for the last three Fridays in four assembly plants. Does this sample allow us to conclude that there is a difference in average absenteeism for different plants? (LO 3)
   Absences

	Plant 1	Plant 2	Plant 3	Plant 4
March 4	19	18	27	22
March 11	22	20	32	27
March 18	20	16	28	26

11.7   Engineers are testing company fleet vehicle fuel economy (miles per gallon, or mpg) performance by using different types of fuel. One vehicle of each size is tested. Does this sample allow us to conclude that there is a difference in average mpg for different types of fuel? (LO 3)   **MPG2**

	87 Octane	89 Octane	91 Octane	Ethanol 5%	Ethanol 10%
Compact	27.2	30.0	30.3	26.8	25.8
Mid-Size	23.0	25.6	28.6	26.6	23.3
Full-Size	21.4	22.5	22.2	18.9	20.8
SUV	18.7	24.1	22.1	18.7	17.4

11.8 Five statistics professors are using the same textbook with the same syllabus and common exams. At the end of the semester, the department committee on instruction looked at average exam scores. Does this sample allow us to conclude a difference in average exam scores for different professors? (LO 3)   **ExamScores**

	Prof. Argand	Prof. Blague	Prof. Clagmire	Prof. Dross	Prof. Ennuyeux
Exam 1	80.9	72.3	84.9	81.2	70.9
Exam 2	75.5	74.6	78.7	76.5	70.3
Exam 3	79.0	76.0	79.6	75.0	73.7
Final	69.9	78.0	77.8	74.1	73.9

11.9 A beer distributor is comparing quarterly sales of Molson Canadian (number of six-packs sold) at three beer stores in the Toronto area. Does this sample allow us to conclude a difference in average quarterly sales at the different stores? (LO 3)   **BeerSales**

	Store 1	Store 2	Store 3
Qtr 1	1,521	1,298	1,708
Qtr 2	1,396	1,492	1,382
Qtr 3	1,178	1,052	1,132
Qtr 4	1,730	1,659	1,851

11.10 Getting to work each day is not much fun if you happen to live in Mississauga and work in Pickering. One such individual who has recently assumed that role has analyzed the traffic situation and has determined that there are three possible routes that he would consider taking from home to work. To help him decide which route would be his route of choice, he conducted an experiment in the belief that the day of the week may affect travelling times to work. Taking this belief into account, he randomly selected three Mondays, three Tuesdays, and so on, during his first month on the job and then he randomly assigned one route to take on one of these Mondays, another route on another Monday, the third route on the third Monday, and so on through the week, measuring his travelling times (in minutes) as follows.

Day	Route A	Route B	Route C
Monday	73	71	75
Tuesday	77	75	78
Wednesday	82	79	82
Thursday	79	74	77
Friday	74	69	73

At the 0.05 level of significance, can this commuter conclude that the average commuting times are not all the same along the three routes? LO 3)

11.4   Two-Factor ANOVA with Replication (Full Factorial Model)

What Does Replication Accomplish?

In a two-factor model, suppose that each factor combination is observed m times. With an equal number of observations in each cell (*balanced data*) we have a two-factor ANOVA model *with replication*. Replication allows us to test not only the factors' **main effects** but also an **interaction effect.** This model is often called the **full factorial** model. In linear model format it may be written

$$y_{ijk} = \mu + A_j + B_k + AB_{jk} + \varepsilon_{ijk} \tag{11.13}$$

where

y_{ijk} = observation i for row j and column k ($i = 1, 2, \ldots, m$)

μ = common mean for all treatments

A_j = effect attributed to factor A in row j ($j = 1, 2, \ldots, r$)

B_k = effect attributed to factor B in column k ($k = 1, 2, \ldots, c$)

AB_{jk} = effect attributed to interaction between factors A and B

ε_{ijk} = random error (normally distributed, zero mean, same variance for all treatments)

Interaction effects can be important. For example, an agribusiness researcher might postulate that corn yield is related to seed type (A), soil type (B), interaction between seed type and soil type (AB), or all three. In the absence of any factor effects, all variation about the mean μ is purely random.

Format of Hypotheses

For a *fixed-effects* ANOVA model (i.e., the levels of each of the two factors are arbitrarily selected as opposed to being randomly selected), the hypotheses that could be tested in the two-factor ANOVA model with replicated observations are

Factor *A:* Row Effect

H_0: $A_1 = A_2 = \cdots = A_r = 0$ (row means are the same)

H_1: Not all the A_j are equal to zero (row means are not all the same)

Factor *B:* Column Effect

H_0: $B_1 = B_2 = \cdots = B_c = 0$ (column means are the same)

H_1: Not all the B_k are equal to zero (column means are not all the same)

Interaction Effect

H_0: All the AB_{jk} are equal to zero (there is no interaction effect)

H_1: Not all the AB_{jk} are equal to zero (there is an interaction effect)

If none of the proposed factors has anything to do with Y, then the model collapses to

$$y_{ijk} = \mu + \varepsilon_{ijk} \tag{11.14}$$

Format of Data

Table 11.7 shows the format of a data set with two factors and a balanced (equal) number of observations per treatment (each row/column intersection is a treatment). To avoid

TABLE 11.7   Data Format of Replicated Two-Factor ANOVA

Level of Factor A	Level of Factor B				Row Mean
	B_1	B_2	...	B_c	
A_1	yyy	yyy	...	yyy	$\bar{y}_{1.}$
	yyy	yyy	...	yyy	
	...	...	...	...	
	yyy	yyy	...	yyy	
A_2	yyy	yyy	...	yyy	$\bar{y}_{2.}$
	yyy	yyy	...	yyy	
	...	...	...	...	
	yyy	yyy	...	yyy	
...	...	...	...	...	
A_r	yyy	yyy	...	yyy	$\bar{y}_{r.}$
	yyy	yyy	...	yyy	
	...	...	...	...	
	yyy	yyy	...	yyy	
Col Mean	$\bar{y}_1$	$\bar{y}_2$	...	$\bar{y}_{.c}$	$\bar{y}$

TABLE 11.8 **Two-Factor ANOVA with Replication**

Source of Variation	Sum of Squares	Degrees of Freedom	Mean Square	F Ratio
Factor A (row effect)	$SSA = cm \sum_{j=1}^{r} (\bar{y}_j - \bar{y})^2$	$r - 1$	$MSA = \dfrac{SSA}{r - 1}$	$F_A = \dfrac{MSA}{MSE}$
Factor B (column effect)	$SSB = rm \sum_{k=1}^{c} (\bar{y}_k - \bar{y})^2$	$c - 1$	$MSB = \dfrac{SSB}{c - 1}$	$F_B = \dfrac{MSB}{MSE}$
Interaction ($A \times B$)	$SSI = m \sum_{j=1}^{r} \sum_{k=1}^{c} (\bar{y}_{jk} - \bar{y}_j - \bar{y}_k + \bar{y})^2$	$(r - 1)(c - 1)$	$MSI = \dfrac{SSI}{(r - 1)(c - 1)}$	$F_I = \dfrac{MSI}{MSE}$
Error	$SSE = \sum_{i=1}^{m} \sum_{j=1}^{r} \sum_{k=1}^{c} (y_{ijk} - \bar{y}_{jk})^2$	$rc(m - 1)$	$MSE = \dfrac{SSE}{rc(m - 1)}$	
Total	$SST = \sum_{i=1}^{m} \sum_{j=1}^{r} \sum_{k=1}^{c} (y_{ijk} - \bar{y})^2$	$rcm - 1$		

needless subscripts, the m observations in each treatment are represented simply as *yyy*. Except for the replication within cells, the format is the same as the non-replicated two-factor ANOVA.

Sources of Variation

There are now three F tests that could be performed: one for each main effect (factors A and B) and a third F test for interaction. The total sum of squares is partitioned into four components:

$$SST = SSA + SSB + SSI + SSE \qquad (11.15)$$

where

SST = total sum of squared deviations about the mean

SSA = between rows sum of squares (effect of factor A)

SSB = between columns sum of squares (effect of factor B)

SSI = interaction sum of squares (effect of AB)

SSE = error sum of squares (residual variation)

For an experiment with r rows, c columns, and m replications per treatment, the sums of squares and ANOVA calculations may be presented in a table, shown in Table 11.8.

If SSE is relatively high compared to SST, we expect that we would fail to reject H_0 for the various hypotheses. Conversely, if SSE is relatively small, it is likely that at least one of the factors (row effect, column effect, or interaction) is a relevant predictor of Y. Before doing the F test, each sum of squares must be divided by its degrees of freedom to obtain its *mean square*. Degrees of freedom sum to $n - 1$ (note that $n = rcm$).

A Closer Look

If the model was a *random-effects model* (i.e., the levels of each factor are randomly selected), the test statistics for testing the individual factors would differ from above and if the model was a *mixed-effects model* (i.e., the levels of one factor are randomly selected while the levels of the other factor are arbitrarily selected), the test statistic for one of the factors would differ from above.

EXAMPLE 4
Further House Hunting

Suppose, when comparing house prices, we were interested in determining whether house prices differed among Toronto, Edmonton, and Montreal, and also whether they differed among high-rise condos, townhouses, ranch-style houses, and multi-level houses. We randomly select three recently sold homes from each of the 12 location-type combinations (e.g., three high-rise condos in Toronto), and the samples produce the following selling prices (in $1000s).

House Prices (in $1000s)			
	Toronto	*Edmonton*	*Montreal*
High-rise Condos	315	325	360
	325	340	325
	295	310	330
Townhouses	285	360	350
	310	315	355
	290	345	370
Ranch-style Houses	420	380	400
	455	340	410
	480	360	395
Multi-level Houses	420	430	360
	430	450	375
	410	430	360

Concept Check

Suppose we summarized this data by determining average prices within each housing type, average prices within each city, and average prices within each combination of type and city, and then plotted their results as follows. By looking at Figures 11.22 through 11.24, created from the above house prices data, and without doing any calculations, do you believe that (1) location has an effect on house prices, (2) type of housing unit has an effect on house prices, or (3) there is an interaction effect of type of housing and location on house prices? Explain your answers.

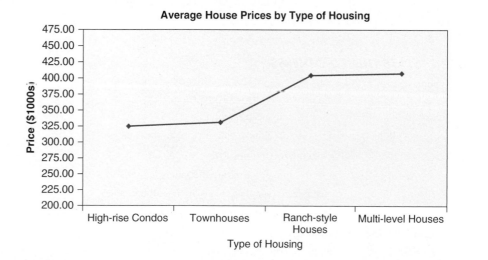

FIGURE 11.22
Average House Prices by Type of Housing

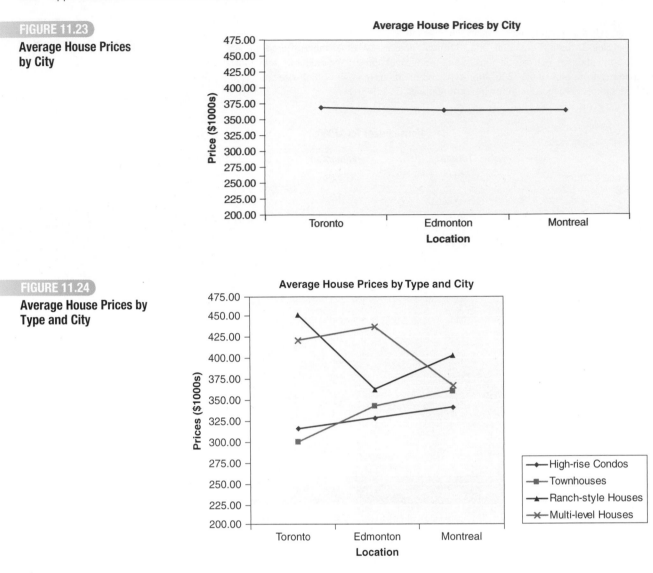

FIGURE 11.23

Average House Prices by City

FIGURE 11.24

Average House Prices by Type and City

EXAMPLE 5

Delivery Time

A regional hospital in the greater Toronto area orders weekly medical supplies for its four clinics from five different suppliers. Delivery times (in days) for four recent weeks are shown in Table 11.9.

Using short variable names, the two-factor ANOVA model has the general form

$$Delivery\ Time = f(Clinic, Supplier, Clinic \times Supplier)$$

The effects are assumed additive. The linear model is

$$y_{ijk} = \mu + A_j + B_k + AB_{jk} + \varepsilon_{ijk}$$

STEP 1: STATE THE HYPOTHESES

The hypotheses are

Factor A: Row Effect (*Clinic*)

$H_0: A_1 = A_2 = \ldots = A_r = 0$ (clinic means are the same)

$H_1:$ Not all the A_j are equal to zero (clinic means are not all the same)

Factor B: Column Effect (*Supplier*)

$H_0: B_1 = B_2 = \ldots = B_c = 0$ (supplier means are the same)

$H_1:$ Not all the B_k are equal to zero (supplier means are not all the same)

Interaction Effect (*Clinic $\times$ Supplier*)

$H_0:$ All the AB_{jk} are equal to zero (there is no interaction effect)

$H_1:$ Not all AB_{jk} are equal to zero (there is an interaction effect)

TABLE 11.9 Delivery Times (in days)

	Supplier 1	Supplier 2	Supplier 3	Supplier 4	Supplier 5
Clinic A	8	14	10	8	17
	8	9	15	7	12
	10	14	10	13	9
	13	11	7	10	10
Clinic B	13	9	12	6	15
	14	9	10	10	12
	12	7	10	12	12
	13	8	11	8	10
Clinic C	11	8	12	10	14
	10	9	10	11	13
	12	11	13	7	10
	14	12	10	10	12
Clinic D	7	8	7	8	14
	10	13	5	5	13
	10	9	6	11	8
	13	12	5	4	11

STEP 2: STATE THE DECISION RULE

Each F test may require a different right-tail critical value because the numerator degrees of freedom depend on the number of factor levels, while denominator degrees of freedom (error SSE) are the same for all three tests:

> Factor A: $v_1 = r - 1 = 4 - 1 = 3$ ($r = 4$ clinics)
> Factor B: $v_1 = c - 1 = 5 - 1 = 4$ ($c = 5$ suppliers)
> Interaction (AB): $v_1 = (r - 1)(c - 1) = (4 - 1)(5 - 1) = 12$
> Error $v_2 = rc(m - 1) = 4 \times 5 \times (4 - 1) = 60$

Excel provides the right-tail F critical values for $\alpha = 0.05$, which we can verify using Appendix F:

> $F_{3,60} = 2.76$ for Factor A
> $F_{4,60} = 2.53$ for Factor B
> $F_{12,60} = 1.92$ for Factor AB

We reject the null hypothesis if an F test statistic exceeds its critical value.

STEP 3: PERFORM THE CALCULATIONS

Excel provides tables of row and column sums and means (not shown here because they are lengthy). The ANOVA table in Figure 11.25 summarizes the partitioning of variation into its component sums of squares, degrees of freedom, mean squares, F test statistics, p values, and critical F values for $\alpha = 0.05$.

Excel's Two-Factor ANOVA with Replication
Deliveries

ANOVA						
Source of Variation	SS	df	MS	F	P-value	F crit
Sample	51.350	3	17.1167	3.434783	0.022424	2.758078
Columns	104.425	4	26.1063	5.238712	0.001097	2.525215
Interaction	102.775	12	8.5646	1.718645	0.085176	1.917396
Within	299.000	60	4.9833			
Total	557.550	79				

STEP 4: MAKE THE DECISION

For the row variable (*Clinic*), the test statistic $F = 3.435$ and its p value ($p = 0.0224$) lead us to conclude that the mean delivery times among clinics are not the same at $\alpha = 0.05$. For the column variable (*Supplier*), the test statistic $F = 5.239$ and its p value ($p = 0.0011$) lead us to conclude that the mean delivery times from suppliers are not the same at $\alpha = 0.05$. For the interaction effect, the test statistic $F = 1.719$ and its p value ($p = 0.0852$) lack significance at $\alpha = 0.05$. The p values permit a more flexible interpretation because α need not be specified in advance. In summary:

Variable	p Value	Interpretation
Clinic	0.0224	Clinic means differ (significant at $\alpha = 0.05$)
Supplier	0.0011	Supplier means differ (significant at $\alpha = 0.01$)
Clinic $\times$ *Supplier*	0.0852	Weak interaction effect (significant at $\alpha = 0.10$)

Using MegaStat

MegaStat's two-factor ANOVA results, shown in Figure 11.26, are similar to Excel's except that the table of treatment means is more compact, the results are rounded, and significant p values are highlighted (orange for $\alpha = 0.01$, light pink for $\alpha = 0.05$).

Interaction Effect

The statistical test for interaction is just like any other F test. But you might still wonder: What *is* an interaction, anyway? Although it was briefly mentioned before, it is worthwhile mentioning it again. You may be familiar with the idea of drug interaction. If you consume a few ounces of vodka, it has an effect on you. If you take an allergy pill, it has an effect on you. But if you combine the two, the effect may be much more dramatic (and possibly dangerous) than just adding the effects of the individual drugs themselves. That is why many medications carry a warning like, "Avoid alcohol while using this medication."

To visualize an interaction, we plot the treatment means for one factor against the levels of the other factor. Within each factor level, we connect the means. In the absence of an interaction, the lines will be roughly parallel or will tend to move in the same direction at the same time. If there is a strong interaction, the lines will have differing slopes and will tend to cross one another.

Figure 11.27 illustrates several possible situations, using a hypothetical two-factor ANOVA model in which factor A has three levels and factor B has two levels. For the delivery time example, a significant *interaction effect* would mean that suppliers have different mean delivery times for different clinics. However, Figure 11.28 shows that, while the interaction plot lines do cross, there is no consistent pattern, and the lines tend to be parallel more than crossing. The visual indications of interaction are, therefore, weak for the delivery time data. This conclusion is consistent with the interaction p value ($p = 0.085$) for the F test of $A \times B$.

FIGURE 11.26

MegaStat's Two-Factor ANOVA Deliveries

Two factor ANOVA

Means:

		Factor 2					
		Supplier 1	Supplier 2	Supplier 3	Supplier 4	Supplier 5	
	Clinic A	9.8	12.0	10.5	9.5	12.0	10.8
Factor 1	Clinic B	13.0	8.3	10.8	9.0	12.3	10.7
	Clinic C	11.8	10.0	11.3	9.5	12.3	11.0
	Clinic D	10.0	10.5	5.8	7.0	11.5	9.0
		11.1	10.2	9.6	8.8	12.0	10.3

ANOVA table

Source	SS	df	MS	F	p-value
Factor 1	51.35	3	17.117	3.43	0.0224
Factor 2	104.43	4	26.106	5.24	0.0011
Interaction	102.78	12	8.565	1.72	0.0852
Error	299.00	60	4.983		
Total	557.56	79			

Possible Interaction Patterns   FIGURE 11.27

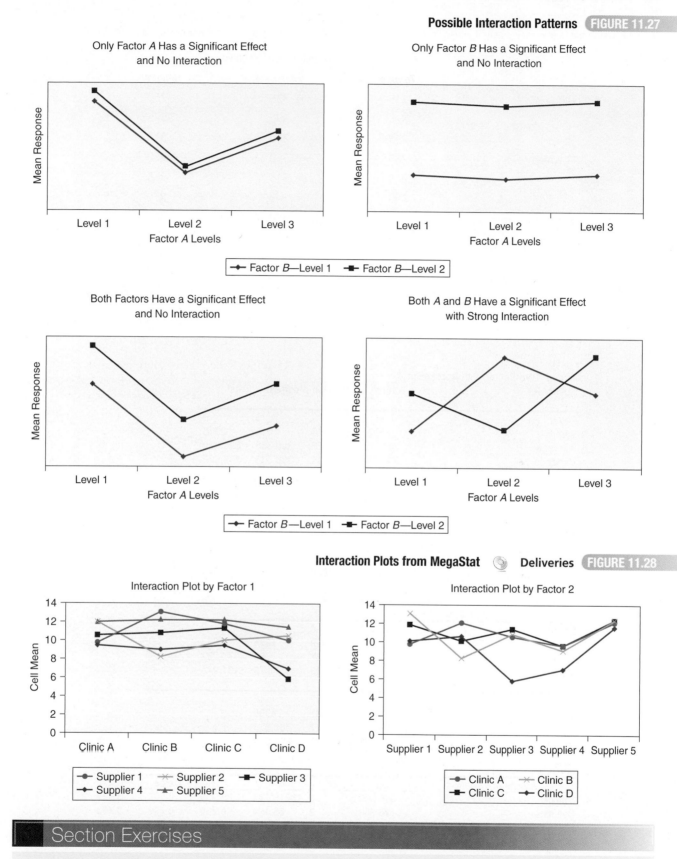

Only Factor *A* Has a Significant Effect
and No Interaction

Only Factor *B* Has a Significant Effect
and No Interaction

Both Factors Have a Significant Effect
and No Interaction

Both *A* and *B* Have a Significant Effect
with Strong Interaction

Interaction Plots from MegaStat   Deliveries   FIGURE 11.28

Interaction Plot by Factor 1

Interaction Plot by Factor 2

Section Exercises

Instructions: For each data set: (a) State the hypotheses. (b) Use Excel's Data > Data Analysis (or MegaStat or MINITAB) to perform the two-factor ANOVA with replication, using $\alpha = 0.05$. (c) State your conclusions about the main effects and interaction effects. (d) Interpret the *p* values carefully. (e) Create interaction plots and interpret them.

11.11 Using the house price example, answer the above questions. The Excel output is shown below this data set. (LO 3)

House Prices (in $1000s)

	Toronto	Edmonton	Montreal
High-rise Condos	315	325	360
	325	340	325
	295	310	330
Townhouses	285	360	350
	310	315	355
	290	345	370
Ranch-style Houses	420	380	400
	455	340	410
	480	360	395
Multi-level Houses	420	430	360
	430	450	375
	410	430	360

Anova: Two-Factor With Replication

SUMMARY	Toronto	Edmonton	Montreal	Total		
high-rise condos						
Count	3	3	3	9		
Sum	935	975	1015	2925		
Average	311.667	325	338.333	325.000		
Variance	233.333	225	358.333	337.500		
townhouses						
Count	3	3	3	9		
Sum	885	1020	1075	2980		
Average	295	340	358.333	331.111		
Variance	175	525	108.333	998.611		
ranch-style houses						
Count	3	3	3	9		
Sum	1355	1080	1205	3640		
Average	451.667	360	401.667	404.444		
Variance	908.333	400	58.333	1921.528		
multi-level houses						
Count	3	3	3	9		
Sum	1260	1310	1095	3665		
Average	420	436.667	365	407.2222		
Variance	100	133.333	75	1131.944		
Total						
Count	12	12	12			
Sum	4435	4385	4390			
Average	369.583	365.417	365.833			
Variance	5220.265	2247.538	681.061			

ANOVA

Source of Variation	SS	df	MS	F	P-value	F crit
Sample	54647.2	3	18215.741	66.239	0.000	3.009
Columns	126.389	2	63.194	0.230	0.796	3.403
Interaction	28390.3	6	4731.713	17.206	0.000	2.508
Within	6600	24	275			
Total	89763.9	35				

11.12 A small independent stock broker has created four sector portfolios for her clients. Each portfolio always has five stocks that may change from year to year. The volatility (coefficient of variation) of each stock is recorded for each year. Are the main effects significant? Is there an interaction? (LO 3) **Volatility**

	Stock Portfolio Type			
Year	Health	Energy	Retail	Leisure
2004	14.5	23.0	19.4	17.6
	18.4	19.9	20.7	18.1
	13.7	24.5	18.5	16.1
	15.9	24.2	15.5	23.2
	16.2	19.4	17.7	17.6
2005	21.6	22.1	21.4	25.5
	25.6	31.6	26.5	24.1
	21.4	22.4	21.5	25.9
	26.6	31.3	22.8	25.5
	19.0	32.5	27.4	26.3
2006	12.6	12.8	22.0	12.9
	13.5	14.4	17.1	11.1
	13.5	13.1	24.8	4.9
	13.0	8.1	13.4	13.3
	13.6	14.7	22.2	12.7

11.13 Petro-Canada has three interdisciplinary project development teams that function on an ongoing basis. Team members rotate from time to time. Every four months (three times a year) each department head rates the performance of each project team (using a 0 to 100 scale, where 100 is the best rating). Are the main effects significant? Is there an interaction? (LO 3) **Rating**

Year	Marketing	Engineering	Finance
2004	90	69	96
	84	72	86
	80	78	86
2005	72	73	89
	83	77	87
	82	81	93
2006	92	84	91
	87	75	85
	87	80	78

11.14 A market research firm is testing consumer reaction to a new shampoo on four age groups in four regions. There are five consumers in each test panel. Each consumer completes a 10-question product satisfaction instrument with a 5-point scale (5 is the highest rating) and the average score is recorded. Are the main effects significant? Is there an interaction? (LO 3) **Satisfaction**

	Atlantic Provinces	Ontario	Prairies	B.C./Alberta
Youth (under 18)	3.9	3.9	3.6	3.9
	4.0	4.2	3.9	4.4
	3.7	4.4	3.9	4.0
	4.1	4.1	3.7	4.1
	4.3	4.0	3.3	3.9
University (18–25)	4.0	3.8	3.6	3.8
	4.0	3.7	4.1	3.8
	3.7	3.7	3.0	3.6
	3.8	3.6	3.9	3.6
	3.8	3.7	4.0	4.1
Adult (26–64)	3.2	3.5	3.5	3.8
	3.8	3.3	3.8	3.6
	3.7	3.4	3.8	3.4
	3.4	3.5	4.0	3.7
	3.4	3.4	3.7	3.1
Senior (65+)	3.4	3.6	3.3	3.4
	2.9	3.4	3.3	3.2
	3.6	3.6	3.1	3.5
	3.7	3.6	3.1	3.3
	3.5	3.4	3.1	3.4

11.15 Petro-Canada has three suppliers of catalysts. Orders are placed with each supplier every 15 working days, or about once every three weeks. The delivery time (days) is recorded for each order over one year. Are the main effects significant? Is there an interaction? (LO 3)   **Deliveries 2**

	Supplier 1	Supplier 2	Supplier 3
Qtr 1	12	10	16
	15	13	13
	11	11	14
	11	9	14
Qtr 2	13	10	14
	11	10	11
	13	13	12
	12	11	12
Qtr 3	12	11	13
	8	9	8
	8	8	13
	13	6	6
Qtr 4	8	8	11
	10	10	11
	13	10	10
	11	10	11

TABLE 11.10   Turbofan Engine Thrust Test Results

Oil Pressure	Turbine Temperature			
	T_1	T_2	T_3	T_4
P_1	1,945.0	1,942.3	1,934.2	1,916.7
	1,933.0	1,931.7	1,930.0	1,943.0
	1,942.4	1,946.0	1,944.0	1,948.8
	1,948.0	1,959.0	1,941.0	1,928.0
	1,930.0	1,939.9	1,942.0	1,946.0
P_2	1,939.4	1,922.0	1,950.6	1,929.6
	1,952.8	1,936.8	1,947.9	1,930.0
	1,940.0	1,928.0	1,950.0	1,934.0
	1,948.0	1,930.7	1,922.0	1,923.0
	1,925.0	1,939.0	1,918.0	1,914.0
P_3	1,932.0	1,939.0	1,952.0	1,960.4
	1,955.0	1,932.0	1,963.0	1,946.0
	1,949.7	1,933.1	1,923.0	1,931.0
	1,933.0	1,952.0	1,965.0	1,949.0
	1,936.5	1,943.0	1,944.0	1,906.0
P_4	1,960.2	1,937.0	1,940.0	1,924.0
	1,909.3	1,941.0	1,984.0	1,906.0
	1,950.0	1,928.2	1,971.0	1,925.8
	1,920.0	1,938.9	1,930.0	1,923.0
	1,964.9	1,919.0	1,944.0	1,916.7

Source: Research project by three engineering students enrolled in an MBA program. Data are disguised.

Mini Case   **11.1**

Turbine Engine Thrust

Engineers testing turbofan aircraft engines wanted to know if oil pressure and turbine temperature are related to engine thrust (pounds). They chose four levels for each factor and observed each combination five times, using the two-factor replicated ANOVA model *Thrust = f(OilPres, TurbTemp, OilPres × TurbTemp)*. The test data are shown in Table 11.10.

The ANOVA results in Figure 11.29 indicate that only turbine temperature is significantly related to thrust. The table of means suggests that because mean thrust varies only over a tiny range, the effect may not be very important. The lack of interaction is revealed by the nearly parallel interaction plots. Levene's test for equal variances (not shown) shows a p value of $p = 0.42$ indicating that variances may be assumed equal, as is desirable for an ANOVA test.

FIGURE 11.29

MegaStat Two-Factor ANOVA Results

Means:

		Temperature				
		T1	T2	T3	T4	
Pressure	P1	1,939.68	1,943.78	1,938.24	1,936.50	1,939.55
	P2	1,941.04	1,931.30	1,937.70	1,926.12	1,934.04
	P3	1,941.24	1,939.82	1,949.40	1,938.48	1,942.24
	P4	1,940.88	1,932.82	1,953.80	1,919.10	1,936.65
		1,940.71	1,936.93	1,944.79	1,930.05	1,938.12

ANOVA table: Two-Factor with Replication

Source	SS	df	MS	F	p-value
Pressure	755.708	3	251.9028	1.32	0.2756
Temperature	2,353.426	3	784.4755	4.11	0.0099
Interaction	1,989.095	9	221.0106	1.16	0.3367
Error	12,212.052	64	190.8133		
Total	17,310.282	79			

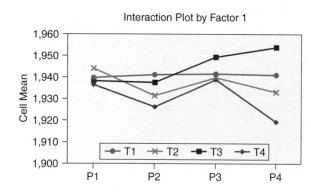

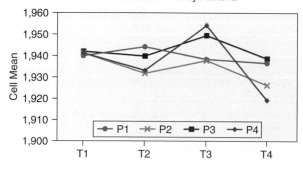

CHAPTER SUMMARY

ANOVA tests whether a numerical dependent variable (**response variable**) is associated with one or more categorical independent variables (**factors**) with several **levels.** Each level or combination of levels is a treatment. A **one-factor ANOVA** compares means in c columns of data. It is a generalization of a two-tailed t test for two independent sample means. Fisher's **F statistic** is a ratio of two variances (treatment versus error). It is compared with a right-tailed critical value from an F table or from Excel for appropriate numerator and denominator degrees of freedom. Alternatively, we compare the p value for the F test statistic with the desired level of significance (p less than α is significant). A **non-replicated two-factor ANOVA** can be viewed as a **randomized block model** if only one factor is of research interest. A **replicated two-factor ANOVA** (or full factorial model) has more than one observation per treatment, permitting inclusion of an interaction test in addition to tests for the **main effects. Interaction effects** can be seen as crossing lines on plots of factor means. Other general advice follows:

- ANOVA may be helpful even if those who collected the data did not utilize a formal experimental design (often the case in real-world business situations).

- ANOVA calculations are tedious because of the sums required, so computers are generally used.

- One-factor ANOVA is the most common and suffices for many business situations.

- Although real-life data may not perfectly meet the normality and equal-variance assumptions, ANOVA is reasonably robust (and alternative tests do exist).

KEY TERMS

analysis of variance (ANOVA), 454	interaction plots, 489	randomized block design model, 471
explained variance, 457	main effects, 478	replication, 478
factors, 457	mean squares, 462	response variable, 457
fixed-effects model, 461	mixed-effects model, 469	treatment, 457
full factorial, 478	one-factor ANOVA, 460	two-factor ANOVA without replication, 471
interaction, 458	partitioned sum of squares, 462	
interaction effect, 478	random-effects model, 469	unexplained variance, 457

CHAPTER REVIEW

Note: Questions labelled * are based on optional material from this chapter.

1. Explain each term: (a) explained variation; (b) unexplained variation; (c) factor; (d) treatment. (LO 1)

2. (a) Explain the difference between one-factor and two-factor ANOVA. (b) Write the linear model form of one-factor ANOVA. (c) State the hypotheses for a one-factor ANOVA in two different ways. (d) Why is one-factor ANOVA used a lot? (LO 1)

3. (a) State three assumptions of ANOVA. (b) What do we mean when we say that ANOVA is fairly robust to violations of these assumptions? (LO 4)

4. (a) Sketch the format of a one-factor ANOVA data set (completely randomized model). (b) Must group sizes be the same for one-factor ANOVA? Is it better if they are? (c) Explain the concepts of variation *between treatments* and variation *within treatments.* (d) What is the F statistic? (e) State the degrees of freedom for the F test in one-factor ANOVA. (LO 1)

5. (a) Sketch the format of a two-factor ANOVA data set without replication. (b) State the hypotheses for a two-factor ANOVA without replication. (c) What is the difference between a randomized block model and a two-factor ANOVA without replication? (d) What do the two F statistics represent in a two-factor ANOVA without replication? (e) What are their degrees of freedom? (LO 2)

6. (a) Sketch the format of a two-factor ANOVA data set with replication. (b) What is gained by replication? (c) State the hypotheses for a two-factor ANOVA with replication. (d) What do the three F statistics represent in a two-factor ANOVA with replication? (e) What are their degrees of freedom? (LO 2)

CHAPTER EXERCISES

Instructions: You may use Excel, MegaStat, MINITAB, or another computer package of your choice. Attach appropriate copies of the output or capture the screens, tables, and relevant graphs and include them in a written report. Try to state your conclusions succinctly in language that would be clear to a decision maker who is a non-statistician. Exercises marked * are based on optional material. Answer the following questions, or those your instructor assigns.

a. Choose an appropriate ANOVA model. State the hypotheses to be tested.
b. Display the data visually (e.g., dot plots or MegaStat's line plots). What do the displays show?
c. Do the ANOVA calculations using the computer.
d. State the decision rule for $\alpha = 0.05$ and make the decision. Interpret the p value.

e. In your judgment, are the observed differences in treatment means (if any) large enough to be of practical importance?

f. Do you think the sample size is sufficient? Explain. Could it be increased? Given the nature of the data, would more data collection be costly?

11.16 Below are grade point averages for 25 randomly chosen university business students during a recent semester. *Research question:* Are the mean grade point averages not all the same for students in these four class levels? (LO 2 & 3) **GPA2**

Grade Point Averages of 25 Business Students

First-Year (5 students)	Second-Year (7 students)	Third-Year (7 students)	Fourth-Year (6 students)
1.91	3.89	3.01	3.32
2.14	2.02	2.89	2.45
3.47	2.96	3.45	3.81
2.19	3.32	3.67	3.02
2.71	2.29	3.33	3.01
	2.82	2.98	3.17
	3.11	3.26	

11.17 The XYZ Corporation is interested in possible differences in days worked by salaried employees in three departments in the financial area. A survey of 23 randomly chosen employees reveals the data shown below. Because of the casual sampling methodology in this survey, the sample sizes are unequal. *Research question:* Are the mean annual attendance rates not all the same for employees in these three departments? (LO 2 & 3) **DaysWorked**

Days Worked Last Year by 23 Employees

Department	Days Worked									
Budgets (5 workers)	278	260	265	245	258					
Payables (10 workers)	205	270	220	240	255	217	266	239	240	228
Pricing (8 workers)	240	258	233	256	233	242	244	249		

11.18 Mean output of solar cells of three types are measured six times under random light intensity over a period of five minutes, yielding the results shown. *Research question:* Is the mean solar cell output not all the same for all cell types? (LO 2 & 3) **SolarWatts**

Solar Cell Output (watts)

Cell Type	Output (watts)					
A	123	121	123	124	125	127
B	125	122	122	121	122	126
C	126	128	125	129	131	128

11.19 In a bumper test, three types of autos were deliberately crashed into a barrier at 5 mph, and the resulting damage (in dollars) was estimated. Five test vehicles of each type were crashed, with the results shown below. *Research question:* Are the mean crash damages not all the same for these three vehicles? (LO 2 & 3) **Crash1**

Crash Damage ($)

Goliath	Varmint	Weasel
1,600	1,290	1,090
760	1,400	2,100
880	1,390	1,830
1,950	1,850	1,250
1,220	950	1,920

11.20 The waiting time (in minutes) for emergency room patients with non-life-threatening injuries was measured at four hospitals for all patients who arrived between 6:00 and 6:30 p.m. on a certain Wednesday. The results are shown below. *Research question:* Are the mean waiting times not all the same for emergency patients in these four hospitals? (LO 2 & 3) **ERWait**

Emergency Room Waiting Time (minutes)

Hospital A (5 patients)	Hospital B (4 patients)	Hospital C (7 patients)	Hospital D (6 patients)
10	8	5	0
19	25	11	20
5	17	24	9
26	36	16	5
11		18	10
		29	12
		15	

11.21 The results shown below are mean productivity measurements (average number of assemblies completed per hour) for a random sample of workers at each of three plants. *Research question:* Are the mean hourly productivity levels not all the same for workers in these three plants? (LO 2 & 3) **Productivity**

Hourly Productivity of Assumblers in the Plants

Plant	Finished Units Produced Per Hour									
A (9 workers)	3.6	5.1	2.8	4.6	4.7	4.1	3.4	2.9	4.5	
B (6 workers)	2.7	3.1	5.0	1.9	2.2	3.2				
C (10 workers)	6.8	2.5	5.4	6.7	4.6	3.9	5.4	4.9	7.1	8.4

11.22 Below are results of braking tests of the Ford Explorer on glare ice, packed snow, and split traction (one set of wheels on ice, the other on dry pavement), using three braking methods. *Research questions:* Is the mean stopping distance affected by braking method and/or by surface type? (LO 2 & 3) **Braking**

Stopping Distance from 65 km/h to 0 km/h

Method	Ice	Split Traction	Packed Snow
Pumping	441	223	149
Locked	455	148	146
ABS	460	183	167

11.23 An MBA director examined GMAT scores for the first 10 MBA applicants (assumed to be a random sample of early applicants) for four academic quarters. *Research question:* Do the mean GMAT scores for early applicants differ by quarter? (LO 2 & 3) **GMAT**

GMAT Scores of First 10 Applicants

Fall	490	580	440	580	430	420	640	470	530	640
Winter	310	590	730	710	540	450	670	390	500	470
Spring	500	450	510	570	610	490	450	590	640	650
Summer	450	590	710	240	510	670	610	550	540	540

11.24 An ANOVA study was conducted to compare dental offices in five small towns. The response variable was the number of days each dental office was open last year. *Research question:* Is there a difference in the means among these five towns? (LO 2 & 3) **DaysOpen**

Dental Clinic Days Open During the Last Year in Five Towns

Chalmers	Greenburg	Villa Nueve	Ulysses	Hazeltown
230	194	206	198	214
215	193	200	186	196
221	208	208	206	194
205	198	206	189	190
232		232	181	203
210		208		

11.25 The U.S. Environmental Protection Agency (EPA) advocates a maximum arsenic level in water of 10 micrograms per litre. Below are results of EPA tests on randomly chosen wells in a suburban Michigan county. *Research question:* Is the mean arsenic level affected by well depth and/or age of well? (LO 2 & 3) **Arsenic**

Arsenic Level in Wells (micrograms per litre)

Well Depth	Age of Well (years)		
	Under 10	10 to 19	20 and Over
Shallow	5.4	6.1	6.8
	4.3	4.1	5.4
	6.1	5.8	5.7
Medium	3.4	5.1	4.5
	3.7	3.7	5.5
	4.3	4.4	4.6
Deep	2.4	3.8	3.9
	2.9	2.7	2.9
	2.7	3.4	4.0

11.26 In a bumper test, three test vehicles of each of three types of autos were crashed into a barrier at 10 km/h, and the resulting damage was estimated. Crashes were from three angles: head-on, slanted, and rear-end. The results are shown below. *Research questions:* Is the mean repair cost affected by crash type and/or vehicle type? Are the observed effects (if any) large enough to be of practical importance (as opposed to statistical significance)? (LO 2 & 3) **Crash2**

10 km/h Collision Damage ($)

Crash Type	Goliath	Varmint	Weasel
Head-On	700	1,700	2,280
	1,400	1,650	1,670
	850	1,630	1,740
Slant	1,430	1,850	2,000
	1,740	1,700	1,510
	1,240	1,650	2,480
Rear-end	700	860	1,650
	1,250	1,550	1,650
	970	1,250	1,240

11.27 As a volunteer for a consumer research group, Monique was assigned to analyze the freshness of three brands of tortilla chips. She examined four randomly chosen bags of chips for four brands of chips from three different stores. She recorded the number of days from the current date until the "fresh until" expiration date printed on the package. *Research question:* Do mean days until the expiration date differ by brand or store? *Note:* Some data values are negative. (LO 2 & 3) **Freshness**

Days Until Expiration Date on Package

	Store 1	Store 2	Store 3
Brand A	−1	25	17
	−1	24	18
	20	10	21
	22	27	6
Brand B	−7	15	29
	30	−8	40
	24	6	24
	23	31	50
Brand C	16	11	41
	7	16	17
	16	30	27
	19	21	18
Brand D	21	42	31
	11	32	30
	10	38	39
	19	28	45

11.28 Three samples of each of three types of PVC pipe of equal wall thickness are tested to failure under three temperature conditions, yielding the results shown below. *Research questions:* Is mean burst strength affected by temperature and/or by pipe type? Is there a "best" brand of PVC pipe? Explain. (LO 2 & 3) **PVCPipe**

Burst Strength of PVC Pipes (psi)

Temperature	PVC_1	PVC_2	PVC_3
Hot (70°C)	250	301	235
	273	285	260
	281	275	279
Warm (40°C)	321	342	302
	322	322	315
	299	339	301
Cool (10°C)	358	375	328
	363	355	336
	341	354	342

11.29 Below are data on truck production (number of vehicles completed) during the second shift at five truck plants for each day in a randomly chosen week. *Research question:* Are the mean production rates the same by plant and by day? (LO 2 & 3) **Trucks**

Trucks Produced During Second Shift

	Mon	Tue	Wed	Thu	Fri
Plant A	130	157	208	227	216
Plant B	204	230	252	250	196
Plant C	147	208	234	213	179
Plant D	141	200	288	260	188

11.30 To check pain-relieving medications for potential side effects on blood pressure, it is decided to give equal doses of each of four medications to test subjects. To control for the potential effect of weight, subjects are classified by weight groups. Subjects are approximately the same age and are in general good health. Two subjects in each category are chosen at random from a large group of male prison volunteers. Subjects' blood pressures 15 minutes after the dose are shown below. *Research question:* Is mean blood pressure affected by body weight and/or by medication type? (LO 2 & 3) **Systolic**

Systolic Blood Pressure of Subjects (mmHg)

Ratio of Subject's Weight to Normal Weight	Medication M1	Medication M2	Medication M3	Medication M4
Under 1.1	131	146	140	130
	135	136	132	125
1.1 to 1.3	136	138	134	131
	145	145	147	133
1.3 to 1.5	145	149	146	139
	152	157	151	141

11.31 To assess the effects of instructor and student gender on student course scores, an experiment was conducted in 11 sections of managerial accounting classes ranging in size from 25 to 66 students. The factors were instructor gender (M, F) and student gender (M, F). There were 11 instructors (7 male, 4 female). Steps were taken to eliminate subjectivity in grading, such as common exams and sharing exam grading responsibility among all instructors so that no one instructor could influence exam grades unduly. (a) What type of ANOVA is this? (b) What conclusions can you draw? (c) Discuss sample size and raise any questions you think may be important. (LO 2 & 3)

Analysis of Variance for Students' Course Scores

Source of Variation	Sum of Squares	Degrees of Freedom	Mean Square	F Ratio	p Value
Instructor gender (I)	97.84	1	97.84	0.61	0.43
Student gender (S)	218.23	1	218.23	1.37	0.24
Interaction ($I \times S$)	743.84	1	743.84	4.66	0.03
Error	63,358.90	397	159.59		
Total	64,418.81	400			

Source: Marlys Gascho Lipe, "Further Evidence on the Performance of Female Versus Male Accounting Students," *Issues in Accounting Education* 4, no. 1 (Spring 1989), pp. 144–50.

11.32 In a market research study, members of a consumer test panel are asked to rate the visual appeal (on a 1 to 10 scale) of the texture of dashboard plastic trim in a mock-up of a new fuel cell car. The manufacturer is testing four finish textures. Panelists are assigned randomly to evaluate each texture. The test results are shown below. Each cell shows the average rating by panelists who evaluated each texture. *Research question:* Is mean rating affected by age group and/or by surface type? (LO 2 & 3)

Mean Ratings of Dashboard Surface Texture

Age Group	Shiny	Satin	Pebbled	Pattern
Youth (under 21)	6.7	6.6	5.5	4.3
Adult (21 to 39)	5.5	5.3	6.2	5.9
Middle-age (40 to 61)	4.5	5.1	6.7	5.5
Senior (62 and over)	3.9	4.5	6.1	4.1

www.mcgrawhillconnect.ca

11.33   This table shows partial results for a one-factor ANOVA, (a) Calculate the F test statistic. (b) Calculate the p value using Excel's function $=\text{FDIST}(F,\nu_1,\nu_2)$. (c) Find the critical value $F_{0.05}$ from Appendix F or using Excel's function $=\text{FINV}(0.05,\nu_1,\nu_2)$. (d) Interpret the results. (LO 2 & 3)

ANOVA

Source of Variation	SS	df	MS	F	p value	$F_{0.05}$
Between groups	3207.5	3	1069.17			
Within groups	441730	36	12270.28			
Total	444937.5	39				

11.34   (a) What kind of ANOVA is this (one-factor, two-factor, or two-factor with replication)? (b) Calculate each F test statistic. (b) Calculate the p value for each F test using Excel's function $=\text{FDIST}(F,\nu_1,\nu_2)$. (c) Interpret the results. (LO 2 & 3)

ANOVA

Source of Variation	SS	df	MS	F	p value
Factor A	36,598.56	3	12,199.52		
Factor B	22,710.29	2	11,355.15		
Interaction	177,015.38	6	29,502.56		
Error	107,561.25	36	2,987.81		
Total	343,885.48	47			

11.35   Here is an Excel ANOVA table for an experiment to assess the effects of ambient noise level and plant location on worker productivity. (a) What kind of ANOVA is this (one-factor, two-factor, two-factor replicated)? (b) Describe the original data format (i.e., how many rows, columns, and observations per cell). (c) At $\alpha = 0.05$ what are your conclusions? (LO 2 & 3)

ANOVA

Source of Variation	SS	df	MS	F	p value	$F_{0.05}$
Plant location	3.0075	3	1.0025	2.561	0.1200	3.863
Noise level	8.4075	3	2.8025	7.16	0.0093	3.863
Error	3.5225	9	0.3914			
Total	14.9375					

11.36   Several friends go bowling a few times per month. They keep track of their scores over several months. An ANOVA was performed. (a) What kind of ANOVA is this (one-factor, two-factor, etc.)? (b) How many friends were there? How many months were observed? How many observations per bowler per month? Explain how you know. (c) What are your conclusions about bowling scores? Explain, referring either to the F tests or p values. (LO 2 & 3)

ANOVA

Source of Variation	SS	df	MS	F	p value	F_{crit}
Month	1,702.389	2	851.194	11.9793	0.0002	3.4028
Bowler	4,674.000	3	1,558.000	21.9265	0.0000	3.0088
Interaction	937.167	6	156.194	2.1982	0.0786	2.5082
Within	1,705.333	24	71.056			
Total	9,018.889	35				

11.37 Air pollution (micrograms of particulate per ml of air) was measured along four highways at each of five different times of day, with the results shown below. (a) What kind of ANOVA is this (one-factor, two-factor, etc.)? (b) What is your conclusion about air pollution? Explain, referring either to the *F* tests or *p* values. (c) Do you think the variances can be assumed equal? Explain your reasoning. Why does it matter? (LO 2 & 3)

SUMMARY	Count	Sum	Average	Variance
Chrysler	5	1,584	316.8	14,333.7
Davidson	5	1,047	209.4	3,908.8
Reuther	5	714	142.8	2,926.7
Lodge	5	1,514	302.8	11,947.2
12 a.m.–6 a.m.	4	505	126.25	872.9
6 a.m.–10 a.m.	4	1,065	266.25	11,060.3
10 a.m.–3 p.m.	4	959	239.75	5,080.3
3 p.m.–7 p.m.	4	1,451	362.75	14,333.6
7 p.m.–12 a.m.	4	879	219.75	7,710.9

ANOVA

Source of Variation	SS	df	MS	F	p value	F_{crit}
Freeway	100,957.4	3	33,652.45	24.903	0.000	3.490
Time of Day	116,249.2	4	29,062.3	21.506	0.000	3.259
Error	16,216.4	12	1,351.367			
Total	233,423.0	19				

11.38 A company has several suppliers of office supplies. It receives several shipments each quarter from each supplier. The time (days) between order and delivery was recorded for several randomly chosen shipments from each supplier in each quarter, and an ANOVA was performed. (a) What kind of ANOVA is this (one-factor, two-factor, etc.)? (b) How many suppliers were there? How many quarters? How many observations per supplier per quarter? Explain how you know. (c) What are your conclusions about shipment time? Explain, referring either to the *F* tests or *p* values. (LO 2 & 3)

ANOVA

Source of Variation	SS	df	MS	F	p value	F_{crit}
Quarter	148.04	3	49.34667	6.0326	0.0009	2.7188
Supplier	410.14	4	102.535	12.5348	0.0000	2.4859
Interaction	247.06	12	20.5883	2.5169	0.0073	1.8753
Within	654.40	80	8.180			
Total	1,459.64	99				

11.39 Several friends go bowling a few times per month. They keep track of their scores over several months. An ANOVA was performed. (a) What kind of ANOVA is this (one-factor, two-factor, etc.)? (b) How could you tell how many friends there were in the sample just from the ANOVA table? Explain. (c) What are your conclusions about bowling scores? Explain, referring either to the F test or p value. (LO 2 & 3)

SUMMARY

Bowler	Count	Sum	Average	Variance
Mary	15	1,856	123.733	77.067
Bill	14	1,599	114.214	200.797
Sally	12	1,763	146.917	160.083
Robert	15	2,211	147.400	83.686
Tom	11	1,267	115.182	90.164

ANOVA

Source of Variation	SS	df	MS	F	p value	F_{crit}
Between Groups	14,465.63	4	3,616.408	29.8025	0.0000	2.5201
Within Groups	7,523.444	62	121.3459			
Total	21,989.07	66				

11.40 Are large companies more profitable *per dollar of assets?* The largest 500 companies in the world in 2000 were ranked according to their number of employees, with groups defined as follows: Small = under 25,000 employees, Medium = 25,000 to 49,999 employees, Large = 50,000 to 99,000 employees, Huge = 100,000 employees or more. An ANOVA was performed using the company's profit-to-assets ratio (percent) as the dependent variable. (a) What kind of ANOVA is this (one-factor, two-factor, etc.)? (b) What is your conclusion about the research question? Explain, referring either to the F test or p value. (LO 2 & 3)

11.41* It has recently been argued that younger students today learn differently than older students and that professors should at least offer their students more than one format for conveying information to their students. To test whether students do rely on different formats for learning, a small study was conducted in an introductory business course. Four different age groups and three different formats were arbitrarily selected for this study. Groups of two randomly selected students within each of the age groups were randomly assigned to each of the different formats of instruction and their final marks were recorded as follows:

	Format		
Age Group	Lecture	Online	Seminar
20–29	53	74	64
	55	76	61
30–39	75	73	74
	78	70	77
40–49	68	65	70
	67	64	72
50–59	62	52	69
	64	53	67

(a) Using Excel, plot the mean marks for each format, the mean marks for each age group, and the mean marks for each format-age combination, and then comment on your findings. (b) Using Excel, run ANOVA on this set of data and answer the following questions using the 0.05 level of significance. Do average marks vary among the four age groups? Do average marks vary among the three formats? Do different age groups react differently to certain formats than other age groups? Explain your answers to each question. Should more than one format be offered to students? Explain. (LO 2, 3 & 5)

LearningStats Unit 11   Analysis of Variance   LS

LearningStats Unit 11 gives examples of the three most common ANOVA tests (one-factor, two-factor, full factorial), including a simulation and tables of critical values. Your instructor may assign specific modules, or you may pursue those that sound interesting.

Topic	Learing States Modules
Overview	One-Factor ANOVA
	Two-Factor ANOVA
	ANOVA Case Studies
Format and Excel examples	Examples: ANOVA Tests
	Stacked versus Unstacked Data
Simulation	One-Factor ANOVA
	ANOVA Data Set Generator
Case studies	One Factor: Car Braking and Noise
	Two Factors: Car Braking and Noise
	Two-Factor Replicated: ATM Data
	Student Project: Call Centre Times
	One Factor: Drug Prices (details)
	Two Factors: Car Noise (details)
	Two-Factor Replicated: Braking (details)
General linear model	Insurance Claims Case Study
Tables	Appendix F—Critical Values of *F*

Key: ⬛ = PowerPoint ⬛ = Word ⬛ = Excel

Visual Statistics   VS

Visual Statistics Modules on Two-Sample Tests

Module	Module Name
12	VS Visualizing Analysis of Variance

Visual Statistics Module 12 (included on your CD) is designed to help you

- Become familiar with situations in which one-factor ANOVA is applicable.
- Understand how much difference must exist between groups to be detected using an *F* test.
- Appreciate the role of sample size in determining power.
- Know the ANOVA assumptions and the effects of violating them.

The worktext (included on the CD in PDF format) contains lists of concepts covered, objectives of the modules, overviews of concepts, illustrations of concepts, orientations to module features, learning exercises (basic, intermediate, advanced), learning projects (individual, team), self-evaluation quizzes, glossaries of terms, and solutions to self-evaluation quizzes.

For solutions to odd-numbered exercises, Exam Review questions, and additional study tools to help you succeed in this course, visit *Connect* at www.mcgrawhillconnect.ca.

www.mcgrawhillconnect.ca

Chapter

12

Chi-Square Tests

Chapter Learning Objectives

When you finish this chapter you should be able to

1. Recognize when to use an appropriate chi-square test.

2. Perform a chi-square test for independence on a contingency table.

3. Perform a goodness-of-fit (GOF) test for any specified distribution.

4. Perform a GOF test for a uniform distribution.

5. Use computer software to perform a chi-square GOF test for normality.

In Chapter 9, we tested the proportion of successes in a single population by testing, for example, H_0: $\pi = 0.30$ versus H_1: $\pi \neq 0.30$ using the z test of a single proportion. To conduct this test, there were only two categories (i.e., success and failure) for the qualitative variable of interest. But suppose there are more than two categories, and we want to test, for example, whether the proportions of the population falling into the various categories are not the same as we had earlier or initially hypothesized. For example, suppose we are interested in comparing consumers' preferences for various types of televisions between this year and last year, where we categorized TVs as belonging to one of four categories (HD plasma, HD LCD, HD projection, and other). Suppose last year, 15 percent of TVs sold in Canada were HD plasma, 45 percent were HD LCD, 25 percent were HD projection, and the remaining

15 percent fit into the "Other" category. Extending the two-category test, we may want to test, using sample results from this year, whether these percentages or proportions have changed, that is, we want to test

H_0: $\pi_1 = 0.15$, $\pi_2 = 0.45$, $\pi_3 = 0.25$, $\pi_4 = 0.15$

H_1: not all π_j's have the above values

where the π's represent this year's unknown proportions purchasing the various types of TVs. The test we will use on this pair of hypotheses is referred to as a goodness-of-fit test, which will be discussed in Section 12.2 of this chapter.

In Chapter 10, we compared the proportion of successes of two populations by testing, for example, H_0: $\pi_1 = \pi_2$ versus H_1: $\pi_1 \neq \pi_2$, using the two-sample z test of proportions. Suppose, we now want to extend this test to more than two categories and/or to more than two populations. For example, suppose we want to compare consumer's preferences for various types of televisions among British Columbians, Quebecers, and Nova Scotians using the same four categories of TVs as with our previous example. Here the test could be stated as

H_0: Consumers in these three provinces have the same preferences for TVs.

H_1: Consumers in these three provinces don't have the same preferences for TVs.

This test is referred to as a **test for independence** and will be discussed in the following section.

12.1   Chi-Square Test for Independence

Not all information pertaining to business can be summarized numerically. We are often interested in answers to questions such as: Do consumers prefer red, yellow, or blue package lettering on their bread bags? Does the name of a new lawn mower influence how we perceive the quality? Answers to such questions are not measurements on a numerical scale. Rather, the variables that we are interested in may be *categorical*. The variable *package lettering colour* would have categories red, yellow, and blue, and the variable *perceived quality* might have categories excellent, satisfactory, and poor.

We can collect observations on these variables to answer the types of questions posed either by surveying our customers and employees or by conducting carefully designed experiments. Once our data have been collected, we summarize by tallying response frequencies on a table that we call a *contingency table*. A **contingency table** is a cross-tabulation of *n* paired observations into categories. Each cell shows the count of observations that fall into the category defined by its row and column heading.

Chapter 13

EXAMPLE 1

Consumers' Television Preferences

Continuing with our introductory example, suppose we want to determine whether consumers' preferences for different types of televisions vary among three specific provinces. To gather evidence, suppose we randomly sampled consumers in each of these provinces who recently purchased TVs and determined the type of TVs they purchased. Suppose the results were tabulated and summarized in the following contingency table.

	British Columbia	*Quebec*	*Nova Scotia*	*Totals*
HD plasma	23	43	24	90
HD LCD	64	83	43	190
HD projection	22	25	13	60
Other	16	24	20	60
Totals	125	175	100	400

In this particular example, we can interpret the information in one of two ways. We can consider the provinces as three separate populations and consumer preferences as the qualitative variable of interest and test:

H_0: Distributions of consumer preferences are the same among the three provinces.

H_1: Distributions of consumer preferences are not the same among the three provinces.

In this case, we would have randomly selected three samples, one from each province, and recorded their consumer preferences. Or we can treat the provinces as categories of the qualitative variable "where one lives" and the types of TV purchased as categories of the qualitative variable "consumer preference" and test:

H_0: Consumer preference is independent of where one lives.

H_1: Consumer preference is not independent of where one lives.

In this case, we would have randomly selected one combined sample from the three provinces and recorded the consumers' preferences and the provinces in which they lived. No matter how we treated the provinces and how we sampled, the value of the test statistic and the decision rule would be the same. The only difference may be in the wording of our conclusion.

EXAMPLE 2

Web Pages (4 × 3 *Table*)

As online shopping has grown, opportunity has also grown for personal data collection and invasion of privacy. Mainstream online retailers have policies known as "privacy disclaimers" that define the rules regarding their uses of information collected, the customer's right to refuse third-party promotional offers, and so on. You can access these policies through a Web link, found either on the Web site's home page, on the order page (i.e., as you enter your credit card information), on a client Web page, or on some other Web page. In North America, such links are voluntary, while in the European Union (EU) they are mandated by law. Location of the privacy disclaimer is considered to be a measure of the degree of consumer protection (the farther the link is from the home page, the less likely it is to be noticed). Marketing researchers did a survey of 291 Web sites in three nations (France, U.K., U.S.) and obtained the *contingency table* shown here as Table 12.1. Is location of the privacy disclaimer *independent* of the Web site's nationality? This question can be answered by using a test based on the frequencies in this contingency table.

TABLE 12.1 Privacy Disclaimer Location and Web Site Nationality   WebSites

	Nationality of Web Site			
Location of Disclaimer	France	U.K.	U.S.	Row Total
Home page	56	68	35	159
Order page	19	19	28	66
Client page	6	10	16	32
Other page	12	9	13	34
Col Total	93	106	92	291

Source: Calin Gurau, Ashok Ranchhod, and Claire Gauzente, "To Legislate or Not to Legislate: A Comparative Exploratory Study of Privacy/Personalisation Factors Affecting French, UK, and US Web Sites," *Journal of Consumer Marketing* 20, no. 7 (2003), p. 659. Used with permission, Emerald Group Publishing Limited.

TABLE 12.2 Table of Observed Frequencies

	Variable B				
Variable A	1	2	...	c	Row Total
1	f_{11}	f_{12}	...	f_{1c}	R_1
2	f_{21}	f_{22}	...	f_{2c}	R_2
⋮	⋮	⋮	⋮	⋮	⋮
r	f_{r1}	f_{r2}	...	f_{rc}	R_r
Col Total	C_1	C_2	...	C_c	n

Table 12.2 illustrates the terminology of a contingency table. Variable A has r levels (rows) and variable B has c levels (columns), so we call this an $r \times c$ contingency table. Each cell shows the observed frequency f_{jk} in row j and column k.

Chi-Square Test

In a test of independence for an $r \times c$ contingency table, the hypotheses may be stated as

H_0: Variable A is independent of variable B.

H_1: Variable A is not independent of variable B.

To test these hypotheses, we use the **chi-square test** *for independence,* developed by Karl Pearson (1857–1936). It is a test based on comparing the **observed frequencies** (f_{jk}), obtained from the sample or samples, and what we would have expected the frequencies to be, or the **expected frequencies** (e_{jk}), if the null hypothesis was true. Through this comparison, we end up with a chi-square test. The chi-square test for independence is a distribution-free test (i.e., it does not require the data to have any specific distribution). The only operation performed is classifying the n data pairs into r rows (variable A) and c columns (variable B) as in the above examples, and making the comparison between the f_{jk} and its corresponding e_{jk}. How to determine these e_{jk}'s will be discussed shortly. The resulting chi-square test statistic is

$$\chi^2_{\text{calc}} = \sum_{j=1}^{r} \sum_{k=1}^{c} \frac{[f_{jk} - e_{jk}]^2}{e_{jk}} \tag{12.1}$$

If the two variables are **independent** (i.e., the null hypothesis is true), then all the f_{jk}'s should be close to their respective e_{jk}'s, resulting in a chi-square test statistic whose value is small. Conversely, if the null hypothesis is not true, we would expect some large differences between the f_{jk}'s and their respective e_{jk}'s, resulting in a chi-square test statistic whose value is somewhat large. Because we expect the test statistic to be small if the null hypothesis is true and large if the alternative hypothesis is true, we will reject the hypothesis of independence if the test statistic is somewhat large or far enough in the right tail of the chi-square distribution.

A Closer Look

Why do we use the above test statistic to test for independence instead of some simpler version (e.g., by removing the denominator, e_{jk}, from this test statistic)? As with all other test statistics, we need to know its distribution in order to derive a decision rule. We use the above test statistic because it has a known distribution—it follows approximately a chi-square distribution if each e_{jk} is large enough (a common rule of thumb is that all e_{jk}'s ≥ 5).

FIGURE 12.1 **Various Chi-Square Distributions**

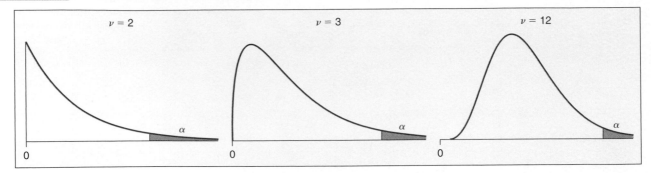

Chi-Square Distribution

The test statistic is compared with a critical value from the **chi-square probability distribution**. It has one parameter ν called **degrees of freedom**. For the $r \times c$ contingency table, the degrees of freedom are

$$\nu = \text{degrees of freedom} = (r - 1)(c - 1) \tag{12.2}$$

where

r = the number of rows in the contingency table

c = the number of columns in the contingency table

The parameter ν (Greek letter read as "nu") is the number of non-redundant cells in the contingency table (see *LearningStats* Unit 15 "Degrees of Freedom" for further explanation). There is a different chi-square distribution for each value of ν. Appendix E contains critical values for right-tail areas of the chi-square distribution. Its mean is ν and its variance is 2ν. As illustrated in Figure 12.1, all chi-square distributions are skewed to the right, but become more symmetric as ν increases. As ν increases, the shape begins to resemble a normal, bell-shaped curve. However, for any contingency table you are likely to encounter, degrees of freedom will not be large enough to assume normality.

Expected Frequencies

Assuming that H_0 is true, the expected frequency of row j and column k is

$$e_{jk} = R_j C_k / n \quad \text{(expected frequency in row } j \text{ and column } k) \tag{12.3}$$

where

R_j = total for row j ($j = 1, 2, \ldots, r$)

C_k = total for column k ($k = 1, 2, \ldots, c$)

n = sample size (or number of responses)

This formula for expected frequencies stems from the definition of independent events (see Chapter 5). When two events are independent, their *joint* probability is the product of their marginal probabilities, so for a cell in row j and column k the joint probability would be $(R_j/n)(C_k/n)$. To get the expected cell frequency, we multiply this joint probability by the sample size n to obtain $e_{jk} = R_j C_k / n$. The e_{jk} always sum to the same row and column frequencies as the observed frequencies. Expected frequencies will not, in general, be integers.

A Closer Look

In general, if we have a sample of size, n, and if the probability of belonging to a particular category is π, the expected number in the sample that should belong to that category is $n\pi$. To expand on this notation, if the probability of belonging to category (j, k)

is symbolized by π_{jk}, the expected number in a sample of size n that should fall in this category is $n\pi_{jk}$. But if the null hypothesis is true, $\pi_{jk} = \pi_j \pi_k$ (or $P(A \cap B) = P(A)P(B)$, another way of symbolizing the multiplication rule for independent events) and $e_{jk} = n\pi_j\pi_k$. Because the true probabilities are unknown, we must estimate them in order to determine the e_{jk}'s. As before, we use their best estimates, which are the proportions in the sample that belong to each of the respective categories. For variable A (the row variable), these proportions are the R_j/n's, and for variable B (the column variable), these proportions are the C_k/n's. Using these estimates,

$$e_{jk} = n\pi_j\pi_k \rightarrow n\left(\frac{R_j}{n}\right)\left(\frac{C_k}{n}\right) \rightarrow e_{jk} = \frac{R_jC_k}{n}$$

Concept Check

Treating variable B as representing different populations and variable A as representing some characteristic, show how you will arrive at the same formula for the e_{jk}'s.

Illustration of the Chi-Square Calculations

We will illustrate the chi-square test by using the Web page frequencies from the contingency table (Table 12.1). We follow the usual five-step hypothesis testing procedure:

Step 1: State the Hypotheses   For the Web page example, the hypotheses are

H_0: Privacy disclaimer location is independent of Web site nationality.

H_1: Privacy disclaimer location is dependent on Web site nationality.

Step 2: Specify the Decision Rule   For the Web page contingency table, we have $r = 4$ rows and $c = 3$ columns, so degrees of freedom are $\nu = (r - 1)(c - 1) = (4 - 1)(3 - 1) = 6$. We will choose $\alpha = 0.05$ for the test. Figure 12.2 shows that the right-tail critical value from Appendix E with $\nu = 6$ is $\chi^2_{0.05} = 12.59$. This critical value could also be obtained from Excel using =CHIINV(.05,6).

For $\alpha = 0.05$ in this right-tailed test, the decision rule is

Reject H_0 if $\chi^2_{calc} > 12.59$

Otherwise do not reject H_0

The decision rule is illustrated in Figure 12.3.

Critical Values of Chi-Square for Area A

FIGURE 12.2
Critical Value of Chi-Square from Appendix E

ν	0.995	0.99	0.975	0.95	0.9	0.1	0.05	0.025	0.01	0.005	ν
1	0.00	0.00	0.00	0.00	0.02	2.71	3.84	5.02	6.63	7.88	1
2	0.01	0.02	0.05	0.10	0.21	4.61	5.99	7.38	9.21	10.60	2
3	0.07	0.11	0.22	0.35	0.58	6.25	7.81	9.35	11.34	12.84	3
4	0.21	0.30	0.48	0.71	1.06	7.78	9.49	11.14	13.28	14.86	4
5	0.41	0.55	0.83	1.15	1.61	9.24	11.07	12.83	15.09	16.75	5
6	0.68	0.87	1.24	1.64	2.20	10.64	12.59	14.45	16.81	18.55	6
7	0.99	1.24	1.69	2.17	2.83	12.02	14.07	16.01	18.48	20.28	7
8	1.34	1.65	2.18	2.73	3.49	13.36	15.51	17.53	20.09	21.95	8
9	1.73	2.09	2.70	3.33	4.17	14.68	16.92	19.02	21.67	23.59	9
10	2.16	2.56	3.25	3.94	4.87	15.99	18.31	20.48	23.21	25.19	10

Right-Tailed Chi-Square Test for $\nu = 6$

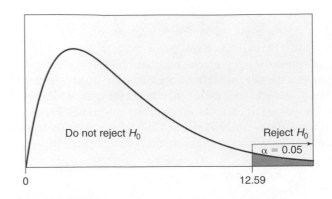

TABLE 12.3 Observed and Expected Frequencies   WebSites

	Observed Frequencies			
Location	*France*	*U.K.*	*U.S*	*Row Total*
Home	56	68	35	159
Order	19	19	28	66
Client	6	10	16	32
Other	12	9	13	34
Col Total	93	106	92	291

	Expected Frequencies (assuming independence)			
Location	*France*	*U.K.*	*U.S*	*Row Total*
Home	(159 × 93)/291 = 50.81	(159 × 106)/291 = 57.92	(159 × 92)/291 = 50.27	159
Order	(66 × 93)/291 = 21.09	(66 × 106)/291 = 24.04	(66 × 92)/291 = 20.87	66
Client	(32 × 93)/291 = 10.23	(32 × 106)/291 = 11.66	(32 × 92)/291 = 10.12	32
Other	(34 × 93)/291 = 10.87	(34 × 106)/291 = 12.38	(34 × 92)/291 = 10.75	34
Col Total	93	106	92	291

Step 3: Calculate the Expected Frequencies The expected frequency in row j and column k is $e_{jk} = R_j C_k/n$. The calculations are illustrated in Table 12.3. The expected frequencies (lower part of Table 12.3) must sum to the same row and column frequencies as the observed frequencies (upper part of Table 12.3). However, due to round-off errors, these sums may not be exactly identical.

Step 4: Calculate the Test Statistic The chi-square test statistic is

$$\chi^2_{\text{calc}} = \sum_{j=1}^{r}\sum_{k=1}^{c} \frac{[f_{jk} - e_{jk}]^2}{e_{jk}} = \frac{(56 - 50.81)^2}{50.81} + \cdots + \frac{(13 - 10.75)^2}{10.75}$$

$$= 0.53 + \cdots + 0.47 = 17.54$$

Even for this simple problem, the calculations are too lengthy to show in full. In fact, few would choose to do the calculations of the expected frequencies and chi-square test statistic without a spreadsheet. Fortunately, any statistical package will do a chi-square test. MegaStat's set-up and output are shown in Figure 12.4. As you can see, MegaStat's calculations are arranged in a tabular form. (**Hint:** It may be easier to show the observed frequencies and expected frequencies in a single table. For example, for the upper left cell, instead of 56 and 50.81 in two different tables, create just one table with an upper left cell with these two values side by side, e.g., 56 (50.81)).

Step 5: Make the Decision Because the test statistic $\chi^2_{\text{calc}} = 17.54$ exceeds 12.59, we conclude that the observed differences between expected and observed frequencies differ significantly at the 5 percent level of significance ($\alpha = 0.05$). The p value (0.0075) indicates that

MegaStat's Chi-Square Test for Web Page Data FIGURE 12.4

H_0 should be firmly rejected at $\alpha = 0.05$. You can obtain this same p value using Excel's function =CHIDIST(χ^2, ν) or in this case =CHIDIST(17.54,6), which gives a right-tail area of 0.0075. This p value indicates that privacy disclaimer location is *not* independent of nationality at $\alpha = 0.05$, based on this sample of 291 Web sites.

Discussion MegaStat rounds things off for display purposes, though it maintains full internal accuracy in the calculations (as you must, if you do these calculations by hand). Differences between observed (O) and expected (E) frequencies, written as ($O - E$), must sum to zero across each row and down each column. If you are doing these calculations by hand, check these sums (if they are not zero, you have made an error). From Figure 12.4 we see that only three cells (column 3, rows 1, 2, and 3) contribute a majority (4.64, 2.44, 3.42) of the chi-square sum (17.54). The hypothesis of independence fails largely because of these three cells.

EXAMPLE 3

Night Flying (2 × 2 *Table*)

After the accident in which John F. Kennedy, Jr., died while piloting his airplane at night from New York to Cape Cod, a random telephone poll was taken in which 409 New Yorkers were asked, "Should private pilots be allowed to fly at night without an instrument rating?" The same question was posed to 70 aviation experts. Results are shown in Table 12.4. The totals exclude those who had "No Opinion" (1 expert and 25 general public).

TABLE 12.4 Should Noninstrument Rated Pilots Fly at Night? 🔘 Pilots

Opinion	Experienced Pilots	General Public	Row Total
Yes	40	61	101
No	29	323	352
Col Total	69	384	453

Source: Siena College Research Institute.

The hypotheses are

H_0: Opinion is independent of aviation expertise.

H_1: Opinion is not independent of aviation expertise.

The test results from MegaStat are shown in Figure 12.5. The degrees of freedom are $\nu = (r - 1)(c - 1) = (2 - 1)(2 - 1) = 1$. Appendix E shows that the critical value of chi-square for $\alpha = 0.005$ is 7.879. Because the test statistic $\chi^2 = 59.80$ greatly exceeds 7.879, we firmly reject the hypothesis. The p value (0.0000) confirms that opinion is *not* independent of aviation experience.

FIGURE 12.5 MegaStat Chi-Square Test with $\nu = 1$

Chi-square Contingency Table Test for Independence

	Col 1	Col 2	Total
Row 1 Observed	**40**	**61**	101
Expected	15.38	85.62	101.00
$O - E$	24.62	−24.62	0.00
$(O - E)^2/E$	39.39	7.08	46.47
Row 2 Observed	**29**	**323**	352
Expected	53.62	298.38	352.00
$O - E$	−24.62	24.62	0.00
$(O - E)^2/E$	11.30	2.03	13.33
Total Observed	69	384	453
Expected	69.00	384.00	453.00
$O - E$	0.00	0.00	0.00
$(O - E)^2/E$	50.69	9.11	59.80

59.80	chi-square
1	df
1.05E-14	p value
1.38E-12	Fisher Exact Probability

Small Expected Frequencies

The chi-square test is unreliable if the *expected* frequencies are too small. As you can see from the formula for the test statistic, when e_{jk} in the denominator is small, the chi-square statistic may be inflated. A commonly used rule of thumb known as **Cochran's Rule** requires that $e_{jk} \geq 5$ for all cells. Computer packages may offer warnings or refuse to proceed when expected frequencies are too small. When this happens, it may be possible to salvage the test by combining adjacent rows or columns to enlarge the expected frequencies. In the Web page example, all the expected frequencies are safely greater than 5.

Concept Check

Suppose we have the following contingency table showing each e_{jk} (in brackets) beside its respective f_{jk}. Assuming that the greater the degrees of freedom, the more information we have, would it be better to combine rows or combine columns in order that all resulting e_{jk}'s are greater than or equal to 5? Explain. Show the resulting contingency table after you do this combining.

			Column		
Row	*1*	*2*	*3*	*4*	*5*
1	13 (7.1)	3 (6.7)	4 (7.9)	4 (6.7)	6 (2.4)
2	15 (18.9)	18 (16.8)	20 (21.1)	22 (16.8)	5 (6.3)
3	17 (18.9)	19 (16.8)	26 (21.1)	14 (16.8)	4 (6.3)

Cross-Tabulating Raw Data

Chi-square tests for independence are quite flexible. Although most often used with nominal data such as gender (male, female), we can also analyze quantitative variables (such as salary) by coding them into categories (e.g., under $25,000, $25,000 to $50,000, $50,000 and over). Open-ended classes are acceptable. We can mix data types as required (nominal, ordinal, interval, ratio) by defining the bins appropriately. Few statistical tests are so versatile. Continuous data may be classified into any categories that make sense. To tabulate a continuous variable into two classes, we would make the cut at the median. For three bins, we would use the 33rd and 67th percentiles as cutpoints. For four bins, we would use the 25th, 50th, and 75th percentiles as cutpoints. We prefer classes that yield approximately equal frequencies for each cell to help protect against small expected frequencies (recall that Cochran's Rule requires expected frequencies be at least 5). Our bin choices are limited when we have integer data with a small range (e.g., a Likert scale with responses 1, 2, 3, 4, 5), but we can still define classes however we wish (e.g., 1 or 2, 3, 4 or 5).

EXAMPLE 4

Doctors and Infant Mortality

Doctors

Let X = doctors per 100,000 residents of a province and Y = infant deaths per 1,000 births in the province. We might reasonably hypothesize that provinces with more doctors relative to population would have lower infant mortality, but do they? We are reluctant to assume normality and equal variances, so we prefer to avoid a t test (for two populations), or an ANOVA (for more than two populations). Instead, we hypothesize

H_0: Infant mortality rate is independent of the number of doctors per 100,000 population.

H_1: Infant mortality rate is not independent of the number of doctors per 100,000 population.

Depending on how we form the contingency table, we could get different results. Figure 12.6 shows 2×2 and 3×3 tables created using Visual Statistics. Each table shows both actual and expected frequencies assuming the null hypothesis. Neither p value indicates a very strong relationship. Because we cannot reject H_0 at any customary level of significance, we conclude that number of doctors and infant mortality are not strongly related.

Three-Way Tables and Higher

There is no conceptual reason to limit ourselves to two-way contingency tables comparing two variables. However, such tables become rather hard to visualize, even when they are "sliced" into a series of two-way tables. A table comparing three variables can be visualized as a *cube* or as a stack of tiled two-way contingency tables. Major computer packages (SAS, SPSS, and others) permit three-way contingency tables. For four or more variables, there is no physical analogue to aid us, and their cumbersome nature would suggest analytical methods other than chi-square tests.

Visual Statistics Contingency Tables   FIGURE 12.6

Infant Deaths per 1,000	2 × 2 Table Doctors per 100,000				3 × 3 Table Doctors per 100,000			
	Low	High	Total	Infant Deaths per 1,000	Low	Med	High	Total
High	15/13.0	11/13.0	26	High	8/5.4	4/5.4	4/5.1	16
Low	10/12.0	14/12.0	24	Med	4/5.4	6/5.4	6/5.1	16
Total	25	25	50	Low	5/6.1	7/6.1	6/5.8	18
				Total	17	17	16	50

Chi-square test statistic = 1.282 ($p = 0.258$)

Chi-square test statistic = 2.762 ($p = 0.598$)

A Closer Look

1. ANOVA examines the relationship between a quantitative and a qualitative variable. We can consider the test for independence to examine the relationship between two qualitative variables. If the two variables are independent, there is no relationship. If the two variables are not independent, there is a relationship. In the next chapter, we will examine the relationship, more specifically the linear relationship, between two quantitative variables.

2. In Chapter 10, we tested $H_0: \pi_1 = \pi_2$ versus $H_1: \pi_1 \neq \pi_2$ using the appropriate z test statistic. We can also test these hypotheses using the chi-square test for independence. Comparing the two test statistics, you would notice that $\chi^2_{calc} = (z_{calc})^2$, and by comparing the rejection regions, you would notice that $\chi^2_{crit} = (z_{crit})^2$. These observations would lead you to conclude that if you reject the null hypothesis using the z test statistic, you would also reject the null hypothesis using the chi-square test statistic, and vice versa.

Section Exercises

Instructions: For each exercise, include MegaStat or Excel exhibits to support your chi-square calculations. (a) State the hypotheses. (b) Show how the degrees of freedom are calculated for the contingency table. (c) Using the level of significance specified in the exercise, find the critical value of chi-square from Appendix E or from Excel's function =CHIINV(α, deg_freedom). (d) Carry out the calculations for a chi-square test for independence and draw a conclusion. (e) Which cells of the contingency table contribute the most to the chi-square test statistic? (f) Are any of the expected frequencies too small? (g) Interpret the p value. If necessary, you can calculate the p value using Excel's function =CHIDIST(test statistic, deg_freedom). *(h) If it is a 2×2 table, perform a two-tailed two-sample z test for $\pi_1 = \pi_2$ and verify that z^2 is the same as your chi-square statistic. *Note:* Exercises marked with an asterisk (*) are more difficult.

12.1 Using the data from a previous example, at the 0.01 level of significance ($\alpha = 0.01$), is there sufficient evidence to conclude that consumers in these three provinces have different preferences for different types of televisions. How would your conclusions affect the purchasing behaviour of a large chain with electronic stores in each of these provinces? Explain. (LO 1 & 2)

	British Columbia	Quebec	Nova Scotia	Totals
HD plasma	23	43	24	90
HD LCD	64	83	43	190
HD projection	22	25	13	60
Other	16	24	20	60
Totals	125	175	100	400

12.2 In a study of how managers attempt to manage earnings, researchers analyzed a sample of 515 earnings-management attempts from a survey of experienced auditors. The frequency of effects is summarized in the table shown. *Research question:* At $\alpha = 0.01$, does the effect on earnings depend on the approach used? (Data are from Mark W. Nelson, John A. Elliott, and Robin L. Tarpley, "How Are Earnings Managed? Examples from Auditors," *Accounting Horizons,* Supplement, 2003, pp. 17–35.) (LO 1 & 2) **Earnings**

Current-Period Income Effect of Four Earnings Management Approaches

Approach Used	Increase	Decrease	No Clear Effect	Row Total
Expenses and Other Losses	133	113	23	269
Revenue and Other Gains	86	20	8	114
Business Combinations	12	22	33	67
Other Approaches	41	4	20	65
Col Total	272	159	84	515

12.3 Teenagers make up a large percentage of the market for clothing. Below are data on running shoe ownership in four world regions (excluding China). *Research question:* At $\alpha = 0.01$, does this sample show that running shoe ownership depends on world region? (See J. Paul Peter and Jerry C. Olson, *Consumer Behavior and Marketing Strategy,* 9th ed. [McGraw-Hill, 2004], p. 64.) (LO 1 & 2) 🔊 **Running**

Running Shoe Ownership in World Regions

Owned by	U.S.	Europe	Asia	Latin America	Row Total
Teens	80	89	69	65	303
Adults	20	11	31	35	97
Col Total	100	100	100	100	400

12.4 Students applying for admission to an MBA program must submit scores from the GMAT test, which includes a verbal and a quantitative component. Shown here are raw scores for 100 randomly chosen MBA applicants at a public, AACSB-accredited business school in the U.S. Midwest. *Research question:* At $\alpha = 0.005$, is there a relationship between the quantitative scores and the verbal scores? (LO 1 & 2) 🔊 **GMAT**

	Quantitative			
Verbal	Under 25	25 to 35	35 or More	Row Total
Under 25	25	9	1	35
25 to 35	4	28	18	50
35 or More	1	3	11	15
Col Total	30	40	30	100

12.5 Computer abuse by employees is an ongoing worry to businesses. A study revealed the data shown below. *Research question:* At $\alpha = 0.01$, does the frequency of disciplinary action depend on the abuser's level of privilege? (Data are from Detmar W. Straub and William D. Nance, "Discovering and Disciplining Computer Abuse in Organizations," *MIS Quarterly* 14, no. 1 [Mar. 1990], pp. 45–60.) (LO 1 & 2) 🔊 **Abuse**

Computer Abuse Incidents Cross-Tabulated by Privilege and Punishment

Level of Privilege	Disciplined	Not Disciplined	Row Total
Low	20	11	31
Medium	42	3	45
High	33	3	36
Col Total	95	17	112

12.6 Marketing researchers prepared an advance notification card announcing an upcoming mail survey and describing the purpose of their research. Half the target customers received the advanced notification, followed by the survey. The other half received only the survey. The survey return rates are shown below. *Research question:* At $\alpha = 0.025$, does the return rate depend on advanced notification? (Data are from Paul R. Murphy, Douglas R. Dalenberg, and James M. Daley, "Improving Survey Responses with Postcards," *Industrial Marketing Management* 19, no. 4 [Nov. 1990], pp. 349–355.) (LO 1 & 2) 🔊 **Advance**

Cross-Tabulation of Returns by Notification

Pre-notified?	Returned	Not Returned	Row Total
Yes	39	155	194
No	22	170	192
Col Total	61	325	386

 Mini Case 12.1

Student Work and Car Age

Do students work longer hours to pay for newer cars? This hypothesis was tested using data from a survey of introductory business statistics students at a large university campus. The survey contained these two fill-in-the-blank questions:

About how many hours per week do you expect to work at an outside job this semester?
What is the age (in years) of the car you usually drive?

The contingency table shown in Table 12.5 summarizes the responses of 162 students. Very few students worked less than 15 hours, and a majority worked 25 hours or more. Most drove cars less than 3 years old, although a few drove cars 10 years old or more. Neither variable was normally distributed (and there were outliers), so a chi-square test was preferable to a correlation or regression model (to be discussed in Chapter 13). The hypotheses to be tested are

H_0: Car age is independent of work hours.

H_1: Car age is not independent of work hours.

Figure 12.7 shows MegaStat's analysis of the 3×4 contingency table. Two expected frequencies (upper right) are below 5, so Cochran's Rule is not quite met. MegaStat has highlighted these cells to call attention to this concern. But

TABLE 12.5 Frequency Classification for Work Hours and Car Age   CarAge

| Hours of Outside Work per Week | Age of Car Usually Driven | | | | |
	Less than 3	3 to 6	6 to 10	10 or More	Row Total
Under 15	9	8	8	4	29
15 to 25	34	17	11	9	71
25 or More	28	20	8	6	62
Col Total	71	45	27	19	162

FIGURE 12.7

MegaStat's Analysis of Car Age Data

Chi-square Contingency Table Test for Independence

		Less than 3	3 to 6	6 to 10	10 or More	Total
Under 15	Observed	9	8	8	4	29
	Expected	12.71	8.06	4.83	3.40	29.00
	$O - E$	−3.71	−0.06	3.17	0.60	0.00
	$(O - E)^2/E$	1.08	0.00	2.07	0.11	3.26
15 to 25	Observed	34	17	11	9	71
	Expected	31.12	19.72	11.83	8.33	71.00
	$O - E$	2.88	−2.72	−0.83	0.67	0.00
	$(O - E)^2/E$	0.27	0.38	0.06	0.05	0.76
25 or More	Observed	28	20	8	6	62
	Expected	27.17	17.22	10.33	7.27	62.00
	$O - E$	0.83	2.78	−2.33	−1.27	0.00
	$(O - E)^2/E$	0.03	0.45	0.53	0.22	1.22
Total	Observed	71	45	27	19	162
	Expected	71.00	45.00	27.00	19.00	162.00
	$O - E$	0.00	0.00	0.00	0.00	0.00
	$(O - E)^2/E$	1.38	0.82	2.66	0.38	5.24

5.24 chi-square
6 df
0.5132 p value

the most striking feature of this table is that almost all of the actual frequencies are very close to the frequencies expected under the hypothesis of independence, leading to a very small chi-square test statistic (5.24). The test requires six degrees of freedom, i.e., $\nu = (r - 1)(c - 1) = (3 - 1)(4 - 1) = 6$. From Appendix E we obtain the right-tail critical value $\chi^2_{0.10} = 10.64$ at $\alpha = 0.10$. Even at this rather weak level of significance, we cannot reject H_0. MegaStat's p value (0.5132) says that a test statistic of this magnitude could arise by chance more than half the time in samples from a population in which the two variables really were independent. Hence, the data lend no support to the hypothesis that students work longer hours to support newer cars.

12.2   Chi-Square Tests for Goodness-of-Fit

Chapter 13

Purpose of the Test

A **goodness-of-fit test** (or **GOF test**) is used to help you decide whether your sample resembles a particular kind of population. This chi-square test can be used to compare sample frequencies with any probability distribution. Tests for goodness-of-fit are easy to understand, but until spreadsheets came along, the calculations were tedious. Today, computers make it easy, and tests for departure from normality or any other distribution are routine. We will first illustrate the GOF test using the most general type of distribution. A **multinomial distribution** is defined by any k probabilities $\pi_1, \pi_2, \ldots, \pi_k$ that sum to one. You can apply this same technique for the three familiar distributions we have already studied (uniform, Poisson, and normal). Although there are many tests for goodness-of-fit, the chi-square test is attractive because it is versatile and easy to understand.

Example of Multinomial GOF Test: M&M Colours

According to the "official" M&M Web site* the distribution of M&M colours is as follows:

Brown (13%)	Red (13%)	Blue (24%)
Orange (20%)	Yellow (16%)	Green (14%)

But do bags of M&Ms shipped to retailers actually follow this distribution? We will use a sample of four bags of candy and conduct a chi-square GOF test. We will assume the distribution is the same as stated on the Web site *unless the sample shows us otherwise.*

Hypotheses

The hypotheses are

H_0: $\pi_{\text{brown}} = 0.13$, $\pi_{\text{red}} = 0.13$, $\pi_{\text{blue}} = 0.24$, $\pi_{\text{orange}} = 0.20$, $\pi_{\text{yellow}} = 0.16$, $\pi_{\text{green}} = 0.14$

H_1: At least one of the π's differs from the hypothesized values.

To test these hypotheses, statistics students opened four bags of M&Ms ($n = 220$ pieces) and counted the number of each colour, with the results shown in Table 12.6. We assign an index to each of the six colours ($j = 1, 2, \ldots, 6$) and define

f_j = the actual frequency of M&Ms of colour j

e_j = the expected frequency of M&Ms of colour j assuming that H_0 is true

Similar to other expected value calculations, each expected frequency (e_j) is calculated by multiplying the sample size (n) by the hypothesized proportion (π_j) or $e_j = n\pi_j$. We can now calculate a chi-square test statistic that compares the actual and expected frequencies:

$$\chi^2_{\text{calc}} = \sum_{j=1}^{c} \frac{[f_j - e_j]^2}{e_j} \tag{12.4}$$

*The official Web site for M&M candies is http://us.mms.com/us/about/products/milkchocolatemms/. These proportions were taken from their Web site during June 2006.

TABLE 12.6 Hypothesis Test of M&M Proportions 🔘 MM

Colour	Official π_j	Observed f_j	Expected $e_j = n \times \pi_j$	$f_j - e_j$	$(f_j - e_j)^2/e_j$
Brown	0.13	38	28.6	+9.4	3.0895
Red	0.13	30	28.6	+1.4	0.0685
Blue	0.24	44	52.8	−8.8	1.4667
Orange	0.20	52	44.0	+8.0	1.4545
Green	0.16	30	35.2	−5.2	0.7682
Yellow	0.14	26	30.8	−4.8	0.7481
Sum	1.00	220	220.0	0.0	$\chi^2_{calc} = 7.5955$

If the null hypothesis is true, the f_j's should be close to their respective e_j's and the chi-square statistic should be small. Conversely, if the alternative hypothesis is true, not all the calculated e_j's are correct, thus not all f_j's should be close to their respective e_j's, and the resulting chi-square statistic should be large. Thus we will reject the null hypothesis when χ^2_{calc} is large, resulting in a right-tail test. That is, we will reject H_0 if the test statistic exceeds the chi-square critical value chosen from Appendix E. For any GOF test, the rule for degrees of freedom is

$$\nu = c - m - 1 \qquad (12.5)$$

where c is the number of classes used in the test and m is the number of parameters estimated.

Results of the Test

Table 12.6 summarizes the calculations in a worksheet. No parameters were estimated ($m = 0$) and we have six classes ($c = 6$), so degrees of freedom are

$$\nu = c - m - 1 = 6 - 0 - 1 = 5$$

From Appendix E, the critical value of chi-square for $\alpha = 0.01$ is $\chi^2_{.01} = 15.09$. Because the test statistic $\chi^2_{calc} = 7.5955$ (from Table 12.6) is smaller than the critical value, we cannot reject the hypothesis that the M&M's colour distribution is as stated on the M&M's Web site. Notice that the f_j and e_j *always* sum exactly to the sample size ($n = 220$ in this example), and the differences $f_j - e_j$ must sum to zero. If not, you have made a mistake in your calculations—a useful way to check your work.

Small Expected Frequencies

The goodness-of-fit test is not very reliable in small samples. The minimum necessary sample size depends on the type of test being employed. As a guideline, a chi-square goodness-of-fit test should be avoided if $n < 25$ (some experts would suggest a higher number). Cochran's Rule that expected frequencies should be at least 5 (i.e., all $e_j \geq 5$) also provides a guideline, although some experts would weaken the rule to require only $e_j \geq 2$. In the M&M's example, the expected frequencies are all large, so there is no reason to doubt the test. No matter what rule of thumb you use for the e_j's, if the rule is violated you would combine categories until all resulting expected values are at least 5. From a mathematical standpoint, it doesn't make a difference which categories are combined as long as the resulting degrees of freedom are as great as possible. From an aesthetic standpoint, it may make a difference. For example, if the expected number of A+'s and the expected number of F's in a course are both less than 5, it would make better sense to combine the A+'s with the A's and the F's with the D's than to combine the A+'s with the F's.

Concept Check

In the game of craps, two dice are rolled and the resulting sum of the dots on the top faces of the two dice determines the outcome of the game (for most bets). If you wanted to test whether the pair of dice were fair, what would the two hypotheses be, stated in terms of the individual π_j's? What would the minimum number of rolls have to be in order that all e_j's are greater than or equal to 5 for this test?

GOF Tests for Other Distributions

We can also use the chi-square GOF test to compare a sample of data with a familiar distribution such as the uniform, Poisson, or normal. We would state the hypotheses as below:

H_0: The population follows a _____ distribution.

H_1: The population doesn't follow a _____ distribution.

The blank may contain the name of any theoretical distribution. Assuming that we have n observations, we group the observations into c classes and then find the *chi-square test statistic* using Equation 12.4. In a GOF test, if we use sample data to *estimate* the distribution's parameters, then our degrees of freedom would be as follows:

$$\textbf{Uniform: } \nu = c - m - 1 = c - 0 - 1 = c - 1 \text{ (no parameters are estimated)} \quad \textbf{(12.6)}$$

$$\textbf{Poisson: } \nu = c - m - 1 = c - 1 - 1 = c - 2 \text{ (if } \lambda \text{ is estimated)} \quad \textbf{(12.7)}$$

$$\textbf{Normal: } \nu = c - m - 1 = c - 2 - 1 = c - 3 \text{ (if } \mu \text{ and } \sigma \text{ are estimated)} \quad \textbf{(12.8)}$$

Section Exercises

12.7 In previous years, exams in a particular statistics course were set by the professor such that 15 percent of students received a grade of A, 25 percent received a grade of B, 30 percent received a grade of C, 20 percent received a grade of D, and 10 percent received a grade of F. This year, the professor decided to change the types of exams he set and the results for a class of 250 students showed that 30 received a grade of A, 55 received a grade of B, 83 received a grade of C, 55 received a grade of D, and 27 received a grade of F. Assuming that these 250 students represent a random sample of students who would be taking this course, is there sufficient evidence, at the 0.05 level of significance, that this new type of exam has affected the grade distribution in this course? (LO 1 & 3)

12.8 Since 9/11, Canadians crossing the U.S. border have seen American Customs and Immigration officers spending more time questioning individuals. Suppose that last year a very extensive study at a particular border crossing revealed that 33 percent of the questioning times lasted between 0 and 2 minutes, 40 percent lasted between 2 and 4 minutes, 22 percent between 4 and 6 minutes, and 5 percent more than 6 minutes. This year, a random sample of 120 cars revealed that 35 were exposed to questioning times of between 0 and 2 minutes, 45 were between 2 and 4 minutes, 35 were between 4 and 6 minutes, and the remaining cars were exposed to times in excess of 6 minutes. At the 0.10 level of significance, can we conclude that the distribution of questioning times has changed from last year? (LO 1 & 3)

12.3   Uniform GOF Test

For those of you who have had the opportunity to visit one of Canada's many casinos and have watched the dice game called craps, the dealers are constantly looking at the dice especially if they fall off the craps table. They look at them because if the dice are fair or balanced, they know that, in the long run, the casino will be making a profit on this game. If the dice are not balanced due to the dice having some substance on them or because one of the corners is deformed, the certainty of making a profit may be in doubt. If a die is balanced or fair, we are saying that the probability of each face landing as the top face is the same ($= 1/6$) (general method), or that the distribution for the top face follows a discrete **uniform distribution.** In fact, the uniform GOF test is simply a special case of the multinomial distribution in which every value has the same chance of occurrence.

The chi-square test for a uniform distribution is a generalization of the test for equality of two proportions. The hypotheses are

$H_0: \pi_1 = \pi_2 = \cdots = \pi_c = 1/c$

H_1: Not all the π_j's are equal.

The chi-square test compares all c groups *simultaneously.* Each discrete outcome should have probability $1/c$, so the test is very easy to perform. Evidence against H_0 would consist of sample frequencies that were not the same for all categories.

Referring to the craps game, we might want to test if a given die is fair. Our hypotheses would then be

$H_0: \pi_1 = \pi_2 = \pi_3 = \pi_4 = \pi_5 = \pi_6 = 1/6$

H_1: Not all the π_j's are equal.

Classes need not represent numerical values. For example, we might compare the total number of items scanned per hour by four supermarket checkers (Bob, Frieda, Sam, and Wanda). The uniform test is quite versatile. For numerical variables, bins do not have to be of equal width and can be open-ended. For example, we might be interested in the ages of X-ray machines in a hospital (under 2 years, 2 to 5 years, 5 to 10 years, 10 years and over). In a uniform population, each category would be expected to have $e_j = n/c$ observations, so the calculation of expected frequencies is simple.

Uniform GOF Test: Grouped Data

The test is easiest if data are already tabulated into groups, which saves us the effort of defining the groups. For example, one year, a certain province had 756 traffic fatalities. Table 12.7 suggests that fatalities are not uniformly distributed by day of week, being higher on weekends. Can we reject the hypothesis of a uniform distribution, say, at $\alpha = 0.005$? The hypotheses are:

H_0: Traffic fatalities are uniformly distributed by day of the week.

H_1: Traffic fatalities are not uniformly distributed by day of the week.

Under H_0 the expected frequency for each weekday is $e_j = n/c = 756/7 = 108$. The expected frequencies happen to be integers, although this is not true in general. Because no parameters were estimated ($m = 0$) to form the seven classes ($c = 7$), the chi-square test will have $\nu = c - m - 1 = 7 - 0 - 1 = 6$ degrees of freedom. From Appendix E, the critical value of chi-square for the 0.5 percent level of significance is $\chi^2_{0.005,6} = 18.55$, so the hypothesis of a rectangular or uniform population can be rejected. The p value (0.0035) can be obtained from the Excel function =CHIDIST(19.426,6). The p value tells us that such a sample result

TABLE 12.7 Traffic Fatalities by Day of Week ⊙ Traffic

Day	f_j	e_j	$f_j - e_j$	$(f_j - e_j)^2$	$(f_j - e_j)^2/e_j$
Sun	121	108	13	169	1.565
Mon	96	108	−12	144	1.333
Tue	91	108	−17	289	2.676
Wed	92	108	−16	256	2.370
Thu	96	108	−12	144	1.333
Fri	122	108	14	196	1.815
Sat	138	108	30	900	8.333
Total	756	756	0		$\chi^2_{calc} = 19.426$

Source: Based on http://www-nrd.nhtsa.dot.gov.

TABLE 12.8   100 Consecutive Winning Three-Digit Lottery Numbers   Lottery-A

367	865	438	437	596	567	121	244	036	337
152	260	470	821	452	606	417	674	786	311
739	611	359	739	184	229	418	565	547	403
103	344	303	531	054	496	167	550	403	785
341	237	913	991	656	661	178	983	431	472
315	792	676	299	738	080	450	991	673	846
500	001	016	581	154	677	457	617	261	807
452	048	052	018	037	517	760	522	711	898
294	605	135	333	886	257	533	119	882	899
814	490	490	885	329	033	033	707	551	651

would occur by chance only about 35 times in 10,000 tests. There is a believable underlying causal mechanism at work (e.g., people may drink and drive more often on weekends).

Uniform GOF Test: Raw Data

When we are using raw data, we must form c bins of equal width and create our own frequency distribution. For example, suppose an auditor is checking the fairness of a province's "Daily 3" lottery. Table 12.8 shows winning three-digit lottery numbers for 100 consecutive days. All numbers from 000 to 999 are supposed to be equally likely, so the auditor is testing these hypotheses:

H_0: Lottery numbers are uniformly distributed.

H_1: Lottery numbers are not uniformly distributed.

We know that three-digit lottery numbers must lie in the range 000 to 999, so there are many ways we could define our classes (e.g., 5 bins of width 200, 10 bins of width 100, 20 bins of width 50, etc.). We will use 10 bins, with the realization that we might get a different result if we chose different bins. The steps are as follows:

- Step 1: Divide the range into 10 bins of equal width.
- Step 2: Calculate the observed frequency, f_j, for each bin.
- Step 3: Define $e_j = n/c = 100/10 = 10$.
- Step 4: Perform the chi-square calculations (see Table 12.9).
- Step 5: Make the decision.

TABLE 12.9   Uniform GOF Test for Lottery Numbers

Bin	f_j	e_j	$f_j - e_j$	$(f_j - e_j)^2$	$(f_j - e_j)^2/e_j$
0 to < 100	11	10	1	1	0.100
100 to < 200	9	10	−1	1	0.100
200 to < 300	8	10	−2	4	0.400
300 to < 400	10	10	0	0	0.000
400 to < 500	16	10	6	36	3.600
500 to < 600	12	10	2	4	0.400
600 to < 700	11	10	1	1	0.100
700 to < 800	9	10	−1	1	0.100
800 to < 900	10	10	0	0	0.000
900 to < 1,000	4	10	−6	36	3.600
Total	100	100	0		$\chi^2_{calc} = 8.400$

Because no parameters were estimated ($m = 0$) to form the 10 classes ($c = 10$), we have $\nu = c - m - 1 = 10 - 0 - 1 = 9$ degrees of freedom. From Appendix E, the critical value of chi-square for the 10 percent level of significance is $\chi^2_{0.10,9} = 14.684$. The test's p value is calculated using the Excel formula =CHIDIST(8.4,9) and equals 0.4944. The null hypothesis of a uniform distribution cannot be rejected.

A Closer Look

The above example used 10 bins to make the calculations less tedious. We should have used 20 bins to keep as much information as possible or to improve the power of the test. Creating 20 equal width intervals, 000–049, 050–099, . . . , 950–999, would result in $\chi^2_{calc} = 18$. Again, from Appendix E, the critical chi-square value for $\alpha = 0.10$ is $\chi^2_{0.10,19} = 27.204$. The test's p value is 0.5224.

A general rule to follow is to use as many bins of equal width as possible as long as all resulting e_j's (expected frequencies) are at least 5.

The histograms in Figures 12.8 and 12.9 suggest too many winning lottery numbers in the middle and too few at the top. But histogram appearance is affected by the way we define our bins and the number of classes, so the chi-square test is a more reliable guide. Humans are adept at finding patterns in sample distributions that actually are within the realm of chance.

FIGURE 12.8

Ten-Bin Histogram

FIGURE 12.9

Five-Bin Histogram

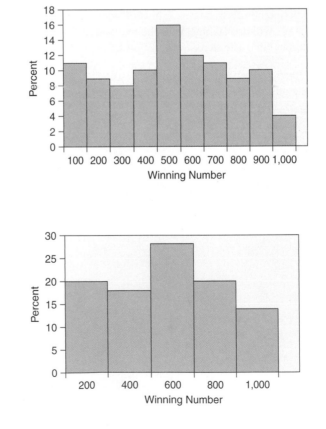

Section Exercises

12.9 To check whether dice manufactured by a particular supplier are still balanced after being exposed to three hours of wear and tear at a craps table, a casino randomly selected one of these dice and rolled it 420 times and recorded the number of times each face appeared on top as follows:

Face	Frequency
1	67
2	68
3	74
4	66
5	75
6	70

At the 0.05 level of significance, is there sufficient evidence to indicate that this die is no longer balanced? (LO 1 & 4)

12.10 Advertisers need to know which age groups are likely to see their ads. Purchasers of 120 copies of *Cosmopolitan* are shown by age group. (a) Make a bar chart and describe it. (b) Calculate expected frequencies for each class. (c) At $\alpha = 0.01$, does this sample contradict the assumption that readership is uniformly distributed among these six age groups? (See J. Paul Peter and Jerry C. Olson, *Consumer Behavior and Marketing Strategy,* 9th ed. [McGraw-Hill, 2004], p. 300.) (LO 1 & 4)   **Cosmo**

Purchaser Age Group	Units Sold
18–24	38
25–34	28
35–44	19
45–54	16
55–64	10
65+	9
Total	120

12.11 One-year sales volume of four similar 590-ml beverages on a university campus is shown. (a) Make a bar chart and describe it. (b) Calculate expected frequencies for each class. (c) Perform the chi-square test for a uniform distribution. At $\alpha = 0.05$, does this sample contradict the assumption that sales are the same for each beverage? (LO 1 & 4)   **Frapp**

Beverage	Sales (Cases)
Frappuccino Coffee	18
Frappuccino Mocha	23
Frappuccino Vanilla	23
Frappuccino Caramel	20
Total	84

12.12 In a three-digit lottery, each of the three digits is supposed to have the same probability of occurrence (counting initial blanks as zeros, e.g., 32 is treated as 032). The table shows the frequency of occurrence of each digit for 90 consecutive daily three-digit drawings. (a) Make a bar chart and describe it. (b) Calculate expected frequencies for each class. (c) Perform the chi-square test for a uniform distribution. At $\alpha = 0.05$, can you reject the hypothesis that the digits are from a uniform population? (LO 1 & 4) **Lottery3**

Digit	Frequency
0	33
1	17
2	25
3	30
4	31
5	28
6	24
7	25
8	32
9	25
Total	270

12.13 Ages of 56 attendees of a *Harry Potter* movie are shown. (a) Form seven age classes (10 to 19, 20 to 29, etc.). Tabulate the frequency of attendees in each class. (b) Calculate expected frequencies for each class. (c) Perform a chi-square GOF test for a uniform distribution, using the 5 percent level of significance. (LO 1 & 4)   **Harry**

10	22	58	11	73	22	57
35	33	33	59	54	55	75
79	24	13	73	52	69	30
71	64	17	50	72	67	50
72	35	26	59	47	65	35
64	34	39	66	37	41	58
51	43	29	74	73	50	62
58	34	50	27	13	67	67

Chapter 13

12.4 Normal Chi-Square Goodness-of-Fit Test

Normal Data-Generating Situations

Any normal population is fully described by the two parameters μ and σ. Many data-generating situations could be compatible with a **normal distribution,** if the data possess a reasonable degree of central tendency and are not badly skewed. Measurements of continuous variables such as physical attributes (e.g., weight, size, travel time) may have a constant mean and variance if the underlying process is stable and the population is homogeneous. The normal model might apply to discrete or integer data if the range is relatively large, such as the number of successes in a large binomial sample or Poisson occurrences if the mean is large. Unless μ and σ parameters are known *a priori* (a rare circumstance), they must be estimated from a sample by using $\bar{x}$ and s. Using these statistics, we can set up the chi-square goodness-of-fit test. Although there are several ways this could be done, we describe three basic ways.

Method 1 (General)

* **Step 1:** Collect the data and create a histogram (frequency distribution) using number of bins (c) based on this data set (or use an already created frequency table or histogram if the raw data are not available). These c bins do not have to be of equal width to conduct this test. So we start with observed frequency of each bin.

* **Step 2:** Calculate this data set's mean and standard deviation (or estimate their values if all you have is a frequency table or histogram to start with; in this case, step 1 is not needed).

* **Step 3:** Using the estimated mean and standard deviation and the bin limits, calculate the probability using the Normal Table in Appendix C (or Excel) of an observation falling into each of the bins. Let these probabilities be $p_1, p_2, \ldots, p_c$.

* **Step 4:** Calculate the expected frequency of each bin using $e_j = np_j$ with the p_j's calculated in Step 3.

* **Step 5:** Calculate the value of the GOF chi-square test statistic and compare it with the decision rule based on $\nu = c - 2 - 1$ degrees of freedom.

Method 2 (Equal Bin Width)

* **Step 1:** For the collected n data values, find mean $\bar{x}$ and standard deviation s of the sample data.

* **Step 2:** Create six intervals for z values ($c = 6$): $z < -2$, $-2 \leq z < -1$, $-1 \leq z < 0$, $0 \leq z < 1$, $1 \leq z < 2$, $z \geq 2$.

* **Step 3:** Find the expected frequency of each interval. Because $P(z < -2) = P(z \geq 2)$ $= 0.5 - 0.4772 = 0.0228$, due to symmetry, the expected frequency of the first and sixth class is $0.0228n$ each. Because $P(-2 < z < -1) = P(1 < z < 2) = 0.4772 - 0.3413$ $= 0.1359$, the expected frequency of the second and fifth classes is $0.1359n$ each. Similarly, the expected frequency of the third and fourth classes is $0.3413n$ each.

* **Step 4:** Convert each z interval to the corresponding x interval by using the transformation $z = (x - \bar{x})/s$. With this transformation, interval $a < z < b$ is converted to the interval $\bar{x} + as < x < \bar{x} + bs$. Thus, corresponding to the six z intervals in Step 2, the six x intervals are $x < \bar{x} - 2s$, $\bar{x} - 2s < x < \bar{x} - s$, $\bar{x} - s < x < \bar{x}$, $\bar{x} < x < \bar{x} + s$, $\bar{x} + s < x < \bar{x} + 2s$, and $x > \bar{x} + 2s$.

* **Step 5:** Using the original data, find the observed frequency of each of the six intervals obtained above in Step 4.

* **Step 6:** Calculate the value of the GOF chi-square test statistic and compare it with the decision rule based on $\nu = c - 2 - 1$ degrees of freedom.

Method 3 (Equal Expected Frequency)

* **Step 1:** Same as Step 1 of Method 2, above.

* **Step 2:** We define intervals so that the expected frequency of each interval is the same. That is, define c interval limits so that the expected frequency of each interval is n/c. To illustrate this method, let us assume that we have 30 observations ($n = 30$), and we decide to have 6 intervals ($c = 6$). The expected frequency of each interval then would be $5 (= 30/6)$, and the normal probability of an observation to be in each interval would be $1/6$. The first and the last interval will be open-ended, each containing an area of $1/6$. So we want a z value such that the area to its left is $1/6$, or 0.1667. From the Normal Table in Appendix C, we see that $P(Z > 0.97) = 0.1660$. This is close to 0.1667. So we could use $z < -0.97$ and $z > 0.97$ to be the two open-ended intervals or bins (used in Excel). If we want an exact area of 0.1667, we could use the Excel formula =NORMSINV(0.1667) and get the answer -0.967. So the two classes, more precisely, will be $z < -0.967$ and $z > 0.967$. To get the next two classes, we need to find the z value so that the cumulative area up to this z value is $2/6$, or 0.3333. Using the Excel formula =NORMSINV(0.3333), we get a value of -0.431. So the next two classes are $-0.967 < z < -0.431$ and $0.431 < z < 0.967$. It is easy to see that each one of these two classes has an area of $1/6$. The final two classes are trivially obtained: $-0.431 < z < 0$ and $0 < z < 0.431$.

* **Step 3:** Convert these z intervals to x intervals as in Step 4 of Method 2.

* **Step 4:** Find the observed frequency of each of these c intervals.

Let us compare the three methods. If all we are given is a frequency distribution, then we must use Method 1, and base our analysis on the classes already defined. If we are given raw data, then it may be easier to use Method 2 or Method 3.

It is very easy to find expected frequencies using Method 2. Using exactly these six classes in this method, however, we need a sample size of at least 200 to ensure that all classes have expected frequency of at least 5. If we have a smaller sample size, we might consider different set of classes. For example, we may consider 5 classes as

$$z < -1.5, -1.5 \leq z < -0.5, -0.5 \leq z < 0.5, 0.5 \leq z < 1.5, z \geq 1.5$$

A sample size of at least 75 observations would ensure that the expected frequency of each one of these 5 classes is at least 5. It is easy to verify that for these 5 classes, the expected frequencies will be $0.0668n$, $0.2417n$, $0.3829n$, $0.2417n$, and $0.0668n$, respectively.

Method 3 has the advantage over Method 2 in that if we decide on 6 bins, we need only 30 observations to ensure that the expected frequency of each class is at least 5. With 30 observations and 6 bins, we have found the 6 classes, each one of which has an expected frequency of exactly 5. The drawback of this method is that it takes a bit more effort to find the bins, or class limits.

We will illustrate all these methods with examples.

A Closer Look

The degrees of freedom are based on the number of intervals or bins (in this case, that number is c), and the number of parameters to be estimated before calculating the appropriate statistics. In this example, to calculate values of z necessary to determine the e_j's, we first have to estimate the population mean, μ, and standard deviation, σ, resulting in a loss of two degrees of freedom ($m = 2$).

EXAMPLE 5

Exam Completion Times

In the past, the time that it took students to complete a professor's exam has been (approximately) normally distributed. Using a new testing procedure, this professor wants to determine whether these times still follow a normal distribution. By recording the times it took her students ($n = 100$) to complete her three-hour exam, she developed the following frequency table. Do these exam completion times come from a normal population?

Time	Number of Students
< 60 minutes	10
60 to 90 minutes	18
90 to 120 minutes	37
120 to 150 minutes	21
> 150 minutes	14

We set up our hypotheses as follows:

H_0: Exam completion times come from a normal population.

H_1: Exam completion times do not come from a normal population.

Because the data is given in the form of a histogram, to conduct the goodness-of-fit test we must use Method 1 and proceed as follows. Using the method described in Section 4.7, we first estimate the mean and standard deviation from this frequency distribution and find that $\bar{x} = 106.8$, $s = 37.607$.

The following Excel worksheet shows the calculations for Steps 3, 4, and 5 of Method 1.

From	To	Freq. f_i	Prob. p_i	Exp. Freq. e_i	$(f_i - e_i)^2/e_i$
0	60	10	0.1067	10.667	0.0416
60	90	18	0.2209	22.087	0.7563
90	120	37	0.3097	30.967	1.1753
120	150	21	0.2375	23.746	0.3176
150	180	14	0.1253	12.533	0.1716
				Chi-Square =	2.4624

To find the probability p_i for the interval 60 to 90 minutes, for example, we use the Excel formula =NORMDIST(90,106.8,37.607,1) − NORMDIST(60,106.8,37.607,1). From this table, we see that $\chi^2_{calc} = 2.4624$. The degrees of freedom for the test are $c - m - 1 = 5 - 2 - 1 = 2$. Using $\alpha = 0.10$, the critical χ^2 value is $\chi^2_{0.10,2} = 4.605$. Thus we cannot reject the null hypothesis of data following a normal distribution.

A random sample of 70 Nestlé Smarties was taken and each candy weighed. The weights are shown below. Can we claim that these weights come from a normal population?

EXAMPLE 6

Weighing Smarties

4.666	4.854	4.868	4.849	4.700	4.683	5.064
4.800	4.694	4.760	5.075	4.780	4.781	5.103
4.568	4.983	5.076	4.808	5.084	4.749	5.092
4.783	4.520	4.698	5.084	4.880	4.883	4.880
4.928	4.651	4.797	4.682	4.756	5.041	4.906
4.808	4.667	4.694	4.732	4.695	5.001	4.659
4.482	5.049	4.754	4.886	4.917	5.091	4.854
4.621	4.494	4.651	4.742	5.077	4.761	5.073
4.852	4.806	4.866	4.877	4.934	4.675	4.995
4.811	4.974	4.742	5.043	5.030	5.069	4.869

Thus, our hypotheses are as follows:

H_0: Smarties weights come from a normal population.

H_1: Smarties weights do not come from a normal population.

Because we have raw data, we can use Method 2 to conduct the goodness-of-fit test. Because we have only 70 observations, we consider five classes for z values. The mean and standard deviation for these 70 weights are $\bar{x} = 4.8397$ and $s = 0.1628$. The Excel output is shown below.

z-values		x-values					
From	To	From	To	Freq. f_i	Prob. P_i	Exp. Freq. e_i	$(f_i-e_i)^2/e_i$
-3	-1.5	4.3514	4.5955	4	0.067	4.677	0.098
-1.5	-0.5	4.5955	4.7583	20	0.242	16.921	0.560
-0.5	0.5	4.7583	4.9210	25	0.383	26.805	0.122
0.5	1.5	4.9210	5.0838	16	0.242	16.921	0.050
1.5	3	5.0838	5.3279	5	0.067	4.677	0.022
			Total	70	1	70	0.852

$$\chi^2_{calc} =$$

So our $\chi^2_{calc} = 0.852$. The test's p value is calculated through Excel as =CHIDIST(0.852,2) and yields a p value of 0.65. Thus, again, we cannot reject the null hypothesis for any reasonable level of significance.

Let us use Method 3 now with this example. Because there are 70 observations, we can have as many as 14 classes. We develop an Excel worksheet with these 14 classes with the following output. As in Method 2, we use the estimates of μ and σ and standardize our data to obtain the observed frequency of each class. For example, there were four observations whose standardized value was between -3 and -1.465. Degrees of freedom equal $14 - 2 - 1 = 11$. The computed chi-square value equals 20. The p value of the test is given by the Excel formula $=$CHIDIST(20,11) and equals 0.045. If $\alpha = 0.05$, we will reject the null hypothesis and claim that data does not follow a normal distribution, contradicting the conclusion made using Method 2. Because Method 3 is more powerful (it has 14 classes as opposed to 5 in Method 2), we will more likely reject the null hypothesis of normality, and perhaps use additional tests (see the topics in the optional Section 12.5) to verify this conclusion.

z-values		x-values					
From	To	From	To	Freq. f_i	Prob. P_i	Exp. Freq. e_i	$(f_i - e_i)^2 / e_i$
-3	-1.465	4.3514	4.6012	4	1/14	5	0.2
-1.465	-1.068	4.6012	4.6659	4	1/14	5	0.2
-1.068	-0.792	4.6659	4.7108	10	1/14	5	5
-0.792	-0.566	4.7108	4.7476	3	1/14	5	0.8
-0.566	-0.366	4.7476	4.7801	6	1/14	5	0.2
-0.366	-0.180	4.7801	4.8104	7	1/14	5	0.8
-0.180	0.000	4.8104	4.8397	1	1/14	5	3.2
0.000	0.180	4.8397	4.8690	6	1/14	5	0.2
0.180	0.366	4.8690	4.8993	6	1/14	5	0.2
0.366	0.566	4.8993	4.9318	3	1/14	5	0.8
0.566	0.792	4.9318	4.9685	1	1/14	5	3.2
0.792	1.068	4.9685	5.0134	4	1/14	5	0.2
1.068	1.465	5.0134	5.0781	10	1/14	5	5
1.465	3	5.0781	5.3279	5	1/14	5	0
			Total	70	1	70	20

$$\chi^2_{calc} =$$

Section Exercises

Note: Exercises marked with an asterisk (*) are more difficult.

12.14 Exam scores of 40 students in a statistics class are shown. (a) Calculate the mean and standard deviation from the sample. (b) Assuming that the data are from a normal distribution, define bins by using Method 3 (equal expected frequencies). Use eight bins. (c) Set up an Excel worksheet for your chi-square calculations, with a column showing the expected frequency for each bin (they must add to 40). (d) Tabulate the observed frequency for each bin and record it in the next column. (e) Carry out the chi-square test, using $\alpha = 0.05$. Can you reject the hypothesis that the exam scores came from a normal population? *(f) Enter the data into the Visual Statistics data editor in Module 13 (Goodness-of-Fit Tests) and do chi-square tests with varying options. Was Visual Statistics helpful? (LO 1 & 5) **ExamScores**

79	75	77	57	81	70	83	66
81	89	59	83	75	60	96	86
78	76	71	78	78	70	54	60
71	81	79	88	77	82	75	68
77	69	83	79	79	76	78	71

12.15 One Friday night, there were 42 carry-out orders at Ashoka Curry Express. (a) Calculate the mean and standard deviation from the sample. (b) Assuming that the data are from a normal distribution, define bins by using Method 3 (equal expected frequencies). Use eight bins. (c) Set up an Excel worksheet for your chi-square calculations, with a column showing the expected frequency for each bin (they must add to 42). (d) Tabulate the observed frequency for each bin and record it in the next column. (e) Do the chi-square test at $\alpha = 0.025$. Can you reject the hypothesis that carry-out orders follow a normal population? *(f) Enter the data into the Visual Statistics data editor in Module 13 (Goodness-of-Fit Tests) and do chi-square tests with varying options. Was Visual Statistics helpful? (LO 1 & 5) **TakeOut**

18.74	21.05	31.19	23.06	20.17	25.12	24.30
46.04	33.96	45.04	34.63	35.24	30.13	29.93
52.33	26.52	19.68	19.62	32.96	42.07	47.82
38.62	31.88	44.97	36.35	21.50	41.42	33.87
26.43	35.28	21.88	24.80	27.49	18.30	44.47
28.40	36.72	26.30	47.08	34.33	13.15	15.51

*12.16 When travelling from Vancouver to Seattle by car, one would not necessarily expect travelling times to follow a normal distribution because of the possibility of lengthy delays at the border crossing. When travelling from Calgary to Edmonton, one should not expect such delays and it is reasonable to assume that travelling times follow a normal distribution. To test whether a normal distribution is appropriate along the route between the Calgary International Airport and the Edmonton International Airport, a limousine service recorded the times for a random sample of 50 of its trips between the two airports and summarized them in the following table:

Times (in minutes)	No. of Trips
120–130	2
130–140	8
140–150	13
150–160	11
160–170	9
170–180	7

(a) Estimate the mean and standard deviation in travelling times. (b) Using the appropriate method, at the 0.05 level of significance is there sufficient evidence to indicate that travelling times between these two airports are not normally distributed? (LO 1 & 5)

12.5 ECDF Tests (Optional)

Kolmogorov-Smirnov and Lilliefors Tests

There are many alternatives to the chi-square test, based on the **empirical cumulative distribution function (ECDF)**. One such test is the **Kolmogorov-Smirnov (K-S) test.** The K-S test statistic D is the largest absolute difference between the actual and expected cumulative relative frequency of the n data values:

$$D = \text{Max}|F_a - F_e| \qquad\qquad (12.9)$$

The K-S test is not recommended for grouped data, as it may be less powerful than the chi-square test.

F_a is the actual cumulative frequency at observation i, and F_e is the expected cumulative frequency at observation i under the assumption that the data came from the hypothesized distribution. The K-S test assumes that no parameters are estimated. If they are (e.g., the mean and variance may be estimated), we use a **Lilliefors test,** whose test statistic is the same, but with a different table of critical values. Because these tests are always done by computer (F_e requires the inverse CDF for the hypothesized distribution), we will omit further details and merely illustrate the test visually. Because observations are treated individually, information is not lost by combining categories, as in a chi-square test. Thus, ECDF tests may surpass the chi-square test in their ability to detect departures from the distribution specified in the null hypothesis, if raw data are available.

Illustrations: Lottery Numbers and Kiss Weights

Figure 12.10 shows a Visual Statistics screen displaying the K-S test for *uniformity* in the 100 lottery numbers tested earlier in a chi-square test. The largest difference (0.087) occurs

FIGURE 12.10

K-S Test for Uniformity

Chapter 13

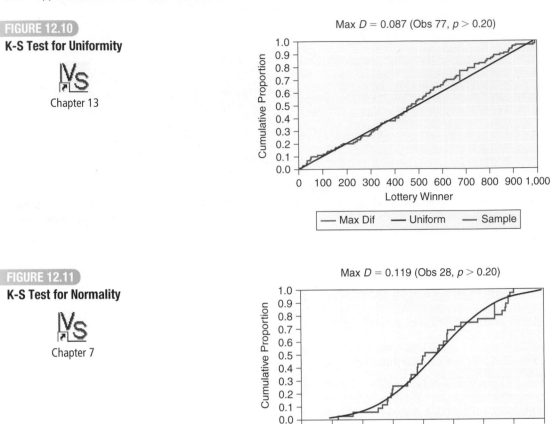

Max $D = 0.087$ (Obs 77, $p > 0.20$)

— Max Dif — Uniform — Sample

FIGURE 12.11

K-S Test for Normality

Chapter 7

Max $D = 0.119$ (Obs 28, $p > 0.20$)

— Max Dif — Normal — Sample

at observation 77, but the large p value does not warrant rejection of the hypothesis of a uniform distribution. The CDF under the hypothesis of uniformity is a straight line, while for a normal distribution, the CDF would be *S*-shaped. Figure 12.11 shows a *normality* test for weights of Hershey's Kisses. The largest difference occurs at observation 28, but the p value does not warrant rejection of the hypothesis of normality. For this data set, the K-S test lacks sufficient power to reject *either* a uniform *or* a normal distribution.

Anderson-Darling Test

The **Anderson-Darling (A-D) test,** another ECDF test, is perhaps the most widely used test for non-normality because of its power. It is always done on a computer as it requires the inverse CDF for the hypothesized distribution. The A-D test is based on a **probability plot.** When the data fit the hypothesized distribution closely, the probability plot will be close to a straight line. The A-D test statistic measures the overall distance between the actual and the hypothesized distributions, using a weighted squared distance. It provides a p value to complement the visual plot. The A-D statistic is not difficult to calculate, but its formula is rather complex, so it is omitted. Figure 12.12 shows a graph displaying the probability plot and A-D statistic for the Hershey's Kiss data using MINITAB's Stats > Basic Statistics > Normality Test. The p value (0.091) suggests a departure from normality at the 10 percent level of significance, but not at the 5 percent level. This result is consistent with our previous findings. The A-D test is more powerful than a chi-square test if raw data are available, because it treats the observations individually. Also, the probability plot has the attraction of revealing discrepancies between the sample and the hypothesized distribution, and it is usually easy to spot outliers.

MINITAB's Probability Plot and Anderson-Darling Test for Kiss Weights FIGURE 12.12

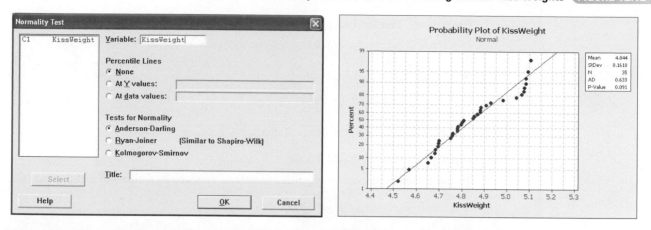

Section Exercises

*12.17 (a) Use MINITAB's Stat > Basic Statistics > Normality Test to obtain a probability plot for the exam score data (see Exercise 12.14). Interpret the probability plot and Anderson-Darling statistic. Was MINITAB easier to use than the chi-square test? (b) Enter the data into the Visual Statistics data editor in Module 13 (Goodness-of-Fit Tests) and create an ECDF plot with the Kolmogorov-Smirnov statistic. Describe the ECDF plot. Was Visual Statistics helpful?   **ExamScores**

*12.18 (a) Use MINITAB's Stat > Basic Statistics > Normality Test to obtain a probability plot for the Ashoka Curry House carry-out order data (see Exercise 12.15). Interpret the probability plot and Anderson-Darling statistic. Was MINITAB easier to use than the chi-square test? (b) Enter the data into the Visual Statistics data editor in Module 13 (Goodness-of-Fit Tests) and create an ECDF plot with the Kolmogorov-Smirnov statistic. Describe the ECDF plot. Was Visual Statistics helpful?   **TakeOut**

CHAPTER SUMMARY

A **chi-square test of independence** requires an $r \times c$ **contingency table** that has r rows and c columns. Degrees of freedom for the chi-square test will be $(r - 1)(c - 1)$. In this test, the **observed frequencies** are compared with the **expected frequencies** under the hypothesis of independence. The test assumes categorical data (attribute data) but can also be used with numerical data grouped into classes. **Cochran's rule** requires that expected frequencies be at least 5 in each cell, although this rule is often relaxed. A test for **goodness-of-fit (GOF)** uses the chi-square statistic to decide whether a sample is from a specified distribution (e.g., multinomial, uniform, Poisson, normal). The **parameters** of the fitted distribution (e.g., the mean) may be specified *a priori,* but more often are estimated from the sample. Degrees of freedom for the GOF test are $c - m - 1$ where c is the number of categories and m is the number of parameters estimated. The **Kolmogorov-Smirnov** and **Lilliefors** tests are **ECDF-based tests** that look at differences between the sample's empirical cumulative distribution function (ECDF) and the hypothesized distribution. They are best used with n individual observations. The **Anderson-Darling** test and the **probability plot** are the most common ECDF tests, most often used to test for normality.

KEY TERMS

Anderson-Darling (A-D) test, *526*
chi-square probability distribution, *504*
chi-square test, *503*
Cochran's rule, *508*
contingency table, *501*
degrees of freedom, *504*

empirical cumulative distribution function (ECDF), *525*
expected frequency, *503*
goodness-of-fit (GOF) test, *513*
independent, *503*
Kolmogorov-Smirnov (K-S) test, *525*

Lilliefors test, *525*
multinomial distribution, *513*
normal distribution, *520*
observed frequency, *503*
probability plot, *526*
test for independence, *501*
uniform distribution, *516*

Commonly Used Formulas

Chi-Square Test for Independence

Test statistic for independence in a contingency table with r rows and c columns:

$$\chi^2_{calc} = \sum_{j=1}^{r} \sum_{k=1}^{c} \frac{[f_{jk} - e_{jk}]^2}{e_{jk}}$$

Degrees of freedom for a contingency table with r rows and c columns:

$$\nu = (r - 1)(c - 1)$$

Expected frequency in row j and column k: $e_{jk} = R_j C_k / n$

Chi-Square Goodness-of-Fit Test

Test statistic for observed frequencies in c classes under a hypothesized distribution H_0

(e.g., uniform, normal): $\chi^2_{calc} = \sum_{j=1}^{c} \frac{[f_j - e_j]^2}{e_j}$

where

f_j = the observed frequency in class j

e_j = the expected frequency in class $j = n\pi_j$ or np_j (if π_j's are unknown)

Degrees of freedom for the chi-square GOF test: $\nu = c - m - 1$

where

c = the number of classes used in the test

m = the number of parameters estimated

CHAPTER REVIEW

Note: Questions labelled * are based on optional material from this chapter.

1. (a) What are the hypotheses in a chi-square test for independence? (b) Why do we call it a test of frequencies? (c) What distribution is used in this test? (d) How do we calculate the degrees of freedom for an $r \times c$ contingency table? (LO 1)

2. How do we calculate the expected frequencies for each cell of the contingency table? (LO 2)

3. What is Cochran's rule, and why is it needed? Why do we call it a "rule of thumb"? (LO 1)

4. (a) Explain why the 2×2 table is analogous to a z test for two proportions. (b) What is the relationship between z and χ^2 in the 2×2 table? (LO 2)

5. (a) What are the hypotheses for a GOF test? (b) Explain how a chi-square GOF test is carried out in general. (LO 3)

6. What is the general formula for degrees of freedom in a chi-square GOF test? (LO 3)

7. (a) In a uniform GOF test, how do we calculate the expected frequencies? (b) Why is the test easier if the data are already grouped? (LO 4)

8. (a) Very briefly describe three ways of calculating expected frequencies for a normal GOF test. (b) Name advantages and disadvantages of each way. (c) Why is a normal GOF test almost always done on a computer? (LO 5)

* 9. What is an ECDF test? Give an example.

*10. (a) Name potential advantages of the Kolmogorov-Smirnov or Lilliefors tests. (b) Why would this type of test almost always be done on a computer?

*11. (a) What does a probability plot show? (b) If the hypothesized distribution is a good fit to the data, what would be the appearance of the probability plot? (c) What are the advantages and disadvantages of a probability plot?

*12. (a) Name two advantages of the Anderson-Darling test. (b) Why is it almost always done on a computer?

CHAPTER EXERCISES

Instructions: In all exercises, include MegaStat, Excel, or MINITAB exhibits to support your calculations. State the hypotheses, show how the degrees of freedom are calculated, find the critical value of chi-square from Appendix E or from Excel's function =CHIINV(alpha, deg_freedom), and interpret the p value. Tell whether the conclusion is sensitive to the level of significance chosen, identify cells that contribute the most to the chi-square test statistic, and check for small expected frequencies. If necessary, you can calculate the *p* value by using Excel's function =CHIDIST(test statistic,deg_free-dom). *Note:* Exercises marked * are harder or require optional material.

12.19 Employees of Axolotl Corporation were sampled at random from pay records and asked to complete an anonymous job satisfaction survey, yielding the tabulation shown. *Research question:* At $\alpha = 0.05$, is job satisfaction not independent of pay category? (LO 1 & 2) 🔘 **Employees**

Pay Type	Satisfied	Neutral	Dissatisfied	Total
Salaried	20	13	2	35
Hourly	135	127	58	320
Total	155	140	60	355

12.20 Sixty-four students in an introductory university economics class were asked how many credits they had earned in university, and how certain they were about their choice of major. *Research question:* At $\alpha = 0.01$, is the degree of certainty not independent of credits earned? (LO 1 & 2) 🔘 **Certainty**

Credits Earned	Very Uncertain	Somewhat Certain	Very Certain	Row Total
0–9	12	8	3	23
10–59	8	4	10	22
60 or more	1	7	11	19
Col Total	21	19	24	64

12.21 To see whether students who finish an exam first get the same grades as those who finish later, a professor kept track of the order in which papers were handed in. Of the first 25 papers, 10 received a grade of B or better compared with 8 of the last 24 papers handed in. *Research question:* At $\alpha = 0.10$, is the grade not independent of the order handed in? Because it is a 2×2 table, try also a two-tailed two-sample *z* test for $\pi_1 = \pi_2$ (see Chapter 10) and verify that z^2 is the same as your chi-square statistic. Which test do you prefer? Why? (LO 1 & 2) 🔘 **Grades**

Grade	Earlier Hand-In	Later Hand-In	Row Total
B or better	10	8	18
C or worse	15	16	31
Col Total	25	24	49

12.22 From 74 of its restaurants, Noodles & Company managers collected data on per-person sales and the percent of sales due to potstickers (a popular food item). Both numerical variables failed tests for normality, so they tried a chi-square test. Each variable was converted into ordinal categories (low, medium, high) using cutoff points that produced roughly equal group sizes. *Research question:* At $\alpha = 0.05$, is per-person spending not independent of percent of sales from potstickers? (LO 1 & 2) 🔘 **Noodles**

	Potsticker Percent of Sales			
Per Person Spending	Low	Medium	High	Row Total
Low	14	7	3	24
Medium	7	15	6	28
High	3	4	15	22
Col Total	24	26	24	74

12.23 A Web-based anonymous survey of students asked for a self-rating on proficiency in a language other than English and the student's frequency of newspaper reading. *Research question:* At $\alpha = 0.10$, is frequency of newspaper reading not independent of foreign language proficiency? (LO 1 & 2) 🔘 **WebSurvey**

Daily Newspaper Reading

Non-English Proficiency	Never	Occasionally	Regularly	Row Total
None	4	13	5	22
Slight	11	45	9	65
Moderate	6	33	7	46
Fluent	5	19	1	25
Col Total	26	110	22	158

12.24 A student team examined parked cars in four different suburban shopping malls. One hundred vehicles were examined in each location. *Research question:* At $\alpha = 0.05$, does vehicle type vary by mall location? (Data are from a project by MBA students Steve Bennett, Alicia Morais, Steve Olson, and Greg Corda.) (LO 1 & 2) **Vehicles**

Vehicle Type	Somerset	Oakland	Great Lakes	Jamestown	Row Total
Car	44	49	36	64	193
Minivan	21	15	18	13	67
Full-sized Van	2	3	3	2	10
SUV	19	27	26	12	84
Truck	14	6	17	9	46
Col Total	100	100	100	100	400

12.25 High levels of cockpit noise in an aircraft can damage the hearing of pilots who are exposed to this hazard for many hours. A Boeing 727 co-pilot collected 61 noise observations using a handheld sound meter. Noise level is defined as "Low" (under 88 decibels), "Medium" (88 to 91 decibels), or "High" (92 decibels or more). There are three flight phases (climb, cruise, descent). *Research question:* At $\alpha = 0.05$, is the cockpit noise level not independent of flight phase? (Data are from Capt. Robert E. Hartl, retired.) (LO 1 & 2) **Noise**

Noise Level	Climb	Cruise	Descent	Row Total
Low	6	2	6	14
Medium	18	3	8	29
High	1	3	14	18
Col Total	25	8	28	61

12.26 Forecasters' interest rate predictions over the period 1982 to 1990 were studied to see whether the predictions corresponded to what actually happened. The 2×2 contingency table below shows the frequencies of actual and predicted interest rate movements. *Research question:* At $\alpha = 0.10$, is the actual change not independent of the predicted change? (Data are from R. A. Kolb and H. O. Steckler, "How Well Do Analysts Forecast Interest Rates?" *Journal of Forecasting* 15, no. 15 [1996], pp. 385–394.) (LO 1 & 2) **Forecasts**

Forecasted Change	Rates Fell	Rates Rose	Row Total
Rates would fall	7	12	19
Rates would rise	9	6	15
Col Total	16	18	34

12.27 In a study of childhood asthma, 4,317 observations were collected on education and smoking during pregnancy, shown in the 4×3 contingency table below. *Research question:* At $\alpha = 0.005$, is smoking during pregnancy not independent of education level? (Data are from Michael

Weitzman and Deborah Klein Walker, "Maternal Smoking and Asthma," *Pediatrics* 85, no. 4 [Apr. 1990], p. 507.) (LO 1 & 2)   **Pregnancy**

Education	No Smoking	$< \frac{1}{2}$ pack	$\geq \frac{1}{2}$ pack	Row Total
< High School	641	196	196	1,033
High School	1,370	290	270	1,930
Some Postsecondary	635	68	53	756
Postsecondary	550	30	18	598
Col Total	3,196	584	537	4,317

12.28   Two contingency tables below show return on investment (ROI) and percent of sales growth over the previous five years for 85 U.S. firms. ROI is defined as percentage of return on a combination of stockholders' equity (both common and preferred) plus capital from long-term debt including current maturities, minority stockholders' equity in consolidated subsidiaries, and accumulated deferred taxes and investment tax credits. *Research question:* At $\alpha = 0.05$, is ROI not independent of sales growth? Would you expect it to be? Do the two tables (2 × 2 and 3 × 3) agree? Are small expected frequencies a problem? (Data are adapted from a research project by MBA student B. J. Oline.) (LO 1 & 2)   **ROI**

2 × 2 Cross-Tabulation of Companies

ROI	Low Growth	High Growth	Row Total
Low ROI	24	16	40
High ROI	14	31	45
Col Total	38	47	85

3 × 3 Cross-Tabulation of Companies

ROI	Low Growth	Medium Growth	High Growth	Row Total
Low ROI	9	12	7	28
Medium ROI	6	14	7	27
High ROI	1	12	17	30
Col Total	16	38	31	85

12.29   Can people really identify their favourite brand of cola? Volunteers tasted Coca-Cola Classic, Pepsi, Diet Coke, and Diet Pepsi, with the results shown below. *Research question:* At $\alpha = .05$, is the correctness of the prediction different for the two types of cola drinkers? Could *you* identify your favourite brand in this kind of test? Because it is a 2 × 2 table, also try a two-tailed two-sample z test for $\pi_1 = \pi_2$ (see Chapter 10) and verify that z^2 is the same as your chi-square statistic. Which test do you prefer? Why? (Data are from *Consumer Reports* 56, no. 8 [Aug. 1991], p. 519.) (LO 1 & 2)   **Cola**

Correct	Regular Cola	Diet Cola	Row Total
Yes, got it right	7	7	14
No, got it wrong	12	20	32
Col Total	19	27	46

12.30   A survey of randomly chosen new students at a certain university revealed the data below concerning the main reason for choosing this university instead of another. *Research question:* At $\alpha = 0.01$, is the main reason for choosing the university independent of student type? (LO 1 & 2)   **Students**

New Student	Tuition	Location	Reputation	Row Total
First-year Students	50	30	35	115
Transfers	15	29	20	64
MBAs	5	20	60	85
Col Total	70	79	115	264

12.31 A survey of 189 statistics students asked the age of car usually driven and the student's political orientation. The car age was a numerical variable, which was converted into ordinal categories. *Research question:* At $\alpha = 0.10$, are students' political views not independent of the age of car they usually drive? (LO 1 & 2) **Politics**

	Age of Car Usually Driven			
Politics	**Under 3**	**3–6**	**7 or More**	**Row Total**
Liberal	19	12	13	44
Middle-of-Road	33	31	28	92
Conservative	16	24	13	53
Col Total	68	67	54	189

12.32 Prof. Green's multiple-choice exam had 50 questions with the distribution of correct answers shown below. *Research question:* At $\alpha = 0.05$, can you reject the hypothesis that Green's exam answers came from a uniform population? (LO 1 & 4) **Correct**

Correct Answer	Frequency
A	8
B	8
C	9
D	11
E	14
Total	50

12.33 In a four-digit lottery, each of the four digits is supposed to have the same probability of occurrence. The table shows the frequency of occurrence of each digit for 89 consecutive daily four-digit drawings. *Research question:* At $\alpha = 0.01$, can you reject the hypothesis that the digits are from a uniform population? Why do the frequencies add to 356? (LO 1 & 4) **Lottery4**

Digit	Frequency
0	39
1	27
2	35
3	39
4	35
5	35
6	27
7	42
8	36
9	41
Total	356

12.34 A student rolled a supposedly fair die 60 times, resulting in the distribution of dots shown. *Research question:* At $\alpha = 0.10$, can you reject the hypothesis that the die is fair? (LO 1 & 4) **Dice**

	Number of Dots						
	1	*2*	*3*	*4*	*5*	*6*	*Total*
Frequency	7	14	9	13	7	10	60

12.35 Pick *one* Excel data set (A through D) and investigate whether the data could have come from a normal population using $\alpha = 0.01$. Use any test you wish, including a chi-square test in MegaStat, the various GOF tests offered by Visual Statistics (using the data editor to paste the data from Excel), or MINITAB's Stats > Basic Statistics > Normality Test to obtain a probability plot with the Anderson-Darling test. Interpret the *p* value from your tests. For larger data sets, only the first three and last three observations are shown. (LO 1 & 5)

DATA SET A   **Kentucky Derby Winning Time (Seconds), 1950–2006 ($n = 57$)**   **Derby**

Year	Derby Winner	Time
1950	Middleground	121.6
1951	Count Turf	122.6
1952	Hill Gail	121.6
⋮	⋮	⋮
2004	Smarty Jones	124.1
2005	Giacomo	122.8
2006	Barbaro	121.4

Source: *Information Please Sports Almanac* (ESPN Books, 1998), *Facts on File, Detroit Free Press, and The New York Times,* selected issues.

DATA SET B   **National League Runs Scored Leader, 1900–2004 ($n = 105$)**   **Runs**

Year	Player	Runs
1900	Roy Thomas, Phil	131
1901	Jesse Burkett, StL	139
1902	Honus Wagner, Pitt	105
⋮	⋮	⋮
2002	Sammy Sosa, Chi	122
2003	Albert Pujols, StL	137
2004	Albert Pujols, StL	133

Source: *Sports Illustrated 2003 Almanac,* pp. 100–113, www.baseball-almanac.com, and www.hickoksports.com.

DATA SET C   **Weight (in grams) of Pieces of Halloween Candy ($n = 78$)**   **Candy**

1.6931	1.8320	1.3167	0.5031	0.7097	1.4358
1.8851	1.6695	1.6101	1.6506	1.2105	1.4074
1.5836	1.1164	1.2953	1.4107	1.3212	1.6353
1.5435	1.7175	1.3489	1.1688	1.5543	1.3566
1.4844	1.4636	1.1701	1.5238	1.7346	1.1981
1.6601	1.8359	1.1334	1.7030	1.2481	1.4356
1.3756	1.3172	1.3700	1.0145	1.0062	0.9409
1.4942	1.2316	1.6505	1.7088	1.1850	1.3583
1.5188	1.3460	1.3928	1.6522	0.5303	1.6301
1.0474	1.4664	1.2902	1.9638	1.9687	1.2406
1.6759	1.6989	1.4959	1.4180	1.5218	2.1064
1.3213	1.1116	1.4535	1.4289	1.9156	1.8142
1.3676	1.7157	1.4493	1.4303	1.2912	1.7137

Source: Independent project by statistics student Frances Williams. Weighed on an American Scientific Model S/P 120 analytical balance accurate to 0.0001 gram.

DATA SET D		Weights of 31 Randomly Chosen Circulated Nickels ($n = 31$)					Nickels
5.043	4.980	4.967	5.043	4.956	4.999	4.917	4.927
4.893	5.003	4.951	5.040	5.043	5.004	5.014	5.035
4.883	5.022	4.932	4.998	5.032	4.948	5.001	4.983
4.912	4.796	4.970	4.956	5.036	5.045	4.801	

Note: Weighed by statistics student Dorothy Duffy as an independent project. Nickels were weighed on a Mettler PE 360 Delta Range scale, accurate to 0.001 gram.

LearningStats Unit 15 Chi-Square Tests

LS

LearningStats Unit 15 explains the chi-square test for independence in contingency tables and illustrates goodness-of-fit tests for uniform, Poisson, and normal distributions. Attention is also given to other tests for normality based on ECDF plots. Your instructor may assign a specific module, but you can work on the others if they sound interesting.

Topic	LearningStats Modules
Overview	Chi-Square Test for Independence
	Goodness-of-Fit Tests
Chi-square tests on contingency tables	Effects of Table Size
	Simulation and Type I Error
	Using Raw Data
Goodness-of-fit tests	Normal and Uniform Tests
	Uniform Tests: Choosing Letters
	Uniform Tests: World Series Runs
	ECDF Plots Illustrated
	Probability Plots: A Simulation
	CDF Normality Test
	Degrees of Freedom
	How Big a Sample
	Student GOF Project
Risk Projects	Table of Chi-Square Critical Values

Key: = PowerPoint; = Word; = Excel

Visual Statistics

Visual Statistics Goodness-of-Fit and Independence Tests

Module	Module Name
13	Visualizing Goodness-of-Fit Tests
14	Visualizing Bivariate Data Analysis

Visual Statistics Modules 13 and 14 (included on your CD) are designed to help you

- Know how to use and interpret a chi-square test for independence in cross-tabulated data.
- Recognize characteristics of data-generating situations that suggest appropriate distributions to fit.
- Interpret common data displays that may reveal whether a specified distribution is appropriate.
- Learn how the chi-square goodness-of-fit test works and how class formation affects it.
- Recognize limitations of the chi-square goodness-of-fit test and alternatives that are available.
- Use visual and analytical ECDF-based tests for goodness-of-fit and compare them with chi-square.

The work text (included on the CD in PDF format) contains a list of concepts covered, objectives of the module, overview of concepts, illustration of concepts, orientation to module features, learning exercises (basic, intermediate, advanced), learning projects (individual, team), self-evaluation quiz, glossary of terms, and solutions to self-evaluation quiz.

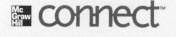

For solutions to odd-numbered exercises, Exam Review questions, and additional study tools to help you succeed in this course, visit *Connect* at www.mcgrawhillconnect.ca.

Chapter

13

Bivariate (Simple Linear) Regression

Chapter Learning Objectives

When you finish this chapter you should be able to

1. Calculate and test a correlation coefficient for significance.

2. Use the appropriate formulas to calculate and interpret the slope and intercept of a regression line and its R^2 in a problem context.

3. Fit a simple regression line on an Excel scatter plot.

4. Perform regression analysis using Excel and interpret its output in a problem context.

5. Test hypotheses about the slope by using the appropriate t test and interpret the findings in a problem context.

6. Interpret the ANOVA table and use and interpret its F test in a problem context.

7. Distinguish between confidence and prediction intervals and perform and interpret the appropriate calculations in a problem context.

8. Recognize the implications of violating the assumptions of regression analysis.

13.1 Visual Displays and Correlation Analysis

Chapter 13

In Chapter 11, we used ANOVA to test for a relationship between a quantitative research variable and a qualitative predictor variable (e.g., the relationship between the price of a house and where that house is located). In Chapter 12, we used the chi-square test for independence to test for the relationship between two qualitative variables (e.g., the relationship between preferences for different types of televisions and where one lives). To complete our study of the relationship between two variables, this chapter will explore the relationship between two quantitative variables where it is assumed that, if any relationship does exist, it is an imperfect linear relationship. (If the relationship is perfect, such as the relationship between degrees in Fahrenheit and degrees in Celsius, there would no need for what will be covered in this chapter.)

Examples of quantitative variables that might be related to each other include: spending on advertising and sales revenue, produce delivery time and percentage of spoiled produce, premium and regular gasoline prices, preventive maintenance spending, and manufacturing productivity rates. It may be that with some of these pairs there is one variable that we would like to be able to *predict* based on the values of the other variable (e.g., we would like to predict sales revenue based on the amount spent on advertising). But first we must learn how to *visualize, describe,* and *quantify* the relationships between variables such as these.

Visual Displays

Analysis of **bivariate data** (i.e., two variables) typically begins with a **scatter plot** that displays each observed data pair (x_i, y_i) as a dot on an $X-Y$ grid. This diagram provides a visual indication of the strength of the relationship or association between the two random variables. This simple display requires no assumptions or computation. A scatter plot is typically the precursor to more complex analytical techniques. Figure 13.1 shows a scatter plot comparing the price per gallon of regular unleaded gasoline to the price per gallon of premium gasoline.

We look at scatter plots to get an initial idea of the relationship between two random variables. Is there an evident pattern to the data? Is the pattern linear or non-linear? Are there data points that are not part of the overall pattern? We would characterize the fuel price relationship as linear (although not perfectly linear) and positive (as premium prices increase, so do regular unleaded prices). We see one pair of values set slightly apart from the rest, above and to the right. This happens to be the state of Hawaii.

Correlation Coefficient

A visual display is a good first step in analysis but we would also like to quantify the strength of the association between two variables. Therefore, accompanying the scatter plot is the **sample correlation coefficient** (also called the Pearson correlation coefficient). This statistic measures the degree of linearity in the relationship between X and Y and is denoted r. Its range is $-1 \le r \le +1$. When r is near 0, there is little or no linear relationship between X and Y in the sample. An r value near $+1$ indicates a strong positive relationship, while an r value near -1 indicates a strong negative relationship in the sample.

$$r = \frac{\sum_{i=1}^{n}(x_i - \bar{x})(y_i - \bar{y})}{\sqrt{\sum_{i=1}^{n}(x_i - \bar{x})^2}\sqrt{\sum_{i=1}^{n}(y_i - \bar{y})^2}} \quad \text{(sample correlation coefficient)} \quad \textbf{(13.1)}$$

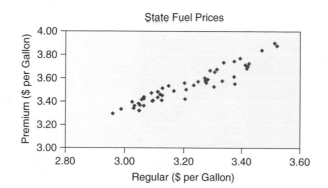

FIGURE 13.1

Fuel Prices
FuelPrices

Source: AAA Fuel Gauge Report, May 27, 2007, www.fuelgaugereport.com

To simplify the notation here and elsewhere in this chapter, we define three terms called **sums of squares:**

$$SS_{xx} = \sum_{i=1}^{n}(x_i - \bar{x})^2 \qquad SS_{yy} = \sum_{i=1}^{n}(y_i - \bar{y})^2 \qquad SS_{xy} = \sum_{i=1}^{n}(x_i - \bar{x})(y_i - \bar{y}) \quad (13.2)$$

Using this notation, the formula for the sample correlation coefficient can be written

$$r = \frac{SS_{xy}}{\sqrt{SS_{xx}}\sqrt{SS_{yy}}} \qquad (13.3)$$

Excel Tip

To calculate a sample correlation coefficient, use Excel's function =CORREL(array1, array2), where array1 is the range for X and array2 is the range for Y. Data may be in rows or columns. Arrays must be the same length.

The correlation coefficient for the variables shown in Figure 13.1 is $r = 0.947$, which is not surprising. We would expect to see a strong positive linear relationship between regular unleaded gasoline prices and premium gasoline prices. Figure 13.2 shows prototype scatter plots. We see that a correlation of 0.500 implies a great deal of random variation, and even a correlation of 0.900 is far from "perfect" linearity. The last scatter plot shows $r = 0.00$ despite an obvious *curvilinear* (non-linear) relationship between X and Y. This illustrates the fact that a correlation coefficient only measures the degree of *linear* relationship between X and Y.

Correlation analysis has many business applications. For example

- Financial planners study correlations between different asset classes over time in order to help their clients diversify their portfolios.

- Marketing analysts study correlations between customers' different online purchases in order to develop new Web advertising strategies.

- Human resources experts study correlations between different measures of employee performance in order to devise new job-training programs.

FIGURE 13.2

Scatter Plots Showing Various Correlation Coefficient Values

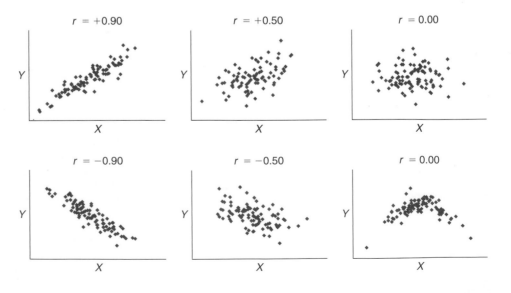

Tests for Significance

The sample correlation coefficient r is an estimate of the **population correlation coefficient,** or ρ (the Greek letter *rho*). There is no flat rule for a "high" correlation because sample size must be taken into consideration. There are two ways to test a correlation coefficient for significance. To test the hypothesis $H_0: \rho = 0$ (no linear relationship), the test statistic is

$$t_{calc} = r\sqrt{\frac{n-2}{1-r^2}} \quad \text{(test for zero correlation)} \tag{13.4}$$

if we assume that the distribution of (X, Y) has a bivariate normal distribution (i.e., a three-dimensional bell-shaped distribution). If it does have a bivariate normal distribution, we can compare this t test statistic with a critical value of t for a one-tailed or two-tailed test from Appendix D using $\nu = n - 2$ degrees of freedom and any desired α. After calculating the *t* **statistic,** we can find its *p* value by using Excel's function =TDIST(t,deg_freedom,tails). MINITAB directly calculates the *p* value for a two-tailed test without displaying the *t* statistic.

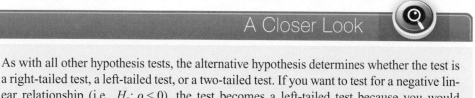

A Closer Look

As with all other hypothesis tests, the alternative hypothesis determines whether the test is a right-tailed test, a left-tailed test, or a two-tailed test. If you want to test for a negative linear relationship (i.e., $H_1: \rho < 0$), the test becomes a left-tailed test because you would expect r, and thus t, to be negative if H_1 was true. The decision rule in this case would be to reject H_0 if $t_{calc} < -t_{\alpha,n-2}$. If you simply want to test for a linear relationship (i.e., $H_1: \rho \neq 0$), the test becomes a two-tailed test because you would expect r, and thus t, to be either somewhat less or somewhat greater than zero if H_1 were true. Here, the decision rule would be to reject H_0 if $t_{calc} < -t_{\alpha/2,n-2}$ or if $t_{calc} > t_{\alpha/2,n-2}$. And if you want to test for a positive linear relationship (i.e., $H_1: \rho > 0$), the test becomes a right-tailed test because you would expect r, and thus t, to be positive if H_1 were true. Now, the decision rule would be to reject H_1 if $t_{calc} > t_{\alpha,n-2}$. The test you decide to use is based on what belief you are trying to support with evidence and what decision you would make based on this evidence. For example, if a restaurant owner could determine that there was sufficient evidence of a positive linear relationship between the amount a customer drinks and the amount of money he or she spends on food, the owner may decide to lower the price of drinks, which would be more than recovered through the sale of more food. Simply determining that there was a linear relationship would not allow the owner to make such a decision.

Concept Check

For each of the following, would you believe the relationship between the two stated variables to be non-existent, a negative relationship, a positive relationship, or a relationship that may be positive or negative? Explain.

(a) Temperature in Calgary and temperature in Edmonton

(b) Temperature in Halifax and temperature in Beijing

(c) Interest rates on car loans and number of cars sold

(d) Number of Hondas sold and number of Toyotas sold

(e) Number of winter coats sold and number of winter hats sold

FIGURE 13.3   Scatter Plots for 30 MBA Applicants   MBA

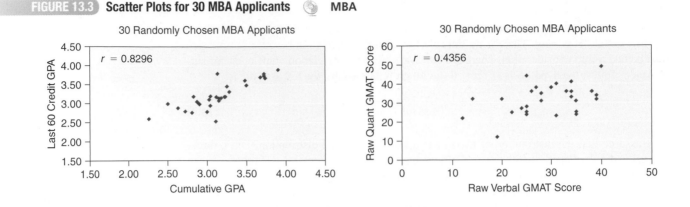

In its admission decision process, a university's MBA program examines an applicant's cumulative undergraduate GPA, as well as the applicant's GPA in the last 60 credits taken. They also examine scores on the GMAT (Graduate Management Aptitude Test), which has both verbal and quantitative components. Figure 13.3 shows two scatter plots with sample correlation coefficients for 30 MBA applicants randomly chosen from 1,961 MBA applicant records at a public university in the U.S. Midwest. Is the correlation ($r = 0.8296$) between cumulative and last 60 credit GPA statistically significant? Is the correlation ($r = 0.4356$) between verbal and quantitative GMAT scores statistically significant?

STEP 1: STATE THE HYPOTHESES

We will use a two-tailed test for significance at $\alpha = 0.05$. The hypotheses are

$$H_0: \rho = 0$$
$$H_1: \rho \neq 0$$

STEP 2: SPECIFY THE DECISION RULE

For a two-tailed test using $\nu = n - 2 = 30 - 2 = 28$ degrees of freedom, Appendix D gives $t_{0.025,28} = 2.048$. The decision rule is

Reject H_0 if $t_{calc} > 2.048$ or if $t_{calc} < -2.048$.

This rule is the same for testing the correlation between either pair of variables since the number of paired observations is the same.

STEP 3: CALCULATE THE TEST STATISTIC

To calculate the test statistic we first need to find the values for r. Using Excel's function =CORREL(array1, array2) we find $r = 0.8296$ for the variables *Cumulative GPA* and *Last 60 Credit GPA*. We find $r = 0.4356$ for the variables *Quant GMAT* and *Verbal GMAT*. We must then calculate two values of t_{calc}. For GPA,

$$t_{calc} = r\sqrt{\frac{n-2}{1-r^2}} = 0.8296\sqrt{\frac{30-2}{1-(0.8296)^2}} = 7.862$$

and for GMAT score,

$$t_{calc} = r\sqrt{\frac{n-2}{1-r^2}} = 0.4356\sqrt{\frac{30-2}{1-(0.4356)^2}} = 2.561$$

STEP 4: MAKE A DECISION

Both test statistic values ($t_{calc} = 7.862$ and $t_{calc} = 2.561$) exceed the critical value $t_{0.025,28} = 2.048$, so we reject the hypothesis of zero correlation at $\alpha = 0.05$ in both cases. Notice that t_{calc} is much greater for the GPA variables, leading to a stronger rejection of zero correlation than in the case of the GMAT score variables.

We can also find the p value for each test using the Excel function =TDIST(t,deg_freedom,tails). For example, for the two-tailed p value for GPA, =TDIST(7.862,28,2) gives 0.0000, and for the two-tailed p value for GMAT score, =TDIST(2.561,28,2) gives 0.0161. We would reject $\rho = 0$ in both cases as $p < 0.05$.

A Closer Look

In this particular example, you could argue that the test for the correlation between the two GPAs should be a right-tailed test because, if there was a relationship, you would expect it to be a positive one. You could not argue the same when looking at the relationship between Verbal and Quant GMAT.

Concept Check

Using the data in Example 1, at the 0.05 level of significance is there sufficient evidence of a positive relationship between a student's GPA and his or her GPA in the last 60 credits taken?

Section Exercises

Instructions for Exercises 13.1 and 13.2: (a) Using common sense, determine whether you would expect a negative relationship, a positive relationship, or simply a relationship. (b) Make an Excel scatter plot. Does this plot support your common sense conclusion? (c) Make an Excel worksheet to calculate SS_{xx}, SS_{yy}, and SS_{xy}. Use these sums to calculate the sample correlation coefficient. Check your work by using Excel's function =CORREL(array1,array2). (d) At $\alpha = 0.05$, is there sufficient evidence to support your expectations concerning the relationship between X and Y? (e) Use Excel's function =TDIST(t,deg_freedom,tails) to calculate the appropriate p value. (LO 1)

13.1 Part-Time Weekly Earnings ($) by University Students  **WeekPay**

Hours Worked (X)	Weekly Pay (Y)
10	93
15	171
20	204
20	156
35	261

13.2 Telephone Hold Time (min.) for Concert Tickets  **CallWait**

Operators (X)	Wait Time (Y)
4	385
5	335
6	383
7	344
8	288

Instructions for Exercises 13.3–13.5: (a) Make a scatter plot of the data. What does it suggest about the correlation between X and Y? (b) Use Excel, MegaStat, or MINITAB to calculate the correlation coefficient. (c) Use Excel or Appendix D to find $t_{0.025}$ for a two-tailed test at $\alpha = 0.05$. (d) Calculate the t test statistic. (e) Can you reject $\rho = 0$? (LO 1)

13.3 Moviegoer Spending ($) on Snacks **Movies**

Age (X)	Spent (Y)
30	2.85
50	6.50
34	1.50
12	6.35
37	6.20
33	6.75
36	3.60
26	6.10
18	8.35
46	4.35

13.4 Portfolio Returns on Selected Mutual Funds **Portfolio**

Last Year (X)	This Year (Y)
11.9	15.4
19.5	26.7
11.2	18.2
14.1	16.7
14.2	13.2
5.2	16.4
20.7	21.1
11.3	12.0
−1.1	12.1
3.9	7.4
12.9	11.5
12.4	23.0
12.5	12.7
2.7	15.1
8.8	18.7
7.2	9.9
5.9	18.9

13.5 Number of Orders and Shipping Cost ($) **ShipCost**

Orders (X)	Shipping Cost (Y)
1,068	4,489
1,026	5,611
767	3,290
885	4,113
1,156	4,883
1,146	5,425
892	4,414
938	5,506
769	3,346
677	3,673
1,174	6,542
1,009	5,088

13.6   (a) Use Excel, MegaStat, or MINITAB to calculate a matrix of correlation coefficients. (b) Calculate the critical value of r_α. (c) Highlight the correlation coefficients that led you to reject $\rho = 0$ in a two-tailed test. (d) What conclusions can you draw about rates of return? (LO 1)  **Construction**

Average Annual Returns for 12 Home Construction Companies

Company Name	1-Year	3-Year	5-Year	10-Year
Beazer Homes USA	50.3	26.1	50.1	28.9
Centex	23.4	33.3	40.8	28.6
D.R. Horton	41.4	42.4	52.9	35.8
Hovnanian Ent	13.8	67.0	73.1	33.8
KB Home	46.1	38.8	35.3	24.9
Lennar	19.4	39.3	50.9	36.0
M.D.C. Holdings	48.7	41.6	53.2	39.7
NVR	65.1	55.7	74.4	63.9
Pulte Homes	36.8	42.4	42.1	27.9
Ryland Group	30.5	46.9	59.0	33.3
Standard Pacific	33.0	39.5	44.2	27.8
Toll Brothers	72.6	46.2	49.1	29.9

Source: *The Wall Street Journal,* Feb. 28, 2005. *Note:* Data are intended for educational purposes only.

Mini Case   13.1

Do Loyalty Cards Promote Sales Growth?   Noodles & Company   noodles & company

A business can achieve sales growth by increasing the number of new customers. Another way is by increasing business from existing customers. Loyal customers visit more often, thus contributing to sales growth. Loyalty cards are used by many companies to foster positive relationships with their customers. Customers carry a card that records the number of purchases or visits they make. They are rewarded with a free item or discount after so many visits. But do these loyalty cards provide incentive to repeat customers to visit more often? Surprisingly, Noodles & Company found out that this wasn't happening in some markets. After several years of running a loyalty card program without truly measuring their impact on the business, in 2005, Noodles performed a correlation analysis on the variables "Sales Growth Percentage" and "Loyalty Card Sales Percentage." The results showed that in some markets there was no significant correlation, meaning the loyalty cards weren't associated with increased sales revenue. However, in other markets there was actually *a statistically significant negative correlation.* In other words, loyalty cards were associated with a decrease in sales growth. Why? Ultimately, the free visits that customers had earned were replacing visits that they would have otherwise paid full price for. Moreover, the resources the company was devoting to the program were taking away from more proven sales-building techniques, such as holding non-profit fundraisers or tastings for local businesses. Based on this analysis, Noodles & Company made the decision to discontinue its loyalty card program and focused on other approaches to building loyal customers.

13.2   Bivariate (Simple Linear) Regression

What Is Bivariate Regression?

Correlation coefficients and scatter plots provide clues about relationships among variables and may suffice for some purposes. But often, the analyst would like to model the relationship for prediction purposes. For example, a business might hypothesize that

- Advertising expenditures predict quarterly sales revenue.
- Number of dependants predicts employee prescription drug expenses.

- Apartment size predicts monthly rent.
- Number of diners predicts business lunch expense.
- Assembly line speed predicts number of product defects.

A **bivariate regression** model specifies one *dependent* variable (sometimes called the *response*) and one *independent* variable (sometimes called the *predictor*). Understanding how the independent variable is related to the dependent variable would allow business to explore policy questions such as the following:

- How much extra sales will be generated, on average, by a $1 million increase in advertising expenditures? What would expected sales be with no advertising?
- How much do prescription drug costs per employee rise, on average, with each extra dependant? What would be the expected cost if the employee had no dependants?
- How much extra rent, on average, is paid per extra square foot?
- How much extra luncheon cost, on average, is generated by each additional member of the group? How much could be saved by restricting luncheon groups to three persons?
- If the assembly line speed is increased by 20 units per hour, what would happen to the mean number of product defects?

Only the dependent variable (not the independent variable) is treated as a random variable.

Concept Check

For each of the following pairs of variables, which variable is the dependent or response variable and which is the independent or predictor variable? Explain your answer.

(a) Number of hours studied and exam mark
(b) Exam mark and probability of getting a scholarship
(c) Gasoline used and kilometres travelled
(d) If driving, price of gasoline per litre and distance to vacation destination
(e) The number of 6/49 tickets sold and projected value of grand prize

Model Form

The hypothesized bivariate relationship may be linear, quadratic, or whatever you want. The examples in Figure 13.4 illustrate situations in which it might be necessary to consider non-linear model forms. For now we will mainly focus on the simple linear (straight-line) model. The bivariate linear model is often just referred to as a *simple linear regression* model. We will examine non-linear relationships later in the chapter.

FIGURE 13.4 **Possible Model Forms**

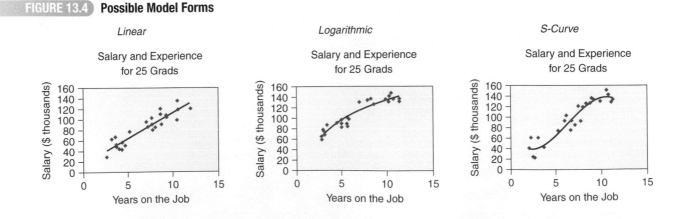

Interpreting a Fitted Regression

The intercept and slope of a **fitted regression** can provide useful information. For example:

Sales = 268 + 7.37 (*Ads*)	Each extra $1 million of advertising will generate $7.37 million of sales on average. The firm would average $268 million of sales with zero advertising. However, the intercept may not be meaningful because *Ads* = 0 may be outside the range of observed data.
DrugCost = 410 + 550 (*Dependants*)	Each extra dependant raises the mean annual prescription drug cost by $550. An employee with zero dependants averages $410 in prescription drugs.
Rent = 150 + 1.05 (*SqFt*)	Each extra square foot adds $1.05 to monthly apartment rent. The intercept is not meaningful because no apartment can have *SqFt* = 0.
Cost = 15.22 + 19.96 (*Persons*)	Each additional diner increases the mean lunch cost by $19.96. The intercept is not meaningful because *Persons* = 0 would not be observable.
Defects = 3.2 + 0.045 (*Speed*)	Each unit increase in assembly line speed adds an average of 0.045 defects per million. The intercept is not meaningful because zero assembly line speed implies no production at all.

When we propose a regression model, we have a causal mechanism in mind, but cause-and-effect is not proven by a simple regression. We should not read too much into a fitted equation.

Prediction Using Regression

One of the main uses of regression is to make predictions. Once we have a fitted regression equation that shows the estimated relationship between X (the independent variable) and Y (the dependent variable), we can plug in any value of X to obtain the prediction for Y. For example:

Sales = 268 + 7.37 (*Ads*)	If the firm spends $10 million on advertising, its expected sales are $341.7 million, that is, *Sales* = 268 + 7.37(10) = 341.7.
DrugCost = 410 + 550 (*Dependants*)	If an employee has four dependants, the expected annual drug cost is $2,610, that is, *DrugCost* = 410 + 550(4) = 2,610.
Rent = 150 + 1.05 (*SqFt*)	The expected rent on an 800-square-foot apartment is $990, that is, *Rent* = 150 + 1.05(800) = 990.
Cost = 15.22 + 19.96 (*Persons*)	The expected cost of lunch for two couples is $95.06, that is, *Cost* = 15.22 + 19.96(4) = 95.06.
Defects = 3.2 + 0.045 (*Speed*)	If 100 units per hour are produced, the expected defect rate is 7.7 defects per million, that is, *Defects* = 3.2 + 0.045(100) = 7.7.

Section Exercises

13.7 (a) Interpret the slope of the fitted regression *Sales* = 842 − 37.5 (*Price*). (b) If *Price* = 20, what is the prediction for *Sales*? (c) Would the intercept be meaningful if this regression represents DVD sales at Blockbuster? (LO 2)

13.8 (a) Interpret the slope of the fitted regression *HomePrice* = 125,000 + 150 (*SquareFeet*). (b) What is the prediction for *HomePrice* if *SquareFeet* = 2,000? (c) Would the intercept be meaningful if this regression applies to home sales in a certain subdivision? (LO 2)

13.3   Regression Terminology

Models and Parameters

The model's *unknown parameters* are denoted by Greek letters β_0 (the **intercept**) and β_1 (the **slope**). The *assumed model* for a linear relationship is

$$Y = \beta_0 + \beta_1 X + \varepsilon \qquad \text{(assumed linear relationship)} \qquad \textbf{(13.5)}$$

This relationship is assumed to hold for all observations ($i = 1, 2, \ldots, n$). Inclusion of a random error ε is necessary because other unspecified variables may also affect Y and also because there may be measurement error in Y. The error is not observable.

We assume that the error term ε is a normally distributed random variable with mean 0 and standard deviation σ. Thus, the regression model actually has three unknown parameters: β_0, β_1, and σ.

Before we describe how we estimate these unknown parameters, let us understand the model assumptions by a hypothetical model whose parameters are known:

$$Y = 9.5 + 2.1X + \varepsilon, \; \varepsilon \sim N(0, 3)$$

That is, $\beta_0 = 9.5$, $\beta_1 = 2.1$, and $\sigma = 3$. The figure below illustrates this population regression model:

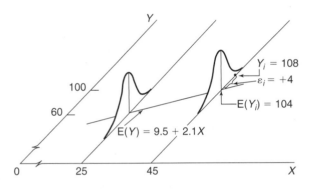

For example, if $X = 25$, then the model becomes $Y = 9.5 + 2.1(25) + \varepsilon = 62 + \varepsilon$. Now, using the law of addition of expectations, $E(Y) = 62 + E(\varepsilon) = 62$. Because the variance of a random variable is not affected by adding a constant, $V(Y) = V(62 + \varepsilon) = V(\varepsilon) = \sigma^2$. Thus, Y follows a normal distribution with mean of 62 and standard deviation of 3. Similarly, if $X = 45$, then the model becomes $Y = 9.5 + 2.1(45) + \varepsilon = 104 + \varepsilon$, and Y now follows a normal distribution with mean of 104 but the same standard deviation of 3. Thus, though $E(Y)$ changes as X changes, the variability of the y value around its mean remains the same.

Because $E(\varepsilon) = 0$, an equivalent way of writing our regression model is

$$E(Y) = \beta_0 + \beta_1 X$$

To estimate the unknown parameters β_0, β_1, and σ, we take a random sample from this population. From the sample, we estimate the **fitted model** and use it to predict the *expected* value of Y for a given value of X:

$$\hat{y} = b_0 + b_1 x \qquad \text{(fitted linear regression model)} \qquad \textbf{(13.6)}$$

Roman letters denote the *fitted coefficients* b_0 (the estimated intercept) and b_1 (the estimated slope). For a given value x, the *fitted* value (or estimated value) of the dependent variable is $\hat{y}$. (You can read this as "y-hat.") The difference between the observed value y_i and the fitted value $\hat{y}$ is the **residual** and is denoted e_i. A residual will always be calculated as the observed value minus the estimated value.

$$e_i = y_i - \hat{y}_i \qquad \text{(residual)} \qquad \textbf{(13.7)}$$

As we will see later, these residuals will be used to estimate σ, the unknown standard deviation of the random error ε that appears in Equation 13.5.

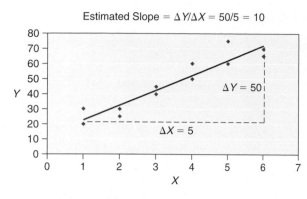

Estimated Slope $= \Delta Y/\Delta X = 50/5 = 10$

FIGURE 13.5

"Eyeball" Regression Line Fitting

Estimating a Regression Line by Eye

From a scatter plot, you can visually estimate the slope and intercept, as illustrated in Figure 13.5. In this graph, the approximate slope is 10 and the approximate intercept (when $X = 0$) is around 15 (i.e., $\hat{y}_i = 15 + 10x_i$). This method, of course, is inexact. However, experiments suggest that people are pretty good at "eyeball" line fitting. You intuitively try to adjust the line so as to ensure that the residuals sum to zero (i.e., the positive residuals offset the negative residuals) and to ensure that no other values for the slope or intercept would give a better "fit."

Fitting a Regression on a Scatter Plot in Excel

A more precise method is to let Excel do the estimates. We enter observations on the independent variable $x_1, x_2, \ldots, x_n$ and the dependent variable $y_1, y_2, \ldots, y_n$ into separate columns, and let Excel fit the regression equation.* The easiest way to find the equation of the regression line is to have Excel add the line onto a scatter plot, using the following steps:

- Step 1: Highlight the data columns.
- Step 2: Click on **Insert** and choose **Scatter** to create a graph.
- Step 3: Click on the scatter plot points to select the data.
- Step 4: Right-click and choose **Add Trendline**.
- Step 5: Choose **Options** and check **Display equation on chart**.

The menus are shown in Figure 13.6. (The R-squared statistic is actually the correlation coefficient squared. It tells us what proportion of the variation in Y is explained by X. We will more fully define R^2 in Section 13.4.) Excel will choose the regression coefficients so as to produce a good fit. In this case, Excel's fitted regression $\hat{y}_i = 13 + 9.857x_i$ is close to our "eyeball" regression equation.

Note: When creating a scatter plot, a standard practice is to plot the dependent variable along the vertical axis and the independent variable along the horizontal axis.

Excel's Trendline Menus FIGURE 13.6

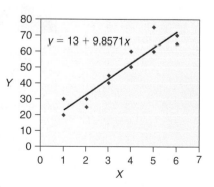

*Excel calls its regression equation a "trendline," although actually that would refer to a time-series trend.

TABLE 13.1   Piper Cheyenne Fuel Usage

Flight Hours	Fuel Used (lbs.)
2.3	145
4.2	258
3.6	219
4.7	276
4.9	283

Source: *Flying* 130, no. 4 (Apr. 2003), p. 99.

Fitted Regression

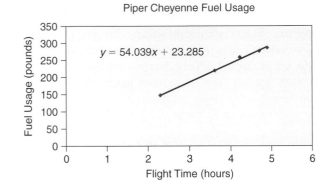

Illustration: Piper Cheyenne Fuel Consumption

Table 13.1 shows a sample of fuel consumption and flight hours for five legs of a cross-country test flight in a Piper Cheyenne, a twin-engine piston business aircraft. Figure 13.7 displays the Excel graph and its fitted regression equation.   **Cheyenne**

Slope Interpretation   The fitted regression is $\hat{y} = 23.285 + 54.039x$. The slope ($b_1 = 54.039$) says that for each additional hour of flight, the Piper Cheyenne consumed about 54 pounds of fuel (1 gallon $\approx$ 6 pounds). This estimated slope is a *statistic,* as a different sample might yield a different estimate of the slope. Bear in mind also that the sample size is very small.

Intercept Interpretation   The intercept ($b_0 = 23.285$) suggests that even if the plane is not flying ($X = 0$) some fuel would be consumed. However, the intercept has little meaning in this case, not only because zero flight hours makes no logical sense, but also because extrapolating to $X = 0$ is beyond the range of the observed data.

Regression Caveats

- The "fit" of the regression does *not* depend on the sign of its slope. The sign of the fitted slope merely tells whether X has a positive or negative association with Y.
- View the intercept with skepticism unless $X = 0$ is logically possible and was actually observed in the data set.
- Regression does not demonstrate cause-and-effect between X and Y. A good fit only shows that X and Y vary together. Both could be affected by another variable or by the way the data are defined.

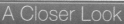

A Closer Look

We use simple linear regression when we believe that there is a linear relationship between the dependent variable, *Y*, and the independent variable, *X*. We draw a scatter plot to check whether this belief is reasonable. This scatter plot can only support our belief over the range of the values of *X* in our sample. Outside of this range, we don't know what type of relationship exists or whether the relationship is still linear but with a different slope. Because we don't know anything about the relationship outside of the range of the values of *X* in our sample, any inferences we make should only apply for values of *X* within this range. To do otherwise may be very risky.

Section Exercises

13.9   The regression equation *NetIncome* = 2,277 + 0.0307 (*Revenue*) was fitted from a sample of 100 leading world companies (variables are in millions of dollars). (a) Interpret the slope. (b) Is the intercept meaningful? Explain. (c) Make a prediction of *NetIncome* when *Revenue* = 1,000. (Data are from www.forbes.com and *Forbes* 172, no. 2 [July 21, 2003], pp. 108–110.) (LO 2)   **Global 100**

13.10   The regression equation *HomePrice* = 51.3 + 2.61 (*Income*) was fitted from a sample of 34 cities in the eastern United States. Both variables are in thousands of dollars. *HomePrice* is the median selling price of homes in the city, and *Income* is median family income for the city. (a) Interpret the slope. (b) Is the intercept meaningful? Explain. (c) Make a prediction of *HomePrice* when *Income* = 50 and also when *Income* = 100. (Data are from *Money Magazine* 32, no. 1 [Jan. 2004], pp. 102–103.) (LO 2)   **HomePrice1**

13.11   The regression equation *Credits* = 15.4 − 0.07 (*Work*) was fitted from a sample of 21 statistics students. *Credits* is the number of university credits taken and *Work* is the number of hours worked per week at an outside job. (a) Interpret the slope. (b) Is the intercept meaningful? Explain. (c) Make a prediction of *Credits* when *Work* = 0 and when *Work* = 40. What do these predictions tell you? (LO 2)   **Credits**

13.12   Below are fitted regressions for *Y* = asking price of a used vehicle and *X* = the age of the vehicle. The observed range of *X* was 1 to 8 years. The sample consisted of all vehicles listed for sale in a particular week in 2005. (a) Interpret the slope of each fitted regression. (b) Interpret the intercept of each fitted regression. Does the intercept have meaning? (c) Predict the price of a 5-year-old Chevy Blazer. (d) Predict the price of a 5-year-old Chevy Silverado. (Data are from *AutoFocus* 4, Issue 38 [(Sept. 17–23, 2004] and are for educational purposes only.) (LO 2)   **CarPrices**

Chevy Blazer: *Y* = 16,189 − 1,050*X* (*n* = 21 vehicles, observed *X* range was 1 to 8 years).
Chevy Silverado: *Y* = 22,951 − 1,339*X* (*n* = 24 vehicles, observed *X* range was 1 to 10 years).

13.13   These data are for a sample of 10 university students who work at weekend jobs in restaurants. (a) Fit an "eyeball" regression equation to this scatter plot of *Y* = tips earned last weekend and *X* = hours worked. (b) Interpret the slope. (c) Interpret the intercept. Would the intercept have meaning in this example? (LO 2)

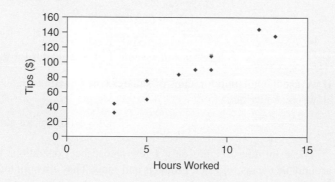

13.14 These data are for a sample of 10 different vendors in a large airport. (a) Fit an "eyeball" regression equation to this scatter plot of Y = bottles of Evian water sold and X = price of the water. (b) Interpret the slope. (c) Interpret the intercept. Would the intercept have meaning in this example? (LO 2)

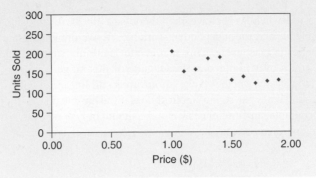

13.4 Ordinary Least Squares Formulas

Slope and Intercept

The **ordinary least squares** method (or **OLS** method for short) is used to estimate a regression so as to ensure the best fit if the errors have constant variance. (The assumptions that are assumed throughout simple linear regression will be discussed toward the end of this chapter.) "Best" fit in this case means that we have selected the slope and intercept so that sum of squares of our residuals is as small as possible. However, it is a characteristic of the OLS estimation method that the residuals around the regression line always sum to zero. That is, the positive residuals exactly cancel the negative ones:

$$\sum_{i=1}^{n} (y_i - \hat{y}_i) = 0 \qquad \text{(OLS residuals always sum to zero)} \qquad \textbf{(13.8)}$$

Therefore, to work with an equation that has a non-zero sum, we square the residuals, just as we squared the deviations from the mean when we developed the equation for variance back in Chapter 4. The fitted coefficients b_0 and b_1 are chosen so that the fitted linear model $\hat{y}_i = b_0 + b_1 x_i$ has the smallest possible sum of squared residuals (*SSE*):

$$SSE = \sum_{i=1}^{n} (y_i - \hat{y}_i)^2 = \sum_{i=1}^{n} (y_i - b_0 - b_1 x_i)^2 \qquad \text{(sum to be minimized)} \qquad \textbf{(13.9)}$$

This is an optimization problem that can be solved for b_0 and b_1 by using Excel's Solver Add-In. However, we can also use calculus (see derivation in *LearningStats* Unit 12) to solve for b_0 and b_1:

$$b_1 = \frac{\sum_{i=1}^{n} (x_i - \bar{x})(y_i - \bar{y})}{\sum_{i=1}^{n} (x_i - \bar{x})^2} \qquad \text{(OLS estimator for slope)} \qquad \textbf{(13.10)}$$

$$b_0 = \bar{y} - b_1 \bar{x} \qquad \text{(OLS estimator for intercept)} \qquad \textbf{(13.11)}$$

If we use the notation for sums of squares (see Equation 13.2), then the OLS formula for the slope can be written

$$b_1 = \frac{SS_{xy}}{SS_{xx}} \qquad \text{(OLS estimator for slope)} \qquad \textbf{(13.12)}$$

These formulas require only a few spreadsheet operations to find the means, deviations around the means, and their products and sums. They are built into Excel and many calculators. The OLS formulas give unbiased estimates of β_0 and β_1. That is, $E(b_0) = \beta_0$, $E(b_1) = \beta_1$.

The OLS regression line always passes through the point $(\bar{x}, \bar{y})$ for any data, as illustrated in Figure 13.8.

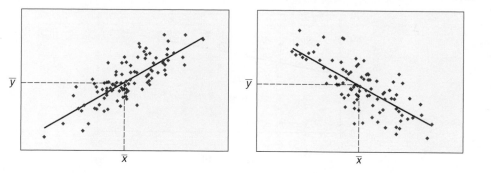

FIGURE 13.8

OLS Regression Line Always Passes through $\bar{x}, \bar{y}$

TABLE 13.2 Study Time and Exam Scores ExamScores

Student	Study Hours	Exam Score
Tom	1	53
Mary	5	74
Sarah	7	59
Oscar	8	43
Cullyn	10	56
Jaime	11	84
Theresa	14	96
Knut	15	69
Jin-Mae	15	84
Courtney	19	83
Sum	105	701
Mean	$\bar{x} = 10.5$	$\bar{y} = 70.1$

Illustration: Exam Scores and Study Time

Table 13.2 shows study time and exam scores for 10 students. The worksheet in Table 13.3 shows the calculations of the sums needed for the slope and intercept. Figure 13.9 shows a fitted regression line. The vertical line segments in the scatter plot show the differences

TABLE 13.3 Worksheet for Slope and Intercept Calculations ExamScores

Student	x_i	y_i	$x_i - \bar{x}$	$y_i - \bar{y}$	$(x_i - \bar{x})(y_i - \bar{y})$	$(x_i - \bar{x})^2$
Tom	1	53	−9.5	−17.1	162.45	90.25
Mary	5	74	−5.5	3.9	−21.45	30.25
Sarah	7	59	−3.5	−11.1	38.85	12.25
Oscar	8	43	−2.5	−27.1	67.75	6.25
Cullyn	10	56	−0.5	−14.1	7.05	0.25
Jaime	11	84	0.5	13.9	6.95	0.25
Theresa	14	96	3.5	25.9	90.65	12.25
Knut	15	69	4.5	−1.1	−4.95	20.25
Jin-Mae	15	84	4.5	13.9	62.55	20.25
Courtney	19	83	8.5	12.9	109.65	72.25
Sum	105	701	0	0	$SS_{xy} = 519.50$	$SS_{xx} = 264.50$
Mean	$\bar{x} = 10.5$	$\bar{y} = 70.1$				

FIGURE 13.9

Scatter Plot with Fitted Line and Residuals Shown as Vertical Line Segments

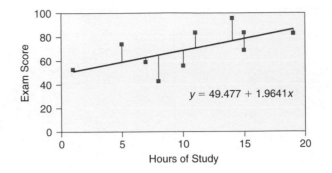

$y = 49.477 + 1.9641x$

between the actual and fitted exam scores (i.e., residuals). The OLS residuals always sum to zero. We have

$$b_1 = \frac{SS_{xy}}{SS_{xx}} = \frac{519.50}{264.50} = 1.9641 \quad \text{(fitted slope)}$$

$$b_0 = \bar{y} - b_1\bar{x} = 70.1 - (1.9641)(10.5) = 49.477 \quad \text{(fitted intercept)}.$$

Interpretation The fitted regression *Score* = 49.477 + 1.9641 (*Study*) says that, on average, each additional hour of study yields a little less than two additional exam points (the slope). A student who did not study (*Study* = 0) would expect a score of about 49 (the intercept). In this example, the intercept is somewhat meaningful because zero study time is not only possible (though hopefully uncommon) but also almost within the range of observed data. The scatter plot shows an imperfect fit, because not all of the variation in exam scores can be explained by study time. The remaining *unexplained* variation in exam scores reflects other factors (e.g., previous night's sleep, class attendance, test anxiety). We can use the fitted regression equation $\hat{y}_i = 1.9641x_i + 49.477$ to find each student's *expected* exam score. Each prediction is a *conditional mean,* given the student's study hours. For example

Student and Study Time	Expected Exam Score
Oscar, 8 hours	$\hat{y}_i = 49.48 + 1.964(8) = 65.19$ (65 to nearest integer)
Theresa, 14 hours	$\hat{y}_i = 49.48 + 1.964(14) = 76.98$ (77 to nearest integer)
Courtney, 19 hours	$\hat{y}_i = 49.48 + 1.964(19) = 86.79$ (87 to nearest integer)

Oscar's actual exam score was only 43, so he did worse than his predicted score of 65. Theresa scored 96, far above her predicted score of 77. Courtney, who studied the longest (19 hours), scored 83, fairly close to her predicted score of 87. These examples show that study time is not a perfect predictor of exam scores.

Assessing Fit

Consider the previous illustration, "Exam Scores and Study Time." Suppose we had no information about how much time each of the 10 students spent studying for the exam. Then the best guess for any student's score would be $\bar{y}$. Then a measure of the total error in our estimating scores of all these students would be $\sum(y_i - \bar{y})^2$. This quantity is called *total sum of squares* and denoted as *SST*:

$$SST = \sum_{i=1}^{n}(y_i - \bar{y})^2 \quad \text{(total sum of squares)} \quad \textbf{(13.13)}$$

In a regression, we seek to explain the variation in the dependent variable by using the value of the independent variable *x*. For observation (x_i, y_i), our fitted regression would estimate the *y* value as $\hat{y}_i = b_0 + b_1x_i$. So the residual $e_i = y_i - \hat{y}_i$ is a measure of the estimation error using regression. As mentioned in Equation 13.8, the sum of residuals is always 0. That is, $\Sigma e_i = 0$. The *unexplained variation* in *Y* (denoted *SSE*) is the sum of *squared* residuals, sometimes referred to as the **error sum of squares.**

TABLE 13.4 **Calculations of Sums of Squares** ExamScores

Student	Hours x_i	Score y_i	Estimated Score $\hat{y}_i = 1.96x_i + 49.48$	Residual $y_i - \hat{y}_i$	$(y_i - \hat{y}_i)^2$	$(\hat{y}_i - \bar{y})^2$	$(y_i - \bar{y})^2$
Tom	1	53	51.441	1.559	2.43	348.15	292.41
Mary	5	74	59.298	14.702	216.15	116.68	15.21
Sarah	7	59	63.226	−4.226	17.86	47.25	123.21
Oscar	8	43	65.190	−22.190	492.40	24.11	734.41
Cullyn	10	56	69.118	−13.118	172.08	0.96	198.81
Jaime	11	84	71.082	12.918	166.87	0.96	193.21
Theresa	14	96	76.974	19.026	361.99	47.25	670.81
Knut	15	69	78.939	−9.939	98.78	78.13	1.21
Jin-Mae	15	84	78.939	5.061	25.61	78.13	193.21
Courtney	19	83	86.795	−3.795	14.40	278.72	166.41
					SSE	SSR	SST
					= 1,568.57	= 1,020.34	= 2,588.90

$$SSE = \sum_{i=1}^{n}(y_i - \hat{y}_i)^2 \quad (\textit{error} \text{ sum of squares, unexplained}) \qquad \textbf{(13.14)}$$

The total variation can, therefore, be split into two parts:

$$\begin{array}{ccc} SST\ (\textit{total} \text{ variation} & = & SSR\ (\text{variation explained} \\ \text{around the mean}) & & \text{by the } \textit{regression}) \end{array} + \begin{array}{c} SSE\ (\text{unexplained or} \\ \textit{error} \text{ variation}) \end{array}$$

The *explained variation* in Y (denoted *SSR*) is the difference between *SST* and *SSE*, and can also be computed as the sum of the squared differences between the conditional mean $\bar{y}_i$ (conditioned on a given value x_i) and the unconditional mean $\bar{y}$ (same for all x_i):

$$SSR = \sum_{i=1}^{n}(\hat{y}_i - \bar{y})^2 \quad (\textit{regression} \text{ sum of squares, explained}) \qquad \textbf{(13.15)}$$

If the fit is good, *SSE* will be relatively small compared to *SST*. If each observed data value y_i is exactly the same as its estimate $\hat{y}_i$ (i.e., a perfect fit), then *SSE* will be zero. Table 13.4 shows the calculation of *SSE* for the exam scores.

Concept Check

For each of the following scenarios, state which of *SST*, *SSR*, and *SSE* equal zero; which have some positive value; and which, if any, are equal to one another. Explain.

(a) All values of Y in the sample have exactly the same value.

(b) Not all values of Y in the sample have the same value, and there is no linear relationship between X and Y in the sample.

(c) Not all values of Y in the sample have the same value, and all values of Y lie along a straight line.

Coefficient of Determination

Because the magnitude of *SSE* is dependent on sample size and on the units of measurement (e.g., dollars, kilograms, ounces), we need a *unit-free* benchmark. The **coefficient of**

determination, or R^2, is a measure of *relative fit* based on a comparison of *SSR* and *SST*. Excel calculates this statistic automatically. It may be calculated in either of two ways:

$$R^2 = 1 - \frac{SSE}{SST} \text{ or } R^2 = \frac{SSR}{SST}$$ (13.16)

The range of the coefficient of determination is $0 \leq R^2 \leq 1$. The highest possible R^2 is 1 because if the regression gives a perfect fit, then $SSE = 0$:

$$R^2 = 1 - \frac{SSE}{SST} = 1 - \frac{0}{SST} = 1 - 0 = 1 \text{ if } SSE = 0 \text{ (perfect fit)}$$

The lowest possible R^2 is 0 because if knowing the value of X does not help predict the value of Y, then $SSE = SST$:

$$R^2 = 1 - \frac{SSE}{SST} = 1 - \frac{SST}{SST} = 1 - 1 = 0 \text{ if } SSE = SST \text{ (worst fit)}$$

For the exam scores, the coefficient of determination is

$$R^2 = 1 - \frac{SSE}{SST} = 1 - \frac{1,568.57}{2,588.90} = 1 - 0.6059 = 0.3941$$

Because a coefficient of determination always lies in the range $0 \leq R^2 \leq 1$, it is often expressed as a *percent of variation explained*. Because the exam score regression yields $R^2 = 0.3941$, we could say that X (hours of study) "explains" 39.41 percent of the variation in Y (exam scores) in our sample. On the other hand, 60.59 percent of the variation in exam scores is *not* explained by study time. The *unexplained variation* reflects factors not included in our model (e.g., reading skills, hours of sleep, hours of work at a job, physical health) or just plain random variation. Although the word "explained" does not necessarily imply causation, in this case we have *a priori* reason to believe that causation exists, and study time improves exam scores.

A Closer Look

In a bivariate regression, R^2 is the square of the correlation coefficient r. Knowing this, we can calculate R^2 by modifying one of the formulas for r, resulting in

$$R^2 = \frac{SS_{xy}^2}{SS_{xx}SS_{yy}}$$

Thus, if $r = \pm 0.50$, then $R^2 = 0.25$. For this reason, MegaStat (and some textbooks) denotes the coefficient of determination as r^2 instead of R^2. In this textbook, the uppercase notation R^2 is used to indicate the difference in their definitions. It is tempting to think that a low R^2 indicates that the model is not useful. Yet in some applications (e.g., predicting crude oil future prices), even a slight improvement in predictive power can translate into millions of dollars.

Concept Check

If $R^2 = 0.81$, what is the value of r? Are you absolutely certain? Explain.

Section Exercises

Instructions for Exercises 13.15 and 13.16: (a) Make an Excel worksheet to calculate SS_{xx}, SS_{yy}, and SS_{xy} (the same worksheet you used in Exercises 13.1 and 13.2). (b) Use the formulas to calculate the slope and intercept. (c) Use your estimated slope and intercept to make a worksheet to calculate *SSE, SSR,* and *SST.* (d) Use these sums to calculate R^2. (e) To check your answers, make an Excel scatter plot of *X* and *Y,* select the data points, right-click, select **Add Trendline,** select the **Options** tab, and choose **Display equation on chart** and **Display R-squared value on chart.** (LO 2 & 3)

13.15 Part-Time Weekly Earnings by University Students   **WeekPay**

Hours Worked (X)	Weekly Pay (Y)
10	93
15	171
20	204
20	156
35	261

13.16 Seconds of Telephone Hold Time for Concert Tickets   **CallWait**

Operators on Duty (X)	Wait Time (Y)
4	385
5	335
6	383
7	344
8	288

Instructions for Exercises 13.17–13.19: (a) Use Excel to make a scatter plot of the data. (b) Select the data points, right-click, select **Add Trendline,** select the **Options** tab, and choose **Display equation on chart** and **Display R-squared value on chart.** (c) Interpret the fitted slope. (d) Is the intercept meaningful? Explain. (e) Interpret R^2. (LO 3)

13.17 Portfolio Returns (%) on Selected Mutual Funds   **Portfolio**

Last Year (X)	This Year (Y)
11.9	15.4
19.5	26.7
11.2	18.2
14.1	16.7
14.2	13.2
5.2	16.4
20.7	21.1
11.3	12.0
−1.1	12.1
3.9	7.4
12.9	11.5
12.4	23.0
12.5	12.7
2.7	15.1
8.8	18.7
7.2	9.9
5.9	18.9

13.18   Number of Orders and Shipping Cost   ◎   **ShipCost**

Orders (X)	Shipping Cost (Y) ($)
1,068	4,489
1,026	5,611
767	3,290
885	4,113
1,156	4,883
1,146	5,425
892	4,414
938	5,506
769	3,346
677	3,673
1,174	6,542
1,009	5,088

13.19   Moviegoer Spending ($) on Snacks   ◎   **Movies**

Age (X)	Spent (Y)
30	2.85
50	6.50
34	1.50
12	6.35
37	6.20
33	6.75
36	3.60
26	6.10
18	8.35
46	4.35

13.20   An experiment was conducted to study the effect of alcoholic consumption (the number of bottles of beer) the night before an exam on a student's performance during the exam. Eight average-performing students were randomly selected from a particular class, with each randomly assigned to drink a specific number of bottles of beer. The results of this experiment were as follows:

Bottles of Beer	Exam Mark
0	79
1	74
2	76
3	65
4	55
5	58
6	45
7	62
8	51

Using Excel, create a scatter plot of this data and comment on the relationship between marks obtained and drinks consumed. Using a calculator or Excel, estimate the linear relationship between marks obtained and bottles of beer consumed and interpret your findings. Calculate R^2 and interpret its value. Check your calculations using the trendline option and the options of including the regression equation and R^2 available with the scatter plot. (LO 2 & 3)

13.21 In a previous chapter, you looked at data on health care costs for various countries. Using the following data and treating the selected countries as a random sample of countries, create a scatter plot of this data using Excel and comment on the relationship between per capita expenditure on health and the percentage of health costs paid by private insurance. Using a calculator or Excel, estimate the linear relationship between these two variables and interpret your findings. Using a calculator or Excel, calculate R^2 and interpret its value. Check your calculations using the trendline option and the options of including the regression equation and R^2 available with the scatter plot. Without doing any calculations, what do you think the trendline would look like and what would you think the value of R^2 would be if the data from the U.S. was not included in this study? (LO 2 & 3)

Country	Per Capita Expenditure on Health (USD)	% of Health Costs Paid by Private Insurance
Japan	2,662	0.4
Sweden	3,149	0.0
Canada	2,669	12.6
Australia	2,519	7.4
Germany	3,204	8.8
France	2,981	12.6
U.K.	2,428	0.0
U.S.	5,711	36.8

13.5 Tests for Significance

Standard Error of Regression

A measure of overall fit is the **standard error** of the estimate:

$$s = \sqrt{\frac{SSE}{n-2}} \quad \text{(standard error)} \tag{13.17}$$

If the fitted model's predictions are perfect ($SSE = 0$), the standard error s will be zero. In general, a smaller value of s indicates a better fit. For the exam scores, we can use SSE from Table 13.4 to find s:

$$s = \sqrt{\frac{SSE}{n-2}} = \sqrt{\frac{1,568.57}{10-2}} = \sqrt{\frac{1,568.57}{8}} = 14.002$$

The standard error s is an estimate of σ (the standard deviation of the unobservable error ε). Because it measures overall fit, the standard error s serves somewhat the same function as the coefficient of determination. However, unlike R^2, the magnitude of s depends on the units of measurement of the dependent variable (e.g., dollars, kilograms, ounces) and on the data magnitude. For this reason, R^2 is usually the preferred measure of overall fit because its scale is always 0 to 1. The main use of the standard error s is to construct confidence intervals and test hypotheses that use s in their formulas.

Confidence Interval for the Slope

Once we have the standard error s, we can construct a confidence interval for the slope from the formulas shown below. Excel, MegaStat, and MINITAB find them automatically.

$$s_{b_1} = \frac{s}{\sqrt{\sum_{i=1}^{n}(x_i - \bar{x})^2}} \quad \text{(standard error of slope)} \tag{13.18}$$

For the exam score data, plugging in the sum from Table 13.3, we get

$$s_{b_1} = \frac{s}{\sqrt{\sum_{i=1}^{n}(x_i - \bar{x})^2}} = \frac{14.002}{\sqrt{264.50}} = 0.86095$$

If the errors are normally distributed, the distribution of b_1 is also normally distributed and this distribution can be expressed as

$$t = \frac{b_1 - \beta_1}{s_{b_1}}$$

where t has a t-distribution with $\nu = n - 2$.

Using this relationship between b_1 and β_1, and the same mathematical manipulations as were previously used to calculate confidence intervals involving the t-distribution, the formula for the confidence interval for β_1 becomes

$$b_1 - t_{\alpha/2, n-2}s_{b_1} \leq \beta_1 \leq b_1 + t_{\alpha/2, n-2}s_{b_1} \qquad \text{(CI for true slope)} \qquad \textbf{(13.19)}$$

A Closer Look

As with previous estimations that use the t-distribution, the formula for calculating this confidence interval is

best estimate $\pm t_{\alpha/2}$ (estimated standard deviation of the best estimator)

Some software packages (e.g., Excel and MegaStat) provide confidence interval automatically, while others do not (e.g., MINITAB).

For the exam scores, the degrees of freedom are $n - 2 = 10 - 2 = 8$. From Appendix D we get, for 95 percent confidence, $t_{\alpha/2, n-2} = t_{0.025,8} = 2.306$. The 95 percent confidence interval for the slope is:

$$b_1 - t_{\alpha/2, n-2}s_{b_1} \leq \beta_1 \leq b_1 + t_{\alpha/2, n-2}s_{b_1}$$
$$= 1.9641 - (2.306)(0.86095) \leq \beta_1 \leq 1.9641 + (2.306)(0.86095)$$
$$\text{or } -0.0213 \leq \beta_1 \leq 3.9495$$

This confidence interval is fairly wide. The width of any confidence interval can be reduced by obtaining a larger sample, partly because the t value would shrink (toward the normal z value) but mainly because the standard errors shrink as n increases. For the exam scores, the slope includes zero, suggesting that the true slope could be zero.

Concept Check

Looking at the formulas for s and s_{b_1}, how else can the width of the confidence interval be smaller other than through a larger sample?

Hypothesis Tests for the Slope

While the relationship between X and Y includes both an intercept and a slope, testing hypotheses (or calculating confidence intervals) for the intercept rarely has any practical applications. The slope is important because it determines the effect that X has on Y, information that we may want to know when making a decision. If $\beta_1 = 0$, it tells us that X has no effect on Y. If $\beta_1 > 0$, we know that X has a positive effect on Y. Conversely, if $\beta_1 < 0$, we know that X has a negative effect on Y. And if $\beta_1 \neq 0$, we know that X has some effect on Y, but we don't know whether it has a positive or negative effect. In addition to testing whether X has a positive, negative, or simply an effect on Y, we can also test whether X has some specific effects on Y.

Examples

- As a student deciding whether to put in additional time studying, you may want to know whether time studying has a positive effect on marks, in which case you would be interested in knowing whether $\beta_1 > 0$. Or you may decide that it is not worthwhile studying unless your marks will go up by more than three marks for each additional hour studied, in which case you would be interested in knowing whether $\beta_1 > 3$.

- As an employer deciding whether to increase the number of vacation days, you may want to know whether increasing the number of vacation days will decrease the number of sick days taken by your employees, in which case you would be interested in knowing whether $\beta_1 < 0$. Or, you may decide that it is not worthwhile increasing the number of vacation days unless the number of sick days is decreased by more than 1.5 days, in which case you would be interested in knowing whether $\beta_1 < 1.5$.

Concept Check

What would the regression model look like if X has no effect on Y?

As with previous hypothesis testing situations, the test statistic is simply the relationship between what is being tested, β_1, and its best estimator, b_1, assuming H_0 is true. The relationship is

$$t = \frac{b_1 - \beta_1}{s_{b_1}}$$

assuming the errors are normally distributed. If $H_0: \beta_1 = 0$ (the most common value of β_1 that is tested), the value of the test statistic becomes

$$t_{\text{calc}} = \frac{b_1}{s_{b_1}}$$

If $H_0: \beta_1 = \beta_1^0$ (where β_1^0 can be any value), the value of the test statistic is

$$t_{\text{calc}} = \frac{b_1 - \beta_1^0}{s_{b_1}}$$

where either test statistic has $n - 2$ degrees of freedom.

As with previous hypothesis tests, the null hypothesis will either be rejected or not rejected by comparing its value with the decision rule. Based on comparing your expectations concerning the value of the test statistic if H_0 is true with your expectations if H_1 is true, the decision rules for testing β_1 are similar to other decision rules involving the t-distribution. These rules are

- If $H_1: \beta_1 < 0$ or if $H_1: \beta_1 < \beta_1^0$, reject the null hypothesis if $t_{\text{calc}} < -t_{\alpha,n-2}$
- If $H_1: \beta_1 \neq 0$ or if $H_1: \beta_1 \neq \beta_1^0$, reject the null hypothesis if $t_{\text{calc}} < -t_{\alpha/2,n-2}$ or if $t_{\text{calc}} > t_{\alpha/2,n-2}$
- If $H_1: \beta_1 > 0$ or if $H_1: \beta_1 > \beta_1^0$, reject the null hypothesis if $t_{\text{calc}} > t_{\alpha,n-2}$

The critical value of $t_{\alpha/2,n-2}$ or $t_{\alpha,n-2}$ is obtained from Appendix D or from Excel's function =TDIST(t,deg_freedom,tails) where tails is 1 (one-tailed test) or 2 (two-tailed test).

The test for zero slope is the same as the test for zero correlation. That is, the t test for zero slope $\left(t_{calc} = \dfrac{b_1}{s_{b_1}} \right)$ will always yield *exactly* the same t_{calc} as the t test for zero correlation (Equation 13.4), and the decision rules will also be the same.

Test for Zero Slope: Exam Scores   ExamScores

For the exam scores, we would anticipate a positive slope (i.e., more study hours should improve exam scores), so we will use a right-tailed test:

Hypotheses	Test Statistic		Critical Value	Decision
H_0: $\beta_1 = 0$ H_1: $\beta_1 > 0$	$t_{calc} = \dfrac{b_1 - 0}{s_{b_1}} = \dfrac{1.9641 - 0}{0.86095}$	$= 2.281$	$t_{0.05,8} = 1.860$	Reject H_0 (i.e., slope is positive)

We can reject the hypothesis of a zero slope in a right-tailed test. (We would be unable to do so in a two-tailed test because the critical value of our t statistic would be 2.306.) Once we have the test statistic for the slope or intercept, we can find the p value by using Excel's function =TDIST(t,deg_freedom,tails). The p value method is preferred by researchers, because it obviates the need for prior specification of α.

Parameter	Excel Function	p Value
Slope	=TDIST(2.281,8,1)	0.025995 (right-tailed test)

Using Excel: Exam Scores   ExamScores

These calculations are normally done by computer (we have demonstrated the calculations only to illustrate the formulas). The Excel menu to accomplish these tasks is shown in Figure 13.10. The resulting output, shown in Figure 13.11, can be used to verify our calculations. Excel always does two-tailed tests, so you must halve the p value if you need the p value for a one-tailed test. You may specify the confidence level, but Excel's default is 95 percent confidence.

Excel's regression function gives us a two-tailed p value. For a one-tailed test, the p value would be half the quoted p value only if the slope of the regression line corresponds to what we would expect if the alternative hypothesis was true. For example, if our alternative hypothesis was H_1: $\beta_1 > 0$, we would expect b_1 to be greater than zero. If b_1 was greater than zero, the actual p value would be half the quoted p value. But if b_1 was less than zero, which is not what we would have expected if the alternative hypothesis was true, the actual p value would not be half the quoted p value. The actual p value would be greater than 0.5, or more precisely, it would be

$$1 - \frac{\text{quoted } p \text{ value}}{2}$$

FIGURE 13.10

Excel's Regression Menu

FIGURE 13.11

Excel's Regression Results for Exam Scores

SUMMARY OUTPUT

Regression Statistics

Multiple R	0.627790986
R Square	0.394121523
Adjusted R Square	0.318386713
Standard Error	14.00249438
Observations	10

Variable	Coefficient	Standard Error	t Stat	P-value	Lower 95%	Upper 95%
Intercept	49.47712665	10.06646125	4.915047	0.001171	26.26381038	72.69044293
Study Hours	1.964083176	0.86097902	2.281221	0.051972	−0.021339288	3.94950564

Tip

Avoid checking the Constant is Zero box in Excel's menu. This would force the intercept through the origin, changing the model drastically. Leave this option to the experts.

Using MegaStat: Exam Scores  **ExamScores**

Figure 13.12 shows MegaStat's menu, and Figure 13.13 shows MegaStat's regression output for this data. The output format is similar to Excel's, except that MegaStat highlights coefficients that differ significantly from zero at $\alpha = 0.05$ in a two-tailed test.

Using MINITAB: Exam Scores **ExamScores**

Figure 13.14 shows MINITAB's regression menus, and Figure 13.15 shows MINITAB's regression output for this data. MINITAB gives you the same general output as Excel, but with strongly rounded results.*

---

*You may have noticed that both Excel and MINITAB calculated something called "adjusted R-Square." For a bivariate regression, this statistic is of little interest, but in the next chapter it becomes important.

FIGURE 13.12

MegaStat's Regression Menu

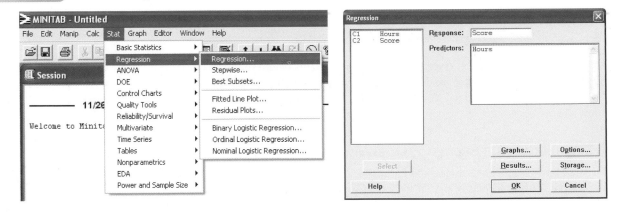

FIGURE 13.13

MegaStat's Regression Results for Exam Scores

Regression Analysis

	r^2	0.394	n	10
	r	0.628	k	1
Std. Error	14.002	Dep. Var.	Exam Score

Regression output — confidence interval

variables	coefficients	std. error	t (df = 8)	p-value	95% lower	95% upper
Intercept	49.4771	10.0665	4.915	0.0012	26.2638	72.6904
Study Hours	1.9641	0.8610	2.281	0.0520	−0.0213	3.9495

FIGURE 13.14 **MINITAB's Regression Menus**

FIGURE 13.15

MINITAB's Regression Results for Exam Scores

The regression equation is
Score = 49.5 + 1.96 Hours

Predictor	Coef	SE Coef	T	P
Constant	49.48	10.07	4.92	0.001
Hours	1.9641	0.8610	2.28	0.052

S = 14.00   R-Sq = 39.4%   R-Sq(adj) = 31.8%

Excel, MegaStat, and MINITAB only calculate test statistics assuming the hypothesized value of β_1 is zero. For any other hypothesized value, you must calculate your own test statistic using the output's b_1 and s_{b_1} and the hypothesized value, β_1^0. For example, to test whether each additional hour will add more than one mark to your score, the test statistic would be

$$t = \frac{1.9641 - 1}{0.8610} = 1.120$$

and the null hypothesis would not be rejected because $1.120 < 1.860$.

So, although studying more will increase a student's mark, there is not enough evidence that it would be worthwhile for a student to study more if he or she wants to see an improvement of more than one mark for each additional hour of study time.

As previously mentioned, any inferences that you make should only apply over the range of X's in the sample. In the exam score example, the amount of hours studied ranged between 1 and 19 hours. Therefore, you should only conclude a positive linear relationship for study times between 1 and 19 hours. It could happen that if a student studies much more than 19 hours, the student's mark may actually go down, especially if he/she doesn't get enough rest and falls asleep during the exam.

Application: Retail Sales   RetailSales

Table 13.5 shows data for gross leasable area (X) and retail sales (Y) in shopping malls in $n = 24$ randomly chosen U.S. states. We will assume a linear relationship between X and Y:

$$Sales = \beta_0 + \beta_1 (Area) + \varepsilon_i$$

We anticipate a positive slope (more leasable area permits more retail sales) and an intercept near zero (zero leasable space would imply no retail sales). Because retail sales do not depend solely on leasable area, the random error term will reflect all other factors that influence retail sales as well as possible measurement error.

TABLE 13.5   Leasable Area and Retail Sales   RetailSales

State	Leasable Area (millions of square feet)	Retail Sales (billions of dollars)	State	Leasable Area (millions of square feet)	Retail Sales (billions of dollars)
AK	8	3.3	MT	10	3.0
AR	41	10.2	ND	10	3.2
AZ	150	36.8	NM	32	9.1
CA	755	182.8	NY	266	65.2
CO	125	35.3	OH	270	59.9
FL	488	144.5	OK	63	17.8
IL	282	63.4	RI	24	5.6
KS	62	16.7	SD	8	1.9
MA	123	35.7	TX	410	127.0
MI	155	37.0	VA	187	47.9
MN	76	20.7	VT	9	2.8
MO	129	33.0	WI	82	21.7

FIGURE 13.16

Leasable Area and Retail Sales RetailSales

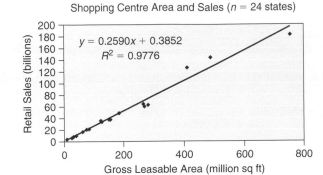

Shopping Centre Area and Sales (n = 24 states)

$y = 0.2590x + 0.3852$
$R^2 = 0.9776$

FIGURE 13.17

MegaStat Regression Results for Retail Sales RetailSales

Regression output

Variables	Coefficients	Std. Error	t (df = 26)	p value	Confidence Interval 95% lower	95% upper
Intercept	0.3852	1.9853	0.194	0.8479	−3.7320	4.5023
Area	0.2590	0.0084	30.972	1.22E-19	0.2417	0.2764

Based on the scatter plot and Excel's fitted linear regression, displayed in Figure 13.16, the linear model seems justified. The very high R^2 says that *Area* "explains" about 98 percent of the variation in *Sales*. Although it is reasonable to assume causation between *Area* and *Sales* in this model, the high R^2 alone does not prove cause-and-effect.

Using MegaStat For a more detailed look, we examine MegaStat's regression output for this data, shown in Figure 13.17. On average, each extra million square feet of leasable space yields an extra $259.4 million in retail sales ($b_1 = 0.2590$). The slope is non-zero in MegaStat's two-tailed test ($t = 30.972$) as indicated by its tiny p value ($p = 1.22 \times 10^{-19}$). MegaStat's highlight indicates that the slope differs significantly from zero at $\alpha = 0.01$, and the narrow confidence interval for the slope (0.2417 to 0.2764) does not enclose zero. We conclude that this sample result (non-zero slope) did not arise by chance—rarely will you see such small p values (except perhaps in time-series data). But the intercept ($b_0 = 0.3852$) does not differ significantly from zero ($p = 0.8479$, $t = 0.194$), and the confidence interval for the intercept (−3.7320 to +4.5023) includes zero. These conclusions are in line with our prior expectations.

Section Exercises

13.22 A regression was performed using data on 32 NFL teams in 2003. The variables were Y = current value of team (millions of dollars) and X = total debt held by the team owners (millions of dollars). (a) Write the fitted regression equation. (b) Construct a 95 percent confidence interval for the slope. (c) Perform a right-tailed t test for zero slope (i.e., test for a positive linear relationship between current value and total debt) at $\alpha = 0.05$. State the hypotheses clearly. (d) Use Excel to find the p value for the t statistic for the slope. (Data are from *Forbes* 172, no. 5, pp. 82–83.) (LO 2 & 5)
NFL

Variables	Coefficients	Std. Error
Intercept	557.4511	25.3385
Debt	3.0047	0.8820

13.23 A regression was performed using data on 16 randomly selected charities in 2003. The variables were Y = expenses (millions of dollars) and X = revenue (millions of dollars). (a) Write the fitted regression equation. (b) Construct a 95 percent confidence interval for the slope. (c) Perform a right-tailed t test for zero slope (i.e., test for a positive linear relationship between expense and revenue) at $\alpha = 0.05$. State the hypotheses clearly. (d) Use Excel to find the p value for the t statistic for the slope. (Data are from *Forbes* 172, no. 12, p. 248, and www.forbes.com.) (LO 2 & 5)   **Charities**

Variables	Coefficients	Std. Error
Intercept	7.6425	10.0403
Revenue	0.9467	0.0936

13.24   Continuing with Exercise 13.21 (health care study), use the results of Excel's regression function to construct a 95 percent confidence interval for the true effect that percent of health care costs paid by private insurance has on per capita expenditure on health. Americans are usually of the opinion that the free market (i.e., private enterprise) is better than government when it comes to efficiency and effectiveness. Without doing any additional calculations, is there sufficient evidence to indicate that the more involved private insurance is in health care, the cheaper the cost of health care? Explain why no additional calculations are required. At the 0.05 level of significance, is there sufficient evidence to indicate that the more involved private insurance is in health care, the more expensive the cost of health care? Determine the p value of this test. If the U.S. were not included in the study, do you think that you would arrive at the same conclusion? Explain without doing any additional calculations. (LO 2 & 5)

13.6   Analysis of Variance: Overall Fit

Decomposition of Variance

A regression seeks to explain variation in the dependent variable around its mean. A simple way to see this is to express the deviation of y_i from its mean $\bar{y}$ as the sum of the deviation of y_i from the regression estimate $\hat{y}_i$ plus the deviation of the regression estimate $\hat{y}_i$ from the mean $\bar{y}$.

$$y_i - \bar{y} = (y_i - \hat{y}_i) + (\hat{y}_i - \bar{y}) \qquad \text{(adding and subtracting } \hat{y}_i) \qquad \textbf{(13.20)}$$

This is also seen graphically by the following diagram in Excel with five plotted points: $\{(1, 8.4), (2, 7.02), (3, 11.42), (4, 14.85), (5, 13.66)\}$:

$$y_4 - \bar{y} = (y_4 - \hat{y}_4) + (\hat{y}_4 - \bar{y})$$

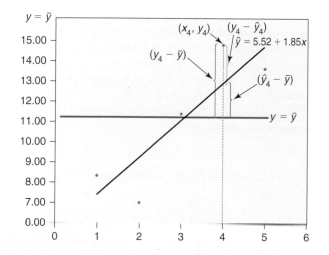

It can be shown that this same decomposition also holds for the *sums of squares:*

$$\sum_{i=1}^{n} (y_i - \bar{y})^2 = \sum_{i=1}^{n} (y_i - \hat{y}_i)^2 + \sum_{i=1}^{n} (\hat{y}_i - \bar{y})^2 \qquad \text{(sums of squares)} \qquad \textbf{(13.21)}$$

As we saw earlier in Section 13.4, this *decomposition of variance* may be written as

SST (*total* variation around the mean)	=	SSE (unexplained or *error* variation)	+	SSR (variation explained by the *regression*)

TABLE 13.6 **ANOVA Table for a Simple Regression**

Source of Variation	Sum of Squares	df	Mean Square	F	Excel p value
Regression (explained)	$SSR = \sum_{i=1}^{n} (\hat{y}_i - \bar{y})^2$	1	$MSR = \dfrac{SSR}{1}$	$F_{calc} = \dfrac{MSR}{MSE}$	$=\text{FDIST}(F_{calc}, 1, n-2)$
Residual (unexplained)	$SSE = \sum_{i=1}^{n} (y_i - \hat{y}_i)^2$	$n - 2$	$MSE = \dfrac{SSE}{n-2}$		
Total	$SST = \sum_{i=1}^{n} (y_i - \bar{y})^2$	$n - 1$			

F Statistic for Overall Fit

To test a regression for overall significance or whether the model is useful for explaining *Y,* we use an *F* test to compare the explained (*SSR*) and unexplained (*SSE*) sums of squares. We divide each sum by its respective degrees of freedom to obtain *mean squares* (*MSR* and *MSE*). The *F statistic* is the ratio of these two mean squares. Calculations of the *F* statistic are arranged in a table called the *analysis of variance* or ANOVA table (see Table 13.6). The ANOVA table also contains the sums required to calculate $R^2 = SSR/SST$. An ANOVA table is provided automatically by any regression software (e.g., Excel, MegaStat).

To test for the usefulness of the model, the two hypotheses are

H_0: *X* (or the model) is not useful in explaining *Y.*

H_1: *X* (or the model) is useful in explaining *Y.*

And the formula for the *F* test statistic is

$$F_{calc} = \frac{MSR}{MSE} = \frac{SSR/1}{SSE/(n-2)} = (n-2)\frac{SSR}{SSE} \quad (F \text{ statistic for simple regression}) \quad \textbf{(13.22)}$$

We use this formula for the test statistic for the same reason we used a similar formula when using ANOVA in Chapter 11. If there is no relationship between *X* and *Y,* or if the model is not useful, *MSR* is an estimate of the true variance, σ^2, of the errors. *MSE* is an unbiased estimator of σ^2 no matter which hypothesis is true. If the null hypothesis is true, then *MSR* is also an unbiased estimator of σ^2 and we would therefore expect F_{calc} to be close to 1 if H_0 is true. Conversely, if H_1 is true, we would expect *MSR* to be larger than σ^2, or equivalently, we would expect F_{calc} to be greater than 1. Based on these expectations and based on the test statistic comparing two estimated variances, the decision rule would be to reject the null hypothesis when F_{calc} is greater than 1, or to

Reject H_0 if $F_{calc} > F_{\alpha, 1, n-2}$

where 1 is the degrees of freedom associated with *MSR* and $n - 2$ is that with *MSE*.

A Closer Look

The *F* statistic reflects both the sample size and the ratio of *SSR* to *SSE*. For a given sample size, a large *F* statistic indicates a better fit (larger *SSR* relative to *SSE*), while a small *F* indicates a poor fit (smaller *SSR* relative to *SSE*). A better fit would be an indication that the model is useful while a poor fit would be an indication that the model may not be useful.

ANOVA table

Source	SS	df	MS	F	p-value
Regression	1,020.3412	1	1,020.3412	5.20	0.0520
Residual	1,568.5588	8	196.0698		
Total	2,588.9000	9			

FIGURE 13.18

MegaStat's ANOVA Table for Exam Data

Figure 13.18 shows MegaStat's ANOVA table for the exam scores. The F statistic is

$$F_{calc} = \frac{MSR}{MSE} = \frac{1020.3412}{196.0698} = 5.20$$

EXAMPLE 2

Exam Scores: *F* Statistic

ExamScores

From Appendix F, the critical value of $F_{0.05,1,8}$ is 5.32, so the exam score regression is not quite significant at $\alpha = 0.05$. The p value of 0.052 says a sample such as ours would be expected about 52 times in 1,000 sample tests if X and Y were unrelated. In other words, if we reject the hypothesis of no relationship between X and Y, we face a Type I error risk of 5.2 percent. This p value might be called *marginally significant*.

From the ANOVA table, we can calculate the standard error from the mean square for the residuals:

$$s = \sqrt{MSE} = \sqrt{196.0698} = 14.002 \quad \text{(standard error for exam scores)}$$

A Closer Look

In a bivariate regression, the F test always yields the same p value as testing $\beta_1 \neq 0$, which in turn always gives the same p value as testing $\rho \neq 0$. The relationship between the test statistics is $F_{calc} = (t_{calc})^2$ and the relationship between the critical values is $F_{crit} = (t_{crit})^2$.

Section Exercises

13.25 Below is a regression using X = home price (000), Y = annual taxes (000), n = 20 homes. (a) Write the fitted regression equation. (b) Write the formula for each t statistic and verify the t statistics shown below. (c) State the degrees of freedom for the t tests and find the two-tail critical value for t by using Appendix D. (d) Use Excel's function =TDIST(t,deg_freedom,tails) to verify the p value shown for each t statistic (slope, intercept). (e) Verify that $F = t^2$ for the slope. (f) In your own words, describe the fit of this regression. (LO 2, 4, 5 & 6)

R²	0.452
Std. Error	0.454
n	12

ANOVA table

Source	SS	df	MS	F	p-value
Regression	1.6941	1	1.6941	8.23	0.0167
Residual	2.0578	10	0.2058		
Total	3.7519	11			

Regression output

variables	coefficients	std. error	t (df =10)	p-value	confidence interval 95% lower	95% upper
Intercept	1.8064	0.6116	2.954	0.0144	0.4438	3.1691
Slope	0.0039	0.0014	2.869	0.0167	0.0009	0.0070

13.26 Below is a regression using X average price, $Y =$ units sold, $n = 20$ stores. (a) Write the fitted regression equation. (b) Write the formula for each t statistic and verify the t statistics shown below. (c) State the degrees of freedom for the t tests and find the two-tail critical value for t by using Appendix D. (d) Use Excel's function =TDIST(t,deg_freedom,tails) to verify the p value shown for each t statistic (slope, intercept). (e) Verify that $F = t^2$ for the slope. (f) In your own words, describe the fit of this regression. (LO 2, 4, 5 & 6)

R^2	0.200
Std. Error	26.128
n	20

ANOVA table

Source	SS	df	MS	F	p-value
Regression	3,080.89	1	3,080.89	4.51	0.0478
Residual	12,288.31	18	682.68		
Total	15,369.20	19			

Regression output   confidence interval

variables	coefficients	std. error	t (df = 18)	p-value	95% lower	95% upper
Intercept	614.9300	51.2343	12.002	0.0000	507.2908	722.5692
Slope	−109.1120	51.3623	−2.124	0.0478	−217.0202	−1.2038

Instructions for Exercises 13.27–13.29: (a) Use Excel's **Data > Data Analysis > Regression** (or MegaStat or MINITAB) to obtain regression estimates. (b) Interpret the 95 percent confidence interval for the slope. Does it contain zero? (c) Interpret the t test for the slope and its p value. (d) Interpret the F statistic. (e) Verify that the p value for F is the same as for the slope's t statistic, and show that $t^2 = F$. (f) Describe the fit of the regression. (LO 4)

13.27 Portfolio Returns (%) on Selected Mutual Funds ($n = 17$ funds)   **Portfolio**

Last Year (X)	This Year (Y)
11.9	15.4
19.5	26.7
11.2	18.2
14.1	16.7
14.2	13.2
5.2	16.4
20.7	21.1
11.3	12.0
−1.1	12.1
3.9	7.4
12.9	11.5
12.4	23.0
12.5	12.7
2.7	15.1
8.8	18.7
7.2	9.9
5.9	18.9

13.28 Number of Orders and Shipping Cost ($n = 12$ orders) **ShipCost**

Orders (X)	Shipping Cost (Y)
1,068	4,489
1,026	5,611
767	3,290
885	4,113
1,156	4,883
1,146	5,425
892	4,414
938	5,506
769	3,346
677	3,673
1,174	6,542
1,009	5,088

13.29 Moviegoer Spending ($) on Snacks ($n = 10$ purchases) **Movies**

Age (X)	Spent (Y)
30	2.85
50	6.50
34	1.50
12	6.35
37	6.20
33	6.75
36	3.60
26	6.10
18	8.35
46	4.35

13.30 Using the results of the Excel output for Exercise 13.24, at the 0.05 level of significance, can we conclude that percentage of health care costs paid by private insurance is useful in explaining per capita expenditure on health? Without doing any additional calculations, do you believe that your conclusions would be the same if the U.S. data were not included in the analysis? Explain. (LO 6)

Mini Case 13.2

Airplane Cockpit Noise **Cockpit**

Career airline pilots face the risk of progressive hearing loss, due to the noisy cockpits of most jet aircraft. Much of the noise comes not from engines but from air roar, which increases at high speeds. To assess this workplace hazard, a pilot measured cockpit noise at randomly selected points during the flight by using a handheld meter. Noise level (in decibels) was measured in seven different aircraft at the first officer's left ear position using a handheld meter. For reference, 60 dB is a normal conversation, 75 is a typical vacuum cleaner, 85 is city traffic, 90 is a typical hair dryer, and 110 is a chain saw. Table 13.7 shows 61 observations on cockpit noise (decibels) and airspeed (knots indicated air speed, or KIAS) for a Boeing 727, an older type of aircraft lacking design improvements in newer planes.

The scatter plot in Figure 13.19 suggests that a linear model provides a reasonable description of the data. The fitted regression shows that each additional knot of airspeed increases the noise level by 0.0765 dB. Thus, a 100-knot increase in airspeed would add about 7.65 dB of noise. The intercept of 64.229 suggests that if the plane were not flying ($KIAS = 0$), the noise level would be only slightly greater than a normal conversation.

The regression results in Figure 13.20 show that the fit is very good ($R^2 = 0.895$) and that the regression is highly significant ($F = 501.16$, $p < 0.001$). Both the slope and intercept have p values below 0.001, indicating that the true parameters are non-zero. Thus, the regression is significant, as well as having practical value.

TABLE 13.7 Cockpit Noise Level and Airspeed for B-727 ($n = 61$) 💿 Cockpit

Speed	Noise	Speed	Noise	Speed	Noise	Speed	Noise	Speed	Noise	Speed	Noise
250	83	380	93	340	90	330	91	350	90	272	84.5
340	89	380	91	340	91	360	94	380	92	310	88
320	88	390	94	380	96	370	94.5	310	88	350	90
330	89	400	95	385	96	380	95	295	87	370	91
346	92	400	96	420	97	395	96	280	86	405	93
260	85	405	97	230	82	365	91	320	88	250	82
280	84	320	89	340	91	320	88	330	90		
395	92	310	88.5	250	86	250	85	320	88		
380	92	250	82	320	89	250	82	340	89		
400	93	280	87	340	90	320	88	350	90		
335	91	320	89	320	90	305	88	270	84		

FIGURE 13.19

Scatter Plot of Cockpit Noise Data (Courtesy of Capt. R. E. Hartl (ret) of Delta Airlines)

Cockpit Noise in B-727 ($n = 61$)

$y = 0.0765x + 64.229$
$R^2 = 0.8947$

(Scatter plot: Noise Level (decibels) on y-axis from 80 to 98, Air Speed (KIAS) on x-axis from 200 to 450)

FIGURE 13.20

Regression Results of Cockpit Noise

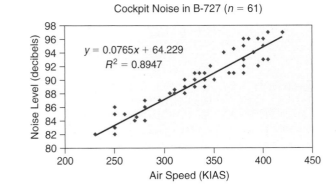

Regression Analysis

r^2	0.895	n	61
r	0.946	k	1
Std. Error	1.292	Dep. Var.	Noise

ANOVA table

Source	SS	df	MS	F	p-value
Regression	836.9817	1	836.9817	501.16	1.60E-30
Residual	98.5347	59	1.6701		
Total	935.5164	60			

Regression output   *confidence interval*

variables	coefficients	std. error	t (df = 59)	p-value	95% lower	95% upper
Intercept	64.2294	1.1489	55.907	8.29E-53	61.9306	66.5283
Speed	0.0765	0.0034	22.387	1.60E-30	0.0697	0.0834

13.7 Confidence and Prediction Intervals for *Y*

How to Construct an Interval Estimate for *Y*

The regression line is an estimate of the *conditional mean* of *Y* (i.e., the expected value of *Y* for a given value of *X*, x_g). But the estimate may be too high or too low. To make this *point estimate* more useful, we need an *interval estimate* to show a range of likely values. To do this, we insert the x_g value into the fitted regression equation and calculate the estimated $\hat{y}$, and use the formulas shown below to obtain intervals that most likely contain the true values being estimated. The first formula gives a **confidence interval** for the conditional mean of *Y* or the expected value of *Y* for the given value of *X*, x_g, while the second is a **prediction interval** for individual values of *Y* for the same x_g. The formulas are similar, except that prediction intervals are wider because there is a lot more uncertainly in predicting *individual y* values than in estimating the *mean* of *Y*.

$$\hat{y} \pm t_{\alpha/2, n-2} s \sqrt{\frac{1}{n} + \frac{(x_g - \bar{x})^2}{\sum_{i=1}^{n}(x_i - \bar{x})^2}} \quad \text{(confidence interval for mean of } Y) \qquad \textbf{(13.23)}$$

$$\hat{y} \pm t_{\alpha/2, n-2} s \sqrt{1 + \frac{1}{n} + \frac{(x_g - \bar{x})^2}{\sum_{i=1}^{n}(x_i - \bar{x})^2}} \quad \text{(prediction interval for individual } Y) \qquad \textbf{(13.24)}$$

In both formulas, $\hat{y} = b_0 + b_1 x_g$, where x_g is the value of *X* for which *Y* or *E(Y)* is to be determined.

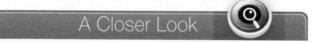

A Closer Look

Although these formulas look more complicated than previous interval formulas using the *t*-distribution, they are similar to these previous formulas in that each interval's calculation is simply

best estimate $\pm\, t_{\alpha/2}$ (estimated standard deviation of the best estimator)

Let's use Equation 13.24 to predict the exam score for a student who studies four hours, using the regression model developed in Section 13.4. What is the 95 percent prediction interval? The student's predicted exam score (see Table 13.4) would be $\hat{y} = 1.9641(4) + 49.477 = 57.333$. For 95 percent confidence with $\nu = n - 2 = 10 - 2 = 8$, we use $t_{0.025,8} = 2.306$. Using the sums from Table 13.4, the 95 percent prediction interval is

$$57.333 \pm (2.306)(14.002)\sqrt{1 + \frac{1}{10} + \frac{(4 \quad 10.5)^2}{264.5}} = 57.333 \pm 36.24$$

If we ask the question, "Estimate the expected exam score for students who study for four hours, using the same regression model," we are now interested in a confidence interval and will use Equation 13.23 instead. So we want to find a 95 percent confidence interval now for the mean of *Y* when *x* = 4:

$$57.333 \pm (2.306)(14.002)\sqrt{\frac{1}{10} + \frac{(4 - 10.5)^2}{264.5}} = 57.333 \pm 16.46$$

FIGURE 13.21 MegaStat's Confidence and Prediction Intervals

Predicted values for Exam Scores

X	Predicted	95% Confidence Intervals		95% Prediction Intervals	
		lower	upper	lower	upper
0	49.477	26.264	72.690	9.709	89.245
2	53.405	33.681	73.130	15.568	91.243
4	57.333	40.877	73.790	21.092	93.575
6	61.262	47.694	74.829	26.237	96.286
8	65.190	53.836	76.543	30.962	99.417
10	69.118	58.859	79.377	35.238	102.998
12	73.046	62.410	83.682	39.050	107.043
14	76.974	64.623	89.325	42.403	111.546
16	80.902	65.952	95.853	45.320	116.485
18	84.831	66.775	102.886	47.836	121.826
20	88.759	67.311	110.207	49.995	127.523

A Closer Look

Based on the above formulas and the results obtained by applying these formulas to the above example, the following observations can be made. For a given confidence level and *x* value, the prediction interval is wider than the confidence interval. This agrees with our intuition that it is easier to accurately predict an average value than a single value. The wide prediction interval in this example implies that we cannot make useful predictions of the exam score for a student who studies four hours. This is not surprising as the fit for the exam score data ($R^2 = 0.3941$) was not very high. Finally, interval width varies with the value of x_g, being narrowest when x_g is near its mean (note that when $x_g = \bar{x}$, the last term under the square root disappears completely). For some data sets, the degree of narrowing near $\bar{x}$ is almost indiscernible, while for other data sets it is quite pronounced. These calculations are usually done by computer (see Figure 13.21). Both MegaStat and MINITAB, for example, will let you type in the x_g value and will give both confidence and prediction intervals *only* for that x_g value, but you must make your own graphs.

Concept Check

In addition to the widths of the intervals being narrower than when value of x_g is closer to $\bar{x}$, looking at the above interval formulas, the intervals would also be narrower

- The lower or higher the level of confidence?
- The better or worse the data fit the regression line?
- The smaller or larger the sample size?
- The more or less spread out the values of *X* in the sample?

Two Illustrations: Exam Scores and Retail Sales ⊙ ExamScores, RetailSales

Because there will be a different interval for every *X* value, it is helpful to see confidence and prediction intervals over the entire range of *X*. Figure 13.22 shows confidence and prediction intervals for exam scores and retail sales. The contrast between the two graphs is striking. Confidence and prediction intervals for exam scores are wide and clearly narrower

Confidence and Prediction Intervals Illustrated FIGURE 13.22

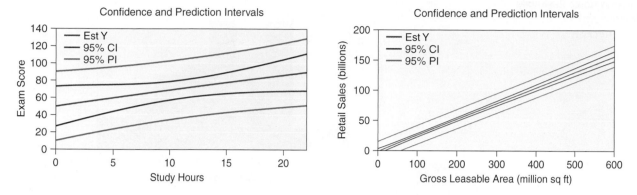

for X values near the mean. The prediction bands for exam scores for large X values (e.g., $X = 20$ hours of study) even extend above 100 points (presumably the upper limit for an exam score). In contrast, the intervals for retail sales appear narrow and only slightly wider for X values below or above the mean. While the prediction bands for retail sales seem narrow, they still represent billions of dollars (e.g., for $X = 500$ the retail sales prediction interval has a width of about $33 billion). This shows that a high R^2 does not guarantee precise predictions.

Section Exercise

13.31 Referring back to the health cost study and the information provided by your previous Excel output (Exercise 13.24), (a) predict, with 95 percent confidence, the per capita expenditure on health for a country where 10 percent of health care costs are paid by private insurance, and (b) estimate, with 95 percent confidence, the expected per capita expenditure on health for countries where 10 percent of health care costs are paid by private insurance. Are you surprised by the results? Explain. (LO 7)

13.8 Violations of Assumptions

Three Important Assumptions

Recall that the dependent variable is a random variable that has an error component, ε. The OLS method makes several assumptions, some of which were previously mentioned, about the random error term ε. Although ε is unobservable, clues may be found in the residuals e_i. Three important assumptions can be tested:

- Assumption 1: The errors are normally distributed.
- Assumption 2: The errors have constant variance (i.e., they are *homoscedastic*).
- Assumption 3: The errors are independent (i.e., they are *nonautocorrelated*).

Because we cannot observe the error ε we must rely on the residuals e_i from the fitted regression for clues about possible violations of these assumptions. Regression residuals often violate one or more of these assumptions. Fortunately, regression is fairly robust in the face of moderate violations of these assumptions. We will examine each violation, explain its consequences, show how to check it, and discuss possible remedies.

Non-Normal Errors

Non-normality of errors is usually considered a mild violation, as the regression parameter estimates b_0 and b_1 and their variances remain unbiased and consistent. The main ill consequence is that confidence intervals and hypothesis tests may be untrustworthy, because the normality assumption is used to justify using Student's t to construct confidence intervals and test statistics.

**Cockpit Noise Residuals
(Histogram)**

Cockpit

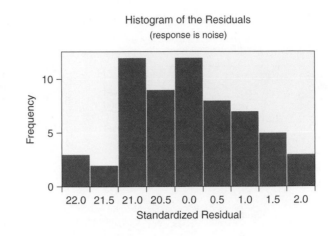

Histogram of the Residuals
(response is noise)

However, if the sample size is large (say, $n > 30$), the results should be okay. An exception would be if outliers exist, posing a serious problem that cannot be cured by large sample size. Three simple methods to check for the normality assumptions are: plotting a histogram of residuals, plotting a normal probabability plot, and using a goodness-of-fit test for testing normality.

Histogram of Residuals   You can visually check for non-normality by creating a histogram of the actual residuals or **standardized residuals.** (A *standardized residual* is obtained by dividing each residual by its standard error.) Histogram shapes will be the same, but standardized residuals offer the advantage of a predictable scale (between -3 and $+3$ unless there are outliers). A simple "eyeball test" can usually reveal outliers or serious asymmetry. Figure 13.23 shows a standardized residual histogram for Mini Case 13.2. There are no outliers and the histogram is roughly symmetric.

Normal Probability Plot   Normal probability plots produced by many regression packages also allow you to check for normality. If the null hypothesis is true (i.e., errors are normally distributed), the residual probability plot should be linear. When testing for normality, the hypotheses are

H_0: Errors are normally distributed.

H_1: Errors are not normally distributed.

If the null hypothesis is true, the residual probability plot should be linear. For example in Figure 13.24 we see slight deviations from linearity at the lower and upper ends of the residual probability plot for Mini Case 13.2 (cockpit noise). But overall, the residuals seem to be consistent with the hypothesis of normality. There are more tests for normality, but the histogram and probability plot suffice for most purposes.

Goodness-of-Fit Test   The goodness-of-fit test for normality, discussed in Chapter 12, would give you a more objective way of testing normality. Here, the hypotheses are

H_0: Errors are normally distributed with a mean of zero.

H_1: Errors are not normally distributed with a mean of zero.

**Cockpit Noise Residuals
(Normal Probability Plot)**

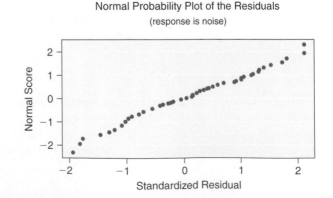

Normal Probability Plot of the Residuals
(response is noise)

The chi-square test statistic is used, and we would reject the null hypothesis if the value of the test statistic exceeds χ^2_{crit}, where $\chi^2_{\text{crit}} = \chi_{\alpha,c-2}$ and c is the created number of classes or bins.

Concept Check

The test for normality in Chapter 12 had $c - 3$ degrees of freedom. Why does this test have $c - 2$ degrees of freedom?

As with all other violations of the regression assumptions, there are ways of eliminating or reducing the impact of these violations. However, these techniques are better left to more experienced statisticians. Non-normality is not considered a major violation, so don't worry too much about it *unless* you have major outliers.

Heteroscedastic Errors (Non-constant Variance)

The regression should fit equally well for all values of X. If the error magnitude is constant for all X, the errors are called **homoscedastic** (the ideal condition). If the errors increase or decrease with X, they are **heteroscedastic.** The most common implication of non-constant variance (when variance increases with the values of X) is to produce test statistics with values that are larger than they should be and confidence intervals that are narrower than they should be. This would make you believe that the results of your regression analysis are more significant than they really are. For a bivariate regression, you can see if heteroscedasticity is present on the XY scatter plot, but a more general visual test is to plot the residuals against their x-values. Ideally, there should be no pattern of increasing or decreasing residuals as we move from left to right.

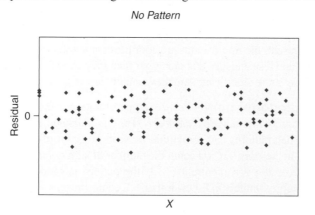

Notice that the residuals *always* have a mean of zero. Although many patterns of non-constant variance might exist, the "fan-out" pattern (increasing residual variance) is most common:

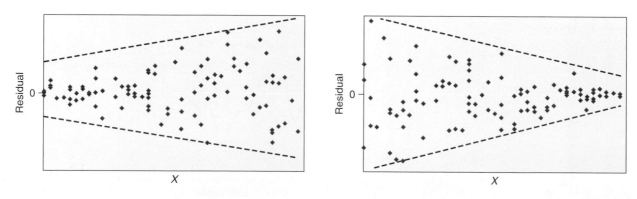

FIGURE 13.25

Cockpit Noise Residual Plot

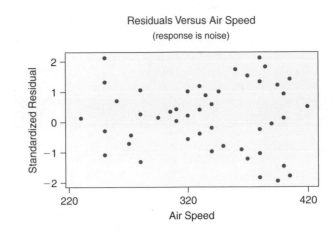

Residuals Versus Air Speed
(response is noise)

Residual plots provide a fairly sensitive "eyeball test" for heteroscedasticity. The residual plot is therefore considered an important tool in the statistician's diagnostic kit. The hypotheses are

H_0: Errors have constant variance (homoscedastic).

H_1: Errors have non-constant variance (heteroscedastic).

Figure 13.25 shows a residual plot for Mini Case 13.2 (cockpit noise). In the residual plot, we see residuals of the same magnitude as we look from left to right. A random pattern like this is consistent with the hypothesis of homoscedasticity (constant variance), although some observers might see a hint of a "fan-out" pattern.

Autocorrelated Errors

Autocorrelation is a pattern of non-independent errors, mainly found in time-series data. In a time-series regression, each residual e_t should be independent of its predecessors $e_{t-1}, e_{t-2}, \ldots,$ e_{t-n}. Violations of this assumption can show up in different ways. In the simple model of *first-order autocorrelation,* we would find that e_t is correlated with the prior residual e_{t-1}. If positive autocorrelation is present, the implications are confidence intervals that are narrower than they should normally be and test statistics that are larger than they should be, resulting in you thinking that the results are more significant than they actually are.

Runs Test for Autocorrelation   *Positive* autocorrelation is indicated by runs of residuals with the *same* sign, while *negative autocorrelation* is indicated by runs of residuals with *alternating* signs. Such patterns can sometimes be seen in a plot of the residuals against the order of data entry. In the *runs test,* we count the number of sign reversals (i.e., how often does the residual plot cross the zero centreline?). If the pattern is random, the number of sign changes should be approximately $n/2$. Fewer than $n/2$ centreline crossings would suggest positive autocorrelation, while more than $n/2$ centreline crossings would suggest negative autocorrelation. For example, if $n = 50$, we would expect about 25 centreline crossings. In the first illustration, there are only 11 crossings (positive autocorrelation) while in the second illustration there are 36 crossings (negative autocorrelation). Positive autocorrelation is common in economic time-series regressions, due to the cyclical nature of the economy. It is harder to envision logical reasons for negative autocorrelation, and in fact it is rarely observed.

Positive Autocorrelation (Common)

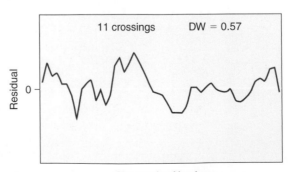

Observation Number

Negative Autocorrelation (Unusual)

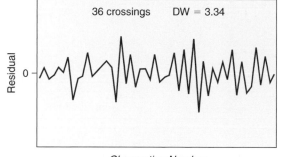

Durbin-Watson Test The most widely used test for autocorrelation is the **Durbin-Watson test.** The hypotheses are

H_0: Errors are non-autocorrelated.

H_1: Errors are autocorrelated.

The Durbin-Watson test statistic for autocorrelation is

$$DW = \frac{\sum_{t=2}^{n}(e_t - e_{t-1})^2}{\sum_{t=1}^{n}e_t^2} \quad \text{(Durbin-Watson test statistic)} \tag{13.25}$$

When there is no autocorrelation, the DW statistic will be near 2, though its range is from 0 to 4. For a formal hypothesis test, a special table is required. For now, we simply note that, in general,

$DW < 2$ suggests positive autocorrelation (common).

$DW \approx 2$ suggests no autocorrelation (ideal).

$DW > 2$ suggests negative autocorrelation (rare).

In a regression, we look for observations that are unusual. An observation could be unusual because its Y value is poorly predicted by the regression model (*unusual residual*) or because its unusual X value greatly affects the regression line (*high leverage*). Tests for unusual residuals and high leverage are important diagnostic tools in evaluating the fitted regression.

13.9 Unusual Observations

Standardized Residuals: Excel

Excel's Data > Data Analysis > Regression provides residuals as an option, as shown in Figure 13.26. Because every regression may have different Y units (e.g., stock price in dollars, shipping time in days) it is helpful to *standardize* the residuals by dividing each residual by its standard error. As a rule of thumb (the Empirical Rule), any *standardized residual* whose absolute value is 2 or more is unusual and any residual whose absolute value is 3 or more would be considered an outlier. Excel obtains its "standardized residuals" by dividing each residual by the standard deviation of the column of residuals. This procedure is not quite correct, as explained below, but generally suffices to identify unusual residuals. Using the Empirical Rule, there are no unusual standardized residuals in Figure 13.26.

Studentized Residuals: MINITAB

MINITAB gives you the same general output as Excel, but with rounded results and more detailed residual information. Its menus are shown in Figure 13.27. MINITAB uses **studentized residuals,** obtained by dividing each residual by its *true standard error.* This calculation requires a unique adjustment for each residual, based on the observation's distance from the mean. Studentized residuals usually are close to Excel's "standardized" residuals.

FIGURE 13.26 Excel's Exam Score Regression with Residuals ExamScores

SUMMARY OUTPUT

Regression Statistics	
Multiple R	0.627790986
R Square	0.394121523
Adjusted R Square	0.318386713
Standard Error	14.00249438
Observations	10

ANOVA

	df	SS	MS	F	Significance F
Regression	1	1020.34121	1020.34121	5.203967954	0.051972204
Residual	8	1568.55879	196.0698488		
Total	9	2588.9			

	Coefficients	Standard Error	t Stat	P-value	Lower 95%	Upper 95%
Intercept	49.47712665	10.06646125	4.915046652	0.001171307	26.26381038	72.69044293
Study Hours	1.964083176	0.86097902	2.281220716	0.051972204	-0.021339288	3.94950564

RESIDUAL OUTPUT

Observation	Predicted Score	Residuals	Standard Residuals
1	51.44120983	1.55879017	0.118075152
2	59.29754253	14.70245747	1.113680937
3	63.22570888	-4.225708885	-0.320088764
4	65.18979206	-22.18979206	-1.680831145
5	69.11795841	-13.11795841	-0.99365839
6	71.08204159	12.91795841	0.978508801
7	76.97429112	19.02570888	1.441158347
8	78.93837429	-9.938374291	-0.752811428
9	78.93837429	5.061625709	0.383407745
10	86.79470699	-3.794706994	-0.287441256

MINITAB's results confirm that there are no unusual residuals in the exam score regression. An attractive feature of MINITAB is that actual and fitted Y values are displayed (Excel shows only the fitted Y values). MINITAB also gives the standard error for the mean of Y (the output column labelled SE Fit), which you can multiply by t to get the confidence interval width.

Studentized Residuals: MegaStat

MegaStat gives you the same general output as Excel and MINITAB. Its regression menu is shown in Figure 13.28. Like MINITAB, it offers studentized residuals, as well as several other residual diagnostics that we will discuss shortly. Also like MINITAB, MegaStat rounds off things to make the output more readable. It also highlights significant items.

FIGURE 13.27 MINITAB's Regression with Residuals ExamScores

Regression Analysis: Score versus Hours

The regression equation is
Score = 49.5 + 1.96 Hours

Predictor	Coef	SE Coef	T	P
Constant	49.48	10.07	4.92	0.001
Hours	1.9641	0.8610	2.28	0.052

S = 14.0025   R-Sq = 39.4%   R-Sq(adj) = 31.8%

Analysis of Variance

Source	DF	SS	MS	F	P
Regression	1	1020.3	1020.3	5.20	0.052
Residual Error	8	1568.6	196.1		
Total	9	2588.9			

Obs	Hours	Score	Fit	SE Fit	Residual	St Resid
1	1.0	53.00	51.44	9.30	1.56	0.15
2	5.0	74.00	59.30	6.48	14.70	1.18
3	7.0	59.00	63.23	5.36	-4.23	-0.33
4	8.0	43.00	65.19	4.92	-22.19	-1.69
5	10.0	56.00	69.12	4.45	-13.12	-0.99
6	11.0	84.00	71.08	4.45	12.92	0.97
7	14.0	96.00	76.97	5.36	19.03	1.47
8	15.0	69.00	78.94	5.88	-9.94	-0.78
9	15.0	84.00	78.94	5.88	5.06	0.40
10	19.0	83.00	86.79	8.55	-3.79	-0.34

MegaStat's Regression with Residuals ExamScores FIGURE 13.28

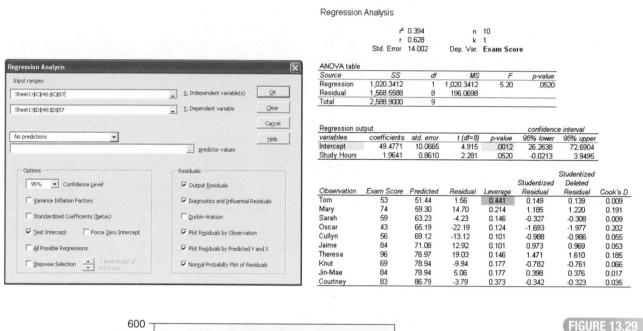

Regression Analysis

r²	0.394	n	10
r	0.628	k	1
Std. Error	14.002	Dep. Var.	**Exam Score**

ANOVA table

Source	SS	df	MS	F	p-value
Regression	1,020.3412	1	1,020.3412	5.20	.0520
Residual	1,568.5588	8	196.0698		
Total	2,588.9000	9			

Regression output

variables	coefficients	std. error	t (df=8)	p-value	confidence interval 95% lower	95% upper
Intercept	49.4771	10.0665	4.915	.0012	26.2638	72.6904
Study Hours	1.9641	0.8610	2.281	.0520	-0.0213	3.9495

Observation	Exam Score	Predicted	Residual	Leverage	Studentized Residual	Studentized Deleted Residual	Cook's D
Tom	53	51.44	1.56	0.441	0.149	0.139	0.009
Mary	74	59.30	14.70	0.214	1.185	1.220	0.191
Sarah	59	63.23	-4.23	0.146	-0.327	-0.308	0.009
Oscar	43	65.19	-22.19	0.124	-1.693	-1.977	0.202
Cullyn	56	69.12	-13.12	0.101	-0.988	-0.986	0.055
Jaime	84	71.08	12.92	0.101	0.973	0.969	0.053
Theresa	96	76.97	19.03	0.146	1.471	1.610	0.185
Knut	69	78.94	-9.94	0.177	-0.782	-0.761	0.066
Jin-Mae	84	78.94	5.06	0.177	0.398	0.376	0.017
Courtney	83	86.79	-3.79	0.373	-0.342	-0.323	0.035

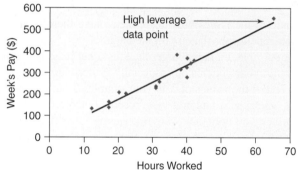

FIGURE 13.29

Illustration of High Leverage Leverage

Leverage and Influence

A high **leverage** statistic indicates that the observation is far from the mean of X. Such observations have great influence on the regression estimates, because they are at the "end of the lever." Figure 13.29 illustrates this concept. One individual worked 65 hours, while the others worked between 12 and 42 hours. This individual will have a big effect on the slope estimate, because he is so far above the mean of X. Yet this highly leveraged data point is *not* an outlier (i.e., the fitted regression line comes very close to the data point, so its residual will be small).

The leverage for observation i is denoted h_i and is calculated as

$$h_i = \frac{1}{n} + \frac{(x_i - \bar{x})^2}{\sum_{i=1}^{n}(x_i - \bar{x})^2} \tag{13.26}$$

As a rule of thumb, a leverage statistic that exceeds $4/n$ is unusual (note that if $x_i = \bar{x}$ the leverage statistic h_i is $1/n$, so the rule of thumb is just four times this value).

We see from Figure 13.30 that two data points (Tom and Courtney) are likely to have high leverage because Tom studied for only 1 hour (far below the mean) while Courtney studied for 19 hours (far above the mean). Using the information in Table 13.4, we can calculate their leverages:

ExamScores

$$h_{\text{Tom}} = \frac{1}{10} + \frac{(1 - 10.5)^2}{264.50} = 0.441 \quad (\text{Tom's leverage})$$

EXAMPLE 3

Exam Scores: Leverage and Influence

$$h_{\text{Courtney}} = \frac{1}{10} + \frac{(19 - 10.5)^2}{264.50} = 0.373 \quad \text{(Courtney's leverage)}$$

Leverage values for both Tom and Courtney are large, so these two observations are *influential*. Yet despite their high leverages, the regression fits Tom's and Courtney's actual exam scores well, so their *residuals* are not unusual. This illustrates that *high leverage* and *unusual residuals* are two different concepts.

Scatter Plot for Exam Data
  ExamScores

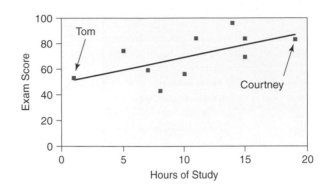

13.10 Another Regression Problem

In addition to some of the issues previously mentioned, there is another problem that may cause you to reach conclusions that are problematic.

Outliers (residuals that are much larger than the other residuals in the model) may have a significant impact on your conclusions especially if these large residuals occur at the lower end or the upper end of the values of X in your sample. If outliers do occur, you should first check to see if the values of X and/or Y were recorded incorrectly. If so, correct the values. If the values are correct, you may then want to check whether this observation could be eliminated for some legitimate reason. For example, if you were studying the relationship between starting salaries after graduation and GPA, and you find that most residuals lie within $\pm\$10,000$ and there is one residual whose value is \$3,500,000, you should look at this individual more closely. If his starting salary was recorded correctly but the student is 7 feet tall, can make three-point shots 80 percent of the time, and has just signed a multi-year contract with the Toronto Raptors, you would have a legitimate reason for removing this individual from your study. *But you should not remove individual observations without justifiable and defendable reasons.*

A Closer Look

When you run a simple linear regression model to study the true effect of X has on Y, you assume some relationship between X and Y. If this assumption is incorrect, you are using the wrong model, or you are misspecifying the model, and the resulting conclusions have a good chance of being meaningless. For example, you may assume that there is only one variable that has an effect on Y when there are other variables that also affect Y. This is a misspecification of the model and you may, for example, conclude that X has a positive effect on Y when it may really have a negative impact. You may assume that Y is linearly related to X when it is actually linearly related to X^2. This is another way of misspecifying the model. For your results to be reliable and defendable, your model must be correctly specified. How do you know that your model is correctly specified? You may never know! (That is why different studies may reach different conclusions.) To reduce the chances of misspecification, your model should have some sound theoretical background.

CHAPTER SUMMARY

The **sample correlation coefficient** r measures linear association between X and Y, with values near 0 indicating a lack of linearity while values near -1 (negative correlation) or $+1$ (positive correlation) suggest linearity. The **t test** is used to test hypotheses about the **population correlation** ρ. In **bivariate regression** there is an assumed linear relationship between the independent variable X (the **predictor**) and the dependent variable Y (the **response**). The slope (β_1) and intercept (β_0) are unknown **parameters** that are estimated from a sample. **Residuals** are the differences between **observed** and **fitted** Y values. The **ordinary least squares** (OLS) method yields **regression coefficients** for the slope (b_1) and intercept (b_0) that minimize the sum of squared residuals. The **coefficient of determination** (R^2) measures the overall fit of the regression, with R^2 near 1 signifying a good fit and R^2 near 0 indicating a poor fit. The **F statistic** in the **ANOVA table** is used to test for significant overall regression, while the **t statistics** (and their p values) are used to test hypotheses about the slope and intercept. The **standard error** of the regression is used to create **confidence intervals** or **prediction intervals** for Y. Regression assumes that the errors are independent and normally distributed random variables with constant variance σ^2. **Residual tests** identify possible **violations** of assumptions (**non-normality, autocorrelation, heteroscedasticity**). Data values with high **leverage** (unusual X values) have strong influence on the regression. Unusual **standardized residuals** indicate cases where the regression gives a poor fit.

KEY TERMS

autocorrelation, *576*
bivariate data, *537*
bivariate regression, *544*
coefficient of determination
  (R^2), *553*
confidence interval, *571*
Durbin-Watson test, *577*
error sum of squares, *552*
fitted model, *546*
fitted regression, *545*
heteroscedastic, *575*

homoscedastic, *575*
intercept, *546*
leverage, *579*
non-normality, *573*
ordinary least squares
  (OLS), *550*
outliers, *580*
population correlation
  coefficient (ρ), *539*
prediction interval, *571*
residual, *546*

sample correlation coefficient
  (r), *537*
scatter plot, *537*
slope, *546*
standard error, *557*
standardized residuals, *574*
studentized residuals, *577*
sums of squares, *538*
t statistic, *539*

Commonly Used Formulas in Simple Regression

Sample correlation coefficient: $r = \dfrac{\sum_{i=1}^{n}(x_i - \bar{x})(y_i - \bar{y})}{\sqrt{\sum_{i=1}^{n}(x_i - \bar{x})^2}\sqrt{\sum_{i=1}^{n}(y_i - \bar{y})^2}}$

Test statistic for zero correlation: $t_{\text{calc}} = r\sqrt{\dfrac{n-2}{1-r^2}}$

True regression line: $y_i = \beta_0 + \beta_1 x_i + \varepsilon_i$

Fitted regression line: $\hat{y}_i = b_0 + b_1 x_i$

Slope of fitted regression: $b_1 = \dfrac{\sum_{i=1}^{n}(x_i - \bar{x})(y_i - \bar{y})}{\sum_{i=1}^{n}(x_i - \bar{x})^2}$

Intercept of fitted regression: $b_0 = \bar{y} - b_1\bar{x}$

Sum of squared residuals: $SSE = \sum_{i=1}^{n}(y_i - \hat{y}_i)^2 = \sum_{i=1}^{n}(y_i - b_0 - b_1 x_i)^2$

Coefficient of determination: $R^2 = 1 - \dfrac{\sum_{i=1}^{n}(y_i - \hat{y}_i)^2}{\sum_{i=1}^{n}(y_i - \bar{y})^2} = 1 - \dfrac{SSE}{SST} = \dfrac{SSR}{SST}$

$$\text{Standard error of the estimate: } s = \sqrt{\frac{\sum_{i=1}^{n}(y_i - \hat{y}_i)^2}{n-2}} = \sqrt{\frac{SSE}{n-2}}$$

$$\text{Standard error of the slope: } s_{b_1} = \frac{s}{\sqrt{\sum_{i=1}^{n}(x_i - \bar{x})^2}}$$

$$\text{Test for zero slope: } t_{\text{calc}} = \frac{b_1}{s_{b_1}}$$

$$\text{Confidence interval for true slope: } b_1 - t_{\alpha/2, n-2} s_{b_1} \leq \beta_1 \leq b_1 + t_{\alpha/2, n-2} s_{b_1}$$

$$\text{Confidence interval for conditional mean of } Y: \hat{y} \pm t_{\alpha/2, n-2}\, s \sqrt{\frac{1}{n} + \frac{(x_g - \bar{x})^2}{\sum_{i=1}^{n}(x_i - \bar{x})^2}}$$

$$\text{Prediction interval for } Y: \hat{y} \pm t_{\alpha/2, n-2} s \sqrt{1 + \frac{1}{n} + \frac{(x_g - \bar{x})^2}{\sum_{i=1}^{n}(x_i - \bar{x})^2}}$$

CHAPTER REVIEW

1. (a) How does correlation analysis differ from regression analysis? (b) What does a correlation coefficient reveal (c) What sums are needed to calculate a correlation coefficient? (LO 1)

2. (a) What is a bivariate regression model? Must it be linear? (b) State three caveats about regression. (c) What does the random error component in a regression model represent? (d) What is the difference between a regression residual and the true random error? (LO 1)

3. (a) Explain how you fit a regression to an Excel scatter plot. (b) What are the limitations of Excel's scatter plot fitted regression? (LO 3)

4. (a) Explain the logic of the ordinary least squares (OLS) method. (b) How are the least squares formulas for the slope and intercept derived? (c) What sums are needed to calculate the least squares estimates? (LO 2)

5. (a) Why can't we use the sum of the residuals to assess fit? (b) What sums are needed to calculate R^2? (c) Name an advantage of using the R^2 statistic instead of the standard error s to measure fit. (d) Why do we need the standard error s? (LO 2)

6. (a) Explain why a confidence interval for the slope or intercept would be equivalent to a two-tailed hypothesis test. (b) Why is it especially important to test for a zero slope? (LO 2)

7. (a) What does the F statistic show? (b) What is its range? (c) What is the relationship between the F test and the t tests for the slope and correlation coefficient? (LO 6)

8. (a) For a given X, explain the distinction between a confidence interval for the conditional mean of Y and a prediction interval for an individual Y value. (b) Why is the individual prediction interval wider? (c) Why are these intervals narrowest when X is near its mean? (LO 7)

9. (a) What is a residual? (b) What is a standardized residual and why is it useful? (c) Name two alternative ways to identify unusual residuals. (LO 7)

10. (a) When does a data point have high leverage (refer to the scatter plot)? (b) Name one test for unusual leverage. (LO 8)

11. (a) Name three assumptions about the random error term in the regression model. (b) Why are the residuals important in testing these assumptions? (LO 8)

12. (a) What are the consequences of non-normal errors? (b) Explain two tests for non-normality. (c) What can we do about non-normal residuals? (LO 8)

13. (a) What is heteroscedasticity? Identify its two common forms. (b) What are its consequences? (c) How do we test for it?

14. (a) What is autocorrelation? Identify two main forms of it. (b) What are its consequences? (c) Name two ways to test for it. (d) What can we do about it? (LO 8)

15. (a) Why might there be outliers in the residuals? (b) What actions could be taken? (LO 8)

CHAPTER EXERCISES

Instructions: Choose one or more of the data sets A–G below, or as assigned by your instructor. Choose the dependent variable (the *response variable* to be "explained") and the independent variable (the *predictor* or *explanatory variable*) as you judge appropriate. Use a spreadsheet or a statistical package (e.g., MegaStat or MINITAB) to obtain the bivariate regression and required graphs. Write your answers to Exercise 13.32 (a) through (p) (or those assigned by your instructor) in a concise report, labelling your answers to each question. Insert tables and graphs in your report as appropriate.

13.32 (a) Are the variables cross-sectional data or time-series data?

(b) How do you imagine the data were collected?

(c) Is the sample size sufficient to yield a good estimate? If not, do you think more data could easily be obtained, given the nature of the problem?

(d) State your *a priori* hypothesis about the sign of the slope. Is it reasonable to suppose a cause and effect relationship?

(e) Make a scatter plot of Y against X. Discuss what it tells you.

(f) Use Excel's Add Trendline feature to fit a linear regression to the scatter plot. Is a linear model credible?

(g) Interpret the slope. Does the intercept have meaning, given the range of the data?

(h) Use Excel, MegaStat, or MINITAB to fit the regression model, including residuals and standardized residuals.

(i) (i) Does the 95 percent confidence interval for the slope include zero? What does it mean? (ii) Do a two-tailed t test for zero slope at $\alpha = 0.05$. State the hypotheses, degrees of freedom, and critical value for your test. (iii) Interpret the p value for the slope. (iv) Which approach do you prefer, the t test or the p value? Why? (v) Did the sample support your hypothesis about the sign of the slope?

(j) (i) Based on R^2 and the ANOVA table for your model, how would you assess the fit? (ii) Interpret the p value for the F statistic. (iii) Would you say that your model's fit is good enough to be of practical value?

(k) Study the table of residuals. Identify as *outliers* any standardized residuals that exceed 3 and identify as *unusual* any that exceed 2. Can you suggest any reasons for these unusual residuals?

(l) (i) Make a histogram (or normal probability plot) of the residuals and discuss its appearance. (ii) Do you see evidence that your regression may violate the assumption of normal errors?

(m) Inspect the residual plot to check for heteroscedasticity and report your conclusions.

(n) Is an autocorrelation test appropriate for your data? If so, perform one or more tests of the residuals (eyeball inspection of residual plot against observation order, runs test, and/or Durbin-Watson test).

(o) Use MegaStat or MINITAB to generate 95 percent confidence and prediction intervals for various X values.

(p) Use MegaStat or MINITAB to identify observations with high leverage.

DATA SET A **Employees and Revenue in Large Automotive Companies in 1999 ($n = 24$ companies) CarFirms**

Company	Employees	Revenue
BMW	119.9	35.9
DaimlerChrysler	441.5	154.6
Dana	86.4	12.8
⋮	⋮	⋮
TRW	78.0	11.9
Volkswagen	297.9	76.3
Volvo	70.3	26.8

Source: Project by statistics students Paul Ruskin, Kristy Bielewski, and Linda Stengel.

Note: Employees are in thousands and *Revenue* is in billions.

DATA SET B Estimated and Actual Length of Stay in Months ($n = 16$ patients) Hospital

Patient	ELOS	ALOS
1	10.5	10
2	4.5	2
3	7.5	4
⋮	⋮	⋮
14	6	10
15	7.5	7
16	3	5.5

Source: Records of a hospital outpatient cognitive retraining clinic.
Note: ELOS used a 42-item assessment instrument combined with expert team judgment. Patients had suffered head trauma, stroke, or other medical conditions affecting cognitive function.

DATA SET C Single-Engine Aircraft Performance ($n = 52$ airplanes) Airplanes

Mfgr/Model	Cruise	TotalHP
AMD CH 2000	100	116
Beech Baron 58	200	600
Beech Baron 58P	241	650
⋮	⋮	⋮
Sky Arrow 650 TC	98	81
Socata TB20 Trinidad	163	250
Tiger AG-5B	143	180

Source: New and used airplane reports in *Flying* (various issues).
Note: Cruise is in knots (nautical miles per hour). Data are for educational purposes only and should not be used as a guide to aircraft performance. *TotalHP* is total horsepower.

DATA SET D Mileage and Vehicle Weight ($n = 43$ vehicles) MPG

Vehicle	City MPG	Weight
Acura CL	20	3,450
Accura TSX	23	3,320
BMW 3-Series	19	3,390
⋮	⋮	⋮
Toyota Sienna	19	4,120
Volkswagen Jetta	34	3,045
Volvo C70	20	3,690

Source: *Consumer Reports New Car Buying Guide 2003–2004* (Consumers Union, 2003).
Note: Sample is the first vehicle on every 5th page starting at page 40. Data are for statistical education only and should not be viewed as a guide to vehicle performance.

DATA SET E Pasta Sauce per Gram Total Calories and Fat Calories ($n = 20$ products) Pasta

Product	Cal/g	Fat Cal/g
Barilla Roasted Garlic & Onion	0.64	0.20
Barilla Tomato & Basil	0.56	0.12
Classico Tomato & Basil	0.40	0.08
⋮	⋮	⋮
Ragu Roasted Garlic	0.70	0.19
Ragu Traditional	0.56	0.20
Sutter Home Tomato & Garlic	0.64	0.16

Source: Independent project by statistics students Donna Bennett, Nicole Cook, Latrice Haywood, and Robert Malcolm.
Note: Data are intended for educational purposes only and should not be viewed as a nutrition guide.

DATA SET F Electric Bills and Consumption for a Residence (*n* = 24 months) Electric

Month	Usage (kWh)	Avg Temp (°F)
1	436	62
2	464	71
3	446	76
⋮	⋮	⋮
22	840	25
23	867	38
24	606	48

Source: Electric bills for a residence and NOAA weather data.

DATA SET G Life Expectancy and Birth Rates (*n* = 153 nations) BirthRates

Nation	Life Expectancy	Birth Rate
Afghanistan	46.6	41.03
Albania	72.1	18.59
Algeria	70.2	22.34
⋮	⋮	⋮
Yemen	60.6	43.30
Zambia	37.4	41.01
Zimbabwe	36.5	24.59

Source: Central Intelligence Agency, *The World Factbook, 2003.*

13.33 Researchers found a correlation coefficient of $r = 0.50$ on personality measures for identical twins. A reporter interpreted this to mean that "the environment orchestrated one-half of their personality differences." Do you agree with this interpretation? Discuss. (See *Science News* 140 [Dec. 7, 1991], p. 377.) (LO 1)

13.34 A study of the role of spreadsheets in planning in 55 small firms defined Y = "satisfaction with sales growth" and X = "executive commitment to planning." Analysis yielded an overall correlation of $r = 0.3043$. Do a two-tailed test for zero correlation at $\alpha = 0.05$. (LO 1)

13.35 In a study of stock prices from 1970 to 1994, the correlation between Nasdaq closing prices on successive days (i.e., with a one-day lag) was $r = 0.13$ with a t statistic of 5.47. Interpret this result. (See David Nawrocki, "The Problems with Monte Carlo Simulation," *Journal of Financial Planning* 14, no. 11 [Nov. 2001], p. 96.) (LO 1)

13.36 Regression analysis of free throws by 29 NBA teams during the 2002–2003 season revealed the fitted regression $Y = 55.2 + 0.73X$ ($R^2 = 0.874$, $s = 53.2$) where Y = total free throws made and X = total free throws attempted. The observed range of X was from 1,620 (New York Knicks) to 2,382 (Golden State Warriors). (a) Find the expected number of free throws made for a team that shoots 2,000 free throws. (b) Do you think that the intercept is meaningful? *Hint:* Make a scatter plot and let Excel fit the line. (LO 3) **FreeThrows**

13.37 In the following regression, X = weekly pay, Y = income tax withheld, and n = 35 McDonald's employees. (a) Write the fitted regression equation. (b) State the degrees of freedom for a two-tailed test for zero slope, and use Appendix D to find the critical value at $\alpha = 0.05$. (c) What is your conclusion about the slope? (d) Interpret the 95 percent confidence limits for the slope. (e) Verify that $F = t^2$ for the slope. (f) In your own words, describe the fit of this regression. (g) Why might a one-tailed test be more appropriate in this case? If it is more appropriate, should it be a left-tailed or a right-tailed test? Explain. (LO 4)

R²	0.202
Std. Error	6.816
n	35

ANOVA table

Source	SS	df	MS	F	p-value
Regression	387.6959	1	387.6959	8.35	0.0068
Residual	1,533.0614	33	46.4564		
Total	1,920.7573	34			

Regression output

variables	coefficients	std. error	t (df = 33)	p-value	confidence interval 95% lower	95% upper
Intercept	30.7963	6.4078	4.806	0.0000	17.7595	43.8331
Slope	0.0343	0.0119	2.889	0.0068	0.0101	0.0584

13.38 In the following regression, $X =$ monthly maintenance spending (dollars), $Y =$ monthly machine downtime (hours), and $n = 15$ copy machines. (a) Write the fitted regression equation. (b) State the degrees of freedom for a two-tailed test for zero slope, and use Appendix D to find the critical value at $\alpha = 0.05$. (c) What is your conclusion about the slope? (d) Interpret the 95 percent confidence limits for the slope. (e) Verify that $F = t^2$ for the slope. (f) In your own words, describe the fit of this regression. (g) Why might a one-tailed test be more appropriate in this case? If it is more appropriate, should it be a left-tailed or a right-tailed test? Explain. (LO 4)

R²	0.370
Std. Error	286.793
n	15

ANOVA table

Source	SS	df	MS	F	p-value
Regression	628,298.2	1	628,298.2	7.64	0.0161
Residual	1,069,251.8	13	82,250.1		
Total	1,697,550.0	14			

Regression output

variables	coefficients	std. error	t (df = 13)	p-value	confidence interval 95% lower	95% upper
Intercept	1,743.57	288.82	6.037	0.0000	1,119.61	2,367.53
Slope	−1.2163	0.4401	−2.764	0.0161	−2.1671	−0.2656

13.39 In the following regression, $X =$ total assets ($ billions), $Y =$ total revenue ($ billions), and $n = 64$ large banks. (a) Write the fitted regression equation. (b) State the degrees of freedom for a two-tailed test for zero slope, and use Appendix D to find the critical value at $\alpha = 0.05$. (c) What is your conclusion about the slope? (d) Interpret the 95 percent confidence limits for the slope. (e) Verify that $F = t^2$ for the slope. (f) In your own words, describe the fit of this regression. (g) Why might a one-tailed test be more appropriate in this case? If it is more appropriate, should it be a left-tailed or a right-tailed test? Explain. (LO 4)

R²	0.519				
Std. Error	6.977				
n	64				

ANOVA table

Source	SS	df	MS	F	p-value
Regression	3,260.0981	1	3,260.0981	66.97	1.90E-11
Residual	3,018.3339	62	48.6828		
Total	6,278.4320	63			

Regression output   *confidence interval*

variables	coefficients	std. error	t (df = 62)	p-value	95% lower	95% upper
Intercept	6.5763	1.9254	3.416	0.0011	2.7275	10.4252
X1	0.0452	0.0055	8.183	1.90E-11	0.0342	0.0563

13.40 Do stock prices of competing companies move together? Below are daily closing prices of two computer services firms (IBM = International Business Machines Corporation, EDS = Electronic Data Systems Corporation). (a) Calculate the sample correlation coefficient (e.g., using Excel or MegaStat). (b) At $\alpha = 0.01$ can you conclude that the true correlation coefficient is greater than zero? (c) Make a scatter plot of the data. What does it say? (Data are from The Center for Research and Security Prices, University of Chicago.) (LO 1)   **StockPrices**

Daily Closing Price ($) of Two Stocks in October and November 2004 ($n = 42$ days)

Date	IBM	EDS
9/1/04	84.22	19.31
9/2/04	84.57	19.63
9/3/04	84.39	19.19
⋮	⋮	⋮
10/27/04	90.00	21.26
10/28/04	89.50	21.41
10/29/04	89.75	21.27

13.41 Below are percentages for *annual sales growth* and *net sales attributed to loyalty card usage* at 74 Noodles & Company restaurants. (a) Make a scatter plot. (b) Find the correlation coefficient and interpret it. (c) Test the correlation coefficient for significance (at $\alpha = 0.05$), clearly stating the degrees of freedom. (d) Does it appear that loyalty card usage is associated with increased sales growth? (LO 1)   **Loyalty Card**   **Noodles & Company**

Annual Sales Growth (%) and Loyalty Card Usage (% of Net Sales) ($n = 74$ restaurants)

Store	Growth %	Loyalty %
1	−8.3	2.1
2	−4.0	2.5
3	−3.9	1.7
⋮	⋮	⋮
72	20.8	1.1
73	25.5	0.6
74	28.8	1.8

Source: Noodles & Company

13.42   Below are fertility rates (average children born per woman) in 15 EU nations for 2 years. (a) Make a scatter plot. (b) Find the correlation coefficient and interpret it. (c) Test the correlation coefficient for significance (at $\alpha = 0.05$), clearly stating the degrees of freedom. (Data are from the World Health Organization.) (LO 1)   **Fertility**

Fertility Rates for EU Nations ($n = 15$)

Nation	1990	2000
Austria	1.5	1.3
Belgium	1.6	1.5
Denmark	1.6	1.7
⋮	⋮	⋮
Spain	1.4	1.1
Sweden	2.0	1.4
U.K.	1.8	1.7

13.43   Consider the following prices and accuracy ratings for 27 stereo speakers. (a) Make a scatter plot of accuracy rating as a function of price. (b) Calculate the correlation coefficient. At $\alpha = 0.05$, does the correlation differ from zero? (c) In your own words, describe the scatter plot. (Data are from *Consumer Reports* 68, no. 11 [Nov. 2003], p. 31. Data are intended for statistical education and not as a guide to speaker performance.) (LO 1)   **Speakers**

Price and Accuracy of Selected Stereo Speakers ($n = 27$)

Brand and Model	Type	Price ($)	Accuracy
BIC America Venturi DV62si	Shelf	200	91
Bose 141	Shelf	100	86
Bose 201 Series V	Shelf	220	89
⋮	⋮	⋮	⋮
Sony SS-MB350H	Shelf	100	92
Sony SS-MF750H	Floor	280	91
Sony SS-X30ED	Shelf	500	83

13.44   Choose *one* of these three data sets. (a) Make a scatter plot. (b) Let Excel estimate the regression line, with fitted equation and R^2. (c) Describe the fit of the regression. (d) Write the fitted regression equation and interpret the slope. (e) Do you think that the estimated intercept is meaningful? Explain. (LO 3 & 4)

Commercial Real Estate (X = assessed value, $000; Y = floor space, sq. ft.) ($n = 15$)
Assessed

Assessed	Size
1,796	4,790
1,544	4,720
2,094	5,940
⋮	⋮
1,678	4,880
710	1,620
678	1,820

Salaries

Employee	Salary
Mary	28.6
Frieda	53.3
Alicia	73.8
⋮	⋮
Marcia	75.8
Ellen	79.8
Iggy	70.2

Poway Big Homes, Ltd. (X = home size, sq. ft.; Y = selling price, $000) ($n = 20$)
HomePrice2

SqFt	Price
3,570	861
3,410	740
2,690	563
⋮	⋮
3,020	720
2,320	575
3,130	785

13.45 Bivariate regression was employed to establish the effects of childhood exposure to lead. The effective sample size was about 122 subjects. The independent variable was the level of dentin lead (parts per million). Below are regressions using various dependent variables. (a) Calculate the t statistic for each slope. (b) From the p values, which slopes differ from zero at $\alpha = 0.01$? (c) Do you feel that cause and effect can be assumed? *Hint:* Do a Web search for information about effects of childhood lead exposure. (Data are from H. L. Needleman et al., *The New England Journal of Medicine* 322, no. 2 [Jan. 1990], p. 86.) (LO 5)

Dependent Variable	R^2	Estimated Slope	Std Error	p Value
Highest grade achieved	0.061	−0.027	0.009	0.008
Reading grade equivalent	0.121	−0.070	0.018	0.000
Class standing	0.039	−0.006	0.003	0.048
Absence from school	0.071	4.8	1.7	0.006
Grammatical reasoning	0.051	0.159	0.062	0.012
Vocabulary	0.108	−0.124	0.032	0.000
Hand-eye coordination	0.043	0.041	0.018	0.020
Reaction time	0.025	11.8	6.66	0.080
Minor antisocial behaviour	0.025	−0.639	0.36	0.082

13.46 Consider the following data on 20 chemical reactions, with Y = chromatographic retention time (seconds) and X = molecular weight (g/mole). (a) Make a scatter plot. (b) Use Excel to fit the regression, with fitted equation and R^2. (c) In your own words, describe the fit. (Data provided by John Seeley of Oakland University.) (LO 3) **Chemicals**

Retention Time and Molecular Weight (*n* = 20)

Name	Retention Time	Molecular Weight
alpha-pinene	234.50	136.24
cyclopentene	95.27	68.12
p-diethylbenzene	284.00	134.22
⋮	⋮	⋮
pentane	78.00	72.15
isooctane	136.90	114.23
hexane	106.00	86.18

13.47 A common belief among faculty is that teaching ratings are lower in large classes. Below are MINITAB results from a regression using Y = mean student evaluation of the professor and X = class size for 364 business school classes taught during the 2002–2003 academic year. Ratings are on a scale of 1 (lowest) to 5 (highest). (a) What do these regression results tell you about the relationship between class size and faculty ratings? (b) Is a bivariate model adequate? If not, suggest additional predictors to be considered. (LO 5)

Predictor	Coef	SE Coef	T	P
Constant	4.18378	0.07226	57.90	0.000
Enroll	0.000578	0.002014	0.29	0.774
S = 0.5688	R-Sq = 0.0%	R-Sq(adj) = 0.0%		

13.48 Below are revenue and profit (both in $ billions) for nine large entertainment companies. (a) Make a scatter plot of profit as a function of revenue. (b) Use Excel to fit the regression, with fitted equation and R^2. (c) In your own words, describe the fit. (Data are from *Fortune* 149, no. 7 [Apr. 5, 2005], p. F-50.) (LO 3) **Entertainment**

Revenue and Profit of Entertainment Companies (*n* = 9)

Company	Revenue	Profit
AMC Entertainment	1.792	−0.020
Clear Channel Communication	8.931	1.146
Liberty Media	2.446	−0.978
⋮	⋮	⋮
Univision Communications	1.311	0.155
Viacom	26.585	1.417
Walt Disney	27.061	1.267

13.49 Below are fitted regressions based on used vehicle ads. Observed ranges of X are shown. The assumed regression model is $AskingPrice = f(VehicleAge)$. (a) Interpret the slopes. (b) Are the intercepts meaningful? Explain. (c) Assess the fit of each model. (d) Is a bivariate model adequate to explain vehicle prices? If not, what other predictors might be considered? (Data are from *Detroit's AutoFocus* 4, Issue 38 [Sept. 17–23, 2004]. Data are for educational purposes only and should not be viewed as a guide to vehicle prices.) (LO 5)

Vehicle	n	Intercept	Slope	R^2	Min Age	Max Age
Ford Explorer	31	22,252	−2,452	0.643	2	6
Ford F-150 Pickup	43	26,164	−2,239	0.713	1	37
Ford Mustang	33	21,308	−1,691	0.328	1	10
Ford Taurus	32	13,160	−906	0.679	1	14

13.50 Below are results of a regression of Y = average stock returns (in percent) as a function of X = average price/earnings ratios for the period 1949–1997 (49 years). Separate regressions were done for various holding periods (sample sizes are therefore variable). (a) Summarize what the regression results tell you. (b) Would you anticipate autocorrelation in this type of data? Explain. (Data are from Ruben Trevino and Fiona Robertson, "P/E Ratios and Stock Market Returns," *Journal of Financial Planning* 15, no. 2 [Feb. 2002], p. 78.) (LO 4 & 8)

Holding Period	Intercept	Slope	t	R²	p
1-Year	28.10	−0.92	1.86	0.0688	0.0686
2-Year	26.11	−0.86	2.57	0.1252	0.0136
5-Year	20.67	−0.57	2.99	0.1720	0.0046
8-Year	24.73	−0.94	6.93	0.5459	0.0000
10-Year	24.51	−0.95	8.43	0.6516	0.0000

13.51 Adult height is somewhat predictable from average height of both parents. For females, a commonly used equation is $YourHeight = ParentHeight - 2.5$ while for males the equation is $YourHeight = ParentHeight + 2.5$. (a) Test these equations on yourself (or on somebody else). (b) How well did the equations predict your height? (c) How do you suppose these equations were derived? (LO 2)

13.52 Looking at the health cost study in previous exercises, what type of problem or problems exist that may have a dramatic effect on your results? Explain. (LO 8)

13.53* Quantity discounts are a common feature in many commercial transactions. But when one builds a house, is the price a buyer pays per square metre lower the larger the size of the house? A random sample of 10 similar-style houses in a community north of Toronto was priced and the price per square metre was calculated as follows:

House	Size (m²)	Price/m²
A	150	$1,170
B	172	$1,150
C	183	$1,275
D	145	$1,300
E	225	$1,020
F	252	$1,035
G	197	$1,195
H	250	$1,132
I	289	$1,085
J	305	$900

(a) Plot the data on a scatter plot and comment on the relationship between the price per square metre and the size of the house.

(b) Using Excel, run regression analysis and state the best estimate of the linear relationship between price/m² and the size of the house. Interpret the results.

(c) Calculate the strength of this linear relationship and interpret its value.

(d) Estimate, with 95 percent confidence, the true effect that house size has on price per square metre.

(e) At $\alpha = 0.01$, is there sufficient evidence to indicate that the larger the house, the lower the price per square metre.

(f) Predict the price per square metre for a house that is 200 m².

(g) Estimate the expected price per square metre for houses that are 200 m².

(h) If similar-sized houses were built in a community north of Quebec City, would the same findings for parts (c) through (g) apply? Why or why not?

(i) Should you use this data set to predict a house's price per square metre, or the expected price per square metre, for a house or houses in that same community north of Toronto that are 400 m²? Would you reach the same conclusion that you reached in part (e) for houses in the range of 400 to 600 m²? Explain your answers to both questions.

(j) Looking at the scatter plot or a plot of the residuals, is there anything about the data that should concern you? Why or why not? (LO 2, 4, 5 & 7)

LearningStats Unit 12 Regression I

LearningStats Unit 12 covers correlation and simple bivariate regression. It includes demonstrations of the least squares method, regression formulas, effects of model form and range of *X*, confidence and prediction intervals, violations of assumptions, and examples of student projects. Your instructor may assign specific modules, or you may decide to check them out because the topic sounds interesting.

Topic	LearningStats Modules
Correlation	Overview of Correlation
	Correlation Analysis
Regression	Overview of Simple Regression
	Using Excel for Regression
Ordinary least squares estimators	Least Squares Method Demonstration
	Doing Regression Calculations
	Effect of Model Form
	Effect of *X* Range
Confidence and prediction intervals	Confidence and Prediction Intervals
	Calculations for Confidence Intervals
	Superimposing Many Fitted Regressions
Violations of assumptions	Non-Normal Errors
	Heteroscedastic Errors
	Autocorrelated Errors
	Cochrane-Orcutt Transform
Formulas	Derivation of OLS Estimators
	Formulas for Significance Tests
Student presentations	Birth Rates
	Effects of Urbanization
Tables of critical values	Appendix D—Student's *t*
	Appendix F—*F* Distribution

Key: = PowerPoint = Word = Excel

Visual Statistics

Visual Statistics Modules on Describing Data

Module	Module Name
14	Bivariate Data Analysis
15	Simple Regression
16	Regression Assumptions
18	Regression Models

Visual Statistics modules 14, 15, 16, and 18 (included on your CD) are designed with the following objectives:

Module 14
- Become familiar with ways to display bivariate data.
- Understand measures of association in bivariate data.
- Be able to interpret bivariate regression statistics and assess their significance.

Module 15
- Understand OLS terminology.
- Understand how sample size, standard error, and range of X affect estimation accuracy.
- Understand confidence intervals for $E(y/x)$ and prediction intervals for y/x.

Module 16
- Learn the regression assumptions required to ensure desirable properties for OLS estimators.
- Learn to recognize violations of the regression assumptions.
- Be able to identify the effects of assumption violations.

Module 18
- Know the common variable transformations and their purposes.
- Learn the effects of variable transformations on the fitted regression and statistics of fit.
- Understand polynomial models.

The worktext chapter (included on the CD in PDF format) contains a list of concepts covered, objectives of the module, overview of concepts, illustration of concepts, orientation to module features, learning exercises (basic, intermediate, advanced), learning projects (individual, team), self-evaluation quiz, glossary of terms, and solutions to self-evaluation quiz.

 For solutions to odd-numbered exercises, Exam Review questions, and additional study tools to help you succeed in this course, visit *Connect* at www.mcgrawhillconnect.ca.

Chapter

14

Multiple Regression

Chapter Learning Objectives

When you finish this chapter you should be able to

1. Use Excel to create output for multiple linear regression models.

2. Interpret multiple linear regression outputs in a problem context.

3. Test for the overall usefulness of the model and for individual effects.

4. Incorporate binary variables in regression models and interpret their effects.

5. Detect multicollinearity and assess its effects.

6. Analyze the residuals to check for violations of regression assumptions.

14.1 Multiple Regression

Bivariate or Multivariate?

Chapter 17

Multiple regression extends bivariate regression to include two or more independent variables (or *predictors*). Everything you learned about *bivariate (simple linear) regression* is a special case of multiple regression. The interpretation of multiple regression is similar, except that two-dimensional *X-Y* scatter plots are of limited value in higher-dimensional models. Because all calculations are done by computer, there is no extra computational burden. In fact, statisticians make no distinction between bivariate and multivariate regression—they just call it *regression.*

Multiple regression is required when a single-predictor model is inadequate to describe the true relationship between the dependent variable Y (the response variable) and its potential predictors ($X_1, X_2, X_3, \ldots$). Because multiple predictors usually are relevant, bivariate regression is only used when there is a compelling need for a simple model, or when other predictors have only modest effects and a single logical predictor stands out as doing a very good job all by itself.

Regression Terminology

The **response variable** (Y) is a random variable that is assumed to be related to the k predictors ($X_1, X_2, \ldots, X_k$) by a linear equation called the *population regression model:*

$$Y = \beta_0 + \beta_1 X_1 + \beta_2 X_2 + \cdots + \beta_k X_k + \varepsilon \qquad (14.1)$$

Each value of Y is assumed to differ from the *conditional mean* $E(Y) = \beta_0 + \beta_1 X_1 + \beta_2 X_2 + \cdots + \beta_k X_k$ by a *random error* ε representing everything that is not part of the model. The unknown regression coefficients $\beta_0, \beta_1, \beta_2, \ldots, \beta_k$ are *parameters* and are denoted by Greek letters. Each coefficient β_j (except the intercept β_0) shows the change in the expected value of Y for a unit change in X_j while holding everything else constant (*all else remaining the same*). The errors are assumed to be unobservable, independent random disturbances that are normally distributed with zero mean and constant variance, that is, $\varepsilon \sim N(0, \sigma^2)$. Under these assumptions, the ordinary least squares (OLS) estimation method yields unbiased, consistent, efficient estimates of the unknown parameters. The *sample estimates* of the regression coefficients are denoted by Roman letters $b_0, b_1, b_2, \ldots, b_k$. The *predicted* value of the response variable is denoted $\hat{y}$ and is calculated by inserting the values of the predictors into the *fitted regression equation:*

$$\hat{y} = b_0 + b_1 x_1 + b_2 x_2 + \cdots + b_k x_k \quad \text{(predicted value of } Y) \qquad (14.2)$$

In this chapter, we will not show formulas for the estimated coefficients $b_0, b_1, b_2, \ldots, b_k$ because they entail matrix algebra. All regressions are fitted by computer software (Excel, MegaStat, MINITAB, etc.) utilizing the appropriate formulas.

Figure 14.1 illustrates the idea of a multiple regression model. Some of the proposed predictors may be useful, while others may not. We won't know until the regression is actually fitted. If an estimated coefficient has a positive (+) sign, then higher X values are associated with higher Y values, and conversely if an estimated coefficient has a negative sign.

In a bivariate regression (one predictor), the fitted regression is a *line,* while in multiple regression (with two predictors), the fitted regression is a *surface* or *plane* as illustrated in Figure 14.2. If there are more than two predictors, no diagram can be drawn, and the fitted regression is represented by a hyperplane.

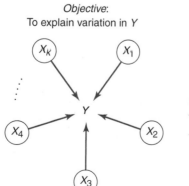

Objective:
To explain variation in Y

Potential explanatory
variables (predictors)
$X_1, X_2, X_3, \ldots, X_k$

FIGURE 14.1

Visualizing a Multiple Regression

FIGURE 14.2   **Fitted Regression: Bivariate versus Multivariate**

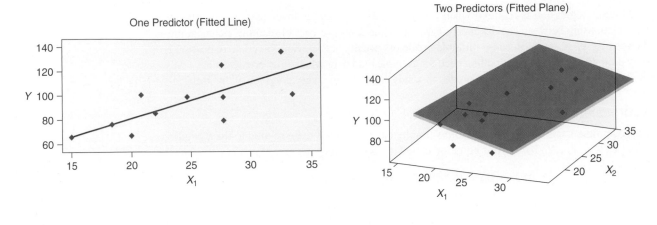

FIGURE 14.3

Data for a Multiple Regression

Response	Predictors			
Y	X_1	X_2	$\cdots$	X_k
y_1	x_{11}	x_{12}	$\cdots$	x_{1k}
y_2	x_{21}	x_{22}	$\cdots$	x_{2k}
$\vdots$	$\vdots$	$\vdots$	$\vdots$	$\vdots$
y_n	x_{n1}	x_{n2}	$\cdots$	x_{nk}

Data Format

To obtain a fitted regression we need n observed values of the response variable Y and its proposed predictors $X_1, X_2, \ldots, X_k$. A multivariate data set is a single column of Y values and k columns of X values. The form of this $n \times k$ matrix of observations is shown in Figure 14.3.

In Excel's **Data > Data Analysis > Regression**, you are required to have the X data in contiguous columns. However, MegaStat and MINITAB permit non-adjacent columns of X data. Flexibility in choosing data columns is useful if you decide to omit one or more X data columns and re-run the regression (e.g., to seek parsimony).

Illustration: Home Prices

Table 14.1 shows sales of 30 new homes in an upscale development. Although the selling price of a home (the *response variable*) may depend on many factors, we will examine three potential *explanatory variables (predictors)*.

Definition of Variable	Short Name
Y = selling price of a home (thousands of dollars)	*Price*
X_1 = home size (square feet)	*SqFt*
X_2 = lot size (thousand square feet)	*LotSize*
X_3 = number of bathrooms	*Baths*

TABLE 14.1 Characteristics of 30 New Homes ⊚ **NewHomes**

Home	Price	SqFt	LotSize	Baths	Home	Price	SqFt	LotSize	Baths
1	505.5	2,192	16.4	2.5	16	675.1	3,076	19.8	3.0
2	784.1	3,429	24.7	3.5	17	710.4	3,259	20.8	3.5
3	649.0	2,842	17.7	3.5	18	674.7	3,162	19.4	4.0
4	689.8	2,987	20.3	3.5	19	663.6	2,885	23.2	3.0
5	709.8	3,029	22.2	3.0	20	606.6	2,550	20.2	3.0
6	590.2	2,616	20.8	2.5	21	758.9	3,380	19.6	4.5
7	643.3	2,978	17.3	3.0	22	723.7	3,131	22.5	3.5
8	789.7	3,595	22.4	3.5	23	621.8	2,754	19.2	2.5
9	683.0	2,838	27.4	3.0	24	622.4	2,710	21.6	3.0
10	544.3	2,591	19.2	2.0	25	631.3	2,616	20.8	2.5
11	822.8	3,633	26.9	4.0	26	574.0	2,608	17.3	3.5
12	637.7	2,822	23.1	3.0	27	863.8	3,572	29.0	4.0
13	618.7	2,994	20.4	3.0	28	652.7	2,924	21.8	2.5
14	619.3	2,696	22.7	3.5	29	844.2	3,614	25.5	3.5
15	490.5	2,134	13.4	2.5	30	629.9	2,600	24.1	3.5

Using short variable names instead of Y and X we may write the regression model in an intuitive form:

$$Price = \beta_0 + \beta_1 \, (SqFt) + \beta_2 \, (LotSize) + \beta_3 \, (Baths) + \varepsilon$$

Logic of Variable Selection

Before doing the estimation, it is desirable to state our hypotheses about the sign of the coefficients in the model. In so doing, we force ourselves to think about our motives for including each predictor, instead of just throwing predictors into the model willy-nilly. Sometimes, of course, we may include a predictor as a "wild card" without any clear expectation about its sign. In the home price example, each predictor is expected to contribute positively to the selling price.

Predictor	Anticipated Sign	Reasoning
SqFt	> 0	Larger homes cost more to build and give greater utility to the buyer.
LotSize	> 0	Larger lots are desirable for privacy, gardening, and play.
Baths	> 0	Additional baths give more utility to the purchaser with a family.

Explicit *a priori* reasoning about cause-and-effect permits us to compare the regression estimates with our expectation and to recognize any surprising results that may occur. However, we would not abandon a predictor whose relevance is grounded solidly in existing theory or common sense simply because it was not a "significant" predictor of Y.

Fitted Regression

A regression can be fitted by using Excel, MegaStat, MINITAB, or any other statistical package. Using the sample of $n = 30$ home sales, we obtain the following Excel (partial) output, following the path Data > Data Analysis > Regression:

Regression Statistics	
Multiple R	0.978
R Square	0.956
Adjusted R Square	0.951
Standard Error	20.306
Observations	30

ANOVA

	df	SS	MS	F	Significance F
Regression	3	232450.090	77483.363	187.922	0.000
Residual	26	10720.249	412.317		
Total	29	243170.339			

	Coefficients	Standard Error	t Stat	P-value	Lower 95%	Upper 95%
Intercept	-28.848	29.711	-0.971	0.341	-89.921	32.225
SqFt	0.171	0.015	11.064	0.000	0.139	0.203
LotSize	6.778	1.421	4.769	0.000	3.856	9.699
Baths	15.535	9.208	1.687	0.104	-3.393	34.463

From this output we see the fitted regression and its statistics of fit (R^2 is the coefficient of determination, s is the standard error of estimate):

$$Price = -28.848 + 0.171\ (SqFt) + 6.778\ (LotSize) + 15.535\ (Baths)\ (R^2 = 0.956, s = 20.306)$$

The intercept is not meaningful, as there can be no home with $SqFt = 0$, $LotSize = 0$, and $Baths = 0$. Each additional square foot seems to add about 0.171 (i.e., $171, as *Price* is measured in thousands of dollars) to the average selling price, *all else remaining the same.* The coefficient of *LotSize* implies that, on average, each additional thousand square feet of lot size adds 6.778 (i.e., $6,778) to the selling price, *all else remaining the same.* The coefficient of *Baths* says that, on average, each additional bathroom adds 15.535 (i.e., $15,535) to the selling price, *all else remaining the same.* Although the three-predictor model's fit ($R^2 = 0.956$) is good, its standard error (20.306, or $20,306) suggests that prediction intervals will be rather wide.

A Closer Look

In interpreting each of the above coefficients, we added the phrase "*all else remaining the same.*" What does this mean? It means, for example, if we have two houses, each of which is 2,500 square feet on a 20,000-square-foot lot, the house with one more bathroom would have an estimated expected selling price of $15,535 more than the similar house without this extra bathroom. It doesn't mean, for example, that a house with one more bathroom would have an estimated expected selling price of $15,535 more than any house without this extra bathroom.

Predictions from a Fitted Regression

We can use the fitted regression model to make predictions for various assumed predictor values. For example, what would be the expected selling price of a 2,800-square-foot home with 2½ baths on a lot with 18,500 square feet? In the fitted regression equation, we simply plug in $SqFt = 2,800$, $LotSize = 18.5$, and $Baths = 2.5$ to get the predicted selling price:

$$SqFt = 2,800 \qquad LotSize = 18.5 \qquad Baths = 2.5$$

$$Price = -28.848 + 0.171(2,800) + 6.778(18.5) + 15.535(2.5) = 614.183 \text{ or } \$614,183$$

Although we could plug in any desired values of the predictors (*SqFt, LotSize, Baths*), as with bivariate regression, it is risky to use predictor values outside the predictor value ranges in the data set used to estimate the fitted regression. For example, it would be risky to choose *SqFt* = 4,000 because no home this large was seen in the original data set. Although the prediction might turn out to be reasonable, we would be extrapolating beyond the range of observed data.

Common Misconceptions about Fit

A common mistake is to assume that the model with the best fit is preferred. Sometimes a model with a slightly lower R^2 may give useful predictions, while a model with a high R^2 and more variables may conceal problems, as we will explain later. For example, a bivariate model using only *SqFt* as a predictor does a pretty good job of predicting *Price* and has an attractive simplicity:

$$Price = 15.47 + 0.222 \; (SqFt) \; (R^2 = 0.914, s = 27.28)$$

Should we perhaps prefer the simpler model? The principle of **Occam's Razor** says that a complex model that is only slightly better may not be preferred if a simpler model will do the job. However, in this case the three-predictor model is not very complex and is based on solid *a priori* logic.

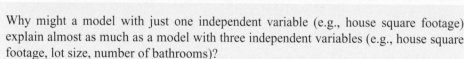

Principle of Occam's Razor

When two explanations are otherwise equivalent, we prefer the simpler, more parsimonious one.

Concept Check

Why might a model with just one independent variable (e.g., house square footage) explain almost as much as a model with three independent variables (e.g., house square footage, lot size, number of bathrooms)?

A Closer Look

When comparing the above two models,

$$Price = -28.848 + 0.171 \; (SqFt) + 6.778 \; (LotSize) + 15.535 \; (Baths)$$
$$(R^2 = 0.956, s = 20.306)$$
$$Price = 15.47 + 0.222 \; (SqFt) \; (R^2 = 0.914, s = 27.28)$$

you will notice that the values of the intercepts differ and the values of the slope for *SqFt* also differ. This can become a major problem if estimated slopes differ substantially when different models are used. Therefore, when using models for making inferences and subsequent decisions, the selection of the correct model can be extremely important.

Section Exercises

14.1 Observations are taken on net revenue from sales of a certain plasma TV at 50 retail outlets. The regression model was Y = net revenue (thousands of dollars), X_1 = shipping cost (dollars per unit), X_2 = expenditures on print advertising (thousands of dollars), X_3 = expenditure on electronic media ads (thousands of dollars), and X_4 = rebate rate (percent of retail price). (a) Write the fitted regression equation. (b) Interpret each coefficient. (c) Would the intercept be likely to have meaning in this regression? (d) Use the fitted equation to make a prediction for *NetRevenue* when *ShipCost* = 10, *PrintAds* = 50, *WebAds* = 40, and *Rebate%* = 15. (LO 2) 　**PlasmaTV**

Predictor	Coefficient
Intercept	4.306
ShipCost	−0.082
PrintAds	2.265
WebAds	2.498
Rebate%	16.697

14.2 Observations are taken on sales of a certain mountain bike in 30 sporting goods stores. The regression model was Y = total sales (thousands of dollars), X_1 = display floor space (square metres), X_2 = competitors' advertising expenditures (thousands of dollars), and X_3 = advertised price (dollars per unit). (a) Write the fitted regression equation. (b) Interpret each coefficient. (c) Would the intercept seem to have meaning in this regression? (d) Make a prediction for *Sales* when *FloorSpace* = 80, *CompetingAds* = 100, and *Price* = 1,200. (LO 2) 　**Bikes**

Predictor	Coefficient
Intercept	1,225.44
FloorSpace	11.52
CompetingAds	−6.935
Price	−0.1496

14.2　Assessing Overall Fit

As in bivariate regression, there is one residual for every observation in a multiple regression:

$$e_i = y_i - \hat{y}_i \quad \text{for } i = 1, 2, \ldots, n$$

Figure 14.4 illustrates the residual for one data value in a two-predictor regression. Each estimated value of Y is a point on the fitted regression plane for a given pair of X values (x_1, x_2). The residual is the vertical distance from the actual y-value for those particular X values (x_1, x_2) to $\hat{y}$. Just as in bivariate regression, we can use the sum of squared residuals (SSE) as a measure of "fit" of the model. A small value for SSE suggests a good overall fit of the model. Proper assessment of the usefulness of the model is done through the F test described next.

F Test for Significance (Usefulness of Model)

The overall fit of a regression is assessed using the F test. For a regression with k predictors, the hypotheses to be tested are

$H_0: \beta_1 = \beta_2 = \cdots = \beta_k = 0$ (model is not useful)

H_1: At least one of the above coefficients is non-zero (model is useful).

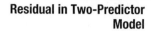

In a multiple regression, each residual is a vertical distance from the actual Y value to the expected (predicted) Y on the regression plane

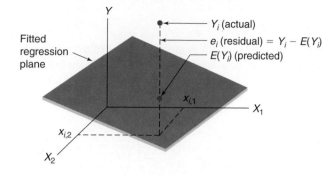

Residual in Two-Predictor Model

FIGURE 14.4

The basis for the *F* test is the **ANOVA table,** which decomposes variation of the response variable around its mean into two parts:

$$SST \quad = \quad SSE \quad + \quad SSR$$

| Total variation | Unexplained error | Explained by regression |

$$\sum_{i=1}^{n}(y_i - \bar{y})^2 = \sum_{i=1}^{n}(\hat{y}_i - \bar{y})^2 + \sum_{i=1}^{n}(y_i - \hat{y}_i)^2 \qquad (14.3)$$

SSE is the sum of the squared residuals, just as it was in a simple regression (Chapter 13), except now each predicted value $\hat{y}_i$ is based on a fitted regression equation with k predictors. The ANOVA calculations for a k-predictor model can be summarized in a table like Table 14.2, and are shown in the Excel output following.

The hypotheses to be tested are

H_0: All the coefficients are zero ($\beta_1 = \beta_2 = \beta_3 = 0$).

H_1: At least one coefficient is non-zero.

ANOVA

	df	SS	MS	F	Significance F
Regression	3	232450.090	77483.363	187.922	0.000
Residual	26	10720.249	412.317		
Total	29	243170.339			

Calculation of the ANOVA table is shown in the Excel output above. The *F* test statistic is $F_{calc} = MSR/MSE = 77{,}483/412.32 = 187.92$. Degrees of freedom are $k = 3$ for the numerator and $n - k - 1 = 30 - 3 - 1 = 26$ for the denominator. For $\alpha = 0.05$, Appendix F gives

TABLE 14.2 ANOVA Table Format

Source of Variation	Sum of Squares	df	Mean Square	F	Excel p Value
Regression (explained)	$SSR = \sum_{i=1}^{n}(\hat{y}_i - \bar{y})^2$	k	$MSR = \dfrac{SSR}{k}$	$F_{calc} = \dfrac{MSR}{MSE}$	=FDIST(Fcalc, k, n − k − 1)
Residual (unexplained)	$SSE = \sum_{i=1}^{n}(y_i - \hat{y}_i)^2$	$n - k - 1$	$MSE = \dfrac{SSE}{n - k - 1}$		
Total	$SST = \sum_{i=1}^{n}(y_i - \bar{y})^2$	$n - 1$			

a critical value of $F_{0.05,3,26} = 2.98$, so the regression is highly significant overall. The p value ($p = 0.000$) for the F statistic is given under the heading "Significance F." Alternatively, we can also use Excel's function =FDIST(187.92, 3, 26) to verify the p value ($p = 0.000$).

Coefficient of Determination (R^2)

The most common measure of overall fit is the **coefficient of determination** or R^2, which is based on the ANOVA table's sums of squares. It can be calculated in two equivalent ways by using the error sum of squares (SSE), regression sum of squares (SSR), and total sum of squares (SST). The formulas are illustrated using the three-predictor regression of home prices:

$$R^2 = 1 - \frac{SSE}{SST} = 1 - \frac{\sum_{i=1}^{n}(y_i - \hat{y}_i)^2}{\sum_{i=1}^{n}(y_i - \bar{y})^2} = 1 - \frac{10,720}{243,170} = 1 - 0.044 = 0.956 \qquad \textbf{(14.4)}$$

or, equivalently,

$$R^2 = \frac{SSR}{SST} = \frac{\sum_{i=1}^{n}(\hat{y}_i - \bar{y})^2}{\sum_{i=1}^{n}(y_i - \bar{y})^2} = \frac{232,450}{243,170} = 0.956 \qquad \textbf{(14.5)}$$

This value is shown as "R Square" in the Excel output below. For the home price data, the R^2 statistic indicates that 95.6 percent of the variation in selling price is "explained" by our three predictors. While this indicates a very good fit, there is still some unexplained variation. Adding more predictors can *never* decrease R^2, and generally will raise R^2. However, when R^2 is already high, there is little room for improvement.

Regression Statistics	
Multiple R	0.978
R Square	0.956
Adjusted R Square	0.951
Standard Error	20.306
Observations	30

Adjusted R^2

In multiple regression, it is almost always possible to raise the coefficient of determination R^2 by including additional predictors, whether these predictors actually have any effects on Y or not. This may tempt you to imagine that we should always include many predictors to get a "better fit." To discourage this tactic (called *overfitting* the model), an adjustment can be made in the R^2 statistic to penalize the inclusion of useless predictors. The **adjusted coefficient of determination** (R_{adj}^2) using n observations and k predictors is

$$R_{adj}^2 = 1 - (1 - R^2)\left(\frac{n - 1}{n - k - 1}\right) \qquad \text{(adjusted } R^2\text{)} \qquad \textbf{(14.6)}$$

R_{adj}^2 is always less than or equal to R^2. As you add predictors, R^2 cannot decline, but R_{adj}^2 may rise, remain the same, or fall, depending on whether the added predictors actually have effects on Y and thus are able to increase R^2 sufficiently. If R_{adj}^2 is substantially smaller than R^2, it suggests that the model contains useless predictors. For the home price data with three predictors, the two statistics are similar ($R^2 = 0.956$ and $R_{adj}^2 = 0.951$), which suggests that the model does not contain useless predictors. The value of

$$R_{adj}^2 = 1 - (1 - 0.956)\left(\frac{30 - 1}{30 - 3 - 1}\right) = 0.951$$

is shown as "Adjusted R Square" in the Excel output. There is no fixed rule of thumb for comparing R^2 and R^2_{adj}. A smaller gap between R^2 and R^2_{adj} indicates a more parsimonious model. A large gap would suggest that if some weak predictors were deleted, a better model would be obtained without losing very much predictive power.

Section Exercises

14.3   Refer to the ANOVA table for this regression. (a) State the degrees of freedom for the F test for overall significance. (b) Use Appendix F to look up the critical value of F for $\alpha = 0.05$. (c) Calculate the F statistic. Is the regression significant overall? (d) Calculate R^2 and R^2_{adj}, showing your formulas clearly. (LO 3)   **Plasma TV**

Source	d.f.	SS	MS
Regression	4	259,412	64,853
Error	45	224,539	4,990
Total	49	483,951	

14.4   Refer to the ANOVA table for this regression. (a) State the degrees of freedom for the F test for overall significance. (b) Use Appendix F to look up the critical value of F for $\alpha = 0.05$. (c) Calculate the F statistic. Is the regression significant overall? (d) Calculate R^2 and R^2_{adj}, showing your formulas clearly. (LO 3)   **Bikes**

Source	d.f.	SS	MS
Regression	3	1,196,410	398,803
Error	26	379,332	14,590
Total	29	1,575,742	

14.3   Predictor Significance

Hypothesis Tests

Chapter 17

Each estimated coefficient shows the change in the conditional mean of Y associated with a one-unit change in an explanatory variable, holding the other explanatory variables constant. We are usually interested in testing each fitted coefficient to find out whether it is significantly different from zero. If there is an *a priori* reason to anticipate a particular direction of association, we could choose a right-tailed or left-tailed test. For example, we would expect *SqFt* to have a positive effect on *Price,* so a right-tailed test might be used. However, the default choice is a two-tailed test because if the null hypothesis can be rejected in a two-tailed test, it will also be rejected in a one-tailed test at the same level of significance. This statement assumes that the value of the test statistic or the value of the estimated slope is consistent with the alternative hypothesis. For example, the two-tailed p value for *SqFt* is approximately 0.000 and thus we would conclude that *SqFt* has an effect on *Price* no matter what level of significance we use. Because the coefficient associated with *SqFt* is positive, which is consistent with the alternative hypothesis of a positive effect, we would also be able to reject the null hypothesis in a right-tailed test and conclude that *SqFt* has a positive effect on *Price.* (The one-tailed p value in this case would be 0.000/2.) If the value of the coefficient or the value of the test statistic is not consistent with the alternative hypothesis, the null hypothesis would not be rejected even if it was rejected in a two-tailed test. (The one-tailed p value in this case would be 1 − [quoted p value/2].)

Hypothesis Tests for Coefficient of Predictor X_j		
Left-Tailed Test	**Two-Tailed Test**	**Right-Tailed Test**
H_0: $\beta_j = 0$	H_0: $\beta_j = 0$	H_0: $\beta_j = 0$
H_1: $\beta_j < 0$	H_1: $\beta_j \neq 0$	H_1: $\beta_j > 0$

Tip

Software packages like Excel, MegaStat, or MINITAB report two-tailed p values by default because if you can reject H_0 in a two-tailed test, you can also reject H_0 in a one-tailed test at the same α as long as the coefficient or test statistic is consistent with the alternative hypothesis.

If we cannot reject the hypothesis that a coefficient is zero, then the corresponding predictor does not contribute to the prediction of Y. For example, consider a three-predictor model:

$$Y = \beta_0 + \beta_1 X_1 + \beta_2 X_2 + \beta_3 X_3 + \varepsilon$$

Does X_2 help us to predict Y? To find out, we might choose a two-tailed test:

H_0: $\beta_2 = 0$ (X_2 is *not* related to Y)

H_1: $\beta_2 \neq 0$ (X_2 *is* related to Y)

If we are unable to reject H_0, we may decide to exclude X_2 from our model, leaving us with the model:

$$Y = \beta_0 + \beta_1 X_1 + \beta_3 X_3 + \varepsilon$$

but we must be cautious when doing so. If you recall from the introductory discussion of hypothesis testing, not rejecting H_0 does not mean that we can conclude that the null hypothesis is true. It just means that we don't have sufficient evidence to indicate that it is not true. So not rejecting H_0: $\beta_2 = 0$ does not necessarily mean that X_2 has no effect on Y.

Test Statistic

Rarely would a fitted coefficient be *exactly* zero, so we use a t test to test whether the difference from zero is *significant*. For predictor X_j, the test statistic for k predictors is Student's t with $n - k - 1$ degrees of freedom. To test for a zero coefficient, we take the ratio of the fitted coefficient b_j to its standard error s_{b_j}:

$$t_{\text{calc}} = \frac{b_j}{s_{b_j}} \quad \text{(test statistic for coefficient of predictor } X_j) \quad \text{(14.7)}$$

We can use Appendix D to find a critical value of t for a chosen level of significance α, or we could find the p value for the t statistic using Excel's function =TDIST(t, deg_freedom, tails). All computer packages report the t statistic and the p value for each predictor, so we actually do not need tables. To test for a zero coefficient, we could alternatively construct a confidence interval for the true coefficient β_j, and see whether the interval includes zero is given by the following formula:

$$b_j - t_{\alpha/2, n-k-1} s_{b_j} \leq \beta_j \leq b_j + t_{\alpha/2, n-k-1} s_{b_j}$$

where s_{b_j} is the standard error of estimator b_j. Excel (as well as MegaStat) output provides the standard error, test statistic values, and confidence intervals (95 percent default).

EXAMPLE 1

Home Prices Continued

To test the effects of individual variables on housing prices, we use the following table of the Excel output.

	Coefficients	Standard Error	t Stat	p Value
Intercept	−28.85	29.711	−0.971	0.341
SqFt	0.171	0.015	11.064	0.000
LotSize	6.78	1.421	4.769	0.000
Baths	15.53	9.208	1.687	0.104

Suppose we want to test if the independent (predictor) variable *SqFt* is a useful variable in the model. We will set up the following hypotheses:

$$H_0: \beta_1 = 0$$
$$H_1: \beta_1 \neq 0$$

The test statistic value is calculated using Equation 14.7 above. From the regression output, we see that

$$b_1 = 0.171, s_{b_1} = 0.015$$

So,

$$t_{calc} = \frac{0.171}{0.015} = 11.4$$

Note that this value is different from the *t* value of 11.064 in the Excel output above. This is due to the round-off errors. This will happen several times when you calculate results with computer output.

For $\alpha = 0.05$, the critical *t* values are $\pm t_{\alpha/2, n-k-1} = \pm t_{0.025, 30-3-1} = \pm t_{0.025, 26} = \pm 2.056$. Thus, the decision rule says that we should reject the null hypothesis if t_{calc} is either less than −2.056 or more than 2.056. Because the calculated value of the test statistic is 11.064, we reject the null hypothesis and claim that *SqFt* is a useful variable to have in the model. The Excel output shows the corresponding *p* value = 0.000.

We can arrive at the same conclusion by computing the confidence interval for β_1:

$$b_1 - t_{\alpha/2, n-k-1} s_{b_1} \leq \beta_1 \leq b_1 + t_{\alpha/2, n-k-1} s_{b_1}$$
$$0.171 - 2.056(0.015) \leq \beta_1 \leq 0.171 + 2.056(0.015)$$
$$0.140 \leq \beta_1 \leq 0.202$$

which is the same as shown in the original Excel output in Section 14.1 (except for rounding). Note that zero is not in this interval. Using similar analysis, we see that *LotSize* is a useful variable (*p* value = 0.000), whereas *Baths* is not.

A Closer Look

1. Occasionally, you may want to test whether a particular effect has some specific values. For example, we may want to test

$$H_0: \beta_2 = 3$$
$$H_1: \beta_2 > 3$$

In this situation neither the *t* statistic nor the *p* value calculated by the computer program is correct; the test statistic must be calculated as in this example, $t_{calc} = \dfrac{b_2 - 3}{s_{b_2}}$; and the *p* value must be determined using the program's function for determining *p* values.

2. As previously mentioned, when conducting a one-tailed test for a particular X, the actual p value would be one-half the quoted p value as long as the sign for the coefficient of that particular X is the sign we would expect if the alternative hypothesis is true. For example, if $H_1: \beta_2 > 0$, and the quoted p value is 0.0842, the actual p value would be one-half of 0.0842, or 0.0421, as long as $b_2 > 0$. If b_2 was negative, the p value would be greater than 0.5 (or 0.9579 in this case).

3. When the regression model consists of several predictor variables, testing each variable independently at some level of significance and reaching conclusions based on these independent tests is problematic. The actual level of significance could be significantly higher than the level of significance you thought you were using. Why? The more tests you conduct, the more likely it is that you will eventually reject a null hypothesis even though all null hypotheses are true.

Concept Check

For the above example (no. 2 under A Closer Look), why is the p value 0.9579?

Section Exercises

14.5 Observations are taken on net revenue from sales of a certain plasma TV at 50 retail outlets. The regression model is $Y =$ net revenue (thousands of dollars), $X_1 =$ shipping cost (dollars per unit), $X_2 =$ expenditures on print advertising (thousands of dollars), $X_3 =$ expenditure on electronic media ads (thousands), and $X_4 =$ rebate rate (percent of retail price). (a) Calculate the t statistic for each coefficient to test for $\beta = 0$. (b) Look up the critical value of Student's t in Appendix D for a two-tailed test at $\alpha = 0.01$. Which coefficients differ significantly from zero? (c) Use Excel to find the p value for each coefficient. (LO 3)
 **PlasmaTV**

Predictor	Coefficient	SE
Intercept	4.310	70.82
ShipCost	−0.0820	4.678
PrintAds	2.265	1.050
WebAds	2.498	0.8457
Rebate%	16.697	3.570

14.6 Observations are taken on sales of a certain mountain bike in 30 sporting goods stores. The regression model is $Y =$ total sales (thousands of dollars), $X_1 =$ display floor space (square metres), $X_2 =$ competitors' advertising expenditures (thousands of dollars), and $X_3 =$ advertised price (dollars per unit). (a) Calculate the t statistic for each coefficient to test for $\beta = 0$. (b) Look up the critical value of Student's t in Appendix D for a two-tailed test at $\alpha = 0.01$. Which coefficients differ significantly from zero? (c) Use Excel to find the p value for each coefficient. (LO 3) **Bikes**

Predictor	Coefficient	SE
Intercept	1225.4	397.3
FloorSpace	11.522	1.330
CompetingAds	−6.935	3.905
Price	−0.14955	0.08927

14.4   Confidence Intervals for *Y*

Standard Error

Another important measure of fit is the **standard error (*s*) of the regression,** derived from the sum of squared residuals (*SSE*) for *n* observations and *k* predictors:

$$s = \sqrt{\frac{\sum_{i=1}^{n} (y_i - \hat{y}_i)^2}{n - k - 1}} = \sqrt{\frac{SSE}{n - k - 1}} = \sqrt{MSE} \ \text{(standard error of the regression)} \ \textbf{(14.8)}$$

The standard error is measured in the same units as the response variable *Y* (dollars, square feet, etc). A smaller *s* indicates a relatively better fit. If all predictions were perfect (i.e., if $y_i = \hat{y}_i$ for all observations), then *s* would be zero. However, perfect predictions are unlikely.

> From the ANOVA table for the three-predictor home price model, we obtain $SSE = 10{,}720$, so
>
> $$s = \sqrt{\frac{SSE}{n - k - 1}} = \sqrt{\frac{10{,}720}{30 - 3 - 1}} = 20.31$$
>
> $s = 20.31$ (i.e., \$20,310 as *Y* is measured in thousands of dollars) suggests that the model has room for improvement, despite its good fit ($R^2 = 0.956$). Forecasters find the standard error more useful than R^2 because *s* tells more about the *practical utility* of the forecasts, especially when it is used to make confidence or prediction intervals.

EXAMPLE 2

Home Prices II

Approximate Confidence and Prediction Intervals for *Y*

We can use the standard error to create approximate confidence or prediction intervals for values of $X_1, X_2, \ldots, X_k$ that are not far from their respective means.* Although these approximate intervals somewhat understate the interval widths, they are helpful when you only need a general idea of the accuracy of your model's predictions.

$$\hat{y}_i \pm t_{\alpha/2, n-k-1} \frac{s}{\sqrt{n}} \qquad \text{(approximate confidence interval for conditional mean of *Y*)} \ \textbf{(14.9)}$$

$$\hat{y}_i \pm t_{\alpha/2, n-k-1}(s) \qquad \text{(approximate prediction interval for individual *Y* value)} \qquad \textbf{(14.10)}$$

> For home prices using the three-predictor model ($SE = 20.31$), the 95 percent confidence interval would require $n - k - 1 = 30 - 3 - 1 = 26$ degrees of freedom. From Appendix D, we obtain $t_{0.025,26} = 2.056$, so the *approximate* intervals are
>
> $$\hat{y}_i \pm (2.056)\frac{20.31}{\sqrt{30}} = \hat{y}_i \pm 7.62 \quad \text{(95 percent confidence interval for conditional mean)}$$
>
> $$\hat{y}_i \pm (2.056)(20.31) = \hat{y}_i \pm 41.76 \quad \text{(95 percent prediction interval for individual home price)}$$
>
> Exact 95 percent confidence and prediction intervals for a home with *SqFt* = 2,950, *LotSize* = 21, and *Baths* = 3 (these values are very near the predictor means for our sample) are $\hat{y}_i \pm 8.55$ and $\hat{y}_i \pm 42.61$, respectively.

EXAMPLE 3

Home Prices III

---

*The exact formulas for a confidence or prediction interval for $\mu_{Y|X}$ or *Y* require matrix algebra. If you need exact intervals, you should use MINITAB or a similar computer package. You must specify the value of *each predictor* for which the confidence interval or prediction is desired.

Section Exercises

14.7 A regression of accountants' starting salaries in a large firm was estimated using 40 new hires and five predictors (university GPA, gender, score on CA exam, years' prior experience, size of graduating class). The standard error was \$3,620. Find the approximate width of a 95 percent prediction interval for an employee's salary, assuming that the predictor values for the individual are near the means of the sample predictors. Would the quick rule give similar results? (LO 2)

14.8 An agribusiness performed a regression of wheat yield (bushels per acre) using observations on 25 test plots with four predictors (rainfall, fertilizer, soil acidity, hours of sun). The standard error was 1.17 bushels. Find the approximate width of a 95 percent prediction interval for wheat yield, assuming that the predictor values for a test plot are near the means of the sample predictors. Would the quick rule give similar results? (LO 2)

Mini Case 14.1

Birth Rates and Life Expectancy BirthRates1

Table 14.3 shows the birth rate (Y = births per 1,000 population), life expectancy (X_1 = life expectancy at birth), and literacy (X_2 = percent of population that can read and write) for a random sample of 49 world nations.

From Figure 14.5, the fitted regression equation is *BirthRate* = 65.879 − 0.362 (*LifeExp*) − 0.233 (*Literate*), which says, *ceteris paribus,* that one year's increase in *LifeExp* is associated with 0.362 fewer babies per 1,000 persons, while one extra percent of *Literate* is associated with 0.233 fewer babies per 1,000 persons. The coefficient of determination is fairly high (R^2 = 0.743) and the overall regression is significant (F_{calc} = 66.42, p = 0.000). Because both predictors are significant (t_{calc} = −5.431 and t_{calc} = −5.610, p values near 0.000) the evidence favours the hypothesis that birth rates tend to fall as nations achieve higher life expectancy and greater literacy. Although cause-and-effect is unproven, the conclusions are consistent with what we know about nutrition, health, and education.

FIGURE 14.5

MegaStat's Output for Birth Rate Data

Source: Central Intelligence Agency, *The World Factbook, 2003.*

Regression Analysis: Birth Rates

R^2	0.743	n	49
Adjusted R^2	0.732	k	2
Std. Error	5.190	Dep. Var.	**BirthRate**

ANOVA table

Source	SS	df	MS	F	p-value
Regression	3,578.2364	2	1,789.1182	66.42	0.0000
Residual	1,239.1479	46	26.9380		
Total	4,817.3843	48			

Regression output

					confidence interval	
variables	coefficients	std. error	t(df = 46)	p-value	95% lower	95% upper
Intercept	65.8790	3.8513	17.106	0.0000	58.1268	73.6312
LifeExp	−0.3618	0.0666	−5.431	0.0000	−0.4960	−0.2277
Literate	−0.2330	0.0415	−5.610	0.0000	−0.3166	−0.1494

TABLE 14.3 **Birth Rates, Life Expectancy, and Literacy in Selected World Nations**

Nation	BirthRate	LifeExp	Literate
Albania	18.59	72.1	93
Algeria	22.34	70.2	62
Australia	12.71	80.0	100
⋮	⋮	⋮	⋮
Yemen	43.30	60.6	38
Zambia	41.01	37.4	79
Zimbabwe	24.59	36.5	85

14.5 Binary Predictors

What Is a Binary Predictor?

Chapter 19

So far we have included only quantitative predictors (independent variables) in our regression model. In many instances it appears that a *categorical* variable may improve the regression model. Although we cannot directly include a categorical variable (qualitative data) as a predictor in a regression, because regression requires *numerical* data (quantitative data), we can, through simple data coding, convert categorical data into useful predictors. A binary predictor has two values, denoting the presence or absence of a condition (usually coded 0 and 1). Statisticians like to use intuitive names for the binary variable. For example:

For *n* Graduates from an MBA Program

Employed = 1	(if the individual is currently employed)
Employed = 0	(otherwise)

For *n* Quarters of Sales Data

Recession = 1	(if the sales data are for a recession year)
Recession = 0	(otherwise)

For *n* Business Schools

AACSB = 1	(if the school is accredited by the AACSB)
AACSB = 0	(otherwise)

For *n* Provinces

West = 1	(if the province is west of Ontario)
West = 0	(otherwise)

Binary predictors are easy to create and are extremely important, because they allow us to capture the effects of non-quantitative (categorical) variables such as gender (female, male) or stock fund type (load, no-load). Such variables are also called dummy or indicator variables.

Tip

Name the binary variable for the characteristic that is present when the variable is 1 (e.g., *Male*) so that others can immediately see what the "1" stands for.

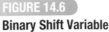

Binary Shift Variable Illustrated

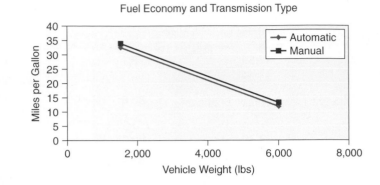

Effects of a Binary Predictor

A binary predictor is sometimes called a **shift variable** because it shifts the regression plane up or down. Suppose that we have a two-predictor fitted regression $Y = b_0 + b_1 X_1 + b_2 X_2$ where X_1 is a binary predictor. Because the only values that X_1 can take on are 0 and 1, its contribution to the regression is either b_1 or nothing, as seen in this example:

If $X_1 = 0$, then $Y = b_0 + b_1(0) + b_2 X_2$, so $Y = b_0 + b_2 X_2$.

If $X_1 = 1$, then $Y = b_0 + b_1(1) + b_2 X_2$, so $Y = (b_0 + b_1) + b_2 X_2$.

The slope of the regression plane on the X_2 axis (b_2) is the same, regardless of the value of X_1, but the intercept is either b_0 (when $X_1 = 0$) or $b_0 + b_1$ (when $X_1 = 1$).

For example, suppose we have a fitted regression of fuel economy based on a sample of 43 cars:

$$MPG = 39.5 - 0.00463\,(Weight) + 1.51\,(Manual)$$

where

$Weight$ = vehicle curb weight as tested (pounds)

$Manual$ = 1 if manual transmission, 0 if automatic

If $Manual = 0$, then

$$MPG = 39.5 - 0.00463\,(Weight) + 1.51(0)$$
$$= 39.5 - 0.00463\,(Weight)$$

If $Manual = 1$, then

$$MPG = 39.5 - 0.00463\,(Weight) + 1.51(1)$$
$$= 41.01 - 0.00463\,(Weight)$$

Thus, the binary variable shifts the intercept, leaving the slope unchanged. The situation is illustrated in Figure 14.6. In this case, we see that, although a manual transmission raises *MPG* slightly (by 1.51 miles per gallon, on average) the change in the intercept is rather small (i.e., manual transmission did not have a very large effect). A different sample could, of course, yield a different result. Many experts feel that the choice of automatic versus manual transmission makes very little difference in fuel economy today.

Testing a Binary Variable for Significance

We test the degree of significance of the binary predictor just as we would test any other predictor, using a *t* test. In multiple regression, binary predictors require no special treatment.

EXAMPLE 4

Subdivision Home Prices
OakKnoll

We know that location is an important determinant of home price. But how can we include "location" in a regression? The answer is to code it as a binary predictor. Table 14.4 shows 20 home sales in two different subdivisions, Oak Knoll and Hidden Hills. We create a binary predictor, arbitrarily designating $OakKnoll = 1$ if the home is in the Oak Knoll subdivision, and $OakKnoll = 0$ otherwise. We then do an ordinary regression, shown in Figure 14.7.

The model has a rather good fit ($R^2 = 0.922$) and is significant overall ($F_{calc} = 100.94$, $p = 0.0000$). Both predictors have a significant effect on *Price* at $\alpha = 0.05$, although *SqFt* ($t_{calc} = 14.008$, $p = 0.0000$) is a much stronger predictor than *OakKnoll* ($t_{calc} = 2.340$, $p = 0.0317$).

The fitted coefficient of *OakKnoll* tells us that, on average, a home in the Oak Knoll subdivision sells for 33.538 more than a home in Hidden Hills (i.e., $33,538 as *Price* is in thousands of dollars). Rounded off a bit, the fitted regression equation is *Price* = 10.6 + 0.199 (*SqFt*) + 33.5 (*OakKnoll*).

TABLE 14.4 **Home Prices with Binary Predictor** ⊙ **OakKnoll**

Obs	Price ($000)	SqFt	OakKnoll	Subdivision
1	615.6	3,055	0	Hidden Hills
2	557.4	2,731	0	Hidden Hills
3	472.6	2,515	0	Hidden Hills
4	595.3	3,011	0	Hidden Hills
5	696.9	3,267	1	Oak Knoll
6	409.2	2,061	1	Oak Knoll
7	814.2	3,842	1	Oak Knoll
8	592.4	2,777	1	Oak Knoll
9	695.5	3,514	0	Hidden Hills
10	495.3	2,145	1	Oak Knoll
11	488.4	2,277	1	Oak Knoll
12	605.4	3,200	0	Hidden Hills
13	635.7	3,065	0	Hidden Hills
14	654.8	2,998	0	Hidden Hills
15	565.6	2,875	0	Hidden Hills
16	642.2	3,000	0	Hidden Hills
17	568.9	2,374	1	Oak Knoll
18	686.5	3,393	1	Oak Knoll
19	724.5	3,457	0	Hidden Hills
20	749.7	3,754	0	Hidden Hills

FIGURE 14.7

Oak Knoll Regression for 20 Home Sales

Regression Analysis: Subdivision Binary (n = 20)

R^2	0.922		
Adjusted R^2	0.913	n	20
R	0.960	k	2
Std. Error	29.670	Dep. Var.	**Price (000)**

ANOVA table

Source	SS	df	MS	F	p-value
Regression	177,706.7957	2	88,853.3979	100.94	0.0000
Residual	14,964.9538	17	880.2914		
Total	192,671.7495	19			

Regression output   confidence interval

variables	coefficients	std. error	t(df = 17)	p-value	95% lower	95% upper
Intercept	10.6185	44.7725	0.237	0.8154	−83.8433	105.0803
SqFt	0.1987	0.0142	14.008	0.0000	0.1688	0.2286
OakKnoll	33.5383	14.3328	2.340	0.0317	3.2986	63.7780

A binary variable not only can shift the regression plane either up or down, it can also change its slope if you believe that the slopes are different for different categories. For example, suppose you believe that average prices are not only different in Oak Knoll and Hidden Hills, but also that what they charge per square foot is also different in the two communities. To incorporate this in your model, you would not only include the dummy variable *OakKnoll* as a stand-alone variable, you would also include the variable (*OakKnoll SqFt*) in the model, resulting in the model

$$Price = \beta_0 + \beta_1\,(SqFt) + \beta_2\,(OakKnoll) + \beta_3\,(OakKnoll\ SqFt) + \varepsilon$$

Note: Allowing the intercepts and slopes to be different does not force them to be different. If $\beta_2 = 0$, the intercepts would be the same for the two subdivisions, and/or if $\beta_3 = 0$, the effect of square footage on price would be the same for the two subdivisions.

Concept Check

Using the above model, show why not only the intercepts can be different for the two subdivisions but also that the effect that square footage has on prices can also be different for the two subdivisions.

More Than Two Categories

A variable like gender (male, female) requires only one binary predictor (e.g., *Male*) because *Male* = 0 would indicate a female. But what if there are more than two categories? For example, we might have home sales in five subdivisions, or quarterly Walmart profits, or student GPA by class level:

Home sales by subdivision: OakKnoll, HiddenHills, RockDale, Lochmoor, KingsRidge

Walmart profit by quarter: *Qtr1, Qtr2, Qtr3, Qtr4*

GPA by class level: First year, Second year, Third year, Fourth year, Master's, Doctoral

To handle such situations, *we need to create one less dummy variable than there are categories* in order to determine the category to which each observation belongs. Thus, if there are *c* categories, we need to create *c* − 1 dummy variables. For example, when there are six class levels, we would create five dummy variables such as the following:

First year = 1 if the student is a first-year student, 0 otherwise

Second year = 1 if the student is a second-year student, 0 otherwise

Third year = 1 if the student is a third-year student, 0 otherwise

Fourth year = 1 if the student is a fourth-year student, 0 otherwise

Master's = 1 if the student is a master's candidate, 0 otherwise

By creating these five dummy variables, we can identify, for example, a first-year student because he or she has a value of 1 for that dummy variable and a value of 0 for the other dummy variables. We can identify the other categories in which a dummy variable was created in the same way. But, how do we identify a doctoral student? Very simply! Doctoral

TABLE 14.5   Why We Need Only $c - 1$ Binaries to Code c Categories

Name	First Year	Second Year	Third Year	Fourth Year	Master's
Jaime	0	0	1	0	0
Fritz	0	1	0	0	0
Mary	0	0	0	0	0
Jean	0	0	0	1	0
Otto	0	0	0	0	1
Gail	1	0	0	0	0
etc.	. . .	. . .	. . .	. . .	. . .

students would be those students with a value of 0 for each of the created dummy variables. Table 14.5 identifies Mary as the doctoral student.

Similarly, we might not create a dummy variable specifically for *KingsRidge,* or for *Qtr4* column for the Walmart time series.

Home sales: OakKnoll, HiddenHills, RockDale, Lochmoor, KingsRidge

Walmart profit: Qtr1, Qtr2, Qtr3, Qtr4

Again, there is nothing special about omitting the last category. We can omit any other single binary instead. The omitted binary becomes the base reference point for the regression; that is, it is part of the intercept. No information is lost.

Note: An important point to note is that if our categorical variable has c categories then we *must* use only $c - 1$ binary variables to represent this categorical variable. Regression analysis cannot, for mathematical reasons, handle all c binary variables.

Mini Case   14.2

Age or Gender Bias?   Oxnard

We can't use simple t tests to compare employee groups based on gender or age or job classification because they fail to take into account relevant factors such as education and experience. A simplistic salary equity study that fails to account for such control variables would be subject to criticism. Instead, we can use binary variables to study the effects of age, experience, gender, and education on salaries within a corporation. Gender and education can be coded as binary variables, and age can be forced into a binary variable that defines older employees explicitly, rather than assuming that age has a linear effect on salary.

Table 14.6 shows salaries for 25 employees in the advertising department at Petro-Canada. As an initial step in a salary equity study, the human resources consultant performed a linear regression using the proposed model $Salary = \beta_0 + \beta_1 (Male) + \beta_2 (Exper) + \beta_3 (Ovr50) + \beta_4 (MBA)$. *Exper* is the employee's experience in years; *Salary* is in thousands of dollars. Binaries are used for gender ($Male = 0, 1$), age ($Ovr50 = 0, 1$), and MBA degree ($MBA = 0, 1$). Can we reject the hypothesis that the coefficients of *Male* and *Ovr50* are zero? If so, it would suggest salary inequity based on gender and/or age.

The coefficients in Figure 14.8 suggest that, *ceteris paribus,* a male ($Male = 1$) makes \$3,013 more on average than a female. However, the coefficient of *Male* does not differ significantly from zero even at $\alpha = 0.10$ ($t_{calc} = 0.86$, $p = 0.399$). The evidence for age discrimination is a little stronger. Although an older employee ($Ovr50 = 1$) makes \$8,598 less than others, on average, the p value for *Ovr50* ($t_{calc} = -1.36$, $p = 0.189$) is not convincing at $\alpha = 0.10$. The coefficient of *MBA* indicates that, *ceteris paribus,* MBA degree holders earn \$9,587 more than others, and the coefficient differs from zero at $\alpha = 0.10$ ($t_{calc} = 1.92$, $p = 0.070$). Salaries at Petro-Canada are dominated by *Exper* ($t_{calc} = 12.08$, $p = 0.000$). Each additional year of experience adds \$3,019, on average, to an employee's salary. The regression is significant overall ($F_{calc} = 52.62$, $p = 0.000$) and has a good fit ($R^2 = 0.913$).

The above analysis suggests a simpler model where we have only one predictor variable, *Exper*, years of experience. Following is the Excel output of this simple model. Using Occam's Razor principle, we would select this simpler model with $R^2 = 0.893$.

Regression Statistics	
Multiple R	0.945
R Square	0.893
Adjusted R Square	0.888
Standard Error	7.705
Observations	25

ANOVA					
	df	SS	MS	F	Significance F
Regression	1	11405.994	11405.994	192.103	0.000
Residual	23	1365.612	59.374		
Total	24	12771.606			

	Coefficients	Standard Error	t Stat	P-value	Lower 95%	Upper 95%	Upper 95.0%
Intercept	36.472	2.873	12.695	0.000	30.529	42.415	42.415
Exper	2.659	0.192	13.860	0.000	2.262	3.055	3.055

TABLE 14.6 Salaries of Advertising Staff of Petro-Canada

Obs	Employee	Salary	Male	Exper	Ovr50	MBA
1	Mary	28.6	0	0	0	1
2	Frieda	53.3	0	4	0	1
3	Alicia	73.8	0	12	0	0
4	Tom	26.0	1	0	0	0
5	Nicole	77.5	0	19	0	0
6	Xihong	95.1	1	17	0	0
7	Ellen	34.3	0	1	0	1
8	Bob	63.5	1	9	0	0
9	Vivian	96.4	0	19	0	0
10	Cecil	122.9	1	31	0	0
11	Barry	63.8	1	12	0	0
12	Jaime	111.1	1	29	1	0
13	Wanda	82.5	0	12	0	1
14	Sam	80.4	1	19	1	0
15	Saundra	69.3	0	10	0	0
16	Pete	52.8	1	8	0	0
17	Steve	54.0	1	2	0	1
18	Juan	58.7	1	11	0	0
19	Dick	72.3	1	14	0	0
20	Lee	88.6	1	21	0	0
21	Judd	60.2	1	10	0	0
22	Sunil	61.0	1	7	0	0
23	Marcia	75.8	0	18	0	0
24	Vivian	79.8	0	19	0	0
25	Igor	70.2	1	12	0	0

FIGURE 14.8

MINITAB Results for Petro-Canada Salary Equity Study

```
The regression equation is
Salary = 28.9 + 3.01 Male − 8.60 Ovr50 + 3.02 Exper + 9.59 MBA

Predictor      Coef     SE Coef       T       P
Constant     28.878      4.925     5.86    0.000
Male          3.013      3.496     0.86    0.399
Ovr50        −8.598      6.324    −1.36    0.189
Exper        3.0190     0.2499    12.08    0.000
MBA           9.587      5.003     1.92    0.070

S = 7.44388     R-Sq = 91.3%    R-Sq(adj) = 89.6%
```

FIGURE 14.9

Four Regional Binaries

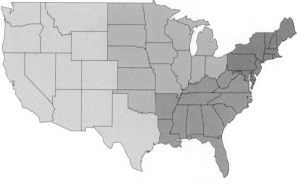

Regional Binaries

One very common use of binaries is to code regions. Figure 14.9 shows how the 50 states of the United States could be divided into four regions (Alaska and Hawaii are included in the West region) by using these binaries:

Midwest = 1 if state is in the Midwest, 0 otherwise

Neast = 1 if state is in the Northeast, 0 otherwise

Seast = 1 if state is in the Southeast, 0 otherwise

West = 1 if state is in the West, 0 otherwise

These are the same regional binaries that are used in the *LearningStats* state databases (cross-sectional data). For example, we can use regression to analyze the U.S. voting patterns in the 2000 U.S. presidential election. Binary predictors could permit us to analyze the effects of region (a qualitative variable) on voting patterns.

 Mini Case   **14.3**

Regional Voting Patterns   Election2000

Table 14.7 shows abbreviated data for the 50 U.S. states from the *LearningStats* 2000 database. There are four regional binaries. Arbitrarily, we omit the *Seast* column, which becomes the baseline for the regression to examine a hypothesis about the effects of population age, urbanization, college graduation rates, unionization, and region on voting patterns in the 2000 U.S. presidential election. The dependent variable (*Bush%*) is the percentage vote for George W. Bush, and the proffered hypothesis to be investigated is

$$Bush\% \approx \beta_0 + \beta_1 (Age65\%) + \beta_2 (Urban\%) + \beta_3 (ColGrad\%) + \beta_4 (Union\%) + \beta_5 (Midwest) + \beta_6 (Neast) + \beta_7 (West)$$

The fitted regression shown in Figure 14.10 has four quantitative predictors and three binaries. The regression is significant overall ($F_{calc} = 22.92, p = 0.000$). It suggests that, *ceteris paribus,* the percent of voters choosing Bush was lower in states with older citizens, greater urbanization, higher percentage of college graduates, and more unionization. The Bush vote was, *ceteris paribus,* significantly higher in the Midwest ($t_{calc} = 2.79, p = 0.008$) and, to a lesser extent, in the West ($t_{calc} = 1.87, p = 0.069$). The coefficient of *Neast* suggests less Bush support in the Northeast ($t_{calc} = -0.65$, $p = 0.522$) but the coefficient of *Neast* is not statistically significant (perhaps masked by quantitative variables such as *Urban%* and *Union%,* which tend to distinguish the northeastern states). Using regional binaries allows us to analyze the effects of these *qualitative* factors. Those who say statistics can only deal with numbers must think again.

TABLE 14.7 **Characteristics of U.S. States in 2000 Election**

State	Bush%	Age65%	Urban%	ColGrad%	Union%	Midwest	Neast	Omitted Seast	West
AL	56.5	13.0	69.9	20.4	9.6	0	0	1	0
AK	58.6	5.7	41.5	28.1	21.9	0	0	0	1
AZ	51.0	13.0	88.2	24.6	6.4	0	0	0	1
AR	51.3	14.0	49.9	18.4	5.8	0	0	1	0
CA	41.7	10.6	96.7	27.5	16.0	0	0	0	1
CO	50.8	9.7	83.9	34.6	9.0	0	0	0	1
CT	38.4	13.8	95.6	31.6	16.3	0	1	0	0
⋮	⋮	⋮	⋮	⋮	⋮	⋮	⋮	⋮	⋮
etc.	etc.	etc.	etc.	etc.	etc.	etc.	etc.	etc.	etc.

FIGURE 14.10

MINITAB Output for Voting Patterns

The regression equation is
Bush% = 94.6 − 1.29 Age65% − 0.0983 Urban% − 0.582 ColGrad% − 0.728 Union%
      + 5.67 Midwest − 1.61 Neast + 3.75 West

Predictor	Coef	SE Coef	T	P	VIF
Constant	94.550	7.525	12.56	0.000	
Age65%	−1.2869	0.4010	−3.21	0.003	1.6
Urban%	−0.09827	0.03476	−2.83	0.007	1.4
ColGrad%	−0.5815	0.1933	−3.01	0.004	1.9
Union%	−0.7281	0.1327	−5.49	0.000	1.5
Midwest	5.671	2.034	2.79	0.008	2.2
Neast	−1.606	2.490	−0.65	0.522	2.9
West	3.748	2.007	1.87	0.069	2.2

$S = 4.28656$ R-Sq = 79.3%   R-Sq(adj) = 75.8%

Analysis of Variance

Source	DF	SS	MS	F	P
Regression	7	2948.11	421.16	22.92	0.000
Residual Error	42	771.73	18.37		
Total	49	3719.84			

Chapter 18

14.6 Tests for Nonlinearity and Interaction

Tests for Nonlinearity

Sometimes the effect of a predictor is non-linear. A simple example would be estimating the volume of lumber to be obtained from a tree. This is a practical problem facing a timber farm because the manager can inventory the trees and measure their heights and diameters without cutting any trees. In addition to improving the accuracy of asset valuation on the balance sheet, the manager can decide the best time to cut the trees, based on their expected growth rates.

The volume of lumber that can be milled from a tree depends on the height of the tree and its radius, that is, *Volume* = *f*(*Height, Radius*). But what is the appropriate model form? Figure 14.11 shows the MINITAB regression output for two regressions of *Volume* on *Height* and *Radius:*

Model 1: *Volume* = −58.0 + 0.3393 (*Height*) + 9.4163 (*Radius*) ($R^2 = 0.948, s = 3.88$)

Model 2: *Volume* = −27.5 + 0.3488 (*Height*) + 0.6738 (*Radius^2*) ($R^2 = 0.973, s = 2.78$)

```
Model 1: The regression equation is
Volume = −58.0 + 0.339 Height + 9.42 Radius

Predictor       Coef      SE Coef        T         P
Constant     −57.988       8.638     −6.71     0.000
Height        0.3393      0.1302      2.61     0.014
Radius        9.4163      0.5285     17.82     0.000

S = 3.88183      R-Sq = 94.8%      R-Sq(adj) = 94.4%
```

```
Model 2: The regression equation is
Volume = −27.5 + 0.349 Height + 0.674 Radius2

Predictor       Coef      SE Coef        T         P
Constant     −27.512       6.558     −4.20     0.000
Height       0.34881      0.09315      3.74     0.001
Radius2      0.67383      0.02672     25.22     0.000

S = 2.79946      R-Sq = 97.3%      R-Sq(adj) = 97.1%
```

FIGURE 14.11

**Regression Results for
Tree Data**

If we regard a log as a cylinder, we would prefer the second regression because the usable volume of a cylinder is proportional to the square of its radius.[*] The t statistics for both *Height* and *Radius* are improved in model 2, and the higher R^2 and reduced standard errors indicate a better fit. Note that this is still a linear regression, except that one of the predictors happens to be the square of another predictor. No special estimation is needed to introduce this type of non-linearity into the model. This example illustrates the importance of model specification.

To test for suspected non-linearity of any predictor, we can include its square in the regression. For example, instead of

$$Y = \beta_0 + \beta_1 X_1 + \beta_2 X_2 + \varepsilon \tag{14.11}$$

we would estimate

$$Y = \beta_0 + \beta_1 X_1 + \beta_2 X_1^2 + \beta_3 X_2 + \beta_4 X_2^2 + \varepsilon \tag{14.12}$$

If the linear model is the correct one, the estimated coefficients of the squared predictors (β_2 and β_4) would not be expected to differ significantly from zero, that is, the model will collapse to a linear model. On the other hand, rejection of the hypothesis H_0: $\beta_2 = 0$ would suggest a quadratic relationship between Y and X_1, and similarly for Y and X_2. Inclusion of squared predictors merely gives the regression a chance to be non-linear. Some researchers include squared predictors as a matter of course in large studies where there is no *a priori* reason to assume linearity. Squared predictors add model complexity and impose a cost of reduced degrees of freedom for significance tests (we lose 1 degree of freedom for each squared predictor), but the potential reward is a more appropriate model specification.

For example, rising total U.S. petroleum consumption from 1980 through 2004 can be fairly well described by a linear time trend model ($R^2 = 0.8691$). Yet, adding a squared predictor (making it a quadratic model) gives an even better fit ($R^2 = 0.9183$) and the x_t^2 term is significant ($t_{calc} = 3.640$). This suggests a non-linear trend, using $x_t = 1, 2, \ldots, 25$ to represent the year.

Linear: $\hat{y}_t = 0.2012 x_t + 15.029$ ($R^2 = 0.8691$)

Quadratic: $y_t = 0.0074 x_t^2 + 0.0078 x_t + 15.899$ ($R^2 = 0.9183$)

---

[*]$V = \pi h r^2$ describes the relationship between the tree's radius (r), height (h), and volume (V). A logarithmic model $\ln(Volume) = \beta_0 + \beta_1 \ln(Height) + \beta_2 \ln(Radius)$ might be even more appropriate, although the resulting R^2 and s would not be comparable to the models shown above because the dependent variable would be in different units.

Tests for Interaction

We can test for **interaction** between two predictors by including their product in the regression. For example, we might hypothesize that Y depends on X_1, X_2, and X_1X_2. To test for interaction, we estimate the model

$$Y = \beta_0 + \beta_1 X_1 + \beta_2 X_2 + \beta_3 X_1 X_2 + \varepsilon \qquad (14.13)$$

If the t test for β_3 allows us to reject the hypothesis $H_0: \beta_3 = 0$, then we conclude that there is a significant interaction effect that transcends the roles of X_1 and X_2 separately (similar to the two-factor ANOVA tests for interaction in Chapter 11). Interaction effects require careful interpretation and cost 1 degree of freedom per interaction. However, if the interaction term improves the model specification, it is well worth the cost. For example, a bank's lost revenue (*Loss*) due to loan defaults depends on the loan size (*Size*) and the degree of risk (*Risk*). Small loans may be risky but may not contribute much to the total losses. Large loans may be less risky but potentially represent a large loss. An interaction term (*Size* × *Risk*) would be large if either predictor is large, thereby capturing the effect of both predictors. Thus, the interaction term might be a significant predictor in the model

$$Loss = b_0 + b_1\,(Size) + b_2\,(Risk) + b_3\,(Size \times Risk)$$

Mini Case 14.4

Cockpit Noise **CockpitNoise**

Cockpit sound level was measured 61 times at various flight phases for seven different B-727 aircraft (an older model) at the first officer's left ear position using a handheld meter. Sound level was measured in decibels. For reference, 60 dB is a normal conversation, 75 is a typical vacuum cleaner, 85 is city traffic, 90 is a typical hair dryer, and 110 is a chain saw. The proposed regression model is $Noise = \beta_0 + \beta_1\,(Climb) + \beta_2\,(Descent) + \beta_3\,(Speed) + \beta_4\,(Speed^2) + \beta_5\,(Alt) + \beta_6\,(Alt^2)$. The airspeed (*Speed*) is in KIAS (knots indicated air speed) or nautical miles per hour. Altitude (*Alt*) is in thousands of feet above MSL (mean sea level). Squared predictors (*SpeedSqr* and *AltSqr*) are included for tests of non-linearity (*SpeedSqr* is divided by 1,000 to improve data conditioning). There are three flight phases, represented by binaries (*Climb, Cruise, Descent*), but *Cruise* is omitted from the regression as it is implied by the other two binaries (i.e., if *Climb* = 0 and *Descent* = 0, then necessarily *Cruise* = 1). Table 14.8 shows a partial data list.

Regression results are shown in Figure 14.12. The coefficient of *Climb* indicates a slight average reduction in *Noise* of 0.814 decibels during the climb flight phase (relative to the baseline of *Cruise*). The coefficient of *Descent* indicates a significant reduction of 1.66 decibels during the descent flight phase. *Speed* and *Alt* have non-linear effects, as indicated by the significance of *SpeedSqr* ($t_{calc} = 2.336$, $p = 0.0232$) and *AltSqr* ($t_{calc} = -2.348$, $p = 0.0226$).

TABLE 14.8   Cockpit Noise in B-727 Aircraft

Obs	Noise	Climb	Cruise	Descent	Speed	Alt	SpeedSqr	AltSqr
1	83	1	0	0	250	10	62.50	100
2	89	1	0	0	340	15	115.60	225
3	88	1	0	0	320	18	102.40	324
4	89	0	1	0	330	24	108.90	576
5	92	0	1	0	346	27	119.72	729
...	...	...	...	...	...	...	...	...
61	82	0	0	1	250	4.5	62.50	20.25

Regression Analysis: Cockpit Noise (*n* = flights)

R²	0.920		
Adjusted R²	0.911	n	61
R	0.959	k	6
Std. Error	1.179	Dep. Var.	**Noise**

ANOVA table

Source	SS	df	MS	F	p-value
Regression	860.4680	6	143.4113	103.19	0.0000
Residual	75.0484	54	1.3898		
Total	935.5164	60			

Regression output

variables	coefficients	std. error	t(df = 54)	p-value	95% lower	95% upper
Intercept	83.0833	8.0747	10.289	0.0000	66.8946	99.2721
Climb	−0.8140	0.5649	−1.441	0.1553	−1.9465	0.3185
Descent	−1.6612	0.5557	−2.989	0.0042	−2.7754	−0.5471
Speed	−0.0492	0.0525	−0.936	0.3533	−0.1545	0.0561
Alt	0.3134	0.1328	2.361	0.0219	0.0472	0.5796
SpeedSqr	0.1867	0.0799	2.336	0.0232	0.0265	0.3470
AltSqr	−0.0074	0.0031	−2.348	0.0226	−0.0137	−0.0011

Source: Capt. R. E. Hartl (ret).

FIGURE 14.12

**MegaStat's Regression
Results for Cockpit Noise**

14.7   Multicollinearity

What Is Multicollinearity?

When the independent variables $X_1, X_2, \ldots, X_m$ are intercorrelated instead of being independent, we have a condition known as **multicollinearity.** If only two predictors are correlated, we have **collinearity.** Almost any data set will have some degree of correlation among the predictors. The depth of our concern would depend on the *degree* of multicollinearity. The higher the degree of multicollinearity, the less reliable is the estimated regression equation.

EXAMPLE 5

**More Home Prices,
Different Neighbourhood**

Consider 30 new homes in another neighbourhood, as shown in Table 14.9.
Following is the Excel multiple regression output.

Regression Statistics	
Multiple R	0.870769
R Square	0.75824
Adjusted R Square	0.740331
Standard Error	42.14143
Observations	30

ANOVA

	df	SS	MS	F	Significance F
Regression	2	150384.6	75192.32	42.34039	0.0000
Residual	27	47949.31	1775.9		
Total	29	198333.9			

	Coeff.	Std Error	t Stat	P-value
Intercept	178.8887	58.213	3.073003	0.0048005
SqFt	0.110242	0.103656	1.063544	0.2969554
LotSize	5.199862	10.41381	0.499324	0.6215959

TABLE 14.9 Home Prices in Different Neighbourhoods

Obs	Price	SqFt	LotSize	Obs	Price	SqFt	LotSize
1	684.8	3,499	36.3	16	674.9	2,968	30.7
2	594.5	2,319	26.0	17	503.1	2,180	23.4
3	615.7	2,935	31.9	18	638.9	3,055	33.0
4	690.5	2,835	29.1	19	720.9	3,390	36.0
5	772.9	3,377	34.7	20	636.1	2,721	28.1
6	668.3	3,339	35.3	21	633.7	2,681	29.0
7	721.4	2,868	31.3	22	683.4	2,851	31.1
8	659.7	3,141	33.7	23	705.0	3,111	31.7
9	570.0	2,330	25.9	24	724.5	3,451	37.3
10	759.7	3,313	35.3	25	724.3	3,094	32.3
11	505.5	2,270	22.9	26	744.8	3,563	36.8
12	768.0	3,261	34.0	27	724.5	3,542	36.5
13	827.8	3,589	38.6	28	538.6	2,495	27.3
14	551.0	2,239	25.1	29	588.1	2,250	24.5
15	760.4	3,120	33.3	30	675.7	3,044	32.6

Let us examine this output closely. Clearly, the regression model is very useful because from the ANOVA table output we see that the F value $= 42.34$ with the p value practically zero. Now let us look at each independent (predictor) variable to see if it is useful in the model. We see that neither $SqFt$ nor $LotSize$ is a useful variable as both have very high p values. That does not make sense. Recall our regression model:

$$E(Y) = \beta_0 + \beta_1 X_1 + \beta_2 X_2$$

where X_1 is the $SqFt$ variable and X_2 is the $LotSize$ variable. If both $\beta_1 = 0$ and $\beta_2 = 0$, as shown by the Excel output, then the model reduces to $E(Y) = \beta_0$. So how could the model be useful? The two parts of the output seem to contradict each other. To further understand, let us consider the two simple linear regression models—one with only X_1 ($SqFt$) as the predictor variable, and the other with X_2 ($LotSize$) as the independent variable with the following Excel outputs, respectively:

Summary output with SqFT as a predictor

Regression Statistics	
Multiple R	0.869
R Square	0.756
Adjusted R Square	0.747
Standard Error	41.573
Observations	30

ANOVA

	df	SS	MS	F	Significance F
Regression	1	149941.860	149941.860	86.757	0.000
Residual	28	48392.087	1728.289		
Total	29	198333.947			

	Coeff.	Std Error	t Stat	P-value
Intercept	191.415	51.821	3.694	0.001
SqFt	0.161	0.017	9.314	0.000

Summary output with LotSize as a predictor

Regression Statistics	
Multiple R	0.865
R Square	0.748
Adjusted R Square	0.739
Standard Error	42.240
Observations	30

ANOVA

	df	SS	MS	F	Significance F
Regression	1	148375.869	148375.869	83.160	0.000
Residual	28	49958.078	1784.217		
Total	29	198333.947			

	Coeff.	Std Error	t Stat	P-value
Intercept	161.949	56.123	2.886	0.007
LotSize	16.116	1.767	9.119	0.000

Both simpler models are useful and provide practically the same R^2 value as the multiple regression model. So the multiple regression model does not add much to either of the two simpler models. The contradictory results that we see in the multiple regression output arise because the two predictor variables are highly correlated. The correlation coefficient, calculated in Excel by Data > Data Analysis > Correlation is $r = 0.9856$. Clearly, both variables essentially provide the same relationship with the dependent variable *Price*. So it does not make sense to have both *SqFt* and *LotSize* in our model.

A Closer Look

Without going into a mathematical explanation of why, with a high degree of collinearity or multicollinearity, the test for the usefulness of the model is significant while none of the predictor variables appear to be significant, let's look at this problem intuitively. When two or more predictor variables are highly correlated, thus tending to move together, it is difficult for regression analysis to determine which of the variables affect Y and which don't, the result of which are t statistics that are not significant. An analogy of this would be when three people are locked in a room and one is murdered. We know that at least one of the remaining two committed the murder but we don't necessarily know which one. Similarly, with collinearity or multicollinearity, we know that at least one variable affects Y but we don't necessarily know which one. Conversely, we may not conclude that the model is useful yet; when looking at the tests for individual effects, one or more of the tests may be rejected, indicating that one or more particular independent variables do have an effect on Y. As previously mentioned, when several tests are conducted, the actual level of significance for each test is greater than the quoted level of significance. Therefore, we may be rejecting individual tests using a higher level of significance than we used to test the overall usefulness of the model. And as mentioned in our initial discussion of hypothesis testing, it is easier to reject a null hypothesis when the level of significance is higher.

Chapter 16

14.8 Violations of Assumptions

Recall that the least squares method makes several assumptions about random errors ε_i. Although ε_i is unobservable, clues may be found in the residuals e_i. We routinely test three important assumptions:

- *Assumption* 1: The errors are normally distributed.
- *Assumption* 2: The errors have constant variance (i.e., they are homoscedastic).
- *Assumption* 3: The errors are independent (i.e., they are non-autocorrelated).

These are the same assumptions that we made in the simple linear regression (bivariate regression) that we made in Chapter 13, and the methods to detect violation of these assumptions were discussed there.

14.9 Other Multiple Regression Topics

Binary Dependent Variable

We have seen that categorical independent variables pose no special problem. However, when the response variable Y is binary (0, 1), the least squares estimation method is no longer appropriate. Specialized regression methods such as "Logit" and "Probit" are called for. MINITAB and other software packages handle this situation easily, but a different interpretation is required. See *LearningStats* Unit 20 for a case study with binary Y.

Stepwise and Best Subsets Regression

It may have occurred to you that there ought to be a way to automate the task of fitting the "best" regression using k predictors. The *stepwise regression* procedure uses the power of the computer to fit the best model using 1, 2, 3, . . . , k predictors. For example, aerospace engineers had a large data set of 469 observations on *Thrust* (takeoff thrust of a jet turbine) along with seven potential predictors (*TurbTemp, AirFlow, TurbSpeed, OilTemp, OilPres, RunTime, ThermCyc*). In the absence of a theoretical model, a stepwise regression was run, with the results shown in Figure 14.13. Only p values are shown for each predictor, along with R^2, R^2_{adj}, and standard error. You can easily assess the effect of adding more predictors. In this example, most p values are tiny due to the large n. While stepwise regression is an efficient way to identify the "best" model for each number of predictors (1, 2, . . . , k), it is appropriate only when there is no theoretical model that specifies which predictors *should* be used. A further degree of automation of the regression task is to perform *best subsets* regression using all possible combinations of predictors. This option is offered by many computer packages, but is not recommended because it yields too much output and too little additional insight.

FIGURE 14.13 **MegaStat's Stepwise Regression of Turbine Data**   Turbines

Regression Analysis—Stepwise Selection displaying the best model of each size

469 observations
Thrust is the dependent variable

Nvar	TurbTemp	Airflow	TurbSpeed	OilTemp	OilPres	RunTime	ThermCyc	s	Adj R²	R²
		p values for the coefficients								
1		0.0000						12.370	0.252	0.254
2		0.0000			0.0004			12.219	0.270	0.273
3	0.0003	0.0000					0.0005	12.113	0.283	0.287
4		0.0000		0.0081	0.0000		0.0039	12.041	0.291	0.297
5	0.0010	0.0000		0.0009	0.0003		0.0006	11.914	0.306	0.314
6	0.0010	0.0000	0.1440	0.0037	0.0005		0.0010	11.899	0.308	0.317
7	0.0008	0.0000	0.1624	0.0031	0.0007	0.2049	0.0006	11.891	0.309	0.319

www.mcgrawhillconnect.ca

CHAPTER SUMMARY

Multivariate regression extends bivariate regression to include multiple **predictors** of the **response variable.** Using too many predictors violates the principle of **Occam's Razor,** which favours a simpler model if it is adequate. If the R^2 differs greatly from R^2_{adj}, the model may contain unhelpful predictors. The ANOVA table and F **test** measure overall significance, while the t **test** is used to test hypotheses about individual predictors. A **confidence interval** for each unknown **parameter** is equivalent to a two-tailed hypothesis test for $\beta = 0$. The **standard error** of the regression is used to create **confidence intervals** or **prediction intervals** for Y. A **binary predictor** (also called a **dummy variable** or an **indicator**) has value 1 if the condition of interest is present, 0 otherwise. For c categories, we only include $c - 1$ binaries or the regression will fail. Including a squared predictor provides a test for **non-linearity.** Including the product of two predictors is a test for **interaction. Collinearity** (correlation between *two* predictors) can be detected by examining the correlation coefficients between each pair of predictor variables. Regression assumes that the errors are normally distributed, independent random variables with constant variance. Residual tests, not covered in this text, are available to identify possible **non-normality, autocorrelation,** or **heteroscedasticity** problems.

KEY TERMS

adjusted coefficient of determination (R^2_{adj}), *602*
ANOVA table, *601*
binary predictor, *609*
coefficient of determination (R^2), *602*
collinearity, *619*

dummy variable, *609*
F test, *600*
indicator variable, *609*
interaction, *618*
multicollinearity, *619*
multiple regression, *594*
Occam's Razor, *599*

predictors, *595*
response variable, *595*
shift variable, *610*
standard error (s) of the regression, *607*

Commonly Used Formulas

Population regression model for k predictors: $Y = \beta_0 + \beta_1 x_1 + \cdots + \beta_k x_k + \varepsilon$

Fitted regression equation for k predictors: $\hat{y} = b_0 + b_1 x_1 + \cdots + \beta_k x_k$

ANOVA sums: $SST = SSR + SSE$

SST (total sum of squares): $\displaystyle\sum_{i=1}^{n} (y_i - \bar{y})^2$

SSR (regression sum of squares): $\displaystyle\sum_{i=1}^{n} (\hat{y}_i - \bar{y})^2$

SSE (error sum of squares): $\displaystyle\sum_{i=1}^{n} (y_i - \hat{y}_i)^2$

MSR (regression mean square): $MSR = SSR/k$

MSE (error mean square): $MSE = SSE/(n - k - 1)$

F test statistic for overall significance: $F_{calc} = MSR/MSE$

Coefficient of determination: $R^2 = 1 - \dfrac{SSE}{SST}$ or $R^2 = \dfrac{SSR}{SST}$

Adjusted R^2: $R^2_{adj} = 1 - (1 - R^2)\left(\dfrac{n-1}{n-k-1}\right)$

Test statistic for coefficient of predictor X_j: $t_{calc} = \dfrac{b_j}{s_{b_j}}$ where s_{b_j} is the standard error of b_j

Confidence interval for coefficient β_j: $b_j \pm t_{\alpha/2, n-k-1} \, s_{b_j}$

Estimated standard error of the regression: $s = \sqrt{\dfrac{\displaystyle\sum_{i=1}^{n}(y_i - \hat{y}_i)^2}{n-k-1}} = \sqrt{\dfrac{SSE}{n-k-1}}$

Approximate confidence interval for Y: $\hat{y}_i \pm t_{\alpha/2n-k-1}\dfrac{s}{\sqrt{n}}$

Approximate prediction interval for Y: $\hat{y}_i \pm t_{\alpha/2n-k-1}(s)$

CHAPTER REVIEW

1. (a) What does ε represent in the regression model? (b) What assumptions do we make about ε? (c) What is the distinction between Greek letters (β) and Roman letters (b) in representing a regression equation? (LO 2)

2. (a) Describe the format of a multiple regression data set. (b) Why is it a good idea to write down our *a priori* reasoning about a proposed regression? (LO 2)

3. (a) Why does a higher R^2 not always indicate a good model? (b) State the principle of Occam's Razor. (LO 2)

4. (a) What is the role of the F test in multiple regression? (b) How is the F statistic calculated from the ANOVA table? (c) Why are tables rarely needed for the F test? (LO 3)

5. (a) Why is testing $H_0: \beta = 0$ a very common test for a predictor? (b) How many degrees of freedom do we use in a t test for an individual predictor's significance? (LO 3)

6. (a) Explain why a confidence interval for a predictor coefficient is equivalent to a two-tailed test of significance. (b) Why are t tables rarely needed in performing significance tests? (LO 3)

7. (a) What does a coefficient of determination (R^2) measure? (b) When R^2 and R_{adj}^2 differ considerably, what does it indicate? (LO 3)

8. State some guidelines to prevent inclusion of too many predictors in a regression. (LO 3)

9. (a) State the formula for the standard error of the regression. (b) Why is it sometimes preferred to R^2 as a measure of "fit"? (c) What is the formula for a quick prediction interval for individual Y values? (d) When you need an exact prediction, what must you do? (LO 3)

10. (a) What is a binary predictor? (b) Why is a binary predictor sometimes called a "shift variable"? (c) How do we test a binary predictor for significance? (LO 4)

11. If we have c categories for an attribute, why do we only use $c - 1$ binaries to represent them in a fitted regression? (LO 4)

12. (a) Explain why it might be useful to include a quadratic term in a regression. (b) Explain why it might be useful to include an interaction term between two predictors in a regression. (c) Name a drawback to including quadratic or interaction terms in a regression. (LO 2)

13. (a) What is multicollinearity? (b) What are its potential consequences? (c) Why is it a matter of degree? (d) Why might it be ignored? (LO 5)

14. How does multicollinearity differ from collinearity? (LO 5)

15. If multicollinearity is severe, what might its symptoms be? (LO 5)

CHAPTER EXERCISES

Instructions for Data Sets: Choose one of the data sets A to I below or as assigned by your instructor. Only the first three and last three observations are shown for each data set (files are on the CD). In each data set, the dependent variable (*response*) is the first variable. Choose the independent variables (*predictors*) as you judge appropriate. Use a spreadsheet or a statistical package (e.g., MegaStat or MINITAB) to perform the necessary regression calculations and to obtain the required graphs. Write a concise report answering questions 14.9 (a) through (h) (or a subset of these questions assigned by your instructor). Label sections of your report to correspond to the questions. Insert tables and graphs in your report as appropriate. (LO 1, 2, 3, 5 & 6)

14.9 (a) Is this cross-sectional data or time-series data? What is the unit of observation (e.g., firm, individual, year)?

(b) State your *a priori* hypotheses about the sign (+ or −) of each predictor and your reasoning about cause and effect. Would the intercept have meaning in this problem? Explain.

(c) Perform the regression and write the estimated regression equation (round off to 3 or 4 significant digits for clarity). Do the coefficient signs agree with your *a priori* expectations?

(d) Does the 95 percent confidence interval for each predictor coefficient include zero? What conclusion can you draw? *Note:* Skip this question if you are using MINITAB, as predictor confidence intervals are not shown.

(e) Do a two-tailed t test for zero slope for each predictor coefficient at $\alpha = 0.05$. State the degrees of freedom and look up the critical value in Appendix D (or from Excel).

(f) (a) Which p values indicate predictor significance at $\alpha = 0.05$? (b) Do the p values support the conclusions you reached from the t tests? (c) Do you prefer the t test or the p value approach? Why?

(g) Based on the R^2 and ANOVA table for your model, how would you describe the fit?

(h) Use the standard error to construct an *approximate* prediction interval for Y. Based on the width of this prediction interval, would you say the predictions are good enough to have practical value?

Data Set A   Mileage and Other Characteristics of Randomly Selected Vehicles (*n* = 43, *k* = 4)
Mileage

Obs	Vehicle	City	Length	Width	Weight	Japan
1	Acura CL	20	192	69	3,450	1
2	Acura TSX	23	183	59	3,320	1
3	BMW 3-Series	19	176	69	3,390	0
⋮	⋮	⋮	⋮	⋮	⋮	⋮
41	Toyota Sienna	19	200	77	4,120	1
42	Volkswagen Jetta	34	172	68	3,045	0
43	Volvo C70	20	186	72	3,690	0

City = EPA miles per gallon in city driving, *Length* = vehicle length (inches), *Width* = vehicle width (inches), *Weight* = weight (pounds), *Japan* = 1 if carmaker is Japanese, 0 otherwise.

Source: *Consumer Reports New Car Buying Guide 2003–2004* (Consumers Union, 2003). Sampling methodology was to select the vehicle on every fifth page starting at page 40. Data are intended for purposes of statistical education and should not be viewed as a guide to vehicle performance.

Data Set B   Noodles & Company Sales, Seating, and Demographic Data (*n* = 74, *k* = 5)
Noodles2

Obs	Sales/SqFt	Seats-Inside	Seats-Patio	MedIncome	MedAge	BachDeg%
1	702	66	18	45.2	34.4	31
2	210	69	16	51.9	41.2	20
3	365	67	10	51.4	40.3	24
⋮	⋮	⋮	⋮	⋮	⋮	⋮
72	340	63	28	60.9	43.5	21
73	401	72	15	73.8	41.6	29
74	327	76	24	64.2	31.4	15

Sales/SqFt = sales per square foot of floor space, *Seats − Inside* = number of interior seats, *Seats − Patio* = number of outside seats. The three demographic variables refer to a three-mile radius of the restaurant: *MedIncome* = median family income, *MedAge* = median age, and *BachDeg%* = percentage of population with at least a bachelor's degree.

Source: Noodles & Company.

Data Set C   Assessed Value of Small Medical Office Buildings (*n* = 32, *k* = 5)   Assessed

Obs	Assessed	Floor	Offices	Entrances	Age	Freeway
1	1,796	4,790	4	2	8	0
2	1,544	4,720	3	2	12	0
3	2,094	5,940	4	2	2	0
⋮	⋮	⋮	⋮	⋮	⋮	⋮
30	1,264	3,580	3	2	27	0
31	1,162	3,610	2	1	8	1
32	1,447	3,960	3	2	17	0

Assessed = assessed value (thousands of dollars), *Floor* = square feet of floor space, *Offices* = number of offices in the building, *Entrances* = number of customer entrances (excluding service doors), *Age* = age of the building (years), *Freeway* = 1 if within one mile of freeway, 0 otherwise.

Data Set D   **Changes in Consumer Price Index, Capacity Utilization, Changes in Money Supply Components, and Unemployment ($n = 41$, $k = 4$)**   **Money**

Year	ChgCPI	CapUtil	ChgM1	ChgM2	Unem
1966	2.9	91.1	2.5	4.6	3.8
1967	3.1	87.2	6.6	9.3	3.8
1968	4.2	87.1	7.7	8.0	3.6
⋮	⋮	⋮	⋮	⋮	⋮
2004	2.7	76.6	5.3	5.8	5.5
2005	3.4	78.8	−0.2	4.0	5.1
2006	3.2	80.4	−0.5	5.3	4.6

ChCPI = percent change in the Consumer Price Index (CPI) over previous year, *CapUtil* = percent utilization of manufacturing capacity in current year, *ChgM1* = percent change in currency and demand deposits (M1) over previous year, *ChgM2* = percent change in small time deposits and other near-money (M2) over previous year, *Unem* = civilian unemployment rate in percent.

Source: *Economic Report of the President, 2007.* These variables are selected from *LearningStats* (Time-Series Data).

Data Set E   **Characteristics of Selected Piston Aircraft ($n = 55$, $k = 4$)**   **CruiseSpeed**

Obs	Mfgr/Model	Cruise	Year	TotalHP	NumBlades	Turbo
1	Cessna Turbo Stationair TU206	148	1981	310	3	1
2	Cessna 310 R	194	1975	570	3	0
3	Piper 125 Tri Pacer	107	1951	125	2	0
⋮	⋮	⋮	⋮	⋮	⋮	⋮
53	OMF Aircraft Symphony	128	2002	160	2	0
54	Liberty XL-2	132	2003	125	2	0
55	Piper 6X	148	2004	300	3	0

Cruise = best cruise speed (knots indicated air speed) at 65–75 percent power, *Year* = year of manufacture, *TotalHP* = total horsepower (both engines if twin), *NumBlades* = number of propeller blades, *Turbo* = 1 if turbocharged, 0 otherwise.

Source: *Flying Magazine* (various issues). Data are for educational purposes only and not as a guide to performance. These variables are selected from *LearningStats* (Technology Data).

Data Set F   **Characteristics of Randomly Chosen Hydrocarbons ($n = 35$, $k = 7$)**   **Retention**

Obs	Name	Ret	MW	BP	RI	H1	H2	H3	H4	H5
1	2,4,4-trimethyl-2-pentene	153.57	112.215	105.06	1.4135	0	1	0	0	0
2	1,5-cyclooctadiene	237.56	108.183	150.27	1.4905	0	0	0	1	0
3	methylcyclohexane	153.57	98.188	101.08	1.4206	0	0	1	0	0
⋮	⋮	⋮	⋮	⋮	⋮	⋮	⋮	⋮	⋮	⋮
33	ethylbenzene	209.700	106.170	136.000	1.4950	0	0	0	0	1
34	m-ethyl toluene	247.800	120.194	161.480	1.4941	0	0	0	0	1
35	3-methylhexane	132.320	100.204	92.000	1.3861	1	0	0	0	0

Ret = Chromatographic retention time (seconds), *MW* = molecular weight (gm/mole), *BP* = boiling point in °C, *RI* = refractive index (dimensionless), *Class* = hydrocarbon class (*H1* = acyclic saturated, *H2* = acyclic unsaturated, *H3* = cyclic saturated, *H4* = cyclic unsaturated, *H5* = aromatic).

Source: Data are courtesy of John Seeley of Oakland University. This is a 50 percent sample of the full data set found in *LearningStats* (Technology Data).

Data Set G   Price and Percent Metal Content of Recovered Metal (*n* = 33, *k* = 6)   Metals

Obs	Price/lb	Al	Si	Cr	Ti	Zn	Pb
1	0.87000	94.2248	0.6079	0.1203	0.0327	0.2316	0.0000
2	0.89240	91.5803	0.2496	0.1006	0.0213	0.1094	0.0594
3	0.91526	91.4810	0.1850	0.1031	0.0227	0.0793	0.0691
⋮	⋮	⋮	⋮	⋮	⋮	⋮	⋮
31	0.94350	94.3890	0.3646	0.0904	0.0321	0.0640	0.0249
32	0.94490	93.9500	0.3001	0.0832	0.0281	0.0697	0.0265
33	0.94790	94.1019	0.2813	0.0915	0.0259	0.1443	0.0290

Each observation shows the selling price per pound and percent metal content of one shipment of metal alloy recovered and processed by a metal recovery firm. *Al* = percent aluminum, *Si* = percent silicon, *Cr* = percent titanium, *Zn* = percent zinc, *Pb* = percent lead.

Source: Confidential.

Data Set H   Body Fat and Personal Measurements for Males (*n* = 50, *k* = 8)   BodyFat2

Obs	Fat%	Age	Weight	Height	Neck	Chest	Abdomen	Hip	Thigh
1	12.6	23	154.25	67.75	36.2	93.1	85.2	94.5	59.0
2	6.9	22	173.25	72.25	38.5	93.6	83.0	98.7	58.7
3	24.6	22	154.00	66.25	34.0	95.8	87.9	99.2	59.6
⋮	⋮	⋮	⋮	⋮	⋮	⋮	⋮	⋮	⋮
48	6.4	39	148.50	71.25	34.6	89.8	79.5	92.7	52.7
49	13.4	45	135.75	68.50	32.8	92.3	83.4	90.4	52.0
50	5.0	47	127.50	66.75	34.0	83.4	70.4	87.2	50.6

Fat% = percent body fat, *Age* = age (yrs.), *Weight* = weight (lbs.), *Height* = height (in.), *Neck* = neck circumference (cm), *Chest* = chest circumference (cm), *Abdomen* = abdomen circumference (cm), *Hip* = hip circumference (cm), *Thigh* = thigh circumference (cm).

Data are a subsample of 252 males analyzed in Roger W. Johnson (1996), "Fitting Percentage of Body Fat to Simple Body Measurements," *Journal of Statistics Education* 4, no. 1.

Data Set I   Used Vehicle Prices (*n* = 637, *k* = 4)   Vehicles

Obs	Model	Price	Age	Car	Truck	SUV
1	Astro GulfStream Conversion	12,988	3	0	0	0
2	Astro LS 4.3L V6	5,950	9	0	0	0
3	Astro LS V6	19,995	4	0	0	0
⋮	⋮	⋮	⋮	⋮	⋮	⋮
635	DC 300M Autostick	10,995	6	1	0	0
636	DC 300M Special Edition	22,995	1	1	0	0
637	GM 3500 4 × 4 w/8ft bed and plow	17,995	5	0	1	0

Price = asking price ($), *Age* = vehicle age (yrs), *Car* = 1 if passenger car, 0 otherwise, *Truck* = 1 if truck, 0 otherwise, *SUV* = 1 if sport utility vehicle, 0 otherwise. (*Van* is the omitted fourth binary).

Source: *DetroitAutoFocus* 4, Issue 38 (Sept. 17–23, 2004). Data are for educational purposes only and should not be used as a guide to depreciation.

GENERAL EXERCISES

14.10 In a model of Ford's quarterly revenue, $TotalRevenue, = \beta_0 + \beta_1 (CarSales) + \beta_2 (TruckSales) + \beta_3 (SUVSales) + \varepsilon$, the three predictors are measured in number of units sold (not dollars). (a) Interpret each slope. (b) Would the intercept be meaningful? (c) What factors might be reflected in the error term? Explain. (LO 2)

14.11 In a study of paint peel problems, a regression was suggested to predict defects per million (the response variable). The intended predictors were supplier (four suppliers, coded as binaries) and substrate (four materials, coded as binaries). There were 11 observations. Explain why regression is impractical in this case, and suggest a remedy. (LO 4)

14.12 A hospital emergency room analyzed $n = 17,664$ hourly observations on its average occupancy rates using six binary predictors representing days of the week and two binary predictors representing the 8-hour work shift (12 midnight–8 a.m., 8 a.m.–4 p.m., 4 p.m.–12 midnight) when the ER census was taken. The fitted regression equation was $AvgOccupancy = 11.2 + 1.19 (Mon) - 0.187 (Tue) - 0.785 (Wed) - 0.580 (Thu) - 0.451 (Fri) - 0.267 (Sat) - 4.58 (Shift1) - 1.65 (Shift2)$ $(SE = 6.18, R^2 = 0.094, R^2_{adj} = 0.093)$. (a) Why did the analyst use only six binaries for days when there are seven days in a week? (b) Why did the analyst use only two work shift binaries when there are three work shifts? (c) Which is the busiest day? (d) Which is the busiest shift? (e) Interpret the intercept. (f) Assess the regression's fit. (LO 4)

14.13 Using test data on 20 types of laundry detergent, an analyst fitted a regression to predict $CostPerLoad$ (average cost per load in cents per load) using binary predictors $TopLoad$ (1 if washer is a top-loading model, 0 otherwise) and $Powder$ (if detergent was in powder form, 0 otherwise). Interpret the results. (Data are from *Consumer Reports* 68, no. 8 [Nov. 2003], p. 42.) (LO 4) **Laundry**

R^2	0.117		
Adjusted R^2	0.006	n	19
R	0.341	k	2
Std. Error	5.915	Dep. Var.	**Cost Per Load**

ANOVA table

Source	SS	df	MS	F	p-value
Regression	73.8699	2	36.9350	1.06	0.3710
Residual	559.8143	16	34.9884		
Total	633.6842	18			

	Regression output				Confidence interval	
variables	coefficients	std. error	t(df = 16)	p-value	95% lower	95% upper
Intercept	26.0000	4.1826	6.216	1.23E-05	17.1333	34.8667
Top-load	−6.3000	4.5818	−1.375	0.1881	−16.0130	3.4130
Powder	−0.2714	2.9150	−0.093	0.9270	−6.4509	5.9081

14.14 A researcher used stepwise regression to create regression models to predict *BirthRate* (births per 1,000) using five predictors: *LifeExp* (life expectancy in years), *InfMort* (infant mortality rate), *Density* (population density per square kilometre), *GDPCap* (gross domestic product per capita), and *Literate* (literacy percent). Interpret these results. (LO 2) **BirthRates2**

Regression Analysis—Stepwise Selection (best model of each size)

   153   observations

   BirthRate is the dependent variable

			***p* values for the coefficients**					
Nvar	**LifeExp**	**InfMort**	**Density**	**GDPCap**	**Literate**	**S**	**Adj R^2**	**R^2**
1		0.0000				6.318	0.722	0.724
2		0.0000			0.0000	5.334	0.802	0.805
3		0.0000		0.0242	0.0000	5.261	0.807	0.811
4	0.5764	0.0000		0.0311	0.0000	5.273	0.806	0.812
5	0.5937	0.0000	0.6289	0.0440	0.0000	5.287	0.805	0.812

14.15   A sports enthusiast created an equation to predict *Victories* (the team's number of victories in the National Basketball Association regular season play) using predictors *FGP* (team field goal percentage), *FTP* (team free throw percentage), *Points* = (team average points per game), *Fouls* (team average number of fouls per game), *TrnOvr* (team average number of turnovers per game), and *Rbnds* (team average number of rebounds per game). The fitted regression was *Victories* = $-281 + 523$ (*FGP*) $+ 3.12$ (*FTP*) $+ 0.781$ (*Points*) $- 2.90$ (*Fouls*) $+ 1.60$ (*TrnOvr*) $+ 0.649$ (*Rbnds*) ($R^2 = 0.802$, $F = 10.80$, $SE = 6.87$). The strongest predictors were *FGP* ($t = 4.35$) and *Fouls* ($t = -2.146$). The other predictors were only marginally significant and *FTP* and *Rbnds* were not significant. The matrix of correlations is shown below. At the time of this analysis, there were 23 NBA teams. (a) Do the regression coefficients make sense? (b) Is the intercept meaningful? Explain. (c) Why might collinearity account for the lack of significance of some predictors? (Data are from a research project by MBA student Michael S. Malloy.) (LO 4 & 5)

	FGP	**FTP**	**Points**	**Fouls**	**TrnOvr**	**Rbnds**
FGP	1.000					
FTP	−0.039	1.000				
Points	0.475	0.242	1.000			
Fouls	−0.014	0.211	0.054	1.000		
TrnOvr	0.276	0.028	0.033	0.340	1.000	
Rbnds	0.436	0.137	0.767	−0.032	0.202	1.000

14.16   An expert witness in a case of alleged racial discrimination in a university school of nursing introduced a regression of the determinants of *Salary* of each professor for each year during an eight-year period ($n = 423$) with the following results, with dependent variable *Salary* and predictors *Year* (year in which the salary was observed), *YearHire* (year when the individual was hired), *Race* (1 if individual is black, 0 otherwise), and *Rank* (1 if individual is an assistant professor, 0 otherwise). Interpret these results. (LO 4)

Variable	**Coefficient**	**t**	**p**
Intercept	−3,816,521	−29.4	0.000
Year	1,948	29.8	0.000
YearHire	−826	−5.5	0.000
Race	−2,093	−4.3	0.000
Rank	−6,438	−22.3	0.000
	$R^2 = 0.811$	$R^2_{adj} = 0.809$	$s = 3,318$

14.17 Analysis of a Detroit Marathon ($n = 1,015$ men, $n = 150$ women) produced the regression results shown below, with dependent variable *Time* (the marathon time in minutes) and predictors *Age* (runner's age), *Weight* (runner's weight in pounds), *Height* (runner's height in inches), and *Exp* (1 if runner had prior marathon experience, 0 otherwise). (a) Interpret the coefficient of *Exp*. (b) Does the intercept have any meaning? (c) Why do you suppose squared predictors were included? (d) Plug in your own *Age, Height, Weight,* and *Exp* to predict your own running time. Do you believe it? (Data courtesy of Detroit Striders.) (LO 2)

	Men (n = 1,015)		Women (n = 150)	
Variable	**Coefficient**	**t**	**Coefficient**	**t**
Intercept	−366		−2,820	
Age	−4.827	−6.1	−3.593	−2.5
Age2	0.07671	7.1	0.05240	2.6
Weight	−1.598	−1.9	3.000	0.7
Weight2	0.008961	3.4	−0.004041	−2.0
Height	24.65	1.5	96.13	1.6
Height2	−0.2074	−1.7	−0.8040	−1.8
Exp	−41.74	−17.0	−28.65	−4.3
	$R^2 = 0.423$		$R^2 = 0.334$	

14.18 Using test data on 43 vehicles, an analyst fitted a regression to predict *CityMPG* (miles per gallon in city driving) using as predictors *Length* (length of car in inches), *Width* (width of car in inches), and *Weight* (weight of car in pounds). Interpret the results. Do you see evidence that some predictors were unhelpful? (LO 2)   **CityMPG**

R^2	0.682		
Adjusted R^2	0.658	n	43
R	0.826	k	3
Std. Error	2.558	Dep. Var.	**CityMPG**

ANOVA table

Source	SS	df	MS	F	p-value
Regression	547.3722	3	182.4574	27.90	8.35E−10
Residual	255.0929	39	6.5408		
Total	802.4651	42			

	Regression output				confidence interval		
variables	**coefficients**	**std. error**	**t(df = 39)**	**p-value**	**95% lower**	**95% upper**	**VIF**
Intercept	39.4492	8.1678	4.830	0.0000	22.9283	55.9701	
Length (in)	−0.0016	0.0454	−0.035	0.9725	−0.0934	0.0902	2.669
Width (in)	−0.0463	0.1373	−0.337	0.7379	−0.3239	0.2314	2.552
Weight (lbs)	−0.0043	0.0008	−5.166	0.0000	−0.0060	−0.0026	2.836

14.19 A researcher used stepwise regression to create regression models to predict *CarTheft* (thefts per 1,000) using four predictors: *Income* (per capita income), *Unem* (unemployment percent), *Pupil/Tea* (pupil-to-teacher ratio), and *Divorce* (divorces per 1,000 population) for the 50 U.S. states. Interpret these results. (LO 2)   **CarTheft**

Regression Analysis—Stepwise Selection (best model of each size)

　　　50　observations

　　　CarTheft is the dependent variable

	p values for the coefficients						
Nvar	*Income*	*Unem*	*Pupil/Tea*	*Divorce*	*Std. Err*	*Adj R²*	*R²*
1			0.0004		167.482	0.218	0.234
2	0.0018		0.0000		152.362	0.353	0.379
3	0.0013	0.0157	0.0001		144.451	0.418	0.454
4	0.0007	0.0323	0.0003	0.1987	143.362	0.427	0.474

14.20* A popular night spot in Windsor, Ontario, caters to the younger crowds (19 to 40 years of age) from the Detroit and Windsor areas. To help management plan its radio advertising strategy, it wants to obtain some information on the amount of money American and Canadian customers of different ages spend when visiting their establishment. If they determine that there is no difference either due to nationality or age, they would use one radio ad in both countries on radio stations listened to by younger adults. If they find spending habits differ either by age or by nationality, they would modify that strategy. American and Canadian customers of different ages were randomly selected and the amounts they spent in an evening were recorded as follows: (LO 1, 2, 3 & 4)

Canadian Customers		**American Customers**	
Sales	*Age*	*Sales*	*Age*
$18	19	$10	19
$13	21	$12	21
$15	23	$10	23
$12	25	$15	25
$14	27	$13	27
$11	29	$16	29
$12	31	$15	31
$ 9	33	$17	33
$12	35	$14	35
$10	37	$21	37
$8	39	$19	39

Using this data set, three regression models were estimated. These models (where Citizenship = 1 if Canadian) were as follows:

1. $Sales = \beta_0 + \beta_1(Age) + \varepsilon$
2. $Sales = \beta_0 + \beta_1(Age) + \beta_2(Citizenship) + \varepsilon$
3. $Sales = \beta_0 + \beta_1(Age) + \beta_2(Citizenship) + \beta_3(Age)(Citizenship) + \varepsilon$

Using Excel, the following outputs were obtained:

Model 1

Regression Statistics

Multiple R	0.0879
R Square	0.0077
Adjusted R Square	−0.0419
Standard Error	3.4179
Observations	22

ANOVA

	df	SS	MS	F	Significance F
Regression	1	1.8182	1.8182	0.1556	0.6974
Residual	20	233.6364	11.6818		
Total	21	235.4545			

	Coefficients	Standard Error	t Stat	P-value	Lower 95%	Upper 95%
Intercept	12.1364	3.4198	3.5488	0.0020	5.0028	19.2700
Age	0.0455	0.1152	0.3945	0.6974	−0.1949	0.2858

Model 2

Regression Statistics

Multiple R	0.3988
R Square	0.1591
Adjusted R Square	0.0706
Standard Error	3.2282
Observations	22

ANOVA

	df	SS	MS	F	Significance F
Regression	2	37.4545	18.7273	1.7971	0.1928
Residual	19	198.0000	10.4211		
Total	21	235.4545			

	Coefficients	Standard Error	t Stat	P-value	Lower 95%	Upper 95%
Intercept	13.4091	3.3025	4.0603	0.0007	6.4969	20.3213
Age	0.0455	0.1088	0.4177	0.6809	−0.1823	0.2732
Citizenship	−2.5455	1.3765	−1.8492	0.0800	−5.4265	0.3356

Model 3

Regression Statistics

Multiple R	0.8779
R Square	0.7707
Adjusted R Square	0.7325
Standard Error	1.7318
Observations	22

ANOVA

	df	SS	MS	F	Significance F
Regression	3	181.4727	60.4909	20.1704	0.0000
Residual	18	53.9818	2.9990		
Total	21	235.4545			

	Coefficients	Standard Error	t Stat	P-value	Lower 95%	Upper 95%
Intercept	1.6773	2.4505	0.6845	0.5024	−3.4710	6.8255
Age	0.4500	0.0826	5.4507	0.0000	0.2766	0.6234
Citizenship	20.9182	3.4655	6.0361	0.0000	13.6375	28.1989
Age · Citizenship	−0.8091	0.1168	−6.9298	0.0000	−1.0544	−0.5638

(a) Using Excel, create three scatter plots—using Canadian data only, using American data only, and using both data sets combined—and comment on your findings.

(b) Using Excel, duplicate the above outputs.

(c) For each model, write out the estimated relationship. Comment on your findings.

(d) Compare the R^2's and Adjusted R^2's across the three models and comment on your findings.

(e) For models 2 and 3, write separate equations for Canadians and Americans and comment on your findings. Are these findings supported by the scatter plots? Explain.

(f) For each model, test its usefulness and test whether each of the model's predictor variables have an effect on sales. Comment on your findings. (Use $\alpha = 0.05$.)

(g) Is it important that the correct model is used before any advertising decisions are made? Explain.

(h) Based on your findings, what should the advertising strategy be? Explain.

LearningStats Unit 13   Multiple Regression

LearningStats Unit 13 illustrates uses of multiple regression, assessing fit (e.g., R^2 and R^2_{adj}), tests for significance (e.g., ANOVA, t tests), and model adequacy (e.g., residual tests). Binary predictors and tests for non-linearity are illustrated. Special attention is given to the issue of multicollinearity and its effects on tests for significance of individual predictors. Your instructor may assign specific modules, or you may pursue those that sound interesting.

Topic	LearningStats Modules
Multiple regression overview	Multiple Regression Overview
	Violations of Assumptions
Using Excel and MINITAB	Regression Using Excel
	Regression Using MINITAB
Simulation	Effects of Collinearity
	Effects of Multicollinearity
	Salary Data Modelling
Case studies	Binary Predictors
	Variance Inflation
	Stepwise Regression
	Squared Predictors
Student presentations	Murder Rates
	Birth Weight
	Cancer Deaths
	Birth Rates
	Car Theft
Student reports	Income per Capita
	Teen Moms by State
	Student Worksheets
Formulas	Useful Regression Formulas
Tables	Appendix D—Student's t
	Appendix F—Critical Values of F

Key   = PowerPoint   = Word   = Excel

Visual Statistics

Visual Statistics Modules on Multiple Regression

Module	Module Name
17	Visualizing Multiple Regression Analysis
18	Visualizing Regression Models
19	Visualizing Binary Predictors in Regression

Visual Statistics Modules 17, 18, and 19 (included on your CD) are designed to help you:

- Recognize and use the terminology of multiple regression.
- Be able to perform significance tests and interpret confidence intervals for model parameters.
- Understand the importance of data conditioning and the potential effects of ill-conditioned data.
- Detect multicollinearity and recognize its common symptoms.
- Learn when a model may be overfitted and why that can be a problem.
- Use visual displays to check residuals for non-normality, autocorrelation, and heteroscedasticity.
- Know the commonly used variable transformations and their purposes.
- Understand how to use polynomial models and interaction tests.
- Be able to interpret regressions with intercept binaries or slope binaries.

The worktext (included on the CD in PDF format) contains lists of concepts covered, objectives of the modules, overviews of concepts, illustrations of concepts, orientations to module features, learning exercises (basic, intermediate, advanced), learning projects (individual, team), self-evaluation quizzes, glossaries of terms, and solutions to self-evaluation quizzes.

EXAM REVIEW QUESTIONS FOR CHAPTERS 11–14

1. Which statement is *correct* concerning one-factor ANOVA? Why not the others?
   a. The ANOVA is a test to see whether the variances of c groups are the same.
   b. In ANOVA, the k groups are compared two at a time, not simultaneously.
   c. ANOVA depends on the assumption of normality of the populations sampled.

2. Given the following ANOVA table, find the F statistic and the critical value of $F_{0.05}$.

Source	Sum of Squares	df	Mean Square	F
Treatment	744.00	4		
Error	751.50	15		
Total	1,495.50	19		

3. Given the following ANOVA: (a) How many ABM locations were there? (b) What was the sample size? (c) At $\alpha = 0.05$, is there a significant effect due to *Day of Week*? (d) At $\alpha = 0.05$, is there a significant interaction?

Source of Variation	SS	df	MS	F	p Value	F Crit
ABM Location	41,926.67	2	20,963.33	9.133	0.0002	3.044
Day of Week	4,909.52	6	818.25	0.356	0.9055	2.147
Interaction	29,913.33	12	2,492.78	1.086	0.3740	1.804
Error	433,820.00	189	2,295.34			
Total	510,569.52	209				

4. Which statement or statements are *incorrect*? If incorrect, what is the correct answer?

    a. In the chi-square goodness-of-fit test with six categories and no estimated parameters, the critical value of χ^2 when $\alpha = 0.05$ is 1.1455.

    b. In the chi-square goodness-of-fit test with five categories and no estimated parameters, the critical value of χ^2 when $\alpha = 0.05$ is 9.4877.

    c. In the chi-square goodness-of-fit test with eight categories and no estimated parameters, the critical value of χ^2 when $\alpha = 0.05$ is 17.5345.

    d. In the chi-square goodness-of-fit test with seven categories and two estimated parameters, the critical value of χ^2 when $\alpha = 0.10$ is 7.7794.

5. Which statement or statements are *incorrect*? If incorrect, what is the correct answer?

    a. In the chi-square test for independence, with 5 rows and 4 columns, the degrees of freedom are 20.

    b. In the chi-square test for independence, when $n = 280$, $R_2 = 60$, and $C_4 = 50$, $e_{24} \approx 10.7$.

    c. In the chi-square test for independence, with 3 rows and 4 columns, the critical value χ^2 when $\alpha = 0.05$ is 14.4494.

6. Given a sample correlation coefficient $r = 0.373$ with $n = 30$, can you reject the hypothesis $= 0$ for the population at $\alpha = 0.01$? Explain, stating the critical value you are using in the test.

7. Which statement is *incorrect?* Explain.

    a. Correlation uses a t test with $n - 2$ degrees of freedom.

    b. Correlation analysis assumes that X is independent and Y is dependent.

    c. Correlation analysis is a test for the degree of linearity between X and Y.

8. Based on the information in this ANOVA table, the coefficient of determination R^2 is

    a. 0.499

    b. 0.501

    c. 0.382

ANOVA Table

Source	Sum of Squares	df	Mean Square	F	p Value
Regression	158.3268	1	158.3268	24.88	0.00004
Residual	159.0806	25	6.3632		
Total	317.4074	26			

9. In a test of the regression model $Y = \beta_0 + \beta_1 X$ with 27 observations, what is the critical value of t to test the hypothesis that $\beta_1 = 0$ using $\alpha = 0.05$ in a two-tailed test?

    a. 1.960   b. 2.060   c. 1.708

10. Which statement is *correct* for a bivariate regression? Why not the others?

    a. A 95% confidence interval (CI) for the mean of Y is wider than the 95% CI for the predicted Y.

    b. A confidence interval for the predicted Y is widest when $X = \bar{x}$.

    c. The t test for zero slope always gives the same t_{calc} as the correlation test for $\rho = 0$.

11. Tell if each statement is *true* or *false* for a bivariate regression. If false, explain.

    a. If the standard error is $s_{yx} = 3,207$, then a residual $e_i = 4,327$ would be an outlier.

    b. In a regression with $n = 50$, a leverage statistic $h_i = 0.10$ indicates unusual leverage.

    c. A decimal change is often used to improve data conditioning.

12. Which *predictor coefficients* differ significantly from zero at $= 0.05$?

    a. X_3 and X_5 b. X_5 only   c. all but X_1 and X_3

	Coefficients	Std. Error	Lower 95%	Upper 95%
Intercept	22.47427	6.43282	9.4012	35.54733
X_1	−0.243035	0.162983	−0.574256	0.088186
X_2	0.187555	0.278185	−0.377784	0.752895
X_3	−0.339730	0.063168	−0.468102	−0.211358
X_4	0.001902	0.008016	−0.014389	0.018193
X_5	1.602511	0.723290	0.132609	3.072413

13. Which predictors differ significantly from zero at $\alpha = 0.05$?

   a. X_3 only

   b. X_4 only

   c. both X_3 and X_4

	Coefficients	Std. Error	p Value
Intercept	23.3015	4.1948	0.0000
X_1	−0.227977	0.178227	0.2100
X_2	0.218970	0.300784	0.4719
X_3	−0.343658	0.059742	0.0000
X_4	1.588353	0.742737	0.0402

14. In this regression with $n = 40$, which *predictor* differs significantly from zero at $\alpha = 0.01$?

   a. X_2 b. X_3 c. X_5

	Coefficients	Std. Error
Intercept	3.210610	0.918974
X_1	−0.034719	0.023283
X_2	0.026794	0.039741
X_3	−0.048533	0.009024
X_4	0.000272	0.001145
X_5	0.228930	0.103327

McGraw Hill **connect**™

For solutions to odd-numbered exercises, Exam Review questions, and additional study tools to help you succeed in this course, visit *Connect* at www.mcgrawhillconnect.ca.

Chapter

15

Time-Series Analysis

Chapter Learning Objectives

When you finish this chapter you should be able to

1. Demonstrate an understanding of time-series data and its various components.

2. Create and interpret linear, exponential, or quadratic trend model and use them for forecasting.

3. Demonstrate an understanding of, and interpret, common fit measures (R^2, MAPE, MAD, MSD).

4. Interpret moving averages and create them manually and using Excel.

5. Use exponential smoothing to forecast trendless data.

6. Create deseasonalized time series manually and using software.

7. Use regression with seasonal binaries to make forecasts.

8. Interpret index numbers.

Chapter 20

15.1 Time-Series Components

Time-Series Data

Businesses must track their performance. By looking at their output over time businesses can tell where they've been, whether they are performing poorly or satisfactorily, and how much improvement is needed, both in the short term and the long term. A **time-series variable** (denoted Y) consists of data observed over n periods of time. Consider a clothing retailer that specializes in blue jeans. Examples of time-series data this company might be interested in tracking would be the number of jeans sold and the company's market share. Or from the manufacturing perspective, the company might track cost of raw materials over time.

Businesses also use time-series data to monitor whether a particular process is stable or unstable. And they use time-series data to help predict the future, a process we call *forecasting.* In addition to business time-series data we see economic time-series data in *Report on Business, The Wall Street Journal, BusinessWeek,* or *The Financial Post,* as well as in *Maclean's* or *Time,* or even when we browse the Web. Although business and economic time-series data are most common, we can see time-series data for population, health, crime, sports, and social problems. Usually, time-series data are presented in a graph, as in Figures 15.1 and 15.2.

It is customary to plot time-series data either as a line graph or a bar graph, with time on the horizontal *X*-axis and the variable of interest on the vertical *Y*-axis to reveal how the variable changes over time. In a line graph, the *X-Y* data points are connected with line segments to make it easier to see fluctuations. While anyone can understand time-series graphs in a

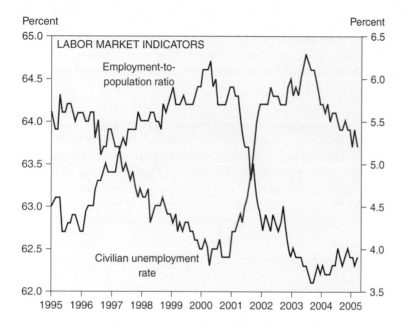

FIGURE 15.1

U.S. Employment (monthly)

Source: www.clevelandfed.org.

FIGURE 15.2

Exchange Rates (daily)

Source: www.clevelandfed.org.

general way, this chapter explains how to interpret time-series data *statistically* and to make defensible forecasts. Our analysis begins with sample observations $y_1, y_2, \ldots, y_n$ covering n time periods. The following notation is used:

- y_t is the value of the time series in period t.
- t is an index denoting the time period ($t = 1, 2, \ldots, n$).
- n is the number of time periods.
- $y_1, y_2, \ldots, y_n$ is the data set for analysis.

To distinguish time-series data from cross-sectional data, we use y_t instead of x_i for an individual observation, and a subscript t instead of i.

Time-series data may be measured *at a point in time* or *over an interval of time*. For example, in accounting, balance sheet data are measured at the end of the fiscal year, while income statement data are measured over an entire fiscal year. The gross domestic product (GDP) is a flow of goods and services measured *over an interval of time*, while the prime rate of interest is measured *at a point in time*. Your GPA is measured *at a point in time* while your weekly pay is measured *over an interval of time*. The distinction is sometimes vague in reported data, but a little thought will usually clarify matters. For example, Canada's 2006 unemployment rate (6.3 percent) would be measured at a point in time (e.g., at year's end) while Canada's 2006 hydroelectric production (341 terawatt-hours) would be measured over the entire year.

Periodicity

The **periodicity** is the time interval over which data are collected (decade, year, quarter, month, week, day, and hour). For example, the Canadian population is measured every five years, your personal income tax is calculated *annually,* GDP is reported *quarterly,* the unemployment rate is estimated *monthly,* and the *National Post* reports the closing price of BCE stock *daily* (although stock prices are also monitored continuously on the Web). Firms typically report profits by quarter, but pension liabilities only at year's end. Any periodicity is possible, but the principles of time-series modelling can be understood with these three common data types:

- Annual data (1 observation per year)
- Quarterly data (4 observations per year)
- Monthly data (12 observations per year)

Additive versus Multiplicative Models

Time-series *decomposition* seeks to separate a time-series Y into four components: trend (T), cycle (C), seasonal (S), and irregular (I). These components are assumed to follow either an additive or a multiplicative model, as shown in Table 15.1.

The additive form is attractive for its simplicity, but the multiplicative model is often more useful for forecasting financial data, particularly when the data vary over a range of magnitudes. Especially in the short run, it may not matter greatly which form is assumed. In fact, the model forms are fundamentally equivalent because the multiplicative model becomes additive if logarithms are taken (as long as the data are non-negative):

$$\log(Y) = \log(T \times C \times S \times I) = \log(T) + \log(C) + \log(S) + \log(I)$$

TABLE 15.1 Components of a Time Series

Model	Components	Used For
Additive	$Y = T + C + S + I$	Data of similar magnitude (short-run or trend-free data) with constant *absolute* growth or decline.
Multiplicative	$Y = T \times C \times S \times I$	Data of increasing or decreasing magnitude (long-run or trended data) with constant *percent* growth or decline.

Four Components of a Time Series `FIGURE 15.3`

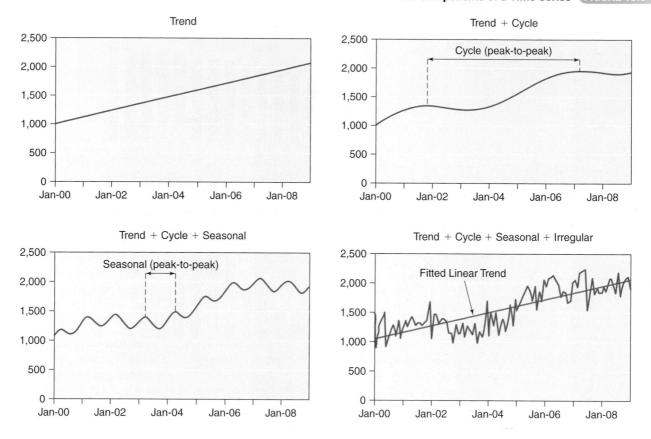

A Graphical View

Figure 15.3 illustrates these four components in a hypothetical time series. The four components may be thought of as layering atop one another to produce the actual time series. In this example, the irregular component (I) is large enough to obscure the cycle (C) and seasonal (S) components, but not the trend (T). However, we can usually extract the original components from the time series by using statistical methods.

Trend

Trend (T) is a general movement over all years ($t = 1, 2, \ldots, n$). Change over a few years is not a trend. Some trends are steady and predictable. For example, the data may be steadily growing (e.g., total Canadian population), neither growing nor declining (e.g., your current car's fuel efficiency), or steadily declining (infant mortality rates in a developing nation). Most of us think of three general patterns: growth, stability, or decline. But there are subtler trends within each category. A time series can increase at a steady *linear* rate (e.g., the number of books you have read in your lifetime), at an *increasing* rate (e.g., medical costs for an aging population), or at a *decreasing* rate (e.g., number of active bowlers). It can grow for a while and then level off (e.g., sales of HDTV) or grow toward an asymptote or a limit (e.g., percent of adults owning a camera phone). A mathematical trend can be fitted to any data, but its predictive value depends on the situation.

For example, to predict future organ transplants (Figure 15.4) a mathematical trend might be useful, but a mathematical model might not be very helpful for predicting space launches (Figure 15.5).

Cycle

Cycle (C) is a repetitive up-and-down movement around the trend that covers *several years*. For example, industry analysts have studied cycles for sales of new automobiles, new home

FIGURE 15.4

Steady Trend

Transplants

Source: www.gsds.org. © Golden State
Donor Services

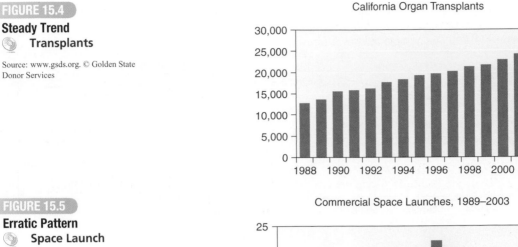

California Organ Transplants

FIGURE 15.5

Erratic Pattern

Space Launch

Source: http://ast.faa.gov.

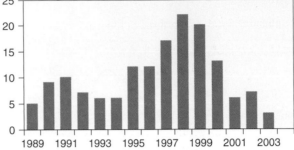

Commercial Space Launches, 1989–2003

construction, inventories, and business investment. These cycles are based primarily on product life and replacement cycles. In any market economy there are broad business cycles that affect employment and production. After we have extracted the trend and seasonal components of a time series, a cycle may be detected as autocorrelation in the residuals (see Chapter 13, Section 13.8). Although cycles are important, there is no general theory of cycles, and even those cycles that have been identified in specific industries have erratic timing and complex causes that defy generalization. Over a small number of time periods (a typical forecasting situation), cycles are undetectable or may resemble a trend. For this reason cycles are not discussed further in this chapter.

Seasonal

Seasonal (*S*) is a repetitive cyclical pattern *within a year*.* For example, many retail businesses experience strong sales during the fourth quarter because of Christmas. Automobile sales rise when new models are released. Peak demand for airline flights to Europe occurs during summer vacation travel. Although often imagined as sine waves, seasonal patterns may not be smooth. Peaks and valleys can occur in any month or quarter, and each industry may face its own unique seasonal pattern. For example, June weddings tend to create a "spike" in bridal sales, but there is no "sine wave" pattern in bridal sales. By definition, annual data have no seasonality.

Irregular

Irregular (*I*) is a random disturbance that follows no apparent pattern. It is also called the *error* component or *random noise* reflecting all factors other than trend, cycle, and seasonality. Large error components are not unusual. For example, daily prices of many common stocks fluctuate greatly. When the irregular component is large, it may be difficult to isolate other individual model components. Some data are pure *I* (lacking meaningful *T* or *S* or *C* components). In such cases, we use special techniques (e.g., moving average or exponential

---

*Repetitive patterns within a week, day, or other time period may also be considered seasonal. For example, mail volume at Canada Post is higher on Monday. Emergency arrivals at hospitals are lower during the first shift (midnight and 6:00 a.m.). In this chapter, we will discuss only *monthly* and *quarterly* seasonal patterns, because these are most typical of business data.

smoothing) to make short-run forecasts. Faced with erratic data, experts may use their own knowledge of a particular industry to make *judgment forecasts.* For example, monthly sales forecasts of a particular automobile may combine judgment forecasts from dealers, financial staff, and economists.

15.2 Trend Forecasting

Chapter 20

There are many forecasting methods designed for specific situations. Much of this chapter deals with *trend models* because they are so common in business. You will also learn to use *decomposition* to make adjustments for *seasonality,* and how to use *smoothing models.* The important topics of *ARIMA models* and *causal models* using regression are reserved for a more specialized class in forecasting. Figure 15.6 summarizes the main categories of forecasting models.

Three Trend Models

There are many possible trend models, but three of them are especially useful in business:

$$y_t = a + bt \qquad \text{for } t = 1, 2, \ldots, n \text{ (linear trend)} \qquad \textbf{(15.1)}$$

$$y_t = ae^{bt} \qquad \text{for } t = 1, 2, \ldots, n \text{ (exponential trend)} \qquad \textbf{(15.2)}$$

$$y_t = a + bt + ct^2 \quad \text{for } t = 1, 2, \ldots, n \text{ (quadratic trend)} \qquad \textbf{(15.3)}$$

The linear and exponential models are widely used because they have only two parameters and are familiar to most business audiences. The quadratic model may be useful when the data have a turning point. All three can be fitted by Excel, MegaStat, or MINITAB. Each model will be examined in turn.

Linear Trend Model

The **linear trend** model has the form $y_t = a + bt$. It is useful for a time series that grows or declines by the same amount (*b*) in each period (not the same *rate*), as shown in Figure 15.7. It is the simplest model and may suffice for short-run forecasting. It is generally preferred in

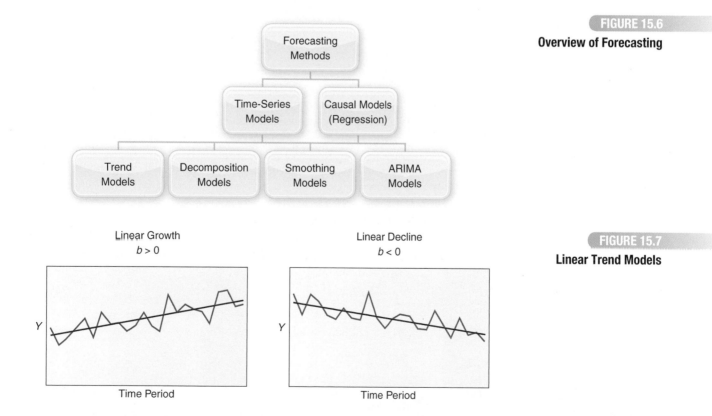

FIGURE 15.6

Overview of Forecasting

FIGURE 15.7

Linear Trend Models

Excel's Linear Trend

CarDealers

Source: *Statistical Abstract of the United States, 2003.*

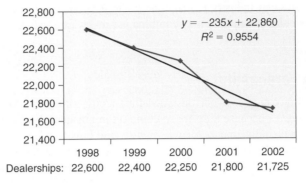

Number of Franchised U.S. New Car Dealerships

$y = -235x + 22,860$
$R^2 = 0.9554$

	1998	1999	2000	2001	2002
Dealerships:	22,600	22,400	22,250	21,800	21,725

business as a baseline forecasting model unless there are compelling reasons to consider a more complex model.

Illustration: Linear Trend

In recent years, the number of U.S. franchised new car dealerships has been declining due to phasing out of low-volume dealerships and consolidation of market areas. What has been the average annual decline? Based on the line graph in Figure 15.8, the linear model seems appropriate to describe this trend in the late 1990s and early 2000s. The slope of Excel's fitted trend indicates that during that period, on average, 235 dealerships were lost annually.

Linear Trend Calculations

The linear trend is fitted in the usual way by using the ordinary least squares formulas, as illustrated in Table 15.2. These formulas were developed in the simple linear regression chapter (Chapter 13). Because you are already familiar with regression, we will only point out the use of the index $t = 1, 2, 3, 4, 5$ as the independent variable (instead of using the years 1998, 1999, 2000, 2001, 2002). We use this time index to simplify the calculations and keep the data magnitudes under control (Excel uses this method too).

$$\text{Slope:} \quad b = \frac{\sum_{t=1}^{n}(t - \bar{t})(y_t - \bar{y})}{\sum_{t=1}^{n}(t - \bar{t})^2} = \frac{-2,350}{10} = -235$$

$$\text{Intercept:} \quad a = \bar{y} - b\bar{t} = 22,155 - (-235)(3) = 22,860$$

The *slope* of the fitted trend $y_t = 22,860 - 235t$ is -235, and it says that we expect to lose 235 dealerships each year. The *intercept* has no real meaning except that it allows us, along with the *slope*, to estimate y_t.

TABLE 15.2 **Sums for Least Squares Calculations**

Year	t	y_t	$t - \bar{t}$	$y_t - \bar{y}$	$(t - \bar{t})^2$	$(t - \bar{t})(y_t - \bar{y})$
1998	1	22,600	−2	445	4	−890
1999	2	22,400	−1	245	1	−245
2000	3	22,250	0	95	0	0
2001	4	21,800	1	−355	1	−355
2002	5	21,725	2	−430	4	−860
Sum	15	110,775	0	0	10	−2,350
Mean	3	22,155	0	0	2	−470

Fitting and Interpreting an Annual Trend

In fitting a trend to annual data, the years (1998, 1999, 2000, 2001, 2002) are merely used as labels for the X-axis. The yearly labels should *not* be used in fitting the trend or calculating the forecast. To fit a trend to annual data, convert the labels to a time index ($t = 1, 2, \ldots$, etc.) To make a forecast, insert a value for the time index ($t = 1, 2, \ldots$, etc.) into Excel's fitted trend.

Forecasting a Linear Trend

We can make a forecast for any future year by using the fitted model $y_t = 22{,}860 - 235t$. In the car dealer example, the fitted trend equation is based on only five years' data, so we should be wary of extrapolating too far ahead:

For 2003 ($t = 6$): $y_6 = 22{,}860 - 235(6) = 21{,}450$

For 2004 ($t = 7$): $y_7 = 22{,}860 - 235(7) = 21{,}215$

For 2005 ($t = 8$): $y_8 = 22{,}860 - 235(8) = 20{,}980$

Linear Trend: Calculating R^2

The worksheet shown in Table 15.3 shows the calculation of the coefficient of determination. In this illustration, the linear model gives a good fit ($R^2 = 0.9554$) to the *past* data. However, a good fit to the past data does not guarantee good *future* forecasts. A deeper analysis of underlying causes of dealership consolidation is needed. What is causing the trend? Are the causal forces likely to remain the same in subsequent years? Could the current trend continue indefinitely, or will it approach an asymptote or limit of some kind? These are questions that forecasters must ask. The forecast is simply a projection of current trend assuming that nothing changes.

$$\text{Coefficient of determination: } R^2 = 1 - \frac{\sum_{t-1}^{n}(y_t - \hat{y}_t)^2}{\sum_{t-1}^{n}(y_t - \bar{y})^2} = 1 - \frac{25{,}750}{578{,}000} = 0.9554$$

Concept Check

Why might the trend line for automobile dealerships based on 1998 through 2002 data not be appropriate to forecast the number of new car dealerships in the years 2009 and beyond?

TABLE 15.3   Sums for R^2 Calculations

Year	t	y_t	$\hat{y}_t = 22{,}860 - 235t$	$y_t - \hat{y}_t$	$(y_t - \hat{y}_t)^2$	$(y_t - \bar{y})^2$
1998	1	22,600	22,625	−25	625	198,025
1999	2	22,400	22,390	10	100	60,025
2000	3	22,250	22,155	95	9,025	9,025
2001	4	21,800	21,920	−120	14,400	126,025
2002	5	21,725	21,685	40	1,600	184,900
Sum	15		110,775	0	25,750	578,000

FIGURE 15.9

Exponential Trend Models

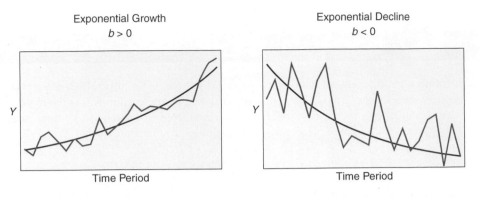

Exponential Trend Model

The **exponential trend** model has the form $y_t = ae^{bt}$. It is useful for a time series that grows or declines at the same *rate* (b) in each period, as shown in Figure 15.9. When the growth rate is positive ($b > 0$), then Y grows by an *increasing* amount each period (unlike the linear model, which assumes a *constant* increment each period). If the growth rate is negative ($b < 0$), then Y declines by a *decreasing* amount each period (unlike the linear model, which assumes a *constant* decrement each period).

When to Use the Exponential Model

The exponential model is often preferred for financial data or data that cover a longer period of time. When you invest money in a commercial bank savings account, interest accrues at a given percent. Your savings grow faster than a linear rate because you earn interest on the accumulated interest. Banks use the exponential formula to calculate interest on CDs. Financial analysts often find the exponential model attractive because costs, revenue, and salaries are best projected under assumed *percent* growth rates.

Another nice feature of the exponential model is that you can compare two growth rates in two time-series variables with dissimilar data units (i.e., a percent growth rate is *unit-free*). For example, between 1990 and 2000 the number of U.S. Medicare enrollees grew from 34.3 million persons to 39.6 million persons (1.45 percent growth per annum), while Medicare payments to hospitals grew from $65.7 billion to $126.0 billion (6.73 percent growth per annum). Comparing the percents, we see that Medicare insurance payments have been growing more than four times as fast as the Medicare head count. These facts underlie the ongoing debate about Medicare spending in the United States.

There may not be much difference between a linear and exponential model when the growth rate is small and the data set covers only a few time periods. For example, suppose your starting salary is $50,000. Table 15.4 compares salary increases of $2,500 each year ($y_t = 50,000 + 2,500t$) with a continuously compounded 4.879 percent salary growth ($y_t = 50,000e^{0.04879t}$). Over the first few years, there is little difference. But after 20 years, the

TABLE 15.4 Two Models of Salary Growth

T	$y_t = 50,000 + 2,500t$ Linear	$y_t = 50,000e^{0.04879t}$ Exponential
0	50,000	50,000
5	62,500	63,814
10	75,000	81,445
15	87,500	103,946
20	100,000	132,664

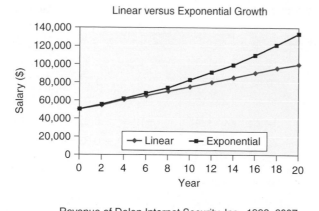

FIGURE 15.10

Linear and Exponential Growth Compared

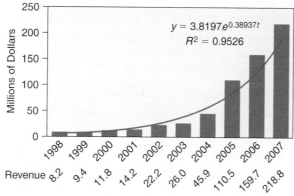

FIGURE 15.11

Excel's Exponential Trend DolonCorp

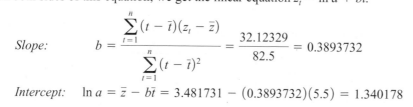

difference is obvious, as shown in Figure 15.10. Despite its attractive simplicity,* the linear model's assumptions may be inappropriate for some financial variables.

Illustration: Exponential Trend

Spending on Internet security has shown explosive growth, as indicated in Figure 15.11. Clearly, a linear trend (constant *dollar* growth) would be inadequate. It is more reasonable to assume a constant *percent* rate of growth and fit an exponential model. For the Dolon company's revenue (shown in Figure 15.11), the fitted exponential trend is $y_t = 3.8197e^{0.3894t}$. The value of b in the exponential model $y_t = ae^{bt}$ is the continuously compounded growth rate, so we can say that Dolon's revenue is growing at an astonishing rate of 38.94 percent per year. A negative value of b in the equation $y_t = ae^{bt}$ would indicate *decline* instead of growth. The intercept a is the "starting point" in period $t = 0$. For example, $y_0 = 3.8197e^{0.3894(0)} = 3.8197$.

Exponential Trend Calculations

Table 15.5 shows the worksheet for the required sums. Calculations of the exponential trend are done by using a transformed variable $z_t = \ln(y_t)$ instead of y_t to produce a linear equation so that we can use the least squares formulas. Note that when $y_t = ae^{bt}$, taking the natural logarithm on both sides of this equation, we get the linear equation $z_t = \ln a + bt$.

$$\text{Slope:} \qquad b = \frac{\sum_{t=1}^{n}(t - \bar{t})(z_t - \bar{z})}{\sum_{t=1}^{n}(t - \bar{t})^2} = \frac{32.12329}{82.5} = 0.3893732$$

$$\text{Intercept:} \quad \ln a = \bar{z} - b\bar{t} = 3.481731 - (0.3893732)(5.5) = 1.340178$$

---

*In a sense, the linear model ($y_t = a + bt$) and the exponential model ($y_t = ae^{bt}$) are equally simple because they are two-parameter models, and a log-transformed exponential model $\ln(y_t) = \ln(a) + bt$ is actually linear.

TABLE 15.5   Least Squares Sums for the Exponential Model   DolonCorp

Year	t	y_t	$z_t = \ln(y_t)$	$t - \bar{t}$	$z_t - \bar{z}$	$(t - \bar{t})^2$	$(t - \bar{t})(z_t - \bar{z})$
1998	1	8.2	2.10413	−4.5	−1.37760	20.25	6.19919
1999	2	9.4	2.24071	−3.5	−1.24102	12.25	4.34357
2000	3	11.8	2.46810	−2.5	−1.01363	6.25	2.53408
2001	4	14.2	2.65324	−1.5	−0.82849	2.25	1.24273
2002	5	22.2	3.10009	−0.5	−0.38164	0.25	0.19082
2003	6	26.0	3.25810	0.5	−0.22363	0.25	−0.11182
2004	7	45.9	3.82647	1.5	0.34473	2.25	0.51710
2005	8	110.5	4.70502	2.5	1.22328	6.25	3.05821
2006	9	159.7	5.07330	3.5	1.59157	12.25	5.57048
2007	10	218.8	5.38816	4.5	1.90643	20.25	8.57892
Sum	55	626.7	34.81731	0.0	0.00000	82.5	32.12329
Mean	5.5	62.67	3.481731				

When the least squares calculations are completed, we must transform the intercept back to the original units by exponentiation to get the correct intercept $a = e^{1.340178} = 3.8197$. In final form, the fitted trend equation is

$$y_t = ae^{bt} = 3.8197e^{0.38937t}$$

This equation is easily obtained in Excel by drawing a scatter plot of these 10 (t, y_t) points, right-clicking on any point in the scatter plot, choosing the option Add Trendline, and then checking on the options shown below.

t	y_t
1	8.2
2	9.4
3	11.8
4	14.2
5	22.2
6	26
7	45.9
8	110.5
9	159.7
10	218.8

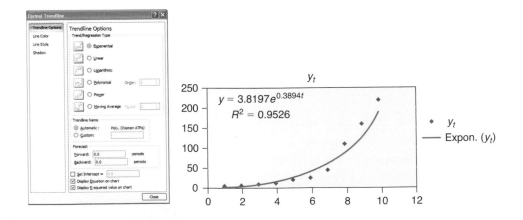

Forecasting an Exponential Trend

We can make a forecast of Dolon's revenue for any future year by using the fitted model:*

For 2008 ($t = 11$): $y_{11} = 3.8197e^{0.38937(11)} = 276.8$

For 2009 ($t = 12$): $y_{12} = 3.8197e^{0.38937(12)} = 408.5$

For 2010 ($t = 13$): $y_{13} = 3.8197e^{0.38937(13)} = 603.0$

Can Dolon's revenue actually continue to grow at a rate of 38.937 percent? It seems unlikely. Typically, when a new product is introduced, its growth rate at first is very strong, but eventually slows down as the market becomes saturated and/or as competitors arise.

Exponential Trend: Calculating R^2

As shown in Table 15.6, we calculate R^2 in the same way as for the linear trend, except that we replace the dependent variable y_t with $z_t = \ln(y_t)$ and the fitted value with $\hat{z}_t = 1.340178 + 0.389373t$. This is necessary because Excel's trend-fitting calculations are done in logarithms in an exponential model:

$$\text{Coefficient of determination: } R^2 = 1 - \frac{\sum_{t=1}^{n}(z_t - \hat{z}_t)^2}{\sum_{t=1}^{n}(z_t - \bar{z})^2} = 1 - \frac{0.62227}{13.13022} = 0.9526$$

In this example, the exponential trend gives a very good fit ($R^2 = 0.9526$) to the past data. Although a high R^2 does not guarantee good forecasts, Internet security protection is expected to reach a wider consumer audience in the future, so the high growth rate could continue if the firm is able to manage its expansion.

TABLE 15.6   Sums for R^2 Calculations in Exponential Model   DolonCorp

t	$z_t = \ln(y_t)$	$\hat{z}_t = 1.340178 + 0.38937t$	$z_t - \hat{z}_t$	$(z_t - \hat{z}_t)^2$	$(z_t - \bar{z})^2$
1	2.10413	1.72955	0.37458	0.14031	1.89777
2	2.24071	2.11892	0.12179	0.01483	1.54013
3	2.46810	2.50830	−0.04020	0.00162	1.02745
4	2.65324	2.89767	−0.24443	0.05975	0.68639
5	3.10009	3.28704	−0.18695	0.03495	0.14565
6	3.25810	3.67642	−0.41832	0.17499	0.05001
7	3.82647	4.06579	−0.23932	0.05728	0.11884
8	4.70502	4.45516	0.24985	0.06243	1.49643
9	5.07330	4.84454	0.22876	0.05233	2.53308
10	5.38816	5.23391	0.15425	0.02379	3.63446
Sum	34.81731	34.81731	0.00001	0.62227	13.13022
Mean	3.48173				

*Excel uses the exponential formula $y_t = ae^{bt}$ in which the coefficient b is the *continuously compounded* growth rate. But MINITAB uses an equivalent formula $y_t = y_0(1 + r)^t$, which you may recognize as the formula for compound interest. Although the formulas appear different, they give identical forecasts. For example, for the Dolon company revenue data, MINITAB's fitted trend is $y_t = 3.81972(1.47606)^t$, so the forecasts are as follows:

For 2008 ($t = 11$): $y_{11} = 3.81972(1.47606)^{11} = 276.8$

For 2009 ($t = 12$): $y_{12} = 3.81972(1.47606)^{12} = 408.6$

For 2010 ($t = 13$): $y_{13} = 3.81972(1.47606)^{13} = 603.1$

To convert MINITAB's fitted equation to Excel's, set $a = y_0$ and $b = \ln(1 + r)$. To convert Excel's fitted equation to MINITAB's, set $y_0 = a$ and $r = e^b - 1$.

FIGURE 15.12

Four Quadratic Trend Models

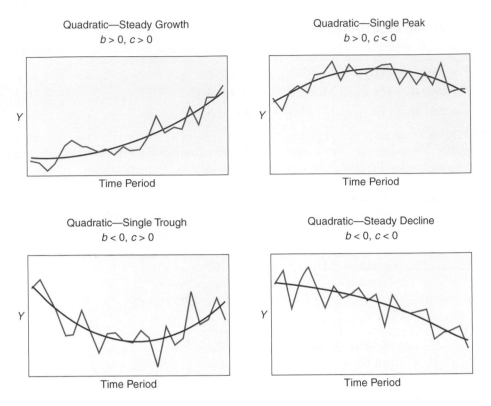

Quadratic—Steady Growth
$b > 0, c > 0$

Quadratic—Single Peak
$b > 0, c < 0$

Quadratic—Single Trough
$b < 0, c > 0$

Quadratic—Steady Decline
$b < 0, c < 0$

Quadratic Trend Model

The **quadratic trend** model has the form $y_t = a + bt + ct^2$. The t^2 term allows a non-linear shape. It is useful for a time series that has a turning point or that is not captured by the exponential model. If $c = 0$, the quadratic model $y_t = a + bt + ct^2$ becomes a linear model because the term ct^2 drops out of the equation (i.e., the linear model is a special case of the quadratic model). Some forecasters fit a quadratic model as a way of checking for non-linearity. If the coefficient c does not differ significantly from zero, then the linear model will suffice. Depending on the values of b and c, the quadratic model can assume any of four shapes, as shown in Figure 15.12.

Illustration: Quadratic Trend

The number of hospital beds (Table 15.7) in the United States declined during the late 1990s, showed signs of levelling out, and then declined again. What trend would we choose if the objective is to make a realistic one-year forecast?

Figure 15.13 shows one-year projections using the linear and quadratic models. Many observers would think that the quadratic model offers a more believable prediction, because the quadratic model is able to capture the slight curvature in the data pattern. But this gain in

TABLE 15.7 **U.S. Hospital Beds (thousands), 1995–2004**   **HospitalBeds**

Year	Beds	Year	Beds
1995	1,081	2000	984
1996	1,062	2001	987
1997	1,035	2002	976
1998	1,013	2003	965
1999	994	2004	956

Source: *Statistical Abstract of the United States, 2007,* p. 114.

Two Trend Models for U.S. Hospital Beds   HospitalBeds   FIGURE 15.13

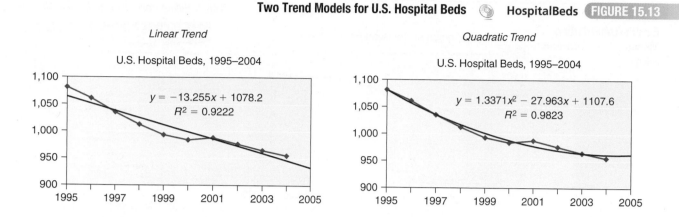

forecast credibility must be weighed against the added complexity of the quadratic model. It appears that the forecasts would turn upward if projected more than one year ahead. We should be especially skeptical of any polynomial model that is projected more than one or two periods into the future.

Because the quadratic trend model $y_t = a + bt + ct^2$ is a multiple regression with two predictors (t and t^2), the least squares calculations are not shown. However, Figure 15.14 shows the MINITAB fitted regression. Note that both t and t^2 are significant predictors (large t, small p).

Using Excel for Trend Fitting

Plot the data, right-click on the data, and choose a trend. Figure 15.15 shows Excel's menu of six trend options. The menu includes a sketch of each trend type. Click the Options tab if you want to display the R^2 and fitted equation on the graph, or if you want to plot forecasts (trend extrapolations) on the graph. The quadratic model is a **polynomial model** of order 2. Despite the many choices, some patterns cannot be captured by any of the common trend models. By default, Excel only reports four-decimal accuracy. However, you can click on Excel's fitted trend equation, choose Format Data Labels, choose Number, and set the number of decimal places you want to see.

Principle of Occam's Razor

Given two *sufficient* explanations, we prefer the simpler one.
  —*William of Occam (1285–1347)*

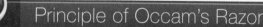

The regression equation is
Beds = 1108 − 28.0 Time + 1.34 Time2

Predictor	Coef	SE Coef	T	P
Constant	1107.62	7.42	149.37	0.000
Time	−27.963	3.097	−9.03	0.000
Time2	1.3371	0.2744	4.87	0.002

S = 6.30473   R-Sq = 98.2%   R-Sq(adj) = 97.7%

FIGURE 15.14

MINITAB's Quadratic Regression
HospitalBeds

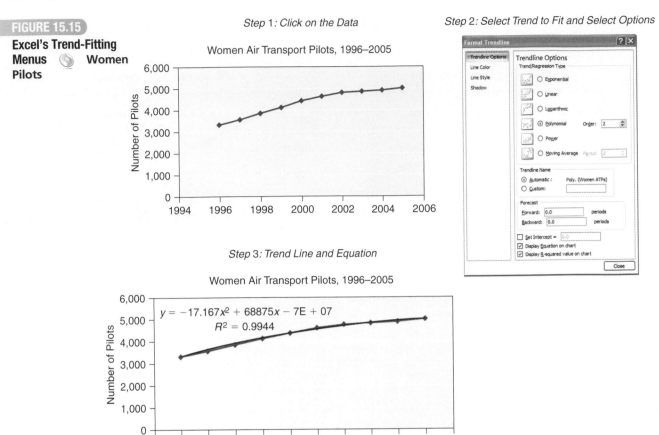

FIGURE 15.15

Excel's Trend-Fitting Menus ⊚ Women Pilots

Step 1: Click on the Data

Women Air Transport Pilots, 1996–2005

Step 2: Select Trend to Fit and Select Options

Step 3: Trend Line and Equation

Women Air Transport Pilots, 1996–2005

$y = -17.167x^2 + 68875x - 7E + 07$
$R^2 = 0.9944$

Trend-Fitting Criteria

It is so easy to fit a trend in Excel that it is tempting to "shop around" for the best fit. But forecasters prefer the simplest trend model that adequately matches the trend. Simple models are easier to interpret and explain to others. Criteria for selecting a trend model for forecasting include the following:

Criterion	Ask Yourself
• Occam's Razor	Would a simpler model suffice?
• Overall fit	How does the trend fit the past data?
• Believability	Does the extrapolated trend "look right"?
• Fit to recent data	Does the fitted trend match the last few data points?

EXAMPLE 1

Comparing Trends

You can usually increase the R^2 by choosing a more complex model. But if you are making a *forecast,* this is not the only relevant issue, because R^2 measures the fit to the *past* data. Figure 15.16 shows four fitted trends using the same data, with three-period forecasts. For this data set, the linear model may be inadequate because its fit to recent periods is marginal (we prefer the simplest model *only if* it "does the job"). Here, the cubic trend yields the highest R^2, but the fitted equation is nonintuitive and would be hard to explain or defend. Also, its forecasts appear to be increasing too rapidly. In this example, the exponential model has the lowest R^2, yet matches the recent data fairly well and its forecasts appear credible when projected a few periods ahead.

Any trend model's forecasts become less reliable as they are extrapolated farther into the future. The quadratic trend, the simplest of Excel's polynomial models, is sometimes acceptable for short-term forecasting. However, forecasters avoid higher-order polynomial models (cubic and higher) not only because they are complex but also because they can give bizarre forecasts when extrapolated more than one period ahead. Table 15.8 compares the features of the three most common trend models.

Four Fitted Trends Using the Same Data FIGURE 15.16

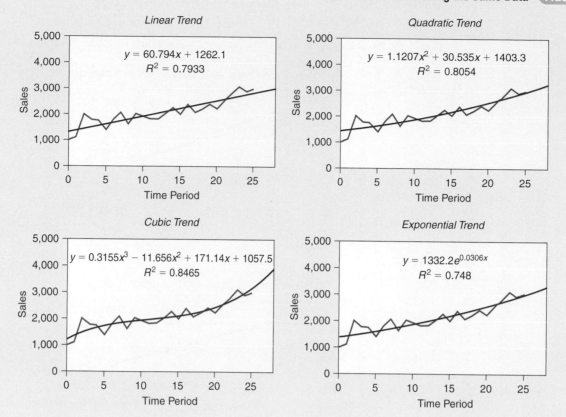

TABLE 15.8   Comparison of Three Trend Models

Model	Pro	Con
Linear	1. Simple, familiar to everyone.	1. Assumes constant slope.
	2. May suffice for short-run data.	2. Cannot capture non-linear change.
Exponential	1. Familiar to financial analysts.	1. Some managers are unfamiliar with e^x.
	2. Shows compound percent growth rate.	2. Data values must be positive.
Quadratic	1. Useful for data with a turning point.	1. Complex and no intuitive interpretation.
	2. Useful test for non-linearity.	2. Can give untrustworthy forecasts if extrapolated too far.

A Closer Look

Not only must you decide which of the above three trend models best fits the data, you must also decide the time frame that is most appropriate when developing your model. For example, using the full 10 years of available data for the U.S. hospital bed example, the forecast for the number of beds in 2005 using the linear trend model would be

$$y_{11} = -13.255(11) + 1078.2 \approx 932.4 \ (1000s)$$

and the forecast for 2005 using the quadratic trend model would be

$$y_{11} = 1.3371(11^2) - 27.963(11) + 1107.6 \approx 961.8\,(1000s)$$

If only the latest five years were used, the line graphs would look like this:

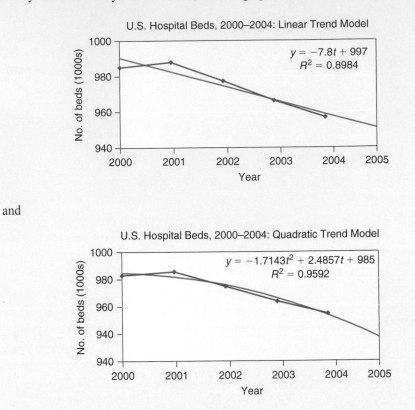

U.S. Hospital Beds, 2000–2004: Linear Trend Model

$$y = -7.8t + 997$$
$$R^2 = 0.8984$$

and

U.S. Hospital Beds, 2000–2004: Quadratic Trend Model

$$y = -1.7143t^2 + 2.4857t + 985$$
$$R^2 = 0.9592$$

Using these models, the forecasts for the number of hospital beds in 2005 ($t = 6$) would be

$$y_6 = -7.8(6) + 997 \approx 950.2\,(1000s) \text{ using the linear trend model}$$

and

$$y_6 = -1.7143(6^2) + 2.4857(6) + 985 \approx 938.2\,(1000s) \text{ using the quadratic trend model}$$

If the above differences between either the linear and quadratic trend models and/or between the models using different time frames are thought to be significant, it is important to determine which is the best model and which is the appropriate time frame to use. When determining the appropriate time frame, generally the more data you have the better, unless something happened that made the earlier data irrelevant or misleading. For example, the Windsor Spitfires of the OHL recently moved into the new WFCU arena. To use attendance figures from their previous venue may be irrelevant when trying to forecast attendance in their new facility.

Concept Check

Looking at the results of the four different models and their forecasts for the U.S. hospital bed example, what are some observations that you can make other than the forecasts are different? What observations could you make if forecasts were made for 2006?

15.1   For the U.S. hospital bed study, use only the last four years of data to create graphs of the linear trend and quadratic trend models. Use the results to forecast the number of beds for 2005 and comment on the results not only between these models but also between these models and the previous models created for this study. (LO 2)

15.2   (a) Make an Excel graph of the data on U.S. diesel new car sales. (b) Discuss the underlying causes that might explain the trend. (c) Use Excel, MegaStat, or MINITAB to fit three trends (linear, quadratic, and exponential) to the time series. (d) Which trend model do you think is best to make forecasts for the next three years? Why? (e) Use *each* of the three fitted trend equations to make numerical forecasts for 2004, 2005, and 2006. How much difference does the choice of model make? Which forecasts do you trust the most, and why? (f) If you have access to *Ward's Automotive Yearbook,* check your forecasts. How accurate were they? (LO 2)   **Diesel**

U.S. Diesel New Car Sales, 1993–2003

Year	Sales
1993	2,800
1994	3,577
1995	3,139
1996	8,469
1997	7,331
1998	10,972
1999	13,573
2000	22,634
2001	15,077
2002	31,430
2003	38,524

Source: *Ward's Automotive Yearbook, 2004,* 66th ed., p. 40.

15.3   (a) Make an Excel graph of the data on U.S. online advertising spending. (b) Discuss the underlying causes that might explain the trend or pattern. (c) Use Excel, MegaStat, or MINITAB to fit three trends (linear, quadratic, exponential) to the time series. (d) Which trend model do you think is best to make forecasts for the next three years? Why? (e) Use *each* of the three fitted trend equations to make a numerical forecast for 2007. How similar are the three models' forecasts? (LO 2)   **Online**

U.S. Online Advertising, 2000–2006 (billions)

Year	Spending
2000	$8.1
2001	7.1
2002	6.0
2003	6.3
2004	6.8
2005	7.2
2006	8.1

Source: William F. Arens, *Contemporary Advertising,* 9th ed. (McGraw-Hill, 2004), p. 549.

15.4 (a) Make an Excel line graph of the data on employee work stoppages. (b) Discuss the underlying causes that might explain the trend or pattern. (c) Fit three trends (linear, exponential, quadratic). (d) Which trend model is best, and why? If none is satisfactory, explain. (e) Make a forecast for 2007, using a trend model of your choice or a judgment forecast. (LO 2)

Strikers

U.S. Workers Involved in Work Stoppages (thousands)

Year	Strikers	Year	Strikers
1997	339	2002	46
1998	387	2003	129
1999	73	2004	171
2000	394	2005	100
2001	99	2006	70

Source: http://data.bls.gov.

15.5 (a) Make an Excel line graph of the pilots' data. (b) Discuss the underlying causes that might explain the trend or pattern. (c) Fit three trends (linear, exponential, quadratic). (d) Which trend model is best, and why? If none is satisfactory, explain. (e) Make a forecast for 2006, using a trend model of your choice or a judgment forecast. (f) Repeat parts (a) through (e) using the latest five years of data. (LO 2) **WomenPilots**

Active Women Air Transport Pilots, 1996–2005

Year	Women ATPs
1996	3,346
1997	3,572
1998	3,848
1999	4,126
2000	4,411
2001	4,630
2002	4,792
2003	4,850
2004	4,908
2005	5,008

Source: www.faa.gov.

15.6 (a) Plot the data on fruit and vegetable consumption. (b) Discuss the underlying causes that might explain the trend or pattern. (c) Fit a linear trend to the data. (d) Interpret the trend equation. What are its implications for producers? (e) Make a forecast for 2010. *Note:* Time increments are five years, so use $t = 7$ for your 2010 forecast. (LO 2) **Fruits**

U.S. per Capita Consumption of Commercially Produced Fruits and Vegetables (pounds)

Year	Total
1980	608.8
1985	632.2
1990	660.2
1995	692.5
2000	711.7
2005	694.3

Source: *Statistical Abstract of the United States, 2007*, p. 134.

15.3 Assessing Fit

Five Measures of Fit

In time-series analysis, you are likely to encounter several different measures of "fit" that show how well the estimated trend model matches the observed time series. "Fit" refers to historical data, and you should bear in mind that a good fit is no guarantee of good forecasts—the usual goal. Five common measures of fit are shown in Table 15.9.

TABLE 15.9 Five Measures of Fit

Statistic	Description	Pro	Con
$R^2 = 1 - \dfrac{\sum_{t=1}^{n}(y_t - \hat{y}_t)^2}{\sum_{t=1}^{n}(y_t - \bar{y}_t)^2}$ (15.4)	Coefficient of Determination	1. Unit-free measure. 2. Very common.	1. Often interpreted incorrectly (e.g., "percent of correct predictions").
$MAPE = \dfrac{100}{n}\sum_{t=1}^{n}\dfrac{|y_t - \hat{y}_t|}{y_t}$ (15.5)	Mean Absolute Percent Error (MAPE)	1. Unit-free measure (%). 2. Intuitive meaning.	1. Requires $y_t > 0$. 2. Lacks nice math properties.
$MAD = \dfrac{1}{n}\sum_{t=1}^{n}|y_t - \hat{y}_t|$ (15.6)	Mean Absolute Deviation (MAD)	1. Intuitive meaning. 2. Same units as y_t.	1. Not unit-free. 2. Lacks nice math properties.
$MSD = \dfrac{1}{n}\sum_{t=1}^{n}(y_t - \hat{y}_t)^2$ (15.7)	Mean Squared Deviation (MSD)	1. Nice math properties. 2. Penalizes big errors more.	1. Non-intuitive 2. Rarely reported.
$SE = \sqrt{\dfrac{\sum_{i=1}^{n}(y_t - \hat{y}_t)^2}{n-2}}$ (15.8)	Standard Error (SE)	1. Same units as y_t. 2. For confidence intervals.	1. Non-intuitive meaning.

Figure 15.17 shows a MINITAB graph with fitted linear trend and three-year forecasts for aggregate U.S. fire losses between 1997 and 2007. Notice that, instead of R^2, MINITAB displays *MAPE, MAD,* and *MSD* statistics. Table 15.10 shows the calculations for these statistics of fit. Because the residuals $y_t - \hat{y}_t$ sum to zero, we see why it's necessary to sum either their absolute values or their squares to obtain a measure of fit. *MAPE, MAD, MSD,* and *SE* would be zero if the trend provided a perfect fit to the time series.

EXAMPLE 2
Fire Losses

FIGURE 15.17

MINITAB's Time-Series Trend—Linear Model
FireLosses

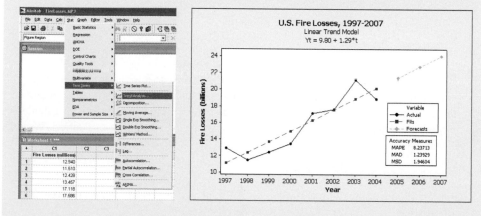

TABLE 15.10 Sums for *MAD, MAPE, MSD,* and Standard Error 🔘   Fire Losses

Period	Year	Losses	$\hat{y}_t = 9.8034 + 1.2949t$	$y_t - \hat{y}_t$	$\lvert y_t - \hat{y}_t \rvert$	$\lvert y_t - \hat{y}_t \rvert / y_t$	$(y_t - \hat{y}_t)^2$
1	1997	12.940	11.0983	1.8417	1.8417	0.1423	3.3919
2	1998	11.510	12.3932	−0.8832	0.8832	0.0767	0.7800
3	1999	12.428	13.6881	−1.2601	1.2601	0.1014	1.5879
4	2000	13.457	14.9830	−1.5260	1.5260	0.1134	2.3287
5	2001	17.118	16.2779	0.8401	0.8401	0.0491	0.7058
6	2002	17.586	17.5728	0.0132	0.0132	0.0008	0.0002
7	2003	21.129	18.8677	2.2613	2.2613	0.1070	5.1135
8	2004	18.874	20.1626	−1.2886	1.2886	0.0683	1.6605
			Sum	0.00	9.9142	0.6590	15.5683
			Mean	0.00	1.2393	0.0824	1.9460

Source: *Statistical Abstract of the United States, 2007,* p. 212. Losses are in billions of dollars.

Calculations

Using the sums in Table 15.10, we can apply the formulas for each fit statistic:

$$MAPE = \frac{100}{n} \sum_{t=1}^{n} \frac{\lvert y_t - \hat{y}_t \rvert}{y_t} = \frac{100}{8}(0.6590) = 8.24\%$$

$$MAD = \frac{1}{n} \sum_{t=1}^{n} \lvert y_t - \hat{y}_t \rvert = \frac{1}{8}(9.9142) = 1.239$$

$$MSD = \frac{1}{n} \sum_{t=1}^{n} (y_t - \hat{y}_t)^2 = \frac{1}{8}(15.5683) = 1.946$$

$$SE = \sqrt{\sum_{t=1}^{n} \frac{(y_t - \hat{y}_t)^2}{n - 2}} = \sqrt{\frac{15.5683}{8 - 2}} = 1.611$$

Interpretation

The *MAPE* says that our fitted trend has a mean absolute error of 8.24 percent. The *MAD* says that the average error is 1.239 billion dollars (ignoring the sign). The *MSD* lacks a simple interpretation. These fit statistics are most useful in comparing different trend models for the same data. All the statistics (especially the *MSD*) are affected by the unusual residual in 2003, when fire losses greatly exceeded the trend. The standard error is useful if we want to make a prediction interval for a forecast, using Equation 15.9. It is the same formula you saw in Chapter 13.

$$\hat{y}_t \pm t_{\alpha/2,\,n-2}SE \sqrt{1 + \frac{1}{n} + \frac{(t - \bar{t})^2}{\sum_{t=1}^{n}(t - \bar{t})^2}} \quad \text{(prediction interval for future } y_t\text{)} \quad \textbf{(15.9)}$$

15.4 Moving Averages

Trendless or Erratic Data

What if the time series $y_1, y_2, \ldots, y_n$ is erratic or has no consistent trend? In such cases, there may be little point in fitting a trend, and if the mean is changing over time, we cannot just "take the average" over the entire data set. Instead, a conservative approach is to calculate a *moving average*. There are two main types of moving averages: trailing or centred. We will illustrate each.

Trailing Moving Average (*TMA*)

The simplest kind of moving average is the **trailing moving average (*TMA*)** over the last *m* periods.

$$\hat{y}_t = \frac{y_t + y_{t-1} + \cdots + y_{t-m+1}}{m} \quad \text{(trailing moving average over } m \text{ periods)} \quad \textbf{(15.10)}$$

The *TMA* smoothes the past fluctuations in the time series, helping us see the pattern more clearly. The choice of *m* depends on the situation. A larger *m* yields a "smoother" *TMA,* but requires more data. The value of $\hat{y}_t$ may also be used as a forecast for period $t + 1$. Beyond the range of the observed data $y_1, y_2, \ldots, y_n$ there is no way to update the moving average, so it is best regarded as a *one-period-ahead forecast.*

Centred Moving Average (*CMA*)

Another moving average is the **centred moving average (*CMA*).** Equation 15.11 shows a *CMA* for $m = 3$ periods. The formula looks both forward *and* backward in time, to express the current "forecast" as the mean of the current observation *and* observations on either side of the current data.

$$\hat{y}_t = \frac{y_{t-1} + y_t + y_{t+1}}{3} \quad \text{(centred moving average over } m \text{ periods)} \quad \textbf{(15.11)}$$

This is not really a forecast at all, but merely a way of smoothing the data.

When *m* is odd ($m = 3$, 5, etc.) the *CMA* is easy to calculate. When *m* is even, the formula is more complex, because the mean of an even number of data points would lie *between* two data points and would not be correctly centred. Instead, we take a double moving average to get the resulting *CMA* centred properly. For example, for $m = 4$, we would average y_{t-2} through y_{t+1}, then average y_{t-1} through y_{t+2}, and finally average the two averages! You need not worry about this formula for now. It will be illustrated shortly in the context of seasonal data.

Using Excel for a *TMA*

Excel offers a *TMA* in its **Add Trendline** option when you click on a time-series line graph or bar chart. Its menus are displayed in Figure 15.18. The *TMA* is a conservative choice whenever you doubt that one of Excel's five other trend models (linear, logarithmic, polynomial, power, exponential) would be appropriate. However, Excel does *not* give you the option of making any forecasts with its moving average model.

15.5   Exponential Smoothing

Excel's Moving Average Menu   FIGURE 15.18

Section Exercises

15.7 A Harvey's restaurant, located adjacent to an Ontario university, relies on students for most of its business. The following table lists the number of hamburgers sold over a 14-day period. Create a line graph using Excel for sales over this period and describe the pattern. Use the *TMA* method to manually calculate three-day and seven-day moving averages and plot these moving averages on a line graph. Interpret and compare these two moving averages and, if noticeable differences occur, explain why they may exist. (LO 4)

Day	Date	Sales	Day	Date	Sales
Saturday	Oct-13	150	Saturday	Oct-20	160
Sunday	Oct-14	173	Sunday	Oct-21	176
Monday	Oct-15	247	Monday	Oct-22	237
Tuesday	Oct-16	272	Tuesday	Oct-23	226
Wednesday	Oct-17	264	Wednesday	Oct-24	258
Thursday	Oct-18	291	Thursday	Oct-25	279
Friday	Oct-19	198	Friday	Oct-26	185

15.8 (a) Make an Excel line graph of the exchange rate data. Describe the pattern. (b) Click on the data and choose Add Trendline > Moving Average. Describe the effect of increasing m (e.g., $m = 2, 4, 6$, etc.). Include a copy of each graph with your answer. (c) Discuss how this moving average might help a currency speculator. (LO 4) **DollarEuro**

Daily Dollar/Euro Exchange Rate for First Three Months of 2005 ($n = 64$ days)

Date	Rate	Date	Rate	Date	Rate	Date	Rate
3-Jan	1.3476	25-Jan	1.2954	16-Feb	1.2994	10-Mar	1.3409
4-Jan	1.3295	26-Jan	1.3081	17-Feb	1.3083	11-Mar	1.3465
5-Jan	1.3292	27-Jan	1.3032	18-Feb	1.3075	14-Mar	1.3346
6-Jan	1.3187	28-Jan	1.3033	21-Feb	1.3153	15-Mar	1.3315
7-Jan	1.3062	31-Jan	1.3049	22-Feb	1.3230	16-Mar	1.3423
10-Jan	1.3109	1-Feb	1.3017	23-Feb	1.3208	17-Mar	1.3373
11-Jan	1.3161	2-Feb	1.3015	24-Feb	1.3205	18-Mar	1.3311
12-Jan	1.3281	3-Feb	1.2959	25-Feb	1.3195	21-Mar	1.3165
13-Jan	1.3207	4-Feb	1.2927	28-Feb	1.3274	22-Mar	1.3210
14-Jan	1.3106	7-Feb	1.2773	1-Mar	1.3189	23-Mar	1.3005
17-Jan	1.3075	8-Feb	1.2783	2-Mar	1.3127	24-Mar	1.2957
18-Jan	1.3043	9-Feb	1.2797	3-Mar	1.3130	25-Mar	1.2954
19-Jan	1.3036	10-Feb	1.2882	4-Mar	1.3244	28-Mar	1.2877
20-Jan	1.2959	11-Feb	1.2864	7-Mar	1.3203	29-Mar	1.2913
21-Jan	1.3049	14-Feb	1.2981	8-Mar	1.3342	30-Mar	1.2944
24-Jan	1.3041	15-Feb	1.2986	9-Mar	1.3384	31-Mar	1.2969

Source: www.federalreserve.gov.

Forecast Updating

The *exponential smoothing* model is a special kind of moving average. It is used for ongoing one-period-ahead forecasting for data that has up-and-down movements but no consistent trend. For example, a retail outlet may place orders for thousands of different stock-keeping units (SKUs) each week, so as to maintain its inventory of each item at the desired level (to avoid emergency calls to warehouses or suppliers). For such forecasts, many firms choose exponential smoothing, a simple forecasting model with only two inputs and one constant. The updating formula for the forecasts is

$$F_{t+1} = \alpha y_t + (1 - \alpha)F_t \quad \text{(smoothing update)} \qquad (15.12)$$

where

F_{t+1} = the forecast for the next period

α = the "smoothing constant" $(0 \le \alpha \le 1)$

y_t = the actual data value in period t

F_t = the previous forecast for period t

Smoothing Constant (α)

The next forecast F_{t+1} is a weighted average of y_t (the current data) and F_t (the previous fore-cast). The value of α, called the **smoothing constant,** is the weight given to the latest data. A small value of α would give low weight to the most recent observation and heavy weight $1 - \alpha$ to the previous forecast (a "heavily smoothed" series). The larger the value of α, the more quickly the forecasts adapt to recent data. For example,

If $\alpha = 0.05$, then $F_{t+1} = 0.05y_t + 0.95F_t$ (heavy smoothing, slow adaptation)

If $\alpha = 0.20$, then $F_{t+1} = 0.20y_t + 0.80F_t$ (moderate smoothing, moderate adaptation)

If $\alpha = 0.50$, then $F_{t+1} = 0.50y_t + 0.50F_t$ (little smoothing, quick adaptation)

Choosing the Value of α

If $\alpha = 1$, there is no smoothing at all, and the forecast for next period is the same as the latest data point, which basically defeats the purpose of exponential smoothing. MINITAB uses $\alpha = 0.20$ (i.e., moderate smoothing) as its default, which is a fairly common choice of α. The fit of the forecasts to the data will change as you try different values of α. Most computer packages can, as an option, solve for the "best" α using a criterion such as minimum *SSE.*

Over time, earlier data values have less effect on the exponential smoothing forecasts than more recent y values. To see this, we can replace F_t in Equation 15.12 with the prior forecast F_{t-1}, and repeat this type of substitution indefinitely to obtain this result:

$$F_{t+1} = \alpha y_t + \alpha(1 - \alpha)y_{t-1} + \alpha(1 - \alpha)^2 y_{t-2} + \alpha(1 - \alpha)^3 y_{t-3} + \cdots \qquad (15.13)$$

We see that the next forecast F_{t+1} depends on *all* the prior data (y_{t-1}, y_{t-2}, etc). As long as $\alpha < 1$, as we go farther into the past, each prior data value has less and less impact on the current forecast.

Initializing the Process

From Equation 15.12, we see that F_{t+1} depends on F_t, which in turn depends on F_{t-1}, and so on, all the way back to F_1. But where do we get F_1 (the initial forecast)? There are many ways to initialize the forecasting process. For example, Excel simply sets the initial forecast equal to the first actual data value:

Method *A*

Set $F_1 = y_1$ (use the first data value).

This method has the advantage of simplicity, but if y_1 happens to be unusual, it could take a few iterations for the forecasts to stabilize. Another approach is to set the initial forecast equal to the average of the first several observed data values. For example, MINITAB uses the first six data values:

Method B

Set $F_1 = \dfrac{y_1 + y_2 + \cdots + y_6}{6}$ (average of first six data values).

This method tends to iron out the effects of unusual y values, but it consumes more data and is still vulnerable to unusual y values.

Method C

Set F_1 = prediction from *backcasting* (backward extrapolation).

You may think of this method as fitting a trend to the data *in reverse time order* and extrapolating the trend to "predict" the initial value in the series. This method is common because it tends to generate a more appropriate initial forecast F_1. However, backcasting requires special software, so it will not be discussed here.

EXAMPLE 3

Weekly Sales Data

Table 15.11 shows weekly sales of deck sealer (a paint product sold in gallon containers) at a large do-it-yourself warehouse-style retailer. For exponential smoothing forecasts, the company uses $\alpha = 0.10$. Its choice of α is based on experience. Because α is fairly small, it will provide strong smoothing. The last two columns compare the two methods of initializing the forecasts. Unusually high sales in week 5 have a strong effect on method B's starting point. At first, the difference in forecasts is striking, but over time the methods converge.

TABLE 15.11   Deck Sealer Sales: Exponential Smoothing ($n = 18$ weeks)
   DeckSealer

Week	Sales in Gallons	Method A: $F_1 = y_1$	Method B: $F_1 = $ Average (1st six)
1	106	106.000	127.833
2	110	106.000	125.650
3	108	106.400	124.085
4	97	106.560	122.477
5	210	105.604	119.929
6	136	116.044	128.936
7	128	118.039	129.642
8	134	119.035	129.478
9	107	120.532	129.930
10	123	119.179	127.637
11	139	119.561	127.174
12	140	121.505	128.356
13	144	123.354	129.521
14	94	125.419	130.969
15	108	122.277	127.272
16	168	120.849	125.345
17	179	125.564	129.610
18	120	130.908	134.549

Smoothed forecasts using $\alpha = 0.10$.

Using Method A:

$$F_2 = \alpha y_1 + (1 - \alpha)F_1 = (0.10)(106) + (0.90)(106) = 106$$
$$F_3 = \alpha y_2 + (1 - \alpha)F_2 = (0.10)(110) + (0.90)(106) = 106.4$$
$$F_4 = \alpha y_3 + (1 - \alpha)F_3 = (0.10)(108) + (0.90)(106.4) = 106.56$$
$$\vdots$$
$$F_{19} = \alpha y_{18} + (1 - \alpha)F_{18} = (0.10)(120) + (0.90)(130.908) = 129.82$$

Using Method B:

$$F_2 = \alpha y_1 + (1 - \alpha)F_1 = (0.10)(106) + (0.90)(127.833) = 125.650$$
$$F_3 = \alpha y_2 + (1 - \alpha)F_2 = (0.10)(110) + (0.90)(125.650) = 124.085$$
$$F_4 = \alpha y_3 + (1 - \alpha)F_3 = (0.10)(108) + (0.90)(124.085) = 122.477$$
$$\vdots$$
$$F_{19} = \alpha y_{18} + (1 - \alpha)F_{18} = (0.10)(120) + (0.90)(134.549) = 133.094$$

Despite their different starting points, the forecasts for period 19 do not differ greatly. Rounding to the next higher integer, for week 19, the firm would order 130 gallons (using method *A*) or 134 gallons (using method *B*). Figures 15.19 and 15.20 show the similarity in *patterns* of the forecasts, although the *level* of forecasts is always higher in method *B* because of its higher initial value. This demonstrates that the choice of starting values *does* affect the forecasts.

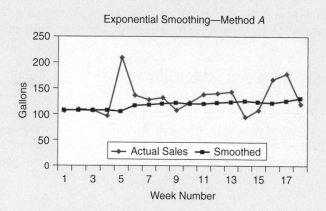

FIGURE 15.19

Using the First *y* Value

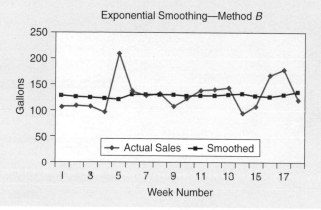

FIGURE 15.20

Averaging the First Six *y* Values

Using MINITAB

Figure 15.21 shows MINITAB's single exponential smoothing and four weeks' forecasts. After week 18, the exponential smoothing method cannot be updated with actual data, so the forecasts are constant. The wide 95 percent confidence intervals reflect the rather erratic past sales pattern.

FIGURE 15.21   MINITAB's Exponential Smoothing

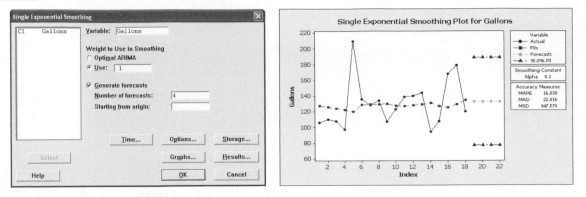

Using Excel

Excel also has an exponential smoothing option. It is found in Data Analysis under the Data menu. One difference to be noted is that Excel asks for a *damping factor,* which is equal to $1 - \alpha$. Excel uses method *A* to initialize the exponential smoothing forecasts. Figure 15.22 shows Excel's exponential smoothing dialogue box and a line chart of the actual values and forecast values. Notice that there are no forecast values beyond period 18 and that there are no confidence intervals as with MINITAB. Excel's default chart doesn't show the original data, so you should expect to make your own "improved" line chart, like the one shown in Figure 15.22.

Smoothing with Trend and Seasonality

Single exponential smoothing is intended for *trendless* data. If your data have a trend, you can try *Holt's method* with *two* smoothing constants (one for *trend,* one for *level*). If you have both trend and seasonality, you can try *Winters's method* with *three* smoothing constants (one for *trend,* one for *level,* one for *seasonality*). These advanced methods are similar to single smoothing in that they use simple formulas to update the forecasts, and you may use them

FIGURE 15.22

Excel's Exponential Smoothing

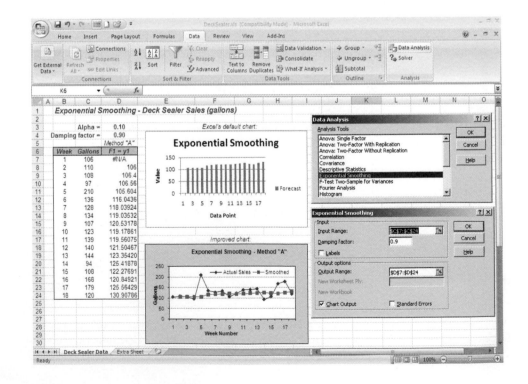

without special caution. *LearningStats* contains examples, explanations, and applications of these methods. Because these topics are usually reserved for a class in forecasting, they will not be explained here.

Mini Case   15.1

Exchange Rates

We have data for March 1 to March 30 and want to forecast one day ahead to March 31 by using exponential smoothing. We choose a smoothing constant value of $\alpha = 0.20$ and set the initial forecast F_1 to the average of the first six data values. Table 15.12 shows the actual data (y_t) and MINITAB's forecasts (F_t) for each date. The March 31 forecast is $F_{23} = \alpha y_{22} + (1 - \alpha)F_{22} = (0.20)(1.2164) + (0.80)(1.21395) = 1.2144$.

Figure 15.23 shows MINITAB's plot of the data and forecasts. The forecasts adapt, but always with a lag. The actual exchange rate on March 31 was 1.2094, slightly lower than the forecast, but well within the 95 percent prediction limits.

TABLE 15.12   Exchange Rate Canada/U.S. Dollar ⊙ Canada

t	Date	y_t	F_t
1	1-Mar-05	1.2425	1.23450
2	2-Mar-05	1.2395	1.23610
3	3-Mar-05	1.2463	1.23678
4	4-Mar-05	1.2324	1.23868
5	7-Mar-05	1.2300	1.23743
6	8-Mar-05	1.2163	1.23594
7	9-Mar-05	1.2064	1.23201
8	10-Mar-05	1.2050	1.22689
9	11-Mar-05	1.2041	1.22251
10	14-Mar-05	1.2087	1.21883
11	15-Mar-05	1.2064	1.21680
12	16-Mar-05	1.2038	1.21472
13	17-Mar-05	1.2028	1.21254
14	18-Mar-05	1.2027	1.21059
15	21-Mar-05	1.2110	1.20901
16	22-Mar-05	1.2017	1.20941
17	23-Mar-05	1.2133	1.20787
18	24-Mar-05	1.2150	1.20895
19	25-Mar-05	1.2180	1.21016
20	28-Mar-05	1.2234	1.21173
21	29-Mar-05	1.2135	1.21406
22	30-Mar-05	1.2164	1.21395
23	31-Mar-05		1.21444

Source: www.federalreserve.gov.

MINITAB's Exponential Smoothing ($\alpha = 0.20$)

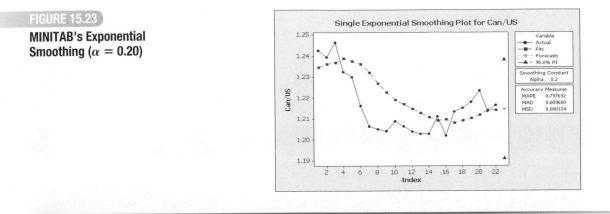

Section Exercises

15.9 (a) Make an Excel line graph of the following bond yield data. Describe the pattern. Is there a consistent trend? (b) Use exponential smoothing (MegaStat, MINITAB, or Excel) with $\alpha = 0.20$. Use both methods *A* and *B* to initialize the forecast (the default in both MegaStat and MINITAB). (c) Record the statistics of fit (MegaStat uses *MSE* and *MSD*; MINITAB uses *MSD* and *MAPE*). With Excel you will have to calculate these by creating cell formulas. (d) Do the smoothing again with $\alpha = 0.10$ and then with $\alpha = 0.30$, recording the statistics of fit. (e) Compare the statistics of fit for the three values of α. (f) Make a one-period forecast (i.e., $t = 53$) using each of the three α values. How did α affect your forecasts? (LO 5) **BondYield**

U.S. Treasury 10-Year Bond Yields at Week's End ($n = 52$ weeks)

Week	Yield	Week	Yield	Week	Yield	Week	Yield
4/2/04	3.95	7/2/04	4.63	10/1/04	4.10	12/31/04	4.29
4/9/04	4.21	7/9/04	4.49	10/8/04	4.20	1/7/05	4.28
4/16/04	4.36	7/16/04	4.47	10/15/04	4.08	1/14/05	4.25
4/23/04	4.43	7/23/04	4.46	10/22/04	4.03	1/21/05	4.19
4/30/04	4.49	7/30/04	4.56	10/29/04	4.05	1/28/05	4.19
5/7/04	4.62	8/6/04	4.41	11/5/04	4.12	2/4/05	4.14
5/14/04	4.81	8/13/04	4.28	11/12/04	4.22	2/11/05	4.06
5/21/04	4.74	8/20/04	4.23	11/19/04	4.17	2/18/05	4.16
5/28/04	4.68	8/27/04	4.25	11/26/04	4.20	2/25/05	4.28
6/4/04	4.74	9/3/04	4.19	12/3/04	4.35	3/4/05	4.37
6/11/04	4.80	9/10/04	4.21	12/10/04	4.19	3/11/05	4.45
6/18/04	4.75	9/17/04	4.14	12/17/04	4.16	3/18/05	4.51
6/25/04	4.69	9/24/04	4.04	12/24/04	4.21	3/25/05	4.59

Source: www.federalreserve.gov.

15.6 Seasonality

When and How to Deseasonalize

When the data periodicity is monthly or quarterly we should calculate a seasonal (monthly or quarterly) index and use it to **deseasonalize** the data (annual data have no seasonality). For a multiplicative model (the usual assumption) a seasonal index is a *ratio*. For example, if the seasonal index for July is 1.25, it means that July is, on average, 125 percent of all the monthly averages. If the seasonal index for January is 0.84, it means that January is, on average, 84 percent of all the monthly average. If the seasonal index for October is 1.00, it means that

TABLE 15.13 **Sales of Floor Covering Materials ($ thousands)** FloorSales

Quarter	2002	2003	2004	2005	2006	2007
1	259	306	379	369	515	626
2	236	300	262	373	373	535
3	164	189	242	255	339	397
4	222	275	296	374	519	488

October is an average month. The seasonal indices must sum to 12 or average 1 for monthly data or sum to 4 or average 1 for quarterly data. The following steps are used to deseasonalize data for time-series observations:

- Step 1 Calculate a centred moving average (*CMA*) for each month (quarter).
- Step 2 Divide each observed y_t value by the *CMA* to obtain seasonal ratios.
- Step 3 Average the seasonal ratios by month (quarter) to get raw seasonal indices.
- Step 4 Adjust the raw seasonal indices so they sum to 12 (monthly) or 4 (quarterly).
- Step 5 Divide each y_t by its seasonal index to get deseasonalized data.

In step 1, we lose 12 observations (monthly data) or 4 observations (quarterly data) because of the centring process. We will illustrate this technique for quarterly data.

Illustration of Calculations

Table 15.13 shows six years' data on quarterly revenue from sales of carpeting, tile, wood, and vinyl flooring by a floor-covering retailer. The data have an upward trend (see Figure 15.24), perhaps due to a boom in consumer spending on home improvement and new homes. There also appears to be seasonality, with lower sales in the third quarter (summer) and higher sales in the first quarter (winter).

The seasonal decomposition of this data is shown in Table 15.14 and Figure 15.24. Calculations are handled automatically by MegaStat, so it's actually easy to perform the decomposition. Because the number of subperiods (quarters) is even ($m = 4$), each value of the *CMA* is the average of two averages. For example, the first *CMA* value 226.125 is the average of $(259 + 236 + 164 + 222)/4$ and $(236 + 164 + 222 + 306)/4$. Table 15.15 shows how the indices are averaged. When calculating the *CMA*'s using quarterly data over a six-year period, *CMA*'s for the first two quarters and the last two quarters cannot be determined, resulting in each seasonal index being an average of only five quarters (instead of six). Each seasonal index is then adjusted to force their sum to be 4.000, and these become the seasonal

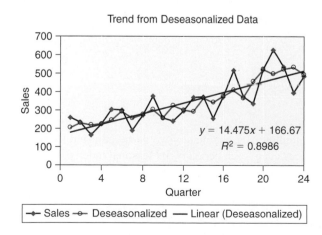

FIGURE 15.24

MegaStat's Deseasonalized Trend

TABLE 15.14 Calculation of Deseasonalized Sales ($n = 24$ quarters) 🔵 FloorSales

Obs	Year	Quarter	Sales	CMA	Sales/CMA	Seasonal Index	Deseasonalized
1	2002	1	259			1.252	206.9
2		2	236			1.021	231.1
3		3	164	226.125	0.725	0.740	221.7
4		4	222	240.000	0.925	0.987	224.9
5	2003	1	306	251.125	1.219	1.252	244.4
6		2	300	260.875	1.150	1.021	293.8
7		3	189	276.625	0.683	0.740	255.5
8		4	275	281.000	0.979	0.987	278.6
9	2004	1	379	282.875	1.340	1.252	302.7
10		2	262	292.125	0.897	1.021	256.6
11		3	242	293.500	0.825	0.740	327.2
12		4	296	306.125	0.967	0.987	299.8
13	2005	1	369	321.625	1.147	1.252	294.7
14		2	373	333.000	1.120	1.021	365.3
15		3	255	361.000	0.706	0.740	344.7
16		4	374	379.250	0.986	0.987	378.8
17	2006	1	515	389.750	1.321	1.252	411.3
18		2	373	418.375	0.892	1.021	365.3
19		3	339	450.375	0.753	0.740	458.3
20		4	519	484.500	1.071	0.987	525.7
21	2007	1	626	512.000	1.223	1.252	500.0
22		2	535	515.375	1.038	1.021	524.0
23		3	397			0.740	536.7
24		4	488			0.987	494.3

TABLE 15.15 Calculation of Seasonal Indices 🔵 FloorSales

Quarter	2002	2003	2004	2005	2006	2007	Mean	Adjusted
1		1.219	1.340	1.147	1.321	1.223	1.250	1.252
2		1.150	0.897	1.120	0.892	1.038	1.019	1.021
3	0.725	0.683	0.825	0.706	0.753		0.738	0.740
4	0.925	0.979	0.967	0.986	1.071		0.986	0.987
						Sum:	3.993	4.000

Due to rounding, details may not yield the result shown.

indices. If we had monthly data, the indices would be adjusted so that their sum would be 12.000. Dividing sales data of each period by its seasonal index provides deseasonalized data for each period.

After the data have been deseasonalized, the trend is fitted. Figure 15.24 shows the fitted trend from MegaStat, based on the deseasonalized data. The sharper peaks and valleys in the original time series (Y) have been smoothed by removing the seasonality (S). Any remaining variation about the trend (T) is irregular (I) or "random noise."

Using MINITAB to Deseasonalize

MINITAB performs its deseasonalization in a similar way, although it averages the seasonal factors using *medians* instead of *means,* so the results are not exactly the same as MegaStat's. For example, using the same floor covering sales data gives the following:

Quarter	MegaStat's Seasonal Index	MINITAB's Seasonal Index
1	1.252	1.234
2	1.021	1.047
3	0.740	0.732
4	0.987	0.987
Sum	4.000	4.000
Fitted trend	$y_t = 166.67 + 14.475t$	$y_t = 166.62 + 14.483t$

MINITAB offers nice graphical displays for decomposition, as well as forecasts, as shown in Figure 15.25. MINITAB also offers additive as well as multiplicative seasonality. In an additive model, the *CMA* is calculated in the same way, but the raw seasonals are *differences* (instead of ratios) and the seasonal indices are forced to sum to *zero* (e.g., months with higher sales must exactly balance months with lower sales). Because most analysts prefer multiplicative models (assuming trended data) the additive model is not discussed in detail here.

A Closer Look

Six years of data (2002 through 2007) were used to calculate the seasonal indices for the floor-covering retailer. Would the same indices be used to determine seasonally adjusted sales for sales beyond the year 2007, or should new indices be updated based on previous data and the newly obtained data? If we assume that the impact of seasonality is constant or approximately constant from year to year, the same seasonal indices can be used for quite a while. The impact of seasonality would be the same if average sales for each season remain constant over the years or if average sales for each season grow or shrink at the same rate. For example, if we assume that car sales are expected to shrink by the same percentage no matter what the quarter, the previous indices can be used. Conversely, if we believe that there is a shift in sales from one season to another (e.g., up in some quarters, down in others), the seasonal indices should be adjusted to reflect the changes in purchasing behaviour.

MINITAB's Graphs for Floor Covering Sales **FIGURE 15.25**

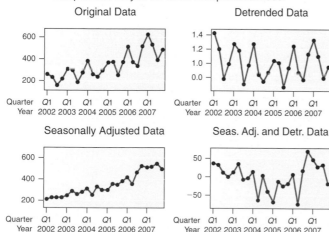
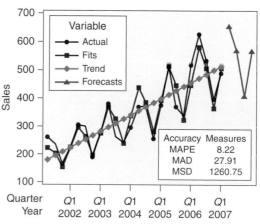

Concept Check

Can seasonally adjusted sales (i.e., deseasonalized sales) go up while actual sales go down in that particular season? Explain.

Chapter 19

Seasonal Forecasts Using Binary Predictors

Another way to address seasonality is to estimate a regression model using **seasonal binaries** as predictors. For quarterly data, for example, the data set would look as shown in Table 15.16. When we have four binaries (i.e., four quarters) we must exclude one binary to prevent perfect multicollinearity (see Chapter 14, Section 14.7). Arbitrarily, we exclude the fourth quarter binary $Qtr4$ (it will be a portion of the intercept when $Qtr1 = 0$ and $Qtr2 = 0$ and $Qtr3 = 0$).

TABLE 15.16 Sales Data with Seasonal Binaries FloorSales

Year	Quarter	Sales	Time	Qtr1	Qtr2	Qtr3
2002	1	259	1	1	0	0
	2	236	2	0	1	0
	3	164	3	0	0	1
	4	222	4	0	0	0
2003	1	306	5	1	0	0
	2	300	6	0	1	0
	3	189	7	0	0	1
	4	275	8	0	0	0
2004	1	379	9	1	0	0
	2	262	10	0	1	0
	3	242	11	0	0	1
	4	296	12	0	0	0
2005	1	369	13	1	0	0
	2	373	14	0	1	0
	3	255	15	0	0	1
	4	374	16	0	0	0
2006	1	515	17	1	0	0
	2	373	18	0	1	0
	3	339	19	0	0	1
	4	519	20	0	0	0
2007	1	626	21	1	0	0
	2	535	22	0	1	0
	3	397	23	0	0	1
	4	488	24	0	0	0

FIGURE 15.26

MINITAB's Fitted Regression for Seasonal Binaries

The regression equation is
Sales = 161 + 14.4 Time + 89.8 Qtr1 + 12.9 Qtr2 − 83.6 Qtr3

Predictor	Coef	SE Coef	T	P
Constant	161.21	24.33	6.62	0.000
Time	14.366	1.244	11.55	0.000
Qtr1	89.76	24.32	3.69	0.002
Qtr2	12.90	24.16	0.53	0.600
Qtr3	−83.63	24.07	−3.47	0.003

S = 41.6313   R-Sq = 90.0%   R-Sq(adj) = 87.9%

We assume a linear trend, and specify the regression model *Sales* = *f*(*Time, Qtr1, Qtr2, Qtr3*). MINITAB's estimated regression is shown in Figure 15.26. This is an additive model of the form $Y = T + S + I$ (recall that we omit the cycle C in practice). The fitted equation is

$$Sales = 161 + 14.4(Time) + 89.8(Qtr1) + 12.9(Qtr2) - 83.6(Qtr3)$$

Time is a significant predictor ($p = 0.000$) indicating significant linear trend. Two of the binaries are significant: *Qtr1* ($p = 0.002$) and *Qtr3* ($p = 0.003$). The second quarter binary *Qtr2* ($p = 0.600$) is not significant. The model gives a good overall fit ($R^2 = 0.90$). The main virtue of the seasonal regression model is its versatility. We can plug in future values of *Time* and the seasonal binaries to create forecasts as far ahead as we wish. For example, the forecasts for four quarters of 2008 are

Period 25: *Sales* = 161 + 14.4(25) + 89.8(1) + 12.9(0) − 83.6(0) = 610.8
Period 26: *Sales* = 161 + 14.4(26) + 89.8(0) + 12.9(1) − 83.6(0) = 548.3
Period 27: *Sales* = 161 + 14.4(27) + 89.8(0) + 12.9(0) − 83.6(1) = 466.2
Period 28: *Sales* = 161 + 14.4(28) + 89.8(0) + 12.9(0) − 83.6(0) = 564.2

Section Exercises

15.10 (a) Use MegaStat or MINITAB to deseasonalize the quarterly data on PepsiCo's revenues and fit a trend. Interpret the results. (b) Use MegaStat or MINITAB to perform a regression using seasonal binaries. Interpret the results. (c) Use the regression equation to make a prediction for each quarter in 2007. (d) If you have access to *Standard & Poor's Stock Reports, 2008,* check your forecasts. How accurate were they? (LO 6)   **PepsiCo**

PepsiCo Revenues ($ millions), 2001–2006

Quarter	2001	2002	2003	2004	2005	2006
Qtr1	5,330	5,101	5,530	6,131	6,585	7,205
Qtr2	6,713	6,178	6,538	7,070	7,697	8,599
Qtr3	6,906	6,376	6,830	7,257	8,184	8,950
Qtr4	7,986	7,457	8,073	8,803	10,096	10,383

Source: *Standard & Poor's Stock Reports,* February 2007.

15.11 (a) Manually and using MegaStat or MINITAB, deseasonalize the monthly Corvette sales data and fit a trend. Interpret the results. (b) Use MegaStat or MINITAB to perform a regression using seasonal binaries. Interpret the results. (c) Use the regression equation to make a prediction for each month in 2004. (d) If you have access to *Ward's Automotive Yearbook, 2005* (67th edition), check your forecasts. How accurate were they? (LO 6) **Corvette**

U.S. Corvette Sales, 2000–2004 (number of cars sold)

Month	2000	2001	2002	2003
Jan	1,863	2,252	2,443	1,468
Feb	2,765	2,766	3,354	1,724
Mar	3,440	2,923	1,877	2,792
Apr	3,018	2,713	2,176	6,249
May	2,725	2,847	3,049	2,441
Jun	2,538	2,521	2,708	2,272
Jul	1,598	2,000	2,960	2,007
Aug	2,861	2,789	2,912	2,107
Sep	2,942	3,639	2,960	1,615
Oct	2,748	4,647	3,094	1,878
Nov	2,376	2,910	2,163	1,596
Dec	2,334	1,648	2,859	1,825
Total	31,208	33,655	32,555	27,974

Source: *Ward's Automotive Yearbook, 2001–2004.*

Concept Check

Given the following Excel regression output on the sales of sporting equipment (in $ millions) at a large Canadian sporting goods chain where Q1 = 1 for sales in quarter 1, Q2 = 1 for sales in quarter 2, and Q3 = 1 for sales in quarter 3, answer the following questions. (a) Write down the regression equation. (b) At $\alpha = 0.05$, which variables, if any, are not significant in explaining sales? If any are insignificant, explain what that means in the context of this study. (c) In which quarter are sales the highest? In which quarter are sales the lowest? Explain. (d) Forecast sales for the next quarter (i.e., quarter 1 and $t = 13$).

	Coefficients	Standard Error	t Stat	p Value
Intercept	129.2500	6.3734	20.2796	0.0000
t	1.4688	0.6171	2.3801	0.0489
Q1	−31.5938	5.9936	−5.2712	0.0012
Q2	−21.3958	5.8326	−3.6683	0.0080
Q3	−12.1979	5.7338	−2.1274	0.0709

15.7 Index Numbers

A simple way to measure changes over time (and especially to compare two or more variables) is to convert time-series data into **index numbers.** The idea is to create an index that starts at 100 in a *base period,* so we can see *relative changes* in the data regardless of the original data

TABLE 15.17   U.S. Foreign Exchange Rates, 2000–2006    Currency

	Foreign Currency per Dollar			Index Numbers (Jan 3, 2000 = 100)		
Date	*U.K.*	*Mexico*	*Canada*	*U.K.*	*Mexico*	*Canada*
3-Jan-00	0.61463	9.4015	1.4465	100.0	100.0	100.0
4-Jan-00	0.61087	9.4570	1.4518	99.4	100.6	100.4
5-Jan-00	0.60920	9.5350	1.4518	99.1	101.4	100.4
⋮	⋮	⋮	⋮	⋮	⋮	⋮
27-Dec-06	0.51109	10.8820	1.1610	83.2	115.7	80.3
28-Dec-06	0.50966	10.8740	1.1599	82.9	115.7	80.2
29-Dec-06	0.51057	10.7995	1.1652	83.1	114.9	80.6

Source: www.federalreserve.gov.

units. Indices are most often used for financial data (e.g., prices, wages, costs) but can be used with any numerical data (e.g., number of units sold, warranty claims, computer spam).

Relative Indices

To convert a time series $y_1, y_2, \ldots, y_n$ into a *relative index* (sometimes called a *simple index*), we divide each data value y_t by the data value y_1 in a base period and multiply by 100. The relative index I_t for period t is

$$I_t = 100 \times \frac{y_t}{y_1} \qquad (15.14)$$

The index in the base period is always $I_1 = 100$, so the index $I_1, I_2, \ldots, I_n$ makes it easy to see *relative changes* in the data, regardless of the original data units. For example, Table 15.17 shows six years of daily U.S. dollar exchange rates (on the left) and the corresponding index numbers (on the right) using January 3, 2000 = 100 as a base period. By the end of 2006, we see that the U.S. dollar fell to 83.1 percent of its starting value versus the British pound, rose to 114.9 percent versus the Mexican peso, and dropped to 80.6 percent versus the Canadian dollar.

A graph like Figure 15.27 allows us to display seven years (1,759 days) of data. Because each index starts at the same point (100), we can easily see the fluctuations and trends. We could fit a moving average, if we wanted to smooth the data. Speculators who engage in currency arbitrage would use even more-sophisticated tools to analyze movements in currency indices.

Weighted Indices

A different calculation is required for a *weighted index* such as the Consumer Price Index. The CPI is a measure of the relative prices paid by consumers for a market basket of goods and services, based on prices of hundreds of goods and services in eight major groups. The goal is to make the CPI representative of the prices paid for all goods and services purchased

FIGURE 15.27

U.S. Foreign Exchange Rates, 2000–2006

Currency

by all consumers. This requires assigning weights to each consumer good or service to reflect its importance relative to all the other goods and services in the market basket (e.g., housing gets a higher weight because it is a larger proportion of total spending). The basic formula for a simple weighted price index is

$$I_t = 100 \times \frac{\sum_{i=1}^{m} p_{it} q_i}{\sum_{i=1}^{m} p_{i1} q_i} = 100 \times \frac{p_{1t} q_1 + p_{2t} q_2 + \cdots + p_{mt} q_m}{p_{11} q_1 + p_{21} q_2 + \cdots + p_{m1} q_m} \qquad (15.15)$$

where

I_t = weighted index for period t ($t = 1, 2, \ldots, n$)

p_{it} = price of good i in period t ($t = 1, 2, \ldots, n$)

q_i = weight assigned to good i ($i = 1, 2, \ldots m$)

The numerator is the cost of buying a given market basket of goods and services at today's prices (period t) relative to the cost of the same market basket in the base period (period 1). The weight q_i represents the relative quantity of the item in the consumer's budget. For example, suppose there is a price increase of 5 percent for food and beverages and a 10 percent increase for medical care costs, with no price changes for the other expenditure categories. This would result in an increase of 1.4 percent in the CPI, as shown in Table 15.18.

From Table 15.18, the price index rose from 100.0 to 101.4, or a 1.4 percent increase:

$$I_2 = 100 \times \frac{\sum_{i=1}^{n} p_{i2} q_i}{\sum_{i=1}^{n} p_{i1} q_i} = 100 \times \frac{101.4}{100.0} = 101.4$$

Equation 15.15 is called a *Laspeyres index*. It treats the base year quantity weights as constant. Weights are based on the *Survey of Consumer Expenditures*. In your economics classes, you may learn more sophisticated methods that take into account the fact that expenditure weights do change over time. One such method is the *Paasche index,* which uses a formula similar to the Laspeyres index, except that quantity weights are adjusted for each period.

TABLE 15.18   Illustrative Calculation of Price Index

Expenditure Category	Weight (q_i)		Relative Price (p_{i1})		Relative Spending $(p_{i1}q_i)$	Weight (q_i)		Relative Price (p_{i2})		Relative Spending $(p_{i2}q_i)$
Food and beverages	15.7	×	1.00	=	15.7	15.7	×	1.05	=	16.5
Housing	40.9	×	1.00	=	40.9	40.9	×	1.00	=	40.9
Apparel	4.4	×	1.00	=	4.4	4.4	×	1.00	=	4.4
Transportation	17.1	×	1.00	=	17.1	17.1	×	1.00	=	17.1
Medical care	5.8	×	1.00	=	5.8	5.8	×	1.10	=	6.4
Recreation	6.0	×	1.00	=	6.0	6.0	×	1.00	=	6.0
Education/ communication	5.8	×	1.00	=	5.8	5.8	×	1.00	=	5.8
Other goods and services	4.3	×	1.00	=	4.3	4.3	×	1.00	=	4.3
Sum	100.0				$\sum_{i=1}^{n} p_{i1} q_i = 100.0$	100.0				$\sum_{i=1}^{n} p_{i2} q_i = 101.4$

Concept Check

For each of the following situations, should the weights assigned to each good (assuming each good is included in the price index) remain the same or change when calculating the price index. Explain.

- The price of each item has increased by 25 percent over the base year's prices.
- The price of steak has increased by 20 percent over its base year's price while the price of chicken has gone down by 15 percent over its base year's price.

Importance of Index Numbers

The CPI affects nearly all of us because it can be used to adjust things like retirement benefits and tax brackets. The CPI could be compared with an index of salary growth for workers, or to measure current-dollar salaries in "real dollars." Statistics Canada publishes indices on a number of goods and services that give valuable insight into Canada's economy. For example, excerpts from a table published by Statistics Canada (www40.statcan.gc.ca/l01/cst01/cpis01a-eng.htm) give us some insight into how much prices for various items have changed between the years 2002 and 2009 (data for the month of March). Using March 2002's index to equal 100, the table reveals that all items (adjusted by the weights that determine the CPI) have increased in price by 14 percent (index = 114.00); food prices have increased by 21.5 percent; shelter has increased by 22.6 percent; clothing and footwear have decreased by 4.3 percent (index = 95.7); and alcoholic beverages and tobacco products have increased by 29.7 percent, closely followed by energy (an increase of 27.1 percent). These results can be reviewed to determine whether any serious issues must be addressed. For example, the increase in the cost of alcoholic beverages and tobacco products may be of concern to those who purchase these products, but they are probably of much less concern to policy makers, whereas the increase in the cost of energy should be of concern to both consumers and policy makers.

Other familiar price indices, such as the Toronto Stock Exchange and the Dow Jones Industrial Average (DJIA), have their own unique methodologies. Originally a simple arithmetic mean of stock prices, the DJIA now is the sum of the 30 stock prices divided by a "divisor" to compensate for stock splits and other changes over time. The divisor is revised periodically. Because high-priced stocks comprise a larger proportion of the sum, the DJIA is more strongly affected by changes in high-priced stocks. A little Web research can tell you a lot about how stock price indices are calculated, their strengths and weaknesses, and some alternative indices that finance experts have invented.

15.8   Forecasting: Final Thoughts

Role of Forecasting

In many ways, forecasting resembles planning. *Forecasting* is an analytical way to describe a "what-if" future that might confront the organization. *Planning* is the organization's attempt to determine actions it will take under each foreseeable contingency. Forecasts help decision makers become aware of trends or patterns that require a response. Actions taken by the decision makers may actually head off the contingency envisioned in the forecast. Thus, forecasts tend to be self-defeating because they trigger homeostatic organizational responses.

Behavioural Aspects of Forecasting

Forecasts can facilitate organizational communication. The forecast (or even just a nicely prepared time-series chart) lets everyone examine the same facts concurrently, and perhaps argue with the data or the assumptions that underlie the forecast or its relevance to the organization.

A quantitative forecast helps *make assumptions explicit*. Those who prepare the forecast must explain and defend their assumptions, while others must challenge them. In the process, everyone gains understanding of the data, the underlying realities, and the imperfections in the data. Forecasts *focus the dialogue* and can make it more productive.

Of course, this assumes a certain maturity among the individuals around the table. Strong leaders (or possibly meeting facilitators) can play a role in guiding the discourse to produce a positive result. The danger is that people may try to find scapegoats (yes, they do tend to blame the forecaster), deny facts, or avoid responsibility for tough decisions. But one premise of this book is that statistics, when done well, can strengthen any dialogue and lead to better decisions.

Forecasts Are Always Wrong

We discussed several measures to use to determine if a forecast model fits the time series. Successful forecasters understand that a forecast is never precise. There is always some error, but we can *use* the error measures to track forecast error. Many companies use several different forecasting models and rely on the model that has had the least error over some time period. We have described simple models in this chapter. You may take a class specifically focusing on forecasting in which you will learn about other time-series models including AR (autoregressive) and ARIMA (autoregressive integrated moving average) models. Such models take advantage of the dependency that might exist between values in the time series.

To ensure good forecast outcomes

- Maintain up-to-date databases of *relevant* data.
- Allow sufficient lead time to analyze the data.
- State several alternative forecasts or scenarios.
- Track forecast errors over time.
- State your assumptions and qualifications and consider your time horizon.
- Don't underestimate the power of a good graph.

 Mini Case 15.2

How Does Noodles & Company Ensure Its Ingredients Are as Fresh as Possible?   **Noodles & Company**

Using only fresh ingredients is key for great food and success for restaurants like Noodles & Company. To be sure that the restaurants are serving only the freshest ingredients, while also reducing food waste, Noodles & Company turned to statistical forecasting for ordering ingredients and daily food preparation. The challenge was to create a forecast that is sophisticated enough to be accurate, yet simple enough for new restaurant employees to understand.

Noodles & Company uses a food management software system to forecast the demand for its menu items based on the moving average of the previous four weeks' sales. This simple forecasting technique has been very accurate. The automated process also uses the forecast of each item to estimate how many ingredients to order as well as how much to prepare each day. For example, the system might forecast that during next Wednesday's lunch, the location in Longmont, Colorado, will sell 55 Pesto Cavatappi's. After forecasting the demand for each menu item, the system then specifies exactly how much of each ingredient to prepare for that lunch period.

For the restaurant teams, the old manual process of estimating and guessing how much of each ingredient to prepare is now replaced with an automated prep sheet. Noodles & Company has reduced food waste because restaurants are less likely to over-order ingredients and over-prepare menu items. The restaurant teams are more efficient and customers are served meals made with the freshest ingredients possible.

A **time series** is assumed to have four components. For most business data, **trend** is the general pattern of change over all years observed while **cycle** is a repetitive pattern of change around the trend over several years and **seasonality** is a repetitive pattern within a year. The **irregular** component is a random disturbance that follows no pattern. The **additive model** is adequate in the short run because the four components' magnitude does not change much, but for observations over longer periods of time, the **multiplicative model** is preferred. Common trend models include **linear** (constant slope and no turning point), **quadratic** (one turning point), and **exponential** (constant percent growth or decline). Higher polynomial models are untrustworthy and liable to give strange forecasts, though any trend model is less reliable the farther out it is projected. In forecasting, forecasters use fit measures besides R^2, such as mean absolute percent error (*MAPE*), mean absolute deviation (*MAD*), and mean squared deviation (*MSD*). For trendless or erratic data, we use a **moving average** over m periods or **exponential smoothing**. Forecasts adapt rapidly to changing data when the **smoothing constant** α is large (near 1) and conversely for a small α (near 0). For monthly or quarterly data, a **seasonal adjustment** is required before extracting the trend. Alternatively, regression with **seasonal binaries** can be used to capture seasonality and make forecasts. **Index numbers** are used to show changes relative to a base period.

CHAPTER SUMMARY

KEY TERMS

centred moving average
  (*CMA*), *659*
coefficient of
  determination, *657*
cycle, *641*
deseasonalize, *666*
exponential smoothing, *642*
exponential trend, *646*
index numbers, *672*
irregular, *642*

linear trend, *643*
mean absolute deviation
  (*MAD*), *657*
mean absolute percent error
  (*MAPE*), *657*
moving average, *642*
mean squared deviation
  (*MSD*), *657*
Occam's Razor, *651*
periodicity, *640*

polynomial model, *651*
quadratic trend, *650*
seasonal, *642*
seasonal binaries, *670*
smoothing constant, *661*
standard error (*SE*), *657*
time-series variable, *638*
trailing moving average
  (*TMA*), *658*
trend, *641*

Commonly Used Formulas

Additive time-series model: $Y = T + C + S + I$

Multiplicative time-series model: $Y = T \times C \times S \times I$

Linear trend model: $y_t = a + bt$

Exponential trend model: $y_t = ae^{bt}$

Quadratic trend model: $y_t = a + bt + ct^2$

Coefficient of determination: $R^2 = 1 - \dfrac{\sum\limits_{t=1}^{n}(y_t - \hat{y}_t)^2}{\sum\limits_{t=1}^{n}(y_t - \bar{y})^2}$

Mean absolute percent error: $MAPE = \dfrac{100}{n}\sum\limits_{t=1}^{n}\dfrac{|y_t - \hat{y}_t|}{y_t}$

Mean absolute deviation: $MAD = \dfrac{1}{n}\sum\limits_{t=1}^{n}|y_t - \hat{y}_t|$

Mean squared deviation: $MSD = \dfrac{1}{n}\sum\limits_{t=1}^{n}(y_t - \hat{y}_t)^2$

Standard error: $SE = \sqrt{\sum\limits_{t=1}^{n}\dfrac{(y_t - \hat{y}_t)^2}{n-2}}$

Forecast updating equation for exponential smoothing: $F_{t+1} = \alpha y_t + (1 - \alpha)F_t$

CHAPTER REVIEW

1. Explain the difference between (a) stocks and flows; (b) cross-sectional and time-series data; (c) additive and multiplicative models. (LO 1)

2. (a) What is periodicity? (b) Give original examples of data with different periodicity. (LO 1)

3. (a) What are the distinguishing features of each component of a time series (trend, cycle, seasonal, irregular)? (b) Why is cycle usually ignored in time-series modelling? (LO 1)

4. Name four criteria for assessing a trend forecast. (LO 2)

5. Name two advantages and two disadvantages of each of the common trend models (linear, exponential, quadratic). (LO 2)

6. When would the exponential trend model be preferred to a linear trend model? (LO 2)

7. Explain how to obtain the compound percent growth rate from a fitted exponential model. (LO 2)

8. (a) When might a quadratic model be useful? (b) What precautions must be taken when forecasting with a quadratic model? (c) Why are higher-order polynomial models dangerous? (LO 2)

9. Name five measures of fit for a trend, and state their advantages and disadvantages. (LO 3)

10. (a) When do we use a moving average? (b) Name two types of moving averages. (c) When is a centred moving average harder to calculate? (LO 4)

11. (a) When is exponential smoothing most useful? (b) Interpret the smoothing constant α. What is its range? (c) What does a small α say about the degree of smoothing? A large α? (LO 5)

12. (a) Explain two ways to initialize the forecasts in an exponential smoothing process. (b) Name an advantage and a disadvantage of each method. (LO 5)

13. (a) Why is seasonality irrelevant for annual data? (b) List the steps in deseasonalizing a monthly time series. (c) What is the sum of a monthly seasonal index? A quarterly index? (LO 6)

14. (a) How can forecasting improve communication within an organization? (b) List five tips for ensuring effective forecasting outcomes. (LO 7)

15. (a) Explain how seasonal binaries can be used to model seasonal data. (b) What is the advantage of using seasonal binaries? (LO 7)

16. Explain the equivalency between the two forms of an exponential trend model. (LO 2)

17. What is the purpose of index numbers? (LO 8)

CHAPTER EXERCISES

Instructions: For each exercise, use Excel, MegaStat, or MINITAB to make an attractive, well-labelled time-series line chart. Adjust the *Y*-axis scale if necessary to show more detail (as Excel usually starts the scale at zero). If a fitted trend is called for, use Excel's option to display the equation and R^2 statistic (or *MAPE, MAD,* and *MSD* in MINITAB). Include printed copies of all relevant graphs with your answers to each exercise.

Note: Problems marked * rely on optional material from this chapter.

15.12 (a) Make a line chart for JetBlue's revenue. (b) Describe the trend (if any) and discuss possible causes. (c) Fit both a linear and an exponential trend to the data. (d) Which model is preferred? Why? (e) Make a forecast for 2007, using a trend model of your choice (or a judgment forecast). (LO 2) 🔘 **JetBlue**

JetBlue Airlines Revenue, 2002–2006 (millions)	
Year	*Revenue*
2002	635
2003	998
2004	1,265
2005	1,701
2006	2,363

Source: *Standard & Poor's Stock Reports,* Feb. 2007.

15.13   (a) Plot both Swiss watch time series on the same graph. (b) Describe the trend (if any) and discuss possible causes. (c) Fit an exponential trend to each time series. (d) Interpret each fitted trend carefully. What conclusion do you draw? (e) Make forecasts for 2003, using the linear trend model. Do you feel confident in your forecasts? Explain. (LO 2)   **Swiss**

Swiss Watch Exports (thousands of units), 1998–2003

Year	Mechanical	Electronic
1998	2,558	29,678
1999	2,526	28,766
2000	2,549	27,313
2001	2,580	23,811
2002	2,722	24,107
2003	2,718	21,864

Source: Fédération de L'Industrie Horlogère Suisse, Swiss Watch Exports, www.fhs.ch.

15.14   (a) Plot the total minutes of TV viewing time per household. (b) Describe the trend (if any) and discuss possible causes. (c) Fit a linear trend to the data. (d) Would this model give reasonable forecasts? Would another trend model be better? Explain. (e) Make a forecast for 2010. Check the forecast if you have access to the Web. Show the forecast calculations. (f) Would this data ever approach an asymptote? Explain. *Note:* Time is in five-year increments, so use $t = 13$ for the 2010 forecast. (LO 2)   **Television**

Average Daily TV Viewing Time per U.S. Household

Year	Hours	Minutes	Total Minutes
1950	4	35	275
1955	4	51	291
1960	5	6	306
1965	5	29	329
1970	5	56	356
1975	6	7	367
1980	6	36	396
1985	7	10	430
1990	6	53	413
1995	7	17	437
2000	7	35	455
2005	8	11	491

Source: As published by the TVB based on Nielsen Media Research data. Used with permission.

15.15   (a) Plot the market-share data. (b) Describe the trend (if any) and discuss possible causes. (c) Fit three trends (linear, exponential, quadratic). (d) Which trend model is best, and why? If none is satisfactory, explain. (e) Make a forecast for 2004 by using a trend model of your choice or a judgment forecast. (LO 2)   **Trucks**

Asian and European Share of U.S. Light Truck Sales, 1990–2003

Year	Percent	Year	Percent
1990	16.4	1997	15.4
1991	17.1	1998	16.2
1992	14.3	1999	18.4
1993	13.7	2000	21.2
1994	14.2	2001	23.1
1995	13.6	2002	23.9
1996	13.6	2003	26.6

Source: *Detroit Free Press*, Nov. 19, 2003, p. 1A.

15.16 (a) Choose *one* category of consumer credit and plot it. (b) Describe the trend (if any) and discuss possible causes. (c) Fit a trend model of your choice. (d) Make a forecast for 2006, using a trend model of your choice. *Note:* Revolving credit is mostly credit card and home equity loans, while non-revolving credit is for a specific purchase such as a car. (LO 2) **Consumer**

Consumer Credit Outstanding, 2000–2005 ($ billions)

Year	Total	Revolving	Non-revolving
2000	1,722	683	1,039
2001	1,872	716	1,155
2002	1,984	749	1,235
2003	2,088	771	1,317
2004	2,202	801	1,401
2005	2,296	827	1,469

Source: *Economic Report of the President*, 2007.

15.17 (a) Choose *one* beverage category and plot the data. (b) Describe the trend (if any) and discuss possible causes. (c) Would a fitted trend be helpful? Explain. (d) Fit several trend models. Which is best, and why? If none is satisfactory, explain. (e) Make a forecast for 2005, using a trend model of your choice or a judgment forecast. Discuss. *Note:* Time increments are five years, so use $t = 6$ for your 2005 forecast. (LO 2) **Beverages**

U.S. per Capita Annual Consumption of Selected Beverages (gallons)

Beverage	1980	1985	1990	1995	2000
Milk	27.6	26.7	25.7	23.9	22.5
Whole	17.0	14.3	10.5	8.6	8.1
Reduced-fat	10.5	12.3	15.2	15.3	14.4
Carbonated soft drinks	35.1	35.7	46.2	47.4	49.3
Diet	5.1	7.1	10.7	10.9	11.6
Regular	29.9	28.7	35.6	36.5	37.7
Fruit juices	7.4	7.8	7.8	8.3	8.7
Alcoholic	28.3	28.0	27.5	24.7	24.9
Beer	24.3	23.8	23.9	21.8	21.7
Wine	2.1	2.4	2.0	1.7	2.0
Distilled spirits	2.0	1.8	1.5	1.2	1.3

Source: *Statistical Abstract of the United States, 2003.*

15.18   (a) Plot both men's and women's winning times on the same graph. (b) Fit a linear trend model to each series. From the fitted trends, will the times eventually converge? *Hint:* Ask Excel for forecasts (e.g., 20 years ahead). (c) Make a copy of your graph, and click each fitted trend and change it to a moving average trend type. (d) Would a moving average be a reasonable approach to modelling these data sets? *Note:* The data file has the data converted to decimal minutes. (LO 2)   **Boston**

Boston Marathon Champions, 1980–2005

	Men		Women	
Year	Name of Winner	Time	Name of Winner	Time
1980	Bill Rodgers	2:12:11	Jacqueline Gareau	2:34:28
1981	Toshihiko Seko	2:09:26	Allison Roe	2:26:46
1982	Alberto Salazar	2:08:52	Charlotte Teske	2:29:33
1983	Greg Meyer	2:09:00	Joan Benoit	2:22:43
1984	Geoff Smith	2:10:34	Lorraine Moller	2:29:30
1985	Geoff Smith	2:14:05	Lisa Larsen Weidenbach	2:34:10
1986	Robert de Castella	2:07:51	Ingrid Kristiansen	2:24:55
1987	Toshihiko Seko	2:11:50	Rosa Mota	2:25:21
1988	Ibrahim Hussein	2:08:43	Rosa Mota	2:24:30
1989	Abebe Mekonnen	2:09:06	Ingrid Kristiansen	2:24:33
1990	Gelindo Bordin	2:08:19	Rosa Mota	2:25:24
1991	Ibrahim Hussein	2:11:06	Wanda Panfil	2:24:18
1992	Ibrahim Hussein	2:08:14	Olga Markova	2:23:43
1993	Cosmas Ndeti	2:09:33	Olga Markova	2:25:27
1994	Cosmas Ndeti	2:07:15	Uta Pippig	2:21:45
1995	Cosmas Ndeti	2:09:22	Uta Pippig	2:25:11
1996	Moses Tanui	2:09:15	Uta Pippig	2:27:12
1997	Lameck Aguta	2:10:34	Fatuma Roba	2:26:23
1998	Moses Tanui	2:07:34	Fatuma Roba	2:23:21
1999	Joseph Chebet	2:09:52	Fatuma Roba	2:23:25
2000	Elijah Lagat	2:09:47	Catherine Ndereba	2:26:11
2001	Lee Bong-Ju	2:09:43	Catherine Ndereba	2:23:53
2002	Rodgers Rop	2:09:02	Margaret Okayo	2:20:43
2003	Robert Kipkoech Cheruiyot	2:10:11	Svetlana Zakharova	2:25:20
2004	Timothy Cherigat	2:10:37	Catherine Ndereba	2:24:27
2005	Hailu Negussie	2:11:45	Catherine Ndereba	2:25:13

Source: www.boston.com/marathon/history.

15.19   (a) Plot the data on leisure and hospitality employment. (b) Describe the trend (if any) and discuss possible causes. (c) Fit the linear and exponential trends. Would these trend models give credible forecasts? Explain. (d) Make a forecast for 2008, using any method (including your own judgment). (LO 2)   **Leisure**

Leisure and Hospitality Employment, 1998–2007 (thousands)

Year	Employees	Year	Employees
1998	11,232	2003	12,173
1999	11,544	2004	12,495
2000	11,860	2005	12,814
2001	12,032	2006	13,139
2002	11,986	2007	13,448

Source: http://data.bls.gov.

15.20 (a) Plot the data on law enforcement officers killed. (b) Describe the trend (if any) and discuss possible causes. (c) Would a fitted trend be helpful? Explain. (d) Make a forecast for 2005 using any method you like (including judgment). (LO 2) **LawOfficers**

U.S. Law Enforcement Officers Killed, 1994–2004

Year	Killed	Year	Killed
1994	141	2000	134
1995	133	2001	218
1996	113	2002	132
1997	133	2003	133
1998	142	2004	139
1999	107		

Source: *Statistical Abstract of the United States, 2007*, p. 205.

15.21 (a) Plot the data on lightning deaths. (b) Describe the trend (if any) and discuss possible causes. (c) Fit an exponential trend to the data. Interpret the fitted equation. (d) Make a forecast for 2010, using a trend model of your choice (or a judgment forecast). Explain the basis for your forecast. *Note:* Time is in five-year increments, so use $t = 15$ for your 2010 forecast. (LO 2) **Lightning**

U.S. Lightning Deaths, 1940–2005

Year	Deaths	Year	Deaths
1940	340	1975	91
1945	268	1980	74
1950	219	1985	74
1955	181	1990	74
1960	129	1995	85
1965	149	2000	51
1970	122	2005	38

Source: *Statistical Abstract of the United States, 2007*, p. 228; and www.nws.noaa.gov.

15.22 (a) Plot the data on full-time mathematics graduate students. (b) Would a fitted trend be helpful? Explain. (c) Make a forecast for 2006, using a trend model of your choice (or a judgment forecast). (LO 2) **MathGrads**

Full-Time Mathematics Graduate Students, 1993–2005

Year	Students	Year	Students
1993	10,525	2000	9,637
1994	10,185	2001	9,361
1995	9,761	2002	9,972
1996	9,476	2003	10,444
1997	9,003	2004	10,707
1998	8,791	2005	10,565
1999	8,838		

Source: American Mathematical Association (www.ams.org).

15.23 (a) Plot both men's and women's winning times on the same graph. (b) Fit a linear trend model to each series (men, women). (c) Use Excel's option to forecast each trend graphically to 2040 (i.e., to period $t = 27$ periods, as observations are in four-year increments). From these projections, does it appear that the times will eventually converge? *(d) Set the fitted trends equal, solve for x (the time period when the trends will cross), and convert x to a year. Is the result plausible? Explain. (e) Use the Web to check your 2004 and 2008 forecasts. (LO 2) **Olympic**

Summer Olympics 100-Metre Winning Times

Year	Men's 100-Metre Winner	Seconds	Women's 100-Metre Winner	Seconds
1928	Percy Williams, Canada	10.80	Elizabeth Robinson, United States	12.20
1932	Eddie Tolan, United States	10.30	Stella Walsh, Poland	11.90
1936	Jesse Owens, United States	10.30	Helen Stephens, United States	11.50
1948	Harrison Dillard, United States	10.30	Fanny Blankers-Koen, Netherlands	11.90
1952	Lindy Remigino, United States	10.40	Marjorie Jackson, United States	11.50
1956	Bobby Morrow, United States	10.50	Betty Cuthbert, Australia	11.50
1960	Armin Hary, West Germany	10.20	Wilma Rudolph, United States	11.00
1964	Bob Hayes, United States	10.00	Wyomia Tyus, United States	11.40
1968	Jim Hines, United States	9.95	Wyomia Tyus, United States	11.00
1972	Valery Borzov, USSR	10.14	Renate Stecher, East Germany	11.07
1976	Hasely Crawford, Trinidad	10.06	Annegret Richter, West Germany	11.08
1980	Allan Wells, Great Britain	10.25	Lyudmila Kondratyeva, USSR	11.06
1984	Carl Lewis, United States	9.99	Evelyn Ashford, United States	10.97
1988	Carl Lewis, United States	9.92	Florence Griffith-Joyner, United States	10.54
1992	Linford Christie, Great Britain	9.96	Gail Devers, United States	10.82
1996	Donovan Bailey, Canada	9.84	Gail Devers, United States	10.94
2000	Maurice Greene, United States	9.87	Marion Jones, United States	10.75

Source: Summer Olympics 100-metre times, *The World Almanac, 2002*, pp. 900–904.

15.24 (a) Use Excel, MegaStat, or MINITAB to fit an m-period moving average to the exchange rate data shown below with $m = 2, 3, 4$, and 5 periods. Make a line chart. (b) Which value of m do you prefer? Why? (c) Is a moving average appropriate for this kind of data? Include a chart for each value of m. (LO 4) **Sterling**

Daily Spot Exchange Rate, U.S. Dollars per Pound Sterling

Date	Rate	Date	Rate	Date	Rate	Date	Rate
1-Apr-04	1.8564	16-Apr-04	1.8004	3-May-04	1.7720	18-May-04	1.7695
2-Apr-04	1.8293	19-Apr-04	1.8055	4-May-04	1.7907	19-May-04	1.7827
5-Apr-04	1.8140	20-Apr-04	1.7914	5-May-04	1.7932	20-May-04	1.7710
6-Apr-04	1.8374	21-Apr-04	1.7720	6-May-04	1.7941	21-May-04	1.7880
7-Apr-04	1.8410	22-Apr-04	1.7684	7-May-04	1.7842	24-May-04	1.7908
8-Apr-04	1.8325	23-Apr-04	1.7674	10-May-04	1.7723	25-May-04	1.8135
9-Apr-04	1.8322	26-Apr-04	1.7857	11-May-04	1.7544	26-May-04	1.8142
12-Apr-04	1.8358	27-Apr-04	1.7925	12-May-04	1.7743	27-May-04	1.8369
13-Apr-04	1.8160	28-Apr-04	1.7720	13-May-04	1.7584	28-May-04	1.8330
14-Apr-04	1.7902	29-Apr-04	1.7751	14-May-04	1.7572		
15-Apr-04	1.7785	30-Apr-04	1.7744	17-May-04	1.7695		

Source: Federal Reserve Board of Governors.

15.25 Refer to exercise 15.24. (a) Plot the dollar/pound exchange rate data. Make the graph nice, then copy and paste it so that you have four copies. (b) Use MegaStat or MINITAB to perform a simple exponential smoothing using $\alpha = 0.05, 0.10, 0.20,$ and 0.50, using a different line chart for each. (c) Which value of α do you prefer? Why? (d) Is an exponential smoothing process appropriate for this kind of data? (LO 5) **Sterling**

15.26 (a) Plot the data on gas bills. (b) Can you see seasonal patterns? Explain. (c) Use MegaStat or MINITAB to calculate estimated seasonal indices and trend. (d) Which months are the most expensive? The least expensive? Can you explain this pattern? (e) Is there a trend in the deseasonalized data? *(f) Use MegaStat or MINITAB to perform a regression using seasonal binaries. Interpret the results. (LO 2 & 8) **GasBills**

Natural Gas Bills for a Residence, 2000–2003

Month	2000	2001	2002	2003
Jan	78.98	118.86	101.44	155.37
Feb	84.44	111.31	122.20	148.77
Mar	65.54	75.62	99.49	115.12
Apr	62.60	77.47	55.85	85.89
May	29.24	29.23	44.94	46.84
Jun	18.10	17.10	19.57	24.93
Jul	91.57	16.59	15.98	20.84
Aug	6.48	27.64	14.97	26.94
Sep	19.35	28.86	18.03	34.17
Oct	29.02	48.21	56.98	88.58
Nov	94.09	67.15	115.27	100.63
Dec	101.65	125.18	130.95	174.63

Source: Homeowner's records.

15.27 (a) Plot the data on air travel delays. (b) Can you see seasonal patterns? Explain. (c) Use MegaStat or MINITAB to calculate estimated seasonal indices and trend. (d) Which months have the most permits? The fewest? Is this logical? (e) Is there a trend in the deseasonalized data? (LO 2 & 8) **Delays**

U.S. Airspace Total System Delays, 2002–2006

Month	2002	2003	2004	2005	2006
Jan	14,158	16,159	28,104	32,121	29,463
Feb	13,821	18,260	32,274	30,176	24,705
Mar	20,020	25,387	34,001	34,633	37,218
Apr	24,027	17,474	32,459	25,887	35,132
May	28,533	26,544	50,800	30,920	40,669
Jun	33,770	27,413	52,121	48,922	48,096
Jul	32,304	32,833	46,894	58,471	47,606
Aug	29,056	37,066	43,770	45,328	46,547
Sep	24,493	28,882	30,412	32,949	48,092
Oct	25,266	21,422	37,271	34,221	51,053
Nov	17,712	34,116	35,234	34,273	43,482
Dec	22,489	31,332	32,446	29,766	39,797

Source: www.faa.gov.

15.28   (a) Plot the data on revolving credit (credit cards and home equity lines of credit are the two major types of revolving credit). (b) Use MegaStat or MINITAB to calculate estimated seasonal indices and trend. Is there a trend in the deseasonalized data? (c) Which months have the most borrowing? The least? Is this logical? (LO 2 & 8)   **Revolving**

U.S. Consumers' Revolving Credit ($ billions)

Month	2001	2002	2003	2004
Jan	223.2	232.5	240.6	276.7
Feb	221.5	229.7	239.7	272.8
Mar	220.1	230.2	234.0	268.3
Apr	227.7	235.6	235.4	270.6
May	229.1	233.1	240.4	278.0
Jun	225.7	231.0	240.7	275.6
Jul	222.1	229.9	238.6	278.7
Aug	219.6	241.1	240.7	286.4
Sep	216.3	243.1	239.9	286.7
Oct	223.3	242.4	235.8	286.1
Nov	233.2	244.2	269.5	285.8
Dec	238.3	250.2	284.7	315.8

Source: www.federalreserve.gov.

15.29   (a) In Excel, convert each time-series variable into index numbers (1990 = 100). (b) What is the 2004 index value for each time series? What does this tell you? (c) Plot all four series of index numbers on the same graph. Describe what you see. (d) What is the advantage of using index numbers in plotting and comparing these data over time? (LO 2 & 8)   **Prisons**

U.S. Adults on Probation, in Jail or Prison, or on Parole, 1990–2004 (thousands)

Year	Probation	Jail	Prison	Parole
1990	2,670	403	743	531
1991	2,728	424	793	590
1992	2,812	442	851	659
1993	2,903	456	909	676
1994	2,981	480	990	690
1995	3,078	507	1,079	679
1996	3,165	510	1,128	680
1997	3,297	558	1,177	695
1998	3,670	584	1,224	696
1999	3,780	596	1,287	714
2000	3,826	621	1,316	724
2001	3,932	631	1,330	732
2002	4,024	665	1,368	751
2003	4,145	691	1,393	745
2004	4,151	714	1,422	765

Source: *Statistical Abstract of the United States, 2007*, p. 209.

15.30 (a) Plot the data on M1 money stock. (b) Use MegaStat or MINITAB to calculate estimated seasonal indices and trend. Is there a trend in the deseasonalized data? (c) Make monthly forecasts for 2007. *Note:* M1 includes currency, travellers cheques, demand deposits, and other checkable deposits. (LO 2 & 8) **MoneyStock**

U.S. Money Stock M1 Component, 2000–2006 ($ billions)

Month	2000	2001	2002	2003	2004	2005	2006
Jan	1,127	1,100	1,191	1,225	1,302	1,361	1,375
Feb	1,097	1,090	1,178	1,225	1,306	1,355	1,362
Mar	1,109	1,111	1,196	1,245	1,338	1,382	1,394
Apr	1,126	1,127	1,197	1,259	1,343	1,369	1,393
May	1,100	1,115	1,186	1,266	1,333	1,369	1,391
Jun	1,102	1,126	1,194	1,284	1,348	1,384	1,378
Jul	1,103	1,140	1,200	1,287	1,339	1,365	1,367
Aug	1,094	1,145	1,182	1,292	1,352	1,377	1,370
Sep	1,089	1,194	1,185	1,286	1,349	1,363	1,347
Oct	1,092	1,159	1,196	1,288	1,351	1,365	1,360
Nov	1,092	1,169	1,205	1,293	1,371	1,373	1,368
Dec	1,112	1,208	1,245	1,332	1,401	1,396	1,388

Source: Federal Reserve Board of Governors, www.federalreserve.gov. Data not seasonally adjusted.

15.31 (a) Use MegaStat or MINITAB to deseasonalize the quarterly data on Coca-Cola's revenues and fit a trend. Interpret the results. (b) Use MegaStat or MINITAB to perform a regression using seasonal binaries. Interpret the results. (c) Use the regression equation to make a prediction for each quarter in 2007. (d) If you have access to *Standard & Poor's Stock Reports, 2008*, check your forecasts. How accurate were they? (LO 6 & 7) **CocaCola**

Coca-Cola Revenues ($ millions), 2001–2006

Quarter	2001	2002	2003	2004	2005	2006
1	4,479	4,079	4,502	5,078	5,206	5,226
2	5,293	5,368	5,695	5,965	6,310	6,476
3	5,397	5,322	5,671	5,622	6,037	6,454
4	4,923	4,795	5,176	5,257	5,551	5,932

Source: *Standard & Poor's Stock Reports,* Feb. 2007.

15.32 (a) Use MegaStat or MINITAB to perform a regression using seasonal binaries. Interpret the results. (b) Make monthly forecasts for 2006. If you can find data on the Web, check your forecasts. (LO 7) 🔘 **StudentPilots**

Student Pilot Certificates Issued by Month, 2000–2005

Month	2000	2001	2002	2003	2004	2005
Jan	4,248	4,747	5,346	4,954	4,883	4,234
Feb	3,824	4,317	4,114	4,602	4,442	5,846
Mar	4,687	4,853	4,306	4,897	5,273	5,063
Apr	4,486	4,616	4,294	5,313	4,584	4,001
May	4,706	4,613	4,982	5,196	5,644	4,697
Jun	5,509	5,485	5,531	6,197	6,560	5,182
Jul	5,306	6,130	6,046	7,151	6,560	5,037
Aug	6,284	6,145	6,216	7,278	7,355	6,401
Sep	4,698	5,524	5,592	6,204	4,643	5,216
Oct	3,985	4,800	5,201	5,621	5,029	4,958
Nov	3,443	4,353	3,818	4,287	4,095	4,130
Dec	2,400	2,779	2,990	3,721	2,771	3,277

Source: www.faa.gov/data_statistics/aviation_data_statistics.

15.33 Translate each of the following fitted exponential trend models into a compound interest model of the form $y_t = y_0(1 + r)^t$. *Hint:* See *LearningStats* Unit 14 or footnote on p. 649. (LO 2)

    a. $y_t = 456e^{0.123t}$ b. $y_t = 228e^{0.075t}$ c. $y_t = 456e^{-0.038t}$

15.34 Translate each of the following fitted compound interest trend models into an exponential model of the form $y_t = ae^{bt}$. *Hint:* See *LearningStats* Unit 14 or footnote on p. 649. (LO 2)

    a. $y_t = 123(1.089)^t$ b. $y_t = 654(1.217)^t$ c. $y_t = 308(0.942)^t$

LearningStats Unit   14 Time-Series Analysis   LS

LearningStats Unit 14 contains simulations to generate quarterly and monthly data, case studies of various kinds of fitted trends, illustrations of the components of a time series, and examples of student projects using fitted trends. Modules are designed for self-study, so you can concentrate on material that is new, and pass quickly over things that you already know or do not find interesting. Your instructor may assign specific modules, or you may decide to check them out because the topic sounds interesting. In addition to helping you learn about statistics, they may be useful as references later on.

Topic	*LearningStats Modules*
Trends and forecasting	Time-Series Components
	Trend Fitting
	Trend Forecasting
Using Excel	Excel logo
	Excel Trends—1
	Excel Trends—2
	Exponential Trend
	Dissimilar Magnitudes
	Exponential Smoothing
Simulations	Time-Series Components
	Trend Simulator
	Seasonal Time-Series Generator
Fit and seasonality	Trend Fit Measures
	Seasonal Factors
Case studies	Health Trends
	Olympic Times
	Federal Budget
	Male/Female Income
	Brad's Bowling Scores
Student projects	Gas Prices
	Investing
	Government Spending
	Olympic Times

Key: = PowerPoint   = Word   = Excel

Visual Statistics

Visual Statistics Modules on Time Series

Module	Module Name
20	 Visualizing Time-Series Data

Visual Statistics Module 20 is designed to help you

*   Understand the importance of the data collection period.

*   Recognize the difficulty in separating trend, seasonality.

*   See why sample size is important.

*   Understand the difference between additive and multiplicative seasonality.

*   Understand common statistics of fit (*MAPE*, R^2, standard error).

The worktext (included on the CD in PDF format) contains lists of concepts covered, objectives of the modules, overviews of concepts, illustrations of concepts, orientations to module features, learning exercises (basic, intermediate, advanced), learning projects (individual, team), self-evaluation quizzes, glossaries of terms, and solutions to self-evaluation quizzes.

For solutions to odd-numbered exercises, Exam Review questions, and additional study tools to help you succeed in this course, visit *Connect* at www.mcgrawhillconnect.ca.

Nonparametric Tests

Chapter Learning Objectives

When you finish this chapter you should be able to

1. Explain what a nonparametric test is and when it may have advantages over a parametric test.

2. Demonstrate an understanding of when and how to use several common nonparametric tests in a problem context.

3. Use computer software to perform the tests and obtain p values.

16.1 Why Use Nonparametric Tests?

The hypothesis tests in previous chapters required the estimation of one or more unknown parameters (for example, the population mean, proportion, or variance). These tests often made sometimes unrealistic assumptions about the normality of the underlying population or require large samples to invoke the Central Limit Theorem. In contrast, **nonparametric tests** or distribution-free tests usually focus on the sign or rank of the data rather than the exact numerical value of the variable, do not specify the shape of the parent population, can often be used in smaller samples, and can be used for ordinal data (when the measurement scale is not interval or ratio). Table 16.1 highlights the advantages and disadvantages of nonparametric tests.

TABLE 16.1 Advantages and Disadvantages of Nonparametric Tests

Advantages	Disadvantages
1. Can often be used in small samples.	1. Require special tables for small samples.
2. Generally more powerful than parametric tests when normality cannot be assumed.	2. If normality *can* be assumed, parametric tests are generally more powerful.
3. Can be used for ordinal data.	

Some Common Nonparametric Tests FIGURE 16.1

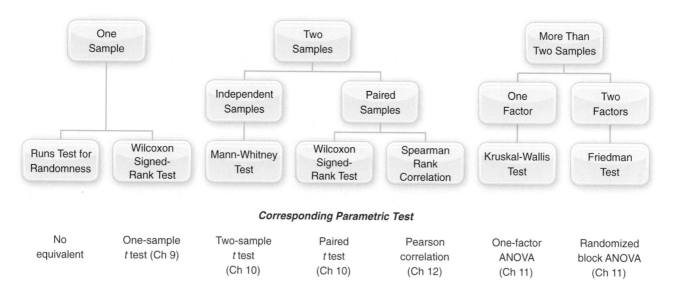

Rejection of a hypothesis using a nonparametric test is especially convincing, because nonparametric tests generally make fewer assumptions about the population. If two methods are justified and have similar **power,** the principle of Occam's Razor favours the simpler method. For this reason, statisticians have long been attracted to nonparametric tests, particularly in applications where data are likely to be ill-behaved and when samples are small.

You might expect that nonparametric tests would primarily be used in areas of business where nominal or ordinal data are common (e.g., human resources, marketing). Yet business analysts who mostly use ratio data (e.g., accounting, finance) may encounter skewed populations that render parametric tests unreliable. These analysts might use nonparametric tests as a *complement* to their customary **parametric tests.** Figure 16.1 shows common nonparametric tests and their parametric counterparts, which you have seen in earlier chapters.

This chapter illustrates only a few of the many nonparametric techniques that are available. The selections are those you are most likely to encounter. Small-sample nonparametric tests are omitted, but references are shown at the end of the chapter for those who need them.

16.2 One-Sample Runs Test

The one-sample **runs test** is also called the **Wald-Wolfowitz test** after its inventor Abraham Wald (1902–1950) and his student Jacob Wolfowitz (1910–1981). Its purpose is to detect non-randomness. A non-random pattern suggests that the observations are not *independent*— a fundamental assumption of many statistical tests. We are asking whether each observation in a sequence is independent of its predecessor. In a time series, a non-random pattern of residuals indicates *autocorrelation* (as in Chapters 14 and 15). In quality control, a non-random pattern of deviations from the design specification may indicate an *out-of-control* process. We will illustrate only the large sample version of this test (as a rule of thumb, defined as samples of 10 or more).

> ### Runs Test
>
> This test is to determine whether a sequence of binary events follows a random pattern. A non-random sequence suggests non-independent observations.

The hypotheses are

H_0: Events follow a random pattern.

H_1: Events do not follow a random pattern.

To test the hypothesis of randomness, we first count the number of outcomes of each type:

n_1 = number of outcomes of the first type (e.g., number of positive residuals, number of successes)

n_2 = number of outcomes of the second type (e.g., number of negative residuals, number of failures)

n = total sample size = $n_1 + n_2$

Application: Quality Inspection Defects

Inspection of 44 computer chips reveals the following sequence of defective (D) and acceptable (A) chips:

> *DAAAAAAADDDDAAAAAAAADDAAAAAAAADDDDAAAAAAAAAA*

Do defective chips appear at random? A pattern could indicate that the assembly process has a cyclic problem due to unknown causes. The hypotheses are

H_0: Defects follow a random sequence.

H_1: Defects follow a non-random sequence.

A *run* is a series of consecutive outcomes of the same type, surrounded by a sequence of outcomes of the other type. We group sequences of similar outcomes and count the runs:

D	*AAAAAAA*	*DDDD*	*AAAAAAAA*	*DD*	*AAAAAAAA*	*DDDD*	*AAAAAAAAAA*
1	2	3	4	5	6	7	8

A run can be a single outcome if it is preceded and followed by outcomes of the other type. There are eight runs in our sample ($R = 8$). The number of outcomes of each type is as follows:

n_1 = number of defective chips (D) = 11

n_2 = number of acceptable chips (A) = 33

n = total sample size = $n_1 + n_2 = 11 + 33 = 44$

In a large-sample situation (when $n_1 \geq 10$ and $n_2 \geq 10$), the number of runs R may be assumed to be normally distributed with mean μ_R and standard deviation σ_R:

$$Z_{\text{calc}} = \frac{R - \mu_R}{\sigma_R} \quad \text{(test statistic comparing } R \text{ with its expected value } \mu_R) \qquad \textbf{(16.1)}$$

$$\mu_R = \frac{2n_1 n_2}{n} + 1 \quad \text{(expected value of } R \text{ if } H_0 \text{ is true)} \qquad \textbf{(16.2)}$$

$$\sigma_R = \sqrt{\frac{2n_1 n_2 (2n_1 n_2 - n)}{n^2(n - 1)}} \quad \text{(standard error of } R \text{ if } H_0 \text{ is true)} \qquad \textbf{(16.3)}$$

For our data, the expected number of runs would be

$$\mu_R = \frac{2n_1 n_2}{n} + 1 = \frac{2(11)(33)}{44} + 1 = 17.5$$

Because the actual number of runs ($R = 8$) is less than expected ($\mu_R = 17.5$) our sample suggests that the null hypothesis may be false, depending on the standard deviation. For our data, the standard deviation is

$$\sigma_R = \sqrt{\frac{2n_1 n_2 (2n_1 n_2 - n)}{n^2(n-1)}} = \sqrt{\frac{2(11)(33)[2(11)(33) - 44]}{44^2(44-1)}} = 2.438785$$

Because the actual number of runs is $R = 8$, the test statistic is

$$z_{calc} = \frac{R - \mu_R}{\sigma_R} = \frac{8 - 17.5}{2.438785} = -3.90$$

Because either too many runs or too few runs would be non-random, we choose a two-tailed test. The critical value $z_{0.005}$ for a two-tailed test at $\alpha = 0.01$ is ± 2.576, so the decision rule is

Reject the hypothesis of a random pattern if $z < -2.576$ or $z > +2.576$.

Otherwise, assume the observed difference is attributable to chance.

Because the test statistic $z = -3.90$ is well below the lower critical limit, as shown in Figure 16.2, we can easily reject the hypothesis of randomness. The difference between the observed number of runs and the expected number of runs is too great to be due to chance ($p = 0.0001$).

Figure 16.3 shows the MegaStat output for this problem, which also includes the p value and the entire distribution for various values of R, not shown because it is lengthy. (MegaStat uses a continuity correction factor, resulting in a value of $z = -3.69$ instead of our manually calculated value of $z = -3.90$.) As with any hypothesis test, the smaller the p value, the stronger is the evidence against H_0. Here, the small p value provides very strong evidence that H_0 is false (i.e., that the sequence is not random).

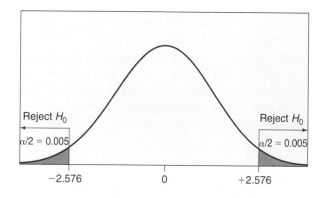

FIGURE 16.2

Decision Rule for Large-Sample Runs Test

Runs Test for Random Sequence

Number of Defects

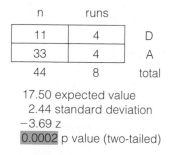

n	runs	
11	4	D
33	4	A
44	8	total

17.50 expected value
2.44 standard deviation
−3.69 z
0.0002 p value (two-tailed)

FIGURE 16.3

MegaStat's Runs Test

Concept Check

Assume that there is an equal number of each type of outcome. What is the minimum number of runs that are possible? What is the maximum number of runs that are possible? What is the expected number of runs if H_0 is true (i.e., no pattern in the outcomes)? What, if any, is the relationship between the minimum and maximum number of runs and the expected number of runs? If these outcomes represent the residuals in a time-series regression analysis, would you expect a small or larger number of runs if there was positive autocorrelation?

A Closer Look

Previously, when using the z-distribution to test hypotheses, the decision rules were

- To reject the null hypothesis if $z_{crit} < -z_\alpha$ when the alternative hypothesis tested for $<$
- To reject the null hyptheis if $z_{crit} < -z_{\alpha/2}$ or $z_{crit} > z_{\alpha/2}$ when the alternative hypothesis tested for $\neq$
- To reject the null hypothesis if $z_{crit} > z_\alpha$ when the alternative hypothesis tested for $>$

The same decision rules also apply here. For example, if you were testing for a positive autocorrelation, you would expect a small number of runs if the alternative hypothesis is true, which is equivalent to your alternative hypothesis testing for $<$ and you would reject the null hypothesis if $z_{crit} < -z_\alpha$.

Small Samples

There are tables of critical values that extend the test to small samples ($n < 10$). The problem with small samples is that they lack power. That is, in a small sample, it would take an extremely small or large number of runs to convince us that the sequence is non-random. While some researchers must deal with small samples, business analysts (e.g., quality control) often have hundreds of observations, so small samples rarely pose a problem.

Section Exercises

16.1 Using $\alpha = 0.05$, perform a runs test for randomness on the sample data ($n = 27$). (LO 2)

   $A\,A\,B\,B\,A\,A\,B\,B\,A\,B\,A\,B\,A\,A\,B\,B\,B\,A\,A\,B\,B\,B\,B\,A\,A\,B\,A\,B\,B$

16.2 Using $\alpha = 0.10$, perform a runs test for randomness on the sample data ($n = 24$). (LO 2)

   $X\,O\,X\,X\,X\,X\,O\,O\,O\,O\,X\,O\,O\,O\,X\,O\,O\,O\,X\,O\,O\,X\,X\,O$

16.3 On a professional certifying exam there are 25 true-false questions. The correct answers are $T\,F\,T\,T\,F\,F\,F\,T\,T\,F\,T\,F\,T\,T\,T\,F$ $F\,T\,T\,F\,F\,T\,T\,F\,T$. *Research question:* At $\alpha = 0.05$, is the T/F pattern random? (LO 2)    **TrueFalse**

16.4 A baseball player was at bat 33 times during preseason exhibition games. His pattern of hits including walks (H) and non-hits (N) is shown. *Research question:* At $\alpha = 0.01$, is the pattern of hits random? (LO 2)   **Hits**

   $N\,N\,N\,H\,N\,H\,N\,N\,H\,N\,N\,H\,H\,N\,N\,N\,N\,H\,N\,H\,N\,N\,N\,H\,N\,N\,H\,N\,H\,N\,N\,H\,H$

16.3   Wilcoxon Signed-Rank Test

The **Wilcoxon signed-rank test** was developed by Frank Wilcoxon (1892–1965) to compare a single sample with a benchmark using only **ranks** of the data instead of the original observations, as in a one-sample *t* test. It is more often used to compare *paired* observations, as an alternative to the paired-sample *t* test, which is a special case of the one-sample *t* test. The advantages of the Wilcoxon test are its freedom from the normality assumption, its robustness to outliers, and its applicability to ordinal data. Although the test does require the population to be roughly symmetric, it has fairly good power over a range of possible non-normal population shapes. It is slightly less powerful than the one-sample *t* test when the population is normal.

> ### Wilcoxon Signed-Rank Test
>
> The Wilcoxon signed-rank test is a nonparametric test to compare a sample median with a benchmark or to test the median difference in paired samples. It does not require normality but does assume symmetric populations.

If we denote the hypothesized benchmark median as M_0, the hypotheses about the population median *M* are as follows:

Left-Tailed Test	*Two-Tailed Test*	*Right-Tailed Test*
$H_0: M = M_0$	$H_0: M = M_0$	$H_0: M = M_0$
$H_1: M < M_0$	$H_1: M \neq M_0$	$H_1: M > M_0$

When the variable of interest is the median difference between paired observations, the test is the same, but we use the symbol M_d for the population median *difference* and (generally) use zero as the benchmark:

Left-Tailed Test	*Two-Tailed Test*	*Right-Tailed Test*
$H_0: M_d = 0$	$H_0: M_d = 0$	$H_0: M_d = 0$
$H_1: M_d < 0$	$H_1: M_d \neq 0$	$H_1: M_d > 0$

We calculate the difference between each observation and the hypothesized median (or the differences between the paired observations), rank them from smallest to largest by absolute value, and add the ranks of the *positive* differences to obtain the Wilcoxon signed-rank test statistic *W*. Its expected value if the null hypothesis is true and variance depend only on the sample size *n*.

$$W = \sum_{i=1}^{n} R^+ \text{ (the sum of all positive ranks)} \tag{16.4}$$

$$\mu_W = \frac{n(n + 1)}{4} \text{ (expected value of the } W \text{ statistic)} \tag{16.5}$$

$$\sigma_W = \sqrt{\frac{n(n + 1)(2n + 1)}{24}} \text{ (standard deviation of the } W \text{ statistic)} \tag{16.6}$$

For large samples ($n \geq 20$) the test statistic is approximately normal:

$$Z = \frac{W - \mu_W}{\sigma_W} = \frac{W - \dfrac{n(n + 1)}{4}}{\sqrt{\dfrac{n(n + 1)(2n + 1)}{24}}} \text{ (Wilcoxon test statistic for large } n) \tag{16.7}$$

Concept Check

1. If $H_1: M < M_0$ is true, what would you expect z_{crit} to be (i.e., positive or negative) and what would your decision rule be? Answer the same question if $H_1: M \neq M_0$ and if $H_1: M > M_0$.

2. Why would you expect W to equal $\dfrac{n(n+1)}{4}$ if the null hypothesis of equality is true? Explain.

A Closer Look

A more basic, but less powerful, test to compare data with a benchmark or to compare a set of paired data is the **sign test.** The sign test simply counts the number of positive differences, D^+ and compares it with $0.5n$ (where n is the number of observations after eliminating any observations with zero differences), which is what would be expected of D^+ if H_0 is true. This comparison is then converted to the test statistic,

$$Z = \frac{D^+ - 0.5n}{\sqrt{0.25n}}$$

which is then compared with z_{crit} using the same reasoning as all other tests involving the z-distribution.

Concept Check

Show how $Z = \dfrac{D^+ - 0.5n}{\sqrt{0.25n}}$ is derived from the formula $Z = \dfrac{X - np}{\sqrt{np(1-p)}}$ when the null hypothesis of equality is true.

Application: Median versus Benchmark

Are price-earnings (P/E) ratios of stocks in *specialty* retail stores (e.g., Abercrombie & Fitch) the same as P/E ratios for stocks of *multiline* retail stores (e.g., Zellers)? Table 16.2 shows P/E ratios for a random sample of 21 specialty stores. The median P/E ratio for all multiline retail stores for the same date was $M_0 = 20.2$ (our benchmark). Our hypotheses are as follows:

$H_0: M = 20.2$ (the median P/E ratio for specialty stores is 20.2)

$H_1: M \neq 20.2$ (the median P/E ratio for specialty stores is not 20.2)

To perform the test, we subtract 20.2 (the benchmark) from each specialty store's P/E ratio, take absolute values, convert to ranks, and sum the *positive* ranks. Negative ranks are shown, but are not used. We assign tie ranks so that the sum of the tied values is the same as if they were not tied. For example, 3.4 occurs twice (Abercrombie & Fitch and AutoZone). If not tied, these data values would have ranks 8 and 9, so we assign a "tie" rank of 8.5 to each. Companies are shown in rank order of absolute differences.

TABLE 16.2   Wilcoxon Signed-Rank Test of P/E Ratios ($n = 21$ firms) 🔘 **WilcoxonA**

Company	X	X − 20.2	|X − 20.2|	Rank	R⁺	R⁻
Bebe Stores Inc	19.8	−0.4	0.4	2		2
Barnes & Noble Inc	19.8	−0.4	0.4	2		2
Aeropostale Inc	20.6	0.4	0.4	2	2	
Deb Shops	18.7	−1.5	1.5	4		4
Gap Inc	22.0	1.8	1.8	5	5	
PETsMART Inc	17.9	−2.3	2.3	6		6
Payless Shoesource	17.0	−3.2	3.2	7		7
Abercrombie & Fitch Co	16.8	−3.4	3.4	8.5		8.5
AutoZone Inc	16.8	−3.4	3.4	8.5		8.5
Lithia Motors Inc A	16.3	−3.9	3.9	10		10
Genesco Inc	24.3	4.1	4.1	11	11	
Sherwin-Williams Co	16.0	−4.2	4.2	12		12
CSK Auto Corp	14.5	−5.7	5.7	13		13
Tiffany & Co	26.2	6.0	6.0	14	14	
Rex Stores	14.0	−6.2	6.2	15		15
Casual Male Retail Group	12.6	−7.6	7.6	16		16
Sally Beauty Co Inc	28.9	8.7	8.7	17	17	
Syms Corp	32.1	11.9	11.9	18	18	
Zale Corp	40.4	20.2	20.2	19	19	
Coldwater Creek Inc	41.0	20.8	20.8	20	20	
Talbots Inc	124.7	104.5	104.5	21	21	
			Sum	231.0	127	104.0

Source: http://investing.businessweek.com, accessed on June 19, 2007. Companies are sorted by rank of absolute differences.

Thus *w*, the value of the random variable *W*, equals 127. Because $n = 21$, we have

$$\mu_W = \frac{n(n+1)}{4} = \frac{21(22)}{4} = 115.5, \; \sigma_W = \sqrt{\frac{n(n+1)(2n+1)}{24}} = \sqrt{\frac{21(22)43}{24}} = 28.77$$

The test statistic is calculated as

$$z_{\text{calc}} = \frac{w - \mu_W}{\sigma_W} = \frac{127 - 115.5}{28.77} = 0.4$$

The two-tailed *p* value is $p = 0.6892$. At any customary level of significance, we cannot reject the hypothesis that specialty retail stores have the same median P/E as multiline retail stores. Although we use the *z* table for the *test statistic* (because $n \geq 20$), the P/E *data* do not seem to be from a normal population (for example, look at Talbot's extreme P/E ratio of 124.7). Thus, Wilcoxon's nonparametric test of the *median* is preferred to a one-sample *t* test of the *mean* (Chapter 9).

Application: Paired Data

Did P/E ratios decline between 2003 and 2007? We will perform a Wilcoxon test for *paired data* using a random sample of 23 common stocks. The parameter of interest is the median difference (M_d). Because the P/E ratios do not appear to be normally distributed (e.g., Rohm & Haas Co.'s 2003 P/E ratio), the Wilcoxon test of *medians* is attractive (instead of the paired

TABLE 16.3 **Wilcoxon Signed-Rank Paired Test ($n = 23$ firms)** WilcoxonB

Company (Ticker Symbol)	2007 P/E	2003 P/E	D	∣d∣	Rank	R⁺	R⁻
FirstEnergy Corp (FE)	14	14	0	0	—		
Whirlpool Corp (WHR)	18	18	0	0	—		
Burlington/Santa (BNI)	14	14	0	0	—		
Constellation Energy (CEG)	16	15	1	1	1	1	
Mellon Financial (MEL)	17	19	−2	2	2.5		2.5
Yum! Brands Inc (YUM)	18	16	2	2	2.5	2.5	
Baxter International (BAX)	20	23	−3	3	5		5
Fluor Corp (FLR)	22	19	3	3	5	5	
Allied Waste Ind (AW)	21	18	3	3	5	5	
Ingersoll-Rand-A (IR)	12	16	−4	4	7.5		7.5
Lexmark Intl A (LXK)	17	21	−4	4	7.5		7.5
Moody's Corp (MCO)	29	24	5	5	9	9	
Electronic Data (EDS)	17	23	−6	6	10		10
Freeport-Mcmor-B (FCX)	11	18	−7	7	11		11
Family Dollar Stores (FDO)	19	27	−8	8	12.5		12.5
Leggett & Platt (LEG)	13	21	−8	8	12.5		12.5
Wendy's Intl Inc (WEN)	24	15	9	9	14	14	
Sara Lee Corp (SLE)	25	13	12	12	15	15	
Bed Bath & Beyond (BBBY)	20	37	−17	17	16		16
Ace Ltd (ACE)	8	26	−18	18	17.5		17.5
ConocoPhillips (COP)	8	26	−18	18	17.5		17.5
Baker Hughes Inc (BHI)	13	55	−42	42	19		19
Rohm & Haas Co (ROH)	15	68	−53	53	20		20
					Sum	210.0	51.5	158.5

Source: *The Wall Street Journal,* July 31, 2003, and Standard & Poors, *Security Owner's Stock Guide,* Feb. 2007. P/E ratios were reported as integers in these publications. Companies are sorted by rank of absolute differences.

t test for *means* in Chapter 10). Using $d = X_{2007} − X_{2003}$, the median of these differences defined as M_d, a left-tailed test is appropriate:

$H_0: M_d \geq 0$ (the median difference is zero or positive)

$H_1: M_d < 0$ (the median difference is negative, i.e., 2007 is less than 2003)

Table 16.3 shows the calculations for the Wilcoxon signed-rank statistic, with the companies in rank order of absolute differences. Because the first three have zero difference (neither positive nor negative), these three observations (highlighted) are *excluded* from the analysis.

Despite losing three observations due to zero differences, we still have $n \geq 20$, so we can use the large-sample test statistic:

$$z_{calc} = \frac{W - \dfrac{n(n+1)}{4}}{\sqrt{\dfrac{n(n+1)(2n+1)}{24}}} = \frac{51.5 - \dfrac{20(20+1)}{4}}{\sqrt{\dfrac{20(20+1)(40+1)}{24}}} = \frac{51.5 - 105.0}{26.7862} = -1.9973$$

Using Excel, we find the left-tailed p value to be $p = 0.0229$ (or $p = 0.0228$ if we use Appendix C with $z = -2.00$), so at $\alpha = 0.05$ we conclude that P/E ratios did decline between 2003 and 2007. Figure 16.4 shows that MegaStat confirms our calculations.

Wilcoxon Signed-Rank Test

variables: 2007 P/E-2003 P/E
    51.5 sum of positive ranks
  158.5 sum of negative ranks

    20 n
105.00 expected value
 26.79 standard deviation
 −2.00 z
 0.0229 p value (one-tailed, lower)

FIGURE 16.4

**MegaStat Signed-Rank
Test for Paired Data**

A Closer Look

If we used the sign test to test for the above example, we would simply add up the positive differences giving us $D^+ = 7$ and $n = 20$ (after eliminating the three zero differences). Using this D^+ and n, we calculate the test statistic to be

$$z_{calc} = \frac{D^+ - 0.5n}{\sqrt{0.25n}} = \frac{7 - 0.5(20)}{\sqrt{0.25(20)}} = -1.34$$

resulting in a p value of 0.0901.

Because $0.0901 > 0.05$, we would not reject the null hypothesis at $\alpha = 0.05$ and not conclude that the P/E ratios declined between 2003 and 2007. (By comparing z_{calc} with z_{crit} of -1.645, we would also not have rejected the null hypothesis at $\alpha = 0.05$.) In this particular example, this conclusion contradicts the conclusion using the Wilcoxon signed-rank pair test, which could happen if the null hypothesis is rejected using the Wilcoxon test. The sign test is not as powerful as the Wilcoxon test, making it easier to make a Type II error.

Section Exercises

16.5 A sample of 28 student scores on a chemistry midterm exam is shown. (a) At $\alpha = 0.10$, does the population median differ from 50? Make a worksheet in Excel for your calculations. (b) Make a histogram of the data. Would you be justified in using a parametric t test that assumes normality? Explain. (LO 2)   **Chemistry**

74	60	7	97	62	2	100
5	99	78	93	32	43	64
87	37	70	54	60	62	17
26	45	84	24	66	7	48

16.6 Final exam scores for a sample of 20 students in a managerial accounting class are shown. (a) At $\alpha = 0.05$, is there a difference in the population median scores on the two exams? Make an Excel worksheet for your Wilcoxon signed-rank test calculations and check your work by using MegaStat or a similar computer package. (b) Perform a two-tailed parametric t test for paired two-sample means by using Excel or MegaStat. Do you get the same decision? (LO 2 & 3)   **Accounting**

Student	Exam 1	Exam 2	Student	Exam 1	Exam 2	Student	Exam 1	Exam 2
1	70	81	8	71	69	15	59	68
2	74	89	9	52	53	16	54	47
3	65	59	10	79	84	17	75	84
4	60	68	11	84	96	18	92	100
5	63	75	12	95	96	19	70	81
6	58	77	13	83	99	20	54	58
7	72	82	14	81	76			

16.7 Canadians crossing the border into the United States from Canada often become very frustrated when they get into a line in which the Customs and Border Protection (CBP) officer seems to be spending more time with each car than a CBP officer in another line. But is this officer spending more time because the occupants in the cars are not prepared to properly answers the questions or are not prepared with the proper documents, or is it because this Officer tends to demand more information from these occupants? As an experiment, 21 subjects were sent across the border on two different occasions. On one occasion they were sent to Officer A's booth, and on the other occasion they were sent to officer B's booth. Each time, they carried the same documentation and were prepared with the same answers. The times (in minutes) that the officers spent with them were recorded below. Using the Wilcoxon signed-rank test at the 0.05 level of significance, is there sufficient evidence to indicate that the demands differ between these two officers? (LO 2)

Subject	Officer A	Officer B	Subject	Officer A	Officer B	Subject	Officer A	Officer B
1	3.45	4.21	8	2.17	2.34	15	4.16	4.01
2	1.47	1.60	9	4.10	3.35	16	5.24	6.31
3	6.32	7.45	10	2.42	3.06	17	3.41	3.98
4	2.65	1.80	11	0.50	1.25	18	2.57	3.05
5	1.98	2.45	12	3.42	4.31	19	3.52	3.31
6	9.40	8.65	13	4.17	3.68	20	2.95	5.00
7	4.47	5.25	14	2.35	2.55	21	1.05	1.41

16.4 Mann-Whitney Test

The **Mann-Whitney test,** named after Henry B. Mann (1905–2000) and D. Ransom Whitney (1915–2007), is a nonparametric test that compares two populations when the samples are independent. The Mann-Whitney test does not assume normality. Assuming that the populations differ only in centrality (i.e., location) it is a test for equality of *medians*. It is analogous to the *t* test for two independent sample means.

Mann-Whitney Test

The Mann-Whitney test is a nonparametric test to compare two populations, utilizing only the ranks of the data from two independent samples. It does not require normality, but does assume equal variances.

Studies suggest that the Mann-Whitney test has only slightly less power in distinguishing between centrality of two populations than the *t* test for two independent sample means, which you studied in Chapter 10. The Mann-Whitney test requires independent samples from populations with equal variances,* but the populations need not be normal. To avoid the use of special tables, we will illustrate only a large-sample version of this test (defined as samples of 10 or more).

Assuming that the only difference in the populations is in location, the hypotheses for a two-tailed test of the population medians would be

$H_0: M_1 = M_2$ (no difference in satisfaction)

$H_1: M_1 \neq M_2$ (satisfaction differs for the two groups)

---

* If populations are normal but have unequal variances, the unpooled two-sample *t*-test with Welch's correction is preferred to the Mann-Whitney test. You can test for equal variances by using the *F* test discussed in Chapter 10.

TABLE 16.4 Satisfaction and Ranks for 29 Chain Restaurants   Restaurants

Obs	Satisfaction	Rank	Price	Obs	Satisfaction	Rank	Price
1	73	1	Low	16	81	16.5	Low
2	76	2.5	Low	17	81	16.5	Low
3	76	2.5	High	18	82	18.5	High
4	77	4.5	Low	19	82	18.5	High
5	77	4.5	Low	20	83	20.5	Low
6	78	7	Low	21	83	20.5	Low
7	78	7	High	22	84	22.5	High
8	78	7	High	23	84	22.5	High
9	79	10	Low	24	85	25	High
10	79	10	Low	25	85	25	High
11	79	10	Low	26	85	25	High
12	80	13.5	Low	27	86	28	High
13	80	13.5	Low	28	86	28	High
14	80	13.5	Low	29	86	28	High
15	80	13.5	High				

Source: © 2003 by Consumers Union of U.S., Inc., Yonkers, NY 10703-1057, excerpted or adapted with permission from the July 2003 issue of *Consumer Reports* for educational purposes only.

Application: Restaurant Quality   Restaurants

Does spending more at a restaurant lead to greater customer satisfaction? Readers of *Consumer Reports* rated 29 American, Italian, and Mexican chain restaurants on a scale of 0 to 100, based mainly on the taste of the food. Results are shown in Table 16.4, sorted by satisfaction rating (note that, in this test, the lowest data value is assigned a rank of 1, which is rather counterintuitive for restaurant ratings). Each restaurant is assigned to one of two price groups: *Low* (under $15 per person) and *High* ($15 or more per person). Is there a significant difference in satisfaction between the higher-priced restaurants and the lower-priced ones? The parametric *t* test for two means would require that the variable be measured on a ratio or interval level. Because the satisfaction ratings are solely based on human perception, we are unwilling to assume the strong measurement properties associated with ratio or interval data. Instead, we treat these measurements as ordinal data (i.e., ranked data).

In Table 16.4, we convert the customer satisfaction ratings into ranks by sorting the *combined* samples from lowest to highest satisfaction, and then assigning a rank to each satisfaction score. If values are tied, the average of the ranks is assigned to each. Restaurants are then separated into two groups based on the price category (*Low, High*) as displayed in Table 16.5.

The ranks are summed for each column to get $T_1 = 164$ and $T_2 = 271$. The sum $T_1 + T_2$ must be $n(n+1)/2$ where $n = n_1 + n_2 = 15 + 14 = 29$. Because $n(n+1)/2 = (29)(30)/2 = 435$ and the sample sums are $T_1 + T_2 = 164 + 271 = 435$, our calculations check.* Next, we calculate the mean rank sums $\overline{T}_1$ and $\overline{T}_2$. If there is no difference between groups, we would expect $\overline{T}_1 - \overline{T}_2$ to be near zero. For large samples ($n_1 \geq 10$, $n_2 \geq 10$) we can use a z test. The test statistic is

$$z_{calc} = \frac{\overline{T}_1 - \overline{T}_2}{(n_1 + n_2)\sqrt{\dfrac{n_1 + n_2 + 1}{12n_1n_2}}} \tag{16.8}$$

*If the sum $T_1 + T_2$ does not check, you have made an error in calculating the ranks. It is more reliable to use MINITAB's Calc function RANK() to convert a column of data into ranks. Avoid Excel's =RANK() function, because it does not adjust for ties.

TABLE 16.5   Chain Restaurant Customer Satisfaction Score

Low-Priced Restaurants ($n_1 = 15$)		High-Priced Restaurants ($n_2 = 14$)	
Satisfaction	Rank	Satisfaction	Rank
73	1	76	2.5
76	2.5	78	7
77	4.5	78	7
77	4.5	80	13.5
78	7	82	18.5
79	10	82	18.5
79	10	84	22.5
79	10	84	22.5
80	13.5	85	25
80	13.5	85	25
80	13.5	85	25
81	16.5	86	28
81	16.5	86	28
83	20.5	86	28
83	20.5		

Rank sum:	$T_1 = 164$	Rank sum:	$T_2 = 271$
Sample size:	$n_1 = 15$	Sample size:	$n_2 = 14$
Mean rank:	$\bar{T}_1 = 164/15 = 10.93333$	Mean rank:	$\bar{T}_2 = 271/14 = 19.35714$

For our data,

$$z_{\text{calc}} = \frac{10.93333 - 19.35714}{(15 + 14)\sqrt{\dfrac{15 + 14 + 1}{(12)(15)(14)}}} = -2.662$$

At $\alpha = 0.01$, rejection in a two-tailed test requires $z > +2.576$ or $z < -2.576$, so we would reject the hypothesis that the population medians are the same. From Appendix C, the two-tailed p value is 0.0078, which says that a sample difference of this magnitude would be expected only about 8 times in 1,000 samples if the populations were the same. MegaStat uses a different version of this test,* but obtains a similar result, as shown in Figure 16.5.

FIGURE 16.5

MegaStat's Mann-Whitney Test

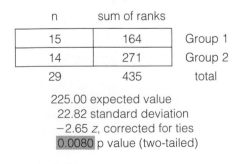

Wilcoxon Mann/Whitney Test

n	sum of ranks	
15	164	Group 1
14	271	Group 2
29	435	total

225.00 expected value
22.82 standard deviation
−2.65 z, corrected for ties
0.0080 p value (two-tailed)

---

* The *Mann-Whitney test* is also called the *Wilcoxon rank-sum test,* hence MegaStat's heading. When statistical tests were developed or popularized independently by more than one statistician, the names may vary.

Section Exercises

16.8   Bob and Tom are "paper investors." They each "buy" stocks they think will rise in value and "hold" them for a year. At the end of the year, they compare their stocks' appreciation (percent). (a) At $\alpha = 0.05$, is there a difference in the medians (assume these are samples of Bob's and Tom's stock-picking skills). Use MegaStat or a similar computer package for the Mann-Whitney (Wilcoxon rank-sum test) calculations. (b) Perform a two-tailed parametric t test for two independent sample means (assuming equal variances) by using Excel or MegaStat. Do you get the same decision? (LO 2 & 3)   **Investors**

| Bob's Portfolio (10 stocks) | 7.0, 2.5, 6.2, 4.4, 4.2, 8.5, 10.0, 6.4, 3.6, 7.6 |
| Tom's Portfolio (12 stocks) | 5.2, 0.4, 2.6, −0.2, 4.0, 5.2, 8.6, 4.3, 3.0, 0.0, 8.6, 7.5 |

16.9   An experimental bumper was designed to reduce damage in low-speed collisions. This bumper was installed on an experimental group of vans in a large fleet, but not on a control group. At the end of a trial period, there were 12 repair incidents (a "repair incident" is an accident that resulted in a repair invoice) for the experimental group and 9 repair incidents for the control group. The dollar cost per repair incident is shown below. (a) Use MegaStat or MINITAB to perform a two-tailed Mann-Whitney test at $\alpha = 0.05$. (b) Perform a two-tailed parametric t test for two independent sample means by using Excel or MegaStat. Do you get the same decision? (Data are from Floyd G. Willoughby and Thomas W. Lauer, confidential case study.) (LO 2 & 3)   **Damage**

Old bumper: 1,185   885   2,955   815   2,852   1,217   1,762   2,592   1,632
New bumper: 1,973   403   509   2,103   1,153   292   1,916   1,602   1,559   547   801   359

16.5   Kruskal-Wallis Test for Independent Samples

William H. Kruskal (1919–2005) and W. Allen Wallis (1912–1998) proposed a test to compare c independent samples. It may be viewed as a generalization of the Mann-Whitney test, which compares two independent samples. Groups can be of different sizes if each has five or more observations. If we assume that the populations differ only in centrality (i.e., location), the **Kruskal-Wallis test (K-W test)** compares the medians of c independent samples. It is analogous to one-factor ANOVA (completely randomized model). The K-W test requires that the populations be of similar shape, but does not require normal populations as in ANOVA, making it an attractive alternative for applications in finance, engineering, and marketing.

> ### Kruskal-Wallis Test
>
> The K-W test compares the medians of c independent samples. It may be viewed as a generalization of the Mann-Whitney test and is a nonparametric alternative to one-factor ANOVA.

Assuming that the populations are otherwise similar, the hypotheses to be tested are

H_0: All c population medians are the same.

H_1: Not all the population medians are the same.

In testing for equality of location, the K-W test may be almost as powerful as one-factor ANOVA. It can even be useful for ratio or interval data when there are outliers or unequal group variances, or if the population is thought to be non-normal. For a completely randomized design with c groups, the test statistic is

$$H_{\text{calc}} = \frac{12}{n\,(n+1)} \sum_{j=1}^{c} \frac{T_j^2}{n_j} - 3(n+1) \quad (\text{Kruskal-Wallis test statistic}) \qquad (16.9)$$

TABLE 16.6 Annual Days Worked by Department ◉ Days

Department	Days Worked								
Budgets	278	260	265	245	258				
Payables	205	270	220	240	255	217	266	239	240	228
Pricing	240	258	233	256	233	242	244	249		

where

$$n = n_1 + n_2 + \cdots + n_c$$

n_j = number of observations in group j

T_j = sum of ranks for group j

Application: Employee Absenteeism

The *XYZ* Corporation is interested in possible differences in days worked by salaried employees in three departments in the financial area. Table 16.6 shows annual days worked by 23 randomly chosen employees from these departments. Because the sampling methodology reflects the department sizes, the sample sizes are unequal.

To get the test statistic, we combine the samples and assign a rank to each observation in each group, as shown in Table 16.7. We use a column worksheet so that the calculations are easier to follow. When a tie occurs, each observation is assigned the average of the ranks.

TABLE 16.7 Merged Data Converted to Ranks

Obs	Rank	Days	Dept
1	1	205	Payables
2	2	217	Payables
3	3	220	Payables
4	4	228	Payables
5	5.5	233	Pricing
6	5.5	233	Pricing
7	7	239	Payables
8	9	240	Payables
9	9	240	Payables
10	9	240	Pricing
11	11	242	Pricing
12	12	244	Pricing
13	13	245	Budgets
14	14	249	Pricing
15	15	255	Payables
16	16	256	Pricing
17	17.5	258	Budgets
18	17.5	258	Pricing
19	19	260	Budgets
20	20	265	Budgets
21	21	266	Payables
22	22	270	Payables
23	23	278	Budgets

TABLE 16.8   Worksheet for Rank Sums

Budgets	Rank	Payables	Rank	Pricing	Rank
245	13	205	1	233	5.5
258	17.5	217	2	233	5.5
260	19	220	3	240	9
265	20	228	4	242	11
278	23	239	7	244	12
		240	9	249	14
		240	9	256	16
		255	15	258	17.5
		266	21		
		270	22		
Sum of ranks	92.5	Sum of ranks	93	Sum of ranks	90.5
Sample size	$n_1 = 5$	Sample size	$n_2 = 10$	Sample size	$n_3 = 8$

Next, the data are arranged by groups, as shown in Table 16.8, and the ranks are summed to give T_1, T_2, and T_3. As a check on our work, the sum of the ranks must be $n(n + 1)/2 = (23)(23 + 1)/2 = 276$. This is easily verified as $T_1 + T_2 + T_3 = 92.5 + 93.0 + 90.5 = 276$. The value of the test statistic is

$$H_{\text{calc}} = \frac{12}{n(n + 1)} \sum_{j=1}^{c} \frac{T_j^2}{n_j} - 3(n + 1)$$

$$= \frac{12}{(23)(23 + 1)} \left[\frac{92.5^2}{5} + \frac{93^2}{10} + \frac{90.5^2}{8} \right] - 3(23 + 1) = 6.259$$

The H test statistic follows a chi-square distribution with degrees of freedom $\nu = c - 1 = 3 - 1 = 2$. This is a right-tailed test (i.e., we will reject the null hypothesis of equal medians if H exceeds its critical value) because it can be shown that H_{calc} should be large if H_1 is true. Using $\nu = 2$, from Appendix E we obtain critical values for various levels of significance:

α	χ_α^2	**Interpretation**
0.10	4.605	Reject H_0—conclude that the medians differ
0.05	5.991	Reject H_0—conclude that the medians differ
0.025	7.378	Do not reject H_0—conclude that the medians are not different

In this instance, our decision is sensitive to the level of significance chosen. The p value is between 0.05 and 0.025, so it seems appropriate to conclude that the difference among the three groups is not overwhelming. MegaStat gives the exact p value (0.0437) as shown in Figure 16.6. We could also obtain this p value from Excel's function $=$CHIDIST(6.259,2). The stacked dot plots in Figure 16.7 reveal that the three distributions overlap quite a bit, so there may be little practical difference in the distributions. The MINITAB K-W test is similar, but requires unstacked data (one column for the data, one column for the group name). MINITAB warns you if the sample size is too small.

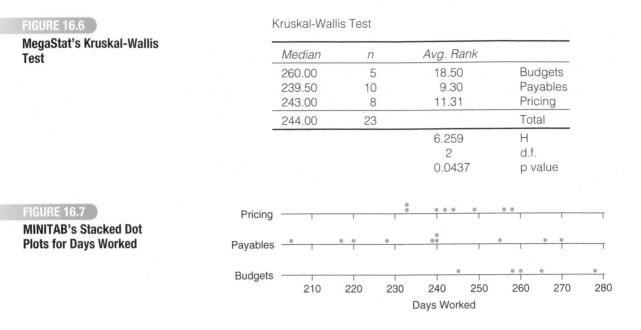

FIGURE 16.6

MegaStat's Kruskal-Wallis Test

Kruskal-Wallis Test

Median	n	Avg. Rank	
260.00	5	18.50	Budgets
239.50	10	9.30	Payables
243.00	8	11.31	Pricing
244.00	23		Total
		6.259	H
		2	d.f.
		0.0437	p value

FIGURE 16.7

MINITAB's Stacked Dot Plots for Days Worked

Section Exercises

16.10 Samples are shown of volatility (coefficient of variation) for sector stocks over a certain period of time. (a) At $\alpha = 0.05$, is there a difference in median volatility in these four portfolios? Use MegaStat, MINITAB, or a similar computer package for the calculations. (b) Use a one-factor ANOVA to compare the means. Do you reach the same conclusion? (c) Make a histogram or other display of each sample. Would you be willing to assume normality? (LO 2 & 3) ⊙ **Volatile**

Health	Energy	Retail	Leisure
14.5	23.0	19.4	17.6
18.4	19.9	20.7	18.1
13.7	24.5	18.5	16.1
16.9	24.2	15.5	23.2
16.2	19.4	17.7	17.6
21.6	22.1	21.4	25.5
25.6	31.6	26.5	24.1
21.4	22.4	21.5	25.9
26.6	31.3	22.8	25.5
19.0	32.5	27.4	26.3
12.6	12.8	22.0	12.9
13.5	14.4	17.1	11.1
13.5		24.8	4.9
13.0		13.4	
13.6			

16.11 The results shown below are mean productivity measurements (average number of assemblies completed per hour) for a random sample of workers at each of three workstations. (a) At $\alpha = 0.05$, is there a difference in median productivity? Use MegaStat, MINITAB, or a similar computer package for the calculations. (b) Use a one-factor ANOVA to compare the means. Do you reach the same conclusion? (c) Make a histogram or other display of the pooled data. Does the assumption of normality seem justified? (LO 2 & 3) **Workers**

Work Station	Finished Units Produced per Hour								
A (9 workers)	3.6	5.1	2.8	4.6	4.7	4.1	3.4	2.9	4.5
B (6 workers)	2.7	3.1	5.0	1.9	2.2	3.2			
C (10 workers)	6.8	2.5	5.4	6.7	4.6	3.9	5.4	4.9	7.1	8.4

Mini Case **16.1**

Price/Earnings Ratios

A price/earnings ratios different for firms in the five sectors shown in Table 16.9? Because the data are interval, we could try either one-factor ANOVA or a Kruskal-Wallis test. How can we decide?

TABLE 16.9 Common Stock P/E Ratios of Selected Companies PERatios

Automotive and Components (*n* = 17)

9	13	14	29	10	32	16	14	9
21	17	21	10	7	20	13	17	

Energy Equipment and Services (*n* = 12)

31	22	39	25	46	7	29	36	42
36	49	35						

Food and Staples Retailing (*n* = 22)

25	22	18	24	27	21	66	30	24
22	21	9	11	16	13	32	15	25
36	29	25	18					

Hotels, Restaurants, and Leisure (*n* = 18)

34	26	74	24	17	19	22	34	30
22	24	19	23	19	21	31	16	19

Multiline Retail Firms (*n* = 18)

16	29	22	19	20	14	22	18	28
13	16	20	21	23	20	3	14	27

Source: *BusinessWeek*, Nov. 22, 2004.

Combining the samples, the histogram in Figure 16.8 and the probability plot in Figure 16.9 suggest non-normality, so instead of one-factor ANOVA we would prefer the nonparametric Kruskal-Wallis test with $\nu = c - 1 = 5 - 1 = 4$ degrees of freedom. MINITAB's output in Figure 16.10 shows that the medians differ ($p = 0.000$). The test statistic ($H = 25.32$) exceeds the chi-square critical value for $\alpha = 0.01$ (13.28). We conclude that the median P/E ratios are *not* the same for these five sectors.

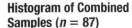

FIGURE 16.8

Histogram of Combined Samples ($n = 87$)

Histogram of PERatio
Normal

Mean	23.18
StDev	11.37
n	87

FIGURE 16.9

Probability Plot of Combined Samples ($n = 87$)

Probability Plot of PERatio
Normal

Mean	23.18
StDev	11.37
n	87
AD	2.163
p Value	<0.005

FIGURE 16.10

MINITAB's Kruskal-Wallis Test

Kruskal-Wallis Test: PERatio versus Sector

Sector	N	Median	Ave Rank	z
Auto	17	14.00	24.4	−3.58
EnergyEq	12	35.50	68.5	3.62
FoodDrug	22	23.00	46.9	0.62
Leisure	18	22.50	51.1	1.34
Retail	18	20.00	35.6	−1.58
Overall	87		44.0	

H = 25.27   DF = 4   P = 0.000
H = 25.32   DF = 4   P = 0.000   (adjusted for ties)

16.6 Friedman Test for Related Samples

The **Friedman test** is a nonparametric test that will reveal whether c treatments have the same central tendency when there is a second factor with r levels. If the populations are assumed the same except for centrality (location), the test is a comparison of medians. The test is analogous to two-factor ANOVA without replication (or randomized block design) with one observation for each cell. The groups must be of the same size, treatments should be randomly assigned within the blocks, and data should be at least interval scale.

Friedman Test

The Friedman test is a nonparametric procedure to discover whether c population medians are the same or different when classification is based on two factors. It is analogous to randomized block ANOVA (two-factor without replication) but without the normality assumption.

The Friedman test resembles the Kruskal-Wallis test except that, in addition to the c treatment levels that define the columns of the observation matrix, it also specifies r block factor levels to define each row of the observation matrix. The hypotheses to be tested are

H_0: All c populations have the same median.

H_1: Not all the populations have the same median.

The Friedman test may be almost as powerful as two-way ANOVA without replication (randomized block design) and may be used with ratio or interval data when there is concern for outliers or non-normality of the underlying populations. It is a rare population that meets the normality requirement, so Friedman's test is quite useful.

Test Statistic

The test statistic is

$$F_{calc} = \frac{12}{rc(c + 1)} \sum_{j=1}^{c} T_j^2 - 3r(c + 1) \quad \text{(Friedman test statistic)} \qquad \textbf{(16.10)}$$

where

r = the number of blocks (rows)

c = the number of treatments (columns)

T_j = the sum of ranks for treatment j

Although the Friedman formula resembles the Kruskal-Wallis formula, there is a difference: The ranks are computed *within each block* rather than within a pooled sample.

Application: Braking Effectiveness

Experiments are being conducted to test the effect of brake pad composition on stopping distance. Five prototype brake pads are prepared. Each pad is installed on the same automobile, which is accelerated to 100 km/h and then braked to the shortest possible stop without loss of control. This test is repeated four times in rapid succession to reveal brake fade due to heating and lining abrasion. Car weight and balance are identical in all tests, and the same expert driver performs all tests. The pavement is dry and the outside air temperature is the same for all tests. To eliminate potential bias, the driver has no information about which pad is installed for a given test. The results are shown in Table 16.10.

The Friedman test requires that either the number of blocks or the number of treatments be at least 5. Our matrix meets this requirement as $r = 4$ and $c = 5$. Ranks are computed *within each row*. As a check on our arithmetic, we may utilize the fact that the ranks must sum to $rc(c + 1)/2 = (4)(5)(5 + 1)/2 = 60$. We see that our sums are correct because $T_1 + T_2 + T_3 + T_4 + T_5 = 15 + 14 + 5 + 19 + 7 = 60$.

We now compute the test statistic:

$$F_{calc} = \frac{12}{rc(c + 1)} \sum_{j=1}^{c} T_j^2 - 3r(c + 1)$$

$$= \frac{12}{(4)(5)(5 + 1)} [15^2 + 14^2 + 5^2 + 19^2 + 7^2] - 3(4)(5 + 1) = 13.6$$

TABLE 16.10   Stopping Distance from 100 km/h   Braking

	Pad 1		Pad 2		Pad 3		Pad 4		Pad 5	
	Feet	*Rank*	*Feet*	*Rank*	*Feet*	*Rank*	*Feet*	*Rank*	*Feet*	*Rank*
Trial 1	166	3	176	4	152	2	198	5	148	1
Trial 2	174	4	170	3	148	1	206	5	152	2
Trial 3	184	3	186	4	160	1	212	5	168	2
Trial 4	220	5	204	3	184	1	216	4	196	2
Rank sum	$T_1 = 15$		$T_2 = 14$		$T_3 = 5$		$T_4 = 19$		$T_5 = 7$	

FIGURE 16.11

**MegaStat's Friedman Test
for Brake Pads**

Friedman Test

Sum of Ranks	Avg. Rank	
15.00	3.75	
14.00	3.50	
5.00	1.25	
19.00	4.75	
7.00	1.75	
60.00	3.00	Total

4 n
13.600 chi-square
4 d.f.
0.0087 p value

The Friedman test statistic follows a chi-square distribution with degrees of freedom $v = c - 1$ $= 5 - 1 = 4$ and we would reject the null hypothesis when F_{calc} is large because we expect it to be large if H_1 is true. Using $v = 4$, from Appendix E we obtain the critical values for various α levels:

α	χ_α^2	*Interpretation*
0.025	11.143	Reject H_0—conclude that the medians differ
0.01	13.277	Reject H_0—conclude that the medians differ
0.005	14.861	Do not reject H_0—the medians do not differ

The p value is between 0.01 and 0.005, so we conclude that there is a significant difference in brake pads except at very strict Type I error levels. The results from MegaStat shown in Figure 16.11 show the exact p value (0.0087). We could also obtain this p value by using Excel's function =CHIDIST(13.6,4).

Section Exercises

16.12 Consumers are asked to rate the attractiveness of four potential dashboard surface textures on an interval scale (1 = least attractive, 10 = most attractive). Use MegaStat or another software package to perform a Friedman test to see whether the median ratings of surfaces differ at $\alpha = 0.05$, using age as the blocking factor. (LO 2 & 3) **Texture**

	Shiny	Satin	Pebbled	Pattern	Embossed
Youth (under 21)	6.7	6.6	5.5	4.3	4.4
Adult (21–39)	5.5	5.3	6.2	5.9	6.2
Middle-Age (40–61)	4.5	5.1	6.7	5.5	5.4
Senior (62 and over)	3.9	4.5	6.1	4.1	4.9

16.13 JavaMax is a neighbourhood take-out coffee shop that offers three sizes. Yesterday's sales are shown. Use MegaStat or another software package to perform a Friedman test to see whether the median sales of coffee sizes differ at $\alpha = 0.05$, using time of day as the blocking factor. (LO 2 & 3) **Coffee**

	Small	Medium	Large
6 a.m.–8 a.m.	60	77	85
8 a.m.–11 a.m.	65	74	76
11 a.m.–3 p.m.	70	70	70
3 p.m.–7 p.m.	61	60	55
7 p.m.–11 p.m.	55	50	48

16.7 Spearman's Rank Correlation Test

An overall nonparametric test of association between two variables can be performed by using **Spearman's rank correlation** coefficient (sometimes called **Spearman's rho**). This statistic is useful when it is inappropriate to assume an interval scale (a requirement of the Pearson correlation coefficient you learned in Chapter 13). The statistic is named for Charles E. Spearman (1863–1945), a British behavioural psychologist who was interested in assessment of human intelligence. The research question was the extent of agreement between different I.Q. tests (e.g., Stanford-Binet and Wechsler's WAIS). However, ordinal data are also common in business. For example, Moody's bond ratings (e.g., Aaa, Aa, A, Baa, Ba, B, etc.), bank safety ratings (e.g., by Veribanc or BankRate.com), or Morningstar's mutual fund ratings (e.g., 5/5, 5/4, 4/4, etc.) are ordinal (not interval) measurements. We could use Spearman's rank correlation to answer questions like these:

- When *n* corporate bonds are assigned a quality rating by two different agencies (e.g., Moody and Dominion), to what extent do the ratings agree?

- When creditworthiness scores are assigned to *n* individuals by different credit-rating agencies (e.g., Equifax and TransUnion), to what extent do the scores agree?

In cases like these, we would expect strong agreement, because presumably the rating agencies are trying to measure the same thing. In other cases, we may have ratio or interval data, but prefer to rely on rank-based tests because of serious non-normality or outliers. For example:

- To what extent do rankings of *n* companies based on revenues agree with their rankings based on profits?

- To what extent do rankings of *n* mutual funds based on one-year rates of return agree with their rankings based on five-year rates of return?

> ### Spearman Rank Correlation
>
> Spearman rank correlation is a nonparametric test that measures the strength of the association, if any, between two variables using only ranks. It does not assume interval measurement.

The formula for Spearman's rank correlation coefficient for a sample is

$$r_s = 1 - \frac{6 \sum_{i=1}^{n} d_i^2}{n(n^2 - 1)} \quad \text{(Spearman rank correlation)} \tag{16.11}$$

where

d_i = difference in ranks for case *i*

n = sample size

The sample rank correlation coefficient r_s must fall in the range $-1 \le r_s \le +1$. Its sign tells whether the relationship is direct (ranks tend to vary in the same direction) or inverse (ranks tend to vary in opposite directions). If r_s is near zero, there is little or no agreement between the rankings. If r_s is near $+1$, there is strong agreement between the ranks; if r_s is near -1, there is strong *inverse* agreement between the ranks.

Application: Calories and Fat

Calories come from fat, but also from carbohydrates. How closely related are fat calories and total calories? As an experiment, a student team examined a sample of 20 brands of pasta sauce, obtaining the data shown in Table 16.11. Because the serving sizes (in grams) varied,

TABLE 16.11 Calories per Gram for 20 Pasta Sauces 🔘 **Pasta**

Product	Total Calories Per Gram	Total Calories Rank	Fat Calories Per Gram	Fat Calories Rank	d_i	d_i^2
Barilla Roasted Garlic & Onion	0.64	10	0.20	8	2	4
Barilla Tomato & Basil	0.56	13	0.12	13.5	−0.5	0.25
Classico Tomato & Basil	0.40	19.5	0.08	17	2.5	6.25
Del Monte Mushroom	0.48	17	0.04	19	−2	4
Five Bros. Tomato & Basil	0.64	10	0.12	13.5	−3.5	12.25
Healthy Choice Traditional	0.40	19.5	0.00	20	−0.5	0.25
Master Choice Chunky Garden Veg.	0.56	13	0.08	17	−4	16
Meijer All Natural Meatless	0.55	15	0.08	17	−2	4
Newman's Own Traditional	0.48	17	0.12	13.5	3.5	12.25
Paul Newman Venetian	0.48	17	0.12	13.5	3.5	12.25
Prego Fresh Mushrooms	1.25	1	0.38	1	0	0
Prego Hearty Meat—Pepperoni	1.00	3.5	0.33	2.5	1	1
Prego Hearty Meat—Hamburger	1.00	3.5	0.29	4	−0.5	0.25
Prego Traditional	1.17	2	0.33	2.5	−0.5	0.25
Prego Roasted Red Pepper & Garlic	0.92	5	0.25	5.5	−0.5	0.25
Ragu Old World Style w/meat	0.67	8	0.25	5.5	2.5	6.25
Ragu Roasted Red Pepper & Onion	0.86	6	0.20	8	−2	4
Ragu Roasted Garlic	0.70	7	0.19	10	−3	9
Ragu Traditional	0.56	13	0.20	8	5	25
Sutter Home Tomato & Garlic	0.64	10	0.16	11	−1	1
Column Sum		210		210	0	118.5

Source: This data set was created by statistics students Donna Bennett, Nicole Cook, Latrice Haywood, and Robert Malcolm. It is intended for training purposes only and should not be viewed as a nutrition guide.

each product's total calories and fat calories were divided by serving size to obtain a per-gram measurement. Ranks were then calculated for each measure of calories. If more than one value was the same, they were assigned the average of the ranks. As a check, the sums of ranks within each column must always be $n(n + 1)/2$, which in our case is $(20)(20 + 1)/2 = 210$. After checking the ranks, the difference in ranks d_i is computed for each observation. As a further check on our calculations, we verify that the rank differences sum to zero (if not, we have made an error somewhere). The sample rank correlation coefficient $r_s = 0.9109$ indicates positive agreement:

$$r_s = 1 - \frac{6\sum_{i=1}^{n} d_i^2}{n(n^2 - 1)} = 1 - \frac{(6)(118.5)}{(20)(20^2 - 1)} = 0.9109$$

Our sample correlation r_s is 0.9109. For a right-tailed test, the hypotheses are as follows:

H_0: True rank correlation is zero ($\rho_s = 0$).

H_1: True rank correlation is positive ($\rho_s > 0$).

In this case we choose a right-tailed test because *a priori* we would expect positive agreement. That is, a pasta sauce that ranks high in fat calories would be expected also to rank high in total calories. If the sample size is small, a special table is required. If n is large (usually defined as at least 20 observations), then r_s may be assumed to follow the Student's t distribution with degrees of freedom $\nu = n - 2$ using the test statistic

$$t_{calc} = r_s \sqrt{\frac{n-2}{1-r_s^2}} \qquad (16.12)$$

To illustrate this formula, we will plug in our previous sample result:

$$t_{calc} = 0.9109 \sqrt{\frac{20-2}{1-0.9109^2}} = 9.366$$

Using Appendix D we obtain one-tail critical values of Student's t for 18 degrees of freedom for various levels of significance:

α	t_α	Interpretation
0.025	2.101	Reject H_0
0.01	2.552	Reject H_0
0.005	2.878	Reject H_0

Clearly, we can reject the hypothesis of no correlation at any of the customary α levels. Using MegaStat, we can obtain equivalent results, as shown in Figure 16.12, except that the critical value of r_s is shown instead of the t statistic.

A Closer Look

As with all other t-distribution tests, our decision rule is based on the direction of the inequality when H_1 is true. In this case, our decision rules are

- Reject H_0 if $t_{calc} < -t_{\alpha, \nu}$ for H_1: $\rho_s < 0$
- Reject H_0 if $t_{calc} < -t_{\alpha/2, \nu}$ or if $t_{calc} > t_{\alpha/2, \nu}$ for H_1: $\rho_s \neq 0$
- Reject H_0 if $t_{calc} > t_{\alpha, \nu}$ for H_1: $\rho_s > 0$

These decision rules are based on our expectations about t_{calc} if H_1 is true.

Correlation versus Causation

One final word of caution: You should remember that correlation does not prove causation. Countless examples can be found of correlations that are "significant" even when there is no causal relation between the two variables. On the other hand, causation is not ruled out. More than one scientific discovery has occurred because of an unexpected correlation. Just bear in mind that if you look at 1,000 correlation coefficients in samples drawn from uncorrelated populations, approximately 50 will be "significant" at $\alpha = 0.05$, approximately 10 will be "significant" at $\alpha = 0.01$, and so on. Testing for significance is just one step in the scientific process.

Bear in mind also that multiple causes may be present. Correlation between X and Y could be caused by an unspecified third variable Z. Even more complex systems of causation may exist. Bivariate correlations of any kind must be regarded as potentially out of context if the true relationship is *multivariate* rather than *bivariate*.

Spearman Coefficient of Rank Correlation

	Total Calories/gram	Fat Calories/gram
Total Calories/gram	1.000	
Fat Calories/gram	0.911	1.000

20 sample size

±0.444 critical value 0.05 (two-tail)
±0.561 critical value 0.01 (two-tail)

FIGURE 16.12

MegaStat's Rank Correlation Test

16.14 Profits of 20 consumer food companies are shown. (a) Convert the data to ranks. Check the column sums. (b) Calculate Spearman's rank correlation coefficient. Show your calculations. (c) At $\alpha = 0.01$ can you reject the hypothesis of zero rank correlation? (d) Check your work by using MegaStat. (e) Calculate the Pearson correlation coefficient (using Excel). (f) Why might the rank correlation be preferred? (LO 2 & 3) **Food-B**

Company	2004	2005
Campbell Soup	595	647
ConAgra Foods	775	880
Dean Foods	356	285
Del Monte Foods	134	165
Dole Food	105	134
Flowers Foods	15	51
General Mills	917	1,055
H. J. Heinz	566	804
Hershey Foods	458	591
Hormel Foods	186	232
Interstate Bakeries	27	−26
J. M. Smucker	96	111
Kellogg	787	891
Land O'Lakes	107	21
McCormick	211	215
PepsiCo	3,568	4,212
Ralcorp Holdings	7	65
Sara Lee	1,221	1,272
Smithfield Foods	26	227
Wm. Wrigley, Jr.	446	493

16.15 Rates of return on 24 mutual funds are shown. (a) Convert the data to ranks. Check the column sums. (b) Calculate Spearman's rank correlation coefficient. Show your calculations. (c) At $\alpha = 0.01$ can you reject the hypothesis of zero rank correlation? (d) Check your work by using MegaStat. (e) Calculate the Pearson correlation coefficient (using Excel). (f) In this case, why might either test be used? (LO 2 & 3) **Funds**

Rates of Return on 24 Selected Mutual Funds (percent)

Fund	12-Mo.	5-Yr.	Fund	12-Mo.	5-Yr.
1	11.2	10.5	13	14.0	9.7
2	−2.4	5.0	14	11.6	14.7
3	8.6	8.6	15	13.2	11.8
4	3.4	3.7	16	−1.0	2.3
5	3.9	−2.9	17	6.2	10.5
6	10.3	9.6	18	21.1	9.0
7	16.1	14.1	19	−1.2	3.0
8	6.7	6.2	20	8.7	7.1
9	6.5	7.4	21	9.7	10.2
10	11.1	14.0	22	0.4	9.3
11	8.0	7.3	23	0.9	6.0
12	11.2	14.2	24	12.7	10.0

16.16 As was discussed in exercise 16.7, Canadians crossing the border into the United States from Canada often become very frustrated when they get into a line in which the Customs and Border Protection (CBP) officer seems to be spending more time with each car than a CBP officer in another line. But, is this officer spending more time because the occupants in the cars are not prepared to properly answers the questions or are not prepared with the proper documents, or is it because this officer tends to demand more information from these occupants? In exercise 16.7, we tested whether the demands differed between the two officers. Here, using the same data from the same experiment, we want to determine whether there is a positive correlation between the times spent by Officer A and the times spent by Officer B. Using the times listed below and Spearman's rank correlation coefficient, test at the 0.05 level of significance. Is there sufficient evidence to indicate that there is a positive correlation between the two sets of times? If there is such a correlation, what could cause this conclusion? Explain. (LO 2)

Subject	Officer A	Officer B	Subject	Officer A	Officer B	Subject	Officer A	Officer B
1	3.45	4.21	8	2.17	2.34	15	4.16	4.01
2	1.47	1.60	9	4.10	3.35	16	5.24	6.31
3	6.32	7.45	10	2.42	3.06	17	3.41	3.98
4	2.65	1.80	11	0.50	1.25	18	2.57	3.05
5	1.98	2.45	12	3.42	4.31	19	3.52	3.31
6	9.40	8.65	13	4.17	3.68	20	2.95	5.00
7	4.47	5.25	14	2.35	2.55	21	1.05	1.41

CHAPTER SUMMARY

Statisticians are attracted to **nonparametric tests** because they avoid the restrictive assumption of normality, although often there are still assumptions to be met (e.g., similar population shape). Many nonparametric tests have **similar power** to their **parametric** counterparts (and superior power when samples are small). The **runs test** (or **Wald-Wolfowitz** test) checks for random order in binary data. The **Wilcoxon signed-rank test** resembles a parametric one-sample t test, most often being used as a substitute for the parametric paired-difference t test. The **Mann-Whitney test** (also called the **Wilcoxon rank sum test**) compares medians in independent samples, resembling a parametric two-sample t test. The **Kruskal-Wallis test** is a c-sample comparison of medians (similar to one-factor ANOVA). The **Friedman test** resembles a randomized block ANOVA except that it compares medians instead of means. **Spearman's rank correlation** is like the usual Pearson correlation except the data are ranks. Calculations of these tests are usually done by computer. Special tables are required when samples are small.

KEY TERMS

Friedman test, *708*
Kruskal-Wallis test (K-W test), *703*
Mann-Whitney test, *700*
nonparametric tests, *690*
parametric tests, *691*

power, *691*
ranks, *695*
runs test, *691*
sign test, *696*
Spearman's rank correlation, *711*

Spearman's rho, *711*
Wald-Wolfowitz test, *691*
Wilcoxon signed-rank test, *695*

Commonly Used Formulas

Wald-Wolfowitz one-sample runs test for randomness (for $n_1 \geq 10$, $n_2 \geq 10$):

$$z_{\text{calc}} = \frac{R - \left(\frac{2n_1 n_2}{n} + 1\right)}{\sqrt{\frac{2n_1 n_2 (2n_1 n_2 - n)}{n^2(n-1)}}}$$

where

R = number of runs

n = total sample size = $n_1 + n_2$

Wilcoxon signed-rank test for one sample median (for $n \geq 20$):

$$z_{calc} = \frac{W - \dfrac{n(n+1)}{4}}{\sqrt{\dfrac{n(n+1)(2n+1)}{24}}}$$

where

W = sum of positive ranks

Mann-Whitney test for equality of two medians (for $n_1 \geq 10$, $n_2 \geq 10$):

$$z_{calc} = \frac{\overline{T}_1 - \overline{T}_2}{(n_1 + n_2)\sqrt{\dfrac{n_1 + n_2 + 1}{12 n_1 n_2}}}$$

where

T_1 = mean rank for sample 1

T_2 = mean rank for sample 2

Kruskal-Wallis test for equality of c medians:

$$H_{calc} = \frac{12}{n(n+1)} \sum_{j=1}^{c} \frac{T_j^2}{n_j} - 3(n+1)$$

where

n_j = number of observations in group j

T_j = sum of ranks for group j

$n = n_1 + n_2 + \cdots + n_c$

Friedman test for equality of medians in an array with r rows and c columns:

$$F_{calc} = \frac{12}{rc(c+1)} \sum_{j=1}^{c} T_j^2 - 3r(c+1)$$

where

r = the number of blocks (rows)

c = the number of treatments (columns)

T_j = the sum of ranks for treatment j

Spearman's rank correlation coefficient for n paired observations:

$$r_s = 1 - \frac{6 \sum\limits_{i=1}^{n} d_i^2}{n(n^2 - 1)}$$

CHAPTER REVIEW

1. (a) Name three advantages of nonparametric tests. (b) Name two deficiencies in data that might cause us to prefer a nonparametric test. (c) Why is significance in a nonparametric test especially convincing? (LO 1)

2. (a) What is the purpose of a runs test? (b) How many runs of each type are needed for a large-sample runs test? (c) Give an example of a sequence containing runs and count the runs. (d) What distribution do we use for the large-sample runs test? (LO 2)

3. (a) What is the purpose of a Wilcoxon signed-rank test? (b) How large a sample is needed to use a normal table for the test statistic? (c) The Wilcoxon signed-rank test resembles which parametric test(s)? (LO 2)

4. (a) What is the purpose of a Mann-Whitney test? (b) The Mann-Whitney test is a test of two medians under what assumption? (c) What sample sizes are needed for the large-sample Mann-Whitney test? (d) The Mann-Whitney test is analogous to which parametric test? (LO 2)

5. (a) In the Mann-Whitney test, how are ranks assigned when there is a tie? (b) What distribution do we use for the large-sample Mann-Whitney test? (LO 2)

6. (a) What is the purpose of a Kruskal-Wallis test? (b) The K-W test is a test of c medians under what assumption? (c) The K-W test is analogous to which parametric test? (LO 2)

7. (a) In the Kruskal-Wallis test, what is the procedure for assigning ranks to observations in each group? (b) What distribution do we use for the K-W test? (c) What are the degrees of freedom for the K-W test? (LO 2)

8. (a) What is the purpose of a Friedman test? (b) The Friedman test is analogous to what parametric test? (c) How does the Friedman test differ from the ANOVA test in the way it handles the blocking factor? (LO 2)

9. (a) Describe the assignment of ranks in the Friedman test. (b) What distribution do we use for the Friedman test? (c) What are the degrees of freedom for the Friedman test? (LO 2)

10. (a) What is the purpose of the Spearman rank correlation? (b) Describe the way in which ranks are assigned in calculating the Spearman rank correlation. (LO 2)

11. (a) Why is a significant correlation not proof of causation? (b) When would a bivariate correlation be misleading? (LO 2)

CHAPTER EXERCISES

Instructions: In all exercises, use a computer package (e.g., MegaStat, MINITAB) or show the calculations in a worksheet, depending on your instructor's wishes. If you use the computer, include relevant output or screen shots. If you do the calculations manually, show your work. State the hypotheses and give the test statistic and its two-tailed p value. Make the decision. If the decision is close, say so. Are there issues of sample size? Is non-normality a concern?

16.17   A supplier of laptop PC power supplies uses a control chart to track the output (in watts) of each unit produced. The pattern below shows whether each unit's output was above (A) or below (B) the desired specification. *Research question:* At $\alpha = 0.05$, do the deviations follow a random pattern? (LO 2 & 3)   **Watts**

$B A A B B B A B A B A A B A A B B A B B A A B A B A$
$A A B B A A A A B B A A B A A A A B B A A B A A$

16.18   A basketball player took 35 free throws during the season. Her sequence of hits (H) and misses (M) is shown. *Research question:* At $\alpha = 0.01$, is her hit/miss sequence random? (LO 2 & 3)   **FreeThrows**

$H M M H H M H M M H H H H H M M H H M M H M H H H M H H H H M M M H H$

16.19   Thirty-four customers at Starbucks either ordered coffee (C) or did not order coffee (X). *Research question:* At $\alpha = 0.05$, is the sequence random? (LO 2 & 3)   **Starbucks**

$C X C X C C C C X X X X C X C X C X C C C X C X C C X C X X X C C X$

16.20   The price of a particular stock over a period of 60 days rises ($+$) or declines ($-$) in the following pattern: *Research question:* At $\alpha = 0.05$, is the pattern random? (LO 2 & 3)   **Stock**

$+ + - - + + + + + + + - - - - + + - + - + - + - - - - + + + +$
$- + + + + - + + + - + - + - + + + - - - - - - + + + + + - -$

16.21   A forecasting model is fitted to sales data over 24 months. Forecasting errors are tabulated to reveal whether the model provides an overestimate ($+$) or an underestimate ($-$) for each month's sales. The results are $- - + + + - + - - + + - - - - - - + + + + + - -$. *Research question:* At $\alpha = 0.05$, is the pattern random? (LO 2 & 3)   **Forecast**

16.22   A cognitive retraining clinic assists outpatient victims of head injury, anoxia, or other conditions that result in cognitive impairment. Each incoming patient is evaluated to establish an appropriate treatment program and estimated length of stay (ELOS); ELOS is always a multiple of four weeks because treatment sessions are scheduled on a monthly basis. To see if there is any difference in ELOS between the two clinics, a sample is taken, consisting of all patients evaluated at each clinic during October, with the results shown. *Research question:* At $\alpha = 0.10$, do the medians differ? (LO 2 & 3)   **Cognitive**

Clinic A (10 patients): 24, 24, 52, 30, 40, 40, 18, 30, 18, 40

Clinic B (12 patients): 20, 20, 52, 36, 36, 36, 24, 32, 16, 40, 24, 16

16.23 Two manufacturing facilities produce 1280 × 1024 LED (light-emitting diode) displays. Twelve shipments are tested at random from each lab, and the number of bad pixels per billion is noted for each shipment. *Research question:* At $\alpha = 0.05$, do the medians differ? (LO 2 & 3)   **LED**

Defects in Randomly Inspected LED Displays

Facility	Number of Bad Pixels per Billion											
Lab *A*	422	319	326	410	393	368	497	381	515	472	423	355
Lab *B*	497	421	408	375	410	489	389	418	447	429	404	477

16.24 In the 1996 Super Bowl, Dallas beat Pittsburgh 27–17. The weights in pounds of the linemen on each team are shown below. *Research question:* At $\alpha = 0.01$, do the medians differ? (LO 2 & 3)   **Linemen**

Weights of Linemen in 1996 Super Bowl

Dallas Cowboys		Pittsburgh Steelers	
Player	**Weight**	**Player**	**Weight**
Derek Kennard	300	Kendall Gammon	288
Nate Newton	320	Dermontti Dawson	288
Ron Stone	309	John Jackson	297
Russell Maryland	279	Thomas Newberry	285
Michael Batiste	305	Brenden Stai	297
George Hegamin	338	Ariel Solomon	290
Dale Hellestrae	286	Leon Searcy	304
Mark Tuinei	305	Justin Strzelczyk	302
Larry Allen	326	Taase Faumui	278
Leon Lett	288	James Parrish	310
Erik Williams	322	Bill Johnson	300
Darren Benson	308	Joel Steed	300
Chad Hennings	288	Oliver Gibson	283
Hurvin McCormack	274		

Source: *Detroit Free Press,* Jan. 28, 1996, pp. 6D–7D.

16.25 Does a class break stimulate the pulse? Here are heart rates for a sample of 30 students before and after a class break. *Research question:* At $\alpha = 0.05$, do the medians differ? (LO 2 & 3)   **HeartRate**

Heart Rate before and after Class Break

Student	Before	After	Student	Before	After
1	60	62	16	70	64
2	70	76	17	69	66
3	77	78	18	64	69
4	80	83	19	70	73
5	82	82	20	59	58
6	82	83	21	62	65
7	41	66	22	66	68
8	65	63	23	81	77
9	58	60	24	56	57
10	50	54	25	64	62
11	82	93	26	78	79
12	56	55	27	75	74
13	71	67	28	66	67
14	67	68	29	59	63
15	66	75	30	98	82

Thanks to colleague Gene Fliedner for having his evening students take their own pulses before and after the 10-minute class break.

16.26 An experimental bumper was designed to reduce damage in low-speed collisions. This bumper was installed on an experimental group of vans in a large fleet, but not on a control group. At the end of a trial period, accident data showed 12 repair incidents for the experimental group and 9 repair incidents for the control group. The vehicle downtime (in days) per repair incident is shown. *Research question:* At $\alpha = 0.05$, do the medians differ? (Data are from Floyd G. Willoughby and Thomas W. Lauer, confidential case study.) (LO 2 & 3)   **Downtime**

New bumper: 9, 2, 5, 12, 5, 4, 7, 5, 11, 3, 7, 1

Old bumper: 7, 5, 7, 4, 18, 4, 8, 14, 13

16.27 The square footage of each of the last 11 homes sold in each of two suburban neighbourhoods is noted. *Research question:* At $\alpha = 0.01$, do the medians differ? (LO 2 & 3)   **SqFt**

Square Footage of Homes Sold

Grosse Hills (Built in 1985)	Haut Nez Estates (Built in 2003)
3,220	3,850
3,450	3,560
3,270	4,300
3,200	4,100
4,850	3,750
3,150	3,450
2,800	3,400
3,050	3,550
2,950	3,750
3,430	4,150
3,220	3,850

16.28 Below are grade point averages for 25 randomly chosen university business students during a recent semester. *Research question:* At $\alpha = 0.01$, are the median grade point averages the same for students in these four class levels? (LO 2 & 3) **GPA**

Grade Point Averages of 25 Business Students

1st Year (5 students)	2nd Year (7 students)	3rd Year (7 students)	4th Year (6 students)
1.91	3.89	3.01	3.32
2.14	2.02	2.89	2.45
3.47	2.96	3.45	3.81
2.19	3.32	3.67	3.02
2.71	2.29	3.33	3.01
	2.82	2.98	3.17
	3.11	3.26	

16.29 In a bumper test, three types of autos were deliberately crashed into a barrier at 5 mph, and the resulting damage (in dollars) was estimated. Five test vehicles of each type were crashed, with the results shown below. *Research question:* At $\alpha = 0.01$, are the median crash damages the same for these three vehicles? (LO 2 & 3) **Crash**

Crash Damage in Dollars

Goliath	Varmint	Weasel
1,600	1,290	1,090
760	1,400	2,100
880	1,390	1,830
1,950	1,850	1,250
1,220	950	1,920

16.30 The waiting time (in minutes) for emergency room patients with non-life-threatening injuries was measured at four hospitals for all patients who arrived between 6:00 and 6:30 p.m. on a certain Wednesday. The results are shown below. *Research question:* At $\alpha = 0.05$, are the median waiting times the same for emergency patients in these four hospitals? (LO 2 & 3) **Emergency**

Emergency Room Waiting Time (minutes)

Hospital A (5 patients)	Hospital B (4 patients)	Hospital C (7 patients)	Hospital D (6 patients)
10	8	5	0
19	25	11	20
5	17	24	9
26	36	16	5
11		18	10
		29	12
		15	

16.31 Mean output of arrays of solar cells of three types are measured four times under random light intensity over a period of five minutes, yielding the results shown below. *Research question:* At $\alpha = 0.05$, is the median solar cell output the same for all three types? (LO 2 & 3) **Solar**

Solar Cell Output (Watts)

Cell Type	Output (Watts)					
A	123	121	123	124	125	127
B	125	122	122	121	122	126
C	126	128	125	129	131	128

16.32 Below are results of braking tests of the Ford Explorer on glare ice, packed snow, and split traction (one set of wheels on ice, the other on dry pavement), using three braking methods. *Research question:* At $\alpha = 0.01$, is braking method related to stopping distance? (LO 2 & 3)

   Stopping

Stopping Distance from 40 mph to Zero

Road Condition	Pumping	Locked	ABS
Glare Ice	441	455	460
Split Traction	223	148	183
Packed Snow	149	146	167

Source: *Popular Science* 252, no. 6 (June 1998), p. 78.

16.33 In a call centre, the average waiting time for an answer (in seconds) is shown below by time of day. *Research question:* At $\alpha = 0.01$, does the waiting time differ by day of the week? *Note:* Only the first three and last three observations are shown. (LO 2 & 3)   **Wait**

Average Waiting Time (in Seconds) for Answer ($n = 26$)

Time	Mon	Tue	Wed	Thu	Fri
06:00	34	71	33	39	39
06:30	52	70	88	53	49
07:00	36	103	47	32	91
.	.	.	.	.	.
.	.	.	.	.	.
.	.	.	.	.	.
17:30	28	31	27	22	26
18:00	35	14	115	26	22
18:30	25	34	9	5	47

16.34 The table below shows annual financial data for a sample of 20 companies in the food consumer products sector. *Research question:* At $\alpha = 0.01$, is there a significant correlation between revenue and profit? Why is a rank correlation preferred? What factors might result in a less-than-perfect correlation? *Note:* Only the first three and last three companies are shown. (LO 2 & 3)   **Food-A**

Food Consumer Products Companies' 2004 Revenue and Profit (millions)

Obs	Company	Revenue	Profit
1	Campbell Soup	7,109	647
2	ConAgra Foods	18,179	880
3	Dean Foods	10,822	285
.	.	.	.
.	.	.	.
.	.	.	.
18	Sara Lee	19,556	1,272
19	Smithfield Foods	10,107	227
20	Wm. Wrigley, Jr.	3,649	493

Source: *Fortune* 151, no. 8, Apr. 18, 2005, p. F-52.

Football Ratings in *ESPN/USA Today Coaches Poll* (*n* = 20)

Team	Week 7	Week 8
Oklahoma	1,575	1,622
Southern California	1,502	1,470
Florida State	1,412	1,320
LSU	1,337	1,241
Virginia Tech	1,281	1,026
Miami	1,263	1,563
Ohio State	1,208	1,226
Michigan	1,135	938
Georgia	951	1,378
Iowa	932	762
Texas	881	605
TCU	875	727
Washington State	827	1,260
Purdue	667	487
Michigan State	645	1,041
Nebraska	558	924
Tennessee	544	449
Minnesota	490	149
Florida	480	246
Bowling Green	369	577

Source: *Detroit Free Press.*

16.40 In an example in a previous chapter, you were given data concerning the number of medals won by the top 20 medal-winning countries at the 2008 Beijing Olympics and their approximate population sizes. A condensed version of this table is repeated below. Create a scatter plot of this data and comment on your findings. Calculate Pearson's correlation coefficient and the rank correlation coefficient between number of medals won and population size and, assuming the results are random, use each measure to test, at the 0.05 level of significance, whether there is a positive correlation between the two variables. (LO 2 & 3)

Country	Total Medals	Approx. Pop'n (M)	Country	Total Medals	Approx. Pop'n (M)
United States	110	305.3	Japan	25	127.7
China	100	1326.4	Cuba	24	11.3
Russia	72	141.9	Belarus	19	9.7
Great Britain	47	61.2	Canada	18	33.4
Australia	46	21.4	Spain	18	46.0
Germany	41	82.0	Netherlands	16	16.4
France	40	64.5	Brazil	15	187.8
South Korea	31	48.2	Kenya	14	37.5
Italy	28	59.6	Kazakhstan	13	15.4
Ukraine	27	46.0	Jamaica	11	2.7

LearningStats Unit 16 Nonparametric Tests

connect

For solutions to odd-numbered exercises, Exam Review questions, and additional study tools to help you succeed in this course, visit *Connect* at www.mcgrawhillconnect.ca.

Chapter

17

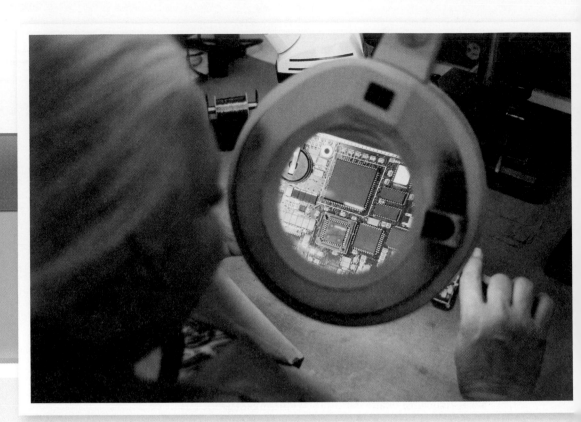

Quality Management

Chapter Learning Objectives

When you finish this chapter you should be able to

1. Define quality and explain how it may be measured and improved.

2. Distinguish between common cause variation and special cause variation.

3. State the purposes of common control charts ($\bar{x}$, R, p, etc.) and how to construct and interpret them.

4. Recognize abnormal patterns in control charts and their potential causes.

5. Assess the capability of a process.

17.1 Quality and Variation

What Is Quality?

Quality has been defined in many ways by well-known researchers and organizations dealing with quality. The American Society for Quality (ASQ) defines quality as the characteristics of a product or service that bear on its ability to satisfy stated or implied needs. ISO 9000 defines quality as the degree to which a set of inherent characteristics fulfill needs or expectations. Perhaps the best definition for our purpose is one by Genichi Taguchi who defines quality as uniformity around a target value. The basic idea of quality is to lower variability in outcomes.

TABLE 17.1 Typical Quality Indicators

Manufacturing	Services
Proportion of nonconforming output	Proportion of satisfied customers
Warranty claim costs	Average customer waiting time
Repeat purchase rate (loyalty)	Repeat client base (loyalty)

Quality can be measured in many ways. Quality may be a *physical* metric, such as the number of bad sectors on a computer hard disk or the quietness of an air-conditioning fan. Quality may be an *aesthetic* attribute such as the ripeness of a banana or cleanliness of a clinic waiting room. (Does the fig bar turned in the wrong direction in Figure 17.1 affect the aesthetic quality of the product?) Quality may be a *functional* characteristic such as ergonomic accessibility of car radio controls or convenience of hours that a bank is open. It may be a *personal* attribute such as friendliness of service at a restaurant or diligence of follow-up by a veterinary clinic. It may be an *efficiency* attribute such as promptness in delivery of an order or the waiting time at a dentist's. Quality is generally understood to include these attributes:

- Conformance to specifications
- Performance in the intended use
- As near to zero defects as possible

- Reliability and durability
- Serviceability when needed
- Favourable customer perceptions

Measurement of quality is specific to the organization and its products. To improve quality, we must undertake systematic data collection and careful measurement of key metrics that describe the product or service that is valued by customers. In manufacturing, the focus is likely to be on physical characteristics (e.g., defects, reliability, consistency), while in services, the focus is likely to be on customer perceptions (e.g., courtesy, responsiveness, competence). Table 17.1 lists some typical quality indicators that might be important to firms engaged in manufacturing as compared to firms that deliver services.

Productivity, Processes, and Quality

Productivity (output per unit of input) is a measure of efficiency. High productivity lowers cost per unit, increases profit, and supports higher wages and salaries. Productivity, like quality, can be measured in various ways. In service industries, productivity is difficult to define. What is the productivity of an investment banker, a CEO, a kindergarten teacher, a university professor, a tax analyst, or a design engineer? Service organizations often rely on quasi-financial measurements, such as average daily sales per field representative, hours billed per attorney, or patients seen by a physician. These are imperfect proxies for productivity, but may be the best that can be devised.

In the past, manufacturing companies assumed an inverse relationship between quality and productivity. This view was based on a short-term perspective. The belief was that the only way to truly improve quality was to slow down and put more time into each product. While

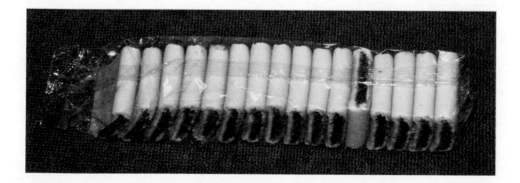

FIGURE 17.1

Unopened Fig Bars: Quality as an Aesthetic Attribute

slowing or stopping an assembly line does imply less output today, defective products lead to waste, rework, and lost customers. In the modern view, quality and productivity move in the same direction, because doing it right the first time saves time and money in the long run. Similarly, in services (e.g., health care) reducing delays and avoiding errors will make customers happier and will reduce the burden of follow-up to fix problems. Our focus in the 21st century is on designing and operating effective business processes to meet customer requirements consistently.

A process is a sequence of interconnected tasks that result in the creation of a product or in the delivery of a service. Manufacturing, assembly, or packaging operations usually come to mind when we hear the term "process." Yet service operations such as filling mail orders, providing customer support, handling loan applications, delivering health services, and meeting payrolls are also processes. Because a majority of workers are in the service sector, it is reasonable to say that non-manufacturing processes are predominant in today's economy. Quality control refers to methods used by organizations to ensure that their products and services meet customer expectations and to ensure that there is improvement over time.

Variance Reduction

Where does statistics enter the quality picture? Statistics can help the company choose appropriate metrics (characteristics measured), set up a system to collect valid data, track variation in the chosen metric(s), and tell when variation is increasing or decreasing. Statistics focuses on the phenomenon of *variation*. Processes that produce, package, and deliver supposedly identical products and services cannot eliminate all sources of variation around the target specification(s). Although some degree of variation is normal and expected, firms do try to attain consistency in their products and services, because excessive variation is often a sign of poor quality. Although slight variation may not affect customer satisfaction, variation that affects real or perceived performance of the product or service clearly requires attention. The quest for reduced variation is a never-ending activity for any firm or not-for-profit organization. *Zero variation* is an elusive goal that can be approached only asymptotically, as each successive improvement usually comes at an increasing cost.

Common Cause versus Special Cause

Statisticians define two categories of variation. Common cause variation (random "noise") is normal and expected, and is present in any stable, in-control process. Special cause variation is due to factors that are abnormal and require investigation. Special cause variation will produce observations that are not from the same population as the majority of observations. Until special cause variation is eliminated, a process is not in control.

Sources of variation in processes include human abilities, training, motivation, technology, materials, management, and organization. Some of these factors are under the control of the organization, while others are fixed and cannot be changed. Most factors are fixed in the short run but may be changed in the long run. For example, technology can be changed through research and development and capital spending on new equipment, but such changes may take years. Human performance can change over time through education and training, but usually not in hours or days.

Role of Management

Management is expected to find ways to maintain process control in the short run and to reduce variation in the long run. The degree to which variance can be reduced depends on equipment, technology, and worker training. Managers may call upon statistical specialists for advice and to train non-statisticians who comprise the majority of the workforce. Training requirements depend on the type of organization. A manufacturing firm may require broad-based statistical training for engineers, plant managers, supervisors, and even assembly workers. But financial, purchasing, marketing, and sales managers must also understand statistics, because they interact with technical experts on cost control, waste management, and quality improvement. Even in banks or health care, broad-based training in statistical methods can be helpful in increasing efficiency and improving quality.

Role of Statisticians

We use statistics to measure variation, set attainable limits for variation, and establish rules to decide whether processes are in control. Trained statisticians may perceive problems that are not immediately apparent to those who are involved in day-to-day business activities. Statisticians have made many contributions to quality management and play an active role as quality consultants.

Section Exercises

17.1   Define (a) process, (b) quality, and (c) variation. (LO 1)

17.2   Distinguish between common cause variation and special cause variation. (LO 2)

17.3   Can zero variation be achieved? Explain. (LO 2)

17.2   Customer Orientation

Who Is a Customer?

One initial step in setting up a quality management system is defining the clients or customers who are being served. A **customer** is whoever consumes what you produce. *Internal customers* are employees of another branch of your organization. For example, the Accounts Payable Department provides services consumed by the Cost Department and the Purchasing Department. *External customers* are outside the organization. Vendors get paid, thereby consuming services provided by the Accounts Payable Department. Employees may be less aware of external customers because most of their dealings are with other employees of the company, but it is the external customers who provide the revenue that supports the organization.

TABLE 17.2   Examples of Customers and Measurable Aspects of Quality

Department or Process	Possible Customers (Type)	Measurable Aspects
Payroll department in a large hospital	Hourly and salaried employees who are to be paid on time (internal)	Percent of employees paid incorrectly or late each month
	Federal and provincial tax agencies that withhold taxes (external)	Percent of employees with insufficient taxes withheld each year
	Creditors and courts seeking to garnish employee wages for child support (external)	Number of weekly creditor telephone complaints
Aluminum beverage container manufacturing plant	Bottling plant awaiting shipments of containers (internal)	Monthly hours of downtime due to delayed shipments
	Staff design engineers seeking to reduce can weight while maintaining strength (internal)	Thickness and weight of alloy or number of structurally defective cans per 100,000
	Federal and provincial health and safety agencies	Number of worker injuries per month
Retail pharmacy	Individuals needing prescription filled (external)	Percent of prescriptions filled within 15 minutes
	Doctors, and customers phoning in prescriptions (external)	Average wait for phone to be answered or percent of callers getting a busy signal
	Cashier waiting for pharmacist to fill prescription (internal)	Time (in minutes) a cashier must wait for pharmacist

Measuring Quality

Each customer category has its own viewpoint, so we may have to measure several aspects of the product or service to assess quality. Different customer groups may require unique quality measurements, while sometimes a single quality measurement may apply to several customer groups. Observers may not agree on the interpretation of quality measures, so planning and training are essential to ensure that employees collect meaningful data. Table 17.2 gives examples of customers and measurable aspects of quality.

Section Exercises

17.4 Distinguish between internal and external customers, giving an example of each within an organization with which you are familiar. (LO 1)

17.5 Define a measurable aspect of quality for (a) the car dealership where you bought your car; (b) the bank or credit union where you usually make personal transactions; and (c) the movie theatre where you usually go. (LO 1)

17.3 Behavioural Aspects of Quality

Blame versus Solutions

Employees tend to think about their own job performance problems or the immediate demands of co-workers and internal customers, losing sight of the fact that their jobs and department budget ultimately depend on serving customers well. To succeed, management must create an atmosphere and incentives that support and reward customer orientation. Employees must take seriously quality indicators that tell whether they are doing a good job. Sometimes this is painful, as it means acknowledging bad outcomes and signs of weakening quality.

In a quality-driven organization, problems do not lead to *blame,* but to a search for *solutions.* What happens if a manager blames an employee for a quality problem? That employee is likely to quit reporting quality problems. Other employees will hear about it and adopt a negative attitude toward quality tracking. If quality problems are covered up, matters can only get worse.

W. Edwards Deming, a famous quality expert, believed that most employees want to do a good job. He found that most of quality problems do not stem from willful disregard of quality, but from flaws in the process or system, such as the following:

- Inadequate equipment
- Inadequate maintenance
- Inadequate training
- Inadequate supervision
- Inadequate support systems
- Inadequate task design

Employee Involvement

Good solutions to quality problems will be more likely if employee representatives from each area are brought together as a *team* to address the quality problem. Team-building activities can help establish group goals, values, and communication. The team then begins the process of problem solving as a group. Teamwork is an important part of the strategy of the quality-driven organization. This goes far beyond statistics.

But organizations have finite resources. Not all problems can be solved. Which problems are most urgent? Which ones can we live with for awhile? Which solutions would have the greatest impact on improving customer satisfaction? Trade-offs must be made. This is an economic problem. There is also a behavioural aspect of resource constraints. Research shows that employee involvement is necessary to create changes that will be accepted, to ensure "buy-in" to change, and to ensure that viable options are not overlooked. Top-down decisions without employee input can create new problems, such as resentment or unworkable processes. That is why we must study organizational behaviour, as well as statistics.

Section Exercises

17.6   Name five barriers to quality improvement. (LO 1)

17.7   What did Deming say about blaming employees for poor quality? (LO 1)

17.4   Pioneers in Quality Management

Brief History of Quality Control

During the early 1900s, quality control took the form of improved inspection and improvement in the methods of mass production, under the leadership of American experts. From about 1920 to just after World War II, techniques such as process control charts (Walter A. Shewhart) and acceptance sampling from lots (Harold F. Dodge and Harry G. Romig) were perfected and were widely applied in North America. But during the 1950s and 1960s, Japanese manufacturers (particularly automotive) shed their previous image as low-quality producers and began to apply American quality control techniques. The Japanese based their efforts largely on ideas and training from American statisticians W. Edwards Deming and Joseph M. Juran, as well as Japanese statisticians Genichi Taguchi and Kaoru Ishikawa. They developed new approaches that focused on customer satisfaction and costs of quality. By the 1970s, despite exhortation by Deming and others, North American firms had lost their initial leadership in quality control, while the Japanese devised and perfected new quality improvement methods, soon adopted by the Europeans.

During the 1980s, North American firms began a process of recommitment to quality improvement, as well as an acceptance of Japanese lean manufacturing methods. In their quest for quality improvement, these firms sought training and advice by experts such as Deming, Juran, and Armand Feigenbaum. The Japanese, however, continued to push the quality frontier forward, under the teachings of Taguchi and the perfection of the *Kaizen* philosophy of continuous improvement. The Europeans articulated the ISO 9000 standards, now adopted by most world-class firms. North American firms have implemented their own style of total quality management. Manufacturers now seek to build *quality* into their products and services, all the way down the supply chain. Quality is best viewed as a *management system* rather than purely as an application of statistics.

W. Edwards Deming

The late **W. Edwards Deming** (1900–1993) deserves special mention as an influential thinker. He was widely honoured in his lifetime. Many know him primarily for his contributions to improving productivity and quality in Japan. In 1950, at the invitation of the Union of Japanese Scientists and Engineers, Deming gave a series of lectures to 230 leading Japanese industrialists who together controlled 80 percent of Japan's capital. His message was the same as to Americans he had taught during the previous decades. The Japanese listened carefully to his message, and their success in implementing Deming's ideas is a matter of historical record.

Deming said that *profound knowledge* of a system is needed for an individual to become a good listener who can teach others. He emphasized that all people are different, that management is not about ranking people, and that anyone's performance is governed largely by the system that he/she works in. He said that fear invites presentation of bad data. If bearers of bad news fare badly, the boss will hear only good news—guaranteeing bad management decisions.

It is difficult to encapsulate Deming's many ideas succinctly, but most observers would agree that his philosophy is reflected in his widely reproduced *14 Points,* which can be found in full on the Web (www.deming.org) or in abbreviated form here. The 14 Points are primarily statements about management, not statistics. They ask that management take responsibility for improving quality and avoid blaming workers. Deming spent much of his long life explaining these and other ideas of his, through a series of seminars aimed initially at management, an activity that continues today through the work of his followers at the W. Edwards Deming Institute. Deming's impact was a function of his philosophy, his stature as a statistician, and his absorbing personal presence, not just his list of 14 Points.

Deming's 14 Points (abbreviated)
 1. Maintain constancy of purpose.
 2. Adopt a new philosophy.
 3. Don't rely on inspection—design quality in.
 4. Don't award contracts just on the basis of price.
 5. Continuous improvement.
 6. Institute training on the job.
 7. Supervision should help people do a better job.
 8. Drive out fear and create trust.
 9. Break down barriers between departments.
10. Eliminate slogans, exhortations, and targets.
11. Eliminate numerical goals.
12. Remove barriers to pride in work.
13. Continuing education for all.
14. Act to accomplish the transformation.

Source: W. Edwards Deming, *Out of the Crisis,* copyright © 1986 W. Edwards Deming. Reprinted by permission of MIT Press.

Modern business students may find some of his recommendations simplistic. For example, "drive out fear" is an elusive goal in a large, complex organization. Deming was not unaware of the behavioural difficulty of achieving his goals. He believed that one major difficulty lay in obtaining commitment from the top leadership, and was impatient when organizations did not demonstrate sufficient resolve to implement his ideas. Deming's ideas are a required subset of the broader principles of quality management.

Other Influential Thinkers

Walter A. Shewhart (1891–1967) invented the control chart and the concepts of special cause and common cause (assignable cause). Shewhart's charts were adopted by the American Society for Testing Materials (ASTM) in 1933 and were used to improve production during World War II. Joseph M. Juran (1904–2008) also taught quality education in Japan, contemporaneously with Deming. Like Deming, he became more influential with North American management in the 1980s. He felt that 80 percent of quality defects arise from management actions, and therefore that quality control was management's responsibility. This may seem obvious today, but before the 1980s there was a tendency to blame labour for quality problems and to assume that not much could be done about it. Juran articulated the idea of the *vital few*—a handful of causes that account for a vast majority of quality problems (the principle behind the **Pareto chart**). Effort, he said, should be concentrated on key problems, rather than diffused over many less-important problems.

Kaoru Ishikawa (1915–1989) was a Japanese quality expert who is associated with the idea of *quality circles,* which characterize the Japanese approach. He also pioneered the idea of companywide quality control and was influential in popularizing statistical tools for quality control. His textbook on statistical methods still is used in training, though many competitors now exist. He taught that elementary statistical tools (Pareto charts, histograms, scatter diagrams, and control charts) should be understood by everyone, while advanced tools (experimental design, regression) might best be left to specialists.

Armand V. Feigenbaum (b. 1922) first used the term *total quality control* in 1951. He favoured broad sharing of responsibility for quality assurance. This was at a time when many companies assumed that quality was the responsibility of the Quality Assurance Department alone. He felt that quality is an essential element of modern management, like marketing or finance. Philip B. Crosby (1926–2001) authored an important book that argues that efforts at improving quality pay for themselves, and was among the first to popularize the catch-phrase "zero defects." Genichi Taguchi (b. 1924) is a pioneer whose contributions are discussed further at the end of this chapter.

Other quality gurus include Claus Moller (b. 1942), whose European company specializes in management training. Moller believes that people can be inspired to do their best through development of the individual's self-esteem. Moller is known for his 12 Golden Rules and 17 hallmarks of a quality company. Shigeo Shingo (1909–1990) had great impact on Japanese industry. His basic idea (the "poka-yoke" system) is to stop a process whenever a defect occurs, define the cause, and prevent future occurrences. If source inspections are used, statistical sampling becomes unnecessary, because the worker is prevented from making errors in the first place. Tom Peters (b. 1942) is an American who studied successful American companies to define a philosophy of quality improvement that discards "management" in favour of "leadership." He emphasizes customer orientation and his 12 keys to a quality revolution.

Section Exercises

17.8 Name five influential thinkers in quality control and briefly state their contributions. (LO 1)

17.9 List 5 of Deming's 14 Points. Look them up on the Internet and explain their meaning. (LO 1)

17.5 Quality Improvement

Acronyms abound in quality management (TQM, BPR, SQC, SPC, etc.). The following are only a few that you should know before you enter the workplace.

Total Quality Management (TQM)

Total quality management or **TQM** requires that all business activities should be oriented toward meeting and exceeding customer needs, empowering employees, eliminating waste or rework, and ensuring the long-run viability of the enterprise through continuous quality improvement. TQM encompasses a broad spectrum of behavioural, managerial, and technical approaches. It includes diverse but complementary elements such as statistics, benchmarking, process redesign, team building, group communications, quality function deployment, and cross-functional management.

Business Process Redesign (BPR)

Like TQM, **business process redesign** or **BPR** has a cross-functional orientation. But instead of focusing on incremental change and gradual improvement of processes, BPR seeks radical redesign of processes to achieve breakthrough improvement in performance measures—a lofty goal that is easier to state than to achieve. Business schools typically incorporate TQM and/or BPR concepts into a variety of non-statistics core classes.

Statistical Quality Control (SQC)

Statistical quality control or **SQC** refers to a subset of quality improvement techniques that rely on statistics. A few of the descriptive tools (see Figure 17.2) have already been covered in earlier chapters, while others (e.g., control charts) will be discussed in this chapter.

FIGURE 17.2 **Three Descriptive SQC Tools**

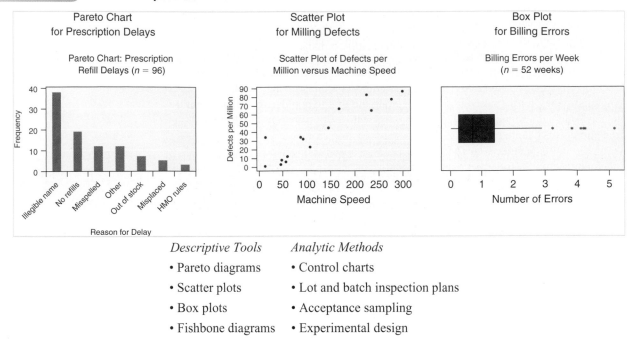

Descriptive Tools	Analytic Methods
• Pareto diagrams	• Control charts
• Scatter plots	• Lot and batch inspection plans
• Box plots	• Acceptance sampling
• Fishbone diagrams	• Experimental design
• Check sheets	• Taguchi robust design

A *check sheet* is a form for counting the frequency of sources of nonconformance. The **fishbone chart** (also called a *cause-and-effect diagram*) is a visual display that summarizes the factors that increase process variation or adversely affect achievement of the target. For example, Figure 17.3 shows a fishbone chart for factors affecting patient length of stay in a hospital. The six main categories (materials, methods, people, management, measurement, technology) are general and may apply to almost any process. You can insert as many verbal descriptions ("fishbones") as you need to identify the causes of variation. The fishbone chart is not, strictly speaking, a statistical tool, but is helpful in thinking about root causes. MINITAB will make fishbone charts.

Statistical Process Control (SPC)

Statistical process control or **SPC** refers specifically to the monitoring of ongoing repetitive processes to ensure conformance to standards by using methods of statistics. Its main tools are *capability analysis* and *control charts.* Because this is a statistics textbook, we will focus on SPC tools, leaving SQC and TQM to other courses that you may take.

FIGURE 17.3

Fishbone (Cause-and-Effect) Chart for Patient Length of Stay

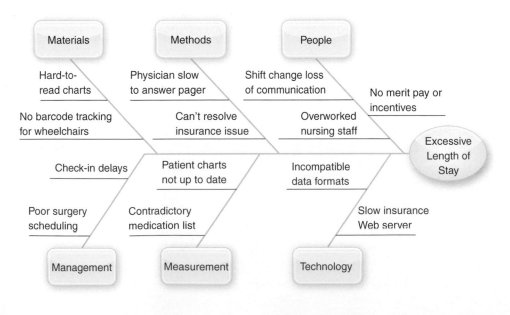

Continuous Quality Improvement (CQI)

This concept has its origin in Japan. The Japanese word for broad continuous improvement in all aspects of life is *Kaizen*. When applied to the workplace, *Kaizen* activities continually try to improve all functions of a business, from manufacturing to management and from CEO to the assembly line workers. By improving standardized activities and practices, *Kaizen's* approach is to eliminate waste.

Quality improvement begins with measurement of a *variable* (e.g., dimensions of an automobile door panel) or an *attribute* (e.g., number of emergency patients who wait more than 30 minutes). For a variable, quality improvement means reducing variation from the target specification. For an attribute, quality improvement means decreasing the rate of nonconformance. Statistical methods are used to ensure that the process is stable and in control by eliminating sources of *special cause* (non-random) variation, as opposed to *common cause* (random) variation that is normal and inherent in the process. We change the process whenever a way is discovered to reduce variation or to decrease nonconformance (especially if the process is incapable of meeting the target specifications). We continue to seek ways to reduce variation and/or nonconformance to even lower levels. The never-ending cycle is repeated indefinitely, giving rise to the concept of **continuous quality improvement** or **CQI**. In business process improvement, this cycle is referred to as the *PDCA cycle* (plan, do, check, and act), also known as the *Deming Wheel*. In the **Six Sigma** school of thought (see Section 17.12), the steps to quality improvement are abbreviated as **DMAIC** (define, measure, analyze, improve, control).

Steps to Continuous Quality Improvement

- Step 1: Define a relevant, measurable parameter of the product or service.
- Step 2: Establish targets or desired specifications for the product or service parameter defined in Step 1.
- Step 3: Monitor the process to be sure it is stable and in control.
- Step 4: Is the process capable of meeting the desired specifications?
- Step 5: Identify sources of variation or nonconformance.
- Step 6: Change the process (technology, training, management, materials).
- Step 7: Repeat Steps 3–6 indefinitely.

The Japanese are credited with perfecting and implementing the philosophy of continuous improvement, along with the related concepts of quality circles, just-in-time inventory, and robust design of products and processes (the **Taguchi method**). Different social, economic, and geographic factors prevent adoption of some Japanese approaches by North American firms, but there is general agreement on their main points. Continuous improvement now is a guiding principle for automobile manufacturers, health care providers, insurance companies, computer software designers, fast-food restaurants, and even universities, churches, entertainment, and sports teams. Permanent change and a continuous search for better ways of doing things cascade down the organizational chart and across departmental lines.

Section Exercises

17.10 How does SPC differ from TQM and CQI? (LO 1)

17.11 List the steps in CQI. (LO 1)

17.6 Control Charts: Overview

What Is a Control Chart?

A **control chart** is a visual display used to study how a process changes over time. Data are plotted in time order. It compares the statistic with limits showing the range of expected common cause variation in the data. Control charts are tools for monitoring process stability and for alerting managers if the process changes. In some processes, inspection of every item may be possible. But random sampling is needed when measurements are costly, time-consuming,

FIGURE 17.4   **Three Common Control Charts (from MINITAB)**

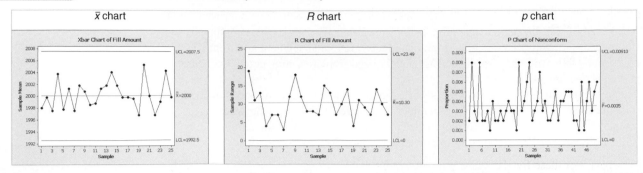

or destructive. For example, we can't test every cellphone battery's useful life, trigger every air bag to see whether it will deploy correctly, or cut open every watermelon to test for pesticide. Sample size and sampling frequency vary with the problem. In SPC the sample size n is referred to as the *subgroup size*.

Two Data Types

For *numerical* data (sometimes called *variable* data) the control chart displays a measure of central tendency (e.g., the sample mean) and/or a measure of variation (e.g., the sample range or standard deviation). A *variable control chart* is used for measurable quantities like weight, length, width, diameter, or time. Typically, such data are found in manufacturing (e.g., dimensions of a metal fastener) but sometimes also in services (e.g., client waiting time). The subgroup size for numerical data may be quite small (e.g., under 10) or even a single item.

For *attribute* data (sometimes called *qualitative* data), the focus is on counting nonconforming or defective items (those that do not meet the target specification). An *attribute control chart* may show the proportion nonconforming (assumed binomial process) or the total number nonconforming (assumed binomial or Poisson process). Attribute control charts are important in service or manufacturing environments when physical measurements are not appropriate. Subgroup size for attribute data may be large (e.g., over 100) depending on the rate of nonconformance. Because modern manufacturing processes may have very low nonconformance rates (e.g., 0.00001 or 0.0000001), even larger samples are needed.

Three Common Control Charts

For a sample mean, the control chart is called an $\bar{x}$ **chart.** For a sample range, it is called an *R* **chart.** For a sample proportion, it is called a *p* **chart.** These three charts are illustrated in Figure 17.4. Each chart plots a sample statistic over time, as well as upper and lower *control limits* that define the expected range of the sample statistic (assuming the process is in control). In these illustrations, all samples fall within the control limits. Control limits are based on the sampling distribution of the statistic. While there are many others, the basic concepts of SPC and setting control limits can be illustrated with these three chart types.

Section Exercises

17.12   What is the difference between an attribute control chart and a variable control chart? (LO 3)

17.13   (a) What determines sampling frequency? (b) Why are variable samples often small? (c) Why are attribute samples often large? (LO 3)

Chapter 21

17.7   Control Charts for a Mean

$\bar{x}$ Charts: Bottle-Filling Example

A bottling plant is filling 2-litre (2,000-ml) soft drink bottles. It is important that the equipment neither overfill nor underfill the bottle. Assume the filling process is stable and in control with mean fill μ and standard deviation σ. The degree of variation depends on the process technology used in the plant. Every 10 minutes, n bottles are chosen at random and their fill is measured. The unit of measurement is millilitres. For a subgroup of size $n = 5$ the sample might look like this:

$$x_1 = 2{,}001 \qquad x_2 = 1{,}998 \qquad x_3 = 2{,}001 \qquad x_4 = 2{,}001 \qquad x_5 = 1{,}997$$

The mean fill for these five bottles is $\bar{x} = 1999.6$. Each time we take a sample of five bottles we expect a different value of the sample mean due to random variation inherent in the process. From previous chapters, we know that the sample mean is an unbiased estimator of the true process mean (i.e., its expected value is μ):

$$E(\bar{X}) = \mu \qquad (\bar{X} \text{ tends toward the true process mean}) \qquad \textbf{(17.1)}$$

The standard deviation of sample mean $\bar{X}$, also called the standard error of the sample mean, is

$$\sigma_{\bar{X}} = \frac{\sigma}{\sqrt{n}} \qquad (\text{larger } n \text{ implies smaller variance of } \bar{X}) \qquad \textbf{(17.2)}$$

The sample mean follows a normal distribution if the population is normal, or if the sample is large enough to assure normality by the Central Limit Theorem.

Control Limits: Known μ and σ

Sample means from a process that is in control should be near the process mean μ, which is the *centreline* of the control chart. The **upper control limit (UCL)** and **lower control limit (LCL)** are set at ± 3 standard errors from the centreline, using the Empirical Rule, which says that almost all the sample means (actually 99.73 percent) will fall within "3-sigma" limits:

$$\text{UCL} = \mu + 3\frac{\sigma}{\sqrt{n}} \qquad (\text{upper control limit for } \bar{X}, \text{ known } \mu \text{ and } \sigma)$$
$$\textbf{(17.3)}$$

$$\text{LCL} = \mu - 3\frac{\sigma}{\sqrt{n}} \qquad (\text{lower control limit for } \bar{X}, \text{ known } \mu \text{ and } \sigma) \qquad \textbf{(17.4)}$$

The $\bar{x}$ chart provides a kind of visual hypothesis test. Sample means will vary, sometimes above the centreline and sometimes below the centreline, but they should stay within the control limits about 99.73 percent of the time, and be symmetrically distributed on either side of the centreline, assuming the process is in control. You will recognize the similarity between *control limits* and *confidence limits* covered in previous chapters. The idea is that if a sample mean falls outside these limits, we suspect that the sample may be from a different population (or the process is out of control) from the one we have specified.

EXAMPLE 1

Bottle Filling

Table 17.3 shows 25 samples from a bottling process with $\mu = 2{,}000$ and $\sigma = 4$. For each sample, the mean and range are calculated. The control limits are

$$\text{UCL} = \mu + 3\frac{\sigma}{\sqrt{n}} = 2{,}000 + 3\frac{4}{\sqrt{5}} = 2{,}000 + 5.367 = 2{,}005.37$$

$$\text{LCL} = \mu - 3\frac{\sigma}{\sqrt{n}} = 2{,}000 - 3\frac{4}{\sqrt{5}} = 2{,}000 - 5.367 = 1{,}994.63$$

TABLE 17.3 **Twenty-Five Samples of Bottle Fill with $n = 5$** ⊙ **BottleFill**

Sample	Bottle 1	Bottle 2	Bottle 3	Bottle 4	Bottle 5	Mean	Range
1	2,001	1,998	2,001	2,001	1,997	1,999.6	4
2	1,997	2,004	2,001	2,000	2,002	2,000.8	7
3	2,001	2,000	2,003	1,995	1,994	1,998.6	9
4	2,007	2,007	2,001	2,000	1,997	2,002.4	10
5	1,999	2,001	1,998	2,001	1,996	1,999.0	5
6	2,002	2,002	1,988	1,995	2,004	1,998.2	16
7	2,003	1,998	1,998	1,996	2,001	1,999.2	7
8	2,005	2,000	1,991	1,996	1,996	1,997.6	14
9	1,999	1,997	2,006	1,999	1,999	2,000.0	9
10	2,005	1,999	1,998	2,002	2,000	2,000.8	7
11	2,001	1,997	2,002	2,004	2,007	2,002.2	10
12	2,002	1,995	1,995	1,997	2,000	1,997.8	7
13	2,006	2,006	1,997	1,998	1,994	2,000.2	12
14	2,003	1,997	2,000	2,003	2,004	2,001.4	7
15	2,003	2,008	1,994	1,998	1,999	2,000.4	14
16	1,998	1,997	1,999	2,001	1,994	1,997.8	7
17	1,988	1,996	2,001	2,002	2,002	1,997.8	14
18	2,003	2,003	1,997	1,995	2,001	1,999.8	8
19	2,003	2,004	1,998	1,998	2,006	2,001.8	8
20	2,005	2,001	2,005	2,000	2,004	2,003.0	5
21	2,004	1,996	2,003	2,002	1,993	1,999.6	11
22	1,998	1,996	2,005	1,997	1,999	1,999.0	9
23	2,002	2,001	1,995	2,004	2,007	2,001.8	12
24	2,002	2,002	1,997	1,995	2,002	1,999.6	7
25	2,002	1,999	2,001	1,992	1,993	1,997.4	10
Average over 25 samples of 5 bottles:						1,999.832	9.160

Figure 17.5 shows a MINITAB $\bar{x}$ chart for these 25 samples, with MINITAB's option to specify μ and σ instead of estimating them from the data. This chart shows a process that is *in control*. If a sample mean exceeds UCL or is below LCL, we suspect that the process may be *out of control*. More complex rules for detecting an out-of-control process will be explained shortly.

Empirical Control Limits

When the process mean μ and standard deviation are unknown (as they often are), we can estimate them from sample data, replacing μ with $\bar{\bar{x}}$ (the average of the means of many samples) and replacing σ with the standard deviation s from a pooled sample of individual X values. Generally, the centreline and control limits are based on *past* data, but are to be used on *future* data to monitor the process. It is desirable to set the control limits from samples taken independently, rather than using the same data to create the control limits and to plot the control chart. However, this is not always possible.

$$\text{UCL} = \bar{\bar{x}} + 3\frac{s}{\sqrt{n}} \quad \text{(upper control limit for } \overline{X}, \text{ unknown } \mu \text{ and } \sigma) \qquad \textbf{(17.5)}$$

MINITAB's $\bar{x}$ Chart with Known Control Limits   FIGURE 17.5

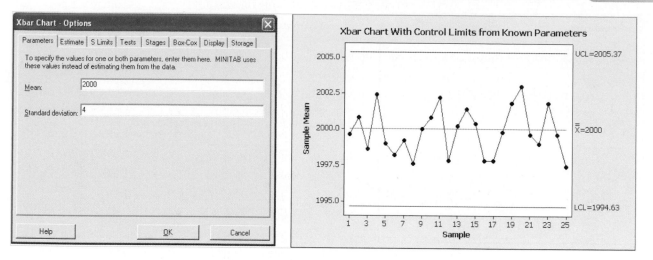

$$\text{LCL} = \bar{\bar{x}} - 3\frac{s}{\sqrt{n}} \quad (\text{lower control limit for } \bar{X}, \text{ unknown } \mu \text{ and } \sigma) \qquad \textbf{(17.6)}$$

There are other ways to estimate the process standard deviation σ. For example, we could use $\bar{s}$, the mean of the standard deviations over many subgroups of size n, with an adjustment for bias. Or we could replace σ with an estimate $\bar{R}/d_2$, where $\bar{R}$ is the average range for many samples and d_2 is a control chart factor that depends on the subgroup size (see Table 17.4). If the number of samples is large enough, any of these methods should give reliable control limits. The $\bar{R}$ method is still common for historical reasons (easier to use prior to the advent of computers) and for the sake of convenience. If the $\bar{R}$ method is used, the formulas become

$$\text{UCL} = \bar{\bar{x}} + 3\frac{\bar{R}}{d_2\sqrt{n}} \quad (\text{upper control limit for } \bar{X}, \text{ unknown } \mu \text{ and } \sigma) \qquad \textbf{(17.7)}$$

$$\text{LCL} = \bar{\bar{x}} - 3\frac{\bar{R}}{d_2\sqrt{n}} \quad (\text{lower control limit for } \bar{X}, \text{ unknown } \mu \text{ and } \sigma) \qquad \textbf{(17.8)}$$

Figure 17.6 shows MINITAB's menu options for estimating control limits from a sample. By default, MINITAB uses the pooled standard deviation, an attractive choice because it directly estimates σ. In Figure 17.6, using the $\bar{R}$ method, the $\bar{x}$ chart is similar to the chart in Figure 17.5, where σ was known, except that the LCL and UCL values are slightly different.

TABLE 17.4   Control Chart Factors

Subgroup Size	d_2	D_3	D_4
2	1.128	0	3.267
3	1.693	0	2.574
4	2.059	0	2.282
5	2.326	0	2.114
6	2.534	0	2.004
7	2.704	0.076	1.924
8	2.847	0.136	1.864
9	2.970	0.184	1.816

Source: See Laythe C. Alwan, *Statistical Process Analysis* (Irwin/McGraw-Hill, 2000), p. 740.

FIGURE 17.6   **MINITAB's $\bar{x}$ Chart with Estimated Control Limits**

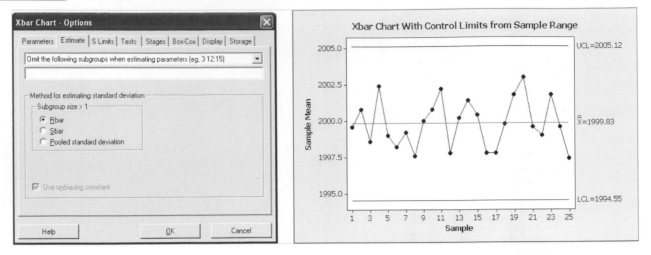

Control Chart Factors

Table 17.4 can be used to set up the control limits from sample data. We only need the first factor (d_2) for the $\bar{x}$ chart (the table also shows D_3 and D_4, which are used to construct control limits for an R chart, to be discussed shortly). The table only goes to $n = 9$ for purposes of illustration (larger tables are available in more specialized textbooks). These factors are built into MINITAB, MegaStat, Visual Statistics, and other computer packages.

To calculate $\bar{\bar{x}}$ and $\bar{R}$ we use averages over 25 samples (see Table 17.3):

$$\bar{\bar{x}} = \frac{\bar{x}_1 + \bar{x}_2 + \cdots + \bar{x}_{25}}{25} = \frac{1{,}999.6 + 2{,}000.8 + \cdots + 1{,}997.4}{25} = 1{,}999.832 \qquad \textbf{(17.9)}$$

$$\bar{R} = \frac{R_1 + R_2 + \cdots + R_{25}}{25} = \frac{4 + 7 + \cdots + 10}{25} = 9.160 \qquad \textbf{(17.10)}$$

Using the sample estimates $\bar{\bar{x}} = 1{,}999.832$ and $\bar{R} = 9.160,$ along with $d_2 = 2.326$ for $n = 5$ from Table 17.4, the estimated empirical control limits are

$$UCL = \bar{\bar{x}} + 3\frac{\bar{R}}{d_2\sqrt{n}} = 1{,}999.832 + 3\frac{9.160}{2.326\sqrt{5}} = 1{,}999.832 + 5.284 = 2{,}005.12$$

and

$$LCL = \bar{\bar{x}} - 3\frac{\bar{R}}{d_2\sqrt{n}} = 1{,}999.832 - 5.284 = 1{,}994.55$$

Note that these *empirical* control limits (2,005.12 and 1,994.55) differ somewhat from the *theoretical* control limits (2,005.37 and 1,994.63) that we obtained using $\mu = 2{,}000$ and $\sigma = 4$, and the *empirical* centreline (1,999.83) differs from $\mu = 2{,}000$. In practice, it would be necessary to take more than 25 samples to ensure a good estimate of the true process mean and standard deviation. Indeed, engineers may run a manufacturing process for days or weeks before its characteristics are well understood. Figure 17.7 shows MegaStat's $\bar{x}$ chart using the sample data to estimate the control limits. MegaStat *always* uses estimated control limits by the $\bar{R}$ method, and does not permit you to specify known parameters. Also, MegaStat expects the observed data to be arranged as a rectangle, with each subgroup's observations comprising a *row* (like Table 17.3). MegaStat's $\bar{x}$-chart is similar to MINITAB's except for details of scaling.

Detecting Abnormal Patterns

Sample means observed beyond or outside the control limits are strong indicators of an out-of-control process. However, more subtle patterns can also indicate problems. Experts have

MegaStat x̄ Chart with Estimated Control Limits   FIGURE 17.7

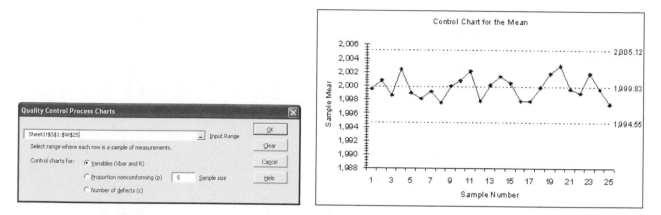

developed many "rules of thumb" to check for patterns that might indicate an out-of-control process. Here are four of them (the "sigma" refers to the *standard error of the mean*):

- *Rule 1.* Single point outside 3 sigma.
- *Rule 2.* Two (or more) of three successive points outside 2 sigma on same side of centreline.
- *Rule 3.* Four (or more) of five successive points outside 1 sigma on same side of centreline.
- *Rule 4.* Nine successive points on same side of centreline.

Violations of Rules 1 and 2 can usually be seen from "eyeball inspection" of control charts. Violations of the other rules are more subtle. A computer may be required to monitor a process to be sure that control chart violations are detected. Figure 17.8 illustrates these four rules, applied to a service organization (a clinic conducting physical exams for babies).

A Closer Look

Why would these rules indicate that the process is out-of-control? If we assume normality, we can argue that any of the above occurrences are highly unlikely to occur if the process is in control. So, if any one of the above occurs, we can reject our assumption about the process being in control. For example, the probability that a single point is outside 3 sigma limits from the mean is 0.0027 ($= 2[0.5 - 0.49865]$ from the z-table) if the process is in control. So, if a single point is outside of 3 sigma limits from the mean, we can conclude that the process is out of control. To determine the other probabilities associated with rules 2, 3, and 4, it is necessary to use probability rules.

Concept Check

Using probability rules from previous chapters, what is the probability that, if a random variable is normally distributed:

- At least two of three successive points will lie outside of 2 sigmas on the same side of the mean?

- At least four of five successive points will lie outside of 1 sigma on the same side of the mean?

- Nine successive points will lie on the same side of the mean?

FIGURE 17.8 **Red Dots indicate Rule Violations (from Visual Statistics)**

Rule 1: 1 Beyond 3 Sigma

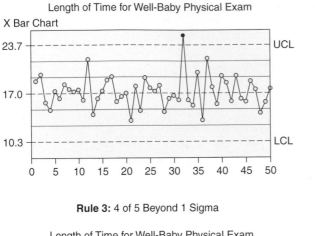

Rule 2: 2 of 3 Beyond 2 Sigma

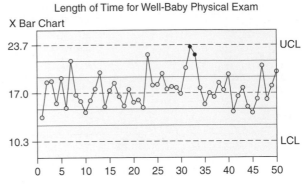

Rule 3: 4 of 5 Beyond 1 Sigma

Rule 4: 9 Successive Same Side

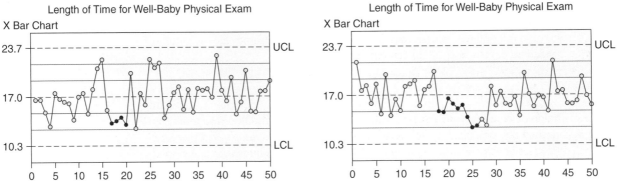

Multiple rule violations are possible. Figure 17.9 shows a MINITAB $\bar{x}$ chart with these four rules applied (note that MINITAB includes many other tests and uses a different numbering system for its rules). In this illustration, an out-of-control process is shown, with eight rule violations (each violation is numbered and highlighted in red).

Histograms

The normal curve is the reference point for variation inherent in the process or due to random sampling. UCL and LCL are set at ± 3 standard errors from the mean, but we could

FIGURE 17.9 **Violations of Rules of Thumb (from MINITAB)**

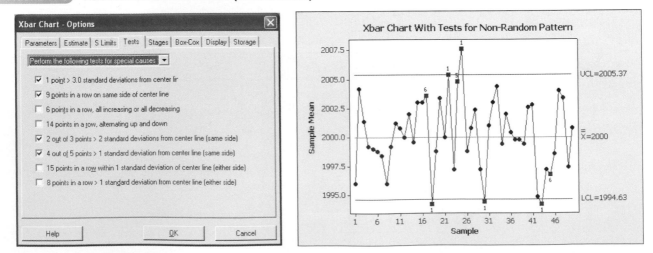

Visual Statistics $\bar{x}$ Chart and Histogram FIGURE 17.10

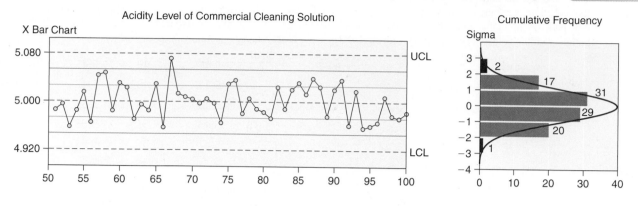

(and should) also examine ± 2 and ± 1 standard error ranges to see whether the percentage of sample means follows the normal distribution. Recall that the expected percent of samples within various distances from the centreline can be stated as normal areas or percentages:

- Within ± 1 standard deviation or 68.26 percent of the time.
- Within ± 2 standard deviations or 95.44 percent of the time.
- Within ± 3 standard deviations or 99.73 percent of the time.

The distribution of sample means can be scrutinized for symmetry and/or deviations from the expected normal percentages. Figure 17.10 shows a Visual Statistics $\bar{x}$ chart and histogram for 100 samples of acidity for a commercial cleaning product. The histogram is roughly symmetric, with 60 sample means between -1 and $+1$ and 97 sample means between -2 and $+2$, while the normal distribution would predict 68 and 95, respectively.

Section Exercises

17.14 To construct control limits for an $\bar{x}$ chart, name three ways to estimate σ empirically. Why is the $\bar{R}$ method often used? Why is the s method the default in MINITAB? (LO 3)

17.15 For an $\bar{x}$ chart, what percent of sample means should be (a) within 1 sigma of the centreline; (b) within 2 sigmas of the centreline; (c) within 3 sigmas of the centreline; (d) outside 2 sigmas of the centreline; (e) outside 3 sigmas of the centreline? *Note:* "sigma" denotes the standard error of the mean. (LO 3)

17.16 List four rules for detecting abnormal (special cause) observations in a control chart. (LO 4)

17.17 Set up control limits for an $\bar{x}$ chart, given $\bar{\bar{x}} = 12.50$, $\bar{R} = 0.42$, and $n = 5$. (LO 3)

17.18 Set up control limits for an $\bar{x}$ chart, given $\bar{\bar{x}} = 400$, $\bar{R} = 5$, and $n = 4$. (LO 3)

17.19 Time (in seconds) to serve an early-morning customer at a fast-food restaurant is normally distributed. Set up a control chart for the mean serving time, assuming that serving times were sampled in random subgroups of four customers. *Note:* Use this sample of 36 observations to estimate μ and σ. (LO 3) 🔘 **ServeTime**

Sample 1	Sample 2	Sample 3	Sample 4	Sample 5	Sample 6	Sample 7	Sample 8	Sample 9
65	56	84	69	75	87	87	99	102
51	87	67	81	80	84	90	61	61
94	84	71	59	76	80	65	84	88
79	70	85	75	88	52	61	79	78

17.20 To print 8.5 × 5.5 note pads, a copy shop uses standard 8.5 × 11 paper, glues the long edge, then cuts the pads in half so that the pad width is 5.5 inches. However, there is variation in the cutting process. Set up a control chart for the mean width of a note pad, assuming that, in the future, pads will be sampled in random subgroups of five pads. Use this sample of 40 observations (widths in inches) to estimate μ and σ. (LO 3)   **NotePads**

5.52	5.57	5.44	5.47	5.52	5.46	5.43	5.45
5.49	5.47	5.48	5.51	5.53	5.53	5.48	5.47
5.59	5.51	5.43	5.48	5.53	5.50	5.49	5.52
5.46	5.46	5.56	5.54	5.47	5.44	5.53	5.58
5.55	5.56	5.47	5.44	5.55	5.42	5.45	5.54

Mini Case   17.1

Control Limits for Jelly Beans   JellyBeans

The manufacture of jelly beans is a high-volume operation that is tricky to manage, with strict standards for food purity, worker safety, and environmental controls. Each bean's jelly core is soft and sticky, and must be coated with a harder sugar shell of the appropriate colour. Hundreds of thousands of beans must be cooled and bagged, with approximately the desired colour proportions. To meet consumer expectations, the surface finish of each bean and its weight must be as uniform as possible. Because jelly beans are a low-priced item, and because the market is highly competitive (i.e., there are many substitutes and many producers), it is not cost-effective to spend millions to achieve the same level of precision that might be used, say, in manufacturing a prescription drug.

So, how do we measure jelly bean quality? One obvious metric is weight. To set control limits, we need estimates of μ and σ. From a local grocery, a bag of Brach's jelly beans was purchased (see Figure 17.11). Each bean was weighed on a precise scale (the full data set is in *LearningStats*). The resulting sample of 182 jelly beans weights showed a bell-shaped distribution, except for three high outliers, easily visible in Figure 17.12. Once the outliers are removed, the sample presents a satisfactory normal probability plot, shown in Figure 17.13. The sample mean and standard deviation ($\bar{x} = 3.352$ grams and $s = 0.3622$ grams) can now be used to set control limits. Referring back to Figure 17.11, some differences in size are visible. Can you spot the three oversized beans? Some consumers may regard "double" beans as a treat, rather than as a product defect. But manufacturers always strive for the most consistent product possible, subject to constraints of time, technology, and budget.

FIGURE 17.11   **The Data Set (*n* = 182)**

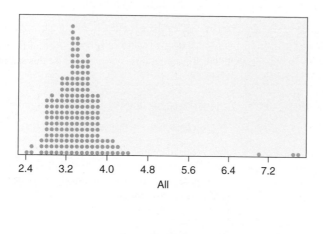

FIGURE 17.12

Dot Plot for All Data
($n = 182$)

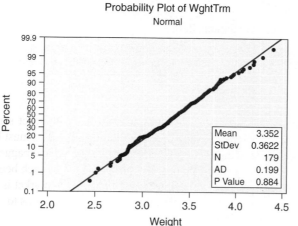

FIGURE 17.13

Normal Plot for Trimmed
Data ($n = 179$)

17.8   Control Charts for a Range

The $\bar{x}$ chart of sample means by itself is insufficient to tell whether a process is in control, because it reveals only *centrality*. We also should examine a chart showing *variation* around the mean. We could track the sample standard deviations (using an *s chart*), but it is more traditional to track the *sample range* (the difference between the largest and smallest item in each sample) using the *R chart*. The sample range is sensitive to extreme values. Nonetheless, its behaviour can be predicted statistically, and control limits can be established. The *R* chart has asymmetric control limits, as the sample range does not follow a normal distribution, even when the sample size is large or the data comes from a normal population.

Chapter 21

Control Limits for the Range

The centreline is obtained by calculating the average range $\bar{R}$ over many samples taken from the process. Estimation of $\bar{R}$ ideally would precede construction of the control chart, using a large number of independent samples, though this is not always possible in practice. Control limits based on samples may not be a good representation of the true process. It depends on the number of samples and the "luck of the draw." The control limits for the *R* chart can be set using the average sample range:

$$\text{UCL} = D_4\bar{R} \quad \text{(upper control limit of sample range)} \tag{17.11}$$

$$\text{LCL} = D_3\bar{R} \quad \text{(lower control limit of sample range)} \tag{17.12}$$

EXAMPLE 2

Bottle Filling: R Chart

The control limits depend upon factors that must be obtained from a table. For the bottle fill data with $n = 5$, we have $D_4 = 2.114$ and $D_3 = 0$ (from Table 17.4). Using $\bar{R} = 9.16$ from the 25 samples (from Table 17.3), the control limits are

$$\bar{R} = 9.16 \qquad \text{(centreline for } R \text{ chart)}$$

$$\text{UCL} = D_4\bar{R} = (2.114)(9.160) = 19.37 \quad \text{(upper control limit)}$$

$$\text{LCL} = D_3\bar{R} = (0)(9.160) = 0 \qquad \text{(lower control limit)}$$

Figure 17.14 shows MINITAB's R chart for the data in Table 17.3. Note that the R chart control limits could also be based on a pooled standard deviation. Using the Parameters tab, MINITAB also offers an option (not shown) to specify σ yourself (e.g., from historical experience). In this illustration, the process variation remains within the control limits.

FIGURE 17.14 **MINITAB's R Chart with Control Limits from Sample Data**

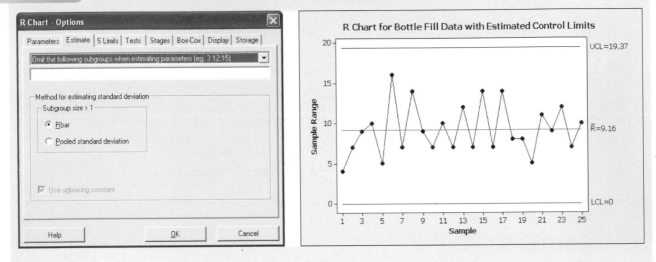

Figure 17.15 shows MegaStat's R chart using the same data to estimate the control limits. The MINITAB and MegaStat charts are similar except for scaling. However, MegaStat always uses estimated control limits (whereas MINITAB gives you the option).

FIGURE 17.15 **MegaStat's R Chart with Control Limits from Sample Data**

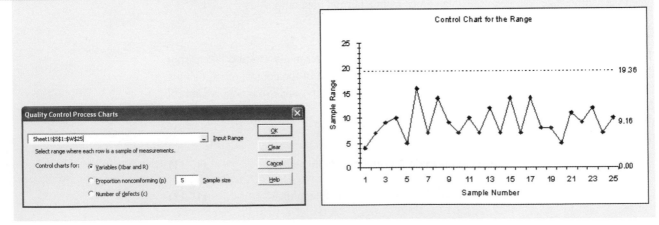

Section Exercises

17.21 Set up limits for the *R* chart, given $\overline{R} = 0.82$ and $n = 6$. (LO 3)

17.22 Set up limits for the *R* chart, given $\overline{R} = 12$ and $n = 3$. (LO 3)

17.9 Patterns in Control Charts

The Overadjustment Problem

Chapter 21

The $\bar{x}$ chart is a visual hypothesis test for μ, while the *R* chart is a visual hypothesis test for σ. In manufacturing, a control chart is used to guide decisions to continue the process or halt the process to make adjustments. *Overadjustment* or stopping to make unnecessary process corrections (Type I error) can lead to loss of production, downtime, unnecessary expense, forgone profit, delayed deliveries, stockout, or employee frustration. On the other hand, failing to make timely process corrections (Type II error) can lead to poor quality, excess scrap, rework, customer dissatisfaction, adverse publicity or litigation, and employee cynicism.

Statistics allows managers to balance these Type I and II errors. It has been shown that, in the absence of statistical decision rules, manufacturing process operators tend toward overadjustment (i.e., adjust the process even when it is in control), which will actually *increase* variation above the level the process is capable of attaining.

The actions to be taken when a control chart violation is detected will depend on the consequences of Type I and II error. For example, if a health insurer notices that processing times for claim payments are out of control (i.e., relative to target benchmarks), the only action may be an investigation into the problem because the immediate consequences are not severe. But in car manufacturing, an out-of-control metal-forming process could require immediate shutdown of the assembly process to prevent costly rework or product liability.

Abnormal Patterns

Quality experts have given names to some of the more common abnormal control chart patterns, that is, patterns that indicate assignable causes:

- **Cycle**   Samples tend to follow a cyclic pattern.
- **Oscillation**   Samples tend to alternate (high-low-high-low) in saw-toothed fashion.
- **Instability**   Samples vary more than expected.
- **Level shift**   Samples shift abruptly either above or below centreline.
- **Trend**   Samples drift slowly either upward or downward.
- **Mixture**   Samples come from two different populations (increased variation).

These names are intended to help you recognize symptoms that may be associated with known causes. These concepts extend to any time-series pattern (not just control charts).

Symptoms and Assignable Causes

Each $\bar{x}$ chart in Figure 17.16 displays 100 samples, which is a long enough run to show the patterns clearly. However, the $\bar{x}$ charts shown are exaggerated to emphasize the essential features of each pattern. Abnormal patterns like these would generate violations of Rule 1, 2, 3, or 4 (or multiple rule violations), so the process would actually have been stopped *before* the pattern developed to the degree shown in Figure 17.16. Although many patterns are discussed in terms of the $\bar{x}$ chart, the *R* chart and histogram of sample means may also reveal abnormal

FIGURE 17.16 **Common Abnormal Patterns**

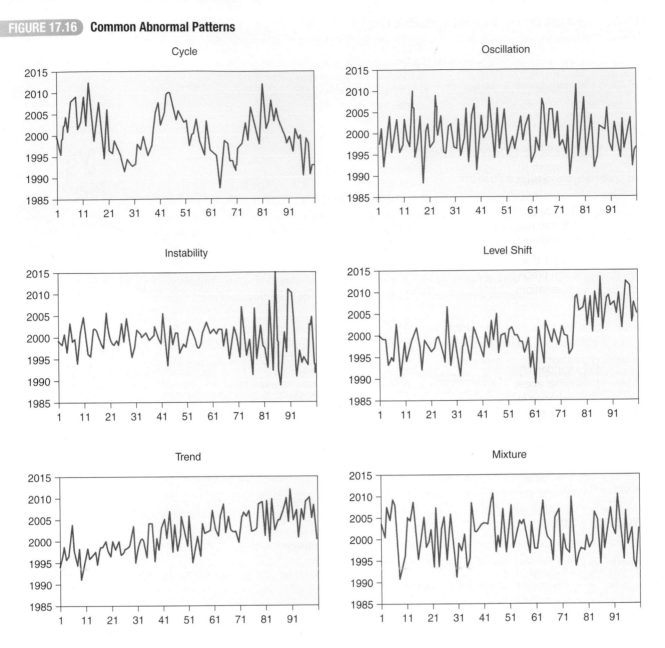

patterns. It may be impossible to identify a pattern or its assignable cause(s) if the period of observation is short. Table 17.5 summarizes the symptoms and likely underlying causes of abnormal patterns.

17.10 Process Capability

A business must translate *customer requirements* into an **upper specification limit (USL)** and **lower specification limit (LSL)** of a quality metric. These limits do *not* depend on the process. Whether the process is *capable* of meeting these requirements depends on the magnitude of the process variation (σ) and whether the process is correctly centred (μ).

C_p Index

The *process capability index* C_p is a ratio that compares the interval between the specification limits with the expected process range (defined as six times the process standard deviation). If the process range is small relative to the specification range, the capability index will be high,

TABLE 17.5 **Pattern Descriptions and Assignable Causes**

Pattern Description	Likely Assignable Causes	Detected How?
Cycle is a repeated series of high measurements followed by a series of low measurements (+ + + + − − − + + + − − − − + + + +, etc.) relative to the centreline. Equivalent to positive autocorrelation in regression residuals.	*Industry:* worn threads or gears, humidity or temperature fluctuations, operator fatigue, voltage changes, overadjustment. *Services:* duty rotations, employee fatigue, poor scheduling, periodic distractions.	May be detected visually (fewer than $m/2$ centreline crossings in m samples) or by a runs test (see Chapter 16) or higher-than-expected tail frequencies in a histogram. Look for violations of Rule 4.
Oscillation is a pattern of alternating high and low measurements (+ − + − + − + −, etc.) relative to the centreline (a zigzag or saw-toothed pattern). Equivalent to negative autocorrelation in regression residuals.	*Industry:* alternating sampling of two machines, two settings, two inspectors, or two gauges. *Services:* attempts to compensate for performance variation on the last task, alternating task between two workers.	May be detected visually (more than $m/2$ centreline crossings in m samples) or by a runs test (see Chapter 16). Process mean stays near the centreline, though process variance may increase. May not violate any rules.
Instability is a larger than normal amount of variation preceded by a period of normal, stable variation.	*Industry:* untrained operators, overadjustment, equipment in need of repair, tool wear, defective material. *Services:* distractions, poor job design, untrained employees, flawed sampling process, samples from only one source, forms filled out from memory.	May be detectable on the $\bar{x}$ chart, but shows up most clearly on the R chart and in higher-than-expected frequencies in the tails of the histogram. Violations of Rules 1, 2, and 3 are likely.
Level shift is a sudden change in measurements either above or below the centreline. It is a change in the actual process mean. Easily confused with trend.	*Industry:* new workers, change in equipment, new inspector, new machine setting, new lot of material. *Services:* changed environment, new supervisor, new work rules.	Centre of the histogram shifts but with no change in variation. Violation of Rule 4 is likely, and perhaps others. May be too few centreline crossings (fewer than $m/2$).
Trend is a slow, continuous drifting of measurements either up or down from the chart centreline. Detectable visually if enough measurements are taken. Easily confused with level shift.	*Industry:* tool wear, inadequate maintenance, worker fatigue, gradual clogging (dirt, shavings, etc.), drying out of lubricant. *Services:* slow relaxing of attention, increasing task flow, bottlenecks.	Process variance may be unchanged, but the histogram grows skewed in one tail. May be too few centreline crossings (fewer than $m/2$). Violation of Rule 4 is likely, and perhaps others.
Mixture is sampling from two or more separate processes. Both may be in control, but with different means, resulting in a bimodal histogram (if the means differ) or no detectable difference (if the means are similar). With merged output from many machines, the overall process variance is increased.	*Industry:* two machines, two gauges, two shifts (day, night), two inspectors, different lots of material. *Services:* different supervisors, two work teams, two shifts.	Difficult to detect, either visually or statistically, especially if more than two processes are mixed. Histogram may be bimodal. Use same tests as for instability.

and vice versa. A higher C_p index (a *more capable* process) is always better. The higher the C_p index, the higher the capability of the process to meet specification limits.

$$C_p = \frac{\text{USL} - \text{LSL}}{6\sigma} \text{ (process capability index } C_p)$$ **(17.13)**

A C_p value of 1.00 would indicate that the process is just barely capable of staying within the specifications *if* precisely centred. But managers typically require $C_p > 1.33$ (i.e., "leeway" of 2σ) to allow flexibility in case the process drifts off centre. In manufacturing, a higher capability index may be required (in some applications even $C_p > 2.67$ might not be good enough, that is, leeway of 10σ).

C_{pk} Index

The index C_p is easy to understand, but fails to show whether the process is well-centred. A process with acceptable variation could be off-centreline and yet have a high C_p capability

FIGURE 17.17

Individual Safety Margins for C_{pk} Index

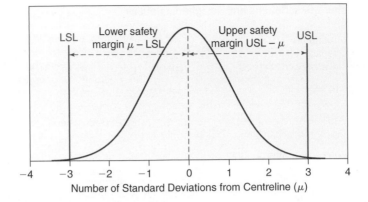

index. To remedy this weakness, we define another more conservative process capability index called C_{pk}, which looks at each *separate* "safety margin" (the distance between each specification limit and the process centreline) as illustrated in Figure 17.17.

The process capability index C_{pk} simply is the smaller of these two distances (USL $- \mu$ and $\mu -$ LSL) expressed as a fraction of the 3σ distance above or below μ:

$$C_{pk} = \frac{\min(\mu - \text{LSL}, \text{USL} - \mu)}{3\sigma} \quad \text{(process capability index } C_{pk}) \quad \textbf{(17.14)}$$

We are assuming that LSL $< \mu <$ USL. If both "safety margins" USL $- \mu$ and $\mu -$ LSL are exactly 3σ, then $C_{pk} = 1.00$. A C_{pk} index of 1.00 is the minimum capability, but much higher values are preferred. Note that $C_{pk} \le C_p$ always. If both "safety margins" ($\mu -$ LSL and USL $- \mu$) are the same, then C_{pk} will be identical to C_p. In contrast to the C_p index, the C_{pk} index imposes a penalty when the process is off-centre.

EXAMPLE 3

Cookie Baking

A bakery is supposed to produce cookies whose average weight, after baking, is 31 grams. To meet quality requirements, it has been decided that USL = 35.0 grams and LSL = 28.0 grams. The process standard deviation is 0.8 grams and the process centreline is set at $\mu = 31$ grams. The company requires a capability index of at least 1.33.

C_p *index:*

$$C_p = \frac{\text{USL} - \text{LSL}}{6\sigma} = \frac{35.0 - 28.0}{(6)(0.8)} = 1.46$$

C_{pk} *index:*

$$C_{pk} = \frac{\min(\mu - \text{LSL}, \text{USL} - \mu)}{3\sigma} = \frac{\min(31.0 - 28.0, 35.0 - 31.0)}{(3)(0.8)} = \frac{3.0}{2.4} = 1.25$$

According to the C_p index, the process capability is barely acceptable ($C_p = 1.46$), but using the C_{pk} index ($C_{pk} = 1.25$) the process capability is unacceptable. Actually, the process capability is doubtful regardless of index used, as both indexes are uncomfortably close to the company's chosen minimum (1.33). The situation is illustrated in Figure 17.18. In cookie making, management is less concerned about oversized cookies than undersized ones (customers will not complain if a cookie is too big), so the limits are not symmetric, as can be seen in Figure 17.18. Note that their process is correctly centred at $\mu = 31$, even though the specification limits are asymmetric.

FIGURE 17.18

Process Capability for Cookie Making

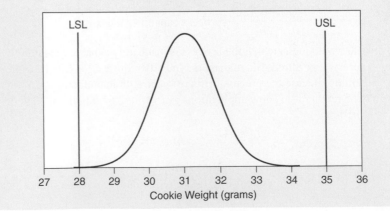

Process Variation versus Specification Limits FIGURE 17.19

Situation A	Situation B	Situation C
Process is capable of meeting specifications even if poorly centred.	Process is barely capable of meeting specifications only if well centred.	Process is incapable of meeting specifications even if well centred.

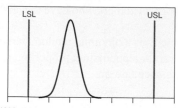 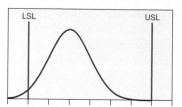 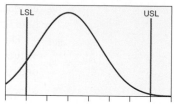

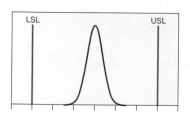 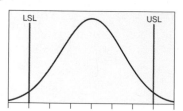

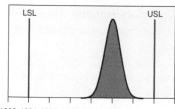 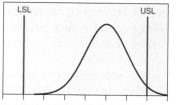 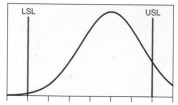

Bottle Filling Revisited

Figure 17.19 illustrates several possible situations, using the bottle filling scenario with symmetric specification limits LSL = 1,994 and USL = 2,006 and a target μ = 2,000. Remember that specification limits are based on customer demands (or engineering requirements) and not on the process itself. *There is no guarantee that the extant process is capable of meeting the requirements.* If it is not, there is no choice but to find ways to improve the process (i.e., by reducing σ) through improved technology, worker training, or capital investment.

Section Exercises

17.23 Find the C_p and C_{pk} indexes for a process with μ = 720, σ = 1.0, LSL = 715, and USL = 725. How would you rate the capability of this process? Explain. (LO 5)

17.24 Find the C_p and C_{pk} indexes for a process with μ = 0.426, σ = 0.001, LSL = 0.423, and USL = 0.432. How would you rate the capability of this process? Explain. (LO 5)

17.25 Find the C_p and C_{pk} indexes for a process with μ = 55.4, σ = 0.1, LSL = 55.2, and USL = 55.9. How would you rate the capability of this process? Explain. (LO 5)

17.11   Other Control Charts

Attribute Data: *p* Charts

The *p chart* for attribute data plots the *proportion* of nonconforming items using the familiar sample proportion *p*:

$$p = \frac{\text{number of nonconforming items}}{\text{sample size}} = \frac{x}{n} \qquad (17.15)$$

In manufacturing, p used to be referred to as a "defect rate," but the term "nonconforming items" is preferred because it is more neutral and better adapted to applications outside manufacturing, such as service environments. For example, for a retailer, p might refer to the proportion of customers who return their purchases for a refund. For a bank, p might refer to the proportion of chequing account customers who have insufficient funds to cover one or more cheques. For Ticketmaster, p might refer to the proportion of customers who have to wait "on hold" more than five minutes to obtain concert tickets.

The number of nonconforming items in a sample of n items is a binomial random variable, so the control limits are constructed as a confidence interval for a population proportion using one of several methods to state the *population* nonconformance rate π:

- An assumed value of π (e.g., a target rate of nonconformance).
- An empirical estimate of π based on a large number of trials.
- An estimate p from the samples being tested (if no other choice).

If n is large enough to assume normality,* the control limits would be

$$\text{UCL} = \pi + 3\sqrt{\frac{\pi(1 - \pi)}{n}} \quad (\pi \text{ is the process centreline}) \tag{17.16}$$

$$\text{LCL} = \pi - 3\sqrt{\frac{\pi(1 - \pi)}{n}} \quad (\pi \text{ is the process centreline}) \tag{17.17}$$

The logic is similar to a two-tailed hypothesis test of a proportion. The choice of 3 standard deviations is conventional, though there are applications where a different choice would be appropriate. If the LCL is negative, it is assumed to be zero. In manufacturing, the rate of nonconformance is likely to be a very small fraction (e.g., 0.02 or even smaller), so it is quite likely that LCL will be zero.

*If n is not large enough to assume normality, the binomial distribution may be used to set up control limits. MINITAB will handle this situation, although the resulting control limits may be quite wide.

EXAMPLE 4

Cellphone Manufacture

A manufacturer of cellphones has a 0.002 historical rate of nonconformance to specifications (i.e., 2 nonconforming phones per 1,000). All phones are tested, and the nonconformance rates are plotted on a p chart, using an assumed value $\pi = 0.002$. Thus, the control limits are

$$\text{UCL} = 0.002 + 3\sqrt{\frac{(0.002)(0.998)}{n}} \quad \text{and LCL} = 0.002 - 3\sqrt{\frac{(0.002)(0.998)}{n}}$$

Table 17.6 shows inspection data for 100 days of production (this table is abbreviated, but *LearningStats* has the full data set). Each production run (n) is around 2,000 phones per day, but does vary. Hence, the control limits are not constant, as shown in the p chart in Figure 17.20.

TABLE 17.6 Nonconforming Cellphones Cellphones

Day	Nonconforming (x)	Production (n)	x/n
1	3	2,056	0.00146
2	1	1,939	0.00052
3	4	2,079	0.00192
4	5	2,079	0.00241
5	4	1,955	0.00205
⋮	⋮	⋮	⋮
96	4	1,967	0.00203
97	6	2,077	0.00289
98	3	2,075	0.00145
99	5	1,908	0.00262
100	2	2,045	0.00098

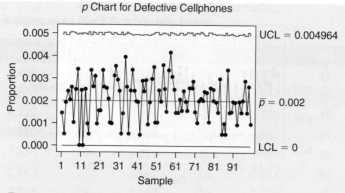

FIGURE 17.20

MINITAB *p* Chart for Cellphones

Notice that p stays within the control limits, although it touches the LCL twice (not a problem because zero defects is ideal). Although n varies, we can illustrate the control limit calculation by using $\pi = 0.002$ and $n = 2,000$:

$$UCL = 0.002 + 3\sqrt{\frac{(0.002)(0.998)}{2,000}} = 0.004997$$

$$LCL = 0.002 - 3\sqrt{\frac{(0.002)(0.998)}{2,000}} = -0.000997$$

Because a negative proportion is impossible, we just set LCL = 0. You will notice that MINITAB's UCL is not quite the same as the calculation above, because MINITAB uses a binomial calculation rather than the normal approximation. The difference may be noticeable when $n < 9\dfrac{(1 - \pi)}{\pi}$ (one of the criteria for a normal approximation to the binomial). In this example, $9\dfrac{(1 - \pi)}{\pi} = \dfrac{9(0.998)}{0.002} = 4{,}491$, the minimum sample size needed to use normal approximation, so the binomial method is preferred (but is too complex to explain here).

Application: Emergency Patients

Instead of being a rate of *nonconformance* to specifications, p could be a rate of *conformance* to specifications. Then

$$p = \frac{\text{number of conforming items}}{\text{sample size}} = \frac{x}{n} \tag{17.18}$$

Ardmore Hospital's emergency facility advertises that its goal is to ensure that, on average, 90 percent of patients receive treatment within 30 minutes of arrival. Table 17.7 shows data

TABLE 17.7   Emergency Patients Seen within 30 Minutes   ER Patients

Day	Seen in 30 Minutes (x)	Patient Volume (n)	x/n
1	87	97	0.900
2	113	122	0.924
3	106	115	0.920
4	84	90	0.928
5	82	92	0.896
⋮	⋮	⋮	⋮
96	128	142	0.900
97	101	112	0.900
98	123	135	0.908
99	128	141	0.908
100	141	149	0.944

improve the design tomorrow, even better solutions are likely to be found later on. Successful organizations try to create a climate in which employees are encouraged to suggest new ways of doing things.

Taguchi's Robust Design

The prominence of Japanese quality expert Genichi Taguchi is mainly due to his contributions in the field of *robust design,* which uses statistically planned experiments to identify process control parameter settings that reduce a process's sensitivity to manufacturing variation. In Taguchi's taxonomy, we identify the functional characteristics that measure the final product's performance, the control parameters that can be specified by process engineers, and the sources of noise that are expensive or impossible to control. By varying control parameters in a planned experiment, we can use the results to predict control parameter settings that would make the process insensitive to noise. Parameter settings are first varied simultaneously in a few experimental runs. Then, a fractional factorial experimental design is selected (see Chapter 11), using a balancing property to choose pairs of parameter settings. Finally, predictions of improved parameter settings are made and verified through a confirming experiment.

Taguchi's methods are especially useful in manufacturing situations with many process control parameters, which imply complex experimental designs. Once the problem is defined, we rely on well-known experimental design methods. In addition, Taguchi is known for explicitly including in quality measures the total loss incurred from the time the product is shipped, using a quadratic loss penalty based on the squared difference between actual and target quality. His inclusion of customers in the model is considered a major innovation.

Six Sigma and Lean Six Sigma

Six Sigma is a broad philosophy to reduce cost, eliminate variability, and improve customer satisfaction through improved design and better management strategy. *Lean Six Sigma* integrates Six Sigma with supply-chain management to optimize resource flows, while also lowering cost and raising quality. Most of us have heard of the Six Sigma goal of 3.4 defects per million through reduced process variation (i.e., extremely high C_p and C_{pk} indexes), essentially using the tools outlined in this chapter and the DMAIC steps for process improvement. However, there is more to it than statistics, and Six Sigma experts must be certified (Green Belts, Black Belts, Master Black Belts) through advanced training. Six Sigma implementation varies according to the organization, with health care being perhaps the latest major application. Six Sigma knowledge goes beyond the bounds of an introductory statistics class, but if you take a job that requires it, your company will give you advanced training.

ISO 9000

Since 1992, firms wishing to sell their products globally have had to comply with a series of ISO standards, first articulated in 1987 in Europe. These standards have continued to evolve. Now, ISO 9000 and ISO audits (both internal and of suppliers) have become a de facto quality system standard for any company wanting to be a world-class competitor. ISO 9001 includes customer service as well as design of products and services (not just manufacturing). The broad scope of ISO 9000, ISO 14000 (environmental management standards), and QS 9000 (quality standard developed by a joint effort of the American automakers) requires special training that is not normally part of an introductory statistics class.

Advanced MINITAB Features

A glance at MINITAB's extensive menus (see Figure 17.25) will tell you that quality tools are one of its strengths. In addition to all types of control charts and cause-and-effect diagrams (fishbone or Ishikawa diagrams), MINITAB offers capability analysis, variable transformations to achieve normality, alternative distributions where the assumption of normality is inappropriate, and gage study for variables and attributes. If you want further study of statistical

More MINITAB Menus FIGURE 17.25

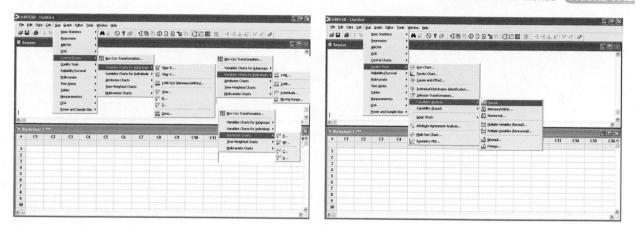

quality tools, you could explore MINITAB's menus, help system, and data sets. Many other general-purpose software packages (e.g., SAS, SPSS) offer similar capabilities.

Future of Statistical Process Control

Automation, numerical control, and continuous process monitoring have changed the meaning of SPC in manufacturing. The integration of manufacturing and factory floor quality monitoring systems in manufacturing planning and control, materials requirements planning (MRP), computer-aided design and manufacturing (CAD/CAM), order entry, and financial, customer service, and support systems have continued to redefine the role of SPC. Automation has made 100 percent testing and inspection attainable in some applications where it was previously thought to be either impossible or uneconomical.

It may be that SPC itself will become part of the background that is built in to every manufacturing organization, allowing managers to focus on higher-level issues. As an analogy, consider that only a few decades ago chart-making required specialists who were skilled in drafting. Now, anyone with access to a computer can make excellent charts. In the service sector of the economy, quality improvement is still at an early level of implementation. In health care, financial services, and retailing, processes are harder to define and tasks are often not as repetitive or as standardized as in manufacturing. Thus, the role of SPC is still unfolding, and every business student needs to know its basic principles.

Quality is measured by a set of attributes that affect **customer satisfaction. Quality improvement** is aimed at **variance reduction. Common cause** variation is normal and expected, while **special cause** variation is abnormal and requires action, such as adjusting the **process** for producing a good or service. Quality is affected by management, resources, technology, and human factors (e.g., training, employee involvement). **Statistical process control** (SPC) involves using **control charts** of key quality metrics to make sure that the processes are **in control**. The **upper control limit** (UCL) and **lower control limit** (LCL) define the range of allowable variation. These limits are usually set **empirically** by observing a process over time. Control charts are used to track the **mean** ($\bar{x}$ chart), **range** (R chart), **proportion** (p chart), and other statistics. Samples may be taken by **subgroups** of n items, or by continuous monitoring with **individual charts** (I charts) and **moving range** (MR charts). There are **rules of thumb** to identify out-of-control patterns (instability, trend, level shift, cycle, oscillation) and their likely causes. A **capable** process is one whose variability (σ) is small in relation to the **upper and lower specification limits** (USL and LSL). SPC concepts were first applied to manufacturing, but can be adapted to service environments such as finance, health care, and retailing. **ISO standards** now guide companies selling in world markets, and Six Sigma techniques are widely used to improve quality in service organizations, as well as in manufacturing.

CHAPTER SUMMARY

www.mcgrawhillconnect.ca

KEY TERMS

acceptance sampling, *756*
business process redesign
  (BPR), *733*
C_p, *748*
C_{pk}, *750*
common cause variation, *728*
control chart, *735*
continuous quality
  improvement (CQI), *735*
customer, *729*
cycle, *747*
Deming, W. Edwards, *731*
DMAIC, *735*
fishbone chart, *734*
I charts, *754*
instability, *747*

ISO 9000, *758*
level shift, *747*
lower control limit (LCL), *737*
lower specification limit
  (LSL), *748*
mixture, *747*
MR charts, *754*
oscillation, *747*
p chart, *736*
Pareto chart, *732*
process, *728*
productivity, *727*
quality, *727*
quality control, *728*
R chart, *736*
reduced variation, *728*

Six Sigma, *735*
special cause variation, *728*
statistical process control
  (SPC), *734*
statistical quality control
  (SQC), *733*
Taguchi method, *735*
total quality management
  (TQM), *733*
trend, *747*
upper control limit (UCL), *737*
upper specification limit
  (USL), *748*
$\bar{x}$ chart, *736*

Commonly Used Formulas

Control limits for $\bar{x}$ chart (known or historical σ): $\mu \pm 3\dfrac{\sigma}{\sqrt{n}}$

Control limits for $\bar{x}$ chart (sample estimate of σ): $\bar{\bar{x}} \pm 3\dfrac{s}{\sqrt{n}}$

Control limits for $\bar{x}$ chart (using average range): $\bar{\bar{x}} \pm 3\dfrac{\bar{R}}{d_2\sqrt{n}}$

Control limits for R chart (using average range or sample standard deviation with control chart factors from a table):

$$\text{UCL} = D_4\bar{R}$$
$$\text{LCL} = D_3\bar{R}$$

Capability index (ignores centring): $C_p = \dfrac{\text{USL} - \text{LSL}}{6\sigma}$

Capability index (tests for centring): $C_{pk} = \dfrac{\min(\mu - \text{LSL}, \text{USL} - \mu)}{3\sigma}$

Control limits for p chart: $\pi \pm 3\sqrt{\dfrac{\pi(1 - \pi)}{n}}$

CHAPTER REVIEW

Note: Questions with * are based on optional material.

1. Define (a) quality, (b) process, and (c) productivity. Why are they hard to define? (LO 1)

2. List six general attributes of quality. (LO 1)

3. Distinguish between common cause and special cause variation. (LO 2)

4. In quality improvement, list three roles played by (a) statisticians and (b) managers. (LO 1)

5. Distinguish between (a) internal versus external customers, (b) assigning blame versus seeking solutions, and (c) employee involvement versus top-down decisions. (LO 1)

6. In chronological order, list important phases in the evolution of the quality movement in North America. What is the main change in emphasis over the last 100 years? (LO 1)

7. (a) Who was W. Edwards Deming and why is he remembered? (b) List three of Deming's major ideas and explain them in your own terms. (LO 1)

8. List three influential thinkers other than Deming who made contributions to the quality movement and state their contributions. (LO 1)

9. (a) Briefly explain each acronym: TQM, BPR, SQC, SPC, CQI, DMAIC. (b) List the steps in the continuous quality improvement model. (LO 1)

10. (a) What is shown on the $\bar{x}$ chart? (b) Name three ways to set the control limits on the $\bar{x}$ chart. (c) How can we obtain good empirical control limits for the $\bar{x}$ chart? (d) Why are quality control samples sometimes small? (LO 3)

11. Explain the four rules of thumb for identifying an out-of-control process. (LO 4)

12. (a) What is shown on the R chart? (b) How do we set control limits for the R chart? (LO 3)

13. Name the six abnormal control chart patterns and tell (a) how they may be recognized, and (b) what their likely causes might be. (LO 4)

14. (a) State the formulas for the two capability indexes C_p and C_{pk}. (b) Why isn't C_p alone sufficient? (c) What is considered an acceptable value for these indexes? (d) Why is an *in-control* process not necessarily *capable?* (LO 5)

15. (a) What is shown on the p chart? (b) How do we set control limits for the p chart? (c) Why might the p chart control limits vary from sample to sample? (LO 3)

*16. Briefly explain (a) the overadjustment problem, (b) *ad hoc* control charts, (c) acceptance sampling, (d) supply-chain management, (e) Taguchi's robust design, (f) the Six Sigma philosophy, and (g) ISO 9000.

Instructions: You may use MINITAB, MegaStat, or similar software to assist you in the control chart questions. Data sets for the exercises are on the CD.

CHAPTER EXERCISES

17.30 Explain each chart's purpose and the parameters that must be known or estimated to establish its control limits. (LO 3)
   a. $\bar{x}$ chart
   b. R chart
   c. p chart
   d. I chart

17.31 Define three possible quality metrics (not necessarily the ones actually used) to describe and monitor: (a) your performance in your university classes; (b) effectiveness of the professors in your university classes; (c) your effectiveness in managing your personal finances; (d) your textbook's effectiveness in helping you learn in a university statistics class. (LO 1)

17.32 Define three quality metrics that might be used to describe quality and performance for the following services: (a) your cellular phone service (e.g., Telus); (b) your Internet service provider (e.g., Shaw); (c) your dry cleaning and laundry service; (d) your physician's office; (e) your hairdresser; (f) your favourite fast-food restaurant. Do you think these data are actually collected or used? Why, or why not? (LO 1)

17.33 Define three quality metrics that might be used to describe quality and performance in the following consumer products: (a) your personal vehicle (e.g., car, SUV, truck, bicycle, motorcycle); (b) the printer on your computer; (c) the toilet in your bathroom; (d) a smartphone (e.g., BlackBerry); (e) an HDTV display screen; (f) a light bulb. Do you think these data are actually collected or used? Why, or why not? (LO 1)

17.34 Based on the cost of sampling and the presumed accuracy required, would sampling or 100 percent inspection be used to collect data on (a) the horsepower of each engine being installed in new cars; (b) the fuel consumption per seat mile of each Air Canada flight; (c) the daily percent of customers who order low-carb menu items for each McDonald's restaurant; (d) the life in hours of each lithium ion battery installed in new laptop computers; (e) the number of medication errors per month in a large hospital. (LO 1)

17.35 Why are the control limits for an R chart asymmetric, while those of an $\bar{x}$-chart are symmetric? (LO 3)

17.36 Bob said, "We use the normal distribution to set the control limits for the $\bar{x}$-chart because samples from processes follow a normal distribution." Is Bob right? Explain. (LO 3)

17.37 Bob said, "They must not be using quality control in automobile manufacturing. Just look at the J.D. Power data showing that new cars all seem to have defects." (a) Discuss Bob's assertion, focusing on the concept of variation. (b) Can you think of processes where zero defects *could* be attained on a regular basis? Explain. (c) Can you think of processes where zero defects *cannot* be attained on a regular basis? *Hint:* Consider activities like pass completion by a football quarterback, three-point shots by a basketball player, or multiple-choice exams taken by a university student. (LO 1)

17.38 Use your favourite Internet search engine to look up any four of the following quality experts. Write a one-paragraph biographical sketch *in your own words* that lists his contributions to quality improvement. (LO 1)
   a. Walter A. Shewhart
   b. Harold F. Dodge
   c. Harry G. Romig
   d. Joseph M. Juran
   e. Genichi Taguchi
   f. Kaoru Ishikawa
   g. Armand V. Feigenbaum

17.39 Make a fishbone chart (cause-and-effect diagram) like the following for the reasons you have ever been (or could be) late to class. Use as many branches as necessary. Which factors are most important? Which are most easily controlled? (LO 3)

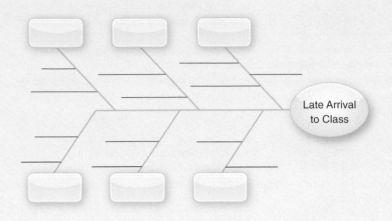

7.40 Make a fishbone chart (cause-and-effect diagram) for the reasons your end-of-month chequebook balance may not match your bank statement. Use as many branches as necessary. Which factors are most important? Which are most easily controlled? (LO 3)

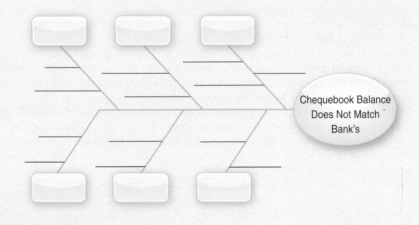

7.41 Make a fishbone chart (cause-and-effect diagram) for the reasons an airline flight might be late to arrive. Use as many branches as necessary. Which factors are most important? Which are most easily controlled? (LO 3)

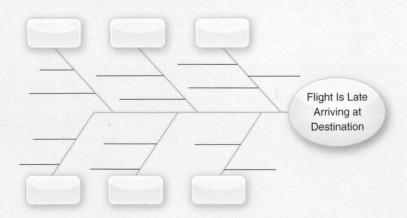

CAPABILITY

17.42 In painting an automobile, the thickness of the colour coat has a lower specification limit of 0.80 mils and an upper specification limit of 1.20 mils. Find the C_p and C_{pk} capability indexes if (a) the process mean is 1.00 mils and the process standard deviation is 0.07 mils; and (b) the process mean is 1.00 mils and the process standard deviation is 0.05 mils. (c) What was the point of this exercise? (LO 5)

17.43 In painting an automobile, the thickness of the colour coat has a lower specification limit of 0.80 mils and an upper specification limit of 1.20 mils. Find the C_p and C_{pk} capability indexes if (a) the process mean is 1.00 mils and the process standard deviation is 0.05 mils; and (b) the process mean is 0.90 mils and the process standard deviation is 0.05 mils. (c) What was the point of this exercise? (LO 5)

17.44 Moisture content per gram of a certain baked product has specification limits of 120 mg and 160 mg. Find the C_p and C_{pk} capability indexes if (a) the process mean is 140 mg and the process standard deviation is 5 mg; and (b) the process mean is 140 mg and the process standard deviation is 3 mg. (c) What was the point of this exercise? (LO 5)

$\bar{x}$ CHARTS

17.45 The yield strength of a metal bolt has a mean of 6,050 pounds with a standard deviation of 100 pounds. Twenty samples of three bolts were tested, resulting in the means shown below. (a) Construct upper and lower control limits for the $\bar{x}$ chart, using the given product parameters. (b) Plot the data on the control chart. (c) Is this process in control? Explain your reasoning. (LO 3)   **Bolts-M**

6,107	6,031	6,075	6,115	6,039	6,079	5,995	6,097	6,114	6,039
6,154	6,054	6,028	6,002	6,062	6,094	6,051	6,031	5,965	6,082

17.46 Refer to the bolt strength problem 17.45. Assume $\mu = 6,050$ and $\sigma = 100$. Use the following 24 *individual* bolt strength observations to answer the questions posed. (a) Prepare a histogram and/or normal probability plot for the sample. (b) Does the sample support the view that yield strength is a normally distributed random variable? (c) Are the sample mean and standard deviation about where they are expected to be? (LO 3)   **Bolts-I**

6,121	6,100	6,007	6,166	6,164	6,032	6,276	6,151
6,054	5,836	6,024	6,105	6,033	6,066	6,079	6,192
6,028	6,087	5,983	6,040	6,062	6,054	6,100	5,983

17.47 In painting an automobile at the factory, the thickness of the colour coat has a process mean of 1.00 mils and a process standard deviation of 0.07 mils. Twenty samples of five cars were tested, resulting in the mean paint thicknesses shown below. (a) Construct upper and lower control limits for the $\bar{x}$ chart, using the given process parameters. (b) Plot the data on the control chart. (c) Is this process in control? Explain your reasoning. (LO 3)   **Paint-M**

0.996	0.960	1.016	1.017	1.001	0.988	1.006	1.073	1.032	1.021
0.984	1.019	0.997	1.024	1.033	1.030	0.994	0.980	0.977	1.037

17.48 Refer to the paint thickness problem 17.47. Assume $\mu = 1.00$ and $\sigma = 0.07$. Use the following 35 *individual* observations on paint thickness to answer the questions posed. (a) Prepare a histogram and/or normal probability plot for the sample. (b) Does the sample support the view that paint thickness is a normally distributed random variable? (c) Are the mean and standard deviation about as expected? (LO 3)   **Paint-I**

1.026	0.949	1.069	1.105	0.995	0.955	1.080
0.932	1.014	0.899	1.031	1.042	1.022	1.082
1.111	0.995	1.005	1.004	0.964	1.065	0.909
0.912	0.978	1.037	0.992	1.010	0.974	0.977
0.905	1.008	0.971	0.951	1.200	1.065	0.972

17.49 The temperature control unit on a commercial freezer in a 24-hour grocery store is set to maintain a mean temperature of -5 degrees Celsius. The temperature varies, because people are constantly opening the freezer door to remove items, but the thermostat is capable of maintaining temperature with a standard deviation of 1 degree Celsius. The desired range is -8 to -2 degrees Celsius. (a) Find the C_p and C_{pk} capability indexes. (b) In words, how would you describe the process capability? (c) If improvement is desired, what might be some obstacles to increasing the capability? (LO 5)

17.50 Refer to the freezer problem 17.49 with $\mu = -5$ and $\sigma = 1$. Temperature measurements are recorded four times a day (at midnight, 0600, 1200, and 1800). Twenty samples of four observations are shown below. (a) Construct upper and lower control limits for the $\bar{x}$ chart, using the given process parameters. (b) Plot the data on the control chart. (c) Is this process in control? Explain your reasoning. (LO 3 & 4) 🎙 **Freezer**

Sample	Midnight	At 0600	At 1200	At 1800	Mean
1	−3.9	−3.3	−5.0	−5.0	−4.3
2	−5.6	−5.0	−2.2	−5.6	−4.6
3	−6.7	−4.4	−3.9	−6.1	−5.3
4	−6.1	−3.9	−5.6	−5.0	−5.1
5	−6.1	−5.0	−6.1	−5.0	−5.6
6	−3.3	−3.9	−2.8	−3.3	−3.3
7	−6.1	−5.0	−3.9	−6.7	−5.4
8	−3.9	−5.0	−5.6	−3.9	−4.6
9	−5.6	−4.4	−4.4	−5.6	−5.0
10	−2.8	−5.0	−3.3	−3.9	−3.8
11	−4.4	−5.0	−6.7	−6.1	−5.6
12	−3.9	−6.1	−5.0	−6.7	−5.4
13	−3.3	−6.1	−6.1	−5.0	−5.1
14	−3.3	−5.6	−3.3	−5.6	−4.4
15	−6.1	−4.4	−6.7	−7.2	−6.1
16	−5.0	−3.3	−5.0	−5.0	−4.6
17	−5.0	−6.1	−4.4	−6.1	−5.4
18	−3.9	−5.6	−5.6	−5.0	−5.0
19	−4.4	−6.7	−6.1	−5.6	−5.7
20	−4.4	−6.1	−5.0	−6.1	−5.4

17.51 Refer to the freezer data's 80 *individual* temperature observations in problem 17.50. (a) Prepare a histogram and/or normal probability plot for the sample. (b) Does the sample support the view that freezer temperature is a normally distributed random variable? (c) Are the sample mean and standard deviation about where they are expected to be? (LO 4)

17.52   A Nabisco Fig Newton has a process mean weight of 14.00 grams with a standard deviation of 0.10 grams. The lower specification limit is 13.40 grams and the upper specification limit is 14.60 grams. (a) Describe the capability of this process, using the techniques you have learned. (b) Would you think that further variance reduction efforts would be a good idea? Explain the pros and cons of such an effort. *Hint:* Use the economic concept of opportunity cost. (LO 5)

17.53   A new type of smoke detector battery is developed. From laboratory tests under standard conditions, the half-life (defined as less than 50 percent of full charge) of 20 batteries are shown below. (a) Make a histogram of the data and/or a probability plot. Do you think that battery half-life can be assumed normal? (b) The engineers say that the mean battery half-life will be 8,760 hours with a standard deviation of 200 hours. Using these parameters (not the sample), set up the centreline and control limits for the $\bar{x}$ chart for a subgroup size of $n = 5$ batteries to be sampled in future production runs. (c) Repeat the previous exercise, but this time, use the sample mean and standard deviation. (d) Do you think that the control limits from this sample would be reliable? Explain, and suggest alternatives. (LO 3)   **Battery**

| 8,502 | 8,660 | 8,785 | 8,778 | 8,804 | 9,069 | 8,516 | 9,048 | 8,628 | 9,213 |
| 8,511 | 8,965 | 8,688 | 8,892 | 8,638 | 8,440 | 8,900 | 8,993 | 8,958 | 8,707 |

17.54   A box of Wheat Chex cereal is to be filled to a mean weight of 466 grams. The lower specification limit is 453 grams (the labelled weight is 453 grams) and the upper specification limit is 477 grams (so as not to overfill the box). The process standard deviation is 2 grams. (a) Find the C_p and C_{pk} capability indexes. (b) Assess the process capability. (c) Why might it be difficult to reduce the variance in this process to raise the capability indices? *Hint:* A single Wheat Chex weighs 0.3 grams (30 mg). (LO 5)

17.55   Refer to the Wheat Chex problem 17.54 with $\mu = 465$ and $\sigma = 3$. During production, samples of three boxes are weighed every five minutes. (a) Find the upper and lower control limit for the $\bar{x}$ chart. (b) Plot the following 20 sample means on the chart. Is the process in control? (LO 3)   **Chex-M**

| 465.7 | 463.7 | 466.0 | 466.3 | 463.0 | 468.3 | 465.0 | 463.3 | 462.0 | 463.0 |
| 465.7 | 467.0 | 463.3 | 466.0 | 465.3 | 465.3 | 463.0 | 466.7 | 466.3 | 466.3 |

17.56   Refer to the Wheat Chex box fill problem 17.54 with $\mu = 465$ and $\sigma = 3$. Below are 30 *individual* observations on box fill. (a) Prepare a histogram and/or normal probability plot for the sample. Does the sample support the view that box fill is a normally distributed random variable? Explain. (b) Is the mean of these 20 same means where it should be? (LO 4)   **Chex-I**

461	465	462	469	463	465	462	465	467	467
460	467	466	466	465	465	462	458	470	460
465	466	464	460	465	465	466	464	465	461

17.57   Each gum drop in two bags of Sathers Gum Drops was weighed (to the nearest 0.001 g) on a sensitive Mettler PE 360 Delta Range scale. After removing one outlier (to improve normality), there were 84 gum drops in the sample, yielding an overall mean $\bar{x} = 11.988$ grams and a pooled standard deviation $s = 0.2208$ grams. (a) Use these sample statistics to construct control limits for an $\bar{x}$ chart, using a subgroup size $n = 6$. (b) Plot the means shown below on your control chart. Is the process in control? (c) Prepare a histogram and/or normal probability plot for the pooled sample. Does the sample support the view that gum drop weight is a normally distributed random variable? Explain. (LO 3)   **GumDrops**

Sample	x_1	x_2	x_3	x_4	x_5	x_6	Mean
1	11.741	11.975	11.985	12.163	12.317	12.032	12.036
2	12.206	11.970	12.179	12.182	11.756	11.975	12.045
3	12.041	12.120	11.855	12.036	11.750	11.870	11.945
4	12.002	11.800	12.092	12.017	12.340	12.488	12.123
5	12.305	12.134	11.949	12.050	12.246	11.839	12.087
6	11.862	12.049	12.105	11.894	11.995	11.722	11.938
7	11.979	12.124	12.171	12.093	12.224	11.965	12.093
8	11.941	11.855	11.587	11.574	11.752	12.345	11.842
9	12.297	12.078	12.137	11.869	11.609	11.732	11.954
10	11.677	11.879	11.926	11.852	11.781	11.932	11.841
11	12.113	12.129	12.156	12.284	12.207	12.247	12.189
12	12.510	11.904	11.675	11.880	12.086	12.458	12.086
13	12.193	11.975	12.173	11.635	11.549	11.744	11.878
14	11.880	11.784	11.696	11.804	11.823	11.693	11.780

p CHARTS

17.58   Past experience indicates that the probability of a post-surgical complication in a certain procedure is 6 percent. A hospital typically performs 200 such surgeries per month. (a) Find the control limits for the monthly p chart. (b) Would it be reasonably safe to assume that the sample proportion X/n is normally distributed? Explain. (LO 3)

17.59   A large retail toy store finds that, on average, a certain cheap (under $20) electronic toy has a 5 percent damage rate during shipping. From each incoming shipment, a sample of 100 is inspected. (a) Find the control limits for a p chart. (b) Plot the 10 samples below on the p chart. Is the process in control? (c) Is the sample size large enough to assume normality of the sample proportion? Explain. (LO 3)   **Toys**

Sample	X	n	X/n
1	3	100	0.03
2	5	100	0.05
3	4	100	0.04
4	7	100	0.07
5	2	100	0.02
6	2	100	0.02
7	0	100	0.00
8	2	100	0.02
9	7	100	0.07
10	6	100	0.06

PATTERNS IN CONTROL CHARTS

17.60   Which abnormal pattern (cycle, instability, level shift, oscillation, trend, mixture), if any, exists in each of the following $\bar{x}$ charts? If you see none, say so. If you see more than one possibility, say so. Explain your reasoning. (LO 4)

Chart A

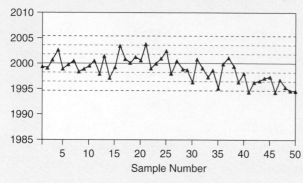

Chart B

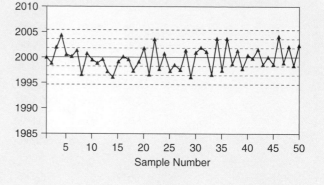

Chart C

Chart D

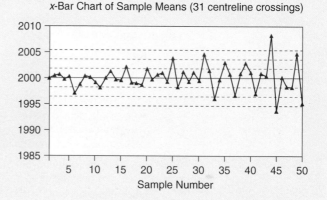

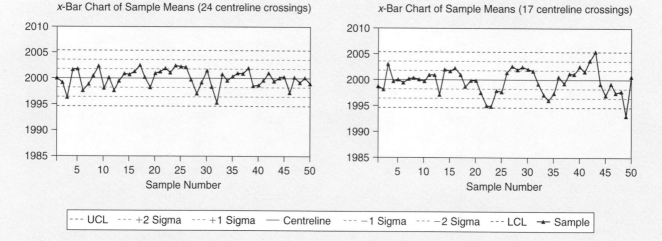

17.61   Referring to Charts A–F, which Rules (1, 2, 3, 4) are violated in each chart? Make a photocopy and circle the points that violate each rule. (LO 4)

17.62   Refer to the bolt strength problem 17.45. Assuming $\mu = 6{,}050$ and $\sigma = 100$ with $n = 3$, then LCL $= 5{,}876.8$ and UCL $= 6{,}223.2$. Below are five sets of 20 sample means using $n = 3$. Test each set of means for the pattern suggested in the column heading. This is a visual judgment question, though you can apply Rules 1–4 if you wish. (LO 4)   **Bolts-P**

Up Trend?	Down Trend?	Unstable?	Cycle?	Oscillate?
5,907	6,100	6,048	6,079	6,122
6,060	6,009	5,975	6,029	5,983
5,987	6,145	6,092	6,006	6,105
5,919	6,049	5,894	6,012	6,024
6,029	6,039	6,083	6,098	6,123
6,114	5,956	6,069	6,124	6,022
6,063	6,103	6,073	6,092	6,082
6,084	6,140	5,972	6,114	6,018
5,980	6,054	6,112	6,071	6,031
6,056	6,062	5,988	6,097	6,107
6,078	6,042	6,006	6,038	6,031
6,118	6,152	6,226	6,099	6,047
6,051	5,961	5,989	6,000	6,055
6,021	5,926	6,111	6,004	6,041
6,068	6,109	6,026	6,054	5,972
6,157	5,904	6,057	6,083	5,987
6,041	6,049	6,098	6,148	6,043
6,129	6,042	6,082	6,071	6,137
6,026	5,847	6,050	6,095	5,930
6,174	6,033	6,084	6,092	6,057

17.63 Refer to the paint problem 17.47 with $\mu = 1.00$ and $\sigma = 0.07$. With $n = 5$, LCL = 0.906 and UCL = 1.094. Below are five sets of 20 sample means using $n = 5$. Test each set of means for the pattern suggested in the column heading. This is a visual judgment question, though you can apply Rules 1–4 if you wish. (LO 4) 　**Paint-P**

No Pattern?	Up Trend?	Down Trend?	Unstable?	Cycle?
0.996	0.995	1.007	0.999	0.964
0.960	0.942	1.000	0.986	1.025
1.016	0.947	1.011	0.950	0.988
1.017	1.011	0.989	0.982	1.000
1.001	0.983	0.999	0.967	1.023
0.988	0.989	1.000	0.972	1.019
1.006	0.978	1.025	0.977	1.035
1.073	0.958	0.963	1.015	1.043
1.032	1.034	1.060	0.970	1.044
1.021	1.058	1.020	1.016	0.993
0.984	1.058	0.977	0.979	0.994
1.019	0.958	0.985	0.934	0.988
0.997	1.030	1.033	0.975	0.991
1.024	1.022	0.975	1.100	1.001
1.033	0.976	0.939	0.976	1.011
1.030	1.024	1.007	0.976	1.015
0.994	1.032	0.994	1.029	1.000
0.980	0.994	0.990	0.987	1.010
0.977	1.016	0.925	0.954	1.061
1.037	1.039	0.907	1.011	1.001

DO IT YOURSELF

17.64   Buy a bag of M&Ms. (a) As a measure of quality, take a sample of 100 M&Ms and count the number with incomplete or illegible "M" printed on them. (b) Calculate the sample proportion with defects. (c) What ambiguity (if any) did you encounter in this task? (d) Do you feel that your sample was large enough? Explain. (LO 3)

17.65   Examine a square metre (or another convenient unit) of paint on your car's driver door. Be sure the area is clean. (a) Tally the number of paint defects (scratch, abrasion, embedded dirt, chip, dent, rust, other). You may add your own defect categories. (b) Repeat, using a friend's car that is either older or newer than yours. (c) State your findings succinctly. (LO 3)

17.66   Buy a box of Cheerios (or your favourite breakfast cereal). (a) As a measure of quality, take a sample of 100 Cheerios, and count the number of Cheerios that are broken. (b) Calculate the sample proportion with defects. (c) What ambiguity (if any) did you encounter in this task? (d) Do you feel that your sample was truly random? Explain. (LO 3)

LearningStats Unit 17   Quality   LS

LearningStats Unit 17 illustrates the tools and applications of statistical process control, capability analysis, and control chart patterns. Your instructor may assign specific modules, or you may pursue those that sound interesting.

Topic	LearningStats Modules
Quality overview	Quality Overview
	Process Control Overview
Terminology	Terminology of Quality
Control charts	Basic Control Charts
	Other Control Charts
Capability	Capability Explained
	Capability Indexes
	Moving Range
Control chart patterns and rules	Control Chart Patterns
Student reports	Level Shift and Trend
	Cycle and Oscillation
	Mixtures and Instability
Other	What Is Six Sigma?

Key: = PowerPoint   = Excel

Visual Statistics   VS

Visual Statistics Modules on Quality

Module	Module Name
21	Visualizing Statistical Process Control
13	Visualizing Goodness-of-Fit Tests

Visual Statistics Modules 21 and 13 are designed to help you

- Understand how control limits are constructed.
- Be able to interpret simple control charts.
- Recognize out-of-control processes and their typical causes.
- Apply pattern recognition rules to control charts.
- Test a sample for normality.

The worktext (included on the CD in PDF format) contains lists of concepts covered, objectives of the modules, overviews of concepts, illustrations of concepts, orientations to module features, learning exercises (basic, intermediate, advanced), learning projects (individual, team), self-evaluation quizzes, glossaries of terms, and solutions to self-evaluation quizzes.

APPENDIX A

Cumulative Binomial Probabilities

$$P(X \le k) = \sum_{x=1}^{k} P(x)$$

n = 3

k	P												
	0.01	0.05	0.1	0.2	0.3	0.4	0.5	0.6	0.7	0.8	0.9	0.95	0.99
0	0.9703	0.8574	0.7290	0.5120	0.3430	0.2160	0.1250	0.0640	0.0270	0.0080	0.0010	0.0001	0.0000
1	0.9997	0.9928	0.9720	0.8960	0.7840	0.6480	0.5000	0.3520	0.2160	0.1040	0.0280	0.0073	0.0003
2	1.0000	0.9999	0.9990	0.9920	0.9730	0.9360	0.8750	0.7840	0.6570	0.4880	0.2710	0.1426	0.0297
3	1.0000	1.0000	1.0000	1.0000	1.0000	1.0000	1.0000	1.0000	1.0000	1.0000	1.0000	1.0000	1.0000

n = 5

k	P												
	0.01	0.05	0.1	0.2	0.3	0.4	0.5	0.6	0.7	0.8	0.9	0.95	0.99
0	0.9510	0.7738	0.5905	0.3277	0.1681	0.0778	0.0313	0.0102	0.0024	0.0003	0.0000	0.0000	0.0000
1	0.9990	0.9774	0.9185	0.7373	0.5282	0.3370	0.1875	0.0870	0.0308	0.0067	0.0005	0.0000	0.0000
2	1.0000	0.9988	0.9914	0.9421	0.8369	0.6826	0.5000	0.3174	0.1631	0.0579	0.0086	0.0012	0.0000
3	1.0000	1.0000	0.9995	0.9933	0.9692	0.9130	0.8125	0.6630	0.4718	0.2627	0.0815	0.0226	0.0010
4	1.0000	1.0000	1.0000	0.9997	0.9976	0.9898	0.9688	0.9222	0.8319	0.6723	0.4095	0.2262	0.0490
5	1.0000	1.0000	1.0000	1.0000	1.0000	1.0000	1.0000	1.0000	1.0000	1.0000	1.0000	1.0000	1.0000

n = 6

k	P												
	0.01	0.05	0.1	0.2	0.3	0.4	0.5	0.6	0.7	0.8	0.9	0.95	0.99
0	0.9415	0.7351	0.5314	0.2621	0.1176	0.0467	0.0156	0.0041	0.0007	0.0001	0.0000	0.0000	0.0000
1	0.9985	0.9672	0.8857	0.6554	0.4202	0.2333	0.1094	0.0410	0.0109	0.0016	0.0001	0.0000	0.0000
2	1.0000	0.9978	0.9842	0.9011	0.7443	0.5443	0.3438	0.1792	0.0705	0.0170	0.0013	0.0001	0.0000
3	1.0000	0.9999	0.9987	0.9830	0.9295	0.8208	0.6563	0.4557	0.2557	0.0989	0.0159	0.0022	0.0000
4	1.0000	1.0000	0.9999	0.9984	0.9891	0.9590	0.8906	0.7667	0.5798	0.3446	0.1143	0.0328	0.0015
5	1.0000	1.0000	1.0000	0.9999	0.9993	0.9959	0.9844	0.9533	0.8824	0.7379	0.4686	0.2649	0.0585
6	1.0000	1.0000	1.0000	1.0000	1.0000	1.0000	1.0000	1.0000	1.0000	1.0000	1.0000	1.0000	1.0000

n = 7

k	P												
	0.01	0.05	0.1	0.2	0.3	0.4	0.5	0.6	0.7	0.8	0.9	0.95	0.99
0	0.9321	0.6983	0.4783	0.2097	0.0824	0.0280	0.0078	0.0016	0.0002	0.0000	0.0000	0.0000	0.0000
1	0.9980	0.9556	0.8503	0.5767	0.3294	0.1586	0.0625	0.0188	0.0038	0.0004	0.0000	0.0000	0.0000
2	1.0000	0.9962	0.9743	0.8520	0.6471	0.4199	0.2266	0.0963	0.0288	0.0047	0.0002	0.0000	0.0000
3	1.0000	0.9998	0.9973	0.9667	0.8740	0.7102	0.5000	0.2898	0.1260	0.0333	0.0027	0.0002	0.0000
4	1.0000	1.0000	0.9998	0.9953	0.9712	0.9037	0.7734	0.5801	0.3529	0.1480	0.0257	0.0038	0.0000
5	1.0000	1.0000	1.0000	0.9996	0.9962	0.9812	0.9375	0.8414	0.6706	0.4233	0.1497	0.0444	0.0020
6	1.0000	1.0000	1.0000	1.0000	0.9998	0.9984	0.9922	0.9720	0.9176	0.7903	0.5217	0.3017	0.0679
7	1.0000	1.0000	1.0000	1.0000	1.0000	1.0000	1.0000	1.0000	1.0000	1.0000	1.0000	1.0000	1.0000

n = 8

k	0.01	0.05	0.1	0.2	0.3	0.4	P 0.5	0.6	0.7	0.8	0.9	0.95	0.99
0	0.9227	0.6634	0.4305	0.1678	0.0576	0.0168	0.0039	0.0007	0.0001	0.0000	0.0000	0.0000	0.0000
1	0.9973	0.9428	0.8131	0.5033	0.2553	0.1064	0.0352	0.0085	0.0013	0.0001	0.0000	0.0000	0.0000
2	0.9999	0.9942	0.9619	0.7969	0.5518	0.3154	0.1445	0.0498	0.0113	0.0012	0.0000	0.0000	0.0000
3	1.0000	0.9996	0.9950	0.9437	0.8059	0.5941	0.3633	0.1737	0.0580	0.0104	0.0004	0.0000	0.0000
4	1.0000	1.0000	0.9996	0.9896	0.9420	0.8263	0.6367	0.4059	0.1941	0.0563	0.0050	0.0004	0.0000
5	1.0000	1.0000	1.0000	0.9988	0.9887	0.9502	0.8555	0.6846	0.4482	0.2031	0.0381	0.0058	0.0001
6	1.0000	1.0000	1.0000	0.9999	0.9987	0.9915	0.9648	0.8936	0.7447	0.4967	0.1869	0.0572	0.0027
7	1.0000	1.0000	1.0000	1.0000	0.9999	0.9993	0.9961	0.9832	0.9424	0.8322	0.5695	0.3366	0.0773
8	1.0000	1.0000	1.0000	1.0000	1.0000	1.0000	1.0000	1.0000	1.0000	1.0000	1.0000	1.0000	1.0000

n = 9

k	0.01	0.05	0.1	0.2	0.3	0.4	P 0.5	0.6	0.7	0.8	0.9	0.95	0.99
0	0.9135	0.6302	0.3874	0.1342	0.0404	0.0101	0.0020	0.0003	0.0000	0.0000	0.0000	0.0000	0.0000
1	0.9966	0.9288	0.7748	0.4362	0.1960	0.0705	0.0195	0.0038	0.0004	0.0000	0.0000	0.0000	0.0000
2	0.9999	0.9916	0.9470	0.7382	0.4628	0.2318	0.0898	0.0250	0.0043	0.0003	0.0000	0.0000	0.0000
3	1.0000	0.9994	0.9917	0.9144	0.7297	0.4826	0.2539	0.0994	0.0253	0.0031	0.0001	0.0000	0.0000
4	1.0000	1.0000	0.9991	0.9804	0.9012	0.7334	0.5000	0.2666	0.0988	0.0196	0.0009	0.0000	0.0000
5	1.0000	1.0000	0.9999	0.9969	0.9747	0.9006	0.7461	0.5174	0.2703	0.0856	0.0083	0.0006	0.0000
6	1.0000	1.0000	1.0000	0.9997	0.9957	0.9750	0.9102	0.7682	0.5372	0.2618	0.0530	0.0084	0.0001
7	1.0000	1.0000	1.0000	1.0000	0.9996	0.9962	0.9805	0.9295	0.8040	0.5638	0.2252	0.0712	0.0034
8	1.0000	1.0000	1.0000	1.0000	1.0000	0.9997	0.9980	0.9899	0.9596	0.8658	0.6126	0.3698	0.0865
9	1.0000	1.0000	1.0000	1.0000	1.0000	1.0000	1.0000	1.0000	1.0000	1.0000	1.0000	1.0000	1.0000

n = 10

k	0.01	0.05	0.1	0.2	0.3	0.4	P 0.5	0.6	0.7	0.8	0.9	0.95	0.99
0	0.9044	0.5987	0.3487	0.1074	0.0282	0.0060	0.0010	0.0001	0.0000	0.0000	0.0000	0.0000	0.0000
1	0.9957	0.9139	0.7361	0.3758	0.1493	0.0464	0.0107	0.0017	0.0001	0.0000	0.0000	0.0000	0.0000
2	0.9999	0.9885	0.9298	0.6778	0.3828	0.1673	0.0547	0.0123	0.0016	0.0001	0.0000	0.0000	0.0000
3	1.0000	0.9990	0.9872	0.8791	0.6496	0.3823	0.1719	0.0548	0.0106	0.0009	0.0000	0.0000	0.0000
4	1.0000	0.9999	0.9984	0.9672	0.8497	0.6331	0.3770	0.1662	0.0473	0.0064	0.0001	0.0000	0.0000
5	1.0000	1.0000	0.9999	0.9936	0.9527	0.8338	0.6230	0.3669	0.1503	0.0328	0.0016	0.0001	0.0000
6	1.0000	1.0000	1.0000	0.9991	0.9894	0.9452	0.8281	0.6177	0.3504	0.1209	0.0128	0.0010	0.0000
7	1.0000	1.0000	1.0000	0.9999	0.9984	0.9877	0.9453	0.8327	0.6172	0.3222	0.0702	0.0115	0.0001
8	1.0000	1.0000	1.0000	1.0000	0.9999	0.9983	0.9893	0.9536	0.8507	0.6242	0.2639	0.0861	0.0043
9	1.0000	1.0000	1.0000	1.0000	1.0000	0.9999	0.9990	0.9940	0.9718	0.8926	0.6513	0.4013	0.0956
10	1.0000	1.0000	1.0000	1.0000	1.0000	1.0000	1.0000	1.0000	1.0000	1.0000	1.0000	1.0000	1.0000

n = 12

k	P 0.01	0.05	0.1	0.2	0.3	0.4	0.5	0.6	0.7	0.8	0.9	0.95	0.99
0	0.8864	0.5404	0.2824	0.0687	0.0138	0.0022	0.0002	0.0000	0.0000	0.0000	0.0000	0.0000	0.0000
1	0.9938	0.8816	0.6590	0.2749	0.0850	0.0196	0.0032	0.0003	0.0000	0.0000	0.0000	0.0000	0.0000
2	0.9998	0.9804	0.8891	0.5583	0.2528	0.0834	0.0193	0.0028	0.0002	0.0000	0.0000	0.0000	0.0000
3	1.0000	0.9978	0.9744	0.7946	0.4925	0.2253	0.0730	0.0153	0.0017	0.0001	0.0000	0.0000	0.0000
4	1.0000	0.9998	0.9957	0.9274	0.7237	0.4382	0.1938	0.0573	0.0095	0.0006	0.0000	0.0000	0.0000
5	1.0000	1.0000	0.9995	0.9806	0.8822	0.6652	0.3872	0.1582	0.0386	0.0039	0.0001	0.0000	0.0000
6	1.0000	1.0000	0.9999	0.9961	0.9614	0.8418	0.6128	0.3348	0.1178	0.0194	0.0005	0.0000	0.0000
7	1.0000	1.0000	1.0000	0.9994	0.9905	0.9427	0.8062	0.5618	0.2763	0.0726	0.0043	0.0002	0.0000
8	1.0000	1.0000	1.0000	0.9999	0.9983	0.9847	0.9270	0.7747	0.5075	0.2054	0.0256	0.0022	0.0000
9	1.0000	1.0000	1.0000	1.0000	0.9998	0.9972	0.9807	0.9166	0.7472	0.4417	0.1109	0.0196	0.0002
10	1.0000	1.0000	1.0000	1.0000	1.0000	0.9997	0.9968	0.9804	0.9150	0.7251	0.3410	0.1184	0.0062
11	1.0000	1.0000	1.0000	1.0000	1.0000	1.0000	0.9998	0.9978	0.9862	0.9313	0.7176	0.4596	0.1136
12	1.0000	1.0000	1.0000	1.0000	1.0000	1.0000	1.0000	1.0000	1.0000	1.0000	1.0000	1.0000	1.0000

n = 15

k	P 0.01	0.05	0.1	0.2	0.3	0.4	0.5	0.6	0.7	0.8	0.9	0.95	0.99
0	0.8601	0.4633	0.2059	0.0352	0.0047	0.0005	0.0000	0.0000	0.0000	0.0000	0.0000	0.0000	0.0000
1	0.9904	0.8290	0.5490	0.1671	0.0353	0.0052	0.0005	0.0000	0.0000	0.0000	0.0000	0.0000	0.0000
2	0.9996	0.9638	0.8159	0.3980	0.1268	0.0271	0.0037	0.0003	0.0000	0.0000	0.0000	0.0000	0.0000
3	1.0000	0.9945	0.9444	0.6482	0.2969	0.0905	0.0176	0.0019	0.0001	0.0000	0.0000	0.0000	0.0000
4	1.0000	0.9994	0.9873	0.8358	0.5155	0.2173	0.0592	0.0093	0.0007	0.0000	0.0000	0.0000	0.0000
5	1.0000	0.9999	0.9978	0.9389	0.7216	0.4032	0.1509	0.0338	0.0037	0.0001	0.0000	0.0000	0.0000
6	1.0000	1.0000	0.9997	0.9819	0.8689	0.6098	0.3036	0.0950	0.0152	0.0008	0.0000	0.0000	0.0000
7	1.0000	1.0000	1.0000	0.9958	0.9500	0.7869	0.5000	0.2131	0.0500	0.0042	0.0000	0.0000	0.0000
8	1.0000	1.0000	1.0000	0.9992	0.9848	0.9050	0.6964	0.3902	0.1311	0.0181	0.0003	0.0000	0.0000
9	1.0000	1.0000	1.0000	0.9999	0.9963	0.9662	0.8491	0.5968	0.2784	0.0611	0.0022	0.0001	0.0000
10	1.0000	1.0000	1.0000	1.0000	0.9993	0.9907	0.9408	0.7827	0.4845	0.1642	0.0127	0.0006	0.0000
11	1.0000	1.0000	1.0000	1.0000	0.9999	0.9981	0.9824	0.9095	0.7031	0.3518	0.0556	0.0055	0.0000
12	1.0000	1.0000	1.0000	1.0000	1.0000	0.9997	0.9963	0.9729	0.8732	0.6020	0.1841	0.0362	0.0004
13	1.0000	1.0000	1.0000	1.0000	1.0000	1.0000	0.9995	0.9948	0.9647	0.8329	0.4510	0.1710	0.0096
14	1.0000	1.0000	1.0000	1.0000	1.0000	1.0000	1.0000	0.9995	0.9953	0.9648	0.7941	0.5367	0.1399
15	1.0000	1.0000	1.0000	1.0000	1.0000	1.0000	1.0000	1.0000	1.0000	1.0000	1.0000	1.0000	1.0000

n = 20

k	P 0.01	0.05	0.1	0.2	0.3	0.4	0.5	0.6	0.7	0.8	0.9	0.95	0.99
0	0.8179	0.3585	0.1216	0.0115	0.0008	0.0000	0.0000	0.0000	0.0000	0.0000	0.0000	0.0000	0.0000
1	0.9831	0.7358	0.3917	0.0692	0.0076	0.0005	0.0000	0.0000	0.0000	0.0000	0.0000	0.0000	0.0000
2	0.9990	0.9245	0.6769	0.2061	0.0355	0.0036	0.0002	0.0000	0.0000	0.0000	0.0000	0.0000	0.0000
3	1.0000	0.9841	0.8670	0.4114	0.1071	0.0160	0.0013	0.0000	0.0000	0.0000	0.0000	0.0000	0.0000
4	1.0000	0.9974	0.9568	0.6296	0.2375	0.0510	0.0059	0.0003	0.0000	0.0000	0.0000	0.0000	0.0000
5	1.0000	0.9997	0.9887	0.8042	0.4164	0.1256	0.0207	0.0016	0.0000	0.0000	0.0000	0.0000	0.0000
6	1.0000	1.0000	0.9976	0.9133	0.6080	0.2500	0.0577	0.0065	0.0003	0.0000	0.0000	0.0000	0.0000
7	1.0000	1.0000	0.9996	0.9679	0.7723	0.4159	0.1316	0.0210	0.0013	0.0000	0.0000	0.0000	0.0000
8	1.0000	1.0000	0.9999	0.9900	0.8867	0.5956	0.2517	0.0565	0.0051	0.0001	0.0000	0.0000	0.0000
9	1.0000	1.0000	1.0000	0.9974	0.9520	0.7553	0.4119	0.1275	0.0171	0.0006	0.0000	0.0000	0.0000

k	0.01	0.05	0.1	0.2	0.3	0.4	0.5	0.6	0.7	0.8	0.9	0.95	0.99
10	1.0000	1.0000	1.0000	0.9994	0.9829	0.8725	0.5881	0.2447	0.0480	0.0026	0.0000	0.0000	0.0000
11	1.0000	1.0000	1.0000	0.9999	0.9949	0.9435	0.7483	0.4044	0.1133	0.0100	0.0001	0.0000	0.0000
12	1.0000	1.0000	1.0000	1.0000	0.9987	0.9790	0.8684	0.5841	0.2277	0.0321	0.0004	0.0000	0.0000
13	1.0000	1.0000	1.0000	1.0000	0.9997	0.9935	0.9423	0.7500	0.3920	0.0867	0.0024	0.0000	0.0000
14	1.0000	1.0000	1.0000	1.0000	1.0000	0.9984	0.9793	0.8744	0.5836	0.1958	0.0113	0.0003	0.0000
15	1.0000	1.0000	1.0000	1.0000	1.0000	0.9997	0.9941	0.9490	0.7625	0.3704	0.0432	0.0026	0.0000
16	1.0000	1.0000	1.0000	1.0000	1.0000	1.0000	0.9987	0.9840	0.8929	0.5886	0.1330	0.0159	0.0000
17	1.0000	1.0000	1.0000	1.0000	1.0000	1.0000	0.9998	0.9964	0.9645	0.7939	0.3231	0.0755	0.0010
18	1.0000	1.0000	1.0000	1.0000	1.0000	1.0000	1.0000	0.9995	0.9924	0.9308	0.6083	0.2642	0.0169
19	1.0000	1.0000	1.0000	1.0000	1.0000	1.0000	1.0000	1.0000	0.9992	0.9885	0.8784	0.6415	0.1821
20	1.0000	1.0000	1.0000	1.0000	1.0000	1.0000	1.0000	1.0000	1.0000	1.0000	1.0000	1.0000	1.0000

n = 25

k	0.01	0.05	0.1	0.2	0.3	0.4	0.5	0.6	0.7	0.8	0.9	0.95	0.99
0	0.7778	0.2774	0.0718	0.0038	0.0001	0.0000	0.0000	0.0000	0.0000	0.0000	0.0000	0.0000	0.0000
1	0.9742	0.6424	0.2712	0.0274	0.0016	0.0001	0.0000	0.0000	0.0000	0.0000	0.0000	0.0000	0.0000
2	0.9980	0.8729	0.5371	0.0982	0.0090	0.0004	0.0000	0.0000	0.0000	0.0000	0.0000	0.0000	0.0000
3	0.9999	0.9659	0.7636	0.2340	0.0332	0.0024	0.0001	0.0000	0.0000	0.0000	0.0000	0.0000	0.0000
4	1.0000	0.9928	0.9020	0.4207	0.0905	0.0095	0.0005	0.0000	0.0000	0.0000	0.0000	0.0000	0.0000
5	1.0000	0.9988	0.9666	0.6167	0.1935	0.0294	0.0020	0.0001	0.0000	0.0000	0.0000	0.0000	0.0000
6	1.0000	0.9998	0.9905	0.7800	0.3407	0.0736	0.0073	0.0003	0.0000	0.0000	0.0000	0.0000	0.0000
7	1.0000	1.0000	0.9977	0.8909	0.5118	0.1536	0.0216	0.0012	0.0000	0.0000	0.0000	0.0000	0.0000
8	1.0000	1.0000	0.9995	0.9532	0.6769	0.2735	0.0539	0.0043	0.0001	0.0000	0.0000	0.0000	0.0000
9	1.0000	1.0000	0.9999	0.9827	0.8106	0.4246	0.1148	0.0132	0.0005	0.0000	0.0000	0.0000	0.0000
10	1.0000	1.0000	1.0000	0.9944	0.9022	0.5858	0.2122	0.0344	0.0018	0.0000	0.0000	0.0000	0.0000
11	1.0000	1.0000	1.0000	0.9985	0.9558	0.7323	0.3450	0.0778	0.0060	0.0001	0.0000	0.0000	0.0000
12	1.0000	1.0000	1.0000	0.9996	0.9825	0.8462	0.5000	0.1538	0.0175	0.0004	0.0000	0.0000	0.0000
13	1.0000	1.0000	1.0000	0.9999	0.9940	0.9222	0.6550	0.2677	0.0442	0.0015	0.0000	0.0000	0.0000
14	1.0000	1.0000	1.0000	1.0000	0.9982	0.9656	0.7878	0.4142	0.0978	0.0056	0.0000	0.0000	0.0000
15	1.0000	1.0000	1.0000	1.0000	0.9995	0.9868	0.8852	0.5754	0.1894	0.0173	0.0001	0.0000	0.0000
16	1.0000	1.0000	1.0000	1.0000	0.9999	0.9957	0.9461	0.7265	0.3231	0.0468	0.0005	0.0000	0.0000
17	1.0000	1.0000	1.0000	1.0000	1.0000	0.9988	0.9784	0.8464	0.4882	0.1091	0.0023	0.0000	0.0000
18	1.0000	1.0000	1.0000	1.0000	1.0000	0.9997	0.9927	0.9264	0.6593	0.2200	0.0095	0.0002	0.0000
19	1.0000	1.0000	1.0000	1.0000	1.0000	0.9999	0.9980	0.9706	0.8065	0.3833	0.0334	0.0012	0.0000
20	1.0000	1.0000	1.0000	1.0000	1.0000	1.0000	0.9995	0.9905	0.9095	0.5793	0.0980	0.0072	0.0000
21	1.0000	1.0000	1.0000	1.0000	1.0000	1.0000	0.9999	0.9976	0.9668	0.7660	0.2364	0.0341	0.0001
22	1.0000	1.0000	1.0000	1.0000	1.0000	1.0000	1.0000	0.9996	0.9910	0.9018	0.4629	0.1271	0.0020
23	1.0000	1.0000	1.0000	1.0000	1.0000	1.0000	1.0000	0.9999	0.9984	0.9726	0.7288	0.3576	0.0258
24	1.0000	1.0000	1.0000	1.0000	1.0000	1.0000	1.0000	1.0000	0.9999	0.9962	0.9282	0.7226	0.2222
25	1.0000	1.0000	1.0000	1.0000	1.0000	1.0000	1.0000	1.0000	1.0000	1.0000	1.0000	1.0000	1.0000

APPENDIX B

Cumulative Poisson Probabilities

$$P(X \le k) = \sum_{x=0}^{k} P(x)$$

k	λ 0.1	0.2	0.3	0.4	0.5	0.6	0.7	0.8	0.9	1	1.1	1.2
0	0.9048	0.8187	0.7408	0.6703	0.6065	0.5488	0.4966	0.4493	0.4066	0.3679	0.3329	0.3012
1	0.9953	0.9825	0.9631	0.9384	0.9098	0.8781	0.8442	0.8088	0.7725	0.7358	0.6990	0.6626
2	0.9998	0.9989	0.9964	0.9921	0.9856	0.9769	0.9659	0.9526	0.9371	0.9197	0.9004	0.8795
3	1.0000	0.9999	0.9997	0.9992	0.9982	0.9966	0.9942	0.9909	0.9865	0.9810	0.9743	0.9662
4		1.0000	1.0000	0.9999	0.9998	0.9996	0.9992	0.9986	0.9977	0.9963	0.9946	0.9923
5				1.0000	1.0000	1.0000	0.9999	0.9998	0.9997	0.9994	0.9990	0.9985
6							1.0000	1.0000	1.0000	0.9999	0.9999	0.9997
7										1.0000	1.0000	1.0000

k	λ 1.3	1.4	1.5	1.6	1.7	1.8	1.9	2	2.1	2.2	2.3	2.4
0	0.2725	0.2466	0.2231	0.2019	0.1827	0.1653	0.1496	0.1353	0.1225	0.1108	0.1003	0.0907
1	0.6268	0.5918	0.5578	0.5249	0.4932	0.4628	0.4337	0.4060	0.3796	0.3546	0.3309	0.3084
2	0.8571	0.8335	0.8088	0.7834	0.7572	0.7306	0.7037	0.6767	0.6496	0.6227	0.5960	0.5697
3	0.9569	0.9463	0.9344	0.9212	0.9068	0.8913	0.8747	0.8571	0.8386	0.8194	0.7993	0.7787
4	0.9893	0.9857	0.9814	0.9763	0.9704	0.9636	0.9559	0.9473	0.9379	0.9275	0.9162	0.9041
5	0.9978	0.9968	0.9955	0.9940	0.9920	0.9896	0.9868	0.9834	0.9796	0.9751	0.9700	0.9643
6	0.9996	0.9994	0.9991	0.9987	0.9981	0.9974	0.9966	0.9955	0.9941	0.9925	0.9906	0.9884
7	0.9999	0.9999	0.9998	0.9997	0.9996	0.9994	0.9992	0.9989	0.9985	0.9980	0.9974	0.9967
8	1.0000	1.0000	1.0000	1.0000	0.9999	0.9999	0.9998	0.9998	0.9997	0.9995	0.9994	0.9991
9					1.0000	1.0000	1.0000	1.0000	0.9999	0.9999	0.9999	0.9998
10									1.0000	1.0000	1.0000	1.0000

k	λ 2.5	2.6	2.7	2.8	2.9	3	3.1	3.2	3.3	3.4	3.5	3.6
0	0.0821	0.0743	0.0672	0.0608	0.0550	0.0498	0.045	0.0408	0.0369	0.0334	0.0302	0.0273
1	0.2873	0.2674	0.2487	0.2311	0.2146	0.1991	0.1847	0.1712	0.1586	0.1468	0.1359	0.1257
2	0.5438	0.5184	0.4936	0.4695	0.4460	0.4232	0.4012	0.3799	0.3594	0.3397	0.3208	0.3027
3	0.7576	0.7360	0.7141	0.6919	0.6696	0.6472	0.6248	0.6025	0.5803	0.5584	0.5366	0.5152
4	0.8912	0.8774	0.8629	0.8477	0.8318	0.8153	0.7982	0.7806	0.7626	0.7442	0.7254	0.7064
5	0.9580	0.9510	0.9433	0.9349	0.9258	0.9161	0.9057	0.8946	0.8829	0.8705	0.8576	0.8441
6	0.9858	0.9828	0.9794	0.9756	0.9713	0.9665	0.9612	0.9554	0.9490	0.9421	0.9347	0.9267
7	0.9958	0.9947	0.9934	0.9919	0.9901	0.9881	0.9858	0.9832	0.9802	0.9769	0.9733	0.9692
8	0.9989	0.9985	0.9981	0.9976	0.9969	0.9962	0.9953	0.9943	0.9931	0.9917	0.9901	0.9883

	λ											
k	2.5	2.6	2.7	2.8	2.9	3	3.1	3.2	3.3	3.4	3.5	3.6
9	0.9997	0.9996	0.9995	0.9993	0.9991	0.9989	0.9986	0.9982	0.9978	0.9973	0.9967	0.9960
10	0.9999	0.9999	0.9999	0.9998	0.9998	0.9997	0.9996	0.9995	0.9994	0.9992	0.9990	0.9987
11	1.0000	1.0000	1.0000	1.0000	0.9999	0.9999	0.9999	0.9999	0.9998	0.9998	0.9997	0.9996
12					1.0000	1.0000	1.0000	1.0000	1.0000	0.9999	0.9999	0.9999
13										1.0000	1.0000	1.0000

	λ											
k	3.7	3.8	3.9	4	4.1	4.2	4.3	4.4	4.5	4.6	4.7	4.8
0	0.0247	0.0224	0.0202	0.0183	0.0166	0.0150	0.0136	0.0123	0.0111	0.0101	0.0091	0.0082
1	0.1162	0.1074	0.0992	0.0916	0.0845	0.0780	0.0719	0.0663	0.0611	0.0563	0.0518	0.0477
2	0.2854	0.2689	0.2531	0.2381	0.2238	0.2102	0.1974	0.1851	0.1736	0.1626	0.1523	0.1425
3	0.4942	0.4735	0.4532	0.4335	0.4142	0.3954	0.3772	0.3594	0.3423	0.3257	0.3097	0.2942
4	0.6872	0.6678	0.6484	0.6288	0.6093	0.5898	0.5704	0.5512	0.5321	0.5132	0.4946	0.4763
5	0.8301	0.8156	0.8006	0.7851	0.7693	0.7531	0.7367	0.7199	0.7029	0.6858	0.6684	0.6510
6	0.9182	0.9091	0.8995	0.8893	0.8786	0.8675	0.8558	0.8436	0.8311	0.8180	0.8046	0.7908
7	0.9648	0.9599	0.9546	0.9489	0.9427	0.9361	0.9290	0.9214	0.9134	0.9049	0.8960	0.8867
8	0.9863	0.9840	0.9815	0.9786	0.9755	0.9721	0.9683	0.9642	0.9597	0.9549	0.9497	0.9442
9	0.9952	0.9942	0.9931	0.9919	0.9905	0.9889	0.9871	0.9851	0.9829	0.9805	0.9778	0.9749
10	0.9984	0.9981	0.9977	0.9972	0.9966	0.9959	0.9952	0.9943	0.9933	0.9922	0.9910	0.9896
11	0.9995	0.9994	0.9993	0.9991	0.9989	0.9986	0.9983	0.9980	0.9976	0.9971	0.9966	0.9960
12	0.9999	0.9998	0.9998	0.9997	0.9997	0.9996	0.9995	0.9993	0.9992	0.9990	0.9988	0.9986
13	1.0000	1.0000	0.9999	0.9999	0.9999	0.9999	0.9998	0.9998	0.9997	0.9997	0.9996	0.9995
14			1.0000	1.0000	1.0000	1.0000	1.0000	0.9999	0.9999	0.9999	0.9999	0.9999
15								1.0000	1.0000	1.0000	1.0000	1.0000

	λ											
k	4.9	5	5.1	5.2	5.3	5.4	5.5	5.6	5.7	5.8	5.9	6
0	0.0074	0.0067	0.0061	0.0055	0.0050	0.0045	0.0041	0.0037	0.0033	0.0030	0.0027	0.0025
1	0.0439	0.0404	0.0372	0.0342	0.0314	0.0289	0.0266	0.0244	0.0224	0.0206	0.0189	0.0174
2	0.1333	0.1247	0.1165	0.1088	0.1016	0.0948	0.0884	0.0824	0.0768	0.0715	0.0666	0.0620
3	0.2793	0.2650	0.2513	0.2381	0.2254	0.2133	0.2017	0.1906	0.1800	0.1700	0.1604	0.1512
4	0.4582	0.4405	0.4231	0.4061	0.3895	0.3733	0.3575	0.3422	0.3272	0.3127	0.2987	0.2851
5	0.6335	0.6160	0.5984	0.5809	0.5635	0.5461	0.5289	0.5119	0.4950	0.4783	0.4619	0.4457
6	0.7767	0.7622	0.7474	0.7324	0.7171	0.7017	0.6860	0.6703	0.6544	0.6384	0.6224	0.6063
7	0.8769	0.8666	0.8560	0.8449	0.8335	0.8217	0.8095	0.7970	0.7841	0.7710	0.7576	0.7440
8	0.9382	0.9319	0.9252	0.9181	0.9106	0.9027	0.8944	0.8857	0.8766	0.8672	0.8574	0.8472
9	0.9717	0.9682	0.9644	0.9603	0.9559	0.9512	0.9462	0.9409	0.9352	0.9292	0.9228	0.9161
10	0.9880	0.9863	0.9844	0.9823	0.9800	0.9775	0.9747	0.9718	0.9686	0.9651	0.9614	0.9574
11	0.9953	0.9945	0.9937	0.9927	0.9916	0.9904	0.9890	0.9875	0.9859	0.9841	0.9821	0.9799
12	0.9983	0.9980	0.9976	0.9972	0.9967	0.9962	0.9955	0.9949	0.9941	0.9932	0.9922	0.9912
13	0.9994	0.9993	0.9992	0.9990	0.9988	0.9986	0.9983	0.9980	0.9977	0.9973	0.9969	0.9964
14	0.9998	0.9998	0.9997	0.9997	0.9996	0.9995	0.9994	0.9993	0.9991	0.9990	0.9988	0.9986
15	0.9999	0.9999	0.9999	0.9999	0.9999	0.9998	0.9998	0.9998	0.9997	0.9996	0.9996	0.9995
16	1.0000	1.0000	1.0000	1.0000	1.0000	0.9999	0.9999	0.9999	0.9999	0.9999	0.9999	0.9998
17						1.0000	1.0000	1.0000	1.0000	1.0000	1.0000	0.9999
18												1.0000

k	6.1	6.2	6.3	6.4	6.5	6.6	6.7	6.8	6.9	7	7.1	7.2
0	0.0022	0.0020	0.0018	0.0017	0.0015	0.0014	0.0012	0.0011	0.0010	0.0009	0.0008	0.0007
1	0.0159	0.0146	0.0134	0.0123	0.0113	0.0103	0.0095	0.0087	0.0080	0.0073	0.0067	0.0061
2	0.0577	0.0536	0.0498	0.0463	0.0430	0.0400	0.0371	0.0344	0.0320	0.0296	0.0275	0.0255
3	0.1425	0.1342	0.1264	0.1189	0.1118	0.1052	0.0988	0.0928	0.0871	0.0818	0.0767	0.0719
4	0.2719	0.2592	0.2469	0.2351	0.2237	0.2127	0.2022	0.1920	0.1823	0.1730	0.1641	0.1555
5	0.4298	0.4141	0.3988	0.3837	0.3690	0.3547	0.3406	0.3270	0.3137	0.3007	0.2881	0.2759
6	0.5902	0.5742	0.5582	0.5423	0.5265	0.5108	0.4953	0.4799	0.4647	0.4497	0.4349	0.4204
7	0.7301	0.7160	0.7017	0.6873	0.6728	0.6581	0.6433	0.6285	0.6136	0.5987	0.5838	0.5689
8	0.8367	0.8259	0.8148	0.8033	0.7916	0.7796	0.7673	0.7548	0.7420	0.7291	0.7160	0.7027
9	0.9090	0.9016	0.8939	0.8858	0.8774	0.8686	0.8596	0.8502	0.8405	0.8305	0.8202	0.8096
10	0.9531	0.9486	0.9437	0.9386	0.9332	0.9274	0.9214	0.9151	0.9084	0.9015	0.8942	0.8867
11	0.9776	0.9750	0.9723	0.9693	0.9661	0.9627	0.9591	0.9552	0.9510	0.9467	0.9420	0.9371
12	0.9900	0.9887	0.9873	0.9857	0.9840	0.9821	0.9801	0.9779	0.9755	0.9730	0.9703	0.9673
13	0.9958	0.9952	0.9945	0.9937	0.9929	0.9920	0.9909	0.9898	0.9885	0.9872	0.9857	0.9841
14	0.9984	0.9981	0.9978	0.9974	0.9970	0.9966	0.9961	0.9956	0.9950	0.9943	0.9935	0.9927
15	0.9994	0.9993	0.9992	0.9990	0.9988	0.9986	0.9984	0.9982	0.9979	0.9976	0.9972	0.9969
16	0.9998	0.9997	0.9997	0.9996	0.9996	0.9995	0.9994	0.9993	0.9992	0.9990	0.9989	0.9987
17	0.9999	0.9999	0.9999	0.9999	0.9998	0.9998	0.9998	0.9997	0.9997	0.9996	0.9996	0.9995
18	1.0000	1.0000	1.0000	1.0000	0.9999	0.9999	0.9999	0.9999	0.9999	0.9999	0.9998	0.9998
19					1.0000	1.0000	1.0000	1.0000	1.0000	1.0000	0.9999	0.9999
20											1.0000	1.0000

k	7.3	7.4	7.5	7.6	7.7	7.8	7.9	8	8.5	9	9.5	10
0	0.0007	0.0006	0.0006	0.0005	0.0005	0.0004	0.0004	0.0003	0.0002	0.0001	0.0001	0.0000
1	0.0056	0.0051	0.0047	0.0043	0.0039	0.0036	0.0033	0.0030	0.0019	0.0012	0.0008	0.0005
2	0.0236	0.0219	0.0203	0.0188	0.0174	0.0161	0.0149	0.0138	0.0093	0.0062	0.0042	0.0028
3	0.0674	0.0632	0.0591	0.0554	0.0518	0.0485	0.0453	0.0424	0.0301	0.0212	0.0149	0.0103
4	0.1473	0.1395	0.1321	0.1249	0.1181	0.1117	0.1055	0.0996	0.0744	0.0550	0.0403	0.0293
5	0.2640	0.2526	0.2414	0.2307	0.2203	0.2103	0.2006	0.1912	0.1496	0.1157	0.0885	0.0671
6	0.4060	0.3920	0.3782	0.3646	0.3514	0.3384	0.3257	0.3134	0.2562	0.2068	0.1649	0.1301
7	0.5541	0.5393	0.5246	0.5100	0.4956	0.4812	0.4670	0.4530	0.3856	0.3239	0.2687	0.2202
8	0.6892	0.6757	0.6620	0.6482	0.6343	0.6204	0.6065	0.5925	0.5231	0.4557	0.3918	0.3328
9	0.7988	0.7877	0.7764	0.7649	0.7531	0.7411	0.7290	0.7166	0.6530	0.5874	0.5218	0.4579
10	0.8788	0.8707	0.8622	0.8535	0.8445	0.8352	0.8257	0.8159	0.7634	0.7060	0.6453	0.5830
11	0.9319	0.9265	0.9208	0.9148	0.9085	0.9020	0.8952	0.8881	0.8487	0.8030	0.7520	0.6968
12	0.9642	0.9609	0.9573	0.9536	0.9496	0.9454	0.9409	0.9362	0.9091	0.8758	0.8364	0.7916
13	0.9824	0.9805	0.9784	0.9762	0.9739	0.9714	0.9687	0.9658	0.9486	0.9261	0.8981	0.8645
14	0.9918	0.9908	0.9897	0.9886	0.9873	0.9859	0.9844	0.9827	0.9726	0.9585	0.9400	0.9165
15	0.9964	0.9959	0.9954	0.9948	0.9941	0.9934	0.9926	0.9918	0.9862	0.9780	0.9665	0.9513
16	0.9985	0.9983	0.9980	0.9978	0.9974	0.9971	0.9967	0.9963	0.9934	0.9889	0.9823	0.9730
17	0.9994	0.9993	0.9992	0.9991	0.9989	0.9988	0.9986	0.9984	0.9970	0.9947	0.9911	0.9857
18	0.9998	0.9997	0.9997	0.9996	0.9996	0.9995	0.9994	0.9993	0.9987	0.9976	0.9957	0.9928
19	0.9999	0.9999	0.9999	0.9999	0.9998	0.9998	0.9998	0.9997	0.9995	0.9989	0.9980	0.9965
20	1.0000	1.0000	1.0000	1.0000	0.9999	0.9999	0.9999	0.9999	0.9998	0.9996	0.9991	0.9984
21					1.0000	1.0000	1.0000	1.0000	0.9999	0.9998	0.9996	0.9993
22									1.0000	0.9999	0.9999	0.9997
23										1.0000	0.9999	0.9999
24											1.0000	1.0000

							λ					
k	11	12	13	14	15	16	17	18	19	20	25	30
0	0.0000	0.0000	0.0000	0.0000	0.0000	0.0000	0.0000	0.0000	0.0000	0.0000	0.0000	0.0000
1	0.0002	0.0001	0.0000	0.0000	0.0000	0.0000	0.0000	0.0000	0.0000	0.0000	0.0000	0.0000
2	0.0012	0.0005	0.0002	0.0001	0.0000	0.0000	0.0000	0.0000	0.0000	0.0000	0.0000	0.0000
3	0.0049	0.0023	0.0011	0.0005	0.0002	0.0001	0.0000	0.0000	0.0000	0.0000	0.0000	0.0000
4	0.0151	0.0076	0.0037	0.0018	0.0009	0.0004	0.0002	0.0001	0.0000	0.0000	0.0000	0.0000
5	0.0375	0.0203	0.0107	0.0055	0.0028	0.0014	0.0007	0.0003	0.0002	0.0001	0.0000	0.0000
6	0.0786	0.0458	0.0259	0.0142	0.0076	0.0040	0.0021	0.0010	0.0005	0.0003	0.0000	0.0000
7	0.1432	0.0895	0.0540	0.0316	0.0180	0.0100	0.0054	0.0029	0.0015	0.0008	0.0000	0.0000
8	0.2320	0.1550	0.0998	0.0621	0.0374	0.0220	0.0126	0.0071	0.0039	0.0021	0.0001	0.0000
9	0.3405	0.2424	0.1658	0.1094	0.0699	0.0433	0.0261	0.0154	0.0089	0.0050	0.0002	0.0000
10	0.4599	0.3472	0.2517	0.1757	0.1185	0.0774	0.0491	0.0304	0.0183	0.0108	0.0006	0.0000
11	0.5793	0.4616	0.3532	0.2600	0.1848	0.1270	0.0847	0.0549	0.0347	0.0214	0.0014	0.0001
12	0.6887	0.5760	0.4631	0.3585	0.2676	0.1931	0.1350	0.0917	0.0606	0.0390	0.0031	0.0002
13	0.7813	0.6815	0.5730	0.4644	0.3632	0.2745	0.2009	0.1426	0.0984	0.0661	0.0065	0.0004
14	0.8540	0.7720	0.6751	0.5704	0.4657	0.3675	0.2808	0.2081	0.1497	0.1049	0.0124	0.0009
15	0.9074	0.8444	0.7636	0.6694	0.5681	0.4667	0.3715	0.2867	0.2148	0.1565	0.0223	0.0019
16	0.9441	0.8987	0.8355	0.7559	0.6641	0.5660	0.4677	0.3751	0.2920	0.2211	0.0377	0.0039
17	0.9678	0.9370	0.8905	0.8272	0.7489	0.6593	0.5640	0.4686	0.3784	0.2970	0.0605	0.0073
18	0.9823	0.9626	0.9302	0.8826	0.8195	0.7423	0.6550	0.5622	0.4695	0.3814	0.0920	0.0129
19	0.9907	0.9787	0.9573	0.9235	0.8752	0.8122	0.7363	0.6509	0.5606	0.4703	0.1336	0.0219
20	0.9953	0.9884	0.9750	0.9521	0.9170	0.8682	0.8055	0.7307	0.6472	0.5591	0.1855	0.0353
21	0.9977	0.9939	0.9859	0.9712	0.9469	0.9108	0.8615	0.7991	0.7255	0.6437	0.2473	0.0544
22	0.9990	0.9970	0.9924	0.9833	0.9673	0.9418	0.9047	0.8551	0.7931	0.7206	0.3175	0.0806
23	0.9995	0.9985	0.9960	0.9907	0.9805	0.9633	0.9367	0.8989	0.8490	0.7875	0.3939	0.1146
24	0.9998	0.9993	0.9980	0.9950	0.9888	0.9777	0.9594	0.9317	0.8933	0.8432	0.4734	0.1572
25	0.9999	0.9997	0.9990	0.9974	0.9938	0.9869	0.9748	0.9554	0.9269	0.8878	0.5529	0.2084
26	1.0000	0.9999	0.9995	0.9987	0.9967	0.9925	0.9848	0.9718	0.9514	0.9221	0.6294	0.2673
27		0.9999	0.9998	0.9994	0.9983	0.9959	0.9912	0.9827	0.9687	0.9475	0.7002	0.3329
28		1.0000	0.9999	0.9997	0.9991	0.9978	0.9950	0.9897	0.9805	0.9657	0.7634	0.4031
29			1.0000	0.9999	0.9996	0.9989	0.9973	0.9941	0.9882	0.9782	0.8179	0.4757
30				0.9999	0.9998	0.9994	0.9986	0.9967	0.9930	0.9865	0.8633	0.5484
31				1.0000	0.9999	0.9997	0.9993	0.9982	0.9960	0.9919	0.8999	0.6186
32					1.0000	0.9999	0.9996	0.9990	0.9978	0.9953	0.9285	0.6845
33						0.9999	0.9998	0.9995	0.9988	0.9973	0.9502	0.7444
34						1.0000	0.9999	0.9998	0.9994	0.9985	0.9662	0.7973
35							1.0000	0.9999	0.9997	0.9992	0.9775	0.8426
36								0.9999	0.9998	0.9996	0.9854	0.8804
37								1.0000	0.9999	0.9998	0.9908	0.9110
38									1.0000	0.9999	0.9943	0.9352
39										0.9999	0.9966	0.9537
40										1.0000	0.9980	0.9677
41											0.9988	0.9779
42											0.9993	0.9852
43											0.9996	0.9903
44											0.9998	0.9937
45											0.9999	0.9960
46											0.9999	0.9975
47											1.0000	0.9985
48												0.9991
49												0.9995

APPENDIX C

Standard Normal Curve Areas: $P(0 < Z < z_0)$

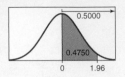

This table shows the normal area between 0 and z_0. Example: $P(0 < Z < 1.96) = \mathbf{0.4750}$

z_0	0	0.01	0.02	0.03	0.04	0.05	0.06	0.07	0.08	0.09
0.0	0.0000	0.0040	0.0080	0.0120	0.0160	0.0199	0.0239	0.0279	0.0319	0.0359
0.1	0.0398	0.0438	0.0478	0.0517	0.0557	0.0596	0.0636	0.0675	0.0714	0.0753
0.2	0.0793	0.0832	0.0871	0.0910	0.0948	0.0987	0.1026	0.1064	0.1103	0.1141
0.3	0.1179	0.1217	0.1255	0.1293	0.1331	0.1368	0.1406	0.1443	0.1480	0.1517
0.4	0.1554	0.1591	0.1628	0.1664	0.1700	0.1736	0.1772	0.1808	0.1844	0.1879
0.5	0.1915	0.1950	0.1985	0.2019	0.2054	0.2088	0.2123	0.2157	0.2190	0.2224
0.6	0.2257	0.2291	0.2324	0.2357	0.2389	0.2422	0.2454	0.2486	0.2517	0.2549
0.7	0.2580	0.2611	0.2642	0.2673	0.2704	0.2734	0.2764	0.2794	0.2823	0.2852
0.8	0.2881	0.2910	0.2939	0.2967	0.2995	0.3023	0.3051	0.3078	0.3106	0.3133
0.9	0.3159	0.3186	0.3212	0.3238	0.3264	0.3289	0.3315	0.3340	0.3365	0.3389
1.0	0.3413	0.3438	0.3461	0.3485	0.3508	0.3531	0.3554	0.3577	0.3599	0.3621
1.1	0.3643	0.3665	0.3686	0.3708	0.3729	0.3749	0.3770	0.3790	0.3810	0.3830
1.2	0.3849	0.3869	0.3888	0.3907	0.3925	0.3944	0.3962	0.3980	0.3997	0.4015
1.3	0.4032	0.4049	0.4066	0.4082	0.4099	0.4115	0.4131	0.4147	0.4162	0.4177
1.4	0.4192	0.4207	0.4222	0.4236	0.4251	0.4265	0.4279	0.4292	0.4306	0.4319
1.5	0.4332	0.4345	0.4357	0.4370	0.4382	0.4394	0.4406	0.4418	0.4429	0.4441
1.6	0.4452	0.4463	0.4474	0.4484	0.4495	0.4505	0.4515	0.4525	0.4535	0.4545
1.7	0.4554	0.4564	0.4573	0.4582	0.4591	0.4599	0.4608	0.4616	0.4625	0.4633
1.8	0.4641	0.4649	0.4656	0.4664	0.4671	0.4678	0.4686	0.4693	0.4699	0.4706
1.9	0.4713	0.4719	0.4726	0.4732	0.4738	0.4744	0.4750	0.4756	0.4761	0.4767
2.0	0.4772	0.4778	0.4783	0.4788	0.4793	0.4798	0.4803	0.4808	0.4812	0.4817
2.1	0.4821	0.4826	0.4830	0.4834	0.4838	0.4842	0.4846	0.4850	0.4854	0.4857
2.2	0.4861	0.4864	0.4868	0.4871	0.4875	0.4878	0.4881	0.4884	0.4887	0.4890
2.3	0.4893	0.4896	0.4898	0.4901	0.4904	0.4906	0.4909	0.4911	0.4913	0.4916
2.4	0.4918	0.4920	0.4922	0.4925	0.4927	0.4929	0.4931	0.4932	0.4934	0.4936
2.5	0.4938	0.4940	0.4941	0.4943	0.4945	0.4946	0.4948	0.4949	0.4951	0.4952
2.6	0.4953	0.4955	0.4956	0.4957	0.4959	0.4960	0.4961	0.4962	0.4963	0.4964
2.7	0.4965	0.4966	0.4967	0.4968	0.4969	0.4970	0.4971	0.4972	0.4973	0.4974
2.8	0.4974	0.4975	0.4976	0.4977	0.4977	0.4978	0.4979	0.4979	0.4980	0.4981
2.9	0.4981	0.4982	0.4982	0.4983	0.4984	0.4984	0.4985	0.4985	0.4986	0.4986
3.0	0.4987	0.4987	0.4987	0.4988	0.4988	0.4989	0.4989	0.4989	0.4990	0.4990

APPENDIX D

t Distribution Critical Values

This table shows the t value that defines the given right-tail area for the stated degrees of freedom (ν). Example: $t_{0.05,15} = 1.753$

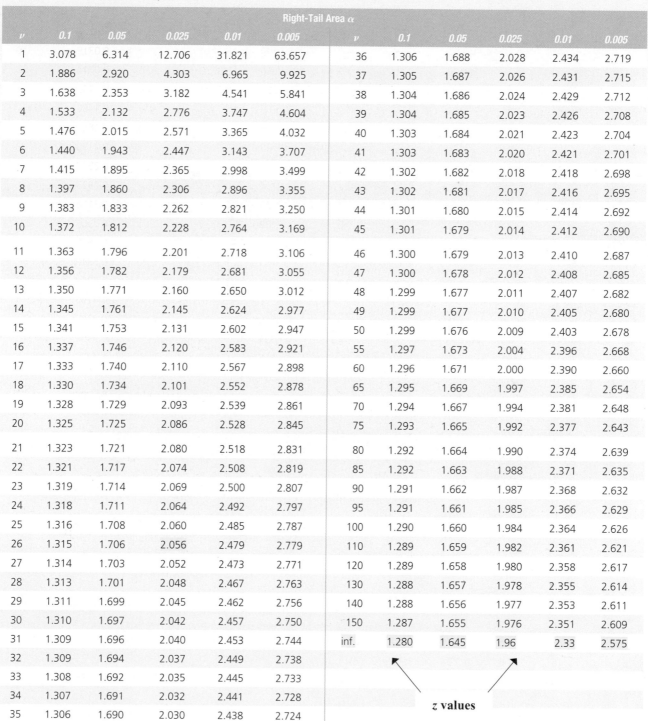

ν	0.1	0.05	0.025	0.01	0.005	ν	0.1	0.05	0.025	0.01	0.005
1	3.078	6.314	12.706	31.821	63.657	36	1.306	1.688	2.028	2.434	2.719
2	1.886	2.920	4.303	6.965	9.925	37	1.305	1.687	2.026	2.431	2.715
3	1.638	2.353	3.182	4.541	5.841	38	1.304	1.686	2.024	2.429	2.712
4	1.533	2.132	2.776	3.747	4.604	39	1.304	1.685	2.023	2.426	2.708
5	1.476	2.015	2.571	3.365	4.032	40	1.303	1.684	2.021	2.423	2.704
6	1.440	1.943	2.447	3.143	3.707	41	1.303	1.683	2.020	2.421	2.701
7	1.415	1.895	2.365	2.998	3.499	42	1.302	1.682	2.018	2.418	2.698
8	1.397	1.860	2.306	2.896	3.355	43	1.302	1.681	2.017	2.416	2.695
9	1.383	1.833	2.262	2.821	3.250	44	1.301	1.680	2.015	2.414	2.692
10	1.372	1.812	2.228	2.764	3.169	45	1.301	1.679	2.014	2.412	2.690
11	1.363	1.796	2.201	2.718	3.106	46	1.300	1.679	2.013	2.410	2.687
12	1.356	1.782	2.179	2.681	3.055	47	1.300	1.678	2.012	2.408	2.685
13	1.350	1.771	2.160	2.650	3.012	48	1.299	1.677	2.011	2.407	2.682
14	1.345	1.761	2.145	2.624	2.977	49	1.299	1.677	2.010	2.405	2.680
15	1.341	1.753	2.131	2.602	2.947	50	1.299	1.676	2.009	2.403	2.678
16	1.337	1.746	2.120	2.583	2.921	55	1.297	1.673	2.004	2.396	2.668
17	1.333	1.740	2.110	2.567	2.898	60	1.296	1.671	2.000	2.390	2.660
18	1.330	1.734	2.101	2.552	2.878	65	1.295	1.669	1.997	2.385	2.654
19	1.328	1.729	2.093	2.539	2.861	70	1.294	1.667	1.994	2.381	2.648
20	1.325	1.725	2.086	2.528	2.845	75	1.293	1.665	1.992	2.377	2.643
21	1.323	1.721	2.080	2.518	2.831	80	1.292	1.664	1.990	2.374	2.639
22	1.321	1.717	2.074	2.508	2.819	85	1.292	1.663	1.988	2.371	2.635
23	1.319	1.714	2.069	2.500	2.807	90	1.291	1.662	1.987	2.368	2.632
24	1.318	1.711	2.064	2.492	2.797	95	1.291	1.661	1.985	2.366	2.629
25	1.316	1.708	2.060	2.485	2.787	100	1.290	1.660	1.984	2.364	2.626
26	1.315	1.706	2.056	2.479	2.779	110	1.289	1.659	1.982	2.361	2.621
27	1.314	1.703	2.052	2.473	2.771	120	1.289	1.658	1.980	2.358	2.617
28	1.313	1.701	2.048	2.467	2.763	130	1.288	1.657	1.978	2.355	2.614
29	1.311	1.699	2.045	2.462	2.756	140	1.288	1.656	1.977	2.353	2.611
30	1.310	1.697	2.042	2.457	2.750	150	1.287	1.655	1.976	2.351	2.609
31	1.309	1.696	2.040	2.453	2.744	inf.	1.280	1.645	1.96	2.33	2.575
32	1.309	1.694	2.037	2.449	2.738						
33	1.308	1.692	2.035	2.445	2.733						
34	1.307	1.691	2.032	2.441	2.728						
35	1.306	1.690	2.030	2.438	2.724						

z values

APPENDIX E

Critical Values of Chi-Square for Area *A*

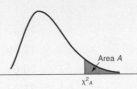

ν	0.995	0.99	0.975	0.95	0.9	0.1	0.05	0.025	0.01	0.005	ν
1	0.00	0.00	0.00	0.00	0.02	2.71	3.84	5.02	6.63	7.88	1
2	0.01	0.02	0.05	0.10	0.21	4.61	5.99	7.38	9.21	10.60	2
3	0.07	0.11	0.22	0.35	0.58	6.25	7.81	9.35	11.34	12.84	3
4	0.21	0.30	0.48	0.71	1.06	7.78	9.49	11.14	13.28	14.86	4
5	0.41	0.55	0.83	1.15	1.61	9.24	11.07	12.83	15.09	16.75	5
6	0.68	0.87	1.24	1.64	2.20	10.64	12.59	14.45	16.81	18.55	6
7	0.99	1.24	1.69	2.17	2.83	12.02	14.07	16.01	18.48	20.28	7
8	1.34	1.65	2.18	2.73	3.49	13.36	15.51	17.53	20.09	21.95	8
9	1.73	2.09	2.70	3.33	4.17	14.68	16.92	19.02	21.67	23.59	9
10	2.16	2.56	3.25	3.94	4.87	15.99	18.31	20.48	23.21	25.19	10
11	2.60	3.05	3.82	4.57	5.58	17.28	19.68	21.92	24.72	26.76	11
12	3.07	3.57	4.40	5.23	6.30	18.55	21.03	23.34	26.22	28.30	12
13	3.57	4.11	5.01	5.89	7.04	19.81	22.36	24.74	27.69	29.82	13
14	4.07	4.66	5.63	6.57	7.79	21.06	23.68	26.12	29.14	31.32	14
15	4.60	5.23	6.26	7.26	8.55	22.31	25.00	27.49	30.58	32.80	15
16	5.14	5.81	6.91	7.96	9.31	23.54	26.30	28.85	32.00	34.27	16
17	5.70	6.41	7.56	8.67	10.09	24.77	27.59	30.19	33.41	35.72	17
18	6.26	7.01	8.23	9.39	10.86	25.99	28.87	31.53	34.81	37.16	18
19	6.84	7.63	8.91	10.12	11.65	27.20	30.14	32.85	36.19	38.58	19
20	7.43	8.26	9.59	10.85	12.44	28.41	31.41	34.17	37.57	40.00	20
21	8.03	8.90	10.28	11.59	13.24	29.62	32.67	35.48	38.93	41.40	21
22	8.64	9.54	10.98	12.34	14.04	30.81	33.92	36.78	40.29	42.80	22
23	9.26	10.20	11.69	13.09	14.85	32.01	35.17	38.08	41.64	44.18	23
24	9.89	10.86	12.40	13.85	15.66	33.20	36.42	39.36	42.98	45.56	24
25	10.52	11.52	13.12	14.61	16.47	34.38	37.65	40.65	44.31	46.93	25
26	11.16	12.20	13.84	15.38	17.29	35.56	38.89	41.92	45.64	48.29	26
27	11.81	12.88	14.57	16.15	18.11	36.74	40.11	43.19	46.96	49.64	27
28	12.46	13.56	15.31	16.93	18.94	37.92	41.34	44.46	48.28	50.99	28
29	13.12	14.26	16.05	17.71	19.77	39.09	42.56	45.72	49.59	52.34	29
30	13.79	14.95	16.79	18.49	20.60	40.26	43.77	46.98	50.89	53.67	30
31	14.46	15.66	17.54	19.28	21.43	41.42	44.99	48.23	52.19	55.00	31
32	15.13	16.36	18.29	20.07	22.27	42.58	46.19	49.48	53.49	56.33	32

ν	0.995	0.99	0.975	0.95	0.9	0.1	0.05	0.025	0.01	0.005	ν
33	15.82	17.07	19.05	20.87	23.11	43.75	47.40	50.73	54.78	57.65	32
34	16.50	17.79	19.81	21.66	23.95	44.90	48.60	51.97	56.06	58.96	34
35	17.19	18.51	20.57	22.47	24.80	46.06	49.80	53.20	57.34	60.27	33
36	17.89	19.23	21.34	23.27	25.64	47.21	51.00	54.44	58.62	61.58	36
37	18.59	19.96	22.11	24.07	26.49	48.36	52.19	55.67	59.89	62.88	34
38	19.29	20.69	22.88	24.88	27.34	49.51	53.38	56.90	61.16	64.18	38
39	20.00	21.43	23.65	25.70	28.20	50.66	54.57	58.12	62.43	65.48	35
40	20.71	22.16	24.43	26.51	29.05	51.81	55.76	59.34	63.69	66.77	40
50	27.99	29.71	32.36	34.76	37.69	63.17	67.50	71.42	76.15	79.49	50
60	35.53	37.48	40.48	43.19	46.46	74.40	79.08	83.30	88.38	91.95	60
70	43.28	45.44	48.76	51.74	55.33	85.53	90.53	95.02	100.43	104.21	70
80	51.17	53.54	57.15	60.39	64.28	96.58	101.88	106.63	112.33	116.32	80
90	59.20	61.75	65.65	69.13	73.29	107.57	113.15	118.14	124.12	128.30	90
100	67.33	70.06	74.22	77.93	82.36	118.50	124.34	129.56	135.81	140.17	100

Critical Values of $F_{0.01}$

Bottom d.f. = v_2	\ Top d.f. = v_1 → 1	2	3	4	5	6	7	8	9	10	11	12	13	14	15	16	17	18	19	20
1	4052.18	4999.50	5403.35	5624.58	5763.65	5858.99	5928.36	5981.07	6022.47	6055.85	6083.32	6106.32	6125.86	6142.67	6157.28	6170.10	6181.43	6191.53	6200.58	6208.73
2	98.50	99.00	99.17	99.25	99.30	99.33	99.36	99.37	99.39	99.40	99.41	99.42	99.42	99.43	99.43	99.44	99.44	99.44	99.45	99.45
3	34.12	30.82	29.46	28.71	28.24	27.91	27.67	27.49	27.35	27.23	27.13	27.05	26.98	26.92	26.87	26.83	26.79	26.75	26.72	26.69
4	21.20	18.00	16.69	15.98	15.52	15.21	14.98	14.80	14.66	14.55	14.45	14.37	14.31	14.25	14.20	14.15	14.11	14.08	14.05	14.02
5	16.26	13.27	12.06	11.39	10.97	10.67	10.46	10.29	10.16	10.05	9.96	9.89	9.82	9.77	9.72	9.68	9.64	9.61	9.58	9.55
6	13.75	10.92	9.78	9.15	8.75	8.47	8.26	8.10	7.98	7.87	7.79	7.72	7.66	7.60	7.56	7.52	7.48	7.45	7.42	7.40
7	12.25	9.55	8.45	7.85	7.46	7.19	6.99	6.84	6.72	6.62	6.54	6.47	6.41	6.36	6.31	6.28	6.24	6.21	6.18	6.16
8	11.26	8.65	7.59	7.01	6.63	6.37	6.18	6.03	5.91	5.81	5.73	5.67	5.61	5.56	5.52	5.48	5.44	5.41	5.38	5.36
9	10.56	8.02	6.99	6.42	6.06	5.80	5.61	5.47	5.35	5.26	5.18	5.11	5.05	5.01	4.96	4.92	4.89	4.86	4.83	4.81
10	10.04	7.56	6.55	5.99	5.64	5.39	5.20	5.06	4.94	4.85	4.77	4.71	4.65	4.60	4.56	4.52	4.49	4.46	4.43	4.41
11	9.65	7.21	6.22	5.67	5.32	5.07	4.89	4.74	4.63	4.54	4.46	4.40	4.34	4.29	4.25	4.21	4.18	4.15	4.12	4.10
12	9.33	6.93	5.95	5.41	5.06	4.82	4.64	4.50	4.39	4.30	4.22	4.16	4.10	4.05	4.01	3.97	3.94	3.91	3.88	3.86
13	9.07	6.70	5.74	5.21	4.86	4.62	4.44	4.30	4.19	4.10	4.02	3.96	3.91	3.86	3.82	3.78	3.75	3.72	3.69	3.66
14	8.86	6.51	5.56	5.04	4.69	4.46	4.28	4.14	4.03	3.94	3.86	3.80	3.75	3.70	3.66	3.62	3.59	3.56	3.53	3.51
15	8.68	6.36	5.42	4.89	4.56	4.32	4.14	4.00	3.89	3.80	3.73	3.67	3.61	3.56	3.52	3.49	3.45	3.42	3.40	3.37
16	8.53	6.23	5.29	4.77	4.44	4.20	4.03	3.89	3.78	3.69	3.62	3.55	3.50	3.45	3.41	3.37	3.34	3.31	3.28	3.26
17	8.40	6.11	5.18	4.67	4.34	4.10	3.93	3.79	3.68	3.59	3.52	3.46	3.40	3.35	3.31	3.27	3.24	3.21	3.19	3.16
18	8.29	6.01	5.09	4.58	4.25	4.01	3.84	3.71	3.60	3.51	3.43	3.37	3.32	3.27	3.23	3.19	3.16	3.13	3.10	3.08
19	8.18	5.93	5.01	4.50	4.17	3.94	3.77	3.63	3.52	3.43	3.36	3.30	3.24	3.19	3.15	3.12	3.08	3.05	3.03	3.00
20	8.10	5.85	4.94	4.43	4.10	3.87	3.70	3.56	3.46	3.37	3.29	3.23	3.18	3.13	3.09	3.05	3.02	2.99	2.96	2.94
21	8.02	5.78	4.87	4.37	4.04	3.81	3.64	3.51	3.40	3.31	3.24	3.17	3.12	3.07	3.03	2.99	2.96	2.93	2.90	2.88
22	7.95	5.72	4.82	4.31	3.99	3.76	3.59	3.45	3.35	3.26	3.18	3.12	3.07	3.02	2.98	2.94	2.91	2.88	2.85	2.83
23	7.88	5.66	4.76	4.26	3.94	3.71	3.54	3.41	3.30	3.21	3.14	3.07	3.02	2.97	2.93	2.89	2.86	2.83	2.80	2.78
24	7.82	5.61	4.72	4.22	3.90	3.67	3.50	3.36	3.26	3.17	3.09	3.03	2.98	2.93	2.89	2.85	2.82	2.79	2.76	2.74
25	7.77	5.57	4.68	4.18	3.85	3.63	3.46	3.32	3.22	3.13	3.06	2.99	2.94	2.89	2.85	2.81	2.78	2.75	2.72	2.70

26	7.72	5.53	4.64	4.14	3.82	3.59	3.42	3.29	3.18	3.09	3.02	2.96	2.90	2.86	2.81	2.78	2.75	2.72	2.69	2.66
27	7.68	5.49	4.60	4.11	3.78	3.56	3.39	3.26	3.15	3.06	2.99	2.93	2.87	2.82	2.78	2.75	2.71	2.68	2.66	2.63
28	7.64	5.45	4.57	4.07	3.75	3.53	3.36	3.23	3.12	3.03	2.96	2.90	2.84	2.79	2.75	2.72	2.68	2.65	2.63	2.60
29	7.60	5.42	4.54	4.04	3.73	3.50	3.33	3.20	3.09	3.00	2.93	2.87	2.81	2.77	2.73	2.69	2.66	2.63	2.60	2.57
30	7.56	5.39	4.51	4.02	3.70	3.47	3.30	3.17	3.07	2.98	2.91	2.84	2.79	2.74	2.70	2.66	2.63	2.60	2.57	2.55
35	7.42	5.27	4.40	3.91	3.59	3.37	3.20	3.07	2.96	2.88	2.80	2.74	2.69	2.64	2.60	2.56	2.53	2.50	2.47	2.44
40	7.31	5.18	4.31	3.83	3.51	3.29	3.12	2.99	2.89	2.80	2.73	2.66	2.61	2.56	2.52	2.48	2.45	2.42	2.39	2.37
45	7.23	5.11	4.25	3.77	3.45	3.23	3.07	2.94	2.83	2.74	2.67	2.61	2.55	2.51	2.46	2.43	2.39	2.36	2.34	2.31
50	7.17	5.06	4.20	3.72	3.41	3.19	3.02	2.89	2.78	2.70	2.63	2.56	2.51	2.46	2.42	2.38	2.35	2.32	2.29	2.27
60	7.08	4.98	4.13	3.65	3.34	3.12	2.95	2.82	2.72	2.63	2.56	2.50	2.44	2.39	2.35	2.31	2.28	2.25	2.22	2.20
70	7.01	4.92	4.07	3.60	3.29	3.07	2.91	2.78	2.67	2.59	2.51	2.45	2.40	2.35	2.31	2.27	2.23	2.20	2.18	2.15
80	6.96	4.88	4.04	3.56	3.26	3.04	2.87	2.74	2.64	2.55	2.48	2.42	2.36	2.31	2.27	2.23	2.20	2.17	2.14	2.12
90	6.93	4.85	4.01	3.53	3.23	3.01	2.84	2.72	2.61	2.52	2.45	2.39	2.33	2.29	2.24	2.21	2.17	2.14	2.11	2.09
100	6.90	4.82	3.98	3.51	3.21	2.99	2.82	2.69	2.59	2.50	2.43	2.37	2.31	2.27	2.22	2.19	2.15	2.12	2.09	2.07
120	6.85	4.79	3.95	3.48	3.17	2.96	2.79	2.66	2.56	2.47	2.40	2.34	2.28	2.23	2.19	2.15	2.12	2.09	2.06	2.03
140	6.82	4.76	3.92	3.46	3.15	2.93	2.77	2.64	2.54	2.45	2.38	2.31	2.26	2.21	2.17	2.13	2.10	2.07	2.04	2.01
160	6.80	4.74	3.91	3.44	3.13	2.92	2.75	2.62	2.52	2.43	2.36	2.30	2.24	2.20	2.15	2.11	2.08	2.05	2.02	1.99
180	6.78	4.73	3.89	3.43	3.12	2.90	2.74	2.61	2.51	2.42	2.35	2.28	2.23	2.18	2.14	2.10	2.07	2.04	2.01	1.98
200	6.76	4.71	3.88	3.41	3.11	2.89	2.73	2.60	2.50	2.41	2.34	2.27	2.22	2.17	2.13	2.09	2.06	2.03	2.00	1.97
300	6.72	4.68	3.85	3.38	3.08	2.86	2.70	2.57	2.47	2.38	2.31	2.24	2.19	2.14	2.10	2.06	2.03	1.99	1.97	1.94
100000	6.64	4.61	3.78	3.32	3.02	2.80	2.64	2.51	2.41	2.32	2.25	2.18	2.13	2.08	2.04	2.00	1.97	1.93	1.90	1.88

Top d.f. = v_1

Bottom d.f. = v_2	22	24	26	28	30	40	45	50	60	70	80	90	100	120	140	160	180	200	300	100000
1	6222.84	6234.63	6244.62	6253.20	6260.65	6286.78	6295.52	6302.52	6313.03	6320.55	6326.20	6330.59	6334.11	6339.39	6343.17	6346.00	6348.20	6349.97	6355.26	6365.83
2	99.45	99.46	99.46	99.46	99.47	99.47	99.48	99.48	99.48	99.48	99.48	99.49	99.49	99.49	99.49	99.49	99.49	99.49	99.50	99.50
3	26.64	26.60	26.56	26.53	26.50	26.41	26.38	26.35	26.32	26.29	26.27	26.25	26.24	26.22	26.21	26.20	26.19	26.18	26.16	26.13
4	13.97	13.93	13.89	13.86	13.84	13.75	13.71	13.69	13.65	13.63	13.61	13.59	13.58	13.56	13.54	13.53	13.53	13.52	13.50	13.46
5	9.51	9.47	9.43	9.40	9.38	9.29	9.26	9.24	9.20	9.18	9.16	9.14	9.13	9.11	9.10	9.09	9.08	9.08	9.06	9.02
6	7.35	7.31	7.28	7.25	7.23	7.14	7.11	7.09	7.06	7.03	7.01	7.00	6.99	6.97	6.96	6.95	6.94	6.93	6.92	6.88
7	6.11	6.07	6.04	6.02	5.99	5.91	5.88	5.86	5.82	5.80	5.78	5.77	5.75	5.74	5.72	5.72	5.71	5.70	5.68	5.65
8	5.32	5.28	5.25	5.22	5.20	5.12	5.09	5.07	5.03	5.01	4.99	4.97	4.96	4.95	4.93	4.92	4.92	4.91	4.89	4.86
9	4.77	4.73	4.70	4.67	4.65	4.57	4.54	4.52	4.48	4.46	4.44	4.43	4.41	4.40	4.39	4.38	4.37	4.36	4.35	4.31
10	4.36	4.33	4.30	4.27	4.25	4.17	4.14	4.12	4.08	4.06	4.04	4.03	4.01	4.00	3.98	3.97	3.97	3.96	3.94	3.91
11	4.06	4.02	3.99	3.96	3.94	3.86	3.83	3.81	3.78	3.75	3.73	3.72	3.71	3.69	3.68	3.67	3.66	3.66	3.64	3.60
12	3.82	3.78	3.75	3.72	3.70	3.62	3.59	3.57	3.54	3.51	3.49	3.48	3.47	3.45	3.44	3.43	3.42	3.41	3.40	3.36
13	3.62	3.59	3.56	3.53	3.51	3.43	3.40	3.38	3.34	3.32	3.30	3.28	3.27	3.25	3.24	3.23	3.23	3.22	3.20	3.17
14	3.46	3.43	3.40	3.37	3.35	3.27	3.24	3.22	3.18	3.16	3.14	3.12	3.11	3.09	3.08	3.07	3.06	3.06	3.04	3.00
15	3.33	3.29	3.26	3.24	3.21	3.13	3.10	3.08	3.05	3.02	3.00	2.99	2.98	2.96	2.95	2.94	2.93	2.92	2.91	2.87
16	3.22	3.18	3.15	3.12	3.10	3.02	2.99	2.97	2.93	2.91	2.89	2.87	2.86	2.84	2.83	2.82	2.81	2.81	2.79	2.75
17	3.12	3.08	3.05	3.03	3.00	2.92	2.89	2.87	2.83	2.81	2.79	2.78	2.76	2.75	2.73	2.72	2.72	2.71	2.69	2.65
18	3.03	3.00	2.97	2.94	2.92	2.84	2.81	2.78	2.75	2.72	2.70	2.69	2.68	2.66	2.65	2.64	2.63	2.62	2.60	2.57
19	2.96	2.92	2.89	2.87	2.84	2.76	2.73	2.71	2.67	2.65	2.63	2.61	2.60	2.58	2.57	2.56	2.55	2.55	2.53	2.49
20	2.90	2.86	2.83	2.80	2.78	2.69	2.67	2.64	2.61	2.58	2.56	2.55	2.54	2.52	2.50	2.49	2.49	2.48	2.46	2.42
21	2.84	2.80	2.77	2.74	2.72	2.64	2.61	2.58	2.55	2.52	2.50	2.49	2.48	2.46	2.44	2.43	2.43	2.42	2.40	2.36
22	2.78	2.75	2.72	2.69	2.67	2.58	2.55	2.53	2.50	2.47	2.45	2.43	2.42	2.40	2.39	2.38	2.37	2.36	2.35	2.31
23	2.74	2.70	2.67	2.64	2.62	2.54	2.51	2.48	2.45	2.42	2.40	2.39	2.37	2.35	2.34	2.33	2.32	2.32	2.30	2.26
24	2.70	2.66	2.63	2.60	2.58	2.49	2.46	2.44	2.40	2.38	2.36	2.34	2.33	2.31	2.30	2.29	2.28	2.27	2.25	2.21
25	2.66	2.62	2.59	2.56	2.54	2.45	2.42	2.40	2.36	2.34	2.32	2.30	2.29	2.27	2.26	2.25	2.24	2.23	2.21	2.17

26	2.62	2.58	2.55	2.53	2.50	2.42	2.39	2.36	2.33	2.30	2.28	2.26	2.25	2.23	2.22	2.21	2.20	2.19	2.17	2.13
27	2.59	2.55	2.52	2.49	2.47	2.38	2.35	2.33	2.29	2.27	2.25	2.23	2.22	2.20	2.18	2.17	2.17	2.16	2.14	2.10
28	2.56	2.52	2.49	2.46	2.44	2.35	2.32	2.30	2.26	2.24	2.22	2.20	2.19	2.17	2.15	2.14	2.13	2.13	2.11	2.06
29	2.53	2.49	2.46	2.44	2.41	2.33	2.30	2.27	2.23	2.21	2.19	2.17	2.16	2.14	2.12	2.11	2.10	2.10	2.08	2.03
30	2.51	2.47	2.44	2.41	2.39	2.30	2.27	2.25	2.21	2.18	2.16	2.14	2.13	2.11	2.10	2.09	2.08	2.07	2.05	2.01
35	2.40	2.36	2.33	2.30	2.28	2.19	2.16	2.14	2.10	2.07	2.05	2.03	2.02	2.00	1.98	1.97	1.96	1.96	1.94	1.89
40	2.33	2.29	2.26	2.23	2.20	2.11	2.08	2.06	2.02	1.99	1.97	1.95	1.94	1.92	1.90	1.89	1.88	1.87	1.85	1.80
45	2.27	2.23	2.20	2.17	2.14	2.05	2.02	2.00	1.96	1.93	1.91	1.89	1.88	1.85	1.84	1.83	1.82	1.81	1.79	1.74
50	2.22	2.18	2.15	2.12	2.10	2.01	1.97	1.95	1.91	1.88	1.86	1.84	1.82	1.80	1.79	1.77	1.76	1.76	1.73	1.68
60	2.15	2.12	2.08	2.05	2.03	1.94	1.90	1.88	1.84	1.81	1.78	1.76	1.75	1.73	1.71	1.70	1.69	1.68	1.65	1.60
70	2.11	2.07	2.03	2.01	1.98	1.89	1.85	1.83	1.78	1.75	1.73	1.71	1.70	1.67	1.65	1.64	1.63	1.62	1.60	1.54
80	2.07	2.03	2.00	1.97	1.94	1.85	1.82	1.79	1.75	1.71	1.69	1.67	1.65	1.63	1.61	1.60	1.59	1.58	1.55	1.49
90	2.04	2.00	1.97	1.94	1.92	1.82	1.79	1.76	1.72	1.68	1.66	1.64	1.62	1.60	1.58	1.57	1.55	1.55	1.52	1.46
100	2.02	1.98	1.95	1.92	1.89	1.80	1.76	1.74	1.69	1.66	1.63	1.61	1.60	1.57	1.55	1.54	1.53	1.52	1.49	1.43
120	1.99	1.95	1.92	1.89	1.86	1.76	1.73	1.70	1.66	1.62	1.60	1.58	1.56	1.53	1.51	1.50	1.49	1.48	1.45	1.38
140	1.97	1.93	1.89	1.86	1.84	1.74	1.70	1.67	1.63	1.60	1.57	1.55	1.53	1.50	1.48	1.47	1.46	1.45	1.42	1.35
160	1.95	1.91	1.88	1.85	1.82	1.72	1.68	1.66	1.61	1.58	1.55	1.53	1.51	1.48	1.46	1.45	1.43	1.42	1.39	1.32
180	1.94	1.90	1.86	1.83	1.81	1.71	1.67	1.64	1.60	1.56	1.53	1.51	1.49	1.47	1.45	1.43	1.42	1.41	1.37	1.30
200	1.93	1.89	1.85	1.82	1.79	1.69	1.66	1.63	1.58	1.55	1.52	1.50	1.48	1.45	1.43	1.42	1.40	1.39	1.36	1.28
300	1.89	1.85	1.82	1.79	1.76	1.66	1.62	1.59	1.55	1.51	1.48	1.46	1.44	1.41	1.39	1.37	1.36	1.35	1.31	1.22
100000	1.83	1.79	1.76	1.72	1.70	1.59	1.55	1.52	1.47	1.43	1.40	1.38	1.36	1.32	1.30	1.28	1.26	1.25	1.20	1.01

Critical Values of $F_{0.025}$

v_2 \ v_1	1	2	3	4	5	6	7	8	9	10	11	12	13	14	15	16	17	18	19	20
1	647.79	799.50	864.16	899.58	921.85	937.11	948.22	956.66	963.28	968.63	973.03	976.71	979.84	982.53	984.87	986.92	988.73	990.35	991.80	993.10
2	38.51	39.00	39.17	39.25	39.30	39.33	39.36	39.37	39.39	39.40	39.41	39.41	39.42	39.43	39.43	39.44	39.44	39.44	39.45	39.45
3	17.44	16.04	15.44	15.10	14.88	14.73	14.62	14.54	14.47	14.42	14.37	14.34	14.30	14.28	14.25	14.23	14.21	14.20	14.18	14.17
4	12.22	10.65	9.98	9.60	9.36	9.20	9.07	8.98	8.90	8.84	8.79	8.75	8.71	8.68	8.66	8.63	8.61	8.59	8.58	8.56
5	10.01	8.43	7.76	7.39	7.15	6.98	6.85	6.76	6.68	6.62	6.57	6.52	6.49	6.46	6.43	6.40	6.38	6.36	6.34	6.33
6	8.81	7.26	6.60	6.23	5.99	5.82	5.70	5.60	5.52	5.46	5.41	5.37	5.33	5.30	5.27	5.24	5.22	5.20	5.18	5.17
7	8.07	6.54	5.89	5.52	5.29	5.12	4.99	4.90	4.82	4.76	4.71	4.67	4.63	4.60	4.57	4.54	4.52	4.50	4.48	4.47
8	7.57	6.06	5.42	5.05	4.82	4.65	4.53	4.43	4.36	4.30	4.24	4.20	4.16	4.13	4.10	4.08	4.05	4.03	4.02	4.00
9	7.21	5.71	5.08	4.72	4.48	4.32	4.20	4.10	4.03	3.96	3.91	3.87	3.83	3.80	3.77	3.74	3.72	3.70	3.68	3.67
10	6.94	5.46	4.83	4.47	4.24	4.07	3.95	3.85	3.78	3.72	3.66	3.62	3.58	3.55	3.52	3.50	3.47	3.45	3.44	3.42
11	6.72	5.26	4.63	4.28	4.04	3.88	3.76	3.66	3.59	3.53	3.47	3.43	3.39	3.36	3.33	3.30	3.28	3.26	3.24	3.23
12	6.55	5.10	4.47	4.12	3.89	3.73	3.61	3.51	3.44	3.37	3.32	3.28	3.24	3.21	3.18	3.15	3.13	3.11	3.09	3.07
13	6.41	4.97	4.35	4.00	3.77	3.60	3.48	3.39	3.31	3.25	3.20	3.15	3.12	3.08	3.05	3.03	3.00	2.98	2.96	2.95
14	6.30	4.86	4.24	3.89	3.66	3.50	3.38	3.29	3.21	3.15	3.09	3.05	3.01	2.98	2.95	2.92	2.90	2.88	2.86	2.84
15	6.20	4.77	4.15	3.80	3.58	3.41	3.29	3.20	3.12	3.06	3.01	2.96	2.92	2.89	2.86	2.84	2.81	2.79	2.77	2.76
16	6.12	4.69	4.08	3.73	3.50	3.34	3.22	3.12	3.05	2.99	2.93	2.89	2.85	2.82	2.79	2.76	2.74	2.72	2.70	2.68
17	6.04	4.62	4.01	3.66	3.44	3.28	3.16	3.06	2.98	2.92	2.87	2.82	2.79	2.75	2.72	2.70	2.67	2.65	2.63	2.62
18	5.98	4.56	3.95	3.61	3.38	3.22	3.10	3.01	2.93	2.87	2.81	2.77	2.73	2.70	2.67	2.64	2.62	2.60	2.58	2.56
19	5.92	4.51	3.90	3.56	3.33	3.17	3.05	2.96	2.88	2.82	2.76	2.72	2.68	2.65	2.62	2.59	2.57	2.55	2.53	2.51
20	5.87	4.46	3.86	3.51	3.29	3.13	3.01	2.91	2.84	2.77	2.72	2.68	2.64	2.60	2.57	2.55	2.52	2.50	2.48	2.46
21	5.83	4.42	3.82	3.48	3.25	3.09	2.97	2.87	2.80	2.73	2.68	2.64	2.60	2.56	2.53	2.51	2.48	2.46	2.44	2.42
22	5.79	4.38	3.78	3.44	3.22	3.05	2.93	2.84	2.76	2.70	2.65	2.60	2.56	2.53	2.50	2.47	2.45	2.43	2.41	2.39
23	5.75	4.35	3.75	3.41	3.18	3.02	2.90	2.81	2.73	2.67	2.62	2.57	2.53	2.50	2.47	2.44	2.42	2.39	2.37	2.36
24	5.72	4.32	3.72	3.38	3.15	2.99	2.87	2.78	2.70	2.64	2.59	2.54	2.50	2.47	2.44	2.41	2.39	2.36	2.35	2.33
25	5.69	4.29	3.69	3.35	3.13	2.97	2.85	2.75	2.68	2.61	2.56	2.51	2.48	2.44	2.41	2.38	2.36	2.34	2.32	2.30

Top d.f. = v_1

Bottom d.f. = v_2

df																			
26	5.66	4.27	3.67	3.33	3.10	2.94	2.82	2.73	2.65	2.59	2.54	2.49	2.45	2.42	2.39	2.36	2.34	2.31	2.29	2.28
27	5.63	4.24	3.65	3.31	3.08	2.92	2.80	2.71	2.63	2.57	2.51	2.47	2.43	2.39	2.36	2.34	2.31	2.29	2.27	2.25
28	5.61	4.22	3.63	3.29	3.06	2.90	2.78	2.69	2.61	2.55	2.49	2.45	2.41	2.37	2.34	2.32	2.29	2.27	2.25	2.23
29	5.59	4.20	3.61	3.27	3.04	2.88	2.76	2.67	2.59	2.53	2.48	2.43	2.39	2.36	2.32	2.30	2.27	2.25	2.23	2.21
30	5.57	4.18	3.59	3.25	3.03	2.87	2.75	2.65	2.57	2.51	2.46	2.41	2.37	2.34	2.31	2.28	2.26	2.23	2.21	2.20
35	5.48	4.11	3.52	3.18	2.96	2.80	2.68	2.58	2.50	2.44	2.39	2.34	2.30	2.27	2.23	2.21	2.18	2.16	2.14	2.12
40	5.42	4.05	3.46	3.13	2.90	2.74	2.62	2.53	2.45	2.39	2.33	2.29	2.25	2.21	2.18	2.15	2.13	2.11	2.09	2.07
45	5.38	4.01	3.42	3.09	2.86	2.70	2.58	2.49	2.41	2.35	2.29	2.25	2.21	2.17	2.14	2.11	2.09	2.07	2.04	2.03
50	5.34	3.97	3.39	3.05	2.83	2.67	2.55	2.46	2.38	2.32	2.26	2.22	2.18	2.14	2.11	2.08	2.06	2.03	2.01	1.99
60	5.29	3.93	3.34	3.01	2.79	2.63	2.51	2.41	2.33	2.27	2.22	2.17	2.13	2.09	2.06	2.03	2.01	1.98	1.96	1.94
70	5.25	3.89	3.31	2.97	2.75	2.59	2.47	2.38	2.30	2.24	2.18	2.14	2.10	2.06	2.03	2.00	1.97	1.95	1.93	1.91
80	5.22	3.86	3.28	2.95	2.73	2.57	2.45	2.35	2.28	2.21	2.16	2.11	2.07	2.03	2.00	1.97	1.95	1.92	1.90	1.88
90	5.20	3.84	3.26	2.93	2.71	2.55	2.43	2.34	2.26	2.19	2.14	2.09	2.05	2.02	1.98	1.95	1.93	1.91	1.88	1.86
100	5.18	3.83	3.25	2.92	2.70	2.54	2.42	2.32	2.24	2.18	2.12	2.08	2.04	2.00	1.97	1.94	1.91	1.89	1.87	1.85
120	5.15	3.80	3.23	2.89	2.67	2.52	2.39	2.30	2.22	2.16	2.10	2.05	2.01	1.98	1.94	1.92	1.89	1.87	1.84	1.82
140	5.13	3.79	3.21	2.88	2.66	2.50	2.38	2.28	2.21	2.14	2.09	2.04	2.00	1.96	1.93	1.90	1.87	1.85	1.83	1.81
160	5.12	3.78	3.20	2.87	2.65	2.49	2.37	2.27	2.19	2.13	2.07	2.03	1.99	1.95	1.92	1.89	1.86	1.84	1.82	1.80
180	5.11	3.77	3.19	2.86	2.64	2.48	2.36	2.26	2.19	2.12	2.07	2.02	1.98	1.94	1.91	1.88	1.85	1.83	1.81	1.79
200	5.10	3.76	3.18	2.85	2.63	2.47	2.35	2.26	2.18	2.11	2.06	2.01	1.97	1.93	1.90	1.87	1.84	1.82	1.80	1.78
300	5.07	3.73	3.16	2.83	2.61	2.45	2.33	2.23	2.16	2.09	2.04	1.99	1.95	1.91	1.88	1.85	1.82	1.80	1.77	1.75
100000	5.02	3.69	3.12	2.79	2.57	2.41	2.29	2.19	2.11	2.05	1.99	1.94	1.90	1.87	1.83	1.80	1.78	1.75	1.73	1.71

Top d.f. = v_1

v_2	100000	300	200	180	160	140	120	100	90	80	70	60	50	45	40	30	28	26	24	22
1	1018.25	1016.56	1015.71	1015.43	1015.08	1014.62	1014.02	1013.17	1012.61	1011.91	1011.00	1009.80	1008.12	1007.00	1005.60	1001.41	1000.22	998.85	997.25	995.36
2	39.50	39.49	39.49	39.49	39.49	39.49	39.49	39.49	39.49	39.49	39.48	39.48	39.48	39.48	39.47	39.46	39.46	39.46	39.46	39.45
3	13.90	13.92	13.93	13.93	13.94	13.94	13.95	13.96	13.96	13.97	13.98	13.99	14.01	14.02	14.04	14.08	14.09	14.11	14.12	14.14
4	8.26	8.28	8.29	8.29	8.30	8.30	8.31	8.32	8.33	8.33	8.35	8.36	8.38	8.39	8.41	8.46	8.48	8.49	8.51	8.53
5	6.02	6.04	6.05	6.05	6.06	6.06	6.07	6.08	6.09	6.10	6.11	6.12	6.14	6.16	6.18	6.23	6.24	6.26	6.28	6.30
6	4.85	4.87	4.88	4.89	4.89	4.90	4.90	4.92	4.92	4.93	4.94	4.96	4.98	4.99	5.01	5.07	5.08	5.10	5.12	5.14
7	4.14	4.17	4.18	4.18	4.18	4.19	4.20	4.21	4.22	4.23	4.24	4.25	4.28	4.29	4.31	4.36	4.38	4.39	4.41	4.44
8	3.67	3.69	3.70	3.71	3.71	3.72	3.73	3.74	3.75	3.76	3.77	3.78	3.81	3.82	3.84	3.89	3.91	3.93	3.95	3.97
9	3.33	3.36	3.37	3.37	3.38	3.38	3.39	3.40	3.41	3.42	3.43	3.45	3.47	3.49	3.51	3.56	3.58	3.59	3.61	3.64
10	3.08	3.10	3.12	3.12	3.13	3.13	3.14	3.15	3.16	3.17	3.18	3.20	3.22	3.24	3.26	3.31	3.33	3.34	3.37	3.39
11	2.88	2.91	2.92	2.92	2.93	2.94	2.94	2.96	2.96	2.97	2.99	3.00	3.03	3.04	3.06	3.12	3.13	3.15	3.17	3.20
12	2.73	2.75	2.76	2.77	2.77	2.78	2.79	2.80	2.81	2.82	2.83	2.85	2.87	2.89	2.91	2.96	2.98	3.00	3.02	3.04
13	2.60	2.62	2.63	2.64	2.64	2.65	2.66	2.67	2.68	2.69	2.70	2.72	2.74	2.76	2.78	2.84	2.85	2.87	2.89	2.92
14	2.49	2.51	2.53	2.53	2.54	2.54	2.55	2.56	2.57	2.58	2.60	2.61	2.64	2.65	2.67	2.73	2.75	2.77	2.79	2.81
15	2.40	2.42	2.44	2.44	2.44	2.45	2.46	2.47	2.48	2.49	2.51	2.52	2.55	2.56	2.59	2.64	2.66	2.68	2.70	2.73
16	2.32	2.34	2.36	2.36	2.37	2.37	2.38	2.40	2.40	2.42	2.43	2.45	2.47	2.49	2.51	2.57	2.58	2.60	2.63	2.65
17	2.25	2.27	2.29	2.29	2.30	2.31	2.32	2.33	2.34	2.35	2.36	2.38	2.41	2.42	2.44	2.50	2.52	2.54	2.56	2.59
18	2.19	2.21	2.23	2.23	2.24	2.25	2.26	2.27	2.28	2.29	2.30	2.32	2.35	2.36	2.38	2.44	2.46	2.48	2.50	2.53
19	2.13	2.16	2.18	2.18	2.19	2.19	2.20	2.22	2.23	2.24	2.25	2.27	2.30	2.31	2.33	2.39	2.41	2.43	2.45	2.48
20	2.09	2.11	2.13	2.13	2.14	2.15	2.16	2.17	2.18	2.19	2.20	2.22	2.25	2.27	2.29	2.35	2.37	2.39	2.41	2.43
21	2.04	2.07	2.09	2.09	2.10	2.10	2.11	2.13	2.14	2.15	2.16	2.18	2.21	2.23	2.25	2.31	2.33	2.34	2.37	2.39
22	2.00	2.03	2.05	2.05	2.06	2.07	2.08	2.09	2.10	2.11	2.13	2.14	2.17	2.19	2.21	2.27	2.29	2.31	2.33	2.36
23	1.97	2.00	2.01	2.02	2.02	2.03	2.04	2.06	2.07	2.08	2.09	2.11	2.14	2.15	2.18	2.24	2.26	2.28	2.30	2.33
24	1.94	1.97	1.98	1.99	1.99	2.00	2.01	2.02	2.03	2.05	2.06	2.08	2.11	2.12	2.15	2.21	2.23	2.25	2.27	2.30

Bottom d.f. = v_2

25	2.27	2.24	2.22	2.20	2.18	2.12	2.10	2.08	2.05	2.03	2.02	2.01	2.00	1.98	1.97	1.96	1.96	1.95	1.94	1.91
26	2.24	2.22	2.19	2.17	2.16	2.09	2.07	2.05	2.03	2.01	1.99	1.98	1.97	1.95	1.94	1.94	1.93	1.92	1.91	1.88
27	2.22	2.19	2.17	2.15	2.13	2.07	2.05	2.03	2.00	1.98	1.97	1.95	1.94	1.93	1.92	1.91	1.90	1.90	1.88	1.85
28	2.20	2.17	2.15	2.13	2.11	2.05	2.03	2.01	1.98	1.96	1.94	1.93	1.92	1.91	1.90	1.89	1.88	1.88	1.86	1.83
29	2.18	2.15	2.13	2.11	2.09	2.03	2.01	1.99	1.96	1.94	1.92	1.91	1.90	1.89	1.88	1.87	1.86	1.86	1.84	1.81
30	2.16	2.14	2.11	2.09	2.07	2.01	1.99	1.97	1.94	1.92	1.90	1.89	1.88	1.87	1.86	1.85	1.84	1.84	1.82	1.79
35	2.09	2.06	2.04	2.02	2.00	1.93	1.91	1.89	1.86	1.84	1.82	1.81	1.80	1.79	1.77	1.77	1.76	1.75	1.74	1.70
40	2.03	2.01	1.98	1.96	1.94	1.88	1.85	1.83	1.80	1.78	1.76	1.75	1.74	1.72	1.71	1.70	1.70	1.69	1.67	1.64
45	1.99	1.96	1.94	1.92	1.90	1.83	1.81	1.79	1.76	1.74	1.72	1.70	1.69	1.68	1.66	1.66	1.65	1.64	1.62	1.59
50	1.96	1.93	1.91	1.89	1.87	1.80	1.77	1.75	1.72	1.70	1.68	1.67	1.66	1.64	1.63	1.62	1.61	1.60	1.58	1.55
60	1.91	1.88	1.86	1.83	1.82	1.74	1.72	1.70	1.67	1.64	1.63	1.61	1.60	1.58	1.57	1.56	1.55	1.54	1.52	1.48
70	1.88	1.85	1.82	1.80	1.78	1.71	1.68	1.66	1.63	1.60	1.59	1.57	1.56	1.54	1.53	1.52	1.51	1.50	1.48	1.44
80	1.85	1.82	1.79	1.77	1.75	1.68	1.65	1.63	1.60	1.57	1.55	1.54	1.53	1.51	1.49	1.48	1.47	1.47	1.45	1.40
90	1.83	1.80	1.77	1.75	1.73	1.66	1.63	1.61	1.58	1.55	1.53	1.52	1.50	1.48	1.47	1.46	1.45	1.44	1.42	1.37
100	1.81	1.78	1.76	1.74	1.71	1.64	1.61	1.59	1.56	1.53	1.51	1.50	1.48	1.46	1.45	1.44	1.43	1.42	1.40	1.35
120	1.79	1.76	1.73	1.71	1.69	1.61	1.59	1.56	1.53	1.50	1.48	1.47	1.45	1.43	1.42	1.41	1.40	1.39	1.36	1.31
140	1.77	1.74	1.72	1.69	1.67	1.60	1.57	1.55	1.51	1.48	1.46	1.45	1.43	1.41	1.39	1.38	1.37	1.36	1.34	1.28
160	1.76	1.73	1.70	1.68	1.66	1.58	1.55	1.53	1.50	1.47	1.45	1.43	1.42	1.39	1.38	1.36	1.35	1.35	1.32	1.26
180	1.75	1.72	1.69	1.67	1.65	1.57	1.54	1.52	1.48	1.46	1.43	1.42	1.40	1.38	1.36	1.35	1.34	1.33	1.31	1.24
200	1.74	1.71	1.68	1.66	1.64	1.56	1.53	1.51	1.47	1.45	1.42	1.41	1.39	1.37	1.35	1.34	1.33	1.32	1.29	1.23
300	1.72	1.69	1.66	1.64	1.62	1.54	1.51	1.48	1.45	1.42	1.39	1.38	1.36	1.34	1.32	1.31	1.29	1.28	1.25	1.18
100000	1.67	1.64	1.61	1.59	1.57	1.48	1.45	1.43	1.39	1.36	1.33	1.31	1.30	1.27	1.25	1.23	1.22	1.21	1.17	1.01

Critical Values of $F_{0.05}$

Bottom d.f. = v_2	Top d.f. = v_1																			
	1	2	3	4	5	6	7	8	9	10	11	12	13	14	15	16	17	18	19	20
1	161.45	199.50	215.71	224.58	230.16	233.99	236.77	238.88	240.54	241.88	242.98	243.91	244.69	245.36	245.95	246.46	246.92	247.32	247.69	248.01
2	18.51	19.00	19.16	19.25	19.30	19.33	19.35	19.37	19.38	19.40	19.40	19.41	19.42	19.42	19.43	19.43	19.44	19.44	19.44	19.45
3	10.13	9.55	9.28	9.12	9.01	8.94	8.89	8.85	8.81	8.79	8.76	8.74	8.73	8.71	8.70	8.69	8.68	8.67	8.67	8.66
4	7.71	6.94	6.59	6.39	6.26	6.16	6.09	6.04	6.00	5.96	5.94	5.91	5.89	5.87	5.86	5.84	5.83	5.82	5.81	5.80
5	6.61	5.79	5.41	5.19	5.05	4.95	4.88	4.82	4.77	4.74	4.70	4.68	4.66	4.64	4.62	4.60	4.59	4.58	4.57	4.56
6	5.99	5.14	4.76	4.53	4.39	4.28	4.21	4.15	4.10	4.06	4.03	4.00	3.98	3.96	3.94	3.92	3.91	3.90	3.88	3.87
7	5.59	4.74	4.35	4.12	3.97	3.87	3.79	3.73	3.68	3.64	3.60	3.57	3.55	3.53	3.51	3.49	3.48	3.47	3.46	3.44
8	5.32	4.46	4.07	3.84	3.69	3.58	3.50	3.44	3.39	3.35	3.31	3.28	3.26	3.24	3.22	3.20	3.19	3.17	3.16	3.15
9	5.12	4.26	3.86	3.63	3.48	3.37	3.29	3.23	3.18	3.14	3.10	3.07	3.05	3.03	3.01	2.99	2.97	2.96	2.95	2.94
10	4.96	4.10	3.71	3.48	3.33	3.22	3.14	3.07	3.02	2.98	2.94	2.91	2.89	2.86	2.85	2.83	2.81	2.80	2.79	2.77
11	4.84	3.98	3.59	3.36	3.20	3.09	3.01	2.95	2.90	2.85	2.82	2.79	2.76	2.74	2.72	2.70	2.69	2.67	2.66	2.65
12	4.75	3.89	3.49	3.26	3.11	3.00	2.91	2.85	2.80	2.75	2.72	2.69	2.66	2.64	2.62	2.60	2.58	2.57	2.56	2.54
13	4.67	3.81	3.41	3.18	3.03	2.92	2.83	2.77	2.71	2.67	2.63	2.60	2.58	2.55	2.53	2.51	2.50	2.48	2.47	2.46
14	4.60	3.74	3.34	3.11	2.96	2.85	2.76	2.70	2.65	2.60	2.57	2.53	2.51	2.48	2.46	2.44	2.43	2.41	2.40	2.39
15	4.54	3.68	3.29	3.06	2.90	2.79	2.71	2.64	2.59	2.54	2.51	2.48	2.45	2.42	2.40	2.38	2.37	2.35	2.34	2.33
16	4.49	3.63	3.24	3.01	2.85	2.74	2.66	2.59	2.54	2.49	2.46	2.42	2.40	2.37	2.35	2.33	2.32	2.30	2.29	2.28
17	4.45	3.59	3.20	2.96	2.81	2.70	2.61	2.55	2.49	2.45	2.41	2.38	2.35	2.33	2.31	2.29	2.27	2.26	2.24	2.23
18	4.41	3.55	3.16	2.93	2.77	2.66	2.58	2.51	2.46	2.41	2.37	2.34	2.31	2.29	2.27	2.25	2.23	2.22	2.20	2.19
19	4.38	3.52	3.13	2.90	2.74	2.63	2.54	2.48	2.42	2.38	2.34	2.31	2.28	2.26	2.23	2.21	2.20	2.18	2.17	2.16
20	4.35	3.49	3.10	2.87	2.71	2.60	2.51	2.45	2.39	2.35	2.31	2.28	2.25	2.22	2.20	2.18	2.17	2.15	2.14	2.12
21	4.32	3.47	3.07	2.84	2.68	2.57	2.49	2.42	2.37	2.32	2.28	2.25	2.22	2.20	2.18	2.16	2.14	2.12	2.11	2.10
22	4.30	3.44	3.05	2.82	2.66	2.55	2.46	2.40	2.34	2.30	2.26	2.23	2.20	2.17	2.15	2.13	2.11	2.10	2.08	2.07
23	4.28	3.42	3.03	2.80	2.64	2.53	2.44	2.37	2.32	2.27	2.24	2.20	2.18	2.15	2.13	2.11	2.09	2.08	2.06	2.05
24	4.26	3.40	3.01	2.78	2.62	2.51	2.42	2.36	2.30	2.25	2.22	2.18	2.15	2.13	2.11	2.09	2.07	2.05	2.04	2.03
25	4.24	3.39	2.99	2.76	2.60	2.49	2.40	2.34	2.28	2.24	2.20	2.16	2.14	2.11	2.09	2.07	2.05	2.04	2.02	2.01

26	4.23	3.37	2.98	2.74	2.59	2.47	2.39	2.32	2.27	2.22	2.18	2.15	2.12	2.09	2.07	2.05	2.03	2.02	2.00	1.99
27	4.21	3.35	2.96	2.73	2.57	2.46	2.37	2.31	2.25	2.20	2.17	2.13	2.10	2.08	2.06	2.04	2.02	2.00	1.99	1.97
28	4.20	3.34	2.95	2.71	2.56	2.45	2.36	2.29	2.24	2.19	2.15	2.12	2.09	2.06	2.04	2.02	2.00	1.99	1.97	1.96
29	4.18	3.33	2.93	2.70	2.55	2.43	2.35	2.28	2.22	2.18	2.14	2.10	2.08	2.05	2.03	2.01	1.99	1.97	1.96	1.94
30	4.17	3.32	2.92	2.69	2.53	2.42	2.33	2.27	2.21	2.16	2.13	2.09	2.06	2.04	2.01	1.99	1.98	1.96	1.95	1.93
35	4.12	3.27	2.87	2.64	2.49	2.37	2.29	2.22	2.16	2.11	2.07	2.04	2.01	1.99	1.96	1.94	1.92	1.91	1.89	1.88
40	4.08	3.23	2.84	2.61	2.45	2.34	2.25	2.18	2.12	2.08	2.04	2.00	1.97	1.95	1.92	1.90	1.89	1.87	1.85	1.84
45	4.06	3.20	2.81	2.58	2.42	2.31	2.22	2.15	2.10	2.05	2.01	1.97	1.94	1.92	1.89	1.87	1.86	1.84	1.82	1.81
50	4.03	3.18	2.79	2.56	2.40	2.29	2.20	2.13	2.07	2.03	1.99	1.94	1.92	1.89	1.86	1.85	1.83	1.81	1.80	1.78
60	4.00	3.15	2.76	2.53	2.37	2.25	2.17	2.10	2.04	1.99	1.95	1.92	1.89	1.86	1.84	1.82	1.80	1.78	1.76	1.75
70	3.98	3.13	2.74	2.50	2.35	2.23	2.14	2.07	2.02	1.97	1.93	1.89	1.86	1.84	1.81	1.79	1.77	1.75	1.74	1.72
80	3.96	3.11	2.72	2.49	2.33	2.21	2.13	2.06	2.00	1.95	1.91	1.88	1.84	1.82	1.79	1.77	1.75	1.73	1.72	1.70
90	3.95	3.10	2.71	2.47	2.32	2.20	2.11	2.04	1.99	1.94	1.90	1.86	1.83	1.80	1.78	1.76	1.74	1.72	1.70	1.69
100	3.94	3.09	2.70	2.46	2.31	2.19	2.10	2.03	1.97	1.93	1.89	1.85	1.82	1.79	1.77	1.75	1.73	1.71	1.69	1.68
120	3.92	3.07	2.68	2.45	2.29	2.18	2.09	2.02	1.96	1.91	1.87	1.83	1.80	1.78	1.75	1.73	1.71	1.69	1.67	1.66
140	3.91	3.06	2.67	2.44	2.28	2.16	2.08	2.01	1.95	1.90	1.86	1.82	1.79	1.76	1.74	1.72	1.70	1.68	1.66	1.65
160	3.90	3.05	2.66	2.43	2.27	2.16	2.07	2.00	1.94	1.89	1.85	1.81	1.78	1.75	1.73	1.71	1.69	1.67	1.65	1.64
180	3.89	3.05	2.65	2.42	2.26	2.15	2.06	1.99	1.93	1.88	1.84	1.81	1.77	1.75	1.72	1.70	1.68	1.66	1.64	1.63
200	3.89	3.04	2.65	2.42	2.26	2.14	2.06	1.98	1.93	1.88	1.84	1.80	1.77	1.74	1.72	1.69	1.67	1.66	1.64	1.62
300	3.87	3.03	2.63	2.40	2.24	2.13	2.04	1.97	1.91	1.86	1.82	1.78	1.75	1.72	1.70	1.68	1.66	1.64	1.62	1.61
100000	3.84	3.00	2.60	2.37	2.21	2.10	2.01	1.94	1.88	1.83	1.79	1.75	1.72	1.69	1.67	1.64	1.62	1.60	1.59	1.57

Top d.f. = v_1

v_2	22	24	26	28	30	40	45	50	60	70	80	90	100	120	140	160	180	200	300	100000
1	248.58	249.05	249.45	249.80	250.10	251.14	251.49	251.77	252.20	252.50	252.72	252.90	253.04	253.25	253.40	253.52	253.61	253.68	253.89	254.31
2	19.45	19.45	19.46	19.46	19.46	19.47	19.47	19.48	19.48	19.48	19.48	19.48	19.49	19.49	19.49	19.49	19.49	19.49	19.49	19.50
3	8.65	8.64	8.63	8.62	8.62	8.59	8.59	8.58	8.57	8.57	8.56	8.56	8.55	8.55	8.55	8.54	8.54	8.54	8.54	8.53
4	5.79	5.77	5.76	5.75	5.75	5.72	5.71	5.70	5.69	5.68	5.67	5.67	5.66	5.66	5.65	5.65	5.65	5.65	5.64	5.63
5	4.54	4.53	4.52	4.50	4.50	4.46	4.45	4.44	4.43	4.42	4.41	4.41	4.41	4.40	4.39	4.39	4.39	4.39	4.38	4.37
6	3.86	3.84	3.83	3.82	3.81	3.77	3.76	3.75	3.74	3.73	3.72	3.72	3.71	3.70	3.70	3.70	3.69	3.69	3.68	3.67
7	3.43	3.41	3.40	3.39	3.38	3.34	3.33	3.32	3.30	3.29	3.29	3.28	3.27	3.27	3.26	3.26	3.25	3.25	3.24	3.23
8	3.13	3.12	3.10	3.09	3.08	3.04	3.03	3.02	3.01	2.99	2.99	2.98	2.97	2.97	2.96	2.96	2.95	2.95	2.94	2.93
9	2.92	2.90	2.89	2.87	2.86	2.83	2.81	2.80	2.79	2.78	2.77	2.76	2.76	2.75	2.74	2.74	2.73	2.73	2.72	2.71
10	2.75	2.74	2.72	2.71	2.70	2.66	2.65	2.64	2.62	2.61	2.60	2.59	2.59	2.58	2.57	2.57	2.57	2.56	2.55	2.54
11	2.63	2.61	2.59	2.58	2.57	2.53	2.52	2.51	2.49	2.48	2.47	2.46	2.46	2.45	2.44	2.44	2.43	2.43	2.42	2.40
12	2.52	2.51	2.49	2.48	2.47	2.43	2.41	2.40	2.38	2.37	2.36	2.36	2.35	2.34	2.33	2.33	2.33	2.32	2.31	2.30
13	2.44	2.42	2.41	2.39	2.38	2.34	2.33	2.31	2.30	2.28	2.27	2.27	2.26	2.25	2.25	2.24	2.24	2.23	2.23	2.21
14	2.37	2.35	2.33	2.32	2.31	2.27	2.25	2.24	2.22	2.21	2.20	2.19	2.19	2.18	2.17	2.17	2.16	2.16	2.15	2.13
15	2.31	2.29	2.27	2.26	2.25	2.20	2.19	2.18	2.16	2.15	2.14	2.13	2.12	2.11	2.11	2.10	2.10	2.10	2.09	2.07
16	2.25	2.24	2.22	2.21	2.19	2.15	2.14	2.12	2.11	2.09	2.08	2.07	2.07	2.06	2.05	2.05	2.04	2.04	2.03	2.01
17	2.21	2.19	2.17	2.16	2.15	2.10	2.09	2.08	2.06	2.05	2.03	2.03	2.02	2.01	2.00	2.00	1.99	1.99	1.98	1.96
18	2.17	2.15	2.13	2.12	2.11	2.06	2.05	2.04	2.02	2.00	1.99	1.98	1.98	1.97	1.96	1.96	1.95	1.95	1.94	1.92
19	2.13	2.11	2.10	2.08	2.07	2.03	2.01	2.00	1.98	1.97	1.96	1.95	1.94	1.93	1.92	1.92	1.91	1.91	1.90	1.88
20	2.10	2.08	2.07	2.05	2.04	1.99	1.98	1.97	1.95	1.93	1.92	1.91	1.91	1.90	1.89	1.88	1.88	1.88	1.86	1.84
21	2.07	2.05	2.04	2.02	2.01	1.96	1.95	1.94	1.92	1.90	1.89	1.88	1.88	1.87	1.86	1.85	1.85	1.84	1.83	1.81
22	2.05	2.03	2.01	2.00	1.98	1.94	1.92	1.91	1.89	1.88	1.86	1.86	1.85	1.84	1.83	1.82	1.82	1.82	1.81	1.78
23	2.02	2.01	1.99	1.97	1.96	1.91	1.90	1.88	1.86	1.85	1.84	1.83	1.82	1.81	1.81	1.80	1.79	1.79	1.78	1.76
24	2.00	1.98	1.97	1.95	1.94	1.89	1.88	1.86	1.84	1.83	1.82	1.81	1.80	1.79	1.78	1.78	1.77	1.77	1.76	1.73
25	1.98	1.96	1.95	1.93	1.92	1.87	1.86	1.84	1.82	1.81	1.80	1.79	1.78	1.77	1.76	1.75	1.75	1.75	1.73	1.71

Bottom d.f. = v_2

26	1.97	1.95	1.93	1.91	1.90	1.85	1.84	1.82	1.80	1.79	1.78	1.77	1.76	1.75	1.74	1.73	1.73	1.73	1.71	1.69
27	1.95	1.93	1.91	1.90	1.88	1.84	1.82	1.81	1.79	1.77	1.76	1.75	1.74	1.73	1.72	1.72	1.71	1.71	1.70	1.67
28	1.93	1.91	1.90	1.88	1.87	1.82	1.80	1.79	1.77	1.75	1.74	1.73	1.73	1.71	1.71	1.70	1.69	1.69	1.68	1.65
29	1.92	1.90	1.88	1.87	1.85	1.81	1.79	1.77	1.75	1.74	1.73	1.72	1.71	1.70	1.69	1.68	1.68	1.67	1.66	1.64
30	1.91	1.89	1.87	1.85	1.84	1.79	1.77	1.76	1.74	1.72	1.71	1.70	1.70	1.68	1.68	1.67	1.66	1.66	1.65	1.62
35	1.85	1.83	1.82	1.80	1.79	1.74	1.72	1.70	1.68	1.66	1.65	1.64	1.63	1.62	1.61	1.61	1.60	1.60	1.58	1.56
40	1.81	1.79	1.77	1.76	1.74	1.69	1.67	1.66	1.64	1.62	1.61	1.60	1.59	1.58	1.57	1.56	1.55	1.55	1.54	1.51
45	1.78	1.76	1.74	1.73	1.71	1.66	1.64	1.63	1.60	1.59	1.57	1.56	1.55	1.54	1.53	1.52	1.52	1.51	1.50	1.47
50	1.76	1.74	1.72	1.70	1.69	1.63	1.61	1.60	1.58	1.56	1.54	1.53	1.52	1.51	1.50	1.49	1.49	1.48	1.47	1.44
60	1.72	1.70	1.68	1.66	1.65	1.59	1.57	1.56	1.53	1.52	1.50	1.49	1.48	1.47	1.46	1.45	1.44	1.44	1.42	1.39
70	1.70	1.67	1.65	1.64	1.62	1.57	1.55	1.53	1.50	1.49	1.47	1.46	1.45	1.44	1.42	1.42	1.41	1.40	1.39	1.35
80	1.68	1.65	1.63	1.62	1.60	1.54	1.52	1.51	1.48	1.46	1.45	1.44	1.43	1.41	1.40	1.39	1.38	1.38	1.36	1.32
90	1.66	1.64	1.62	1.60	1.59	1.53	1.51	1.49	1.46	1.44	1.43	1.42	1.41	1.39	1.38	1.37	1.36	1.36	1.34	1.30
100	1.65	1.63	1.61	1.59	1.57	1.52	1.49	1.48	1.45	1.43	1.41	1.40	1.39	1.38	1.36	1.35	1.35	1.34	1.32	1.28
120	1.63	1.61	1.59	1.57	1.55	1.50	1.47	1.46	1.43	1.41	1.39	1.38	1.37	1.35	1.34	1.33	1.32	1.32	1.30	1.25
140	1.62	1.60	1.57	1.56	1.54	1.48	1.46	1.44	1.41	1.39	1.38	1.36	1.35	1.33	1.32	1.31	1.30	1.30	1.28	1.23
160	1.61	1.59	1.57	1.55	1.53	1.47	1.45	1.43	1.40	1.38	1.36	1.35	1.34	1.32	1.31	1.30	1.29	1.28	1.26	1.21
180	1.60	1.58	1.56	1.54	1.52	1.46	1.44	1.42	1.39	1.37	1.35	1.34	1.33	1.31	1.30	1.29	1.28	1.27	1.25	1.20
200	1.60	1.57	1.55	1.53	1.52	1.46	1.43	1.41	1.39	1.36	1.35	1.33	1.32	1.30	1.29	1.28	1.27	1.26	1.24	1.19
300	1.58	1.55	1.53	1.51	1.50	1.43	1.41	1.39	1.36	1.34	1.32	1.31	1.30	1.28	1.27	1.26	1.24	1.23	1.21	1.15
100000	1.54	1.52	1.50	1.48	1.46	1.39	1.37	1.35	1.32	1.29	1.27	1.26	1.24	1.22	1.20	1.20	1.19	1.18	1.14	1.01

Critical Values of $F_{0.10}$

Bottom d.f. = v_2	Top d.f. = v_1																			
	1	2	3	4	5	6	7	8	9	10	11	12	13	14	15	16	17	18	19	20
1	39.86	49.50	53.59	55.83	57.24	58.20	58.91	59.44	59.86	60.19	60.47	60.71	60.90	61.07	61.22	61.35	61.46	61.57	61.66	61.74
2	8.53	9.00	9.16	9.24	9.29	9.33	9.35	9.37	9.38	9.39	9.40	9.41	9.41	9.42	9.42	9.43	9.43	9.44	9.44	9.44
3	5.54	5.46	5.39	5.34	5.31	5.28	5.27	5.25	5.24	5.23	5.22	5.22	5.21	5.20	5.20	5.20	5.19	5.19	5.19	5.18
4	4.54	4.32	4.19	4.11	4.05	4.01	3.98	3.95	3.94	3.92	3.91	3.90	3.89	3.88	3.87	3.86	3.86	3.85	3.85	3.84
5	4.06	3.78	3.62	3.52	3.45	3.40	3.37	3.34	3.32	3.30	3.28	3.27	3.26	3.25	3.24	3.23	3.22	3.22	3.21	3.21
6	3.78	3.46	3.29	3.18	3.11	3.05	3.01	2.98	2.96	2.94	2.92	2.90	2.89	2.88	2.87	2.86	2.85	2.85	2.84	2.84
7	3.59	3.26	3.07	2.96	2.88	2.83	2.78	2.75	2.72	2.70	2.68	2.67	2.65	2.64	2.63	2.62	2.61	2.61	2.60	2.59
8	3.46	3.11	2.92	2.81	2.73	2.67	2.62	2.59	2.56	2.54	2.52	2.50	2.49	2.48	2.46	2.45	2.45	2.44	2.43	2.42
9	3.36	3.01	2.81	2.69	2.61	2.55	2.51	2.47	2.44	2.42	2.40	2.38	2.36	2.35	2.34	2.33	2.32	2.31	2.30	2.30
10	3.29	2.92	2.73	2.61	2.52	2.46	2.41	2.38	2.35	2.32	2.30	2.28	2.27	2.26	2.24	2.23	2.22	2.22	2.21	2.20
11	3.23	2.86	2.66	2.54	2.45	2.39	2.34	2.30	2.27	2.25	2.23	2.21	2.19	2.18	2.17	2.16	2.15	2.14	2.13	2.12
12	3.18	2.81	2.61	2.48	2.39	2.33	2.28	2.24	2.21	2.19	2.17	2.15	2.13	2.12	2.10	2.09	2.08	2.08	2.07	2.06
13	3.14	2.76	2.56	2.43	2.35	2.28	2.23	2.20	2.16	2.14	2.12	2.10	2.08	2.07	2.05	2.04	2.03	2.02	2.01	2.01
14	3.10	2.73	2.52	2.39	2.31	2.24	2.19	2.15	2.12	2.10	2.07	2.05	2.04	2.02	2.01	2.00	1.99	1.98	1.97	1.96
15	3.07	2.70	2.49	2.36	2.27	2.21	2.16	2.12	2.09	2.06	2.04	2.02	2.00	1.99	1.97	1.96	1.95	1.94	1.93	1.92
16	3.05	2.67	2.46	2.33	2.24	2.18	2.13	2.09	2.06	2.03	2.01	1.99	1.97	1.95	1.94	1.93	1.92	1.91	1.90	1.89
17	3.03	2.64	2.44	2.31	2.22	2.15	2.10	2.06	2.03	2.00	1.98	1.96	1.94	1.93	1.91	1.90	1.89	1.88	1.87	1.86
18	3.01	2.62	2.42	2.29	2.20	2.13	2.08	2.04	2.00	1.98	1.95	1.93	1.92	1.90	1.89	1.87	1.86	1.85	1.84	1.84
19	2.99	2.61	2.40	2.27	2.18	2.11	2.06	2.02	1.98	1.96	1.93	1.91	1.89	1.88	1.86	1.85	1.84	1.83	1.82	1.81
20	2.97	2.59	2.38	2.25	2.16	2.09	2.04	2.00	1.96	1.94	1.91	1.89	1.87	1.86	1.84	1.83	1.82	1.81	1.80	1.79
21	2.96	2.57	2.36	2.23	2.14	2.08	2.02	1.98	1.95	1.92	1.90	1.87	1.86	1.84	1.83	1.81	1.80	1.79	1.78	1.78
22	2.95	2.56	2.35	2.22	2.13	2.06	2.01	1.97	1.93	1.90	1.88	1.86	1.84	1.83	1.81	1.80	1.79	1.78	1.77	1.76
23	2.94	2.55	2.34	2.21	2.11	2.05	1.99	1.95	1.92	1.89	1.87	1.84	1.83	1.81	1.80	1.78	1.77	1.76	1.75	1.74
24	2.93	2.54	2.33	2.19	2.10	2.04	1.98	1.94	1.91	1.88	1.85	1.83	1.81	1.80	1.78	1.77	1.76	1.75	1.74	1.73
25	2.92	2.53	2.32	2.18	2.09	2.02	1.97	1.93	1.89	1.87	1.84	1.82	1.80	1.79	1.77	1.76	1.75	1.74	1.73	1.72

df																			
26	2.91	2.52	2.31	2.17	2.08	2.01	1.96	1.92	1.88	1.86	1.83	1.81	1.79	1.77	1.76	1.75	1.73	1.72	1.71	1.71
27	2.90	2.51	2.30	2.17	2.07	2.00	1.95	1.91	1.87	1.85	1.82	1.80	1.78	1.76	1.75	1.74	1.72	1.71	1.70	1.70
28	2.89	2.50	2.29	2.16	2.06	2.00	1.94	1.90	1.87	1.84	1.81	1.79	1.77	1.75	1.74	1.73	1.71	1.70	1.69	1.69
29	2.89	2.50	2.28	2.15	2.06	1.99	1.93	1.89	1.86	1.83	1.80	1.78	1.76	1.75	1.73	1.72	1.71	1.69	1.68	1.68
30	2.88	2.49	2.28	2.14	2.05	1.98	1.93	1.88	1.85	1.82	1.79	1.77	1.75	1.74	1.72	1.71	1.70	1.69	1.68	1.67
35	2.85	2.46	2.25	2.11	2.02	1.95	1.90	1.85	1.82	1.79	1.76	1.74	1.72	1.70	1.69	1.67	1.66	1.65	1.64	1.63
40	2.84	2.44	2.23	2.09	2.00	1.93	1.87	1.83	1.79	1.76	1.74	1.71	1.70	1.68	1.66	1.65	1.64	1.62	1.61	1.61
45	2.82	2.42	2.21	2.07	1.98	1.91	1.85	1.81	1.77	1.74	1.72	1.70	1.68	1.66	1.64	1.63	1.62	1.60	1.59	1.58
50	2.81	2.41	2.20	2.06	1.97	1.90	1.84	1.80	1.76	1.73	1.70	1.68	1.66	1.64	1.63	1.61	1.60	1.59	1.58	1.57
60	2.79	2.39	2.18	2.04	1.95	1.87	1.82	1.77	1.74	1.71	1.68	1.66	1.64	1.62	1.60	1.59	1.58	1.56	1.55	1.54
70	2.78	2.38	2.16	2.03	1.93	1.86	1.80	1.76	1.72	1.69	1.66	1.64	1.62	1.60	1.59	1.57	1.56	1.55	1.54	1.53
80	2.77	2.37	2.15	2.02	1.92	1.85	1.79	1.75	1.71	1.68	1.65	1.63	1.61	1.59	1.57	1.56	1.55	1.53	1.52	1.51
90	2.76	2.36	2.15	2.01	1.91	1.84	1.78	1.74	1.70	1.67	1.64	1.62	1.60	1.58	1.56	1.55	1.54	1.52	1.51	1.50
100	2.76	2.36	2.14	2.00	1.91	1.83	1.78	1.73	1.69	1.66	1.64	1.61	1.59	1.57	1.56	1.54	1.53	1.52	1.50	1.49
120	2.75	2.35	2.13	1.99	1.90	1.82	1.77	1.72	1.68	1.65	1.63	1.60	1.58	1.56	1.55	1.53	1.52	1.50	1.49	1.48
140	2.74	2.34	2.12	1.99	1.89	1.82	1.76	1.71	1.68	1.64	1.62	1.59	1.57	1.55	1.54	1.52	1.51	1.50	1.48	1.47
160	2.74	2.34	2.12	1.98	1.88	1.81	1.75	1.71	1.67	1.64	1.61	1.59	1.57	1.55	1.53	1.52	1.50	1.49	1.48	1.47
180	2.73	2.33	2.11	1.98	1.88	1.81	1.75	1.70	1.67	1.63	1.61	1.58	1.56	1.54	1.53	1.51	1.50	1.49	1.48	1.46
200	2.73	2.33	2.11	1.97	1.88	1.80	1.75	1.70	1.66	1.63	1.60	1.58	1.56	1.54	1.52	1.51	1.49	1.48	1.47	1.46
300	2.72	2.32	2.10	1.96	1.87	1.79	1.74	1.69	1.65	1.62	1.59	1.57	1.55	1.53	1.51	1.49	1.48	1.47	1.46	1.45
100000	2.71	2.30	2.08	1.94	1.85	1.77	1.72	1.67	1.63	1.60	1.57	1.55	1.52	1.50	1.49	1.47	1.46	1.44	1.43	1.42

Top d.f. = v_1

Bottom d.f. = v_2	22	24	26	28	30	40	45	50	60	70	80	90	100	120	140	160	180	200	300	100000
1	61.88	62.00	62.10	62.19	62.26	62.53	62.62	62.69	62.79	62.87	62.93	62.97	63.01	63.06	63.10	63.13	63.15	63.17	63.22	63.33
2	9.45	9.45	9.45	9.46	9.46	9.47	9.47	9.47	9.47	9.48	9.48	9.48	9.48	9.48	9.48	9.48	9.49	9.49	9.49	9.49
3	5.18	5.18	5.17	5.17	5.17	5.16	5.16	5.15	5.15	5.15	5.15	5.15	5.14	5.14	5.14	5.14	5.14	5.14	5.14	5.13
4	3.84	3.83	3.83	3.82	3.82	3.80	3.80	3.80	3.79	3.79	3.78	3.78	3.78	3.78	3.77	3.77	3.77	3.77	3.77	3.76
5	3.20	3.19	3.18	3.18	3.17	3.16	3.15	3.15	3.14	3.14	3.13	3.13	3.13	3.12	3.12	3.12	3.12	3.12	3.11	3.11
6	2.83	2.82	2.81	2.81	2.80	2.78	2.77	2.77	2.76	2.76	2.75	2.75	2.75	2.74	2.74	2.74	2.74	2.73	2.73	2.72
7	2.58	2.58	2.57	2.56	2.56	2.54	2.53	2.52	2.51	2.51	2.50	2.50	2.50	2.49	2.49	2.49	2.49	2.48	2.48	2.47
8	2.41	2.40	2.40	2.39	2.38	2.36	2.35	2.35	2.34	2.33	2.33	2.32	2.32	2.32	2.31	2.31	2.31	2.31	2.30	2.29
9	2.29	2.28	2.27	2.26	2.25	2.23	2.22	2.22	2.21	2.20	2.20	2.19	2.19	2.18	2.18	2.18	2.18	2.17	2.17	2.16
10	2.19	2.18	2.17	2.16	2.16	2.13	2.12	2.12	2.11	2.10	2.09	2.09	2.09	2.08	2.08	2.08	2.07	2.07	2.07	2.06
11	2.11	2.10	2.09	2.08	2.08	2.05	2.04	2.04	2.03	2.02	2.01	2.01	2.01	2.00	2.00	1.99	1.99	1.99	1.98	1.97
12	2.05	2.04	2.03	2.02	2.01	1.99	1.98	1.97	1.96	1.95	1.95	1.94	1.94	1.93	1.93	1.93	1.92	1.92	1.92	1.90
13	1.99	1.98	1.97	1.96	1.96	1.93	1.92	1.92	1.90	1.90	1.89	1.89	1.88	1.88	1.87	1.87	1.87	1.86	1.86	1.85
14	1.95	1.94	1.93	1.92	1.91	1.89	1.88	1.87	1.86	1.85	1.84	1.84	1.83	1.83	1.82	1.82	1.82	1.82	1.81	1.80
15	1.91	1.90	1.89	1.88	1.87	1.85	1.84	1.83	1.82	1.81	1.80	1.80	1.79	1.79	1.78	1.78	1.78	1.77	1.77	1.76
16	1.88	1.87	1.86	1.85	1.84	1.81	1.80	1.79	1.78	1.77	1.77	1.76	1.76	1.75	1.75	1.74	1.74	1.74	1.73	1.72
17	1.85	1.84	1.83	1.82	1.81	1.78	1.77	1.76	1.75	1.74	1.74	1.73	1.73	1.72	1.71	1.71	1.71	1.71	1.70	1.69
18	1.82	1.81	1.80	1.79	1.78	1.75	1.74	1.74	1.72	1.71	1.71	1.70	1.70	1.69	1.69	1.68	1.68	1.68	1.67	1.66
19	1.80	1.79	1.78	1.77	1.76	1.73	1.72	1.71	1.70	1.69	1.68	1.68	1.67	1.67	1.66	1.66	1.65	1.65	1.65	1.63
20	1.78	1.77	1.76	1.75	1.74	1.71	1.70	1.69	1.68	1.67	1.66	1.65	1.65	1.64	1.64	1.63	1.63	1.63	1.62	1.61
21	1.76	1.75	1.74	1.73	1.72	1.69	1.68	1.67	1.66	1.65	1.64	1.63	1.63	1.62	1.62	1.61	1.61	1.61	1.60	1.59
22	1.74	1.73	1.72	1.71	1.70	1.67	1.66	1.65	1.64	1.63	1.62	1.62	1.61	1.60	1.60	1.60	1.59	1.59	1.58	1.57
23	1.73	1.72	1.70	1.69	1.69	1.66	1.64	1.64	1.62	1.61	1.61	1.60	1.59	1.59	1.58	1.58	1.57	1.57	1.56	1.55
24	1.71	1.70	1.69	1.68	1.67	1.64	1.63	1.62	1.61	1.60	1.59	1.58	1.58	1.57	1.57	1.56	1.56	1.56	1.55	1.53
25	1.70	1.69	1.68	1.67	1.66	1.63	1.62	1.61	1.59	1.58	1.58	1.57	1.56	1.56	1.55	1.55	1.54	1.54	1.53	1.52

26	1.50	1.52	1.53	1.53	1.53	1.54	1.54	1.55	1.56	1.56	1.57	1.58	1.59	1.60	1.61	1.65	1.66	1.67	1.68	1.69
27	1.49	1.51	1.52	1.52	1.52	1.53	1.53	1.54	1.54	1.55	1.56	1.57	1.58	1.59	1.60	1.64	1.64	1.65	1.67	1.68
28	1.48	1.50	1.50	1.51	1.51	1.51	1.52	1.53	1.53	1.54	1.55	1.56	1.57	1.58	1.59	1.63	1.63	1.64	1.66	1.67
29	1.47	1.48	1.49	1.50	1.50	1.50	1.51	1.52	1.52	1.53	1.54	1.55	1.56	1.57	1.58	1.62	1.62	1.63	1.65	1.66
30	1.46	1.47	1.48	1.49	1.49	1.49	1.50	1.51	1.51	1.52	1.53	1.54	1.55	1.56	1.57	1.61	1.62	1.63	1.64	1.65
35	1.41	1.43	1.44	1.44	1.45	1.45	1.46	1.47	1.47	1.48	1.49	1.50	1.51	1.52	1.53	1.57	1.58	1.59	1.60	1.62
40	1.38	1.40	1.41	1.41	1.41	1.42	1.42	1.43	1.44	1.45	1.46	1.47	1.48	1.49	1.51	1.54	1.55	1.56	1.57	1.59
45	1.35	1.37	1.38	1.38	1.39	1.39	1.40	1.41	1.41	1.42	1.43	1.44	1.46	1.47	1.48	1.52	1.53	1.54	1.55	1.57
50	1.33	1.35	1.36	1.36	1.37	1.37	1.38	1.39	1.39	1.40	1.41	1.42	1.44	1.45	1.46	1.50	1.51	1.52	1.54	1.55
60	1.29	1.32	1.33	1.33	1.33	1.34	1.35	1.36	1.36	1.37	1.38	1.40	1.41	1.42	1.44	1.48	1.49	1.50	1.51	1.53
70	1.27	1.29	1.30	1.31	1.31	1.32	1.32	1.34	1.34	1.35	1.36	1.37	1.39	1.40	1.42	1.46	1.47	1.48	1.49	1.51
80	1.24	1.27	1.28	1.29	1.29	1.30	1.31	1.32	1.33	1.33	1.34	1.36	1.38	1.39	1.40	1.44	1.45	1.47	1.48	1.49
90	1.23	1.26	1.27	1.27	1.28	1.28	1.29	1.30	1.31	1.32	1.33	1.35	1.36	1.38	1.39	1.43	1.44	1.45	1.47	1.48
100	1.21	1.24	1.26	1.26	1.27	1.27	1.28	1.29	1.30	1.31	1.32	1.34	1.35	1.37	1.38	1.42	1.43	1.45	1.46	1.48
120	1.19	1.22	1.24	1.24	1.25	1.26	1.26	1.28	1.28	1.29	1.31	1.32	1.34	1.35	1.37	1.41	1.42	1.43	1.45	1.46
140	1.18	1.21	1.22	1.23	1.24	1.24	1.25	1.26	1.27	1.28	1.29	1.31	1.33	1.34	1.36	1.40	1.41	1.42	1.44	1.45
160	1.16	1.20	1.21	1.22	1.23	1.23	1.24	1.26	1.26	1.27	1.29	1.30	1.32	1.33	1.35	1.39	1.40	1.42	1.43	1.45
180	1.15	1.19	1.21	1.21	1.22	1.22	1.23	1.25	1.26	1.27	1.28	1.29	1.32	1.33	1.34	1.39	1.40	1.41	1.43	1.44
200	1.14	1.18	1.20	1.20	1.21	1.22	1.23	1.24	1.25	1.26	1.27	1.29	1.31	1.32	1.34	1.38	1.39	1.41	1.42	1.44
300	1.12	1.16	1.18	1.18	1.19	1.20	1.21	1.22	1.23	1.24	1.26	1.27	1.29	1.31	1.32	1.37	1.38	1.39	1.41	1.43
100000	1.01	1.11	1.13	1.14	1.15	1.16	1.17	1.19	1.20	1.21	1.22	1.24	1.26	1.28	1.30	1.34	1.35	1.37	1.38	1.40

Answers to Concept Checks

Chapter 4
Page 116

Data set A: $\bar{x} = \dfrac{\sum x_i}{n} = \dfrac{60}{6} = 10$ median $= \dfrac{10 + 10}{2} = 10$ mode $= 10$

Distribution is symmetrical and unimodal (mean = median = mode).

Data set B: $\bar{x} = \dfrac{\sum x_i}{n} = \dfrac{110}{11} = 10$ median $= 10$ no mode

Distribution is symmetrical (mean = median) and uniform (no mode).

Data set C: $\bar{x} = \dfrac{\sum x_i}{n} = \dfrac{56}{6} = 9.333$ median $= \dfrac{9 + 11}{2} = 10$ mode $= 15$

Distribution is left-skewed (mean < median) and unimodal.

Data set D: $\bar{x} = \dfrac{\sum x_i}{n} = \dfrac{52}{6} = 8.667$ median $= \dfrac{7 + 7}{2} = 7$ modes $= 5$ and 7

Distribution is right-skewed (mean > median) and bimodal.
Corrected data sets:

Data set A: $\bar{x} = \dfrac{\sum x_i}{n} = \dfrac{80}{6} = 13.333$ median $= \dfrac{10 + 10}{2} = 10$ mode $= 10$

Data set B: $\bar{x} = \dfrac{\sum x_i}{n} = \dfrac{130}{11} = 11.818$ median $= 10$ no mode

Data set C: $\bar{x} = \dfrac{\sum x_i}{n} = \dfrac{76}{6} = 12.667$ median $= \dfrac{9 + 11}{2} = 10$ mode $= 15$

Data set D: $\bar{x} = \dfrac{\sum x_i}{n} = \dfrac{72}{6} = 12$ median $= \dfrac{7 + 7}{2} = 7$ modes $= 5$ and 7

Observations:

Extreme values or changes in extreme values have no effect on either the median or mode.

Extreme values or changes in extreme values have a greater effect on the mean when there are fewer observations.

Chapter 5
Page 174

Number of ways $= 3^{10} = 59{,}049$

$P(\text{one specific set of toppings}) = \dfrac{1}{59{,}049} = 0.00001694$

Page 183

By definition, if event B occurs, A cannot occur. Therefore, $P(A|B) = 0$.

Page 191

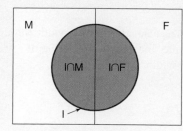

$$P(I) = P(I \cap M) + P(I \cap F)$$
$$= P(M)P(I|M) + P(F)P(I|F)$$
$$= (0.519)(0.316) + (0.481)(0.294)$$
$$= 0.305$$

Chapter 6
Page 225

x	P(x)	xP(x)
1	0.1	0.1
2	0.2	0.4
3	0.4	1.2
4	0.2	0.8
5	0.1	0.5
15		3.0

$$\bar{x} = \frac{\sum x_i}{n} = \frac{15}{5} = 3 \qquad E(X) = \sum x_i P(x_i) = 3.0$$

Page 234
Probability distribution of profits (y) earned:

y	P(y)	yP(y)
−$ 50	0.064	−$ 3.20
$ 50	0.288	$ 14.40
$150	0.432	$ 64.80
$250	0.216	$ 54.00
	1.000	$130.00

$$E(Y) = \sum y_i P(y_i) = \$130$$

Using the expected value rules:
$$Y = -\$50 + \$100X \rightarrow E(Y) = -\$50 + \$100E(X)$$
$$= -\$50 + \$100(1.800) = \$130$$

Page 243
a) All the characteristics of the binomial distribution apply.

b) Not all the characteristics of the binomial distribution apply. The probability of a ticket winning changes from draw to draw depending on which tickets were previously selected.

c) Not all the characteristics of the binomial distribution apply. The number of successes is not limited by the sample size or the number of trials. Theoretically, there can be an infinite number of successes.

d) Not all the characteristics of the binomial distribution necessarily apply. Pitchers have their good days and their bad days, and they may have a better chance of striking out some batters than other batters. Therefore, the probability of a strikeout may not necessarily be the same from game to game or from batter to batter.

Chapter 7
Page 274

$$Z = \frac{X - \mu}{\sigma} \rightarrow Z = \frac{X}{\sigma} - \frac{\mu}{\sigma} \rightarrow Z = \left(\frac{1}{\sigma}\right)X - \frac{\mu}{\sigma}$$

$$E(aX + b) = aE(X) + b \rightarrow E(Z)$$
$$= E\left(\left(\frac{1}{\sigma}\right)X + \left(-\frac{\mu}{\sigma}\right)\right)$$

$$\rightarrow E(Z) = \frac{1}{\sigma}E(X) + \left(-\frac{\mu}{\sigma}\right) = \frac{1}{\sigma}\mu - \frac{\mu}{\sigma} = 0$$

$$V(aX + b) = a^2 V(X) \rightarrow V(Z) = \left(\frac{1}{\sigma}\right)^2 \sigma^2$$
$$= 1 \rightarrow \sigma_Z = \sqrt{V(Z)} = 1$$

Page 276
$$P(0 < Z < 1.32)$$

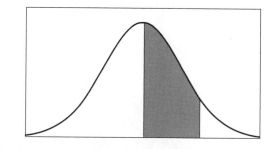

The probability can be directly read from the table.

$$P(Z > 1.32)$$

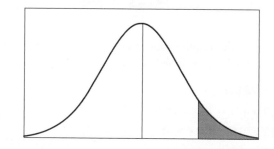

The probability requires you to subtract the probability read from the table from 0.5.

$P(Z > -1.32)$

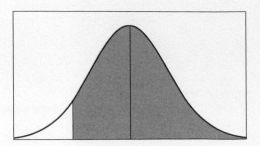

The probability requires you to add 0.5 to the probability read from the table.
$P(1.32 < Z < 1.47)$

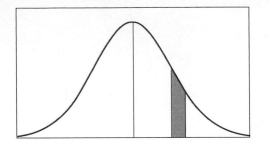

The probability requires you to subtract the lower probability read in the table from the higher probability read from the table.

$P(-1.32 < Z < 1.47)$

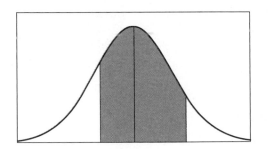

The probability requires you to add together the two probabilities read from the table.

Page 289

a. $P(X > 15) = P(X > 15.5)$

b. $P(X \geq 15) = P(X > 14.5)$

c. $P(X = 15) = P(14.5 < X < 15.5)$

d. $P(X < 18) = P(X < 17.5)$

e. $P(X \leq 18) = P(X < 18.5)$

f. $P(15 < X < 18) = P(15.5 < X < 17.5)$

g. $P(15 \leq X \leq 18) = P(14.5 < X < 18.5)$

Chapter 8

Page 324

The sample size also affects the width through $t_{\alpha/2}$. The larger the sample, the smaller the value of $t_{\alpha/2}$, resulting in even a smaller width.

Page 327

$$P = \frac{X}{n} = \frac{1}{n}X$$

$$E(aX) = aE(X) \rightarrow E(P) = \frac{1}{n}E(X) = \frac{1}{n}n\pi = \pi$$

$$V(aX) = a^2V(X) \rightarrow V(P) = \left(\frac{1}{n}\right)^2 V(X)$$

$$= \frac{1}{n^2}n\pi(1 - \pi) = \frac{\pi(1 - \pi)}{n}$$

$$\sigma_P = \sqrt{V(P)} = \sqrt{\frac{\pi(1 - \pi)}{n}}$$

Page 334

You would take a larger sample when you want to be more accurate (i.e., smaller margin of error or smaller confidence interval width required). You would also be able to take a smaller sample, when the population is more homogeneous. Blood tests require the insertion of a needle in only one spot on your body because your blood is the same throughout your body, or $\sigma = 0$. (Although using the formula for the sample size when $\sigma = 0$ would tell you that n must be greater than or equal to 0, you would need a sample size of at least 1.)

Chapter 9

Page 357

The psychological cost to the jury of having an innocent person put to death should be quite severe, although not as severe as the cost to the innocent person. Therefore, the jury should be less willing to find an innocent person guilty if he or she would be put to death. Thus, the jury would need stronger evidence indicating guilt before it would find the person guilty. As a result, more guilty people would be found not guilty, not exactly a deterrent for committing murder. On the other hand, the severe penalty for being found guilty may be somewhat of a deterrent to the individual contemplating murder.

Page 358

Professor Plum:	H_0: deserves to pass
	H_1: deserves to fail
Professor Wine:	H_0: deserves to fail
	H_1: deserves to pass

It is more costly to students if they fail when they deserve to pass. Therefore, they would like the two hypotheses to be as follows:

H_0: deserves to pass

H_1: deserves to fail

Page 371

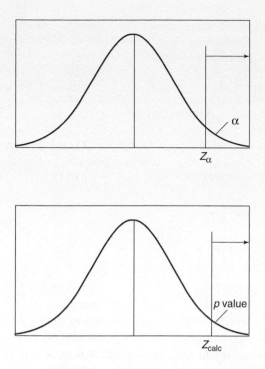

From the two diagrams, we can see that if z_{calc} falls in the rejection region (reject H_0), the p value $< \alpha$ (reject H_0). Conversely, if z_{calc} does not fall in the rejection region (do not reject H_0), the p value $> \alpha$ (do not reject H_0).

Page 383
Professor Plum's student:

H_0: deserves to pass ($\pi \geq 0.5$)

H_1: deserves to fail ($\pi < 0.5$)

$\alpha = 0.05$

Test statistic

$$Z = \frac{p - \pi_0}{\sqrt{\dfrac{\pi_0(1 - \pi_0)}{n}}} = \frac{\dfrac{96}{200} - 0.5}{\sqrt{\dfrac{0.5(1 - 0.5)}{200}}} = -0.566$$

Rejection region (decision rule)

$R: Z < -z_\alpha$

$Z < -1.645$

As $-0.566 > -1.645$, we don't reject H_0 at $\alpha = 0.05$. There is insufficient evidence that this student deserves to fail. Therefore, Professor Plum will pass this student.

Professor Wine's student:

H_0: deserves to fail ($\pi \leq 0.5$)

H_1: deserves to pass ($\pi > 0.5$)

$\alpha = 0.05$

Test statistic

$$Z = \frac{p - \pi_0}{\sqrt{\dfrac{\pi_0(1 - \pi_0)}{n}}} = \frac{\dfrac{105}{200} - 0.5}{\sqrt{\dfrac{0.5(1 - 0.5)}{200}}} = 0.707$$

Rejection region (decision rule)

$R: Z > z_\alpha$

$Z > 1.645$

As $0.707 < 1.645$, we don't reject H_0 at $\alpha = 0.05$. There is insufficient evidence that this student deserves to pass. Therefore, Professor Wine will fail this student.

To pass Professor Plum's course:

$$Z > -1.645 \rightarrow \frac{p - 0.5}{\sqrt{\dfrac{0.5(1 - 0.5)}{200}}} > -1.645$$

$$\rightarrow p > 0.5 - 1.645\sqrt{\frac{0.5(1 - 0.5)}{200}} \rightarrow p > 0.4418$$

To pass, a student of Professor Plum would need more than 44.18% to pass his course (or he or she would need to correctly answer at least 89 of the 200 questions).

To pass Professor Wine's course:

$$Z > 1.645 \rightarrow \frac{p - 0.5}{\sqrt{\dfrac{0.5(1 - 0.5)}{200}}} > 1.645$$

$$\rightarrow p > 0.5 + 1.645\sqrt{\frac{0.5(1 - 0.5)}{200}} \rightarrow p > 0.5582$$

To pass, a student of Professor Wine would need more than 55.82% to pass his course (or he or she would need to correctly answer at least 112 of the 200 questions).

Chapter 10
Page 413
Sample 1 (and population 1) = American:

H_0: $\mu_1 - \mu_2 = 20$ (or ≤ 20)

H_1: $\mu_1 - \mu_2 > 20$

Sample 1 (and population 1) = Canadian:

H_0: $\mu_1 - \mu_2 = -20$ (or ≥ 20)

H_1: $\mu_1 - \mu_2 < -20$

Page 420
The numerator would still be -240 because the difference in the two averages, $\bar{x}_1 - \bar{x}_2$, using independent samples equals the average difference, $\bar{d}$, using matched paired samples.

The numerator should be much larger than 103.495 using independent samples because the values within each sample are much more variable than the difference in values within the pairs resulting a relatively large s_p^2. This relatively large s_p^2 would result in $\sqrt{\dfrac{s_p^2}{n_1} + \dfrac{s_p^2}{n_2}}$ being larger than $s_d/\sqrt{n}$.

Page 420

We paired our samples because we believed that there is some characteristic within the population that influences the values of X. And this influence results in the values within each pair to tend to move in the same direction (e.g., we believe that amount overweight influences weight loss, and the more a person is overweight, the more he or she should lose). Or we believe that there is a positive relationship between the X's. Pearson's Correlation coefficient (the statistic r in Chapter 4) measures this relationship (although it assumes a linear relationship), and it being positive supports our belief and our decision to pair the samples.

Page 425

$$\bar{p} = \frac{n_1 p_1 + n_2 p_2}{n_1 + n_2} = \frac{n_1 \dfrac{x_1}{n_1} + n_2 \dfrac{x_2}{n_2}}{n_1 + n_2} = \frac{x_1 + x_2}{n_1 + n_2}$$

Chapter 11

Page 462

a) All houses in the study sold at exactly the same price.

$SST = SSA = SSE = 0$

b) Not all houses in the study sold at exactly the same price but the houses within each city sold at the same price.

$SST > 0,\ SSA > 0,\ SSE = 0$

c) Not all houses within one or more of the cities sold at exactly the same price and housing prices in Montreal tended to be lower than the housing prices in either Toronto or Edmonton.

$SST > 0,\ SSA > 0,\ SSE > 0$

d) Not all houses within one or more of the cities sold at exactly the same price although the average selling prices were the same for the three cities

$SST > 0,\ SSA = 0,\ SSE > 0$

Page 464

In Chapter 8, we were told that the degrees of freedom tell us how many observations we used to calculate s less the number of intermediate estimates we used in our calculation. *SSA, SSE,* and *SST* are measures of variability as s is, and, thus, the determination of degrees of freedom is similar to s.

$SSA = \sum n_j(\bar{y}_j - \bar{y})^2$ measures how variable the c treatment means, $\bar{y}_j$'s (i.e., observations), are. But to calculate *SSA,* we first have to estimate the overall true average μ with $\bar{y}$. Therefore, the degrees of freedom for *SSA* are $c - 1$.

$SSE = \sum \sum (y_{ij} - \bar{y}_j)$ measures how variable the n individual values, y_{ij}'s (i.e., observations), are within each treatment. But to calculate *SSE,* we first have to estimate the c true means, μ_j's, with the $\bar{y}_j$'s. Therefore, the degrees of freedom for *SSE* are $n - c$.

$SST = \sum \sum (y_{ij} - \bar{y})^2$ measures how variable the n individual values, y_{ij}'s (i.e., observations), are within the entire sample. But to calculate *SST,* we first have to estimate the overall true average μ with $\bar{y}$. Therefore, the degrees of freedom for *SST* are $n - 1$.

Page 477

SST would not change because it simply measures how different the n values are. As long as the values don't change, *SST* would not change whether or not we recognized that the samples were matched.

   SSA would also not change because it simply measures how different the sample means are among the treatments. As long as the values don't change, the treatment means don't change and, thus, *SSA* would not change whether or not we recognized that the samples were matched.

It is almost certain that *SSE* would be smaller if we recognized that the samples were matched. It would definitely not increase. It should be smaller because there is another identifiable factor, the characteristic on which the matching was based, which would explain some of the original unexplained variation (i.e., the original *SSE*). The *SSE* would be reduced by the amount of variation explained by this additional factor.

F_{crit} when matching is not recognized has degrees of freedom $\nu_1 = c - 1$ and $\nu_2 = n - c$. When matching is recognized, F_{crit} has degrees of freedom $\nu_1 = c - 1$ and $\nu_2 = n - c - r + 1$ (or, equivalently, $(r - 1)(c - 1)$). It is easy to see that the ν_2, when recognizing matching, is less than the ν_2, when not recognizing matching. A quick examination of an *F* table tells us that the smaller the ν_2, the larger the F_{crit}, when ν_1 remains the same. Therefore, F_{crit} would be larger if matching was recognized.

Because F_{crit} is larger when matching is recognized, the value of the test statistic *F* would need to be larger before the null hypothesis could be rejected. On the other hand, the value of the test statistic should be substantially larger if we were correct when we decided to match our samples. If we were not correct when we decided to match, it should be more difficult to reject the null hypothesis.

Page 481

Looking at the middle graph, there doesn't appear to be strong evidence to indicate that location has an effect on housing prices because the sample means across cities are very similar. Looking at the top graph, there is substantial evidence that type of housing has an effect on housing prices. The sample means for ranch-style and multi-level style houses are quite a bit higher than the sample means for high-rise condos and townhouses. Looking at the bottom graph, there appears to be an interaction effect on housing prices. The four sets of lines are not close to being parallel except for the high-rise condo and townhouse lines.

Chapter 12

Page 505

Treating variable *B* as representing *c* populations and variable *A* as a characteristic with *r* categories, the null and alternative hypotheses could be stated as follows:

H_0: Variable *A* has the same distribution across the *c* populations.

H_1: Variable *A* does not have the same distribution across the *c* populations.

These two hypotheses are equivalent to

$$H_0: \pi_1 = \pi_2 \ (\text{or } \pi_1 - \pi_2 = 0)$$
$$H_1: \pi_1 \neq \pi_2 \ (\text{or } \pi_1 - \pi_2 \neq 0)$$

when we had only two populations with two categories (success and failure).

When arriving at the test statistic for these hypotheses, we used a common estimate of both population proportions by simply summing the number of successes in both samples combined and dividing that sum by the number of observations in both samples combined. We use the same procedure here. For each category of variable *A*, we add up the total number of observations belonging to the category (which we have symbolized by R_j) and divide that by the total number of observations (which we have symbolized by *n*). By doing so, our estimates of the π_j's are

$$\frac{R_j}{n}$$

To obtain the expected values, e_{jk}'s, we simply multiply these estimates by the number of observations in each of the *c* populations (which we have symbolized by C_k's, resulting in each e_{jk} being, as before

$$e_{jk} = \frac{R_j}{n} C_k \text{ or } e_{jk} = \frac{R_j C_k}{n}$$

Page 508

Row	Column 1	2	3	4	5
1	13 (7.1)	3 (6.7)	4 (7.9)	4 (6.7)	6 (2.4)
2	15 (18.9)	18 (16.8)	20 (21.1)	22 (16.8)	5 (6.3)
3	17 (18.9)	19 (16.8)	26 (21.1)	14 (16.8)	4 (6.3)

Currently, there is only one e_{jk} with an expected value less than 5 ($e_{15} = 2.4$). To eliminate this problem, we either have to combine Row 1 with another row (assume that row to be Row 2) or to combine Column 5 with another column (assume that column to be Column 4). Given that the degrees of freedom are

$$\nu = (r - 1)(c - 1)$$

combining rows would result in degrees of freedom

$$\nu = (r - 1)(c - 1) = (2 - 1)(5 - 1) = 4$$

or combining columns would result in degrees of freedom

$$\nu = (r - 1)(c - 1) = (3 - 1)(4 - 1) = 6$$

Therefore, we should combine Column 5 with Column 4, resulting in the following new contingency table:

Row	Column 1	2	3	4
1	13 (7.1)	3 (6.7)	4 (7.9)	10 (9.1)
2	15 (18.9)	18 (16.8)	20 (21.1)	27 (23.1)
3	17 (18.9)	19 (16.8)	26 (21.1)	18 (23.1)

Note: The sum of the e_{jk}'s along each row and down each column don't necessarily equal the sums of the respective f_{jk}'s because of rounding errors.

Page 515

Letting π_2 equal the probability that the sum of dots equals 2, π_3 equal the probability that the sum of dots equals 3, etc.,

$$H_0 : \pi_2 = \frac{1}{36}, \pi_3 = \frac{2}{36}, \pi_4 = \frac{3}{36}, \pi_5 = \frac{4}{36}, \pi_6 = \frac{5}{36}, \pi_7 = \frac{6}{36}, \pi_8 = \frac{5}{36}, \pi_9 = \frac{4}{36}, \pi_{10} = \frac{3}{36},$$

$$\pi_{11} = \frac{2}{36}, \pi_{12} = \frac{1}{36}$$

H_1 : Not all the π_j's as above.

To insure that all e_j's ≥ 5, we have to make certain that the category or categories with the smallest π_j (categories labelled 2 and 12) have an $e_j \geq 5$. Solving for the minimum number of rolls, n,

$$e_j = n\pi_j \rightarrow n = \frac{e_j}{\pi_j} \rightarrow n = \frac{5}{1/36} = 180$$

The minimum number of rolls to insure that all e_j's ≥ 5 is 180.

Chapter 13

Page 539

(a) Being somewhat close to each other, the temperature in Calgary and temperature in Edmonton should have a positive relationship.

(b) Being very far from one another, there should be no relationship between the temperature in Halifax and temperature in Beijing.

(c) Because cars are cheaper to purchase when interest rates are low, there should be a negative relationship between interest rates on car loans and number of cars sold. (However, one could argue that interest rates on car loans are low to encourage people to buy more cars because few cars are currently being sold. In this situation, there would be a positive relationship.)

(d) As with the previous example, one could argue that the relationship between the number of Hondas sold and the number of Toyotas sold could either be positive or negative. The relationship would be positive if people are buying more or less cars in general, no matter what the car is. The relationship would be negative if people are switching from Hondas to Toyotas, or vice versa.

(e) The number of winter coats sold and number of winter hats sold should have a positive relationship because people, as a group, tend to buy less of each when it is warmer and more of each when it is colder.

Page 541

Testing for a positive relationship, the two hypotheses become

$H_0: \rho = 0$ (or ≤ 0)

$H_1: \rho > 0$

The test statistic remains the same:

$$t_{calc} = r\sqrt{\frac{n-2}{1-r^2}} = 0.8296\sqrt{\frac{30-2}{1-(0.8296)^2}} = 7.862$$

but the rejection region changes to

$R: t_{calc} > t_{0.05,28}$ or $t_{calc} > 1.701$

As $7.862 > 1.701$, we would reject H_0 at $\alpha = 0.05$ and conclude that there is a positive (linear) relationship between a student's GPA and his or her GPA in the last 60 credits taken.

Page 544

(a) The dependent variable is exam mark and the independent variable is amount of hours studied because exam marks should depend, to some extent, on how many hours a student studies.

(b) The probability of getting a scholarship is the dependent variable and the exam mark is the independent variable as most scholarships depend on a student's academic performance.

(c) The amount of gasoline used is dependent on the number of kilometres travelled because kilometres travelled affects the amount of gasoline used.

(d) Distance to the vacation destination should be the dependent variable because the price of gasoline could affect how far someone is willing to drive.

(e) The number of 6/49 tickets sold should be the dependent variable and the projected value of the grand prize should be the independent variable because more tickets are sold when the grand prize increases in value. As with previous answers, we could argue that the projected value of the grand prize is the dependent variable because the value depends on the number of tickets sold.

Page 553

(a) In this case, because all values of Y are the same, there is no variation in the values of Y; therefore, $SST = 0$. There is also no relationship between Y and X and there are no random fluctuations about the regression line. Therefore, SSR and SSE are also equal to zero and $SST = SSR = SSE$.

(b) Because there is some variation in the values of Y, $SST > 0$. Because there is no linear relationship between Y and X in the sample, $SSR = 0$. Because $SSR = 0$ and $SST = SSR + SSE$, $SSE > 0$ and $SSE = SST$.

(c) Because there is some variation in the values of Y, $SST > 0$. Because there is some variation in the values of Y and because the values of Y all lie along a straight line, this straight line must either have a positive or negative slope. Therefore, $SSR > 0$. Because all the values lie along this straight line, $SSE = 0$. And because $SST = SSR + SSE$, $SSR = SSE$.

Page 554

When we normally take the square root of a number, we only consider the positive square root. But there are always two square roots: a positive square root and a negative square root. So the square root of 0.81 could be $+0.9$ and -0.9. When determining the correlation r between two random variables by taking the square root of R^2, it is very important that we determine the correct sign for r. This can be easily determined by looking at the slope of the regression line. If the slope is positive, r is positive square root of R^2. If the slope is negative, r is the negative square root of R^2.

Page 558

Because

$$SSE = \sum (y_i - \hat{y}_i), \; s = \sqrt{\frac{SSE}{n-2}}, \text{ and } s_{b_1} = \frac{s}{SS_{xx}}$$

and the confidence interval for β_1 is $b_1 \pm t_{\alpha/2} s_{b_1}$, the width of the confidence interval would be smaller the more closely the values of Y fit the regression line (the smaller the SSE), and the more variable the values of X are in the sample (the larger the SS_{xx}).

Page 559

The true model would be $y_i = \beta_0 + \varepsilon$.

Page 572

The intervals would be narrower in the following circumstances:

- The lower the level of confidence
- The better the data fit the regression line
- The larger the sample
- The more spread out the values of X in the sample

Page 575

In Chapter 12, when testing for normality, we had to estimate both μ and σ, causing us to lose 2 additional degrees of freedom beyond the normal loss of 1 degree of freedom. When testing normality here, we assume that $\mu = 0$, requiring us to just have to estimate σ. Therefore, we lose only 1 degree of freedom beyond the normal loss of 1 degree of freedom.

Chapter 14

Page 599

There could be two primary reasons with the first reason being that the two additional variables do not affect the dependent variable. The second primary reason is that although these two additional variables do affect the dependent variable, they are also closely related to the original independent variable. Because they are closely related, the effects that these two variables have on the dependent variable have already been measured through the original variable.

Page 606

When testing $H_1: \beta_2 > 0$, and when the quoted p value is 0.0842, the area in each tail for that particular value of the test statistic is 0.0842/2, or 0.0421. If the value of b_2 happened to be positive, the p value would be 0.0421. But if the value of b_2 was negative, the correct p value would be $P(t > -t_{calc})$, which is obviously greater than 0.5 if one were to sketch the appropriate diagram. Because the area in the left-hand tail, or because $P(t < t_{calc}) = 0.0421$, the area to the right of t_{calc}, or the p value would equal $1 - 0.0421 = 0.9579$.

Page 612

The model

$$Price = \beta_0 + \beta_1(SqFt) + \beta_2(OakKnoll) + \beta_3(OakKnoll \cdot SqFt) + \varepsilon$$

includes the dummy variable *Oak Knoll*, which has a value of 1 if the home is located in Oak Knoll and a value of 0 if the home is located in Hidden Hills. Therefore, if the home is located in Hidden Hills, the model becomes

$$Price = \beta_0 + \beta_1(SqFt) + \beta_2(O) + \beta_3(0) \cdot (SqFt) + \varepsilon$$

or

$$Price = \beta_0 + \beta_1(SqFt) + \varepsilon$$

and the effect that square footage has on price is measured by β_1.

If the home is located in Oak Knoll, the model becomes

$$Price = \beta_0 + \beta_1(SqFt) + \beta_2(1) + \beta_3(1) \cdot (SqFt) + \varepsilon$$

or, rearranging terms,

$$Price = (\beta_0 + \beta_2) + (\beta_1 + \beta_3)(SqFt) + \varepsilon$$

and the effect that square footage has on price is now measured by $\beta_1 + \beta_3$.

Chapter 15

Page 645

With the beginning of the recession in 2009 having a great impact on the automobile industry, the way the automobile industry does business has changed. One way it has changed is to reduce the number of car dealerships. Thus, what happened up to 2009 as far as car dealerships are concerned should not be used to forecast the number of new car dealerships in the future.

Page 654

For the linear trend model using 1995–2004 data, the model indicates that the number of beds will be decreasing in 2005 and 2006.

For the quadratic trend model using 1995–2004 data, the model indicates that the number of beds will be increasing in 2005 and 2006.

For the linear trend model using 2000–2004 data, the model indicates that the number of beds will be decreasing in 2005 and 2006, but not as quickly as if the forecast was based on the 1995–2004 data.

For the quadratic trend using 2000–2004 data, the model indicates that the number of beds will be decreasing in 2005 and 2006, with the decrease being greater than that forecast by the linear trend model using the same data.

Page 670

If the seasonally adjusted sales were, for example, predicted to decrease by 10 percent over the previous season's sales, and the sales only decrease by, for example, 5 percent, the seasonally adjusted sales will show an increase while actual sales will have gone down.

Page 672

(a) Sales $= 129.2500 + 1.4688t - 31.5938(Q1) - 21.3958(Q2) - 12.1979(Q3) + e$

(b) Q3 is not significant in explaining sales because its p value > 0.05. This means that there isn't sufficient evidence that Q3 sales are significantly different than the sales in Q4.

(c) Q4 has the highest sales because the coefficients for all other quarters are negative and its coefficient could be considered to be zero as there is essentially no dummy variable for Q4. Sales in Q1 are the lowest because the most negative coefficient is associated with Q1.

(d) Forecast sales $= 129.2500 + 1.4688(13) - 31.5938(1) = 116.7506$ ($ millions)

Page 675

If the price of each item has increased by 25 percent over the base year's prices, individuals, on average, should probably not change their preferences for the various items and, thus, the weights assigned to each good should remain the same.

If the price of steak has increased by 20 percent while the price of chicken has decreased by 15 percent, individuals, on average, should tend to buy relatively more chicken now and relatively less steak now than they did in the base year. Therefore, the weights assigned should be adjusted to better reflect the amount of money consumers are actually spending now.

Chapter 16

Page 694

The minimum number of runs that are possible is two. This results when all of one type occurs first, followed by all of the other type.

The maximum number of runs would occur if the pattern is one of each type occurs followed by one of the other type. This would result in a total of $2n_1$ or $2n_2$ runs where $n_1 = n_2$ (the number of each type of outcome).

The expected number of runs is, in general,

$$\mu_R = \frac{2n_1 n_2}{n} + 1$$

When $n_1 = n_2$, this expected number becomes

$$\mu_R = \frac{2n_1 n_1}{n_1 + n_1} + 1 = \frac{2n_1^2}{2n_1} + 1 = n_1 + 1$$

or the expected number of runs is the number of outcomes of either type plus 1.

Page 696

1. If H_1: $M < M_0$, we would expect more negative ranks and these negative ranks should be of a higher order of magnitude than the positive ranks. Therefore, $W = \Sigma R^+$ should be less than $\frac{n(n + 1)}{4}$ and, thus, Z should be less than 0 if H_1 is true. Therefore, we would want to reject H_0 if Z is somewhat less than zero, or z_{crit} would be negative and we would reject the null hypothesis when $z_{calc} < -z_\alpha$.

   If H_1: $M \neq M_0$, we would either expect more negative ranks of higher order of magnitude or more positive ranks of higher order of magnitude. Thus, we would expect Z to be either less than zero or greater than zero if H_1 were true. Therefore, there would be both a positive and negative z_{crit}, and the decision rule would be to reject the null hypothesis if $z_{calc} < -z_{\alpha/2}$ or $z_{calc} > z_{\alpha/2}$.

   If H_1: $M > M_0$, we would expect more positive ranks and these positive ranks should be of a higher order of magnitude than the negative ranks. Therefore, we would want to reject H_0 if Z is somewhat greater than zero, or z_{crit} would be positive and we would reject the null hypothesis when $z_{calc} > z_\alpha$.

2. The sum of integers from 1 to n equals $\frac{n(n + 1)}{2}$. Thus, the sum of the ranks from 1 to n also equals $\frac{n(n + 1)}{2}$. If the null hypothesis of equality is true, you would expect half of this sum to be positive and half to be negative, or you would expect the sum of the positive ranks to be

$$\frac{1}{2}\left(\frac{n(n + 1)}{2}\right) \text{ or } \frac{n(n + 1)}{4}$$

Page 696

If the null hypothesis is true, the probability of a positive difference should equal the probability of a negative difference or the probability of a positive difference, $\pi = 0.5$. Therefore, substituting D^+ for X and 0.5 for π

$$Z = \frac{X - n\pi}{\sqrt{n\pi(1 - \pi)}} = \frac{D^+ - n(0.5)}{\sqrt{n(0.5)(1 - 0.5)}} = \frac{D^+ - 0.5n}{\sqrt{0.25n}}$$

Chapter 17

Page 741

- At least two of three successive points will lie outside of 2 sigmas on the same side of the mean?

$$P(Z > 2) = 0.5 - 0.4772 = 0.0228$$

$$P(Z < -2) = 0.5 - 0.4772 = 0.0228$$

P(one point will lie outside of 2 sigmas on the same side of the mean) $= P(Z > 2)$ or $P(Z < -2)$
$= 0.0228 + 0.0228 = 0.0456$ (addition rule for mutually exclusive events)
To calculate the probability of at least two of three successive points lying outside of 2 sigmas on the same size of the mean, we use the binomial distribution with $n = 3$ and $\pi = 0.0056$.

$$
\begin{aligned}
P(X \geq 2) &= P(X = 2) + P(X = 3) \\
&= \frac{3!}{2!1!}(0.0456^2)(0.9544^1) + \frac{3!}{3!0!}(0.0456^3)(0.9544^0) \\
&\approx 0.005954 + 0.000095 \\
&\approx 0.00605
\end{aligned}
$$

- At least four of five successive points will lie outside of 1 sigma on the same side of the mean?

$$P(Z > 1) = 0.5 - 0.3413 = 0.1587$$

$$P(Z < -1) = 0.5 - 0.3413 = 0.1587$$

Or P(one point will lie outside of 1 sigma on the same side of the mean) $= 2(0.1587) = 0.3174$ (addition rule for mutually exclusive events)

Again, we use the binomial distribution to calculate at least four of five points lying outside of 1 sigma on the same side of the mean. Here, $n = 5$ and $\pi = 0.3174$.

$$
P(X \geq 4) = P(X = 4) + P(X = 5) = \frac{5!}{4!1!}(0.3174^4)(0.6826^1) + \frac{5!}{5!0!}(0.3174^5)(0.6826^0)
$$
$$
\approx 0.034639 + 0.003221 \approx 0.03786
$$

- Nine successive points will lie on the same side of the mean?

P(nine successive points on the same side of the mean) $= P$(nine successive points below the mean) $+ P$(nine successive points above the mean) (addition rule for mutually exclusive events)

P(nine successive points above the mean) $= 0.5^9 \approx 0.001953$

P(nine successive points below the mean) $= 0.5^9 \approx 0.001953$

P(nine successive points on the same side of the mean) $\approx 0.001953 + 0.001953 \approx 0.003906$

Index